THE BROADVIEW
Introduction to
Literature

THE BROADVIEW
Introduction to
Literature

General Editors
Lisa Chalykoff
Neta Gordon
Paul Lumsden

broadview press

Library and Archives Canada Cataloguing in Publication

The Broadview introduction to literature / general editors, Lisa Chalykoff, Neta Gordon, Paul Lumsden.

Includes index.
ISBN 978-1-55481-078-9 (pbk.)

1. Literature—Collections. I. Lumsden, Paul, 1961-, editor of compilation II. Chalykoff, Lisa, editor of compilation III. Gordon, Neta, 1971-, editor of compilation IV. Title: Introduction to literature.

PN6014.B76 2013   808   C2013-903879-5

Broadview Press is an independent, international publishing house, incorporated in 1985. We welcome comments and suggestions regarding any aspect of our publications—please feel free to contact us at the addresses below or at broadview@broadviewpress.com.

North America	PO Box 1243, Peterborough, Ontario, Canada K9J 7H5
	2215 Kenmore Ave., Buffalo, New York, USA 14207
	Tel: (705) 743-8990; Fax: (705) 743-8353
	email: customerservice@broadviewpress.com
UK, Europe, Central Asia,	Eurospan Group,
Middle East, Africa, India,	3 Henrietta St., London WC2E 8LU, United Kingdom
and Southeast Asia	Tel: 44 (0) 1767 604972; Fax: 44 (0) 1767 601640
	email: eurospan@turpin-distribution.com
Australia and	NewSouth Books c/o TL Distribution,
New Zealand	15-23 Helles Ave., Moorebank, NSW, Australia 2170
	Tel: (02) 8778 9999; Fax: (02) 8778 9944
	email: orders@tldistribution.com.au

www.broadviewpress.com

Broadview Press acknowledges the financial support of the Government of Canada through the Canada Book Fund for our publishing activities.

PRINTED IN CANADA

Contributors to *The Broadview Introduction to Literature*

MANAGING EDITORS	Don LePan
	Marjorie Mather
DEVELOPMENTAL AND TEXTUAL EDITOR	Laura Buzzard
EDITORIAL COORDINATORS	Tara Bodie
	Bryanne Miller
CONTRIBUTING EDITORS AND TRANSLATORS	Lisa Chalykoff
	Neta Gordon
	Ian Johnston
	David Swain
CONTRIBUTING WRITERS	Laura Buzzard
	Paul Johnston Byrne
	Tara Bodie

EDITORIAL ASSISTANTS

Tara Bodie	Amanda Mullen
Alicia Christianson	Virginia Philipson
Joel DeShaye	Anja Pujic
Victoria Duncan	Andrew Reszitnyk
Rose Eckert-Jantzie	David Ross
Emily Farrell	Nora Ruddock
Travis Grant	Kate Sinclair
Karim Lalani	Jack Skeffington
Phil Laven	Kaitlyn Till
Kellen Loewen	Morgan Tunzelmann

PRODUCTION COORDINATOR   Tara Lowes
PRODUCTION ASSISTANT   Allison LaSorda
COPY EDITOR   Colleen Franklin
PROOFREADERS   Joe Davies
                                           Judith Earnshaw
DESIGN AND TYPESETTING   Eileen Eckert
PERMISSIONS COORDINATOR   Merilee Atos
COVER DESIGN   Michel Vrana

Contents

DRAMA

POETRY

LITERARY NON-FICTION

Preface

On hearing that Broadview was planning a new anthology designed to provide an overview of literature at the first-year level, more than a few people have expressed surprise. What could a new anthology have to offer that really is different—that gives something new and valuable to academics and students alike? We hope that you will find your own answers to that question once you have looked through this volume. Certainly our intent has been to offer something that is in many ways different. We have brought fresh eyes to the process of choosing a table of contents; from Charles Mungoshi's "The Setting Sun and the Rolling World" to Lydia Millet's "Love in Infant Monkeys," from Alice Oswald's "Wedding" to R.W. Gray's "How this begins," from Sharon Harris's "Where Do Poems Come From?" to Hannah Moscovitch's *Essay*, you'll find selections here that have not been widely anthologized elsewhere. You'll also find more visual material than in competing anthologies—including author-illustrated works such as Shaun Tan's "The Nameless Holiday" and Alasdair Gray's "The Star." You'll find a short section on poetry in translation. You'll also find a selection of literary non-fiction—a form that is increasingly being taken seriously as a literary genre, but that is passed over in most anthologies which purport to offer an overview of literature. (It would be difficult to read an essay such as Miriam Toews's "A Father's Faith" and not be persuaded that literary non-fiction is indeed an important literary genre.)

Although the emphasis of the anthology is very much on literature in English (in recognition of the reality that most "introduction to literature" courses in Canada are taught in English departments), we have included rather more literature in translation than is to be found in most competing anthologies. Particularly noteworthy is the special section on Poetry in Translation that discusses some of the many issues involved and provides a concise but wide-ranging sample of poems in translation, with the original offered for comparison.

Not everything about *The Broadview Introduction to Literature* is entirely new, of course. Many of the selections will, we hope, be familiar to instructors; as to which of the "old chestnuts" continue to work well in a teaching context we have in large part been guided by the advice provided to us by academics at a variety of institutions across Canada. But even where familiar authors and selections are concerned, we think you'll find quite a bit here that is different. We have worked hard to pitch both the author introductions and the explanatory notes at a consistent level throughout—and, in both introductions and notes, to give students more by way of background.

Finally, you'll find fresh material posted on the companion website associated with the anthology. The site <http://sites.broadviewpress.com/BIL/> features additional material on many literary sub-genres and movements (from the sonnet to sound poetry, and from speculative fiction to microfiction); material on reading poetry (including exercises that will help those unfamiliar with the patterns of accentual-syllabic metre in English); material on writing essays about literature—and on referencing and citation; a much fuller glossary of literary terms than it is possible to include in these pages; self-test quizzes on the information provided in the introductions to the various genres; and several additional selections that we were unable to find space for in the bound book. We have included Rossetti's "Goblin Market" in its entirety here; those looking to incorporate more long poems into a course will find several options on the website (including Milton's "Lycidas" and Coleridge's "The Rime of the Ancient Mariner"). Similarly, those looking to explore the borders of short fiction may find further examples of long short stories (or short novels) on the website—including Kafka's "Metamorphosis," Conrad's "The Secret Sharer," and Joyce's "The Dead." All are introduced and annotated according to the same principles and presented in the same format as the selections in the bound-book anthology. Those wishing to go beyond these choices for fiction—or for drama—may assign any one of the more than 300 volumes in the acclaimed Broadview Editions series, and we can arrange to have that volume bundled together with the bound book anthology in a shrink-wrapped package, at little or no additional charge to the student.

Any of the genre volumes of the anthology may also be bundled together in special-price shrink-wrapped packages; whatever genres your course covers, and whatever works you would like to cover within those genres, we will do our best to put together a package that will suit your needs. (Instructors should note that, in addition to the main companion website of materials that may be of interest both to students and to instructors, we have posted instructor-related materials on a separate website.)

I do hope you will like what you see—and I hope as well that you will be in touch with any questions or suggestions; we will always be on the lookout for good ideas as to what we should add to the anthology's companion website—and/or for what we should look to include in the next edition of *The Broadview Introduction to Literature*.

[D.L.]

Acknowledgements

The general editors, managing editors, and all of us at Broadview owe a debt of gratitude to the academics who have offered assistance and feedback at various stages of the project:

Rhonda Anderson
Trevor Arkell
Veronica Austen
John Ball
David Bentley
Shashi Bhat
Nicholas Bradley
Jocelyn Coates
Richard Cole
Alison Conway
Heidi J. Tiedemann Darroch
Celeste Daphne Derksen
Lorraine DiCicco
Kerry Doyle
Monique Dumontet
Michelle Faubert
Rebecca Gagan
Jay Gamble
Dana Hansen
Alexander Hart
Linda Harwood
Chandra Hodgson
Kathryn Holland
Ashton Howley
Renee Hulan
Kathleen James-Cavan
Karl Jirgens
Diana Frances Lobb

Kathyrn MacLennan
Shelley Mahoney
Joanna Mansbridge
Mark McDayter
Lindsey McMaster
Susan McNeill-Bindon
Craig Melhoff
Bob Mills
Stephanie Morley
Andrew Murray
Russell Perkin
Allan Pero
Mike Perschon
John Pope
Phyllis Rozendal
Cory Rushton
Laura Schechter
Stephen Schryer
Peter Slade
Marjorie Stone
Daniel Tysdal
Linda Van Netten Blimke
Molly Wallace
David Watt
Nanci White
David Wilson
Dorothy Woodman
Gena Zuroski-Jenkins

The Study of Literature

The Nobel prize-winning physicist Paul Dirac reportedly said, "The aim of science is to make difficult things understandable in a simple way; the aim of poetry is to state simple things in an incomprehensible way." More recently, noted Language poet Charles Bernstein—whose work typically challenges the limits of simple comprehension—published the poem "Thank you for saying thank you," in which he explicitly takes up the issue of how poetry "states" things:

> This is a totally
> accessible poem.
> There is nothing
> in this poem
> that is in any
> way difficult.
> All the words
> are simple &
> to the point.

Though Bernstein's work is undoubtedly meant to register as ironic, both his poem and Dirac's comment draw attention to the idea that literature uses language in a peculiar way, and that one of the most fundamental questions readers of literature must ask themselves is: "How is this said?" Or—with apologies to Dirac—the question might be: "How do the language choices in this text make a seemingly simple thing—for example, a statement about love, or family, or justice, or grief—not incomprehensible, but rather more than just something simple?"

Another way of approaching the question of how literature works is to consider the way this anthology of literature is organized around the idea of genre, with texts chosen and categorized according to the way they fit into the classifications of poetry, short fiction, drama, and literary non-fiction. One way of organizing an introductory anthology of literature is the historical, in which selections are sorted from oldest to most recent, usually grouped together according to what have become acknowledged as distinctive historical periods of literary output. Another is the topical or thematic, in which historically and generically diverse selections are grouped together according to subject matter, so that students may compare differing attitudes toward, for example, gender relations, personal loss, particular historical events, or the process of growing up. The decision by an editor of an anthology—or the instructor of a course—to select one organizing principle over another is not arbitrary, but reflects a choice in terms of teaching students how to approach the reading of literature. In very simple terms, one might regard the three options thus: the historical configuration emphasizes discovering the "what" and "when" of literature—what is the body of written work that has come to be considered "literature" (especially in terms of tracing the outlines of a national literature), and when were examples from this distinguished corpus written? The thematic configuration emphasizes sorting through the "why" of literature—why do writers turn to literature to work through complex ideas, and what can we make of our complex responses to differing, often compet- ing, stances on various topics? The generic configuration, finally, emphasizes the "how" of literature—how is the text put together? What are its working parts? How does an attention to the formal attributes of a literary piece help the reader understand the way it achieves its intellectual and emotional—its more than just simple—effects?

What do literary critics mean when they refer to genre? The word was introduced into the English language sometime in the late eighteenth century, borrowed from the French word *genre*, which meant "kind" or "style" of art, as when the British agricultural reformer Arthur Young refers in his travel narra- tives to the "genre" of Dutch painting, which he finds wanting in comparison to the work of the Italian masters. We can look back further to the Latin root *genus*, or even the Greek γένος (*génos*), a term which also refers to the idea of a distinct family or clan; thus, the notion of "kind" might helpfully be thought of as a way of thinking about resemblances, relationships, and keys to recogni- tion among the literary genres. Another helpful analogy is the way biologists have taken up the term *genus* as part of the taxonomy of organisms. The term *genus felis*, for example, refers to a particular order of small cats, including such species as the domestic cat (*felis catus*) and the wildcat (*felis silvestris*); both species share common generic attributes, such as a similar size and a preferred diet of small rodents. For biologists and literary critics alike, the concept of genus or genre, respectively, is used to group things together according to a system of shared, identifiable features, with both terms allowing for the idea that larger groupings can be further broken down into even more specific ones (thus we can refer to the various breeds of domestic cats, or the distinctions among the Petrarchan, Shakespearian, and Spenserian sonnets).

Biologists tend to use the word "characteristics" to designate the features of a genus; literary critics, on the other hand, make use of the word "convention," a somewhat more complicated term. Like *characteristics*, the term *conventions* refers to distinguishing elements of a genre, which is why the study of literature requires a thorough understanding of the specialized descriptive vocabulary used to discuss such elements as a text's metre, its narrative point of view, its use of figurative language, etc. The introductions to each section of this anthology will draw attention to this specialized vocabulary, and students will also want to refer to the extensive glossary of literary terms located at the end of the anthology. The idea of convention, though, has additional conceptual importance relating to the way texts are built to be read. While a domestic cat is simply born with retractable claws and a taste for mice, a literary text is constructed, written in a particular way, often with the aim of eliciting a particular response from a reader. The word convention, in this sense, harks back to the legal concept of agreement, so that when writers make use of conventions associated with a genre, they set up a kind of contract with the reader whereby the reader has a sense of what to expect from the text. For example: when the first five minutes of a film include a long shot of the Pentagon, along with a few quickly edited shots of grim-looking military personnel moving quickly through underground hallways, and perhaps a shot of someone in a dark suit yelling into a cellphone, "Operation Silvestris has been aborted!" the audience understands that they are in for some sort of political thriller. They need not know anything about the details of Operation Silvestris to make this interpretive leap, as the presence of a few conventions of the political thriller (the shot of the Pentagon, the phrase "Operation [blank] has been aborted!") are enough to provide the general outline of a contract entered into between film and audience. Likewise, recognizing that a poem has 14 lines and makes use of a rhyming couplet at the end will provide knowledgeable readers of literature with an inkling as to what they should expect, as these readers will be familiar with the structural conventions of the Shakespearean sonnet.

Whereas a legal contract is a fairly straightforward affair—it outlines the terms of agreement for both sides and more or less explicitly refers to the penalties for undermining those terms—the contract between text and reader is multifaceted. One of the most fascinating things about the way writers make use of literary convention is that the terms of agreement are constantly subject to further consideration, thoughtful challenge, or outright derision. Thus, when the speaker of Shakespeare's sonnet 130 refers to his lady's "dun" breasts and "reek[ing]" breath, the point is not to insult his mistress, or even to admire her in a new, more realistic way; rather, the point is to ridicule the way other poets slavishly adhere to the convention that sonnets glorify a woman's beauty, comparing her eyes to the sun and her breath to the smell of roses. This reading is available for the reader who knows that by the time Shakespeare decided to try his hand at the genre, translations and imitations of the Petrarchan sonnet had been circulating at the Elizabethan court for many decades. Like organisms, or even laws, conventions of literature evolve over time as writers seek to rethink the rules of the form they wish to explore. In the prologue to her recent collection *XEclogue*, Lisa Robertson declares, "I needed a genre to gloss my ancestress' complicity with a socially expedient code"; she explains how, in turning to the conventions of the eclogue—a collection of pastoral poems, often satiric—she has found a suitable formal framework for her exploration of the way social insiders and outsiders are marked by class and gender.

Is it somehow problematic to inquire too tenaciously into the working parts of a literary text? Does one risk undermining the emotional force of a poem, the sharp wit of a play, or the exciting plot of an adventure tale if one pays too much attention to seemingly mundane issues of plot structure or metre? To paraphrase a common grievance of the distressed student: by examining the way literature works, are we, somehow, just wrecking it? These questions might, paradoxically, recall Dirac's complaint that literature makes simple things incomprehensible: while we know that literature can manage to communicate difficult notions, making what is mysterious more comprehensible, it is often difficult to articulate or make a viable argument about how it does so. By paying attention to the way a text is built and to the way an author constructs his or her end of the contract, the reader can begin to understand and respond explicitly to the question of how literature produces its particular effects.

Consider the following two textual excerpts:

> Come live with me and be my love,
> And we shall all the pleasures prove.
> (Christopher Marlowe, 1590)

> Boom, boom, boom, let's go back to my room,
> And we can do it all night, and I can make you feel right.
> (Paul Lekakis, 1987)

Based on a quick reading: which excerpt is more appropriate for inclusion in a Valentine's Day card? A poll of employees at Hallmark, not to mention the millions of folks invested in the idea that Valentine's Day is a celebration of romance, would likely make an overwhelming case for the Marlowe excerpt. But why? Answering that question might involve a methodological inquiry into how each excerpt produces a particular response, one which might be broken down into five stages:

Level One: Evaluation—Do I like this text? What is my gut reaction to it?
No doubt, most students of literature have heard an instructor proclaim, with
more or less vitriol, "It doesn't matter if you like the poem/story/play! This
is a literature class, not a book club!" And, while it is true that the evaluative
response does not constitute an adequate final critical response to a text, it's
important to acknowledge one's first reaction. After all, the point of literature
is to produce an effect, sometimes an extreme response. When a text seems
confusing, or hilarious, or provocative, or thrilling, it prompts questions: How
are such effects produced using mere words in particular combinations? Why
would an author want to generate feelings of confusion, hilarity, provocation,
etc.? How am I—the reader—being positioned on the other end of such effects?

Level Two: Interpretation—What is the text about? This is a trickier level
of reading than it might seem. Students sometimes think, mistakenly, that
all literature—and especially poetry—is "open to interpretation," and that
all interpretations are therefore correct. This line of thinking leads to snap,
top-down interpretations, in which the general "mood" of the text is felt
at a gut level (see above), and the ensuing reading of the poem is wrangled
into shape to match that feeling. It is sometimes helpful to think about interpretation as a kind of translation, as in the way those who work at the
United Nations translating talking points from Arabic to Russian are called
"interpreters." Though no translation is flawless, the goal of simultaneous
translation is to get as close as possible to the meaning of the original. Thus,
an interpretation should be thought of as a carefully paraphrased summary
or, for particularly dense works, a line by line explication of the literary text,
both of which may require several rereadings and some meticulous use of
a dictionary. As with reading for evaluation, reading for interpretation can
help generate useful critical questions, such as: How does the way this text
is written affect my attitude toward the subject matter? What is the point of
all the fancy language, which makes this text more or less difficult to interpret? Now that I've figured out what this text is about—at least in terms of
its subject matter—can I begin to determine what sorts of themes are being
tackled?

A note about the distinction between subject matter and **theme**: while
these terms are sometimes used interchangeably, the notion of theme differs
from subject matter in that it implies an idea about or attitude toward the
subject matter. A good rule of thumb to remember is that theme can never be
summed up in just one word (so, there is no such thing as the theme of "Love"
or "Family" or "Women"). Whereas the subject matter of Shakespeare's sonnet
"Shall I compare thee to a summer's day" is admiration or the nature of beauty,

one theme of the poem, arguably, is that the beloved's good qualities are best made apparent in poetry, and that art is superior to nature. Another theme of the poem, arguably, is that the admiration of youth is best accomplished by someone older. Thus, identifying a text's subject matter via interpretation aims to pinpoint a general topic, while the process of contemplating a text's theme is open to elaboration and argumentation.

Level Three: Description—What does the text look like, at least at first glance? Can you give a quick account of its basic formal features? At this level of reading, one starts to think about how a text is built, especially in terms of basic generic features. For example, are we dealing with poetry? Short fiction? Drama? If poetry, can we identify a sub-genre the text fits into—for instance, the sonnet, the ode, or the elegy—and can we begin to assess whether the author is following or challenging conventions associated with that genre? Of course, answering these questions requires prior knowledge of what, for example, a conventional ode is supposed to look like, which is why the student of literature must have a thorough understanding of the specific terminology associated with the discipline. At this level of reading, one might also begin to think about and do some preliminary research on when and where the text was written, so that the issues of literary history and cultural context are broached; likewise, one might begin to think about who is writing the poem, as the matter of the author's societal position might prove a fruitful avenue for further investigation. Thus, a consequent objective at this level of reading is to map the terrain of inquiry, establishing some general facts about the text as building blocks that underpin critical analysis.

Level Four: Analysis—How are particular formal features working, especially as they interact with content? The word analysis comes from the Greek terms ἀνά- (ana-), meaning "throughout," and λύειν (lysis), meaning "to loose." Thus, the procedure for analysis involves taking a text and shaking it apart in order to see more clearly all its particular bits and pieces. This level of reading is akin to putting a text under a microscope. First, one has to identify individual formal features of the text. Then one needs to consider how all the parts fit together. It is at this level that one's knowledge of generic conventions and particular literary techniques—the way figurative language works, the ways in which rhythm and rhyme affect our response to language, the way plotting and point of view can be handled, and so on—is crucial. It may be the case that not everything one notices will find its way into an essay. But the goal at this level of reading should be to notice as much as possible (and it is usually when working at this level that an instructor will be accused of "reading too much into a text," as if that image of a moth beating its wings against a window means nothing more than that the moth is trapped, and that it just happens to have been included in a work). Careful analysis shows that nothing in a text "just happens" to be there. A text is constructed out of special uses of language that beg to be "read into." Reading at this level takes time and a certain amount of expertise so as to tease out how the work is built and begin to understand the connections between form and content.

Level Five: Critical Analysis—How do the formal elements of a literary work connect with what the work has to say to the reader? It is at this level of reading that one begins to make an argument, to develop a thesis. In order to construct a viable thesis, one needs to answer a question, perhaps one of the questions that arose at an earlier level of reading. For example, why does this poem, which seems on the surface to be about love, make use of so many images that have to do with science? What is up with this narrator, who seems to be addressing another character without in any way identifying who he is speaking to? What is significant about the fact that the climax of this play hangs on the matter of whether a guy is willing to sell a portrait? It is at this level of reading, rather than at the level of interpretation, that the literary critic is able to flex his or her creative muscles, as a text poses any number of viable questions and suggests any number of viable arguments. Note, however, that the key word here is "viable." In order to make an argument—in order to convincingly answer a question posed—one must have the textual evidence to make the case, evidence that has been gleaned through careful, meticulous, and thoughtful reading.

Returning now to the two texts, let's see if we can come up with one viable argument as to why Marlowe's text seems more likely to show up in a Valentine's Day card, going through each level of reading to build the foundation—the case—for making that argument.

Level One: Evaluation. At first glance, the Marlowe text just seems more romantic than the Lekakis text: it uses flowery words and has a nice flow to it, while the phrase "do it all night" is kind of blunt and unromantic. On a gut level, one might feel that a Valentine's Day card should avoid such blunt language (although this gut reaction might suggest a first useful research question: why should romance be associated with flowery language rather than blunt expressions?).

Moving on to **Level Two: Interpretation.** Well, the Lekakis text is certainly the more straightforward one when it comes to interpretation, though one has to know that the phrase "do it" refers to having sex as opposed to some other activity (and it is interesting to note that even in the more straightforward text, the author has used a common euphemism). The phrase "Boom boom boom" seems to be untranslatable, which begs the question of why the author used it. Is the phrase still meaningful, even if it's just a series of sounds?

As for the Marlowe text, a careful paraphrase would go something like this: "Move in with me and be my lover, and we can enjoy all kinds of pleasures together." Hmmm—wait a minute: what does the author mean by "pleasures"? Eating good food? Playing card games? Though the word is arguably vague, the references in the first line to moving in together and love make it pretty clear that "pleasures" is another euphemism for having sex (though perhaps a more elegant one than "doing it").

If both texts can be interpreted similarly—both are the words of a would-be lover trying to convince the object of his/her affection to have sex—why does it matter which phrase ends up in a Valentine's Day card? What are the significant differences between each text that cause them to generate distinct gut responses?

Level Three: Description. The Marlowe text, at least this piece of it, is a **couplet**, written in iambic **tetrameter** (or eight syllables in each line that follow the rhythmic pattern of unstressed/stressed). The language is flowery, or, to use a slightly more technical phrase, the **diction** is elevated, which means that this is not the way people normally talk in everyday life. In fact, there seems to have been a lot of attention paid to making the words sound pleasing to the ear, through patterns of rhythm and rhyme, and also through patterns of alliteration in the consonants (of the soft "l" sound in the first line, and then of powerful plosives at the end of the second).

The Lekakis text also makes use of rhyme, but in a different way: each line includes an **internal rhyme**, so that "boom" rhymes with "room" and "night" rhymes with "right." The rhythmic pattern is harder to make sense of, as there are a different number of syllables in each line and a lot of short, sharp words that undermine a sing-song effect. The sound effects of the text are comparatively harsher than in the Marlowe text, with many "b" and "k" and "t" sounds.

The Marlowe text was written in the 1590s, while the Lekakis text is a popular dance song from the 1980s; it might be interesting to follow up on the distinct cultural contexts out of which each work emerges. It might also be interesting to examine how each text thematizes the subject of having sex: whereas the Marlowe text seems to promote the attitude that the "pleasures" of sex should be tried out (to "prove" in sixteenth-century English meant to test or to try out) within the context of "living with" someone, or that love and sex go hand-in-hand, the Lekakis text seems to suggest that even sex on one "night" in someone's "room" can make one feel "right." Or, good sex has nothing at all to do with love.

Because these texts are so short and are fairly simple, much of the work of **Level Four: Analysis** has already been touched on. A closer inspection of the use of rhyme and **alliteration** in the Marlowe text demonstrates the way the poem insists on the idea that love can be "proved" by sex, while the internal rhyming of the words "me," "be," and "we" further indicates a strong emphasis on how the joining of two people represents a significant change. The use of elevated diction is consistent, suggesting that discussions of love and sex are worthy of serious consideration.

As for the Lekakis text, a major point to analyze is the phrase "boom boom boom." Is this **onomatopoeia**? If so, what "sense" is the sound trying to express? The sound of sex? If so, what kind of sex are we talking about here? Or is it the sound of something else, perhaps dancing (as is suggested by the cultural context of which the text emerges)? Maybe the phrase is simply meant to express excitement? What do we make of the plain speech the text employs? Does the use of such diction debase notions of sex, or is it simply more candid about the way sex and love might be separated?

As you can see, the level of **Critical Analysis**, or argument, is quickly and organically developing. If the research question one decides on is, What is interesting about the distinct way each text thematizes the relationship between love and sex?, a viable argument, based on evidence gleaned from close reading, might be: "Whereas Marlowe's text suggests that the pleasures of sex are best discovered within the context of a stable, long-term relationship, the text by Lekakis asserts that sex can be enjoyed in and of itself, undermining the importance of the long-term relationship." One might take this argument further. Why is what you have noted significant or particularly interesting? A possible answer to that question—and an even more sophisticated thesis—might be: "Thus, while the Lekakis text is, on the surface, less romantic, its attitude toward sex is much less confining than the attitude presented in Marlowe's text." Or, one might pursue an entirely different argument: "Whereas Marlowe's text indicates that sex is to be enjoyed mutually by two people, the Lekakis text implies that sex is something one 'does' to another person. Further, it implies that sex is a fairly meaningless and potentially aggressive activity."

The above description of the steps taken toward critical analysis shows how students of literature are meant to approach the works they read. What the description does not convey is why one would bother to make the effort at all, or why the process of critical literary analysis is thought to be a meaningful activity. In order to answer that question, it is helpful to consider how the discipline of literary studies came to be considered a worthwhile course of study for university and college students.

The history of literary studies is both very old and, in terms of the study of English literature, very fresh. In the fifth century, Martianus Capella wrote the allegory *De nuptiis Philologiae et Mercurii* ("The Marriage of Philology and Mercury"), in which he described the seven pillars of learning: grammar, dialectic, rhetoric, geometry, arithmetic, astronomy, and musical harmony. Collectively, such subjects came to be referred to as the liberal arts; as such, they were taken up by many of the high medieval universities as constituting the core curriculum. During the Early Modern period, the study of the so-called *trivium* (grammar, dialectic, rhetoric) was transformed to include the critical analysis of classical texts, i.e., the study of literature. As universities throughout Europe, and later in North America, proliferated and flourished between the sixteenth and nineteenth centuries, the focus remained on classical texts. As Gerald Graff explains, "In theory, the study of Greek and Latin was supposed to inspire the student with the nobility of his cultural heritage." (Somewhat paradoxically, classical texts were studied primarily in terms of their language use as opposed to their literary quality, perhaps because no one read or spoke Greek or Latin outside the classroom.) Until the late nineteenth century, the university system did not consider literary works written in English (or French or German or Italian) to be worthy of rigorous study, but only of *appreciation*. As Terry Eagleton notes in *Literary Theory: An Introduction*, the reading of works of English Literature was thought best left to working-class men, who might attend book clubs or public lectures, and to women; it was "a convenient sort of non-subject to palm off on the ladies, who were in any case excluded from science and the professions." It was only in the early twentieth century—hundreds of years after the founding of the great European universities—that literature came to be taken seriously as a university or college subject.

Over the past century and more, the discipline of literary studies has undergone a number of shifts. In the very early twentieth century, literature was studied largely for the way in which it embodied cultural tradition; one would learn something about being American or British by reading so-called great works of literature. (As British subjects, Canadians were also taught what it was to be a part of the British tradition.) By mid-century the focus had shifted to the aesthetic properties of the work itself. This fresh approach was known as Formalism and/or the New Criticism. Its proponents advocated paying close attention to literary form—in some cases, for an almost scientific approach to close reading. They tended to de-emphasize authorial biography and literary history. The influence of this approach continues to be felt in university and college classrooms (giving rise to such things as, for example, courses organized around the concept of literary genre). But it is important to keep in mind here that the emphasis on form—on generic conventions, on literary terminology, on the aesthetic as opposed to the cultural, philosophical, or moral qualities of literature—is not the only way to approach the study of literature, but was, rather, institutionalized as the best, most scholarly way. The work of close reading and producing literary criticism is not in any way "natural," but is how the study of literature has been "disciplined"; thus the student in a literature classroom should not feel discouraged if the initial steps of learning what it is he or she is supposed to be doing are challenging or seem strange.

The most recent important shift to have occurred in the "disciplining" of literary studies was the rise in the 1960s and 1970s of what became known as "literary theory." There is not room enough here to adequately elucidate the range of theories that have been introduced into literary studies, but a crude comparison between how emerging methods were set in opposition to New Criticism (which is itself a type of literary theory) may be useful. John Crowe Ransom's *The World's Body*—a sort of manifesto for New Criticism—argues that the work of the literary critic must strenuously avoid, among other things, "Any other special studies which deal with some abstract or prose content taken out of the work … [such as] Chaucer's command of medieval sciences … [or] Shakespeare's understanding of the law." In other words, the New Critic should focus solely on the text itself. In contrast, those today who make use of such theoretical frameworks as New Historicism, Gender Studies, or Postcolonial Studies will strenuously *embrace* all manner of "special studies" in order to consider how the text interacts with context. As Graff puts it, "Theory is what is generated when some aspect of literature, its nature, its history, its place in society, its conditions for production and reception, its meaning in general … ceases to be a given and becomes a question to be argued." What this means for the student of literature trying to work out what to do with a text is that the question "Why is what I have noticed in the text significant?" can be approached from an almost limitless set of knowledge contexts. How might a particular poem illuminate historical notions of class divisions? How might a particular play tell us something about how technological advances have changed the way humans think about identity? And, though it might seem that the focus on form that so defines the New Critical approach becomes irrelevant once Literary Theory arrives on the disciplinary scene, the fact is that most field practitioners (i.e., writers of literary criticism) still depend heavily on the tools of close reading; formal analysis becomes the foundation on which a more theoretical analysis is built.

Thus, we might consider a sixth level of reading: advanced critical analysis. At this level the stakes are raised as arguments about why a text's formal construction is meaningful are set within a larger conceptual framework. The work of advanced critical analysis requires that the literary critic think about and research whatever conceptual framework is being pursued. For example, after noticing that the Marlowe text and the Lekakis text are written about 400 years apart, one might further research cultural attitudes toward sex in the two time periods to come up with another, even more sophisticated, layer of argumentation, one which would not only provide insight into two literary texts, but show how the comparative analysis of such texts tells us something about how viewpoints on sex have shifted. Or, after noticing that both texts are written by male authors, one might further research and consider what they reveal about masculine approaches to sex and seduction. Or, after discovering that Marlowe's poem follows the conventions of **pastoral** poetry, or that "Boom boom boom (let's go back to my room)" became popular within the LGBT community, one might contemplate and develop an argument about the implications of the way sex is idealized and/or becomes part of a complex cultural fantasy. Or, after discovering that Marlowe presented homoerotic material frequently in his other writing (in his poem "Hero and Leander," for example, he writes of one of the male protagonists that "in his looks were all that men desire"), one might inquire into the ways in which the author's or narrator's sexual orientation may or may not be relevant to a discussion of a love poem. To put it bluntly (and anachronistically), does it matter if Marlowe was gay?

Because the reading of literature entails a painstaking, thoughtful interaction with some of the most multifaceted, evocative, and provocative uses of language humans have produced, thinking about such work critically may tell us something about what it means to be human.

[N.G.]

Short Fiction

History

The literary genre we call short fiction is perhaps the purest incarnation of the basic human impulse to tell stories. And writing that loosely resembles this genre has been produced literally for millennia. Egyptian papyri dating before Christian times make reference to the sons of Cheops telling tales to their father; and the Bible itself offers all kinds of stories—stories such as that of Jonah and the whale or Daniel in the lions' den. Petronius, a Roman courtier during the reign of Nero (54–68), is believed to have written the *Satyricon*, which contains a series of satirical sketches that aren't too far from what we now think of as short fiction. In the medieval period Chaucer's *Canterbury Tales* and Boccaccio's *Decameron* appeared, each of which bring together a wide range of short tales within a longer work. In the 1700s the informal essays of Addison and Steele became popular; many of these contain short sketches describing individuals and their deeds and misdeeds. All of these are what we'd call precursors or antecedents to the short story—stories, sometimes oral and sometimes written, sometimes in verse and sometimes in prose, that narrate events to listeners or readers.

Yet the short story—as a genre of prose fiction that authors have been conscious of producing and trying to understand—has a much shorter history. It came into being quite rapidly in the nineteenth century, in both America and Europe, with writers such as Washington Irving, Nathaniel Hawthorne, and Edgar Allan Poe (in America), and Honoré de Balzac, Anton Chekhov, and E.T.A. Hoffman (in Europe). Why would this change have occurred so suddenly in both America and Europe? For one thing, more and more people were learning to read, and were reading for pleasure; not surprisingly, easily accessible and affordable forms of writing, such as newspapers and magazines, rose to meet this new reading public's hunger. The short story was ideally suited to these venues: it's compact, discrete, and entertaining. This history reflects the fact that short fiction is a dynamic literary form, one that quickly echoes social and cultural change.

The flexibility of short fiction may also explain why this genre has, from its earliest years, accommodated so many literary styles and forms of experimentation. In the early 1800s Hoffman used it as a means of giving expression to surrealism—a movement that sought to give priority to the unconscious mind, with its myriad images and seemingly nonsensical connections. The modernists Virginia Woolf and Katherine Mansfield both used short fiction as a venue for the close study of the many levels of perception—conscious, unconscious, sensual, emotional—in a style of writing that sought to capture the full "stream" of human consciousness, as the philosopher William James put it (see "The Garden Party" and "Kew Gardens" for examples of this form of writing). The French writer Guy de Maupassant used short fiction to give expression to naturalism, a style of writing most famously associated with Émile Zola and based on a belief that the human being is an animal like any other, governed by physiological impulses and environmental stimuli (see "The False Gems," for example). Another form of literary expression that has deep roots in short fiction is regionalism, a kind of writing that focuses on the particular characteristics of a place and the human culture it helps to form. Some of the best-loved examples of literary regionalism are short stories; William Faulkner's "A Rose for Emily" and Alistair MacLeod's "As Birds Bring Forth the Sun" are two excellent examples. Authors have also used this genre to think through and ask us to imagine worlds other than our own—a kind of writing broadly termed speculative fiction. We include two examples here: Ursula Le Guin's "The Ones Who Walk Away from Omelas" takes us into a seemingly utopian world that we discover has something horrific at its core, and in "Terminal Avenue," Eden Robinson presents us with a more contemporary postcolonial dystopia in which the trope of "the dying Indian" is brought to life in a nightmarish future world. Both works are chilling, and while neither actually represents the world as it is, both inferentially offer critiques of contemporary society. These are just five of the many styles and kinds of literary endeavour that short fiction has accommodated.

Short Fiction: Some Defining Characteristics

You'd think that, if we're able to identify the many roots of short fiction, point out its earliest examples and discuss its stylistic variability, it would be a snap to define the short story. But this isn't the case. No one has ever fixed on a tidy definition of short fiction (or the novel), and this is largely because of the genre's diversity. The only characteristics a piece of writing *must* have to be classified as short fiction are the two captured in its name: it must be relatively *short*, and it must be *fiction*.

How short is short? There is no rule for this, but there is a great rule of thumb, one that Poe introduced in his review of Hawthorne's *Twice-Told Tales* in the genre's early days: one of the quintessential features of short fiction is that readers can consume it in a single sitting; if we can't read a story all at once (barring breaks to answer the telephone or make a cup of tea), then it isn't really a short story: it's moving toward the novella or, more typically, the novel. The longest story we've included here is Jhumpa Lahiri's "Interpreter of Maladies," at about 10,000 words. At the other extreme we've included two very short works, known as microfictions: John Gould's "What You're Ready For" and James Kelman's "Acid," both under 200 words.

The brevity of short fiction also helps to explain what many—including Poe—see as another crucial characteristic of a successful short story: it should possess a certain singularity of purpose. Poe thought that a proper short story should be crafted from its first sentence to create a very specific effect on the reader. As he put it back in 1842,

> A skilful literary artist has constructed a tale. If wise, he has not fashioned his thoughts to accommodate his incidents; but having conceived, with deliberate care, a certain unique or single effect to be wrought out, he then invents such incidents—he then combines such events as may best aid him in establishing this preconceived effect. If his very initial sentence tend [sic] not to the out-bringing of this effect, then he has failed in his first step. In the whole composition there should be no word written, of which the tendency, direct or indirect, is not to the one pre-established design.

These days few would claim that *all* short story writers begin with an effect they want to create and then choose characters, events, and language to bring it about. And we're certainly less preoccupied with an author's intentions these days than people were back in Poe's time (critics now being more likely to think of a text as a thing with a life of its own that extends beyond the author's thoughts about it). But there is something in Poe's statement that remains as true today as it was then: good short stories tend to have a certain singularity of focus. While a novel can develop many characters and many plot lines, the brevity of the short story encourages a much tidier approach. To give just one example, many short stories focus on the development of a single human relationship over time; in this collection, Edith Wharton's "Atrophy," Raymond Carver's "Cathedral," William Trevor's "Folie à Deux," Emma Donoghue's "Seven Pictures Not Taken," Jhumpa Lahiri's "Interpreter of Maladies," and Madeleine Thien's "Simple Recipes" all have a relationship at their centre. Sometimes stories seem to be exploring a certain state of mind or belief system: this is one way we might describe James Joyce's "Araby," Lydia Millet's "Love in Infant Monkeys," Ursula Le Guin's "The Ones Who Walk Away from Omelas," or Chinua Achebe's "Dead Men's Path."

It's always an act of critical judgment to say "this story is about x," because there is virtually always more than one way to articulate the focus of a short story. Efforts to pinpoint a story's focus are really attempts to pinpoint a central theme in a work, a **theme** being a concept that is explored through characters, events, and images. In order to be fully developed, however, a theme must go beyond naming the concept (e.g., "love") and assert what the work is saying about it (e.g., "love hurts"). Though some themes are more central than others, it's important to note that no work of literature has just one. To illustrate this, let's take another look at two of the stories discussed above. While many might argue that the haunting nature of early relationships is central to "Folie à Deux," others might well prioritize themes relating to guilt, isolation, or the connections between human and non-human animals; all four concepts are being explored through event, character, and image. Similarly, while Raymond Carver certainly explores the dynamic nature of human relationships in the way he relates the three characters in "Cathedral," he's also using characters, events, and images to ask us to think about jealousy, disability, communication, and prejudice, for instance. In sum, though short stories often gain some of their elegance through a singularity of focus, the business of articulating this focus very quickly moves us from description to thematic analysis.

We've now considered some of the ways the "short" of "short fiction" gives this genre certain distinctive characteristics. The "fiction" element of "short fiction" clearly isn't as important in trying to understand the distinctive features of this genre—novels are fiction, too. But the fictional element is at least as important in helping us understand how short stories create meaning and inspire responses in readers. A key element in almost all prose **fiction**, whether we're dealing with a novel or a short story, is that it tells a story, and an invented one at that. For many years fictional narratives were defined in opposition to non-fictional narratives: while fiction tells us made-up stories, the theory went, non-fiction is based on real historical events. Over the last few decades, literary critics and historians alike have become more aware of how much is shared by fictional and non-fictional narratives: for example, both fictional and non-fictional narratives rely on the author's imagination to select, arrange, and prioritize events and the "characters" who enact them in very particular ways. In other words, there is much invention at play in all narratives, whether based on real or made-up events. This doesn't mean that they're identical; rather, it suggests that all writing uses imagination, but that some, such as fiction, utilizes more than others, such as non-fiction. Let us now turn to thinking in more detail about how authors utilize imagination to shape event into story.

Making Short Stories:
The Selection and Manipulation of Events

Most of us have probably encountered friends who aren't particularly good storytellers; maybe they leave out necessary details or, conversely, they might ramble on at such length, and give us so much detail, that we lose interest in the story. Writers of short stories need many of the same skills shared by good oral storytellers. They need to be particularly adept at two things: selecting the events to include and ordering these events in a way that sparks and sustains a reader's interest.

Over the years authors and scholars have developed a number of terms and distinctions to name the ways writers organize narratives. For example, novelist E.M. Forster came up with the useful distinction between **story** and **plot** to help us think about the use of time in organizing narrative information: while a story is the chronological unfolding of the events that compose a narrative, the plot is the result of an author's manipulation of these events. Thus we say that the events of a narrative are *plotted*. Sometimes the plot follows the chronological order of the story. This is the case in Katherine Mansfield's "The Garden Party": we follow the day's happenings as they unfold, beginning with breakfast and preparations for the party, proceeding to the party itself (which gets quite brief treatment, interestingly), and ending with Laura's evening trip to the grieving widow (notice how wonderfully the fading of day coincides with the darkening of mood here). In contrast, Madeleine Thien's "Simple Recipes" veers dramatically from chronological ordering: our narrator moves us repeatedly between her present position as an adult and her memories of childhood events. Such plotting almost always has the effect of controlling and emphasizing causality—of using the past to in some way *explain* the present. Such causation can be established very suddenly, to great dramatic effect. This is the case in Thien's story, where it isn't until the final paragraphs that we learn of the father's present state, and the state of the narrator's feelings for him; these final bits of narrative information enable a sudden realization that these two people are as they are because of the past we've just been told about: these past events have had profound consequences for both of them.

Another effect that can be created by manipulating the order in which we receive information is **suspense**, our anticipation of an outcome of events. Think of how Flannery O'Connor's "A Good Man Is Hard to Find" pulls readers along by first presenting The Misfit as a notorious figure in the newspaper—hardly more than an idea, really—and slowly but surely propelling him into the lives of the Grandmother and her family. As is often the case, ambiguity is a key ingredient in the creation of suspense here: it's our uncertainty, first about the identity of the stranger—*is* he The Misfit? No, surely not—and then about the nature of this man's character—just how good or bad a man is he? Would he do that? No, surely not—that propels us forward in anticipation that answers will be given.

A field of literary criticism called narratology has developed a number of useful terms for naming particular ways that authors organize and present the events in a narrative. **Analepsis**, for example, is a shift backward in time (a technique also known as a flashback) and is routinely used by short story writers to create history for characters and events. Emma Donoghue makes very artful use of analepsis in "Seven Pictures Not Taken," a story in which our narrator very purposefully selects out seven moments, via specific images, over the course of a relationship. The story is composed entirely of instances of analepsis, in other words. What we learn of our narrator we learn through her selection and description of the images and through her decision to imagine her past in this way (what can we infer about a character who chooses to imagine the past as a series of separate photographs, Donoghue seems to be asking us). **Prolepsis**—a sudden movement ahead to future time, also known as flashforward—is used less frequently in short fiction. We see an interesting example of it in Eden Robinson's "Terminal Avenue": as the narrator describes the family's last potlatch on Monkey Beach, this voice states, "This will happen in four hours when they land." In this seemingly simple statement we in fact see analepsis and prolepsis combined—we're being given a flashforward within a memory. Here Robinson provides a great illustration of the paradox that, while it's sometimes complex to clearly express how time is manipulated in narratives, such shifts in time are a simple facet of life: the human mind is wonderfully adept at roving back and forth through time, putting events together for itself.

Sometimes authors choose to embed one story within another, thus creating what is called an **embedded narrative**: a story within a story. Rohinton Mistry's "Squatter" is an embedded narrative: what we encounter in the story is an unidentified narrator telling us the story of Nariman Hansotia, who is himself telling various stories, but centrally the story of the migrant Sarosh, to the boys of Firozsha Baag (an apartment complex in Mumbai). As this description illustrates, embedded narratives are more structurally complex, and this complexity can create certain effects. For example, embedding one narrative within another inevitably makes storytelling itself a theme worth thinking about. Embedding one narrative within another can also reveal information about character: in "Squatter," for instance, we might well ask ourselves why the narrator didn't just take over the telling of Sarosh's stories for himself: why give Nariman such pride of place? If you were to read the full collection from which "Squatter" is taken—*Tales from Firozsha Baag*—you would learn that our narrator is in fact a man named Kersi, who was once one of the boys whom Nariman Hansotia delighted with his tales. Thus the fact that Kersi, our narrator, chooses to weave Nariman's storytelling so closely within his own might suggest, for example, his desire to honour his mentor, thereby giving to a story that uses comedy to advance a biting critique about the effects of racism a gentle emotional richness.

Freytag's Pyramid

Another tool that can enhance our ability to stand back from a story and analyze how authors manipulate narrative information to create plot is **Freytag's Pyramid**. Devised in the late nineteenth century by the German novelist and playwright Gustav Freytag to aid in the analysis of the classical, five-act plays from ancient Greece and Renaissance England, Freytag's Pyramid is today just as commonly used as a reference point in discussing short fiction. In examining these plays Freytag noticed that there was a clear pattern discernible in the way playwrights from these two eras arranged narrative events. The five stages he named correspond to the five acts in many classical plays. Not all short stories—or for that matter, plays—include the five parts and, even when they do, they're sometimes not so tidily or discretely arranged as they used to be. However, Freytag's Pyramid is useful precisely because it gives us a model to apply: whether a short story conforms to the five stages or not, examining its structure against this standard allows us to gain some critical distance from the plotting of events: we can begin to step back from the work and see the choices that have gone into crafting the story.

The five stages Freytag identified were, first, **exposition**, in which some context is established and the conflict that will be examined and resolved in some way over the course of the work is introduced. Second comes the **rising action** in which both the conflict and the central characters are more thoroughly developed; third is the **climax**, which can be understood a couple of ways: it can be the moment of highest drama or tension in a work or, slightly differently, the moment that marks a turning point in the protagonist's life. Fourth comes what Freytag called the **falling action**, where the outcome between protagonist and antagonist is resolved; this often involves a moment of tension during which the protagonist is again tested or altered, though not so dramatically as in the climax. Finally, the fifth element is the **dénouement**, wherein events are concluded.

Stories conform to the expectations of Freytag's Pyramid to differing degrees. An example of a short story that conforms quite nicely to this model is Chekhov's "An Upheaval": as the story begins, we are given some basic information about the protagonist, Mashenka, and introduced to the conflict she will grapple with over the course of the story: a governess in the household, she has had her honour undermined by being included among a list of suspects in the disappearance of a brooch belonging to the mistress of the house. The rising action comes about as Mashenka gradually grasps the extent of the insult she has suffered. Some might locate the climax in that moment during dinner when Mashenka, feeling that all are looking at her accusingly, breaks into tears and exits the dining room awkwardly—a moment of dramatic tension, certainly. But if we think of the climax as the point marking a decisive shift in the protagonist, we might instead isolate the moment when Mashenka determines that, regardless of practical concerns, she must leave the household: an element of her character that was in flux seems to solidify at this moment. The falling action—which, again, should resolve the central conflict—seems quite clearly marked by the master's appearance in Mashenka's room because it is here that she is affirmed as unjustly accused and her accuser is critiqued as unjustly accusing. And indeed, in classic manner, Chekhov includes a final moment of tension here as the master of the house begs Mashenka to stay and attempts to forge a stronger bond with her; while this flattery might be a temptation to some, it hastens Mashenka's departure from the house, thus bringing about the story's dénouement.

It is only in rare cases that all readers would agree on exactly how to apply the stages of Freytag's Pyramid to a story; and indeed, there are certainly cases in which we could argue convincingly that stories lack some of the elements. For example, stories that conclude with a shocking sudden event—known as an "O. Henry" or a "surprise ending"—such as Faulkner's "A Rose for Emily" and Kate Chopin's "The Story of an Hour," could be said to lack both falling action and dénouement: the narrative simply ends with the disclosure of a climactic revelation or event. Alternatively, we might interpret the sudden mention of the odour of decay in "A Rose for Emily" as the climax, which would make the powerful final image we are left with both falling action and dénouement. Similarly, we might argue that "The Story of an Hour" reaches its climax not with the surprising arrival, but with that moment of resolution within the mind of the wife, when she recognizes and embraces her freedom. Thus the point of Freytag's Pyramid is not so much to label the parts of a story as it is to enable us to stand back and recognize that there are discernible stages in the plotting of events, the development of character, and the distribution of narrative tension.

Character and Characterization

There is perhaps no feature of storytelling that more powerfully draws us into a narrative than character: the simple fact is that we human beings find each other (and ourselves) endlessly interesting. Fiction, whether of the long or short variety, gives us an opportunity to indulge and indeed examine this interest. The development of literary characters is quite sensibly termed **characterization**. And for all the power that characters have to pull us out of ourselves, to pull us into stories, and to make us care about the figments of someone else's imagination, they are constructed with surprisingly few tools. Characters are developed in three basic ways: through narrative description (which can include suggestive physical description as well as direct statements about character), through actions (including dialogue) that implicitly suggest traits, and by giving us access to characters' feelings and thought processes.

The basic vocabulary surrounding character is quite simple: characters are said to be **round** when they have enough complexity to give them a three-dimensional likeness to human beings; characters are said to be **flat** when they lack such complexity. It's important to bear in mind that these aren't evaluative terms: flat characters are not inferior to or less useful than round characters; rather, these character types serve different purposes. The characters in fables, for example, are *necessarily* flat because it is their task to stand in for or symbolize things. Had Aesop given his tortoise complexity, the additional traits would only have lessened his capacity both to oppose the hare and stand in for the benefits of slow and steady work. And it isn't just fables that require flat characters to achieve their ends: many short stories require them as well: think of Thomas King's "A Short History of Indians in Canada" and Le Guin's "The Ones Who Walk Away from Omelas": as in Aesop's fable, the flat characters in these stories do the work of standing in for certain social categories. Giving them idiosyncratic characteristics would only detract from their ability to do this work.

One other distinction commonly used to categorize characters is stasis versus dynamism. While **static characters** (whether round or flat) remain essentially unchanged over the course of a work, **dynamic characters** undergo some kind of development, either experiencing a shift in character or revealing new dimensions of their character as the narrative unfolds (it's not always easy to distinguish between these two processes). Static characters can be round or flat: for instance, Flora from Alice Munro's "Friend of My Youth" seems to be a round character since she reveals a number of interesting traits (we might think of cheerfulness, adaptability, competence, fierce independence, a seemingly forgiving nature, patience, and industriousness). And you might say it's the very consistency of these traits in the face of such a remarkable series of life events that makes Flora so compelling a character: we keep waiting for the emotional calculus to complete itself, for some hint of bitterness or anger to exhibit itself—for her to, effectively, become a dynamic character. But does she? In fact, as the story proceeds, Flora's status as a character comes to the fore as the narrator offers different ways Flora's actions might be interpreted and contemplates the varying motivations we might have for "reading" her one way or another.

Setting

Because the events in stories have to occur somewhere, it is inevitable that all fiction has a setting or, more often than not, settings. While this is also the case with drama, it's not with poetry: for example, a lyric can articulate ideas and feelings without specifying a locale. Fiction writers are a little freer to imagine setting than playwrights since they're not constrained by the need to choose settings that can be physically created on a stage. So it's not surprising that writers of short and long fiction craft all kinds of imaginary geographies, which achieve a variety of ends.

The most basic of these ends is to contribute to the creation of a convincing fictional world. This aim is a constant regardless of whether authors are attempting to construct a world that resembles one that exists or has existed or are seeking to create a world that is purposefully different from our own. There are no rules about how much description is necessary to establish setting, or how this material should be incorporated into a story; but more often than not authors avoid overt, sustained descriptions of setting and instead delineate it gradually through the use of small, seemingly unnecessary details. It's rather the accumulation of details that allows the reader's imagination to create the locations in which actions occur. For example, in "A Basket Full of Wallpaper," Colum McCann uses two brief sentences within his first two paragraphs—"He had come to Ireland to forget it all" and "On the beach he walked with his head slung low to the ground, stooping to collect stones"—to indirectly inform us that we are reading of past events that took place on the coast of Ireland. Thus a basic setting is established—without betraying the author's efforts to do so.

Yet the work accomplished by setting goes well beyond the creation of a convincing fictional world. It also does tremendous work of other sorts, in echoing theme, shaping character, establishing mood, and creating symbols, for example. Notice in "A Basket Full of Wallpaper," for instance, that the descriptions of Osobe's room, with its messy array of everyday objects and tools of his trade, does several things: yes, it helps bring this fictional world to life in our minds, but it also helps to establish a sharp contrast between Osobe's simple bachelor existence and the townspeople's desire to see him as exotic, as other than themselves. This is one example of the general fact that authors choose the details of their imaginary geographies carefully, often making them accomplish multiple tasks. Think, for instance, of Joyce's decision in "Araby" to describe the street where the neighbourhood kids play as "blind."

How might we link this diction choice with themes or the development of our narrator's character? Similarly, the house in Poe's "The Black Cat" accomplishes some great work in creating symbols: as our narrator falls further and further from his better nature, so his home undergoes a parallel degradation; in the end, the ugly secret in his heart seems to be disturbingly paralleled by the ugly secret in the cellar. In contrast, in Munro's "Friend of My Youth" it's the stability of Flora's house, echoing the stability and indeed stasis of her own life, that seems to give it symbolic qualities. Not only do the two sides of the house echo the contrasting lives of their inhabitants, they also serve as a social statement that the outside world reads and interprets. In all of these cases setting helps to contribute to mood, whether through the choice of the adjective "blind" or through the use of strong images, of a house quite literally divided in Munro, or of a house undergoing a process of decay in Poe. Kazuo Ishiguro's "A Family Supper" offers an excellent example of how a seemingly minor element of setting can contribute great richness and depth to a short story: think here of the well in the back garden of the family home. Its historical associations—both with haunting and with the denial that haunting occurs—are one of the means by which Ishiguro creates the tense mood that pervades this story but remains beneath the surface of the social encounters. Setting works so effectively to create mood and echo theme because it gives expression to the fact that we can never objectively view or inhabit the places we interact with: what we see is always shaped by our moods and circumstances. Our geographies are always, to some extent, emotional geographies; fiction highlights and intensifies this fact, allowing us to savour it and, if we look closely into the matter, interrogate it.

Point of View and Narration

All short fiction comes from a certain **point of view**, a very roomy expression that generally refers to the perspective from which a story is told. This includes both the kind of narrator an author utilizes and, more challengingly, the narrator's attitude toward events and characters.

The vast majority of short stories utilize either a first- or a third-person narrator (there are a few examples of second-person narration, but they are rare). In the case of **third-person narration**, we usually don't know the identity of the narrator, who refers to all characters in the third person ("he," "she," "Peter," etc.) but generally makes no reference to him or herself (indeed, it's only the demands of English that require us to ascribe a sex to such anonymous voices). The opposite is true of a **first-person narrator**: we typically do know the narrator's identity, and such a voice tends to refer to him or herself in the first person ("I").

One opportunity that comes with third-person narration is an author's ability to use omniscience. We know we have an **omniscient narrator** when we are given access to the thoughts and feelings of different characters. Sometimes it is only one or two characters whose inner worlds we gain access to—this is called **limited omniscience**. Perhaps not surprisingly, omniscient narrators often give priority to the thoughts of the protagonist, as in Chinua Achebe's "Dead Men's Path" or Lahiri's "Interpreter of Maladies," for example. Indeed, giving us access to a character's thoughts is a crucial means by which authors form protagonists.

Determining the narrator's attitude toward events may sometimes be a real challenge for readers. This is especially the case with third-person narrators, who are often imagined to be objective purveyors of information. Though we have little choice but to take the basic facts delivered by third-person narrators as truthful, we should be alert for signs of the particular attitudes such narrators exhibit toward characters and events. As an example, consider Mansfield's "The Garden Party," where some close reading reveals that the narrator gives more sympathetic treatment to Laura, who is initially horrified to carry on with the party after learning of the neighbour's death, than to her sisters or mother, who show impatience with Laura's sensitivity. Notice, for instance, how the narrator's final comment undermines Jose's words as she responds to Laura's horror at continuing with plans for the party:

> "If you're going to stop a band playing every time someone has an
> accident, you'll lead a very strenuous life. I'm every bit as sorry about
> it as you. I feel just as sympathetic." Her eyes hardened.

The narrator's decision to add that last line—"Her eyes hardened"—suggests that this voice isn't simply describing the characters and events (which it is indeed doing): it's also revealing a certain attitude toward them. Jose's eyes could have "glazed over" or "stared at her sister" rather than "harden," a term that so wonderfully suggests her lack of sympathy and the fact that she is not "every bit as sorry" about the man's death as is Laura.

Many readers have an easier time discerning the narrator's attitude toward characters and events in the case of first-person narratives; this is perhaps because there is no guise of objectivity that clings to first-person narrators: it is clear that all of our information is being filtered through a consciousness that has its own particular way of viewing the world. As readers, our task is to try to discern how events and characters might appear to us were we able to correct for the narrator's biases. Sometimes this is relatively easy: in "Cathedral," for instance, Carver makes use of a male narrator whose prejudices toward and jealousy of Robert, his wife's blind friend, are difficult to miss. Such prejudices mean that, when it comes to assessing our narrator's view of characters and events, we must account for the effects of an **unreliable narrator**, a narrator whose understandings or information may be called into question.

Free Indirect Discourse

Though authors have to make decisions about what kind of narrator to use, a specific style of writing, known as **free indirect discourse**, represents something of a middle ground between first- and third-person narration. Developed by nineteenth-century authors (from Jane Austen through to Gustave Flaubert and Anton Chekhov), this style of writing allows a writer to imbue a third-person perspective with some of the characteristics of first-person writing. Flaubert inspired moral outrage for his use of free indirect discourse to give expression to Emma Bovary's adulterous desires precisely because this style of writing makes it difficult to discern whether the ideas we are reading are those of the narrator or those of the character being described by the narrator. Flaubert's reading public objected to this ambiguity, believing that it was the narrator's duty to unequivocally condemn Emma's unfaithfulness. Happily for us, this style of writing has long outlasted Flaubert's initial experimentation and is widely found in third-person writing today. Edith Wharton makes fine use of free indirect discourse to sketch out Nora Frenway's thoughts about her own adulterous desires in "Atrophy":

> Not that she was a woman to be awed by the conventions. She knew she wasn't. She had always taken their measure, smiled at them—and conformed. On account of poor George Frenway, to begin with. Her husband, in a sense, was a man to be pitied; his weak health, his bad temper, his unsatisfied vanity, all made him a rather forlornly comic figure. But it was chiefly on account of the two children that she had always resisted the temptation to do anything reckless. The least self-betrayal would have been the end of everything. Too many eyes were watching her, and her husband's family was so strong, so united—when there was anybody for them to hate—and at all times so influential, that she would have been defeated at every point, and her husband would have kept the children.
>
> At the mere thought she felt herself on the brink of an abyss.

Though we are clearly receiving our information from a third-person narrator in this passage—Nora is referred to as "she", not "I"—it is difficult to determine whether we are accessing Nora's thoughts or the knowledge and opinions of the omniscient narrator. Once we reach the first line of the second paragraph—"At the mere thought she felt herself on the brink of an abyss"—we receive confirmation that at least those ideas coming to us near the end of the first paragraph must have originated in Nora's mind. But ambiguity remains regarding the earlier statements. Also note the stylistic advantages that come from free indirect discourse: Wharton varies the rhythm of some of her sentences to *suggest* that we are accessing Nora's thought processes. Intentionally ungrammatical "run-on" sentences (or comma splices) are often used in free indirect discourse, as are double dashes—the purpose being to try to capture the somewhat chaotic flow of human thought. Here we seem to see Nora adjust her initial claim that the family is united, to the more precise and critical idea that they are united "when there is anybody for them to hate." When we think to ourselves (as opposed to when we write for others), our ideas are often refined through such chaotic processes of self-correction and adjustment.

Metafiction

Metafiction is writing that draws a reader's attention to the fact that he or she is engaged in the process of reading a piece of writing. It's best understood in opposition to the specific style of writing known as realism. When successful, realism induces what is sometimes called the realist illusion, an expression for that delightful way in which a story can allow us to lose awareness of the fact that we are reading, thus enabling us to fall into the textual world the author has created for us. A key characteristic of metafiction is that it disrupts the realist illusion and renders us self-conscious readers.

Readers have differing degrees of sensitivity to metafiction; however, some forms are unmistakeable and virtually unavoidable, as when an author refers to the story we are reading. Ali Smith provides an example of this at the end of "True Short Story" when she tells us that "this story was written in discussion with my friend Kasia." This reference to the production of the very story we are reading cannot help but draw most readers out of the realist illusion and make us conscious of the fact that we are reading a constructed piece of writing. In a piece of fiction called "True Short Story" about a woman with a friend named Kasia, this metafictional reference to how the story was made in consultation with Kasia is but one of several ways Smith is encouraging us to think about the relationship between fiction and non-fiction, between story and autobiography, between literature and life. Metafiction often encourages us to remove our gaze from the work we are reading and think about it within a larger context as Smith does here.

Another way authors encourage self-consciousness within their readers is by making reference to some facet of literature. Smith's story, which we could describe as intensely metafictional, provides two good examples of this technique: first, she ends her story by listing ideas about short fiction expressed by no less than 13 writers; second, she has two men and two women discuss the difference between the novel and the short story. Mistry also makes storytelling itself a theme in "Squatter" both by creating an embedded narrative (see the discussion of this in "Making Short Stories: The Selection and Manipulation of Events" above) and, more boldly, by crafting a character, Jehangir, who discusses the literary styles and techniques (such as humour) used by Nariman, one of the two storytellers we encounter. Margaret Atwood gives us another variation on this kind of metafiction in "Happy Endings" when she discusses endings and plots, even referring at one instance to a weak point in her own story's plotting. Reading a story that itself talks about weak plotting or the use of humour in stories makes many readers conscious of what they themselves are reading and of how it is plotted or makes use of humour, for example. This is one of metafiction's most common impacts: it alters our perspective on the story, encouraging us to regard it more analytically.

Some forms of metafiction are more subtle and might easily be missed by even careful readers. This is the case when authors purposefully disregard literary conventions: if a reader isn't aware of the conventions themselves, they can't be expected to notice an author manipulating them. And this explains one of the great pleasures of learning about literature: it gives us access to a code of conventions authors have relied on to make meaning. When an author alters a literary convention, readers "in the know" become alert to this and start to think about why he or she might have made this gesture. Microfiction provides an interesting example of this. A reader new to short fiction might read Gould's "What You're Ready For" and think, "this is a very short short story indeed," and have it end there. But for readers familiar with this field's history, microfiction's very minimalism might well prompt questions, such as, "Is this a short story?" This question might, in turn, provoke others about the nature of short fiction: "How *do* we define short fiction?" "Which characteristics are necessary and which are merely optional?" These questions, in short, demonstrate that we have been rendered self-conscious readers and have shifted from merely reading the work in front of us to analyzing it.

There is nothing new about metafiction. A famous example is found in Chaucer's medieval verse narrative "Troilus and Criseyde." In his Epilogue, Chaucer addresses the text itself, saying "go litel book," and expresses his hopes that it won't be misunderstood by the world. However, metafiction has become much more popular and experimental since the 1970s and is now a significant component of contemporary fiction, short and long. The question of why authors wish to break the realist illusion and render us self-conscious readers is a complex and difficult one, but one that deserves at least brief consideration here. Some see the popularity of metafiction as an inevitable consequence of the fact that readers are highly literate these days and can become bored by a given set of literary conventions. By definition, conventions become familiar, and they can begin to strike readers as tired and trite. Authors seek to **defamiliarize** fiction—to make that which was familiar *unfamiliar* and fresh—by breaking rules and pushing boundaries. New forms of metafiction come along to renew the literary genre and for a time seem fresh, exciting, challenging.

It is important to realize that there can be metafictional elements even within works that can be broadly classed as realist. And as the above examples have suggested, adding metafictional elements to a text almost always makes for a more challenging story. Munro's "Friend of My Youth" offers a final case in point: as the narrator begins to veer from her task of narrating the story of Flora for us, and to consider the differing ways she and her mother interpreted these characters, and indeed, the motivations they had for "reading" these people in different ways, we're encouraged to think about how the past is made into a story, about the multiple ways the past can be narrated, about the impossibility of a definitive version of events—more generally, about how life is turned into history. By making use of a self-conscious narrator who draws attention to facets of storytelling, in other words, Munro enables her small story to ask rather large questions about neutrality, authority, and history. However briefly, these examples suggest the role metafictional elements can play in making us more critical readers. Many have argued that the rise of metafiction reflects the needs of our own times: in a world in which so many competing interests seek to convince us of the truth of their claims, people need critical skills. Metafiction provides a means by which authors can tell a good story, one that can even move us emotionally, while also offering readers the opportunity to deepen their thinking about story, history, and truth.

—L.C.

Edgar Allan Poe
1809–1849

Designed to produce an atmosphere of terror by laying open to the reader the realm of the irrational, the uncanny, and the macabre, the Gothic tales of Edgar Allan Poe haunt the outskirts of the mind long after the last page is turned. In the "strange medium of his works," Robert Louis Stevenson detected "a certain jarring note, a taint of something that we do not care to dwell upon or find a name for." Poe returns to this nameless "something" again and again in stories like "The Pit and the Pendulum" (1842), "The Tell-Tale Heart" (1843), and "The Black Cat" (1843).

However one defines the "suggestive indefinitiveness" at the core of his most characteristic tales—a fascination with death, the iron grip of the past, or what Poe called "the human thirst for self-torture" perhaps come close— its presence reflects his pursuit of "a unity of effect or impression," a quality he considered the form of short fiction uniquely well suited to support. Poe held that the very brevity of the tale enlarges its power: because such works may be read at a sitting, the soul of the reader is fully at the writer's control, with neither weariness nor distraction to compromise the totality of the effect. But if the compactness of the tale allows the writer to realize "the fulness [sic] of his intention," it also demands perfect craft: for Poe, every word must advance "the one pre-established design."

Although Poe was among the first major theorists of the modern short story, his fictional practice has always been controversial, particularly among fellow American writers. Some object to his baroque prose and highly wrought formalism; others dismiss him as a hack who, having spent much of his life in poverty, indulged a lurid sensationalism in the hope of securing a wider readership. But as D.H. Lawrence observed, Poe was above all "an adventurer into vaults and cellars and horrible underground passages of the human soul," an author who not only founded detective fiction but who invested familiar forms with enormous power and psychological complexity.

The Black Cat

For the most wild, yet most homely narrative which I am about to pen, I neither expect nor solicit belief. Mad indeed would I be to expect it, in a case where my very senses reject their own evidence. Yet, mad am I not—and very surely do I not dream. But to-morrow I die, and to-day I would unburden my soul. My immediate purpose is to place before the world, plainly, succinctly, and without comment, a series of mere household events. In their consequences, these events have terrified—have tortured—have destroyed me. Yet I will not attempt to expound them. To me, they have presented little but Horror—to many they will seem less terrible than *barroques*.[1] Hereafter, perhaps, some intellect may be found which will reduce my phantasm[2] to the common-place—some intellect more calm, more logical, and far less excitable than my own, which will perceive, in the circumstances I detail with awe, nothing more than an ordinary succession of very natural causes and effects.

From my infancy I was noted for the docility and humanity of my disposition. My tenderness of heart was even so conspicuous as to make me the jest of my companions. I was especially fond of animals, and was indulged by my parents with a great variety of pets. With these I spent most of my time, and never was so happy as when feeding and caressing them. This peculiarity of character grew with my growth, and in my manhood, I derived from it one of my principal sources of pleasure. To those who have cherished an affection for a faithful and sagacious dog, I need hardly be at the trouble of explaining the nature or the intensity of the gratification thus derivable. There is something in the unselfish and self-sacrificing love of a brute, which goes directly to the heart of him who has had frequent occasion to test the paltry friendship and gossamer fidelity of mere *Man*.

I married early, and was happy to find in my wife a disposition not un-congenial with my own. Observing my partiality for domestic pets, she lost no opportunity of procuring those of the most agreeable kind. We had birds, gold-fish, a fine dog, rabbits, a small monkey, and *a cat*.

This latter was a remarkably large and beautiful animal, entirely black, and sagacious to an astonishing degree. In speaking of his intelligence, my wife, who at heart was not a little tinctured with superstition, made frequent allusion to the ancient popular notion, which regarded all black cats as witches in disguise. Not that she was ever *serious* upon this point—and I mention the matter at all for no better reason than that it happens, just now, to be remembered.

Pluto[3]—this was the cat's name—was my favourite pet and playmate. I alone fed him, and he attended me wherever I went about the house. It was even with difficulty that I could prevent him from following me through the streets.

Our friendship lasted, in this manner, for several years, during which my general temperament and character—through the instrumentality of the Fiend Intemperance[4]—had (I blush to confess it) experienced a radical alteration for the worse. I grew, day by day, more moody, more irritable, more regardless of the feelings of others. I suffered myself to use intemperate language to my

1   *barroques* French: weird, strange.
2   *phantasm* Delusion or frightening apparition.
3   *Pluto* In Greek mythology, Pluto is the lord of the underworld.
4   *Fiend Intemperance* The narrator demonizes the excessive consumption of alcohol.

wife. At length, I even offered her personal violence. My pets, of course, were made to feel the change in my disposition. I not only neglected, but ill-used them. For Pluto, however, I still retained sufficient regard to restrain me from maltreating him, as I made no scruple of maltreating the rabbits, the monkey, or even the dog, when by accident, or through affection, they came in my way. But my disease grew upon me—for what disease is like Alcohol!—and at length even Pluto, who was now becoming old, and consequently somewhat peevish—even Pluto began to experience the effects of my ill temper.

One night, returning home, much intoxicated, from one of my haunts about town, I fancied that the cat avoided my presence. I seized him; when, in his fright at my violence, he inflicted a slight wound upon my hand with his teeth. The fury of a demon instantly possessed me. I knew myself no longer. My original soul seemed, at once, to take its flight from my body and a more than fiendish malevolence, gin-nurtured, thrilled every fibre of my frame. I took from my waistcoat-pocket a pen-knife, opened it, grasped the poor beast by the throat, and deliberately cut one of its eyes from the socket! I blush, I burn, I shudder, while I pen the damnable atrocity.

When reason returned with the morning—when I had slept off the fumes of the night's debauch—I experienced a sentiment half of horror, half of re-morse, for the crime of which I had been guilty; but it was, at best, a feeble and equivocal feeling, and the soul remained untouched. I again plunged into excess, and soon drowned in wine all memory of the deed.

In the meantime the cat slowly recovered. The socket of the lost eye pre-sented, it is true, a frightful appearance, but he no longer appeared to suffer any pain. He went about the house as usual, but, as might be expected, fled in extreme terror at my approach. I had so much of my old heart left, as to be at first grieved by this evident dislike on the part of a creature which had once so loved me. But this feeling soon gave place to irritation. And then came, as if to my final and irrevocable overthrow, the spirit of PERVERSENESS. Of this spirit philosophy takes no account. Yet I am not more sure that my soul lives, than I am that perverseness is one of the primitive impulses of the human heart—one of the indivisible primary faculties, or sentiments, which give direction to the character of Man. Who has not, a hundred times, found himself committing a vile or a silly action, for no other reason than because he knows he should not? Have we not a perpetual inclination, in the teeth of our best judgment, to violate that which is *Law*, merely because we understand it to be such? This spirit of perverseness, I say, came to my final overthrow. It was this unfathom-able longing of the soul *to vex itself*—to offer violence to its own nature—to do wrong for the wrong's sake only—that urged me to continue and finally to consummate the injury I had inflicted upon the unoffending brute. One morning, in cool blood, I slipped a noose about its neck and hung it to the limb of a tree;—hung it with the tears streaming from my eyes, and with the bitterest remorse at my heart;—hung it *because* I knew that it had loved me, and *because* I felt it had given me no reason of offence;—hung it *because* I knew that in so doing I was committing a sin—a deadly sin that would so jeopardize my immortal soul as to place it—if such a thing were possible—even beyond the reach of the infinite mercy of the Most Merciful and Most Terrible God.

On the night of the day on which this cruel deed was done, I was aroused from sleep by the cry of fire. The curtains of my bed were in flames. The whole house was blazing. It was with great difficulty that my wife, a servant, and myself, made our escape from the conflagration.[1] The destruction was complete. My entire worldly wealth was swallowed up, and I resigned myself thenceforward to despair.

I am above the weakness of seeking to establish a sequence of cause and effect, between the disaster and the atrocity. But I am detailing a chain of facts—and wish not to leave even a possible link imperfect. On the day succeeding the fire, I visited the ruins. The walls, with one exception, had fallen in. This exception was found in a compartment wall, not very thick, which stood about the middle of the house, and against which had rested the head of my bed. The plastering had here, in great measure, resisted the action of the fire—a fact which I attributed to its having been recently spread. About this wall a dense crowd were collected, and many persons seemed to be examining a particular portion of it with very minute and eager attention. The words "strange!" "singular!" and other similar expressions, excited my curiosity. I approached and saw, as if graven in *bas relief*[2] upon the white surface, the figure of a gigantic *cat*. The impression was given with an accuracy truly marvellous. There was a rope about the animal's neck.

When I first beheld this apparition—for I could scarcely regard it as less— my wonder and my terror were extreme. But at length reflection came to my aid. The cat, I remembered, had been hung in a garden adjacent to the house. Upon the alarm of fire, this garden had been immediately filled by the crowd—by some one of whom the animal must have been cut from the tree and thrown, through an open window, into my chamber. This had probably been done with the view of arousing me from sleep. The falling of other walls had compressed the victim of my cruelty into the substance of the freshly-spread plaster; the lime of which, with the flames, and the *ammonia* from the carcass, had then accomplished the portraiture as I saw it.

---

1   *conflagration* Destructive fire.

2   *bas relief* Relief sculpture characterized by slightly raised features that project from a flat background.

Although I thus readily accounted to my reason, if not altogether to my conscience, for the startling fact just detailed, it did not the less fail to make a deep impression upon my fancy. For months I could not rid myself of the phantasm of the cat; and, during this period, there came back into my spirit a half-sentiment that seemed, but was not, remorse. I went so far as to regret the loss of the animal, and to look about me, among the vile haunts which I now habitually frequented, for another pet of the same species, and of somewhat similar appearance, with which to supply its place.

One night as I sat, half stupefied, in a den of more than infamy, my attention was suddenly drawn to some black object, reposing upon the head of one of the immense hogsheads[1] of Gin, or of Rum, which constituted the chief furniture of the apartment. I had been looking steadily at the top of this hogshead for some minutes, and what now caused me surprise was the fact that I had not sooner perceived the object thereupon. I approached it, and touched it with my hand. It was a black cat—a very large one—fully as large as Pluto, and closely resembling him in every respect but one. Pluto had not a white hair upon any portion of his body; but this cat had a large, although indefinite splotch of white, covering nearly the whole region of the breast. Upon my touching him, he immediately arose, purred loudly, rubbed against my hand, and appeared delighted with my notice. This, then, was the very creature of which I was in search. I at once offered to purchase it of the landlord; but this person made no claim to it—knew nothing of it—had never seen it before.

I continued my caresses, and, when I prepared to go home, the animal evinced a disposition to accompany me. I permitted it to do so; occasionally stooping and patting it as I proceeded. When it reached the house it domesticated itself at once, and became immediately a great favourite with my wife.

For my own part, I soon found a dislike to it arising within me. This was just the reverse of what I had anticipated; but—I know not how or why it was—its evident fondness for myself rather disgusted and annoyed. By slow degrees, these feelings of disgust and annoyance rose into the bitterness of hatred. I avoided the creature; a certain sense of shame, and the remembrance of my former deed of cruelty, preventing me from physically abusing it. I did not, for some weeks, strike, or otherwise violently ill use it; but gradually—very gradually—I came to look upon it with unutterable loathing, and to flee silently from its odious presence, as from the breath of a pestilence.

What added, no doubt, to my hatred of the beast, was the discovery, on the morning after I brought it home, that, like Pluto, it also had been deprived of one of its eyes. This circumstance, however, only endeared it to my wife, who, as I have already said, possessed, in a high degree, that humanity of feel-

---

1   *hogsheads* Casks.

ing which had once been my distinguishing trait, and the source of many of my simplest and purest pleasures.

With my aversion to this cat, however, its partiality for myself seemed to increase. It followed my footsteps with a pertinacity which it would be difficult to make the reader comprehend. Whenever I sat, it would crouch beneath my chair, or spring upon my knees, covering me with its loathsome caresses. If I arose to walk it would get between my feet and thus nearly throw me down, or, fastening its long and sharp claws in my dress, clamber, in this manner, to my breast. At such times, although I longed to destroy it with a blow, I was yet withheld from so doing, partly by a memory of my former crime, but chiefly—let me confess it at once—by absolute dread of the beast.

This dread was not exactly a dread of physical evil—and yet I should be at a loss how otherwise to define it. I am almost ashamed to own—yes, even in this felon's cell, I am almost ashamed to own—that the terror and horror with which the animal inspired me, had been heightened by one of the merest chimaeras[1] it would be possible to conceive. My wife had called my attention, more than once, to the character of the mark of white hair, of which I have spoken, and which constituted the sole visible difference between the strange beast and the one I had destroyed. The reader will remember that this mark, although large, had been originally very indefinite; but, by slow degrees—degrees nearly imperceptible, and which for a long time my Reason struggled to reject as fanciful—it had, at length, assumed a rigorous distinctness of outline. It was now the representation of an object that I shudder to name—and for this, above all, I loathed, and dreaded, and would have rid myself of the monster *had I dared*—it was now, I say, the image of a hideous—of a ghastly thing—of the GALLOWS!—oh, mournful and terrible engine of Horror and of Crime—of Agony and of Death!

And now was I indeed wretched beyond the wretchedness of mere Humanity. And a brute beast—whose fellow I had contemptuously destroyed—*a brute beast* to work out for *me*—for me a man, fashioned in the image of the High God—so much of insufferable woe! Alas! neither by day nor by night knew I the blessing of Rest any more! During the former the creature left me no moment alone; and, in the latter, I started, hourly, from dreams of unutterable fear, to find the hot breath of *the thing* upon my face, and its vast weight—an incarnate Night-Mare that I had no power to shake off—incumbent eternally upon my *heart*!

Beneath the pressure of torments such as these, the feeble remnant of the good within me succumbed. Evil thoughts became my sole intimates—the darkest and most evil of thoughts. The moodiness of my usual temper in-

---

1   *chimaeras* Illusory or monstrous things.

creased to hatred of all things and of all mankind; while, from the sudden, frequent, and ungovernable outbursts of a fury to which I now blindly abandoned myself, my uncomplaining wife, alas! was the most usual and the most patient of sufferers.

One day she accompanied me, upon some household errand, into the cellar of the old building which our poverty compelled us to inhabit. The cat followed me down the steep stairs, and, nearly throwing me headlong, exasperated me to madness. Uplifting an axe, and forgetting, in my wrath, the childish dread which had hitherto stayed my hand, I aimed a blow at the animal which, of course, would have proved instantly fatal had it descended as I wished. But this blow was arrested by the hand of my wife. Goaded, by the interference, into a rage more than demoniacal, I withdrew my arm from her grasp and buried the axe in her brain. She fell dead upon the spot, without a groan.

This hideous murder accomplished, I set myself forthwith, and with entire deliberation, to the task of concealing the body. I knew that I could not remove it from the house, either by day or by night, without the risk of being observed by the neighbours. Many projects entered my mind. At one period I thought of cutting the corpse into minute fragments, and destroying them by fire. At another, I resolved to dig a grave for it in the floor of the cellar. Again, I deliberated about casting it in the well in the yard—about packing it in a box, as if merchandize, with the usual arrangements, and so getting a porter to take it from the house. Finally I hit upon what I considered a far better expedient than either of these. I determined to wall it up in the cellar—as the monks of the middle ages are recorded to have walled up their victims.

For a purpose such as this the cellar was well adapted. Its walls were loosely constructed, and had lately been plastered throughout with a rough plaster, which the dampness of the atmosphere had prevented from hardening. Moreover, in one of the walls was a projection, caused by a false chimney, or fireplace, that had been filled up, and made to resemble the red of the cellar. I made no doubt that I could readily displace the bricks at this point, insert the corpse, and wall the whole up as before, so that no eye could detect any thing suspicious. And in this calculation I was not deceived. By means of a crow-bar I easily dislodged the bricks, and, having carefully deposited the body against the inner wall, I propped it in that position, while, with little trouble, I re-laid the whole structure as it originally stood. Having procured mortar, sand, and hair,[1] with every possible precaution, I prepared a plaster which could not be distinguished from the old, and with this I very carefully went over the new brickwork. When I had finished, I felt satisfied that all was right. The wall did

---

1   *hair* The addition of animal hair to mortar increases its durability.

not present the slightest appearance of having been disturbed. The rubbish on the floor was picked up with the minutest care. I looked around triumphantly, and said to myself—"Here at least, then, my labour has not been in vain."

My next step was to look for the beast which had been the cause of so much wretchedness; for I had, at length, firmly resolved to put it to death. Had I been able to meet with it, at the moment, there could have been no doubt of its fate; but it appeared that the crafty animal had been alarmed at the violence of my previous anger, and forbore to present itself in my present mood. It is impossible to describe, or to imagine, the deep, the blissful sense of relief which the absence of the detested creature occasioned in my bosom. It did not make its appearance during the night—and thus for one night at least, since its introduction into the house, I soundly and tranquilly slept; aye, slept even with the burden of murder upon my soul!

The second and the third day passed, and still my tormentor came not. Once again I breathed as a freeman. The monster, in terror, had fled the premises forever! I should behold it no more! My happiness was supreme! The guilt of my dark deed disturbed me but little. Some few inquiries had been made, but these had been readily answered. Even a search had been instituted—but of course nothing was to be discovered. I looked upon my future felicity as secured.

Upon the fourth day of the assassination, a party of the police came, very unexpectedly, into the house, and proceeded again to make rigorous investigation of the premises. Secure, however, in the inscrutability of my place of concealment, I felt no embarrassment whatever. The officers bade me accompany them in their search. They left no nook or corner unexplored. At length, for the third or fourth time, they descended into the cellar. I quivered not in a muscle. My heart beat calmly as that of one who slumbers in innocence. I walked the cellar from end to end. I folded my arms upon my bosom, and roamed easily to and fro. The police were thoroughly satisfied and prepared to depart. The glee at my heart was too strong to be restrained. I burned to say if but one word, by way of triumph, and to render doubly sure their assurance of my guiltlessness.

"Gentlemen," I said at last, as the party ascended the steps, "I delight to have allayed your suspicions. I wish you all health, and a little more courtesy. By the bye, gentlemen, this—this is a very well constructed house." [In the rabid desire to say something easily, I scarcely knew what I uttered at all.]—"I may say an *excellently* well constructed house. These walls—are you going, gentlemen?—these walls are solidly put together;" and here, through the mere phrenzy of bravado, I rapped heavily, with a cane which I held in my hand, upon that very portion of the brick-work behind which stood the corpse of the wife of my bosom.

But may God shield and deliver me from the fangs of the Arch-Fiend! No sooner had the reverberation of my blows sunk into silence, than I was answered by a voice from within the tomb!—by a cry, at first muffled and broken, like the sobbing of a child, and then quickly swelling into one long, loud, and continuous scream, utterly anomalous and inhuman—a howl—a wailing shriek, half of horror and half of triumph, such as might have arisen only out of hell, conjointly from the throats of the dammed in their agony and of the demons that exult in the damnation.

Of my own thoughts it is folly to speak. Swooning, I staggered to the opposite wall. For one instant the party upon the stairs remained motionless, through extremity of terror and of awe. In the next, a dozen stout arms were toiling at the wall. It fell bodily. The corpse, already greatly decayed and clotted with gore, stood erect before the eyes of the spectators. Upon its head, with red extended mouth and solitary eye of fire, sat the hideous beast whose craft had seduced me into murder, and whose informing voice had consigned me to the hangman. I had walled the monster up within the tomb!

—1843

Kate Chopin
1850–1904

Kate Chopin became a writer late in life, beginning her career only after the death of her husband in 1882. The short stories and two published novels of this writer of the American South were often considered transgressive in her day, addressing the subjects of race and class, marriage and divorce, sexuality, and female autonomy. Through her provocative writing, Chopin sought to expose the nature of truth as tied to the limited perspective of the individual, showing that, in her words, "truth rests upon a shifting basis and is apt to be kaleidoscopic."

The controversy that Chopin's ideas incited is perhaps best exemplified by the reception of her most recognized work, *The Awakening* (1899). The novel, which depicts one woman's sensual awakening and her defiance of societal expectations of women, received high praise from a few reviewers, but a larger number dismissed it as "morbid," "sordid," and "sex fiction." It took scholars roughly 50 years after Chopin's death to acknowledge *The Awakening* as a novel of enduring importance—a work of historical value for its critical engagement with the role of women at the turn of the nineteenth century, but also a work that would continue to resonate for generations of readers.

Like *The Awakening*, "The Story of an Hour," first published in the December 1894 issue of *Vogue*, probes the marked tension between what Chopin referred to as the "outward existence which conforms, [and] the inward life which questions."

The Story of an Hour

Knowing that Mrs. Mallard was afflicted with a heart trouble, great care was taken to break to her as gently as possible the news of her husband's death.

It was her sister Josephine who told her, in broken sentences; veiled hints that revealed in half concealing. Her husband's friend Richards was there, too, near her. It was he who had been in the newspaper office when intelligence of the railroad disaster was received, with Brently Mallard's name leading the list of "killed." He had only taken the time to assure himself of its truth by a second telegram, and had hastened to forestall any less careful, less tender friend in bearing the sad message.

She did not hear the story as many women have heard the same, with a paralyzed inability to accept its significance. She wept at once, with sudden, wild abandonment, in her sister's arms. When the storm of grief had spent itself she went away to her room alone. She would have no one follow her.

There stood, facing the open window, a comfortable, roomy armchair. Into this she sank, pressed down by a physical exhaustion that haunted her body and seemed to reach into her soul.

She could see in the open square before her house the tops of trees that were all aquiver with the new spring life. The delicious breath of rain was in the air. In the street below a peddler was crying his wares. The notes of a distant song which someone was singing reached her faintly, and countless sparrows were twittering in the eaves.

There were patches of blue sky showing here and there through the clouds that had met and piled one above the other in the west facing her window.

She sat with her head thrown back upon the cushion of the chair, quite motionless, except when a sob came up into her throat and shook her, as a child who has cried itself to sleep continues to sob in its dreams.

She was young, with a fair, calm face, whose lines bespoke repression and even a certain strength. But now there was a dull stare in her eyes, whose gaze was fixed away off yonder on one of those patches of blue sky. It was not a glance of reflection, but rather indicated a suspension of intelligent thought.

There was something coming to her and she was waiting for it, fearfully. What was it? She did not know; it was too subtle and elusive to name. But she felt it, creeping out of the sky, reaching toward her through the sounds, the scents, the colour that filled the air.

Now her bosom rose and fell tumultuously. She was beginning to recognize this thing that was approaching to possess her, and she was striving to beat it back with her will—as powerless as her two white slender hands would have been.

When she abandoned herself a little whispered word escaped her slightly parted lips. She said it over and over under her breath: "free, free, free!" The vacant stare and the look of terror that had followed it went from her eyes. They stayed keen and bright. Her pulses beat fast, and the coursing blood warmed and relaxed every inch of her body.

She did not stop to ask if it were or were not a monstrous joy that held her. A clear and exalted perception enabled her to dismiss the suggestion as trivial.

She knew that she would weep again when she saw the kind, tender hands folded in death; the face that had never looked save with love upon her, fixed and grey and dead. But she saw beyond that bitter moment a long procession of years to come that would belong to her absolutely. And she opened and spread her arms out to them in welcome.

There would be no one to live for her during those coming years; she would live for herself. There would be no powerful will bending hers in that blind persistence with which men and women believe they have a right to impose a private will upon a fellow-creature. A kind intention or a cruel intention made the act seem no less a crime as she looked upon it in that brief moment of illumination.

And yet she had loved him—sometimes. Often she had not. What did it matter! What could love, the unsolved mystery, count for in face of this possession of self-assertion which she suddenly recognized as the strongest impulse of her being!

"Free! Body and soul free!" she kept whispering.

Josephine was kneeling before the closed door with her lips to the keyhole, imploring for admission. "Louise, open the door! I beg; open the door—you will make yourself ill. What are you doing, Louise? For heaven's sake open the door."

"Go away. I am not making myself ill." No; she was drinking in a very elixir of life through that open window.

Her fancy was running riot along those days ahead of her. Spring days, and summer days, and all sorts of days that would be her own. She breathed a quick prayer that life might be long. It was only yesterday she had thought with a shudder that life might be long.

She arose at length and opened the door to her sister's importunities. There was a feverish triumph in her eyes, and she carried herself unwittingly like a goddess of Victory. She clasped her sister's waist, and together they descended the stairs. Richards stood waiting for them at the bottom.

Some one was opening the front door with a latchkey. It was Brently Mallard who entered, a little travel-stained, composedly carrying his grip-sack and umbrella. He had been far from the scene of accident, and did not even know there had been one. He stood amazed at Josephine's piercing cry; at Richards' quick motion to screen him from the view of his wife.

But Richards was too late.

When the doctors came they said she had died of heart disease—of joy that kills.

—1894

Guy de Maupassant
1850–1893

Guy de Maupassant was a French short story writer and novelist; he is considered one of the nineteenth-century masters of short fiction. The clarity of his plots, his deceptively simple style, and his detached narrative voice have all been formative in the development of the short story.

Born in Normandy, as a youth he abandoned the study of law to serve in the Franco-Prussian war. He settled in Paris, where he worked in the civil service until his writing provided him with a living wage; here, he was introduced to the novelist Gustave Flaubert, who became a close friend and mentor. Through Flaubert, Maupassant became part of a literary circle of Naturalist writers, who strove to observe human nature accurately and to depict it honestly, without moral judgment. Maupassant first achieved recognition when his short story "Boule de Suif" was published in a Naturalist anthology in 1880.

Like other nineteenth-century Naturalist writers, Maupassant often depicted characters unable to control their destinies in a world governed by biological forces and harsh social conditions. His characters are drawn from all walks of life, from aristocrats to prostitutes, though most often they are middle class, either country people or urban civil servants. They are all, however, depicted with Naturalistic attention to their flaws; their stories typically reveal the too-often petty and selfish motives behind human interactions. Émile Zola, a friend of Maupassant's and key proponent of literary Naturalism, said: "We leave his pages looking at ourselves, with the same moral and physical joy that we gain from a walk in the plain light of day."

The False Gems[1]

Monsieur Lantin had met the young girl at a reception at the house of the second head of his department, and had fallen head over heels in love with her.

She was the daughter of a provincial tax collector, who had been dead several years. She and her mother came to live in Paris, where the latter, who made the acquaintance of some of the families in her neighbourhood, hoped to find a husband for her daughter.

They had very moderate means, and were honourable, gentle, and quiet.

The young girl was a perfect type of the virtuous woman in whose hands every sensible young man dreams of one day entrusting his happiness. Her

---

1   *The False Gems* Translation by Albert M.C. McMaster, A.E. Henderson, and Louise Charlotte Garstin Quesada. Maupassant's title, "Les Bijoux," is often translated as "The Jewellery."

simple beauty had the charm of angelic modesty, and the imperceptible smile which constantly hovered about the lips seemed to be the reflection of a pure and lovely soul. Her praises resounded on every side. People never tired of repeating: "Happy the man who wins her love! He could not find a better wife."

Monsieur Lantin, then chief clerk in the Department of the Interior, enjoyed a snug little salary of three thousand five hundred francs, and he proposed to this model young girl, and was accepted.

He was unspeakably happy with her. She governed his household with such clever economy that they seemed to live in luxury. She lavished the most delicate attentions on her husband, coaxed and fondled him; and so great was her charm that six years after their marriage, Monsieur Lantin discovered that he loved his wife even more than during the first days of their honeymoon.

He found fault with only two of her tastes: her love for the theatre, and her taste for imitation jewellery. Her friends (the wives of some petty officials) frequently procured for her a box at the theatre, often for the first representations of the new plays; and her husband was obliged to accompany her, whether he wished it or not, to these entertainments which bored him excessively after his day's work at the office.

After a time, Monsieur Lantin begged his wife to request some lady of her acquaintance to accompany her, and to bring her home after the theatre. She opposed this arrangement, at first; but, after much persuasion, finally consented, to the infinite delight of her husband.

Now, with her love for the theatre, came also the desire for ornaments. Her costumes remained as before, simple, in good taste, and always modest; but she soon began to adorn her ears with huge rhinestones, which glittered and sparkled like real diamonds. Around her neck she wore strings of false pearls, on her arms bracelets of imitation gold, and combs set with glass jewels.

Her husband frequently remonstrated with her, saying:

"My dear, as you cannot afford to buy real jewellery, you ought to appear adorned with your beauty and modesty alone, which are the rarest ornaments of your sex."

But she would smile sweetly, and say:

"What can I do? I am so fond of jewellery. It is my only weakness. We cannot change our nature."

Then she would wind the pearl necklace round her fingers, make the facets of the crystal gems sparkle, and say:

"Look! are they not lovely? One would swear they were real."

Monsieur Lantin would then answer, smilingly:

"You have bohemian[1] tastes, my dear."

---

1   *bohemian* Unconventional.

Sometimes, of an evening, when they were enjoying a tête-à-tête by the fireside, she would place on the tea table the morocco leather box containing the "trash," as Monsieur Lantin called it. She would examine the false gems with a passionate attention, as though they imparted some deep and secret joy; and she often persisted in passing a necklace around her husband's neck, and, laughing heartily, would exclaim: "How droll you look!" Then she would throw herself into his arms, and kiss him affectionately.

One evening, in winter, she had been to the opera, and returned home chilled through and through. The next morning she coughed, and eight days later she died of inflammation of the lungs.

Monsieur Lantin's despair was so great that his hair became white in one month. He wept unceasingly; his heart was broken as he remembered her smile, her voice, every charm of his dead wife.

Time did not assuage his grief. Often, during office hours, while his colleagues were discussing the topics of the day, his eyes would suddenly fill with tears, and he would give vent to his grief in heartrending sobs. Everything in his wife's room remained as it was during her lifetime; all her furniture, even her clothing, being left as it was on the day of her death. Here he was wont to seclude himself daily and think of her who had been his treasure—the joy of his existence.

But life soon became a struggle. His income, which, in the hands of his wife, covered all household expenses, was now no longer sufficient for his own immediate wants; and he wondered how she could have managed to buy such excellent wine and the rare delicacies which he could no longer procure with his modest resources.

He incurred some debts, and was soon reduced to absolute poverty. One morning, finding himself without a cent in his pocket, he resolved to sell something, and immediately the thought occurred to him of disposing of his wife's paste jewels, for he cherished in his heart a sort of rancor against these "deceptions," which had always irritated him in the past. The very sight of them spoiled, somewhat, the memory of his lost darling.

To the last days of her life she had continued to make purchases, bringing home new gems almost every evening, and he turned them over some time before finally deciding to sell the heavy necklace, which she seemed to prefer, and which, he thought, ought to be worth about six or seven francs; for it was of very fine workmanship, though only imitation.

He put it in his pocket, and started out in search of what seemed a reliable jeweller's shop. At length he found one, and went in, feeling a little ashamed to expose his misery, and also to offer such a worthless article for sale.

"Sir," said he to the merchant, "I would like to know what this is worth."

The man took the necklace, examined it, called his clerk, and made some remarks in an undertone; he then put the ornament back on the counter, and looked at it from a distance to judge of the effect.

Monsieur Lantin, annoyed at all these ceremonies, was on the point of saying: "Oh! I know well enough it is not worth anything," when the jeweller said: "Sir, that necklace is worth from twelve to fifteen thousand francs; but I could not buy it, unless you can tell me exactly where it came from."

The widower opened his eyes wide and remained gaping, not comprehending the merchant's meaning. Finally he stammered: "You say—are you sure?" The other replied, drily: "You can try elsewhere and see if anyone will offer you more. I consider it worth fifteen thousand at the most. Come back; here, if you cannot do better."

Monsieur Lantin, beside himself with astonishment, took up the necklace and left the store. He wished time for reflection.

Once outside, he felt inclined to laugh, and said to himself: "The fool! Oh, the fool! Had I only taken him at his word! That jeweller cannot distinguish real diamonds from the imitation article."

A few minutes after, he entered another store, in the Rue de la Paix.[1] As soon as the proprietor glanced at the necklace, he cried out:

"Ah, parbleu![2] I know it well; it was bought here."

Monsieur Lantin, greatly disturbed, asked:

"How much is it worth?"

"Well, I sold it for twenty thousand francs. I am willing to take it back for eighteen thousand, when you inform me, according to our legal formality, how it came to be in your possession."

This time, Monsieur Lantin was dumbfounded. He replied:

"But—but—examine it well. Until this moment I was under the impression that it was imitation."

The jeweller asked:

"What is your name, sir?"

"Lantin—I am in the employ of the Minister of the Interior. I live at number sixteen Rue des Martyrs."

The merchant looked through his books, found the entry, and said: "That necklace was sent to Madame Lantin's address, sixteen Rue des Martyrs, July 20, 1876."

The two men looked into each other's eyes—the widower speechless with astonishment; the jeweller scenting a thief. The latter broke the silence.

1   *Rue de la Paix* Trendy shopping district in Paris.
2   *parbleu* French: Oh, my God!

"Will you leave this necklace here for twenty-four hours?" said he; "I will give you a receipt."

Monsieur Lantin answered hastily: "Yes, certainly." Then, putting the ticket in his pocket, he left the store.

He wandered aimlessly through the streets, his mind in a state of dreadful confusion. He tried to reason, to understand. His wife could not afford to purchase such a costly ornament. Certainly not.

But, then, it must have been a present!—a present!—a present, from whom? Why was it given her?

He stopped, and remained standing in the middle of the street. A horrible doubt entered his mind—She? Then, all the other jewels must have been presents, too! The earth seemed to tremble beneath him—the tree before him to be falling; he threw up his arms, and fell to the ground, unconscious. He recovered his senses in a pharmacy, into which the passers-by had borne him. He asked to be taken home, and, when he reached the house, he shut himself up in his room, and wept until nightfall. Finally, overcome with fatigue, he went to bed and fell into a heavy sleep.

The sun awoke him next morning, and he began to dress slowly to go to the office. It was hard to work after such shocks. He sent a letter to his employer, requesting to be excused. Then he remembered that he had to return to the jeweller's. He did not like the idea; but he could not leave the necklace with that man. He dressed and went out.

It was a lovely day; a clear, blue sky smiled on the busy city below. Men of leisure were strolling about with their hands in their pockets.

Monsieur Lantin, observing them, said to himself: "The rich, indeed, are happy. With money it is possible to forget even the deepest sorrow. One can go where one pleases, and in travel find that distraction which is the surest cure for grief. Oh if I were only rich!"

He perceived that he was hungry, but his pocket was empty. He again remembered the necklace. Eighteen thousand francs! Eighteen thousand francs! What a sum!

He soon arrived in the Rue de la Paix, opposite the jeweller's. Eighteen thousand francs! Twenty times he resolved to go in, but shame kept him back. He was hungry, however—very hungry—and not a cent in his pocket. He decided quickly, ran across the street, in order not to have time for reflection, and rushed into the store.

The proprietor immediately came forward, and politely offered him a chair; the clerks glanced at him knowingly.

"I have made inquiries, Monsieur Lantin," said the jeweller, "and if you are still resolved to dispose of the gems, I am ready to pay you the price I offered."

"Certainly, sir," stammered Monsieur Lantin.

Whereupon the proprietor took from a drawer eighteen large bills, count-ed, and handed them to Monsieur Lantin, who signed a receipt; and, with trembling hand, put the money into his pocket.

As he was about to leave the store, he turned toward the merchant, who still wore the same knowing smile, and lowering his eyes, said:

"I have—I have other gems, which came from the same source. Will you buy them, also?"

The merchant bowed: "Certainly, sir."

Monsieur Lantin said gravely: "I will bring them to you." An hour later, he returned with the gems.

The large diamond earrings were worth twenty thousand francs; the bracelets, thirty-five thousand; the rings, sixteen thousand; a set of emeralds and sapphires, fourteen thousand; a gold chain with solitaire pendant, forty thousand—making the sum of one hundred and forty-three thousand francs.

The jeweller remarked, jokingly:

"There was a person who invested all her savings in precious stones."

Monsieur Lantin replied, seriously:

"It is only another way of investing one's money."

That day he lunched at Voisin's,[1] and drank wine worth twenty francs a bottle. Then he hired a carriage and made a tour of the Bois.[2] He gazed at the various turnouts[3] with a kind of disdain, and could hardly refrain from crying out to the occupants:

"I, too, am rich!—I am worth two hundred thousand francs."

Suddenly he thought of his employer. He drove up to the bureau, and entered gaily, saying:

"Sir, I have come to resign my position. I have just inherited three hundred thousand francs."

He shook hands with his former colleagues, and confided to them some of his projects for the future; he then went off to dine at the Café Anglais.[4]

He seated himself beside a gentleman of aristocratic bearing; and, during the meal, informed the latter confidentially that he had just inherited a fortune of four hundred thousand francs.

For the first time in his life, he was not bored at the theatre, and spent the remainder of the night in a gay frolic.

Six months afterward, he married again. His second wife was a very virtu-ous woman; but had a violent temper. She caused him much sorrow.

—1883

---

1   *Voisin's* Renowned, expensive restaurant.
2   *Bois* Bois de Boulogne, a park on the outskirts of Paris that was frequented by the upper classes in the late nineteenth century.
3   *turnouts* Fashionable carriages.
4   *Café Anglais* Famous high-class Parisian restaurant.

Anton Pavlovich Chekhov
1860–1904

Although well known as the playwright of four major plays, *The Seagull* (1896), *Uncle Vanya* (1897), *Three Sisters* (1901), and *The Cherry Orchard* (1904), Anton Chekhov was also highly acclaimed as a writer of short stories. Raised in the small Russian city of Taganrog, he moved to Moscow after his father's death to attend medical school and to help support his family. He began his writing career while he was still a student—to earn extra money, he sent stories to humour magazines—and continued to write short stories throughout his life, producing over 500 pieces in total. Many of his stories were translated into English in the early twentieth century, and their publication has been described by novelist James T. Farrell as "one of the greatest single literary influences at work in the short story of America, England, and Ireland" in that it encouraged authors in those traditions to "seek in simple and realistic terms to make of the story a form that more seriously reflects life."

Chekhov experimented extensively with narrative voice; in a typical Chekhov story, the governing narrative voice is objective and aloof, but at times also adopts the point of view of one or more of the characters. This technique, which has come to be known as "free indirect discourse," anticipates the more extended "stream of consciousness" narrative techniques adopted by James Joyce, and other modernist writers.

Chekhov also practiced medicine. He said that his experience as a physician was integral to his writing: "My study of medicine significantly broadened the scope of my observations and enriched me with knowledge whose value for me as a writer only a doctor can appreciate.... It seems to me that as a doctor I have described the sicknesses of the soul correctly."

An Upheaval[1]

Mashenka Pavletsky, a young girl who had only just finished her studies at a boarding school, returning from a walk to the house of the Kushkins, with whom she was living as a governess, found the household in a terrible turmoil. Mihailo, the porter who opened the door to her, was excited and red as a crab.

Loud voices were heard from upstairs.

"Madame Kushkin is in a fit, most likely, or else she has quarrelled with her husband," thought Mashenka.

---

1   *An Upheaval* Translation by Constance Garnett.

In the hall and in the corridor she met maid-servants. One of them was crying. Then Mashenka saw, running out of her room, the master of the house himself, Nikolay Sergeitch, a little man with a flabby face and a bald head, though he was not old. He was red in the face and twitching all over. He passed the governess without noticing her, and throwing up his arms, exclaimed:

"Oh, how horrible it is! How tactless! How stupid! How barbarous! Abominable!"

Mashenka went into her room, and then, for the first time in her life, it was her lot to experience in all its acuteness the feeling that is so familiar to persons in dependent positions, who eat the bread of the rich and powerful, and cannot speak their minds. There was a search going on in her room. The lady of the house, Fedosya Vassilyevna, a stout, broad-shouldered, uncouth woman with thick black eyebrows, a faintly perceptible moustache, and red hands, who was exactly like a plain, illiterate cook in face and manners, was standing, without her cap on, at the table, putting back into Mashenka's workbag balls of wool, scraps of materials, and bits of paper.... Evidently the governess's arrival took her by surprise, since, on looking round and seeing the girl's pale and astonished face, she was a little taken aback, and muttered:

"*Pardon.* I ... I upset it accidentally.... My sleeve caught in it...."

And saying something more, Madame Kushkin rustled her long skirts and went out. Mashenka looked round her room with wondering eyes, and, unable to understand it, not knowing what to think, shrugged her shoulders, and turned cold with dismay. What had Fedosya Vassilyevna been looking for in her work-bag? If she really had, as she said, caught her sleeve in it and upset everything, why had Nikolay Sergeitch dashed out of her room so excited and red in the face? Why was one drawer of the table pulled out a little way? The money-box, in which the governess put away ten kopeck[1] pieces and old stamps, was open. They had opened it, but did not know how to shut it, though they had scratched the lock all over. The whatnot with her books on it, the things on the table, the bed—all bore fresh traces of a search. Her linen-basket, too. The linen had been carefully folded, but it was not in the same order as Mashenka had left it when she went out. So the search had been thorough, most thorough. But what was it for? Why? What had happened? Mashenka remembered the excited porter, the general turmoil which was still going on, the weeping servant-girl; had it not all some connection with the search that had just been made in her room? Was not she mixed up in something dreadful? Mashenka turned pale, and feeling cold all over, sank on to her linen-basket.

A maid-servant came into the room.

---

1   *kopeck* Russian currency. One hundred kopecks equals one rouble.

"Liza, you don't know why they have been rummaging in my room?" the governess asked her.

"Mistress has lost a brooch worth two thousand," said Liza.

"Yes, but why have they been rummaging in my room?"

"They've been searching every one, miss. They've searched all my things, too. They stripped us all naked and searched us.… God knows, miss, I never went near her toilet-table, let alone touching the brooch. I shall say the same at the police-station."

"But … why have they been rummaging here?" the governess still wondered.

"A brooch has been stolen, I tell you. The mistress has been rummaging in everything with her own hands. She even searched Mihailo, the porter, herself. It's a perfect disgrace! Nikolay Sergeitch simply looks on and cackles like a hen. But you've no need to tremble like that, miss. They found nothing here. You've nothing to be afraid of if you didn't take the brooch."

"But, Liza, it's vile … it's insulting," said Mashenka, breathless with indignation. "It's so mean, so low! What right had she to suspect me and to rummage in my things?"

"You are living with strangers, miss," sighed Liza. "Though you are a young lady, still you are … as it were … a servant.… It's not like living with your papa and mamma."

Mashenka threw herself on the bed and sobbed bitterly. Never in her life had she been subjected to such an outrage, never had she been so deeply insulted.… She, well-educated, refined, the daughter of a teacher, was suspected of theft; she had been searched like a street-walker! She could not imagine a greater insult. And to this feeling of resentment was added an oppressive dread of what would come next. All sorts of absurd ideas came into her mind. If they could suspect her of theft, then they might arrest her, strip her naked, and search her, then lead her through the street with an escort of soldiers, cast her into a cold, dark cell with mice and woodlice, exactly like the dungeon in which Princess Tarakanov[1] was imprisoned. Who would stand up for her? Her parents lived far away in the provinces; they had not the money to come to her. In the capital she was as solitary as in a desert, without friends or kindred. They could do what they liked with her.

"I will go to all the courts and all the lawyers," Mashenka thought, trembling. "I will explain to them, I will take an oath.… They will believe that I could not be a thief!"

---

1   *Princess Tarakanov* Yelizaveta Alekseyevna (1753–75), an impostor who claimed to be a Russian princess. She was captured in 1775 and died of tuberculosis while in prison.

Mashenka remembered that under the sheets in her basket she had some sweetmeats, which, following the habits of her schooldays, she had put in her pocket at dinner and carried off to her room. She felt hot all over, and was ashamed at the thought that her little secret was known to the lady of the house; and all this terror, shame, resentment, brought on an attack of palpitation of the heart, which set up a throbbing in her temples, in her heart, and deep down in her stomach.

"Dinner is ready," the servant summoned Mashenka.

"Shall I go, or not?"

Mashenka brushed her hair, wiped her face with a wet towel, and went into the dining-room. There they had already begun dinner. At one end of the table sat Fedosya Vassilyevna with a stupid, solemn, serious face; at the other end Nikolay Sergeitch. At the sides there were the visitors and the children. The dishes were handed by two footmen in swallowtails and white gloves. Everyone knew that there was an upset in the house, that Madame Kushkin was in trouble, and everyone was silent. Nothing was heard but the sound of munching and the rattle of spoons on the plates.

The lady of the house, herself, was the first to speak.

"What is the third course?" she asked the footman in a weary, injured voice.

"*Esturgeon à la russe*,"[1] answered the footman.

"I ordered that, Fenya," Nikolay Sergeitch hastened to observe. "I wanted some fish. If you don't like it, *ma chère*,[2] don't let them serve it. I just ordered it...."

Fedosya Vassilyevna did not like dishes that she had not ordered herself, and now her eyes filled with tears.

"Come, don't let us agitate ourselves," Mamikov, her household doctor, observed in a honeyed voice, just touching her arm, with a smile as honeyed. "We are nervous enough as it is. Let us forget the brooch! Health is worth more than two thousand roubles!"

"It's not the two thousand I regret," answered the lady, and a big tear rolled down her cheek. "It's the fact itself that revolts me! I cannot put up with thieves in my house. I don't regret it—I regret nothing; but to steal from me is such ingratitude! That's how they repay me for my kindness...."

They all looked into their plates, but Mashenka fancied after the lady's words that everyone was looking at her. A lump rose in her throat; she began crying and put her handkerchief to her lips.

"*Pardon*," she muttered. "I can't help it. My head aches. I'll go away."

---

1   *Esturgeon à la russe* Russian preparation of sturgeon, a large, freshwater fish; "*à la russe*" translates literally to "in the Russian style."

2   *ma chère* French: my dear.

And she got up from the table, scraping her chair awkwardly, and went out quickly, still more overcome with confusion.

"It's beyond everything!" said Nikolay Sergeitch, frowning. "What need was there to search her room? How out of place it was!"

"I don't say she took the brooch," said Fedosya Vassilyevna, "but can you answer for her? To tell the truth, I haven't much confidence in these learned paupers."

"It really was unsuitable, Fenya…. Excuse me, Fenya, but you've no kind of legal right to make a search."

"I know nothing about your laws. All I know is that I've lost my brooch. And I will find the brooch!" She brought her fork down on the plate with a clatter, and her eyes flashed angrily. "And you eat your dinner, and don't interfere in what doesn't concern you!"

Nikolay Sergeitch dropped his eyes mildly and sighed. Meanwhile Mashenka, reaching her room, flung herself on her bed. She felt now neither alarm nor shame, but she felt an intense longing to go and slap the cheeks of this hard, arrogant, dull-witted, prosperous woman.

Lying on her bed she breathed into her pillow and dreamed of how nice it would be to go and buy the most expensive brooch and fling it into the face of this bullying woman. If only it were God's will that Fedosya Vassilyevna should come to ruin and wander about begging, and should taste all the horrors of poverty and dependence, and that Mashenka, whom she had insulted, might give her alms! Oh, if only she could come in for a big fortune, could buy a carriage, and could drive noisily past the windows so as to be envied by that woman!

But all these were only dreams, in reality there was only one thing left to do—to get away as quickly as possible, not to stay another hour in this place. It was true it was terrible to lose her place, to go back to her parents, who had nothing; but what could she do? Mashenka could not bear the sight of the lady of the house nor of her little room; she felt stifled and wretched here. She was so disgusted with Fedosya Vassilyevna, who was so obsessed by her illnesses and her supposed aristocratic rank, that everything in the world seemed to have become coarse and unattractive because this woman was living in it. Mashenka jumped up from the bed and began packing.

"May I come in?" asked Nikolay Sergeitch at the door; he had come up noiselessly to the door, and spoke in a soft, subdued voice. "May I?"

"Come in."

He came in and stood still near the door. His eyes looked dim and his red little nose was shiny. After dinner he used to drink beer, and the fact was perceptible in his walk, in his feeble, flabby hands.

"What's this?" he asked, pointing to the basket.

"I am packing. Forgive me, Nikolay Sergeitch, but I cannot remain in your house. I feel deeply insulted by this search!"

"I understand.... Only you are wrong to go. Why should you? They've searched your things, but you ... what does it matter to you? You will be none the worse for it."

Mashenka was silent and went on packing. Nikolay Sergeitch pinched his moustache, as though wondering what he should say next, and went on in an ingratiating voice:

"I understand, of course, but you must make allowances. You know my wife is nervous, headstrong; you mustn't judge her too harshly."

Mashenka did not speak.

"If you are so offended," Nikolay Sergeitch went on, "well, if you like, I'm ready to apologize. I ask your pardon."

Mashenka made no answer, but only bent lower over her box. This exhausted, irresolute man was of absolutely no significance in the household. He stood in the pitiful position of a dependent and hanger-on, even with the servants, and his apology meant nothing either.

"H'm! ... You say nothing! That's not enough for you. In that case, I will apologize for my wife. In my wife's name.... She behaved tactlessly, I admit it as a gentleman...."

Nikolay Sergeitch walked about the room, heaved a sigh, and went on: "Then you want me to have it rankling here, under my heart.... You want my conscience to torment me...."

"I know it's not your fault, Nikolay Sergeitch," said Mashenka, looking him full in the face with her big tear-stained eyes. "Why should you worry yourself?"

"Of course, no.... But still, don't you ... go away. I entreat you."

Mashenka shook her head. Nikolay Sergeitch stopped at the window and drummed on the pane with his finger-tips.

"Such misunderstandings are simply torture to me," he said. "Why, do you want me to go down on my knees to you, or what? Your pride is wounded, and here you've been crying and packing up to go; but I have pride, too, and you do not spare it! Or do you want me to tell you what I would not tell as Confession? Do you? Listen; you want me to tell you what I won't tell the priest on my deathbed?"

Mashenka made no answer.

"I took my wife's brooch," Nikolay Sergeitch said quickly. "Is that enough now? Are you satisfied? Yes, I ... took it.... But, of course, I count on your discretion.... For God's sake, not a word, not half a hint to any one!"

Mashenka, amazed and frightened, went on packing; she snatched her things, crumpled them up, and thrust them anyhow into the box and the basket. Now, after this candid avowal on the part of Nikolay Sergeitch, she could not remain another minute, and could not understand how she could have gone on living in the house before.

"And it's nothing to wonder at," Nikolay Sergeitch went on after a pause. "It's an everyday story! I need money, and she … won't give it to me. It was my father's money that bought this house and everything, you know! It's all mine, and the brooch belonged to my mother, and … it's all mine! And she took it, took possession of everything…. I can't go to law with her, you'll admit…. I beg you most earnestly, overlook it … stay on. *Tout comprendre, tout pardonner.*[1] Will you stay?"

"No!" said Mashenka resolutely, beginning to tremble. "Let me alone, I entreat you!"

"Well, God bless you!" sighed Nikolay Sergeitch, sitting down on the stool near the box. "I must own I like people who still can feel resentment, contempt, and so on. I could sit here forever and look at your indignant face…. So you won't stay, then? I understand…. It's bound to be so … Yes, of course…. It's all right for you, but for me—wo-o-o-o! … I can't stir a step out of this cellar. I'd go off to one of our estates, but in every one of them there are some of my wife's rascals … stewards, experts, damn them all! They mortgage and remortgage…. You mustn't catch fish, must keep off the grass, mustn't break the trees."

"Nikolay Sergeitch!" his wife's voice called from the drawing-room. "Agnia, call your master!"

"Then you won't stay?" asked Nikolay Sergeitch, getting up quickly and going towards the door. "You might as well stay, really. In the evenings I could come and have a talk with you. Eh? Stay! If you go, there won't be a human face left in the house. It's awful!"

Nikolay Sergeitch's pale, exhausted face besought her, but Mashenka shook her head, and with a wave of his hand he went out.

Half an hour later she was on her way.

—1886

---

1   *Tout comprendre, tout pardonner* French: To understand all is to forgive all.

Charlotte Perkins Gilman
1860–1935

Charlotte Perkins Gilman was born into a family prominent for activism and reform; her great-aunt was Harriet Beecher Stowe, author of *Uncle Tom's Cabin*. As a young woman she embraced the idea that a single woman could be a useful member of society and she resolved to dedicate her life to her work. Circumstances intervened, however: she fell in love, married, and plunged into a severe depression after the birth of her only child in 1885. She received treatment from the "nerve doctor" S. Weir Mitchell, who prescribed his famous "rest cure"—isolation, quiet domesticity, and abstention from intellectual endeavours—which greatly worsened her condition. In 1892, she published the short story "The Yellow Wallpaper," in which the protagonist is treated according to similar principles.

By this time, Gilman had left her husband, moved to California, and began again to work outside the home, forging a career as a feminist writer and lecturer. She won admiration from women reformers such as Jane Addams (1860–1935) and Elizabeth Cady Stanton (1815–1902). Her non-fiction work *Women and Economics* (1898) was a bestseller. From 1909 to 1916, she wrote for and edited her own magazine, *The Forerunner*; in 1915, the magazine serialized her novel *Herland*, about a utopia populated solely by women. In a statement that she made about the composition of "The Yellow Wallpaper," Gilman expressed the belief that informed all of her writing: "Work, in which is joy and growth and service, without which one is a pauper and a parasite," was essential for women.

The Yellow Wallpaper

It is very seldom that mere ordinary people like John and myself secure ancestral halls for the summer.

A colonial mansion, a hereditary estate, I would say a haunted house and reach the height of romantic felicity—but that would be asking too much of fate!

Still I will proudly declare that there is something queer about it.

Else, why should it be let so cheaply? And why have stood so long untenanted?

John laughs at me, of course, but one expects that.

John is practical in the extreme. He has no patience with faith, an intense horror of superstition, and he scoffs openly at any talk of things not to be felt and seen and put down in figures.

John is a physician, and *perhaps*—(I would not say it to a living soul, of course, but this is dead paper and a great relief to my mind)—*perhaps* that is one reason I do not get well faster.

You see, he does not believe I am sick! And what can one do?

If a physician of high standing, and one's own husband, assures friends and relatives that there is really nothing the matter with one but temporary nervous depression—a slight hysterical tendency—what is one to do?

My brother is also a physician, and also of high standing, and he says the same thing.

So I take phosphates or phosphites—whichever it is—and tonics, and air and exercise, and journeys, and am absolutely forbidden to "work" until I am well again.

Personally, I disagree with their ideas.

Personally, I believe that congenial work, with excitement and change, would do me good.

But what is one to do?

I did write for a while in spite of them, but it *does* exhaust me a good deal—having to be so sly about it, or else meet with heavy opposition.

I sometimes fancy that in my condition, if I had less opposition and more society and stimulus—but John says the very worst thing I can do is to think about my condition, and I confess it always makes me feel bad.

So I will let it alone and talk about the house.

The most beautiful place! It is quite alone, standing well back from the road, quite three miles from the village. It makes me think of English places that you read about, for there are hedges and walls and gates that lock, and lots of separate little houses for the gardeners and people.

There is a *delicious* garden! I never saw such a garden—large and shady, full of box-bordered paths, and lined with long grape-covered arbours with seats under them.

There were greenhouses, but they are all broken now.

There was some legal trouble, I believe, something about the heirs and co-heirs; anyhow, the place has been empty for years.

That spoils my ghostliness, I am afraid, but I don't care—there is something strange about the house—I can feel it.

I even said so to John one moonlight evening, but he said what I felt was a draught, and shut the window.

I get unreasonably angry with John sometimes. I'm sure I never used to be so sensitive. I think it is due to this nervous condition.

But John says if I feel so, I shall neglect proper self-control; so I take pains to control myself—before him, at least, and that makes me very tired.

I don't like our room a bit. I wanted one downstairs that opened on the piazza and had roses all over the window, and such pretty old-fashioned chintz hangings! But John would not hear of it.

He said there was only one window and not room for two beds, and no near room for him if he took another.

He is very careful and loving, and hardly lets me stir without special direction.

I have a schedule prescription for each hour in the day; he takes all care from me, and so I feel basely ungrateful not to value it more.

He said we came here solely on my account, that I was to have perfect rest and all the air I could get. "Your exercise depends on your strength, my dear," said he, "and your food somewhat on your appetite; but air you can absorb all the time." So we took the nursery at the top of the house.

It is a big, airy room, the whole floor nearly, with windows that look all ways, and air and sunshine galore. It was nursery first and then playroom and gymnasium, I should judge; for the windows are barred for little children, and there are rings and things in the walls.

The paint and paper look as if a boys' school had used it. It is stripped off—the paper—in great patches all around the head of my bed, about as far as I can reach, and in a great place on the other side of the room low down. I never saw a worse paper in my life. One of those sprawling flamboyant patterns committing every artistic sin.

It is dull enough to confuse the eye in following, pronounced enough to constantly irritate and provoke study, and when you follow the lame uncertain curves for a little distance they suddenly commit suicide—plunge off at outrageous angles, destroy themselves in unheard-of contradictions.

The colour is repellent, almost revolting; a smouldering unclean yellow, strangely faded by the slow-turning sunlight. It is a dull yet lurid orange in some places, a sickly sulphur tint in others.

No wonder the children hated it! I should hate it myself if I had to live in this room long.

There comes John, and I must put this away—he hates to have me write a word.

We have been here two weeks, and I haven't felt like writing before, since that first day.

I am sitting by the window now, up in this atrocious nursery, and there is nothing to hinder my writing as much as I please, save lack of strength.

John is away all day, and even some nights when his cases are serious.

I am glad my case is not serious!

But these nervous troubles are dreadfully depressing.

John does not know how much I really suffer. He knows there is no reason to suffer, and that satisfies him.

Of course it is only nervousness. It does weigh on me so not to do my duty in any way!

I mean to be such a help to John, such a real rest and comfort, and here I am a comparative burden already!

Nobody would believe what an effort it is to do what little I am able—to dress and entertain, and order things.

It is fortunate Mary is so good with the baby. Such a dear baby!

And yet I *cannot* be with him, it makes me so nervous.

I suppose John never was nervous in his life. He laughs at me so about this wallpaper!

At first he meant to repaper the room, but afterwards he said that I was letting it get the better of me, and that nothing was worse for a nervous patient than to give way to such fancies.

He said that after the wallpaper was changed it would be the heavy bedstead, and then the barred windows, and then that gate at the head of the stairs, and so on.

"You know the place is doing you good," he said, "and really, dear, I don't care to renovate the house just for a three months' rental."

"Then do let us go downstairs," I said. "There are such pretty rooms there."

Then he took me in his arms and called me a blessed little goose, and said he would go down cellar, if I wished, and have it whitewashed into the bargain.

But he is right enough about the beds and windows and things.

It is as airy and comfortable a room as anyone need wish, and, of course, I would not be so silly as to make him uncomfortable just for a whim.

I'm really getting quite fond of the big room, all but that horrid paper.

Out of one window I can see the garden—those mysterious deep-shaded arbours, the riotous old-fashioned flowers, and bushes and gnarly trees.

Out of another I get a lovely view of the bay and a little private wharf belonging to the estate. There is a beautiful shaded lane that runs down there from the house. I always fancy I see people walking in these numerous paths and arbours, but John has cautioned me not to give way to fancy in the least. He says that with my imaginative power and habit of story-making, a nervous weakness like mine is sure to lead to all manner of excited fancies, and that I ought to use my will and good sense to check the tendency. So I try.

I think sometimes that if I were only well enough to write a little it would relieve the press of ideas and rest me.

But I find I get pretty tired when I try.

It is so discouraging not to have any advice and companionship about my work. When I get really well, John says we will ask Cousin Henry and Julia down for a long visit; but he says he would as soon put fireworks in my pillow-case as to let me have those stimulating people about now.

I wish I could get well faster.

But I must not think about that. This paper looks to me as if it *knew* what a vicious influence it had!

There is a recurrent spot where the pattern lolls like a broken neck and two bulbous eyes stare at you upside down.

I get positively angry with the impertinence of it and the everlastingness. Up and down and sideways they crawl, and those absurd unblinking eyes are everywhere. There is one place where two breadths didn't match, and the eyes go all up and down the line, one a little higher than the other.

I never saw so much expression in an inanimate thing before, and we all know how much expression they have! I used to lie awake as a child and get more entertainment and terror out of blank walls and plain furniture than most children could find in a toy-store.

I remember what a kindly wink the knobs of our big old bureau used to have, and there was one chair that always seemed like a strong friend.

I used to feel that if any of the other things looked too fierce I could always hop into that chair and be safe.

The furniture in this room is no worse than inharmonious, however, for we had to bring it all from downstairs. I suppose when this was used as a playroom they had to take the nursery things out, and no wonder! I never saw such ravages as the children have made here.

The wallpaper, as I said before, is torn off in spots, and it sticketh closer than a brother[1]—they must have had perseverance as well as hatred.

Then the floor is scratched and gouged and splintered, the plaster itself is dug out here and there, and this great heavy bed which is all we found in the room, looks as if it had been through the wars.

But I don't mind it a bit—only the paper.

There comes John's sister. Such a dear girl as she is, and so careful of me! I must not let her find me writing.

She is a perfect and enthusiastic housekeeper, and hopes for no better profession. I verily believe she thinks it is the writing which made me sick!

But I can write when she is out, and see her a long way off from these windows.

---

1   *sticketh ... brother* From Proverbs 18.24.

There is one that commands the road, a lovely shaded winding road, and one that just looks off over the country. A lovely country, too, full of great elms and velvet meadows.

This wallpaper has a kind of sub-pattern in a different shade, a particularly irritating one, for you can only see it in certain lights, and not clearly then.

But in the places where it isn't faded and where the sun is just so—I can see a strange, provoking, formless sort of figure that seems to skulk about behind that silly and conspicuous front design.

There's sister on the stairs!

Well, the Fourth of July is over! The people are all gone, and I am tired out. John thought it might do me good to see a little company, so we just had Mother and Nellie and the children down for a week.

Of course I didn't do a thing. Jennie sees to everything now.

But it tired me all the same.

John says if I don't pick up faster he shall send me to Weir Mitchell in the fall.

But I don't want to go there at all. I had a friend who was in his hands once, and she says he is just like John and my brother, only more so!

Besides, it is such an undertaking to go so far.

I don't feel as if it was worthwhile to turn my hand over for anything, and I'm getting dreadfully fretful and querulous.

I cry at nothing, and cry most of the time.

Of course I don't when John is here, or anybody else, but when I am alone.

And I am alone a good deal just now. John is kept in town very often by serious cases, and Jennie is good and lets me alone when I want her to.

So I walk a little in the garden or down that lovely lane, sit on the porch under the roses, and lie down up here a good deal.

I'm getting really fond of the room in spite of the wallpaper. Perhaps because of the wallpaper.

It dwells in my mind so!

I lie here on this great immovable bed—it is nailed down, I believe—and follow that pattern about by the hour. It is as good as gymnastics, I assure you. I start, we'll say, at the bottom, down in the corner over there where it has not been touched, and I determine for the thousandth time that I *will* follow that pointless pattern to some sort of conclusion.

I know a little of the principle of design, and I know this thing was not arranged on any laws of radiation, or alternation, or repetition, or symmetry, or anything else that I ever heard of.

It is repeated, of course, by the breadths, but not otherwise.

Looked at in one way, each breadth stands alone; the bloated curves and flourishes—a kind of "debased Romanesque" with delirium tremens[1]—go waddling up and down in isolated columns of fatuity.

But, on the other hand, they connect diagonally, and the sprawling outlines run off in great slanting waves of optic horror, like a lot of wallowing sea-weeds in full chase.

The whole thing goes horizontally, too, at least it seems so, and I exhaust myself trying to distinguish the order of its going in that direction.

They have used a horizontal breadth for a frieze, and that adds wonderfully to the confusion.

There is one end of the room where it is almost intact, and there, when the crosslights fade and the low sun shines directly upon it, I can almost fancy radiation after all—the interminable grotesque seems to form around a common centre and rush off in headlong plunges of equal distraction.

It makes me tired to follow it. I will take a nap, I guess.

I don't know why I should write this.

I don't want to.

I don't feel able.

And I know John would think it absurd. But I *must* say what I feel and think in some way—it is such a relief!

But the effort is getting to be greater than the relief.

Half the time now I am awfully lazy, and lie down ever so much.

John says I mustn't lose my strength, and has me take cod liver oil and lots of tonics and things, to say nothing of the ale and wine and rare meat.

Dear John! He loves me very dearly, and hates to have me sick. I tried to have a real earnest reasonable talk with him the other day, and tell him how I wish he would let me go and make a visit to Cousin Henry and Julia.

But he said I wasn't able to go, nor able to stand it after I got there; and I did not make out a very good case for myself, for I was crying before I had finished.

It is getting to be a great effort for me to think straight. Just this nervous weakness, I suppose.

And dear John gathered me up in his arms, and just carried me upstairs and laid me on the bed, and sat by me and read to me till it tired my head.

He said I was his darling and his comfort and all he had, and that I must take care of myself for his sake, and keep well.

---

1   *Romanesque* Medieval architectural style involving columns and round arches similar to those found in Roman architecture; *delirium tremens* Condition resulting from extreme alcohol withdrawal; its symptoms include tremors, hallucinations, and random physical movements.

He says no one but myself can help me out of it, that I must use my will and self-control and not let any silly fancies run away with me.

There's one comfort—the baby is well and happy, and does not have to occupy this nursery with the horrid wallpaper.

If we had not used it, that blessed child would have! What a fortunate escape! Why, I wouldn't have a child of mine, an impressionable little thing, live in such a room for worlds.

I never thought of it before, but it is lucky that John kept me here after all, I can stand it so much easier than a baby, you see.

Of course I never mention it to them any more—I am too wise—but I keep watch for it all the same.

There are things in that paper that nobody knows about but me, or ever will.

Behind that outside pattern the dim shapes get clearer every day.

It is always the same shape, only very numerous.

And it is like a woman stooping down and creeping about behind that pattern. I don't like it a bit. I wonder—I begin to think—I wish John would take me away from here!

It is so hard to talk with John about my case, because he is so wise, and because he loves me so.

But I tried it last night.

It was moonlight. The moon shines in all around just as the sun does.

I hate to see it sometimes, it creeps so slowly, and always comes in by one window or another.

John was asleep and I hated to waken him, so I kept still and watched the moonlight on that undulating wallpaper till I felt creepy.

The faint figure behind seemed to shake the pattern, just as if she wanted to get out.

I got up softly and went to feel and see if the paper *did* move, and when I came back John was awake.

"What is it, little girl?" he said. "Don't go walking about like that—you'll get cold."

I thought it was a good time to talk, so I told him that I really was not gaining here, and that I wished he would take me away.

"Why, darling!" said he. "Our lease will be up in three weeks, and I can't see how to leave before.

"The repairs are not done at home, and I cannot possibly leave town just now. Of course if you were in any danger, I could and would, but you really are better, dear, whether you can see it or not. I am a doctor, dear, and I know.

You are gaining flesh and colour, your appetite is better, I feel really much easier about you."

"I don't weigh a bit more," said I, "nor as much; and my appetite may be better in the evening when you are here but it is worse in the morning when you are away!"

"Bless her little heart!" said he with a big hug. "She shall be as sick as she pleases! But now let's improve the shining hours[1] by going to sleep, and talk about it in the morning!"

"And you won't go away?" I asked gloomily.

"Why, how can I, dear? It is only three weeks more and then we will take a nice little trip of a few days while Jennie is getting the house ready. Really, dear, you are better!"

"Better in body perhaps—" I began, and stopped short, for he sat up straight and looked at me with such a stern, reproachful look that I could not say another word.

"My darling," said he, "I beg of you, for my sake and for our child's sake, as well as your own, that you will never for one instant let that idea enter your mind! There is nothing so dangerous, so fascinating, to a temperament like yours. It is a false and foolish fancy. Can you not trust me as a physician when I tell you so?"

So of course I said no more on that score, and we went to sleep before long. He thought I was asleep first, but I wasn't, and lay there for hours trying to decide whether that front pattern and the back pattern really did move together or separately.

On a pattern like this, by daylight, there is a lack of sequence, a defiance of law, that is a constant irritant to a normal mind.

The colour is hideous enough, and unreliable enough, and infuriating enough, but the pattern is torturing.

You think you have mastered it, but just as you get well under way in following, it turns a back-somersault and there you are. It slaps you in the face, knocks you down, and tramples upon you. It is like a bad dream.

The outside pattern is a florid arabesque,[2] reminding one of a fungus. If you can imagine a toadstool in joints, an interminable string of toadstools, budding and sprouting in endless convolutions—why, that is something like it.

That is, sometimes!

---

1   *improve the … hours* See Isaac Watts's popular children's poem "Against Idleness and Mischief" (1715): "How doth the little busy bee / Improve each shining hour."

2   *arabesque* Complex decorative design.

There is one marked peculiarity about this paper, a thing nobody seems to notice but myself, and that is that it changes as the light changes.

When the sun shoots in through the east window—I always watch for that first long, straight ray—it changes so quickly that I never can quite believe it.

That is why I watch it always.

By moonlight—the moon shines in all night when there is a moon—I wouldn't know it was the same paper.

At night in any kind of light, in twilight, candlelight, lamplight, and worst of all by moonlight, it becomes bars! The outside pattern, I mean, and the woman behind it is as plain as can be.

I didn't realize for a long time what the thing was that showed behind, that dim sub-pattern, but now I am quite sure it is a woman.

By daylight she is subdued, quiet. I fancy it is the pattern that keeps her so still. It is so puzzling. It keeps me quiet by the hour.

I lie down ever so much now. John says it is good for me, and to sleep all I can.

Indeed he started the habit by making me lie down for an hour after each meal.

It is a very bad habit I am convinced, for you see, I don't sleep.

And that cultivates deceit, for I don't tell them I'm awake—O no!

The fact is I am getting a little afraid of John.

He seems very queer sometimes, and even Jennie has an inexplicable look.

It strikes me occasionally, just as a scientific hypothesis, that perhaps it is the paper!

I have watched John when he did not know I was looking, and come into the room suddenly on the most innocent excuses, and I've caught him several times *looking at the paper*! And Jennie too. I caught Jennie with her hand on it once.

She didn't know I was in the room, and when I asked her in a quiet, a very quiet voice, with the most restrained manner possible, what she was doing with the paper—she turned around as if she had been caught stealing, and looked quite angry—asked me why I should frighten her so!

Then she said that the paper stained everything it touched, that she had found yellow smooches on all my clothes and John's, and she wished we would be more careful!

Did not that sound innocent? But I know she was studying that pattern, and I am determined that nobody shall find it out but myself!

Life is very much more exciting now than it used to be. You see I have something more to expect, to look forward to, to watch. I really do eat better, and am more quiet than I was.

John is so pleased to see me improve! He laughed a little the other day, and said I seemed to be flourishing in spite of my wallpaper.

I turned it off with a laugh. I had no intention of telling him it was *because* of the wallpaper—he would make fun of me. He might even want to take me away.

I don't want to leave now until I have found it out. There is a week more, and I think that will be enough.

I'm feeling so much better!

I don't sleep much at night, for it is so interesting to watch developments; but I sleep a good deal during the daytime.

In the daytime it is tiresome and perplexing.

There are always new shoots on the fungus, and new shades of yellow all over it. I cannot keep count of them, though I have tried conscientiously.

It is the strangest yellow, that wallpaper! It makes me think of all the yellow things I ever saw—not beautiful ones like buttercups, but old, foul, bad yellow things.

But there is something else about that paper—the smell! I noticed it the moment we came into the room, but with so much air and sun it was not bad. Now we have had a week of fog and rain, and whether the windows are open or not, the smell is here.

It creeps all over the house.

I find it hovering in the dining-room, skulking in the parlour, hiding in the hall, lying in wait for me on the stairs.

It gets into my hair.

Even when I go to ride, if I turn my head suddenly and surprise it—there is that smell!

Such a peculiar odour, too! I have spent hours in trying to analyze it, to find what it smelled like.

It is not bad—at first—and very gentle, but quite the subtlest, most enduring odour I ever met.

In this damp weather it is awful, I wake up in the night and find it hanging over me.

It used to disturb me at first. I thought seriously of burning the house—to reach the smell.

But now I am used to it. The only thing I can think of that it is like is the *colour* of the paper! A yellow smell.

There is a very funny mark on this wall, low down, near the mopboard. A streak that runs round the room. It goes behind every piece of furniture, except the bed, a long, straight, even *smooch*, as if it had been rubbed over and over.

I wonder how it was done and who did it, and what they did it for. Round and round and round—round and round and round—it makes me dizzy!

I really have discovered something at last.

Through watching so much at night, when it changes so, I have finally found out.

The front pattern *does* move—and no wonder! The woman behind shakes it!

Sometimes I think there are a great many women behind, and sometimes only one, and she crawls around fast, and her crawling shakes it all over.

Then in the very bright spots she keeps still, and in the very shady spots she just takes hold of the bars and shakes them hard.

And she is all the time trying to climb through. But nobody could climb through that pattern—it strangles so; I think that is why it has so many heads.

They get through, and then the pattern strangles them off and turns them upside down, and makes their eyes white!

If those heads were covered or taken off it would not be half so bad.

I think that woman gets out in the daytime!

And I'll tell you why—privately—I've seen her!

I can see her out of every one of my windows!

It is the same woman, I know, for she is always creeping, and most women do not creep by daylight.

I see her in that long shaded lane, creeping up and down. I see her in those dark grape arbours, creeping all around the garden.

I see her on that long road under the trees, creeping along, and when a carriage comes she hides under the blackberry vines.

I don't blame her a bit. It must be very humiliating to be caught creeping by daylight!

I always lock the door when I creep by daylight. I can't do it at night, for I know John would suspect something at once.

And John is so queer now that I don't want to irritate him. I wish he would take another room! Besides, I don't want anybody to get that woman out at night but myself.

I often wonder if I could see her out of all the windows at once.

But, turn as fast as I can, I can only see out of one at one time.

And though I always see her, she *may* be able to creep faster than I can turn! I have watched her sometimes away off in the open country, creeping as fast as a cloud shadow in a wind.

If only that top pattern could be gotten off from the under one! I mean to try it, little by little.

I have found out another funny thing, but I shan't tell it this time! It does not do to trust people too much.

There are only two more days to get this paper off, and I believe John is beginning to notice. I don't like the look in his eyes.

And I heard him ask Jennie a lot of professional questions about me. She had a very good report to give.

She said I slept a good deal in the daytime.

John knows I don't sleep very well at night, for all I'm so quiet!

He asked me all sorts of questions, too, and pretended to be very loving and kind.

As if I couldn't see through him!

Still, I don't wonder he acts so, sleeping under this paper for three months.

It only interests me, but I feel sure John and Jennie are affected by it.

Hurrah! This is the last day, but it is enough. John is to stay in town over night, and won't be out until this evening.

Jennie wanted to sleep with me—the sly thing; but I told her I should undoubtedly rest better for a night all alone.

That was clever, for really I wasn't alone a bit! As soon as it was moonlight and that poor thing began to crawl and shake the pattern, I got up and ran to help her.

I pulled and she shook, I shook and she pulled, and before morning we had peeled off yards of that paper.

A strip about as high as my head and half around the room.

And then when the sun came and that awful pattern began to laugh at me, I declared I would finish it today!

We go away tomorrow, and they are moving all my furniture down again to leave things as they were before.

Jennie looked at the wall in amazement, but I told her merrily that I did it out of pure spite at the vicious thing.

She laughed and said she wouldn't mind doing it herself, but I must not get tired.

How she betrayed herself that time!

But I am here, and no person touches this paper but Me—not *alive*!

She tried to get me out of the room—it was too patent! But I said it was so quiet and empty and clean now that I believed I would lie down again and sleep all I could; and not to wake me even for dinner—I would call when I woke.

So now she is gone, and the servants are gone, and the things are gone, and there is nothing left but that great bedstead nailed down, with the canvas mattress we found on it.

We shall sleep downstairs tonight, and take the boat home tomorrow.

I quite enjoy the room, now it is bare again.

How those children did tear about here!

This bedstead is fairly gnawed!

But I must get to work.

I have locked the door and thrown the key down into the front path.

I don't want to go out, and I don't want to have anybody come in, till John comes.

I want to astonish him.

I've got a rope up here that even Jennie did not find. If that woman does get out, and tries to get away, I can tie her!

But I forgot I could not reach far without anything to stand on!

This bed will *not* move!

I tried to lift and push it until I was lame, and then I got so angry I bit off a little piece at one corner—but it hurt my teeth.

Then I peeled off all the paper I could reach standing on the floor. It sticks horribly and the pattern just enjoys it! All those strangled heads and bulbous eyes and waddling fungus growths just shriek with derision!

I am getting angry enough to do something desperate. To jump out of the window would be admirable exercise, but the bars are too strong even to try.

Besides I wouldn't do it. Of course not. I know well enough that a step like that is improper and might be misconstrued.

I don't like to *look* out of the windows even—there are so many of those creeping women, and they creep so fast.

I wonder if they all come out of that wallpaper as I did?

But I am securely fastened now by my well-hidden rope—you don't get me out in the road there!

I suppose I shall have to get back behind the pattern when it comes night, and that is hard!

It is so pleasant to be out in this great room and creep around as I please!

I don't want to go outside. I won't, even if Jennie asks me to.

For outside you have to creep on the ground, and everything is green instead of yellow.

But here I can creep smoothly on the floor, and my shoulder just fits in that long smooch around the wall, so I cannot lose my way.

Why there's John at the door!

It is no use, young man, you can't open it!

How he does call and pound!

Now he's crying to Jennie for an axe.

It would be a shame to break down that beautiful door!

"John dear!" said I in the gentlest voice. "The key is down by the front steps, under a plantain leaf!"

That silenced him for a few moments.

Then he said—very quietly indeed, "Open the door, my darling!"

"I can't," said I. "The key is down by the front door under a plantain leaf!"

And then I said it again, several times, very gently and slowly, and said it so often that he had to go and see, and he got it of course, and came in. He stopped short by the door.

"What is the matter?" he cried. "For God's sake, what are you doing!"

I kept on creeping just the same, but I looked at him over my shoulder.

"I've got out at last," said I, "in spite of you and Jane! And I've pulled off most of the paper, so you can't put me back!"

Now why should that man have fainted? But he did, and right across my path by the wall, so that I had to creep over him every time!

—1892

Edith Wharton
1862–1937

Edith Wharton was born in New York into a life of wealth and privilege, but, from an early age, she perceived that her peers, particularly women, were imprisoned by the social constraints of her class. Her novels and short stories would become known for their keen, often satiric observation of social mores—especially those of the high society world of her youth—and the ways in which those mores complicated and stifled the lives of her characters. As the novelist Francine Prose has said, "no one has written more incisively not just about a historical period and a particular social milieu but about something more timeless—the ardor with which we flee and return to the prison of conditioning and convenience."

Like most girls of her class, Wharton was educated at home by governesses, but she augmented her education by reading widely. As she reveals in her autobiography, *A Backward Glance*, she also loved "making up" stories and began to write when very young, even though her family disapproved of the activity as beneath her class—"something between a black art and a form of manual labor." In fact, she was so strapped for writing paper she was often reduced to using the wrapping from packages for her compositions. In 1879, *The Atlantic Monthly* published some of her poems; 25 novels, 86 short stories, and numerous works of non-fiction were to follow, with her 1920 novel, *The Age of Innocence*, winning a Pulitzer Prize.

By 1913, Wharton had moved permanently to France and, like her good friend, the writer Henry James (1843–1916), she capitalized on her knowledge of the differences between American and European society to write novels like *The Custom of the Country* (1913) with settings on both sides of the Atlantic.

Atrophy

1

Nora Frenway settled down furtively in her corner of the Pullman[1] and, as the express plunged out of the Grand Central Station, wondered at herself for being where she was. The porter came along. "Ticket?" "Westover." She had instinctively lowered her voice and glanced about her. But neither the porter nor her nearest neighbours—fortunately none of them known to her—seemed in the least surprised or interested by the statement that she was travelling to Westover.

---

1   *Pullman* Luxurious railway carriage.

Yet what an earth-shaking announcement it was! Not that she cared, now; not that anything mattered except the one overwhelming fact which had convulsed her life, hurled her out of her easy velvet-lined rut, and flung her thus naked to the public scrutiny.... Cautiously, again, she glanced about her to make doubly sure that there was no one, absolutely no one, in the Pullman whom she knew by sight.

Her life had been so carefully guarded, so inwardly conventional in a world where all the outer conventions were tottering, that no one had ever known she had a lover. No one—of that she was absolutely sure. All the circumstances of the case had made it necessary that she should conceal her real life—her only real life—from everyone about her; from her half-invalid irascible husband, his prying envious sisters, and the terrible monumental old chieftainess, her mother-in-law, before whom all the family quailed and humbugged and fibbed and fawned.

What nonsense to pretend that nowadays, even in big cities, in the world's greatest social centres, the severe old-fashioned standards had given place to tolerance, laxity and ease! You took up the morning paper, and you read of girl bandits, movie-star divorces, "hold-ups" at balls, murder and suicide and elopement, and a general welter of disjointed disconnected impulses and appetites; then you turned your eyes onto your own daily life, and found yourself as cribbed and cabined, as beset by vigilant family eyes, observant friends, all sorts of embodied standards, as any white-muslin novel heroine of the 'sixties![1]

In a different way, of course. To the casual eye Mrs. Frenway herself might have seemed as free as any of the young married women of her group. Poker playing, smoking, cocktail drinking, dancing, painting, short skirts, bobbed hair and the rest—when had these been denied to her? If by any outward sign she had differed too markedly from her kind—lengthened her skirts, refused to play for money, let her hair grow, or ceased to make-up—her husband would have been the first to notice it, and to say: "Are you ill? What's the matter? How queer you look! What's the sense of making yourself conspicuous?" For he and his kind had adopted all the old inhibitions and sanctions, blindly transferring them to a new ritual, as the receptive Romans did when strange gods were brought into their temples....

The train had escaped from the ugly fringes of the city, and the soft spring landscape was gliding past her: glimpses of green lawns, budding hedges, pretty irregular roofs, and miles and miles of alluring tarred roads slipping away into

1   *white-muslin ... sixties* Refers to the 1860s trend of the sensation novel, characterized by lurid plots involving crime and shocking family secrets. Among the most popular of these novels was Wilkie Collins's *The Woman in White* (1860), in which the title character is unjustly committed to an asylum.

mystery. How often she had dreamed of dashing off down an unknown road with Christopher!

Not that she was a woman to be awed by the conventions. She knew she wasn't. She had always taken their measure, smiled at them—and conformed. On account of poor George Frenway, to begin with. Her husband, in a sense, was a man to be pitied; his weak health, his bad temper, his unsatisfied vanity, all made him a rather forlornly comic figure. But it was chiefly on account of the two children that she had always resisted the temptation to do anything reckless. The least self-betrayal would have been the end of everything. Too many eyes were watching her, and her husband's family was so strong, so united—when there was anybody for them to hate—and at all times so influential, that she would have been defeated at every point, and her husband would have kept the children.

At the mere thought she felt herself on the brink of an abyss. "The children are my religion," she had once said to herself; and she had no other.

Yet here she was on her way to Westover.... Oh, what did it matter now? That was the worst of it—it was too late for anything between her and Christopher to matter! She was sure he was dying. The way in which his cousin, Gladys Brincker, had blurted it out the day before at Kate Salmer's dance: "You didn't know—poor Kit?[1] Thought you and he were such pals! Yes, awfully bad, I'm afraid. Return of the old trouble! I know there've been two consultations—they had Knowlton down. They say there's not much hope; and nobody but that forlorn frightened Jane mounting guard...."

Poor Christopher! His sister Jane Aldis, Nora suspected, forlorn and frightened as she was, had played in his life a part nearly as dominant as Frenway and the children in Nora's. Loyally, Christopher always pretended that she didn't; talked of her indulgently as "poor Jenny." But didn't she, Nora, always think of her husband as "poor George"? Jane Aldis, of course, was much less self-assertive, less demanding, than George Frenway; but perhaps for that very reason she would appeal all the more to a man's compassion. And somehow, under her unobtrusive air, Nora had—on the rare occasions when they met—imagined that Miss Aldis was watching and drawing her inferences. But then Nora always felt, where Christopher was concerned, as if her breast were a pane of glass through which her trembling palpitating heart could be seen as plainly as holy viscera in a reliquary. Her sober after-thought was that Jane Aldis was just a dowdy self-effacing old maid whose life was filled to the brim by looking over the Westover place for her brother, and seeing that the fires were lit and the rooms full of flowers when he brought down his friends for a week-end.

---

1   *Kit* Short for Christopher.

Ah, how often he had said to Nora: "If I could have you to myself for a week-end at Westover"—quite as if it were the easiest thing imaginable, as far as his arrangements were concerned! And they had even pretended to discuss how it could be done. But somehow she fancied he said it because he knew that the plan, for her, was about as feasible as a week-end in the moon. And in reality her only visits to Westover had been made in the company of her husband, and that of other friends, two or three times, at the beginning.... For after that she wouldn't. It was three years now since she had been there.

Gladys Brincker, in speaking of Christopher's illness, had looked at Nora queerly, as though suspecting something. But no—what nonsense! No one had ever suspected Nora Frenway. Didn't she know what her friends said of her? "Nora? No more temperament than a lamp-post. Always buried in her books.... Never very attractive to men, in spite of her looks." Hadn't she said that of other women, who perhaps, in secret, like herself...?

The train was slowing down as it approached a station. She sat up with a jerk and looked at her wrist-watch. It was half-past two, the station was Ockham; the next would be Westover. In less than an hour she would be under his roof, Jane Aldis would be receiving her in that low panelled room full of books, and she would be saying—what would she be saying?

She had gone over their conversation so often that she knew not only her own part in it but Miss Aldis's by heart. The first moments would of course be painful, difficult; but then a great wave of emotion, breaking down the barriers between the two anxious women, would fling them together. She wouldn't have to say much, to explain; Miss Aldis would just take her by the hand and lead her upstairs to the room.

That room! She shut her eyes, and remembered other rooms where she and he had been together in their joy and their strength.... No, not that; she must not think of that now. For the man she had met in those other rooms was dying; the man she was going to was someone so different from that other man that it was like a profanation to associate their images.... And yet the man she was going to was her own Christopher, the one who had lived in her soul; and how his soul must be needing hers, now that it hung alone on the dark brink! As if anything else mattered at such a moment! She neither thought nor cared what Jane Aldis might say or suspect; she wouldn't have cared if the Pullman had been full of prying acquaintances, or if George and all George's family had got in at that last station.

She wouldn't have cared a fig for any of them. Yet at the same moment she remembered having felt glad that her old governess, whom she used to go and see twice a year, lived at Ockham—so that if George did begin to ask questions, she could always say: "Yes, I went to see poor old Fraulein; she's absolutely crippled now. I shall have to get her a Bath chair.[1] Could you get me a catalogue of prices?" There wasn't a precaution she hadn't thought of—and now she was ready to scatter them all to the winds....

Westover—"Junction!"

She started up and pushed her way out of the train. All the people seemed to be obstructing her, putting bags and suit-cases in her way. And the express stopped for only two minutes. Suppose she should be carried on to Albany?

Westover Junction was a growing place, and she was fairly sure there would be a taxi at the station. There was one—she just managed to get to it ahead of a travelling man with a sample case and a new straw hat. As she opened the door a smell of damp hay and bad tobacco greeted her. She sprang in and gasped: "To Oakfield. You know? Mr. Aldis's place near Westover."

2

It began exactly as she had expected. A surprised parlour maid—why surprised?—showed her into the low panelled room that was so full of his presence, his books, his pipes, his terrier dozing on the shabby rug. The parlour maid said she would go and see if Miss Aldis could come down. Nora wanted to ask if she were with her brother—and how he was. But she found herself unable to speak the words. She was afraid her voice might tremble. And why should she question the parlour maid, when in a moment, she hoped, she was to see Miss Aldis?

The woman moved away with a hushed step—the step which denotes illness in the house. She did not immediately return, and the interval of waiting in that room, so strange yet so intimately known, was a new torture to Nora. It was unlike anything she had imagined. The writing table with his scattered pens and letters was more than she could bear. His dog looked at her amicably from the hearth, but made no advances; and though she longed to stroke him, to let her hand rest where Christopher's had rested, she dared not for fear he should bark and disturb the peculiar hush of that dumb watchful house. She stood in the window and looked out at the budding shrubs and the bulbs pushing up through the swollen earth.

"This way, please."

Her heart gave a plunge. Was the woman actually taking her upstairs to his room? Her eyes filled, she felt herself swept forward on a great wave of passion and anguish.... But she was only being led across the hall into a stiff lifeless drawing-room—the kind that bachelors get an upholsterer to do for them, and then turn their backs on forever. The chairs and sofas looked at her with an undisguised hostility, and then resumed the moping expression

---

1   *Bath chair* Wheelchair.

common to furniture in unfrequented rooms. Even the spring sun slanting in through the windows on the pale marquetry of a useless table seemed to bring no heat or light with it.

The rush of emotion subsided, leaving in Nora a sense of emptiness and apprehension. Supposing Jane Aldis should look at her with the cold eyes of this resentful room? She began to wish she had been friendlier and more cordial to Jane Aldis in the past. In her intense desire to conceal from everyone the tie between herself and Christopher she had avoided all show of interest in his family; and perhaps, as she now saw, excited curiosity by her very affectation of indifference.

No doubt it would have been more politic to establish an intimacy with Jane Aldis; and today, how much easier and more natural her position would have been! Instead of groping about—as she was again doing—for an explanation of her visit, she could have said: "My dear, I came to see if there was anything in the world I could do to help you."

She heard a hesitating step in the hall—a hushed step like a parlour maid's—and saw Miss Aldis pause near the half-open door. How old she had grown since their last meeting! Her hair, untidily pinned up, was grey and lanky. Her eyelids, always reddish, were swollen and heavy, her face sallow with anxiety and fatigue. It was odd to have feared so defenceless an adversary. Nora, for an instant, had the impression that Miss Aldis had wavered in the hall to catch a glimpse of her, take the measure of the situation. But perhaps she had only stopped to push back a strand of hair as she passed in front of a mirror.

"Mrs. Frenway—how good of you!" She spoke in a cool detached voice, as if her real self were elsewhere and she were simply an automaton wound up to repeat the familiar forms of hospitality. "Do sit down," she said.

She pushed forward one of the sulky arm-chairs, and Nora seated herself stiffly, her hand-bag clutched on her knee, in the self-conscious attitude of a country caller.

"I came——"

"So good of you," Miss Aldis repeated. "I had no idea you were in this part of the world. Not the slightest."

Was it a lead she was giving? Or did she know everything, and wish to extend to her visitor the decent shelter of a pretext? Or was she really so stupid—

"You're staying with the Brinckers, I suppose. Or the Northrups? I remember the last time you came to lunch here you motored over with Mr. Frenway from the Northrups'. That must have been two years ago, wasn't it?" She put the question with an almost sprightly show of interest.

"No—three years," said Nora mechanically.

"Was it? As long ago as that? Yes—you're right. That was the year we moved the big fern-leaved beech. I remember Mr. Frenway was interested in tree moving, and I took him out to show him where the tree had come from. He IS interested in tree moving, isn't he?"

"Oh, yes; very much."

"We had those wonderful experts down to do it. 'Tree doctors,' they call themselves. They have special appliances, you know. The tree is growing better than it did before they moved it. But I suppose you've done a great deal of transplanting on Long Island."

"Yes. My husband does a good deal of transplanting."

"So you've come over from the Northrups'? I didn't even know they were down at Maybrook yet. I see so few people."

"No; not from the Northrups'."

"Oh—the Brinckers'? Hal Brincker was here yesterday, but he didn't tell me you were staying there."

Nora hesitated. "No. The fact is, I have an old governess who lives at Ockham. I go to see her sometimes. And so I came on to Westover——" She paused, and Miss Aldis interrogated her brightly: "Yes?" as if prompting her in a lesson she was repeating.

"Because I saw Gladys Brincker the other day, and she told me that your brother was ill."

"Oh." Miss Aldis gave the syllable its full weight, and set a full stop after it. Her eyebrows went up, as if in a faint surprise. The silent room seemed to close in on the two speakers, listening. A resuscitated fly buzzed against the sunny window pane. "Yes; he's ill," she conceded at length.

"I'm so sorry; I ... he has been ... such a friend of ours ... so long...."

"Yes; I've often heard him speak of you and Mr. Frenway." Another full stop sealed this announcement. ("No, she knows nothing," Nora thought.) "I remember his telling me that he thought a great deal of Mr. Frenway's advice about moving trees. But then you see our soil is so different from yours. I suppose Mr. Frenway has had your soil analyzed?"

"Yes; I think he has."

"Christopher's always been a great gardener."

"I hope he's not—not very ill? Gladys seemed to be afraid——"

"Illness is always something to be afraid of, isn't it?"

"But you're not—I mean, not anxious ... not seriously?"

"It's so kind of you to ask. The doctors seem to think there's no particular change since yesterday."

"And yesterday?"

"Well, yesterday they seemed to think there might be."

"A change, you mean?"

"Well, yes."

"A change—I hope for the better?"

"They said they weren't sure; they couldn't say."

The fly's buzzing had become so insistent in the still room that it seemed to be going on inside of Nora's head, and in the confusion of sound she found it more and more difficult to regain a lead in the conversation. And the minutes were slipping by, and upstairs the man she loved was lying. It was absurd and lamentable to make a pretense of keeping up this twaddle. She would cut through it, no matter how.

"I suppose you've had—a consultation?"

"Oh, yes; Dr. Knowlton's been down twice."

"And what does he——"

"Well; he seems to agree with the others."

There was another pause, and then Miss Aldis glanced out of the window. "Why, who's that driving up?" she enquired. "Oh, it's your taxi, I suppose, coming up the drive."

"Yes, I got out at the gate." She dared not add: "For fear the noise might disturb him."

"I hope you had no difficulty in finding a taxi at the Junction?"

"Oh, no; I had no difficulty."

"I think it was so kind of you to come—not even knowing whether you'd find a carriage to bring you out all this way. And I know how busy you are. There's always so much going on in town, isn't there, even at this time of year?"

"Yes; I suppose so. But your brother——"

"Oh, of course my brother won't be up to any sort of gaiety; not for a long time."

"A long time; no. But you do hope——"

"I think everybody about a sick bed ought to hope, don't you?"

"Yes; but I mean——"

Nora stood up suddenly, her brain whirling. Was it possible that she and that woman had sat thus facing each other for half an hour, piling up this conversational rubbish, while upstairs, out of sight, the truth, the meaning of their two lives hung on the frail thread of one man's intermittent pulse? She could not imagine why she felt so powerless and baffled. What had a woman who was young and handsome and beloved to fear from a dowdy and insignificant old maid? Why, the antagonism that these very graces and superiorities would create in the other's breast, especially if she knew they were all spent in charming the being on whom her life depended. Weak in herself, but powerful from her circumstances, she stood at bay on the ruins of all that Nora had ever loved. "How she must hate me—and I never thought of it," mused Nora, who had imagined that she had thought of everything where her relation to her lover was concerned. Well, it was too late now to remedy her omission; but at least she must assert herself, must say something to save the precious minutes that remained and break through the stifling web of platitudes which her enemy's tremulous hand was weaving around her.

"Miss Aldis—I must tell you—I came to see——"

"How he was? So very friendly of you. He would appreciate it, I know. Christopher is so devoted to his friends."

"But you'll—you'll tell him that I——"

"Of course. That you came on purpose to ask about him. As soon as he's a little bit stronger."

"But I mean—now?"

"Tell him now that you called to enquire? How good of you to think of that too! Perhaps tomorrow morning, if he's feeling a little bit brighter...."

Nora felt her lips drying as if a hot wind had parched them. They would hardly move. "But now—now—today." Her voice sank to a whisper as she added: "Isn't he conscious?"

"Oh, yes; he's conscious; he's perfectly conscious." Miss Aldis emphasized this with another of her long pauses. "He shall certainly be told that you called." Suddenly she too got up from her seat and moved toward the window. "I must seem dreadfully inhospitable, not even offering you a cup of tea. But the fact is, perhaps I ought to tell you—if you're thinking of getting back to Ockham this afternoon there's only one train that stops at the Junction after three o'clock." She pulled out an old-fashioned enamelled watch with a wreath of roses about the dial, and turned almost apologetically to Mrs. Frenway. "You ought to be at the station by four o'clock at the latest; and with one of those old Junction taxis.... I'm so sorry; I know I must appear to be driving you away." A wan smile drew up her pale lips.

Nora knew just how long the drive from Westover Junction had taken, and understood that she was being delicately dismissed. Dismissed from life—from hope—even from the dear anguish of filling her eyes for the last time with the face which was the one face in the world to her! ("But then she does know everything," she thought.)

"I mustn't make you miss your train, you know."

"Miss Aldis, is he—has he seen any one?" Nora hazarded in a painful whisper.

"Seen any one? Well, there've been all the doctors—five of them! And then the nurses. Oh, but you mean friends, of course. Naturally." She seemed to reflect. "Hal Brincker, yes; he saw our cousin Hal yesterday—but not for very long."

Hal Brincker! Nora knew what Christopher thought of his Brincker cousins—blighting bores, one and all of them, he always said. And in the extremity of his illness the one person privileged to see him had been—Hal Brincker! Nora's eyes filled; she had to turn them away for a moment from Miss Aldis's timid inexorable face.

"But today?" she finally brought out.

"No. Today he hasn't seen any one; not yet." The two women stood and looked at each other; then Miss Aldis glanced uncertainly about the room. "But couldn't I—Yes, I ought at least to have asked if you won't have a cup of tea. So stupid of me! There might still be time. I never take tea myself." Once more she referred anxiously to her watch. "The water is sure to be boiling, because the nurses' tea is just being taken up. If you'll excuse me a moment I'll go and see."

"Oh, no, no!" Nora drew in a quick sob. "How can you?... I mean, I don't want any...."

Miss Aldis looked relieved. "Then I shall be quite sure that you won't reach the station too late." She waited again, and then held out a long stony hand. "So kind—I shall never forget your kindness. Coming all this way, when you might so easily have telephoned from town. Do please tell Mr. Frenway how I appreciated it. You will remember to tell him, won't you? He sent me such an interesting collection of pamphlets about tree moving. I should like him to know how much I feel his kindness in letting you come." She paused again, and pulled in her lips so that they became a narrow thread, a mere line drawn across her face by a ruler. "But, no; I won't trouble you; I'll write to thank him myself." Her hand ran out to an electric bell on the nearest table. It shrilled through the silence, and the parlour maid appeared with a stage-like promptness.

"The taxi, please? Mrs. Frenway's taxi."

The room became silent again. Nora thought: "Yes; she knows everything." Miss Aldis peeped for the third time at her watch, and then uttered a slight unmeaning laugh. The blue-bottle banged against the window, and once more it seemed to Nora that its sonorities were reverberating inside her head. They were deafeningly mingled there with the explosion of the taxi's reluctant starting-up and its convulsed halt at the front door. The driver sounded his horn as if to summon her.

"He's afraid too that you'll be late!" Miss Aldis smiled.

The smooth slippery floor of the hall seemed to Nora to extend away in front of her for miles. At its far end she saw a little tunnel of light, a miniature maid, a toy taxi. Somehow she managed to travel the distance that separated her from them, though her bones ached with weariness, and at every step she seemed to be lifting a leaden weight. The taxi was close to her now, its door open, she was getting in. The same smell of damp hay and bad tobacco greeted her. She saw her hostess standing on the threshold. "To the Junction, driver—back to the Junction," she heard Miss Aldis say. The taxi began to roll toward the gate. As it moved away Nora heard Miss Aldis calling: "I'll be sure to write and thank Mr. Frenway."

—1927

James Joyce
1882–1941

James Joyce was born in Dublin, and although he left the city for good in 1904, it provided the background for all his major works. His best-known novel, *Ulysses* (1922), describes a day in the life of three of the city's inhabitants, with the various incidents paralleling episodes from Homer's *Odyssey*. It is written in an intricately constructed combination of literary styles, including long sections of stream-of-consciousness narration.

Joyce and Nora Barnacle, a woman whom he met on a Dublin street and who would become his wife and lifelong companion, lived in Trieste, Zurich, and Paris, where Joyce made his living by teaching English. In 1914, the modernist poet Ezra Pound arranged for Joyce's autobiographical novel *A Portrait of the Artist as a Young Man* to be serialized in *The Egoist*, a British magazine. The same year, Joyce's collection of short stories, *Dubliners*, was published. In each story, the protagonist experiences what Joyce called an "epiphany," a moment of revelation that he described as "a sudden spiritual manifestation, whether in the vulgarity of speech or of gesture or in a memorable phase of the mind itself."

Shortly after, Joyce began work on *Ulysses*. In 1918, *The Egoist* and an American magazine, *The Little Review*, began serializing the work, but charges that passages were obscene led to the suspension of serialization. Joyce is said to have retorted, "If *Ulysses* isn't fit to read, life isn't fit to live." It was finally published in book form in Paris in 1922.

By this time, friends and admirers were supporting Joyce financially, allowing him to concentrate on his writing; he began work on his last book, *Finnegans Wake*, an extremely complex work of dream imaginings and linguistic invention, which was published in 1939.

Araby[1]

North Richmond Street, being blind,[2] was a quiet street except at the hour when the Christian Brothers' School set the boys free. An uninhabited house of two storeys stood at the blind end, detached from its neighbours in a square ground. The other houses of the street, conscious of decent lives within them, gazed at one another with brown imperturbable faces.

The former tenant of our house, a priest, had died in the back drawing-room. Air, musty from having been long enclosed, hung in all the rooms, and

---

1   *Araby* Charity bazaar held in Dublin in 1894; it was advertised as a "grand, Oriental fête."

2   *being blind* I.e., being a dead-end street.

the waste room behind the kitchen was littered with old useless papers. Among these I found a few paper-covered books, the pages of which were curled and damp: *The Abbot*, by Walter Scott, *The Devout Communicant* and *The Memoirs of Vidocq*.[1] I liked the last best because its leaves were yellow. The wild garden behind the house contained a central apple-tree and a few straggling bushes under one of which I found the late tenant's rusty bicycle-pump. He had been a very charitable priest; in his will he had left all his money to institutions and the furniture of his house to his sister.

When the short days of winter came dusk fell before we had well eaten our dinners. When we met in the street the houses had grown sombre. The space of sky above us was the colour of ever-changing violet and towards it the lamps of the street lifted their feeble lanterns. The cold air stung us and we played till our bodies glowed. Our shouts echoed in the silent street. The career of our play brought us through the dark muddy lanes behind the houses where we ran the gantlet of the rough tribes from the cottages, to the back doors of the dark dripping gardens where odours arose from the ash-pits, to the dark odorous stables where a coachman smoothed and combed the horse or shook music from the buckled harness. When we returned to the street light from the kitchen windows had filled the areas.[2] If my uncle was seen turning the corner we hid in the shadow until we had seen him safely housed. Or if Mangan's sister came out on the doorstep to call her brother in to his tea we watched her from our shadow peer up and down the street. We waited to see whether she would remain or go in and, if she remained, we left our shadow and walked up to Mangan's steps resignedly. She was waiting for us, her figure defined by the light from the half-opened door. Her brother always teased her before he obeyed and I stood by the railings looking at her. Her dress swung as she moved her body and the soft rope of her hair tossed from side to side.

Every morning I lay on the floor in the front parlour watching her door. The blind was pulled down to within an inch of the sash so that I could not be seen. When she came out on the doorstep my heart leaped. I ran to the hall, seized my books and followed her. I kept her brown figure always in my eye and, when we came near the point at which our ways diverged, I quickened my pace and passed her. This happened morning after morning. I had never spoken to her, except for a few casual words, and yet her name was like a summons to all my foolish blood.

---

1   *The Abbot* 1820 historical novel by Sir Walter Scott about Mary, Queen of Scots; *The Devout Communicant* Title common to several nineteenth-century religious tracts; *The Memoirs of Vidocq* Autobiography of François Vidocq, a nineteenth-century Parisian criminal turned police detective.

2   *areas* Spaces between the railings and the fronts of houses, below street level.

Her image accompanied me even in places the most hostile to romance. On Saturday evenings when my aunt went marketing I had to go to carry some of the parcels. We walked through the flaring streets, jostled by drunken men and bargaining women, amid the curses of labourers, the shrill litanies of shop-boys who stood on guard by the barrels of pigs' cheeks, the nasal chanting of street-singers, who sang a *come-all-you* about O'Donovan Rossa,[1] or a ballad about the troubles in our native land. These noises converged in a single sensation of life for me: I imagined that I bore my chalice safely through a throng of foes. Her name sprang to my lips at moments in strange prayers and praises which I myself did not understand. My eyes were often full of tears (I could not tell why) and at times a flood from my heart seemed to pour itself out into my bosom. I thought little of the future. I did not know whether I would ever speak to her or not or, if I spoke to her, how I could tell her of my confused adoration. But my body was like a harp and her words and gestures were like fingers running upon the wires.

One evening I went into the back drawing-room in which the priest had died. It was a dark rainy evening and there was no sound in the house. Through one of the broken panes I heard the rain impinge upon the earth, the fine incessant needles of water playing in the sodden beds. Some distant lamp or lighted window gleamed below me. I was thankful that I could see so little. All my senses seemed to desire to veil themselves and, feeling that I was about to slip from them, I pressed the palms of my hands together until they trembled, murmuring: *O love! O love!* many times.

At last she spoke to me. When she addressed the first words to me I was so confused that I did not know what to answer. She asked me was I going to *Araby*. I forget whether I answered yes or no. It would be a splendid bazaar, she said; she would love to go.

—And why can't you? I asked.

While she spoke she turned a silver bracelet round and round her wrist. She could not go, she said, because there would be a retreat that week in her convent.[2] Her brother and two other boys were fighting for their caps and I was alone at the railings. She held one of the spikes, bowing her head towards me. The light from the lamp opposite our door caught the white curve of her neck, lit up her hair that rested there and, falling, lit up the hand upon the railing. It fell over one side of her dress and caught the white border of a petticoat, just visible as she stood at ease.

—It's well for you, she said.

---

1   *come-all-you* Ballad, so called because many ballads started with this phrase; *O'Donovan Rossa* Jeremiah O'Donovan Rossa (1831–1915), an activist for Irish independence.
2   *convent* I.e., convent school.

—If I go, I said, I will bring you something.

What innumerable follies laid waste my waking and sleeping thoughts after that evening! I wished to annihilate the tedious intervening days. I chafed against the work of school. At night in my bedroom and by day in the classroom her image came between me and the page I strove to read. The syllables of the word *Araby* were called to me through the silence in which my soul luxuriated and cast an Eastern enchantment over me. I asked for leave to go to the bazaar on Saturday night. My aunt was surprised and hoped it was not some Freemason[1] affair. I answered few questions in class. I watched my master's face pass from amiability to sternness; he hoped I was not beginning to idle. I could not call my wandering thoughts together. I had hardly any patience with the serious work of life which, now that it stood between me and my desire, seemed to me child's play, ugly monotonous child's play.

On Saturday morning I reminded my uncle that I wished to go to the bazaar in the evening. He was fussing at the hallstand, looking for the hat-brush, and answered me curtly:

—Yes, boy, I know.

As he was in the hall I could not go into the front parlour and lie at the window. I left the house in bad humour and walked slowly towards the school. The air was pitilessly raw and already my heart misgave me.

When I came home to dinner my uncle had not yet been home. Still it was early. I sat staring at the clock for some time and, when its ticking began to irritate me, I left the room. I mounted the staircase and gained the upper part of the house. The high cold empty gloomy rooms liberated me and I went from room to room singing. From the front window I saw my companions playing below in the street. Their cries reached me weakened and indistinct and, leaning my forehead against the cool glass, I looked over at the dark house where she lived. I may have stood there for an hour, seeing nothing but the brown-clad figure cast by my imagination, touched discreetly by the lamplight at the curved neck, at the hand upon the railings and at the border below the dress.

When I came downstairs again I found Mrs. Mercer sitting at the fire. She was an old garrulous woman, a pawnbroker's widow, who collected used stamps for some pious purpose. I had to endure the gossip of the tea-table. The meal was prolonged beyond an hour and still my uncle did not come. Mrs. Mercer stood up to go: she was sorry she couldn't wait any longer, but it was after eight o'clock and she did not like to be out late, as the night air was bad for her. When she had gone I began to walk up and down the room, clenching my fists. My aunt said:

1   *Freemason* In reference to the Freemasons, a secret society believed by many in Ireland to be anti-Catholic.

—I'm afraid you may put off your bazaar for this night of Our Lord.

At nine o'clock I heard my uncle's latchkey in the halldoor. I heard him talking to himself and heard the hallstand rocking when it had received the weight of his overcoat. I could interpret these signs. When he was midway through his dinner I asked him to give me the money to go to the bazaar. He had forgotten.

—The people are in bed and after their first sleep now, he said.

I did not smile. My aunt said to him energetically:

—Can't you give him the money and let him go? You've kept him late enough as it is.

My uncle said he was very sorry he had forgotten. He said he believed in the old saying: *All work and no play makes Jack a dull boy.* He asked where I was going and, when I had told him a second time he asked me did I know *The Arab's Farewell to his Steed.*[1] When I left the kitchen he was about to recite the opening lines of the piece to my aunt.

I held a florin tightly in my hand as I strode down Buckingham Street towards the station. The sight of the streets thronged with buyers and glaring with gas recalled to me the purpose of my journey. I took my seat in a third-class carriage of a deserted train. After an intolerable delay the train moved out of the station slowly. It crept onward among ruinous houses and over the twinkling river. At Westland Row Station a crowd of people pressed to the carriage doors; but the porters moved them back, saying that it was a special train for the bazaar. I remained alone in the bare carriage. In a few minutes the train drew up beside an improvised wooden platform. I passed out on to the road and saw by the lighted dial of a clock that it was ten minutes to ten. In front of me was a large building which displayed the magical name.

I could not find any sixpenny entrance and, fearing that the bazaar would be closed, I passed in quickly through a turnstile, handing a shilling to a weary-looking man. I found myself in a big hall girdled at half its height by a gallery. Nearly all the stalls were closed and the greater part of the hall was in darkness. I recognized a silence like that which pervades a church after a service. I walked into the centre of the bazaar timidly. A few people were gathered about the stalls which were still open. Before a curtain, over which the words *Café Chantant* were written in coloured lamps, two men were counting money on a salver.[2] I listened to the fall of the coins.

Remembering with difficulty why I had come I went over to one of the stalls and examined porcelain vases and flowered tea-sets. At the door of the

---

1 *The Arab's ... his Steed* Popular Romantic poem by Caroline Norton (1808–77).
2 *Café Chantant* Café that provides musical entertainment; *salver* Tray.

stall a young lady was talking and laughing with two young gentlemen. I remarked their English accents and listened vaguely to their conversation.

—O, I never said such a thing!

—O, but you did!

—O, but I didn't!

—Didn't she say that?

—Yes. I heard her.

—O, there's a ... fib!

Observing me the young lady came over and asked me did I wish to buy anything. The tone of her voice was not encouraging; she seemed to have spoken to me out of a sense of duty. I looked humbly at the great jars that stood like eastern guards at either side of the dark entrance to the stall and murmured:

—No, thank you.

The young lady changed the position of one of the vases and went back to the two young men. They began to talk of the same subject. Once or twice the young lady glanced at me over her shoulder.

I lingered before her stall, though I knew my stay was useless, to make my interest in her wares seem the more real. Then I turned away slowly and walked down the middle of the bazaar. I allowed the two pennies to fall against the sixpence in my pocket. I heard a voice call from one end of the gallery that the light was out. The upper part of the hall was now completely dark.

Gazing up into the darkness I saw myself as a creature driven and derided by vanity; and my eyes burned with anguish and anger.

—1914

Eveline

She sat at the window watching the evening invade the avenue. Her head was leaned against the window curtains and in her nostrils was the odour of dusty cretonne.[1] She was tired.

Few people passed. The man out of the last house passed on his way home; she heard his footsteps clacking along the concrete pavement and afterwards crunching on the cinder path before the new red houses. One time there used to be a field there in which they used to play every evening with other people's children. Then a man from Belfast bought the field and built houses in it—not like their little brown houses but bright brick houses with shining roofs. The children of the avenue used to play together in that field—the Devines, the Waters, the Dunns, little Keogh the cripple, she and her brothers and sisters.

---

1   *cretonne* Thick cotton fabric often used for chair coverings or curtains.

Ernest, however, never played: he was too grown up. Her father used often to hunt them in out of the field with his blackthorn stick; but usually little Keogh used to keep *nix*[1] and call out when he saw her father coming. Still they seemed to have been rather happy then. Her father was not so bad then; and besides, her mother was alive. That was a long time ago; she and her brothers and sisters were all grown up; her mother was dead. Tizzie Dunn was dead, too, and the Waters had gone back to England. Everything changes. Now she was going to go away like the others, to leave her home.

Home! She looked round the room, reviewing all its familiar objects which she had dusted once a week for so many years, wondering where on earth all the dust came from. Perhaps she would never see again those familiar objects from which she had never dreamed of being divided. And yet during all those years she had never found out the name of the priest whose yellowing photograph hung on the wall above the broken harmonium beside the coloured print of the promises made to Blessed Margaret Mary Alacoque.[2] He had been a school friend of her father. Whenever he showed the photograph to a visitor her father used to pass it with a casual word:

—He is in Melbourne now.

She had consented to go away, to leave her home. Was that wise? She tried to weigh each side of the question. In her home anyway she had shelter and food; she had those whom she had known all her life about her. Of course she had to work hard both in the house and at business. What would they say of her in the Stores when they found out that she had run away with a fellow? Say she was a fool, perhaps; and her place would be filled up by advertisement. Miss Gavan would be glad. She had always had an edge on her, especially whenever there were people listening.

—Miss Hill, don't you see these ladies are waiting?

—Look lively, Miss Hill, please.

She would not cry many tears at leaving the Stores.

But in her new home, in a distant unknown country, it would not be like that. Then she would be married—she, Eveline. People would treat her with respect then. She would not be treated as her mother had been. Even now, though she was over nineteen, she sometimes felt herself in danger of her father's violence. She knew it was that that had given her the palpitations. When they were growing up he had never gone for her, like he used to go for Harry and Ernest, because she was a girl; but latterly he had begun to threaten her and say what he would do to her only for her dead mother's sake. And

1   *keep nix* Keep watch.
2   *harmonium* Reed instrument similar to an organ; *Blessed Margaret Mary Alacoque* Marguerite Marie Alacoque (1647–90), a French Catholic nun and religious mystic who had visions of Christ. She was made a saint in 1920.

now she had nobody to protect her. Ernest was dead and Harry, who was in the church decorating business, was nearly always down somewhere in the country. Besides, the invariable squabble for money on Saturday nights had begun to weary her unspeakably. She always gave her entire wages—seven shillings—and Harry always sent up what he could but the trouble was to get any money from her father. He said she used to squander the money, that she had no head, that he wasn't going to give her his hard-earned money to throw about the streets, and much more, for he was usually fairly bad of a Saturday night. In the end he would give her the money and ask her had she any intention of buying Sunday's dinner. Then she had to rush out as quickly as she could and do her marketing, holding her black leather purse tightly in her hand as she elbowed her way through the crowds and returning home late under her load of provisions. She had hard work to keep the house together and to see that the two young children who had been left to her charge went to school regularly and got their meals regularly. It was hard work—a hard life—but now that she was about to leave it she did not find it a wholly undesirable life.

She was about to explore another life with Frank. Frank was very kind, manly, open-hearted. She was to go away with him by the night-boat to be his wife and to live with him in Buenos Ayres where he had a home waiting for her. How well she remembered the first time she had seen him; he was lodging in a house on the main road where she used to visit. It seemed a few weeks ago. He was standing at the gate, his peaked cap pushed back on his head and his hair tumbled forward over a face of bronze. Then they had come to know each other. He used to meet her outside the Stores every evening and see her home. He took her to see *The Bohemian Girl*[1] and she felt elated as she sat in an unaccustomed part of the theatre with him. He was awfully fond of music and sang a little. People knew that they were courting and, when he sang about the lass that loves a sailor, she always felt pleasantly confused. He used to call her Poppens out of fun. First of all it had been an excitement for her to have a fellow and then she had begun to like him. He had tales of distant countries. He had started as a deck boy at a pound a month on a ship of the Allan Line[2] going out to Canada. He told her the names of the ships he had been on and the names of the different services. He had sailed through the Straits of Magellan and he told her stories of the terrible Patagonians.[3] He

1   *The Bohemian Girl* 1843 opera by Irish composer Michael Balfe.
2   *Allan Line* Steamship company that made weekly sailings between Liverpool and western Canada via South America.
3   *Straits of Magellan* Sea route near the tip of South America; *terrible Patagonians* Refers either to the strong, unpredictable Patagonian winds in the Strait of Magellan, or to a group of South American natives that early explorers had claimed were giants. By the beginning of the nineteenth century, this rumour was discredited.

had fallen on his feet in Buenos Ayres, he said, and had come over to the old country just for a holiday. Of course, her father had found out the affair and had forbidden her to have anything to say to him.

—I know these sailor chaps, he said.

One day he had quarrelled with Frank and after that she had to meet her lover secretly.

The evening deepened in the avenue. The white of two letters in her lap grew indistinct. One was to Harry; the other was to her father. Ernest had been her favourite but she liked Harry too. Her father was becoming old lately, she noticed; he would miss her. Sometimes he could be very nice. Not long before, when she had been laid up for a day, he had read her out a ghost story and made toast for her at the fire. Another day, when their mother was alive, they had all gone for a picnic to the Hill of Howth.[1] She remembered her father putting on her mother's bonnet to make the children laugh.

Her time was running out but she continued to sit by the window, leaning her head against the window curtain, inhaling the odour of dusty cretonne. Down far in the avenue she could hear a street organ playing. She knew the air. Strange that it should come that very night to remind her of the promise to her mother, her promise to keep the home together as long as she could. She remembered the last night of her mother's illness; she was again in the close dark room at the other side of the hall and outside she heard a melancholy air of Italy. The organ-player had been ordered to go away and given sixpence. She remembered her father strutting back into the sickroom saying:

—Damned Italians! coming over here!

As she mused the pitiful vision of her mother's life laid its spell on the very quick of her being—that life of commonplace sacrifices closing in final craziness. She trembled as she heard again her mother's voice saying constantly with foolish insistence:

—Derevaun Seraun! Derevaun Seraun![2]

She stood up in a sudden impulse of terror. Escape! She must escape! Frank would save her. He would give her life, perhaps love, too. But she wanted to live. Why should she be unhappy? She had a right to happiness. Frank would take her in his arms, fold her in his arms. He would save her.

She stood among the swaying crowd in the station at the North Wall. He held her hand and she knew that he was speaking to her, saying something about the passage over and over again. The station was full of soldiers with brown

---

1   *Hill of Howth* Hill located northeast of Dublin, on the Howth peninsula.
2   *Derevaun … Seraun!* The meaning of this phrase is uncertain; it may be garbled Irish or simply gibberish.

baggages. Through the wide doors of the sheds she caught a glimpse of the black mass of the boat, lying in beside the quay wall, with illumined portholes. She answered nothing. She felt her cheek pale and cold and, out of a maze of distress, she prayed to God to direct her, to show her what was her duty. The boat blew a long mournful whistle into the mist. If she went, to-morrow she would be on the sea with Frank, steaming towards Buenos Ayres. Their passage had been booked. Could she still draw back after all he had done for her? Her distress awoke a nausea in her body and she kept moving her lips in silent fervent prayer.

A bell clanged upon her heart. She felt him seize her hand:

—Come!

All the seas of the world tumbled about her heart. He was drawing her into them: he would drown her. She gripped with both hands at the iron railing.

—Come!

No! No! No! It was impossible. Her hands clutched the iron in frenzy. Amid the seas she sent a cry of anguish!

—Eveline! Evvy!

He rushed beyond the barrier and called to her to follow. He was shouted at to go on but he still called to her. She set her white face to him, passive, like a helpless animal. Her eyes gave him no sign of love or farewell or recognition.

—1914

Virginia Woolf
1882–1941

It is no accident that the life of Virginia Woolf, one of the most innovative writers of the twentieth century, coincides very nearly with the emergence and flourishing of literary modernism. Many of her highly experimental novels—notably *Mrs Dalloway* (1925), *To the Lighthouse* (1927), and *The Waves* (1931)—are key landmarks in the modernist revolt against conventional modes of literary representation. In contrast to what she described as the superficial, "materialist" fixation of Edwardian novelists on external details, Woolf set out to convey the essence of lived experience, the incessant influx of impressions—"trivial, fantastic, evanescent, or engraved with the sharpness of steel"—that stream through and light up the mind from moment to crowded moment with all manner of fugitive, seemingly random images, thoughts, feelings, memories, and associations.

For Woolf, life does not form an orderly, linear chronicle of events, like "a series of gig lamps symmetrically arranged." Rather, "life is a luminous halo, a semi-transparent envelope surrounding us from the beginning of consciousness to the end." In order to faithfully render some semblance of this "uncircumscribed spirit," Woolf followed writers like James Joyce in developing a fluid stream-of-consciousness technique that subordinates the action of plot to the subjective interplay of perception, recollection, emotion, and understanding. This essentially lyrical method is used to great effect in stories like "Kew Gardens" (1919).

The circumstances of Woolf's own life were often deeply troubled. Although born into an illustrious British family with an impressive literary pedigree, Woolf received no formal education, an injustice that occupies a central place in much of her social and political writing. The loss of her parents and several siblings exacted a heavy emotional and psychological toll, and periodic fits of mental instability and depression ultimately led her to suicide. But though her hauntingly beautiful, intricately crafted novels and stories are written in a predominantly elegiac key, they also explore the rich multiplicity of connections between individuals, memories, and moments in time that persist across the years.

Vanessa Bell, woodcut illustration for "Kew Gardens," 1919. Vanessa Bell was Virginia Woolf's sister and fellow member of the Bloomsbury Group, a social circle of talented avant-garde writers, artists, and intellectuals that flourished in London in the first half of the twentieth century. Best known as a post-impressionist painter, Bell was also a designer, and she produced book covers and illustrations for Hogarth Press, the publishing house Virginia Woolf operated with her husband. The above illustration appeared in a Hogarth Press edition of "Kew Gardens."

Kew Gardens[1]

From the oval-shaped flower-bed there rose perhaps a hundred stalks spreading into heart-shaped or tongue-shaped leaves half way up and unfurling at the tip red or blue or yellow petals marked with spots of colour raised upon the surface; and from the red, blue or yellow gloom of the throat emerged a straight bar, rough with gold dust and slightly clubbed at the end. The petals were voluminous enough to be stirred by the summer breeze, and when they moved, the red, blue, and yellow lights passed one over the other, staining an inch of the brown earth beneath with a spot of the most intricate colour. The light fell either upon the smooth grey back of a pebble, or the shell of a snail with its brown circular veins, or, falling into a raindrop, it expanded with such intensity of red, blue, and yellow the thin walls of water that one expected them to burst and disappear. Instead, the drop was left in a second silver grey once more, and the light now settled upon the flesh of a leaf, revealing the branching thread of fibre beneath the surface, and again it moved on and spread its illumination in the vast green spaces beneath the dome of the heart-shaped and tongue-shaped leaves. Then the breeze stirred rather more briskly overhead and the colour was flashed into the air above, into the eyes of the men and women who walk in Kew Gardens in July.

The figures of these men and women straggled past the flower-bed with a curiously irregular movement not unlike that of the white and blue butterflies who crossed the turf in zig-zag flights from bed to bed. The man was about six inches in front of the woman, strolling carelessly, while she bore on with greater purpose, only turning her head now and then to see that the children were not too far behind. The man kept this distance in front of the woman purposely, though perhaps unconsciously, for he wanted to go on with his thoughts.

"Fifteen years ago I came here with Lily," he thought. "We sat somewhere over there by a lake, and I begged her to marry me all through the hot afternoon. How the dragon-fly kept circling round us: how clearly I see the dragon-fly and her shoe with the square silver buckle at the toe. All the time I spoke I saw her shoe and when it moved impatiently I knew without looking up what she was going to say: the whole of her seemed to be in her shoe. And my love, my desire, were in the dragon-fly; for some reason I thought that if it settled there, on that leaf, the broad one with the red flower in the middle of it, if the dragonfly settled on the leaf she would say 'Yes' at once. But the dragon-fly went round and round: it never settled anywhere—of course not,

---

1   *Kew Gardens* Royal Botanic Gardens in Kew, a district of Greater London.

happily not, or I shouldn't be walking here with Eleanor and the children—
Tell me, Eleanor, d'you ever think of the past?"

"Why do you ask, Simon?"

"Because I've been thinking of the past. I've been thinking of Lily, the woman I might have married ... Well, why are you silent? Do you mind my thinking of the past?"

"Why should I mind, Simon? Doesn't one always think of the past, in a garden with men and women lying under the trees? Aren't they one's past, all that remains of it, those men and women, those ghosts lying under the trees ... one's happiness, one's reality?"

"For me, a square silver shoe-buckle and a dragon-fly—"

"For me, a kiss. Imagine six little girls sitting before their easels twenty years ago, down by the side of a lake, painting the water-lilies, the first red water-lilies I'd ever seen. And suddenly a kiss, there on the back of my neck. And my hand shook all the afternoon so that I couldn't paint. I took out my watch and marked the hour when I would allow myself to think of the kiss for five minutes only—it was so precious—the kiss of an old grey-haired woman with a wart on her nose, the mother of all my kisses all my life. Come Caroline, come Hubert."

They walked on past the flower-bed, now walking four abreast, and soon diminished in size among the trees and looked half transparent as the sunlight and shade swam over their backs in large trembling irregular patches.

In the oval flower-bed the snail, whose shell had been stained red, blue, and yellow for the space of two minutes or so, now appeared to be moving very slightly in its shell, and next began to labour over the crumbs of loose earth which broke away and rolled down as it passed over them. It appeared to have a definite goal in front of it, differing in this respect from the singular high-stepping angular green insect who attempted to cross in front of it, and waited for a second with its antennae trembling as if in deliberation, and then stepped off as rapidly and strangely in the opposite direction. Brown cliffs with deep green lakes in the hollows, flat blade-like trees that waved from root to tip, round boulders of grey stone, vast crumpled surfaces of a thin crackling texture—all these objects lay across the snail's progress between one stalk and another to his goal. Before he had decided whether to circumvent the arched tent of a dead leaf or to breast it there came past the bed the feet of other human beings.

This time they were both men. The younger of the two wore an expression of perhaps unnatural calm; he raised his eyes and fixed them very steadily in front of him while his companion spoke, and directly his companion had done speaking he looked on the ground again and sometimes opened his lips only after a long pause and sometimes did not open them at all. The elder man had a curiously uneven and shaky method of walking, jerking his hand forward and throwing up his head abruptly, rather in the manner of an impatient carriage horse tired of waiting outside a house; but in the man these gestures were ir-resolute and pointless. He talked almost incessantly; he smiled to himself and again began to talk, as if the smile had been an answer. He was talking about spirits—the spirits of the dead, who, according to him, were even now telling him all sorts of odd things about their experiences in Heaven.

"Heaven was known to the ancients as Thessaly, William, and now, with this war,[1] the spirit matter is rolling between the hills like thunder." He paused, seemed to listen, smiled, jerked his head and continued:—

"You have a small electric battery and a piece of rubber to insulate the wire—isolate?—insulate?—well, we'll skip the details, no good going into details that wouldn't be understood—and in short the little machine stands in any convenient position by the head of the bed, we will say, on a neat ma-hogany stand. All arrangements being properly fixed by workmen under my direction, the widow applies her ear and summons the spirit by sign as agreed. Women! Widows! Women in black—"

Here he seemed to have caught sight of a woman's dress in the distance, which in the shade looked a purple black. He took off his hat, placed his hand upon his heart, and hurried towards her muttering and gesticulating feverishly. But William caught him by the sleeve and touched a flower with the tip of his walking-stick in order to divert the old man's attention. After looking at it for a moment in some confusion the old man bent his ear to it and seemed to answer a voice speaking from it, for he began talking about the forests of Uruguay which he had visited hundreds of years ago in company with the most beautiful young woman in Europe. He could be heard murmuring about forests of Uruguay blanketed with the wax petals of tropical roses, nightingales, sea beaches, mermaids and women drowned at sea, as he suffered himself to be moved on by William, upon whose face the look of stoical patience grew slowly deeper and deeper.

Following his steps so closely as to be slightly puzzled by his gestures came two elderly women of the lower middle class, one stout and ponderous, the other rosy-cheeked and nimble. Like most people of their station[2] they were frankly fascinated by any signs of eccentricity betokening a disordered brain, especially in the well-to-do; but they were too far off to be certain whether the gestures were merely eccentric or genuinely mad. After they had scrutinized the

1   *Thessaly* Region of ancient Greece; a large, fertile plain surrounded by mountains; *this war* I.e., World War I (1914–18).
2   *their station* I.e., their position in English society.

old man's back in silence for a moment and given each other a queer, sly look, they went on energetically piecing together their very complicated dialogue:

"Nell, Bert, Lot, Cess, Phil, Pa, he says, I says, she says, I says, I says, I says—"

"My Bert, Sis, Bill, Grandad, the old man, sugar,

    Sugar, flour, kippers, greens

    Sugar, sugar, sugar."

The ponderous woman looked through the pattern of falling words at the flowers standing cool, firm and upright in the earth, with a curious expression. She saw them as a sleeper waking from a heavy sleep sees a brass candlestick reflecting the light in an unfamiliar way, and closes his eyes and opens them, and seeing the brass candlestick again, finally starts broad awake and stares at the candlestick with all his powers. So the heavy woman came to a standstill opposite the oval-shaped flower-bed, and ceased even to pretend to listen to what the other woman was saying. She stood there letting the words fall over her, swaying the top part of her body slowly backwards and forwards, looking at the flowers. Then she suggested that they should find a seat and have their tea.

The snail had now considered every possible method of reaching his goal without going round the dead leaf or climbing over it. Let alone the effort needed for climbing a leaf, he was doubtful whether the thin texture which vibrated with such an alarming crackle when touched even by the tip of his horns would bear his weight; and this determined him finally to creep beneath it, for there was a point where the leaf curved high enough from the ground to admit him. He had just inserted his head in the opening and was taking stock of the high brown roof and was getting used to the cool brown light when two other people came past outside on the turf. This time they were both young, a young man and a young woman. They were both in the prime of youth, or even in that season which precedes the prime of youth, the season before the smooth pink folds of the flower have burst their gummy case, when the wings of the butterfly, though fully grown, are motionless in the sun.

"Lucky it isn't Friday," he observed.

"Why? D'you believe in luck?"

"They make you pay sixpence on Friday."

"What's sixpence anyway? Isn't it worth sixpence?"

"What's 'it'—what do you mean by 'it'?"

"O anything—I mean—you know what I mean."

Long pauses came between each of these remarks: they were uttered in toneless and monotonous voices. The couple stood still on the edge of the flower-bed, and together pressed the end of her parasol deep down into the soft earth. The action and the fact that his hand rested on the top of hers expressed their feelings in a strange way, as these short insignificant words also expressed something, words with short wings for their heavy body of meaning, inadequate to carry them far and thus alighting awkwardly upon the very common objects that surrounded them and were to their inexperienced touch so massive: but who knows (so they thought as they pressed the parasol into the earth) what precipices aren't concealed in them, or what slopes of ice don't shine in the sun on the other side? Who knows? Who has ever seen this before? Even when she wondered what sort of tea they gave you at Kew, he felt that something loomed up behind her words, and stood vast and solid behind them; and the mist very slowly rose and uncovered—O Heavens,—what were those shapes?—little white tables, and waitresses who looked first at her and then at him; and there was a bill that he would pay with a real two shilling piece, and it was real, all real, he assured himself, fingering the coin in his pocket, real to everyone except to him and to her; even to him it began to seem real; and then—but it was too exciting to stand and think any longer, and he pulled the parasol out of the earth with a jerk and was impatient to find the place where one had tea with other people, like other people.

"Come along, Trissie; it's time we had our tea."

"Wherever does one have one's tea?" she asked with the oddest thrill of excitement in her voice, looking vaguely round and letting herself be drawn on down the grass path, trailing her parasol, turning her head this way and that way, forgetting her tea, wishing to go down there and then down there, remembering orchids and cranes among wild flowers, a Chinese pagoda and a crimson-crested bird; but he bore her on.

Thus one couple after another with much the same irregular and aimless movement passed the flower-bed and were enveloped in layer after layer of green-blue vapour, in which at first their bodies had substance and a dash of colour, but later both substance and colour dissolved in the green-blue atmosphere. How hot it was! So hot that even the thrush chose to hop, like a mechanical bird, in the shadow of the flowers, with long pauses between one movement and the next; instead of rambling vaguely the white butterflies danced one above another, making with their white shifting flakes the outline of a shattered marble column above the tallest flowers; the glass roofs of the palm house shone as if a whole market full of shiny green umbrellas had opened in the sun; and in the drone of the aeroplane the voice of the summer sky murmured its fierce soul. Yellow and black, pink and snow white, shapes of all these colours, men, women, and children, were spotted for a second upon the horizon, and then, seeing the breadth of yellow that lay upon the grass, they wavered and sought shade beneath the trees, dissolving like drops of water in the yellow and green atmosphere, staining it faintly with red and blue. It seemed as if all gross and heavy bodies had sunk down in the heat motionless and lay huddled upon the ground, but their voices went wavering from them as if they were flames lolling from the thick waxen bodies of candles. Voices, yes, voices, wordless voices, breaking the silence suddenly with such depth of contentment, such passion of desire, or, in the voices of children, such freshness of surprise; breaking the silence? But there was no silence; all the time the motor omnibuses were turning their wheels and changing their gear; like a vast nest of Chinese boxes[1] all of wrought steel turning ceaselessly one within another the city murmured; on the top of which the voices cried aloud and the petals of myriads of flowers flashed their colours into the air.

—1921

---

1   *Chinese boxes* Boxes that fit inside one another.

Katherine Mansfield
1888–1923

In her short life, Katherine Mansfield managed to secure a reputation as one of the world's most gifted writers of short fiction. Her later stories in particular are important for their experimentation with style and atmosphere; instead of a conventional storyline, these stories present a series of loosely linked moments, portraying the small details of human life as a means of illuminating a specific character at a specific point of crisis or epiphany. Through such small details, Mansfield addresses grand themes such as the evolution of the self and the reality of death. Malcolm Cowley, a contemporary of Mansfield, wrote that her stories "have a thesis: namely, that life is a very wonderful spectacle, but disagreeable for the actors."

Born as Kathleen Mansfield Beauchamp in Wellington, New Zealand, in 1908 Mansfield moved permanently to Europe, where she could live the bohemian life she craved. In London, she cultivated several close—if sometimes tumultuous—friendships within literary circles, most notably with D.H. Lawrence, Virginia Woolf, and Aldous Huxley.

Mansfield grieved profoundly when her youngest brother Leslie was killed in 1915 as a soldier in France. In an effort to console herself she began writing stories about her childhood in New Zealand; thus began her most productive and successful period as a writer. Her long story *Prelude*, first published by Woolf's Hogarth Press in 1918, draws on her memories of New Zealand, as do several of her other stories, some of which return to the characters she introduces in *Prelude*. *Prelude* was reprinted in *Bliss and Other Stories* (1920); this and her following collection, *The Garden Party and Other Stories* (1922), established her importance as a modernist writer.

Troubled by ill health for most of her adult life, Mansfield died of tuberculosis at 34. After her death, her husband John Middleton Murry published two more collections of her stories, as well as editions of her poems, journals, and letters; her letters in particular are valued almost as highly as her short stories for their wit, perceptiveness, and sincerity.

The Garden Party

And after all the weather was ideal. They could not have had a more perfect day for a garden party if they had ordered it. Windless, warm, the sky without a cloud. Only the blue was veiled with a haze of light gold, as it is sometimes in early summer. The gardener had been up since dawn, mowing the lawns and sweeping them, until the grass and the dark flat rosettes where the daisy plants had been seemed to shine. As for the roses, you could not help feeling they understood that roses are the only flowers that impress people at garden parties; the only flowers that everybody is certain of knowing. Hundreds, yes, literally hundreds, had come out in a single night; the green bushes bowed down as though they had been visited by archangels.

Breakfast was not yet over before the men came to put up the marquee.[1]

"Where do you want the marquee put, mother?"

"My dear child, it's no use asking me. I'm determined to leave everything to you children this year. Forget I am your mother. Treat me as an honoured guest."

But Meg could not possibly go and supervise the men. She had washed her hair before breakfast, and she sat drinking her coffee in a green turban, with a dark wet curl stamped on each cheek. Jose, the butterfly, always came down in a silk petticoat and a kimono jacket.

"You'll have to go, Laura, you're the artistic one."

Away Laura flew, still holding her piece of bread-and-butter. It's so delicious to have an excuse for eating out of doors and, besides, she loved having to arrange things; she always felt she could do it so much better than anybody else.

Four men in their shirt-sleeves stood grouped together on the garden path. They carried staves[2] covered with rolls of canvas, and they had big tool-bags slung on their backs. They looked impressive. Laura wished now that she was not holding that piece of bread-and-butter, but there was nowhere to put it, and she couldn't possibly throw it away. She blushed and tried to look severe and even a little bit short-sighted as she came up to them.

"Good morning," she said, copying her mother's voice. But that sounded so fearfully affected that she was ashamed, and stammered like a little girl, "Oh—er—have you come—is it about the marquee?"

"That's right, miss," said the tallest of the men, a lanky, freckled fellow, and he shifted his tool-bag, knocked back his straw hat, and smiled down at her. "That's about it."

His smile was so easy, so friendly, that Laura recovered. What nice eyes he had, small, but such a dark blue! And now she looked at the others, they were smiling too. "Cheer up, we won't bite," their smile seemed to say. How very nice workmen were! And what a beautiful morning! She mustn't mention the morning; she must be businesslike. The marquee.

"Well, what about the lily-lawn? Would that do?"

And she pointed to the lily-lawn with the hand that didn't hold the bread-and-butter. They turned, they stared in the direction. A little fat chap thrust out his underlip, and the tall fellow frowned.

---

1   *marquee* Tent.
2   *staves* Rods.

"I don't fancy it," said he. "Not conspicuous enough. You see, with a thing like a marquee," and he turned to Laura in his easy way, "you want to put it somewhere where it'll give you a bang slap in the eye, if you follow me."

Laura's upbringing made her wonder for a moment whether it was quite respectful of a workman to talk to her of bangs slap in the eye. But she did quite follow him.

"A corner of the tennis court," she suggested. "But the band's going to be in one corner."

"H'm, going to have a band, are you?" said another of the workmen. He was pale. He had a haggard look as his dark eyes scanned the tennis court. What was he thinking?

"Only a very small band," said Laura gently. Perhaps he wouldn't mind so much if the band was quite small. But the tall fellow interrupted.

"Look here, miss, that's the place. Against those trees. Over there. That'll do fine."

Against the karakas. Then the karaka trees would be hidden. And they were so lovely, with their broad, gleaming leaves, and their clusters of yellow fruit. They were like trees you imagined growing up on a desert island, proud, solitary, lifting their leaves and fruits to the sun in a kind of silent splendour. Must they be hidden by a marquee?

They must. Already the men had shouldered their staves and were making for the place. Only the tall fellow was left. He bent down, pinched a sprig of lavender, put his thumb and forefinger to his nose and snuffed up the smell. When Laura saw that gesture she forgot all about the karakas in her wonder at him caring for things like that—caring for the smell of lavender. How many men that she knew would have done such a thing. *Oh, how extraordinarily nice workmen were*, she thought. Why couldn't she have workmen for friends rather than the silly boys she danced with and who came to Sunday night supper? She would get on much better with men like these.

It's all the fault, she decided, as the tall fellow drew something on the back of an envelope, something that was to be looped up or left to hang, of these absurd class distinctions. Well, for her part, she didn't feel them. Not a bit, not an atom.... And now there came the chock-chock of wooden hammers. Someone whistled, someone sang out, "Are you right there, matey?" "Matey!" The friendliness of it, the—the—Just to prove how happy she was, just to show the tall fellow how at home she felt, and how she despised stupid conventions, Laura took a big bite of her bread-and-butter as she stared at the little drawing. She felt just like a work-girl.

"Laura, Laura, where are you? Telephone, Laura!" a voice cried from the house.

"Coming!" Away she skimmed, over the lawn, up the path, up the steps, across the veranda, and into the porch. In the hall her father and Laurie were brushing their hats ready to go to the office.

"I say, Laura," said Laurie very fast, "you might just give a squiz[1] at my coat before this afternoon. See if it wants pressing."

"I will," said she. Suddenly she couldn't stop herself. She ran at Laurie and gave him a small, quick squeeze. "Oh, I do love parties, don't you?" gasped Laura.

"Ra-ther," said Laurie's warm, boyish voice, and he squeezed his sister too, and gave her a gentle push. "Dash off to the telephone, old girl."

The telephone. "Yes, yes; oh yes. Kitty? Good morning, dear. Come to lunch? Do, dear. Delighted of course. It will only be a very scratch[2] meal—just the sandwich crusts and broken meringue-shells and what's left over. Yes, isn't it a perfect morning? Your white? Oh, I certainly should. One moment—hold the line. Mother's calling." And Laura sat back. "What, mother? Can't hear."

Mrs. Sheridan's voice floated down the stairs. "Tell her to wear that sweet hat she had on last Sunday."

"Mother says you're to wear that *sweet* hat you had on last Sunday. Good. One o'clock. Bye-bye."

Laura put back the receiver, flung her arms over her head, took a deep breath, stretched, and let them fall. "Huh," she sighed, and the moment after the sigh she sat up quickly. She was still, listening. All the doors in the house seemed to be open. The house was alive with soft, quick steps and running voices. The green baize door[3] that led to the kitchen regions swung open and shut with a muffled thud. And now there came a long, chuckling absurd sound. It was the heavy piano being moved on its stiff castors. But the air! If you stopped to notice, was the air always like this? Little faint winds were playing chase in at the tops of the windows, out at the doors. And there were two tiny spots of sun, one on the inkpot, one on a silver photograph frame, playing too. Darling little spots. Especially the one on the inkpot lid. It was quite warm. A warm little silver star. She could have kissed it.

The front door bell pealed, and there sounded the rustle of Sadie's print skirt on the stairs. A man's voice murmured; Sadie answered, careless, "I'm sure I don't know. Wait. I'll ask Mrs. Sheridan."

"What is it, Sadie?" Laura came into the hall.

"It's the florist, Miss Laura."

---

1   *squiz* New Zealand slang: a quick, close look.

2   *scratch* Quickly thrown together.

3   *green baize door* Swinging door that separated the servants' quarters from the rest of the house. Baize, a felt-like fabric, was often tacked to the inside of doors to insulate against noise.

It was, indeed. There, just inside the door, stood a wide, shallow tray full of pots of pink lilies. No other kind. Nothing but lilies—canna lilies, big pink flowers, wide open, radiant, almost frighteningly alive on bright crimson stems.

"O-oh, Sadie!" said Laura, and the sound was like a little moan. She crouched down as if to warm herself at that blaze of lilies; she felt they were in her fingers, on her lips, growing in her breast.

"It's some mistake," she said faintly. "Nobody ever ordered so many. Sadie, go and find mother."

But at that moment Mrs. Sheridan joined them.

"It's quite right," she said calmly. "Yes, I ordered them. Aren't they lovely?" She pressed Laura's arm. "I was passing the shop yesterday, and I saw them in the window, and I suddenly thought for once in my life I shall have enough canna lilies. The garden party will be a good excuse."

"But I thought you said you didn't mean to interfere," said Laura. Sadie had gone. The florist's man was still outside at his van. She put her arm round her mother's neck and gently, very gently, she bit her mother's ear.

"My darling child, you wouldn't like a logical mother, would you? Don't do that. Here's the man."

He carried more lilies still, another whole tray.

"Bank them up, just inside the door, on both sides of the porch, please," said Mrs. Sheridan. "Don't you agree, Laura?"

"Oh, I *do*, mother."

In the drawing room Meg, Jose, and good little Hans had at last succeeded in moving the piano.

"Now, if we put this chesterfield against the wall and move everything out of the room except the chairs, don't you think?"

"Quite."

"Hans, move these tables into the smoking room, and bring a sweeper to take these marks off the carpet and—one moment, Hans—" Jose loved giving orders to the servants, and they loved obeying her. She always made them feel they were taking part in some drama. "Tell Mother and Miss Laura to come here at once."

"Very good, Miss Jose."

She turned to Meg. "I want to hear what the piano sounds like, just in case I'm asked to sing this afternoon. Let's try over 'This Life is Weary'."

Pom! Ta-ta-ta *Tee*-ta! The piano burst out so passionately that Jose's face changed. She clasped her hands. She looked mournfully and enigmatically at her mother and Laura as they came in.

This Life is *Wee*-ary,
A Tear—a Sigh.

A Love that *Chan*-ges,
    This Life is *Wee*-ary,
A Tear—a Sigh.
A Love that *Chan*-ges,
And then ... Good-bye!

But at the word "Good-bye", and although the piano sounded more desperate than ever, her face broke into a brilliant, dreadfully unsympathetic smile.

"Aren't I in good voice, mummy?" she beamed.

This Life is *Wee*-ary,
Hope comes to Die,
A Dream—a *Wa*-kening.

But now Sadie interrupted them. "What is it, Sadie?"

"If you please, m'm, cook says have you got the flags for the sandwiches?"

"The flags for the sandwiches, Sadie?" echoed Mrs. Sheridan dreamily. And the children knew by her face that she hadn't got them. "Let me see." And she said to Sadie firmly, "Tell cook I'll let her have them in ten minutes."

Sadie went.

"Now, Laura," said her mother quickly, "come with me into the smoking room. I've got the names somewhere on the back of an envelope. You'll have to write them out for me. Meg, go upstairs this minute and take that wet thing off your head. Jose, run and finish dressing this instant. Do you hear me, children, or shall I have to tell your father when he comes home tonight? And—and, Jose, pacify cook if you do go into the kitchen, will you? I'm terrified of her this morning."

The envelope was found at last behind the dining-room clock, though how it had got there Mrs. Sheridan could not imagine.

"One of you children must have stolen it out of my bag, because I remember vividly—cream-cheese and lemon-curd. Have you done that?"

"Yes."

"Egg and—" Mrs. Sheridan held the envelope away from her. "It looks like mice. It can't be mice, can it?"

"Olive, pet," said Laura, looking over her shoulder.

"Yes, of course, olive. What a horrible combination it sounds. Egg and olive."

They were finished at last, and Laura took them off to the kitchen. She found Jose there pacifying the cook, who did not look at all terrifying.

"I have never seen such exquisite sandwiches," said Jose's rapturous voice. "How many kinds did you say there were, cook? Fifteen?"

"Fifteen, Miss Jose."

"Well, cook, I congratulate you."

Cook swept up crusts with the long sandwich knife, and smiled broadly.

"Godber's has come," announced Sadie, issuing out of the pantry. She had seen the man pass the window.

That meant that cream puffs had come. Godber's were famous for their cream puffs. Nobody ever thought of making them at home.

"Bring them in and put them on the table, my girl," ordered cook.

Sadie brought them in and went back to the door. Of course Laura and Jose were far too grown-up to really care about such things. All the same, they couldn't help agreeing that the puffs looked very attractive. Very. Cook began arranging them, shaking off the extra icing sugar.

"Don't they carry one back to all one's parties?" said Laura.

"I suppose they do," said practical Jose, who never liked to be carried back. "They look beautifully light and feathery, I must say."

"Have one each, my dears," said cook in her comfortable voice. "Yer ma won't know."

Oh, impossible. Fancy cream puffs so soon after breakfast. The very idea made one shudder. All the same, two minutes later Jose and Laura were licking their fingers with that absorbed inward look that only comes from whipped cream.

"Let's go into the garden, out by the back way," suggested Laura. "I want to see how the men are getting on with the marquee. They're such awfully nice men."

But the back door was blocked by cook, Sadie, Godber's man and Hans. Something had happened.

"Tuk-tuk-tuk," clucked cook like an agitated hen. Sadie had her hand clapped to her cheek as though she had a toothache. Hans's face was screwed up in the effort to understand. Only Godber's man seemed to be enjoying himself; it was his story.

"What's the matter? What happened?"

"There's been a horrible accident," said cook. "A man killed."

"A man killed! Where? How? When?"

But Godber's man wasn't going to have his story snatched from under his very nose.

"Know those little cottages just below here, miss?" Know them? Of course, she knew them. "Well, there's a young chap living there, name of *Scott*, a carter.[1] His horse shied at a traction-engine,[2] corner of Hawke Street this morning, and he was thrown out on the back of his head. Killed."

---

1   *carter* Driver of a horse-drawn vehicle used to transport goods.

2   *traction-engine* Steam locomotive used on roads.

"Dead!" Laura stared at Godber's man.

"Dead when they picked him up," said Godber's man with relish. "They were taking the body home as I come up here." And he said to the cook, "He's left a wife and five little ones."

"Jose, come here." Laura caught hold of her sister's sleeve and dragged her through the kitchen to the other side of the green baize door. There she paused and leaned against it. "Jose!" she said, horrified, "however are we going to stop everything?"

"Stop everything, Laura!" cried Jose in astonishment. "What do you mean?"

"Stop the garden party, of course." Why did Jose pretend?

But Jose was still more amazed. "Stop the garden party? My dear Laura, don't be so absurd. Of course we can't do anything of the kind. Nobody expects us to. Don't be so extravagant."

"But we can't possibly have a garden party with a man dead just outside the front gate."

That really was extravagant, for the little cottages were in a lane to themselves at the very bottom of a steep rise that led up to the house. A broad road ran between. True, they were far too near. They were the greatest possible eyesore and they had no right to be in that neighbourhood at all. They were little mean dwellings painted a chocolate brown. In the garden patches there was nothing but cabbage stalks, sick hens and tomato cans. The very smoke coming out of their chimneys was poverty-stricken. Little rags and shreds of smoke, so unlike the great silvery plumes that uncurled from the Sheridans' chimneys. Washerwomen lived in the lane and sweeps and a cobbler and a man whose house-front was studded all over with minute bird-cages. Children swarmed. When the Sheridans were little they were forbidden to set foot there because of the revolting language and of what they might catch. But since they were grown up, Laura and Laurie on their prowls sometimes walked through. It was disgusting and sordid. They came out with a shudder. But still one must go everywhere; one must see everything. So through they went.

"And just think of what the band would sound like to that poor woman," said Laura.

"Oh, Laura!" Jose began to be seriously annoyed. "If you're going to stop a band playing every time someone has an accident, you'll lead a very strenuous life. I'm every bit as sorry about it as you. I feel just as sympathetic." Her eyes hardened. She looked at her sister just as she used to when they were little and fighting together. "You won't bring a drunken workman back to life by being sentimental," she said softly.

"Drunk! Who said he was drunk?" Laura turned furiously on Jose. She said just as they had used to say on those occasions, "I'm going straight up to tell mother."

"Do, dear," cooed Jose.

"Mother, can I come into your room?" Laura turned the big glass door-knob.

"Of course, child. Why, what's the matter? What's given you such a colour?" And Mrs. Sheridan turned round from her dressing-table. She was trying on a new hat.

"Mother, a man's been killed," began Laura.

"*Not* in the garden?" interrupted her mother.

"No, no!"

"Oh, what a fright you gave me!" Mrs. Sheridan sighed with relief, and took off the big hat and held it on her knees.

"But listen, mother," said Laura. Breathless, half-choking, she told the dreadful story. "Of course, we can't have our party, can we?" she pleaded. "The band and everybody arriving. They'd hear us, mother; they're nearly neighbours!"

To Laura's astonishment her mother behaved just like Jose; it was harder to bear because she seemed amused. She refused to take Laura seriously. "But, my dear child, use your common sense. It's only by accident we've heard of it. If someone had died there normally—and I can't understand how they keep alive in those poky little holes—we should still be having our party, shouldn't we?"

Laura had to say "yes" to that, but she felt it was all wrong. She sat down on her mother's sofa and pinched the cushion frill.

"Mother, isn't it really terribly heartless of us?" she asked.

"Darling!" Mrs. Sheridan got up and came over to her, carrying the hat. Before Laura could stop her she had popped it on. "My child!" said her mother, "the hat is yours. It's made for you. It's much too young for me. I have never seen you look such a picture. Look at yourself!" And she held up her hand-mirror.

"But, mother," Laura began again. She couldn't look at herself; she turned aside.

This time Mrs. Sheridan lost patience just as Jose had done.

"You are being very absurd, Laura," she said coldly. "People like that don't expect sacrifices from us. And it's not very sympathetic to spoil everybody's enjoyment as you're doing now."

"I don't understand," said Laura, and she walked quickly out of the room into her own bedroom. There, quite by chance, the first thing she saw was this charming girl in the mirror, in her black hat trimmed with gold daisies and a long black velvet ribbon. Never had she imagined she could look like that. Is mother right? she thought. And now she hoped her mother was right. Am I being extravagant? Perhaps it was extravagant. Just for a moment she had another glimpse of that poor woman and those little children, and the body being carried into the house. But it all seemed blurred, unreal, like a picture in the newspaper. I'll remember it again after the party's over, she decided. And somehow that seemed quite the best plan....

Lunch was over by half-past one. By half-past two they were all ready for the fray. The green-coated band had arrived and was established in a corner of the tennis court.

"My dear!" trilled Kitty Maitland, "aren't they too like frogs for words? You ought to have arranged them round the pond with the conductor in the middle on a leaf."

Laurie arrived and hailed them on his way to dress. At the sight of him Laura remembered the accident again. She wanted to tell him. If Laurie agreed with the others, then it was bound to be all right. And she followed him into the hall.

"Laurie!"

"Hallo!" He was halfway upstairs, but when he turned round and saw Laura he suddenly puffed out his cheeks and goggled his eyes at her. "My word, Laura! You do look stunning," said Laurie. "What an absolutely topping hat!"

Laura said faintly "Is it?" and smiled up at Laurie, and didn't tell him after all.

Soon after that people began coming in streams. The band struck up; the hired waiters ran from the house to the marquee. Wherever you looked there were couples strolling, bending to the flowers, greeting, moving on over the lawn. They were like bright birds that had alighted in the Sheridans' garden for this one afternoon, on their way to—where? Ah, what happiness it is to be with people who all are happy, to press hands, press cheeks, smile into eyes.

"Darling Laura, how well you look!"

"What a becoming hat, child!"

"Laura, you look quite Spanish. I've never seen you look so striking."

And Laura, glowing, answered softly, "Have you had tea? Won't you have an ice? The passion-fruit ices really are rather special." She ran to her father and begged him: "Daddy darling, can't the band have something to drink?"

And the perfect afternoon slowly ripened, slowly faded, slowly its petals closed.

"Never a more delightful garden party ..." "The greatest success ..." "Quite the most ..."

Laura helped her mother with the good-byes. They stood side by side on the porch till it was all over.

"All over, all over, thank heaven," said Mrs. Sheridan. "Round up the others, Laura. Let's go and have some fresh coffee. I'm exhausted. Yes, it's been very successful. But oh, these parties, these parties! Why will you children insist on giving parties!" And they all of them sat down in the deserted marquee.

"Have a sandwich, daddy dear. I wrote the flag."

"Thanks." Mr. Sheridan took a bite and the sandwich was gone. He took another. "I suppose you didn't hear of a beastly accident that happened today?" he said.

"My dear," said Mrs. Sheridan, holding up her hand, "we did. It nearly ruined the party. Laura insisted we should put it off."

"Oh, mother!" Laura didn't want to be teased about it.

"It was a horrible affair all the same," said Mr. Sheridan. "The chap was married too. Lived just below in the lane, and leaves a wife and half a dozen kiddies, so they say."

An awkward little silence fell. Mrs. Sheridan fidgeted with her cup. Really, it was very tactless of father....

Suddenly she looked up. There on the table were all those sandwiches, cakes, puffs, all uneaten, all going to be wasted. She had one of her brilliant ideas.

"I know," she said. "Let's make up a basket. Let's send that poor creature some of this perfectly good food. At any rate, it will be the greatest treat for the children. Don't you agree? And she's sure to have neighbours calling in and so on. What a point to have it all ready prepared. Laura!" She jumped up. "Get me the big basket out of the stairs cupboard."

"But, mother, do you really think it's a good idea?" said Laura.

Again, how curious, she seemed to be different from them all. To take scraps from their party. Would the poor woman really like that?

"Of course! What's the matter with you today? An hour or two ago you were insisting on us being sympathetic."

Oh well! Laura ran for the basket. It was filled, it was now heaped by her mother.

"Take it yourself, darling," said she. "Run down just as you are. No, wait, take the arum lilies too. People of that class are so impressed by arum lilies."

"The stems will ruin her lace frock," said practical Jose.

So they would. Just in time. "Only the basket, then. And, Laura!"—her mother followed her out of the marquee—"don't on any account—"

"What, mother?"

No, better not put such ideas into the child's head! "Nothing! Run along."

It was just growing dusky as Laura shut their garden gates. A big dog ran by like a shadow. The road gleamed white, and down below in the hollow the little cottages were in deep shade. How quiet it seemed after the afternoon. Here she was going down the hill to somewhere where a man lay dead, and she couldn't realize it. Why couldn't she? She stopped a minute. And it seemed to her that kisses, voices, tinkling spoons, laughter, the smell of crushed grass were somehow inside her. She had no room for anything else. How strange!

She looked up at the pale sky, and all she thought was, "Yes, it was the most successful party."

Now the broad road was crossed. The lane began, smoky and dark. Women in shawls and men's tweed caps hurried by. Men hung over the palings; the children played in the doorways. A low hum came from the mean little cottages. In some of them there was a flicker of light, and a shadow, crab-like, moved across the window. Laura bent her head and hurried on. She wished now she had put on a coat. How her frock shone! And the big hat with the velvet streamer—if only it was another hat! Were the people looking at her? They must be. It was a mistake to have come; she knew all along it was a mistake. Should she go back even now?

No, too late. This was the house. It must be. A dark knot of people stood outside. Beside the gate an old, old woman with a crutch sat in a chair, watching. She had her feet on a newspaper. The voices stopped as Laura drew near. The group parted. It was as though she was expected, as though they had known she was coming here.

Laura was terribly nervous. Tossing the velvet ribbon over her shoulder, she said to a woman standing by, "Is this Mrs. Scott's house?" and the woman, smiling queerly, said, "It is, my lass."

Oh, to be away from this! She actually said, "Help me, God," as she walked up the tiny path and knocked. To be away from those staring eyes, or to be covered up in anything, one of those women's shawls even. I'll just leave the basket and go, she decided. I shan't even wait for it to be emptied.

Then the door opened. A little woman in black showed in the gloom.

Laura said, "Are you Mrs. Scott?" But to her horror the woman answered, "Walk in, please, miss," and she was shut in the passage.

"No," said Laura, "I don't want to come in. I only want to leave this basket. Mother sent—"

The little woman in the gloomy passage seemed not to have heard her. "Step this way, please, miss," she said in an oily voice, and Laura followed her.

She found herself in a wretched little low kitchen, lighted by a smoky lamp. There was a woman sitting before the fire.

"Em," said the little creature who had let her in. "Em! It's a young lady." She turned to Laura. She said meaningly, "I'm 'er sister, miss. You'll excuse 'er, won't you?"

"Oh, but of course!" said Laura. "Please, please don't disturb her. I—I only want to leave—"

But at that moment the woman at the fire turned round. Her face, puffed up, red, with swollen eyes and swollen lips, looked terrible. She seemed as though she couldn't understand why Laura was there. What did it mean? Why was this stranger standing in the kitchen with a basket? What was it all about? And the poor face puckered up again.

"All right, my dear," said the other. "I'll thenk the young lady."

And again she began, "You'll excuse her, miss, I'm sure," and her face, swollen too, tried an oily smile.

Laura only wanted to get out, to get away. She was back in the passage. The door opened. She walked straight through into the bedroom where the dead man was lying.

"You'd like a look at 'im, wouldn't you?" said Em's sister, and she brushed past Laura over to the bed. "Don't be afraid, my lass,"—and now her voice sounded fond and sly, and fondly she drew down the sheet—"'e looks a picture. There's nothing to show. Come along, my dear."

Laura came.

There lay a young man, fast asleep—sleeping so soundly, so deeply, that he was far, far away from them both. Oh, so remote, so peaceful. He was dreaming. Never wake him up again. His head was sunk in the pillows, his eyes were closed; they were blind under the closed eyelids. He was given up to his dream. What did garden parties and baskets and lace frocks matter to him? He was far from all those things. He was wonderful, beautiful. While they were laughing and while the band was playing, this marvel had come to the lane. Happy ... happy.... All is well, said that sleeping face. This is just as it should be. I am content.

But all the same you had to cry, and she couldn't go out of the room without saying something to him. Laura gave a loud childish sob.

"Forgive my hat," she said.

And this time she didn't wait for Em's sister. She found her way out of the door, down the path, past all those dark people. At the corner of the lane she met Laurie.

He stepped out of the shadow. "Is that you, Laura?"

"Yes."

"Mother was getting anxious. Was it all right?"

"Yes, quite. Oh, Laurie!" She took his arm, she pressed up against him.

"I say, you're not crying, are you?" asked her brother.

Laura shook her head. She was.

Laurie put his arm round her shoulder. "Don't cry," he said in his warm, loving voice. "Was it awful?"

"No," sobbed Laura. "It was simply marvellous. But, Laurie—" She stopped, she looked at her brother. "Isn't life," she stammered, "isn't life—" But what life was she couldn't explain. No matter. He quite understood.

"*Isn't* it, darling?" said Laurie.

—1922

William Faulkner
1897–1962

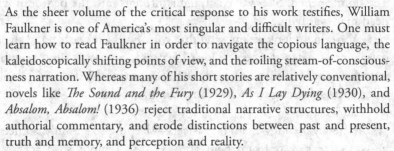

As the sheer volume of the critical response to his work testifies, William Faulkner is one of America's most singular and difficult writers. One must learn how to read Faulkner in order to navigate the copious language, the kaleidoscopically shifting points of view, and the roiling stream-of-consciousness narration. Whereas many of his short stories are relatively conventional, novels like *The Sound and the Fury* (1929), *As I Lay Dying* (1930), and *Absalom, Absalom!* (1936) reject traditional narrative structures, withhold authorial commentary, and erode distinctions between past and present, truth and memory, and perception and reality.

Today Faulkner is recognized for his masterful ability to create "flesh-and-blood, living, suffering, anguishing human beings," but for much of his career he was regarded as a regional Southern writer of small importance. Though he would eventually receive the 1949 Nobel Prize in Literature, all his major novels were out of print just a few years before. In part this is because of their difficulty, but critics also objected to the "pathological delinquency" and "pageant of degeneracy" that they found in his work. But in Faulkner's view, the writer must suppress no tendency or tangent of human behaviour; it is not for him to judge, preach, or proselytize but only to show human beings "in the furious motion of being alive," to tell about "man in his constant struggle with his own heart, with the hearts of others, or with his environment."

"A Rose for Emily" (1930), Faulkner's best-known story, exemplifies his interest in the outer limits of human nature. Yet it is more than a tale of horror or a case study in abnormal psychology: like much of his fiction, it is also concerned with the grip of the myths and memories of a dead but unburied Southern past.

A Rose for Emily

I

When Miss Emily Grierson died, our whole town went to her funeral: the men through a sort of respectful affection for a fallen monument, the women mostly out of curiosity to see the inside of her house, which no one save an old manservant—a combined gardener and cook—had seen in at least ten years.

It was a big, squarish frame house that had once been white, decorated with cupolas and spires and scrolled balconies in the heavily lightsome style of the seventies, set on what had once been our most select street. But garages and cotton gins had encroached and obliterated even the august names of that neighbourhood; only Miss Emily's house was left, lifting its stubborn and coquettish decay above the cotton wagons and the gasoline pumps—an eyesore among eyesores. And now Miss Emily had gone to join the representatives of those august names where they lay in the cedar-bemused cemetery among the ranked and anonymous graves of Union and Confederate soldiers who fell at the battle of Jefferson.[1]

Alive, Miss Emily had been a tradition, a duty, and a care; a sort of hereditary obligation upon the town, dating from that day in 1894 when Colonel Sartoris, the mayor—he who fathered the edict that no Negro woman should appear on the streets without an apron—remitted her taxes, the dispensation dating from the death of her father on into perpetuity. Not that Miss Emily would have accepted charity. Colonel Sartoris invented an involved tale to the effect that Miss Emily's father had loaned money to the town, which the town, as a matter of business, preferred this way of repaying. Only a man of Colonel Sartoris' generation and thought could have invented it, and only a woman could have believed it.

When the next generation, with its more modern ideas, became mayors and aldermen, this arrangement created some little dissatisfaction. On the first of the year they mailed her a tax notice. February came, and there was no reply. They wrote her a formal letter, asking her to call at the sheriff's office at her convenience. A week later the mayor wrote her himself, offering to call or to send his car for her, and received in reply a note on paper of an archaic shape, in a thin, flowing calligraphy in faded ink, to the effect that she no longer went out at all. The tax notice was also enclosed, without comment.

They called a special meeting of the Board of Aldermen. A deputation waited upon her, knocked at the door through which no visitor had passed since she ceased giving china-painting lessons eight or ten years earlier. They were admitted by the old Negro into a dim hall from which a stairway mounted into still more shadow. It smelled of dust and disuse—a close, dank smell. The Negro led them into the parlour. It was furnished in heavy, leather-covered furniture. When the Negro opened the blinds of one window, a faint dust rose sluggishly about their thighs, spinning with slow motes in the single sun-ray. On a tarnished gilt easel before the fireplace stood a crayon portrait of Miss Emily's father.

They rose when she entered—a small, fat woman in black, with a thin gold chain descending to her waist and vanishing into her belt, leaning on an ebony cane with a tarnished gold head. Her skeleton was small and spare; perhaps that was why what would have been merely plumpness in another was obesity in her. She looked bloated, like a body long submerged in motionless water, and of that pallid hue. Her eyes, lost in the fatty ridges of her face, looked like

---

1   *Union and … Jefferson* I.e., casualties of the American Civil War (1861–65).

two small pieces of coal pressed into a lump of dough as they moved from one face to another while the visitors stated their errand.

She did not ask them to sit. She just stood in the door and listened quietly until the spokesman came to a stumbling halt. Then they could hear the invisible watch ticking at the end of the gold chain.

Her voice was dry and cold. "I have no taxes in Jefferson. Colonel Sartoris explained it to me. Perhaps one of you can gain access to the city records and satisfy yourselves."

"But we have. We are the city authorities, Miss Emily. Didn't you get a notice from the sheriff, signed by him?"

"I received a paper, yes," Miss Emily said. "Perhaps he considers himself the sheriff.... I have no taxes in Jefferson."

"But there is nothing on the books to show that, you see. We must go by the—"

"See Colonel Sartoris. I have no taxes in Jefferson."

"But Miss Emily—"

"See Colonel Sartoris." (Colonel Sartoris had been dead almost ten years.) "I have no taxes in Jefferson. Tobe!" The Negro appeared. "Show these gentlemen out."

II

So she vanquished them, horse and foot, just as she had vanquished their fathers thirty years before about the smell. That was two years after her father's death and a short time after her sweetheart—the one we believed would marry her—had deserted her. After her father's death she went out very little; after her sweetheart went away, people hardly saw her at all. A few of the ladies had the temerity to call, but were not received, and the only sign of life about the place was the Negro man—a young man then—going in and out with a market basket.

"Just as if a man—any man—could keep a kitchen properly," the ladies said; so they were not surprised when the smell developed. It was another link between the gross, teeming world and the high and mighty Griersons.

A neighbour, a woman, complained to the mayor, Judge Stevens, eighty years old.

"But what will you have me do about it, madam?" he said.

"Why, send her word to stop it," the woman said. "Isn't there a law?"

"I'm sure that won't be necessary," Judge Stevens said. "It's probably just a snake or a rat that nigger[1] of hers killed in the yard. I'll speak to him about it."

---

[1]   *nigger* This pejorative term remained in frequent use by many white Americans in the South until well into the 1960s.

The next day he received two more complaints, one from a man who came in diffident deprecation. "We really must do something about it, Judge. I'd be the last one in the world to bother Miss Emily, but we've got to do something." That night the Board of Aldermen met—three grey-beards and one younger man, a member of the rising generation.

"It's simple enough," he said. "Send her word to have her place cleaned up. Give her a certain time to do it in, and if she don't...."

"Dammit, sir," Judge Stevens said, "will you accuse a lady to her face of smelling bad?"

So the next night, after midnight, four men crossed Miss Emily's lawn and slunk about the house like burglars, sniffing along the base of the brickwork and at the cellar openings while one of them performed a regular sowing motion with his hand out of a sack slung from his shoulder. They broke open the cellar door and sprinkled lime there, and in all the outbuildings. As they recrossed the lawn, a window that had been dark was lighted and Miss Emily sat in it, the light behind her, and her upright torso motionless as that of an idol. They crept quietly across the lawn and into the shadow of the locusts that lined the street. After a week or two the smell went away.

That was when people had begun to feel really sorry for her. People in our town, remembering how old lady Wyatt, her great-aunt, had gone completely crazy at last, believed that the Griersons held themselves a little too high for what they really were. None of the young men were quite good enough for Miss Emily and such. We had long thought of them as a tableau; Miss Emily a slender figure in white in the background, her father a spraddled silhouette in the foreground, his back to her and clutching a horsewhip, the two of them framed by the backflung front door. So when she got to be thirty and was still single, we were not pleased exactly, but vindicated; even with insanity in the family she wouldn't have turned down all of her chances if they had really materialized.

When her father died, it got about that the house was all that was left to her; and in a way, people were glad. At last they could pity Miss Emily. Being left alone, and a pauper, she had become humanized. Now she too would know the old thrill and the old despair of a penny more or less.

The day after his death all the ladies prepared to call at the house and offer condolence and aid, as is our custom. Miss Emily met them at the door, dressed as usual and with no trace of grief on her face. She told them that her father was not dead. She did that for three days, with the ministers calling on her, and the doctors, trying to persuade her to let them dispose of the body. Just as they were about to resort to law and force, she broke down, and they buried her father quickly.

We did not say she was crazy then. We believed she had to do that. We remembered all the young men her father had driven away, and we knew that with nothing left, she would have to cling to that which had robbed her, as people will.

III

She was sick for a long time. When we saw her again, her hair was cut short, making her look like a girl, with a vague resemblance to those angels in coloured church windows—sort of tragic and serene.

The town had just let the contracts for paving the sidewalks, and in the summer after her father's death they began to work. The construction company came with niggers and mules and machinery, and a foreman named Homer Barron, a Yankee[1]—a big, dark, ready man, with a big voice and eyes lighter than his face. The little boys would follow in groups to hear him cuss the niggers, and the niggers singing in time to the rise and fall of picks. Pretty soon he knew everybody in town. Whenever you heard a lot of laughing anywhere about the square, Homer Barron would be in the centre of the group. Presently we began to see him and Miss Emily on Sunday afternoons driving in the yellow-wheeled buggy and the matched team of bays from the livery stable.

At first we were glad that Miss Emily would have an interest, because the ladies all said, "Of course a Grierson would not think seriously of a Northerner, a day labourer." But there were still others, older people, who said that even grief could not cause a real lady to forget *noblesse oblige*[2]—without calling it *noblesse oblige*. They just said, "Poor Emily. Her kinsfolk should come to her." She had some kin in Alabama; but years ago her father had fallen out with them over the estate of old lady Wyatt, the crazy woman, and there was no communication between the two families. They had not even been represented at the funeral.

And as soon as the old people said, "Poor Emily," the whispering began. "Do you suppose it's really so?" they said to one another. "Of course it is. What else could...." This behind their hands; rustling of craned silk and satin behind jalousies[3] closed upon the sun of Sunday afternoon as the thin, swift clop-clop-clop of the matched team passed: "Poor Emily."

She carried her head high enough—even when we believed that she was fallen. It was as if she demanded more than ever the recognition of her dignity as the last Grierson; as if it had wanted that touch of earthiness to reaffirm her imperviousness. Like when she bought the rat poison, the arsenic. That was over a year after they had begun to say "Poor Emily," and while the two female cousins were visiting her.

---

1   *Yankee* Person from the Northern states.
2   *noblesse oblige* French: nobility obliges. In this case, the obligation of social élites to take an interest in those "below" them.
3   *jalousies* Shutters.

"I want some poison," she said to the druggist. She was over thirty then, still a slight woman, though thinner than usual, with cold, haughty black eyes in a face the flesh of which was strained across the temples and about the eyesockets as you imagine a lighthouse-keeper's face ought to look. "I want some poison," she said.

"Yes, Miss Emily. What kind? For rats and such? I'd recom—"

"I want the best you have. I don't care what kind."

The druggist named several. "They'll kill anything up to an elephant. But what you want is—"

"Arsenic," Miss Emily said. "Is that a good one?"

"Is ... arsenic? Yes, ma'am. But what you want—"

"I want arsenic."

The druggist looked down at her. She looked back at him, erect, her face like a strained flag. "Why, of course," the druggist said. "If that's what you want. But the law requires you to tell what you are going to use it for."

Miss Emily just stared at him, her head tilted back in order to look him eye for eye, until he looked away and went and got the arsenic and wrapped it up. The Negro delivery boy brought her the package; the druggist didn't come back. When she opened the package at home there was written on the box, under the skull and bones: "For rats."

IV

So the next day we all said, "She will kill herself"; and we said it would be the best thing. When she had first begun to be seen with Homer Barron, we had said, "She will marry him." Then we said, "She will persuade him yet," because Homer himself had remarked—he liked men, and it was known that he drank with the younger men in the Elk's Club—that he was not a marrying man. Later we said, "Poor Emily," behind the jalousies as they passed on Sunday afternoon in the glittering buggy, Miss Emily with her head high and Homer Barron with his hat cocked and a cigar in his teeth, reins and whip in a yellow glove.

Then some of the ladies began to say that it was a disgrace to the town and a bad example to the young people. The men did not want to interfere, but at last the ladies forced the Baptist minister—Miss Emily's people were Episcopal[1]—to call upon her. He would never divulge what happened during that interview, but he refused to go back again. The next Sunday they again drove about the streets, and the following day the minister's wife wrote to Miss Emily's relations in Alabama.

---

1   *Baptist ... Episcopal* In America at this time, aristocratic families were more likely to be Episcopalian and working-class families were more likely to be Baptist.

So she had blood-kin under her roof again and we sat back to watch developments. At first nothing happened. Then we were sure that they were to be married. We learned that Miss Emily had been to the jeweller's and ordered a man's toilet set in silver, with the letters H.B. on each piece. Two days later we learned that she had bought a complete outfit of men's clothing, including a nightshirt, and we said, "They are married." We were really glad. We were glad because the two female cousins were even more Grierson than Miss Emily had ever been.

So we were not surprised when Homer Barron—the streets had been finished some time since—was gone. We were a little disappointed that there was not a public blowing-off, but we believed that he had gone on to prepare for Miss Emily's coming, or to give her a chance to get rid of the cousins. (By that time it was a cabal,[1] and we were all Miss Emily's allies to help circumvent the cousins.) Sure enough, after another week they departed. And, as we had expected all along, within three days Homer Barron was back in town. A neighbour saw the Negro man admit him at the kitchen door at dusk one evening.

And that was the last we saw of Homer Barron. And of Miss Emily for some time. The Negro man went in and out with the market basket, but the front door remained closed. Now and then we would see her at a window for a moment, as the men did that night when they sprinkled the lime, but for almost six months she did not appear on the streets. Then we knew that this was to be expected too: as if that quality of her father which had thwarted her woman's life so many times had been too virulent and too furious to die.

When we next saw Miss Emily, she had grown fat and her hair was turning grey. During the next few years it grew greyer and greyer until it attained an even pepper-and-salt iron-grey, when it ceased turning. Up to the day of her death at seventy-four it was still that vigorous iron-grey, like the hair of an active man.

From that time on her front door remained closed, save for a period of six or seven years, when she was about forty, during which she gave lessons in china-painting. She fitted up a studio in one of the downstairs rooms, where the daughters and grand-daughters of Colonel Sartoris' contemporaries were sent to her with the same regularity and in the same spirit that they were sent on Sundays with a twenty-five cent piece for the collection plate. Meanwhile her taxes had been remitted.

Then the newer generation became the backbone and the spirit of the town, and the painting pupils grew up and fell away and did not send their children to her with boxes of colour and tedious brushes and pictures cut from

---

1   *cabal* Covert group of conspirators.

the ladies' magazines. The front door closed upon the last one and remained closed for good. When the town got free postal delivery Miss Emily alone refused to let them fasten the metal numbers above her door and attach a mailbox to it. She would not listen to them.

Daily, monthly, yearly we watched the Negro grow greyer and more stooped, going in and out with the market basket. Each December we sent her a tax notice, which would be returned by the post office a week later, unclaimed. Now and then we would see her in one of the downstairs windows—she had evidently shut up the top floor of the house—like the carven torso of an idol in a niche, looking or not looking at us, we could never tell which. Thus she passed from generation to generation—dear, inescapable, impervious, tranquil, and perverse.

And so she died. Fell ill in the house filled with dust and shadows, with only a doddering Negro man to wait on her. We did not even know she was sick; we had long since given up trying to get any information from the Negro. He talked to no one, probably not even to her, for his voice had grown harsh and rusty, as if from disuse.

She died in one of the downstairs rooms, in a heavy walnut bed with a curtain, her grey head propped on a pillow yellow and mouldy with age and lack of sunlight.

V

The Negro met the first of the ladies at the front door and let them in, with their hushed, sibilant voices and their quick, curious glances, and then he disappeared. He walked right through the house and out the back and was not seen again.

The two female cousins came at once. They held the funeral on the second day, with the town coming to look at Miss Emily beneath a mass of bought flowers, with the crayon face of her father musing profoundly above the bier and the ladies sibilant and macabre; and the very old men—some in their brushed Confederate uniforms—on the porch and the lawn, talking of Miss Emily as if she had been a contemporary of theirs, believing that they had danced with her and courted her perhaps, confusing time with its mathematical progression, as the old do, to whom all the past is not a diminishing road, but, instead, a huge meadow which no winter ever quite touches, divided from them now by the narrow bottleneck of the most recent decade of years.

Already we knew that there was one room in that region above stairs which no one had seen in forty years, and which would have to be forced. They waited until Miss Emily was decently in the ground before they opened it.

The violence of breaking down the door seemed to fill this room with pervading dust. A thin, acrid pall as of the tomb seemed to lie everywhere upon this room decked and furnished as for a bridal: upon the valance curtains of faded rose colour, upon the rose-shaded lights, upon the dressing table, upon the delicate array of crystal and the man's toilet things backed with tarnished silver, silver so tarnished that the monogram was obscured. Among them lay a collar and tie, as if they had just been removed, which, lifted, left upon the surface a pale crescent in the dust. Upon a chair hung the suit, carefully folded; beneath it the two mute shoes and the discarded socks.

The man himself lay in the bed.

For a long while we just stood there, looking down at the profound and fleshless grin. The body had apparently once lain in the attitude of an embrace, but now the long sleep that outlasts love, that conquers even the grimace of love, had cuckolded him. What was left of him, rotted beneath what was left of the nightshirt, had become inextricable from the bed in which he lay; and upon him and upon the pillow beside him lay that even coating of the patient and biding dust.

Then we noticed that in the second pillow was the indentation of a head. One of us lifted something from it, and leaning forward, that faint and invisible dust dry and acrid in the nostrils, we saw a long strand of iron-grey hair.

—1930

Ernest Hemingway
1899–1961

Ernest Hemingway is considered one of the great American authors of the twentieth century. His influence can be seen in the objective style of writing he propagated, characterized by sparse sentences devoid of embellishment. Hemingway famously argues for his technique in *Death in the Afternoon* (1932): "If a writer of prose knows enough about what he is writing about he may omit things that he knows and the reader, if the writer is writing truly enough, will have a feeling of those things as strongly as though the writer had stated them. The dignity of movement of an iceberg is due to only one-eighth of it being above water." In 1952, Hemingway was awarded the Pulitzer Prize for his novel *The Old Man and the Sea*, the story of a Cuban fisherman's quest to reel in a giant marlin. In 1954, he was awarded the Nobel Prize in Literature for his "mastery of the art of narrative, most recently demonstrated in *The Old Man and the Sea*, and for the influence that he has exerted on contemporary style."

In 1918, Hemingway travelled to Italy as an ambulance driver for the American Red Cross. His injury and recuperation later that year removed him from service, but the experience inspired his 1929 novel, *A Farewell to Arms*. His first novel, *The Sun Also Rises* (1926), drew from his life as an expatriate in Paris in the 1920s. During the Spanish Civil War (1936–39), Hemingway raised money for the Republican cause and travelled throughout Spain as a journalist. This inspired his greatest commercial success, the 1939 novel *For Whom the Bell Tolls*, a semi-autobiographical story of a young American who fights fascism.

Hemingway's writing reflects his passion for pursuits such as bullfighting, fishing, and hunting, and often examines the cruel legacy of war. In presenting the Nobel Prize to Hemingway, Anders Osterling said: "It may be true that Hemingway's earlier writings display brutal, cynical, and callous sides which may be considered at variance with the Nobel Prize's requirement for a work of an ideal tendency. But on the other hand, he also possesses a heroic pathos which forms the basic element in his awareness of life, a manly love of danger and adventure with a natural admiration for every individual who fights the good fight in a world of reality overshadowed by violence and death."

Hemingway committed suicide in Idaho in 1961, after a period of serious depression.

A Clean, Well-Lighted Place

It was very late and every one had left the café except an old man who sat in the shadow the leaves of the tree made against the electric light. In the day time the street was dusty, but at night the dew settled the dust and the old man liked to sit late because he was deaf and now at night it was quiet and he felt the difference. The two waiters inside the café knew that the old man was a little drunk, and while he was a good client they knew that if he became too drunk he would leave without paying, so they kept watch on him.

"Last week he tried to commit suicide," one waiter said.

"Why?"

"He was in despair."

"What about?"

"Nothing."

"How do you know it was nothing?"

"He has plenty of money."

They sat together at a table that was close against the wall near the door of the café and looked at the terrace where the tables were all empty except where the old man sat in the shadow of the leaves of the tree that moved slightly in the wind. A girl and a soldier went by in the street. The street light shone on the brass number on his collar. The girl wore no head covering and hurried beside him.

"The guard will pick him up," one waiter said.

"What does it matter if he gets what he's after?"

"He had better get off the street now. The guard will get him. They went by five minutes ago."

The old man sitting in the shadow rapped on his saucer with his glass. The younger waiter went over to him.

"What do you want?"

The old man looked at him. "Another brandy," he said.

"You'll be drunk," the waiter said. The old man looked at him. The waiter went away.

"He'll stay all night," he said to his colleague. "I'm sleepy now. I never get into bed before three o'clock. He should have killed himself last week."

The waiter took the brandy bottle and another saucer from the counter inside the café and marched out to the old man's table. He put down the saucer and poured the glass full of brandy.

"You should have killed yourself last week," he said to the deaf man. The old man motioned with his finger. "A little more," he said. The waiter poured on into the glass so that the brandy slopped over and ran down the stem into the top saucer of the pile.""Thank you," the old man said. The waiter took the bottle back inside the café. He sat down at the table with his colleague again.

"He's drunk now," he said.

"He's drunk every night."

"What did he want to kill himself for?"

"How should I know."

"How did he do it?"

"He hung himself with a rope."

"Who cut him down?"

"His niece."

"Why did they do it?"

"Fear for his soul."

"How much money has he got?"

"He's got plenty."

"He must be eighty years old."

"Anyway I should say he was eighty."

"I wish he would go home. I never get to bed before three o'clock. What kind of hour is that to go to bed?"

"He stays up because he likes it."

"He's lonely. I'm not lonely. I have a wife waiting in bed for me."

"He had a wife once too."

"A wife would be no good to him now."

"You can't tell. He might be better with a wife."

"His niece looks after him."

"I know. You said she cut him down."

"I wouldn't want to be that old. An old man is a nasty thing."

"Not always. This old man is clean. He drinks without spilling. Even now, drunk. Look at him."

"I don't want to look at him. I wish he would go home. He has no regard for those who must work."

The old man looked from his glass across the square, then over at the waiters.

"Another brandy," he said, pointing to his glass. The waiter who was in a hurry came over.

"Finished," he said, speaking with that omission of syntax stupid people employ when talking to drunken people or foreigners. "No more tonight. Close now."

"Another," said the old man.

"No. Finished." The waiter wiped the edge of the table with a towel and shook his head.

The old man stood up, slowly counted the saucers, took a leather coin purse from his pocket and paid for the drinks, leaving half a peseta tip.

The waiter watched him go down the street, a very old man walking unsteadily but with dignity.

"Why didn't you let him stay and drink?" the unhurried waiter asked. They were putting up the shutters. "It is not half-past two."

"I want to go home to bed."

"What is an hour?"

"More to me than to him."

"An hour is the same."

"You talk like an old man yourself. He can buy a bottle and drink at home."

"It's not the same."

"No, it is not," agreed the waiter with a wife. He did not wish to be unjust. He was only in a hurry.

"And you? You have no fear of going home before your usual hour?"

"Are you trying to insult me?"

"No, hombre,[1] only to make a joke."

"No," the waiter who was in a hurry said, rising from pulling down the metal shutters. "I have confidence. I am all confidence."

"You have youth, confidence, and a job," the older waiter said. "You have everything."

"And what do you lack?"

"Everything but work."

"You have everything I have."

"No. I have never had confidence and I am not young."

"Come on. Stop talking nonsense and lock up."

"I am of those who like to stay late at the café," the older waiter said. "With all those who do not want to go to bed. With all those who need a light for the night."

"I want to go home and into bed."

"We are of two different kinds," the older waiter said. He was now dressed to go home. "It is not only a question of youth and confidence although those things are very beautiful. Each night I am reluctant to close up because there may be some one who needs the café."

"Hombre, there are bodegas[2] open all night long."

"You do not understand. This is a clean and pleasant café. It is well lighted. The light is very good and also, now, there are shadows of the leaves."

---

1   *hombre* Spanish: man, dude.

2   *bodegas* Wine sellers, cheap drinking establishments.

"Good night," said the younger waiter.

"Good night," the other said. Turning off the electric light he continued the conversation with himself. It is the light of course but it is necessary that the place be clean and pleasant. You do not want music. Certainly you do not want music. Nor can you stand before a bar with dignity although that is all that is provided for these hours. What did he fear? It was not a fear or dread. It was a nothing that he knew too well. It was all a nothing and a man was nothing too. It was only that and light was all it needed and a certain cleanness and order. Some lived in it and never felt it but he knew it all was nada y pues nada[1] y nada y pues nada. Our nada who art in nada, nada be thy name thy kingdom nada thy will be nada in nada as it is in nada. Give us this nada our daily nada and nada us our nada as we nada our nadas and nada us not into nada but deliver us from nada; pues nada. Hail nothing full of nothing, nothing is with thee.[2] He smiled and stood before a bar with a shining steam pressure coffee machine.

"What's yours?" asked the barman.

"Nada."

"Otro loco más,"[3] said the barman and turned away.

"A little cup," said the waiter.

The barman poured it for him.

"The light is very bright and pleasant but the bar is unpolished," the waiter said.

The barman looked at him but did not answer. It was too late at night for conversation.

"You want another copita?"[4] the barman asked.

"No, thank you," said the waiter and went out. He disliked bars and bodegas. A clean, well-lighted café was a very different thing. Now, without thinking further, he would go home to his room. He would lie in the bed and finally, with daylight, he would go to sleep. After all, he said to himself, it is probably only insomnia. Many must have it.

—1933

---

1   *nada ... nada* Spanish: nothing and then nothing.
2   *Our nada ... with thee* Parodies the Lord's Prayer, which is included in the New Testament (see Matthew 6:9–13) and used in most Christian churches.
3   *Otro loco más* Spanish: One more madman.
4   *copita* Spanish: glass.

Flannery O'Connor
1925–1964

Born in Savannah, Georgia, Mary Flannery O'Connor spent most of her life in the American South, where her novels and most of her short stories are set. Participating in the tradition of the "Southern Gothic," her writing blends humour and the grotesque, often incorporating bleak or violent events and physically deformed or morally twisted characters. O'Connor approached the "Southern Gothic" through the lens of her intensely deep Catholic faith; indeed, she writes that "the meaning of life is centered in our Redemption by Christ and what I see in the world I see in its relation to that."

After graduating from the Georgia State College for Women in 1945, O'Connor spent three years at the prestigious Writers' Workshop at the University of Iowa. She probably would have remained in the northern United States if she were not struck in 1950 by the first signs of lupus. Weakened by the disease and the debilitating cortisone treatments it required, she went to live with her mother in Milledgeville, Georgia, where she would remain for the rest of her life.

Although O'Connor was a deeply committed Catholic, her fiction is set in the Southern "Bible Belt" where Protestantism was predominant, and her characters are often Protestant fundamentalists who are both materially and spiritually poor. Her stories focus on terrible events befalling such characters, she said, in order to portray "the action of grace in territory held largely by the devil." She described her short story collection *A Good Man Is Hard to Find* (1955), which received the O. Henry first prize for short fiction, as a book of "stories about original sin."

In addition to *A Good Man Is Hard to Find*, O'Connor published two novels—*Wise Blood* (1952) and *The Violent Bear It Away* (1960)—before her early death in 1964 as a result of lupus. Her last short story collection, *Everything that Rises Must Converge*, was published posthumously the following year.

A Good Man Is Hard to Find

The grandmother didn't want to go to Florida. She wanted to visit some of her connections in east Tennessee and she was seizing at every chance to change Bailey's mind. Bailey was the son she lived with, her only boy. He was sitting on the edge of his chair at the table, bent over the orange sports section of the *Journal*. "Now look here, Bailey," she said, "see here, read this," and she stood with one hand on her thin hip and the other rattling the newspaper at his bald head. "Here this fellow that calls himself The Misfit is aloose from the Federal Pen and headed toward Florida and you read here what it says he did to these people. Just you read it. I wouldn't take my children in any direction with a criminal like that aloose in it. I couldn't answer to my conscience if I did."

Bailey didn't look up from his reading so she wheeled around then and faced the children's mother, a young woman in slacks, whose face was as broad and innocent as a cabbage and was tied around with a green head-kerchief that had two points on the top like rabbit's ears. She was sitting on the sofa, feeding the baby his apricots out of a jar. "The children have been to Florida before," the old lady said. "You all ought to take them somewhere else for a change so they would see different parts of the world and be broad. They never have been to east Tennessee."

The children's mother didn't seem to hear her but the eight-year-old boy, John Wesley, a stocky child with glasses, said, "If you don't want to go to Florida, why dontcha stay at home?" He and the little girl, June Star, were reading the funny papers on the floor.

"She wouldn't stay at home to be queen for a day," June Star said without raising her yellow head.

"Yes and what would you do if this fellow, The Misfit, caught you?" the grandmother asked.

"I'd smack his face," John Wesley said.

"She wouldn't stay at home for a million bucks," June Star said. "Afraid she'd miss something. She has to go everywhere we go."

"All right, Miss," the grandmother said. "Just remember that the next time you want me to curl your hair."

June Star said her hair was naturally curly.

The next morning the grandmother was the first one in the car, ready to go. She had her big black valise that looked like the head of a hippopotamus in one corner, and underneath it she was hiding a basket with Pitty Sing, the cat, in it. She didn't intend for the cat to be left alone in the house for three days because he would miss her too much and she was afraid he might brush against one of the gas burners and accidentally asphyxiate himself. Her son, Bailey, didn't like to arrive at a motel with a cat.

She sat in the middle of the back seat with John Wesley and June Star on either side of her. Bailey and the children's mother and the baby sat in front and they left Atlanta at eight forty-five with the mileage on the car at 55890. The grandmother wrote this down because she thought it would be interesting to say how many miles they had been when they got back. It took them twenty minutes to reach the outskirts of the city.

The old lady settled herself comfortably, removing her white cotton gloves and putting them up with her purse on the shelf in front of the back window. The children's mother still had on slacks and still had her head tied up in a green kerchief, but the grandmother had on a navy blue straw sailor hat with a bunch of white violets on the brim and a navy blue dress with a small white dot in the print. Her collars and cuffs were white organdy trimmed with lace and at her neckline she had pinned a purple spray of cloth violets containing a sachet. In case of an accident, anyone seeing her dead on the highway would know at once that she was a lady.

She said she thought it was going to be a good day for driving, neither too hot nor too cold, and she cautioned Bailey that the speed limit was fifty-five miles an hour and that the patrolmen hid themselves behind billboards and small clumps of trees and sped out after you before you had a chance to slow down. She pointed out interesting details of the scenery: Stone Mountain; the blue granite that in some places came up to both sides of the highway; the brilliant red clay banks slightly streaked with purple; and the various crops that made rows of green lace-work on the ground. The trees were full of silver-white sunlight and the meanest of them sparkled. The children were reading comic magazines and their mother had gone back to sleep.

"Let's go through Georgia fast so we won't have to look at it much," John Wesley said.

"If I were a little boy," said the grandmother, "I wouldn't talk about my native state that way. Tennessee has the mountains and Georgia has the hills."

"Tennessee is just a hillbilly dumping ground," John Wesley said, "and Georgia is a lousy state too."

"You said it," June Star said.

"In my time," said the grandmother, folding her thin veined fingers, "children were more respectful of their native states and their parents and everything else. People did right then. Oh look at the cute little pickaninny!"[1] she said and pointed to a Negro child standing in the door of a shack. "Wouldn't that make a picture, now?" she asked and they all turned and looked at the little Negro out of the back window. He waved.

"He didn't have any britches on," June Star said.

"He probably didn't have any," the grandmother explained. "Little niggers[2] in the country don't have things like we do. If I could paint, I'd paint that picture," she said.

The children exchanged comic books.

The grandmother offered to hold the baby and the children's mother passed him over the front seat to her. She set him on her knee and bounced him and told him about the things they were passing. She rolled her eyes and screwed up her mouth and stuck her leathery thin face into his smooth bland

---

1   *pickaninny* Derogatory term for an African American child.
2   *niggers* This pejorative term remained in frequent use by many white Americans in the South until well into the 1960s.

one. Occasionally he gave her a faraway smile. They passed a large cotton field with five or six graves fenced in the middle of it, like a small island. "Look at the graveyard!" the grandmother said, pointing it out. "That was the old family burying ground. That belonged to the plantation."

"Where's the plantation?" John Wesley asked.

"Gone With the Wind," said the grandmother. "Ha. Ha."

When the children finished all the comic books they had brought, they opened the lunch and ate it. The grandmother ate a peanut butter sandwich and an olive and would not let the children throw the box and the paper napkins out the window. When there was nothing else to do they played a game by choosing a cloud and making the other two guess what shape it suggested. John Wesley took one the shape of a cow and June Star guessed a cow and John Wesley said, no, an automobile, and June Star said he didn't play fair, and they began to slap each other over the grandmother.

The grandmother said she would tell them a story if they would keep quiet. When she told a story, she rolled her eyes and waved her head and was very dramatic. She said once when she was a maiden lady she had been courted by a Mr. Edgar Atkins Teagarden from Jasper, Georgia. She said he was a very good-looking man and a gentleman and that he brought her a watermelon every Saturday afternoon with his initials cut in it, E.A.T. Well, one Saturday, she said, Mr. Teagarden brought the watermelon and there was nobody at home and he left it on the front porch and returned in his buggy to Jasper, but she never got the watermelon, she said, because a nigger boy ate it when he saw the initials, E.A.T.! This story tickled John Wesley's funny bone and he giggled and giggled but June Star didn't think it was any good. She said she wouldn't marry a man that just brought her a watermelon on Saturday. The grandmother said she would have done well to marry Mr. Teagarden because he was a gentleman and had bought Coca-Cola stock when it first came out and that he had died only a few years ago, a very wealthy man.

They stopped at The Tower for barbecued sandwiches. The Tower was a part stucco and part wood filling station and dance hall set in a clearing outside of Timothy. A fat man named Red Sammy Butts ran it and there were signs stuck here and there on the building and for miles up and down the highway saying, TRY RED SAMMY'S FAMOUS BARBECUE. NONE LIKE FAMOUS RED SAMMY'S! RED SAM! THE FAT BOY WITH THE HAPPY LAUGH. A VETERAN! RED SAMMY'S YOUR MAN!

Red Sammy was lying on the bare ground outside The Tower with his head under a truck while a grey monkey about a foot high, chained to a small chinaberry tree, chattered nearby. The monkey sprang back into the tree and got on the highest limb as soon as he saw the children jump out of the car and run toward him.

Inside, The Tower was a long dark room with a counter at one end and tables at the other and dancing space in the middle. They all sat down at a board table next to the nickelodeon and Red Sam's wife, a tall burnt-brown woman with hair and eyes lighter than her skin, came and took their order. The children's mother put a dime in the machine and played "The Tennessee Waltz," and the grandmother said that tune always made her want to dance. She asked Bailey if he would like to dance but he only glared at her. He didn't have a naturally sunny disposition like she did and trips made him nervous. The grandmother's brown eyes were very bright. She swayed her head from side to side and pretended she was dancing in her chair. June Star said play something she could tap to so the children's mother put in another dime and played a fast number and June Star stepped out onto the dance floor and did her tap routine.

"Ain't she cute?" Red Sam's wife said, leaning over the counter. "Would you like to come be my little girl?"

"No I certainly wouldn't," June Star said. "I wouldn't live in a broken-down place like this for a million bucks!" and she ran back to the table.

"Ain't she cute?" the woman repeated, stretching her mouth politely.

"Ain't you ashamed?" hissed the grandmother.

Red Sam came in and told his wife to quit lounging on the counter and hurry up with these people's order. His khaki trousers reached just to his hip bones and his stomach hung over them like a sack of meal swaying under his shirt. He came over and sat down at a table nearby and let out a combination sigh and yodel. "You can't win," he said. "You can't win," and he wiped his sweating red face off with a grey handkerchief. "These days you don't know who to trust," he said. "Ain't that the truth?"

"People are certainly not nice like they used to be," said the grandmother.

"Two fellers come in here last week," Red Sammy said, "driving a Chrysler. It was a old beat-up car but it was a good one and these boys looked all right to me. Said they worked at the mill and you know I let them fellers charge the gas they bought? Now why did I do that?"

"Because you're a good man!" the grandmother said at once.

"Yes'm, I suppose so," Red Sam said as if he were struck with this answer.

His wife brought the orders, carrying the five plates all at once without a tray, two in each hand and one balanced on her arm. "It isn't a soul in this green world of God's that you can trust," she said. "And I don't count nobody out of that, not nobody," she repeated, looking at Red Sammy.

"Did you read about that criminal, The Misfit, that's escaped?" asked the grandmother.

"I wouldn't be a bit surprised if he didn't attact this place right here," said the woman. "If he hears about it being here, I wouldn't be none surprised to see him. If he hears it's two cent in the cash register, I wouldn't be a tall surprised if he...."

"That'll do," Red Sam said. "Go bring these people their Co'-Colas," and the woman went off to get the rest of the order.

"A good man is hard to find," Red Sammy said. "Everything is getting terrible. I remember the day you could go off and leave your screen door unlatched. Not no more."

He and the grandmother discussed better times. The old lady said that in her opinion Europe was entirely to blame for the way things were now. She said the way Europe acted you would think we were made of money and Red Sam said it was no use talking about it, she was exactly right. The children ran outside into the white sunlight and looked at the monkey in the lacy china-berry tree. He was busy catching fleas on himself and biting each one carefully between his teeth as if it were a delicacy.

They drove off again into the hot afternoon. The grandmother took cat naps and woke up every few minutes with her own snoring. Outside of Toombsboro she woke up and recalled an old plantation that she had visited in this neighbourhood once when she was a young lady. She said the house had six white columns across the front and that there was an avenue of oaks leading up to it and two little wooden trellis arbours on either side in front where you sat down with your suitor after a stroll in the garden. She recalled exactly which road to turn off to get to it. She knew that Bailey would not be willing to lose any time looking at an old house, but the more she talked about it, the more she wanted to see it once again and find out if the little twin arbours were still standing. "There was a secret panel in this house," she said craftily, not telling the truth but wishing that she were, "and the story went that all the family silver was hidden in it when Sherman[1] came through but it was never found ..."

"Hey!" John Wesley said. "Let's go see it! We'll find it! We'll poke all the woodwork and find it! Who lives there? Where do you turn off at? Hey Pop, can't we turn off there?"

"We never have seen a house with a secret panel!" June Star shrieked. "Let's go to the house with the secret panel! Hey, Pop, can't we go see the house with the secret panel!"

"It's not far from here, I know," the grandmother said. "It wouldn't take over twenty minutes."

Bailey was looking straight ahead. His jaw was as rigid as a horseshoe. "No," he said.

---

1   *Sherman* American Union commander William Tecumseh Sherman marched his troops through Georgia to Atlanta in 1864 during the American Civil War.

The children began to yell and scream that they wanted to see the house with the secret panel. John Wesley kicked the back of the front seat and June Star hung over her mother's shoulder and whined desperately into her ear that they never had any fun even on their vacation, that they could never do what THEY wanted to do. The baby began to scream and John Wesley kicked the back of the seat so hard that his father could feel the blows in his kidney.

"All right!" he shouted and drew the car to a stop at the side of the road. "Will you all shut up? Will you all just shut up for one second? If you don't shut up, we won't go anywhere."

"It would be very educational for them," the grandmother murmured.

"All right," Bailey said, "but get this: this is the only time we're going to stop for anything like this. This is the one and only time."

"The dirt road that you have to turn down is about a mile back," the grandmother directed. "I marked it when we passed."

"A dirt road," Bailey groaned.

After they had turned around and were headed toward the dirt road, the grandmother recalled other points about the house, the beautiful glass over the front doorway and the candle-lamp in the hall. John Wesley said that the secret panel was probably in the fireplace.

"You can't go inside this house," Bailey said. "You don't know who lives there."

"While you all talk to the people in front, I'll run around behind and get in a window," John Wesley suggested.

"We'll all stay in the car," his mother said.

They turned onto the dirt road and the car raced roughly along in a swirl of pink dust. The grandmother recalled the times when there were no paved roads and thirty miles was a day's journey. The dirt road was hilly and there were sudden washes in it and sharp curves on dangerous embankments. All at once they would be on a hill, looking down over the blue tops of trees for miles around, then the next minute, they would be in a red depression with the dust-coated trees looking down on them.

"This place had better turn up in a minute," Bailey said, "or I'm going to turn around."

The road looked as if no one had travelled on it in months.

"It's not much farther," the grandmother said and just as she said it, a horrible thought came to her. The thought was so embarrassing that she turned red in the face and her eyes dilated and her feet jumped up, upsetting her valise in the corner. The instant the valise moved, the newspaper top she had over the basket under it rose with a snarl and Pitty Sing, the cat, sprang onto Bailey's shoulder.

The children were thrown to the floor and their mother, clutching the baby, was thrown out the door onto the ground; the old lady was thrown into the front seat. The car turned over once and landed right-side-up in a gulch off the side of the road. Bailey remained in the driver's seat with the cat—grey-striped with a broad white face and an orange nose—clinging to his neck like a caterpillar.

As soon as the children saw they could move their arms and legs, they scrambled out of the car, shouting, "We've had an ACCIDENT!" The grandmother was curled up under the dashboard, hoping she was injured so that Bailey's wrath would not come down on her all at once. The horrible thought she had had before the accident was that the house she had remembered so vividly was not in Georgia but in Tennessee.

Bailey removed the cat from his neck with both hands and flung it out the window against the side of a pine tree. Then he got out of the car and started looking for the children's mother. She was sitting against the side of the red gutted ditch, holding the screaming baby, but she only had a cut down her face and a broken shoulder. "We've had an ACCIDENT!" the children screamed in a frenzy of delight.

"But nobody's killed," June Star said with disappointment as the grandmother limped out of the car, her hat still pinned to her head but the broken front brim standing up at a jaunty angle and the violet spray hanging off the side. They all sat down in the ditch, except the children, to recover from the shock. They were all shaking.

"Maybe a car will come along," said the children's mother hoarsely.

"I believe I have injured an organ," said the grandmother, pressing her side, but no one answered her. Bailey's teeth were clattering. He had on a yellow sport shirt with bright blue parrots designed in it and his face was as yellow as the shirt. The grandmother decided that she would not mention that the house was in Tennessee.

The road was about ten feet above and they could see only the tops of the trees on the other side of it. Behind the ditch they were sitting in there were more woods, tall and dark and deep. In a few minutes they saw a car some distance away on top of a hill, coming slowly as if the occupants were watching them. The grandmother stood up and waved both arms dramatically to attract their attention. The car continued to come on slowly, disappeared around a bend and appeared again, moving even slower, on top of the hill they had gone over. It was a big black battered hearse-like automobile. There were three men in it.

It came to a stop just over them and for some minutes, the driver looked down with a steady expressionless gaze to where they were sitting, and didn't speak. Then he turned his head and muttered something to the other two and they got out. One was a fat boy in black trousers and a red sweat shirt with a silver stallion embossed on the front of it. He moved around on the right side of them and stood staring, his mouth partly open in a kind of loose grin. The other had on khaki pants and a blue striped coat and a grey hat pulled down very low, hiding most of his face. He came around slowly on the left side. Neither spoke.

The driver got out of the car and stood by the side of it, looking down at them. He was an older man than the other two. His hair was just beginning to grey and he wore silver-rimmed spectacles that gave him a scholarly look. He had a long creased face and didn't have on any shirt or undershirt. He had on blue jeans that were too tight for him and was holding a black hat and a gun. The two boys also had guns.

"We've had an ACCIDENT!" the children screamed.

The grandmother had the peculiar feeling that the bespectacled man was someone she knew. His face was as familiar to her as if she had known him all her life but she could not recall who he was. He moved away from the car and began to come down the embankment, placing his feet carefully so that he wouldn't slip. He had on tan and white shoes and no socks, and his ankles were red and thin. "Good afternoon," he said. "I see you all had you a little spill."

"We turned over twice!" said the grandmother.

"Oncet," he corrected. "We seen it happen. Try their car and see will it run, Hiram," he said quietly to the boy with the grey hat.

"What you got that gun for?" John Wesley asked. "Whatcha gonna do with that gun?"

"Lady," the man said to the children's mother, "would you mind calling them children to sit down by you? Children make me nervous. I want all you all to sit down right together there where you're at."

"What are you telling US what to do for?" June Star asked.

Behind them the line of woods gaped like a dark open mouth. "Come here," said their mother.

"Look here now," Bailey began suddenly, "we're in a predicament! We're in...."

The grandmother shrieked. She scrambled to her feet and stood staring. "You're The Misfit!" she said. "I recognized you at once!"

"Yes'm," the man said, smiling slightly as if he were pleased in spite of himself to be known, "but it would have been better for all of you, lady, if you hadn't of reckernized me."

Bailey turned his head sharply and said something to his mother that shocked even the children. The old lady began to cry and The Misfit reddened.

"Lady," he said, "don't you get upset. Sometimes a man says things he don't mean. I don't reckon he meant to talk to you thataway."

"You wouldn't shoot a lady, would you?" the grandmother said and removed a clean handkerchief from her cuff and began to slap at her eyes with it.

The Misfit pointed the toe of his shoe into the ground and made a little hole and then covered it up again. "I would hate to have to," he said.

"Listen," the grandmother almost screamed, "I know you're a good man. You don't look a bit like you have common blood. I know you must come from nice people!"

"Yes mam," he said, "finest people in the world." When he smiled he showed a row of strong white teeth. "God never made a finer woman than my mother and my daddy's heart was pure gold," he said. The boy with the red sweat shirt had come around behind them and was standing with his gun at his hip. The Misfit squatted down on the ground. "Watch them children, Bobby Lee," he said. "You know they make me nervous." He looked at the six of them huddled together in front of him and he seemed to be embarrassed as if he couldn't think of anything to say. "Ain't a cloud in the sky," he remarked, looking up at it. "Don't see no sun but don't see no cloud neither."

"Yes, it's a beautiful day," said the grandmother. "Listen," she said, "you shouldn't call yourself The Misfit because I know you're a good man at heart. I can just look at you and tell."

"Hush!" Bailey yelled. "Hush! Everybody shut up and let me handle this!" He was squatting in the position of a runner about to sprint forward but he didn't move.

"I pre-chate that, lady," The Misfit said and drew a little circle in the ground with the butt of his gun.

"It'll take a half a hour to fix this here car," Hiram called, looking over the raised hood of it.

"Well, first you and Bobby Lee get him and that little boy to step over yonder with you," The Misfit said, pointing to Bailey and John Wesley. "The boys want to ast you something," he said to Bailey. "Would you mind stepping back in them woods there with them?"

"Listen," Bailey began, "we're in a terrible predicament! Nobody realizes what this is," and his voice cracked. His eyes were as blue and intense as the parrots in his shirt and he remained perfectly still.

The grandmother reached up to adjust her hat brim as if she were going to the woods with him but it came off in her hand. She stood staring at it and after a second she let it fall on the ground. Hiram pulled Bailey up by the arm as if he were assisting an old man. John Wesley caught hold of his father's hand and Bobby Lee followed. They went off toward the woods and just as they reached the dark edge, Bailey turned and supporting himself against a grey naked pine trunk, he shouted, "I'll be back in a minute, Mamma, wait on me!"

"Come back this instant!" his mother shrilled but they all disappeared into the woods.

"Bailey Boy!" the grandmother called in a tragic voice but she found she was looking at The Misfit squatting on the ground in front of her. "I just know you're a good man," she said desperately. "You're not a bit common!"

"Nome, I ain't a good man," The Misfit said after a second as if he had considered her statement carefully, "but I ain't the worst in the world neither. My daddy said I was a different breed of dog from my brothers and sisters. 'You know,' Daddy said, 'it's some that can live their whole life out without asking about it and it's others has to know why it is, and this boy is one of the latters. He's going to be into everything!'" He put on his black hat and looked up suddenly and then away deep into the woods as if he were embarrassed again. "I'm sorry I don't have on a shirt before you ladies," he said, hunching his shoulders slightly. "We buried our clothes that we had on when we escaped and we're just making do until we can get better. We borrowed these from some folks we met," he explained.

"That's perfectly all right," the grandmother said. "Maybe Bailey has an extra shirt in his suitcase."

"I'll look and see terrectly," The Misfit said.

"Where are they taking him?" the children's mother screamed.

"Daddy was a card himself," The Misfit said. "You couldn't put anything over on him. He never got in trouble with the Authorities though. Just had the knack of handling them."

"You could be honest too if you'd only try," said the grandmother. "Think how wonderful it would be to settle down and live a comfortable life and not have to think about somebody chasing you all the time."

The Misfit kept scratching in the ground with the butt of his gun as if he were thinking about it. "Yes'm, somebody is always after you," he murmured.

The grandmother noticed how thin his shoulder blades were just behind his hat because she was standing up looking down on him. "Do you ever pray?" she asked.

He shook his head. All she saw was the black hat wiggle between his shoulder blades. "Nome," he said.

There was a pistol shot from the woods, followed closely by another. Then silence. The old lady's head jerked around. She could hear the wind move through the tree tops like a long satisfied insuck of breath. "Bailey Boy!" she called.

"I was a gospel singer for a while," The Misfit said. "I been most everything. Been in the arm service, both land and sea, at home and abroad, been twict married, been an undertaker, been with the railroads, plowed Mother Earth, been in a tornado, seen a man burnt alive oncet," and he looked up at the children's mother and the little girl who were sitting close together, their faces white and their eyes glassy; "I even seen a woman flogged," he said.

"Pray, pray," the grandmother began, "pray, pray...."

"I never was a bad boy that I remember of," The Misfit said in an almost dreamy voice, "but somewheres along the line I done something wrong and got sent to the penitentiary. I was buried alive," and he looked up and held her attention to him by a steady stare.

"That's when you should have started to pray," she said. "What did you do to get sent to the penitentiary that first time?"

"Turn to the right, it was a wall," The Misfit said, looking up again at the cloudless sky. "Turn to the left, it was a wall. Look up it was a ceiling, look down it was a floor. I forget what I done, lady. I set there and set there, trying to remember what it was I done and I ain't recalled it to this day. Oncet in a while, I would think it was coming to me, but it never come."

"Maybe they put you in by mistake," the old lady said vaguely.

"Nome," he said. "It wasn't no mistake. They had the papers on me."

"You must have stolen something," she said.

The Misfit sneered slightly. "Nobody had nothing I wanted," he said. "It was a head-doctor at the penitentiary said what I had done was kill my daddy but I known that for a lie. My daddy died in nineteen ought nineteen of the epidemic flu and I never had a thing to do with it. He was buried in the Mount Hopewell Baptist churchyard and you can go there and see for yourself."

"If you would pray," the old lady said, "Jesus would help you."

"That's right," The Misfit said.

"Well then, why don't you pray?" she asked trembling with delight suddenly.

"I don't want no hep," he said. "I'm doing all right by myself."

Bobby Lee and Hiram came ambling back from the woods. Bobby Lee was dragging a yellow shirt with bright blue parrots in it.

"Thow me that shirt, Bobby Lee," The Misfit said. The shirt came flying at him and landed on his shoulder and he put it on. The grandmother couldn't name what the shirt reminded her of. "No, lady," The Misfit said while he was buttoning it up, "I found out the crime don't matter. You can do one thing or you can do another, kill a man or take a tire off his car, because sooner or later you're going to forget what it was you done and just be punished for it."

The children's mother had begun to make heaving noises as if she couldn't get her breath. "Lady," he asked, "would you and that little girl like to step off yonder with Bobby Lee and Hiram and join your husband?"

"Yes, thank you," the mother said faintly. Her left arm dangled helplessly and she was holding the baby, who had gone to sleep, in the other. "Hep that lady up, Hiram," The Misfit said as she struggled to climb out of the ditch, "and Bobby Lee, you hold onto that little girl's hand."

"I don't want to hold hands with him," June Star said. "He reminds me of a pig."

The fat boy blushed and laughed and caught her by the arm and pulled her into the woods after Hiram and her mother.

Alone with The Misfit, the grandmother found that she had lost her voice. There was not a cloud in the sky nor any sun. There was nothing around her but woods. She wanted to tell him that he must pray. She opened and closed her mouth several times before anything came out. Finally she found herself saying, "Jesus. Jesus," meaning, Jesus will help you, but the way she was saying it, it sounded as if she might be cursing.

"Yes'm," The Misfit said as if he agreed. "Jesus thown everything off balance. It was the same case with Him as with me except He hadn't committed any crime and they could prove I had committed one because they had the papers on me. Of course," he said, "they never shown me my papers. That's why I sign myself now. I said long ago, you get you a signature and sign everything you do and keep a copy of it. Then you'll know what you done and you can hold up the crime to the punishment and see do they match and in the end you'll have something to prove you ain't been treated right. I call myself The Misfit," he said, "because I can't make what all I done wrong fit what all I gone through in punishment."

There was a piercing scream from the woods, followed closely by a pistol report. "Does it seem right to you, lady, that one is punished a heap and another ain't punished at all?"

"Jesus!" the old lady cried. "You've got good blood! I know you wouldn't shoot a lady! I know you come from nice people! Pray! Jesus, you ought not to shoot a lady. I'll give you all the money I've got!"

"Lady," The Misfit said, looking beyond her far into the woods, "there never was a body that give the undertaker a tip."

There were two more pistol reports and the grandmother raised her head like a parched old turkey hen crying for water and called, "Bailey Boy, Bailey Boy!" as if her heart would break.

"Jesus was the only One that ever raised the dead," The Misfit continued, "and He shouldn't have done it. He thown everything off balance. If He did what He said, then it's nothing for you to do but thow away everything and follow Him, and if He didn't, then it's nothing for you to do but enjoy the few minutes you got left the best way you can—by killing somebody or burning down his house or doing some other meanness to him. No pleasure but meanness," he said and his voice had become almost a snarl.

"Maybe He didn't raise the dead," the old lady mumbled, not knowing what she was saying and feeling so dizzy that she sank down in the ditch with her legs twisted under her.

"I wasn't there so I can't say He didn't," The Misfit said. "I wisht I had of been there," he said, hitting the ground with his fist. "It ain't right I wasn't there because if I had of been there I would of known. Listen lady," he said in a high voice, "if I had of been there I would of known and I wouldn't be like I am now." His voice seemed about to crack and the grandmother's head cleared for an instant. She saw the man's face twisted close to her own as if he were going to cry and she murmured, "Why you're one of my babies. You're one of my own children!" She reached out and touched him on the shoulder. The Misfit sprang back as if a snake had bitten him and shot her three times through the chest. Then he put his gun down on the ground and took off his glasses and began to clean them.

Hiram and Bobby Lee returned from the woods and stood over the ditch, looking down at the grandmother who half sat and half lay in a puddle of blood with her legs crossed under her like a child's and her face smiling up at the cloudless sky.

Without his glasses, The Misfit's eyes were red-rimmed and pale and de-fenceless-looking. "Take her off and thow her where you thown the others," he said, picking up the cat that was rubbing itself against his leg.

"She was a talker, wasn't she?" Bobby Lee said, sliding down the ditch with a yodel.

"She would of been a good woman," The Misfit said, "if it had been some-body there to shoot her every minute of her life."

"Some fun!" Bobby Lee said.

"Shut up, Bobby Lee," The Misfit said. "It's no real pleasure in life."

—1953

William Trevor
b. 1928

From George Moore and James Joyce to Elizabeth Bowen and Frank O'Connor, Ireland has produced a host of writers who have demonstrated a particular aptitude for the short story. Amongst these must surely be counted William Trevor, a prolific author known for minutely observed stories that peer into the loneliness and despair of ordinary people without venturing to intrude a moral perspective on their shortcomings.

A graduate of Trinity College, Dublin, Trevor worked as a schoolteacher, sculptor, and copywriter before wholly devoting himself to fiction after the success of his second novel, *The Old Boys* (1964). Because of its keenly satirical quality, reviewers compared Trevor's early work to that of English writers like Evelyn Waugh and Kingsley Amis. But Trevor's voice and style have more in common with the "scrupulous meanness" of Joyce's *Dubliners* and the Russian writer Anton Chekhov's bleak but humane portrayals of the incidental details of modest lives.

In his novels and short stories, Trevor typically withholds narrative commentary, cultivating an ironic detachment that is nevertheless compassionate in its refusal to condemn the failings of his characters. "I don't believe in the black and white," he has said of this unwillingness to impose judgment; "I believe in the grey shadows and the murkiness." Trevor's protagonists are frequently made to suffer the collapse of cherished illusions as they are confronted by the hollowness of the lies they tell themselves and each other.

Although Trevor's technique resembles mainstream realism, his fiction also manifests a modernist distrust of omniscience. His most characteristic stories, among them "Folie à Deux," rotate between multiple centres of consciousness, juxtaposing contrary points of view to reflect the difficulty of achieving meaningful connections with other human beings. But if these stories accept alienation as a condition of modern society, they also assert the importance of compassion as a means of overcoming it.

Folie à Deux[1]

Aware of a presence close to him, Wilby glances up from the book he has just begun to read. The man standing there says nothing. He doesn't smile. A dishcloth hangs from where it's tucked into grubby apron-strings knotted at the front, and Wilby assumes that the man is an envoy sent from the kitchen to apologize for the delay in the cooking of the fish he has ordered.

---

1   *Folie à Deux* French: mental disorder shared by two closely associated individuals.

The place is modest, in rue Piques off rue de Sèvres:[1] Wilby didn't notice what it is called. A café as much as a brasserie,[2] it is poorly illuminated except for the bar, at which a couple are hunched over their glasses, conversing softly. One of the few tables belonging to the café is occupied by four elderly women playing cards and there are a few people at tables in the brasserie.

Still without communicating, the man who has come from the kitchen turns and goes away, leaving Wilby with the impression that he has been mistaken for someone else. He pours himself more wine and reads again. Wilby reads a lot, and drinks a lot.

He is a spare, sharp-faced man in his forties, clean-shaven, in a grey suit, with a striped blue-and-red tie almost but not quite striking a stylish note. He visits Paris once in a while to make the rounds of salerooms specializing in rare postage stamps, usually spinning out his time when he is there, since he can afford to. Three years ago he inherited his family's wine business in County Westmeath,[3] which he sold eighteen months later, planning to live on the proceeds while he indulged his interest in philately.[4] He occupies, alone now, the house he inherited at that time also, creeper-clad, just outside the Westmeath town where he was born. Marriage failed him there, or he it, and he doubts that he will make another attempt in that direction.

His food is brought to him by a small, old waiter, a more presentable figure than the man who came and went. He is attentive, addressing Wilby in conventional waiter's terms and supplying, when they are asked for, salt and pepper from another table. "*Voilà, monsieur*,"[5] he murmurs, his tone apologetic.

Wilby eats his fish, wondering what fish it is. He knew when he ordered it but has since forgotten, and the taste doesn't tell him much. The bread is the best part of his meal and he catches the waiter's attention to ask for more. His book is a paperback he has read before, *The Hand of Ethelberta*.[6]

He reads another page, orders more wine, finishes the *pommes frites*[7] but not the fish. He likes quiet places, and doesn't hurry. He orders coffee and— though not intending to—a calvados.[8] He drinks too much, he tells himself, and restrains the inclination to have another when the coffee comes. He reads again, indulging the pleasure of being in Paris, in a brasserie where Muzak[9]

---

1   *rue Piques ... de Sèvres* Rue Piques is fictional; all the other streets named in the story are part of the Faubourg Saint-Germain, a district in Paris.
2   *brasserie* French: casual restaurant.
3   *Westmeath* County in Ireland.
4   *philately* Postage stamp collecting.
5   *Voilà, monsieur* French: Here you are, sir.
6   *The Hand of Ethelberta* 1876 novel by Thomas Hardy.
7   *pommes frites* French: fried potatoes.
8   *calvados* Apple brandy.
9   *Muzak* Mediocre recorded background music.

isn't playing, at a small corner table, engrossed in a story that's familiar yet has receded sufficiently to be blurred in places, like something good remembered. He never minds it when the food isn't up to much; wine matters more, and peace. He'll walk back to the Hôtel Merneuil;[1] with luck he'll be successful in the salerooms tomorrow.

He gestures for his bill, and pays. The old waiter has his overcoat ready for him at the door, and Wilby tips him a little for that. Outside, being late November, the night is chilly.

The man who came to look at him is there on the street, dressed as he was then. He stands still, not speaking. He might have come outside to have a cigarette, as waiters sometimes do. But there is no cigarette.

"*Bonsoir*,"[2] Wilby says.

"*Bonsoir*."

Saying that, quite suddenly the man is someone else. A resemblance flickers: the smooth black hair, the head like the rounded end of a bullet, the fringe that is not as once it was but is still a fringe, the dark eyes. There is a way of standing, without unease or agitation and yet awkward, hands lank, open.

"What is all this?" Even as he puts the question, Wilby's choice of words sounds absurd to him. "Anthony?" he says.

There is a movement, a hand's half gesture, meaningless, hardly a response. Then the man turns away, entering the brasserie by another door.

"Anthony," Wilby mutters again, but only to himself.

People have said that Anthony is dead.

• • •

The streets are emptier than they were, the bustle of the pavements gone. Obedient to pedestrian lights at rue de Babylone where there is fast-moving traffic again, Wilby waits with a woman in a pale waterproof coat, her legs slim beneath it, blonde hair brushed up. Not wanting to think about Anthony, he wonders if she's a tart, since she has that look, and for a moment sees her pale coat thrown down in some small room, the glow of an electric fire, money placed on a dressing-table: now and again when he travels he has a woman. But this one doesn't glance at him, and the red light changes to green.

It couldn't possibly have been Anthony, of course it couldn't. Even assuming that Anthony is alive, why would he be employed as a kitchen worker in Paris? "Yes, I'm afraid we fear the worst," his father said on the telephone, years ago now. "He sent a few belongings here, but that's a good while back. A note to you, unfinished, was caught up in the pages of a book. Nothing in it, really. Your name, no more."

---

1   *Hôtel Merneuil* The name is a play on the famous Hôtel Verneuil located in this neighbourhood.
2   *Bonsoir* French: Good evening.

In rue du Bac there is a window Wilby likes, with prints of the Revolution.[1] The display has hardly changed since he was here last: the death of Marie Antoinette, the Girondists on their way to the guillotine, the storming of the Bastille, Danton's death, Robespierre triumphant, Robespierre fallen from grace. Details aren't easy to make out in the dim street-light. Prints he hasn't seen before are indistinguishable at the back.

At a bar he has another calvados. He said himself when people asked him—a few had once—that he, too, imagined Anthony was dead. A disappearance so prolonged, with no reports of even a glimpse as the years advanced, did appear to confirm a conclusion that became less tentative, and in the end wasn't tentative at all.

In rue Montalembert a couple ask for directions to the Metro.[2] Wilby points it out, walking back a little way with them to do so, as grateful for this interruption as he was when the woman at the traffic crossing caught his interest.

"*Bonne nuit, monsieur.*"[3] In the hall of the Hôtel Merneuil the night porter holds open the lift doors. He closes them and the lift begins its smooth ascent. "The will to go on can fall away, you know," Anthony's father said on the telephone again, in touch to find out if there was anything to report.

• • •

Monsieur Jothy shakes his head over the pay packet that hasn't been picked up. It's on the windowsill above the sinks, where others have been ignored too. He writes a message on it and props it against an empty bottle.

At this late hour Monsieur Jothy has the kitchen to himself, a time for assessing what needs to be ordered, for satisfying himself that, in general, the kitchen is managing. He picks up Jean-André's note of what he particularly requires for tomorrow, and checks the shelves where the cleaning materials are kept. He has recently become suspicious of Jean-André, suspecting short-cuts. His risotto, once an attraction on the menu, is scarcely ever ordered now; and with reason in Monsieur Jothy's opinion, since it has lost the intensity of flavour that made it popular, and is often dry. But the kitchen at least is clean, and Monsieur Jothy, examining cutlery and plates, fails to find food clinging anywhere, or a rim left on a cup. Once he employed two dish-washers at the sinks, but now one does it on his own, and half the time forgets his wages. Anxious to keep him, Monsieur Jothy has wondered about finding somewhere for him to sleep on the premises instead of having the long journey to and from his room. But there isn't even a corner of a pantry, and when he asked

---

1   *the Revolution* I.e., the French Revolution (1789–99). The people and events depicted in the display are all from this period.
2   *Metro* Parisian subway system.
3   *Bonne nuit, monsieur* French: Good night, sir.

in the neighbourhood about accommodation near rue Piques he was also unsuccessful.

The dishcloths, washed and rinsed, are draped on the radiators and will be dry by the morning, the soup bowls are stacked; the glasses, in their rows, gleam on the side table. "*Très bon,*[1] *très bon,*" Monsieur Jothy murmurs before he turns the lights out and locks up.

• • •

Wilby does not sleep and cannot read, although he tries to.

"A marvel, isn't it?" Miss Davally said, the memory vivid, as if she'd said it yesterday. You wouldn't think apricots would so easily ripen in such a climate. Even on a wall lined with brick you wouldn't think it. She pointed at the branches sprawled out along their wires, and you could see the fruit in little clusters. "Delphiniums,"[2] she said, pointing again, and one after another named the flowers they passed on their way through the garden. "And this is Anthony," she said in the house.

The boy looked up from the playing cards he had spread out on the floor. "What's his name?" he asked, and Miss Davally said he knew because she had told him already. But even so she did so again. "Why's he called that?" Anthony asked. "Why're you called that?"

"It's my name."

"Shall we play in the garden?"

That first day, and every day afterwards, there were gingersnap biscuits in the middle of the morning. "Am I older than you?" Anthony asked. "Is six older?" He had a house, he said, in the bushes at the end of the garden, and they pretended there was a house. "Jericho he's called," Anthony said of the dog that followed them about, a black Labrador with an injured leg that hung limply, thirteen years old. "Miss Davally is an orphan," Anthony said. "That's why she lives with us. Do you know what an orphan is?"

In the yard the horses looked out over the half-doors of their stables; the hounds were in a smaller yard. Anthony's mother was never at lunch because her horse and the hounds were exercised then. But his father always was, each time wearing a different tweed jacket, his grey moustache clipped short, the olives he liked to see on the lunch table always there, the whiskey he took for his health. "Well, young chap, how are you?" he always asked.

On wet days they played marbles in the kitchen passages, the dog stretched out beside them. "You come to the sea in summer," Anthony said. "They told me." Every July: the long journey from Westmeath to the same holiday cottage on the cliffs above the bay that didn't have a name. It was Miss Davally

---

1   *Très bon* French: Very good.
2   *Delphiniums* Garden plants with blue flowers.

who had told Anthony all that, and in time—so that hospitality might be returned—she often drove Anthony there and back. An outing for her too, she used to say, and sometimes she brought a cake she'd made, being in the way of bringing a present when she went to people's houses. She liked it at the sea as much as Anthony did; she liked to turn the wheel of the bellows in the kitchen of the cottage and watch the sparks flying up; and Anthony liked the hard sand of the shore, and collecting flintstones, and netting shrimps. The dog prowled about the rocks, sniffing the seaweed, clawing at the sea-anemones. "Our house," Anthony called the cave they found when they crawled through an opening in the rocks, a cave no one knew was there.

• • •

Air from the window Wilby slightly opens at the top is refreshing and brings with it, for a moment, the chiming of two o'clock. His book is open, face downward to keep his place, his bedside light still on. But the dark is better, and he extinguishes it.

There was a blue vase in the recess of the staircase wall, nothing else there; and paperweights crowded the shallow landing shelves, all touching one another; forty-six, Anthony said. His mother played the piano in the drawing-room. "Hub," she said, holding out her hand and smiling. She wasn't much like someone who exercised foxhounds: slim and small and wearing scent, she was also beautiful. "Look!" Anthony said, pointing at the lady in the painting above the mantelpiece in the hall.

Miss Davally was a distant relative as well as being an orphan, and when she sat on the sands after her bathe[1] she often talked about her own childhood in the house where she'd been given a home: how a particularly unpleasant boy used to creep up on her and pull a cracker in her ear, how she hated her rib-boned pigtails and persuaded a simple-minded maid to cut them off, how she taught the kitchen cat to dance and how people said they'd never seen the like.

Every lunchtime Anthony's father kept going a conversation about a world that was not yet known to his listeners. He spoke affectionately of the playboy pugilist Jack Doyle,[2] demonstrating the subtlety of his right punch and recalling the wonders of his hell-raising before poverty claimed him. He told of the exploits of an ingenious escapologist, Major Pat Reid.[3] He condemned the first Earl of Inchiquin[4] as the most disgraceful man ever to step out of Ireland.

---

1   *bathe* Swim.
2   *pugilist* Boxer; *Jack Doyle* Famous Irish boxer and wrestler.
3   *Major Pat Reid* British soldier famous for escaping a German prisoner-of-war camp during World War II.
4   *first Earl of Inchiquin* Murrough O'Brien (1614–74), a peer of Ireland reviled for his brutal behaviour toward the Irish Catholics on behalf of the English Protestants during the Irish Confederate War (1642–53).

Much other information was passed on at the lunch table: why aeroplanes flew, how clocks kept time, why spiders spun their webs and how they did it. Information was everything, Anthony's father maintained, and its lunchtime dissemination, with Miss Davally's reminiscences, nurtured curiosity: the unknown became a fascination. "What would happen if you didn't eat?" Anthony wondered; and there were attempts to see if it was possible to create a rainbow with a water hose when the sun was bright, and the discovery made that, in fact, it was. A jellyfish was scooped into a shrimp net to see if it would perish or survive when it was tipped out on to the sand. Miss Davally said to put it back, and warned that jellyfish could sting as terribly as wasps.

A friendship developed between Miss Davally and Wilby's mother—a formal association, first names not called upon, neither in conversation nor in the letters that came to be exchanged from one summer to the next. *Anthony is said to be clever*, Miss Davally's spidery handwriting told. And then, as if that perhaps required watering down, *Well, so they say*. It was reported also that when each July drew near Anthony began to count the days. *He values the friendship so!* Miss Davally commented. *How fortunate for two only children such a friendship is!*

Fortunate indeed it seemed to be. There was no quarrelling, no vying for authority, no competing. When, one summer, a yellow Lilo[1] was washed up, still inflated, it was taken to the cave that no one else knew about, neither claiming that it was his because he'd seen it first. "Someone lost that thing," Anthony said, but no one came looking for it. They didn't know what it was, only that it floated. They floated it themselves, the dog limping behind them when they carried it to the sea, his tail wagging madly, head cocked to one side. In the cave it became a bed for him, to clamber on to when he was tired.

The Lilo was another of the friendship's precious secrets, as the cave itself was. No other purpose was found for it, but its possession was enough to make it the highlight of that particular summer and on the last day of July it was again carried to the edge of the sea. "Now, now," the dog was calmed when he became excited. The waves that morning were hardly waves at all.

• • •

In the dark there is a pinprick glow of red somewhere on the television set. The air that comes into the room is colder and Wilby closes the window he has opened a crack, suppressing the murmur of a distant plane. Memory won't let him go now; he knows it won't and makes no effort to resist it.

Nothing was said when they watched the drowning of the dog. Old Jericho was clever, never at a loss when there was fun. Not moving, he was obedient, as he always was. He played his part, going with the Lilo when

---

1   *Lilo* Inflatable mattress.

it floated out, a deep black shadow, sharp against the garish yellow. They watched as they had watched the hosepipe rainbow gathering colour, as Miss Davally said she'd watched the shaky steps of the dancing cat. Far away already, the yellow of the Lilo became a blur on the water, was lost, was there again and lost again, and the barking began, and became a wail. Nothing was said then either. Nor when they clambered over the shingle and the rocks, and climbed up to the short-cut and passed through the gorse field. From the cliff they looked again, for the last time, far out to the horizon. The sea was undisturbed, glittering in the sunlight. "So what have you two been up to this morning?" Miss Davally asked. The next day, somewhere else, the dog was washed in.

Miss Davally blamed herself, for that was in her nature. But she could not be blamed. It was agreed that she could not be. Unaware of his limitations—more than a little blind, with only three active legs—old Jericho had had a way of going into the sea when he sensed a piece of driftwood bobbing about. Once too often he had done that. His grave was in the garden, a small slate plaque let into the turf, his name and dates.

They did not ever speak to one another about the drowning of the dog. They did not ever say they had not meant it to occur. There was no blame, no accusing. They had not called it a game, only said they wondered what would happen, what the dog would do. The silence had begun before they pushed the Lilo out.

Other summers brought other incidents, other experiences, but there was no such occurrence again. There were adjustments in the friendship, since passing time demanded that, and different games were played, and there were different conversations, and new discoveries.

Then, one winter, a letter from Miss Davally was less cheerful than her letters usually were. *Withdrawn*, she wrote, *and they are concerned*. What she declared, in detail after that, was confirmed when summer came: Anthony was different, and more different still in later summers, quieter, timid, seeming sometimes to be lost. It was a mystery when the dog's gravestone disappeared from the garden.

• • •

In the dark, the bright red dot of the television light still piercingly there, Wilby wonders, as so often he has, what influence there was when without incitement or persuasion, without words, they did what had been done. They were nine years old then, when secrets became deception.

It was snowing the evening he and Anthony met again, both of them waiting in the chapel cloisters for their names, as new boys, to be called out. It was not a surprise that Anthony was there, passing on from the school that years ago had declared him clever; nor was it by chance that they were to be together for what remained of their education. "Nice for Anthony to have someone he knows," his father said on the telephone, and confirmed that Anthony was still as he had become.

In the dim evening light the snow blew softly into the cloisters, and when the roll-call ended and a noisy dispersal began, the solitary figure remained, the same smooth black hair, a way of standing that hadn't changed. "How are you?" Wilby asked. His friend's smile, once so readily there, came as a shadow and then was lost in awkwardness.

Peculiar, Anthony was called at school, but wasn't bullied, as though it had been realized that bullying would yield no satisfaction. He lacked skill at games, avoided all pursuits that were not compulsory, displayed immediate evidence of his cleverness, science and mathematical subjects his forte. Religious boys attempted to befriend him, believing that to be a duty; kindly masters sought to draw him out. "Well, yes, I knew him," Wilby admitted, lamely explaining his association with someone who was so very much not like the friends he made now. "A long time ago," he nearly always added.

Passing by the windows of empty classrooms, he several times noticed Anthony, the only figure among the unoccupied desks. And often—on the drive that ended at the school gates, or often anywhere—there was the same lone figure in the distance. On the golf-course where senior boys were allowed to play, Anthony sometimes sat on a seat against a wall, watching the golfers as they approached, watching them as they walked on. He shied away when conversation threatened, creeping back into his shadowlands.

One day he wasn't there, his books left tidily in his desk, clothes hanging in his dormitory locker, his pyjamas under his pillow. He would be on his way home, since boys who kept themselves to themselves were often homesick. But he had not attempted to go home and was found still within the school grounds, having broken no rules except that he had ignored for a day the summoning of bells.

• • •

Dawn comes darkly, and Wilby sleeps. But his sleep is brief, his dreams forgotten when he wakes. The burden of guilt that came when in silence they clambered over the shingle and the rocks, when they passed through the gorse field, was muddled by bewilderment, a child's tormenting panic not yet constrained by suppression as later it would be. Long afterwards, when first he heard that Anthony was dead—and when he said it himself—the remnants of the shame guilt had become fell away.

He shaves and washes, dresses slowly. In the hall the reception clerks have just come on duty. They nod at him, wish him good-day. No call this morning for an umbrella, one says.

Outside it is not entirely day, or even day at all. The cleaning lorries[1] are on the streets, water pouring in the gutters, but there's no one about in rue du Bac, refuse sacks still waiting to be collected. A bar is open further on, men standing at the counter, disinclined for conversation with one another. A sleeping figure in a doorway has not been roused. What hovel, Wilby wonders as he passes, does a kitchen worker occupy?

In rue Piques the brasserie is shuttered, no lights showing anywhere. Cardboard boxes are stacked close to the glass of three upstairs windows, others are uncurtained; none suggests the domesticity of a dwelling. Le Père Jothy the place is called.

Wilby roams the nearby streets. A few more cafés are opening and in one coffee is brought to him. He sips it, breaking a croissant. There's no one else, except the barman.

He knows he should go away. He should take the train to Passy, to the salerooms he has planned to visit there; he should not ever return to rue Piques. He has lived easily with an aberration, then shaken it off: what happened was almost nothing.

Other men come in, a woman on her own, her face bruised on one side, no effort made to conceal the darkening weals. Her voice is low when she explains this injury to the barman, her fingers now and again touching it. Soundlessly, she weeps when she has taken her cognac to a table.

Oh, this is silly! his unspoken comment was when Miss Davally's letter came, its implications apparent only to him. For heaven's sake! he crossly muttered, the words kept to himself when he greeted Anthony in the cloisters, and again every time he caught sight of him on the golf-course. The old dog's life had been all but over. And Wilby remembers now—as harshly as he has in the night—the bitterness of his resentment when a friendship he delighted in was destroyed, when Anthony's world—the garden, the house, his mother, his father, Miss Davally—was no longer there.

"He has no use for us," his father said. "No use for anyone, we think."

• • •

Turning into rue Piques, Anthony notices at once the figure waiting outside the ribbon shop. It is November the twenty-fourth, the last Thursday of the month. This day won't come again.

"*Bonjour*,"[2] he says.

"How are you, Anthony?"

And Anthony says that Monday is the closed day. Not that Sunday isn't too. If someone waited outside the ribbon shop on a Monday or a Sunday it wouldn't be much good. Not that many people wait there.

---

1   *lorries* Trucks.
2   *Bonjour* French: Good day.

Wind blows a scrap of paper about, close to where they stand. In the window of the ribbon shop coils of ribbon are in all widths and colours, and there are swatches of trimming for other purposes, lace and velvet, and plain white edging, and a display of button cards.[1] Anthony often looks to see if there has been a change, but there never has been.

"How are you, Anthony?"

It is a fragment of a white paper bag that is blown about and Anthony identifies it from the remains of the red script that advertises the *boulangerie*[2] in rue Dupin. When it is blown closer to him he catches it under his shoe.

"People have wondered where you are, Anthony."

"I went away from Ireland."

Anthony bends and picks up the litter he has trapped. He says he has the ovens to do today. A Thursday, and he works in the morning.

"Miss Davally still writes, wondering if there is news of you."

Half past eight is his time on Thursdays. Anthony says that, and adds that there's never a complaint in the kitchen. One speck on the prong of a fork could lead to a complaint, a shred of fish skin could, a cabbage leaf. But there's never a complaint.

"People thought you were dead, Anthony."

• • •

Wilby says he sold the wineshop. He described it once, when they were children: the shelves of bottles, the different shapes, their contents red or white, pink if people wanted that. He tasted wine a few times, he remembers saying.

"Your father has died himself, Anthony. Your mother has. Miss Davally was left the house because there was no one else. She lives there now."

No response comes; Wilby has not expected one. He has become a philatelist, he says.

• • •

Anthony nods, waiting to cross the street. He knows his father died, his mother too. He has guessed Miss Davally inherited the house. The deaths were in the *Irish Times*, which he always read, cover to cover, all the years he was the night porter at the Cliff Castle Hotel in Dalkey.[3]

He doesn't mention the Cliff Castle Hotel. He doesn't say he misses the *Irish Times*, the familiar names, the political news, the photographs of places, the change there is in Ireland now. *Le Monde*[4] is more staid, more circumspect, more serious. Anthony doesn't say that either because he doubts that it's of interest to a visitor to Paris.

---

1   *button cards* Small packages of buttons for sale.
2   *boulangerie* French: bakery.
3   *Dalkey* Coastal village on the outskirts of Dublin.
4   *Le Monde* Major French newspaper.

A gap comes in the stream of cars that has begun to go by; but not trusting this opportunity, Anthony still waits. He is careful on the streets, even though he knows them well.

"I haven't died," he says.

• • •

Perfectly together, they shared an act that was too shameful to commit alone, taking a chance on a sunny morning in order to discover if an old dog's cleverness would see to his survival.

For a moment, while Anthony loses another opportunity to cross the street, Wilby gathers into sentences how he might attempt a denial that this was how it was, how best to put it differently. An accident, a misfortune beyond anticipation, the unexpected: with gentleness, for gentleness is due, he is about to plead. But Anthony crosses the street then, and opens with a key the side door of the brasserie. He makes no gesture of farewell, he does not look back.

• • •

Walking by the river on his way to the salerooms at Passy, Wilby wishes he'd said he was glad his friend was not dead. It is his only thought. The pleasure-boats slip by on the water beside him, hardly anyone on them. A child waves. Raised too late in response, Wilby's own hand drops to his side. The wind that blew the litter about in rue Piques has freshened. It snatches at the remaining leaves on the black-trunked trees that are an orderly line, following the river's course.

The salerooms are on the other bank, near the radio building and the apartment block that change the river's character. Several times he has visited this vast display in which the world's stamps are exhibited behind glass if they are notably valuable, on the tables, country by country, when they are not. That busy image has always excited Wilby's imagination and as he climbs the steps to the bridge he is near he attempts to anticipate it now, but does not entirely succeed.

It is not in punishment that the ovens are cleaned on another Thursday morning. It is not in expiation[1] that soon the first leavings of the day will be scraped from the lunchtime plates. There is no bothering with redemption. Looking down from the bridge at the sluggish flow of water, Wilby confidently asserts that. A morning murkiness, like dusk, has brought some lights on in the apartment block. Traffic crawls on distant streets.

For Anthony, the betrayal matters, the folly, the carelessness that would have been forgiven, the cruelty. It mattered in the silence—while they watched, while they clambered over the shingle and the rocks, while they passed through

---

1   *expiation* Atonement.

the gorse field. It matters now. The haunted sea is all the truth there is for Anthony, what he honours because it matters still.

The buyers move among the tables and Wilby knows that for him, in this safe, second-hand world of postage stamps, tranquillity will return. He knows where he is with all this; he knows what he's about, as he does in other aspects of his tidy life. And yet this morning he likes himself less than he likes his friend.

—2007

Ursula K. Le Guin
b. 1929

Few writers have done more to elevate the standing of science fiction as a recognized literary genre than Ursula K. Le Guin. Together with fellow American authors Philip K. Dick and Samuel R. Delany, Le Guin was instrumental in the emergence of New Wave science fiction, a movement that distinguished itself from the genre's so-called Golden Age of the 1940s and 1950s by a greater attention to style, increasingly nuanced characterization, a mounting interest in experimental narrative, and a more forthright engagement with political and gender issues. Le Guin's finest works—amongst them the Hugo and Nebula Award-winning novels *The Left Hand of Darkness* (1969) and *The Dispossessed* (1974)—are remarkable not only for the fluent evenness of their prose and the conceptual seriousness of their subject matter but also for their political astuteness and the minutely observed social and cultural details of the worlds they imagine into being.

The daughter of a noted anthropologist and psychologist, Le Guin was educated at Radcliffe College and Columbia. Her early interest in cultural anthropology, Jungian psychology, and Taoist philosophy would eventually come to provide a unifying conceptual framework for her writing. In the tradition of J.R.R. Tolkien's world-building, many of Le Guin's novels and stories dramatize a conflict between vividly realized alien cultures that the protagonist—frequently a traveller—observes and participates in as a quasi anthropologist. Archetypal figures and settings such as psychologist Carl Jung believed to symbolize humanity's shared psychic heritage also figure prominently in her work, which often has a richly allegorical dimension. Taoism, a third key element in Le Guin's intellectual framework, is likewise central to many of her texts, particularly the doctrine of inaction, which urges passivity over aggression, and the principle of the relativity of opposites, which posits the interdependence of light and darkness, good and evil, and male and female.

More than a master storyteller, Le Guin has done much to advance the place of science fiction as a literature of ideas. In affirming the importance of imagination to human experience, her work demonstrates that science fiction can reflect the world more faithfully than what conventionally passes for realism.

The Ones Who Walk Away from Omelas

With a clamour of bells that set the swallows soaring, the Festival of Summer came to the city. Omelas, bright-towered by the sea. The rigging of the boats in harbour sparkled with flags. In the streets between houses with red roofs and painted walls, between old moss-grown gardens and under avenues of trees, past great parks and public buildings, processions moved. Some were decorous: old people in long stiff robes of mauve and grey, grave master work-men, quiet, merry women carrying their babies and chatting as they walked. In other streets the music beat faster, a shimmering of gong and tambourine, and the people went dancing, the procession was a dance. Children dodged in and out, their high calls rising like the swallows' crossing flights over the music and the singing. All the processions wound towards the north side of the city, where on the great water-meadow called the Green Fields boys and girls, naked in the bright air, with mud-stained feet and ankles and long, lithe arms, exercised their restive horses before the race. The horses wore no gear at all but a halter without bit. Their manes were braided with streamers of silver, gold, and green. They flared their nostrils and pranced and boasted to one another; they were vastly excited, the horse being the only animal who has adopted our ceremonies as his own. Far off to the north and west the mountains stood up half encircling Omelas on her bay. The air of morning was so clear that the snow still crowning the Eighteen Peaks burned with white-gold fire across the miles of sunlit air, under the dark blue of the sky. There was just enough wind to make the banners that marked the racecourse snap and flutter now and then. In the silence of the broad green meadows one could hear the music winding through the city streets, farther and nearer and ever approaching, a cheerful faint sweetness of the air that from time to time trembled and gathered together and broke out into the great joyous clanging of the bells.

Joyous! How is one to tell about joy? How describe the citizens of Omelas?

They were not simple folk, you see, though they were happy. But we do not say the words of cheer much any more. All smiles have become archaic.[1] Given a description such as this one tends to make certain assumptions. Given a description such as this one tends to look next for the King, mounted on a splendid stallion and surrounded by his noble knights, or perhaps in a golden litter borne by great-muscled slaves. But there was no king. They did not use swords, or keep slaves. They were not barbarians. I do not know the rules and laws of their society, but I suspect that they were singularly few.

---

1   *All smiles … archaic* Reference to the "archaic smile," an expression found on the faces of many sculpted figures from Ancient Greece.

As they did without monarchy and slavery, so they also got on without the stock exchange, the advertisement, the secret police, and the bomb. Yet I repeat that these were not simple folk, not dulcet shepherds, noble savages, bland utopians. They were not less complex than us. The trouble is that we have a bad habit, encouraged by pedants and sophisticates, of considering happiness as something rather stupid. Only pain is intellectual, only evil interesting. This is the treason of the artist: a refusal to admit the banality of evil and the terrible boredom of pain. If you can't lick 'em, join 'em. If it hurts, repeat it. But to praise despair is to condemn delight, to embrace violence is to lose hold of everything else. We have almost lost hold; we can no longer describe a happy man, nor make any celebration of joy. How can I tell you about the people of Omelas? They were not naive and happy children—though their children were, in fact, happy. They were mature, intelligent, passionate adults whose lives were not wretched. O miracle! but I wish I could describe it better. I wish I could convince you. Omelas sounds in my words like a city in a fairy tale, long ago and far away, once upon a time. Perhaps it would be best if you imagined it as your own fancy bids, assuming it will rise to the occasion, for certainly I cannot suit you all. For instance, how about technology? I think that there would be no cars or helicopters in and above the streets; this follows from the fact that the people of Omelas are happy people. Happiness is based on a just discrimination of what is necessary, what is neither necessary nor destructive, and what is destructive. In the middle category, however—that of the unnecessary but undestructive, that of comfort, luxury, exuberance, etc.—they could perfectly well have central heating, subway trains, washing machines, and all kinds of marvellous devices not yet invented here, floating light-sources, fuelless power, a cure for the common cold. Or they could have none of that: it doesn't matter. As you like it. I incline to think that people from towns up and down the coast have been coming in to Omelas during the last days before the Festival on very fast little trains and double-decked trains and that the train station of Omelas is actually the handsomest building in town, though plainer than the magnificent Farmers' Market. But even granted trains, I fear that Omelas so far strikes some of you as goody-goody. Smiles, bells, parades, horses, bleh. If so, please add an orgy. If an orgy would help, don't hesitate. Let us not, however, have temples from which issue beautiful nude priests and priestesses already half in ecstasy and ready to copulate with any man or woman, lover or stranger, who desires union with the deep godhead of the blood, although that was my first idea. But really it would be better not to have any temples in Omelas—at least, not manned temples. Religion yes, clergy no. Surely the beautiful nudes can just wander about, offering themselves like divine soufflés to the hunger of the needy and the rapture of the flesh. Let them join the processions. Let tambourines be struck above the copulations, and the glory of desire be proclaimed upon the gongs, and (a not unimportant point) let the offspring of these delightful rituals be beloved and looked after by all. One thing I know there is none of in Omelas is guilt. But what else should there be? I thought at first there were no drugs, but that is puritanical. For those who like it, the faint insistent sweetness of *drooz* may perfume the ways of the city, *drooz* which first brings a great lightness and brilliance to the mind and limbs, and then after some hours a dreamy languor, and wonderful visions at last of the very arcana and inmost secrets of the Universe, as well as exciting the pleasure 'of sex beyond all belief; and it is not habit-forming. For more modest tastes I think there ought to be beer. What else, what else belongs in the joyous city? The sense of victory, surely, the celebration of courage. But as we did without clergy, let us do without soldiers. The joy built upon successful slaughter is not the right kind of joy; it will not do; it is fearful and it is trivial. A boundless and generous contentment, a magnanimous triumph felt not against some outer enemy but in communion with the finest and fairest in the souls of all men everywhere and the splendour of the world's summer: this is what swells the hearts of the people of Omelas, and the victory they celebrate is that of life. I really don't think many of them need to take *drooz*.

Most of the processions have reached the Green Fields by now. A marvellous smell of cooking goes forth from the red and blue tents of the provisioners. The faces of small children are amiably sticky; in the benign grey beard of a man a couple of crumbs of rich pastry are entangled. The youths and girls have mounted their horses and are beginning to group around the starting line of the course. An old woman, small, fat, and laughing, is passing out flowers from a basket, and tall young men wear her flowers in their shining hair. A child of nine or ten sits at the edge of the crowd, alone, playing on a wooden flute. People pause to listen, and they smile, but they do not speak to him, for he never ceases playing and never sees them, his dark eyes wholly rapt in the sweet, thin magic of the tune.

He finishes, and slowly lowers his hands holding the wooden flute.

As if that little private silence were the signal, all at once a trumpet sounds from the pavilion near the starting line: imperious, melancholy, piercing. The horses rear on their slender legs, and some of them neigh in answer. Soberfaced, the young riders stroke the horses' necks and soothe them, whispering, "Quiet, quiet, there my beauty, my hope...." They begin to form in rank along the starting line. The crowds along the racecourse are like a field of grass and flowers in the wind. The Festival of Summer has begun.

Do you believe? Do you accept the festival, the city, the joy? No? Then let me describe one more thing.

In a basement under one of the beautiful public buildings of Omelas, or perhaps in the cellar of one of its spacious private homes, there is a room. It has one locked door, and no window. A little light seeps in dustily between cracks in the boards, secondhand from a cobwebbed window somewhere across the cellar. In one corner of the little room a couple of mops, with stiff, clotted, foul-smelling heads, stand near a rusty bucket. The floor is dirt, a little damp to the touch, as cellar dirt usually is. The room is about three paces long and two wide: a mere broom closet or disused tool room. In the room a child is sitting. It could be a boy or a girl. It looks about six, but actually is nearly ten. It is feeble-minded. Perhaps it was born defective, or perhaps it has become imbecile through fear, malnutrition, and neglect. It picks its nose and occasionally fumbles vaguely with its toes or genitals, as it sits hunched in the corner farthest from the bucket and the two mops. It is afraid of the mops. It finds them horrible. It shuts its eyes, but it knows the mops are still standing there; and the door is locked; and nobody will come. The door is always locked; and nobody ever comes, except that sometimes—the child has no understanding of time or interval—sometimes the door rattles terribly and opens, and a person, or several people, are there. One of them may come in and kick the child to make it stand up. The others never come close, but peer in at it with frightened, disgusted eyes. The food bowl and the water jug are hastily filled, the door is locked, the eyes disappear. The people at the door never say anything, but the child, who has not always lived in the tool room, and can remember sunlight and its mother's voice, sometimes speaks. "I will be good," it says. "Please let me out. I will be good!" They never answer. The child used to scream for help at night, and cry a good deal, but now it only makes a kind of whining, "eh-haa, eh-haa," and it speaks less and less often. It is so thin there are no calves to its legs; its belly protrudes; it lives on a half-bowl of corn meal and grease a day. It is naked. Its buttocks and thighs are a mass of festered sores, as it sits in its own excrement continually.

They all know it is there, all the people of Omelas. Some of them have come to see it, others are content merely to know it is there. They all know that it has to be there. Some of them understand why, and some do not, but they all understand that their happiness, the beauty of their city, the tenderness of their friendships, the health of their children, the wisdom of their scholars, the skill of their makers, even the abundance of their harvest and the kindly weathers of their skies, depend wholly on this child's abominable misery.

This is usually explained to children when they are between eight and twelve, whenever they seem capable of understanding; and most of those who come to see the child are young people, though often enough an adult comes, or comes back, to see the child. No matter how well the matter has been explained to them, these young spectators are always shocked and sickened at the sight. They feel disgust, which they had thought themselves superior to. They feel anger, outrage, impotence, despite all the explanations. They would like to do something for the child. But there is nothing they can do. If the child were brought up into the sunlight out of that vile place, if it were cleaned and fed and comforted, that would be a good thing, indeed; but if it were done, in that day and hour all the prosperity and beauty and delight of Omelas would wither and be destroyed. Those are the terms. To exchange all the goodness and grace of every life in Omelas for that single, small improvement: to throw away the happiness of thousands for the chance of the happiness of one: that would be to let guilt within the walls indeed.

The terms are strict and absolute; there may not even be a kind word spoken to the child.

Often the young people go home in tears, or in a tearless rage, when they have seen the child and faced this terrible paradox. They may brood over it for weeks or years. But as time goes on they begin to realize that even if the child could be released, it would not get much good of its freedom: a little vague pleasure of warmth and food, no doubt, but little more. It is too degraded and imbecile to know any real joy. It has been afraid too long ever to be free of fear. Its habits are too uncouth for it to respond to humane treatment. Indeed, after so long it would probably be wretched without walls about it to protect it, and darkness for its eyes, and its own excrement to sit in. Their tears at the bitter injustice dry when they begin to perceive the terrible justice of reality and to accept it. Yet it is their tears and anger, the trying of their generosity and the acceptance of their helplessness, which are perhaps the true source of the splendour of their lives. Theirs is no vapid, irresponsible happiness. They know that they, like the child, are not free. They know compassion. It is the existence of the child, and their knowledge of its existence, that makes possible the nobility of their architecture, the poignancy of their music, the profundity of their science. It is because of the child that they are so gentle with children. They know that if the wretched one were not there snivelling in the dark, the other one, the flute-player, could make no joyful music as the young riders line up in their beauty for the race in the sunlight of the first morning of summer.

Now do you believe in them? Are they not more credible? But there is one more thing to tell, and this is quite incredible.

At times one of the adolescent girls or boys who go to see the child does not go home to weep or rage, does not, in fact, go home at all. Sometimes also a man or woman much older falls silent for a day or two, and then leaves home. These people go out into the street, and walk down the street alone. They keep walking, and walk straight out of the city of Omelas, through the beautiful gates. They keep walking across the farmlands of Omelas. Each one goes alone, youth or girl, man or woman. Night falls; the traveller must pass down village streets, between the houses with yellow-lit windows, and on out into the darkness of the fields. Each alone, they go west or north, towards the mountains. They go on. They leave Omelas, they walk ahead into the darkness, and they do not come back. The place they go towards is a place even less imaginable to most of us than the city of happiness. I cannot describe it at all. It is possible that it does not exist. But they seem to know where they are going, the ones who walk away from Omelas.

—1973

Chinua Achebe

1930–2013

Chinua Achebe was born in Nigeria when the country was still a colonial territory of the British Empire. He established his place as an important figure in world literature with the publication of his first novel, *Things Fall Apart*, in 1958. It remains, perhaps, the work for which he is best known, but Achebe was a prolific and wide-ranging writer who steadily published novels, short stories, poetry, essays, and children's books until his death in 2013. In 1989, Achebe was awarded the Nobel Prize in Literature.

While still a student, Achebe read literary accounts of Africa written by Europeans, many of which he found "appalling." This experience taught him that more African voices should represent Africans; Achebe writes that he "decided that the story we had to tell could not be told by anyone else no matter how gifted or well intentioned." For Achebe, telling such stories accurately was of political as well as artistic importance because his writing was "concerned with universal human communication across racial and cultural boundaries as a means of fostering respect for all people" and, he believed, "such respect can only issue from understanding." This aim of understanding across racial and cultural boundaries is one of the reasons he chose to write in English.

As in the selection here, as well as in novels such as *No Longer at Ease* (1960) and *Arrow of God* (1964), Achebe's protagonists are often flawed individuals, recalling the characters of the classical tragedies. He resisted simple tales of good and evil, attempting instead to represent the complexity and uncertainty of the human experience.

Dead Men's Path

Michael Obi's hopes were fulfilled much earlier than he had expected. He was appointed headmaster of Ndume Central School in January 1949. It had always been an unprogressive school, so the Mission authorities[1] decided to send a young and energetic man to run it. Obi accepted this responsibility with enthusiasm. He had many wonderful ideas and this was an opportunity to put them into practice. He had had sound secondary school education which designated him a "pivotal teacher" in the official records and set him apart from the other headmasters in the mission field. He was outspoken in his condemnation of the narrow views of these older and often less-educated ones.

---

1   *Mission authorities* Many schools in African countries formerly colonized by the British were run by Christian missionary organizations.

"We shall make a good job of it, shan't we?" he asked his young wife when they first heard the joyful news of his promotion.

"We shall do our best," she replied. "We shall have such beautiful gardens and everything will be just *modern* and delightful...." In their two years of married life she had become completely infected by his passion for "modern methods" and his denigration of "these old and superannuated people in the teaching field who would be better employed as traders in the Onitsha[1] market." She began to see herself already as the admired wife of the young headmaster, the queen of the school.

The wives of the other teachers would envy her position. She would set the fashion in everything.... Then, suddenly, it occurred to her that there might not be other wives. Wavering between hope and fear, she asked her husband, looking anxiously at him.

"All our colleagues are young and unmarried," he said with enthusiasm which for once she did not share. "Which is a good thing," he continued.

"Why?"

"Why? They will give all their time and energy to the school."

Nancy was downcast. For a few minutes she became skeptical about the new school; but it was only for a few minutes. Her little personal misfortune could not blind her to her husband's happy prospects. She looked at him as he sat folded up in a chair. He was stoop-shouldered and looked frail. But he sometimes surprised people with sudden bursts of physical energy. In his present posture, however, all his bodily strength seemed to have retired behind his deep-set eyes, giving them an extraordinary power of penetration. He was only twenty-six, but looked thirty or more. On the whole, he was not unhandsome.

"A penny for your thoughts, Mike," said Nancy after a while, imitating the woman's magazine she read.

"I was thinking what a grand opportunity we've got at last to show these people how a school should be run."

Ndume School was backward in every sense of the word. Mr. Obi put his whole life into the work, and his wife hers too. He had two aims. A high standard of teaching was insisted upon, and the school compound was to be turned into a place of beauty. Nancy's dream-gardens came to life with the coming of the rains, and blossomed. Beautiful hibiscus and allamanda hedges in brilliant red and yellow marked out the carefully tended school compound from the rank neighbourhood bushes.

---

1   *Onitsha* City in southeastern Nigeria; the Onitsha market is one of the largest in West Africa.

One evening as Obi was admiring his work he was scandalized to see an old woman from the village hobble right across the compound, through a marigold flower-bed and the hedges. On going up there he found faint signs of an almost disused path from the village across the school compound to the bush on the other side.

"It amazes me," said Obi to one of his teachers who had been three years in the school, "that you people allowed the villagers to make use of this footpath. It is simply incredible." He shook his head.

"The path," said the teacher apologetically, "appears to be very important to them. Although it is hardly used, it connects the village shrine with their place of burial."

"And what has that got to do with the school?" asked the headmaster.

"Well, I don't know," replied the other with a shrug of the shoulders. "But I remember there was a big row some time ago when we attempted to close it."

"That was some time ago. But it will not be used now," said Obi as he walked away. "What will the Government Education Officer think of this when he comes to inspect the school next week? The villagers might, for all I know, decide to use the schoolroom for a pagan ritual during the inspection."

Heavy sticks were planted closely across the path at the two places where it entered and left the school premises. These were further strengthened with barbed wire.

Three days later the village priest of *Ani*[1] called on the headmaster. He was an old man and walked with a slight stoop. He carried a stout walking-stick which he usually tapped on the floor, by way of emphasis, each time he made a new point in his argument.

"I have heard," he said after the usual exchange of cordialities, "that our ancestral footpath has recently been closed...."

"Yes," replied Mr. Obi. "We cannot allow people to make a highway of our school compound."

"Look here, my son," said the priest bringing down his walking-stick, "this path was here before you were born and before your father was born. The whole life of this village depends on it. Our dead relatives depart by it and our ancestors visit us by it. But most important, it is the path of children coming in to be born...."

Mr. Obi listened with a satisfied smile on his face.

"The whole purpose of our school," he said finally, "is to eradicate just such beliefs as that. Dead men do not require footpaths. The whole idea is just fantastic. Our duty is to teach your children to laugh at such ideas."

---

1   *Ani* Traditional belief system of the Igbo people of Nigeria, often called Odinani.

"What you say may be true," replied the priest, "but we follow the practices of our fathers. If you reopen the path we shall have nothing to quarrel about. What I always say is: let the hawk perch and let the eagle perch." He rose to go.

"I am sorry," said the young headmaster. "But the school compound cannot be a thoroughfare. It is against our regulations. I would suggest your constructing another path, skirting our premises. We can even get our boys to help in building it. I don't suppose the ancestors will find the little detour too burdensome."

"I have no more words to say," said the old priest, already outside.

Two days later a young woman in the village died in childbed. A diviner was immediately consulted and he prescribed heavy sacrifices to propitiate ancestors insulted by the fence.

Obi woke up next morning among the ruins of his work. The beautiful hedges were torn up not just near the path but right round the school, the flowers trampled to death and one of the school buildings pulled down ... That day, the white Supervisor came to inspect the school and wrote a nasty report on the state of the premises but more seriously about the "tribal-war situation developing between the school and the village, arising in part from the misguided zeal of the new headmaster."

—1953

Alice Munro

b. 1931

Alice Munro is acclaimed as a writer with a keen eye for detail and a fine sense of emotional nuance. In 2009, when she received the Man Booker International Prize, the award panel commented that "she brings as much depth, wisdom, and precision to every story as most novelists bring to a lifetime of novels."

Alice Laidlaw was born into a farming community in Wingham, Ontario. After graduating from high school, she won a partial scholarship to attend the University of Western Ontario. She completed two years towards a degree in English, but she was unable to continue her studies due to strained finances. In 1951, she married James Munro; they moved to Vancouver and then to Victoria, British Columbia, where the couple opened a bookstore. They eventually had three daughters; Munro has often commented that the genre of the short story is well-suited to a working mother whose time for writing is limited.

Munro's work began to receive wide attention with the 1971 publication of *The Lives of Girls and Women*, a collection of interlinked stories (described later by the author as "autobiographical in form but not in fact") that traces the development of Del Jordan as she grows up in the constricting atmosphere of the small town of Jubilee. Everyday concerns over money and class and love and sex are recurrent themes in Munro's stories. Sensational events do happen in her fiction, but, as Alison Lurie has observed, "they usually take place offstage"; the focus of a Munro story is typically on emotion, not on incident.

Friend of My Youth

WITH THANKS TO R.J.T.

I used to dream about my mother, and though the details in the dream varied, the surprise in it was always the same. The dream stopped, I suppose because it was too transparent in its hopefulness, too easy in its forgiveness.

In the dream I would be the age I really was, living the life I was really living, and I would discover that my mother was still alive. (The fact is, she died when I was in my early twenties and she in her early fifties.) Sometimes I would find myself in our old kitchen, where my mother would be rolling out piecrust on the table, or washing the dishes in the battered cream-coloured dish-pan with the red rim. But other times I would run into her on the street, in places where I would never have expected to see her. She might be walking through a handsome hotel lobby, or lining up in an airport. She would be look-ing quite well—not exactly youthful, not entirely untouched by the paralyzing disease that held her in its grip for a decade or more before her death, but so much better than I remembered that I would be astonished. Oh, I just have this little tremor in my arm, she would say, and a little stiffness up this side of my face. It is a nuisance but I get around.

I recovered then what in waking life I had lost—my mother's liveliness of face and voice before her throat muscles stiffened and a woeful, impersonal mask fastened itself over her features. How could I have forgotten this, I would think in the dream—the casual humour she had, not ironic but merry, the lightness and impatience and confidence? I would say that I was sorry I hadn't been to see her in such a long time—meaning not that I felt guilty but that I was sorry I had kept a bugbear in my mind, instead of this reality—and the strangest, kindest thing of all to me was her matter-of-fact reply.

Oh, well, she said, better late than never. I was sure I'd see you someday.

When my mother was a young woman with a soft, mischievous face and shiny, opaque silk stockings on her plump legs (I have seen a photograph of her, with her pupils), she went to teach at a one-room school, called Grieves School, in the Ottawa Valley. The school was on a corner of the farm that belonged to the Grieves family—a very good farm for that country. Well-drained fields with none of the Precambrian rock[1] shouldering through the soil, a little willow-edged river running alongside, a sugar bush, log barns, and a large, unornamented house whose wooden walls had never been painted but had been left to weather. And when wood weathers in the Ottawa Valley, my mother said, I do not know why this is, but it never turns grey, it turns black. There must be something in the air, she said. She often spoke of the Ottawa Valley, which was her home—she had grown up about twenty miles away from Grieves School—in a dogmatic, mystified way, emphasizing things about it that distinguished it from any other place on earth. Houses turn black, maple syrup has a taste no maple syrup produced elsewhere can equal, bears amble within sight of farmhouses. Of course I was disappointed when I finally got to see this place. It was not a valley at all, if by that you mean a cleft between hills; it was a mixture of flat fields and low rocks and heavy bush and little lakes—a scrambled, disarranged sort of country with no easy harmony about it, not yielding readily to any description.

The log barns and unpainted house, common enough on poor farms, were not in the Grieveses' case a sign of poverty but of policy. They had the

---

1   *Precambrian rock* I.e., the rock of the Canadian Shield, a plateau spanning a large portion of Eastern and Central Canada.

money but they did not spend it. That was what people told my mother. The Grieveses worked hard and they were far from ignorant, but they were very backward. They didn't have a car or electricity or a telephone or a tractor. Some people thought this was because they were Cameronians—they were the only people in the school district who were of that religion—but in fact their church (which they themselves always called the Reformed Presbyterian) did not forbid engines or electricity or any inventions of that sort, just card playing, dancing, movies, and, on Sundays, any activity at all that was not religious or unavoidable.

My mother could not say who the Cameronians were or why they were called that. Some freak religion from Scotland, she said from the perch of her obedient and lighthearted Anglicanism. The teacher always boarded with the Grieveses, and my mother was a little daunted at the thought of going to live in that black board house with its paralytic Sundays and coal-oil lamps and primitive notions. But she was engaged by that time, she wanted to work on her trousseau[1] instead of running around the country having a good time, and she figured she could get home one Sunday out of three. (On Sundays at the Grieveses' house, you could light a fire for heat but not for cooking, you could not even boil the kettle to make tea, and you were not supposed to write a letter or swat a fly. But it turned out that my mother was exempt from these rules. "No, no," said Flora Grieves, laughing at her. "That doesn't mean you. You must just go on as you're used to doing." And after a while my mother had made friends with Flora to such an extent that she wasn't even going home on the Sundays when she'd planned to.)

Flora and Ellie Grieves were the two sisters left of the family. Ellie was married, to a man called Robert Deal, who lived there and worked the farm but had not changed its name to Deal's in anyone's mind. By the way people spoke, my mother expected the Grieves sisters and Robert Deal to be middle-aged at least, but Ellie, the younger sister, was only about thirty, and Flora seven or eight years older. Robert Deal might be in between.

The house was divided in an unexpected way. The married couple didn't live with Flora. At the time of their marriage, she had given them the parlour and the dining room, the front bedrooms and staircase, the winter kitchen. There was no need to decide about the bathroom, because there wasn't one. Flora had the summer kitchen, with its open rafters and uncovered brick walls, the old pantry made into a narrow dining room and sitting room, and the two back bedrooms, one of which was my mother's. The teacher was housed with Flora, in the poorer part of the house. But my mother didn't mind. She

---

1   *trousseau* Collection of clothing and household items assembled by a bride in preparation for her wedding.

immediately preferred Flora, and Flora's cheerfulness, to the silence and sick-room atmosphere of the front rooms. In Flora's domain it was not even true that all amusements were forbidden. She had a crokinole[1] board—she taught my mother how to play.

The division had been made, of course, in the expectation that Robert and Ellie would have a family, and that they would need the room. This hadn't happened. They had been married for more than a dozen years and there had not been a live child. Time and again Ellie had been pregnant, but two babies had been stillborn, and the rest she had miscarried. During my mother's first year, Ellie seemed to be staying in bed more and more of the time, and my mother thought that she must be pregnant again, but there was no mention of it. Such people would not mention it. You could not tell from the look of Ellie, when she got up and walked around, because she showed a stretched and ruined though slack-chested shape. She carried a sickbed odour, and she fretted in a childish way about everything. Flora took care of her and did all the work. She washed the clothes and tidied up the rooms and cooked the meals served in both sides of the house, as well as helping Robert with the milking and separating. She was up before daylight and never seemed to tire. During the first spring my mother was there, a great housecleaning was embarked upon, during which Flora climbed the ladders herself and carried down the storm windows, washed and stacked them away, carried all the furniture out of one room after another so that she could scrub the woodwork and varnish the floors. She washed every dish and glass that was sitting in the cupboards sup-posedly clean already. She scalded every pot and spoon. Such need and energy possessed her that she could hardly sleep—my mother would wake up to the sound of stovepipes being taken down, or the broom, draped in a dish towel, whacking at the smoky cobwebs. Through the washed uncurtained windows came a torrent of unmerciful light. The cleanliness was devastating. My mother slept now on sheets that had been bleached and starched and that gave her a rash. Sick Ellie complained daily of the smell of varnish and cleansing powders. Flora's hands were raw. But her disposition remained topnotch. Her kerchief and apron and Robert's baggy overalls that she donned for the climbing jobs gave her the air of a comedian—sportive, unpredictable.

My mother called her a whirling dervish.[2]

"You're a regular whirling dervish, Flora," she said, and Flora halted. She wanted to know what was meant. My mother went ahead and explained, though she was a little afraid lest piety should be offended. (Not piety ex-

---

1   *crokinole* Tabletop game played by flicking small disks toward a target at the centre of the board.

2   *whirling dervish* Islamic mystic whose spiritual practice includes an ecstatic, spinning dance; figuratively, "whirling dervish" refers to an extremely energetic person.

actly—you could not call it that. Religious strictness.) Of course it wasn't. There was not a trace of nastiness or smug vigilance in Flora's observance of her religion. She had no fear of heathens—she had always lived in the midst of them. She liked the idea of being a dervish, and went to tell her sister.

"Do you know what the teacher says I am?"

Flora and Ellie were both dark-haired, dark-eyed women, tall and narrow-shouldered and long-legged. Ellie was a wreck, of course, but Flora was still superbly straight and graceful. She could look like a queen, my mother said—even riding into town in that cart they had. For church they used a buggy or a cutter,[1] but when they went to town they often had to transport sacks of wool—they kept a few sheep—or of produce, to sell, and they had to bring provisions home. The trip of a few miles was not made often. Robert rode in front, to drive the horse—Flora could drive a horse perfectly well, but it must always be the man who drove. Flora would be standing behind holding on to the sacks. She rode to town and back standing up, keeping an easy balance, wearing her black hat. Almost ridiculous but not quite. A gypsy queen, my mother thought she looked like, with her black hair and her skin that always looked slightly tanned, and her lithe and bold serenity. Of course she lacked the gold bangles and the bright clothes. My mother envied her her slenderness, and her cheekbones.

Returning in the fall for her second year, my mother learned what was the matter with Ellie.

"My sister has a growth," Flora said. Nobody then spoke of cancer.

My mother had heard that before. People suspected it. My mother knew many people in the district by that time. She had made particular friends with a young woman who worked in the post office; this woman was going to be one of my mother's bridesmaids. The story of Flora and Ellie and Robert had been told—or all that people knew of it—in various versions. My mother did not feel that she was listening to gossip, because she was always on the alert for any disparaging remarks about Flora—she would not put up with that. But indeed nobody offered any. Everybody said that Flora had behaved like a saint. Even when she went to extremes, as in dividing up the house—that was like a saint.

Robert came to work at Grieveses' some months before the girls' father died. They knew him already, from church. (Oh, that church, my mother said, having attended it once, out of curiosity—that drear building miles on the other side of town, no organ or piano and plain glass in the windows and a doddery old minister with his hours-long sermon, a man hitting a tuning

---

1   *cutter* Sleigh.

fork for the singing.) Robert had come out from Scotland and was on his way west. He had stopped with relatives or people he knew, members of the scanty congregation. To earn some money, probably, he came to Grieveses'. Soon he and Flora were engaged. They could not go to dances or to card parties like other couples, but they went for long walks. The chaperone—unofficially—was Ellie. Ellie was then a wild tease, a long-haired, impudent, childish girl full of lolloping energy. She would run up hills and smite the mullein stalks with a stick, shouting and prancing and pretending to be a warrior on horseback. That, or the horse itself. This when she was fifteen, sixteen years old. Nobody but Flora could control her, and generally Flora just laughed at her, being too used to her to wonder if she was quite right in the head. They were wonderfully fond of each other. Ellie, with her long skinny body, her long pale face, was like a copy of Flora—the kind of copy you often see in families, in which because of some carelessness or exaggeration of features or colouring, the handsomeness of one person passes into the plainness—or almost plainness—of the other. But Ellie had no jealousy about this. She loved to comb out Flora's hair and pin it up. They had great times, washing each other's hair. Ellie would press her face into Flora's throat, like a colt nuzzling its mother. So when Robert laid claim to Flora, or Flora to him—nobody knew how it was—Ellie had to be included. She didn't show any spite toward Robert, but she pursued and waylaid them on their walks; she sprung on them out of the bushes or sneaked up behind them so softly that she could blow on their necks. People saw her do it. And they heard of her jokes. She had always been terrible for jokes and sometimes it had got her into trouble with her father, but Flora had protected her. Now she put thistles in Robert's bed. She set his place at the table with the knife and fork the wrong way around. She switched the milk pails to give him the old one with the hole in it. For Flora's sake, maybe, Robert humoured her.

The father had made Flora and Robert set the wedding day a year ahead, and after he died they did not move it any closer. Robert went on living in the house. Nobody knew how to speak to Flora about this being scandalous, or looking scandalous. Flora would just ask why. Instead of putting the wedding ahead, she put it back—from next spring to early fall, so that there should be a full year between it and her father's death. A year from wedding to funeral—that seemed proper to her. She trusted fully in Robert's patience and in her own purity.

So she might. But in the winter a commotion started. There was Ellie, vomiting, weeping, running off and hiding in the haymow, howling when they found her and pulled her out, jumping to the barn floor, running around in circles, rolling in the snow. Ellie was deranged. Flora had to call the doctor. She told him that her sister's periods had stopped—could the backup of blood be driving her wild? Robert had had to catch her and tie her up, and together he and Flora had put her to bed. She would not take food, just whipped her head from side to side, howling. It looked as if she would die speechless. But somehow the truth came out. Not from the doctor, who could not get close enough to examine her, with all her thrashing about. Probably, Robert confessed. Flora finally got wind of the truth, through all her high-mindedness. Now there had to be a wedding, though not the one that had been planned.

No cake, no new clothes, no wedding trip, no congratulations. Just a shameful hurry-up visit to the manse.[1] Some people, seeing the names in the paper, thought the editor must have got the sisters mixed up. They thought it must be Flora. A hurry-up wedding for Flora! But no—it was Flora who pressed Robert's suit—it must have been—and got Ellie out of bed and washed her and made her presentable. It would have been Flora who picked one geranium from the window plant and pinned it to her sister's dress. And Ellie hadn't torn it out. Ellie was meek now, no longer flailing or crying. She let Flora fix her up, she let herself be married, she was never wild from that day on.

Flora had the house divided. She herself helped Robert build the necessary partitions. The baby was carried full term—nobody even pretended that it was early—but it was born dead after a long, tearing labour. Perhaps Ellie had damaged it when she jumped from the barn beam and rolled in the snow and beat on herself. Even if she hadn't done that, people would have expected something to go wrong, with that child or maybe one that came later. God dealt out punishment for hurry-up marriages—not just Presbyterians but almost everybody else believed that. God rewarded lust with dead babies, idiots, harelips and withered limbs and clubfeet.

In this case the punishment continued. Ellie had one miscarriage after another, then another stillbirth and more miscarriages. She was constantly pregnant, and the pregnancies were full of vomiting fits that lasted for days, headaches, cramps, dizzy spells. The miscarriages were as agonizing as full-term births. Ellie could not do her own work. She walked around holding on to chairs. Her numb silence passed off, and she became a complainer. If anybody came to visit, she would talk about the peculiarities of her headaches or describe her latest fainting fit, or even—in front of men, in front of unmarried girls or children—go into bloody detail about what Flora called her "disappointments." When people changed the subject or dragged the children away, she turned sullen. She demanded new medicine, reviled the doctor, nagged Flora. She accused Flora of washing the dishes with a great clang and clatter, out of spite, of pulling her—Ellie's—hair when she combed it out, of stingily substituting water-and-molasses for her real medicine. No matter what she said, Flora soothed her. Everybody who came into the house had some story

1   *manse* Minister's house.

of that kind to tell. Flora said, "Where's my little girl, then? Where's my Ellie? This isn't my Ellie, this is some crosspatch[1] got in here in place of her!"

In the winter evenings after she came in from helping Robert with the barn chores, Flora would wash and change her clothes and go next door to read Ellie to sleep. My mother might invite herself along, taking whatever sewing she was doing, on some item of her trousseau. Ellie's bed was set up in the big dining room, where there was a gas lamp over the table. My mother sat on one side of the table, sewing, and Flora sat on the other side, reading aloud. Sometimes Ellie said, "I can't hear you." Or if Flora paused for a little rest Ellie said, "I'm not asleep yet."

What did Flora read? Stories about Scottish life—not classics. Stories about urchins and comic grandmothers. The only title my mother could remember was *Wee Macgregor*.[2] She could not follow the stories very well, or laugh when Flora laughed and Ellie gave a whimper, because so much was in Scots dialect or read with that thick accent. She was surprised that Flora could do it—it wasn't the way Flora ordinarily talked, at all.

(But wouldn't it be the way Robert talked? Perhaps that is why my mother never reports anything that Robert said, never has him contributing to the scene. He must have been there, he must have been sitting there in the room. They would only heat the main room of the house. I see him black-haired, heavy-shouldered, with the strength of a plow horse, and the same kind of sombre, shackled beauty.)

Then Flora would say, "That's all of that for tonight." She would pick up another book, an old book written by some preacher of their faith. There was in it such stuff as my mother had never heard. What stuff? She couldn't say. All the stuff that was in their monstrous old religion. That put Ellie to sleep, or made her pretend she was asleep, after a couple of pages.

All that configuration of the elect and the damned, my mother must have meant—all the arguments about the illusion and necessity of free will. Doom and slippery redemption. The torturing, defeating, but for some minds irresistible pileup of interlocking and contradictory notions. My mother could resist it. Her faith was easy, her spirits at that time robust. Ideas were not what she was curious about, ever.

But what sort of thing was that, she asked (silently), to read to a dying woman? This was the nearest she got to criticizing Flora.

The answer—that it was the only thing, if you believed it—never seemed to have occurred to her.

---

1   *crosspatch* Grump.
2   *Wee Macgregor* Comic short story collection by John Joy Bell (1902).

By spring a nurse had arrived. That was the way things were done then. People died at home, and a nurse came in to manage it.

The nurse's name was Audrey Atkinson. She was a stout woman with corsets as stiff as barrel hoops, marcelled[1] hair the colour of brass candlesticks, a mouth shaped by lipstick beyond its own stingy outlines. She drove a car into the yard—her own car, a dark-green coupé, shiny and smart. News of Audrey Atkinson and her car spread quickly. Questions were asked. Where did she get the money? Had some rich fool altered his will on her behalf? Had she exercised influence? Or simply helped herself to a stash of bills under the mattress? How was she to be trusted?

Hers was the first car ever to sit in the Grieveses' yard overnight.

Audrey Atkinson said that she had never been called out to tend a case in so primitive a house. It was beyond her, she said, how people could live in such a way.

"It's not that they're poor, even," she said to my mother. "It isn't, is it? That I could understand. Or it's not even their religion. So what is it? They do not care!"

She tried at first to cozy up to my mother, as if they would be natural allies in this benighted place. She spoke as if they were around the same age—both stylish, intelligent women who liked a good time and had modern ideas. She offered to teach my mother to drive the car. She offered her cigarettes. My mother was more tempted by the idea of learning to drive than she was by the cigarettes. But she said no, she would wait for her husband to teach her. Audrey Atkinson raised her pinkish-orange eyebrows at my mother behind Flora's back, and my mother was furious. She disliked the nurse far more than Flora did.

"I knew what she was like and Flora didn't," my mother said. She meant that she caught a whiff of a cheap life, maybe even of drinking establishments and unsavory men, of hard bargains, which Flora was too unworldly to notice.

Flora started into the great housecleaning again. She had the curtains spread out on stretchers, she beat the rugs on the line, she leapt up on the stepladder to attack the dust on the moulding. But she was impeded all the time by Nurse Atkinson's complaining.

"I wondered if we could have a little less of the running and clattering?" said Nurse Atkinson with offensive politeness. "I only ask for my patient's sake." She always spoke of Ellie as "my patient" and pretended that she was the only one to protect her and compel respect. But she was not so respectful of Ellie herself. "Allee-oop," she would say, dragging the poor creature up on her pillows. And she told Ellie she was not going to stand for fretting and whimpering. "You don't do yourself any good that way," she said. "And you

---

1   *marcelled* Artificially wavy.

certainly don't make me come any quicker. What you just as well might do is learn to control yourself." She exclaimed at Ellie's bedsores in a scolding way, as if they were a further disgrace of the house. She demanded lotions, ointments, expensive soap—most of them, no doubt, to protect her own skin, which she claimed suffered from the hard water. (How could it be hard, my mother asked her—sticking up for the household when nobody else would—how could it be hard when it came straight from the rain barrel?)

Nurse Atkinson wanted cream, too—she said that they should hold some back, not sell it all to the creamery. She wanted to make nourishing soups and puddings for her patient. She did make puddings, and jellies, from packaged mixes such as had never before entered this house. My mother was convinced that she ate them all herself.

Flora still read to Ellie, but now it was only short bits from the Bible. When she finished and stood up, Ellie tried to cling to her. Ellie wept, sometimes she made ridiculous complaints. She said there was a horned cow outside, trying to get into the room and kill her.

"They often get some kind of idea like that," Nurse Atkinson said. "You mustn't give in to her or she won't let you go day or night. That's what they're like, they only think about themselves. Now, when I'm here alone with her, she behaves herself quite nice. I don't have any trouble at all. But after you been in here I have trouble all over again because she sees you and she gets upset. You don't want to make my job harder for me, do you? I mean, you brought me here to take charge, didn't you?"

"Ellie, now, Ellie dear, I must go," said Flora, and to the nurse she said, "I understand. I do understand that you have to be in charge and I admire you, I admire you for your work. In your work you have to have so much patience and kindness."

My mother wondered at this—was Flora really so blinded, or did she hope by this undeserved praise to exhort Nurse Atkinson to the patience and kindness that she didn't have? Nurse Atkinson was too thick-skinned and self-approving for any trick like that to work.

"It is a hard job, all right, and not many can do it," she said. "It's not like those nurses in the hospital, where they got everything laid out for them." She had no time for more conversation—she was trying to bring in "Make-Believe Ballroom"[1] on her battery radio.

My mother was busy with the final exams and the June exercises at the school. She was getting ready for her wedding in July. Friends came in cars and whisked her off to the dressmaker's, to parties, to choose the invitations

---

1   *"Make-Believe Ballroom"* Radio program (1930s–1950s) that broadcast recordings of popular music.

and order the cake. The lilacs came out, the evenings lengthened, the birds were back and nesting, my mother bloomed in everybody's attention, about to set out on the deliciously solemn adventure of marriage. Her dress was to be appliquéd with silk roses, her veil held by a cap of seed pearls. She belonged to the first generation of young women who saved their money and paid for their own weddings—far fancier than their parents could have afforded.

On her last evening, the friend from the post office came to drive her away, with her clothes and her books and the things she had made for her trousseau and the gifts her pupils and others had given her. There was great fuss and laughter about getting everything loaded into the car. Flora came out and helped. This getting married is even more of a nuisance than I thought, said Flora, laughing. She gave my mother a dresser scarf, which she had crocheted in secret. Nurse Atkinson could not be shut out of an important occasion—she presented a spray bottle of cologne. Flora stood on the slope at the side of the house to wave good-bye. She had been invited to the wedding, but of course she had said she could not come, she could not "go out" at such a time. The last my mother ever saw of her was this solitary, energetically waving figure in her housecleaning apron and bandanna, on the green slope by the black-walled house, in the evening light.

"Well, maybe now she'll get what she should've got the first time round," the friend from the post office said. "Maybe now they'll be able to get married. Is she too old to start a family? How old is she, anyway?"

My mother thought that this was a crude way of talking about Flora and replied that she didn't know. But she had to admit to herself that she had been thinking the very same thing.

When she was married and settled in her own home, three hundred miles away, my mother got a letter from Flora. Ellie was dead. She had died firm in her faith, Flora said, and grateful for her release. Nurse Atkinson was staying on for a little while, until it was time for her to go off to her next case. This was late in the summer.

News of what happened next did not come from Flora. When she wrote at Christmas, she seemed to take for granted that information would have gone ahead of her.

"You have in all probability heard," wrote Flora, "that Robert and Nurse Atkinson have been married. They are living on here, in Robert's part of the house. They are fixing it up to suit themselves. It is very impolite of me to call her Nurse Atkinson, as I see I have done. I ought to have called her Audrey."

Of course the post-office friend had written, and so had others. It was a great shock and scandal and a matter that excited the district—the wedding as secret and surprising as Robert's first one had been (though surely not for the same reason), Nurse Atkinson permanently installed in the community, Flora losing out for the second time. Nobody had been aware of any courtship, and they asked how the woman could have enticed him. Did she promise children, lying about her age?

The surprises were not to stop with the wedding. The bride got down to business immediately with the "fixing up" that Flora mentioned. In came the electricity and then the telephone. Now Nurse Atkinson—she would always be called Nurse Atkinson—was heard on the party line lambasting painters and paperhangers and delivery services. She was having everything done over. She was buying an electric stove and putting in a bathroom, and who knew where the money was coming from? Was it all hers, got in her deathbed dealings, in shady bequests? Was it Robert's, was he claiming his share? Ellie's share, left to him and Nurse Atkinson to enjoy themselves with, the shameless pair?

All these improvements took place on one side of the house only. Flora's side remained just as it was. No electric lights there, no fresh wallpaper or new venetian blinds. When the house was painted on the outside—cream with dark-green trim—Flora's side was left bare. This strange open statement was greeted at first with pity and disapproval, then with less sympathy, as a sign of Flora's stubbornness and eccentricity (she could have bought her own paint and made it look decent), and finally as a joke. People drove out of their way to see it.

There was always a dance given in the schoolhouse for a newly married couple. A cash collection—called "a purse of money"—was presented to them. Nurse Atkinson sent out word that she would not mind seeing this custom followed, even though it happened that the family she had married into was opposed to dancing. Some people thought it would be a disgrace to gratify her, a slap in the face to Flora. Others were too curious to hold back. They wanted to see how the newlyweds would behave. Would Robert dance? What sort of outfit would the bride show up in? They delayed a while, but finally the dance was held, and my mother got her report.

The bride wore the dress she had worn at her wedding, or so she said. But who would wear such a dress for a wedding at the manse? More than likely it was bought specially for her appearance at the dance. Pure-white satin with a sweetheart neckline, idiotically youthful. The groom was got up in a new dark-blue suit, and she had stuck a flower in his buttonhole. They were a sight. Her hair was freshly done to blind the eye with brassy reflections, and her face looked as if it would come off on a man's jacket, should she lay it against his shoulder in the dancing. Of course she did dance. She danced with every man present except the groom, who sat scrunched into one of the school desks along the wall. She danced with every man present—they all claimed they had to do it, it was the custom—and then she dragged Robert out to receive the money and to thank everybody for their best wishes. To the ladies in the cloakroom she even hinted that she was feeling unwell, for the usual newlywed reason. Nobody believed her, and indeed nothing ever came of this hope, if she really had it. Some of the women thought that she was lying to them out of malice, insulting them, making them out to be so credulous. But nobody challenged her, nobody was rude to her—maybe because it was plain that she could summon a rudeness of her own to knock anybody flat.

Flora was not present at the dance.

"My sister-in-law is not a dancer," said Nurse Atkinson. "She is stuck in the olden times." She invited them to laugh at Flora, whom she always called her sister-in-law, though she had no right to do so.

My mother wrote a letter to Flora after hearing about all these things. Being removed from the scene, and perhaps in a flurry of importance due to her own newly married state, she may have lost sight of the kind of person she was writing to. She offered sympathy and showed outrage, and said blunt disparaging things about the woman who had—as my mother saw it—dealt Flora such a blow. Back came a letter from Flora saying that she did not know where my mother had been getting her information, but that it seemed she had misunderstood, or listened to malicious people, or jumped to unjustified conclusions. What happened in Flora's family was nobody else's business, and certainly nobody needed to feel sorry for her or angry on her behalf. Flora said that she was happy and satisfied in her life, as she always had been, and she did not interfere with what others did or wanted, because such things did not concern her. She wished my mother all happiness in her marriage and hoped that she would soon be too busy with her own responsibilities to worry about the lives of people that she used to know.

This well-written letter cut my mother, as she said, to the quick. She and Flora stopped corresponding. My mother did become busy with her own life and finally a prisoner in it.

But she thought about Flora. In later years, when she sometimes talked about the things she might have been, or done, she would say, "If I could have been a writer—I do think I could have been; I could have been a writer—then I would have written the story of Flora's life. And do you know what I would have called it? 'The Maiden Lady.'"

The Maiden Lady. She said these words in a solemn and sentimental tone of voice that I had no use for. I knew, or thought I knew, exactly the value she found in them. The stateliness and mystery. The hint of derision turning to reverence. I was fifteen or sixteen years old by that time, and I believed that I could see into my mother's mind. I could see what she would do with Flora, what she had already done. She would make her into a noble figure, one who accepts defection, treachery, who forgives and stands aside, not once but twice. Never a moment of complaint. Flora goes about her cheerful labours, she cleans the house and shovels out the cow byre, she removes some bloody mess from her sister's bed, and when at last the future seems to open up for her—Ellie will die and Robert will beg forgiveness and Flora will silence him with the proud gift of herself—it is time for Audrey Atkinson to drive into the yard and shut Flora out again, more inexplicably and thoroughly the second time than the first. She must endure the painting of the house, the electric lights, all the prosperous activity next door. "Make-Believe Ballroom," "Amos 'n' Andy."[1] No more Scottish comedies or ancient sermons. She must see them drive off to the dance—her old lover and that coldhearted, stupid, by no means beautiful woman in the white satin wedding dress. She is mocked. (And of course she has made over the farm to Ellie and Robert, of course he has inherited it, and now everything belongs to Audrey Atkinson.) The wicked flourish. But it is all right. It is all right—the elect are veiled in patience and humility and lighted by a certainty that events cannot disturb.

That was what I believed my mother would make of things. In her own plight her notions had turned mystical, and there was sometimes a hush, a solemn thrill in her voice that grated on me, alerted me to what seemed a personal danger. I felt a great fog of platitudes and pieties lurking, an incontestable crippled-mother power, which could capture and choke me. There would be no end to it. I had to keep myself sharp-tongued and cynical, arguing and deflating. Eventually I gave up even that recognition and opposed her in silence.

This is a fancy way of saying that I was no comfort and poor company to her when she had almost nowhere else to turn.

I had my own ideas about Flora's story. I didn't think that I could have written a novel but that I would write one. I would take a different tack. I saw through my mother's story and put in what she left out. My Flora would be as black as hers was white. Rejoicing in the bad turns done to her and in her own forgiveness, spying on the shambles of her sister's life. A Presbyterian witch, reading out of her poisonous book. It takes a rival ruthlessness, the comparatively innocent brutality of the thick-skinned nurse, to drive her back, to flourish in her shade. But she is driven back; the power of sex and ordinary greed drive her back and shut her up in her own part of the house with the coal-oil lamps. She shrinks, she caves in, her bones harden and her joints thicken, and—oh, this is it, this is it, I see the bare beauty of the ending I will contrive!—she becomes crippled herself, with arthritis, hardly able to move. Now Audrey Atkinson comes into her full power—she demands the whole house. She wants those partitions knocked out that Robert put up with Flora's help when he married Ellie. She will provide Flora with a room, she will take

---

1   "Amos 'n' Andy" Comedy radio program (1928–58).

care of her. (Audrey Atkinson does not wish to be seen as a monster, and perhaps she really isn't one.) So one day Robert carries Flora—for the first and last
time he carries her in his arms—to the room that his wife Audrey has prepared
for her. And once Flora is settled in her well-lit, well-heated corner Audrey
Atkinson undertakes to clean out the newly vacated rooms, Flora's rooms. She
carries a heap of old books out into the yard. It's spring again, housecleaning
time, the season when Flora herself performed such feats, and now the pale
face of Flora appears behind the new net curtains. She has dragged herself
from her corner, she sees the light-blue sky with its high skidding clouds over
the watery fields, the contending crows, the flooded creeks, the reddening tree
branches. She sees the smoke rise out of the incinerator in the yard, where her
books are burning. Those smelly old books, as Audrey has called them. Words
and pages, the ominous dark spines. The elect, the damned, the slim hopes,
the mighty torments—up in smoke. There was the ending.

To me the really mysterious person in the story, as my mother told it, was
Robert. He never has a word to say. He gets engaged to Flora. He is walking
beside her along the river when Ellie leaps out at them. He finds Ellie's thistles
in his bed. He does the carpentry made necessary by his and Ellie's marriage.
He listens or does not listen while Flora reads. Finally he sits scrunched up in
the school desk while his flashy bride dances by with all the men.

So much for his public acts and appearances. But he was the one who
started everything, in secret. He *did it to* Ellie. He did it to that skinny wild
girl at a time when he was engaged to her sister, and he did it to her again and
again when she was nothing but a poor botched body, a failed childbearer,
lying in bed.

He must have done it to Audrey Atkinson, too, but with less disastrous
results.

Those words, *did it to*—the words my mother, no more than Flora, would
never bring herself to speak—were simply exciting to me. I didn't feel any decent revulsion or reasonable indignation. I refused the warning. Not even the
fate of Ellie could put me off. Not when I thought of that first encounter—the
desperation of it, the ripping and striving. I used to sneak longing looks at
men in those days. I admired their wrists and their necks and any bit of their
chests a loose button let show, and even their ears and their feet in shoes. I
expected nothing reasonable of them, only to be engulfed by their passion. I
had similar thoughts about Robert.

What made Flora evil in my story was just what made her admirable in my
mother's—her turning away from sex. I fought against everything my mother
wanted to tell me on this subject; I despised even the drop in her voice, the
gloomy caution, with which she approached it. My mother had grown up in
a time and in a place where sex was a dark undertaking for women. She knew

that you could die of it. So she honoured the decency, the prudery, the frigid-ity, that might protect you. And I grew up in horror of that very protection, the dainty tyranny that seemed to me to extend to all areas of life, to enforce tea parties and white gloves and all other sorts of tinkling inanities. I favoured bad words and a breakthrough, I teased myself with the thought of a man's recklessness and domination. The odd thing is that my mother's ideas were in line with some progressive notions of her times, and mine echoed the notions that were favoured in my time. This in spite of the fact that we both believed ourselves independent, and lived in backwaters that did not register such changes. It's as if tendencies that seem most deeply rooted in our minds, most private and singular, have come in as spores on the prevailing wind, looking for any likely place to land, any welcome.

Not long before she died, but when I was still at home, my mother got a let-ter from the real Flora. It came from that town near the farm, the town that Flora used to ride to, with Robert, in the cart, holding on to the sacks of wool or potatoes.

Flora wrote that she was no longer living on the farm.

"Robert and Audrey are still there," she wrote. "Robert has some trouble with his back but otherwise he is very well. Audrey has poor circulation and is often short of breath. The doctor says she must lose weight but none of the diets seem to work. The farm has been doing very well. They are out of sheep entirely and into dairy cattle. As you may have heard, the chief thing nowadays is to get your milk quota from the government and then you are set. The old stable is all fixed up with milking machines and the latest modern equipment, it is quite a marvel. When I go out there to visit I hardly know where I am."

She went on to say that she had been living in town for some years now, and that she had a job clerking in a store. She must have said what kind of a store this was, but I cannot now remember. She said nothing, of course, about what had led her to this decision—whether she had in fact been put off her own farm, or had sold out her share, apparently not to much advantage. She stressed the fact of her friendliness with Robert and Audrey. She said her health was good.

"I hear that you have not been so lucky in that way," she wrote. "I ran into Cleta Barnes who used to be Cleta Stapleton at the post office out at home, and she told me that there is some problem with your muscles and she said your speech is affected too. This is sad to hear but they can do such wonderful things nowadays so I am hoping that the doctors may be able to help you."

An unsettling letter, leaving so many things out. Nothing in it about God's will or His role in our afflictions. No mention of whether Flora still went to that church. I don't think my mother ever answered. Her fine legible handwriting, her schoolteacher's writing, had deteriorated, and she had difficulty holding a pen. She was always beginning letters and not finishing them. I would find them lying around the house. *My dearest Mary*, they began. *My darling Ruth, My dear little Joanne (though I realize you are not little anymore), My dear old friend Cleta, My lovely Margaret.* These women were friends from her teaching days, her Normal School days, and from high school. A few were former pupils. I have friends all over the country, she would say defiantly. I have dear, dear friends.

I remember seeing one letter that started out: *Friend of my Youth.* I don't know whom it was to. They were all friends of her youth. I don't recall one that began with *My dear and most admired Flora.* I would always look at them, try to read the salutation and the few sentences she had written, and because I could not bear to feel sadness I would feel an impatience with the flowery language, the direct appeal for love and pity. She would get more of that, I thought (more from myself, I meant), if she could manage to withdraw with dignity, instead of reaching out all the time to cast her stricken shadow.

I had lost interest in Flora by then. I was always thinking of stories, and by this time I probably had a new one on my mind.

But I have thought of her since. I have wondered what kind of a store. A hardware store or a five-and-ten, where she has to wear a coverall, or a drugstore, where she is uniformed like a nurse, or a Ladies' Wear, where she is expected to be genteelly fashionable? She might have had to learn about food blenders or chain saws, negligees, cosmetics, even condoms. She would have to work all day under electric lights, and operate a cash register. Would she get a permanent, paint her nails, put on lipstick? She must have found a place to live—a little apartment with a kitchenette, overlooking the main street, or a room in a boarding house. How could she go on being a Cameronian? How could she get to that out-of-the-way church unless she managed to buy a car and learned to drive it? And if she did that she might drive not only to church but to other places. She might go on holidays. She might rent a cottage on a lake for a week, learn to swim, visit a city. She might eat meals in a restaurant, possibly in a restaurant where drinks were served. She might make friends with women who were divorced.

She might meet a man. A friend's widowed brother, perhaps. A man who did not know that she was a Cameronian or what Cameronians were. Who knew nothing of her story. A man who had never heard about the partial painting of the house or the two betrayals, or that it took all her dignity and innocence to keep her from being a joke. He might want to take her dancing, and she would have to explain that she could not go. He would be surprised but not put off—all that Cameronian business might seem quaint to him, almost charming. So it would to everybody. She was brought up in some weird religion, people would say. She lived a long time out on some godforsaken farm. She is a little bit strange but really quite nice. Nice-looking, too. Especially since she went and got her hair done.

I might go into a store and find her.

No, no. She would be dead a long time now.

But suppose I had gone into a store—perhaps a department store. I see a place with the brisk atmosphere, the straightforward displays, the old-fashioned modern look of the fifties. Suppose a tall, handsome woman, nicely turned out, had come to wait on me, and I had known, somehow, in spite of the sprayed and puffed hair and the pink or coral lips and fingernails—I had known that this was Flora. I would have wanted to tell her that I knew, I knew her story, though we had never met. I imagine myself trying to tell her. (This is a dream now, I understand it as a dream.) I imagine her listening, with a pleasant composure. But she shakes her head. She smiles at me, and in her smile there is a degree of mockery, a faint, self-assured malice. Weariness, as well. She is not surprised that I am telling her this, but she is weary of it, of me and my idea of her, my information, my notion that I can know anything about her.

Of course it's my mother I'm thinking of, my mother as she was in those dreams, saying, It's nothing, just this little tremor; saying with such astonishing lighthearted forgiveness, Oh, I knew you'd come someday. My mother surprising me, and doing it almost indifferently. Her mask, her fate, and most of her affliction taken away. How relieved I was, and happy. But I now recall that I was disconcerted as well. I would have to say that I felt slightly cheated. Yes. Offended, tricked, cheated, by this welcome turnaround, this reprieve. My mother moving rather carelessly out of her old prison, showing options and powers I never dreamed she had, changes more than herself. She changes the bitter lump of love I have carried all this time into a phantom—something useless and uncalled for, like a phantom pregnancy.

The Cameronians, I have discovered, are or were an uncompromising remnant of the Covenanters—those Scots who in the seventeenth century bound themselves, with God, to resist prayer books, bishops, any taint of popery or interference by the King. Their name comes from Richard Cameron, an outlawed, or "field," preacher, soon cut down. The Cameronians—for a long time they have preferred to be called the Reformed Presbyterians—went into battle singing the seventy-fourth and the seventy-eighth Psalms. They hacked the haughty Bishop of St. Andrews to death on the highway and rode their horses over his body. One of their ministers, in a mood of firm rejoicing at his own hanging, excommunicated all the other preachers in the world.

—1990

Alasdair Gray
b. 1934

Alasdair Gray is a novelist, poet, playwright, painter, and illustrator. He was born in 1934 to a working-class family in the suburb of Riddrie, in East Glasgow, Scotland. Gray claims that he began writing and sketching to stave off the doldrums of schoolboy life and to escape his perception of Glasgow as a dull and ordinary place. By his teens, Gray says, he realized that Glasgow "was as full of the materials of Heaven and Hell, of the possibilities of delight and horror, as anywhere else in the world or even the places you could invent." Gray has used Glasgow and Glasgow-like settings as the backdrop for much of his fiction, including *Lanark: A Life in Four Books* (1981)—a novel that he spent the better part of 30 years writing and the literary work for which he is best known.

Gray's parents were avid readers and kept many books in their home. As a child, Gray developed a particular fondness for authors who illustrated their own work, like Rudyard Kipling and William Blake. Gray was also captivated by the colourful and often imaginative artwork contained within volumes of the *Harmsworth Encyclopedia*. These early influences inspired Gray to enroll at the Glasgow School of Art and write fiction on the side. It was during his time as an art student that Gray began work on *Lanark* and wrote some of his finest short stories.

Critical response to Alasdair Gray's work is polarised. Upon reading *Lanark*, Anthony Burgess proclaimed Gray to be "the first major Scottish writer since Walter Scott" but retracted his praise after reading Gray's *1982, Janine* (1984), saying it displayed "the same large talent deployed to a somewhat juvenile end." Peter Levi offered even harsher criticism of *1982, Janine*, calling it "radio-active hogwash." Fellow Scottish author Irvine Welsh, however, is among a contingent of critics who believe that Gray is "one of the most gifted writers who have put pen to paper in the English language."

The Star

A star had fallen beyond the horizon, in Canada perhaps. (He had an aunt in Canada.) The second was nearer, just beyond the iron works, so he was not surprised when the third fell into the backyard. A flash of gold light lit the walls of the enclosing tenements and he heard a low musical chord. The light turned deep red and went out, and he knew that somewhere below a star was cooling in the night air. Turning from the window he saw that no-one else had noticed. At the table his father, thoughtfully frowning, filled in a football coupon, his mother continued ironing under the pulley with its row of underwear. He said in a small voice, "A'm gawn out."

His mother said, "See you're no' long then."

He slipped through the lobby and onto the stairhead,[1] banging the door after him.

The stairs were cold and coldly lit at each landing by a weak electric bulb. He hurried down three flights to the black silent yard and began hunting backward and forward, combing with his fingers the lank grass round the base of the clothes-pole. He found it in the midden[2] on a decayed cabbage leaf. It was smooth and round, the size of a glass marble, and it shone with a light which made it seem to rest on a precious bit of green and yellow velvet. He picked it up. It was warm and filled his cupped palm with a ruby glow. He put it in his pocket and went back upstairs.

That night in bed he had a closer look. He slept with his brother who was not easily wakened. Wriggling carefully far down under the sheets, he opened his palm and gazed. The star shone white and blue, making the space around him like a cave in an iceberg. He brought it close to his eye. In its depth was the pattern of a snow-flake, the grandest thing he had ever seen. He looked through the flake's crystal lattice into an ocean of glittering blue-black waves under a sky full of huge galaxies. He heard a remote lulling sound like the sound in a sea-shell, and fell asleep with the star safely clenched in his hand.

He enjoyed it for nearly two weeks, gazing at it each night below the sheets, sometimes seeing the snow-flake, sometimes a flower, jewel, moon or landscape. At first he kept it hidden during the day but soon took to carrying it

1   *stairhead* Landing above a staircase.
2   *midden* Household garbage heap.

about with him; the smooth rounded gentle warmth in his pocket gave comfort when he felt insulted or neglected.

At school one afternoon he decided to take a quick look. He was at the back of the classroom in a desk by himself. The teacher was among the boys at the front row and all heads were bowed over books. Quickly he brought out the star and looked. It contained an aloof eye with a cool green pupil which dimmed and trembled as if seen through water.

"What have you there, Cameron?"

He shuddered and shut his hand.

"Marbles are for the playground, not the classroom. You'd better give it to me."

"I cannae, sir."

"I don't tolerate disobedience, Cameron. Give me that thing."

The boy saw the teacher's face above him, the mouth opening and shutting under a clipped moustache. Suddenly he knew what to do and put the star in his mouth and swallowed. As the warmth sank toward his heart he felt relaxed and at ease. The teacher's face moved into the distance. Teacher, classroom, world receded like a rocket into a warm, easy blackness leaving behind a trail of glorious stars, and he was one of them.

—1951

Alistair MacLeod
b. 1936

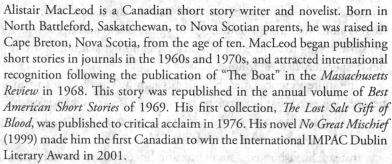

Alistair MacLeod is a Canadian short story writer and novelist. Born in North Battleford, Saskatchewan, to Nova Scotian parents, he was raised in Cape Breton, Nova Scotia, from the age of ten. MacLeod began publishing short stories in journals in the 1960s and 1970s, and attracted international recognition following the publication of "The Boat" in the *Massachusetts Review* in 1968. This story was republished in the annual volume of *Best American Short Stories* of 1969. His first collection, *The Lost Salt Gift of Blood*, was published to critical acclaim in 1976. His novel *No Great Mischief* (1999) made him the first Canadian to win the International IMPAC Dublin Literary Award in 2001.

Much of MacLeod's fiction depicts the psychological, physical, and emotional experience of the mining and fishing communities of Nova Scotia, set against the natural cycles of the seasons, of the sea, and of life and death. He often uses first-person present-tense narration, which lends immediacy to his subjects and themes and foregrounds the experience of memory. Joyce Carol Oates writes that the "single underlying motive" for the stories "is the urge to memorialize, the urge to sanctify." This elegiac tone is reminiscent of the Scottish and English traditions of oral literature, and the lyrical power of MacLeod's prose underscores this association, as does the natural ease of the storytelling.

MacLeod accepted a post at the University of Windsor in 1969, where he taught literature and creative writing. Each summer, he and his family returned to Inverness in Cape Breton, where he wrote his stories. He retired in 2000.

As Birds Bring Forth the Sun

Once there was a family with a highland name who lived beside the sea. And the man had a dog of which he was very fond. She was large and grey, a sort of staghound from another time. And if she jumped up to lick his face, which she loved to do, her paws would jolt against his shoulders with such force that she would come close to knocking him down and he would be forced to take two or three backward steps before he could regain his balance. And he himself was not a small man, being slightly over six feet and perhaps one hundred and eighty pounds.

She had been left, when a pup, at the family's gate in a small handmade box and no one knew where she had come from or that she would eventually grow to such a size. Once, while still a small pup, she had been run over by the steel wheel of a horse-drawn cart which was hauling kelp from the shore to be used as fertilizer. It was in October and the rain had been falling for some weeks and the ground was soft. When the wheel of the cart passed over her, it sunk her body into the wet earth as well as crushing some of her ribs; and apparently the silhouette of her small crushed body was visible in the earth after the man lifted her to his chest while she yelped and screamed. He ran his fingers along her broken bones, ignoring the blood and urine which fell upon his shirt, trying to soothe her bulging eyes and her scrabbling front paws and her desperately licking tongue.

The more practical members of his family, who had seen run-over dogs before, suggested that her neck be broken by his strong hands or that he grasp her by the hind legs and swing her head against a rock, thus putting an end to her misery, but he would not do it.

Instead, he fashioned a small box and lined it with woollen remnants from a sheep's fleece and one of his old and frayed shirts. He placed her within the box and placed the box behind the stove and then he warmed some milk in a small saucepan and sweetened it with sugar. And he held open her small and trembling jaws with his left hand while spooning the sweetened milk with his right, ignoring the needle-like sharpness of her small teeth. She lay in the box most of the remaining fall and into the early winter, watching everything with her large brown eyes.

Although some members of the family complained about her presence and the odour from the box and the waste of time she involved, they gradually adjusted to her; and as the weeks passed by, it became evident that her ribs were knitting together in some form or other and that she was recovering with the resilience of the young. It also became evident that she would grow to a tremendous size, as she outgrew one box and then another and the grey hair began to feather from her huge front paws. In the spring she was outside almost all of the time and followed the man everywhere; and when she came inside during the following months, she had grown so large that she would no longer fit into her accustomed place behind the stove and was forced to lie beside it. She was never given a name but was referred to in Gaelic as *cù mòr glas*, the big grey dog.

By the time she came into her first heat, she had grown to a tremendous height, and although her signs and her odour attracted many panting and highly aroused suitors, none was big enough to mount her and the frenzy of their disappointment and the longing of her unfulfilment were more than the man could stand. He went, so the story goes, to a place where he knew there was a big dog. A dog not as big as she was, but still a big dog, and he brought him home with him. And at the proper time he took the *cù mòr glas* and the big dog down to the sea where he knew there was a hollow in the rock which appeared only at low tide. He took some sacking to provide footing for the male dog and he placed the *cù mòr glas* in the hollow of the rock and knelt beside her and steadied her with his left arm under her throat and helped position the male dog above her and guided his blood-engorged penis. He was a man used to working with the breeding of animals, with the guiding of rams and bulls and stallions and often with the funky smell of animal semen heavy on his large and gentle hands.

The winter that followed was a cold one and ice formed on the sea and frequent squalls and blizzards obliterated the offshore islands and caused the people to stay near their fires much of the time, mending clothes and nets and harness and waiting for the change in season. The *cù mòr glas* grew heavier and even more large until there was hardly room for her around the stove or even under the table. And then one morning, when it seemed that spring was about to break, she was gone.

The man and even his family, who had become more involved than they cared to admit, waited for her but she did not come. And as the frenzy of spring wore on, they busied themselves with readying their land and their fishing gear and all of the things that so desperately required their attention. And then they were into summer and fall and winter and another spring which saw the birth of the man and his wife's twelfth child. And then it was summer again.

That summer the man and two of his teenaged sons were pulling their herring nets about two miles offshore when the wind began to blow off the land and the water began to roughen. They became afraid that they could not make it safely back to shore, so they pulled in behind one of the offshore islands, knowing that they would be sheltered there and planning to outwait the storm. As the prow of their boat approached the gravelly shore they heard a sound above them, and looking up they saw the *cù mòr glas* silhouetted on the brow of the hill which was the small island's highest point.

"*M'eudal cù mòr glas*" shouted the man in his happiness—*m'eudal* meaning something like dear or darling; and as he shouted, he jumped over the side of his boat into the waist-deep water, struggling for footing on the rolling gravel as he waded eagerly and awkwardly towards her and the shore. At the same time, the *cù mòr glas* came hurtling down towards him in a shower of small rocks dislodged by her feet; and just as he was emerging from the water, she met him as she used to, rearing up on her hind legs and placing her huge front paws on his shoulders while extending her eager tongue.

The weight and speed of her momentum met him as he tried to hold his balance on the sloping angle and the water rolling gravel beneath his feet, and he staggered backwards and lost his footing and fell beneath her force. And in that instant again, as the story goes, there appeared over the brow of the hill six more huge grey dogs hurtling down towards the gravelled strand. They had never seen him before; and seeing him stretched prone beneath their mother, they misunderstood, like so many armies, the intention of their leader.

They fell upon him in a fury, slashing his face and tearing aside his lower jaw and ripping out his throat, crazed with blood-lust or duty or perhaps starvation. The *cù mòr glas* turned on them in her own savagery, slashing and snarling and, it seemed, crazed by their mistake; driving them bloodied and yelping before her, back over the brow of the hill where they vanished from sight but could still be heard screaming in the distance. It all took perhaps little more than a minute.

The man's two sons, who were still in the boat and had witnessed it all, ran sobbing through the salt water to where their mauled and mangled father lay; but there was little they could do other than hold his warm and bloodied hands for a few brief moments. Although his eyes "lived" for a small fraction of time, he could not speak to them because his face and throat had been torn away, and of course there was nothing they could do except to hold and be held tightly until that too slipped away and his eyes glazed over and they could no longer feel his hands holding theirs. The storm increased and they could not get home and so they were forced to spend the night huddled beside their father's body. They were afraid to try to carry the body to the rocking boat because he was so heavy and they were afraid that they might lose even what little of him remained and they were afraid also, huddled on the rocks, that the dogs might return. But they did not return at all and there was no sound from them, no sound at all, only the moaning of the wind and the washing of the water on the rocks.

In the morning they debated whether they should try to take his body with them or whether they should leave it and return in the company of older and wiser men. But they were afraid to leave it unattended and felt that the time needed to cover it with protective rocks would be better spent in trying to get across to their home shore. For a while they debated as to whether one should go in the boat and the other remain on the island, but each was afraid to be alone and so in the end they managed to drag and carry and almost float him towards the bobbing boat. They lay him face-down and covered him with what clothes there were and set off across the still-rolling sea. Those who waited on the shore missed the large presence of the man within the boat and some of them waded into the water and others rowed out in skiffs, attempting to hear the tearful messages called out across the rolling waves.

The *cù mòr glas* and her six young dogs were never seen again, or perhaps I should say they were never seen again in the same way. After some weeks, a group of men circled the island tentatively in their boats but they saw no sign. They went again and then again but found nothing. A year later, and grown much braver, they beached their boats and walked the island carefully, looking into the small sea caves and the hollows at the base of the wind-ripped trees, thinking perhaps that if they did not find the dogs, they might at least find their whitened bones; but again they discovered nothing.

The *cù mòr glas*, though, was supposed to be sighted here and there for a number of years. Seen on a hill in one region or silhouetted on a ridge in another or loping across the valleys or glens in the early morning or the shadowy evening. Always in the area of the half perceived. For a while she became rather like the Loch Ness Monster or the Sasquatch on a smaller scale. Seen but not recorded. Seen when there were no cameras. Seen but never taken.

The mystery of where she went became entangled with the mystery of whence she came. There was increased speculation about the handmade box in which she had been found and much theorizing as to the individual or individuals who might have left it. People went to look for the box but could not find it. It was felt she might have been part of a *buidseachd* or evil spell cast on the man by some mysterious enemy. But no one could go much farther than that. All of his caring for her was recounted over and over again and nobody missed any of the ironies.

What seemed literally known was that she had crossed the winter ice to have her pups and had been unable to get back. No one could remember ever seeing her swim; and in the early months at least, she could not have taken her young pups with her.

The large and gentle man with the smell of animal semen often heavy on his hands was my great-great-great-grandfather, and it may be argued that he died because he was too good at breeding animals or that he cared too much about their fulfillment and well-being. He was no longer there for his own child of the spring who, in turn, became my great-great-grandfather, and he was perhaps too much there in the memory of his older sons who saw him fall beneath the ambiguous force of the *cù mòr glas*. The youngest boy in the boat was haunted and tormented by the awfulness of what he had seen. He would wake at night screaming that he had seen the *cù mòr glas a'bhàis*, the big grey dog of death, and his screams filled the house and the ears and minds of the listeners, bringing home again and again the consequences of their loss. One morning, after a night in which he saw the *cù mòr glas a'bhàis* so vividly that his sheets were drenched with sweat, he walked to the high cliff which faced the island and there he cut his throat with a fish knife and fell into the sea.

The other brother lived to be forty, but, again so the story goes, he found himself in a Glasgow pub one night, perhaps looking for answers, deep and sodden with the whiskey which had become his anaesthetic. In the half darkness he saw a large, grey-haired man sitting by himself against the wall and mumbled something to him. Some say he saw the *cù mòr glas a'bhàis* or uttered the name. And perhaps the man heard the phrase through ears equally affected by drink and felt he was being called a dog or a son of a bitch or something of that nature. They rose to meet one another and struggled outside into the cobble-stoned passageway behind the pub where, most improbably, there were supposed to be six other large, grey-haired men who beat him to death on the cobblestones, smashing his bloodied head into the stone again and again before vanishing and leaving him to die with his face turned to the sky. The *cù mòr glas a'bhàis* had come again, said his family, as they tried to piece the tale together.

This is how the *cù mòr glas a'bhàis* came into our lives, and it is obvious that all of this happened a long, long time ago. Yet with succeeding generations it seemed the spectre had somehow come to stay and that it had become *ours*—not in the manner of an unwanted skeleton in the closet from a family's ancient past but more in the manner of something close to a genetic possibility. In the deaths of each generation, the grey dog was seen by some—by women who were to die in childbirth; by soldiers who went forth to the many wars but did not return; by those who went forth to feuds or dangerous love affairs; by those who answered mysterious midnight messages; by those who swerved on the highway to avoid the real or imagined grey dog and ended in masses of crumpled steel. And by one professional athlete who, in addition to his ritualized athletic superstitions, carried another fear or belief as well. Many of the man's descendants moved like careful hemophiliacs, fearing that they carried unwanted possibilities deep within them. And others, while they laughed, were like members of families in which there is a recurrence over the generations of repeated cancer or the diabetes which comes to those beyond middle age. The feeling of those who may say little to others but who may say often and quietly to themselves, "It has not happened to me," while adding always the cautionary "*yet*."

I am thinking all of this now as the October rain falls on the city of Toronto and the pleasant, white-clad nurses pad confidently in and out of my father's room. He lies quietly amidst the whiteness, his head and shoulders elevated so that he is in that hospital position of being neither quite prone nor yet sitting. His hair is white upon his pillow and he breathes softly and sometimes unevenly, although it is difficult ever to be sure.

My five grey-haired brothers and I take turns beside his bedside, holding his heavy hands in ours and feeling their response, hoping ambiguously that he will speak to us, although we know that it may tire him. And trying to read his life and ours into his eyes when they are open. He has been with us for a long time, well into our middle age. Unlike those boys in that boat of so long ago, we did not see him taken from us in our youth. And unlike their youngest brother who, in turn, became our great-great-grandfather, we did not grow into a world in which there was no father's touch. We have been lucky to have this large and gentle man so deep into our lives.

No one in this hospital has mentioned the *cù mòr glas a'bhàis*. Yet as my mother said ten years ago, before slipping into her own death as quietly as a grownup child who leaves or enters her parents' house in the early hours, "It is hard to *not* know what you do know."

Even those who are most skeptical, like my oldest brother who has driven here from Montreal, betray themselves by their nervous actions. "I avoided the Greyhound bus stations in both Montreal and Toronto," he smiled upon his arrival, and then added, "Just in case."

He did not realize how ill our father was and has smiled little since then. I watch him turning the diamond ring upon his finger, knowing that he hopes he will not hear the Gaelic he knows too well. Not having the luxury, as he once said, of some who live in Montreal and are able to pretend they do not understand the "other" language. You cannot *not* know what you do know.

Sitting here, taking turns holding the hands of the man who gave us life, we are afraid for him and for ourselves. We are afraid of what he may see and we are afraid to hear the phrase born of the vision. We are aware that it may become confused with what the doctors call "the will to live" and we are aware that some beliefs are what others would dismiss as "garbage." We are aware that there are men who believe the earth is flat and that the birds bring forth the sun.

Bound here in our own peculiar mortality, we do not wish to see or see others see that which signifies life's demise. We do not want to hear the voice of our father, as did those other sons, calling down his own particular death upon him.

We would shut our eyes and plug our ears, even as we know such actions to be of no avail. Open still and fearful to the grey hair rising on our necks if and when we hear the scrabble of the paws and the scratching at the door.

—1985

Raymond Carver
1938–1988

Born in Clatskanie, Oregon, to working-poor parents, Raymond Carver was raised in an abusive and unstable alcoholic home. By the age of 20, he was married with two children, working menial jobs, and drinking heavily. Struggling to pay the family's bills, he began writing poetry and short stories to earn extra money. Carver's experiences provided him with an intimate understanding of the hard-fought lives of America's struggling classes and he wrote about them with honesty and respect. "They're my people," said Carver. "I could never write down to them."

1977 marked the beginning of what Carver called his "second life." First, his collection of short stories *Will You Please Be Quiet, Please?* (1976) was nominated for a National Book Award; then he quit drinking and remained sober for the rest of his life. His subsequent collection *What We Talk about When We Talk about Love* (1981), which was an enormous success, moved critic Michael Wood to praise Carver's work for its "edges and silences" in which "a good deal of the unsayable gets said." Even greater success followed with the publication of *Cathedral* (1983), a collection that broke from the minimalism of Carver's previous work in favour of a new expansiveness.

Carver's next and final collection, *Where I'm Calling From* (1988), appeared only months before his death. A heavy smoker who once referred to himself as "a cigarette with a body attached to it," Carver succumbed to lung cancer at the age of 50. His grave lies in Port Angeles, Washington, and overlooks the Strait of Juan de Fuca.

Cathedral

This blind man, an old friend of my wife's, he was on his way to spend the night. His wife had died. So he was visiting the dead wife's relatives in Connecticut. He called my wife from his in-laws'. Arrangements were made. He would come by train, a five-hour trip, and my wife would meet him at the station. She hadn't seen him since she worked for him one summer in Seattle ten years ago. But she and the blind man had kept in touch. They made tapes and mailed them back and forth. I wasn't enthusiastic about his visit. He was no one I knew. And his being blind bothered me. My idea of blindness came from the movies. In the movies, the blind moved slowly and never laughed. Sometimes they were led by seeing-eye dogs. A blind man in my house was not something I looked forward to.

That summer in Seattle she had needed a job. She didn't have any money. The man she was going to marry at the end of the summer was in officers' training school. He didn't have any money, either. But she was in love with the guy, and he was in love with her, etc. She'd seen something in the paper: HELP WANTED—*Reading to Blind Man*, and a telephone number. She phoned and went over, was hired on the spot. She'd worked with this blind man all summer. She read stuff to him, case studies, reports, that sort of thing. She helped him organize his little office in the county social-service department. They'd become good friends, my wife and the blind man. How do I know these things? She told me. And she told me something else. On her last day in the office, the blind man asked if he could touch her face. She agreed to this. She told me he touched his fingers to every part of her face, her nose—even her neck! She never forgot it. She even tried to write a poem about it. She was always trying to write a poem. She wrote a poem or two every year, usually after something really important had happened to her.

When we first started going out together, she showed me the poem. In the poem, she recalled his fingers and the way they had moved around over her face. In the poem, she talked about what she had felt at the time, about what went through her mind when the blind man touched her nose and lips. I can remember I didn't think much of the poem. Of course, I didn't tell her that. Maybe I just don't understand poetry. I admit it's not the first thing I reach for when I pick up something to read.

Anyway, this man who'd first enjoyed her favours, the officer-to-be, he'd been her childhood sweetheart. So okay. I'm saying that at the end of the summer she let the blind man run his hands over her face, said goodbye to him, married her childhood etc., who was now a commissioned officer, and she moved away from Seattle. But they'd kept in touch, she and the blind man. She made the first contact after a year or so. She called him up one night from an Air Force base in Alabama. She wanted to talk. They talked. He asked her to send him a tape and tell him about her life. She did this. She sent the tape. On the tape, she told the blind man about her husband and about their life together in the military. She told the blind man she loved her husband but she didn't like it where they lived and she didn't like it that he was a part of the military-industrial thing. She told the blind man she'd written a poem about what it was like to be an Air Force officer's wife. The poem wasn't finished yet. She was still writing it. The blind man made a tape. He sent her the tape. She made a tape. This went on for years. My wife's officer was posted to one base and then another. She sent tapes from Moody AFB, McGuire, McConnell, and finally Travis, near Sacramento, where one night she got to feeling lonely and cut off from people she kept losing in that moving-around life. She got to feeling she couldn't go it another step. She went in and swallowed all the pills and capsules in the medicine chest and washed them down with a bottle of gin. Then she got into a hot bath and passed out.

But instead of dying, she got sick. She threw up. Her officer—why should he have a name? he was the childhood sweetheart, and what more does he want?—came home from somewhere, found her, and called the ambulance. In time, she put it all on a tape and sent the tape to the blind man. Over the years, she put all kinds of stuff on tapes and sent the tapes off lickety-split. Next to writing a poem every year, I think it was her chief means of recreation. On one tape, she told the blind man she'd decided to live away from her officer for a time. On another tape, she told him about her divorce. She and I began going out, and of course she told her blind man about it. She told him every-thing, or so it seemed to me. Once she asked me if I'd like to hear the latest tape from the blind man. This was a year ago. I was on the tape, she said. So I said okay, I'd listen to it. I got us drinks and we settled down in the living room. We made ready to listen. First she inserted the tape into the player and adjusted a couple of dials. Then she pushed a lever. The tape squeaked and someone began to talk in this loud voice. She lowered the volume. After a few minutes of harmless chitchat, I heard my own name in the mouth of this stranger, this blind man I didn't even know! And then this: "From all you've said about him, I can only conclude—" But we were interrupted, a knock at the door, something, and we didn't ever get back to the tape. Maybe it was just as well. I'd heard all I wanted to.

Now this same blind man was coming to sleep in my house.

"Maybe I could take him bowling," I said to my wife. She was at the draining board doing scalloped potatoes. She put down the knife she was us-ing and turned around.

"If you love me," she said, "you can do this for me. If you don't love me, okay. But if you had a friend, any friend, and the friend came to visit, I'd make him feel comfortable." She wiped her hands with the dish towel.

"I don't have any blind friends," I said.

"You don't have *any* friends," she said. "Period. Besides," she said, "god-damn it, his wife's just died! Don't you understand that? The man's lost his wife!"

I didn't answer. She'd told me a little about the blind man's wife. Her name was Beulah. Beulah! That's a name for a coloured woman.

"Was his wife a Negro?" I asked.

"Are you crazy?" my wife said. "Have you just flipped or something?" She picked up a potato. I saw it hit the floor, then roll under the stove. "What's wrong with you?" she said. "Are you drunk?"

"I'm just asking," I said.

Right then my wife filled me in with more detail than I cared to know. I made a drink and sat at the kitchen table to listen. Pieces of the story began to fall into place.

Beulah had gone to work for the blind man the summer after my wife had stopped working for him. Pretty soon Beulah and the blind man had themselves a church wedding. It was a little wedding—who'd want to go to such a wedding in the first place?—just the two of them, plus the minister and the minister's wife. But it was a church wedding just the same. It was what Beulah had wanted, he'd said. But even then Beulah must have been carrying the cancer in her glands. After they had been inseparable for eight years—my wife's word, *inseparable*—Beulah's health went into a rapid decline. She died in a Seattle hospital room, the blind man sitting beside the bed and holding on to her hand. They'd married, lived and worked together, slept together—had sex, sure—and then the blind man had to bury her. All this without his having ever seen what the goddamned woman looked like. It was beyond my under-standing. Hearing this, I felt sorry for the blind man for a little bit. And then I found myself thinking what a pitiful life this woman must have led. Imagine a woman who could never see herself as she was seen in the eyes of her loved one. A woman who could go on day after day and never receive the smallest compliment from her beloved. A woman whose husband could never read the expression on her face, be it misery or something better. Someone who could wear makeup or not—what difference to him? She could, if she wanted, wear green eye-shadow around one eye, a straight pin in her nostril, yellow slacks and purple shoes, no matter. And then to slip off into death, the blind man's hand on her hand, his blind eyes streaming tears—I'm imagining now—her last thought maybe this: that he never even knew what she looked like, and she on an express to the grave. Robert was left with a small insurance policy and half of a twenty-peso Mexican coin. The other half of the coin went into the box with her. Pathetic.

So when the time rolled around, my wife went to the depot to pick him up. With nothing to do but wait—sure, I blamed him for that—I was having a drink and watching the TV when I heard the car pull into the drive. I got up from the sofa with my drink and went to the window to have a look.

I saw my wife laughing as she parked the car. I saw her get out of the car and shut the door. She was still wearing a smile. Just amazing. She went around to the other side to where the blind man was already starting to get out. This blind man, feature this, he was wearing a full beard! A beard on a blind man! Too much, I say. The blind man reached into the back seat and dragged out a suitcase. My wife took his arm, shut the car door, and, talking all the way, moved him down the drive and then up the steps to the front porch. I turned off the TV. I finished my drink, rinsed the glass, dried my hands. Then I went to the door.

My wife said, "I want you to meet Robert. Robert, this is my husband. I've told you all about him." She was beaming. She had this blind man by his coat sleeve.

The blind man let go of his suitcase and up came his hand.

I took it. He squeezed hard, held my hand, and then he let it go.

"I feel like we've already met," he boomed.

"Likewise," I said. I didn't know what else to say. Then I said, "Welcome. I've heard a lot about you." We began to move then, a little group, from the porch into the living room, my wife guiding him by the arm. The blind man was carrying his suitcase in his other hand. My wife said things like, "To your left here, Robert. That's right. Now watch it, there's a chair. That's it. Sit down right here. This is the sofa. We just bought this sofa two weeks ago."

I started to say something about the old sofa. I'd liked that old sofa. But I didn't say anything. Then I wanted to say something else, small-talk, about the scenic ride along the Hudson. How going *to* New York, you should sit on the right-hand side of the train, and coming *from* New York, the left-hand side.

"Did you have a good train ride?" I said. "Which side of the train did you sit on, by the way?"

"What a question, which side!" my wife said. "What's it matter which side?" she said.

"I just asked," I said.

"Right side," the blind man said. "I hadn't been on a train in nearly forty years. Not since I was a kid. With my folks. That's been a long time. I'd nearly forgotten the sensation. I have winter in my beard now," he said. "So I've been told, anyway. Do I look distinguished, my dear?" the blind man said to my wife.

"You look distinguished, Robert," she said. "Robert," she said. "Robert, it's just so good to see you."

My wife finally took her eyes off the blind man and looked at me. I had the feeling she didn't like what she saw. I shrugged.

I've never met, or personally known, anyone who was blind. This blind man was late forties, a heavy-set, balding man with stooped shoulders, as if he carried a great weight there. He wore brown slacks, brown shoes, a light-brown shirt, a tie, a sports coat. Spiffy. He also had this full beard. But he didn't use a cane and he didn't wear dark glasses. I'd always thought dark glasses were a must for the blind. Fact was, I wished he had a pair. At first glance, his eyes looked like anyone else's eyes. But if you looked close, there was something different about them. Too much white in the iris, for one thing, and the pupils seemed to move around in the sockets without his knowing it or being able to stop it. Creepy. As I stared at his face, I saw the left pupil turn in toward his nose while the other made an effort to keep in one place. But it was only an effort, for that eye was on the roam without his knowing it or wanting it to be.

I said, "Let me get you a drink. What's your pleasure? We have a little of everything. It's one of our pastimes."

"Bub, I'm a Scotch man myself," he said fast enough in this big voice.

"Right," I said. Bub! "Sure you are. I knew it."

He let his fingers touch his suitcase, which was sitting alongside the sofa. He was taking his bearings. I didn't blame him for that.

"I'll move that up to your room," my wife said.

"No, that's fine," the blind man said loudly. "It can go up when I go up."

"A little water with the Scotch?" I said.

"Very little," he said.

"I knew it," I said.

He said, "Just a tad. The Irish actor, Barry Fitzgerald? I'm like that fellow. When I drink water, Fitzgerald said, I drink water. When I drink whiskey, I drink whiskey." My wife laughed. The blind man brought his hand up under his beard. He lifted his beard slowly and let it drop.

I did the drinks, three big glasses of Scotch with a splash of water in each. Then we made ourselves comfortable and talked about Robert's travels. First the long flight from the West Coast to Connecticut, we covered that. Then from Connecticut up here by train. We had another drink concerning that leg of the trip.

I remembered having read somewhere that the blind didn't smoke because, as speculation had it, they couldn't see the smoke they exhaled. I thought I knew that much and that much only about blind people. But this blind man smoked his cigarette down to the nubbin and then lit another one. This blind man filled his ashtray and my wife emptied it.

When we sat down at the table for dinner, we had another drink. My wife heaped Robert's plate with cube steak, scalloped potatoes, green beans. I buttered him up two slices of bread. I said, "Here's bread and butter for you." I swallowed some of my drink. "Now let us pray," I said, and the blind man lowered his head. My wife looked at me, her mouth agape. "Pray the phone won't ring and the food doesn't get cold," I said.

We dug in. We ate everything there was to eat on the table. We ate like there was no tomorrow. We didn't talk. We ate. We scarfed. We grazed that table. We were into serious eating. The blind man had right away located his foods, he knew just where everything was on his plate. I watched with admiration as he used his knife and fork on the meat. He'd cut two pieces of meat, fork the meat into his mouth, and then go all out for the scalloped potatoes, the beans next, and then he'd tear off a hunk of buttered bread and eat that.

He'd follow this up with a big drink of milk. It didn't seem to bother him to use his fingers once in a while, either.

We finished everything, including half a strawberry pie. For a few moments, we sat as if stunned. Sweat beaded on our faces. Finally, we got up from the table and left the dirty plates. We didn't look back. We took ourselves into the living room and sank into our places again. Robert and my wife sat on the sofa. I took the big chair. We had us two or three more drinks while they talked about the major things that had come to pass for them in the past ten years. For the most part, I just listened. Now and then I joined in. I didn't want him to think I'd left the room, and I didn't want her to think I was feeling left out. They talked of things that had happened to them—to them!—these past ten years. I waited in vain to hear my name on my wife's sweet lips: "And then my dear husband came into my life"—something like that. But I heard nothing of the sort. More talk of Robert. Robert had done a little of everything, it seemed, a regular blind jack-of-all-trades. But most recently he and his wife had had an Amway[1] distributorship, from which, I gathered, they'd earned their living, such as it was. The blind man was also a ham radio operator. He talked in his loud voice about conversations he'd had with fellow operators in Guam, in the Philippines, in Alaska, and even in Tahiti. He said he'd have a lot of friends there if he ever wanted to go visit those places. From time to time, he'd turn his blind face toward me, put his hand under his beard, ask me something. How long had I been in my present position? (Three years.) Did I like my work? (I didn't.) Was I going to stay with it? (What were the options?) Finally, when I thought he was beginning to run down, I got up and turned on the TV.

My wife looked at me with irritation. She was heading toward a boil. Then she looked at the blind man and said, "Robert, do you have a TV?"

The blind man said, "My dear, I have two TVs. I have a colour set and a black-and-white thing, an old relic. It's funny, but if I turn the TV on, and I'm always turning it on, I turn on the colour set. It's funny, don't you think?"

I didn't know what to say to that. I had absolutely nothing to say to that. No opinion. So I watched the news program and tried to listen to what the announcer was saying.

"This is a colour TV," the blind man said. "Don't ask me how, but I can tell."

"We traded up a while ago." I said.

The blind man had another taste of his drink. He lifted his beard, sniffed it, and let it fall. He leaned forward on the sofa. He positioned his ashtray on the coffee table, then put the lighter to his cigarette. He leaned back on the sofa and crossed his legs at the ankles.

---

1   *Amway* Large pyramid sales company.

My wife covered her mouth, and then she yawned. She stretched. She said, "I think I'll go upstairs and put on my robe. I think I'll change into something else. Robert, you make yourself comfortable," she said.

"I'm comfortable," the blind man said.

"I want you to feel comfortable in this house," she said.

"I am comfortable," the blind man said.

After she'd left the room, he and I listened to the weather report and then to the sports roundup. By that time, she'd been gone so long I didn't know if she was going to come back. I thought she might have gone to bed. I wished she'd come back downstairs. I didn't want to be left alone with a blind man. I asked him if he wanted to smoke some dope with me. I said I'd just rolled a number. I hadn't, but I planned to do so in about two shakes.

"I'll try some with you," he said.

"Damn right," I said. "That's the stuff."

I got our drinks and sat down on the sofa with him. Then I rolled us two fat numbers. I lit one and passed it. I brought it to his fingers. He took it and inhaled.

"Hold it as long as you can," I said. I could tell he didn't know the first thing.

My wife came back downstairs wearing her pink robe and her pink slippers.

"What do I smell?" she said.

"We thought we'd have us some cannabis," I said.

My wife gave me a savage look. Then she looked at the blind man and said, "Robert, I didn't know you smoked."

He said, "I do now, my dear. There's a first time for everything. But I don't feel anything yet."

"This stuff is pretty mellow," I said. "This stuff is mild. It's dope you can reason with," I said. "It doesn't mess you up."

"Not much it doesn't, bub," he said, and laughed.

My wife sat on the sofa between the blind man and me. I passed her the number. She took it and toked and then passed it back to me. "Which way is this going?" she said. Then she said, "I shouldn't be smoking this. I can hardly keep my eyes open as it is. That dinner did me in. I shouldn't have eaten so much."

"It was the strawberry pie," the blind man said. "That's what did it," he said, and he laughed his big laugh. Then he shook his head.

"There's more strawberry pie," I said.

"Do you want some more, Robert?" my wife said.

"Maybe in a little while," he said.

We gave our attention to the TV. My wife yawned again. She said, "Your bed is made up when you feel like going to bed, Robert. I know you must have had a long day. When you're ready to go to bed, say so." She pulled his arm. "Robert?"

He came to and said, "I've had a real nice time. This beats tapes, doesn't it?"

I said, "Coming at you," and I put the number between his fingers. He inhaled, held the smoke, and then let it go. It was like he'd been doing it since he was nine years old.

"Thanks, bub," he said. "But I think this is all for me. I think I'm beginning to feel it," he said. He held the burning roach out for my wife.

"Same here," she said. "Ditto. Me, too." She took the roach and passed it to me. "I may just sit here for a while between you two guys with my eyes closed. But don't let me bother you, okay? Either one of you. If it bothers you, say so. Otherwise, I may just sit here with my eyes closed until you're ready to go to bed," she said. "Your bed's made up, Robert, when you're ready. It's right next to our room at the top of the stairs. We'll show you up when you're ready. You wake me up now, you guys, if I fall asleep." She said that and then she closed her eyes and went to sleep.

The news program ended. I got up and changed the channel. I sat back down on the sofa. I wished my wife hadn't pooped out. Her head lay across the back of the sofa, her mouth open. She'd turned so that her robe had slipped away from her legs, exposing a juicy thigh. I reached to draw her robe back over her, and it was then that I glanced at the blind man. What the hell! I flipped the robe open again.

"You say when you want some strawberry pie," I said.

"I will," he said.

I said, "Are you tired? Do you want me to take you up to your bed? Are you ready to hit the hay?"

"Not yet," he said. "No, I'll stay up with you, bub. If that's all right. I'll stay up until you're ready to turn in. We haven't had a chance to talk. Know what I mean? I feel like me and her monopolized the evening." He lifted his beard and he let it fall. He picked up his cigarettes and lighter.

"That's all right," I said. Then I said, "I'm glad for the company."

And I guess I was. Every night I smoked dope and stayed up as long as I could before I fell asleep. My wife and I hardly ever went to bed at the same time. When I did go to sleep, I had these dreams. Sometimes I'd wake up from one of them, my heart going crazy.

Something about the church and the Middle Ages was on the TV. Not your run-of-the-mill TV fare. I wanted to watch something else. I turned to the other channels. But there was nothing on them, either. So I turned back to the first channel and apologized.

"Bub, it's all right," the blind man said. "It's fine with me. Whatever you want to watch is okay. I'm always learning something. Learning never ends. It won't hurt me to learn something tonight. I got ears," he said.

We didn't say anything for a time. He was leaning forward with his head turned at me, his right ear aimed in the direction of the set. Very disconcerting. Now and then his eyelids dropped and then they snapped open again. Now and then he put his fingers into his beard and tugged, like he was thinking about something he was hearing on the television.

On the screen, a group of men wearing cowls was being set upon and tormented by men dressed in skeleton costumes and men dressed as devils. The men dressed as devils wore devil masks, horns, and long tails. This pageant was part of a procession. The Englishman who was narrating the thing said it took place in Spain once a year. I tried to explain to the blind man what was happening.

"Skeletons," he said. "I know about skeletons," he said and he nodded.

The TV showed this one cathedral. Then there was a long, slow look at another one. Finally, the picture switched to the famous one in Paris, with its flying buttresses and its spires reaching up to the clouds. The camera pulled away to show the whole of the cathedral rising above the skyline.

There were times when the Englishman who was telling the thing would shut up, would simply let the camera move around over the cathedrals. Or else the camera would tour the countryside, men in fields walking behind oxen. I waited as long as I could. Then I felt I had to say something. I said, "They're showing the outside of this cathedral now. Gargoyles. Little statues carved to look like monsters. Now I guess they're in Italy. Yeah, they're in Italy. There's paintings on the walls of this one church."

"Are those fresco paintings, bub?" he asked, and he sipped from his drink.

I reached for my glass. But it was empty. I tried to remember what I could remember. "You're asking me are those frescoes?" I said. "That's a good question. I don't know."

The camera moved to a cathedral outside Lisbon. The differences in the Portuguese cathedral compared with the French and Italian were not that great. But they were there. Mostly the interior stuff. Then something occurred to me, and I said, "Something has occurred to me. Do you have any idea what a cathedral is? What they look like, that is? Do you follow me? If somebody says cathedral to you, do you have any notion what they're talking about? Do you know the difference between that and a Baptist church, say?"

He let the smoke dribble from his mouth. "I know they took hundreds of workers fifty or a hundred years to build," he said. "I just heard the man say that, of course. I know generations of the same families worked on a cathedral. I heard him say that, too. The men who began their life's work on them, they never lived to see the completion of their work. In that wise, bub, they're no different from the rest of us, right?" He laughed. Then his eyelids drooped again. His head nodded. He seemed to be snoozing. Maybe he was imagining himself in Portugal. The TV was showing another cathedral now. This one was in Germany. The Englishman's voice droned on. "Cathedrals," the blind man said. He sat up and rolled his head back and forth. "If you want the truth, bub, that's about all I know. What I just said. What I heard him say. But maybe you could describe one to me? I wish you'd do it. I'd like that. If you want to know, I really don't have a good idea."

I stared hard at the shot of the cathedral on the TV. How could I even begin to describe it? But say my life depended on it. Say my life was being threatened by an insane guy who said I had to do it or else.

I stared some more at the cathedral before the picture flipped off into the countryside. There was no use. I turned to the blind man and said, "To begin with, they're very tall." I was looking around the room for clues. "They reach way up. Up and up. Toward the sky. They're so big, some of them, they have to have these supports. To help hold them up, so to speak. These supports are called buttresses. They remind me of viaducts, for some reason. But maybe you don't know viaducts, either? Sometimes the cathedrals have devils and such carved into the front. Sometimes lords and ladies. Don't ask me why this is," I said.

He was nodding. The whole upper part of his body seemed to be moving back and forth.

"I'm not doing so good, am I?" I said.

He stopped nodding and leaned forward on the edge of the sofa. As he listened to me, he was running his fingers through his beard. I wasn't getting through to him, I could see that. But he waited for me to go on just the same. He nodded, like he was trying to encourage me. I tried to think what else to say. "They're really big," I said. "They're massive. They're built of stone. Marble, too, sometimes. In those olden days, when they built cathedrals, men wanted to be close to God. In those olden days, God was an important part of everyone's life. You could tell this from their cathedral-building. I'm sorry," I said, "but it looks like that's the best I can do for you. I'm just no good at it."

"That's all right, bub," the blind man said. "Hey, listen, I hope you don't mind my asking you. Can I ask you something? Let me ask you a simple question, yes or no. I'm just curious and there's no offence. You're my host. But let me ask if you are in any way religious? You don't mind my asking?"

I shook my head. He couldn't see that, though. A wink is the same as a nod to a blind man. "I guess I don't believe in it. In anything. Sometimes it's hard. You know what I'm saying?"

"Sure, I do," he said.

"Right," I said.

The Englishman was still holding forth. My wife sighed in her sleep. She drew a long breath and went on with her sleeping.

"You'll have to forgive me," I said. "But I can't tell you what a cathedral looks like. It just isn't in me to do it. I can't do any more than I've done."

The blind man sat very still, his head down, as he listened to me.

I said, "The truth is, cathedrals don't mean anything special to me. Nothing. Cathedrals. They're something to look at on late-night TV. That's all they are."

It was then that the blind man cleared his throat. He brought something up. He took a handkerchief from his back pocket. Then he said, "I get it, bub. It's okay. It happens. Don't worry about it," he said. "Hey, listen to me. Will you do me a favour? I got an idea. Why don't you find us some heavy paper? And a pen. We'll do something. We'll draw one together. Get us a pen and some heavy paper. Go on, bub, get the stuff," he said.

So I went upstairs. My legs felt like they didn't have any strength in them. They felt like they did after I'd done some running. In my wife's room, I looked around. I found some ballpoints in a little basket on her table. And then I tried to think where to look for the kind of paper he was talking about.

Downstairs, in the kitchen, I found a shopping bag with onion skins at the bottom of the bag. I emptied the bag and shook it. I brought it into the living room and sat down with it near his legs. I moved some things, smoothed the wrinkles from the bag, spread it out on the coffee table.

The blind man got down from the sofa and sat next to me on the carpet.

He ran his fingers over the paper. He went up and down the sides of the paper. The edges, even the edges. He fingered the corners.

"All right," he said. "All right, let's do her."

He found my hand, the hand with the pen. He closed his hand over my hand. "Go ahead, bub, draw," he said. "Draw. You'll see. I'll follow along with you. It'll be okay. Just begin now like I'm telling you. You'll see. Draw," the blind man said.

So I began. First I drew a box that looked like a house. It could have been the house I lived in. Then I put a roof on it. At either end of the roof, I drew spires. Crazy.

"Swell," he said. "Terrific. You're doing fine," he said. "Never thought anything like this could happen in your lifetime, did you, bub? Well, it's a strange life, we all know that. Go on now. Keep it up."

I put in windows with arches. I drew flying buttresses. I hung great doors. I couldn't stop. The TV station went off the air. I put down the pen and closed and opened my fingers. The blind man felt around over the paper. He moved the tips of his fingers over the paper, all over what I had drawn, and he nodded.

"Doing fine," the blind man said.

I took up the pen again, and he found my hand. I kept at it. I'm no artist. But I kept drawing just the same.

My wife opened up her eyes and gazed at us. She sat up on the sofa, her robe hanging open. She said, "What are you doing? Tell me, I want to know."

I didn't answer her.

The blind man said, "We're drawing a cathedral. Me and him are working on it. Press hard," he said to me. "That's right. That's good," he said. "Sure. You got it, bub. I can tell. You didn't think you could. But you can, can't you? You're cooking with gas now. You know what I'm saying? We're going to really have us something here in a minute. How's the old arm?" he said. "Put some people in there now. What's a cathedral without people?"

My wife said, "What's going on? Robert, what are you doing? What's going on?"

"It's all right," he said to her. "Close your eyes now," the blind man said to me.

I did it. I closed them just like he said.

"Are they closed?" he said. "Don't fudge."

"They're closed," I said.

"Keep them that way," he said. He said, "Don't stop now. Draw."

So we kept on with it. His fingers rode my fingers as my hand went over the paper. It was like nothing else in my life up to now.

Then he said, "I think that's it. I think you got it," he said. "Take a look. What do you think?"

But I had my eyes closed. I thought I'd keep them that way for a little longer. I thought it was something I ought to do.

"Well?" he said. "Are you looking?"

My eyes were still closed. I was in my house. I knew that. But I didn't feel like I was inside anything.

"It's really something," I said.

—1983

Margaret Atwood
b. 1939

Aptly described as "a nationalist who rankles nationalists, a feminist who rankles feminists," and "a political satirist who resists political solutions," Margaret Atwood is a writer who defies traditional categories. Her internationally renowned novels, short stories, and poems span and splice together a multitude of genres and have established her as a germinal figure in Canadian literature.

Atwood was born in Ottawa but spent much of her childhood in the Canadian bush. Educated at the University of Toronto and Radcliffe College, Atwood is a self-consciously Canadian writer, working in a tradition that she characterized in *Survival* (1972), her thematic survey of Canadian literature, as uniquely preoccupied with victimhood.

Although it was the stark, terse, eerily detached poetry in collections like *The Journals of Susanna Moodie* (1970) that made her reputation, Atwood's fiction is astonishing for its variety of tone, mingling seriousness, playful irony, sardonic humour, and even Gothic terror across a similarly diverse range of genres, from the dystopian "speculative fiction" of *The Handmaid's Tale* (1985) and *The Year of the Flood* (2009) to historical novels like *Alias Grace* (1996).

For Atwood, every art form is enclosed by a "set of brackets," conventions that check "the deviousness[,] inventiveness[,] audacity[,] and perversity of the creative spirit." In her work she aims to "expand the brackets," rewriting traditions to deliver the creative spirit from restraint. Though she has written a good deal of realist fiction, her fascination with storytelling has also led her to experiment widely with metafictional techniques, as in the at once open-ended and inexorable plots of "Happy Endings."

Of all the labels critics have applied to her, perhaps "trickster" suits Atwood best, for she is a master fabricator of great wit and imagination whose work refashions the rules to prove that, in the end, "art is what you can get away with."

Happy Endings

John and Mary meet.
What happens next?
If you want a happy ending, try A.

A

John and Mary fall in love and get married. They both have worthwhile and remunerative jobs which they find stimulating and challenging. They buy a charming house. Real estate values go up. Eventually, when they can afford live-in help, they have two children, to whom they are devoted. The children turn out well. John and Mary have a stimulating and challenging sex life and worthwhile friends. They go on fun vacations together. They retire. They both have hobbies which they find stimulating and challenging. Eventually they die. This is the end of the story.

B

Mary falls in love with John but John doesn't fall in love with Mary. He merely uses her body for selfish pleasure and ego gratification of a tepid kind. He comes to her apartment twice a week and she cooks him dinner, you'll notice that he doesn't even consider her worth the price of a dinner out, and after he's eaten the dinner he fucks her and after that he falls asleep, while she does the dishes so he won't think she's untidy, having all those dirty dishes lying around, and puts on fresh lipstick so she'll look good when he wakes up, but when he wakes up he doesn't even notice, he puts on his socks and his shorts and his pants and his shirt and his tie and his shoes, the reverse order from the one in which he took them off. He doesn't take off Mary's clothes, she takes them off herself, she acts as if she's dying for it every time, not because she likes sex exactly, she doesn't, but she wants John to think she does because if they do it often enough surely he'll get used to her, he'll come to depend on her and they will get married, but John goes out the door with hardly so much as a goodnight and three days later he turns up at six o'clock and they do the whole thing over again.

Mary gets run-down. Crying is bad for your face, everyone knows that and so does Mary but she can't stop. People at work notice. Her friends tell her John is a rat, a pig, a dog, he isn't good enough for her, but she can't believe it. Inside John, she thinks, is another John, who is much nicer. This other John will emerge like a butterfly from a cocoon, a Jack from a box, a pit from a prune, if the first John is only squeezed enough.

One evening John complains about the food. He has never complained about the food before. Mary is hurt.

Her friends tell her they've seen him in a restaurant with another woman, whose name is Madge. It's not even Madge that finally gets to Mary: it's the restaurant. John has never taken Mary to a restaurant. Mary collects all the sleeping pills and aspirins she can find, and takes them and a half a bottle of sherry. You can see what kind of a woman she is by the fact that it's not even whiskey. She leaves a note for John. She hopes he'll discover her and get her to the hospital in time and repent and then they can get married, but this fails to happen and she dies.

John marries Madge and everything continues as in A.

C

John, who is an older man, falls in love with Mary, and Mary, who is only twenty-two, feels sorry for him because he's worried about his hair falling out. She sleeps with him even though she's not in love with him. She met him at work. She's in love with someone called James, who is twenty-two also and not yet ready to settle down.

John on the contrary settled down long ago: this is what is bothering him. John has a steady, respectable job and is getting ahead in his field, but Mary isn't impressed by him, she's impressed by James, who has a motorcycle and a fabulous record collection. But James is often away on his motorcycle, being free. Freedom isn't the same for girls, so in the meantime Mary spends Thursday evenings with John. Thursdays are the only days John can get away.

John is married to a woman called Madge and they have two children, a charming house which they bought just before the real estate values went up, and hobbies which they find stimulating and challenging, when they have the time. John tells Mary how important she is to him, but of course he can't leave his wife because a commitment is a commitment. He goes on about this more than is necessary and Mary finds it boring, but older men can keep it up longer so on the whole she has a fairly good time.

One day James breezes in on his motorcycle with some top-grade California hybrid and James and Mary get higher than you'd believe possible and they climb into bed. Everything becomes very underwater, but along comes John, who has a key to Mary's apartment. He finds them stoned and entwined. He's hardly in any position to be jealous, considering Madge, but nevertheless he's overcome with despair. Finally he's middle-aged, in two years he'll be bald as an egg and he can't stand it. He purchases a handgun, saying he needs it for target practice—this is the thin part of the plot, but it can be dealt with later—and shoots the two of them and himself.

Madge, after a suitable period of mourning, marries an understanding man called Fred and everything continues as in A, but under different names.

D

Fred and Madge have no problems. They get along exceptionally well and are good at working out any little difficulties that may arise. But their charming house is by the seashore and one day a giant tidal wave approaches. Real estate values go down. The rest of the story is about what caused the tidal wave and how they escape from it. They do, though thousands drown, but Fred and

Madge are virtuous and lucky. Finally on high ground they clasp each other, wet and dripping and grateful, and continue as in A.

E

Yes, but Fred has a bad heart. The rest of the story is about how kind they both are until Fred dies. Then Madge devotes herself to charity work until the end of A. If you like, it can be "Madge," "cancer," "guilty and confused," and "bird watching."

F

If you think this is all too bourgeois, make John a revolutionary and Mary a counterespionage agent and see how far that gets you. Remember, this is Canada. You'll still end up with A, though in between you may get a lustful brawling saga of passionate involvement, a chronicle of our times, sort of.

You'll have to face it, the endings are the same however you slice it. Don't be deluded by any other endings, they're all fake, either deliberately fake, with malicious intent to deceive, or just motivated by excessive optimism if not by downright sentimentality.
The only authentic ending is the one provided here:
John and Mary die. John and Mary die. John and Mary die.

So much for endings. Beginnings are always more fun. True connoisseurs, however, are known to favour the stretch in between, since it's the hardest to do anything with.
That's about all that can be said for plots, which anyway are just one thing after another, a what and a what and a what.

Now try How and Why.

—1983

Ama Ata Aidoo
b. 1940

Born in a small village in Ghana, Ama Ata Aidoo is a prominent and accomplished author of plays, poetry, novels, and short stories, as well as an activist and academic. Her work often examines cultural and political conflicts between Africa and the West, directing particular attention to the everyday struggles of women in this postcolonial context. As Aidoo has explained, "in so many great literatures of the world, women are nearly always around to service the great male heroes. Since I am a woman it is natural that I not only write about women but with women in more central roles."

Known for her devotion to the cause of women's equality in Africa, Aidoo helped to found the Women's World Organization for Rights Development and Literature in 1994, and in 2000 she founded the Mbaasem Foundation, an NGO that "supports and promotes women's writing in Africa and across Ghana." Regarding the relationship between feminism and African politics, she argues that "every woman and every man should be a feminist—especially if they believe that Africans should take charge of our lands, its wealth, our lives and the burden of our own development. Because it is not possible to advocate independence for our continent without also believing that African women must have the best that the environment can offer."

Aidoo's writing is notable for combining influences from English-language written traditions with influences from West African oral traditions. In her fiction, the immediacy of her storytelling and her emphasis on dialogue combine to produce work that is, as she says, "written to be heard." Although she works in English, critics have remarked that her writing is sensitive to the rhythms and idioms of Ghanaian speech, as well as to the distinct voices of her individual characters.

In 1992, Aidoo was awarded the Commonwealth Writers' Prize for Best Book (Africa) for her novel *Changes* (1991). In addition to proving herself as a talented writer on the world stage, she has held positions at the University of Ghana, the University of Cape Coast, Stanford University, and Brown University.

The Message

"Look here my sister, it should not be said but they say they opened her up."

"They opened her up?"

"Yes, opened her up."

"And the baby removed?"

"Yes, the baby removed."

"Yes, the baby removed."

"I say ..."

"They do not say, my sister."

"Have you heard it?"

"What?"

"This and this and that ..."

"A-a-ah! that is it ..."

"*Meewuo!*"[1]

"They don't say *meewuo* ..."

"And how is she?"

"Am I not here with you? Do I know the highway which leads to Cape Coast?"[2]

"Hmmm ..."

"And anyway how can she live? What is it like even giving birth with a stomach which is whole ... eh? ... I am asking you. And if you are always standing on the brink of death who go to war with a stomach that is whole, then how would she do whose stomach is open to the winds?"

"Oh, *poo*, pity ..."

"I say ..."

My little bundle, come. You and I are going to Cape Coast today.

I am taking one of her own cloths with me, just in case.[3] These people on the coast do not know how to do a thing and I am not going to have anybody mishandling my child's body. I hope they give it to me. Horrible things I have heard done to people's bodies. Cutting them up and using them for instructions. Whereas even murderers still have decent burials.

I see Mensima coming.... And there is Nkama too ... and Adwoa Meenu.... Now they are coming to ... "*poo* pity" me. Witches, witches, witches[4] ... they have picked mine up while theirs prosper around them, children, grandchildren and great-grandchildren—theirs shoot up like mushrooms.

---

1   *Meewuo* Ewe: Dying.

2   *Cape Coast* Port town in southern Ghana, the capital of its Central Region.

3   *just in case* I.e., to use as a shroud if she is dead.

4   *Witches ... witches* In Ghana, witchcraft is a common explanation for misfortune.

"Esi, we have heard of your misfortune ..."

"That our little lady's womb has been opened up ..."

"And her baby removed ..."

Thank you very much.

"Has she lived through it?"

I do not know.

"Esi, bring her here, back home whatever happens."

Yoo, thank you. If the government's people allow it, I shall bring her home.

"And have you got ready your things?"

Yes.... No.

I cannot even think well.

It feels so noisy in my head.... Oh my little child.... I am wasting time.... And so I am going ...

Yes, to Cape Coast.

No, I do not know anyone there now but do you think no one would show me the way to this big hospital ... if I asked around?

Hmmm ... it's me has ended up like this. I was thinking that everything was alright now.... *Yoo*. And thank you too. Shut the door for me when you are leaving. You may stay too long outside if you wait for me, so go home and be about your business. I will let you know when I bring her in.

"Maami Amfoa, where are you going?"

My daughter, I am going to Cape Coast.

"And what is our old mother going to do with such swift steps? Is it serious?"

My daughter, it is very serious.

"Mother, may God go with you."

Yoo, my daughter.

"Eno, and what calls at this hour of the day?"

They want me in Cape Coast.

"Does my friend want to go and see how much the city has changed since we went there to meet the new Wesleyan Chairman,[1] twenty years ago?"

My sister, do you think I have knees to go parading on the streets of Cape Coast?

"Is it heavy?"

Yes, very heavy indeed. They have opened up my grandchild at the hospital, *hi, hi, hi*....

"Eno *due, due, due* ... I did not know. May God go with you...."

---

1   *Wesleyan* Methodist. British Methodists began a missionary effort in Ghana in the nineteenth century, and the Church is now well-established there; *Wesleyan Chairman* Methodist church official responsible for a district.

Thank you. *Yaa.*

"O, the world!"

"It's her grandchild. The only daughter of her only son. Do you remember Kojo Amisa who went to sodja and fell in the great war, overseas?"

"Yes, it's his daughter...."

... O, *poo*, pity.

"Kobina, run to the street, tell Draba Anan to wait for Nana Amfoa."

"... Draba Anan, Draba, my mother says I must come and tell you to wait for Nana Amfoa."

"And where is she?"

"There she comes."

"Just look at how she hops like a bird ... does she think we are going to be here all day? And anyway we are full already ..."

O, you drivers!

"What have drivers done?"

"And do you think it shows respect when you speak in this way? It is only that things have not gone right; but she could, at least have been your mother...."

"But what have I said? I have not insulted her. I just think that only Youth must be permitted to see Cape Coast, the town of the Dear and Expensive...."

"And do you think she is going on a peaceful journey? The only daughter of her only son has been opened up and her baby removed from her womb."

O ... God.

O

O

O

Poo, pity.

"Me ... *poo*—pity, I am right about our modern wives I always say they are useless as compared with our mothers."

"You drivers!"

"Now what have your modern wives done?"

"Am I not right what I always say about them?"

"You go and watch them in the big towns. All so thin and dry as sticks— you can literally blow them away with your breath. No decent flesh anywhere. Wooden chairs groan when they meet with their hard exteriors."

"O you drivers...."

"But of course all drivers ..."

"What have I done? Don't all my male passengers agree with me? These modern girls.... Now here is one who cannot even have a baby in a decent way. But must have the baby removed from her stomach. *Tchiaa!*"

"What ..."

"Here is the old woman."

"Whose grandchild ...?"

"Yes."

"Nana, I hear you are coming to Cape Coast with us."

Yes my master.

"We nearly left you behind but we heard it was you and that it is a heavy journey you are making."

Yes my master ... thank you my master.

"Push up please ... push up. Won't you push up? Why do you all sit look-ing at me with such eyes as if I was a block of wood?"

"It is not that there is nowhere to push up to. Five fat women should go on that seat, but look at you!"

"And our own grandmother here is none too plump herself.... Nana, if they won't push, come to the front seat with me."

"... *Hei*, scholar, go to the back...."

"... And do not scowl on me. I know your sort too well. Something tells me you do not have any job at all. As for that suit you are wearing and looking so grand in, you hired or borrowed it...."

"Oh you drivers!"

Oh you drivers ...

The scholar who read this tengram thing, said it was made about three days ago. My lady's husband sent it.... Three days.... God—that is too long ago. Have they buried her ... where? Or did they cut her up.... I should not think about it ... or something will happen to me. Eleven or twelve ... Efua Panyin, Okuma, Kwame Gyasi and who else? But they should not have left me here. Sometimes ... ah, I hate this nausea. But it is this smell of petrol. Now I have remembered I never could travel in a lorry.[1] I always was so sick. But now I hope at least that will not happen. These young people will think it is because I am old and they will laugh. At least if I knew the child of my child was alive, it would have been good. And the little things she sent me.... Sometimes some people like Mensima and Nkansa make me feel as if I had been a barren woman instead of only one with whom infant-mortality pledged friendship ...

I will give her that set of earrings, bracelet and chain which Odwumfo Ata made for me. It is the most beautiful and the most expensive thing I have.... It docs not hurt me to think that I am going to die very soon and have them and their children gloating over my things. After all what did they swallow my children for? It does not hurt me at all. If I had been someone else, I would have given them all away before I died. But it does not matter. They can share their own curse. Now, that is the end of me and my roots.... Eternal death has

---

1   *lorry* Truck.

worked like a warrior rat, with diabolical sense of duty, to gnaw my bottom. Everything is finished now. The vacant lot is swept and the scraps of old sugar-cane pulp, dry sticks and bunches of hair burnt ... how it reeks, the smoke!

"O, Nana do not weep ..."

"Is the old woman weeping?"

"If the only child of your only child died, won't you weep?"

"Why do you ask me? Did I know her grandchild is dead?"

"Where have you been, not in this lorry? Where were your ears when we were discussing it?"

"I do not go putting my mouth in other people's affairs ..."

"So what?"

"So go and die."

"*Hei, hei*, it is prohibited to quarrel in my lorry."

"Draba, here is me, sitting quiet and this lady of muscles and bones being cheeky to me."

"Look, I can beat you."

"Beat me ... beat me ... let's see."

"*Hei*, you are not civilized, eh?"

"Keep quiet and let us think, both of you, or I will put you down."

"Nana, do not weep. There is God above."

Thank you my master.

"But we are in Cape Coast already."

Meewuo! My God, hold me tight or something will happen to me.

My master, I will come down here.

"O Nana, I thought you said you were going to the hospital.... We are not there yet."

I am saying maybe I will get down here and ask my way around.

"Nana, you do not know these people, eh? They are very impudent here. They have no use for old age. So they do not respect it. Sit down, I will take you there."

Are you going there, my master?

"No, but I will take you there."

Ah, my master, your old mother thanks you. Do not shed a tear when you hear of my death ... my master, your old mother thanks you.

I hear there is somewhere where they keep corpses until their owners claim them ... if she has been buried, then I must find her husband ... Esi Amfoa, what did I come to do under this sky? I have buried all my children and now I am going to bury my only grandchild!

"Nana we are there."

Is this the hospital?

"Yes, Nana. What is your child's name?"

Esi Amfoa. Her father named her after me.

"Do you know her European name?"

No, my master.

"What shall we do?"

"... *Ei* lady, Lady Nurse, we are looking for somebody."

"You are looking for somebody and can you read? If you cannot, you must ask someone what the rules in the hospital are. You can only come and visit people at three o'clock."

Lady, please. She was my only grandchild ...

"Who? And anyway, it is none of our business."

"Nana, you must be patient ... and not cry ..."

"Old woman, why are you crying, it is not allowed here. No one must make any noise ..."

My lady, I am sorry but she was all I had.

"Who? Oh, are you the old woman who is looking for somebody?"

Yes.

"Who is he?"

She was my granddaughter—the only child of my only son.

"I mean, what was her name?"

Esi Amfoa.

"Esi Amfoa ... Esi Amfoa. I am sorry, we do not have anyone whom they call like that here."

Is that it?

"Nana, I told you they may know only her European name here."

My master, what shall we do then?

"What is she ill with?"

She came here to have a child ...

"... And they say, they opened her stomach and removed the baby."

"Oh ... oh, I see."

My Lord, hold me tight so that nothing will happen to me now.

"I see. It is the Caesarean[1] case."

"Nurse, you know her?"

And when I take her back, Anona Ebusuafo will say that I did not wait for them to come with me ...

"Yes. Are you her brother?"

"No. I am only the driver who brought the old woman."

"Did she bring all her clan?"

"No. She came alone."

---

1   *Caesarean* I.e., caesarean section, an operation in which a baby is delivered through an incision in the mother's abdomen.

"Strange thing for a villager to do."

I hope they have not cut her up already.

"Did she bring a whole bag full of cassava and plantain and kenkey?"[1]

"No. She has only her little bundle."

"Follow me. But you must not make any noise. This is not the hour for coming here ..."

My master, does she know her?

"Yes."

I hear it is very cold where they put them ...

• • •

It was feeding time for new babies. When old Esi Amfoa saw young Esi Amfoa, the latter was all neat and nice. White sheets and all. She did not see the beautiful stitches under the sheets. "This woman is a tough bundle," Dr. Gyamfi had declared after the identical twins had been removed, the last stitches had been threaded off and Mary Koomson, alias Esi Amfoa, had come to.

The old woman somersaulted into the room and lay groaning, not screaming, by the bed. For was not her last pot broken? So they lay them in state even in hospitals and not always cut them up for instruction?

The Nursing Sister was furious. Young Esi Amfoa spoke. And this time old Esi Amfoa wept loud and hard—wept all her tears.

Scrappy nurse-under-training, Jessy Treeson, second-generation-Cape-Coaster-her-grandmother-still-remembered-at-Egyaa[2] No. 7 said, "As for these villagers," and giggled.

Draba Anan looked hard at Jessy Treeson, looked hard at her, all of her: her starched uniform, apron and cap ... and then dismissed them all.... "Such a cassava stick ... but maybe I will break my toe if I kicked at her buttocks," he thought.

And by the bed the old woman was trying hard to rise and look at the only pot which had refused to get broken.

—1970

---

1   *cassava* Starchy root vegetable, a staple crop in Ghana; *plantain* Banana-like fruit, eaten cooked; *kenkey* Dumplings made of fermented white corn flour, a traditional Ghanaian dish.

2   *Egyaa* Town on the coast of Ghana.

Thomas King
b. 1943

One of the first Native writers to gain a significant popular and critical following in Canada and the United States, Thomas King has explored Aboriginal identities and experiences in a wide range of forms, genres, and mediums. Though often identified as a comic writer, King considers himself a satirist who uses comedy to deal with serious subjects—the exploitation of cultures, the loss of a way of life, the struggle for self-definition, and the question of authenticity—without descending into polemical denunciations. As King explains, "Tragedy is my topic. Comedy is my strategy."

In novels like *Green Grass, Running Water* (1993) and the stories collected in *A Short History of Indians in Canada* (2005), King often confronts head-on the traumatic legacy of colonization. His characters are not woebegone "solitary figures poised on the brink of extinction" but many-sided individuals bound by a nourishing sense of community. For King, the term *postcolonial* misleadingly implies that European contact was the primary generative impetus of Native literature. As he argues in "Godzilla vs. Post-Colonial" (1990), "the idea of post-colonial writing effectively cuts us off from our traditions, traditions that were in place before colonialism ever became a question, traditions which have come down to us through our cultures in spite of colonialism."

King takes up and carries forward many of these traditions, often fusing the conventions of oral storytelling with those of written narratives. Certain stories, including "A Short History of Indians in Canada," were written as oral performance pieces. In all his work, King aims not only to reclaim Native culture from reductive stereotypical representations but to reinforce "the notion that, in addition to the useable past that the concurrence of oral literature and traditional history provides us with, we also have an active present marked by cultural tenacity and a viable future."

A Short History of Indians in Canada

Can't sleep, Bob Haynie tells the doorman at the King Eddie. Can't sleep, can't sleep.

First time in Toronto? says the doorman.

Yes, says Bob.

Businessman?

Yes.

Looking for some excitement?

Yes.

Bay Street,[1] sir, says the doorman.

Bob Haynie catches a cab to Bay Street at three in the morning. He loves the smell of concrete. He loves the look of city lights. He loves the sound of skyscrapers.

Bay Street.

Smack!

Bob looks up just in time to see a flock of Indians fly into the side of the building.

Smack! Smack!

Bob looks up just in time to get out of the way.

Whup!

An Indian hits the pavement in front of him.

Whup! Whup!

Two Indians hit the pavement behind him.

Holy Cow! shouts Bob, and he leaps out of the way of the falling Indians.

Whup! Whup! Whup!

Bob throws his hands over his head and dashes into the street. And is almost hit by a city truck.

Honk!

Two men jump out of the truck. Hi, I'm Bill. Hi, I'm Rudy.

Hi, I'm Bob.

Businessman? says Bill.

Yes.

First time in Toronto? says Rudy.

Yes.

Whup! Whup! Whup!

Look out! Bob shouts. There are Indians flying into the skyscrapers and falling on the sidewalk.

Whup!

Mohawk, says Bill.

Whup! Whup!

Couple of Cree over here, says Rudy.

Amazing, says Bob. How can you tell?

By the feathers, says Bill. We got a book.

It's our job, says Rudy.

Whup!

Bob looks around. What's this one? he says.

Holy! says Bill. Holy! says Rudy.

Check the book, says Bill. Just to be sure.

Flip, flip, flip.

---

1   *Bay Street* Major street in Toronto's financial district.

Navajo!

Bill and Rudy put their arms around Bob. A Navajo! Don't normally see Navajos this far north. Don't normally see Navajos this far east.

Is she dead? says Bob.

Nope, says Bill. Just stunned.

Most of them are just stunned, says Rudy.

Some people never see this, says Bill. One of nature's mysteries. A natural phenomenon.

They're nomadic you know, says Rudy. And migratory.

Toronto's in the middle of the flyway, says Bill. The lights attract them.

Bob counts the bodies. Seventy-three. No. Seventy-four. What can I do to help?

Not much that anyone can do, says Bill. We tried turning off the lights in the buildings.

We tried broadcasting loud music from the roofs, says Rudy.

Rubber owls? asks Bob.

It's a real problem this time of the year, says Bill.

Whup! Whup! Whup!

Bill and Rudy pull green plastic bags out of their pockets and try to find the open ends.

The dead ones we bag, says Rudy.

The lives ones we tag, says Bill. Take them to the shelter. Nurse them back to health. Release them in the wild.

Amazing, says Bob.

A few wander off dazed and injured. If we don't find them right away, they don't stand a chance.

Amazing, says Bob.

You're one lucky guy, says Bill. In another couple of weeks, they'll be gone.

A family from Alberta came through last week and didn't even see an Ojibway, says Rudy.

Your first time in Toronto? says Bill.

It's a great town, says Bob. You're doing a great job.

Whup!

Don't worry, says Rudy. By the time the commuters show up, you'll never even know the Indians were here.

Bob catches a cab back to the King Eddie and shakes the doorman's hand. I saw the Indians, he says.

Thought you'd enjoy that, sir, says the doorman.

Thank you, says Bob. It was spectacular.

Not like the old days. The doorman sighs and looks up into the night. In the old days, when they came through, they would black out the entire sky.

—2005

James Kelman
b. 1946

▅▅▅ Widely esteemed as one of Scotland's most influential and innovative writers, James Kelman is also a literary iconoclast whose novels and short stories
question the cultural standards by which they are often judged. Although his
work has received and been shortlisted for many awards—including the Man
Booker Prize, which he won amidst great controversy for his novel *How late
it was, how late* (1994)—Kelman remains an outspoken critic of the literary
establishment and what he considers its elitist, bourgeois values.

In his famous Booker Prize acceptance speech, the native Glaswegian
defiantly declared: "My culture and my language have the right to exist,
and no one has the authority to dismiss that right." Many critics have approached Kelman's fictional project as an affirmation of this right in the
face of the dominant norms—linguistic, stylistic, narrative, even grammatical—of traditional British literature. For Kelman, who emerged as a writer
at the height of the British class war in the 1970s, standard written English
and other "genteel" formal conventions deny the validity of working-class
culture, just as they misrepresent the reality of working-class experience.

Kelman rejects traditional realism; many of the stories collected in *Short
Tales from the Night Shift* (1978) and *Not Not While the Giro* (1983) are
highly compressed, essentially plotless, consisting of concrete statements of
fact that allow the working-class subject matter to speak for itself without
commentary from a perspective that pretends superiority. The influence of
such writers as Franz Kafka and Ernest Hemingway on Kelman's work is
evident in its preoccupation with themes of alienation, powerlessness, and
thwarted masculinity.

Acid

In this factory in the north of England acid was essential. It was contained in
large vats. Gangways were laid above them. Before these gangways were made
completely safe a young man fell into a vat feet first. His screams of agony
were heard all over the department. Except for one old fellow the large body
of men was so horrified that for a time not one of them could move. In an
instant this old fellow who was also the young man's father had clambered up
and along the gangway carrying a big pole. Sorry Hughie, he said. And then
ducked the young man below the surface. Obviously the old fellow had had
to do this because only the head and shoulders—in fact, that which had been
seen above the acid was all that remained of the young man.

—1978

Charles Mungoshi

b. 1947

Charles Mungoshi is an award-winning Zimbabwean author who writes in both English and Shona, the native language of the Shona peoples of Zimbabwe and Zambia. He has received both regional and international acclaim. His collection of short stories *The Setting Sun and the Rolling World* (1987) was runner-up for the Commonwealth Prize for Best Book (Africa). Ten years later he won this prize with his short story collection *Walking Still* (1997). He has also received awards for his poetry—*The Milkman Doesn't Only Deliver Milk* (1998) won second place in the Zimbabwean Literary Awards—and for an illustrated collection of children's stories, *One Day, Long Ago: More Stories from a Shona Childhood* (1991), which won the Noma Award for Publishing in Africa. He holds two PEN Awards for his novel *Waiting for the Rain* (1975), which was published in English, and for *Ndiko kupindana kwa mazuva* (1975), a novel written and published in Shona.

Mungoshi's long list of achievements is a testament to the diversity of his writing, which ranges across genres, styles, and subjects. While generally cited as an anti- and post-colonial writer, Mungoshi does not limit his work to the strictly political—and when he does deal with political themes, he does so through finely realized individual characters. His stories are the stories of the ways in which inevitable changes affect the relationships between parents and children, of the pressures of poverty on the ties of family, of tensions between the urban and the rural. Though Mungoshi's stories are often set within systems of colonial oppression, his characters are always, as the critic Maurice Taonezvi Vabe says, "hewn from the hardwood of the lives of ordinary people."

The Setting Sun and the Rolling World

Old Musoni raised his dusty eyes from his hoe and the unchanging stony earth he had been tilling and peered into the sky. The white speck whose sound had disturbed his work and thoughts was far out at the edge of the yellow sky, near the horizon. Then it disappeared quickly over the southern rim of the sky and he shook his head. He looked to the west. Soon the sun would go down. He looked over the sunblasted land and saw the shadows creeping east, blearer and taller with every moment that the sun shed each of its rays. Unconsciously wishing for rain and relief, he bent down again to his work and did not see his son, Nhamo, approaching.

Nhamo crouched in the dust near his father and greeted him. The old man half raised his back, leaning against his hoe, and said what had been bothering him all day long.

"You haven't changed your mind?"

"No, father."

There was a moment of silence. Old Musoni scraped earth off his hoe.

"Have you thought about this, son?"

"For weeks, father."

"And you think that's the only way?"

"There is no other way."

The old man felt himself getting angry again. But this would be the last day he would talk to his son. If his son was going away, he must not be angry. It would be equal to a curse. He himself had taken chances before, in his own time, but he felt too much of a father. He had worked and slaved for his family and the land had not betrayed him. He saw nothing now but disaster and death for his son out there in the world. Lions had long since vanished but he knew of worse animals of prey, animals that wore redder claws than the lion's, beasts that would not leave an unprotected homeless boy alone. He thought of the white metal bird and he felt remorse.

"Think again. You will end dead. Think again, of us, of your family. We have a home, poor though it is, but can you think of a day you have gone without?"

"I have thought everything over, father, I am convinced this is the only way out."

"There is no only way out in the world. Except the way of the land, the way of the family."

"The land is overworked and gives nothing now, father. And the family is almost broken up."

The old man got angry. Yes, the land is useless. True, the family tree is uprooted and it dries in the sun. True, many things are happening that haven't happened before, that we did not think would happen, ever. But nothing is more certain to hold you together than the land and a home, a family. And where do you think you are going, a mere beardless kid with the milk not yet dry on your baby nose? What do you think you will do in the great treacherous world where men twice your age have gone and returned with their backs broken—if they returned at all? What do you know of life? What do you know of the false honey bird[1] that leads you the whole day

---

1   *honey bird* Bird named for its helpful habit of deliberately guiding people to wild bees' nests.

through the forest to a snake's nest? But all he said was: "Look. What have you asked me and I have denied you? What, that I have, have I not given you for the asking?"

"All. You have given me all, father." And here, too, the son felt hampered, patronized and his pent-up fury rolled through him. It showed on his face but stayed under control. You have given me damn all and nothing. You have sent me to school and told me the importance of education, and now you ask me to throw it on the rubbish heap and scrape for a living on this tired cold shell of the moon. You ask me to forget it and muck around in this slow dance of death with you. I have this one chance of making my own life, once in all eternity, and now you are jealous. You are afraid of your own death. It is, after all, your own death. I shall be around a while yet. I will make my way home if a home is what I need. I am armed more than you think and wiser than you can dream of. But all he said, too, was:

"Really, father, have no fear for me. I will be all right. Give me this chance. Release me from all obligations and pray for me."

There was a spark in the old man's eyes at these words of his son. But just as dust quickly settles over a glittering pebble revealed by the hoe, so a murkiness hid the gleam in the old man's eye. Words are handles made to the smith's fancy and are liable to break under stress. They are too much fat on the hard unbreaking sinews of life.

"Do you know what you are doing, son?"

"Yes."

"Do you know what you will be a day after you leave home?"

"Yes, father."

"A homeless, nameless vagabond living on dust and rat's droppings, living on thank-yous, sleeping up a tree or down a ditch, in the rain, in the sun, in the cold, with nobody to see you, nobody to talk to, nobody at all to tell your dreams to. Do you know what it is to see your hopes come crashing down like an old house out of season and your dreams turning to ash and dung without a tang of salt in your skull? Do you know what it is to live without a single hope of ever seeing good in your own lifetime?" And to himself: Do you know, young bright ambitious son of my loins, the ruins of time and the pains of old age? Do you know how to live beyond a dream, a hope, a faith? Have you seen black despair, my son?

"I know it, father. I know enough to start on. The rest I shall learn as I go on. Maybe I shall learn to come back."

The old man looked at him and felt: Come back where? Nobody comes back to ruins. You will go on, son. Something you don't know will drive you on along deserted plains, past ruins and more ruins, on and on until there is only one ruin left: yourself. You will break down, without tears, son. You are human, too. Learn to the *haya*—the rain bird[1] and heed its warning of coming storm: plough no more, it says. And what happens if the storm catches you far, far out on the treeless plain? What, then, my son?

But he was tired. They had taken over two months discussing all this. Going over the same ground like animals at a drinking place until, like animals, they had driven the water far deep into the stony earth, until they had sapped all the blood out of life and turned it into a grim skeleton, and now they were creating a stampede on the dust, grovelling for water. Mere thoughts. Mere words. And what are words? Trying to grow a fruit tree in the wilderness.

"Go son, with my blessings. I give you nothing. And when you remember what I am saying you will come back. The land is still yours. As long as I am alive you will find a home waiting for you."

"Thank you, father."

"Before you go, see Chiremba. You are going out into the world. You need something to strengthen yourself. Tell him I shall pay him. Have a good journey, son."

"Thank you, father."

Nhamo smiled and felt a great love for his father. But there were things that belonged to his old world that were just lots of humbug on the mind, empty load, useless scrap. He would go to Chiremba but he would burn the charms as soon as he was away from home and its sickening environment. A man stands on his feet and guts. Charms were for you—so was God, though much later. But for us now the world is godless, no charms will work. All that is just the opium you take in the dark in the hope of a light. You don't need that now. You strike a match for a light. Nhamo laughed.

He could be so easily light-hearted. Now his brain worked with a fury only known to visionaries. The psychological ties were now broken, only the biological tied him to his father. He was free. He too remembered the aeroplane which his father had seen just before their talk. Space had no bounds and no ties. Floating laws ruled the darkness and he would float with the fiery balls. He was the sun, burning itself out every second and shedding tons of energy which it held in its power, giving it the thrust to drag its brood wherever it wanted to. This was the law that held him. The mystery that his father and ancestors had failed to grasp and which had caused their being wiped off the face of the earth. This thinking reached such a pitch that he began to sing, imitating as intimately as he could Satchmo's[2] voice: "What a wonderful world." It was Satchmo's voice that he turned to when he felt buoyant.

---

1   *haya ... bird* Cuckoo, said in Zimbabwe to sing before it rains.
2   *Satchmo* Louis Armstrong (1901–71), American jazz trumpeter and vocalist.

Old Musoni did not look at his son as he left him. Already, his mind was trying to focus at some point in the dark unforeseeable future. Many things could happen and while he still breathed he would see that nothing terribly painful happened to his family, especially to his stubborn last born, Nhamo. Tomorrow, before sunrise, he would go to see Chiremba and ask him to throw bones over the future of his son. And if there were a couple of ancestors who needed appeasement, he would do it while he was still around.

He noticed that the sun was going down and he scraped the earth off his hoe.

The sun was sinking slowly, bloody red, blunting and blurring all the objects that had looked sharp in the light of day. Soon a chilly wind would blow over the land and the cold cloudless sky would send down beads of frost like white ants over the unprotected land.

—1972

Rohinton Mistry
b. 1952

Rohinton Mistry is a Mumbai-born Canadian novelist and short story writer. In a review in *The New Yorker*, literary critic and fellow novelist John Updike wrote that he "harks back to the nineteenth-century novelists, for whom every detail, every urban alley, every character however lowly added a vital piece to the full social picture, and for whom every incident illustrated the eventually crushing weight of the world."

At 23, Mistry emigrated with his wife to Canada and settled in Toronto. He worked as a bank clerk but studied English literature at the University of Toronto, earning his BA in 1983. In 1987, he published *Tales from Firozsha Baag*, a collection of short stories set in both the writer's own minority Parsi community in Bombay (now Mumbai) and abroad. Each story deals with topics that would recur in Mistry's writing: community, identity, diaspora, poverty, dreams, and human conflict.

His first novel, *Such a Long Journey* (1991), set in Bombay during the Indian-Pakistan War of 1971, won the Governor General's Award and the Commonwealth Writers Prize. Mistry's second novel, *A Fine Balance* (1995), set in India during The Emergency imposed by Indira Ghandi, 1975-77, won a host of awards, including the Giller Prize. *Family Matters* (2002), set in mid-1990s Bombay, was another critical success, garnering the Kiriyama Pacific Rim Book Prize, a third straight Commonwealth Writers Prize, and a third straight appearance on the prestigious Man Booker Prize shortlist. In 2012, Mistry was awarded the Neustadt International Prize in recognition of his contributions to world literature.

Squatter[1]

Whenever Nariman Hansotia returned in the evening from the Cawasji Framji Memorial Library in a good mood the signs were plainly evident.

First, he parked his 1932 Mercedes-Benz (he called it the apple of his eye) outside A Block, directly in front of his ground-floor veranda window, and beeped the horn three long times. It annoyed Rustomji who also had a ground-floor flat in A Block. Ever since he had defied Nariman in the matter of painting the exterior of the building, Rustomji was convinced that nothing

---

1　*Squatter* This story appeared in Mistry's *Tales from Firozsha Baag*, in which all of the short stories are linked to an apartment block in Mumbai, India. Most of the inhabitants of the block are Parsis, members of a Zoroastrian religious minority with Persian roots that has lived in India for the past thousand years.

the old coot did was untainted by the thought of vengeance and harassment, his retirement pastime.

But the beeping was merely Nariman's signal to let Hirabai inside know that though he was back he would not step indoors for a while. Then he raised the hood, whistling "Rose Marie,"[1] and leaned his tall frame over the engine. He checked the oil, wiped here and there with a rag, tightened the radiator cap, and lowered the hood. Finally, he polished the Mercedes star and let the whistling modulate into the march from *The Bridge on the River Kwai*.[2] The boys playing in the compound knew that Nariman was ready now to tell a story. They started to gather round.

"*Sahibji*, Nariman Uncle," someone said tentatively and Nariman nodded, careful not to lose his whistle, his bulbous nose flaring slightly. The pursed lips had temporarily raised and reshaped his Clark Gable[3] moustache. More boys walked up. One called out, "How about a story, Nariman Uncle?" at which point Nariman's eyes began to twinkle, and he imparted increased energy to the polishing. The cry was taken up by others, "Yes, yes, Nariman Uncle, a story!" He swung into a final verse of the march. Then the lips relinquished the whistle, the Clark Gable moustache descended. The rag was put away, and he began.

"You boys know the great cricketers: Contractor, Polly Umrigar, and recently, the young chap, Farokh Engineer.[4] Cricket *aficionados*, that's what you all are." Nariman liked to use new words, especially big ones, in the stories he told, believing it was his duty to expose young minds to as shimmering and varied a vocabulary as possible; if they could not spend their days at the Cawasji Framji Memorial Library then he, at least, could carry bits of the library out to them.

The boys nodded; the names of the cricketers were familiar.

"But does any one know about Savukshaw, the greatest of them all?" They shook their heads in unison.

"This, then, is the story about Savukshaw, how he saved the Indian team from a humiliating defeat when they were touring in England." Nariman sat on the steps of A Block. The few diehards who had continued with their games could not resist any longer when they saw the gathering circle, and ran up to

1   *"Rose Marie"* Popular theme song from a 1924 Broadway musical set in the Rocky Mountains of Canada, remade several times into Hollywood films.

2   *The Bridge ... Kwai* 1957 film about a group of Allied soldiers imprisoned in a Japanese prisoner-of-war camp in World War II.

3   *Clark Gable* American actor, most famous for his performance in the 1939 film *Gone with the Wind*.

4   *great cricketers ... Engineer* Cricket is a bat-and-ball sport popular in the United Kingdom and its past colonies, including India. The cricketers mentioned were all Parsi members of India's national team.

listen. They asked their neighbours in whispers what the story was about, and were told: Savukshaw the greatest cricketer. The whispering died down and Nariman began.

"The Indian team was to play the indomitable MCC as part of its tour of England. Contractor was our captain. Now the MCC being the strongest team they had to face, Contractor was almost certain of defeat. To add to Contractor's troubles, one of his star batsmen, Nadkarni, had caught influenza early in the tour, and would definitely not be well enough to play against the MCC. By the way, does anyone know what those letters stand for? You, Kersi, you wanted to be a cricketer once."

Kersi shook his head. None of the boys knew, even though they had heard the MCC mentioned in radio commentaries, because the full name was hardly ever used.

Then Jehangir Bulsara spoke up, or Bulsara Bookworm, as the boys called him. The name given by Pesi *paadmaroo*[1] had stuck even though it was now more than four years since Pesi had been sent away to boarding-school, and over two years since the death of Dr. Mody. Jehangir was still unliked by the boys in the Baag, though they had come to accept his aloofness and respect his knowledge and intellect. They were not surprised that he knew the answer to Nariman's question: "Marylebone Cricket Club."[2]

"Absolutely correct," said Nariman, and continued with the story. "The MCC won the toss and elected to bat. They scored four hundred and ninety-seven runs in the first inning before our spinners[3] could get them out. Early in the second day's play our team was dismissed for one hundred and nine runs, and the extra who had taken Nadkarni's place was injured by a vicious bumper[4] that opened a gash on his forehead." Nariman indicated the spot and the length of the gash on his furrowed brow. "Contractor's worst fears were coming true. The MCC waived their own second inning and gave the Indian team a follow-on,[5] wanting to inflict an inning's defeat. And this time he had to use the second extra. The second extra was a certain Savukshaw."

The younger boys listened attentively; some of them, like the two sons of the chartered accountant in B Block, had only recently been deemed old

---

1   *paadmaroo* Pesi is given this punning nickname in another story in *Tales from Firozsha Baag*; it is a reference to his pungent flatulence.
2   *Marylebone Cricket Club* Based in London, the MCC is the most famous cricket club in the world. The governing body of international cricket until 1993, the MCC holds the copyright to the sport's official laws.
3   *spinners* Cricket bowlers who use trickery to oust opposing batters, roughly equivalent to changeup pitchers in baseball.
4   *bumper* Ball pitched fast and bounced toward the batter's head.
5   *follow-on* Inning in which the team that has just batted is required to bat again because their score from the first inning is less than half the other team's.

enough by their parents to come out and play in the compound, and had not received any exposure to Nariman's stories. But the others like Jehangir, Kersi, and Viraf were familiar with Nariman's technique.

Once, Jehangir had overheard them discussing Nariman's stories, and he could not help expressing his opinion: that unpredictability was the brush he used to paint his tales with, and ambiguity the palette he mixed his colours in. The others looked at him with admiration. Then Viraf asked what exactly he meant by that. Jehangir said that Nariman sometimes told a funny incident in a very serious way, or expressed a significant matter in a light and playful manner. And these were only two rough divisions, in between were lots of subtle gradations of tone and texture. Which, then, was the funny story and which the serious? Their opinions were divided, but ultimately, said Jehangir, it was up to the listener to decide.

"So," continued Nariman, "Contractor first sent out his two regular openers, convinced that it was all hopeless. But after five wickets were lost[1] for just another thirty-eight runs, out came Savukshaw the extra. Nothing mattered any more."

The street lights outside the compound came on, illuminating the iron gate where the watchman stood. It was a load off the watchman's mind when Nariman told a story. It meant an early end to the hectic vigil during which he had to ensure that none of the children ran out on the main road, or tried to jump over the wall. For although keeping out riff-raff was his duty, keeping in the boys was as important if he wanted to retain the job.

"The first ball Savukshaw faced was wide outside the off stump.[2] He just lifted his bat and ignored it. But with what style! What panache! As if to say, come on, you blighters, play some polished cricket. The next ball was also wide, but not as much as the first. It missed the off stump narrowly. Again Savukshaw lifted his bat, boredom written all over him. Everyone was now watching closely. The bowler was annoyed by Savukshaw's arrogance, and the third delivery was a vicious fast pitch, right down on the middle stump.

"Savukshaw was ready, quick as lightning. No one even saw the stroke of his bat, but the ball went like a bullet towards the square leg.[3]

"Fielding at square leg was a giant of a fellow, about six feet seven, weighing two hundred and fifty pounds, a veritable Brobdingnagian,[4] with arms like branches and hands like a pair of huge *sapaat*, the kind that Dr. Mody

---

1   *five ... lost* I.e., five players were out.
2   *stump* One of the three standing wooden sticks that comprise a wicket. The batter stands in front of the wicket to protect it from the pitcher, who attempts to hit it; if the pitch knocks one of the stumps out of the ground, the player is out.
3   *square leg* Fielder positioned to the side of the batter.
4   *Brobdingnagian* Giant. See Jonathan Swift's *Gulliver's Travels* (1726).

used to wear, you remember what big feet Dr. Mody had." Jehangir was the only one who did; he nodded. "Just to see him standing there was scary. Not one ball had got past him, and he had taken some great catches. Savukshaw purposely aimed his shot right at him. But he was as quick as Savukshaw, and stuck out his huge *sapaat* of a hand to stop the ball. What do you think happened then, boys?"

The older boys knew what Nariman wanted to hear at this point. They asked, "What happened, Nariman Uncle, what happened?" Satisfied, Nariman continued.

"A howl is what happened. A howl from the giant fielder, a howl that rang through the entire stadium, that soared like the cry of a banshee[1] right up to the cheapest seats in the furthest, highest corners, a howl that echoed from the scoreboard and into the pavilion, into the kitchen, startling the chap inside who was preparing tea and scones for after the match, who spilled boiling water all over himself and was severely hurt. But not nearly as bad as the giant fielder at square leg. Never at any English stadium was a howl heard like that one, not in the whole history of cricket. And why do you think he was howling, boys?"

The chorus asked, "Why, Nariman Uncle, why?"

"Because of Savukshaw's bullet-like shot, of course. The hand he had reached out to stop it, he now held up for all to see, and *dhur-dhur, dhur-dhur* the blood was gushing like a fountain in an Italian piazza, like a burst watermain from the Vihar-Powai reservoir, dripping onto his shirt and his white pants, and sprinkling the green grass, and only because he was such a giant of a fellow could he suffer so much blood loss and not faint. But even he could not last forever; eventually, he felt dizzy, and was helped off the field. And where do you think the ball was, boys, that Savukshaw had smacked so hard?"

And the chorus rang out again on the now dark steps of A Block: "Where, Nariman Uncle, where?"

"Past the boundary line, of course. Lying near the fence. Rent asunder. Into two perfect leather hemispheres. All the stitches had ripped, and some of the insides had spilled out. So the umpires sent for a new one, and the game resumed. Now none of the fielders dared to touch any ball that Savukshaw hit. Every shot went to the boundary, all the way for four runs. Single-handedly, Savukshaw wiped out the deficit, and had it not been for loss of time due to rain, he would have taken the Indian team to a thumping victory against the MCC. As it was, the match ended in a draw."

Nariman was pleased with the awed faces of the youngest ones around him. Kersi and Viraf were grinning away and whispering something. From

---

1   *banshee* Fairy woman in Irish folklore whose wail foretells death.

one of the flats the smell of frying fish swam out to explore the night air, and tickled Nariman's nostrils. He sniffed appreciatively, aware that it was in his good wife Hirabai's pan that the frying was taking place. This morning, he had seen the pomfret[1] she had purchased at the door, waiting to be cleaned, its mouth open and eyes wide, like the eyes of some of these youngsters. It was time to wind up the story.

"The MCC will not forget the number of new balls they had to produce that day because of Savukshaw's deadly strokes. Their annual ball budget was thrown badly out of balance. Any other bat would have cracked under the strain, but Savukshaw's was seasoned with a special combination of oils, a secret formula given to him by a *sadhu*[2] who had seen him one day playing cricket when he was a small boy. But Savukshaw used to say his real secret was practice, lots of practice, that was the advice he gave to any young lad who wanted to play cricket."

The story was now clearly finished, but none of the boys showed any sign of dispersing. "Tell us about more matches that Savukshaw played in," they said.

"More nothing. This was his greatest match. Anyway, he did not play cricket for long because soon after the match against the MCC he became a champion bicyclist, the fastest human on two wheels. And later, a pole-vaulter—when he glided over on his pole, so graceful, it was like watching a bird in flight. But he gave that up, too, and became a hunter, the mightiest hunter ever known, absolutely fearless, and so skilful, with a gun he could have, from the third floor of A Block, shaved the whisker of a cat in the backyard of C Block."

"Tell us about that," they said, "about Savukshaw the hunter!"

The fat ayah,[3] Jaakaylee, arrived to take the chartered accountant's two children home. But they refused to go without hearing about Savukshaw the hunter. When she scolded them and things became a little hysterical, some other boys tried to resurrect the ghost she had once seen: "Ayah *bhoot*![4] Ayah *bhoot*!" Nariman raised a finger in warning—that subject was still taboo in Firozsha Baag; none of the adults was in a hurry to relive the wild and rampageous days that Pesi *paadmaroo* had ushered in, once upon a time, with the *bhoot* games.

Jaakaylee sat down, unwilling to return without the children, and whispered to Nariman to make it short. The smell of frying fish which had tickled Nariman's nostrils ventured into and awakened his stomach. But the story of Savukshaw the hunter was one he had wanted to tell for a long time.

---

1   *pomfret* Fish common in southern Asia.
2   *sadhu* Gujarati: monk.
3   *ayah* Nanny.
4   *bhoot* Gujarati: ghost.

"Savukshaw always went hunting alone, he preferred it that way. There are many incidents in the life of Savukshaw the hunter, but the one I am telling you about involves a terrifying situation. Terrifying for us, of course; Savukshaw was never terrified of anything. What happened was, one night he set up camp, started a fire and warmed up his bowl of chicken-*dhansaak*."

The frying fish had precipitated famishment upon Nariman, and the subject of chicken-*dhansaak* suited him well. His own mouth watering, he elaborated: "Mrs. Savukshaw was as famous for her *dhansaak* as Mr. was for hunting. She used to put in tamarind and brinjal, coriander and cumin, cloves and cinnamon, and dozens of other spices no one knows about. Women used to come from miles around to stand outside her window while she cooked it, to enjoy the fragrance and try to penetrate her secret, hoping to identify the ingredients as the aroma floated out, layer by layer, growing more complex and delicious. But always, the delectable fragrance enveloped the women and they just surrendered to the ecstasy, forgetting what they had come for. Mrs. Savukshaw's secret was safe."

Jaakaylee motioned to Nariman to hurry up, it was past the children's dinner-time. He continued: "The aroma of savoury spices soon filled the night air in the jungle, and when the *dhansaak* was piping hot he started to eat, his rifle beside him. But as soon as he lifted the first morsel to his lips, a tiger's eyes flashed in the bushes! Not twelve feet from him! He emerged licking his chops! What do you think happened then, boys?"

"What, what, Nariman Uncle?"

Before he could tell them, the door of his flat opened. Hirabai put her head out and said, "*Chaalo ni,*[1] Nariman, it's time. Then if it gets cold you won't like it."

That decided the matter. To let Hirabai's fried fish, crisp on the outside, yet tender and juicy inside, marinated in turmeric and cayenne—to let that get cold would be something that *Khoedaiji*[2] above would not easily forgive. "Sorry boys, have to go. Next time about Savukshaw and the tiger."

There were some groans of disappointment. They hoped Nariman's good spirits would extend into the morrow when he returned from the Memorial Library, or the story would get cold.

But a whole week elapsed before Nariman again parked the apple of his eye outside his ground-floor flat and beeped the horn three times. When he had raised the hood, checked the oil, polished the star and swung into the "Colonel Bogie March,"[3] the boys began drifting towards A Block.

---

1   *Chaalo ni* Gujarati: Come along now.
2   *Khoedaiji* Gujarati: God.
3   *"Colonel Bogie March"* Marching song of the imprisoned soldiers in *Bridge on the River Kwai*.

Some of them recalled the incomplete story of Savukshaw and the tiger, but they knew better than to remind him. It was never wise to prompt Nariman until he had dropped the first hint himself, or things would turn out badly.

Nariman inspected the faces: the two who stood at the back, always looking superior and wise, were missing. So was the quiet Bulsara boy, the intelligent one. "Call Kersi, Viraf, and Jehangir," he said. "I want them to listen to today's story."

Jehangir was sitting alone on the stone steps of C Block. The others were chatting by the compound gate with the watchman. Someone went to fetch them.

"Sorry to disturb your conference, boys, and your meditation, Jehangir," Nariman said facetiously, "but I thought you would like to hear this story. Especially since some of you are planning to go abroad."

This was not strictly accurate, but Kersi and Viraf did talk a lot about America and Canada. Kersi had started writing to universities there since his final high-school year, and had also sent letters of inquiry to the Canadian High Commission in New Delhi and to the US Consulate at Breach Candy. But so far he had not made any progress. He and Viraf replied with as much sarcasm as their unripe years allowed, "Oh yes, next week, just have to pack our bags."

"Riiiight," drawled Nariman. Although he spoke perfect English, this was the one word with which he allowed himself to take liberties, indulging in a broadness of vowel more American than anything else. "But before we go on with today's story, what did you learn about Savukshaw, from last week's story?"

"That he was a very talented man," said someone.

"What else?"

"He was also a very lucky man, to have so many talents," said Viraf.

"Yes, but what else?"

There was silence for a few moments. Then Jehangir said, timidly: "He was a man searching for happiness, by trying all kinds of different things."

"Exactly! And he never found it. He kept looking for new experiences, and though he was very successful at everything he attempted, it did not bring him happiness. Remember this, success alone does not bring happiness. Nor does failure have to bring unhappiness. Keep it in mind when you listen to today's story."

A chant started somewhere in the back: "We-want-a-story! We-want-a-story!"

"Riiiight," said Nariman. "Now, everyone remembers Vera and Dolly, daughters of Najamai from C Block." There were whistles and hoots; Viraf nudged Kersi with his elbow, who was smiling wistfully. Nariman held up his hand: "Now now, boys, behave yourselves. Those two girls went abroad for studies many years ago, and never came back. They settled there happily.

"And like them, a fellow called Sarosh also went abroad, to Toronto, but did not find happiness there. This story is about him. You probably don't know him, he does not live in Firozsha Baag, though he is related to someone who does."

"Who? Who?"

"Curiosity killed the cat," said Nariman, running a finger over each branch of his moustache, "and what's important is the tale. So let us continue. This Sarosh began calling himself Sid after living in Toronto for a few months, but in our story he will be Sarosh and nothing but Sarosh, for that is his proper Parsi name. Besides, that was his own stipulation when he entrusted me with the sad but instructive chronicle of his recent life." Nariman polished his glasses with his handkerchief, put them on again, and began.

"At the point where our story commences, Sarosh had been living in Toronto for ten years. We find him depressed and miserable, perched on top of the toilet, crouching on his haunches, feet planted firmly for balance upon the white plastic oval of the toilet seat.

"Daily for a decade had Sarosh suffered this position. Morning after morning, he had no choice but to climb up and simulate the squat of our Indian latrines. If he sat down, no amount of exertion could produce success.

"At first, this inability was not more than mildly incommodious. As time went by, however, the frustrated attempts caused him grave anxiety. And when the failure stretched unbroken over ten years, it began to torment and haunt all his waking hours."

Some of the boys struggled hard to keep straight faces. They suspected that Nariman was not telling just a funny story, because if he intended them to laugh there was always some unmistakable way to let them know. Only the thought of displeasing Nariman and prematurely terminating the story kept their paroxysms of mirth from bursting forth unchecked.

Nariman continued: "You see, ten years was the time Sarosh had set himself to achieve complete adaptation to the new country. But how could he claim adaptation with any honesty if the acceptable catharsis[1] continually failed to favour him? Obtaining his new citizenship had not helped either. He remained dependent on the old way, and this unalterable fact, strengthened afresh every morning of his life in the new country, suffocated him.

"The ten-year time limit was more an accident than anything else. But it hung over him with the awesome presence and sharpness of a guillotine.

1   *catharsis* Purgation; usually refers to emotional release, but can also refer to defecation.

Careless words, boys, careless words in a moment of lightheartedness, as is so often the case with us all, had led to it.

"Ten years before, Sarosh had returned triumphantly to Bombay after fulfilling the immigration requirements of the Canadian High Commission in New Delhi. News of his imminent departure spread amongst relatives and friends. A farewell party was organized. In fact, it was given by his relatives in Firozsha Baag. Most of you will be too young to remember it, but it was a very loud party, went on till late in the night. Very lengthy and heated arguments took place, which is not the thing to do at a party. It started like this: Sarosh was told by some what a smart decision he had made, that his whole life would change for the better; others said he was making a mistake, emigration was all wrong, but if he wanted to be unhappy that was his business, they wished him well.

"By and by, after substantial amounts of Scotch and soda and rum and Coke had disappeared, a fierce debate started between the two groups. To this day Sarosh does not know what made him raise his glass and announce: 'My dear family, my dear friends, if I do not become completely Canadian in exactly ten years from the time I land there, then I will come back. I promise. So please, no more arguments. Enjoy the party.' His words were greeted with cheers and shouts of hear! hear! They told him never to fear embarrassment; there was no shame if he decided to return to the country of his birth.

"But shortly, his poor worried mother pulled him aside. She led him to the back room and withdrew her worn and aged prayer book from her purse, saying, 'I want you to place your hand upon the *Avesta*¹ and swear that you will keep that promise.'

"He told her not to be silly, that it was just a joke. But she insisted. '*Kassum khà*²—on the *Avesta*. One last thing for your mother. Who knows when you will see me again?' and her voice grew tremulous as it always did when she turned deeply emotional. Sarosh complied, and the prayer book was returned to her purse.

"His mother continued: 'It is better to live in want among your family and your friends, who love you and care for you, than to be unhappy surrounded by vacuum cleaners and dishwashers and big shiny motor cars.' She hugged him. Then they joined the celebration in progress.

"And Sarosh's careless words spoken at the party gradually forged themselves into a commitment as much to himself as to his mother and the others. It stayed with him all his years in the new land, reminding him every morning

---

1   *Avesta* Sacred text of Zoroastrianism.
2   *Kassum khà* Gujarati: Swear.

of what must happen at the end of the tenth, as it reminded him now while he descended from his perch."

Jehangir wished the titters and chortles around him would settle down, he found them annoying. When Nariman structured his sentences so carefully and chose his words with extreme care as he was doing now, Jehangir found it most pleasurable to listen. Sometimes, he remembered certain words Nariman had used, or combinations of words, and repeated them to himself, enjoying again the beauty of their sounds when he went for his walks to the Hanging Gardens[1] or was sitting alone on the stone steps of C Block. Mumbling to himself did nothing to mitigate the isolation which the other boys in the Baag had dropped around him like a heavy cloak, but he had grown used to all that by now.

Nariman continued: "In his own apartment Sarosh squatted barefoot. Elsewhere, if he had to go with his shoes on, he would carefully cover the seat with toilet paper before climbing up. He learnt to do this after the first time, when his shoes had left telltale footprints on the seat. He had had to clean it with a wet paper towel. Luckily, no one had seen him.

"But there was not much he could keep secret about his ways. The world of washrooms is private and at the same time very public. The absence of his feet below the stall door, the smell of faeces, the rustle of paper, glimpses caught through the narrow crack between stall door and jamb—all these added up to only one thing: a foreign presence in the stall, not doing things in the conventional way. And if the one outside could receive the fetor of Sarosh's business wafting through the door, poor unhappy Sarosh too could detect something malodorous in the air: the presence of xenophobia and hostility."

What a feast, thought Jehangir, what a feast of words! This would be the finest story Nariman had ever told, he just knew it.

"But Sarosh did not give up trying. Each morning he seated himself to push and grunt, grunt and push, squirming and writhing unavailingly on the white plastic oval. Exhausted, he then hopped up, expert at balancing now, and completed the movement quite effortlessly.

"The long morning hours in the washroom created new difficulties. He was late going to work on several occasions, and one such day, the supervisor called him in: 'Here's your time-sheet for this month. You've been late eleven times. What's the problem?'"

Here, Nariman stopped because his neighbour Rustomji's door creaked open. Rustomji peered out, scowling and muttered, "Saala[2] loafers, sitting all

---

1   *Hanging Gardens* Terraced gardens in Bombay (Mumbai) featuring hedges sculpted into animal shapes.
2   *Saala* Hindi swear word.

evening outside people's houses, making a nuisance, and being encouraged by grownups at that."

He stood there a moment longer, fingering the greying chest hair that was easily accessible through his *sudra*, then went inside. The boys immediately took up a soft and low chant: "Rustomji-the-curmudgeon! Rustomji-the-curmudgeon!"

Nariman held up his hand disapprovingly. But secretly, he was pleased that the name was still popular, the name he had given Rustomji when the latter had refused to pay his share for painting the building. "Quiet, quiet!" said he. "Do you want me to continue or not?"

"Yes, yes!" The chanting died away, and Nariman resumed the story.

"So Sarosh was told by his supervisor that he was coming late to work too often. What could poor Sarosh say?"

"What, Nariman Uncle?" rose the refrain.

"Nothing, of course. The supervisor, noting his silence, continued: 'If it keeps up, the consequences could be serious as far as your career is concerned.'

"Sarosh decided to speak. He said embarrassedly, 'It's a different kind of problem. I ... I don't know how to explain ... it's an immigration-related problem.'

"Now this supervisor must have had experience with other immigrants, because right away he told Sarosh, 'No problem. Just contact your Immigrant Aid Society. They should be able to help you. Every ethnic group has one: Vietnamese, Chinese—I'm certain that one exists for Indians. If you need time off to go there, no problem. That can be arranged, no problem. As long as you do something about your lateness, there's no problem.' That's the way they talk over there, nothing is ever a problem.

"So Sarosh thanked him and went to his desk. For the umpteenth time he bitterly rued his oversight. Could fate have plotted it, concealing the western toilet behind a shroud of anxieties which had appeared out of nowhere to beset him just before he left India? After all, he had readied himself meticulously for the new life. Even for the great, merciless Canadian cold he had heard so much about. How could he have overlooked preparation for the western toilet with its matutinal[1] demands unless fate had conspired? In Bombay, you know that offices of foreign businesses offer both options in their bathrooms. So do all hotels with three stars or more. By practising in familiar surroundings, Sarosh was convinced he could have mastered a seated evacuation before departure.

"But perhaps there was something in what the supervisor said. Sarosh found a telephone number for the Indian Immigrant Aid Society and made

---

1   *matutinal* Early-morning.

an appointment. That afternoon, he met Mrs. Maha-Lepate[1] at the Society's office."

Kersi and Viraf looked at each other and smiled. Nariman Uncle had a nerve, there was more *lepate* in his own stories than anywhere else.

"Mrs. Maha-Lepate was very understanding, and made Sarosh feel at ease despite the very personal nature of his problem. She said, 'Yes, we get many referrals. There was a man here last month who couldn't eat Wonder Bread—it made him throw up.'

"By the way, boys, Wonder Bread is a Canadian bread which all happy families eat to be happy in the same way; the unhappy families are unhappy in their own fashion[2] by eating other brands." Jehangir was the only one who understood, and murmured, "Tolstoy," at Nariman's little joke. Nariman noticed it, pleased. He continued.

"Mrs. Maha-Lepate told Sarosh about that case: 'Our immigrant specialist, Dr. No-Ilaaz, recommended that the patient eat cake instead.[3] He explained that Wonder Bread caused vomiting because the digestive system was used to Indian bread only, made with Indian flour in the village he came from. However, since his system was unfamiliar with cake, Canadian or otherwise, it did not react but was digested as a newfound food. In this way he got used to Canadian flour first in cake form. Just yesterday we received a report from Dr. No-Ilaaz. The patient successfully ate his first slice of whole-wheat Wonder Bread with no ill effects. The ultimate goal is pure white Wonder Bread.'

"Like a polite Parsi boy, Sarosh said, 'That's very interesting.' The garrulous Mrs. Maha-Lepate was about to continue, and he tried to interject: 'But I—' but Mrs. Maha-Lepate was too quick for him: 'Oh, there are so many interesting cases I could tell you about. Like the woman from Sri Lanka—referred to us because they don't have their own Society—who could not drink the water here. Dr. No-Ilaaz said it was due to the different mineral content. So he started her on Coca-Cola and then began diluting it with water, bit by bit. Six weeks later she took her first sip of unadulterated Canadian water and managed to keep it down.'

"Sarosh could not halt Mrs. Maha-Lepate as she launched from one case history into another: 'Right now, Dr. No-Ilaaz is working on a very unusual case. Involves a whole Pakistani family. Ever since immigrating to Canada,

---

1   *Maha-Lepate* Hindi: Great Yarn-Teller.
2   *"the unhappy ... own fashion"* See the opening sentence of Leo Tolstoy's classic Russian novel *Anna Karenina* (1873–77): "Happy families are all alike; every unhappy family is unhappy in its own way."
3   *No-Ilaaz* Hindi: No-Cure; *eat cake instead* Reference to a quotation attributed to Marie Antoinette (1755–93), Queen of France. When told that the peasants had no bread to eat, she supposedly declared, "let them eat cake."

none of them can swallow. They choke on their own saliva, and have to spit constantly. But we are confident that Dr. No-Ilaaz will find a remedy. He has never been stumped by any immigrant problems. Besides, we have an information network with other third-world Immigrant Aid Societies. We all seem to share a history of similar maladies, and regularly compare notes. Some of us thought these problems were linked to retention of original citizenship. But this was a false lead.'

"Sarosh, out of his own experience, vigorously nodded agreement. By now he was truly fascinated by Mrs. Maha-Lepate's wealth of information. Reluctantly, he interrupted: 'But will Dr. No-Ilaaz be able to solve my problem?'

"'I have every confidence that he will,' replied Mrs. Maha-Lepate in great earnest. 'And if he has no remedy for you right away, he will be delighted to start working on one. He loves to take up new projects.'"

Nariman halted to blow his nose, and a clear shrill voice travelled the night air of the Firozsha Baag compound from C Block to where the boys had collected around Nariman in A Block: "Jehangoo! O Jehangoo! Eight o'clock! Upstairs now!"

Jehangir stared at his feet in embarrassment. Nariman looked at his watch and said, "Yes, it's eight." But Jehangir did not move, so he continued.

"Mrs. Maha-Lepate was able to arrange an appointment while Sarosh waited, and he went directly to the doctor's office. What he had heard so far sounded quite promising. Then he cautioned himself not to get overly optimistic, that was the worst mistake he could make. But along the way to the doctor's, he could not help thinking what a lovely city Toronto was. It was the same way he had felt when he first saw it ten years ago, before all the joy had dissolved in the acid of his anxieties."

Once again that shrill voice travelled through the clear night: "*Arré* Jehangoo! *Muà*, do I have to come down and drag you upstairs!"

Jehangir's mortification was now complete. Nariman made it easy for him, though: "The first part of the story is over. Second part continues tomorrow. Same time, same place." The boys were surprised, Nariman did not make such commitments. But never before had he told such a long story. They began drifting back to their homes.

As Jehangir strode hurriedly to C Block, falsettos and piercing shrieks followed him in the darkness: "*Arré* Jehangoo! *Muà*, Jehangoo! Bulsara Bookworm! Eight o'clock Jehangoo!" Shaking his head, Nariman went indoors to Hirabai.

Next evening the story punctually resumed when Nariman took his place on the topmost step of A Block: "You remember that we left Sarosh on his way to see the Immigrant Aid Society's doctor. Well, Dr. No-Ilaaz listened patiently to Sarosh's concerns, then said, 'As a matter of fact, there is a remedy which is so new even the IAS does not know about it. Not even that Mrs. Maha-Lepate who knows it all,' he added drolly, twirling his stethoscope like a stunted lasso. He slipped it on around his neck before continuing: 'It involves a minor operation which was developed with financial assistance from the Multicultural Department. A small device, *Crappus Non Interruptus*, or CNI as we call it, is implanted in the bowel. The device is controlled by an external handheld transmitter similar to the ones used for automatic garage door-openers—you may have seen them in hardware stores.'

Nariman noticed that most of the boys wore puzzled looks and realized he had to make some things clearer. "The Multicultural Department is a Canadian invention. It is supposed to ensure that ethnic cultures are able to flourish, so that Canadian society will consist of a mosaic of cultures—that's their favourite word, mosaic—instead of one uniform mix, like the American melting pot. If you ask me, mosaic and melting pot are both nonsense, and ethnic is a polite way of saying bloody foreigner. But anyway, you understand Multicultural Department? Good. So Sarosh nodded, and Dr. No-Ilaaz went on: 'You can encode the hand-held transmitter with a personal ten-digit code. Then all you do is position yourself on the toilet seat and activate your transmitter. Just like a garage door, your bowel will open without pushing or grunting.'"

There was some snickering in the audience, and Nariman raised his eyebrows, whereupon they covered up their mouths with their hands. "The doctor asked Sarosh if he had any questions. Sarosh thought for a moment, then asked if it required any maintenance.

"Dr. No-Ilaaz replied: 'CNI is semi-permanent and operates on solar energy. Which means you would have to make it a point to get some sun periodically, or it would cease and lead to constipation. However, you don't have to strip for a tan. Exposing ten percent of your skin surface once a week during summer will let the device store sufficient energy for year-round operation.'

"Sarosh's next question was: 'Is there any hope that someday the bowels can work on their own, without operating the device?' at which Dr. No-Ilaaz grimly shook his head: 'I'm afraid not. You must think very, very carefully before making a decision. Once CNI is implanted, you can never pass a motion in the natural way—neither sitting nor squatting.'

"He stopped to allow Sarosh time to think it over, then continued: 'And you must understand what that means. You will never be able to live a normal life again. You will be permanently different from your family and friends because of this basic internal modification. In fact, in this country or that, it will set you apart from your fellow countrymen. So you must consider the whole thing most carefully.'

"Dr. No-Ilaaz paused, toyed with his stethoscope, shuffled some papers on his desk, then resumed: 'There are other dangers you should know about.

Just as a garage door can be accidentally opened by a neighbour's transmitter on the same frequency, CNI can also be activated by someone with similar apparatus.' To ease the tension he attempted a quick laugh and said, 'Very embarrassing, eh, if it happened at the wrong place and time. Mind you, the risk is not so great at present, because the chances of finding yourself within a fifty-foot radius of another transmitter on the same frequency are infinitesimal. But what about the future? What if CNI becomes very popular? Sufficient permutations may not be available for transmitter frequencies and you could be sharing the code with others. Then the risk of accidents becomes greater.'"

Something landed with a loud thud in the yard behind A Block, making Nariman startle. Immediately, a yowling and screeching and caterwauling went up from the stray cats there, and the *kuchrawalli*'s[1] dog started barking. Some of the boys went around the side of A Block to peer over the fence into the backyard. But the commotion soon died down of its own accord. The boys returned and, once again, Nariman's voice was the only sound to be heard.

"By now, Sarosh was on the verge of deciding against the operation. Dr. No-Ilaaz observed this and was pleased. He took pride in being able to dissuade his patients from following the very remedies which he first so painstakingly described. True to his name, Dr. No-Ilaaz believed no remedy is the best remedy, rather than prescribing this-mycin and that-mycin for every little ailment. So he continued: 'And what about our sons and daughters? And the quality of their lives? We still don't know about the long-term effects of CNI. Some researchers speculate that it could generate a genetic deficiency, that the offspring of a CNI parent would also require CNI. On the other hand, they could be perfectly healthy toilet seat-users, without any congenital defects. We just don't know at this stage.'

"Sarosh rose from his chair: 'Thank you very much for your time, Dr. No-Ilaaz. But I don't think I want to take such a drastic step. As you suggest, I will think it over carefully.'

"'Good, good,' said Dr. No-Ilaaz, 'I was hoping you would say that. There is one more thing. The operation is extremely expensive, and is not covered by the province's Health Insurance Plan. Many immigrant groups are lobbying to obtain coverage for special immigration-related health problems. If they succeed, then good for you.'

"Sarosh left Dr. No-Ilaaz's office with his mind made up. Time was running out. There had been a time when it was perfectly natural to squat. Now it seemed a grotesquely aberrant thing to do. Wherever he went he was reminded of the ignominy of his way. If he could not be westernized in all respects, he was nothing but a failure in this land—a failure not just in the washrooms

---

1   *kuchrawalli* Garbage collector.

of the nation but everywhere. He knew what he must do if he was to be true
to himself and to the decade-old commitment. So what do you think Sarosh
did next?"

"What, Nariman Uncle?"

"He went to the travel agent specializing in tickets to India. He bought a
fully refundable ticket to Bombay for the day when he would complete exactly
ten immigrant years—if he succeeded even once before that day dawned, he
would cancel the booking.

"The travel agent asked sympathetically, 'Trouble at home?' His name was
Mr. Rawaana, and he was from Bombay too.

"'No,' said Sarosh, 'trouble in Toronto.'

"'That's a shame,' said Mr. Rawaana. 'I don't want to poke my nose into
your business, but in my line of work I meet so many people who are going
back to their homeland because of their problems here. Sometimes I forget
I'm a travel agent, that my interest is to convince them to travel. Instead, I tell
them: don't give up, God is great, stay and try again. It's bad for my profits
but gives me a different, a spiritual kind of satisfaction when I succeed. And
I succeed about half the time. Which means,' he added with a wry laugh, 'I
could double my profits if I minded my own business.'

"After the lengthy sessions with Mrs. Maha-Lepate and Dr. No-Ilaaz,
Sarosh felt he had listened to enough advice and kind words. Much as he
disliked doing it, he had to hurt Mr. Rawaana's feelings and leave his predicament undiscussed: 'I'm sorry, but I'm in a hurry. Will you be able to look after
the booking?'

"'Well, okay,' said Mr. Rawaana, a trifle crestfallen; he did not relish the
travel business as much as he did counselling immigrants. 'Hope you solve
your problem. I will be happy to refund your fare, believe me.'

"Sarosh hurried home. With only four weeks to departure, every spare
minute, every possible method had to be concentrated on a final attempt at
adaptation.

"He tried laxatives, crunching down the tablets with a prayer that these
would assist the sitting position. Changing brands did not help, and neither
did various types of suppositories. He spent long stretches on the toilet seat
each morning. The supervisor continued to reprimand him for tardiness. To
make matters worse, Sarosh left his desk every time he felt the slightest urge,
hoping: maybe this time.

"The working hours expended in the washroom were noted with unflag-
ging vigilance by the supervisor. More counselling sessions followed. Sarosh
refused to extinguish his last hope, and the supervisor punctiliously recorded
'No Improvement' in his daily log. Finally, Sarosh was fired. It would soon
have been time to resign in any case, and he could not care less.

"Now whole days went by seated on the toilet, and he stubbornly refused to relieve himself the other way. The doorbell would ring only to be ignored. The telephone went unanswered. Sometimes, he would awake suddenly in the dark hours before dawn and rush to the washroom like a madman."

Without warning, Rustomji flung open his door and stormed: "Ridiculous nonsense this is becoming! Two days in a row, whole Firozsha Baag gathers here! This is not Chaupatty beach,[1] this is not a squatters' colony, this is a building, people want to live here in peace and quiet!" Then just as suddenly, he stamped inside and slammed the door. Right on cue, Nariman continued, before the boys could say anything.

"Time for meals was the only time Sarosh allowed himself off the seat. Even in his desperation he remembered that if he did not eat well, he was doomed—the downward pressure on his gut was essential if there was to be any chance of success.

"But the ineluctable day of departure dawned, with grey skies and the scent of rain, while success remained out of sight. At the airport Sarosh checked in and went to the dreary lounge. Out of sheer habit he started towards the washroom. Then he realized the hopelessness of it and returned to the cold, clammy plastic of the lounge seats. Airport seats are the same almost anywhere in the world.

"The boarding announcement was made, and Sarosh was the first to step onto the plane. The skies were darker now. Out of the window he saw a flash of lightning fork through the clouds. For some reason, everything he'd learned years ago in St. Xavier's about sheet lightning and forked lightning went through his mind. He wished it would change to sheet, there was some-thing sinister and unpropitious about forked lightning."

Kersi, absorbedly listening, began cracking his knuckles quite uncon-sciously. His childhood habit still persisted. Jehangir frowned at the distur-bance, and Viraf nudged Kersi to stop it.

"Sarosh fastened his seat-belt and attempted to turn his thoughts towards the long journey home: to the questions he would be expected to answer, the sympathy and criticism that would be thrust upon him. But what remained uppermost in his mind was the present moment—him in the plane, dark skies lowering, lightning on the horizon—irrevocably spelling out: defeat.

"But wait. Something else was happening now. A tiny rumble. Inside him. Or was it his imagination? Was it really thunder outside which, in his present disoriented state, he was internalizing? No, there it was again. He had to go.

"He reached the washroom, and almost immediately the sign flashed to 'Please return to seat and fasten seat-belts.' Sarosh debated whether to squat

---

1   *Chaupatty beach* Public beach in Bombay (Mumbai).

and finish the business quickly, abandoning the perfunctory seated attempt. But the plane started to move and that decided him; it would be difficult now to balance while squatting.

"He pushed. The plane continued to move. He pushed again, trembling with the effort. The seat-belt sign flashed quicker and brighter now. The plane moved faster and faster. And Sarosh pushed hard, harder than he had ever pushed before, harder than in all his ten years of trying in the new land. And the memories of Bombay, the immigration interview in New Delhi, the farewell party, his mother's tattered prayer book, all these, of their own accord, emerged from beyond the region of the ten years to push with him and give him newfound strength."

Nariman paused and cleared his throat. Dusk was falling, and the frequency of B.E.S.T. buses plying the main road outside Firozsha Baag had dropped. Bats began to fly madly from one end of the compound to the other, silent shadows engaged in endless laps over the buildings.

"With a thunderous clap the rain started to fall. Sarosh felt a splash under him. Could it really be? He glanced down to make certain. Yes, it was. He had succeeded!

"But was it already too late? The plane waited at its assigned position on the runway, jet engines at full thrust. Rain was falling in torrents and takeoff could be delayed. Perhaps even now they would allow him to cancel his flight, to disembark. He lurched out of the constricting cubicle.

"A stewardess hurried towards him: 'Excuse me, sir, but you must return to your seat immediately and fasten your belt.'

"'You don't understand!' Sarosh shouted excitedly. 'I must get off the plane! Everything is all right. I don't have to go anymore ...'

"'That's impossible, sir!' said the stewardess, aghast. 'No one can leave now. Takeoff procedures are in progress!' The wild look in his sleepless eyes, and the dark rings around them scared her. She beckoned for help.

"Sarosh continued to argue, and a steward and the chief stewardess hurried over: 'What seems to be the problem, sir? You *must* resume your seat. We are authorized, if necessary, to forcibly restrain you, sir.'

"The plane began to move again, and suddenly Sarosh felt all the urgency leaving him. His feverish mind, the product of nightmarish days and tortuous nights, was filled again with the calm which had fled a decade ago, and he spoke softly now: 'That ... that will not be necessary ... it's okay, I understand.' He readily returned to his seat.

"As the aircraft sped down the runway, Sarosh's first reaction was one of joy. The process of adaptation was complete. But later, he could not help wondering if success came before or after the ten-year limit had expired. And since he had already passed through the customs and security check, was he really an immigrant in every sense of the word at the moment of achievement?

"But such questions were merely academic. Or were they? He could not decide. If he returned, what would it be like? Ten years ago, the immigration officer who had stamped his passport had said, 'Welcome to Canada.' It was one of Sarosh's dearest memories, and thinking of it, he fell asleep.

"The plane was flying above the rainclouds. Sunshine streamed into the cabin. A few raindrops were still clinging miraculously to the windows, reminders of what was happening below. They sparkled as the sunlight caught them."

Some of the boys made as if to leave, thinking the story was finally over. Clearly, they had not found this one as interesting as the others Nariman had told. What dolts, thought Jehangir, they cannot recognize a masterpiece when they hear one. Nariman motioned with his hand for silence.

"But our story does not end there. There was a welcome-home party for Sarosh a few days after he arrived in Bombay. It was not in Firozsha Baag this time because his relatives in the Baag had a serious sickness in the house. But I was invited to it anyway. Sarosh's family and friends were considerate enough to wait till the jet lag had worked its way out of his system. They wanted him to really enjoy this one.

"Drinks began to flow freely again in his honour: Scotch and soda, rum and Coke, brandy. Sarosh noticed that during his absence all the brand names had changed—the labels were different and unfamiliar. Even for the mixes. Instead of Coke there was Thums-Up, and he remembered reading in the papers about Coca-Cola being kicked out by the Indian Government for refusing to reveal their secret formula.

"People slapped him on the back and shook his hand vigorously, over and over, right through the evening. They said: 'Telling the truth, you made the right decision, look how happy your mother is to live to see this day;' or they asked: 'Well, bossy, what changed your mind?' Sarosh smiled and nodded his way through it all, passing around Canadian currency at the insistence of some of the curious ones who, egged on by his mother, also pestered him to display his Canadian passport and citizenship card. She had been badgering him since his arrival to tell her the real reason: '*Saachoo kahé*,[1] what brought you back?' and was hoping that tonight, among his friends, he might raise his glass and reveal something. But she remained disappointed.

"Weeks went by and Sarosh found himself desperately searching for his old place in the pattern of life he had vacated ten years ago. Friends who had organized the welcome-home party gradually disappeared. He went walking

---

1   *Saachoo kahé* Gujarati: Tell the truth.

in the evenings along Marine Drive, by the sea-wall, where the old crowd used to congregate. But the people who sat on the parapet while waves crashed behind their backs were strangers. The tetrapods[1] were still there, staunchly protecting the reclaimed land from the fury of the sea. He had watched as a kid when cranes had lowered these cement and concrete hulks of respectable grey into the water. They were grimy black now, and from their angularities rose the distinct stench of human excrement. The old pattern was never found by Sarosh; he searched in vain. Patterns of life are selfish and unforgiving.

"Then one day, as I was driving past Marine Drive, I saw someone sitting alone. He looked familiar, so I stopped. For a moment I did not recognize Sarosh, so forlorn and woebegone was his countenance. I parked the apple of my eye and went to him, saying, 'Hullo, Sid, what are you doing here on your lonesome?' And he said, 'No, no! No more Sid, please, that name reminds me of all my troubles.' Then, on the parapet at Marine Drive, he told me his unhappy and wretched tale, with the waves battering away at the tetrapods, and around us the hawkers screaming about coconut-water and sugar-cane juice and *paan*.[2]

"When he finished, he said that he had related to me the whole sad saga because he knew how I told stories to boys in the Baag, and he wanted me to tell this one, especially to those who were planning to go abroad. 'Tell them,' said Sarosh, 'that the world can be a bewildering place, and dreams and ambitions are often paths to the most pernicious of traps.' As he spoke, I could see that Sarosh was somewhere far away, perhaps in New Delhi at his immigration interview, seeing himself as he was then, with what he thought was a life of hope and promise stretching endlessly before him. Poor Sarosh. Then he was back beside me on the parapet.

"'I pray you, in your stories,' said Sarosh, his old sense of humour returning as he deepened his voice for his favourite *Othello* lines"—and here, Nariman produced a basso profundo of his own—"'when you shall these unlucky deeds relate, speak of me as I am; nothing extenuate, nor set down aught in malice: tell them that in Toronto once there lived a Parsi boy as best as he could. Set you down this; and say, besides, that for some it was good and for some it was bad, but for me life in the land of milk and honey was just a pain in the posterior.'"[3]

And now, Nariman allowed his low-pitched rumbles to turn into chuckles. The boys broke into cheers and loud applause and cries of "Encore!"

1   *tetrapods* Four-pointed concrete shapes placed on the shoreline to prevent erosion.
2   *paan* Preparation of betel leaves, a natural stimulant.
3   *"I pray you ... the posterior"* Parody of Othello's last words in Shakespeare's *Othello*.

and "More!" Finally, Nariman had to silence them by pointing warningly at Rustomji-the-curmudgeon's door.

While Kersi and Viraf were joking and wondering what to make of it all, Jehangir edged forward and told Nariman this was the best story he had ever told. Nariman patted his shoulder and smiled. Jehangir left, wondering if Nariman would have been as popular if Dr. Mody was still alive. Probably, since the two were liked for different reasons: Dr. Mody used to be constantly jovial, whereas Nariman had his periodic story-telling urges.

Now the group of boys who had really enjoyed the Savukshaw story during the previous week spoke up. Capitalizing on Nariman's extraordinarily good mood, they began clamouring for more Savukshaw: "Nariman Uncle, tell the one about Savukshaw the hunter, the one you had started that day."

"What hunter? I don't know which one you mean." He refused to be reminded of it, and got up to leave. But there was a loud protest, and the boys started chanting, "We-want-Savukshaw! We-want-Savukshaw!"

Nariman looked fearfully towards Rustomji's door and held up his hands placatingly: "All right, all right! Next time it will be Savukshaw again. Savukshaw the artist. The story of Parsi Picasso."[1]

—1987

---

1   *Parsi Picasso* Pun on the name of Spanish artist Pablo Picasso (1881–1973).

Kazuo Ishiguro
b. 1954

Kazuo Ishiguro was born in Nagasaki, Japan. He and his family moved to England in 1960, when his father accepted a two-year research post at the National Institute of Oceanography. The family considered their life in England a temporary situation. Ishiguro has said that his parents "didn't have the mentality of immigrants because they always thought they would go home at some stage." The confluence of Ishiguro's memory of Japan—"a few hazy images"—his family's continued observance of Japanese culture in the home, and his growth to maturity in England informs his work, which often speaks of regret, unresolved emotion, and a yearning to recapture the past.

Before the age of 35, Ishiguro wrote three novels that established his credentials as a serious author: *A Pale View of Hills* (1982), which was awarded the Winifred Holtby Memorial Prize; *An Artist of the Floating World* (1986), which was awarded the Whitbread Book of the Year award and was shortlisted for the Man Booker Prize for Fiction; and *The Remains of the Day* (1989), which was awarded the Man Booker Prize for Fiction and was made into a full-length feature film.

Ishiguro's fourth novel, *The Unconsoled* (1995), revealed a change in his artistic direction, previously mischaracterized, he believes, as realist. The novel received mixed reviews and baffled many readers, including the critic James Wood, who said that it "invented its own category of badness." Nevertheless, *The Unconsoled* won the Cheltenham Prize, which is awarded yearly to a book of considerable merit that is overlooked by critics. Since *The Unconsoled*, Ishiguro has continued to produce works that challenge and interrogate the novel's conventions, including *Never Let Me Go* (2005), the second of his novels to be made into a feature film. He has also written two original screenplays, *The Saddest Music in the World* (2003) and *The White Countess* (2005).

A Family Supper

Fugu is a fish caught off the Pacific shores of Japan. The fish has held a special significance for me ever since my mother died through eating one. The poison resides in the sexual glands of the fish, inside two fragile bags. When preparing the fish, these bags must be removed with caution, for any clumsiness will result in the poison leaking into the veins. Regrettably, it is not easy to tell whether or not this operation has been carried out successfully. The proof is, as it were, in the eating.

Fugu poisoning is hideously painful and almost always fatal. If the fish has been eaten during the evening, the victim is usually overtaken by pain during his sleep. He rolls about in agony for a few hours and is dead by morning. The fish became extremely popular in Japan after the war. Until stricter regulations were imposed, it was all the rage to perform the hazardous gutting operation in one's own kitchen, then to invite neighbours and friends round for the feast.

At the time of my mother's death, I was living in California. My relationship with my parents had become somewhat strained around that period, and consequently I did not learn of the circumstances surrounding her death until I returned to Tokyo two years later. Apparently, my mother had always refused to eat fugu, but on this particular occasion she had made an exception, having been invited by an old schoolfriend whom she was anxious not to offend. It was my father who supplied me with the details as we drove from the airport to his house in the Kamakura district. When we finally arrived, it was nearing the end of a sunny autumn day,

"Did you eat on the plane?" my father asked. We were sitting on the tatami[1] floor of his tea-room.

"They gave me a light snack."

"You must be hungry. We'll eat as soon as Kikuko arrives."

My father was a formidable-looking man with a large stony jaw and furious black eyebrows. I think now in retrospect that he much resembled Chou En-lai,[2] although he would not have cherished such a comparison, being particularly proud of the pure samurai blood that ran in the family. His general presence was not one which encouraged relaxed conversation; neither were things helped much by his odd way of stating each remark as if it were the concluding one. In fact, as I sat opposite him that afternoon, a boyhood memory came back to me of the time he had struck me several times around the head for "chattering like an old woman." Inevitably, our conversation since my arrival at the airport had been punctuated by long pauses.

"I'm sorry to hear about the firm," I said when neither of us had spoken for some time. He nodded gravely.

"In fact the story didn't end there," he said. "After the firm's collapse, Watanabe killed himself. He didn't wish to live with the disgrace."

"I see."

"We were partners for seventeen years. A man of principle and honour. I respected him very much."

"Will you go into business again?" I asked.

---

1   *tatami* Straw mat traditionally used as floor covering in Japanese homes.
2   *Chou En-lai* Chinese communist politician (1898–1976).

"I am—in retirement. I'm too old to involve myself in new ventures now. Business these days has become so different. Dealing with foreigners. Doing things their way. I don't understand how we've come to this. Neither did Watanabe." He sighed. "A fine man. A man of principle."

The tea-room looked out over the garden. From where I sat I could make out the ancient well which as a child I had believed haunted. It was just visible now through the thick foliage. The sun had sunk low and much of the garden had fallen into shadow.

"I'm glad in any case that you've decided to come back," my father said. "More than a short visit, I hope."

"I'm not sure what my plans will be."

"I for one am prepared to forget the past. Your mother too was always ready to welcome you back—upset as she was by your behaviour."

"I appreciate your sympathy. As I say, I'm not sure what my plans are."

"I've come to believe now that there were no evil intentions in your mind," my father continued. "You were swayed by certain—influences. Like so many others."

"Perhaps we should forget it, as you suggest."

"As you will. More tea?"

Just then a girl's voice came echoing through the house.

"At last." My father rose to his feet. "Kikuko has arrived."

Despite our difference in years, my sister and I had always been close. Seeing me again seemed to make her excessively excited and for a while she did nothing but giggle nervously. But she calmed down somewhat when my father started to question her about Osaka and her university. She answered him with short formal replies. She in turn asked me a few questions, but she seemed inhibited by the fear that her questions might lead to awkward topics. After a while, the conversation had become even sparser than prior to Kikuko's arrival. Then my father stood up, saying: "I must attend to the supper. Please excuse me for being burdened down by such matters. Kikuko will look after you."

My sister relaxed quite visibly once he had left the room. Within a few minutes, she was chatting freely about her friends in Osaka and about her classes at university. Then quite suddenly she decided we should walk in the garden and went striding out onto the veranda. We put on some straw sandals that had been left along the veranda rail and stepped out into the garden. The daylight had almost gone.

"I've been dying for a smoke for the last half-hour," she said, lighting a cigarette.

"Then why didn't you smoke?"

She made a furtive gesture back towards the house, then grinned mischievously.

"Oh I see," I said.

"Guess what? I've got a boyfriend now."

"Oh yes?"

"Except I'm wondering what to do. I haven't made up my mind yet."

"Quite understandable."

"You see, he's making plans to go to America. He wants me to go with him as soon as I finish studying."

"I see. And you want to go to America?"

"If we go, we're going to hitch-hike." Kikuko waved a thumb in front of my face. "People say it's dangerous, but I've done it in Osaka and it's fine."

"I see. So what is it you're unsure about?"

We were following a narrow path that wound through the shrubs and finished by the old well. As we walked, Kikuko persisted in taking unnecessarily theatrical puffs on her cigarette.

"Well. I've got lots of friends now in Osaka. I like it there. I'm not sure I want to leave them all behind just yet. And Suichi—I like him, but I'm not sure I want to spend so much time with him. Do you understand?"

"Oh perfectly."

She grinned again, then skipped on ahead of me until she had reached the well. "Do you remember," she said, as I came walking up to her, "how you used to say this well was haunted?"

"Yes, I remember."

We both peered over the side.

"Mother always told me it was the old woman from the vegetable store you'd seen that night," she said. "But I never believed her and never came out here alone."

"Mother used to tell me that too. She even told me once the old woman had confessed to being the ghost. Apparently she'd been taking a short cut through our garden. I imagine she had some trouble clambering over these walls."

Kikuko gave a giggle. She then turned her back to the well, casting her gaze about the garden.

"Mother never really blamed you, you know," she said, in a new voice. I remained silent. "She always used to say to me how it was their fault, hers and Father's, for not bringing you up correctly. She used to tell me how much more careful they'd been with me, and that's why I was so good." She looked up and the mischievous grin had returned to her face. "Poor Mother," she said.

"Yes. Poor Mother."

"Are you going back to California?"

"I don't know. I'll have to see."

"What happened to—to her? To Vicki?"

"That's all finished with," I said. "There's nothing much left for me now in California."

"Do you think I ought to go there?"

"Why not? I don't know. You'll probably like it." I glanced towards the house. "Perhaps we'd better go in soon. Father might need a hand with the supper."

But my sister was once more peering down into the well. "I can't see any ghosts," she said. Her voice echoed a little.

"Is Father very upset about his firm collapsing?"

"Don't know. You can never tell with Father." Then suddenly she straightened up and turned to me. "Did he tell you about old Watanabe? What he did?"

"I heard he committed suicide."

"Well, that wasn't all. He took his whole family with him. His wife and his two little girls."

"Oh yes?"

"Those two beautiful little girls. He turned on the gas while they were all asleep. Then he cut his stomach with a meat knife."

"Yes, Father was just telling me how Watanabe was a man of principle."

"Sick." My sister turned back to the well.

"Careful. You'll fall right in."

"I can't see any ghost," she said. "You were lying to me all that time."

"But I never said it lived down the well."

"Where is it, then?"

We both looked around at the trees and shrubs. The light in the garden had grown very dim. Eventually I pointed to a small clearing some ten yards away.

"Just there I saw it. Just there."

We stared at the spot.

"What did it look like?"

"I couldn't see very well. It was dark."

"But you must have seen something."

"It was an old woman. She was just standing there, watching me."

We kept staring at the spot as if mesmerized.

"She was wearing a white kimono," I said. "Some of her hair had come undone. It was blowing around a little."

Kikuko pushed her elbow against my arm. "Oh be quiet. You're trying to frighten me all over again." She trod on the remains of her cigarette, then for a brief moment stood regarding it with a perplexed expression. She kicked some pine needles over it, then once more displayed her grin. "Let's see if supper's ready," she said.

We found my father in the kitchen. He gave us a quick glance, then carried on with what he was doing.

"Father's become quite a chef since he's had to manage on his own," Kikuko said with a laugh. He turned and looked at my sister coldly.

"Hardly a skill I'm proud of," he said. "Kikuko, come here and help."

For some moments my sister did not move. Then she stepped forward and took an apron hanging from a drawer.

"Just these vegetables need cooking now," he said to her. "The rest just needs watching." Then he looked up and regarded me strangely for some seconds. "I expect you want to look around the house," he said eventually. He put down the chopsticks he had been holding. "It's a long time since you've seen it."

As we left the kitchen I glanced back towards Kikuko, but her back was turned.

"She's a good girl," my father said quietly.

I followed my father from room to room. I had forgotten how large the house was. A panel would slide open and another room would appear. But the rooms were all startlingly empty. In one of the rooms the lights did not come on, and we stared at the stark walls and tatami in the pale light that came from the windows.

"This house is too large for a man to live in alone," my father said. "I don't have much use for most of these rooms now."

But eventually my father opened the door to a room packed full of books and papers. There were flowers in vases and pictures on the walls. Then I noticed something on a low table in the corner of the room. I came nearer and saw it was a plastic model of a battleship, the kind constructed by children. It had been placed on some newspaper; scattered around it were assorted pieces of grey plastic.

My father gave a laugh. He came up to the table and picked up the model.

"Since the firm folded," he said, "I have a little more time on my hands." He laughed again, rather strangely. For a moment his face looked almost gentle. "A little more time."

"That seems odd," I said. "You were always so busy."

"Too busy perhaps." He looked at me with a small smile. "Perhaps I should have been a more attentive father."

I laughed. He went on contemplating his battleship. Then he looked up. "I hadn't meant to tell you this, but perhaps it's best that I do. It's my belief that your mother's death was no accident. She had many worries. And some disappointments."

We both gazed at the plastic battleship.

"Surely," I said eventually, "my mother didn't expect me to live here forever."

"Obviously you don't see. You don't see how it is for some parents. Not only must they lose their children, they must lose them to things they don't understand." He spun the battleship in his fingers. "These little gunboats here could have been better glued, don't you think?"

"Perhaps. I think it looks fine."

"During the war I spent some time on a ship rather like this. But my ambition was always the air force. I figured it like this. If your ship was struck by the enemy, all you could do was struggle in the water hoping for a lifeline. But in an aeroplane—well—there was always the final weapon." He put the model back onto the table. "I don't suppose you believe in war."

"Not particularly."

He cast an eye around the room. "Supper should be ready by now," he said. "You must be hungry."

Supper was waiting in a dimly lit room next to the kitchen. The only source of light was a big lantern that hung over the table, casting the rest of the room into shadow. We bowed to each other before starting the meal.

There was little conversation. When I made some polite comment about the food, Kikuko giggled a little. Her earlier nervousness seemed to have returned to her. My father did not speak for several minutes. Finally he said:

"It must feel strange for you, being back in Japan."

"Yes, it is a little strange."

"Already, perhaps, you regret leaving America."

"A little. Not so much. I didn't leave behind much. Just some empty rooms."

"I see."

I glanced across the table. My father's face looked stony and forbidding in the half-light. We ate on in silence.

Then my eye caught something at the back of the room. At first I continued eating, then my hands became still. The others noticed and looked at me. I went on gazing into the darkness past my father's shoulder.

"Who is that? In that photograph there?"

"Which photograph?" My father turned slightly, trying to follow my gaze.

"The lowest one. The old woman in the white kimono."

My father put down his chopsticks. He looked first at the photograph, then at me.

"Your mother." His voice had become very hard. "Can't you recognize your own mother?"

"My mother. You see, it's dark. I can't see it very well."

No one spoke for a few seconds, then Kikuko rose to her feet. She took the photograph down from the wall, came back to the table and gave it to me.

"She looks a lot older," I said.

"It was taken shortly before her death," said my father.

"It was the dark. I couldn't see very well."

I looked up and noticed my father holding out a hand. I gave him the photograph. He looked at it intently, then held it towards Kikuko. Obediently, my sister rose to her feet once more and returned the picture to the wall.

There was a large pot left unopened at the centre of the table. When Kikuko had seated herself again, my father reached forward and lifted the lid. A cloud of steam rose up and curled towards the lantern. He pushed the pot a little towards me.

"You must be hungry," he said. One side of his face had fallen into shadow.

"Thank you." I reached forward with my chopsticks. The steam was almost scalding. "What is it?"

"Fish."

"It smells very good."

In amidst soup were strips of fish that had curled almost into balls. I picked one out and brought it to my bowl.

"Help yourself. There's plenty."

"Thank you." I took a little more, then pushed the pot towards my father. I watched him take several pieces to his bowl. Then we both watched as Kikuko served herself.

My father bowed slightly. "You must be hungry," he said again. He took some fish to his mouth and started to eat. Then I too chose a piece and put it in my mouth. It felt soft, quite fleshy against my tongue.

"Very good," I said. "What is it?"

"Just fish."

"It's very good."

The three of us ate on in silence. Several minutes went by.

"Some more?"

"Is there enough?"

"There's plenty for all of us." My father lifted the lid and once more steam rose up. We all reached forward and helped ourselves.

"Here," I said to my father, "you have this last piece."

"Thank you."

When we had finished the meal, my father stretched out his arms and yawned with an air of satisfaction. "Kikuko," he said. "Prepare a pot of tea, please."

My sister looked at him, then left the room without comment. My father stood up.

"Let's retire to the other room. It's rather warm in here."

I got to my feet and followed him into the tea-room. The large sliding windows had been left open, bringing in a breeze from the garden. For a while we sat in silence.

"Father," I said, finally.

"Yes?"

"Kikuko tells me Watanabe-San took his whole family with him."

My father lowered his eyes and nodded. For some moments he seemed deep in thought. "Watanabe was very devoted to his work," he said at last. "The collapse of the firm was a great blow to him. I fear it must have weakened his judgment."

"You think what he did—it was a mistake?"

"Why, of course. Do you see it otherwise?"

"No, no. Of course not."

"There are other things besides work."

"Yes."

We fell silent again. The sound of locusts came in from the garden. I looked out into the darkness. The well was no longer visible.

"What do you think you will do now?" my father asked. "Will you stay in Japan for a while?"

"To be honest, I hadn't thought that far ahead."

"If you wish to stay here, I mean here in this house, you would be very welcome. That is, if you don't mind living with an old man."

"Thank you. I'll have to think about it."

I gazed out once more into the darkness.

"But of course," said my father, "this house is so dreary now. You'll no doubt return to America before long."

"Perhaps. I don't know yet."

"No doubt you will."

For some time my father seemed to be studying the back of his hands. Then he looked up and sighed.

"Kikuko is due to complete her studies next spring," he said. "Perhaps she will want to come home then. She's a good girl."

"Perhaps she will."

"Things will improve then."

"Yes, I'm sure they will."

We fell silent once more, waiting for Kikuko to bring the tea.

—1982

John Gould
b. 1959

John Gould is a Canadian author and educator known primarily for his short fiction, though he is also a published novelist and the author of a number of non-fiction pieces. A collection of his short stories, *Kilter: 55 Fictions* (2003), was shortlisted for the 2003 Giller Prize; the jury commented that "the enormous inventiveness of these 55 fictions offers the reader an emotional and intellectual gourmet feast." As an educator, Gould has worked with the BC Festival of the Arts and taught writing at the University of Victoria.

Gould's brand of short fiction is particularly short; what he calls his "very short stories," and others have called "microfictions," are composed in the tradition of the Japanese author Yasunari Kawabata's "Palm of the Hand Stories." The Nobel Prize-winning Kawabata developed the form over the course of his whole career, writing stories of roughly one or two pages in length, with some examples so short as to be almost poem-like. Gould invoked this form explicitly in the title of his first collection of short stories, *The Kingdom of Heaven: Eighty-Eight Palm-of-the-Hand Stories* (1996), and exemplifies this practice in *Kilter*, with the stories an average of three to four pages each. Speaking of the "very short stories" in *Kilter*, author Nino Ricci observes that "Gould's fictions manage to combine the compression of poetry with the narrative drive of fiction, creating whole worlds in a few deft strokes and just as deftly bringing them to sharp, often startling resolutions."

The short story included here, "What You're Ready For," appeared in *Kilter*. Author and filmmaker Corey Lee adapted the story into a short film of the same name, which itself received the Best Short Film Award in 2007 at The Edmonton International Film Festival, and, in 2008, won the Alberta Motion Picture Industry's Award for Best Short Film.

What You're Ready For

"Have you ever asked yourself why this moment is called the present?" says Dr. Laird. "I'd like you to think about that now."

Dr. Laird runs a hand intently through his whitecap of neat, wavy hair—the kind of hair you'd expect of an upwardly mobile prophet, the kind of hair Moses might have worn if he hadn't died in the desert but had made it to the promised land, retired and hit the lecture circuit. Edgar O. Laird, PhD, esteemed author, therapist and guru, takes another step towards his studio audience, towards the dazzled eye of the camera. He spreads his hands, palms out—no tricks. "Why is this moment called the present? Can anybody tell me?"

Up and down the raked rows heads shake, faces adopt a flummoxed, expectant look. The answer to Dr. Laird's question, by the way, is yes. Any one of us could tell him exactly why this moment is called the present—Dr. Laird explained it to us just moments ago, before one of the cameras went kaput and we had to start again. Besides, most of us are so steeped in the wise man's writings that he'd have a devil of a time stumping us. His nifty mnemonics help us out, naturally. I'M MORE: I'm Making My Own Reality Everyday. I CAN: I'm Calling for Abundance Now. GIMME: God Is Making More for Everyone. Still, we wear expressions of unfeigned and delighted anticipation. We're enjoying the shtick even more now that we're in on it.

"Let me tell you then," Dr. Laird finally relents. He tugs back the sleeves of his woolen turtleneck, exposing two thick, furry forearms—getting down to business. "This moment, this now"—he effects a scooping motion with his hands, gathering in the instant like a great pile of poker chips—"this *present* is a *gift*." And he clutches it to his chest.

An appreciative murmur ripples through the audience, a collective sigh of wonder and assent. Heads list ever so slightly right or left in wistful rumination. Present ... gift ... This guy's good.

"As a matter of fact," Dr. Laird continues, "now isn't just a gift, it's *the* gift. If you don't take anything else away with you tonight, I'd like you to take this, the knowledge that this moment is your only possession. It's a difficult knowledge, a demanding knowledge, but you're ready for it. How do I know this? I know this because if you weren't ready for what I have to teach you ... *you wouldn't be here tonight!* It's that simple. If you weren't ready, you wouldn't be here. The car would have broken down, the sitter would have cancelled. Do you see what I'm saying? The world gives each one of us just exactly what we're ready for. I have to tell you, I was on a retreat recently in the Catskills with Ben Roshi, the great Jewish Zen master. Incredible man, Ben is, a true Bodhisattva."[1] The doctor's tone has modulated here, from oracular to avuncular—he's ready to share a little anecdote. A cameraman darts forward with a handheld unit to impart an intimate feel to the footage.

"I'd just been meditating for about eighteen hours," Dr. Laird continues, "and I stopped into the hotel's reception area to pick up a fax. Ben was there doing the same thing. We had a good laugh—it's the sages who really see how funny it all is, you know. Anyway—"

"Okay, Dr. Laird," comes a voice over the studio's PA, "we got this bit before. Let's skip ahead, let's take it from memories and hopes."

"Memories and hopes?" says Dr. Laird, momentarily perplexed. "Memories and hopes? Oh, of course. Right." He closes his eyes for a moment, re-

---

1   *Bodhisattva* In Buddhism, an enlightened being.

calibrating the fine instrument of his soul. "What I'm saying," he finally says, "what I'm saying is that you have nothing but this, nothing but the here and now. I go into this at greater length in *The Wisdom of Wealth*, by the way, for those of you who want to take it further. As I say, nothing but the here, the now. What else have you got? You've got nothing. No past, no future. You've got memories, you've got hopes, yes—but only in the present! Don't you see? This moment is all you've got! Live it now! Live it as though it's your last!"

The first bullet smacks Dr. Laird in the left shoulder, spinning him clockwise, twice. He wobbles briefly before tipping onto his side—an exhausted top. Two more bullets thwack into his prostrate form. After an instant of stunned silence—a moment of presence in the purest sense—people leap to their feet, start scrabbling and clawing their way towards the exits. I allow myself to be carried along with them. I walk a dozen blocks or so—breathing deep, really drinking in the air—and turn down an alleyway. I ditch the gun in one dumpster, my gloves in another.

It's not that he deserved it, that's not what it's about. Tanya would have left me anyway, I understand that, I acknowledge that. If it hadn't been Laird it would have been some other smarmy son of a bitch. No, it's not what you deserve—she explained it to me time and again—it's what you're ready for.

—2003

Ali Smith
b. 1962

Praised by critics as a "deliciously quirky postmodern" writer and a "master of stylistic daring," Ali Smith is a British author and a Fellow of the Royal Society of Literature. Smith divides her attention between the genres of short fiction and the novel, with her novels in particular receiving critical acclaim. Her second novel, *Hotel World* (2001), and her third, *The Accidental* (2005), were each shortlisted for both the Orange Prize for Fiction and the Man Booker Prize for Fiction.

Smith was born in Scotland to working-class parents. She came to writing fiction in a roundabout way, and her first short story collection, *Free Love and Other Stories* (1995), was not published until she was in her early thirties. Smith's stories are often centred around the lives of women, but Amanda Thursfield, writing for the British Council's Arts Group, catalogues a wide range of interests: "The themes she chooses to write about are ambitious: love, particularly that between women, death, loss, guilt, grief, illness, time and the chasms of misunderstanding between the generations where affection can become lost in impatience and incomprehension."

Smith's writing is frequently playful and usually in some way experimental, and she is noted for the tight construction and precise language of her work. She considers short stories a challenging genre for readers "because they are hard. They are closer to poetry in their demands. The easiest thing in the world is to read a blockbuster—you can skip and skim in a way that is impossible if every word counts." This tension between the formal qualities of the short story and the novel provides one of the key elements in the work included here.

True Short Story

There were two men in the café at the table next to mine. One was younger, one was older. They could have been father and son, but there was none of that practised diffidence, none of the cloudy anger that there almost always is between fathers and sons. Maybe they were the result of a parental divorce, the father keen to be a father now that his son was properly into his adulthood, the son keen to be a man in front of his father now that his father was opposite him for at least the length of time of a cup of coffee. No. More likely the older man was the kind of family friend who provides a fathership on summer weekends for the small boy of a divorce-family; a man who knows his responsibility, and now look, the boy had grown up, the man was an older man, and there was this unsaid understanding between them, etc.

I stopped making them up. It felt a bit wrong to. Instead, I listened to what they were saying. They were talking about literature, which happens to be interesting to me, though it wouldn't interest a lot of people. The younger man was talking about the difference between the novel and the short story. The novel, he was saying, was a flabby old whore.

A flabby old whore! the older man said looking delighted.

She was serviceable, roomy, warm and familiar, the younger was saying, but really a bit used up, really a bit too slack and loose.

Slack and loose! the older said laughing.

Whereas the short story, by comparison, was a nimble goddess, a slim nymph.[1] Because so few people had mastered the short story she was still in very good shape.

Very good shape! The older man was smiling from ear to ear at this. He was presumably old enough to remember years in his life, and not so long ago, when it would have been at least a bit dodgy to talk like this. I idly wondered how many of the books in my house were fuckable and how good they'd be in bed. Then I sighed, and got my mobile out and phoned my friend, with whom I usually go to this café on Friday mornings.

She knows quite a lot about the short story. She's spent a lot of her life reading them, writing about them, teaching them, even on occasion writing them. She's read more short stories than most people know (or care) exist. I suppose you could call it a lifelong act of love, though she's not very old, was that morning still in her late thirties. A life-so-far act of love. But already she knew more about the short story and about the people all over the world who write and have written short stories than anyone I've ever met.

She was in hospital, on this particular Friday a couple of years ago now, because a course of chemotherapy had destroyed every single one of her tiny white blood cells and after it had she'd picked up an infection in a wisdom tooth.

I waited for the automaton voice of the hospital phone system to tell me all about itself, then to recite robotically back to me the number I'd just called, then to mispronounce my friend's name, which is Kasia, then to tell me exactly how much it was charging me to listen to it tell me all this, and then to tell me how much it would cost to speak to my friend per minute. Then it connected me.

Hi, I said. It's me.

Are you on your mobile? she said. Don't, Ali, it's expensive on this system. I'll call you back.

---

1   *nymph* Sexually desirable young woman; also, in mythology, a beautiful nature spirit.

No worries, I said. It's just a quickie. Listen. Is the short story a goddess and a nymph and is the novel an old whore?

Is what what? she said.

An old whore, kind of Dickensian[1] one, maybe, I said. Like that prostitute who first teaches David Niven[2] how to have sex in that book.

David Niven? she said.

You know, I said. The prostitute he goes to in The Moon's a Balloon when he's about fourteen, and she's really sweet and she initiates him and he loses his virginity, and he's still wearing his socks, or maybe that's the prostitute who's still wearing the socks, I can't remember, anyway, she's really sweet to him and then he goes back to see her in later life when she's an old whore and he's an internationally famous movie star, and he brings her a lot of presents because he's such a nice man and never forgets a kindness. And is the short story more like Princess Diana?[3]

The short story like Princess Diana, she said. Right.

I sensed the two men, who were getting ready to leave the café, looking at me curiously. I held up my phone.

I'm just asking my friend what she thinks about your nymph thesis, I said.

Both men looked slightly startled. Then both men left the café without looking back.

I told her about the conversation I'd just overheard.

I was thinking of Diana because she's a bit nymphy, I suppose, I said. I can't think of a goddess who's like a nymph. All the goddesses that come into my head are, like, Kali, or Sheela-Na-Gig.[4] Or Aphrodite,[5] she was pretty tough. All that deer-slaying. Didn't she slay deer?

Why is the short story like a nymph, Kasia said. Sounds like a dirty joke. Ha.

Okay, I said. Come on then. Why is the short story like a nymph?

I'll think about it, she said. It'll give me something to do in here.

---

1   *Dickensian* Relating to the style or works of Charles Dickens (1812–70), a popular English novelist known for his depictions of harsh social conditions.

2   *David Niven* British actor and novelist, author of *The Moon's a Balloon: Reminiscences* (1971), an account of his early life.

3   *Princess Diana* Diana Frances Spencer (1961–97), former wife of Charles, Prince of Wales. Her charitable efforts and popular public persona attracted immense media coverage.

4   *Kali* Hindu goddess linked with death and violent sexuality. She slays demons and often wears a necklace of skulls; *Sheela-Na-Gig* Irish term for medieval carvings of exaggerated female figures, usually displaying grotesque sexuality. It has been suggested that these figures are linked to a Celtic goddess.

5   *Aphrodite* Ancient Greek goddess of love. In Ovid's *Metamorphoses* (c. 8 CE), she hunts deer with her mortal lover, but refuses to hunt more dangerous animals.

Kasia and I have been friends now for just over twenty years, which doesn't feel at all long, though it sounds quite long. "Long" and "short" are relative. What was long was every single day she was spending in hospital; today was her tenth long day in one of the cancer wards, being injected with a cocktail of antibiotics and waiting for her temperature to come down and her white cell count to go up. When those two tiny personal adjustments happened in the world, then she'd be allowed to go home. Also, there was a lot of sadness round her in the ward. After ten long days the heaviness of that sadness, which might sound bearably small if you're not a person who has to think about it or is being forced by circumstance to address it, but is close to epic if you are, was considerable.

She phoned me back later that afternoon and left a message on the answerphone. I could hear the clanking hospital and the voices of other people in the ward in the recorded air around her voice.

Okay. Listen to this. It depends what you mean by "nymph." So, depending. A short story is like a nymph because satyrs[1] *want to sleep with it all the time. A short story is like a nymph because both like to live on mountains and in groves and by springs and rivers and in valleys and cool grottoes. A short story is like a nymph because it likes to accompany Artemis*[2] *on her travels. Not very funny yet, I know, but I'm working on it.*

I heard the phone being hung up. Message received at three forty-three, my answerphone's robot voice said. I called her back and went through the exact echo of the morning's call to the system. She answered and before I could even say hello she said:

Listen! Listen! A short story is like a nymphomaniac because both like to sleep around—or get into lots of anthologies—but neither accepts money for the pleasure.

I laughed out loud.

Unlike the bawdy old whore, the novel, ha ha, she said. And when I was speaking to my father at lunchtime he told me you can fish for trout with a nymph. They're a kind of fishing fly. He says there are people who carry magnifying glasses around with them all the time in case they get the chance to look at real nymphs,[3] so as to be able to copy them even more exactly in the fishing flies they make.

I tell you, I said. The world is full of astounding things.

I know, she said. What do you reckon to the anthology joke?

---

1   *satyrs* Mythological creatures who are part human, part animal. Satyrs are frequently depicted behaving lecherously toward nymphs.

2   *Artemis* Ancient Greek goddess of virginity and the hunt, who lives in the wilderness with an entourage of maidens.

3   *nymphs* Larvae of some insects, such as dragonflies.

Six out of ten, I said.

Rubbish then, she said. Okay. I'll try and think of something better.

Maybe there's mileage in the nymphs-at-your-flies thing, I said.

Ha ha, she said. But I'll have to leave the nymph thing this afternoon and get back on the Herceptin trail.

God, I said.

I'm exhausted, she said. We're drafting letters.

When is an anti-cancer drug not an anti-cancer drug? I said.

When people can't afford it, she said. Ha ha.

Lots of love, I said.

You too, she said. Cup of tea?

I'll make us one, I said. Speak soon.

I heard the phone go dead. I put my phone down and went through and switched the kettle on. I watched it reach the boil and the steam come out of the spout. I filled two cups with boiling water and dropped the teabags in. I drank my tea watching the steam rise off the other cup.

This is what Kasia meant by "Herceptin trail."

Herceptin is a drug that's been being used in breast cancer treatment for a while now. Doctors had, at the point in time that Kasia and I were having the conversations in this story, very recently discovered that it really helps some women—those who over-produce the HER2 protein—in the early stages of the disease. When given to a receptive case it can cut the risk of the cancer returning by 50 per cent. Doctors all over the world were excited about it because it amounted to a paradigm shift in breast cancer treatment.

I had never heard of any of this till Kasia told me, and she had never heard of any of it until a small truth, less than two centimetres in size, which a doctor found in April that year in one of her breasts, had meant a paradigm shift in everyday life. It was now August. In May her doctor had told her about how good Herceptin is, and how she'd definitely be able to have it at the end of her chemotherapy on the NHS.[1] Then at the end of July her doctor was visited by a member of the PCT, which stands for the words Primary, Care and Trust, and is concerned with NHS funding. The PCT member instructed my friend's doctor not to tell any more of the women affected in the hospital's catchment area about the wonders of Herceptin until a group called NICE[2] had approved its cost-effectiveness. At the time, they thought this might take about nine months or maybe a year (by which time it would be too late for my friend and many other women). Though Kasia knew that if she wanted to buy Herceptin

---

1   *NHS* National Health Service, a mainly publicly funded system of state-provided medical services in the UK.

2   *NICE* National Institute for Health and Clinical Excellence.

on BUPA,[1] right then, for roughly twenty-seven thousand pounds, she could. This kind of thing will be happening to an urgently needed drug right now, somewhere near you.

"Primary." "Care." "Trust." "Nice."

Here's a short story that most people already think they know about a nymph. (It also happens to be one of the earliest manifestations in literature of what we now call anorexia.)

Echo was an Oread, which is a kind of mountain nymph. She was well known among the nymphs and shepherds not just for her glorious garrulousness but for her ability to save her nymph friends from the wrath of the goddess Juno.[2] For instance, her friends would be lying about on the hillside in the sun and Juno would come round the corner, about to catch them slacking, and Echo, who had a talent for knowing when Juno was about to turn up, would leap to her feet and head the goddess off by running up to her and distracting her with stories and talk, talk and stories, until all the slacker nymphs were up and working like they'd never been slacking at all.

When Juno worked out what Echo was doing she was a bit annoyed. She pointed at her with her curse-finger and threw off the first suitable curse that came into her head.

From now on, she said, you will be able only to repeat out loud the words you've heard others say just a moment before. Won't you?

Won't you, Echo said.

Her eyes grew large. Her mouth fell open.

That's you sorted, Juno said.

You sordid, Echo said.

Right. I'm off back to the hunt, Juno said.

The cunt, Echo said.

Actually, I'm making up that small rebellion. There is actually no rebelliousness for Echo in Ovid's[3] original version of the story. It seems that after she's robbed of being able to talk on her own terms, and of being able to watch her friends' backs for them, there's nothing left for her—in terms of story—but to fall in love with a boy so in love with himself that he spends all his days bent over a pool of his own desire and eventually pines to near-death (then transforms, instead of dying, from a boy into a little white flower).[4]

---

1   *BUPA* British United Provident Association, a private healthcare and health insurance company.
2   *garrulousness* Talkativeness; *Juno* Roman goddess of marriage, queen of the Gods, and wife of Jupiter.
3   *Ovid* Echo's story appears in Ovid's *Metamorphoses*.
4   *a boy … flower* The "boy" is Narcissus, whose story is also told in Ovid's *Metamorphoses*.

Echo pined too. Her weight dropped off her. She became fashionably skinny, then she became nothing but bones, then all that was left of her was a whiny, piny voice which floated bodilessly about, saying over and over exactly the same things that everybody else was saying.

Here, by contrast, is the story of the moment I met my friend Kasia, more than twenty years ago.

I was a postgraduate student at Cambridge and I had lost my voice. I don't mean I'd lost it because I had a cold or a throat infection, I mean that two years of a system of hierarchies so entrenched that girls and women were still a bit of a novelty to it had somehow knocked what voice I had out of me.

So I was sitting at the back of a room not even really listening properly any more, and I heard a voice. It was from somewhere up ahead of me. It was a girl's voice and it was directly asking the person giving the seminar and the chair of the seminar a question about the American writer Carson McCullers.[1]

Because it seems to me that McCullers is obviously very relevant at all levels in this discussion, the voice said.

The person and the chair of the meeting both looked a bit shocked that anyone had said anything out loud. The chair cleared his throat.

I found myself leaning forward. I hadn't heard anyone speak like this, with such an open and carefree display of knowledge and forthrightness, for a couple of years. More: earlier that day I had been talking with an undergraduate student who had been unable to find anyone in the whole of Cambridge University English Department to supervise her dissertation on McCullers. It seemed nobody eligible to teach had read her.

Anyway, I venture to say you'll find McCullers not at all of the same stature, the person giving the paper on Literature After Henry James[2] said.

Well, the thing is, I disagree, the voice said.

I laughed out loud. It was a noise never heard in such a room; heads turned to see who was making such an unlikely noise. The new girl carried on politely asking questions which no one answered. She mentioned, I remember, how McCullers had been fond of a maxim: nothing human is alien to me.

At the end of the seminar I ran after that girl. I stopped her in the street. It was winter. She was wearing a red coat.

She told me her name. I heard myself tell her mine.

---

1   *Carson McCullers* American author (1917–67) known for her stories of the American South.

2   *Henry James* American novelist and critic (1843–1916) whose work is a common focus of scholarly interest.

Franz Kafka[1] says that the short story is a cage in search of a bird. (Kafka's been dead for more than eighty years, but I can still say Kafka says. That's just one of the ways art deals with our mortality.)

Tzvetan Todorov[2] says that the thing about a short story is that it's so short it doesn't allow us the time to forget that it's only literature and not actually life.

Nadine Gordimer[3] says short stories are absolutely about the present moment, like the brief flash of a number of fireflies here and there in the dark.

Elizabeth Bowen[4] says the short story has the advantage over the novel of a special kind of concentration, and that it creates narrative every time absolutely on its own terms.

Eudora Welty[5] says that short stories often problematize their own best interests and that this is what makes them interesting.

Henry James says that the short story, being so condensed, can give a particularized perspective on both complexity and continuity.

Jorge Luis Borges[6] says that short stories can be the perfect form for novelists too lazy to write anything longer than fifteen pages.

Ernest Hemingway[7] says that short stories are made by their own change and movement, and that even when a story seems static and you can't make out any movement in it at all it is probably changing and moving regardless, just unseen by you.

William Carlos Williams[8] says that the short story, which acts like the flare of a match struck in the dark, is the only real form for describing the briefness, the brokenness and the simultaneous wholeness of people's lives.

Walter Benjamin[9] says that short stories are stronger than the real, lived moment, because they can go on releasing the real, lived moment after the real, lived moment is dead.

Cynthia Ozick[10] says that the difference between a short story and a novel is that the novel is a book whose journey, if it's a good working novel, actually alters a reader, whereas a short story is more like the talismanic gift given to the protagonist of a fairy tale—something complete, powerful, whose power

---

1   *Franz Kafka* Influential German-language author (1883-1924) best known for his novella *Metamorphosis* (1915).

2   *Tzvetan Todorov* Franco-Bulgarian literary and cultural theorist (b. 1939).

3   *Nadine Gordimer* Nobel Prize-winning South African novelist and short story writer (b. 1923).

4   *Elizabeth Bowen* British novelist and short story writer (1889–1973).

5   *Eudora Welty* American short story writer and novelist (1909–2001).

6   *Jorge Luis Borges* Argentine writer (1899–1986) best known for his fantastic short stories.

7   *Ernest Hemingway* Influential American novelist and short story writer (1899–1961).

8   *William Carlos Williams* American modernist poet and prose author (1883–1963).

9   *Walter Benjamin* German literary and social theorist (1892–1940).

10 *Cynthia Ozick* American novelist, essayist, and short story writer (b. 1928).

may not yet be understood, which can be held in the hands or tucked into the pocket and taken through the forest on the dark journey.

Grace Paley[1] says that she chose to write only short stories in her life because art is too long and life is too short, and that short stories are, by nature, about life, and that life itself is always found in dialogue and argument.

Alice Munro[2] says that every short story is at least two short stories.

There were two men in the café at the table next to mine. One was younger, one was older. We sat in the same café for only a brief amount of time but we disagreed long enough for me to know there was a story in it.

This story was written in discussion with my friend Kasia, and in celebration of her (and all) tireless articulacy—one of the reasons, in this instance, that a lot more people were able to have that particular drug when they needed it.

So when is the short story like a nymph?

When the echo of it answers back.

—2008

---

1   *Grace Paley* American activist, poet, and short story writer (1922–2007).
2   *Alice Munro* Canadian short story writer (b. 1931).

Colum McCann
b. 1965

The novels and short stories of Colum McCann range freely over international borders, from Soviet Russia and the former Czechoslovakia to Northern Ireland and modern-day America; but again and again they return to the concept of home. Like the many Irish-born writers before him who left to seek their country elsewhere, McCann is deeply preoccupied with the conditions and consequences of exile—geographic, psychic, and emotional. Inspired by the work of Beat writers like Jack Kerouac, McCann immigrated to America at 21 to pursue his literary ambitions, but he describes himself as "a man of two countries," for his Irish roots run deep and ramify in complex ways throughout his work.

Few Irish writers can avoid the long shadow of James Joyce, Ireland's most famous literary expatriate, and McCann is no exception. But whereas many of Joyce's characters ultimately fail to break loose of their confined, paralyzed lives, McCann's frequently escape to discover neither a sense of freedom nor of wholeness but only loneliness, disintegration, and despair. In stories like "A Basket Full of Wallpaper," McCann peers into the "dark corners" of untold stories, examining the lives of ordinary men and women who have lost home in their very quest to find it.

For McCann, the idea of home is closely tied to the idea of wholeness, a unified and pristine state that his displaced characters long to recuperate. But if their lives are often broken, it is through the cracks that the light gets in: their search for connection often yields a new identity, restoring what McCann—echoing the Welsh poet Dylan Thomas—calls the "rage to live." The first Irish-born author to receive the National Book Award, McCann considers himself a "poetic realist" whose lyrical, adventurous writing invites "creative reading," prompting the reader to participate in each character's pursuit of meaning.

A Basket Full of Wallpaper

Some people said that he'd been a chicken-sexer during the Forties, a pale and narrow man who had spent his days interned in a camp for the Japanese near the mountains of Idaho. Endless months spent determining whether chickens were male or female. He had come to Ireland to forget it all. At other times, the older men, elbows on the bar counter, invented heinous crimes for him. In Japan, they said, he had attached electrical cords to the testicles of airmen, ritually sliced prisoners with swords, operated slow drip torture on young Marines. They said he had that sort of face. Dark eyes falling down into sunken cheeks, a full mouth without any colour, a tiny scar over his right eye. Even the women created a fantastic history for him. He was the fourth son of an emperor, or a poet, or a general, carrying the baggage of unrequited love. To us boys at school he was a kamikaze pilot[1] who had gotten cold feet, barrelling out in a parachute and somehow drifting to our town, carried by some ferocious, magical wave.

On the beach he walked with his head slung low to the ground, stooping to collect stones. We would sometimes hide in the dunes, parting the long grass to watch him, his trouser pockets filling up with stones. He had a long rambling stride, sometimes walking for hours along the coast, the gulls hurling themselves up from the strand, small fishing boats bobbing on the sea. When I was twelve years old I saw him leap along the beach while a porpoise surfaced and resurfaced in the water, fifty yards away. Once Paul Ryan wrapped a note around a brick and flung it through the window of his cottage, one of a row of fifteen small houses in the centre of our village. *Nip*[2] *go home*, said the note. The following day we noticed that the window had been covered with wallpaper and Paul Ryan went home from school with blood caked under his nose because we could no longer see through Osobe's front window.

Osobe had come to Ireland before I was born, some time in the Fifties. He would have been a curious sight in any Irish town, his black hair sticking out like conifer needles, his eyes shaded by the brim of his brown hat. He had bought the cottage, a dilapidated two-room affair, from an out-of-town landlord who thought that Osobe might stay for just a month or two. But, according to my father, a huge lorry carrying reams and reams of wallpaper pulled up to the cottage during the first summer of his visit. Osobe and two hefty Dubliners lifted all the paper into the house and later he hung a sign on his front window: *Wallpaper for Sale—Ask Inside*. There were mutterings about how the paper had been stolen, how it had been imported from Japan at a ridiculous price, undercutting the Irish wholesalers. Nobody bought any for a month until my Aunt Moira, who was infamous for having gotten drunk with Brendan Behan[3] in a Republican pub in Dublin, knocked on his door and ordered a floral pattern with a touch of pink for her living room.

Osobe rode his black bicycle along the river out to her house. Rolls of paper, cans of glue, knives, and brushes were stuffed into the basket. My aunt said he did a wonderful job, although people muttered about her outside mass on Sunday mornings. "He was as quiet then as he is now," she told me.

---

1   *kamikaze pilot* Pilot who suicidally crashes a plane loaded with explosives into an intended target; this tactic was used by the Japanese during World War II.
2   *Nip* Offensive term for a Japanese person.
3   *Brendan Behan* Irish author (1923–64) known for his alcoholic lifestyle and his involvement with the Irish Republican Army.

"No more noise out of him than a dormouse and we should leave it that way. He's a good man who never done anyone a whit of harm." She laughed at the rumours that hung around him.

By the time I was born he was a fixture around town, no stranger than the newspaper editor whose handkerchiefs drooped from his trouser pockets, the shopkeeper who stole all the footballs that landed in her back garden, the soldier who had lost his right hand fighting for Franco.[1] People nodded to him on the streets and, in Gaffney's pub, he was left alone over his morning pint of Guinness. He had a brisk trade going with the wallpaper and occasionally when Kieran O'Malley, the local handyman, was sick, he was called out to unblock a toilet or fix a crooked door. There was talk that he was seeing a young girl from Galway, a madwoman who walked around with three sleeves sewn on her dresses. But that had about as much truth as all the other rumours—or less, in fact, since he was never seen to leave town, not even on his bicycle.

He spoke English only haltingly and in the shops he would whisper for a packet of cigarettes or a jar of jam. On Sundays he never wore his brown hat. Girls giggled when he passed them in the street, a red Japanese sun umbrella held above his head. I was sixteen years old when he hung a sign on his front door, looking for help with a wallpaper job. It was a hot summer, the ground was bone dry, and there were no seasonal jobs in the fields. My father would moan at the dinner table about the huge toll that emigration was having on his undertaking business. "Everyone's gone somewhere else to die," he'd say. "Even that bloody Mrs. Hynes is hanging on for dear life." One evening my mother came and sat by my bed, mashing her fingers together nervously. She muttered under her breath that I should get some work with the Japanese man, that I was old enough now to put some bread on the table. I had noticed that, in the bread that she baked at home, there were no currants anymore.

The following morning, in a blue wool jumper and old working trousers, I sidled down to his house and knocked on his door.

The cottage was filled with rolls of wallpaper. They were stacked on top of each other all around the room, crowding in toward the small table and two wooden chairs. Most of it was muted in colour, but together they made a strange collage, flowers and vines and odd shapes all meshed together. The walls themselves had been papered with dozens of different types and the smell of paste was heavy in the house. On the ground sat rows and rows of small paper dolls, the faces painted almost comically. An old philosopher, a young

---

1   *Franco* Francisco Franco (1892–1975), a leader of the Nationalist anti-democratic forces during the Spanish Civil War (1936–39), following which he became dictator of Spain. Irish volunteers fought on both sides of the conflict.

girl, a wizened woman, a soldier. A row of Japanese books lay in one corner. On top of them, a pan of sliced bread. Cigarette packages littered the floor. There was a collection of beach stones on the mantelpiece. I noticed lots of change, a few pound notes scattered around the cottage, and a twenty-pound note stuffed under a lamp. A kettle whistled on the stove and he filled up two china cups with tea.

"Welcome," he said. The saucer rattled in my fingers. "There is big job in house. You will help me?"

I nodded and sipped at the tea, which tasted peculiarly bitter. His hands were long and spindly. I noticed the liver spots gathering up from his wrists. A grey shirt slouched on his thin shoulders.

"You will go home and get bicycle, in this afternoon we start. Very good?"

We rode out together to the old Gorman house, which had lain empty for three years. Osobe whistled as we pedalled and people stared at us from their cars and houses. Five rolls of pale green wallpaper were balanced in his front basket and I carried two cans of paste in my right hand, steering the bicycle with the other. I saw Paul Ryan hanging out by the school, smoking a long cigar. "Ya get slanty eyes from wanking too much, Donnelly," he shouted, and I tucked my head down toward the handlebars.

The Gorman House had been bought by an American millionaire just three months before. There were schoolboy rumours that the American drove a huge Cadillac and had five blonde daughters who would be fond of the local disco and, on excellent authority, were known to romp behind haystacks. But there was nobody there when we arrived on our bicycles. Osobe produced a set of keys from his overalls and walked slowly through the house, pointing at the walls, motes of dust kicking up from behind him. We made five trips on the bikes that day, carrying reams of wallpaper and paste each time. At the end of the day, after I had carried a ladder over my shoulder from his house, he produced a brand new ten-pound note and offered it to me.

"Tomorrow we start," he said, and then he bowed slightly. "You are fast on bicycle," he said.

I went outside. The sun was slouching over the town. I heard Osobe humming in the background as I leaped on my bike and rode toward home, the money stuffed down deep in my pocket.

That summer I read books in my bedroom and I wanted Osobe to tell me a fabulous story about his past. I suppose I wanted to own something of him, to make his history belong to me.

It would have something to do with Hiroshima, I had decided, with the children of the pikadon, the flash boom. There would be charred telegraph poles and tree trunks, a wasteland of concrete, a single remaining shell of a building. People with melted faces would run wildly through the streets. Bloated corpses would float down the Ota River. The slates on the roofs of houses would bubble. He would spit on the American and British soldiers as they sat under burnt cherry blossom trees, working the chewing gum over in their mouths. Perhaps, in his story, he would reach out for the festered face of a young girl. Or massage the burnt scalp of a boy. A woman friend of his would see her reflection in a bowl of soup and howl. Maybe he would run off toward the hills and never stop. Or perhaps he would simply just walk away, down narrow roads, in wooden sandals, a begging bowl in his hands. It would be a peculiar Buddhist hell, that story of his, and a B-29[1] would drone in constantly from the clouds.

But Osobe stayed silent almost all the time as he stood in that big old house and rolled paste on the walls in long smooth motions, humming gently as the house began to take on colour. "Sean," he would say to me in comically broken English, with his face cocked into a smile, "some day you will be great wallpaper man. You must think how important this job. We make people happy, or sad if we do bad job."

He would buy big bottles of Club Orange and packets of Gold-grain biscuits, and spread them out on the ground during lunchtime. He brought a radio one morning and his old body swayed with laughter as he tuned in to a pop station from Dublin. Once, for a joke, he swiped a ladder away from me and left me hanging from a ledge. He was deft with a knife, slicing the wall-paper in one smooth motion. At the end of the day he would sit and smoke two cigarettes, allowing me a puff at the end of each. Then he would go back into the house and sit, lotus-legged, in front of the most newly decorated wall and nod, smiling gently, rocking back and forth.

"What is Japan like?" I asked him one evening as we were cycling home, my palms sweaty.

"Like everywhere else. Not as beautiful like this," he said, sweeping his arm around the fields and hills.

"Why did you come here?"

"So long ago." He pointed at his nose. "Don't remember. Sorry."

"Were you in the war?"

"You ask lots of questions."

"Somebody told me you were in Hiroshima."

He laughed uproariously, slapping his thighs. "These questions," he said. "I have no answer." He rode silently for a while. "Hiroshima was sad place. Japanese don't talk about."

---

1   *B-29* Bomber plane used by the American military in attacks on Japan, including the atomic bombing of Hiroshima.

"Were you in Hiroshima?" I asked again.

"No, no," he said. "No, no."

"Do you hate Americans?"

"Why?"

"Because ..."

"You are very young. You shouldn't think these things. You should think of making good job with wallpaper. That's important."

We rode out to the house at eight every morning. The lawn was dry and cracked. The third-floor windows were black with soot. When the radio played it could be heard all over the house. Osobe worked with tremendous energy. In the hot afternoons I could see his sinewy arms under the sleeves of his rolled-up shirts. Once, when the radio told us of an earthquake in Japan, he blanched and said that the country was suffering from too much pain.

In the evenings I started going down to the bridge with my friends to drink flagons of cider with the money I held back from my parents. I began to buy my own cigarettes. I read books about World War II and created fabulous lies about how he had been in that southern Japanese city when the bomb had been dropped, how his family had been left as shadows on the Town Hall walls, all of them vaporized, disappeared. He had been ten miles from the epicentre of the blast, I said, in the shadow of a building, wearing billowy orange carpenter pants and a large straw hat. He was flung to the ground, and when he awoke the city was howling all around him. He had never found his family. They were scattered around the centre, dark patches of people left on broken concrete. He had reeled away from the pain of it all, travelling the world, ending up eventually in the West of Ireland. My friends whistled through their teeth. Under the bridge they pushed the bottle towards me.

Occasionally my mother and father asked me about Osobe, muted questions, probings, which they slid in at dinnertime after I had handed over most of my wages.

"He's a strange one, that one," said my father.

"Hiding something, I'd guess," my mother would respond, the fork clanging against her teeth.

"Bit of a mad fellow, isn't he, Sean?"

"Ah, he's not too bad," I said.

"People say he lived in Brazil for a while."

"God knows, he could have," said my mother.

"He doesn't tell me anything," I said.

For all I really knew, he had just wandered to our town, for no good or sufficient reason, and decided to stay. I had an uncle in Ghana, an older brother in Nebraska, a distant cousin who worked as a well-digger near Melbourne, none of which struck me as peculiar. Osobe was probably just one of their breed, a wanderer, a misfit, although I didn't want him to be.

We worked through that hot summer together, finished the Gorman house, and started on a few others. I grew to enjoy clambering along the roads on our bicycles in the morning, slapping paste on the walls, inventing tales about him for my friends down under the bridge. Some of my friends were working in the chipper,[1] others were bringing in the tired hay, and a couple of them were selling golf balls down at the club. Every evening I continued with Osobe stories for them, their faces lit up by a small fire we kept going. We all nodded and slurped at the bottles, fascinated by the horror and brilliance of it all. Fireballs had raged throughout the city as he fled, I told them. People ran with sacks of rice in their melted hands. A Shinto monk said prayers over the dead. Strange weeds grew in clumps where the plum trees once flowered and Osobe wandered away from the city, half-naked, his throat and eyes burning.

Osobe opened the door to me one morning toward the end of summer. "All the jobs almost done," he said. "We celebrate with cup of tea."

He guided me gently by the arm to the chair in the middle of the room. Looking around I noticed that he had been wallpapering again. He had papered over the paper. But there were no bubbles, no stray ends, no spilt paste around the edges. I imagined him staying up late at night, humming as he watched the patterns close in on him. The rest of the cottage was a riot of odds and ends—dishes and teacups, an oriental fan, wrapped slices of cheese, a futon rolled in the corner. There was a twenty-pound note sitting on the small gas heater near the table. Another ten-pound note lay on the floor, near the table. His brown hat was hung up over the door. There were paintbrushes everywhere.

"You did good job," he said. "Will you go soon school?"

"In a few weeks."

"Will you one day paper? Again. If I find you job?" he said.

Before I could answer he had sprung to his heels to open the front door for a marmalade-coloured cat, which had been scratching at the door. It was a stray. We often saw it slinking around the back of the chipper, waiting for some scraps. John Brogan once tried to catch it with a giant net, but couldn't. It scurried away from everyone. Osobe leaned down on his hunkers and, swooping his arms as if he were going to maul it, he got the cat to come closer. It was almost a windmill motion, smoothly through the air, his thin arms making arcs. The cat stared. Then, with a violent quickness, Osobe scooped it up,

---

1   *chipper* Fish and chip shop.

turned it on its back, pinned it down with one hand and roughly stroked his other hand along it. The cat leaned its head back and purred. Osobe laughed.

For a moment I felt a vicious hatred for him and his quiet ways, his mundane stroll through the summer, his ordinariness, the banality of everything he had become for me. He should have been a hero, or a seer. He should have told me some incredible story that I could carry with me forever. After all, he had been the one who had run along the beach parallel to a porpoise, who filled his pockets full of pebbles, who could lift the stray orange cat in his fingers.

I looked around the room for a moment while he hunched down with the cat, his back to me. I was hoping to find something, a diary, a picture, a drawing, a badge, anything that would tell me a little more about him. Looking over my shoulder I reached across to the gas heater, picked up the twenty-pound note and stuffed it in my sock, then pulled my trousers down over it. I sat at the wooden table, my hand shaking. After a while Osobe turned and came over toward me with the cat in his hands, stroking it with the same harsh motion as before. With his right hand he reached into his overalls and gave me a hundred pounds in ten new notes. "For you school." I could feel the other twenty-pound note riding up in my sock and as I backed out the door a sick feeling rose in my stomach.

"You did very good job," he said. "Come back for visit."

It was only afterward that I realized I never got the cup of tea he offered.

That night, I walked down along the row of houses where Osobe lived. I climbed around the back of the house, through the hedge, along by some flowerpots, rattling an old wheelbarrow as I moved up to the window. He was there, slapping paste on the wall in gentle arcs. I counted five separate sheets and the wall must have come a good quarter of an inch closer to him. I wanted him to be sloppy this time, not to smooth the sheets out, to wield the knife in a slipshod way, but he did the job as always, precise and fluid. The whole time he was humming and I stood, drunk, rattling the change from the twenty-pound note in the bottom of my pocket.

Years later, when I was acquiring an English accent in the East End of London, I got a letter from my father. Business was still slow and a new wave of emigration had left its famous scars. Old Mrs. Hynes still hadn't kicked the bucket. Five of the new council houses were empty now and even the Gorman house had been sold once more. The American in his Cadillac had never arrived with his five blonde daughters. The hurling[1] team had lost all its matches again this year. There was a bumper crop of hay.

---

1   *hurling* Ireland's national sport, similar to field hockey.

On the last page of the letter he told me that Osobe had died. The body was not discovered for three days, until my old Aunt Moira called around with a basket of fruit for him. When my father went into the house he said the stench was so bad that he almost vomited. Children gathered at the front door with their hands held to their noses. But there was a whip-round made in Gaffney's pub that extended out to the streets. People threw generous amounts of money in a big brown hat that the owner of the chipper carried from door to door. My aunt chose him a fine coffin, although someone said that he might have been offended by it, that he should have been sent back to Japan to be cremated. She scoffed at the suggestion and made a bouquet of flowers for him.

There was a party held the night of the funeral and rumours were flung around according to the depths of the whiskey bottle—but more or less everyone was sure now that he had been a victim of Hiroshima. All the young boys who had worked for him in the summer months had heard vivid details of that frightening August morning. He had fled from the city in a pair of wooden sandals. All his family had been killed. They had been vaporized. He was a man in flight. By the late, sober hours of the morning, my father added, the talk was that Osobe was a decent sort, no matter what his history was. Over the years he had employed many young men to work with him, treated them fairly, paid them handsomely, and confided in them about his life. They laughed at how strange his accent had become at the end of it all—when he went to the shop to buy cigarettes, he would lean over the counter and whisper for *pack of fags prease*. The sight of him carrying that big ladder on his bicycle would be sorely missed around town.

But the strangest thing of all, my father said, was that when he had gone into the house to recover the body, the room had seemed very small to him. It was customary to burn the bed sheets and scrape the paper from the walls when someone had been dead that long. But he took a knife to the paper and discovered it was a couple of feet thick though it didn't seem so at first glance. Layers and layers of wallpaper. It looked as if Osobe had been gathering the walls into himself, probably some sort of psychological effect brought on by the bomb. Because the wallpaper had been so dense my father and some members of the town council simply had to knock the house down, burying everything that Osobe owned in the rubble. There had been no clues in the house, no letters, no medical papers, nothing to indicate that he had come from that most horrific of our century's moments.

It was a pathetic gesture, but I rode my bicycle around London that night. I plowed along to no particular place, furious in the pedals. Blood thumped in me. Sweat leapt from my brow. The chain squeaked. A road in Ireland rose up—a road of grass grown ocher in the summer heat, a very thin figure in a brown hat along the river, a cat the colour of the going sun, a certain wall brought forward in slow movements, a road that wound forever through dry fields toward a grey beach, a road long gone, a road flung out elsewhere, a road that was still within me somewhere. I found myself down by the Thames in the early morning—it was rolling along in a desultory grey. I dropped a single twenty-pound note into the water and watched it as it spun away very slowly, very deliberately, with the current, down toward some final sea, to fete the dead, their death, and their dying too.

—1995

Sherman Alexie
b. 1966

Critical assessments of the novels, poems, and short stories of Sherman Alexie frequently begin with a summary statement of his Native American origins and upbringing. In some ways this is fitting: Alexie is a member of the Spokane and Coeur d'Alene tribes, and much of his early work—notably *The Lone Ranger and Tonto Fistfight in Heaven* (1993) and *Reservation Blues* (1995)—unflinchingly confronts the systemic poverty, hopelessness, and alcoholism that marked his own childhood experience of rural reservation life. But Alexie is uncomfortable with the label *Native American writer*, especially the presumption that he is a representative spokesman for "Indian country."

Drawing heavily on irony and satire, Alexie delights in upending stereotypical assumptions about traditional Native "storytelling." His work is strewn with references to mainstream American culture, and, in his more recent fiction, including the story "Flight Patterns" from the collection *Ten Little Indians* (2009), he tends to be less interested in representing a separate and distinct tribal reality than with the urban experience of life beyond the reservation. As he puts it: "I try to write about everyday Indians, the kind of Indian I am, who is just as influenced by *The Brady Bunch* as I am by my tribal traditions, who spends as much time going to the movies as I do going to ceremonies."

Alexie's writing, though preoccupied with trauma, prejudice, and alienation, also enacts and celebrates the redemptive power of humour and imagination to transmute anger into a vital creative force and sow the strength necessary to survive hardship. In his work as in his life, the concept of survival remains uppermost: "Indians fight their way to the end," he writes, "holding onto the last good thing, because our whole lives have to do with survival." Far from succumbing to a sense of what one critic has called "doomed Indianness," many of Alexie's characters are defiant survivors.

Flight Patterns

At 5:05 A.M., Patsy Cline[1] fell loudly to pieces on William's clock radio. He hit the snooze button, silencing lonesome Patsy, and dozed for fifteen more minutes before Donna Fargo[2] bragged about being the happiest girl in the

---

1   *Patsy Cline* American country singer known for sad love ballads such as "I Fall to Pieces" (1961).
2   *Donna Fargo* Stage name of Yvonne Vaughan, American country singer-songwriter best known for her song "The Happiest Girl in the Whole USA" (1972).

whole USA. William wondered what had ever happened to Donna Fargo, whose birth name was the infinitely more interesting Yvonne Vaughn, and wondered *why* he knew Donna Fargo's birth name. Ah, he was the bemused and slightly embarrassed owner of a twenty-first-century American mind. His intellect was a big comfy couch stuffed with sacred and profane trivia. He knew the names of all nine of Elizabeth Taylor's[1] husbands and could quote from memory the entire Declaration of Independence. William knew Donna Fargo's birth name because he *wanted* to know her birth name. He wanted to know all of the great big and tiny little American details. He didn't want to choose between Ernie Hemingway and the Spokane tribal elders, between Mia Hamm and Crazy Horse, between *The Heart Is a Lonely Hunter* and Chief Dan George.[2] William wanted all of it. Hunger was his crime. As for dear Miss Fargo, William figured she probably played the Indian casino circuit along with the Righteous Brothers, Smokey Robinson, Eddie Money, Pat Benatar, RATT, REO Speedwagon, and dozens of other formerly famous rock- and country-music stars. Many of the Indian casino acts were bad, and most of the rest were pure nostalgic entertainment, but a small number made beautiful and timeless music. William knew the genius Merle Haggard[3] played thirty or forty Indian casinos every year, so long live Haggard and long live tribal economic sovereignty. Who cares about fishing and hunting rights? Who cares about uranium mines and nuclear-waste-dump sites[4] on sacred land? Who cares about the recovery of tribal languages? Give me Freddy Fender[5] singing "Before the Next Teardrop Falls" in English and Spanish to 206 Spokane Indians, William thought, and I will be a happy man.

But William wasn't happy this morning. He'd slept poorly—he always slept poorly—and wondered again if his insomnia was a physical or a mental condition. His doctor had offered him sleeping-pill prescriptions, but William declined for philosophical reasons. He was an Indian who didn't smoke or drink or eat processed sugar. He lifted weights three days a week, ran every day,

1   *Elizabeth Taylor* Hollywood movie star (1932–2011) who had a long and prestigious acting career as well as a dramatic romantic life.
2   *Ernie Hemingway* Ernest Hemingway (1899–1961), influential white American author; *Spokane* Native North American people primarily located in Washington; *Mia Hamm* Record-breaking white American soccer player (b. 1972); *Crazy Horse* Famous Sioux war chief and activist (c. 1842–77); *The Heart Is a Lonely Hunter* Acclaimed 1940 novel by white Southern American writer Carson McCullers; *Chief Dan George* Salish chief, author, and film and television actor (1899–1981).
3   *Merle Haggard* Influential country singer and songwriter (b. 1937).
4   *uranium mines ... dump sites* An open-pit uranium mine on the Spokane Reservation closed in 1981; some of the pits were filled in with radioactive waste from the mine.
5   *Freddy Fender* Mexican-American country musician known for bilingual hits such as "Before the Next Teardrop Falls" (1975).

and competed in four triathlons a year. A two-mile swim, a 150-mile bike ride, and a full marathon. A triathlon was a religious quest. If Saint Francis[1] were still around, he'd be a triathlete. Another exaggeration! Theological hyperbole! Rabid self-justification! Diagnostically speaking, William was an obsessive-compulsive workaholic who was afraid of pills. So he suffered sleepless nights and constant daytime fatigue.

This morning, awake and not awake, William turned down the radio, changing Yvonne Vaughn's celebratory anthem into whispered blues, and rolled off the couch onto his hands and knees. His back and legs were sore because he'd slept on the living room couch so the alarm wouldn't disturb his wife and daughter upstairs. Still on his hands and knees, William stretched his spine, using the twelve basic exercises he'd learned from Dr. Adams, that master practitioner of white middle-class chiropractic voodoo. This was all part of William's regular morning ceremony. Other people find God in ornate ritual, but William called out to Geronimo, Jesus Christ, Saint Therese, Buddha, Allah, Billie Holiday, Simon Ortiz, Abe Lincoln, Bessie Smith, Howard Hughes, Leslie Marmon Silko, Joan of Arc and Joan of Collins, John Woo, Wilma Mankiller, and Karl and Groucho Marx[2] while he pumped out fifty push-ups and fifty abdominal crunches. William wasn't particularly religious; he was generally religious. Finished with his morning calisthenics, William showered in the basement, suffering the water that was always too cold down there, and threaded his long black hair into two tight braids—the indigenous businessman's tonsorial[3] special—and dressed in his best travel suit, a navy three-button pinstripe he'd ordered online. He'd worried about the fit, but his tailor was a magician and had only mildly chastised William for such an impulsive purchase. After knotting his blue paisley tie, purchased in person and on sale, William walked upstairs in bare feet and kissed his wife, Marie, good-bye.

---

1   *Saint Francis* Francis of Assisi (c. 1181–1226), mystic and founder of the Franciscan monastic order.

2   *Geronimo* Apache resistance leader (c. 1829–1909); *Saint Therese* Thérèse of Liseux, a devout French nun (1873–97); *Billie Holiday* African American jazz singer (1915–59); *Simon Ortiz* Pueblo poet and prose writer (b. 1941); *Bessie Smith* African American blues singer (1898–1937); *Howard Hughes* White American billionaire (1905–76) who invested in film and aviation; *Leslie Marmon Silko* Laguna-Mexican-Anglo writer (b. 1948); *Joan of Collins* Nickname for English actor and writer Joan Collins (b. 1933); *John Woo* Chinese action filmmaker (b. 1946) who works in Hong Kong and Hollywood; *Wilma Mankiller* Wilma Pearl Mankiller (1945–2010), the first female Cherokee chief; *Karl and Groucho Marx* Karl Marx, German theorist best known for co-authoring *The Communist Manifesto* (1848), and Groucho Marx (1895–1977), member of the American comedy group "The Marx Brothers."

3   *tonsorial* Of hairdressing.

"Cancel your flight," she said. "And come back to bed."

"You're supposed to be asleep," he said.

She was a small and dark woman who seemed to be smaller and darker at that time of the morning. Her long black hair had once again defeated its braids, but she didn't care. She sometimes went two or three days without brushing it. William was obsessive about his mane, tying and retying his ponytail, knotting and reknotting his braids, experimenting with this shampoo and that conditioner. He greased down his cowlicks (inherited from a cowlicked father and grandfather) with shiny pomade, but Marie's hair was always unkempt, wild, and renegade. William's hair hung around the fort, but Marie's rode on the war path! She constantly pulled stray strands out of her mouth. William loved her for it. During sex, they spent as much time readjusting her hair as they did readjusting positions. Such were the erotic dangers of loving a Spokane Indian woman.

"Take off your clothes and get in bed," Marie pleaded now.

"I can't do that," William said. "They're counting on me."

"Oh, the plane will be filled with salesmen. Let some other salesman sell what you're selling."

"Your breath stinks."

"So do my feet, my pits, and my butt, but you still love me. Come back to bed, and I'll make it worth your while."

William kissed Marie, reached beneath her pajama top, and squeezed her breasts. He thought about reaching inside her pajama bottoms. She wrapped her arms and legs around him and tried to wrestle him into bed. Oh, God, he wanted to climb into bed and make love. He wanted to fornicate, to sex, to breed, to screw, to make the beast with two backs. *Oh, sweetheart, be my little synonym*! He wanted her to be both subject and object. Perhaps it was wrong (and unavoidable) to objectify female strangers, but shouldn't every husband seek to objectify his wife at least once a day? William loved and respected his wife, and delighted in her intelligence, humour, and kindness, but he also loved to watch her lovely ass when she walked, and stare down the front of her loose shirts when she leaned over, and grab her breasts at wildly inappropriate times—during dinner parties and piano recitals and uncontrolled intersections, for instance. He constantly made passes at her, not necessarily expecting to be successful, but to remind her he still desired her and was excited by the thought of her. She was his passive and active.

"Come on," she said. "If you stay home, I'll make you Scooby."

He laughed at the inside joke, created one night while he tried to give her sexual directions and was so aroused that he sounded exactly like Scooby-Doo.

"Stay home, stay home, stay home," she chanted and wrapped herself tighter around him. He was supporting all of her weight, holding her two feet off the bed.

"I'm not strong enough to do this," he said.

"Baby, baby, I'll make you strong," she sang, and it sounded like she was writing a Top 40 hit in the Brill Building,[1] circa 1962. How could he leave a woman who sang like that? He hated to leave, but he loved his work. He was a man, and men needed to work. More sexism! More masculine tunnel vision! More need for gender-sensitivity workshops! He pulled away from her, dropping her back onto the bed, and stepped away.

"Willy Loman," she said, "you must pay attention to me."[2]

"I love you," he said, but she'd already fallen back to sleep—a narcoleptic gift William envied—and he wondered if she would dream about a man who never left her, about some unemployed agoraphobic Indian warrior who liked to cook and wash dishes.

William tiptoed into his daughter's bedroom, expecting to hear her light snore, but she was awake and sitting up in bed, and looked so magical and androgynous with her huge brown eyes and crew-cut hair. She'd wanted to completely shave her head: *I don't want long hair, I don't want short hair, I don't want hair at all, and I don't want to be a girl or a boy, I want to be a yellow and orange leaf some little kid picks up and pastes in his scrapbook.*

"Daddy," she said.

"Grace," he said. "You should be asleep. You have school today."

"I know," she said. "But I wanted to see you before you left."

"Okay," said William as he kissed her forehead, nose, and chin. "You've seen me. Now go back to sleep. I love you and I'm going to miss you."

She fiercely hugged him.

"Oh," he said. "You're such a lovely, lovely girl."

Preternaturally serious, she took his face in her eyes and studied his eyes. Morally examined by a kindergartner!

"Daddy," she said. "Go be silly for those people far away."

She cried as William left her room. Already quite sure he was only an adequate husband, he wondered, as he often did, if he was a bad father. During these mornings, he felt generic and violent, like some caveman leaving the fire to hunt animals in the cold and dark. Maybe his hands were smooth and clean, but they felt bloody.

---

1   *Brill Building* New York music industry songwriting headquarters where staff writers composed pop hits in the 1950s and 1960s.

2   *Willy Loman* Title character of Arthur Miller's *Death of a Salesman* (1949); *you must ... to me* In *Death of a Salesman*, Willy Loman's wife says that "attention must be paid" to him.

Downstairs, he put on his socks and shoes and overcoat and listened for his daughter's crying, but she was quiet, having inherited her mother's gift for instant sleep. She had probably fallen back into one of her odd little dreams. While he was gone, she often drew pictures of those dreams, colouring the sky green and the grass blue—everything backward and wrong—and had once sketched a man in a suit crashing an airplane into the bright yellow sun. Ah, the rage, fear, and loneliness of a five-year-old, simple and true! She'd been especially afraid since September 11 of the previous year and constantly quizzed William about what he would do if terrorists hijacked his plane.

"I'd tell them I was your father," he'd said to her before he left for his last business trip. "And they'd stop being bad."

"You're lying," she'd said. "I'm not supposed to listen to liars. If you lie to me, I can't love you."

He couldn't argue with her logic. Maybe she was the most logical person on the planet. Maybe she should be illegally elected president of the United States.

William understood her fear of flying and of his flight. He was afraid of flying, too, but not of terrorists. After the horrible violence of September 11, he figured hijacking was no longer a useful weapon in the terrorist arsenal. These days, a terrorist armed with a box cutter would be torn to pieces by all of the coach-class passengers and fed to the first-class upgrades. However, no matter how much he tried to laugh his fear away, William always scanned the airports and airplanes for little brown guys who reeked of fundamentalism. That meant William was equally afraid of Osama bin Laden and Jerry Falwell[1] wearing the last vestiges of a summer tan. William himself was a little brown guy, so the other travellers were always sniffing around him, but he smelled only of Dove soap, Mennen deodorant, and sarcasm. Still, he understood why people were afraid of him, a brown-skinned man with dark hair and eyes. If Norwegian terrorists had exploded the World Trade Center, then blue-eyed blondes would be viewed with more suspicion. Or so he hoped.

Locking the front door behind him, William stepped away from his house, carried his garment bag and briefcase onto the front porch, and waited for his taxi to arrive. It was a cold and foggy October morning. William could smell the saltwater of Elliott Bay and the freshwater of Lake Washington. Surrounded by grey water and grey fog and grey skies and grey mountains and a grey sun, he'd lived with his family in Seattle for three years and loved it. He couldn't imagine living anywhere else, with any other wife or child, in any other time.

---

1   *Jerry Falwell* White American minister, televangelist, and leader in fundamentalist Christian politics (1932–2007).

William was tired and happy and romantic and exaggerating the size of his familial devotion so he could justify his departure, so he could survive his departure. He did sometimes think about other women and other possible lives with them. He wondered how his life would have been different if he'd married a white woman and fathered half-white children who grew up to complain and brag about their biracial identities: *Oh, the only box they have for me is Other! I'm not going to check any box! I'm not the Other! I am Tiger Woods!*[1] But William most often fantasized about being single and free to travel as often as he wished—maybe two million miles a year—and how much he'd enjoy the benefits of being a platinum frequent flier. Maybe he'd have one-night stands with a long series of travelling saleswomen, all of them thousands of miles away from husbands and children who kept looking up "feminism" in the dictionary. William knew that was yet another sexist thought. In this capitalistic and democratic culture, talented women should also enjoy the freedom to emotionally and physically abandon their families. After all, talented and educated men have been doing it for generations. Let freedom ring!

Marie had left her job as a corporate accountant to be a full-time mother to Grace. William loved his wife for making the decision, and he tried to do his share of the housework, but he suspected he was an old-fashioned bastard who wanted his wife to stay at home and wait, wait, wait for him.

Marie was always waiting for William to call, to come home, to leave messages saying he was getting on the plane, getting off the plane, checking in to the hotel, going to sleep, waking up, heading for the meeting, catching an earlier or later flight home. He spent one third of his life trying to sleep in uncomfortable beds and one third of his life trying to stay awake in airports. He travelled with thousands of other capitalistic foot soldiers, mostly men but increasing numbers of women, and stayed in the same Ramadas, Holiday Inns, and Radissons. He ate the same room-service meals and ran the same exercise-room treadmills and watched the same pay-per-view porn and stared out the windows at the same strange and lonely cityscapes. Sure, he was an enrolled member of the Spokane Indian tribe, but he was also a fully recognized member of the notebook-computer tribe and the security-checkpoint tribe and the rental-car tribe and the hotel-shuttle-bus tribe and the cell-phone-roaming-charge tribe.

William travelled so often, the Seattle-based flight attendants knew him by first name.

At five minutes to six, the Orange Top taxi pulled into the driveway. The driver, a short and thin black man, stepped out of the cab and waved. William

---

1   *Tiger Woods* American professional golfer (b. 1975) whose ancestry is African American, Thai, Chinese, Dutch, and Native American.

rushed down the stairs and across the pavement. He wanted to get away from the house before he changed his mind about leaving.

"Is that everything, sir?" asked the taxi driver, his accent a colonial cocktail of American English, formal British, and French sibilants added to a base of what must have been North African.

"Yes, it is, sir," said William, self-consciously trying to erase any class differences between them. In Spain the previous summer, an elderly porter had cursed at William when he insisted on carrying his own bags into the hotel. "Perhaps there is something wrong with the caste system, sir," the hotel concierge had explained to William. "But all of us, we want to do our jobs, and we want to do them well."

William didn't want to insult anybody; he wanted the world to be a fair and decent place. At least that was what he wanted to want. More than anything, he wanted to stay home with his fair and decent family. He supposed he wanted the world to be fairer and more decent to his family. We are special, he thought, though he suspected they were just one more family on this block of neighbours, in this city of neighbours, in this country of neighbours, in a world of neighbours. He looked back at his house, at the windows behind which slept his beloved wife and daughter. When he travelled, he had nightmares about strangers breaking into the house and killing and raping Marie and Grace. In other nightmares, he arrived home in time to save his family by beating the intruders and chasing them away. During longer business trips, William's nightmares became more violent as the days and nights passed. If he was gone over a week, he dreamed about mutilating the rapists and eating them alive while his wife and daughter cheered for him.

"Let me take your bags, sir," said the taxi driver.

"What?" asked William, momentarily confused.

"Your bags, sir."

William handed him the briefcase but held on to the heavier garment bag. A stupid compromise, thought William, but it's too late to change it now. God, I'm supposed to be some electric aboriginal warrior, but I'm really a wimpy liberal pacifist. *Dear Lord, how much longer should I mourn the death of Jerry Garcia?*[1]

The taxi driver tried to take the garment bag from William.

"I've got this one," said William, then added, "I've got it, sir."

The taxi driver hesitated, shrugged, opened the trunk, and set the briefcase inside. William laid the garment bag next to his briefcase. The taxi driver shut the trunk and walked around to open William's door.

---

1   *Jerry Garcia* American singer and guitarist (1942–95) best known for his leadership of The Grateful Dead, a band associated with the hippie movement.

"No, sir," said William as he awkwardly stepped in front of the taxi driver, opened the door, and took a seat. "I've got it."

"I'm sorry, sir," said the taxi driver and hurried around to the driver's seat. This strange American was making him uncomfortable, and he wanted to get behind the wheel and drive. Driving comforted him.

"To the airport, sir?" asked the taxi driver as he started the meter.

"Yes," said William. "United Airlines."

"Very good, sir."

In silence, they drove along Martin Luther King Jr. Way, the bisector of an African American neighbourhood that was rapidly gentrifying. William and his family were Native American gentry! They were the very first Indian family to ever move into a neighbourhood and bring up the property values! That was one of William's favourite jokes, self-deprecating and politely racist. White folks could laugh at a joke like that and not feel guilty. But how guilty could white people feel in Seattle? Seattle might be the only city in the country where white people lived comfortably on a street named after Martin Luther King, Jr.

No matter where he lived, William always felt uncomfortable, so he enjoyed other people's discomfort. These days, in the airports, he loved to watch white people enduring random security checks. It was a perverse thrill, to be sure, but William couldn't help himself. He knew those white folks wanted to scream and rage: *Do I look like a terrorist?* And he knew the security officers, most often low-paid brown folks, wanted to scream back: *Define terror you Anglo bastard!* William figured he'd been pulled over for pat-down searches about 75 percent of the time. Random, my ass! But that was okay! William might have wanted to irritate other people, but he didn't want to scare them. He wanted his fellow travellers to know exactly who and what he was: *I am a Native American and therefore have ten thousand more reasons to terrorize the US than any of those Taliban[1] jerk-offs, but I have chosen instead to become a civic American citizen, so all of you white folks should be celebrating my kindness and moral decency and awesome ability to forgive!* Maybe William should have worn beaded vests when he travelled. Maybe he should have brought a hand drum and sang "Way, ya, way, ya, hey." Maybe he should have thrown casino chips into the crowd.

The taxi driver turned west on Cherry, drove twenty blocks into downtown, took the entrance ramp onto I-5, and headed south for the airport. The freeway was moderately busy for that time of morning.

"Where are you going, sir?" asked the taxi driver.

---

1   *Taliban* Islamic fundamentalist organization linked to al-Qaeda, the terrorist group responsible for the 11 September 2001 attacks on the World Trade Center and other American targets.

"I've got business in Chicago," William said. He didn't really want to talk. He needed to meditate in silence. He needed to put his fear of flying inside an imaginary safe deposit box and lock it away. We all have our ceremonies, thought William, our personal narratives. He'd always needed to meditate in the taxi on the way to the airport. Immediately upon arrival at the departure gate, he'd listen to a tape he'd made of rock stars who died in plane crashes. Buddy Holly, Otis Redding, Stevie Ray, "Oh Donna," "Chantilly Lace," "(Sittin' on) The Dock of the Bay." William figured God would never kill a man who listened to such a morbid collection of music. Too easy a target, and plus, God could never justify killing a planeful of innocents to punish one minor sinner.

"What do you do, sir?" asked the taxi driver.

"You know, I'm not sure," said William and laughed. It was true. He worked for a think tank and sold ideas about how to improve other ideas. Two years ago, his company had made a few hundred thousand dollars by designing and selling the idea of a better shopping cart. The CGI prototype was amazing. It looked like a mobile walk-in closet. But it had yet to be manufactured and probably never would be.

"You wear a good suit," said the taxi driver, not sure why William was laughing. "You must be a businessman, no? You must make lots of money."

"I do okay."

"Your house is big and beautiful."

"Yes, I suppose it is."

"You are a family man, yes?"

"I have a wife and daughter."

"Are they beautiful?"

William was pleasantly surprised to be asked such a question. "Yes," he said. "Their names are Marie and Grace. They're very beautiful. I love them very much."

"You must miss them when you travel."

"I miss them so much I go crazy," said William. "I start thinking I'm going to disappear, you know, just vanish, if I'm not home. Sometimes I worry their love is the only thing that makes me human, you know? I think if they stopped loving me, I might burn up, spontaneously combust, and turn into little pieces of oxygen and hydrogen and carbon. Do you know what I'm saying?"

"Yes sir, I understand love can be so large."

William wondered why he was being honest and poetic with a taxi driver. There is emotional safety in anonymity, he thought.

"I have a wife and three sons," said the driver. "But they live in Ethiopia with my mother and father. I have not seen any of them for many years."

For the first time, William looked closely at the driver. He was clear-eyed and handsome, strong of shoulder and arm, maybe fifty years old, maybe

older. A thick scar ran from his right ear down his neck and beneath his collar. A black man with a violent history; William thought and immediately
reprimanded himself for racially profiling the driver: *Excuse me, sir, but I pulled
you over because your scar doesn't belong in this neighbourhood.*

"I still think of my children as children," the driver said. "But they are
men now. Taller and stronger than me. They are older now than I was when
I last saw them."

William did the math and wondered how this driver could function with
such fatherly pain. "I bet you can't wait to go home and see them again," he
said, following the official handbook of the frightened American male: *When
confronted with the mysterious you can defend yourself by speaking in obvious
generalities.*

"I cannot go home," said the taxi driver, "and I fear I will never see them
again."

William didn't want to be having this conversation. He wondered if his
silence would silence the taxi driver. But it was too late for that.

"What are you?" the driver asked.

"What do you mean?"

"I mean, you are not white, your skin, it is dark like mine."

"Not as dark as yours."

"No," said the driver and laughed. "Not so dark, but too dark to be white.
What are you? Are you Jewish?"

Because they were so often Muslim, taxi drivers all over the world had
often asked William if he was Jewish. William was always being confused for
something else. He was ambiguously ethnic, living somewhere in the darker
section of the Great American Crayola Box, but he was more beige than
brown, more mauve than sienna.

"Why do you want to know if I'm Jewish?" William asked.

"Oh, I'm sorry, sir, if I offended you. I am not anti-Semitic. I love all of
my brothers and sisters. Jews, Catholics, Buddhists, even the atheists, I love
them all. Like you Americans sing, 'Joy to the world and Jeremiah Bullfrog!'"[1]

The taxi driver laughed again, and William laughed with him.

"I'm Indian," William said.

"From India?"

"No, not jewel-on-the-forehead Indian," said William. "I'm a bows-and-
arrows Indian."

"Oh, you mean ten little, nine little, eight little Indians?"

"Yeah, sort of," said William. "I'm that kind of Indian, but much smarter.
I'm a Spokane Indian. We're salmon people."

---

1   *Joy to ... Bullfrog* Garbled reference to the popular rock song "Joy to the World" (1971).

"In England, they call you Red Indians."

"You've been to England?"

"Yes, I studied physics at Oxford."

"Wow," said William, wondering if this man was a liar.

"You are surprised by this, I imagine. Perhaps you think I'm a liar?"

William covered his mouth with one hand. He smiled this way when he was embarrassed.

"Aha, you do think I'm lying. You ask yourself questions about me. How could a physicist drive a taxi? Well, in the United States, I am a cabdriver, but in Ethiopia, I was a jet-fighter pilot."

By coincidence or magic, or as a coincidence that could wilfully be interpreted as magic, they drove past Boeing Field at that exact moment.

"Ah, you see," said the taxi driver, "I can fly any of those planes. The prop planes, the jet planes, even the very large passenger planes. I can also fly the experimental ones that don't fly. But I could make them fly because I am the best pilot in the world. Do you believe me?"

"I don't know," said William, very doubtful of this man but fascinated as well. If he was a liar, then he was a magnificent liar.

On both sides of the freeway, blue-collared men and women drove trucks and forklifts, unloaded trains, trucks, and ships, built computers, televisions, and airplanes. Seattle was a city of industry, of hard work, of calluses on the palms of hands. So many men and women working so hard. William worried that his job—his selling of the purely theoretical—wasn't a real job at all. He didn't build anything. He couldn't walk into department and grocery stores and buy what he'd created, manufactured, and shipped. William's life was measured by imaginary numbers: the binary code of computer languages, the amount of money in his bank accounts, the interest rate on his mortgage, and the rise and fall of the stock market. He invested much of his money in socially responsible funds. Imagine that! Imagine choosing to trust your money with companies that supposedly made their millions through ethical means. Imagine the breathtaking privilege of such a choice. All right, so maybe this was an old story for white men. For most of American history, who else but a white man could endure the existential crisis of economic success? But this story was original and aboriginal for William. For thousands of years, Spokane Indians had lived subsistence lives, using every last part of the salmon and deer because they'd die without every last part, but William only ordered salmon from menus and saw deer on television. Maybe he romanticized the primal—for thousands of years, Indians also died of ear infections—but William wanted his comfortable and safe life to contain more *wilderness*.

"Sir, forgive me for saying this," the taxi driver said, "but you do not look like the Red Indians I have seen before."

"I know," William said. "People usually think I'm a longhaired Mexican."

"What do you say to them when they think such a thing?"

"*No habla español. Indio de Norteamericanos.*"[1]

"People think I'm black American. They always want to hip-hop rap to me. 'Are you East Coast or West Coast?' they ask me, and I tell them I am Ivory Coast."[2]

"How have things been since September eleventh?"

"Ah, a good question, sir. It's been interesting. Because people think I'm black, they don't see me as a terrorist, only as a crackhead addict on welfare. So I am a victim of only one misguided idea about who I am."

"We're all trapped by other people's ideas, aren't we?"

"I suppose that is true, sir. How has it been for you?"

"It's all backward," William said. "A few days after it happened, I was walking out of my gym downtown, and this big phallic pickup pulled up in front of me in the crosswalk. Yeah, this big truck with big phallic tires and a big phallic flagpole and a big phallic flag flying, and the big phallic symbol inside leaned out of his window and yelled at me, 'Go back to your own country!'"

"Oh, that is sad and funny," the taxi driver said.

"Yeah," William said. "And it wasn't so much a hate crime as it was a crime of irony, right? And I was laughing so hard, the truck was halfway down the block before I could get breath enough to yell back, 'You first!'"

William and the taxi driver laughed and laughed together. Two dark men laughing at dark jokes.

"I had to fly on the first day you could fly," William said. "And I was flying into Baltimore, you know, and D.C. and Baltimore are pretty much the same damn town, so it was like flying into Ground Zero, you know?"

"It must have been terrifying."

"It was, it was. I was sitting in the plane here in Seattle, getting ready to take off, and I started looking around for suspicious brown guys. I was scared of little brown guys. So was everybody else. We were all afraid of the same things. I started looking around for big white guys because I figured they'd be undercover cops, right?"

"Imagine wanting to be surrounded by white cops!"

"Exactly! I didn't want to see some pacifist, vegan, whole-wheat, free-range, organic, progressive, grey-ponytail, communist, liberal, draft-dodging, NPR[3]-listening wimp! What are they going to do if somebody tries to hijack the plane? Throw a Birkenstock at him? Offer him some pot?"

1   *No habla … Norteamericanos* Spanish: Don't speak Spanish. North American Indian.
2   *Ivory Coast* Country in West Africa.
3   *NPR* American public radio network.

"Marijuana might actually stop the violence everywhere in the world," the taxi driver said.

"You're right," William said. "But on that plane, I was hoping for about twenty-five NRA-loving, gun-nut, serial-killing, psychopathic, Ollie North, Norman Schwarzkopf, right-wing, Agent Orange,[1] post-traumatic-stress-disorder, CIA, FBI, automatic-weapon, smart-bomb, laser-sighting bastards!"

"You wouldn't want to invite them for dinner," the taxi driver said. "But you want them to protect your children, am I correct?"

"Yes, but it doesn't make sense. None of it makes sense. It's all contradictions."

"The contradictions are the story, yes?"

"Yes."

"I have a story about contradictions," said the taxi driver. "Because you are a Red Indian, I think you will understand my pain."

"*Su-num-twee*," said William.

"What is that? What did you say?"

"*Su-num-twee*. It's Spokane. My language."

"What does it mean?"

"Listen to me."

"Ah, yes, that's good. *Su-num-twee, su-num-twee.* So, what is your name?"

"William."

The taxi driver sat high and straight in his seat, like he was going to say something important. "William, my name is Fekadu. I am Oromo[2] and Muslim, and I come from Addis Ababa in Ethiopia, and I want you to *su-num-twee*."

There was nothing more important than a person's name and the names of his clan, tribe, city, religion, and country. By the social rules of his tribe, William should have reciprocated and officially identified himself. He should have been polite and generous. He was expected to live by so many rules, he sometimes felt like he was living inside an indigenous version of an Edith Wharton[3] novel.

---

1   *NRA* National Rifle Association, an American organization opposing laws that restrict gun ownership; *Ollie North* American military official Oliver North (b. 1943), a member of the National Security Council who was tried for illegally providing military aid to anticommunist fighters in Nicaragua; *Norman Schwarzkopf* American general who secured a quick victory as commander in the 1991 Gulf War; *Agent Orange* Extremely toxic chemical weapon used by the American military during the Vietnam War (1954–75).

2   *Oromo* Member of the Oromo people, an ethnic group in Ethiopia and Somalia.

3   *Edith Wharton* American Pulitzer Prize-winning author (1862–1937) whose most famous novels satirize the social conventions of high society.

"Mr. William," asked Fekadu, "do you want to hear my story? Do you want to *su-num-twee*?"

"Yes, I do, sure, yes, please," said William. He was lying. He was twenty minutes away from the airport and so close to departure.

"I was not born into an important family," said Fekadu. "But my father worked for an important family. And this important family worked for the family of Emperor Haile Selassie.[1] He was a great and good and kind and terrible man, and he loved his country and killed many of his people. Have you heard of him?"

"No, I'm sorry, I haven't."

"He was magical. Ruled our country for forty-three years. Imagine that! We Ethiopians are strong. White people have never conquered us. We won every war we fought against white people. For all of our history, our emperors have been strong, and Selassie was the strongest. There has never been a man capable of such love and destruction."

"You fought against him?"

Fekadu breathed in so deeply that William recognized it as a religious moment, as the first act of a ceremony, and with the second act, an exhalation, the ceremony truly began.

"No," Fekadu said. "I was a smart child. A genius. A prodigy. It was Selassie who sent me to Oxford. And there I studied physics and learned the math and art of flight. I came back home and flew jets for Selassie's army."

"Did you fly in wars?" William asked.

"Ask me what you really want to ask me, William. You want to know if I was a killer, no?"

William had a vision of his wife and daughter huddling terrified in their Seattle basement while military jets screamed overhead. It happened every August when the US Navy Blue Angels came to entertain the masses with their aerial acrobatics.

"Do you want to know if I was a killer?" asked Fekadu. "Ask me if I was a killer."

William wanted to know the terrible answer without asking the terrible question.

"Will you not ask me what I am?" asked Fekadu.

"I can't."

"I dropped bombs on my own people."

---

1   *Haile Selassie* Emperor of Ethiopia, an internationally respected authoritarian leader who encouraged his country to modernize. He lost popular support toward the end of his reign and was deposed by military coup in 1974.

In the sky above them, William counted four, five, six jets flying in holding patterns while awaiting permission to land.

"For three years, I killed my own people," said Fekadu. "And then, on the third of June in 1974, I could not do it anymore. I kissed my wife and sons good-bye that morning, and I kissed my mother and father, and I lied to them and told them I would be back that evening. They had no idea where I was going. But I went to the base, got into my plane, and flew away."

"You defected?" William asked. How could a man steal a fighter plane? Was that possible? And if possible, how much courage would it take to commit such a crime? William was quite sure he could never be that courageous.

"Yes, I defected," said Fekadu. "I flew my plane to France and was almost shot down when I violated their airspace, but they let me land, and they arrested me, and soon enough, they gave me asylum. I came to Seattle five years ago, and I think I will live here the rest of my days."

Fekadu took the next exit. They were two minutes away from the airport. William was surprised to discover that he didn't want this journey to end so soon. He wondered if he should invite Fekadu for coffee and a sandwich, for a slice of pie, for brotherhood. William wanted to hear more of this man's stories and learn from them, whether they were true or not. Perhaps it didn't matter if any one man's stories were true. Fekadu's autobiography might have been completely fabricated, but William was convinced that somewhere in the world, somewhere in Africa or the United States, a man, a jet pilot, wanted to fly away from the war he was supposed to fight. There must be hundreds, maybe thousands, of such men, and how many were courageous enough to fly away? If Fekadu wasn't describing his own true pain and loneliness, then he might have been accidentally describing the pain of a real and lonely man.

"What about your family?" asked William, because he didn't know what else to ask and because he was thinking of his wife and daughter. "Weren't they in danger? Wouldn't Selassie want to hurt them?"

"I could only pray Selassie would leave them be. He had always been good to me, but he saw me as impulsive, so I hoped he would know my family had nothing to do with my flight. I was a coward for staying and a coward for leaving. But none of it mattered, because Selassie was overthrown a few weeks after I defected."

"A coup?"

"Yes, the Derg[1] deposed him, and they slaughtered all of their enemies and their enemies' families. They suffocated Selassie with a pillow the next year. And now I could never return to Ethiopia because Selassie's people would

---

1   *Derg* Military group that ruled Ethiopia as a socialist state from 1974 until it was defeated by popular uprising in 1991.

always want to kill me for my betrayal and the Derg would always want to kill me for being Selassie's soldier. Every night and day, I worry that any of them might harm my family. I want to go there and defend them. I want to bring them here. They can sleep on my floor! But even now, after democracy has almost come to Ethiopia,[1] I cannot go back. There is too much history and pain, and I am too afraid."

"How long has it been since you've talked to your family?"

"We write letters to each other, and sometimes we receive them. They sent me photos once, but they never arrived for me to see. And for two days, I waited by the telephone because they were going to call, but it never rang."

Fekadu pulled the taxi to a slow stop at the airport curb. "We are here, sir," he said. "United Airlines."

William didn't know how this ceremony was supposed to end. He felt small and powerless against the collected history. "What am I supposed to do now?" he asked.

"Sir, you must pay me thirty-eight dollars for this ride," said Fekadu and laughed. "Plus a very good tip."

"How much is good?"

"You see, sometimes I send cash to my family. I wrap it up and try to hide it inside the envelope. I know it gets stolen, but I hope some of it gets through to my family. I hope they buy themselves gifts from me. I hope."

"You pray for this?"

"Yes, William, I pray for this. And I pray for your safety on your trip, and I pray for the safety of your wife and daughter while you are gone."

"Pop the trunk, I'll get my own bags," said William as he gave sixty dollars to Fekadu, exited the taxi, took his luggage out of the trunk, and slammed it shut. Then William walked over to the passenger-side window, leaned in, and studied Fekadu's face and the terrible scar on his neck.

"Where did you get that?" William asked.

Fekadu ran a finger along the old wound. "Ah," he said. "You must think I got this flying in a war. But no, I got this in a taxicab wreck. William, I am a much better jet pilot than a car driver."

Fekadu laughed loudly and joyously. William wondered how this poor man could be capable of such happiness, however temporary it was.

"Your stories," said William. "I want to believe you."

"Then believe me," said Fekadu.

Unsure, afraid, William stepped back.

"Good-bye, William American," Fekadu said and drove away.

---

1   *democracy ... Ethiopia* Ethiopia had its first multi-party elections in 1995.

Standing at curbside, William couldn't breathe well. He wondered if he was dying. Of course he was dying, a flawed mortal dying day by day, but he felt like he might fall over from a heart attack or stroke right there on the sidewalk. He left his bags and ran inside the terminal. Let a luggage porter think his bags were dangerous! Let a security guard x-ray the bags and find mysterious shapes! Let a bomb-squad cowboy explode the bags as precaution! Let an airport manager shut down the airport and search every possible traveller! Let the FAA[1] president order every airplane to land! Let the American skies be empty of everything with wings! Let the birds stop flying! Let the very air go still and cold! William didn't care. He ran through the terminal, searching for an available pay phone, a landline, something true and connected to the ground, and he finally found one and dropped two quarters into the slot and dialed his home number, and it rang and rang and rang and rang, and William worried that his wife and daughter were harmed, were lying dead on the floor, but then Marie answered.

"Hello, William," she said.

"I'm here," he said.

—2003

---

1   *FAA* Federal Aviation Administration.

Jhumpa Lahiri
b. 1967

Many of the characters in the finely crafted stories of Jhumpa Lahiri—who was born in England to Indian immigrants and raised in the United States— are from different continents and cultures but are at home in none. Those who leave their native land become strangers, forced to rely on their children to help them navigate the language and customs of their vastly changed environments. The sons and daughters are likewise outsiders, fluent in both the ancestral and the adopted ways but more observers than participants, destined to remain at a distance from the world they inhabit by virtue of being its interpreters. As Lahiri has observed, "Almost all my characters are translators insofar as they must make sense of the foreign to survive." This foreignness is by no means strictly cultural, just as the idea of home is not simply geographic: Lahiri's men and women are often as estranged from one another as they are from their surroundings.

Since the appearance of her first collection of short stories, the Pulitzer Prize-winning *Interpreter of Maladies* (1999), critics have approached Lahiri as a postcolonial voice of the South Asian diaspora in the tradition of writers like Salman Rushdie and V.S. Naipaul. Yet Lahiri resists the simplistic notion that, as a prominent author of Bengali descent, she represents and speaks for a particular group. Informed by her early life as a newcomer to upper middle-class New England, much of her work illuminates the immigrant experience, but Lahiri is interested above all in the experience of being human.

Interpreter of Maladies

At the tea stall Mr. and Mrs. Das bickered about who should take Tina to the toilet. Eventually Mrs. Das relented when Mr. Das pointed out that he had given the girl her bath the night before. In the rearview mirror Mr. Kapasi watched as Mrs. Das emerged slowly from his bulky white Ambassador, dragging her shaved, largely bare legs across the back seat. She did not hold the little girl's hand as they walked to the rest room.

They were on their way to see the Sun Temple at Konarak.[1] It was a dry, bright Saturday, the mid-July heat tempered by a steady ocean breeze, ideal weather for sightseeing. Ordinarily Mr. Kapasi would not have stopped so soon along the way, but less than five minutes after he'd picked up the family that

---

1   *Sun Temple at Konarak* Famous Hindu temple (c. 1241) representing the chariot of the sun god Surya. Its location, Konarak, is a town in Orissa, a coastal state in northeastern India.

morning in front of Hotel Sandy Villa, the little girl had complained. The first thing Mr. Kapasi had noticed when he saw Mr. and Mrs. Das, standing with their children under the portico of the hotel, was that they were very young, perhaps not even thirty. In addition to Tina they had two boys, Ronny and Bobby, who appeared very close in age and had teeth covered in a network of flashing silver wires. The family looked Indian but dressed as foreigners did, the children in stiff, brightly coloured clothing and caps with translucent visors. Mr. Kapasi was accustomed to foreign tourists; he was assigned to them regularly because he could speak English. Yesterday he had driven an elderly couple from Scotland, both with spotted faces and fluffy white hair so thin it exposed their sunburnt scalps. In comparison, the tanned, youthful faces of Mr. and Mrs. Das were all the more striking. When he'd introduced himself, Mr. Kapasi had pressed his palms together in greeting, but Mr. Das squeezed hands like an American so that Mr. Kapasi felt it in his elbow. Mrs. Das, for her part, had flexed one side of her mouth, smiling dutifully at Mr. Kapasi, without displaying any interest in him.

As they waited at the tea stall, Ronny, who looked like the older of the two boys, clambered suddenly out of the back seat, intrigued by a goat tied to a stake in the ground.

"Don't touch it," Mr. Das said. He glanced up from his paperback tour book, which said "INDIA" in yellow letters and looked as if it had been published abroad. His voice, somehow tentative and a little shrill, sounded as though it had not yet settled into maturity.

"I want to give it a piece of gum," the boy called back as he trotted ahead.

Mr. Das stepped out of the car and stretched his legs by squatting briefly to the ground. A clean-shaven man, he looked exactly like a magnified version of Ronny. He had a sapphire blue visor, and was dressed in shorts, sneakers, and a T-shirt. The camera slung around his neck, with an impressive telephoto lens and numerous buttons and markings, was the only complicated thing he wore. He frowned, watching as Ronny rushed toward the goat, but appeared to have no intention of intervening. "Bobby, make sure that your brother doesn't do anything stupid."

"I don't feel like it," Bobby said, not moving. He was sitting in the front seat beside Mr. Kapasi, studying a picture of the elephant god taped to the glove compartment.

"No need to worry," Mr. Kapasi said. "They are quite tame." Mr. Kapasi was forty-six years old, with receding hair that had gone completely silver but his butterscotch complexion and his unlined brow, which he treated in spare moments to dabs of lotus-oil balm, made it easy to imagine what he must have looked like at an earlier age. He wore grey trousers and a matching jacket-style shirt, tapered at the waist, with short sleeves and a large pointed collar, made of a thin but durable synthetic material. He had specified both the cut and the fabric to his tailor—it was his preferred uniform for giving tours because it did not get crushed during his long hours behind the wheel. Through the windshield he watched as Ronny circled around the goat, touched it quickly on its side, then trotted back to the car.

"You left India as a child?" Mr. Kapasi asked when Mr. Das had settled once again into the passenger seat.

"Oh, Mina and I were both born in America," Mr. Das announced with an air of sudden confidence. "Born and raised. Our parents live here now, in Assansol.[1] They retired. We visit them every couple years." He turned to watch as the little girl ran toward the car, the wide purple bows of her sundress flopping on her narrow brown shoulders. She was holding to her chest a doll with yellow hair that looked as if it had been chopped, as a punitive measure, with a pair of dull scissors. "This is Tina's first trip to India, isn't it, Tina?"

"I don't have to go to the bathroom anymore," Tina announced.

"Where's Mina?" Mr. Das asked.

Mr. Kapasi found it strange that Mr. Das should refer to his wife by her first name when speaking to the little girl. Tina pointed to where Mrs. Das was purchasing something from one of the shirtless men who worked at the tea stall. Mr. Kapasi heard one of the shirtless men sing a phrase from a popular Hindi love song as Mrs. Das walked back to the car, but she did not appear to understand the words of the song, for she did not express irritation, or embarrassment, or react in any other way to the man's declarations.

He observed her. She wore a red-and-white-checkered skirt that stopped above her knees, slip-on shoes with a square wooden heel, and a close-fitting blouse styled like a man's undershirt. The blouse was decorated at chest-level with a calico appliqué in the shape of a strawberry. She was a short woman, with small hands like paws, her frosty pink fingernails painted to match her lips, and was slightly plump in her figure. Her hair, shorn only a little longer than her husband's, was parted far to one side. She was wearing large dark brown sunglasses with a pinkish tint to them, and carried a big straw bag, almost as big as her torso, shaped like a bowl, with a water bottle poking out of it. She walked slowly, carrying some puffed rice tossed with peanuts and chili peppers in a large packet made from newspapers. Mr. Kapasi turned to Mr. Das.

"Where in America do you live?"

"New Brunswick, New Jersey."

"Next to New York?"

"Exactly. I teach middle school there."

---

1   *Assansol* City in West Bengal, the state north of Orissa.

"What subject?"

"Science. In fact, every year I take my students on a trip to the Museum of Natural History in New York City. In a way we have a lot in common, you could say, you and I. How long have you been a tour guide, Mr. Kapasi?"

"Five years."

Mrs. Das reached the car. "How long's the trip?" she asked, shutting the door.

"About two and a half hours," Mr. Kapasi replied.

At this Mrs. Das gave an impatient sigh, as if she had been travelling her whole life without pause. She fanned herself with a folded Bombay film magazine written in English.

"I thought that the Sun Temple is only eighteen miles north of Puri,"[1] Mr. Das said, tapping on the tour book.

"The roads to Konarak are poor. Actually it is a distance of fifty-two miles," Mr. Kapasi explained.

Mr. Das nodded, readjusting the camera strap where it had begun to chafe the back of his neck.

Before starting the ignition, Mr. Kapasi reached back to make sure the cranklike locks on the inside of each of the back doors were secured. As soon as the car began to move the little girl began to play with the lock on her side, clicking it with some effort forward and backward, but Mrs. Das said nothing to stop her. She sat a bit slouched at one end of the back seat, not offering her puffed rice to anyone. Ronny and Tina sat on either side of her, both snapping bright green gum.

"Look," Bobby said as the car began to gather speed. He pointed with his finger to the tall trees that lined the road. "Look."

"Monkeys!" Ronny shrieked. "Wow!"

They were seated in groups along the branches, with shining black faces, silver bodies, horizontal eyebrows, and crested heads. Their long grey tails dangled like a series of ropes among the leaves. A few scratched themselves with black leathery hands, or swung their feet, staring as the car passed.

"We call them the hanuman," Mr. Kapasi said. "They are quite common in the area."

As soon as he spoke, one of the monkeys leaped into the middle of the road, causing Mr. Kapasi to brake suddenly. Another bounced onto the hood of the car, then sprang away. Mr. Kapasi beeped his horn. The children began to get excited, sucking in their breath and covering their faces partly with their hands. They had never seen monkeys outside of a zoo, Mr. Das explained. He asked Mr. Kapasi to stop the car so that he could take a picture.

---

1   *Puri* Major city in Orissa.

While Mr. Das adjusted his telephoto lens, Mrs. Das reached into her straw bag and pulled out a bottle of colourless nail polish, which she proceeded to stroke on the tip of her index finger.

The little girl stuck out a hand. "Mine too. Mommy, do mine too."

"Leave me alone," Mrs. Das said, blowing on her nail and turning her body slightly. "You're making me mess up."

The little girl occupied herself by buttoning and unbuttoning a pinafore on the doll's plastic body.

"All set," Mr. Das said, replacing the lens cap.

The car rattled considerably as it raced along the dusty road, causing them all to pop up from their seats every now and then, but Mrs. Das continued to polish her nails. Mr. Kapasi eased up on the accelerator, hoping to produce a smoother ride. When he reached for the gearshift the boy in front accommodated him by swinging his hairless knees out of the way. Mr. Kapasi noted that this boy was slightly paler than the other children. "Daddy, why is the driver sitting on the wrong side in this car, too?" the boy asked.

"They all do that here, dummy," Ronny said.

"Don't call your brother a dummy," Mr. Das said. He turned to Mr. Kapasi. "In America, you know ... it confuses them."

"Oh yes, I am well aware," Mr. Kapasi said. As delicately as he could, he shifted gears again, accelerating as they approached a hill in the road. "I see it on *Dallas*,[1] the steering wheels are on the left-hand side."

"What's *Dallas*?" Tina asked, banging her now naked doll on the seat behind Mr. Kapasi.

"It went off the air," Mr. Das explained. "It's a television show."

They were all like siblings, Mr. Kapasi thought as they passed a row of date trees. Mr. and Mrs. Das behaved like an older brother and sister, not parents. It seemed that they were in charge of the children only for the day; it was hard to believe they were regularly responsible for anything other than themselves. Mr. Das tapped on his lens cap, and his tour book, dragging his thumbnail occasionally across the pages so that they made a scraping sound. Mrs. Das continued to polish her nails. She had still not removed her sunglasses. Every now and then Tina renewed her plea that she wanted her nails done, too, and so at one point Mrs. Das flicked a drop of polish on the little girl's finger before depositing the bottle back inside her straw bag.

"Isn't this an air-conditioned car?" she asked, still blowing on her hand. The window on Tina's side was broken and could not be rolled down.

"Quit complaining," Mr. Das said. "It isn't so hot."

---

1   *Dallas* Popular American soap opera (1978–91) set in Dallas, Texas.

"I told you to get a car with air-conditioning," Mrs. Das continued. "Why do you do this, Raj, just to save a few stupid rupees. What are you saving us, fifty cents?"

Their accents sounded just like the ones Mr. Kapasi heard on American television programs, though not like the ones on *Dallas*.

"Doesn't it get tiresome, Mr. Kapasi, showing people the same thing every day?" Mr. Das asked, rolling down his own window all the way. "Hey do you mind stopping the car. I just want to get a shot of this guy."

Mr. Kapasi pulled over to the side of the road as Mr. Das took a picture of a barefoot man, his head wrapped in a dirty turban, seated on top of a cart of grain sacks pulled by a pair of bullocks.[1] Both the man and the bullocks were emaciated. In the back seat Mrs. Das gazed out another window, at the sky, where nearly transparent clouds passed quickly in front of one another.

"I look forward to it, actually," Mr. Kapasi said as they continued on their way. "The Sun Temple is one of my favourite places. In that way it is a reward for me. I give tours on Fridays and Saturdays only. I have another job during the week."

"Oh? Where?" Mr. Das asked.

"I work in a doctor's office."

"You're a doctor?"

"I am not a doctor. I work with one. As an interpreter."

"What does a doctor need an interpreter for?"

"He has a number of Gujarati[2] patients. My father was Gujarati, but many people do not speak Gujarati in this area, including the doctor. And so the doctor asked me to work in his office, interpreting what the patients say."

"Interesting. I've never heard of anything like that," Mr. Das said.

Mr. Kapasi shrugged. "It is a job like any other."

"But so romantic," Mrs. Das said dreamily breaking her extended silence. She lifted her pinkish brown sunglasses and arranged them on top of her head like a tiara. For the first time, her eyes met Mr. Kapasi's in the rearview mirror: pale, a bit small, their gaze fixed but drowsy.

Mr. Das craned to look at her. "What's so romantic about it?"

"I don't know. Something." She shrugged, knitting her brows together for an instant. "Would you like a piece of gum, Mr. Kapasi?" she asked brightly. She reached into her straw bag and handed him a small square wrapped in green-and-white-striped paper. As soon as Mr. Kapasi put the gum in his mouth a thick sweet liquid burst onto his tongue.

"Tell us more about your job, Mr. Kapasi," Mrs. Das said.

---

1   *bullocks* Young bulls.

2   *Gujarati* Member of the Gujarati ethnic group, located primarily in western India.

"What would you like to know, madame?"

"I don't know," again she shrugged, munching on some puffed rice and licking the mustard oil from the corners of her mouth. "Tell us a typical situation." She settled back in her seat, her head tilted in a patch of sun, and closed her eyes. "I want to picture what happens."

"Very well. The other day a man came in with a pain in his throat."

"Did he smoke cigarettes?"

"No. It was very curious. He complained that he felt as if there were long pieces of straw stuck in his throat. When I told the doctor he was able to prescribe the proper medication."

"That's so neat."

"Yes," Mr. Kapasi agreed after some hesitation.

"So these patients are totally dependent on you," Mrs. Das said. She spoke slowly as if she were thinking aloud. "In a way more dependent on you than the doctor."

"How do you mean? How could it be?"

"Well, for example, you could tell the doctor that the pain felt like a burning, not straw. The patient would never know what you had told the doctor, and the doctor wouldn't know that you had told the wrong thing. It's a big responsibility."

"Yes, a big responsibility you have there, Mr. Kapasi," Mr. Das agreed.

Mr. Kapasi had never thought of his job in such complimentary terms. To him it was a thankless occupation. He found nothing noble in interpreting people's maladies, assiduously translating the symptoms of so many swollen bones, countless cramps of bellies and bowels, spots on people's palms that changed colour, shape, or size. The doctor, nearly half his age, had an affinity for bell-bottom trousers and made humourless jokes about the Congress party.[1] Together they worked in a stale little infirmary where Mr. Kapasi's smartly tailored clothes clung to him in the heat, in spite of the blackened blades of a ceiling fan churning over their heads.

The job was a sign of his failings. In his youth he'd been a devoted scholar of foreign languages, the owner of an impressive collection of dictionaries. He had dreamed of being an interpreter for diplomats and dignitaries, resolving conflicts between people and nations, settling disputes of which he alone could understand both sides. He was a self-educated man. In a series of notebooks, in the evenings before his parents settled his marriage, he had listed the common etymologies of words, and at one point in his life he was confident that he could converse, if given the opportunity, in English, French, Russian, Portu-

---

1   *Congress party* One of India's major political parties; after India's independence in 1947, it dominated the government for most of the rest of the century.

guese, and Italian, not to mention Hindi, Bengali, Oriya, and Gujarati. Now only a handful of European phrases remained in his memory, scattered words for things like saucers and chairs. English was the only non-Indian language he spoke fluently anymore. Mr. Kapasi knew it was not a remarkable talent. Sometimes he feared that his children knew better English than he did, just from watching television. Still, it came in handy for the tours.

He had taken the job as an interpreter after his first son, at the age of seven, contracted typhoid—that was how he had first made the acquaintance of the doctor. At the time Mr. Kapasi had been teaching English in a grammar school, and he bartered his skills as an interpreter to pay the increasingly exorbitant medical bills. In the end the boy had died one evening in his mother's arms, his limbs burning with fever, but then there was the funeral to pay for, and the other children who were born soon enough, and the newer, bigger house, and the good schools and tutors, and the fine shoes and the television, and the countless other ways he tried to console his wife and to keep her from crying in her sleep, and so when the doctor offered to pay him twice as much as he earned at the grammar school, he accepted. Mr. Kapasi knew that his wife had little regard for his career as an interpreter. He knew it reminded her of the son she'd lost, and that she resented the other lives he helped, in his own small way, to save. If ever she referred to his position, she used the phrase "doctor's assistant," as if the process of interpretation were equal to taking someone's temperature, or changing a bedpan. She never asked him about the patients who came to the doctor's office, or said that his job was a big responsibility.

For this reason it flattered Mr. Kapasi that Mrs. Das was so intrigued by his job. Unlike his wife, she had reminded him of its intellectual challenges. She had also used the word "romantic." She did not behave in a romantic way toward her husband, and yet she had used the word to describe him. He wondered if Mr. and Mrs. Das were a bad match, just as he and his wife were. Perhaps they too, had little in common apart from three children and a decade of their lives. The signs he recognized from his own marriage were there—the bickering, the indifference, the protracted silences. Her sudden interest in him, an interest she did not express in either her husband or her children, was mildly intoxicating. When Mr. Kapasi thought once again about how she had said "romantic," the feeling of intoxication grew.

He began to check his reflection in the rearview mirror as he drove, feeling grateful that he had chosen the grey suit that morning and not the brown one, which tended to sag a little in the knees. From time to time he glanced through the mirror at Mrs. Das. In addition to glancing at her face he glanced at the strawberry between her breasts, and the golden brown hollow in her throat. He decided to tell Mrs. Das about another patient, and another: the young woman who had complained of a sensation of raindrops in her spine, the gentleman whose birthmark had begun to sprout hairs. Mrs. Das listened attentively, stroking her hair with a small plastic brush that resembled an oval bed of nails, asking more questions, for yet another example. The children were quiet, intent on spotting more monkeys in the trees, and Mr. Das was absorbed by his tour book, so it seemed like a private conversation between Mr. Kapasi and Mrs. Das. In this manner the next half hour passed, and when they stopped for lunch at a roadside restaurant that sold fritters and omelette sandwiches, usually something Mr. Kapasi looked forward to on his tours so that he could sit in peace and enjoy some hot tea, he was disappointed. As the Das family settled together under a magenta umbrella fringed with white and orange tassels, and placed their orders with one of the waiters who marched about in tricornered caps, Mr. Kapasi reluctantly headed toward a neighbouring table.

"Mr. Kapasi, wait. There's room here," Mrs. Das called out. She gathered Tina onto her lap, insisting that he accompany them. And so, together, they had bottled mango juice and sandwiches and plates of onions and potatoes deep-fried in graham-flour batter. After finishing two omelette sandwiches Mr. Das took more pictures of the group as they ate.

"How much longer?" he asked Mr. Kapasi as he paused to load a new roll of film in the camera.

"About half an hour more."

By now the children had gotten up from the table to look at more monkeys perched in a nearby tree, so there was a considerable space between Mrs. Das and Mr. Kapasi. Mr. Das placed the camera to his face and squeezed one eye shut, his tongue exposed at one corner of his mouth. "This looks funny. Mina, you need to lean in closer to Mr. Kapasi."

She did. He could smell a scent on her skin, like a mixture of whiskey and rosewater. He worried suddenly that she could smell his perspiration, which he knew had collected beneath the synthetic material of his shirt. He polished off his mango juice in one gulp and smoothed his silver hair with his hands. A bit of the juice dripped onto his chin. He wondered if Mrs. Das had noticed.

She had not. "What's your address, Mr. Kapasi?" she inquired, fishing for something inside her straw bag.

"You would like my address?"

"So we can send you copies," she said. "Of the pictures." She handed him a scrap of paper which she had hastily ripped from a page of her film magazine. The blank portion was limited, for the narrow strip was crowded by lines of text and a tiny picture of a hero and heroine embracing under a eucalyptus tree.

The paper curled as Mr. Kapasi wrote his address in clear, careful letters. She would write to him, asking about his days interpreting at the doctor's office, and he would respond eloquently choosing only the most entertaining anecdotes, ones that would make her laugh out loud as she read them in her house in New Jersey. In time she would reveal the disappointment of her marriage, and he his. In this way their friendship would grow, and flourish. He would possess a picture of the two of them, eating fried onions under a magenta umbrella, which he would keep, he decided, safely tucked between the pages of his Russian grammar. As his mind raced, Mr. Kapasi experienced a mild and pleasant shock. It was similar to a feeling he used to experience long ago when, after months of translating with the aid of a dictionary he would finally read a passage from a French novel, or an Italian sonnet, and understand the words, one after another, unencumbered by his own efforts. In those moments Mr. Kapasi used to believe that all was right with the world, that all struggles were rewarded, that all of life's mistakes made sense in the end. The promise that he would hear from Mrs. Das now filled him with the same belief.

When he finished writing his address Mr. Kapasi handed her the paper, but as soon as he did so he worried that he had either misspelled his name, or accidentally reversed the numbers of his postal code. He dreaded the possibility of a lost letter, the photograph never reaching him, hovering somewhere in Orissa, close but ultimately unattainable. He thought of asking for the slip of paper again, just to make sure he had written his address accurately but Mrs. Das had already dropped it into the jumble of her bag.

They reached Konarak at two-thirty. The temple, made of sandstone, was a massive pyramid-like structure in the shape of a chariot. It was dedicated to the great master of life, the sun, which struck three sides of the edifice as it made its journey each day across the sky. Twenty-four giant wheels were carved on the north and south sides of the plinth. The whole thing was drawn by a team of seven horses, speeding as if through the heavens. As they approached, Mr. Kapasi explained that the temple had been built between A.D. 1243 and 1255, with the efforts of twelve hundred artisans, by the great ruler of the Ganga dynasty, King Narasimhadeva the First, to commemorate his victory against the Muslim army.

"It says the temple occupies about a hundred and seventy acres of land," Mr. Das said, reading from his book.

"It's like a desert," Ronny said, his eyes wandering across the sand that stretched on all sides beyond the temple.

"The Chandrabhaga River once flowed one mile north of here. It is dry now," Mr. Kapasi said, turning off the engine.

They got out and walked toward the temple, posing first for pictures by the pair of lions that flanked the steps. Mr. Kapasi led them next to one of the wheels of the chariot, higher than any human being, nine feet in diameter.

"'The wheels are supposed to symbolize the wheel of life,'" Mr. Das read. "'They depict the cycle of creation, preservation, and achievement of realization.' Cool." He turned the page of his book. "'Each wheel is divided into eight thick and thin spokes, dividing the day into eight equal parts. The rims are carved with designs of birds and animals, whereas the medallions in the spokes are carved with women in luxurious poses, largely erotic in nature.'"

What he referred to were the countless friezes of entwined naked bodies, making love in various positions, women clinging to the necks of men, their knees wrapped eternally around their lovers' thighs. In addition to these were assorted scenes from daily life, of hunting and trading, of deer being killed with bows and arrows and marching warriors holding swords in their hands.

It was no longer possible to enter the temple, for it had filled with rubble years ago, but they admired the exterior, as did all the tourists Mr. Kapasi brought there, slowly strolling along each of its sides. Mr. Das trailed behind, taking pictures. The children ran ahead, pointing to figures of naked people, intrigued in particular by the Nagamithunas, the half-human, half-serpentine couples who were said, Mr. Kapasi told them, to live in the deepest waters of the sea. Mr. Kapasi was pleased that they liked the temple, pleased especially that it appealed to Mrs. Das. She stopped every three or four paces, staring silently at the carved lovers, and the processions of elephants, and the topless female musicians beating on two-sided drums.

Though Mr. Kapasi had been to the temple countless times, it occurred to him, as he, too, gazed at the topless women, that he had never seen his own wife fully naked. Even when they had made love she kept the panels of her blouse hooked together, the string of her petticoat knotted around her waist. He had never admired the backs of his wife's legs the way he now admired those of Mrs. Das, walking as if for his benefit alone. He had, of course, seen plenty of bare limbs before, belonging to the American and European ladies who took his tours. But Mrs. Das was different. Unlike the other women, who had an interest only in the temple, and kept their noses buried in a guidebook, or their eyes behind the lens of a camera, Mrs. Das had taken an interest in him.

Mr. Kapasi was anxious to be alone with her, to continue their private conversation, yet he felt nervous to walk at her side. She was lost behind her sunglasses, ignoring her husband's requests that she pose for another picture, walking past her children as if they were strangers. Worried that he might disturb her, Mr. Kapasi walked ahead, to admire, as he always did, the three life-sized bronze avatars of Surya, the sun god, each emerging from its own niche on the temple facade to greet the sun at dawn, noon, and evening. They wore elaborate headdresses, their languid, elongated eyes closed, their bare chests draped with carved chains and amulets. Hibiscus petals, offerings from previous visitors, were strewn at their grey-green feet. The last statue, on the northern wall of the temple, was Mr. Kapasi's favourite. This Surya had a tired expression, weary after a hard day of work, sitting astride a horse with folded legs. Even his horse's eyes were drowsy. Around his body were smaller sculptures of women in pairs, their hips thrust to one side.

"Who's that?" Mrs. Das asked. He was startled to see that she was standing beside him.

"He is the Astachala-Surya," Mr. Kapasi said. "The setting sun."

"So in a couple of hours the sun will set right here?" She slipped a foot out of one of her square-heeled shoes, rubbed her toes on the back of her other leg.

"That is correct."

She raised her sunglasses for a moment, then put them back on again. "Neat."

Mr. Kapasi was not certain exactly what the word suggested, but he had a feeling it was a favourable response. He hoped that Mrs. Das had understood Surya's beauty, his power. Perhaps they would discuss it further in their letters. He would explain things to her, things about India, and she would explain things to him about America. In its own way this correspondence would fulfill his dream, of serving as an interpreter between nations. He looked at her straw bag, delighted that his address lay nestled among its contents. When he pictured her so many thousands of miles away he plummeted, so much so that he had an overwhelming urge to wrap his arms around her, to freeze with her, even for an instant, in an embrace witnessed by his favourite Surya. But Mrs. Das had already started walking.

"When do you return to America?" he asked, trying to sound placid.

"In ten days."

He calculated: A week to settle in, a week to develop the pictures, a few days to compose her letter, two weeks to get to India by air. According to his schedule, allowing room for delays, he would hear from Mrs. Das in approximately six weeks' time.

The family was silent as Mr. Kapasi drove them back, a little past four-thirty, to Hotel Sandy Villa. The children had bought miniature granite versions of the chariot's wheels at a souvenir stand, and they turned them round in their hands. Mr. Das continued to read his book. Mrs. Das untangled Tina's hair with her brush and divided it into two little ponytails.

Mr. Kapasi was beginning to dread the thought of dropping them off. He was not prepared to begin his six-week wait to hear from Mrs. Das. As he stole glances at her in the rearview mirror, wrapping elastic bands around Tina's hair, he wondered how he might make the tour last a little longer. Ordinarily he sped back to Puri using a shortcut, eager to return home, scrub his feet and hands with sandalwood soap, and enjoy the evening newspaper and a cup of tea that his wife would serve him in silence. The thought of that silence, something to which he'd long been resigned, now oppressed him. It was then that he suggested visiting the hills at Udayagiri and Khandagiri, where a number of monastic dwellings were hewn out of the ground, facing one another across a defile.[1] It was some miles away but well worth seeing, Mr. Kapasi told them.

"Oh yeah, there's something mentioned about it in this book," Mr. Das said. "Built by a Jain[2] king or something."

"Shall we go then?" Mr. Kapasi asked. He paused at a turn in the road. "It's to the left."

Mr. Das turned to look at Mrs. Das. Both of them shrugged.

"Left, left," the children chanted.

Mr. Kapasi turned the wheel, almost delirious with relief. He did not know what he would do or say to Mrs. Das once they arrived at the hills. Perhaps he would tell her what a pleasing smile she had. Perhaps he would compliment her strawberry shirt, which he found irresistibly becoming. Perhaps, when Mr. Das was busy taking a picture, he would take her hand.

He did not have to worry. When they got to the hills, divided by a steep path thick with trees, Mrs. Das refused to get out of the car. All along the path, dozens of monkeys were seated on stones, as well as on the branches of the trees. Their hind legs were stretched out in front and raised to shoulder level, their arms resting on their knees.

"My legs are tired," she said, sinking low in her seat. "I'll stay here."

"Why did you have to wear those stupid shoes?" Mr. Das said. "You won't be in the pictures."

"Pretend I'm there."

"But we could use one of these pictures for our Christmas card this year. We didn't get one of all five of us at the Sun Temple. Mr. Kapasi could take it."

"I'm not coming. Anyway, those monkeys give me the creeps."

"But they're harmless," Mr. Das said. He turned to Mr. Kapasi. "Aren't they?"

"They are more hungry than dangerous," Mr. Kapasi said. "Do not provoke them with food, and they will not bother you."

Mr. Das headed up the defile with the children, the boys at his side, the little girl on his shoulders. Mr. Kapasi watched as they crossed paths with a Japanese man and woman, the only other tourists there, who paused for a final photograph, then stepped into a nearby car and drove away. As the car disap-

---

1   *defile* Narrow gorge.

2   *Jain* Adherent of Jainism, an Indian religion related to Hinduism and notable for asceticism, belief in the transmigration of souls, and advocating the avoidance of harm to all living creatures.

peared out of view some of the monkeys called out, emitting soft whooping sounds, and then walked on their flat black hands and feet up the path. At one point a group of them formed a little ring around Mr. Das and the children. Tina screamed in delight. Ronny ran in circles around his father. Bobby bent down and picked up a fat stick on the ground. When he extended it, one of the monkeys approached him and snatched it, then briefly beat the ground.

"I'll join them," Mr. Kapasi said, unlocking the door on his side. "There is much to explain about the caves."

"No. Stay a minute," Mrs. Das said. She got out of the back seat and slipped in beside Mr. Kapasi. "Raj has his dumb book anyway." Together, through the windshield, Mrs. Das and Mr. Kapasi watched as Bobby and the monkey passed the stick back and forth between them.

"A brave little boy," Mr. Kapasi commented.

"It's not so surprising," Mrs. Das said.

"No?"

"He's not his."

"I beg your pardon?"

"Raj's. He's not Raj's son."

Mr. Kapasi felt a prickle on his skin. He reached into his shirt pocket for the small tin of lotus-oil balm he carried with him at all times, and applied it to three spots on his forehead. He knew that Mrs. Das was watching him, but he did not turn to face her. Instead he watched as the figures of Mr. Das and the children grew smaller, climbing up the steep path, pausing every now and then for a picture, surrounded by a growing number of monkeys.

"Are you surprised?" The way she put it made him choose his words with care.

"It's not the type of thing one assumes," Mr. Kapasi replied slowly. He put the tin of lotus-oil balm back in his pocket.

"No, of course not. And no one knows, of course. No one at all. I've kept it a secret for eight whole years." She looked at Mr. Kapasi, tilting her chin as if to gain a fresh perspective. "But now I've told you."

Mr. Kapasi nodded. He felt suddenly parched, and his forehead was warm and slightly numb from the balm. He considered asking Mrs. Das for a sip of water, then decided against it.

"We met when we were very young," she said. She reached into her straw bag in search of something, then pulled out a packet of puffed rice. "Want some?"

"No, thank you."

She put a fistful in her mouth, sank into the seat a little, and looked away from Mr. Kapasi, out the window on her side of the car. "We married when we were still in college. We were in high school when he proposed. We went to the same college, of course. Back then we couldn't stand the thought of being separated, not for a day, not for a minute. Our parents were best friends who lived in the same town. My entire life I saw him every weekend, either at our house or theirs. We were sent upstairs to play together while our parents joked about our marriage. Imagine! They never caught us at anything, though in a way I think it was all more or less a setup. The things we did those Friday and Saturday nights, while our parents sat downstairs drinking tea ... I could tell you stories, Mr. Kapasi."

As a result of spending all her time in college with Raj, she continued, she did not make many close friends. There was no one to confide in about him at the end of a difficult day or to share a passing thought or a worry. Her parents now lived on the other side of the world, but she had never been very close to them, anyway. After marrying so young she was overwhelmed by it all, having a child so quickly and nursing, and warming up bottles of milk and testing their temperature against her wrist while Raj was at work, dressed in sweaters and corduroy pants, teaching his students about rocks and dinosaurs. Raj never looked cross or harried, or plump as she had become after the first baby.

Always tired, she declined invitations from her one or two college girl-friends, to have lunch or shop in Manhattan. Eventually the friends stopped calling her, so that she was left at home all day with the baby, surrounded by toys that made her trip when she walked or wince when she sat, always cross and tired. Only occasionally did they go out after Ronny was born, and even more rarely did they entertain. Raj didn't mind; he looked forward to coming home from teaching and watching television and bouncing Ronny on his knee. She had been outraged when Raj told her that a Punjabi[1] friend, someone whom she had once met but did not remember, would be staying with them for a week for some job interviews in the New Brunswick area.

Bobby was conceived in the afternoon, on a sofa littered with rubber teething toys, after the friend learned that a London pharmaceutical company had hired him, while Ronny cried to be freed from his playpen. She made no protest when the friend touched the small of her back as she was about to make a pot of coffee, then pulled her against his crisp navy suit. He made love to her swiftly in silence, with an expertise she had never known, without the meaningful expressions and smiles Raj always insisted on afterward. The next day Raj drove the friend to JFK. He was married now, to a Punjabi girl, and they lived in London still, and every year they exchanged Christmas cards with Raj and Mina, each couple tucking photos of their families into the envelopes. He did not know that he was Bobby's father. He never would.

---

1   *Punjabi* From the Punjab region in northwestern India.

"I beg your pardon, Mrs. Das, but why have you told me this information?" Mr. Kapasi asked when she had finally finished speaking, and had turned to face him once again.

"For God's sake, stop calling me Mrs. Das. I'm twenty-eight. You probably have children my age."

"Not quite." It disturbed Mr. Kapasi to learn that she thought of him as a parent. The feeling he had had toward her, that had made him check his reflection in the rearview mirror as they drove, evaporated a little.

"I told you because of your talents." She put the packet of puffed rice back into her bag without folding over the top.

"I don't understand," Mr. Kapasi said.

"Don't you see? For eight years I haven't been able to express this to anybody, not to friends, certainly not to Raj. He doesn't even suspect it. He thinks I'm still in love with him. Well, don't you have anything to say?"

"About what?"

"About what I've just told you. About my secret, and about how terrible it makes me feel. I feel terrible looking at my children, and at Raj, always terrible. I have terrible urges, Mr. Kapasi, to throw things away. One day I had the urge to throw everything I own out the window, the television, the children, everything. Don't you think it's unhealthy?"

He was silent.

"Mr. Kapasi, don't you have anything to say? I thought that was your job."

"My job is to give tours, Mrs. Das."

"Not that. Your other job. As an interpreter."

"But we do not face a language barrier. What need is there for an interpreter?"

"That's not what I mean. I would never have told you otherwise. Don't you realize what it means for me to tell you?"

"What does it mean?"

"It means that I'm tired of feeling so terrible all the time. Eight years, Mr. Kapasi, I've been in pain eight years. I was hoping you could help me feel better, say the right thing. Suggest some kind of remedy."

He looked at her, in her red plaid skirt and strawberry T-shirt, a woman not yet thirty, who loved neither her husband nor her children, who had already fallen out of love with life. Her confession depressed him, depressed him all the more when he thought of Mr. Das at the top of the path, Tina clinging to his shoulders, taking pictures of ancient monastic cells cut into the hills to show his students in America, unsuspecting and unaware that one of his sons was not his own. Mr. Kapasi felt insulted that Mrs. Das should ask him to interpret her common, trivial little secret. She did not resemble the patients in the doctor's office, those who came glassy-eyed and desperate, unable to sleep or breathe or urinate with ease, unable, above all, to give words to their pains. Still, Mr. Kapasi believed it was his duty to assist Mrs. Das. Perhaps he ought to tell her to confess the truth to Mr. Das. He would explain that honesty was the best policy. Honesty surely would help her feel better, as she'd put it. Perhaps he would offer to preside over the discussion, as a mediator. He decided to begin with the most obvious question, to get to the heart of the matter, and so he asked, "Is it really pain you feel, Mrs. Das, or is it guilt?"

She turned to him and glared, mustard oil thick on her frosty pink lips. She opened her mouth to say something, but as she glared at Mr. Kapasi some certain knowledge seemed to pass before her eyes, and she stopped. It crushed him; he knew at that moment that he was not even important enough to be properly insulted. She opened the car door and began walking up the path, wobbling a little on her square wooden heels, reaching into her straw bag to eat handfuls of puffed rice. It fell through her fingers, leaving a zigzagging trail, causing a monkey to leap down from a tree and devour the little white grains. In search of more, the monkey began to follow Mrs. Das. Others joined him, so that she was soon being followed by about half a dozen of them, their velvety tails dragging behind.

Mr. Kapasi stepped out of the car. He wanted to holler, to alert her in some way but he worried that if she knew they were behind her, she would grow nervous. Perhaps she would lose her balance. Perhaps they would pull at her bag or her hair. He began to jog up the path, taking a fallen branch in his hand to scare away the monkeys. Mrs. Das continued walking, oblivious, trailing grains of puffed rice. Near the top of the incline, before a group of cells fronted by a row of squat stone pillars, Mr. Das was kneeling on the ground, focusing the lens of his camera. The children stood under the arcade, now hiding, now emerging from view.

"Wait for me," Mrs. Das called out. "I'm coming."

Tina jumped up and down. "Here comes Mommy!"

"Great," Mr. Das said without looking up. "Just in time. We'll get Mr. Kapasi to take a picture of the five of us."

Mr. Kapasi quickened his pace, waving his branch so that the monkeys scampered away distracted, in another direction.

"Where's Bobby?" Mrs. Das asked when she stopped.

Mr. Das looked up from the camera. "I don't know. Ronny, where's Bobby?"

Ronny shrugged. "I thought he was right here."

"Where is he?" Mrs. Das repeated sharply. "What's wrong with all of you?"

They began calling his name, wandering up and down the path a bit. Because they were calling, they did not initially hear the boy's screams. When they found him, a little farther down the path under a tree, he was surrounded by a group of monkeys, over a dozen of them, pulling at his T-shirt with their long black fingers. The puffed rice Mrs. Das had spilled was scattered at his feet, raked over by the monkeys' hands. The boy was silent, his body frozen, swift tears running down his startled face. His bare legs were dusty and red with welts from where one of the monkeys struck him repeatedly with the stick he had given to it earlier.

"Daddy, the monkey's hurting Bobby," Tina said.

Mr. Das wiped his palms on the front of his shorts. In his nervousness he accidentally pressed the shutter on his camera; the whirring noise of the advancing film excited the monkeys, and the one with the stick began to beat Bobby more intently. "What are we supposed to do? What if they start attacking?"

"Mr. Kapasi," Mrs. Das shrieked, noticing him standing to one side. "Do something, for God's sake, do something!"

Mr. Kapasi took his branch and shooed them away hissing at the ones that remained, stomping his feet to scare them. The animals retreated slowly, with a measured gait, obedient but unintimidated. Mr. Kapasi gathered Bobby in his arms and brought him back to where his parents and siblings were standing. As he carried him he was tempted to whisper a secret into the boy's ear. But Bobby was stunned, and shivering with fright, his legs bleeding slightly where the stick had broken the skin. When Mr. Kapasi delivered him to his parents, Mr. Das brushed some dirt off the boy's T-shirt and put the visor on him the right way. Mrs. Das reached into her straw bag to find a bandage which she taped over the cut on his knee. Ronny offered his brother a fresh piece of gum. "He's fine. Just a little scared, right, Bobby?" Mr. Das said, patting the top of his head.

"God, let's get out of here," Mrs. Das said. She folded her arms across the strawberry on her chest. "This place gives me the creeps."

"Yeah. Back to the hotel, definitely," Mr. Das agreed.

"Poor Bobby," Mrs. Das said. "Come here a second. Let Mommy fix your hair." Again she reached into her straw bag, this time for her hairbrush, and began to run it around the edges of the translucent visor. When she whipped out the hairbrush, the slip of paper with Mr. Kapasi's address on it fluttered away in the wind. No one but Mr. Kapasi noticed. He watched as it rose, carried higher and higher by the breeze, into the trees where the monkeys now sat, solemnly observing the scene below. Mr. Kapasi observed it too, knowing that this was the picture of the Das family he would preserve forever in his mind.

—1998

Lydia Millet
b. 1968

For all their range of tone and variety of perspective, many of American writer Lydia Millet's novels and short stories are centrally concerned with humanity's potential for exploitation. And yet, although Millet has worked for the Natural Resources Defense Council and the Center for Biological Diversity, she regards herself not as an activist but rather as a writer of fiction that is chiefly philosophical and only secondarily social or political. In her view, "Fiction writers are primarily onlookers whose job is to evoke the beautiful, the painful, the funny, and the sublime in a way that both embraces and transcends individual experience."

All of these qualities are readily to be found—often side by side and where least expected—in the short stories collected in *Love in Infant Monkeys* (2009), a finalist for the 2010 Pulitzer Prize. As in the absurdist satirical novels *George Bush, Dark Prince of Love* (2000), which traces an ex-con's tormented infatuation with the leader of the free world, and *Oh Pure and Radiant Heart* (2005), which transposes the architects of the atomic bomb to contemporary America and imagines them as improbable crusaders against nuclear proliferation, *Love in Infant Monkeys* mingles fact and fiction, often to darkly comic effect. In each thematically linked story, the relationship between animals and celebrities or historical figures—from the actor David Hasselhoff to the infamous psychologist Harry Harlow—reveals a dimension of the protagonist's fundamental nature.

Millet is a writer whose comic vision belies a seriousness of purpose that is grounded in what she describes as "a love of the beasts and growths and forms of this stunning and irreplaceable world, a belief that humans are, in fact, not the sun around which the other planets revolve but mere planets themselves."

Love in Infant Monkeys

Harry Harlow[1] had a general hypothesis: Mothers are useful, in scientific terms. They have an intrinsic value, even beyond their breast milk. Call it their company.

In this hypothesis he was bucking a trend in American psychology. For decades experts on parenting had been advising mothers to show their children

---

1   *Harry Harlow* Harry F. Harlow (1905–81), a psychologist known for his experiments studying the development of young monkeys in isolation from their mothers. Although the following story is fictional, it incorporates accurate information regarding Harlow's life and work.

as little affection as possible. Too much affection was coddling, and coddling weakened a child. "When you are tempted to pet your child," said a president of the American Psychological Association in a speech, "remember that mother love is a dangerous instrument." This school of thought ran counter to what was believed by those not indebted for their child-rearing strategies to a rigorously monitored testing process. But it was dominant in the scholarship. To refute it, Harlow decided, the value of love would have to be demonstrated in a controlled experimental setting.

He worked long hours, seldom leaving his laboratory. With his experiments he made a name for himself, appearing on television programs and travelling the country on speaking engagements. He was seen as a rebel and an iconoclast. He spoke boldly of mother love, calling it "contact comfort." He stressed its value to emotional health.

But he spoke harshly of his test subjects. "The only thing I care about is whether a monkey will turn out a property I can publish," he said. "I don't have any love for them. I never have. How could you love a monkey?"

To know how love works, a scientist must study its absence. This is simple scientific method; Harry admitted it. The suffering of lesser beings is often the price of knowledge. As he put it, "If my work will save only one million human children, I can't get overly concerned about ten monkeys."

Others were doing bold animal experiments at the same time, in the fifties, when Harry started, and after. Rats were dropped in boiling water, cats pinned down for months until their legs withered, dogs irradiated until their skin crisped, monkeys shot in the heads and stomachs or immobilized to have their spinal cords severed. When it came to the treatment of research animals, Harry was squarely in the mainstream. Only his willingness to speak bluntly was avant-garde.

He gathered disciples around him, young women and men who would continue his work, and decades later he would still be revered by psychology. While acknowledging the problem of what some might call animal cruelty, later scholars would view his collateral damage as a necessary unpleasantness. His chief biographer, a woman journalist, described him as a rose in a cornfield.

He was a high-functioning alcoholic, and there were long periods in his life when he was rarely sober. He had wives—first one, then another, then the first one again. He had two sets of children he never saw.

Harry Frederick Harlow had been born Harry Frederick Israel. Around the time of his doctoral dissertation he had changed his last name, not because he was Jewish—for he was not, in fact, Jewish—but because the name Israel sounded Jewish, and this made it hard to secure a good job. He did not dislike Jews; indeed, he admired them for their intelligence and their education. But others in academia had certain prejudices. A famous professor who was also his first mentor did not wish him to continue to be mistaken for a Jew, so Harry deferred to him.

It was a minor accommodation.

One way to prove the hypothesis was to take a newborn monkey away from its mother and never give it back. Put it in a bare box, observe it. Anxiety first, shown in trembling and shaking; then come the screams. Watch it huddle, small limbs clutching. Make careful notations. Next, construct a wire mannequin that holds a milk bottle. See if the baby thinks the mannequin is its mother. When it does not think so, give it a mannequin draped with terry cloth, but no milk. See it cling to this milkless cloth mannequin.

Repeat experiment with numerous infants. Make notations.

Second, place infant monkeys in isolation, with neither monkey nor human contact save the sight of the researchers' hands entering the box to change bedding or food. Leave them there for thirty days. Make careful notations. When the infants are removed, watch two among them starve themselves till they expire. Notations. Repeat with longer isolation periods. First six months, then a year. If necessary, force-feed upon removal from box. Observe: If left in boxes for twelve months, infants will no longer move. Only life signs: pulse and respiration. Upon removal from box, such damaged infants may have to be reisolated for the duration of their short lives. Notations.

Third, attempt to breed the isolated monkeys to produce needed new experimental subjects. When the monkeys show no inclination to mate, inseminate the females. Observe the birth of infants. Observe that the longest-isolated mothers kill infants by chewing off fingers and toes or crushing heads with their teeth. Notations.

Fourth, create bad-mother surrogates: mothers with spikes, mothers that blast cold wind. Put baby monkeys on them. Observe: Time after time, baby monkeys return. Bad mother is better than none.

Only 8:00 pm, and he was already slurring. He would swing by that party. What the hell. Suomi had said he'd be there.

But first, check the experiments.

Walking along the row of vertical chambers, he gave cursory glances inside—one, two, three subjects in a row had given up trying to climb out of their wells of isolation. The pits were designed, of course, to make it impossible to escape.

One subject scrambled and fell back, a weak young female. She looked up with her great round black eyes. Blink blink. She was afraid, but still plucky. Still game to try to get out, change her situation. The others were abject at the bottom of their separate holes, knew by now they could never climb the sides of the wells. As far as they knew, they were in there for good. Plucky got you nowhere if you were a lab monkey.

Then the boxes where Bill had dosed the subjects with reserpine.[1] These monkeys, too, huddled unmoving. Serotonin had been suppressed; this seemed to equate almost uniformly with complete listlessness, complete passivity. Might be other factors, but still: very interesting.

Back past the so-called pits of despair, where the young female—what had they named her? Minestrone?—was still trying to climb the walls and falling repeatedly. She squeaked at him. Well, not at him, technically. She did not know he was there; she could not see him. She could see no one. She was alone.

Harlow got in the car. Drove. Wasn't far. Hated faculty parties, hardly ever went to them: frivolous. Took him away from his work.

He said this to a new female grad student who met him on the walkway, exclaiming at his presence. She had long curly hair and wore no brassiere.

"Dr. Harlow! I can't believe you actually made it!"

"Work allatime," he said, nodding and shrugging at once. Not as easy as he'd thought it would be. Pulled it together, though. "Lucky. Always have smart wives to help me with it."

She shot him a look of pity: Everyone knew the second smart wife was on her cancer deathbed.

"Some of the faculty," he went on, "these guys don't even work on Sundays. Not serious."

She was looking at him like he was a baby bird fallen from its nest. The free-love ones were maternal. Always acting like everyone's little mommy.

Save it up for the kiddies, he thought. Wasted on me.

These days, Peggy dying like this, maybe he should take a break more often—the depression, for one thing. Felt like the top of his head was weighing him down. Headaches constantly. Chest squashed and nervous stomach. Nothing compared to the chemo, but still. Hair and skin greasy. Plus he was tired, face ached with it. Didn't know if he could have kept his head up if he'd stayed at his desk. Fell asleep with a cigarette in his mouth last night, woke up with a stack of papers smouldering. Something smelled wrong. Burned his eyebrow half off, it turned out.

He patted his pocket for his cigarettes. Full pack. His students were going to be here. Chance to talk to Steve again about the chambers. Steve had said not to call them *dungeons*. Bad for public opinion.

Bullshit, but Steve was good at that side of it. Spade a spade, goddammit.

Saw a garden hose sticking out of a spigot against the side of the house. Turned it on, with some difficulty. Wrestled with the hose till cool water sput-

---

1   *reserpine* Sedative and antipsychotic drug.

tered into his mouth. Cleared his head. Tongue felt less mealy. He wiggled the tongue around in his mouth. Testing it.

"Harry!—I can't believe this—Harry!"

Fat woman from the department, what did she do? Personnel? Payroll? Lumbering.

"Ha, ha," he said, dropping the hose, stepping up onto the stoop and lurching into the doorjamb.

"So you're finally out of your cave! Look who's here! It's *Harry*! Can you guys believe this? Come on in!"

There was the good-looking girl from East Germany who was interested in the nuclear-family experiments, smoking in the corner with Jim. Poor Jim, that plagiarism thing with Peggy. Unfair. But nothing he could do about it. Couldn't get in the middle. He shrugged, itchy.

The jacket: How long had he been wearing it? Felt oily. Maybe it was the shirt. Was it supposed to be white? He could not remember. Grey, beige or white? What colour was the shirt to begin with?

"Get you a highball, Harry?"

It was a hard-to-breathe night. Humid, filmy. He squinted. Barely see the kids in the corner, but all of them seemed to be looking at him.

The fat payroll said something about gin. He nodded. Headache getting worse. Bands of light spanning his field of vision.

"Harry," said a guy from the right. "Harry Harlow, right? Hey, I read 'Love in Infant Monkeys.' Great paper."

"Huh," grunted Harry. "Seen Suomi?"

"Steve's not here yet," said the guy, either frowning or leering. No idea who it was. Might be the chancellor, for all he knew. Wished he would disappear.

"Huh," Harry muttered. Guy was already veering toward something out the side door, where a fountain was playing. A twinkle of water? Mermaids?

"Lie down a little," he told the payroll woman, hovering with a heavy tumbler. He accepted it gratefully, drank it down and gave it right back. Good to be prompt. Aftertaste was hinky. "Spare daybed, maybe? Dark room? Cot thing?"

"Certainly," said the woman. "There, there. You poor dear." She leaned close and whispered with obscene intimacy: "How's she *doing*?"

Wasn't a baby bird, for Chrissake. No broken wing. Piece of his mind; tell her straight she resembled a water buffalo. Should be roaming the Serengeti with her quadruped friends. "Holding up, holding up," he mumbled. "Brave girl, Peggy." Hadn't seen her for more than five minutes since what, Tuesday? Busy. She knew; she understood perfectly.

He persevered to the room at the back. Secluded. The water buffalo showed him in. Closed the door in her face. "No buffalos," he said, quietly but firmly.

He fell down on the bed and felt a brief satisfaction.

When he woke, the party was over. Brimming ashtrays everywhere. Skinny kid fast asleep on the couch, legs straight, sneakers splayed on the sofa arm. He stood over the kitchen sink, full of squeezed-out lemon halves and olives. He splashed water on his face and gargled out of a used glass. Didn't see a clean one. Who cared. His mouth was pure alcohol, would neutralize the germs. Made his way out of the bungalow, thirsty as hell. Needed something real to drink.

White light; he blinked on the stoop. It was early morning. Sunday? Legs felt heavy, but he would go to the lab. Still had a faint headache, but bearable now.

Lab was empty. Students must be sitting on their asses this weekend. Pure mediocrity.

Walking the gauntlet of the pits of despair he glanced into Minestrone's setup. Saw the top of her head. She was just sitting there. He kept watching; she did not move. Not a spark animated the creature. Finally given up. Now broken. Her spindly arms hung loose from the sockets, doing nothing. Hunched little figure, staring. Nothing there. It had gone.

Had a flask in a special file cabinet. Headed for it. Deep swig.

In the nightmare, which he'd had in other forms before, he stood beside his beautiful boxes, the boxes of his own design, the boxes that B.F. Skinner[1] himself had admired. He mistook each infant monkey for a beloved soul. In that way the nightmare was confusing. He saw each infant in the heart of its mother, precious, unique, held so close because the mother was willing to die for it. The mother, in the dream, knew what he was doing as he took the infant from her. She was fully aware of what was happening to her and her baby. It was as though she were being forced to watch the infant waste away, left alone in the box—not for the length of its life, perhaps, but for the length of its self, until the self flew out and was forever gone.

In the nightmare it was always the mother monkey he faced, not the infants. The mother, with her wild, desperate eyes. He felt what he could think of only as her passion, like a heat emanating. The mother was crazy with love, mad with a singular devotion. All she wanted was the safety of her infant. She would chew off her feet for it. She would do anything.

But she was trapped, simply trapped. He had put her in a cage, and the cage was too strong for her. When he took the baby from her arms, her panic

---

1   *B.F. Skinner* Burrhus Frederic Skinner (1904–90), an influential American psychologist who advocated the study of behaviour as opposed to internal psychological states. To conduct experiments in behaviour conditioning, he invented the "Skinner box," a cage in which a captive animal is rewarded for performing a specific action, such as pulling a lever.

rose so high it could rise no higher; if she knew how to beg she would beg till the end of the world, scream until her throat split. *Give me my baby back.*

He knew the feeling of loss that would last till she died. He knew it the way he knew a distant country. They had their own customs there.

—2009

Eden Robinson
b. 1968

Eden Robinson, the author of some of the most startling and macabre fiction in contemporary Canadian literature, counts among her major influences Edgar Allan Poe, Stephen King, and filmmaker David Cronenberg. In many of her best-known stories, notably those in her first collection, *Traplines* (1996), extremes of physical and psychological violence are not disruptions of a peaceful norm but rather part of everyday, less to be wondered at than endured as a matter of course.

Much, though not all, of Robinson's work engages with the lives of First Nations people today, and Robinson herself was born to a Heiltsuk mother and a Haisla father on a reserve in northern British Columbia. However, Robinson, like so many writers, is suspicious of labels, including the label of "Native writer." As she has observed: "Once you've been put in the box of being a native writer, then it's hard to get out."

It is difficult to fashion any sort of box to hold Robinson's fiction: it is dark, disturbing, traversed by characters she describes as "flamboyant psychopaths," and yet full of humour. While Robinson gained much acclaim for *Traplines*, her first novel, *Monkey Beach* (2000), became a national bestseller and was nominated for both the Scotiabank Giller Prize and the Governor General's Award. A story that follows the journey of a young Haisla woman as she seeks to unravel the mystery of her missing brother, it is both stylistically bold and intensely readable. Robinson's latest novel is *Blood Sports*, which is again noted for its wide use of violence and focus on sociopathic characters; like *Monkey Beach*, the novel relates back to one of the first stories published in *Traplines*.

Terminal Avenue

His brother once held a peeled orange slice up against the sun. When the light shone through it, the slice became a brilliant amber: the setting sun is this colour, ripe orange. The uniforms of the five advancing Peace Officers are robin's egg blue, but the slanting light catches their visors and sets their faces aflame.

&

In his memory, the water of the Douglas Channel[1] is a hard blue, baked to a glassy translucence by the August sun. The mountains in the distance form a crown; *Gabiswa*, the mountain in the centre, is the same shade of blue as his lover's veins.

She raises her arms to sweep her hair from her face. Her breasts lift. In the cool morning air, her nipples harden to knobby raspberries. Her eyes are widening in indignation: he once saw that shade of blue in a dragonfly's wing, but this is another thing he will keep secret.

&

Say nothing, his mother said, without moving her lips, careful not to attract attention. They waited in their car in silence after that. His father and mother were in the front seat, stiff.

Blood plastered his father's hair to his skull; blood leaked down his father's blank face. In the flashing lights of the patrol car, the blood looked black and moved like honey.

&

A rocket has entered the event horizon[2] of a black hole. To an observer who is watching this from a safe distance, the rocket trapped here, in the black hole's inescapable halo of gravity, will appear to stop.

To an astronaut in the rocket, however, gravity is a rack that stretches his body like taffy, thinner and thinner, until there is nothing left but x-rays.

&

In full body-armour, the five Peace Officers are sexless and anonymous. With their visors down, they look like old-fashioned astronauts. The landscape they move across is the rapid transit line, the Surreycentral Skytrain station, but if they remove their body-armour, it may as well be the moon.

The Peace Officers begin to match strides until they move like a machine. This is an intimidation tactic that works, is working on him even though he knows what it is. He finds himself frozen. He can't move, even as they roll towards him, a train on invisible tracks.

&

---

1   *Douglas Channel* Inlet on the coast of northern British Columbia. At the end of the inlet is Kitamaat Village, the site of a Haisla First Nations community.
2   *event horizon* Boundary at the edge of a black hole where the force of gravity becomes so strong that no light can escape.

Once, when his brother dared him, he jumped off the high diving tower. He wasn't really scared until he stepped away from the platform. In that moment, he realized he couldn't change his mind.

You stupid shit, his brother said when he surfaced.

In his dreams, everything is the same, except there is no water in the swimming pool and he crashes into the concrete like a dropped pumpkin.

&

He thinks of his brother, who is so perfect he wasn't born, but chiselled from stone. There is nothing he can do against that brown Apollo's face, nothing he can say that will justify his inaction. Kevin would know what to do, with doom coming towards him in formation.

But Kevin is dead. He walked through their mother's door one day, wearing the robin's egg blue uniform of the great enemy, and his mother struck him down. She summoned the ghost of their father and put him in the room, sat him beside her, bloody and stunned. Against this Kevin said, I can stop it, Mom. I have the power to change things now.

She turned away, then the family turned away. Kevin looked at him, pleading, before he left her house and never came back, disappeared. Wil closed his eyes, a dark, secret joy welling in him, to watch his brother fall: Kevin never made the little mistakes in his life, never so much as sprouted a pimple. He made up for it though by doing the unforgivable.

Wil wonders if his brother knows what is happening. If, in fact, he isn't one of the Peace Officers, filled himself with secret joy.

&

His lover will wait for him tonight. Ironically, she will be wearing a complete Peace Officer's uniform, bought at great expense on the black market, and very, very illegal. She will wait at the door of her club, Terminal Avenue, and she will frisk clients that she knows will enjoy it. She will have the playroom ready, with its great wooden beams stuck through with hook and cages, with its expensive equipment built for the exclusive purpose of causing pain. On a steel cart, her toys will be spread out as neatly as surgical instruments.

When he walks through the door, she likes to have her bouncers, also dressed as Peace Officers, hurl him against the wall. They let him struggle before they handcuff him. Their uniforms are slippery as rubber. He can't get a grip on them. The uniforms are padded with the latest in wonderfabric so no matter how hard he punches them, he can't hurt them. They will drag him into the back and strip-search him in front of clients who pay for the privilege of watching. He stands under a spotlight that shines an impersonal cone of light from the ceiling. The rest of the room is darkened. He can see reflections of glasses, red-eyed cigarettes, the glint of ice clinking against glass, shadows shifting. He can hear zippers coming undone, low moans; he can smell the cum when he's beaten into passivity.

Once, he wanted to cut his hair, but she wouldn't let him, said she'd never speak to him again if he did. She likes it when the bouncers grab him by his hair and drag him to the exploratory table in the centre of the room. She says she likes the way it veils his face when he's kneeling.

In the playroom though, she changes. He can't hurt her the way she wants him to; she is tiring of him. He whips her half-heartedly until she tells the bouncer to do it properly.

A man walked in one day, in a robin's egg blue uniform, and Wil froze. When he could breathe again, when he could think, he found her watching him, thoughtful.

She borrowed the man's uniform and lay on the table, her face blank and smooth and round as a basketball under the visor. He put a painstick against the left nipple. It darkened and bruised. Her screams were muffled by the helmet. Her bouncers whispered things to her as they pinned her to the table, and he hurt her. When she begged him to stop, he moved the painstick to her right nipple.

He kept going until he was shaking so hard he had to stop.

That's enough for tonight, she said, breathless, wrapping her arms around him, telling the bouncers to leave when he started to cry. My poor virgin. It's not pain so much as it is a cleansing.

Is it, he asked her, one of those whiteguilt things?

She laughed, kissed him. Rocked him and forgave him, on the evening he discovered that it wasn't just easy to do terrible things to another person: it could give pleasure. It could give power.

She said she'd kill him if he told anyone what happened in the playroom. She has a reputation and is vaguely ashamed of her secret weakness. He wouldn't tell, not ever. He is addicted to her pain.

To distinguish it from real uniforms, hers has an inverted black triangle[1] on the left side, just over her heart: asocialism, she says with a laugh, and he doesn't get it. She won't explain it, her blue eyes black with desire as her pupils widened suddenly like a cat's.

The uniforms advancing on him, however, are clean and pure and real.

∞

---

1   *inverted black triangle* Badge given to Nazi concentration camp inmates to mark them as "asocial"—a broad category that included prostitutes, lesbians, and homeless people.

Wil wanted to be an astronaut. He bought the books, he watched the movies and he dreamed. He did well in Physics, Math, and Sciences, and his mother bragged, He's got my brains.

He was so dedicated, he would test himself, just like the astronauts on TV. He locked himself in his closet once with nothing but a bag of potato chips and a bottle of pop. He wanted to see if he could spend time in a small space, alone and deprived. It was July and they had no air conditioning. He fainted in the heat, dreamed that he was floating over the Earth on his way to Mars, weightless.

Kevin found him, dragged him from the closet, and laughed at him.

You stupid shit, he said. Don't you know anything?

When his father slid off the hood leaving a snail's trail of blood, Kevin ran out of the car.

Stop it! Kevin screamed, his face contorted in the headlight's beam. Shadows loomed over him, but he was undaunted. Stop it!

Kevin threw himself on their dad and saved his life.

Wil stayed with their father in the hospital, never left his side. He was there when the Peace Officers came and took their father's statement. When they closed the door in his face and he heard his father screaming. The nurses took him away and he let them. Wil watched his father withdraw into himself after that, never quite healing.

He knew the names of all the constellations, the distances of the stars, the equations that would launch a ship to reach them. He knew how to stay alive in any conditions, except when someone didn't want to stay alive.

No one was surprised when his father shot himself.

At the funeral potlatch, his mother split his father's ceremonial regalia between Wil and Kevin. She gave Kevin his father's frontlet.[1] He placed it immediately on his head and danced. The room became still, the family shocked at his lack of tact. When Kevin stopped dancing, she gave Wil his father's button blanket.[2] The dark wool held his smell. Wil knew then that he would never be an astronaut. He didn't have a backup dream and drifted through school, coasting on a reputation of Brain he'd stopped trying to earn.

Kevin, on the other hand, ran away and joined the Mohawk Warriors.[3] He was at Oka[4] on August 16 when the bombs rained down and the last Canadian reserve was Adjusted.

---

1   *frontlet* Headdress worn on the forehead, used in Haisla regalia.
2   *button blanket* Ceremonial wool blanket decorated with abalone buttons.
3   *Mohawk Warriors* Native activist group.
4   *Oka* Quebec town and site of the 1990 Oka Crisis, a Mohawk protest over disputed land that developed into a violent conflict with government military and police forces. The government used guns and tear gas, but did not bomb the activists.

Wil expected him to come back broken. He was ready with patience, with forgiveness. Kevin came back a Peace Officer.

Why? his aunts, his uncles, cousins, and friends asked.

How could you? his mother asked.

Wil said nothing. When his brother looked up, Wil knew the truth, even if Kevin didn't. There were things that adjusted to rapid change—pigeons, dogs, rats, cockroaches. Then there were things that didn't—panda bears, whales, flamingos, Atlantic cod, salmon, owls.

Kevin would survive the Adjustment. Kevin had found a way to come through it and be better for it. He instinctively felt the changes coming and adapted. I, on the other hand, he thought, am going the way of the dodo bird.

∞

There are rumours in the neighbourhood. No one from the Vancouver Urban Reserve #2 can get into Terminal Avenue. They don't have the money or the connections. Whispers follow him, anyway, but no one will ask him to his face. He suspects that his mother suspects. He has been careful, but he sees the questions in her eyes when he leaves for work. Someday she'll ask him what he really does and he'll lie to her.

To allay suspicion, he smuggles cigarettes and sweetgrass[1] from the downtown core to Surreycentral. This is useful, makes him friends, adds a kick to his evening train ride. He finds that he needs these kicks. Has a morbid fear of becoming dead like his father, talking and breathing and eating, but frightened into vacancy, a living blankness.

His identity card that gets him to the downtown core says *Occupation: Waiter*. He pins it to his jacket so that no one will mistake him for a terrorist and shoot him.

He is not really alive until he steps past the industrial black doors of his lover's club. Until that moment, he is living inside his head, lost in memories. He knows that he is a novelty item, a real living Indian: that is why his prices are so inflated. He knows there will come a time when he is yesterday's condom.

He walks past the club's façade, the elegant dining rooms filled with the glittering people who watch the screens or dance across the dimly-lit ballroom-sized floor. He descends the stairs where his lover waits for him with her games and her toys, where they do things that aren't sanctioned by the Purity laws, where he gets hurt and gives hurt.

1   *sweetgrass* Marijuana; also refers to a herb used in First Nations spiritual ceremonies.

He is greeted by his high priestess. He enters her temple of discipline and submits. When the pain becomes too much, he hallucinates. There is no preparing for that moment when reality shifts and he is free.

ဆ

They have formed a circle around him. Another standard intimidation tactic. The Peace Officer facing him is waiting for him to talk. He stares up at it. This will be different from the club. He is about to become an example.

Wilson Wilson? the Officer says. The voice sounds male but is altered by computers so it won't be recognizable.

He smiles. The name is one of his mother's little jokes, a little defiance. He has hated her for it all his life, but now he doesn't mind. He is in a forgiving mood. *Yes, that's me.*

In the silence that stretches, Wil realizes that he always believed this moment would come. That he has been preparing himself for it. The smiling-faced lies from the TV haven't fooled him, or anyone else. After the Uprisings, it was only a matter of time before someone decided to solve the Indian problem once and for all.

The Peace Officer raises his club and brings it down.

ဆ

His father held a potlatch before they left Kitamaat, before they came to Vancouver to earn a living, after the aluminum smelter closed.

They had to hold it in secret, so they hired three large seiners[1] for the family and rode to Monkey Beach. They left in their old beat-up speedboat, early in the morning, when the Douglas Channel was calm and flat, before the winds blew in from the ocean, turning the water choppy. The seine boats fell far behind them, heavy with people. Kevin begged and begged to steer and his father laughingly gave in.

Wil knelt on the bow and held his arms open, wishing he could take off his lifejacket. In four hours they will land on Monkey Beach and will set up for the potlatch where they will dance and sing and say goodbye. His father will cook salmon around fires, roasted the old-fashioned way: split down the centre and splayed open like butterflies, thin sticks of cedar woven through the skin to hold the fish open, the sticks planted in the sand; as the flesh darkens, the juice runs down and hisses on the fire. The smell will permeate the beach. Camouflage nets will be set up all over the beach so they won't be spotted by planes. Family will lounge under them as if they were beach umbrellas. The

---

1   *seiners* Fishing boats.

more daring of the family will dash into the water, which is still glacier-cold and shocking.

This will happen when they land in four hours, but Wil chooses to remember the boat ride with his mother resting in his father's arm when Wil comes back from the bow and sits beside them. She is wearing a blue scarf and black sunglasses and red lipstick. She can't stop smiling even though they are going to leave home soon. She looks like a movie star. His father has his hair slicked back, and it makes him look like an otter. He kisses her, and she kisses him back.

Kevin is so excited that he raises one arm and makes the Mohawk salute they see on TV all the time. He loses control of the boat, and they swerve violently. His father cuffs Kevin and takes the wheel.

The sun rises as they pass Costi Island, and the water sparkles and shifts. The sky hardens into a deep summer blue.

The wind and the noise of the engine prevent them from talking. His father begins to sing. Wil doesn't understand the words, couldn't pronounce them if he tried. He can see that his father is happy. Maybe he's drunk on the excitement of the day, on the way that his wife touches him, tenderly. He gives Wil the wheel.

His father puts on his button blanket, rests it solemnly on his shoulders. He balances on the boat with the ease of someone who's spent all his life on the water. He does a twirl, when he reaches the bow of the speedboat and the button blanket opens, a navy lotus. The abalone buttons sparkle when they catch the light. She's laughing as he poses. He dances, suddenly inspired, exuberant.

Later he will understand what his father is doing, the rules he is breaking, the risks he is taking, and the price he will pay on a deserted road, when the siren goes off and the lights flash and they are pulled over.

At the time, though, Wil is white-knuckled, afraid to move the boat in a wrong way and toss his father overboard. He is also embarrassed, wishing his father were more reserved. Wishing he was being normal instead of dancing, a whirling shadow against the sun, blocking his view of the Channel.

This is the moment he chooses to be in, the place he goes to when the club flattens him to the Surreycentral tiles. He holds himself there, in the boat with his brother, his father, his mother. The sun on the water makes pale northern lights flicker against everyone's faces, and the smell of the water is clean and salty, and the boat's spray is cool against his skin.

—1996

Emma Donoghue
b. 1969

In her novels, plays, short stories, and nonfiction, Emma Donoghue investigates contemporary and historical gender roles and what she has described as the "fluidity and unpredictability of human sexuality." Influenced by writers such as Jeanette Winterson and Margaret Atwood, much of Donoghue's work is constructed around female characters who find themselves "drifting into attraction rather than discovering a crystal-clear sense of identity." While Donoghue identifies herself as a feminist, she sees herself as a writer first, arguing that "Writers should never be trusted as the political 'voices of the community' because our loyalties are generally to literature."

The daughter of a renowned literary scholar, Donoghue is also an accomplished critic in her own right. After graduating from University College Dublin with a degree in English and French literature, she left her native Ireland to pursue a doctorate at Cambridge and has since published a number of highly regarded critical studies, including *Passions between Women: British Lesbian Culture 1668-1801* (1993) and *Inseparable: Desire between Women in Literature* (2010).

Donoghue has demonstrated a particular talent for fiction based on true events, and meticulously researched novels such as *Slammerkin* (2000), the story of an eighteenth-century prostitute involved in a brutal murder, and *Room* (2010), which recounts the forced confinement of a mother and child from the child's point of view, have won her a large international popular and critical following.

Seven Pictures Not Taken

1: Rhubarb

Climbing up the slope behind your house, returning from the river you've been showing me before your fortieth birthday party begins, digging our feet into the unashamed grassy breast of what you call your back yard (though the word yard to me means a hard paved thing), our eyes meet momentarily (by that I mean for a moment, you would mean in a moment's time). Neither of us is English, and our Englishes will always be a word or two apart. Our bodies talk better than our minds, even that first day, when our eyes are spread wide by sunlight.

I like the look of the few downy whiskers on your chin. We are standing beside the hugely overgrown rhubarb bush, some sticks as tall as us, gone black with age, others still new and pink. We both call it a rhubarb bush, good to know we can agree on something.

Though I have only just met you, I want to give you something, to make you remember me. It all begins with vanity, not generosity.

Later you will tell me that you remembered me making rhubarb crumble for your guests. But if you had not met me again, I am sure you would have forgotten my face in a week, my rhubarb crumble in another. It is only in retrospect that strangers seem instantly memorable. I know I would have remembered you, but mostly because my eyes tend to look for pictures to remember. Maybe I invented you, summoned you up as a holiday vision.

All I know is that for a week after your party I had scalding dreams of lying down together on that particular spot, that curve of sundried grass behind your house. The vertical hold becomes a horizontal flow. So by the time you actually laid hands on me, I had drawn out the whole story already.

2: River

This picture is about light on wet skin. I am watching you but the picture is of both of us. Women troop down to the water in the late afternoon; the midges hover, aroused by our heat. I pull black silk up and over my head, step through satin mud and slide in. Under the meniscus[1] I lose my shyness. I watch you as I tread water, kicking off the years. I am a newborn baby in the slip of hills.

How we met was a web of chance rivers, meandering across three continents. If A had not bumped into B in the hottest country she'd ever been in, after (or was it before?) meeting you on the west coast, then driving south with you this summer she would never have introduced you to B's ex-lover C, who happened to bring me (who had made friends with B and C half a world away) to your birthday party. It scares me that if any one of us had stepped out of any one of those streams, I would never have met you, would never even have known there was a you to meet, but I suppose I have to lie back in the current of coincidence, trusting that it has been shaped for us just as the river has been carved through the mountains to reach your house so that I can bathe in it, treading water, looking up at you. Afterwards, as we all dry ourselves on the bank, you tell me that you only own this bit of river to midstream, which must confuse it.

3: Room

The next picture is taken in the dark. No dark is ever entire, of course, there is always enough light to begin to find out shapes. We are practically strangers,

1   *meniscus* Here, surface of the water.

at this time of sharing a bed in our mutual friend's mother's house. You could always sleep in the other room, but as I have mentioned to you in passing, the bed there is very hard; we are in agreement that it would not be good for your bad back. This is true but also a barefaced lie. In the dark you ask me if I want to cuddle up, and I do.

In this picture, I am lying awake, marvelling at your strange weight against me, much too aware of you to move. I can't catch a breath; my arm is numb; my arthritic hip is screaming to shift position. I inch it backwards. I do not want to disturb you in case you'll twist away, with the selfishness of the half-awake. I want you to keep resting deeply, coiled around me. I decide to find out how little breath I can manage on, how long my muscles will obey me. I am glad to offer you my discomfort, even if you will never know it.

This room is so dark, fifty miles from a city; no way could a picture of this be taken with an ordinary camera. For all I know this is the only night I will ever spend in your arms.

4: Forest

We are twenty years past wasting time.

The ferns are sharp under the purple cloak I have spread for us, Walter Raleigh style.[1] Their dry fingers idly scratch our hips. Sounds of brass and woodwind leak through the woods from the concert we are missing. Sun slithers through the lattice of maples to lie across your back. My lips, drawn across your shoulder bone, find invisible fur. Desire has twitched and bitten and marked us all day as the brazen mosquitoes do now, here on the forest floor where we are lying.

Seen from high above in the canopy of leaves, we must be pale as mushrooms that have pushed up overnight. Two women, two dark heads, two dark triangles, a maze of limbs arranged by the geometry of pleasure. We press close, my hipbone wedded to your thighs, my breast quilting your ribs, to leave as little body exposed to the insects as we can.

It is hot and uncomfortable and exactly where I want to be. At certain moments what your body is doing to mine wipes away all awareness of the insect bites, the concert, the time, the other women in our pasts and futures, the other days in our lives, all other sights there are to be seen.

---

1   *purple cloak … Raleigh style* Sir Walter Ralegh (1552–1618), a prominent courtier to Queen Elizabeth I, is said to have thrown his cloak over a puddle so that the Queen could cross without wetting her shoes.

5: Body

It is what you call fall, in this picture, and I persist in calling autumn, even though I'm back on your territory again. The patches on your back yard where my ecstatic hands ripped out grass in the summer are covered with leaves now.

We are sitting on your sofa looking through your photo albums in chronological order. You find it hard to believe that I am truly interested enough to turn every page. But I want the whole picture, the full hand of decades. I interrogate you through baby snaps, family crises, teenage hairstyles. I pause on one of you in the first week of your uniform, grinning with an innocent gun; it chills me. You remark that you're glad they kicked you out for being a pervert; you're finally glad. You repeat for me a line from a folk song:

> I will not use my body as a weapon of war
> That's not what any body's for.

I look at the photograph to memorize it. I wonder what this body in the albums, that has come through so many changes in front of my browsing eyes, is for. I'm going too fast. I regret, absurdly, that I was not here to see you grow up. I am having to learn it all in a weekend with the leaves dancing by the window, mocking me with their message of phoenix fire. We have so little time, the most careful picture is a snapshot.

6: Real

The last day of that five-day weekend, I say: I don't want to get in the way of your real life.

Life doesn't get any more real than this, you tell me.

I am momentarily content. But neither of us is sure whether any of this is happening. It seems too good to be actual. Too sure, too easy and unmixed, as bliss goes, to be anything other than some kind of trip.

Down by the river you take out your camera. We sit on rocks and lean over the water, taking turns to pose, laughing at the absurdity of our ambition to capture the moment.

But wouldn't it be worse if photos were better than the real thing? Sometimes I shut a book of fabulous pictures, and my own life seems like a puny little after-image. Better this feeling of overflow. Thank god for times like these when I remember: there is too much life to fit into art.

You take a final photo anyway, with a timer, to prove it happened, that we were in this frame together, that there was no space for light between our faces.

I almost expect the pictures to come out blank. But when you airmail them to me they are full of colour. I look at this middle-aged couple embracing against the sun-polished rocks. Already they are not us. Already they are figures in a collage. Already we are not the same.

7: Frame

In this last of the pictures I never took, it is New Year and I am standing at your window again, looking out at the mountains under their shirt of snow. I make a diamond frame with my hands to shape the picture: dark verticals of trees, angles of snow, some silver birch trees to complicate the contrast. The river is frozen black except for some swirls of white near the bank. It is a beautiful picture, but it is flattening into two dimensions already.

Having flown here for green summer and orange leaves and white snow, and not much wanting to see the mud season, I get the feeling that I am not going to be back. And it turns my stomach to watch myself framing this away, folding it over, when it is still good, before anything has actually happened to put an end to it.

I know I'm speeding, way over the limit, slapping down each image as soon as I catch it, dashing on to the next. Why the hell can't I live in the present, like my friends keep telling me to? They say youth is the hasty time, but I've been in the biggest hurry ever since I entered my forties. I have this craving to see everything I've got left.

The snow fills up the window in this picture, kindly and indifferent.

Maybe this thing needs to be over before I can see it. Maybe in my twisted way I am ending it now so that I can understand and represent it, so the story has an ending to match its beginning. Maybe (what bullshit, what cowardly bullshit), maybe this turning of my back is a version of love.

—1996

David Bezmozgis
b. 1973

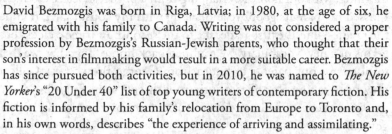

David Bezmozgis was born in Riga, Latvia; in 1980, at the age of six, he emigrated with his family to Canada. Writing was not considered a proper profession by Bezmozgis's Russian-Jewish parents, who thought that their son's interest in filmmaking would result in a more suitable career. Bezmozgis has since pursued both activities, but in 2010, he was named to *The New Yorker*'s "20 Under 40" list of top young writers of contemporary fiction. His fiction is informed by his family's relocation from Europe to Toronto and, in his own words, describes "the experience of arriving and assimilating."

"Tapka" illustrates this focus. It first appeared in a 2003 issue of *The New Yorker* and later became the opening piece in *Natasha and Other Stories* (2004), a collection of seven linked short stories that span the life of their narrator Mark Berman from his childhood to early adulthood. Like Bezmozgis, Mark is a Jewish immigrant who grows up in Toronto. Describing his approach to autobiographical fiction, Bezmozgis says, "It's the game that the author plays and the purpose of the game is to establish a compelling intimacy between the story contained in the narrative and the reader's own life experiences and sensibility." This collection won the Commonwealth Writers Prize for First Book and was also nominated for a Governor General's Award. *The Calgary Herald*'s Meghan O'Rourke notes that Bezmozgis's strength is his "covert subtlety" and likens his immigrant stories to those of Jhumpa Lahiri, Nathan Englander, and Aleksandar Hemon.

Since *Natasha and Other Stories*, Bezmozgis has written his first novel, *The Free World* (2011), the story of a family fleeing the Soviet Union to Rome in 1978 to escape the Iron Curtain. *The Free World* was shortlisted for both the Scotiabank Giller Prize and the Governor General's Award.

Tapka

Goldfinch was flapping clotheslines, a tenement delirious with striving. 6030 Bathurst: insomniac, scheming Odessa. Cedarcroft:[1] reeking borscht in the hallways. My parents, Soviet refugees but Baltic aristocrats,[2] took an apartment at 715 Finch, fronting a ravine and across from an elementary school—one respectable block away from the Russian swarm. We lived on the fifth floor, my cousin, aunt, and uncle directly below us on the fourth. Except for the Nahu-

---

1   *Goldfinch ... Cedarcroft* Streets in the Bathurst-Finch area of northern Toronto, the site of Toronto's largest community of Russian immigrants.

2   *Soviet ... aristocrats* The Soviet Union forcibly occupied the Baltic states—Estonia, Latvia, and Lithuania—from the 1940s until 1991.

movskys, a couple in their fifties, there were no other Russians in the building. For this privilege, my parents paid twenty extra dollars a month in rent.

In March of 1980, near the end of the school year but only three weeks after our arrival in Toronto, I was enrolled in Charles H. Best Elementary. Each morning, with our house key hanging from a brown shoelace around my neck, I kissed my parents goodbye and, along with my cousin Jana, tramped across the ravine—I to the first grade, she to the second. At three o'clock, bearing the germs of a new vocabulary, we tramped back home. Together, we then waited until six for our parents to return from George Brown City College, where they were taking an obligatory six-month course in English—a course that provided them with the rudiments of communication along with a modest government stipend.

In the evenings, we assembled and compiled our linguistic bounty.

Hello, havaryew?
Red, yellow, green, blue.
May I please go to the washroom?
Seventeen, eighteen, nineteen, twenny.

Joining us most nights were the Nahumovskys. They attended the same English classes and travelled with my parents on the same bus. Rita Nahumovsky was a beautician who wore layers of makeup, and Misha Nahumovsky was a tool-and-die maker.[1] They came from Minsk and didn't know a soul in Canada. With abounding enthusiasm, they incorporated themselves into our family. My parents were glad to have them. Our life was tough, we had it hard—but the Nahumovskys had it harder. They were alone, they were older, they were stupefied by the demands of language. Being essentially helpless themselves, my parents found it gratifying to help the more helpless Nahumovskys.

After dinner, with everyone gathered on cheap stools around our table, my mother repeated the day's lessons for the benefit of the Nahumovskys and, to a slightly lesser degree, for the benefit of my father. My mother had always been an exceptional and dedicated student, and she extended this dedication to George Brown City College. My father and the Nahumovskys came to rely on her detailed notes and her understanding of the curriculum. For as long as they could, they listened attentively and groped desperately toward comprehension. When this became too frustrating, my father put on the kettle, Rita painted my mother's nails, and Misha told Soviet *anekdoti*.[2]

---

1   *tool-and-die maker* Machinist who makes tools and moulds for use in manufacturing.
2   *anekdoti* Russian: anecdotes.

In a first-grade classroom a teacher calls on her students and inquires after their nationalities. "Sasha," she says. Sasha says, "Russian." "Very good," says the teacher. "Arnan," she says. Arnan says, "Armenian." "Very good," says the teacher. "Lyubka," she says. Lyubka says, "Ukrainian." "Very good," says the teacher. And then she asks Dima. Dima says, "Jewish." "What a shame," says the teacher. "So young and already a Jew."

The Nahumovskys had no children, only a white Lhasa Apso named Tapka. The dog had lived with them for years before they emigrated and then travelled with them from Minsk to Vienna, from Vienna to Rome, and from Rome to Toronto. During our first month in the building, Tapka was in quarantine, and I saw her only in photographs. Rita had dedicated an entire album to the dog, and, to dampen the pangs of separation, she consulted the album daily. There were shots of Tapka in the Nahumovskys' old Minsk apartment, seated on the cushions of faux-Louis XIV furniture; there was Tapka on the steps of a famous Viennese palace; Tapka at the Vatican, in front of the Colosseum, at the Sistine Chapel, and under the Leaning Tower of Pisa. My mother—despite having grown up with goats and chickens in her yard—didn't like animals and found it impossible to feign interest in Rita's dog. Shown a picture of Tapka, my mother wrinkled her nose and said, "Phoo." My father also couldn't be bothered. With no English, no money, no job, and only a murky conception of what the future held, he wasn't equipped to admire Tapka on the Italian Riviera. Only I cared. Through the photographs, I became attached to Tapka and projected upon her the ideal traits of the dog I did not have. Like Rita, I counted the days until Tapka's liberation.

The day Tapka was to be released from quarantine, Rita prepared an elaborate dinner. My family was invited to celebrate the dog's arrival. While Rita cooked, Misha was banished from their apartment. For distraction, he seated himself at our table with a deck of cards. As my mother reviewed sentence construction, Misha played hand after hand of *durak*[1] with me.

"The woman loves this dog more than me. A taxi to the customs facility is going to cost us ten, maybe fifteen dollars. But what can I do? The dog is truly a sweet little dog."

When it came time to collect the dog, my mother went with Misha and Rita to act as their interpreter. With my nose to the window, I watched the taxi take them away. Every few minutes, I reapplied my nose to the window. Three hours later, the taxi pulled into our parking lot, and Rita emerged from the back seat cradling animated fur. She set the fur down on the pavement where it assumed the shape of a dog. The length of its coat concealed its legs, and, as it hovered around Rita's ankles, it appeared to have either a thousand

---

1   *durak* A popular Russian card game.

tiny legs or none at all. My head ringing "Tapka, Tapka, Tapka," I raced into the hallway to meet the elevator.

That evening, Misha toasted the dog: "This last month, for the first time in years, I have enjoyed my wife's undivided attention. But I believe no man, not even one as perfect as me, can survive so much attention from his wife. So I say, with all my heart, thank God our Tapka is back home with us. Another day and I fear I may have requested a divorce."

Before he drank, Misha dipped his pinkie finger into his vodka glass and offered it to the dog. Obediently, Tapka gave Misha's finger a thorough licking. Impressed, my uncle declared her a good Russian dog. He also gave her a lick of his vodka. I gave her a piece of my chicken. Jana rolled her a pellet of bread. Misha taught us how to dangle food just out of Tapka's reach and thereby induce her to perform a charming little dance. Rita also produced Clonchik, a red-and-yellow rag clown. She tossed Clonchik under the table, onto the couch, down the hallway, and into the kitchen; over and over, Rita called, "Tapka, get Clonchik," and, without fail, Tapka got Clonchik. Everyone delighted in Tapka's antics except my mother, who sat stiffly in her chair, her feet slightly off the floor, as though preparing herself for a mild electric shock.

After the dinner, when we returned home, my mother announced that she would no longer set foot in the Nahumovskys' apartment. She liked Rita, she liked Misha, but she couldn't sympathize with their attachment to the dog. She understood that the attachment was a consequence of their lack of sophistication and also their childlessness. They were simple people. Rita had never attended university. She could derive contentment from talking to a dog, brushing its coat, putting ribbons in its hair, and repeatedly throwing a rag clown across the apartment. And Misha, although very lively and a genius with his hands, was also not an intellectual. They were good people, but a dog ruled their lives.

Rita and Misha were sensitive to my mother's attitude toward Tapka. As a result, and to the detriment of her progress with English, Rita stopped visiting our apartment. Nightly, Misha would arrive alone while Rita attended to the dog. Tapka never set foot in our home. This meant that, in order to see her, I spent more and more time at the Nahumovskys'. Each evening, after I had finished my homework, I went to play with Tapka. My heart soared every time Rita opened the door and Tapka raced to greet me. The dog knew no hierarchy of affection. Her excitement was infectious. In Tapka's presence, I resonated with doglike glee.

Because of my devotion to the dog, and their lack of an alternative, Misha and Rita added their house key to the shoelace hanging around my neck. During our lunch break and again after school, Jana and I were charged with caring for Tapka. Our task was simple: put Tapka on her leash, walk her to the ravine, release her to chase Clonchik, and then bring her home.

Every day, sitting in my classroom, understanding little, effectively friend-less, I counted down the minutes to lunchtime. When the bell rang, I met Jana on the playground and we sprinted across the grass toward our building. In the hall, our approaching footsteps elicited panting and scratching. When I inserted the key into the lock, I felt emanations of love through the door. And once the door was open Tapka hurled herself at us, her entire body consumed with an ecstasy of wagging. Jana and I took turns embracing her, petting her, covertly vying for her favour. Free of Rita's scrutiny, we also satisfied certain anatomical curiosities. We examined Tapka's ears, her paws, her teeth, the roots of her fur, and her doggy genitals. We poked and prodded her, we threw her up in the air, rolled her over and over, and swung her by her front legs. I felt such overwhelming love for Tapka that sometimes, when hugging her, I had to restrain myself from squeezing too hard and crushing her little bones.

It was April when we began to care for Tapka. Snow melted in the ravine; sometimes it rained. April became May. Grass absorbed the thaw, turned green; dandelions and wildflowers sprouted yellow and blue; birds and insects flew, crawled, and made their characteristic noises. Faithfully and reliably, Jana and I attended to Tapka. We walked her across the parking lot and down into the ravine. We threw Clonchik and said, "Tapka, get Clonchik." Tapka always got Clonchik. Everyone was proud of us. My mother and my aunt wiped tears from their eyes while talking about how responsible we were. Rita and Misha rewarded us with praise and chocolates. Jana was seven and I was six; much had been asked of us, but we had risen to the challenge.

Inspired by everyone's confidence, we grew confident. Whereas at first we made sure to walk thirty paces into the ravine before releasing Tapka, we gradually reduced that requirement to ten paces, then five paces, until finally we released her at the grassy border between the parking lot and the ravine. We did this not because of laziness or intentional recklessness but because we wanted proof of Tapka's love. That she came when we called was evidence of her love, that she didn't piss in the elevator was evidence of her love, that she offered up her belly for scratching was evidence of her love, that she licked our faces was evidence of her love. All of this was evidence, but it wasn't proof. Proof could come in only one form. We had intuited an elemental truth: love needs no leash.

That first spring, even though most of what was said around me remained a mystery, a thin rivulet of meaning trickled into my cerebral catch basin and collected into a little pool of knowledge. By the end of May, I could sing the ABC song. Television taught me to say "What's up, Doc?" and "super-duper."

The playground introduced me to "shithead," "mental case," and "gaylord." I seized upon every opportunity to apply my new knowledge.

One afternoon, after spending nearly an hour in the ravine throwing Clonchik in a thousand different directions, Jana and I lolled in sunlit pollen. I called her shithead, mental case, and gaylord, and she responded by calling me gaylord, shithead, and mental case.

"Shithead."

"Gaylord."

"Mental case."

"Tapka, get Clonchik."

"Shithead."

"Gaylord."

"Come, Tapka-lapka."

"Mental case."

We went on like this, over and over, until Jana threw the clown and said, "Shithead, get Clonchik." Initially, I couldn't tell if she had said this on purpose or if it had merely been a blip in her rhythm. But when I looked at Jana her smile was triumphant.

"Mental case, get Clonchik."

For the first time, as I watched Tapka bounding happily after Clonchik, the profanity sounded profane.

"Don't say that to the dog."

"Why not?"

"It's not right."

"But she doesn't understand."

"You shouldn't say it."

"Don't be a baby. Come, shithead, come my dear one."

Her tail wagging with accomplishment, Tapka dropped Clonchik at my feet.

"You see, she likes it."

I held Clonchik as Tapka pawed frantically at my shins.

"Call her shithead. Throw the clown."

"I'm not calling her shithead."

"What are you afraid of, shithead?"

I aimed the clown at Jana's head and missed.

"Shithead, get Clonchik."

As the clown left my hand, Tapka, a white shining blur, oblivious to insult, was already cutting through the grass. I wanted to believe that I had intended the "shithead" exclusively for Jana, but I knew it wasn't true.

"I told you, gaylord, she doesn't care."

I couldn't help thinking, Poor Tapka. I felt moral residue and looked around for some sign of recrimination. The day, however, persisted in unimpeachable brilliance: sparrows winged overhead; bumblebees levitated above flowers; beside a lilac shrub, Tapka clamped down on Clonchik. I was amazed at the absence of consequences.

Jana said, "I'm going home."

As she started for home, I saw that she was still holding Tapka's leash. It swung insouciantly from her hand. I called after her just as, once again, Tapka deposited Clonchik at my feet.

"I need the leash."

"Why?"

"Don't be stupid. I need the leash."

"No, you don't. She comes when we call her. Even shithead. She won't run away."

Jana turned her back on me and proceeded toward our building. I called her again, but she refused to turn around. Her receding back was a blatant provocation. Guided more by anger than by logic, I decided that if Tapka was closer to Jana then the onus of responsibility would be on her. I picked up the doll and threw it as far as I could into the parking lot.

"Tapka, get Clonchik."

Clonchik tumbled through the air. I had put everything in my six-year-old arm behind the throw, which still meant that the doll wasn't going very far. Its trajectory promised a drop no more than twenty feet from the edge of the ravine. Running, her head arched to the sky, Tapka tracked the flying clown. As the doll reached its apex, it crossed paths with a sparrow. The bird veered off toward Finch Avenue, and the clown plummeted to the asphalt. When the doll hit the ground, Tapka raced past it after the bird.

A thousand times we had thrown Clonchik and a thousand times Tapka had retrieved him. But who knows what passes for a thought in the mind of a dog? One moment a Clonchik is a Clonchik, and the next moment a sparrow is a Clonchik.

I shouted at Jana to catch Tapka and then watched in abject horror as the dog, her attention fixed on the sparrow, skirted past Jana and directly into traffic. From my vantage point on the slope of the ravine, I couldn't see what happened. I saw only that Jana broke into a sprint and I heard the caterwauling of tires, followed by Tapka's shrill fractured yip.

By the time I reached the street, a line of cars already stretched a block beyond Goldfinch. At the front of the line were a brown station wagon and a pale-blue sedan blistered with rust. As I neared, I noted the chrome letters on the back of the sedan: D-U-S-T-E-R. In front of the sedan, Jana kneeled in a tight semicircle with a pimply young man and an older woman with very large sunglasses. Tapka lay on her side at the centre of their circle. She panted in quick shallow bursts. She stared impassively at me, at Jana. Except for a hind leg twitching at the sky at an impossible angle, she seemed completely unharmed. She looked much as she did when she rested on the rug at the Nahumovskys' apartment after a vigorous romp in the ravine.

Seeing her this way, barely mangled, I felt a sense of relief. I started to convince myself that things weren't as bad as I had feared, and I tentatively edged forward to pet her. The woman in the sunglasses said something in a restrictive tone that I neither understood nor heeded. I placed my hand on Tapka's head, and she responded by opening her mouth and allowing a trickle of blood to escape onto the asphalt. This was the first time I had ever seen dog blood, and I was struck by the depth of its colour. I hadn't expected it to be red, although I also hadn't expected it to be not-red. Set against the grey asphalt and her white coat, Tapka's blood was the red I envisioned when I closed my eyes and thought: red.

I sat with Tapka until several dozen car horns demanded that we clear the way. The woman with the large sunglasses ran to her station wagon, returned with a blanket, and scooped Tapka off the street. The pimply young man stammered a few sentences, of which I understood nothing except the word "sorry." Then we were in the back seat of the station wagon with Tapka in Jana's lap. The woman kept talking until she finally realized that we couldn't understand her at all. As we started to drive off, Jana remembered something. I motioned for the woman to stop the car and scrambled out. Above the atonal chorus of car horns, I heard: "Mark, get Clonchik."

I ran and got Clonchik.

For two hours, Jana and I sat in the reception area of a small veterinary clinic in an unfamiliar part of town. In another room, with a menagerie of afflicted creatures, Tapka lay in traction, connected to a blinking machine by a series of tubes. Jana and I had been allowed to see her once but were rushed out when we both burst into tears. Tapka's doctor, a woman wearing a white coat and furry slippers resembling bear paws, tried to calm us down. Again, we could neither explain ourselves nor understand what she was saying. We managed only to establish that Tapka was not our dog. The doctor gave us colouring books, stickers, and access to the phone. Every fifteen minutes, we called home. Between phone calls, we absently flipped pages and sniffled for Tapka and for ourselves. We had no idea what would happen to Tapka; all we knew was that she wasn't dead. As for ourselves, we already felt punished and knew only that more punishment was to come.

"Why did you throw Clonchik?"

"Why didn't you give me the leash?"

"You could have held on to her collar."

"You shouldn't have called her shithead."

At six-thirty, my mother picked up the phone. I could hear the agitation in her voice. The ten minutes she had spent at home not knowing where I was had taken their toll. For ten minutes, she had been the mother of a dead child. I explained to her about the dog and felt a twinge of resentment when she said, "So it's only the dog?" Behind her I heard other voices. It sounded as though everyone were speaking at once, pursuing personal agendas, translating the phone conversation from Russian to Russian until one anguished voice separated itself: "My God, what happened?" Rita.

After getting the address from the veterinarian, my mother hung up and ordered another expensive taxi. Within a half hour, my parents, my aunt, and Misha and Rita pulled up at the clinic. Jana and I waited for them on the sidewalk. As soon as the taxi doors opened, we began to sob uncontrollably, partly out of relief but mainly in the hope of engendering sympathy. I ran to my mother and caught sight of Rita's face. Her face made me regret that I also hadn't been hit by a car.

As we clung to our mothers, Rita descended upon us.

"Children, what, oh, what have you done?"

She pinched compulsively at the loose skin of her neck, raising a cluster of pink marks.

While Misha methodically counted individual bills for the taxi-driver, we swore on our lives that Tapka had simply got away from us. That we had minded her as always but, inexplicably, she had seen a bird and bolted from the ravine and into the road. We had done everything in our power to catch her, but she had surprised us, eluded us, been too fast.

Rita considered our story.

"You are liars. Liars!"

She uttered the words with such hatred that we again burst into sobs.

My father spoke in our defence.

"Rita Borisovna, how can you say this? They are children."

"They are liars. I know my Tapka. Tapka never chased birds. Tapka never ran from the ravine."

"Maybe today she did?"

"Liars."

Having delivered her verdict, she had nothing more to say. She waited anxiously for Misha to finish paying the driver.

"Misha, enough already. Count it a hundred times, it will still be the same."

Inside the clinic, there was no longer anyone at the reception desk. During our time there, Jana and I had watched a procession of dyspeptic cats and lethargic parakeets disappear into the back rooms for examination and diagnosis. One after another they had come and gone until, by the time of our parents' arrival, the waiting area was entirely empty and the clinic officially closed. The only people remaining were a night nurse and the doctor in the bear-paw slippers, who had stayed expressly for our sake.

Looking desperately around the room, Rita screamed, "Doctor! Doctor!" But when the doctor appeared she was incapable of making herself understood. Haltingly, with my mother's help, it was communicated to the doctor that Rita wanted to see her dog. Pointing vigorously at herself, Rita asserted, "Tapka. Mine dog."

The doctor led Rita and Misha into the veterinary version of an intensive-care ward. Tapka lay on her little bed, Clonchik resting directly beside her. At the sight of Rita and Misha, Tapka weakly wagged her tail. Little more than an hour had elapsed since I had seen her last, but somehow over the course of that time Tapka had shrunk considerably. She had always been a small dog, but now she looked desiccated. She was the embodiment of defeat. Rita started to cry, grotesquely smearing her mascara. With trembling hands, and with sublime tenderness, she stroked Tapka's head.

"My God, my God, what has happened to you, my Tapkochka?"

Through my mother, and with the aid of pen and paper, the doctor provided the answer. Tapka required two operations. One for her leg. Another to stop internal bleeding. An organ had been damaged. For now, a machine was helping her, but without the machine she would die. On the paper, the doctor drew a picture of a scalpel, of a dog, of a leg, of an organ. She made an arrow pointing at the organ and drew a teardrop and coloured it in to represent blood. She also wrote down a number preceded by a dollar sign. The number was fifteen hundred.

At the sight of the number, Rita let out a low animal moan and steadied herself against Tapka's little bed. My parents exchanged a glance. I looked at the floor. Misha said, "My dear God." The Nahumovskys and my parents each took in less than five hundred dollars a month. We had arrived in Canada with almost nothing, a few hundred dollars, which had all but disappeared on furniture. There were no savings. Fifteen hundred dollars. The doctor could just as well have written a million.

In the middle of the intensive-care ward, Rita slid down to the floor and wailed. Her head thrown back, she appealed to the fluorescent lights: "*Nu*, Tapkochka, what is going to become of us?"

I looked up from my feet and saw horror and bewilderment on the doctor's face. She tried to put a hand on Rita's shoulder, but Rita violently shrugged it off.

My father attempted to intercede.

"Rita Borisovna, I understand that it is painful, but it is not the end of the world."

"And what do you know about it?"

"I know that it must be hard, but soon you will see.... Even tomorrow we could go and help you find a new one."

My father looked to my mother for approval, to insure that he had not promised too much. He needn't have worried.

"A new one? What do you mean, a new one? I don't want a new one. Why don't you get yourself a new son? A new little liar? How about that? New. Everything we have now is new. New everything."

On the linoleum floor, Rita keened, rocking back and forth. She hiccupped, as though hyperventilating. Pausing for a moment, she looked up at my mother and told her to translate for the doctor. To tell her that she would not let Tapka die.

"I will sit here on this floor forever. And if the police come to drag me out I will bite them."

"Ritochka, this is crazy."

"Why is it crazy? My Tapka's life is worth more than a thousand dollars. Because we don't have the money, she should die here? It's not her fault."

Seeking rationality, my mother turned to Misha—Misha who had said nothing all this time except "My dear God."

"Misha, do you want me to tell the doctor what Rita said?"

Misha shrugged philosophically.

"Tell her or don't tell her, you see my wife has made up her mind. The doctor will figure it out soon enough."

"And you think this is reasonable?"

"Sure. Why not? I'll sit on the floor, too. The police can take us both to jail. Besides Tapka, what else do we have?"

Misha sat on the floor beside his wife.

I watched as my mother struggled to explain to the doctor what was happening. With a mixture of words and gesticulations, she got the point across. The doctor, after considering her options, sat down on the floor beside Rita and Misha. Once again, she tried to put her hand on Rita's shoulder. This time, Rita, who was still rocking back and forth, allowed it. Misha rocked in time to his wife's rhythm. So did the doctor. The three of them sat in a line, swaying together, like campers at a campfire. Nobody said anything. We looked at each other. I watched Rita, Misha, and the doctor swaying and swaying. I became mesmerized by the swaying. I wanted to know what would happen to Tapka; the swaying answered me.

The swaying said: Listen, shithead, Tapka will live. The doctor will perform the operation. Either money will be found or money will not be necessary.

I said to the swaying: This is very good. I love Tapka. I meant her no harm. I want to be forgiven.

The swaying replied: There is reality and then there is truth. The reality is that Tapka will live. But, let's be honest, the truth is you killed Tapka. Look at Rita; look at Misha. You see, who are you kidding? You killed Tapka and you will never be forgiven.

—2003

Shaun Tan
b. 1974

Although his assorted picture books are often viewed as works of children's literature, the Australian author-illustrator Shaun Tan insists that his art is for "anyone who is curious, who enjoys strangeness, mystery, and oddity," in short, "who likes asking questions and using their imagination." Playfully combining a host of unlikely objects and ideas to create a unique, often absurd and surreal universe, Tan's drawings, paintings, and stories seek to pose questions rather than to impose answers. For Tan, a work of imagination ought to present itself as a "speculative proposition," juxtaposing pictures and words in an effort to return the reader to a state of unfamiliarity.

After publishing his first drawing at just 16, Tan worked as a freelance illustrator for various small-press magazines and book publishers while studying English and fine arts at the University of Western Australia. Since then, he has emerged from relative obscurity to international acclaim. His work has been honoured with many distinctions, including the 2010 Academy Award for best animated short film, which he received for directing an adaptation of his story *The Lost Thing* (2000), and the 2011 Astrid Lindgren Memorial Award, bestowed in recognition of his outstanding contribution to children's and young-adult literature.

Among his many influences, which include authors like George Orwell, visual artists like Quentin Blake, and filmmakers like Stanley Kubrick, Tan singles out Ray Bradbury as the writer whose short stories inspired him to experiment with science fiction, fantasy, and dreamlike fables of his own. According to Tan, whose short story collection *Tales from Outer Suburbia* (2008) shares a kindred spirit with many tales from outer space, everything "can be seen as science fiction" if we cultivate the visual literacy to recognize the mysteriousness of the mundane and the strangeness of the familiar.

the
nameless
holiday

The nameless holiday happens once a year, usually around late August, sometimes October. It is always anticipated by children and adults alike with mixed emotion: it's not exactly festive, but still a celebration of sorts, the origin of which has been long forgotten.

All that is known are the familiar rituals: the laying out of one's most prized possessions on the bedroom floor; then choosing one special object—exactly the right one—and carrying it carefully up a ladder to the roof and leaving it under the TV aerial[1] (already decorated with small shiny things such as chocolate wrappers, old CDs, and the tops off tubs of yogourt, licked clean and threaded with string, tied with special slip-knots).

Then there is the traditional midnight picnic in the backyard, front lawn, or any place with a good view of one's own roof—across the street if necessary, which is why families sometimes gather by the roadside on blankets. Here are born fond memories of freshly baked gingerbread crows, hot pomegranate juice as tart as a knife and small plastic whistles, inaudible to the ears of both humans and dogs. Not to mention all that excited chatter and giggling, all that polite shushing, everyone struggling to observe the convention of silence.

Those who stay awake long enough are rewarded by a momentary sound that never fails to draw a sharp intake of breath—the delicate tapping of hoofs descending on roof tiles. It is always so startling, so hard to believe at first, like a waking dream or a rumour made solid. But sure enough, there he is,

---

1   *aerial* Antenna.

the reindeer with no name: enormous, blind as a bat, sniffing under the TV aerial with infinite animal patience. He always knows exactly which objects are so loved that their loss will be felt like the snapping of a cord to the heart, and it's only these that he nudges tenderly until they become hooked onto his great antlers. The rest he leaves alone, leaping gracefully back up into the cool darkness.

What a remarkable, unnameable feeling it is, right at the moment of his leaping: something like sadness and regret, of suddenly wanting your gift back and held tight to your chest, knowing that you will certainly never see it again. And then there is the letting go as your muscles release, your lungs exhale, and the backwash of longing leaves behind this one image on the shore of memory: a huge reindeer on your roof, bowing down.

—2008

Madeleine Thien
b. 1974

The youngest of three children of Malaysian-Chinese parents—and the only child born in Canada—Madeleine Thien is a translator of cultural experiences. "I occupy a different kind of place," says Thien. "My sense of place is slightly different. I'm the child of immigrants without being an immigrant. I am the sister of immigrants without being an immigrant. It's a sense of occupying a new world, feeling I could embrace a new place right away, without hesitation." Her perspectives on family unity, immigration, and place inspire much of her fiction, and her stories of family dynamics and regional alliances have met with critical acclaim. She received the Canadian Author's Association award for most promising writer under 30 and the Ethel Wilson Fiction Prize for her first publication, a collection of short stories titled *Simple Recipes* (2001).

Thien was born and educated in Vancouver, British Columbia. She received a Master of Fine Arts in Creative Writing at the University of British Columbia, where she began work on the title story for *Simple Recipes*. Shortly after the success of her inaugural publication, Thien collaborated with Chinese-Canadian filmmaker and illustrator Joe Chang on a children's book adapted from his National Film Board short *The Chinese Violin* (2002). Thien's debut novel *Certainty* (2006), which addresses the complications of familial bonds, received international attention and has been translated into over 15 languages.

Threads of her own family history and life experience are stitched throughout Thien's fiction; her stories are not, however, wholly autobiographical. Instead, Thien's real-life affinities serve as reminders of "what it is to write honestly." Familiar activities and simple memories, such as cooking rice, become the bases for robust, multi-layered stories. These autobiographical markers, Thien remarks, provide a "feeling of writing that reminds you of the feeling of putting down the truth."

Simple Recipes

There is a simple recipe for making rice. My father taught it to me when I was a child. Back then, I used to sit up on the kitchen counter watching him, how he sifted the grains in his hands, sure and quick, removing pieces of dirt or sand, tiny imperfections. He swirled his hands through the water and it turned cloudy. When he scrubbed the grains clean, the sound was as big as a field of insects. Over and over, my father rinsed the rice, drained the water, then filled the pot again.

The instructions are simple. Once the washing is done, you measure the water this way—by resting the tip of your index finger on the surface of the rice. The water should reach the bend of your first knuckle. My father did not need instructions or measuring cups. He closed his eyes and felt for the waterline.

Sometimes I still dream of my father, his bare feet flat against the floor, standing in the middle of the kitchen. He wears old buttoned shirts and faded sweatpants drawn at the waist. Surrounded by the gloss of the kitchen counters, the sharp angles of the stove, the fridge, the shiny sink, he looks out of place. This memory of him is so strong, sometimes it stuns me, the detail with which I can see it.

Every night before dinner, my father would perform this ritual—rinsing and draining, then setting the pot in the cooker. When I was older, he passed this task on to me but I never did it with the same care. I went through the motions, splashing the water around, jabbing my finger down to measure the water level. Some nights the rice was a mushy gruel. I worried that I could not do so simple a task right. "Sorry," I would say to the table, my voice soft and embarrassed. In answer, my father would keep eating, pushing the rice into his mouth as if he never expected anything different, as if he noticed no difference between what he did so well and I so poorly. He would eat every last mouthful, his chopsticks walking quickly across the plate. Then he would rise, whistling, and clear the table, every motion so clean and sure, I would be convinced by him that all was well in the world.

• • •

My father is standing in the middle of the kitchen. In his right hand he holds a plastic bag filled with water. Caught inside the bag is a live fish.

The fish is barely breathing, though its mouth opens and closes. I reach up and touch it through the plastic bag, trailing my fingers along the gills, the soft, muscled body, pushing my finger overtop the eyeball. The fish looks straight at me, flopping sluggishly from side to side.

My father fills the kitchen sink. In one swift motion he overturns the bag and the fish comes sailing out with the water. It curls and jumps. We watch it closely, me on my tiptoes, chin propped up on the counter. The fish is the length of my arm from wrist to elbow. It floats in place, brushing up against the sides of the sink.

I keep watch over the fish while my father begins the preparations for dinner. The fish folds its body, trying to turn or swim, the water nudging overtop. Though I ripple tiny circles around it with my fingers, the fish stays still, bobbing side-to-side in the cold water.

For many hours at a time, it was just the two of us. While my mother worked and my older brother played outside, my father and I sat on the couch, flipping channels. He loved cooking shows. We watched *Wok with Yan*, my father passing judgment on Yan's methods. I was enthralled when Yan transformed orange peels into swans. My father sniffed. "I can do that," he said. "You don't have to be a genius to do that." He placed a sprig of green onion in water and showed me how it bloomed like a flower. "I know many tricks like this," he said. "Much more than Yan."

Still, my father made careful notes when Yan demonstrated Peking Duck. He chuckled heartily at Yan's punning. "Take a wok on the wild side!" Yan said, pointing his spatula at the camera.

"Ha ha!" my father laughed, his shoulders shaking. "*Wok* on the wild side!"

In the mornings, my father took me to school. At three o'clock, when we came home again, I would rattle off everything I learned that day. "The brachiosaurus," I informed him, "eats only soft vegetables."

My father nodded. "That is like me. Let me see your forehead." We stopped and faced each other in the road. "You have a high forehead," he said, leaning down to take a closer look. "All smart people do."

I walked proudly, stretching my legs to match his steps. I was overjoyed when my feet kept time with his, right, then left, then right, and we walked like a single unit. My father was the man of tricks, who sat for an hour mining a watermelon with a circular spoon, who carved the rind into a castle.

My father was born in Malaysia and he and my mother immigrated to Canada several years before I was born, first settling in Montreal, then finally in Vancouver. While I was born into the persistence of the Vancouver rain, my father was born in the wash of a monsoon country. When I was young, my parents tried to teach me their language but it never came easily to me. My father ran his thumb gently over my mouth, his face kind, as if trying to see what it was that made me different.

My brother was born in Malaysia but when he immigrated with my parents to Canada the language left him. Or he forgot it, or he refused it, which is also common, and this made my father angry. "How can a child forget a language?" he would ask my mother. "It is because the child is lazy. Because the child chooses not to remember." When he was twelve years old, my brother stayed away in the afternoons. He drummed the soccer ball up and down the back alley, returning home only at dinner time. During the day, my mother worked as a sales clerk at the Woodward's store downtown, in the building with the red revolving W on top.

In our house, the ceilings were yellowed with grease. Even the air was heavy with it. I remember that I loved the weight of it, the air that was dense with the smell of countless meals cooked in a tiny kitchen, all those good smells jostling for space.

The fish in the sink is dying slowly. It has a glossy sheen to it, as if its skin is made of shining minerals. I want to prod it with both hands, its body tense against the pressure of my fingers. If I hold it tightly, I imagine I will be able to feel its fluttering heart. Instead, I lock eyes with the fish. *You're feeling verrrry sleepy*, I tell it. *You're getting verrrry tired.*

Beside me, my father chops green onions quickly. He uses a cleaver that he says is older than I am by many years. The blade of the knife rolls forward and backward, loops of green onion gathering in a pyramid beside my father's wrist. When he is done, he rolls his sleeve back from his right hand, reaches in through the water and pulls the plug.

The fish in the sink floats and we watch it in silence. The water level falls beneath its gills, beneath its belly. It drains and leaves the sink dry. The fish is lying on its side, mouth open and its body heaving. It leaps sideways and hits the sink. Then up again. It curls and snaps, lunging for its own tail. The fish sails into the air, dropping hard. It twitches violently.

My father reaches in with his bare hands. He lifts the fish out by the tail and lays it gently on the counter. While holding it steady with one hand, he hits the head with the flat of the cleaver. The fish falls still, and he begins to clean it.

• • •

In my apartment, I keep the walls scrubbed clean. I open the windows and turn the fan on whenever I prepare a meal. My father bought me a rice cooker when I first moved into my own apartment, but I use it so rarely it stays in the back of the cupboard, the cord wrapped neatly around its belly. I have no longing for the meals themselves, but I miss the way we sat down together, our bodies leaning hungrily forward while my father, the magician, unveiled plate after plate. We laughed and ate, white steam fogging my mother's glasses until she had to take them off and lay them on the table. Eyes closed, she would eat, crunchy vegetables gripped in her chopsticks, the most vivid green.

• • •

My brother comes into the kitchen and his body is covered with dirt. He leaves a thin trail of it behind as he walks. The soccer ball, muddy from outside, is encircled in one arm. Brushing past my father, his face is tense.

Beside me, my mother sprinkles garlic onto the fish. She lets me slide one hand underneath the fish's head, cradling it, then bending it backwards so that she can fill the fish's insides with ginger. Very carefully, I turn the fish over. It is firm and slippery, and beaded with tiny, sharp scales.

At the stove, my father picks up an old teapot. It is full of oil and he pours the oil into the wok. It falls in a thin ribbon. After a moment, when the oil begins crackling, he lifts the fish up and drops it down into the wok. He adds water and the smoke billows up. The sound of the fish frying is like tires on gravel, a sound so loud it drowns out all other noises. Then my father steps out from the smoke. "Spoon out the rice," he says as he lifts me down from the counter.

My brother comes back into the room, his hands muddy and his knees the colour of dusty brick. His soccer shorts flutter against the backs of his legs. Sitting down, he makes an angry face. My father ignores him.

Inside the cooker, the rice is flat like a pie. I push the spoon in, turning the rice over, and the steam shoots up in a hot mist and condenses on my skin. While my father moves his arms delicately over the stove, I begin dishing the rice out: first for my father, then my mother, then my brother, then myself. Behind me the fish is cooking quickly. In a crockery pot, my father steams cauliflower, stirring it round and round.

My brother kicks at a table leg.

"What's the matter?" my father asks.

He is quiet for a moment, then he says, "Why do we have to eat fish?"

"You don't like it?"

My brother crosses his arms against his chest. I see the dirt lining his arms, dark and hardened. I imagine chipping it off his body with a small spoon.

"I don't like the eyeball there. It looks sick."

My mother tuts. Her nametag is still clipped to her blouse. It says *Woodward's*, and then, *Sales Clerk*. "Enough," she says, hanging her purse on the back of the chair. "Go wash your hands and get ready for supper."

My brother glares, just for a moment. Then he begins picking at the dirt on his arms. I bring plates of rice to the table. The dirt flies off his skin, speckling the tablecloth. "Stop it," I say crossly.

"*Stop it*," he says, mimicking me.

"Hey!" My father hits his spoon against the counter. It *pings*, high-pitched. He points at my brother. "No fighting in this house."

My brother looks at the floor, mumbles something, and then shuffles away from the table. As he moves farther away, he begins to stamp his feet.

Shaking her head, my mother takes her jacket off. It slides from her shoulders. She says something to my father in the language I can't understand. He merely shrugs his shoulders. And then he replies, and I think his words are so familiar, as if they are words I should know, as if maybe I did know them once but then I forgot them. The language that they speak is full of soft vowels, words running together so that I can't make out the gaps where they pause for breath.

My mother told me once about guilt. Her own guilt she held in the palm of her hands, like an offering. But your guilt is different, she said. You do not need to hold on to it. Imagine this, she said, her hands running along my forehead, then up into my hair. Imagine, she said. Picture it, and what do you see?

A bruise on the skin, wide and black.

A bruise, she said. Concentrate on it. Right now, it's a bruise. But if you concentrate, you can shrink it, compress it to the size of a pinpoint. And then, if you want to, if you see it, you can blow it off your body like a speck of dirt.

She moved her hands along my forehead.

I tried to picture what she said. I pictured blowing it away like so much nothing, just these little pieces that didn't mean anything, this complicity that I could magically walk away from. She made me believe in the strength of my own thoughts, as if I could make appear what had never existed. Or turn it around. Flip it over so many times you just lose sight of it, you lose the tail end and the whole thing disappears into smoke.

My father pushes at the fish with the edge of his spoon. Underneath, the meat is white and the juice runs down along the side. He lifts a piece and lowers it carefully onto my plate.

Once more, his spoon breaks skin. Gingerly, my father lifts another piece and moves it towards my brother.

"I don't want it," my brother says.

My father's hand wavers, "Try it," he says, smiling. "Take a wok on the wild side."

"No."

My father sighs and places the piece on my mother's plate. We eat in silence, scraping our spoons across the dishes. My parents use chopsticks, lifting their bowls and motioning the food into their mouths. The smell of food fills the room.

Savouring each mouthful, my father eats slowly, head tuned to the flavours in his mouth. My mother takes her glasses off, the lenses fogged, and lays them on the table. She eats with her head bowed down, as if in prayer.

Lifting a stem of cauliflower to his lips, my brother sighs deeply. He chews, and then his face changes. I have a sudden picture of him drowning, his hair waving like grass. He coughs, spitting the mouthful back onto his plate. Another cough. He reaches for his throat, choking.

My father slams his chopsticks down on the table. In a single movement, he reaches across, grabbing my brother by the shoulder. "I have tried," he is saying. "I don't know what kind of son you are. To be so ungrateful." His other hand sweeps by me and bruises into my brother's face.

My mother flinches. My brother's face is red and his mouth is open. His eyes are wet.

Still coughing, he grabs a fork, tines aimed at my father, and then in an unthinking moment, he heaves it at him. It strikes my father in the chest and drops.

"I hate you! You're just an asshole, you're just a fucking asshole chink!" My brother holds his plate in his hands. He smashes it down and his food scatters across the table. He is coughing and spitting. "I wish you weren't my father! I wish you were dead."

My father's hand falls again. This time pounding downwards. I close my eyes. All I can hear is someone screaming. There is a loud voice. I stand awkwardly, my hands covering my eyes.

"Go to your room," my father says, his voice shaking.

And I think he is talking to me so I remove my hands.

But he is looking at my brother. And my brother is looking at him, his small chest heaving.

A few minutes later, my mother begins clearing the table, face weary as she scrapes the dishes one by one over the garbage.

I move away from my chair, past my mother, onto the carpet and up the stairs.

Outside my brother's bedroom, I crouch against the wall. When I step forward and look, I see my father holding the bamboo pole between his hands. The pole is smooth. The long grains, fine as hair, are pulled together, at intervals, jointed. My brother is lying on the floor, as if thrown down and dragged there. My father raises the pole into the air.

I want to cry out. I want to move into the room between them, but I can't.

It is like a tree falling, beginning to move, a slow arc through the air.

The bamboo drops silently. It rips the skin on my brother's back. I cannot hear any sound. A line of blood edges quickly across his body.

The pole rises and again comes down. I am afraid of bones breaking.

My father lifts his arms once more.

On the floor, my brother cries into the carpet, pawing at the ground. His knees folded into his chest, the crown of his head burrowing down. His back is hunched over and I can see his spine, little bumps on his skin.

The bamboo smashes into bone and the scene in my mind bursts into a million white pieces.

My mother picks me up off the floor, pulling me across the hall, into my bedroom, into bed. Everything is wet, the sheets, my hands, her body, my face, and she soothes me with words I cannot understand because all I can hear is screaming. She rubs her cool hands against my forehead. "Stop," she says. "Please stop," but I feel loose, deranged, as if everything in the known world is ending right here.

In the morning, I wake up to the sound of oil in the pan and the smell of French toast. I can hear my mother bustling around, putting dishes in the cupboards.

No one says anything when my brother doesn't come down for breakfast. My father piles French toast and syrup onto a plate and my mother pours a glass of milk. She takes everything upstairs to my brother's bedroom.

As always, I follow my father around the kitchen. I track his footprints, follow behind him and hide in the shadow of his body. Every so often, he reaches down and ruffles my hair with his hands. We cast a spell, I think. The way we move in circles, how he cooks without thinking because this is the task that comes to him effortlessly. He smiles down at me, but when he does this, it somehow breaks the spell. My father stands in place, hands dropping to his sides as if he has forgotten what he was doing mid-motion. On the walls, the paint is peeling and the floor, unswept in days, leaves little pieces of dirt stuck to our feet.

My persistence, I think, my unadulterated love, confuse him. With each passing day, he knows I will find it harder to ignore what I can't comprehend, that I will be unable to separate one part of him from another. The unconditional quality of my love for him will not last forever, just as my brother's did not. My father stands in the middle of the kitchen, unsure. Eventually, my mother comes downstairs again and puts her arms around him and holds him, whispering something to him, words that to me are meaningless and incomprehensible. But she offers them to him, sound after sound, in a language that was stolen from some other place, until he drops his head and remembers where he is.

Later on, I lean against the door frame upstairs and listen to the sound of a metal fork scraping against a dish. My mother is already there, her voice rising and falling. She is moving the fork across the plate, offering my brother pieces of French toast.

I move towards the bed, the carpet scratchy, until I can touch the wooden bed-frame with my hands. My mother is seated there, and I go to her, reaching my fingers out to the buttons on her cuff and twisting them over to catch the light.

"Are you eating?" I ask my brother.

He starts to cry. I look at him, his face half hidden in the blankets.

"Try and eat," my mother says softly.

He only cries harder but there isn't any sound. The pattern of sunlight on his blanket moves with his body. His hair is pasted down with sweat and his head moves forward and backward like an old man's.

At some point I know my father is standing at the entrance of the room but I cannot turn to look at him. I want to stay where I am, facing the wall. I'm afraid that if I turn around and go to him, I will be complicit, accepting a portion of guilt, no matter how small that piece. I do not know how to prevent this from happening again, though now I know, in the end, it will break us apart. This violence will turn all my love to shame and grief. So I stand there, not looking at him or my brother. Even my father, the magician, who can make something beautiful out of nothing, he just stands and watches.

A face changes over time, it becomes clearer. In my father's face, I have seen everything pass. Anger that has stripped it of anything recognizable, so that it is only a face of bones and skin. And then, at other times, so much pain that it is unbearable, his face so full of grief it might dissolve. How to reconcile all that I know of him and still love him? For a long time, I thought it was not possible. When I was a child, I did not love my father because he was complicated, because he was human, because he needed me to. A child does not know yet how to love a person that way.

How simple it should be. Warm water running over, the feel of the grains between my hands, the sound of it like stones running along the pavement. My father would rinse the rice over and over, sifting it between his fingertips, searching for the impurities, pulling them out. A speck, barely visible, resting on the tip of his finger.

If there were some recourse, I would take it. A cupful of grains in my open hand, a smoothing out, finding the impurities, then removing them piece by piece. And then, to be satisfied with what remains.

Somewhere in my memory, a fish in the sink is dying slowly. My father and I watch as the water runs down.

—2001

Drama

In Tom Stoppard's *Rosencrantz and Guildenstern Are Dead*, the character of The Player contemplates the peculiarity of what it means to be a stage actor: "There we are—demented children mincing about in clothes that no one ever wore, speaking as no man ever spoke, swearing love in wigs and rhymed couplets, killing each other with wooden swords ... Don't you see?! We're actors—we're the opposite of people!" While it is true that texts belonging to other generic categories might more or less explicitly refer to their own status as fictions—think, for example, of Margaret Atwood's short story "Happy Endings"—dramatic texts must foreground the matter of the conventions that go along with fictionality, at least in terms of form. (In referring to "fiction" here, the issue is not genre or "drama" versus "fiction" versus "poetry," but rather that the dramatic text tells a fictitious story, that it is a product of the imagination.) Consider the act of going to see a play: you and several or several hundred other people gather together in a specific place and, at a specific time, quiet down and focus your attention at a specific location. In that location, for a certain length of time, other people say and do things, all the while pretending to be other people and pretending that they have no idea they are being watched by several or several hundred others. For your part, you pretend that the people pretending to be other people are in fact those other people, and that you, and several or several hundred others, are completely invisible. In what other context would such bizarre conduct seem not only reasonable, but absolutely necessary? Daniel MacIvor's play *House Humans* describes an instance when this strange balancing act of reciprocal pretending is threatened: "Harold is an old man who goes to the theatre ... He always sits at the front and claps in all the wrong places and yells out Marxist slogans during the tender moments and calls the actors by their real names. (Once he went to see a play where at one point a watermelon would roll out and surprise the audience, and he went back several times so that just before the watermelon would roll out he could yell: 'Here comes the watermelon!')" No other literary genre is at risk for this type of sabotage. In considering some of the basic conventions of drama, then, it is helpful to think about how they flow from both its central principle and its central constraint: the drama is built around the potentially fragile concept of the willing suspension of disbelief.

The Drama and the Performance

The expression "willing suspension of disbelief" was coined by the poet Samuel Taylor Coleridge in his 1817 autobiography, *Biographia Literaria*. Coleridge explained that, in order for readers to appreciate some of his more fantastical narratives—for example, his ballad *The Rime of the Ancient Mariner*, with its ghostly figures and supernatural events—they would have to temporarily set aside—or suspend—any inclination towards skepticism about the truthfulness of such a tale. Willing suspension of disbelief is a crucial component of what makes the dramatic performance work. In the eighteenth century, Denis Diderot asserted that actors should perform as if the spectator did not exist, as if a "large wall" separated the stage from the audience, and as if "the curtain did not rise."

Diderot's treatise on acting technique followed the development of the **proscenium stage**, as his mention of a "curtain" makes clear; proscenium stages, introduced in Europe during the seventeenth century, make use of an archway or large frame to separate the stage area from the audience area and thus provide for the possibility of hanging a curtain and marking more easily, for example, the beginnings and endings of acts. Before the advent of the proscenium stage, dramatists often wrote plays meant to be performed on a **thrust stage**, a raised platform encircled by the audience on three sides; thus, a play such as Shakespeare's *Twelfth Night* was written before it was possible to use a curtain, and one might consider the different techniques employed to indicate the breaks between scenes and acts. Other popular stage formats are the **arena** or **theatre-in-the-round stage**, in which the audience, sitting in sloped seating, completely (or almost completely) encircles the stage area, or the **found space**, in which the stage area and audience area might be configured in any number of ways. In the contemporary era, directors and stage designers have the opportunity to stage plays along various designs, though unless a found space or a specially built space is being used, they must take into account an existing physical structure, be it an arena, proscenium stage, or otherwise.

What becomes interesting to consider is the way dramatists sometimes make explicit reference to the idea of the willing suspension of disbelief, not only in terms of a clear addressing of the audience—as in Viola's asides in *Twelfth Night*, but also in terms of a thematic concern with the operation of illusion that is so easily observable in drama. Though the **realism** of Henrik Ibsen and Tennessee Williams, whereby everything on stage is meant to register as a potential, everyday activity, has not been entirely abandoned in recent years (witness Hannah Moscovitch's *Essay*), interest in **metafictional** theatre, or plays that call attention to their own fictionality in their content, has also exploded. From an absurdist play such as Samuel Beckett's *Krapp's Last Tape* to Sharon Pollock's incorporation of the figure of the Actress in *Blood Relations*, dramatists have made use of the inherent strangeness at the heart of playgoing to raise such questions as how we believe what we believe, why humans are so engrossed by illusion-making and art, and how our perceptions can be produced and undermined by mere words.

This notion of a reader or audience member's temporary willingness to simply believe things that are patently untrue is a crucial factor in the success of the drama, especially the success of the drama's performance. For the critical analysis of this genre, it is important to distinguish between the notion of the drama or play, that is, the written version of the work, and theatre, which is the live enactment of mutual pretending described above. In his critical work *The Semiotics of Performance*, Marco De Marinis helpfully refines this distinction, referring to the **dramatic text** vs. the **performance text**. The dramatic text—the written play—consists of dialogue and **stage directions**, which are the instructions contained in the written play that specify how characters are supposed to move on, off, and about the stage, and sometimes how they are meant to behave. While the stage directions in some plays, especially older ones, are basically limited to such instructions as "*Enter*" and "*Exit*," they may also provide detailed, evocative information on the mood of the play, as in Tennessee Williams's stage directions for *Cat on a Hot Tin Roof*, or about the arrangement of stage décor, as in those for Stoppard's *Arcadia*. The performance text, on the other hand, consists of the intended or implicit acting out of the written play. Thus, the performance text is not quite the same thing as a specific theatrical production of a given play on a given evening; rather, it is the *potential* of theatrical production that is embedded in the written play, a potential that readers of the dramatic text must somehow imagine in their mind's eye, and that to a large extent limits the type of action that can be portrayed. While it is true that some authors—for example, Mary Sidney and Percy Shelley—have written what are called **closet dramas**, or plays not meant to be performed, most plays are predicated on the idea of being acted out and of requiring a temporary agreement between actors and audience to accept all manner of imitation, impersonation, and active use of the imagination.

Constructing the Drama: Plot, Character, Space, and Speech

In the earliest surviving work of dramatic theory, *The Poetics*, Aristotle compares tragic drama to epic poetry, asserting that, while both genres should be concerned with heroic action, the events portrayed in a tragic drama must "fall within a single revolution of the sun, or slightly exceed this," while the epic is "unlimited in point of time." Later in the work, Aristotle adds that tragic drama should present "an action that is heroic and complete and of a certain magnitude." During the sixteenth and seventeenth centuries, Italian, French, and English neoclassicists expanded upon and refined these remarks, claiming that, ideally, all dramas should adhere to what were termed the **three classical unities**. Italian critic Lodovico Castelvetro explained that a play must have a **unity of action** (a focus on a single incident or two interrelated incidents), a **unity of time**, and a **unity of space**, with the dramatized events taking place within a 24-hour time frame and in a single locale. Later critics noted that exceptions might be made; for example, Pierre Corneille argued that the restricted timeframe of Aeschylus's *Agamemnon* was absurd and that the periods of time represented in a play should not strain verisimilitude (except in the final act, when the audience is more interested in finding out what happens than they are in the likelihood that it might all happen very quickly). In *Of Dramatic Poesy: An Essay*, John Dryden noted that while Ben Jonson "has given us the most correct plays," in which the adherence to the three unities provide "profitable rules for perfecting the stage," Shakespeare's ignorance of such rules might be forgiven because of his great wit.

By the beginning of the nineteenth century, most drama critics and theorists had abandoned the notion of the three unities, at least as a prescriptive set of rules. That said, these foundational conventions are still worth keeping in mind for the student of literature attuned to how the drama is built. It may be helpful to consider how the notion of unity of action is associated with the **plotting** of drama. The terms associated with **Freytag's pyramid**, such as **exposition**, **rising action**, **climax**, **falling action**, and **dénouement/resolution**, are often used to discuss prose narratives, though Gustav Freytag himself was concerned only with the five-act plot structure of classical and Renaissance plays. While few contemporary plays retain the five-act structure, the student of literature should consider how the plotting of dramas tends to retain a sense of tightness, chronological simplicity, and forward momentum, likely because the implied audience of the performance text will experience the performance in real time. For example, though Williams's *Cat on a Hot Tin Roof* is broken down into four acts, the limited timeframe and strict chronology of the action are controlled by the simple fact that the action takes place over the course of a single evening, as the family celebrates Big Daddy's birthday. What, then, might one say about the relationship between this formal choice in structuring the plot of the play and its thematic concern with domestic space, family relationships, and the way humans confront death? Other important plotting techniques associated with drama include **suspense**—or the anticipation about how things will turn out—and suspense's customary partner, **foreshadowing**—or how anticipation is created via hints. In thinking about suspense, one might consider whether the play leaves the audience in the dark as to what might occur in the end, thus leading up to a feeling of surprise, or whether foreshadowing makes it seem as if the resolution to the plot is inevitable.

Moreover, it is often important to think about how the dramatist negotiates breaking the action down into chunks that can be performed, i.e., into **acts** and **scenes**. Whereas a prose narrative can suggest a change in action or space or time using mere words, the convention of the embedded performance text necessitates that the dramatist consider how each unit of action will be made evident, whether by the closing and opening of a curtain, by the dimming of lights, or by some other means. In Pollock's *Blood Relations*, the stage directions indicate that units of action should not be marked, with the exception of a blackout at the end of Act I, despite the fact that various moments in time and space are represented. One might ask how this formal directive is related to the play's emphasis on questioning authority, or on changing attitudes toward women over time. The implicit performance text within a drama also complicates the way one thinks of **characterization**: while all fictional narrative texts might contain characters—that is, represented individuals who have particular personality traits—in a drama the process of defining and indicating those traits cannot be achieved through direct authorial exposition, whereby the author simply tells the reader what the character is like via narration. In a drama, the character reveals his- or herself through speech and action, though it is sometimes the case that dramatists "cheat," as in moments where characters describe one another or when a character describes—sometimes at length—his- or herself. Some characters will go so far as to articulate their **motivations**, the reasons for particular actions or desires, though it is often left to the student of literature to glean a character's motivations based on what that character says and does. And, just as with first-person narrators, it is sometimes the case that the motivations characters give to us, or the way a character might describe his- or herself, is inaccurate; it is the task of the audience member to evaluate the information that is given. Usually, if a character's motivations can be assessed and analyzed, one is dealing with what is called a **round character**, one that is fully developed and whose actions are credible. At the other end of the spectrum is the **flat character**, one defined by a small number of traits, or that functions as a **stock character**, which is a familiar stereotype—for example, the young, naïve female lover, the scheming revenge-seeker, or the bumbling father figure. A character may be thought of as a **foil** if his or her main function is to reflect something important about a main character. For example, Gooper from *Cat on a Hot Tin Roof* is portrayed as conventionally masculine so as to further emphasize his brother Brick's more complex struggle with his gender identity and sexuality. Though it is often the case that a foil is also a flat character, it is certainly possible for such a figure—like Gooper—to be fully and complexly developed.

Castelvetro made his case for the unity of space by drawing attention to "the limitation of the space in which [the play] is acted"; in other words, the theoretical concept and literary convention derive from a practical concern: how many places can one reasonably include in a drama, given the implicit performance text embedded in every play and the necessity of representing those places, live? And what, then, is the significance of the place or places a dramatist chooses to include, especially given that the selections must be limited? Ibsen's *A Doll's House* is set entirely in one room, the living room of the Helmers' apartment, though various other rooms are gestured toward as characters move off stage. Why does Ibsen choose this space—which is both domestic, and yet somehow public—for his exploration of the Helmers' marriage?

The term dramatists and literary critics use to refer to the location of represented action is **setting**, a term also associated with prose narratives, but used in a very specific way for discussions of dramas. The French term **mise en scène** is perhaps a more helpful way to refer to a drama's setting, as it encompasses the scenery, the properties or moveable set pieces, the way everything on stage is arranged, and even the way lighting and sound effects are to be used throughout a performance. The issue of properties (usually called props) is especially interesting, as it is often the case that such items take on **symbolic** meaning, which is not surprising given—again—that there are only so many items a dramatist can reasonably have cluttering up the performance area. Any item that is important enough to be lugged onto a stage thus has the potential to transcend its function as décor—even in a play such as *A Doll's House*, the setting of which is meant to register as a real living room. For example, in Act III, the stage directions inform the reader that, while preparing to open his letter-box, "*Helmer takes his bunch of keys from his pocket and goes into the hall.*" It is perfectly realistic that a man wishing to unlock his letter-box would fish keys out of his pocket. Yet Ibsen's choice to represent this action on the stage—which requires that a fake set of keys be made up and carried by the actor playing Torvald Helmer—leads one to ask whether the keys might have any additional or symbolic significance. Might they indicate, for example, the sort of control Helmer holds over his wife? Similarly, the portrait of Sir

Oliver Surface in Richard Brinsley Sheridan's *The School for Scandal* operates as a complex prop—especially if one considers that for every new production of the play, a portrait of the *actor* playing Sir Oliver Surface must be fabricated. The Surface portrait may thus be seen as a symbolic anchor for the play's exploration of true and false identities.

Another distinguishing convention of the drama is that, unlike a prose or poetry narrative, in which an omniscient narrator or speaker might describe what is happening, in a drama the action must be expressed through what can be physically represented on stage and what the characters in a play say to one another, or to themselves. The term **dialogue**, which comes from the Greek words meaning "through" (dia) and "to speak" (legein), refers to the way conversations between two or more persons on stage work to reveal character and to advance the plot. The drama's formal dependence on dialogue—as opposed to expository or descriptive or figurative writing, such as is used regularly and to great effect in other genres—is often accompanied by explorations within the drama of the power of language. Consider, for example, Moscovitch's play *Essay*, in which the characters deal with the way a footnote in a history textbook becomes the source of a complex power struggle, or how Beckett's *Krapp's Last Tape* explores the way certain words define our identities and memories. It is sometimes the case in a drama that only one person is speaking, either in a **monologue** or in a **soliloquy**. Monologues occur when one person is speaking aloud, for an extended length of time, to one or more listeners, while soliloquies are meant to represent a circumstance in which a character talks to him- or herself. In a prose narrative, such internal musing is common and, arguably, most lyric poems represent this same contemplative activity. In a drama, however, the audience must accept the convention that people do their internal musing aloud, as when, in Act II of *Twelfth Night*, Viola meditates (out loud, in iambic pentameter) on the frailty of women. Another convention of speech used in drama, one that seems to oppose so many of the genre's other conventions, is the **aside**. This is a moment when the spell of mutual pretending is broken and a character directly addresses the audience, with the implicit understanding that the character's words to the audience cannot be heard by anyone else on stage. After Viola swears to Orsino that she—in the guise of Cesario—will help him court Olivia, for example, she then makes an aside to the audience asserting that she wishes Orsino would have her as a wife.

The aside is an example of what is known as "breaking the fourth wall," an expression that references Diderot's assertion about "the large wall." Asides draw attention to the idea that, when an audience is watching a play, they are peeking into a room—a room with one invisible wall—where people are simply going about their business. Other examples of breaking the fourth wall in dramas include the use of prologues or epilogues, the use of a **chorus**, when a group of characters offer commentary on the action, and the inclusion of a song, or even a dance in the middle of the play. In much historical drama, for example Renaissance and Restoration drama, the aside is meant to register as "truth," whereby the character looks through the invisible wall and confesses something genuine to the audience. Contemporary playwrights have often experimented with the convention of character-audience interaction, as when, in *Blood Relations*, Pollock's use of language associated with a courtroom case implicitly asks the audience to "judge" the truth of Lizzie Borden's case. A kind of opposition to the aside is the notion of **dramatic irony**, a type of irony in which the audience knows more about a particular situation than the characters themselves (an archetypal instance occurs in Shakespeare's *Romeo and Juliet*, when the audience knows that Juliet is not really dead but only drugged, but can only watch helplessly as Romeo poisons himself out of grief).

Drama and Mode

Another important effect of the dramatic text being linked with its implicit performance text is that clues about the play's **mode**—whether the play fits into the subgenre of tragedy, comedy, or something else—can be given very efficiently. As with a film, the drama can make use of both words and aspects of the mise en scène, lighting, and music to set up expectations about the treatment of the subject matter. The idea of mode as a defining trait of a subgenre such as the tragic or comedic play derives out of the notion that the same subject can be handled in a variety of ways, and that choices made in the handling will produce different expectations. If, in the first five minutes of a film set in a high school, the audience is faced with grainy images of unhappy teens loitering about the back door and exhausted teachers trying to bring order to unruly classrooms, the audience may reasonably expect a gritty and possibly tragic film about youth. On the other hand, if the opening shots of the high school reveal brightly dressed, laughing teens engaging in back-to-school chatter and hijinks, the audience may reasonably expect a lighthearted and comedic film about youth. The drama has often been crudely considered as being an either/or affair when it comes to mode. Lord Byron summarized it this way: "All tragedies are finished by death, / All comedies are ended by marriage." Aristotle, for his part, saw tragedies as intended to inspire "pity and fear," and comedies as intended to entertain via wit and humour.

Such simplistic divisions do not always make sense. Even the exemplary tragic hero Oedipus doesn't die at the end of Sophocles' play, and some of Shakespeare's romantic comedies, in particular *Measure for Measure* and *The Merchant of Venice*, are not exactly lighthearted (though they do both end with a focus on marriage). Playwrights often make use of the expectations associated with the modes of tragedy or comedy to explore the grey area between the two. For example, in seventeenth- and eighteenth-century France, the idea of tragedy was associated with plays about history or public matters. Such material was considered important enough to warrant serious treatment; the issue of death was not mandatory. In some contemporary tragedies the conventional focus on a hero is set aside, or explicitly challenged. In Arthur Miller's *Death of a Salesman*, Willy Loman is just an ordinary businessman who has a fraught relationship with his sons, and ends up committing suicide. A play such as Ibsen's *A Doll's House* also fits into the mode of tragedy, though it is unclear if the audience is meant to fear or be inspired by Nora's escape from her marriage. Likewise, the comedic mode is made use of in many plays that have nothing to do with marriage. Throughout the Elizabethan and Jacobean periods, both the comedy of humours and the city comedy were popular alternatives to the romantic comedy; both of these subgenres take a satiric view of human behaviour, showing how ordinary humans let the faults in their own nature get the better of them. (Ben Jonson's city comedy *Volpone*, for example, focuses on the greed of various men and the foolish behaviour that greed generates.) In the Restoration period and through the eighteenth century the **comedy of manners** (exemplified by Sheridan's *The School for Scandal*) was likewise focused on human folly, especially in terms of the way particular characteristics were associated with social class. The **farce** may be defined as a comedy that depicts broadly humourous situations, in which plot devices such as mistaken identities, plans gone awry, and surprise endings take precedent over the subtleties of characterization or thematic development. The farce has a very long history, from the Roman comedies of Plautus, which featured all manner of clever servants, braggart warriors, and disguised lovers, to Michael Frayn's 1982 play *Noises Off*, a somewhat metafictional farce about a theatre company's rehearsals and performance of *Nothing On*, a fictional play chiefly about people trying to get in and out of each others' bedrooms.

One of the most interesting grey areas between tragedy and comedy is the subgenre of the **tragicomedy**. In the classical period, the term was used by Plautus to describe the mixing of low- and high-born characters in a single play. Many of Shakespeare's so-called problem plays might also be thought to fit into the idea of tragicomedy as a catch-all category, whereby the marriages at the end of *A Winter's Tale* don't quite make up for the cruelty of Leontes and the suffering of Hermione. In the more contemporary period, playwrights such as Ibsen, Anton Chekhov, and Sean O'Casey experimented with the idea that everyday existence could be both funny and unhappy, often because a character—for example Chekhov's Uncle Vanya—mistakenly perceives him- or herself to be living a noble life. Many plays associated with the **Theatre of**

the Absurd might be considered tragicomedies. In Beckett's *Krapp's Last Tape*, the audience is presented with a man who takes outlandish pleasure in eating bananas and repeating the word "Spool," but who is also faced with the emptiness of his life in old age. The metafictional plays of Pollock and Stoppard are similarly mixed in terms of the expectations they seem to raise, as both playwrights use wit to explore dark or complex themes.

[N.G.]

William Shakespeare
1564–1616

The plays of Shakespeare have influenced literary culture more broadly and more deeply than almost any other group of texts in the English-speaking world. The imagery and poetic facility of his plays; their ways of telling stories; the variety and depth of their characterizations; their innovative dramatic qualities; their complex exploration of ideas—for all these qualities his work has been widely regarded as the highest achievement in English literature.

The son of a glove-maker and alderman, Shakespeare was born in Stratford-upon-Avon in 1564. He was probably educated at the local grammar school, but he did not go on to university; at the time, university attendance would have been highly unusual for a person from the middle class. When Shakespeare was 18, he married Anne Hathaway, with whom he had three children.

Probably in the late 1580s, Shakespeare moved to London and joined the professional theatre. At this time four permanent theatres had recently been established in the London area (all just beyond the city limits, so as to be outside the regulatory authority of the city). Their presence created a steady and ongoing demand for new plays, and helped to shape a new approach to theatre; whereas the travelling troupes of the early Elizabethan era had focused on plays that imitated Roman models (featuring long set-piece speeches, and keeping comedy and tragedy as entirely separate spheres), the new plays were filled with rapid movement and rapid dialogue. Comic characters and scenes were introduced into serious dramatic works, and plays began to depict characters of all sorts—commoners as well as nobles, women as well as men (though the women's roles were played by adolescent males—it was considered unseemly for women to appear on the stage). With remarkable speed the Elizabethan stage became the site of unprecedented vitality, sophistication, and theatrical agility; the list of accomplished playwrights who flourished in the 1590s and the early seventeenth century includes not only Shakespeare but also Christopher Marlowe, Ben Jonson, and dozens of others.

Unlike most other playwrights of the age, Shakespeare wrote in every major dramatic genre: history plays, including *Richard II*; comedies, such as *Much Ado About Nothing*; tragedies, notably *Hamlet* and *King Lear*; a series of tragicomical "romances," such as *The Tempest*; and the "problem plays" or "dark comedies," among them *All's Well That Ends Well*, that ambivalently mingle levity and bitterness.

Shakespeare's work appears to have been extremely well regarded in his own time—when he died Jonson lauded him as "soul of the age" and "the wonder of our stage." Before long a consensus had developed that his work was unrivalled in English literature. Although he often borrowed the basic elements of his stories from other sources, his characters were much more psychologically realistic than any that had previously been represented in English literature. He was also an innovator in his use of the English language, revealing its largely unexplored potential for subtle expression and even expanding its vocabulary—an estimated 1700 English words have their first known usage in Shakespeare's writing.

Twelfth Night has always remained among the most popular of Shakespeare's comedies. Its title alludes to the irreverence, reversals, and general misrule that obtained on the Feast of Epiphany, the culminating twelfth night of traditional Christmas revels. Infused with this festive spirit, *Twelfth Night* satirizes puritanical self-righteousness while playing in a variety of ways with the comedy of sexual identity. But like all of Shakespeare's finest comedies, it is not without serious undercurrents.

Twelfth Night, or What You Will[1]

DRAMATIS PERSONAE

Orsino, *Duke (or Count) of Illyria*[2]
Valentine, *gentleman attending on the Duke*
Curio, *gentleman attending on the Duke*

Viola, *later disguised as Cesario*
Sea Captain, *friend of Viola*
Sebastian, *twin brother of Viola*
Antonio, *a sea captain, friend of Sebastian*

---

1   *Twelfth Night ... Will* The present text has been edited for Broadview Press by David Swain, and is copyright © Broadview Press. *Twelfth Night* appeared in print for the first time in the First Folio of Shakespeare's works (1623). The 1623 text is remarkably clean and free of errors. There is evidence, however, that either the scribe of the copy-text or the compositor himself made some corrections. For instance, Orsino is called a duke four times in Act 1 but a count 13 times throughout, and in scene directions he is always *Duke*. Editors continue to debate inconsistencies in the plot such as that between Viola's stated intention to feign being a eunuch who sings and her actual disguise as a page, or the temporal problem of reconciling Viola and Orsino's three-day acquaintance with Sebastian and Antonio's three-month sojourn, with some arguing that Shakespeare or a printer must have revised the text and others (including the present editor) holding that these contradictions serve the play's deliberate indeterminacy. This edition restores readings from the First Folio that have traditionally been corrected for the sake of consistency. Spelling and punctuation have been modernized except where rhythm and character are better served by contractions and old spelling. Stage directions in square brackets have been inserted by the current editor; those appearing in parentheses derive from the First Folio.

2   *Illyria* Ancient, mysterious region on the Balkan peninsula bordering the Adriatic, although the play occupies an imagined geography and time.

Olivia, *a countess*
Maria, *Olivia's lady-in-waiting*
Sir Toby Belch, *uncle of Olivia*
Sir Andrew Aguecheek, *companion of Sir Toby*
Malvolio, *steward to Olivia*
Fabian, *servant to Olivia*
Feste, *a clown, servant to Olivia*

A Priest
First Officer
Second Officer
Lords, Musicians, Sailors, and other Attendants

ACT 1, SCENE 1

([*Music.*] *Enter Orsino, Duke of Illyria, Curio, and other Lords.*)

ORSINO. If music be the food of love, play on,
    Give me excess of it that,° surfeiting,   *so that*
    The appetite may sicken¹ and so die.
    That strain again, it had a dying fall.²
    O, it came o'er my ear like the sweet sound°   *spring breeze*   5
    That breathes upon a bank of violets,³
    Stealing and giving odour. Enough, no more,
    'Tis not so sweet now as it was before.
    O spirit of love, how quick and fresh° art thou!   *lively and eager*
    That, notwithstanding thy capacity   10
    Receiveth as the sea, nought enters there,
    Of what validity° and pitch° so e'er,   *value / intensity*
    But falls into abatement° and low price⁴   *depreciation*
    Even in a minute. So full of shapes is fancy,°   *imagination*
    That it alone is high fantastical.⁵   15
CURIO. Will you go hunt, my lord?
ORSINO.   What, Curio?

---

1   *surfeiting ... sicken* I.e., exceeding its need (for music), my desire might grow sick of it.
2   *That strain ... fall* He orders the musicians to repeat a melancholy falling cadence.
3   *violets* Considered an antidote for melancholy.
4   *notwithstanding ... low price* I.e., capacious like the sea, love receives all sensations, but
     no matter their excellence, love quickly devalues and tires of them.
5   *So full of ... high fantastical* I.e., imagination is so full of envisioned forms (of love) that
     it alone is supremely creative (compared with the other mental faculties of reason and
     memory).

CURIO.   The hart.

ORSINO. Why, so I do, the noblest that I have.[1]
O, when mine eyes did see Olivia first,
Methought she purged the air of pestilence.[2]
20 That instant was I turned into a hart,
And my desires, like fell° and cruel hounds,   *fierce*
E'er since pursue me.[3]

(*Enter Valentine.*)

How now, what news from her?

VALENTINE. So please my lord, I might not be admitted,[4]
25 But from her handmaid do return this answer:
The element° itself, till seven years' heat,°   *sky / summers*
Shall not behold her face at ample° view,   *full*
But like a cloistress° she will veilèd walk,   *cloistered nun*
And water once a day her chamber round
30 With eye-offending brine°—all this to season°   *tears / preserve*
A brother's dead love, which she would keep fresh
And lasting in her sad remembrance.
ORSINO. O, she that hath a heart of that fine frame°   *exquisite form*
To pay this debt of love but to a brother,
35 How will she love when the rich golden shaft°   *Cupid's arrow*
Hath killed the flock of all affections else[5]
That live in her—when liver, brain, and heart,
These sovereign thrones,[6] are all supplied and filled,
Her sweet perfections, with one selfsame king![7]
40 Away before me to sweet beds of flowers:
Love-thoughts lie rich when canopied with bowers.

(*Exeunt.*)

---

1   *hart ... I have* Punning on "hart" and "heart" (his noblest part).
2   *she purged ... pestilence* I.e., cleansed the air of plague (Renaissance medicine held that disease was propagated by noxious vapours).
3   *was I turned ... pursue me* In Ovid's *Metamorphoses*, after the hunter Actaeon sees Diana bathing, she turns him into a deer pursued by his own hounds.
4   *might not be admitted* I.e., was not allowed in (to see her).
5   *How will ... affections else* I.e., how much more might she love (me) when Cupid's arrow kills all other feelings.
6   *liver ... thrones* In Renaissance psychology, these organs were the respective seats ("thrones") of the faculties of passion, reason, and feeling.
7   *one selfsame king* I.e., myself as king (playing on "thrones"); in the First Folio, "one self king."

ACT 1, SCENE 2

(Enter Viola, a Captain, and Sailors.)

VIOLA. What country, friends, is this?
CAPTAIN.   This is Illyria, lady.
VIOLA. And what should I do in Illyria?
My brother he is in Elysium.[1]
Perchance° he is not drowned. What think you, sailors?   *Perhaps*
CAPTAIN. It is perchance° that you yourself were saved.   *by chance*   5
VIOLA. O my poor brother! And so perchance may he be.
CAPTAIN. True, madam, and to comfort you with chance,°   *possibility*
Assure yourself, after our ship did split,
When you, and those poor number saved with you,
Hung on our driving° boat, I saw your brother,   *drifting* 10
Most provident° in peril, bind himself—   *far-thinking*
Courage and hope both teaching him the practice—
To a strong mast that lived° upon the sea,   *floated*
Where, like Arion on the dolphin's back,
I saw him hold acquaintance with the waves[2]   15
So long as I could see.
VIOLA.   For saying so, there's gold. [*Gives him money.*]
Mine own escape unfoldeth to° my hope,   *encourages*
Whereto thy speech serves for authority,
The like of him.[3] Know'st thou this country?
CAPTAIN. Ay, madam, well, for I was bred and born   20
Not three hours' travel from this very place.
VIOLA. Who governs here?
CAPTAIN. A noble duke, in nature as in name.
VIOLA. What is his name?
CAPTAIN.   Orsino.
VIOLA. Orsino! I have heard my father name him.   25
He was a bachelor then.
CAPTAIN. And so is now, or was so very late,°   *recently*
For but a month ago I went from hence,
And then 'twas fresh in murmur°—as, you know,   *newly rumoured*
What great ones° do, the less° will prattle of—   *nobility / commoners* 30
That he did seek the love of fair Olivia.

---

1   *Elysium* In Greek mythology, the state or place of happiness after death.
2   *Arion ... waves* In Ovid's *Fasti*, the poet Arion escapes murder at sea by jumping over-
    board and playing his lyre for the dolphins, who bear him ashore.
3   *The like of him* I.e., that he also escaped alive.

VIOLA. What's she?[1]

CAPTAIN. A virtuous maid, the daughter of a count
That died some twelvemonth since, then leaving her
35   In the protection of his son, her brother,
Who shortly also died, for whose dear love,
They say, she hath abjured° the sight   *renounced*
And company of men.[2]

VIOLA.   O that I served that lady,
And might not be delivered° to the world   *revealed*
40   Till I had made mine own occasion mellow°   *ripen*
What my estate is.[3]

CAPTAIN.   That were hard to compass,°   *bring about*
Because she will admit no kind of suit,
No, not° the Duke's.   *not even*

VIOLA. There is a fair behaviour° in thee, Captain,   *conduct*
45   And though that nature with a beauteous wall
Doth oft close in pollution,[4] yet of thee
I will believe thou hast a mind that suits
With this thy fair and outward character.°   *appearance*
I prithee°—and I'll pay thee bounteously—   *pray thee*
50   Conceal me what I am,[5] and be my aid
For such disguise as haply shall become°   *suit*
The form of my intent.[6] I'll serve this duke.
Thou shalt present me as an eunuch[7] to him.
It may be worth thy pains, for I can sing,
55   And speak to him in many sorts of music
That will allow° me very worth his service.   *prove*
What else may hap,° to time I will commit,   *happen*
Only shape thou thy silence to my wit.[8]

---

1   *What's she?* I.e., what is her rank and situation?
2   *the sight / And company of men* Some editors alter the First Folio text to read "the com-
     pany / And sight of men."
3   *Till I … estate is* I.e., until I determined the time was right to reveal my rank.
4   *a beauteous wall … pollution* I.e., a wall of beauty often encloses a corrupt nature.
5   *Conceal me what I am* I.e., do not reveal that I am a woman.
6   *form of my intent* I.e., shape of my strategy (and her male appearance).
7   *eunuch* Castrato, a castrated male soprano, which explains "I can sing." But Viola never
     sings and is disguised as a page, leading some editors to argue that the text was revised but
     retains unresolved inconsistencies.
8   *shape thou … my wit* I.e., be prepared to keep quiet where my ingenuity requires
     it; *wit* Mental agility (associated with verbal skill and improvisation).

CAPTAIN. Be you his eunuch, and your mute¹ I'll be.

When my tongue blabs, then let mine eyes not see.²   60

VIOLA. I thank thee. Lead me on.

  (*Exeunt.*)

ACT 1, SCENE 3

(Enter Sir Toby [Belch] and Maria.)

SIR TOBY. What a plague³ means my niece to take the death of her brother
  thus? I am sure care's an enemy to life.⁴

MARIA. By my troth,⁵ Sir Toby, you must come in earlier a-nights. Your
  cousin, my lady, takes great exceptions to your ill⁶ hours.

SIR TOBY. Why, let her except, before excepted.⁷   5

MARIA. Ay, but you must confine yourself within the modest limits of order.

SIR TOBY. Confine? I'll confine myself no finer than I am.⁸ These clothes are
  good enough to drink in, and so be these boots too; an⁹ they be not, let
  them hang themselves in their own straps.

MARIA. That quaffing and drinking will undo you. I heard my lady talk of   10
  it yesterday, and of a foolish knight that you brought in one night here to
  be her wooer.

SIR TOBY. Who, Sir Andrew Aguecheek?¹⁰

MARIA. Ay, he.

SIR TOBY. He's as tall¹¹ a man as any's in Illyria.   15

MARIA. What's that to the purpose?

SIR TOBY. Why, he has three thousand ducats a year.

MARIA. Ay, but he'll have but a year in all these ducats.¹² He's a very fool and
  a prodigal.¹³

---

1   *your mute* Tongueless servant (mutes attended eunuchs who guarded Turkish harems).
2   *When my ... not see* I.e., if I betray you, blind me.
3   *What a plague* Equivalent to "what the devil."
4   *care's an enemy to life* I.e., excessive mourning will drive her to an early grave.
5   *By my troth* I.e., by my faith (a mild oath).
6   *ill* Late.
7   *except ... excepted* I.e., make whatever exceptions (playing on Latin legal jargon, *exceptis excipiendis*, "except for the previously mentioned exceptions").
8   *I'll confine ... I am* I.e., not restrain myself with any more social refinement than is natural to me (literally, bind my figure no thinner).
9   *an* If.
10   *Aguecheek* Suggesting a pale, lean complexion from an ague (fever).
11   *tall* Worthy, but taken literally.
12   *he'll have ... ducats* I.e., he'll soon be broke.
13   *prodigal* Spendthrift.

20 SIR TOBY. Fie that you'll say so! He plays o' the viol-de-gamboys,[1] and speaks three or four languages word for word without book,[2] and hath all the good gifts[3] of nature.

MARIA. He hath indeed, almost natural,[4] for besides that he's a fool, he's a great quarreller, and but that he hath the gift of a coward to allay the gust[5]

25   he hath in quarrelling, 'tis thought among the prudent he would quickly have the gift of a grave.[6]

SIR TOBY. By this hand, they are scoundrels and substractors[7] that say so of him. Who are they?

MARIA. They that add,[8] moreover, he's drunk nightly in your company.

30 SIR TOBY. With drinking healths to my niece; I'll drink to her as long as there is a passage in my throat and drink in Illyria. He's a coward and a coystrill[9] that will not drink to my niece till his brains turn o' the toe like a parish-top.[10] What wench, *Castiliano vulgo*![11] for here comes Sir Andrew Agueface.

(*Enter Sir Andrew [Aguecheek]*.)

SIR ANDREW. Sir Toby Belch! How now, Sir Toby Belch!

35 SIR TOBY. Sweet Sir Andrew.

SIR ANDREW. Bless you, fair shrew.[12]

MARIA. And you too, sir.

SIR TOBY. Accost, Sir Andrew, accost.[13]

SIR ANDREW. What's[14] that?

40 SIR TOBY. My niece's chambermaid.[15]

---

1   *viol-de-gamboys* Viola da gamba, a bass viol held between the legs (with an innuendo on "gamboys").

2   *without book* By memory.

3   *gifts* Talents.

4   *almost natural* I.e., nearly a born simpleton.

5   *gust* Appetite.

6   *but that he ... a grave* I.e., if he were not such a coward his habit of picking fights would earn him a quick death.

7   *substractors* Detractors, slanderers (a tipsy malapropism). "Substract" is an archaic form of "subtract."

8   *add* Playing on "substract."

9   *coystrill* Low fellow (literally, a horse groom).

10   *parish-top* Large top spun with a whip, provided by parishes for exercise and entertainment.

11   *Castiliano vulgo* Equivalent to "speak of the devil" (although the derivation is uncertain, the phrase perhaps means "base Castilian" and draws upon popular stereotypes of evil Spaniards).

12   *shrew* Woman, a generic use intended as a compliment (otherwise meaning "scold").

13   *accost* Address courteously or woo; originally, a naval term for "go alongside."

14   *What's* Who is.

15   *chambermaid* Lady-in-waiting.

SIR ANDREW. Good Mistress Accost, I desire better acquaintance.

MARIA. My name is Mary, sir.

SIR ANDREW. Good Mistress Mary Accost—

SIR TOBY. You mistake, knight. "Accost" is front her, board her, woo her, assail her.[1]   45

SIR ANDREW. By my troth, I would not undertake her[2] in this company. Is
that the meaning of "accost?"

MARIA. Fare you well, gentlemen. [*leaving*]

SIR TOBY. An thou let part so,[3] Sir Andrew, would thou mightst never draw
sword[4] again.   50

SIR ANDREW. An you part so, mistress, I would I might never draw sword
again. Fair lady, do you think you have fools in hand?[5]

MARIA. Sir, I have not you by the hand.

SIR ANDREW. Marry, but you shall have, and here's my hand.

MARIA. [*taking his hand*] Now, sir, thought is free.[6] I pray you, bring your   55
hand to th' buttery-bar[7] and let it drink.

SIR ANDREW. Wherefore, sweetheart? What's your metaphor?[8]

MARIA. It's dry,[9] sir.

SIR ANDREW. Why, I think so. I am not such an ass but I can keep my hand
dry.[10] But what's your jest?   60

MARIA. A dry jest,[11] sir.

SIR ANDREW. Are you full of them?

MARIA. Ay, sir, I have them at my fingers' ends;[12] marry, now I let go your
hand, I am barren.[13]

(*Exit Maria.*)

1   *front her ... assail her* Naval terms of battle (each with innuendo).
2   *undertake her* I.e., take her on (with innuendo).
3   *An thou let part so* I.e., if you let her part like this (without "accosting" her).
4   *draw sword* I.e., be gentlemanly.
5   *fools in hand* I.e., are dealing with fools.
6   *thought is free* Proverbial answer to "do you think I'm a fool?"
7   *buttery-bar* Shelf formed by the open hatch to a butter (or bottle) room (in performance,
she would bring his hand to her breasts).
8   *What's your metaphor* I.e., what does a drinking hand signify?
9   *dry* Thirsty (but also weak or impotent).
10 *an ass ... hand dry* A proverbial response, as in "any fool can keep his head dry."
11 *dry jest* I.e., foolish joke (a joke for a fool).
12 *at my fingers' ends* I.e., always ready (literally, "by the hand").
13 *barren* I.e., empty of jokes (playing on "full," also meaning "pregnant").

65 SIR TOBY. O knight, thou lack'st a cup of canary![1] When did I see thee so put down?[2]

SIR ANDREW. Never in your life, I think, unless you see canary put me down.[3] Methinks sometimes I have no more wit than a Christian[4] or an ordinary man has, but I am a great eater of beef, and I believe that does harm to my wit.[5]

70 SIR TOBY. No question.

SIR ANDREW. An I thought that, I'd forswear it.[6] I'll ride home tomorrow, Sir Toby.

SIR TOBY. *Pourquoi*,[7] my dear knight?

SIR ANDREW. What is "pourquoi?" Do, or not do? I would I had bestowed
75 that time in the tongues[8] that I have in fencing, dancing, and bear-baiting. Oh, had I but followed the arts![9]

SIR TOBY. Then hadst thou had an excellent head of hair.[10]

SIR ANDREW. Why, would that have mended my hair?

SIR TOBY. Past question,[11] for thou seest it will not curl by nature.[12]

80 SIR ANDREW. But it becomes me well enough, does't not?

SIR TOBY. Excellent. It hangs like flax on a distaff,[13] and I hope to see a housewife take thee between her legs and spin it off.[14]

SIR ANDREW. Faith, I'll home to-morrow, Sir Toby. Your niece will not be seen, or if she be, it's four to one she'll none of me. The Count[15] himself
85 here hard by[16] woos her.

---

1   *canary* Sweet wine from the Canary Islands.
2   *so put down* Dejected.
3   *put me down* I.e., make me pass out.
4   *Christian* Common.
5   *great eater … to my wit* Renaissance dietary manuals cautioned that beef made the intellect sluggish.
6   *An I … forswear it* I.e., if I really believed that, I'd swear off beef.
7   *Pourquoi* French: why.
8   *tongues* Languages.
9   *the arts* Liberal arts.
10 *excellent head of hair* Punning on "tongues" (pronounced "tongs") and "curling-tongs."
11 *Past question* Without a doubt.
12 *nature* Playing off *the arts*.
13 *flax on a distaff* Straw-coloured fibre spun (usually by a housewife) on a cleft pole held between the knees; *flax* Flaxen hair was thought to indicate cowardice and anger; *distaff* Woman's work, a wife's duties.
14 *housewife … spin it off* In the First Folio "huswife," suggesting "hussy" or "prostitute"; *spin it off* Make you lose your hair (thought to be a symptom of venereal disease).
15 *Count* Orsino is consistently called a duke in stage directions and speech headings, but in the text he is called a duke only in the first two scenes and in 1.4.1, after which he is always called a count. This inconsistency might be due to scribal errors, but may also reflect Shakespeare's habit of making counts young lovers and dukes older men of authority (Orsino combines both).
16 *hard by* Nearby.

SIR TOBY. She'll none o' the Count. She'll not match above her degree, neither in estate, years, nor wit,[1] I have heard her swear't. Tut, there's life in't,[2]
man.

SIR ANDREW. I'll stay a month longer. I am a fellow o' th' strangest mind in
the world. I delight in masques and revels sometimes altogether.[3]   90

SIR TOBY. Art thou good at these kickshawses,[4] knight?

SIR ANDREW. As any man in Illyria, whatsoever he be, under the degree of
my betters; and yet I will not compare with an old man.[5]

SIR TOBY. What is thy excellence in a galliard,[6] knight?

SIR ANDREW. Faith, I can cut a caper.[7]   95

SIR TOBY. And I can cut the mutton[8] to't.

SIR ANDREW. And I think I have the back-trick[9] simply as strong as any man
in Illyria.

SIR TOBY. Wherefore are these things hid? Wherefore have these gifts a curtain before 'em? Are they like to take dust, like Mistress Mall's[10] picture?   100
Why dost thou not go to church in a galliard and come home in a coranto?[11]
My very walk should be a jig. I would not so much as make water[12] but
in a sink-a-pace.[13] What dost thou mean? Is it a world to hide virtues in? I

---

1   *She'll not match ... wit* She won't marry above her rank, age, or education (Olivia is a coun-
     tess, so Orsino's actual rank must be higher).

2   *there's life in't* Proverbial: "While there is life, there is hope."

3   *masques and revels* Courtly entertainments featuring dancing; *altogether* In all respects.

4   *kickshawses* Dainty dishes (referring to dances), trifles; a corruption of the French *quelque
     chose*, "something."

5   *any man ... old man* I.e., any man who is not above me in rank; but I don't compare to
     an expert (suggesting Toby's experience, but also his age).

6   *galliard* Lively five-step dance in triple time.

7   *caper* Leap before the fifth step in a *galliard*, but also a delicacy used in a sauce for mut-
     ton.

8   *mutton* Slang for prostitute.

9   *back-trick* Back-step in the *galliard*.

10   *Mistress Mall's* Like *Moll*, *Mall* was a nickname for Mary, and here is probably used
     generically as an example of a woman's portrait. At this time, *Moll* is also beginning to
     signify a disgraced woman, especially a prostitute, and many candidates have been pro-
     posed for this allusion, ranging from Olivia's lady-in-waiting, Maria, to Mary Frith (also
     known as Moll Cutpurse), a cross-dressing purse thief first arrested in 1600 and sensa-
     tionalized in Thomas Dekker and Thomas Middleton's play *The Roaring Girl* (1611). In
     combination with *go to church in a galliard*, this may also be a mocking reference to the
     Puritan disapproval of idolatrous images (such as the Virgin Mary) as well as dancing
     and plays.

11   *coranto* Running dance.

12   *make water* Urinate.

13   *sink-a-pace* Cinque pace, a "five-step" dance equivalent to a *galliard* (punning on *sink*,
     sewer).

did think, by the excellent constitution of thy leg, it was formed under the
105   star[1] of a galliard.

SIR ANDREW.   Ay, 'tis strong, and it does indifferent[2] well in dun-coloured
stock.[3] Shall we set about some revels?

SIR TOBY.   What shall we do else? Were we not born under Taurus?

SIR ANDREW.   Taurus? That's sides and heart.

110   SIR TOBY.   No, sir; it is legs and thighs.[4] Let me see the caper. Ha, higher! Ha,
ha, excellent.

(*Exeunt.*)

ACT 1, SCENE 4

(*Enter Valentine, and Viola in man's attire.*)

VALENTINE.   If the Duke continue these favours towards you, Cesario,[5] you
are like to be much advanced.[6] He hath known you but three days,[7] and
already you are no stranger.

VIOLA.   You either fear his humour[8] or my negligence, that you call in ques-
5   tion the continuance of his love. Is he inconstant, sir, in his favours?

VALENTINE.   No, believe me.

(*Enter [Orsino], Curio, and Attendants.*)

VIOLA.   I thank you. Here comes the Count.

ORSINO.   Who saw Cesario, ho?

VIOLA.   On your attendance,° my lord, here.   *at your service*

10   ORSINO.   [*to Curio and Attendants*] Stand you awhile aloof. Cesario,
Thou know'st no less but all.° I have unclasped   *than everything*
To thee[9] the book even of my secret soul.°   *private feelings*
Therefore, good youth, address thy gait[10] unto her.

---

1   *star* Astrological sign.

2   *does indifferent* Does tolerably.

3   *dun-coloured stock* Beige stockings. In the First Folio "dam'd coloured"; some editors substitute "flame-" or "divers-coloured."

4   *born under Taurus ... and thighs* Renaissance anatomy charts assigned the zodiac to parts
of the body; Taurus the bull governed the throat (i.e., a sign for drinkers).

5   *Cesario* Viola's adopted name.

6   *advanced* Promoted.

7   *but three days* This line introduces a double-time problem, for in 5.1.88 three months are
said to have elapsed in the same time-frame as Viola's service to Orsino.

8   *fear his humour* Doubt his character (implying he is "inconstant").

9   *Thou know'st ... To thee* Orsino uses the familiar forms *thou* and *thee*.

10   *address thy gait* Direct your steps.

Be not denied access, stand at her doors,
And tell them there thy fixèd foot shall grow°   take root   15
Till thou have audience.

VIOLA.   Sure,° my noble lord,   But
If she be so abandoned° to her sorrow   given up
As it is spoke, she never will admit me.

ORSINO. Be clamorous and leap all civil bounds,[1]
Rather than make unprofited° return.   unsuccessful   20

VIOLA. Say I do speak with her, my lord, what then?

ORSINO. O, then unfold° the passion of my love,   display
Surprise[2] her with discourse of my dear faith.
It shall become thee well[3] to act my woes,
She will attend it better in thy youth   25
Than in a nuncio's° of more grave aspect.°   messenger's / appearance

VIOLA. I think not so, my lord.

ORSINO.   Dear lad, believe it,
For they shall yet° belie thy happy years°   as yet / youth
That say thou art a man: Diana's lip
Is not more smooth and rubious;° thy small pipe°   ruby red / voice   30
Is as the maiden's organ, shrill° and sound,°   high / unbroken
And all is semblative a woman's part.[4]
I know thy constellation[5] is right apt
For this affair. [*to Curio and Attendants*] Some four or five attend him—
All, if you will, for I myself am best   35
When least in company. Prosper well° in this,   succeed
And thou shalt live as freely° as thy lord,   independently
To call his fortunes thine.

VIOLA.   I'll do my best
To woo your lady. [*aside*] Yet, a barful strife[6]—
Whoe'er I woo, myself would be his wife.   40

1   *leap all civil bounds* I.e., disregard all constraints of politeness.
2   *Surprise* Capture unawares (a military term).
3   *become thee well* I.e., suit your strategy best.
4   *semblative a woman's part* Resembling a woman's voice (or acting role).
5   *constellation* Character and ability (thought to be predetermined by astrology).
6   *barful strife* Conflict full of obstacles ("bars").

ACT 1, SCENE 5

(*Enter Maria and* [*Feste,*[1] *a*] *clown.*)

MARIA. Nay, either tell me where thou hast been, or I will not open my lips so wide as a bristle may enter in way[2] of thy excuse. My lady will hang thee for thy absence.

FESTE. Let her hang me. He that is well hanged in this world needs to fear
5   no colours.[3]

MARIA. Make that good.[4]

FESTE. He shall see none to fear.

MARIA. A good lenten[5] answer. I can tell thee where that saying was born, of "I fear no colours."

10 FESTE. Where, good Mistress Mary?

MARIA. In the wars, and that[6] may you be bold to say in your foolery.

FESTE. Well, God give them wisdom that have it, and those that are fools, let them use their talents.[7]

MARIA. Yet you will be hanged for being so long absent, or to be turned
15   away[8]—is not that as good as a hanging to you?

FESTE. Many a good hanging prevents a bad marriage;[9] and for turning away, let summer bear it out.[10]

MARIA. You are resolute, then?

FESTE. Not so, neither; but I am resolved on two points.[11]

20 MARIA. That if one break, the other will hold; or if both break, your gaskins[12] fall.

FESTE. Apt, in good faith, very apt. Well, go thy way. If Sir Toby would leave drinking, thou wert as witty a piece of Eve's flesh[13] as any in Illyria.

---

1   *Feste* Pronounced "fest-ay," from the Latin or Italian *festa*, "festival."

2   *in way* By way.

3   *He that ... fear no colours* Proverbial: "only the dead have no one to fear"; *colours* Military flags (punning on "collars," hangman's nooses).

4   *Make that good* Explain that.

5   *lenten* Meagre (Lent is a time of fasting).

6   *that* Referring to either "in the wars" or "fear no colours" (i.e., he should be clearer and braver).

7   *God give ... their talents* I.e., let the wise make the most of their wisdom, and fools the most of their comic talents (paraphrasing the parable of the talents in Matthew 25.29).

8   *turned away* Dismissed.

9   *Many a good ... bad marriage* Proverbial: "better to be half hanged than badly married" (with innuendo on "good hanging").

10 *bear it out* Make it endurable; masterless men were considered vagabonds by law and were either imprisoned or forced into homeless wandering.

11 *points* Matters, but also laces that tied breeches to a doublet.

12 *gaskins* Wide breeches.

13 *If Sir Toby ... Eve's flesh* I.e., if Toby were sober, he'd appreciate what a clever woman you are.

MARIA. Peace, you rogue, no more o' that. Here comes my lady. Make your
excuse wisely, you were best.[1]   25

[*Exit.*]

(*Enter Lady Olivia, with Malvolio[2] [and Attendants.*])

FESTE. Wit, an't be thy will,[3] put me into good fooling![4] Those wits that think
they have[5] thee do very oft prove fools, and I that am sure I lack[6] thee may
pass for a wise man. For what says Quinapalus?[7] "Better a witty fool than
a foolish wit." God bless thee, lady.

OLIVIA. Take the fool away.   30

FESTE. Do you not hear, fellows? Take away the lady.

OLIVIA. Go to,[8] y'are a dry[9] fool. I'll no more of you. Besides, you grow
dishonest.[10]

FESTE. Two faults, madonna,[11] that drink and good counsel will amend, for
give the dry fool drink, then is the fool not dry.[12] Bid the dishonest man   35
mend[13] himself: if he mend, he is no longer dishonest; if he cannot, let
the botcher[14] mend him. Anything that's mended is but patched,[15] virtue
that transgresses is but patched with sin, and sin that amends is but
patched with virtue. If that this simple syllogism[16] will serve, so. If it will
not, what remedy? As there is no true cuckold but calamity, so beauty's   40
a flower.[17] The lady bade take away the fool, therefore I say again, take
her away.

OLIVIA. Sir, I bade them take away you.

---

1   *you were best* I.e., if you know what's best.
2   *Malvolio* "Ill-will," from Italian *mal* (bad) and *voglia* (desire).
3   *will* Desire.
4   *Wit, an't be ... good fooling* Mock invocation of his muse, the spirit of ingenuity, to inspire his performance.
5   *have* Outwit.
6   *lack* Fall short of.
7   *Quinapalus* Nonsense classical authority.
8   *Go to* Enough.
9   *dry* Empty.
10 *dishonest* Unfaithful.
11 *madonna* My lady.
12 *dry* Thirsty.
13 *mend* Reform.
14 *botcher* Clothes mender.
15 *patched* Imperfect, but alluding to fools' costumes, which were sewn from mismatched
cloth.
16 *syllogism* Logical argument from two claims (here, regarding "virtue" and "sin").
17 *no true ... a flower* I.e., nothing less faithful than calamity (if you are wedded to it), so
beauty will fade (by the time Olivia is done mourning).

FESTE. Misprision[1] in the highest degree! Lady, "*Cucullus non facit monach-*
45   *um*";[2] that's as much to say as I wear not motley[3] in my brain. Good madonna, give me leave to prove you a fool.

OLIVIA. Can you do it?

FESTE. Dexteriously,[4] good madonna.

OLIVIA. Make your proof.

50   FESTE. I must catechize[5] you for it, madonna. Good my mouse[6] of virtue,
answer me.

OLIVIA. Well, sir, for want of other idleness, I'll bide[7] your proof.

FESTE. Good madonna, why mourn'st thou?

OLIVIA. Good fool, for my brother's death.

55   FESTE. I think his soul is in hell, madonna.

OLIVIA. I know his soul is in heaven, fool.

FESTE. The more fool, madonna, to mourn for your brother's soul, being in
heaven. Take away the fool, gentlemen.

OLIVIA. What think you of this fool, Malvolio? Doth he not mend?[8]

60   MALVOLIO. Yes, and shall do, till the pangs of death shake him. Infirmity,[9]
that decays the wise, doth ever make the better fool.

FESTE. God send you, sir, a speedy infirmity,[10] for the better increasing your
folly. Sir Toby will be sworn that I am no fox, but he will not pass[11] his word
for twopence that you are no fool.[12]

65   OLIVIA. How say you to that, Malvolio?

MALVOLIO. I marvel your ladyship takes delight in such a barren rascal. I
saw him put down the other day with an ordinary fool[13] that has no more
brain than a stone. Look you now, he's out of his guard[14] already. Unless
you laugh and minister[15] occasion to him, he is gagged. I protest I take

---

1   *Misprision* Misunderstanding, wrongful arrest.
2   *Cucullus non facit monachum* Latin: the cowl does not make the monk.
3   *motley* Many-coloured ("patched") costume worn by fools.
4   *Dexteriously* Dextrously.
5   *catechize you* Question you; the Catechism tested the orthodoxy of one's faith through a
     series of formal questions and answers.
6   *Good my mouse* My good mouse (a term of endearment).
7   *idleness* Pastime; *bide* Endure.
8   *mend* I.e., improve his fooling.
9   *Infirmity* Senility.
10   *speedy infirmity* Playing on "speedy recovery."
11   *pass* Give.
12   *no fox ... no fool* I.e., not cunning, but he won't swear you aren't sly.
13   *ordinary fool* Common fool, but also a fool who frequents an ordinary, a commoners'
     tavern (alluding to a popular tavern-fool named Stone).
14   *out of his guard* Off guard.
15   *minister* Provide.

these wise men that crow so at these set[1] kind of fools no better than the   70
fools' zanies.[2]

OLIVIA. O, you are sick of[3] self-love, Malvolio, and taste with a distempered[4]
appetite. To be generous, guiltless, and of free disposition, is to take those
things for bird-bolts that you deem cannon bullets.[5] There is no slander in
an allowed fool, though he do nothing but rail, nor no railing in known   75
discreet man, though he do nothing but reprove.[6]

FESTE. Now Mercury endue thee with leasing,[7] for thou speak'st well of fools.

([*Re-*]*enter Maria.*)

MARIA. Madam, there is at the gate a young gentleman much[8] desires to
speak with you.

OLIVIA. From the Count Orsino, is it?   80

MARIA. I know not, madam. 'Tis a fair young man, and well attended.

OLIVIA. Who of my people hold him in delay?

MARIA. Sir Toby, madam, your kinsman.

OLIVIA. Fetch him off, I pray you, he speaks nothing but madman.[9] Fie on
him. [*Exit Maria.*] Go you, Malvolio; if it be a suit from the Count, I am   85
sick, or not at home—what you will[10] to dismiss it. (*Exit Malvolio.*) Now
you see, sir, how your fooling grows old, and people dislike it.

FESTE. Thou hast spoke for us, madonna, as if thy eldest son should be a
fool,[11] whose skull Jove cram with brains, for—here he comes—

(*Enter Sir Toby.*)

one of thy kin has a most weak *pia mater*.[12]   90

OLIVIA. By mine honour, half drunk. What is he[13] at the gate, cousin?

SIR TOBY. A gentleman.

---

1   *set* Rehearsed.

2   *zanies* Buffoons, from Italian *zanni*: comic sidekicks in *commedia dell'arte*.

3   *of* From.

4   *distempered* Unhealthy.

5   *to take those things … cannon bullets* I.e., to be optimistic where you are pessimistic; *bird-bolts* Blunt crossbow arrows for birding.

6   *no slander … nothing but reprove* Fools traditionally had licence to reprove their masters while stewards were trusted to regulate a household by maintaining decorum among its members.

7   *leasing* Lying (Mercury was the god of deception).

8   *much* Who much.

9   *nothing but madman* Madman's talk.

10   *what you will* Do whatever you like.

11   *thy eldest … a fool* Playing on the parable "a wise man has a foolish son."

12   *pia mater* Latin: brain (literally "tender mother").

13   *What is he* I.e., what is his rank and situation.

OLIVIA. A gentleman? What gentleman?

SIR TOBY. 'Tis a gentleman here. [*Belches.*] A plague o' these pickle-herring!
95   How now, sot!¹

FESTE. Good Sir Toby.

OLIVIA. Cousin, cousin, how have you come so early by this lethargy?²

SIR TOBY. Lechery? I defy lechery. There's one at the gate.³

OLIVIA. Ay, marry,⁴ what is he?

100 SIR TOBY. Let him be the devil an he will, I care not. Give me faith, say I.
Well, it's all one.⁵ (*Exit.*)

OLIVIA. What's a drunken man like, fool?

FESTE. Like a drowned man, a fool, and a madman: one draught above heat⁶
makes him a fool; the second mads him; and a third drowns him.

105 OLIVIA. Go thou and seek the crowner, and let him sit o' my coz⁷ for he's in
the third degree of drink, he's drowned. Go look after him.

FESTE. He is but mad yet, madonna, and the fool shall look to the madman.
[*Exit.*]

(*Enter Malvolio.*)

MALVOLIO. Madam, yond young fellow swears he will speak with you. I told
him you were sick. He takes on him⁸ to understand so much, and therefore
110 comes to speak with you. I told him you were asleep, he seems to have a
foreknowledge of that too, and therefore comes to speak with you. What is
to be said to him, lady? He's fortified against any denial.

OLIVIA. Tell him he shall not speak with me.

MALVOLIO. H'as⁹ been told so, and he says he'll stand at your door like a
115 sheriff's post,¹⁰ and be the supporter¹¹ to a bench, but he'll speak with you.

OLIVIA. What kind o' man is he?

MALVOLIO. Why, of mankind.¹²

---

1   *sot* Fool.
2   *lethargy* Drunken stupor.
3   *There's one at the gate* He resumes announcing the visitor.
4   *marry* Indeed.
5   *Give me faith ... it's all one* Toby winks at two controversies of Reformation faith, the
Protestant doctrine of salvation by faith (not works), and the theory that some theological
debates were indifferent (or "all one") and thus inessential to salvation.
6   *above heat* I.e., beyond normal body temperature; wine was thought to alter personality
by heating the body beyond its temperate state.
7   *crowner ... my coz* Coroner, and let him hold an inquest for my cousin.
8   *takes on him* Claims.
9   *H'as* He has.
10 *sheriff's post* Decorative post placed before the houses of mayors and sheriffs.
11 *supporter* Support.
12 *of mankind* I.e., an ordinary man.

OLIVIA. What manner of man?

MALVOLIO. Of very ill manner—he'll speak with you, will you or no.

OLIVIA. Of what personage and years is he?   120

MALVOLIO. Not yet old enough for a man, nor young enough for a boy, as a squash is before 'tis a peascod, or a codling[1] when 'tis almost an apple. 'Tis with him in standing water,[2] between boy and man. He is very well-favoured,[3] and he speaks very shrewishly.[4] One would think his mother's milk were scarce out of him.[5]   125

OLIVIA. Let him approach. Call in my gentlewoman.

MALVOLIO. Gentlewoman, my lady calls.

(*Exit.*)

(*Enter Maria.*)

OLIVIA. Give me my veil; come, throw it o'er my face.
We'll once more hear Orsino's embassy.[6]

(*Enter [Viola as Cesario.]*)

VIOLA. The honourable lady of the house, which is she?   130

OLIVIA. Speak to me, I shall answer for her. Your will?

VIOLA. Most radiant, exquisite, and unmatchable beauty—[*to Maria*] I pray you tell me if this be the lady of the house, for I never saw her. I would be loath to cast away my speech, for besides that it is excellently well penned, I have taken great pains to con[7] it. Good beauties, let me sustain no scorn; 135 I am very comptible, even to the least sinister usage.[8]

OLIVIA. Whence came you, sir?

VIOLA. I can say little more than I have studied,[9] and that question's out of my part. Good gentle one, give me modest assurance if you be the lady of the house, that I may proceed in my speech.   140

OLIVIA. Are you a comedian?[10]

---

1   *squash* Undeveloped peapod ("peascod");   *codling* Unripe apple.
2   *in standing water* I.e., like the turning tide, midway.
3   *well-favoured* Attractive.
4   *shrewishly* I.e., in a squeaky voice (like a shrew).
5   *mother's milk … him* Barely weaned (proverbial).
6   *embassy* Message.
7   *con* Memorize.
8   *let me sustain … sinister usage* I.e., do not scorn me; I am sensitive, even to the slightest rudeness (addressing Maria and attendants).
9   *than I have studied* I.e., other than what I have rehearsed ("my part").
10   *comedian* Actor.

VIOLA. No, my profound heart;[1] and yet—by the very fangs of malice[2] I swear—I am not that[3] I play. Are you the lady of the house?

OLIVIA. If I do not usurp[4] myself, I am.

145 VIOLA. Most certain, if you are she, you do usurp yourself, for what is yours to bestow is not yours to reserve. But this is from[5] my commission. I will on with my speech in your praise, and then show you the heart of my message.

OLIVIA. Come to what is important in't. I forgive you[6] the praise.

150 VIOLA. Alas, I took great pains to study it, and 'tis poetical.

OLIVIA. It is[7] the more like to be feigned,[8] I pray you keep it in.[9] I heard you were saucy[10] at my gates, and allowed your approach rather to wonder at you than to hear you. If you be mad,[11] be gone. If you have reason, be brief. 'Tis not that time of moon with me to make one in so skipping a

155 dialogue.[12]

MARIA. Will you hoist sail, sir? Here lies your way.

VIOLA. No, good swabber, I am to hull[13] here a little longer. [to Olivia] Some mollification for your giant,[14] sweet lady.

OLIVIA. Tell me your mind.[15]

160 VIOLA. I am a messenger.

OLIVIA. Sure, you have some hideous matter to deliver, when the courtesy[16] of it is so fearful. Speak your office.

---

1   *my profound heart* By my soul.
2   *very fangs of malice* Equivalent to "all that is evil" (a strong oath).
3   *that* The character.
4   *usurp* Misrepresent.
5   *from* Not in.
6   *forgive you* Excuse.
7   *It is* As it is.
8   *and 'tis poetical … feigned* Lyrical and dramatic poetry were considered fiction (unlike history or philosophy), and Renaissance critics of imaginative literature suspected that eloquent ("poetical") language misrepresented ("feigned") truth.
9   *in* To yourself.
10 *saucy* Insolent.
11 *be mad* In the First Folio, "be not mad" (likely a scribal error).
12 *time of moon … skipping a dialogue* I.e., phase of the moon (thought to create lunacy) that I would indulge you in aimless conversation.
13 *hoist sail* Nautical term meaning "leave port"; *swabber* Seaman who cleans the deck; *to hull* To remain at anchor.
14 *Some mollification … giant* I.e., please pacify your protector; *giant* Alluding to legendary giants who protected ladies (and to Maria's small size).
15 *mind* Message.
16 *courtesy* Polite preamble.

VIOLA. It alone concerns your ear. I bring no overture of war, no taxation of
    homage.[1] I hold the olive[2] in my hand. My words are as full of peace as
    matter.   165
OLIVIA. Yet you began rudely. What are you? What would you?
VIOLA. The rudeness that hath appeared in me have I learned from my enter-
    tainment.[3] What I am and what I would are as secret as maidenhead[4]—to
    your ears, divinity;[5] to any other's, profanation.
OLIVIA. Give us the place alone. We will hear this divinity.   170

    [*Exit Maria and Attendants.*]

    Now, sir, what is your text?
VIOLA. Most sweet lady—
OLIVIA. A comfortable[6] doctrine, and much may be said of it. Where lies
    your text?
VIOLA. In Orsino's bosom.   175
OLIVIA. In his bosom? In what chapter of his bosom?
VIOLA. To answer by the method,[7] in the first of his heart.
OLIVIA. O, I have read it. It is heresy. Have you no more to say?
VIOLA. Good madam, let me see your face.
OLIVIA. Have you any commission from your lord to negotiate with my face?   180
    You are now out of[8] your text, but we will draw the curtain and show you
    the picture.[9] [*unveiling*] Look you, sir, such a one I was this present.[10] Is't
    not well done?
VIOLA. Excellently done, if God did all.[11]
OLIVIA. 'Tis in grain, sir, 'twill endure wind and weather.   185
VIOLA. 'Tis beauty truly blent, whose red and white
    Nature's own sweet and cunning hand laid on.[12]
    Lady, you are the cruell'st she° alive,   *woman*

---

1   *overture ... homage* Declaration of war, demand for tribute.
2   *olive* Olive branch (of peace).
3   *entertainment* Reception.
4   *maidenhead* Virginity.
5   *your ears, divinity* I.e., heaven to your ears; love as a secular religion is played upon in
    religious terminology in the lines that follow: "text" (a biblical theme for a sermon), "doc-
    trine" (established belief), and "heresy" (belief against doctrine).
6   *comfortable* Comforting.
7   *by the method* In the same style.
8   *out of* Digressing from.
9   *picture* Portrait; the theme of portraiture is taken up in painting terms in the lines that
    follow: "in grain" (indelible), "blent" (blended), "laid on," and "copy."
10 *this present* Just now.
11 *if God did all* I.e., if your beauty is yours by nature (not painted by art).
12 *'Tis beauty ... laid on* See Shakespeare's Sonnet 20, lines 1–2.

If you will lead these graces to the grave,
190   And leave the world no copy.[1]

OLIVIA.   O, sir, I will not be so hard-hearted. I will give out divers schedules[2]
of my beauty. It shall be inventoried, and every particle and utensil labelled
to my will: as, *item*,[3] two lips indifferent[4] red; *item*, two grey eyes with lids
to them; *item*, one neck, one chin, and so forth. Were you sent hither to
195   praise me?

VIOLA.   I see you what you are. You are too proud;
But, if° you were the devil, you are fair.   *even if*
My lord and master loves you. O, such love
Could be but recompensed, though[5] you were crowned
The nonpareil[6] of beauty!

200   OLIVIA.   How does he love me?

VIOLA.   With adorations, fertile° tears,   *abundant*
With groans that thunder love, with sighs of fire.

OLIVIA.   Your lord does know my mind—I cannot love him.
Yet I suppose him virtuous, know him noble,
205   Of great estate, of fresh and stainless° youth,   *uncorrupted*
In voices well divulged, free,[7] learned, and valiant,
And in dimension and the shape of nature[8]
A gracious person. But yet I cannot love him.
He might have took his answer long ago.

VIOLA.   If I did love you in my master's flame,°   *passion*
210   With such a suffering, such a deadly° life,   *death-like*
In your denial I would find no sense,
I would not understand it.

OLIVIA.   Why, what would you?[9]

VIOLA.   Make me a willow cabin[10] at your gate,
215   And call upon my soul[11] within the house.

---

1   *Lady, you are … no copy* You are the cruellest woman alive if you plan to die childless,
     i.e., without making copies of your beauty; *graces* The three graces—Charm, Grace, and
     Beauty—were goddesses led to Hell by the deceitful god Mercury.
2   *schedules* Various inventories.
3   *item* Latin: likewise (used to indicate articles in a formal list such as a will).
4   *indifferent* Tolerably.
5   *but recompensed, though* Merely repaid, even if.
6   *nonpareil* French: one without equal.
7   *In voices well divulged, free* In the general opinion (he is praised as) generous.
8   *dimension … shape of nature* Synonymous terms for "physical form."
9   *what would you* I.e., what would you do to show me your master's passion.
10   *willow cabin* Small shelter of willow boughs (a willow was an emblem of unrequited
     love).
11   *my soul* I.e., Olivia.

Write loyal cantons of contemned love[1]
And sing them loud even in the dead of night.
Halloo° your name to the reverberate° hills,   *Shout / echoing*
And make the babbling gossip[2] of the air
Cry out "Olivia!" O, you should not rest   220
Between the elements of air and earth[3]
But you should pity me.
OLIVIA. You might do much.[4]
    What is your parentage?
VIOLA. Above my fortunes, yet my state is well.[5]   225
    I am a gentleman.
OLIVIA.   Get you to your lord.
    I cannot love him. Let him send no more—
    Unless, perchance, you come to me again
    To tell me how he takes it. Fare you well.
    I thank you for your pains—spend this for me. [*Offers a purse.*]   230
VIOLA. I am no fee'd post,° lady. Keep your purse.   *paid messenger*
    My master, not myself, lacks recompense.
    Love make his heart of flint that you shall love,[6]
    And let your fervour like my master's be,[7]
    Placed in contempt! Farewell, fair cruelty. (*Exit.*)   235
OLIVIA. "What is your parentage?"
    "Above my fortunes, yet my state is well.
    I am a gentleman." I'll be sworn thou art.
    Thy tongue, thy face, thy limbs, actions, and spirit,
    Do give thee five-fold blazon.[8] Not too fast. Soft, soft—   240
    Unless the master were the man.[9] How now?°   *What then*
    Even so quickly may one catch the plague?[10]
    Methinks I feel this youth's perfections°   *beauties*
    With an invisible and subtle stealth

---

1   *loyal cantons ... love* Faithful songs of unrequited love; *cantons* From Italian *canto*: verse.
2   *babbling gossip* Echo, a nymph who wasted away for love of Narcissus until only her voice
    remained to echo other lovers' complaints.
3   *rest / Between ... and earth* I.e., find peace anywhere.
4   *do much* I.e., persuade me to pity you.
5   *fortunes ... state is well* Present situation (as a servant), but my social standing is high.
6   *Love make ... shall love* May Love (Cupid) harden the heart of the man whom you choose
    to love.
7   *like my master's be* I.e., be treated like (you treat) my master's (with contempt).
8   *blazon* Listing of multiple (i.e., five-fold) physical virtues, a popular device in sonnets
    (literally, a heraldic description of a coat of arms).
9   *Unless ... the man* I.e., but what if the messenger were the one wooing me.
10   *catch the plague* I.e., fall in love.

245   To creep in at mine eyes.[1] Well, let it be.
       What ho, Malvolio!

       (*Enter Malvolio.*)

MALVOLIO.   Here, madam, at your service.
OLIVIA.   Run after that same peevish° messenger,   *obstinate*
       The County's° man. He left this ring behind him,   *Count's*
       Would I or not.[2] Tell him I'll none of it.
250   Desire him not to flatter with his lord,
       Nor hold him up[3] with hopes. I am not for him.
       If that the youth will come this way tomorrow,
       I'll give him reasons for't. Hie thee,° Malvolio.   *Hurry*
MALVOLIO.   Madam, I will. (*Exit.*)
255 OLIVIA.   I do I know not what, and fear to find
       Mine eye too great a flatterer for my mind.[4]
       Fate, show thy force. Ourselves we do not owe.°   *own*
       What is decreed must be, and be this so.[5]

       [*Exit.*]

ACT 2, SCENE 1

(*Enter Antonio and Sebastian.*)

ANTONIO.   Will you stay no longer, nor will you not[6] that I go with you?
SEBASTIAN.   By your patience, no. My stars shine darkly over me; the malig-
       nancy of my fate might perhaps distemper yours.[7] Therefore I shall crave
       of you your leave that I may bear my evils[8] alone. It were a bad recompense
    5 for your love to lay any of them on you.
ANTONIO.   Let me know of you whither you are bound.
SEBASTIAN.   No, sooth, sir; my determinate[9] voyage is mere extravagancy.[10] But
       I perceive in you so excellent a touch of modesty[11] that you will not extort

---

1   *at mine eyes* Love was traditionally thought to enter at the eyes (as in "love at first sight").
2   *Would I or not* Whether I wanted it or not.
3   *flatter with … hold him up* Lead him on or encourage him (synonymous phrases).
4   *Mine eye … mind* I.e., that my eye has misled my judgment.
5   *Fate … be this so* This and line 240 above restate the proverb, "what must be must be,"
    and also echo contemporary religious debates about the doctrine of predestination.
6   *will you not* Do you not wish?
7   *stars shine darkly … distemper yours* Astrological terms for the evil influence of fate, which
    he fears will infect ("distemper") Antonio's fortunes.
8   *evils* Misfortunes.
9   *determinate* Intended.
10 *extravagancy* Aimless wandering.
11 *modesty* Politeness.

from me what I am willing to keep in. Therefore it charges me in manners
the rather to express[1] myself. You must know of me then, Antonio, my   10
name is Sebastian, which I called Roderigo. My father was that Sebastian
of Messaline[2] whom I know you have heard of. He left behind him myself
and a sister, both born in an hour. If the heavens had been pleased, would
we had so ended. But you, sir, altered that, for some[3] hour before you took
me from the breach of the sea[4] was my sister drowned.   15

ANTONIO. Alas the day!

SEBASTIAN. A lady, sir, though it was said she much resembled me, was yet
of many accounted beautiful. But though I could not with such estimable
wonder overfar[5] believe that, yet thus far I will boldly publish[6] her—she
bore a mind that envy could not but call fair. She is drowned already, sir,   20
with salt water, though I seem to drown her remembrance again with more.

ANTONIO. Pardon me, sir, your bad entertainment.[7]

SEBASTIAN. O good Antonio, forgive me your trouble.[8]

ANTONIO. If you will not murder me for my love,[9] let me be your servant.

SEBASTIAN. If you will not undo what you have done—that is, kill him whom   25
you have recovered—desire it not. Fare ye well at once. My bosom is full
of kindness,[10] and I am yet so near the manners of my mother that, upon
the least occasion more, mine eyes will tell tales of me.[11] I am bound to the
Count Orsino's court. Farewell.

> (*Exit.*)

ANTONIO. The gentleness° of all the gods go with thee   *favour*   30
I have many enemies in Orsino's court,
Else° would I very shortly see thee there.   *Otherwise*
But come what may, I do adore thee so
That danger shall seem sport, and I will go.

> (*Exit.*)

---

1   *express* Reveal.
2   *Messaline* A Shakespearean invention, but perhaps derived from Massila (now Marseilles);
     Massilians and Illyrians are mentioned together in Plautus's *Menaechmi* in a passage de-
     scribing one twin's search for his sibling.
3   *some* About an.
4   *breach of the sea* Breakers.
5   *estimable wonder overfar* Exceeding esteem and wonder.
6   *publish* Proclaim.
7   *your bad entertainment* I.e., my poor hospitality.
8   *your trouble* I.e., the trouble I have caused you.
9   *murder … love* I.e., punish me for my act of human kindness (that altered your fate).
10   *kindness* Feeling.
11   *yet so near … tales of me* I.e., still so liable to cry like a woman that, at the least emotion,
     my tears will betray my feelings.

ACT 2, SCENE 2

(*Enter Viola and Malvolio at several*[1] *doors.*)

MALVOLIO. Were you not ev'n now with the Countess Olivia?

VIOLA. Even now, sir, on a moderate pace I have since arrived but hither.[2]

MALVOLIO. She returns this ring to you, sir. You might have saved me my
pains, to have taken it away yourself. She adds, moreover, that you should
5   put your lord into a desperate assurance[3] she will none of him. And one
thing more—that you be never so hardy[4] to come again in his affairs, unless it be to report your lord's taking of this. Receive it so.[5]

VIOLA. She took the ring of[6] me. I'll none of it.

MALVOLIO. Come, sir, you peevishly threw it to her, and her will is it should
10   be so returned. If it be worth stooping for, there it lies in your eye.[7] If not,
be it his that finds it.

(*Exit.*)

VIOLA. I left no ring with her. What means this lady?
Fortune forbid my outside° have not charmed her!   *appearance*
She made good view of me,[8] indeed, so much
15   That methought[9] her eyes had lost her tongue,
For she did speak in starts distractedly.[10]
She loves me, sure. The cunning° of her passion   *craftiness*
Invites me in° this churlish messenger.   *by means of*
None of° my lord's ring! Why, he sent her none.   *Refuse*
20   I am the man.[11] If it be so—as 'tis—
Poor lady, she were better love a dream.
Disguise, I see thou art a wickedness
Wherein the pregnant enemy does much.[12]
How easy is it for the proper false

---

1   *several* Different (suggesting simultaneous arrival at both stage entrances).
2   *hither* This far.
3   *desperate assurance* Hopeless certainty.
4   *hardy* Eager.
5   *Receive it so* I.e., take the ring on these terms.
6   *of* From.
7   *eye* Sight.
8   *made good view of me* Looked me over carefully.
9   *That methought* Some editors mend the rough metre here with "That sure methought."
10   *eyes had ... distractedly* She was so perplexed that she became tongue-tied, for she spoke
in disjointed "fits and starts."
11   *the man* I.e., man she desires.
12   *pregnant ... much* Resourceful enemy (Cupid or the devil) can take advantage.

In women's waxen hearts to set their forms!¹   25
Alas, our frailty is the cause, not we
For such as we are made of, such² we be.
How will this fadge?° My master loves her dearly,   *turn out*
And I, poor monster,³ fond° as much on him,   *dote*
And she, mistaken, seems to dote on me.   30
What will become of this? As I am man,
My state is desperate for my master's love.⁴
As I am woman, now, alas the day,
What thriftless° sighs shall poor Olivia breathe.   *fruitless*
O Time, thou must untangle this, not I.   35
It is too hard a knot for me t'untie!

> [*Exit.*]

ACT 2, SCENE 3

(*Enter Sir Toby and Sir Andrew.*)

SIR TOBY. Approach, Sir Andrew. Not to be abed after midnight is to be up
betimes,⁵ and *diluculo surgere*⁶ thou know'st—

SIR ANDREW. Nay, by my troth, I know not, but I know to be up late is to
be up late.

SIR TOBY. A false conclusion! I hate it as an unfilled can.⁷ To be up after   5
midnight and to go to bed then is early, so that to go to bed after midnight
is to go to bed betimes. Does not our lives consist of the four elements?⁸

SIR ANDREW. Faith, so they say, but I think it rather consists of eating and
drinking.

---

1   *for the … their forms* For handsome deceitful (men) to leave impressions on women's
     hearts (as wax takes the impression of a seal).

2   *our frailty … such* Traditionally, women were considered the "weaker vessel," and suscep-
     tibility to passion was thought to derive from physical weakness.

3   *monster* I.e., being both man and woman; Renaissance medical manuals used "monster"
     for unusual births of all types, particularly those of uncertain or dual gender.

4   *As I am … master's love* I.e., since I am now considered a man, my love for my master is
     hopeless.

5   *betimes* Early.

6   *diluculo surgere* Latin. From the proverb, *Diluculo surgere saluberrimum est* ("to rise at
     dawn is most healthy"), found in popular school texts and medical advice books, which
     urged moderation in food, drink, exercise, and rest to avoid unhealthy imbalances of bod-
     ily humours.

7   *can* Tankard.

8   *four elements* Air, earth, fire, and water; the elements were thought to compose all things
     and corresponded to the four humours of the body (blood, phlegm, choler, and melan-
     choly), which were thought to govern behaviour and health.

10   SIR TOBY. Th'art a scholar, let us therefore eat and drink.
Marian,[1] I say, a stoup[2] of wine.

(*Enter [Feste.]*)

SIR ANDREW. Here comes the fool, i' faith.
FESTE. How now, my hearts! Did you never see the picture of "we three?"[3]
SIR TOBY. Welcome, ass. Now let's have a catch.[4]
15   SIR ANDREW. By my troth, the fool has an excellent breast.[5] I had rather than
forty shillings I had such a leg,[6] and so sweet a breath to sing, as the fool
has. In sooth, thou wast in very gracious fooling last night, when thou
spok'st of Pigrogromitus, of the Vapians passing the equinoctial of Queubus.[7] 'Twas very good, i' faith. I sent thee sixpence for thy leman.[8] Hadst it?
20   FESTE. I did impeticos thy gratility, for Malvolio's nose is no whipstock. My
lady has a white hand, and the Myrmidons are no bottle-ale houses.[9]
SIR ANDREW. Excellent! Why, this is the best fooling, when all is done. Now,
a song.
SIR TOBY. Come on, there is sixpence for you. Let's have a song.
25   SIR ANDREW. There's a testril[10] of me too. If one knight give a—[11]
FESTE. Would you have a love-song, or a song of good life?[12]
SIR TOBY. A love-song, a love-song.
SIR ANDREW. Ay, ay, I care not for good life.

---

1   *Marian* Diminutive of Mary.
2   *stoup* Two-pint tankard.
3   *we three* This caption accompanied illustrations on inn signs depicting two fools or asses;
the third ass was the viewer.
4   *catch* Song sung in a three-part round.
5   *breast* Voice.
6   *leg* Dancing skill.
7   *Pigrogromitus ... Queubus* Sir Andrew is repeating (or perhaps mangling) Feste's exotic
nonsense names, which seem to imitate popular travel literature or the pseudo-classical
names in Rabelais's *Gargantua and Pantagruel* (c. 1532); *equinoctial* Equator.
8   *leman* Mistress.
9   *I did ... bottle-ale houses* Feste's speech mingles near sense with "fooling" illogic; *impeticos
thy gratility* Mock Latin for "pocketed your gratuity"; *whipstock* Handle of a whip (i.e.,
Malvolio can look down his nose at me, but he can't punish me); *My lady ... hand* I.e.,
Olivia is of noble birth and manners; *Myrmidons ... bottle-ale* Myrmidons were fol-
lowers of Achilles, but this is likely a joke on the Mermaid Inn, whose literary clientele
presumably drank no common "bottle-ale."
10   *testril* Diminutive of "tester," a sixpence piece (fools entertained for money).
11   *give a—* In the First Folio this line ends at the margin without punctuation, and perhaps
the next line was dropped from the text; in performance, this provides Feste an opportunity to interrupt Sir Andrew.
12   *love-song ... good life* I.e., a song of courtly love or a drinking song (although Sir Andrew
takes "good" to mean "righteous").

We Three Loggerheads, *early seventeenth century. It is likely that Feste—who refers to this type of "we three" image in Act 2, Scene 3 of* Twelfth Night—*wore jester's clothes in the play's first production. If he did, his costume would have been similar to those worn by the characters in this painting: multicoloured clothes decorated with bells and accompanied by a fool's cap. There were several varieties of fool's cap, but many such caps, like the two shown here, had the ears of an ass or the head of a cock attached. One of the figures in the painting also bears a common fool's accessory called a "marotte," a carved fool's head on a stick with which the possessor could conduct pretend conversations.*

FESTE. (*Sings.*)
O mistress mine,[1] where are you roaming?
30   O, stay and hear, your true love's coming,
    That can sing both high and low.
Trip° no further, pretty sweeting.°   *Go / darling*
Journeys end in lovers meeting,
    Every wise man's son doth know.[2]
35   SIR ANDREW. Excellent good, i' faith.
SIR TOBY. Good, good!
FESTE. [*Sings.*]
What is love? 'Tis not hereafter,
Present mirth hath present laughter.
    What's to come is still° unsure.   *always*
40   In delay there lies no plenty,°   *gain*
Then come kiss me, sweet and twenty.[3]
    Youth's a stuff will not endure.[4]
SIR ANDREW. A mellifluous voice, as I am true knight.
SIR TOBY. A contagious breath.[5]
45   SIR ANDREW. Very sweet and contagious, i' faith.
SIR TOBY. To hear by the nose, it is dulcet in contagion.[6] But shall we make
    the welkin[7] dance indeed? Shall we rouse the night-owl in a catch that will
    draw three souls out of one weaver?[8] Shall we do that?
SIR ANDREW. An you love me, let's do't. I am dog at[9] a catch.
50   FESTE. By'r lady,[10] sir, and some dogs will catch well.
SIR ANDREW. Most certain. Let our catch be "Thou knave."

---

1   *O mistress mine* While the words to this song might be Shakespeare's, what tune was
    played in performance is uncertain; one likely accompaniment is a tune in Thomas Mor-
    ley's *First Book of Consort Lessons* (1599).
2   *wise man's son* Proverbial: "a wise man has a foolish son."
3   *sweet and twenty* I.e., twenty times as sweetly.
4   *Youth's ... endure* I.e., our youth will not last (so let's seize the day).
5   *contagious breath* I.e., infectious voice, playing on "catch" in two senses: it is a "catchy"
    tune easily remembered, and they will "catch" the plague from Feste's foul breath (al-
    though Andrew mistakes "contagious" as a compliment).
6   *To hear ... contagion* I.e., if you could hear through your nose, it would be sweetly con-
    tagious (winking at Andrew's confusion, but also alluding to the plague-time practice of
    breathing through perfumed handkerchiefs).
7   *welkin* Heavens.
8   *draw three ... weaver* Many weavers in London were Calvinist refugees who would have
    sung only Psalms; *three souls* Both a joke on the three-part "catch" and an allusion to the
    three faculties of the soul—reason, feeling, and passion.
9   *dog at* Good at.
10   *By'r lady* By our Lady, the Virgin Mary (a mild oath).

FESTE. "Hold thy peace, thou knave"[1] knight? I shall be constrained[2] in't to
    call thee knave, knight.
SIR ANDREW. 'Tis not the first time I have constrained one to call me knave.[3]
    Begin, fool. It begins "Hold thy peace."   55
FESTE. I shall never begin if I hold my peace.[4]
SIR ANDREW. Good, i' faith. Come, begin. (*Catch sung.*)

    (*Enter Maria.*)

MARIA. What a caterwauling[5] do you keep here! If my lady have not called up
    her steward Malvolio, and bid him turn you out of doors, never trust me.
SIR TOBY. My lady's a Cathayan, we are politicians, Malvolio's a Peg-a-Ramsey,[6] 60
    and (*He sings.*) "Three merry men be we."[7] Am not I consanguineous?[8] Am
    I not of her blood? Tilly-vally. "Lady!"[9] [*Sings.*] "There dwelt a man in
    Babylon, lady, lady."[10]
FESTE. Beshrew me,[11] the knight's in admirable fooling.
SIR ANDREW. Ay, he does well enough if he be disposed, and so do I too. He 65
    does it with a better grace, but I do it more natural.[12]
SIR TOBY. [*Sings.*] "O' the twelfth day of December—"[13]
MARIA. For the love o' God, peace.

    (*Enter Malvolio.*)

---

1   *Hold thy peace, thou knave* In this round each singer in turn is told to be silent and called
    a knave.
2   *constrained* Compelled.
3   *'Tis not ... me knave* Sir Andrew may be recalling how Maria treated him in 1.3, or sim-
    ply admitting he is more knave than knight.
4   *peace* Punning on "piece," slang for "penis."
5   *caterwauling* Crying of cats in heat.
6   *Cathayan, we are ... Peg-a-Ramsey* This sequence mimics Feste's nonsense statements ear-
    lier in this scene; *Cathayan* Literally, an inhabitant of Cathay (China, and perhaps an
    insult), but Toby more likely means Catharan (from *cathari*, Latin for "the pure"), a term
    often used for Puritans (implying she is morally inflexible); *politicians* I.e., shrewd self-
    servers; *Peg-a-Ramsey* Title of a lewd popular song and dance.
7   *Three merry ... be we* Fragment of a song that appeared in George Peele's *The Old Wives*
    Tale (1595); other versions of this song contrast "merry men" with "wise men."
8   *consanguineous* Of the same blood (as Olivia).
9   *Tilly-vally. "Lady!"* Nonsense expression of impatience at Maria's "my lady" above.
10   *There dwelt ... lady* Opening line and refrain from the popular ballad, *Constant Susanna*
    (c. 1562), about Susanna and the Elders in Daniel 13.
11   *Beshrew me* Curse me.
12   *better grace ... natural* More artfully, but I do it like a natural (a born fool).
13   *O' ... December* Possibly the opening line of a popular war ballad, *Musselburgh Field*
    (tune unknown), but it is plausible that Toby is drunkenly misquoting "On the twelfth
    day of Christmas."

MALVOLIO. My masters,[1] are you mad? Or what are you? Have you no wit,
70   manners, nor honesty,[2] but to gabble like tinkers at this time of night? Do
       ye make an ale-house of my lady's house, that ye squeak out your coziers'
       catches[3] without any mitigation or remorse[4] of voice? Is there no respect of
       place, persons, nor time,[5] in you?

SIR TOBY. We did keep time, sir, in our catches. Sneck up.[6]

75   MALVOLIO. Sir Toby, I must be round[7] with you. My lady bade me tell you
       that, though she harbours you as her kinsman, she's nothing allied to your
       disorders.[8] If you can separate yourself and[9] your misdemeanours, you are
       welcome to the house. If not, and it would please you to take leave of her,
       she is very willing to bid you farewell.

80   SIR TOBY. [Sings.] "Farewell, dear heart, since I must needs be gone."[10]

MARIA. Nay, good Sir Toby.[11]

FESTE. [Sings.] "His eyes do show his days are almost done."

MALVOLIO. Is't even so?

SIR TOBY. [Sings.] "But I will never die."

85   FESTE. [Sings.] "Sir Toby, there you lie."[12]

MALVOLIO. This is much credit to you.

SIR TOBY. [Sings.] "Shall I bid him go?"

FESTE. [Sings.] "What and if you do?"

SIR TOBY. [Sings.] "Shall I bid him go, and spare not?"

90   FESTE. [Sings.] "O, no, no, no, no, you dare not."

---

1   *masters* Sir Toby and Sir Andrew are Malvolio's social superiors.

2   *wit* Sense; *honesty* Decency.

3   *gabble like tinkers ... catches* Insulting comparisons to vagrant salesmen (with a reputa-
     tion for drinking and foul language), and to cobblers (who presumably sung as they
     worked).

4   *mitigation or remorse* Moderation or consideration.

5   *place, persons, nor time* I.e., "don't you know your place, who I am, and what time it is"
     (alluding to Aristotle's dramatic unities, which required consistency in setting, characteri-
     zation, and chronology).

6   *Sneck up* Shut up.

7   *round* Direct.

8   *nothing allied to your disorders* I.e., disowns your misconduct.

9   *and* From.

10   *Farewell ... be gone* Toby sings a shortened version of the ballad *Corydon's Farewell to
     Phyllis*, from Robert Jones's *First Book of Songs and Ayres* (1600), sharing lines with Feste.

11   *Nay, good Sir Toby* In performance, Toby may try to embrace Maria after *dear heart*.

12   *will never die ... you lie* Here, Toby might parody a melodramatic death, but "die" also
     means to experience sexual pleasure, a pun Feste trades with "there you lie"; Feste's line in
     the ballad reads "so long as I can spy."

SIR TOBY. [*rising*] Out o' tune,[1] sir? Ye lie. Art any more than a steward? Dost thou think, because thou art virtuous, there shall be no more cakes and ale?[2]

FESTE. Yes, by Saint Anne,[3] and ginger[4] shall be hot i' th' mouth too.[5]

SIR TOBY. Th' art i' th' right. Go, sir, rub your chain with crumbs.[6] A stoup   95
of wine, Maria!

MALVOLIO. Mistress Mary, if you prized my lady's favour at anything more than contempt, you would not give means[7] for this uncivil rule.[8] She shall know of it, by this hand.

(*Exit.*)

MARIA. Go shake your ears.[9]   100

SIR ANDREW. 'Twere as good a deed as to drink when a man's a-hungry,[10] to challenge him the field,[11] and then to break promise with him and make a fool of him.[12]

SIR TOBY. Do't, knight. I'll write thee a challenge, or I'll deliver thy indignation to him by word of mouth.   105

MARIA. Sweet Sir Toby, be patient for to-night. Since the youth of the Count's was to-day with my lady, she is much out of quiet.[13] For Monsieur Malvolio, let me alone with him.[14] If I do not gull him into a nayword,[15] and make

---

1   *Out o' tune* I.e., in disorder (recalling Malovolio's comments before the song). Many edi-
    tors emend the First Folio to read "out o' time" to recall his earlier punning response to
    Malvolio, "we did keep time."

2   *thou art virtuous ... cakes and ale* A common complaint against Puritan reformers who
    agitated for the suppression of traditional parish celebrations of holy-days, among them
    "church-ales," which raised funds for the local parish by selling ale and baked goods.

3   *Saint Anne* Mother of the Virgin Mary (a mild oath).

4   *ginger* Used for spicing Christmas ales and considered an aphrodisiac.

5   *too* Feste has no lines after this point, and most editions have him exit here; however, in
    some modern performances Feste remains on stage in silent detachment.

6   *rub ... crumbs* I.e., exercise your authority on insignificant matters; *chain* Stewards
    wore a ceremonial chain signalling their office.

7   *give means* Provide drink.

8   *uncivil rule* Disorderly conduct.

9   *shake your ears* I.e., like the ass that you are.

10 *'Twere as good ... a-hungry* The first phrase is proverbial ("it's good to drink when you are
    thirsty") but rendered nonsense by the second.

11 *the field* To a duel.

12 *a fool of him* In fact, the code of honour that governed duelling would make a fool of Sir
    Andrew if he then refused to duel.

13 *out of quiet* Troubled.

14 *let me alone with him* Leave him to me.

15 *gull him ... nayword* I.e., trick him into being a byword (for gullibility).

him a common recreation,[1] do not think I have wit enough to lie straight
110   in my bed. I know I can do it.

SIR TOBY. Possess[2] us, possess us, tell us something of him.

MARIA. Marry, sir, sometimes he is a kind of puritan.[3]

SIR ANDREW. O, if I thought that, I'd beat him like a dog.

SIR TOBY. What, for being a puritan? Thy exquisite[4] reason, dear knight?

115   SIR ANDREW. I have no exquisite reason for't, but I have reason good enough.

MARIA. The devil a puritan that he is,[5] or anything constantly but a time-
pleaser;[6] an affectioned[7] ass that cons state without book and utters it by
great swarths;[8] the best persuaded[9] of himself, so crammed, as he thinks,
with excellencies that it is his grounds of faith that all that look on him love
120   him; and on that vice[10] in him will my revenge find notable cause to work.

SIR TOBY. What wilt thou do?

MARIA. I will drop in his way some obscure epistles[11] of love, wherein, by the
colour of his beard, the shape of his leg, the manner of his gait, the expressure[12] of his eye, forehead, and complexion, he shall find himself most feel-
125   ingly personated.[13] I can write very like my lady, your niece. On forgotten
matter[14] we can hardly make distinction of our hands.

SIR TOBY. Excellent! I smell a device.[15]

SIR ANDREW. I have't in my nose too.

SIR TOBY. He shall think, by the letters that thou wilt drop, that they come
130   from my niece, and that she's in love with him.

---

1   *common recreation* Laughingstock.
2   *Possess* Acquaint.
3   *kind of a puritan* I.e., morally rigid, highly scrupled person; the term does not necessarily refer (as Andrew thinks) to Puritans, the radical reformers of the English Protestant
church.
4   *exquisite* Carefully considered.
5   *The devil ... he is* I.e., he is no more a Puritan than the devil.
6   *constantly ... time-pleaser* Consistently except for a time-server (i.e., he serves only his
own interests).
7   *affectioned* Affected.
8   *cons state ... great swarths* Memorizes the rules of decorum and proclaims them at great
length; *swarths* Swaths, amounts of hay or corn that could be cut with one sweep of a
scythe.
9   *best persuaded* Highest opinion.
10   *that vice* I.e., pride, one of the seven deadly sins.
11   *obscure epistles* Ambiguous letters.
12   *expressure* Expression.
13   *feelingly personated* Sensitively portrayed.
14   *forgotten matter* I.e., routine matters either of us could have recorded in a household
book.
15   *device* Stratagem.

MARIA. My purpose is, indeed, a horse of that colour.[1]

SIR ANDREW. And your horse now would make him an ass.

MARIA. Ass,[2] I doubt not.

SIR ANDREW. O, 'twill be admirable!

MARIA. Sport royal,[3] I warrant you. I know my physic[4] will work with him. 135
I will plant you two—and let the fool make a third[5]—where he shall find
the letter. Observe his construction[6] of it. For this night, to bed, and dream
on the event. Farewell.

   (*Exit.*)

SIR TOBY. Good night, Penthesilea.[7]

SIR ANDREW. Before me,[8] she's a good wench.   140

SIR TOBY. She's a beagle[9] true-bred, and one that adores me. What o' that?

SIR ANDREW. I was adored once too.

SIR TOBY. Let's to bed, knight. Thou hadst need send for more money.[10]

SIR ANDREW. If I cannot recover your niece, I am a foul way out.[11]

SIR TOBY. Send for money, knight. If thou hast her not i' th' end, call me cut.[12] 145

SIR ANDREW. If I do not, never trust me, take it how you will.

SIR TOBY. Come, come, I'll go burn some sack.[13] 'Tis too late to go to bed
now. Come, knight, come, knight.

   (*Exeunt.*)

---

1   *horse of that colour* I.e., precisely that (a proverbial expression Andrew doesn't recognize).

2   *Ass* Punning on "as" and "ass," but also suggesting Andrew is an ass.

3   *Sport royal* Entertainment worthy of royalty.

4   *physic* Medicine.

5   *fool make a third* This is usually cited as evidence that Feste has left the scene after his last
     line above, and that Shakespeare originally planned for him to be the third observer (in
     fact, Fabian replaces Feste in 2.5). In performance, Maria may add this as a nod to the
     silent Fool, who replies with a dismissive gesture.

6   *construction* Interpretation.

7   *Penthesilea* Queen of the Amazons.

8   *Before me* On my soul.

9   *beagle* Small hunting dog noted for its tenacity and intelligence.

10   *more money* Of Andrew's annual income of three thousand ducats, Toby has by 3.2 re-
     ceived "some two thousand strong, or so."

11   *foul way out* I.e., I will be in a difficult situation; *out* In debt.

12   *cut* A cart horse (either with a cropped tail or gelded).

13   *burn some sack* I.e., heat up some sherry with spices.

ACT 2, SCENE 4

(*Enter Orsino, Viola, Curio, and others.*)

ORSINO. Give me some music. Now, good morrow, friends. (*Musicians enter.*)
    Now, good Cesario, but° that piece of song,   *sing just*
    That old and antic° song we heard last night.   *rustic and antique*
    Methought it did relieve my passion much,
5   More than light airs[1] and recollected terms[2]
    Of these most brisk and giddy-pacèd° times.   *dizzying*
    Come, but one verse.
CURIO. He is not here, so please your lordship, that should sing it.
ORSINO. Who was it?
10 CURIO. Feste, the jester, my lord, a fool that the Lady Olivia's father took much
    delight in. He is about the house.
ORSINO. Seek him out, and play the tune the while.

    [*Exit Curio.*]

    (*Music plays.*)

    Come hither, boy. If ever thou shalt love,
    In the sweet pangs of it remember me,
15   For such as I am all true lovers are,
    Unstaid° and skittish in all motions° else   *Unsteady / emotions*
    Save in° the constant° image of the creature   *Except for / true*
    That is beloved. How dost thou like this tune?
VIOLA. It gives a very echo to the seat
20   Where Love is throned.[3]
ORSINO.   Thou dost speak masterly.
    My life upon't, young though thou art, thine eye
    Hath stayed° upon some favour° that it loves,   *fixed / face*
    Hath it not, boy?
VIOLA.   A little, by your favour.[4]
ORSINO. What kind of woman is't?
VIOLA.   Of your complexion.°   *temperament*

---

1   *airs* Fashionable courtly songs popularized by John Dowland's *First Book of Songs or Airs*
    (1597).
2   *recollected terms* Rehearsed, artificial language.
3   *It gives ... Love is throned* It perfectly echoes the feelings of the heart (where love was
    thought to have its seat).
4   *by your favour* By your leave, but also punning on "some favour that it loves."

ORSINO. She is not worth thee, then. What years, i' faith?   25
VIOLA. About your years, my lord.
ORSINO. Too old, by heaven! Let still° the woman take   *always*
    An elder than herself. So wears° she to him;   *conforms*
    So sways she level¹ in her husband's heart.
    For, boy, however we do praise ourselves,   30
    Our fancies° are more giddy and unfirm,   *affections*
    More longing, wavering, sooner lost and won,
    Than women's are.
VIOLA.   I think it well, my lord.
ORSINO. Then let thy love be younger than thyself,
    Or thy affection cannot hold the bent.²   35
    For women are as roses, whose fair flower
    Being once displayed, doth fall³ that very hour.
VIOLA. And so they are. Alas, that they are so,
    To die, even when they to perfection grow.

    (*Enter Curio and Feste.*)

ORSINO. O, fellow, come, the song we had last night.   40
    Mark it, Cesario, it is old and plain.
    The spinsters⁴ and the knitters in the sun,
    And the free° maids that weave their thread with bones,⁵   *care-free*
    Do use to chant it. It is silly sooth,°   *simple truth*
    And dallies with° the innocence of love,   *dwells on* 45
    Like the old age.⁶
FESTE. Are you ready, sir?
ORSINO. Ay, prithee, sing.

    (*Music.*)

---

1   *So wears she ... sways she level* Thus she conforms herself to him; thus she maintains a
    balanced influence.
2   *hold the bent* I.e., remain strong and true (a term from archery for a bow's strength under
    tension).
3   *displayed, doth fall* In full bloom, wilts.
4   *spinsters* Women spinning (but hinting at the modern meaning, unmarried women).
5   *weave their ... bones* Make their lace with bone bobbins (often fish bones instead of metal
    pins). The aristocratic taste for fine lace supported a labour-intensive cottage industry in
    which girls and young women contributed to their dowries by lace-making.
6   *old age* Mythic golden age of pastoral simplicity.

FESTE. [*Sings.*]

Come away,° come away, death,[1]   *Come quickly*
50   And in sad cypress[2] let me be laid.
Fie away,° fie away, breath,   *Begone*
        I am slain by a fair cruel maid.
My shroud of white, stuck all with yew,[3]
        O, prepare it.
55 My part of death no one so true
        Did share it.[4]

Not a flower, not a flower sweet,
        On my black coffin let there be strown.
Not a friend, not a friend greet°   *to greet*
60   My poor corpse where my bones shall be thrown.
A thousand thousand to save,
        Lay me, O, where
True[5] lover never° find my grave,   *may never*
        To weep there.

65 ORSINO. There's for thy pains. [*Gives him money.*]
FESTE. No pains, sir. I take pleasure in singing, sir.
ORSINO. I'll pay thy pleasure, then.
FESTE. Truly, sir, and pleasure will be paid one time or another.
ORSINO. Give me now leave to leave thee.[6]
70 FESTE. Now the melancholy god[7] protect thee, and the tailor make thy doublet of changeable taffeta,[8] for thy mind is a very opal.[9] I would have men
of such constancy put to sea,[10] that their business might be everything, and
their intent everywhere,[11] for that's it that always makes a good voyage of
nothing.[12] Farewell.

---

1   *Come away ... death* This song may or may not be Shakespeare's; no contemporary musical setting survives.
2   *sad cypress* A black coffin of cypress.
3   *yew* Sprigs of yew; like the cypress, the yew was associated with death.
4   *My part ... Did share it* No one so true (to love) as I has ever shared my portion of death
(i.e., died of love).
5   *True* Many editions read "Sad true" to correct the metre in this line.
6   *Give me ... leave thee* Allow me to dismiss you.
7   *melancholy god* Saturn (thought to govern moodiness).
8   *changeable taffeta* Shot silk, woven with contrasting thread colours to iridesce in changing light (associated with changes of mind).
9   *opal* Iridescent gemstone (i.e., your mood is changeable).
10 *sea* Traditional image of changeability.
11 *their business ... intent everywhere* Proverbial: "he that is everywhere is nowhere."
12 *that's it ... of nothing* I.e., that changeable attitude makes something out of nothing.

(*Exit* [*Feste*].)

ORSINO. Let all the rest give place.°   *leave*   75

    [*Exit Curio and others.*]

    Once more, Cesario,
    Get thee to yond same sovereign cruelty.°   *cruel lady*
    Tell her my love, more noble than the world,°   *material things*
    Prizes not quantity of dirty lands.
    The parts° that fortune hath bestowed upon her,   *wealth and rank*   80
    Tell her I hold as giddily° as Fortune.   *lightly*
    But 'tis that miracle and queen of gems[1]
    That Nature pranks° her in attracts my soul.   *adorns*

VIOLA. But if she cannot love you, sir?

ORSINO. I cannot be so answered.   85

VIOLA. Sooth,° but you must.   *In truth*
    Say that some lady, as perhaps there is,
    Hath for your love as great a pang of heart
    As you have for Olivia. You cannot love her.
    You tell her so. Must she not then be answered?   90

ORSINO. There is no woman's sides
    Can bide° the beating of so strong a passion   *withstand*
    As love doth give my heart; no woman's heart
    So big to hold so much. They lack retention.[2]
    Alas, their love may be called appetite,   95
    No motion of the liver, but the palate,
    That suffer surfeit, cloyment, and revolt;[3]
    But mine is all as hungry as the sea,
    And can digest as much. Make no compare
    Between that love a woman can bear me   100
    And that I owe° Olivia.   *have for*

VIOLA. Ay, but I know—

ORSINO. What dost thou know?

VIOLA. Too well what love women to men may owe.
    In faith, they are as true of heart as we.   105
    My father had a daughter loved a man,
    As it might be perhaps, were I a woman,
    I should your lordship.

---

1   *that miracle ... gems* A diamond (i.e., her rare and matchless beauty).
2   *retention* In Renaissance medicine, the power to retain the contents of one's body.
3   *No motion ... revolt* A mere hunger, not a deep passion, easily satisfied, but quickly sick-
    ened; *cloyment* Satiety; *revolt* Revulsion.

ORSINO.   And what's her history?

110 VIOLA. A blank, my lord. She never told her love,
        But let concealment, like a worm i' th' bud,°   *rosebud*
        Feed on her damask° cheek. She pined in thought,   *pink and white*
        And with a green and yellow melancholy[1]
        She sat like Patience on a monument,[2]
115   Smiling at grief. Was not this love indeed?
        We men may say more, swear more, but indeed
        Our shows are more than will.[3] For still we prove
        Much in our vows, but little in our love.

ORSINO. But died thy sister of her love, my boy?

120 VIOLA. I am all the daughters of my father's house,
        And all the brothers too, and yet I know not.
        Sir, shall I to this lady?

ORSINO.   Ay, that's the theme.
        To her in haste. Give her this jewel. Say
        My love can give no place, bide no denay.[4]

    (*Exeunt [separately.]*)

ACT 2, SCENE 5

(*Enter Sir Toby, Sir Andrew, and Fabian.*[5])

SIR TOBY. Come thy ways, Signior Fabian.

FABIAN. Nay, I'll come. If I lose a scruple[6] of this sport let me be boiled to
        death with melancholy.[7]

SIR TOBY. Wouldst thou not be glad to have the niggardly[8] rascally sheep-biter[9]
5   come by some notable shame?

FABIAN. I would exult, man. You know he brought me out o' favour with my
        lady about a bear-baiting[10] here.

---

1   *green ... melancholy* Pale and yellow sadness, referring to "green-sickness" (chlorosis), an
    anemia thought to afflict virgins.
2   *Patience on a monument* Minerva, the goddess of patience, was often portrayed on tombs.
3   *Our shows ... will* I.e., our displays of love suggest more than our actual passion.
4   *give no place ... denay* I.e., not hold back, endure no denial.
5   *Fabian* Fabian is introduced to replace Feste as the third observer (see 2.3.136).
6   *a scruple* A bit.
7   *boiled to death with melancholy* Melancholy was in fact a cold humour.
8   *niggardly* Grudging.
9   *sheep-biter* Literally, a guard dog that bites sheep, but figuratively a whore-monger (punning
    on "mutton," meaning "whore") and associated with Puritans by the satirist Thomas Nashe.
10 *bear-baiting* A popular entertainment condemned by Puritans (Shakespeare's Globe
    theatre was located next to a bear-baiting arena).

SIR TOBY. To anger him we'll have the bear again, and we will fool him black
and blue, shall we not, Sir Andrew?

SIR ANDREW. An we do not, it is pity of our lives.   10

(*Enter Maria.*)

SIR TOBY. Here comes the little villain. How now, my metal of India![1]

MARIA. Get ye all three into the box-tree.[2] Malvolio's coming down this walk.
He has been yonder i' the sun practicing behaviour[3] to his own shadow
this half hour. Observe him, for the love of mockery, for I know this letter
will make a contemplative[4] idiot of him. Close,[5] in the name of jesting.   15
[*They hide and she drops a letter.*] Lie thou there, for here comes the trout
that must be caught with tickling.[6] (*Exit.*)

(*Enter Malvolio.*)

MALVOLIO. 'Tis but fortune, all is fortune.[7] Maria once told me she did affect[8] me, and I have heard herself come thus near, that should she fancy, it
should be one of my complexion.[9] Besides, she uses[10] me with a more ex-   20
alted respect than anyone else that follows[11] her. What should I think on't?

SIR TOBY. Here's an overweening rogue.

FABIAN. O, peace! Contemplation makes a rare turkeycock of him, how he
jets under his advanced[12] plumes!

SIR ANDREW. 'Slight,[13] I could so beat the rogue.   25

SIR TOBY. Peace, I say.

MALVOLIO. To be Count Malvolio!

SIR TOBY. Ah, rogue.

SIR ANDREW. Pistol[14] him, pistol him.

SIR TOBY. Peace, peace.   30

---

1   *metal of India* Gold (i.e., my treasure); *India* The West Indies.
2   *box-tree* Boxwood bush, an evergreen (a common stage property).
3   *behaviour* Courtly gestures.
4   *contemplative* Thoughtless.
5   *Close* Keep close.
6   *trout … with tickling* Proverbial: to be duped by flattery (literally, a technique for catch-
     ing trout without tackle).
7   *all is fortune* Everything is subject to changeable fortune.
8   *she did affect* Olivia was fond of.
9   *complexion* Character.
10   *uses* Treats.
11   *follows* Serves, woos.
12   *turkeycock*; Peacock; *jets* Struts; *advanced* Displayed.
13   *'Slight* By God's light.
14   *Pistol* Pistol-whip.

MALVOLIO. There is example[1] for't: the Lady of the Strachy married the yeoman of the wardrobe.[2]

SIR ANDREW. Fie on him, Jezebel.[3]

FABIAN. O, peace, now he's deeply in. Look how imagination blows him.[4]

35 MALVOLIO. Having been three months married to her, sitting in my state[5]—

SIR TOBY. O, for a stone-bow[6] to hit him in the eye!

MALVOLIO. Calling my officers[7] about me, in my branched[8] velvet gown, having come from a day-bed[9] where I have left Olivia sleeping—

SIR TOBY. Fire and brimstone!

40 FABIAN. O, peace, peace.

MALVOLIO. And then to have the humour of state,[10] and after a demure travel of regard,[11] telling them I know my place as I would they should do theirs, to ask for my kinsman Toby[12]—

SIR TOBY. Bolts and shackles![13]

45 FABIAN. O, peace, peace, peace, now, now.

MALVOLIO. Seven of my people, with an obedient start, make out for him. I frown the while, and perchance wind up my watch, or play with my[14]— some rich jewel. Toby approaches, curtsies[15] there to me—

SIR TOBY. Shall this fellow live?

50 FABIAN. Though our silence be drawn from us with cars,[16] yet peace.

MALVOLIO. I extend my hand to him thus, quenching my familiar smile with an austere regard of control[17]—

---

1   *example* Precedent.

2   *Lady of the Strachy ... wardrobe* Like "Mistress Mall's picture" in 1.3.100, this may be a fictional example; however, records indicate that in 1606 a gentleman named William Strachey was a part-owner of the rival Blackfriar's Theatre, whose wardrobe master was David Yeomans, a tailor; *married* Likely a euphemism.

3   *Jezebel* Proverbial: "as proud as Jezebel," the infamous widow of King Ahab in 2 Kings 9.30–37.

4   *blows him* Puffs him up.

5   *state* Chair of state.

6   *stone-bow* Crossbow that fired stones to kill birds.

7   *officers* Attendants.

8   *branched* Embroidered with a pattern of branches.

9   *day-bed* Couch.

10 *state* Stately demeanour.

11 *demure travel of regard* I.e., grave survey of those present.

12 *kinsman Toby* Dropping the "Sir."

13 *Bolts and shackles* Fetters for prisoners.

14 *play with my* Here, he reaches for his steward's chain.

15 *curtsies* Bows.

16 *cars* Horse-drawn carts; prisoners might be tied between carts and "drawn" until they confessed.

17 *regard of control* Gaze of authority.

SIR TOBY. And does not Toby take[1] you a blow o' the lips then?

MALVOLIO. Saying "Cousin Toby, my fortunes, having cast me on your niece, give me this prerogative of speech"—   55

SIR TOBY. What, what!

MALVOLIO. "You must amend your drunkenness."

SIR TOBY. Out, scab![2]

FABIAN. Nay, patience, or we break the sinews of[3] our plot.

MALVOLIO. "Besides, you waste the treasure of your time with a foolish   60
knight"—

SIR ANDREW. That's me, I warrant you.

MALVOLIO. "One Sir Andrew."

SIR ANDREW. I knew 'twas I, for many do call me fool.

MALVOLIO. What employment have we here?   65

[*Picks up the letter.*]

FABIAN. Now is the woodcock near the gin.[4]

SIR TOBY. O, peace! And the spirit of humours intimate reading aloud to him![5]

MALVOLIO. By my life, this is my lady's hand. These be her very c's, her u's, and her t's,[6] and thus makes she her great P's. It is, in contempt of[7] ques-   70
tion, her hand.

SIR ANDREW. Her c's, her u's, and her t's. Why that?

MALVOLIO. [*Reads.*] "To the unknown beloved, this, and my good wishes."
Her very phrases. By your leave, wax.[8] Soft[9]—and the impressure her Lucrece[10] with which she uses to seal—'tis my lady. To whom should this be?   75

FABIAN. This wins him, liver[11] and all.

MALVOLIO. [*Reads.*]

"Jove knows I love,
But who?

---

1   *take* Give.

2   *scab* Scoundrel.

3   *break the sinews of* I.e., disable.

4   *woodcock near the gin* Woodcocks were proverbially foolish birds; *gin* Engine, a snare.

5   *And the spirit … to him* I.e., may his eccentric disposition inspire him to read it aloud.

6   *c's, her u's, and her t's* I.e., cut, slang for female genitals (making an obscene joke with "great P's").

7   *in contempt of* Beyond.

8   *By your leave, wax* He breaks the wax seal.

9   *Soft* Wait.

10   *her Lucrece* Olivia's seal is the emblematic figure of chastity, stabbing herself after being raped (and the subject of Shakespeare's narrative poem, *Lucrece*).

11   *liver* I.e., his passions.

Lips, do not move,
80   No man must know."
"No man must know." What follows? The numbers[1] altered. "No man must know." If this should be thee, Malvolio?
SIR TOBY. Marry, hang thee, brock![2]
MALVOLIO. [*Reads.*]
85   "I may command where I adore,
        But silence, like a Lucrece knife,
     With bloodless stroke my heart doth gore.
        M. O. A. I. doth sway my life."
FABIAN. A fustian[3] riddle.
90 SIR TOBY. Excellent wench, say I.
MALVOLIO. "M. O. A. I. doth sway my life." Nay, but first let me see, let me see, let me see.
FABIAN. What dish o' poison has she dressed[4] him!
SIR TOBY. And with what wing the staniel checks at[5] it!
95 MALVOLIO. "I may command where I adore." Why, she may command me. I serve her, she is my lady. Why, this is evident to any formal capacity,[6] there is no obstruction in this. And the end—what should that alphabetical position[7] portend? If I could make that resemble something in me. Softly,[8] M. O. A. I.—
100 SIR TOBY. O, ay,[9] make up that! He is now at a cold scent.[10]
FABIAN. Sowter will cry upon't for all this, though it be as rank as a fox.[11]
MALVOLIO. "M." Malvolio. "M," why, that begins my name.
FABIAN. Did not I say he would work it out? The cur is excellent at faults.[12]
MALVOLIO. "M." But then there is no consonancy in the sequel; that suffers
105 under probation.[13] "A" should follow, but "O" does.

---

1   *numbers* Metre.
2   *brock* Badger, perhaps alluding to his black-and-white attire.
3   *fustian* Pompous.
4   *dressed* Prepared for.
5   *wing ... checks at* I.e., how quickly the kestrel (a bird of prey) veers to pursue.
6   *capacity* Common sense.
7   *position* Arrangement.
8   *Softly* Slowly.
9   *O, ay* Punning on "O. A."
10 *at a cold scent* I.e., like a hound who has lost its quarry's scent.
11 *Sowter will cry ... as a fox* I.e., he will pick up the trail even though it's been crossed by the strong scent of a fox; *Sowter* Cobbler, but here the traditional name of a hound past his prime.
12 *faults* Lost scents.
13 *consonancy ... under probation* I.e., agreement in what follows; that ("the sequel," conclusion) breaks down when tested. In the First Folio, these phrases are run together without punctuation.

FABIAN. And "O" shall end,[1] I hope.

SIR TOBY. Ay, or I'll cudgel him, and make him cry "O!"

MALVOLIO. And then "I" comes behind.

FABIAN. Ay, an you had any eye behind you, you might see more detraction[2] at your heels than fortunes before you.

MALVOLIO. M. O. A. I. This simulation is not as the former,[3] and yet, to crush this a little, it would bow[4] to me, for every one of these letters are in my name. Soft, here follows prose: [*Reads.*] "If this fall into thy hand, revolve.[5] In my stars I am above thee, but be not afraid of greatness. Some are become great,[6] some achieve greatness, and some have greatness thrust upon 'em. Thy Fates open their hands, let thy blood and spirit embrace them, and to inure[7] thyself to what thou art like to be, cast thy humble slough and appear fresh.[8] Be opposite[9] with a kinsman, surly with servants. Let thy tongue tang[10] arguments of state; put thyself into the trick of singularity.[11] She thus advises thee that sighs for thee. Remember who commended thy yellow stockings, and wished to see thee ever cross-gartered.[12] I say, remember, go to, thou art made,[13] if thou desir'st to be so. If not, let me see thee a steward still, the fellow of servants, and not worthy to touch Fortune's fingers. Farewell. She that would alter services[14] with thee,

> The Fortunate-Unhappy."

---

1   *"O" shall end* I.e., he'll end in the circle of the hangman's noose.

2   *detraction* Misfortune.

3   *This simulation ... the former* I.e., this riddle is not as easy as the former ("I may command where I adore").

4   *crush* Force; *bow* Yield.

5   *revolve* Carefully consider; in performance, Malvolio sometimes takes this literally and spins slowly.

6   *become great* Beginning with Nicolas Rowe's 1714 edition, this famous phrase in the First Folio has traditionally been corrected to "born great" because Malvolio recalls it that way in 3.4.34 and Feste quotes that wording in 5.1.349.

7   *inure* Accustom.

8   *cast thy humble slough* I.e., abandon your humble manner (like a snake "sloughs" its old skin); *fresh* Bold.

9   *opposite* Contrary.

10   *tang* Ring out.

11   *trick of singularity* Habit of eccentricity.

12   *cross-gartered* Wearing stocking garters wrapped above and below the knee so as to cross behind it.

13   *go to ... art made* I.e., be sure, you are a made man.

14   *alter services* I.e., exchange places (by marrying below her rank, and making him her lord).

Daylight and champain discovers[1] not more. This is open.[2] I will be proud, I will read politic authors, I will baffle Sir Toby, I will wash off gross[3] acquaintance, I will be point-device[4] the very man. I do not now fool myself to let imagination jade[5] me, for every reason excites to[6] this, that my lady loves me. She did commend my yellow stockings of late, she did praise my leg being cross-gartered, and in this she manifests herself to my love, and with a kind of injunction drives me to these habits[7] of her liking. I thank my stars, I am happy. I will be strange, stout,[8] in yellow stockings, and cross-gartered, even with the swiftness of putting on. Jove[9] and my stars be praised. Here is yet a postscript: [*Reads.*] "Thou canst not choose but know who I am. If thou entertain'st[10] my love, let it appear in thy smiling, thy smiles become thee well. Therefore in my presence still[11] smile, dear my sweet, I prithee." Jove, I thank thee. I will smile, I will do everything that thou wilt have me.

(*Exit.*)

FABIAN. I will not give my part of this sport for a pension of thousands to be paid from the Sophy.[12]

SIR TOBY. I could marry this wench for this device.

SIR ANDREW. So could I too.

SIR TOBY. And ask no other dowry with her but such another jest.

(*Enter Maria.*)

SIR ANDREW. Nor I neither.

FABIAN. Here comes my noble gull-catcher.[13]

SIR TOBY. Wilt thou set thy foot o' my neck?

SIR ANDREW. Or o' mine either?

---

1   *champain discovers* Open countryside reveals.
2   *open* Obvious.
3   *politic* Political; *baffle* Disgrace; *gross* Common.
4   *point-device* I.e., to the point of perfection.
5   *jade* Trick.
6   *excites to* Urges.
7   *habits* Idiosyncrasies.
8   *strange, stout* Aloof, firm.
9   *Jove* Jupiter, the Roman god of justice.
10   *entertain'st* Accept.
11   *still* Always.
12   *the Sophy* Shah of Persia; in 1598, Sir Anthony Shirley and his brothers travelled to the Shah's court and in 1600 reported his munificence in a popular travel narrative.
13   *gull-catcher* Fool-catcher.

SIR TOBY. Shall I play[1] my freedom at tray-trip,[2] and become thy bond-slave?   150
SIR ANDREW. I' faith, or I either?
SIR TOBY. Why, thou hast put him in such a dream that when the image of
   it leaves him he must run mad.
MARIA. Nay, but say true. Does it work upon him?
SIR TOBY. Like aqua-vita with a midwife.[3]   155
MARIA. If you will then see the fruits of the sport, mark his first approach be-
   fore my lady. He will come to her in yellow stockings, and 'tis a colour she
   abhors, and cross-gartered, a fashion she detests, and he will smile upon
   her, which will now be so unsuitable to her disposition, being addicted to a
   melancholy as she is, that it cannot but turn him into a notable contempt.[4]   160
   If you will see it, follow me.
SIR TOBY. To the gates of Tartar,[5] thou most excellent devil of wit.
SIR ANDREW. I'll make one[6] too.

   (*Exeunt.*)

ACT 3, SCENE 1

(*Enter Viola, and* [*Feste playing on a pipe and tabor.*[7]])

VIOLA. Save[8] thee, friend, and thy music. Dost thou live by[9] thy tabor?
FESTE. No, sir, I live by the church.
VIOLA. Art thou a churchman?
FESTE. No such matter, sir. I do live by the church, for I do live at my house,
   and my house doth stand by the church.   5
VIOLA. So thou mayst say the king lies by a beggar, if a beggar dwell near
   him, or the church stands[10] by thy tabor, if thy tabor stand by the church.
FESTE. You have said, sir. To see this[11] age! A sentence[12] is but a chev'rel[13] glove
   to a good wit. How quickly the wrong side may be turned outward.

---

1   *play* Gamble away.
2   *tray-trip* Dice game in which rolling a three (Old French *treis*) wins.
3   *aqua-vita with a midwife* Likely a stereotype associating distilled spirits with midwives
     and nurses; in *Romeo and Juliet*, for instance, the nurse twice asks for some to calm her.
4   *notable contempt* Object of contempt.
5   *Tartar* Tartarus, a region of hell.
6   *make one* Come along.
7   *tabor* Small drum typically played by jesters while piping.
8   *Save* God save.
9   *live by* I.e., make your living by playing.
10   *stands* I.e., is maintained by.
11   *To see this* Bear witness to this.
12   *sentence* Saying.
13   *chev'rel* Kid leather.

10   VIOLA.   Nay, that's certain. They that dally nicely[1] with words may quickly make them wanton.[2]

FESTE.   I would, therefore, my sister had had[3] no name, sir.

VIOLA.   Why, man?

FESTE.   Why, sir, her name's a word, and to dally with that word might make
15   my sister wanton. But indeed words are very rascals since bonds disgraced them.[4]

VIOLA.   Thy reason, man?

FESTE.   Troth, sir, I can yield you none without words, and words are grown so false I am loath to prove reason with them.

20   VIOLA.   I warrant thou art a merry fellow and car'st for nothing.

FESTE.   Not so, sir, I do care for something. But in my conscience, sir, I do not care for you. If that be to care for nothing, sir, I would it would make you invisible.

VIOLA.   Art not thou the Lady Olivia's fool?

25   FESTE.   No, indeed, sir. The Lady Olivia has no folly. She will keep no fool, sir, till she be married, and fools are as like husbands as pilchards are to herrings—the husband's the bigger.[5] I am indeed not her fool, but her corrupter of words.

VIOLA.   I saw thee late[6] at the Count Orsino's.

30   FESTE.   Foolery, sir, does walk about the orb like the sun[7]—it shines everywhere. I would be sorry, sir, but the fool should be[8] as oft with your master as with my mistress. I think I saw your wisdom there.[9]

VIOLA.   Nay, an thou pass upon me, I'll no more[10] with thee. Hold, there's expenses for thee. [*She gives coins.*]

35   FESTE.   Now Jove in his next commodity[11] of hair send thee a beard.

VIOLA.   By my troth, I'll tell thee, I am almost sick for one, [*aside*] though I would not have it grow on my chin. Is thy lady within?

---

1   *dally nicely* I.e., play subtly.

2   *wanton* I.e., equivocal (but taken to mean "unchaste").

3   *had* Been given.

4   *words are … disgraced them* I.e., words are suspect when they require a legal contract to enforce them (playing on the adage "a man's word is his bond").

5   *fools are as like … the bigger* A double comparison, since pilchards and herrings are similar, yet husbands are greater fools.

6   *late* Recently.

7   *walk about … the sun* The sun was still believed to circle the earth (the "orb").

8   *but the fool should be* I.e., if the fool were not allowed to be.

9   *I think … wisdom there* I.e., I think you are also serving two masters; *there* I.e., at Orsino's.

10   *an thou pass … no more* I.e., if you pass judgment on me, I'll deal no more.

11   *commodity* Shipment.

FESTE. Would not a pair of these have bred,[1] sir?

VIOLA. Yes, being kept together and put to use.[2]

FESTE. I would play Lord Pandarus of Phrygia, sir, to bring a Cressida to this   40
Troilus.[3]

VIOLA. I understand you, sir, 'tis well begged. [*Giving more coins.*]

FESTE. The matter[4] I hope is not great, sir, begging but a beggar:[5] Cressida
was a beggar.[6] My lady is within, sir. I will conster[7] to them whence you
come. Who you are and what you would are out of my welkin—I might   45
say "element" but the word is overworn.[8]

(*Exit [Feste.]*)

VIOLA. This fellow is wise enough to play the fool,[9]
And to do that well craves a kind of wit.
He must observe their mood on whom he jests,
The quality of persons, and the time,   50
And like the haggard, check at every feather
That comes before his eye.[10] This is a practice°   skill
As full of labour as a wise man's art,
For folly that he wisely shows is fit,[11]
But wise men, folly-fall'n, quite taint° their wit.   discredit   55

(*Enter Sir Toby and Sir Andrew.*)

SIR TOBY. Save you, gentleman.

VIOLA. And you, sir.

SIR ANDREW. *Dieu vous garde, monsieur.*

---

1   *pair of these ... bred* Coins have accrued interest.

2   *put to use* I.e., invested.

3   *Lord Pandarus ... to this Troilus* Cressida's uncle acted as their go-between ("pander"),
a story familiar from Chaucer's narrative poem, *Troilus and Criseyde* (c. 1380s); Shakespeare's *Troilus and Cressida* was written soon after *Twelfth Night*.

4   *matter* Amount.

5   *begging but a beggar* Here "beggar" means both servant (i.e., a servant begging from a
servant) and orphan, and may allude to the practice of "begging" the Queen for guardian-
ship of rich wards of the state.

6   *Cressida was a beggar* Pandarus was Cressida's guardian.

7   *conster* Explain.

8   *out of my ... overworn* "Out of my element" was by this time indeed a cliché, and "welkin" was a showy substitute.

9   *wise enough ... fool* Proverbial: "no man can play the fool so well as the wise man."

10   *the haggard ... before his eye* Wild hawks ("haggards") were trained not to shy away from
("check at") the falconer's hand by first touching them with feathers.

11   *For folly ... is fit* I.e., playing the fool with discretion is appropriate.

VIOLA. *Et vous aussi; votre serviteur.*[1]

60 SIR ANDREW. I hope, sir, you are, and I am yours.

SIR TOBY. Will you encounter the house?[2] My niece is desirous you should enter, if your trade[3] be to her.

VIOLA. I am bound to your niece, sir. I mean, she is the list[4] of my voyage.

SIR TOBY. Taste your legs, sir, put them to motion.[5]

65 VIOLA. My legs do better understand me, sir, than[6] I understand what you mean by bidding me taste my legs.

SIR TOBY. I mean, to go, sir, to enter.

VIOLA. I will answer you with gait and entrance.[7] But we are prevented.

(*Enter Olivia and* [*Maria*].)

Most excellent accomplished lady, the heavens rain odours on you.

70 SIR ANDREW. That youth's a rare courtier—"Rain odours"—well.[8]

VIOLA. My matter hath no voice, lady, but to your own most pregnant and vouchsafed[9] ear.

SIR ANDREW. "Odours," "pregnant," and "vouchsafed"—I'll get 'em all three all ready.[10]

75 OLIVIA. Let the garden door be shut,[11] and leave me to my hearing. [*Exeunt all but Olivia and Viola.*] Give me your hand, sir.

VIOLA. My duty, madam, and most humble service.

OLIVIA. What is your name?

VIOLA. Cesario is your servant's name, fair Princess.

80 OLIVIA. My servant, sir? 'Twas never merry world
Since lowly feigning° was called compliment.   *pretended humility*
Y'are servant to the Count Orsino, youth.

VIOLA. And he is yours, and his must needs be yours.
Your servant's servant is your servant, madam.

---

1   *Dieu vous garde … votre serviteur* French: God save you, sir. And you also; (I am) your servant.

2   *encounter the house* I.e., go to meet Olivia (a mock-courtly phrase).

3   *trade* Business.

4   *list* Destination.

5   *Taste your legs … to motion* I.e., test your seafaring legs on land (continuing the nautical metaphors in the previous lines).

6   *than* Better than.

7   *gait and entrance* Her nouns answer Toby's verbs, "go" and "enter."

8   *well* Well said.

9   *pregnant and vouchsafed* I.e., receptive and kindly disposed.

10   *all ready* I.e., ready to use in courtly conversation.

11   *garden door be shut* She is receiving Cesario in a walled, private garden.

OLIVIA. For him, I think not on him. For his thoughts,   85
 Would they were blanks[1] rather than filled with me.
VIOLA. Madam, I come to whet° your gentle thoughts   *encourage*
 On his behalf.
OLIVIA.   O, by your leave, I pray you.
 I bade you never speak again of him,
 But would you undertake another suit,   90
 I had rather hear you to solicit that
 Than music from the spheres.[2]
VIOLA.   Dear lady—
OLIVIA. Give me leave, beseech you. I did send,
 After the last enchantment you did here,
 A ring in chase of you. So did I abuse°   *wrong* 95
 Myself, my servant, and I fear me, you.
 Under your hard construction° must I sit,   *judgment*
 To force that on you in a shameful cunning
 Which you knew none of yours. What might you think?
 Have you not set mine honour at the stake,   100
 And baited it with all th' unmuzzled thoughts[3]
 That tyrannous heart can think? To one of your receiving° *perception*
 Enough is shown: a cypress,[4] not a bosom,
 Hides my heart. So, let me hear you speak.
VIOLA. I pity you.   105
OLIVIA.   That's a degree to love.
VIOLA. No, not a grise,[5] for 'tis a vulgar proof°   *common experience*
 That very oft we pity enemies.
OLIVIA. Why, then, methinks 'tis time to smile again.
 O world, how apt the poor are to be proud.
 If one should be a prey, how much the better   110
 To fall before the lion than the wolf.[6] (*Clock strikes.*)
 The clock upbraids me with the waste of time.[7]
 Be not afraid, good youth, I will not have you,
 And yet, when wit and youth is come to harvest,° *maturity*

---

1 *blanks* Empty sheets of paper.
2 *music ... spheres* I.e., heavenly music said to be produced by the movement of crystalline
 spheres containing the planets, stars, and heavenly firmament.
3 *at the stake ... unmuzzled thoughts* Olivia compares her distress to a chained bear attacked
 by dogs.
4 *cypress* Transparent veil, often black to signal mourning.
5 *grise* Synonym for "step," as is "degree."
6 *To fall ... the wolf* I.e., to be defeated by a noble creature (Cesario) than an ignoble one
 (Orsino).
7 *the waste of time* I.e., my fruitless efforts to win your love.

115 Your wife is like to reap a proper man.
There lies your way, due west.
VIOLA.   Then westward-ho![1]
Grace and good disposition attend your ladyship.
You'll nothing,° madam, to my lord by me?   *say nothing*
OLIVIA. Stay—
120 I prithee tell me what thou[2] think'st of me.
VIOLA. That you do think you are not what you are.[3]
OLIVIA. If I think so, I think the same of you.[4]
VIOLA. Then think you right, I am not what I am.
OLIVIA. I would you were as I would have you be.[5]
125 VIOLA. Would it be better, madam, than I am?
I wish it might, for now I am your fool.[6]
OLIVIA. O, what a deal of scorn looks beautiful
In the contempt and anger of his lip![7]
A murd'rous guilt shows not itself more soon
130 Than love that would seem hid. Love's night is noon.[8]
Cesario, by the roses of the spring,
By maidhood, honour, truth, and everything,
I love thee so that, maugre° all thy pride,   *despite*
Nor wit nor reason can my passion hide.
135 Do not extort thy reasons from this clause:
For that I woo, thou therefore hast no cause.[9]
But rather reason thus with reason fetter:[10]
Love sought is good, but given unsought is better.

---

1   *due west ... westward-ho* In Renaissance humoural theory, west was associated with Ve-
    nus or the Moon and with water, all synonymous with women (i.e., your destiny is to
    find a wife); *westward ho* The cry of Thames watermen taking passengers to Westminster
    from London.
2   *thou* Olivia switches from the formal "you" to the familiar form.
3   *you do think ... what you are* There are several possible readings: you don't see yourself as
    people see you; you won't admit you love beneath your rank; or, you won't admit you love
    a woman.
4   *the same of you* I.e., you are something other than what you seem.
5   *I would you ... have you be* I.e., I wish you could return my love; or, I wish you were the
    right rank (or sex) to be my lover.
6   *I am your fool* I.e., I am performing for you like your fool; or, you are forcing me to
    equivocate with words like your fool.
7   *deal of scorn ... of his lip* The signs of anger only intensify his beauty.
8   *more soon ... night is noon* I.e., love reveals itself in trying to hide.
9   *Do not extort ... hast no cause* Do not draw false conclusions from this premise: that since
    I woo you, you need not woo me.
10 *reason ... reason fetter* Overrule that argument with this one.

VIOLA. By innocence I swear, and by my youth,
   I have one heart, one bosom, and one truth,   140
   And that no woman has, nor never none[1]
   Shall mistress be of it, save I alone.
   And so adieu, good madam. Never more
   Will I my master's tears to you deplore.[2]
OLIVIA. Yet come again, for thou perhaps mayst move   145
   That heart which now abhors, to like his love.

      (*Exeunt.*)

ACT 3, SCENE 2

   (*Enter Sir Toby, Sir Andrew and Fabian.*)

SIR ANDREW. No, faith, I'll not stay a jot longer.
SIR TOBY. Thy reason, dear venom,[3] give thy reason.
FABIAN. You[4] must needs yield your reason, Sir Andrew.
SIR ANDREW. Marry, I saw your niece do more favours[5] to the Count's serv-
   ingman than ever she bestowed upon me. I saw't i' th' orchard.[6]   5
SIR TOBY. Did she see thee the while, old boy? Tell me that.
SIR ANDREW. As plain as I see you now.
FABIAN. This was a great argument[7] of love in her toward you.
SIR ANDREW. 'Slight, will you make an ass o' me?
FABIAN. I will prove it legitimate,[8] sir, upon the oaths of judgment and rea-   10
   son.
SIR TOBY. And they have been grand-jurymen since before Noah was a sailor.[9]
FABIAN. She did show favour to the youth in your sight only to exasperate
   you, to awake your dormouse[10] valour, to put fire in your heart and brim-

---

1 *nor never none* Each term of this triple negative corresponds to her three possessions,
   "heart," "bosom," and "truth."
2 *deplore* I.e., tell with grief.
3 *Thy reason, dear venom* Andrew enters with "venom" (violent intentions) regarding Olivia's attention to Cesario.
4 *You* Fabian's polite "you" contrasts with Toby's familiar "thy."
5 *I saw … more favours* As he left the stage in 3.1, he evidently saw Olivia give Cesario her
   hand.
6 *orchard* Garden.
7 *argument* Proof.
8 *prove it legitimate* I.e., make good my claim (that she does love you).
9 *grand-jurymen … was a sailor* Grand juries decided whether the evidence (i.e., "oaths of
   judgment and reason") merited a trial; *before Noah was a sailor* I.e., since time immemorial.
10 *dormouse* Dormant, timid.

15 stone in your liver.[1] You should then have accosted her, and with some
    excellent jests, fire-new from the mint,[2] you should have banged the youth
    into dumbness. This was looked for at your hand, and this was baulked.
    The double gilt[3] of this opportunity you let time wash off, and you are
    now sailed into the north of my lady's opinion, where you will hang like an
20 icicle on a Dutchman's beard,[4] unless you do redeem it by some laudable
    attempt either of valour or policy.[5]

SIR ANDREW. An't be any way, it must be with valour, for policy I hate. I had
    as lief[6] be a Brownist[7] as a politician.

SIR TOBY. Why, then, build me[8] thy fortunes upon the basis of valour. Chal-
25 lenge me the Count's youth to fight with him. Hurt him in eleven places.[9]
    My niece shall take note of it, and assure thyself there is no love-broker
    in the world can more prevail in man's commendation with woman than
    report of valour.

FABIAN. There is no way but this, Sir Andrew.

30 SIR ANDREW. Will either of you bear me a challenge to him?

SIR TOBY. Go, write it in a martial hand,[10] be curst[11] and brief. It is no matter
    how witty, so it be eloquent and full of invention.[12] Taunt him with the
    license of ink.[13] If thou thou'st him[14] some thrice, it shall not be amiss. And
    as many lies as will lie in thy sheet of paper, although the sheet were big
35 enough for the bed of Ware[15] in England, set 'em down. Go about it. Let
    there be gall enough in thy ink, though thou write with a goose-pen,[16] no
    matter. About it.

---

1   *put fire ... your liver* I.e., give you courage and passion.
2   *fire-new ... mint* I.e., newly forged (blank coins were hammered or "banged" onto a die).
3   *gilt* I.e., high value (higher currency coins were gilded rather than being minted of solid gold).
4   *sailed into the ... Dutchman's beard* You will now suffer her cold indifference (alluding to the Arctic voyage in 1596–97 of the Dutchman, William Barentz).
5   *policy* I.e., cleverness (but taken to mean political position).
6   *lief* Rather.
7   *Brownist* Member of a radical Puritan sect founded by Robert Browne, an advocate for separation of church and state.
8   *build me* Build for me.
9   *eleven places* In addition to the deadly point thrust to the abdomen, Italian fencing manuals described ten potential sabre cuts.
10 *martial hand* Military style.
11 *curst* Forceful.
12 *eloquent and full of invention* Clear and full of substance. Unlike Toby's advice, duelling manuals advised against using insulting language or repeating charges of lying.
13 *license of ink* I.e., freedom of writing (rather than confronting him face to face).
14 *thou thou'st him* Using the familiar form with a stranger was insulting.
15 *bed of Ware* A famous bedstead in Ware nearly eleven feet square.
16 *gall enough ... goose-pen* I.e., write with enough bitterness in your words to hide your cowardice (ink was made from oak galls, pens from goose-feathers).

SIR ANDREW. Where shall I find you?

SIR TOBY. We'll call thee at the cubiculo.[1] Go.

  (*Exit Sir Andrew.*)

FABIAN. This is a dear manikin[2] to you, Sir Toby.   35

SIR TOBY. I have been dear[3] to him, lad, some two thousand strong, or so.

FABIAN. We shall have a rare letter from him, but you'll not deliver't?

SIR TOBY. Never trust me then, and by all means stir on the youth to an answer. I think oxen and wainropes[4] cannot hale them together.[5] For Andrew, if he were opened and you find so much blood in his liver as will clog   40 the foot of a flea, I'll eat the rest of th' anatomy.[6]

FABIAN. And his opposite, the youth, bears in his visage no great presage[7] of cruelty.

  (*Enter Maria.*)

SIR TOBY. Look where the youngest wren of nine[8] comes.

MARIA. If you desire the spleen,[9] and will laugh yourselves into stitches, fol-   45 low me. Yond gull Malvolio is turned heathen, a very renegado,[10] for there is no Christian that means to be saved by believing rightly can ever believe such impossible passages of grossness.[11] He's in yellow stockings.

SIR TOBY. And cross-gartered?

MARIA. Most villainously,[12] like a pedant that keeps a school i' th' church.[13] I   50 have dogged[14] him like his murderer. He does obey every point of the letter that I dropped to betray him. He does smile his face into more lines than

---

1   *cubiculo* Italian: bedchamber.

2   *manikin* Puppet.

3   *dear* Costly.

4   *wainropes* Wagon ropes.

5   *hale them together* I.e., get them to fight.

6   *opened … anatomy* An anatomist opened the body to demonstrate the organs; before William Harvey's *On the Circulation of Blood* (1628), blood was thought to be produced by the liver; *so much blood … a flea* I.e., so little courage; *th' anatomy* Skeleton (implying Andrew is just "skin and bones").

7   *presage* Sign.

8   *youngest wren of nine* I.e., the littlest of the brood.

9   *spleen* The spleen was believed to be the seat of laughter.

10   *renegado* Spanish: deserter of his faith.

11   *passages of grossness* I.e., stupid statements (in the letter, and implying that Malvolio is a credulous literalist).

12   *villainously* Abominably.

13   *pedant … i' th' church* Maria alludes to the obsolescent practice of rural schools meeting in churches; *pedant* Overly formal, dogmatic teacher.

14   *dogged* Followed.

is in the new map with the augmentation of the Indies.[1] You have not seen
such a thing as 'tis. I can hardly forbear hurling things at him. I know my
lady will strike him. If she do, he'll smile and take't for a great favour.

SIR TOBY. Come, bring us, bring us where he is.

     (*Exeunt omnes.*)

ACT 3, SCENE 3

    (*Enter Sebastian and Antonio.*)

SEBASTIAN. I would not by my will have troubled you,	
But since you make your pleasure of your pains,	
I will no further chide you.	
ANTONIO. I could not stay behind you. My desire,	
5 More sharp than filèd° steel, did spur me forth,	*sharpened*
And not all° love to see you—though so much	*only for*
As might have drawn one to a longer voyage—	
But jealousy° what might befall your travel,	*concern*
Being skilless in° these parts, which to a stranger,	*unacquainted with*
10 Unguided and unfriended, often prove	
Rough and unhospitable. My willing love,	
The rather° by these arguments of fear,	*urged*
Set forth in your pursuit.	
SEBASTIAN. My kind Antonio,	
I can no other answer make but thanks,	
15 And thanks, and ever thanks; and oft° good turns	*too often*
Are shuffled off° with such uncurrent° pay.	*dismissed / worthless*
But were my worth as is my conscience firm,[2]	
You should find better dealing. What's to do?	
Shall we go see the relics° of this town?	*antiquities*
20 ANTONIO. Tomorrow, sir, best first go see your lodging.	
SEBASTIAN. I am not weary, and 'tis long to night.	
I pray you, let us satisfy our eyes	
With the memorials and the things of fame	
That do renown this city.	
ANTONIO. Would you'd pardon me.	
25 I do not without danger walk these streets:	

---

1   *new map ... the Indies* Edward Wright's world map, produced in 1599, showed the East Indies in detail and featured longitudinal rhumb lines to aid navigation.

2   *worth ... firm* I.e., wealth as great as my sense of indebtedness.

Once in a sea-fight 'gainst the Count his° galleys   *Count's*
I did some service, of such note indeed
That were I ta'en here it would scarce be answered.[1]
SEBASTIAN. Belike° you slew great number of his people.   *Perhaps*
ANTONIO. Th' offence is not of such a bloody nature,   30
Albeit the quality° of the time and quarrel   *circumstances*
Might well have given us bloody argument.[2]
It might have since been answered in repaying
What we took from them, which for traffic's° sake   *trade's*
Most of our city did. Only myself stood out,   35
For which if I be lapsed° in this place,   *caught*
I shall pay dear.
SEBASTIAN.   Do not then walk too open.
ANTONIO. It doth not fit me.[3] Hold, sir, here's my purse.
In the south suburbs, at the Elephant,[4]
Is best to lodge. I will bespeak our diet[5]   40
Whiles you beguile° the time and feed your knowledge   *pass*
With viewing of the town. There shall you have me.
SEBASTIAN. Why I your purse?
ANTONIO. Haply your eye shall light upon some toy°   *trifle*
You have desire to purchase, and your store   45
I think is not for idle markets,[6] sir.
SEBASTIAN. I'll be your purse-bearer, and leave you for
An hour.
ANTONIO. To th' Elephant.
SEBASTIAN.   I do remember.

(*Exeunt.*)

---

1   *scarce be answered* No reparation I could make would suffice.
2   *bloody argument* Justification for violence.
3   *It doth not fit me* I.e., it's not in my nature to be secretive.
4   *the Elephant* An Elephant Inn existed in Southwark near the Globe theatre around 1599
     (it may have doubled as a brothel).
5   *bespeak our diet* Order our food (parallel to "feed your knowledge").
6   *your store ... idle markets* I.e., you don't have enough money for luxuries.

ACT 3, SCENE 4

(*Enter Olivia and Maria.*)

OLIVIA. [*aside*] I have sent after him, he says[1] he'll come.
How shall I feast him? What bestow of him?
For youth is bought more oft than begged or borrowed.[2]
I speak too loud. [*to Maria*] Where's Malvolio? He is sad and civil,[3]

5   And suits well for a servant with my fortunes.
Where is Malvolio?

MARIA. He's coming, madam, but in very strange manner.
He is sure possessed,[4] madam.

OLIVIA. Why, what's the matter? Does he rave?

10 MARIA. No, madam, he does nothing but smile. Your ladyship were best
to have some guard about you if he come, for sure the man is tainted in's
wits.

OLIVIA. Go call him hither.

([*Maria leaving,*] *enter Malvolio.*)[5]

                         I am as mad as he,
If sad and merry madness equal be.

15   How now, Malvolio!

MALVOLIO. Sweet lady, ho, ho.

OLIVIA. Smil'st thou?
I sent for thee upon a sad[6] occasion.

MALVOLIO. Sad, lady? I could be sad. This does make some obstruction in the

20   blood, this cross-gartering, but what of that? If it please the eye of one, it is
with me as the very true sonnet is, "Please one and please all."[7]

OLIVIA. Why, how dost thou, man? What is the matter with thee?

---

1   *he says* I.e., what if he says.
2   *bought ... borrowed* Proverbial: "Better to buy than to borrow" (or "to beg").
3   *sad and civil* Serious and shows restraint.
4   *possessed* By the devil, insane.
5   *Maria leaving, enter Malvolio* Most editors have Maria exit here, leaving Olivia to speak
her couplet alone, and immediately return with Malvolio; comic timing is better served
with his entrance while Olivia speaks her lines, thinking she is alone.
6   *sad* Serious (as in "sad and civil" above), but Malvolio takes it to mean melancholy caused
by poor circulation, an "obstruction in the blood" caused by his crossed garters.
7   *Please one and please all* A line from a bawdy ballad about wilful women.

A cross-gartered German cavalier, from Omnium pene Europae, Asiae, Aphricae atque Americae gentium habitus, *1581. To wear stockings "cross-gartered" is to hold up each stocking with a ribbon crossed behind the knee and tied with a bow at the front or side. It may be that, by the time* Twelfth Night *was written, cross-gartering was perceived as an out-of-date affectation of pretenders to high class. It is also possible that cross-gartering was still very much in style—but only among fashionable young people. In either case, the fashion would have been wholly inappropriate for Malvolio.*

MALVOLIO. Not black in my mind, though yellow[1] in my legs. It did come to his hands, and commands shall be executed. I think we do know the sweet
25   Roman hand.[2]

OLIVIA. Wilt thou go to bed,[3] Malvolio?

MALVOLIO. To bed? Ay, sweetheart, and I'll come to thee.

OLIVIA. God comfort thee! Why dost thou smile so, and kiss thy hand so oft?

MARIA. How do you, Malvolio?

30 MALVOLIO. At your request? Yes, nightingales answer daws.[4]

MARIA. Why appear you with this ridiculous boldness before my lady?

MALVOLIO. "Be not afraid of greatness." 'Twas well writ.

OLIVIA. What mean'st thou by that, Malvolio?

MALVOLIO. "Some are born great,"—

35 OLIVIA. Ha?

MALVOLIO. "Some achieve greatness,"—

OLIVIA. What say'st thou?

MALVOLIO. "And some have greatness thrust upon them."

OLIVIA. Heaven restore thee!

40 MALVOLIO. "Remember who commended thy yellow stockings,"—

OLIVIA. "Thy yellow stockings?"

MALVOLIO. "And wished to see thee cross-gartered."

OLIVIA. "Cross-gartered?"

MALVOLIO. "Go to, thou art made, if thou desir'st to be so."

45 OLIVIA. Am I made?

MALVOLIO. "If not, let me see thee a servant still."

OLIVIA. Why, this is very midsummer madness.[5]

    (*Enter Servant.*)

SERVANT. Madam, the young gentleman of the Count Orsino's is returned. I could hardly[6] entreat him back. He attends your ladyship's pleasure.

50 OLIVIA. I'll come to him.

    (*Exit* [*Servant.*])

---

1   *black ... yellow* Black and yellow bile corresponded with melancholy and choler, and yellow stockings were thought to indicate jealousy. "Black and Yellow" was also a popular song.

2   *Roman hand* Fashionable italic lettering (rather than common English cursive).

3   *to bed* I.e., to rest and recover from his madness.

4   *nightingales answer daws* I.e., even a nightingale sings at the crowing of a jackdaw.

5   *midsummer madness* Proverbial: "it is midsummer moon with you."

6   *hardly* Only with difficulty (persuade him to return).

Good Maria, let this fellow be looked to. Where's my cousin Toby? Let some of my people have a special care of him. I would not have him mis-carry[1] for the half of my dowry.

(*Exit* [*Olivia and Maria*].)

MALVOLIO. O, ho, do you come near me[2] now? No worse man than Sir Toby to look to me. This concurs directly with the letter; she sends him on 55 purpose, that I may appear stubborn to him, for she incites me to that in the letter. "Cast thy humble slough," says she. "Be opposite with kinsman, surly with servants. Let thy tongue tang with[3] arguments of state, put thy-self into the trick of singularity," and consequently[4] sets down the manner how, as a sad face, a reverend carriage, a slow tongue, in the habit of some 60 sir of note,[5] and so forth. I have limed[6] her, but it is Jove's doing, and Jove make me thankful. And when she went away now—"Let this fellow be looked to"—"fellow," not "Malvolio" nor after my degree,[7] but "fellow." Why, everything adheres together, that no dram of a scruple, no scruple of a scruple,[8] no obstacle, no incredulous[9] or unsafe circumstance—what can 65 be said?—nothing that can be can come between me and the full prospect of my hopes. Well, Jove, not I, is the doer of this, and he is to be thanked.

(*Enter Sir Toby, Fabian, and Maria.*)

SIR TOBY. Which way is he, in the name of sanctity?[10] If all the devils of hell be drawn in little,[11] and Legion[12] himself possessed him, yet I'll speak to him.
FABIAN. Here he is, here he is. How is't with you, sir? 70
SIR TOBY. How is't with you, man?
MALVOLIO. Go off, I discard you. Let me enjoy my private.[13] Go off.

---

1   *miscarry* Come to harm.
2   *come near me* I.e., begin to appreciate my value.
3   *tang with* The First Folio reads "langer with," a printer's error, while the letter in the First Folio reads "tang arguments."
4   *consequently* Subsequently.
5   *sir of note* I.e., distinguished gentleman.
6   *limed* I.e., caught; bird lime is a sticky paste smeared on branches to trap birds.
7   *my degree* I.e., my position as steward.
8   *no dram ... scruple* I.e., without a doubt, even the smallest doubt; drams and scruples were tiny measures used by apothecaries, with a scruple being one third of a dram.
9   *incredulous* Incredible.
10 *in the ... of sanctity* I.e., by God.
11 *drawn in little* Contracted into a space, drawn in miniature.
12 *Legion* Toby mistakenly names a spirit who possessed a man in Mark 5.9 saying, "my name is legion, for we are many."
13 *private* Privacy.

MARIA. Lo, how hollow[1] the fiend speaks within him. Did not I tell you? Sir Toby, my lady prays you to have a care of him.

75 MALVOLIO. Ah ha, does she so?

SIR TOBY. Go to, go to. Peace, peace, we must deal gently with him. Let me alone.[2] How do you, Malvolio? How is't with you? What, man, defy the devil. Consider, he's an enemy to mankind.

MALVOLIO. Do you know what you say?[3]

80 MARIA. La[4] you, an you speak ill of the devil, how he takes it at heart. Pray God he be not bewitched.

FABIAN. Carry his water to th' wise woman.[5]

MARIA. Marry, and it shall be done tomorrow morning,[6] if I live. My lady would not lose him for more than I'll say.

85 MALVOLIO. How now, mistress?

MARIA. O Lord!

SIR TOBY. Prithee hold thy peace, this is not the way. Do you not see you move[7] him? Let me alone with him.

FABIAN. No way but gentleness—gently, gently. The fiend is rough,[8] and will

90 not be roughly used.

SIR TOBY. Why, how now, my bawcock.[9] How dost thou, chuck?[10]

MALVOLIO. Sir!

SIR TOBY. Ay, biddy,[11] come with me. What, man, 'tis not for gravity[12] to play at cherrypit[13] with Satan. Hang him, foul collier.[14]

95 MARIA. Get him to say his prayers, good Sir Toby, get him to pray.

MALVOLIO. My prayers, minx![15]

MARIA. No, I warrant you, he will not hear of godliness.

---

1   *hollow* Insincerely.
2   *alone* Alone with him.
3   *Do you ... say* I.e., how dare you (a drunk) moralize.
4   *La* Look.
5   *Carry his water ... woman* Have his urine examined (for signs of disease); *wise woman* A medical practitioner with knowledge of basic medicine and herbal remedies, but often associated with witchcraft.
6   *tomorrow morning* I.e., after the chamber pot is emptied.
7   *move* Anger.
8   *rough* Violent.
9   *bawcock* Fine bird.
10   *chuck* Chicken.
11   *biddy* Hen (with "bawcock" and "chuck," a term of affection).
12   *gravity* A man of gravity or dignity.
13   *cherrypit* Children's game in which cherry stones are tossed into a hole.
14   *collier* Coalman (i.e., Satan).
15   *minx* Impudent woman.

MALVOLIO. Go, hang yourselves all! You are idle shallow things, I am not of your element.[1] You shall know more hereafter.

(*Exit.*)

SIR TOBY. Is't possible?   100

FABIAN. If this were played upon a stage now, I could condemn it as an improbable fiction.[2]

SIR TOBY. His very genius[3] hath taken the infection of the device,[4] man.

MARIA. Nay, pursue him now, lest the device take air and taint.[5]

FABIAN. Why, we shall make him mad indeed.   105

MARIA. The house will be the quieter.

SIR TOBY. Come, we'll have him in a dark room and bound.[6] My niece is already in the belief that he's mad. We may carry it thus, for our pleasure and his penance till our very pastime, tired out of breath, prompt us to have mercy on him. At which time we will bring the device to the bar and   110 crown thee for a finder of madmen.[7] But see, but see.

(*Enter Sir Andrew.*)

FABIAN. More matter[8] for a May morning.

SIR ANDREW. Here's the challenge, read it. I warrant there's vinegar and pepper in't.

FABIAN. Is't so saucy?[9]   115

SIR ANDREW. Ay, is't, I warrant him. Do but read.

SIR TOBY. Give me. [*Reads.*] "Youth, whatsoever thou art, thou art but a scurvy fellow."

FABIAN. Good, and valiant.

SIR TOBY. [*Reads.*] "Wonder not, nor admire not in thy mind, why I do call   120 thee so, for I will show thee no reason for't."

FABIAN. A good note, that keeps you from the blow of the law.[10]

---

1   *I am … your element* I.e., I am made of better stuff than you.

2   *improbable fiction* Along with immorality, stage plays were condemned for their lack of realism.

3   *genius* Soul.

4   *the device* I.e., the letter trick.

5   *take air and taint* Spoil, grow stale (playing on "taken the infection").

6   *dark room and bound* The customary sixteenth-century treatment of the mad.

7   *to the bar … finder of madmen* Alluding to jury trials where a "finder" demonstrated the defendant's madness.

8   *matter* Entertainment.

9   *saucy* Spicy.

10   *blow of the law* Legal punishment for breaking the peace (the usual punishment for duelling).

SIR TOBY. [*Reads.*] "Thou com'st to the Lady Olivia, and in my sight she uses thee kindly; but thou liest in thy throat, that is not the matter[1] I challenge
125   thee for."

FABIAN. Very brief, and to exceeding good sense [*aside*] –less.

SIR TOBY. [*Reads.*] "I will waylay thee going home, where if it be thy chance to kill me"—

FABIAN. Good.

130 SIR TOBY. "Thou kill'st me like a rogue and a villain."[2]

FABIAN. Still you keep o' th' windy side[3] of the law—good.

SIR TOBY. [*Reads.*] "Fare thee well, and God have mercy upon one of our souls. He may have mercy upon mine, but my hope is better, and so look to thyself. Thy friend, as thou usest[4] him, and thy sworn enemy,
135   Andrew Aguecheek."
If this letter move him not, his legs cannot. I'll give't him.

MARIA. You may have very fit occasion for't. He is now in some commerce[5] with my lady, and will by and by depart.

SIR TOBY. Go, Sir Andrew. Scout me[6] for him at the corner of the orchard,
140   like a bum-baily.[7] So soon as ever thou seest him, draw, and as thou draw'st, swear horrible, for it comes to pass oft that a terrible oath, with a swaggering accent sharply twanged off, gives manhood more approbation than ever proof[8] itself would have earned him. Away.

SIR ANDREW. Nay, let me alone for swearing.[9]

        (*Exit.*)

145 SIR TOBY. Now will not I[10] deliver his letter, for the behaviour of the young gentleman gives him out to be of good capacity and breeding.[11] His employment between his lord and my niece confirms no less. Therefore this letter, being so excellently ignorant, will breed no terror in the youth. He will find it comes from a clodpole.[12] But, sir, I will deliver his challenge by
150   word of mouth, set upon Aguecheek a notable report of valour, and drive

---

1   *thou liest ... not the matter* Andrew's accusation of a deep lie would have meant an automatic challenge, but "not the matter" (like "no reason" above) cancels the accusation.
2   *kill'st me ... villain* Ambiguous, as "rogue and a villain" follows either "thou" or "me."
3   *windy side* Windward (i.e., the safe side).
4   *as thou usest* I.e., to the extent that you consider him a friend.
5   *commerce* Conversation.
6   *Scout me* Look out.
7   *bum-baily* A bailiff (Sheriff's officer) who snuck up behind debtors to arrest them.
8   *horrible* Horribly; *approbation* Credit; *proof* A duel.
9   *let me alone for swearing* Leave the swearing to me.
10 *Now will not I* I will not.
11 *of good ... and breeding* Intelligent and well-bred.
12 *clodpole* Blockhead.

the gentleman—as I know his youth will aptly receive it[1]—into a most hideous opinion of his rage, skill, fury, and impetuosity. This will so fright them both that they will kill one another by the look, like cockatrices.[2]

(*Enter Olivia and Viola.*)

FABIAN. Here he comes with your niece. Give them way[3] till he take leave, and presently after him.   155

SIR TOBY. I will meditate the while upon some horrid[4] message for a challenge.

[*Exeunt Sir Toby, Fabian, and Maria.*]

OLIVIA. I have said too much unto a heart of stone,
And laid mine honour too unchary on't.[5]
There's something in me that reproves my fault,   160
But such a headstrong potent fault it is
That it but mocks reproof.

VIOLA. With the same 'haviour° that your passion bears   *behaviour*
Goes on my master's griefs.[6]

OLIVIA. Here, wear this jewel[7] for me, 'tis my picture.   165
Refuse it not, it hath no tongue to vex you.
And I beseech you come again tomorrow.
What shall you ask of me that I'll deny,
That honour saved may upon asking give?[8]

VIOLA. Nothing but this: your true love for my master.   170

OLIVIA. How with mine honour may I give him that
Which I have given to you?

VIOLA. I will acquit you.[9]

OLIVIA. Well, come again tomorrow. Fare thee well.
A fiend like thee might bear my soul to hell.   175

[*Exit Olivia.*]

(*Enter Sir Toby and Sir Fabian.*)

---

1   *his youth ... receive it* Because of his inexperience, he will readily believe the report.
2   *cockatrices* Basilisks, legendary serpents that could kill on sight.
3   *way* Room.
4   *horrid* Terrifying.
5   *laid mine ... on't* Staked my honour too rashly on it ("a heart of stone"); *on't* In the First Folio, but often emended to "out."
6   *your passion ... master's griefs* Passion and grief were said to be both indications of love-sickness.
7   *jewel* Miniature painting set in a jewelled pendant.
8   *honour saved ... asking give* Honour may grant without yielding (her chastity).
9   *acquit you* I.e., release you (from the love you have given me).

SIR TOBY. Gentleman, God save thee.

VIOLA. And you, sir.

SIR TOBY. That defence thou hast, betake thee to't.[1] Of what nature the wrongs are thou hast done him, I know not, but thy interceptor, full of despite,[2] bloody as the hunter, attends[3] thee at the orchard end.[4] Dismount thy tuck, be yare[5] in thy preparation, for thy assailant is quick, skilful, and deadly.

VIOLA. You mistake, sir. I am sure no man hath any quarrel to me.[6] My remembrance is very free and clear from any image of offence done to any man.

SIR TOBY. You'll find it otherwise, I assure you. Therefore, if you hold your life at any price, betake you to[7] your guard, for your opposite hath in him what youth, strength, skill, and wrath, can furnish man withal.

VIOLA. I pray you, sir, what is he?

SIR TOBY. He is knight, dubbed with unhatched[8] rapier and on carpet consideration,[9] but he is a devil in private brawl. Souls and bodies hath he divorced three, and his incensement[10] at this moment is so implacable that satisfaction can be none but by pangs of death and sepulchre. "Hob-nob" is his word—give't or take't.[11]

VIOLA. I will return again into the house and desire some conduct[12] of the lady. I am no fighter. I have heard of some kind of men that put quarrels purposely on others to taste[13] their valour. Belike[14] this is a man of that quirk.[15]

SIR TOBY. Sir, no. His indignation derives itself out of a very competent[16]

---

1   *That defence ... thee to't* Prepare to use what means of defence you possess.
2   *despite* Defiance.
3   *attends* Awaits.
4   *the orchard end* I.e., at the end of the garden; Sir Andrew awaits Cesario at the corner of the orchard, so the duel may take place outside Olivia's private garden.
5   *Dismount thy tuck ... yare* Draw your rapier ("dismount" usually indicates setting a cannon in place for firing); *yare* Quick.
6   *quarrel to me* I.e., reason to challenge me to a duel.
7   *betake you to* Be on.
8   *unhatched* Unhacked (i.e., ceremonial).
9   *carpet consideration* Courtly merit, not military valour; Andrew is a "carpet knight."
10   *incensement* Wrath.
11   *"Hob-nob" ... take't* "Have or have not" is his motto—kill or be killed; *Hob-nob* From the Middle English *habbe he, nabbe he.*
12   *some conduct* I.e., someone to escort me (or serve as a second).
13   *taste* Test.
14   *Belike* Perhaps.
15   *quirk* Peculiar behaviour, alluding to a fashion among gentlemen for duelling on superficial grounds.
16   *competent* Legally sufficient (and therefore requiring satisfaction).

injury. Therefore, get you on and give him his desire. Back you shall not to   200
the house, unless you undertake that with me which with as much safety
you might answer him.[1] Therefore on, or strip your sword stark naked.[2]
For meddle[3] you must, that's certain, or forswear to wear iron[4] about you.

VIOLA. This is as uncivil as strange. I beseech you do me this courteous office
as to know of[5] the knight what my offence to him is. It is something of my   205
negligence, nothing of my purpose.

SIR TOBY. I will do so. Signior Fabian, stay you by this gentleman till my
return.

(*Exit Toby.*)

VIOLA. Pray you, sir, do you know of this matter?

FABIAN. I know the knight is incensed against you, even to a mortal   210
arbitrement,[6] but nothing of the circumstance more.

VIOLA. I beseech you, what manner of man is he?

FABIAN. Nothing of that wonderful promise, to read him by his form,[7] as
you are like to find him in the proof of his valour. He is indeed, sir, the
most skilful, bloody, and fatal opposite that you could possibly have found   215
in any part of Illyria. Will you[8] walk towards him, I will make your peace
with him if I can.

VIOLA. I shall be much bound to you for't. I am one that would rather go
with Sir Priest than Sir Knight.[9] I care not who knows so much of my
mettle.[10]   220

(*Exeunt.*)

(*Enter Sir Toby and Sir Andrew.*)

SIR TOBY. Why, man, he's a very devil. I have not seen such a firago.[11] I had a
pass with him, rapier, scabbard, and all, and he gives me the stuck in with

---

1   *undertake that ... answer him* I.e., fight a duel with me, who am no less dangerous than
      he.
2   *strip ... naked* I.e., be publicly shamed for cowardice.
3   *meddle* Engage him.
4   *iron* A sword.
5   *know of* Learn from.
6   *mortal arbitrement* Fight to the death.
7   *Nothing of ... his form* Not promising, judging by his appearance.
8   *Will you* If you will.
9   *I am one ... Sir Knight* I.e., I'd rather make peace than fight (priests were called "sir,"
      either by courtesy or to indicate a college degree).
10   *mettle* Disposition.
11   *firago* Virago, a woman warrior (implying Cesario's ferocity is at odds with his feminine
      appearance).

such a mortal motion[1] that it is inevitable. And on the answer, he pays[2] you as surely as your feet hit the ground they step on. They say he has been

225   fencer to the Sophy.

SIR ANDREW. Pox on't. I'll not meddle with him.

SIR TOBY. Ay, but he will not now be pacified. Fabian can scarce hold him yonder.

SIR ANDREW. Plague on't an I thought he had been valiant, and so cunning

230   in fence, I'd have seen him damned ere I'd have challenged him. Let him let the matter slip, and I'll give him my horse, grey Capilet.[3]

SIR TOBY. I'll make the motion.[4] Stand here, make a good show on't, this shall end without the perdition of souls.[5] [aside] Marry, I'll ride your horse as well as I ride[6] you.

       (Enter Fabian and Viola.)

235   [aside to Fabian] I have his horse to take up the quarrel. I have persuaded him the youth's a devil.

FABIAN. [aside to Sir Toby] He is as horribly conceited[7] of him, and pants and looks pale, as if a bear were at his heels.

SIR TOBY. [to Viola] There's no remedy, sir. He will fight with you for's oath[8]

240   sake. Marry, he hath better bethought him of his quarrel,[9] and he finds that now scarce to be worth talking of.[10] Therefore draw for the supportance of his vow. He protests he will not hurt you.

VIOLA. [aside] Pray God defend me. A little thing would make me tell them how much I lack of a man.[11]

245   FABIAN. [to Sir Andrew] Give ground if you see him furious.

SIR TOBY. Come, Sir Andrew, there's no remedy. The gentleman will, for his honour's sake, have one bout with you. He cannot by the duello avoid it,

---

1   *stuck in ... mortal motion* Thrust with such a practiced movement (that it would have inevitable deadly consequences); *stuck* From Italian, *stoccata*.

2   *on the answer, he pays* As you attempt to parry his thrust, he kills.

3   *Capilet* Spelling in the First Folio, although spelled "Capulet" in *Romeo and Juliet*, both variants on the obsolete word "caple," meaning "horse."

4   *motion* Offer.

5   *perdition of souls* I.e., deaths (but alluding to the damnation of murderers).

6   *ride* Make a fool of.

7   *is as horribly conceited* I.e., has as terrifying an image.

8   *for's oath* His oath's.

9   *bethought ... quarrel* Reconsidered the reasons for his challenge.

10   *scarce ... talking of* Duelling code (the duello) required an oath to be upheld even if its motives no longer existed; as Toby explains below, "he cannot by the duello avoid it."

11   *A little thing ... lack of a man* It would not take much (of a threat from Andrew) to expose my fear, or to reveal that I am a woman (with innuendo on "a little thing").

but he has promised me, as he is a gentleman and a soldier, he will not hurt
you. Come on, to't.

SIR ANDREW. Pray God he keep his oath.   250

(*Enter Antonio.*)[1]

VIOLA. I do assure you 'tis against my will. [*Sir Andrew and Viola draw.*]
ANTONIO. Put up your sword. If this young gentleman
    Have done offence, I take the fault on me.
    If you offend him, I for him defy you.[2]
SIR TOBY. You, sir? Why, what are you?   255
ANTONIO. One, sir, that for his love[3] dares yet do more
    Than you have heard him brag to you he will.
SIR TOBY. Nay, if you be an undertaker, I am for you. [*Draws his sword.*]

(*Enter Officers.*)

FABIAN. O good Sir Toby, hold. Here come the officers.
SIR TOBY. [*to Antonio*] I'll be with you anon.   260
VIOLA. Pray, sir, put your sword up, if you please.
SIR ANDREW. Marry, will I, sir. And for that I promised[4] you, I'll be as good
    as my word. He will bear you easily and reins well.
FIRST OFFICER. This is the man, do thy office.
SECOND OFFICER. Antonio, I arrest thee at the suit[5] of Count Orsino.   265
ANTONIO. You do mistake me, sir.
FIRST OFFICER. No, sir, no jot. I know your favour[6] well,
    Though now you have no sea-cap on your head.[7]
    Take him away; he knows I know him well.
ANTONIO. I must obey. [*to Viola*] This comes with seeking you.   270
    But there's no remedy, I shall answer it.[8]
    What will you do, now my necessity
    Makes me to ask you for my purse? It grieves me

---

1   *Enter Antonio* Antonio's sudden entrance, and the arrival of officers below, indicates that
    the duel occurs in a public place, and not in Olivia's garden.
2   *take the fault ... defy you* Antonio offers to act as proxy for Cesario (whom he mistakes
    for Sebastian throughout this scene, since the siblings look alike), a practice that helped
    prevent unevenly matched opponents.
3   *his love* I.e., love of him (Sebastian, but indicating Cesario).
4   *that I promised* His horse, Capilet (Toby has kept Andrew's offer to himself).
5   *suit* Petition.
6   *favour* Face.
7   *Though now ... on your head* This line condenses and confirms Antonio's account in 3.3
    of a sea-battle and piracy.
8   *answer it* I.e., accept the consequences of my former actions.

Much more for what I cannot do for you
275   Than what befalls myself. You stand amazed,°   *bewildered*
        But be of comfort.
SECOND OFFICER. Come, sir, away.
ANTONIO. [*to Viola*] I must entreat of you some of that money.
VIOLA. What money, sir?
280   For the fair kindness you have showed me here,
        And part being prompted by your present trouble,
        Out of my lean and low ability°   *meagre resources*
        I'll lend you something. My having is not much.
        I'll make division of my present¹ with you.
285   Hold, [*offering money*] there's half my coffer.
ANTONIO. [*refuses money*] Will you deny me now?
        Is't possible that my deserts to you
        Can lack persuasion?² Do not tempt my misery,
        Lest that it make me so unsound³ a man
290   As to upbraid you with those kindnesses
        That I have done for you.
VIOLA.   I know of none,
        Nor know I you by voice or any feature.
        I hate ingratitude more in a man
        Than lying, vainness, babbling drunkenness,
295   Or any taint of vice whose strong corruption
        Inhabits our frail blood.
ANTONIO.   O heavens themselves!
SECOND OFFICER. Come, sir, I pray you go.
ANTONIO. Let me speak a little. This youth that you see here
        I snatched one half out of the jaws of death,⁴
300   Relieved him with such sanctity⁵ of love,
        And to his image, which methought did promise
        Most venerable worth,⁶ did I devotion.
FIRST OFFICER. What's that to us? The time goes by away.
ANTONIO. But O, how vile an idol proves this god!
305   Thou hast, Sebastian, done good feature° shame.   *physical perfection*

---

1   *My having* What I own; *my present* My ready money.
2   *deserts … lack persuasion* I.e., services that merit reward do not move you.
3   *unsound* Morally weak (because kindness should expect no reward).
4   *snatched one … jaws of death* Pulled half-dead from the sea.
5   *sanctity* Devotion; this is the first in a series of religious terms: *image, venerable, devotion, idol, god.*
6   *venerable worth* Worthy of devotion.

In nature there's no blemish but the mind.
None can be called deformed but the unkind.[1]
Virtue is beauty, but the beauteous evil
Are empty trunks, o'er-flourished by the devil.[2]
FIRST OFFICER. The man grows mad. Away with him.
  Come, come, sir.   310
ANTONIO. Lead me on.

    (*Exit* [*with Officers.*])

VIOLA. Methinks his words do from such passion fly
  That he believes himself. So do not I.[3]
  Prove true, imagination, O, prove true,
  That I, dear brother, be now ta'en for you!   315
SIR TOBY. Come hither, knight. Come hither, Fabian. We'll whisper o'er a
  couplet or two of most sage saws.[4]
VIOLA. He named Sebastian. I my brother know
  Yet living in my glass.[5] Even such and so
  In favour was my brother. And he went   320
  Still° in this fashion, colour, ornament,   *Always*
  For him I imitate. O, if it prove,°   *proves true*
  Tempests are kind, and salt waves fresh in love!

    [*Exit Viola.*]

SIR TOBY. A very dishonest paltry[6] boy, and more a coward than a hare.[7] His
  dishonesty appears in leaving his friend here in necessity and denying him. 325
  And for his cowardship, ask Fabian.
FABIAN. A coward, a most devout coward, religious in it.
SIR ANDREW. 'Slid,[8] I'll after him again and beat him.
SIR TOBY. Do, cuff him soundly, but never draw thy sword.
SIR ANDREW. An I do not—[9] [*Exit.*]   330

---

1   *unkind* Cruel, unnatural (i.e., morally deformed).
2   *the beauteous evil ... the devil* Those who are beautiful yet evil are like empty chests lav-
     ishly decorated (to tempt desire).
3   *So do not I* I.e., I dare not believe the hope (that Sebastian is alive).
4   *sage saws* Wise sayings; Sir Toby invites Fabian to contemplate the unexpected outcome
     of the duel (but possibly also mocking Viola's preceding couplets).
5   *I my brother ... my glass* I know my brother is mirrored in my disguise.
6   *dishonest paltry* Dishonourable, weak.
7   *more a coward than a hare* Proverbial: "as fearful as a hare."
8   *'Slid* By God's eyelid.
9   *An I do not* I.e., if I don't ("cuff him soundly").

FABIAN. Come, let's see the event.[1]

SIR TOBY. I dare lay any money 'twill be nothing yet.[2]

(*Exit.*)

ACT 4, SCENE 1

(*Enter Sebastian and Feste.*)

FESTE. Will you[3] make me believe that I am not sent for you?

SEBASTIAN. Go to, go to, thou art a foolish fellow. Let me be clear of[4] thee.

FESTE. Well held out,[5] i' faith! No, I do not know you, nor I am not[6] sent
to you by my lady, to bid you come speak with her, nor your name is not
5　　Master Cesario, nor this is not my nose[7] neither. Nothing that is so is so.

SEBASTIAN. I prithee vent thy folly somewhere else. Thou know'st not me.

FESTE. Vent my folly! He has heard that word of some great man, and now
applies it to a fool. Vent my folly—I am afraid this great lubber,[8] the world,
will prove a cockney.[9] I prithee now, ungird thy strangeness,[10] and tell me
10　　what I shall "vent" to my lady. Shall I "vent" to her that thou art coming?

SEBASTIAN. I prithee, foolish Greek,[11] depart from me.
There's money for thee. If you tarry longer I shall give worse payment.[12]

FESTE. By my troth, thou hast an open hand.[13] These wise men that give fools
money get themselves a good report after fourteen years' purchase.[14]

(*Enter [Sir] Andrew, [Sir] Toby, and Fabian.*)

15　SIR ANDREW. Now, sir, have I met you again? [*striking Sebastian*] There's for
you.

1　　*event* Outcome.

2　　*yet* After all.

3　　*Will you* I.e., are you trying to.

4　　*clear of* Free from.

5　　*held out* Insisted (the scene begins mid-conversation).

6　　*I am not* Am I not (establishing a series of double negatives).

7　　*not my nose* Proverbial: "as plain as the nose on my face."

8　　*lubber* Clumsy, lazy fellow.

9　　*cockney* Spoiled child.

10　*ungird thy strangeness* Drop your aloof formality.

11　*Greek* I.e., buffoon.

12　*worse payment* On stage, Sebastian may threaten Feste here by raising his hand.

13　*thou hast an open hand* You are generous (perhaps ironic, but Cesario gave him money in
3.1).

14　*good report ... purchase* I.e., good reputation provided they pay well enough (the typical
price of a plot of land was equal to twelve years' rent).

SEBASTIAN. Why, [*beating Sir Andrew*] there's for thee, and there, and there.
(*Beats Sir Andrew.*) Are all the people mad?

SIR TOBY. [*holding Sebastian*] Hold, sir, or I'll throw your dagger o'er the
house. 20

FESTE. This will I tell my lady straight. I would not be in some of your coats
for two-pence.[1] [*Exit.*]

SIR TOBY. Come on, sir, hold.

SIR ANDREW. Nay, let him alone. I'll go another way to work[2] with him. I'll
have an action of battery[3] against him if there be any law in Illyria. Though 25
I struck him first, yet it's no matter for that.

SEBASTIAN. Let go thy hand.

SIR TOBY. Come, sir, I will not let you go. Come, my young soldier, put up
your iron. You are well fleshed.[4] Come on.

SEBASTIAN. I will be free from thee. What wouldst thou now? 30
If thou dar'st tempt me further, draw thy sword. [*Draws.*]

SIR TOBY. What, what? Nay, then I must have an ounce or two of this malapert[5] blood from you. [*Draws.*]

(*Enter Olivia.*)

OLIVIA. Hold, Toby. On thy life, I charge thee hold.

SIR TOBY. Madam. 35

OLIVIA. Will it be ever thus? Ungracious wretch,
Fit for the mountains and the barbarous caves,
Where manners ne'er were preached. Out of my sight!
Be not offended, dear Cesario—
Rudesby,° be gone! *Ruffian* 40

[*Exeunt Sir Toby, Sir Andrew, and Fabian.*]

I prithee, gentle friend,
Let thy fair wisdom, not thy passion, sway
In this uncivil and unjust extent[6]
Against thy peace. Go with me to my house,
And hear thou there how many fruitless pranks 45

---

1   *two-pence* Either Feste is being ironic or this small sum is significant to him.
2   *go another way to work* Find other means to revenge myself.
3   *action of battery* Lawsuit for armed assault (although "I struck him first" undercuts his
    claim).
4   *young soldier ... well fleshed* Thinking Sebastian is the once-timid Cesario, Toby compares
    him to a soldier who is used to bloodshed; a young hawk or hound was "fleshed" by feed-
    ing on its kill.
5   *malapert* Impudent.
6   *extent* Attack (from the legal term *extendi facias*, to seize goods for the king).

This ruffian hath botched up,° that thou thereby   *clumsily contrived*
Mayst smile at this. Thou shalt not choose but go.
Do not deny. Beshrew° his soul for me.   *Curse*
He started one poor heart of mine in thee.[1]

50   SEBASTIAN.   What relish is in this? How runs the stream?[2]
Or° I am mad, or else this is a dream.   *Either*
Let fancy still my sense in Lethe steep.[3]
If it be thus to dream, still let me sleep.

OLIVIA.   Nay, come, I prithee. Would thou'dst be ruled by me.

55   SEBASTIAN.   Madam, I will.

OLIVIA.   O, say so, and so be!

(*Exeunt.*)

ACT 4, SCENE 2

(*Enter Maria and Feste.*)

MARIA.   Nay, I prithee, put on this gown and this beard. Make him believe
thou art Sir Topaz[4] the curate.[5] Do it quickly. I'll call Sir Toby the whilst.
[*Exit.*]

FESTE.   Well, I'll put it on, and I will dissemble myself in't; and I would I
were the first that ever dissembled[6] in such a gown. I am not tall enough to
5   become the function well nor lean enough to be thought a good student.[7]
But to be said "an honest man and a good housekeeper" goes as fairly as to
say "a careful man and a great scholar." The competitors[8] enter.

(*Enter [Sir] Toby [and Maria].*)

SIR TOBY.   Jove bless thee, Master Parson.[9]

---

1   *started ... in thee* Made my heart leap in fear for you (punning on "start"—to rouse a
resting animal—and "hart," a deer).

2   *What relish ... runs the stream* Both phrases mean, figuratively, "what does this
mean?"; *relish* Flavour.

3   *Let fancy ... Lethe steep* May imagination drown my (confused) senses in oblivion; *Lethe* Mythological river of forgetfulness; *steep* Flowing quickly.

4   *Sir Topaz* "Topas" in the First Folio; *Topaz* Precious stone thought to cure madness (but
associated with changeability like opal in 2.4.71).

5   *curate* Parish priest.

6   *dissembled* Put on false appearances, acted hypocritically.

7   *not tall enough ... good student* Feste alludes to two clerical stereotypes, that tall priests
had more authority, and that scholars of divinity spent more money on books than
food; *function* Priestly office.

8   *competitors* Partners.

9   *Master Parson* This generic title suggests Topaz has earned his "Sir" with a Master of
Divinity degree.

FESTE. *Bonos dies*,[1] Sir Toby, for as the old hermit of Prague,[2] that never saw
pen and ink, very wittily said to a niece of King Gorboduc[3] "that that is,   10
is."[4] So I, being Master Parson, am Master Parson, for what is "that" but
that, and "is" but is?
SIR TOBY. To him,[5] Sir Topaz.
FESTE. What ho, I say, peace in this prison.[6]
SIR TOBY. The knave counterfeits well—a good knave.   15

(*Malvolio within.*)[7]

MALVOLIO. Who calls there?
FESTE. Sir Topaz the curate, who comes to visit Malvolio the lunatic.
MALVOLIO. Sir Topaz, Sir Topaz, good Sir Topaz, go to my lady.
FESTE. Out, hyperbolical fiend,[8] how vexest thou this man! Talkest thou
nothing but of ladies?   20
SIR TOBY. Well said, Master Parson.
MALVOLIO. Sir Topaz, never was man thus wronged. Good Sir Topaz, do not
think I am mad. They have laid me here in hideous darkness.
FESTE. Fie, thou dishonest Satan! I call thee by the most modest[9] terms, for I
am one of those gentle ones[10] that will use the devil himself with courtesy. 25
Say'st thou that house is dark?
MALVOLIO. As hell, Sir Topaz.
FESTE. Why, it hath bay windows transparent as barricadoes, and the clere-
stories toward the south north are as lustrous as ebony,[11] and yet complain-
est thou of obstruction?   30

---

1 *Bonos dies* Good day; Feste makes mock Latin out of the Spanish greeting, *Buenos dias*.
2 *hermit of Prague* Mock authority like "Quinapalus" in 1.5.28.
3 *King Gorboduc* Legendary English king.
4 *that that is, is* Feste is spoofing logical tautologies, things self-evidently evident.
5 *To him* Go to him.
6 *peace in this prison* An allusion to the "Order for the Visitation of the Sick" in the *Book of Common Prayer* (1559), instructing priests to say "peace be in this house" as they enter.
7 *Malvolio within* This stage direction in the First Folio suggests that Malvolio is heard from his dark cell, but not seen; some productions place him off-stage, while some place him in an imaginary cell upstage.
8 *Out, hyperbolical fiend* Feste paraphrases Mark 5.8, "Come out of the man, thou unclean spirit"; *hyperbolical* Outrageous, extreme.
9 *modest* Mildest.
10 *those gentle ones* Methods of exorcism ranged from using physical force to expel the demon to debating the demon on theological matters, hoping to trap it in contradictions, as Feste does below.
11 *transparent as ... as ebony* Oxymorons (along with "south north"), both equivalent to "clear as mud"; *barricadoes* From Spanish: barricades, thick earthen barriers; *clerestories* Upper windows in halls and churches.

MALVOLIO. I am not mad, Sir Topaz. I say to you this house is dark.

FESTE. Madman, thou errest.[1] I say there is no darkness but ignorance, in which thou art more puzzled than the Egyptians in their fog.[2]

MALVOLIO. I say this house is as dark as ignorance, though ignorance were as
35   dark as hell, and I say there was never man thus abused. I am no more mad than you are. Make the trial of it in any constant question.[3]

FESTE. What is the opinion of Pythagoras concerning wild fowl?[4]

MALVOLIO. That the soul of our grandam might haply[5] inhabit a bird.

FESTE. What think'st thou of his opinion?

40   MALVOLIO. I think nobly of the soul,[6] and no way approve his opinion.

FESTE. Fare thee well. Remain thou still in darkness. Thou shalt hold th' opinion of Pythagoras ere I will allow of thy wits,[7] and fear to kill a wood-cock, lest thou dispossess the soul of thy grandam. Fare thee well.

MALVOLIO. Sir Topaz, Sir Topaz!

45   SIR TOBY. My most exquisite[8] Sir Topaz!

FESTE. Nay, I am for all waters.[9]

MARIA. Thou mightst have done this without thy beard and gown. He sees thee not.

SIR TOBY. To[10] him in thine own voice, and bring me word how thou find'st
50   him. I would we were well rid of this knavery. If he may be conveniently delivered,[11] I would he were, for I am now so far in offence with my niece that I cannot pursue with any safety this sport to the upshot.[12] Come by and by to my chamber.[13]

(*Exit* [*with Maria*].)

1   *say to you … thou errest* Malvolio uses the polite "you," Feste the condescending "thou."
2   *Egyptians in their fog* One of the ten plagues on Egypt was described in Exodus 10.21 as a "darkness that may be felt."
3   *Make the trial … constant question* Test my sanity with any logical problem.
4   *Pythagoras concerning wild fowl* This ancient Greek philosopher held that after death a soul could transmigrate to either a newborn child or an animal; one follower of Pythagoras, Empedocles, claimed "before now, I too have been a boy, a girl, a bush, a bird, and a scaly fish in the sea."
5   *haply* Perhaps.
6   *nobly of the soul* Christian philosophers rejected transmigration by asserting the nobility of the soul, arguing that it was indivisible and unique to God's highest creation.
7   *ere … thy wits* Before I accept that you are sane.
8   *exquisite* Perfect.
9   *for all waters* Proverbial: "to have a cloak for all waters" (i.e., prepared for anything).
10   *To* Go to.
11   *delivered* Released.
12   *to the upshot* To its outcome (the "upshot" was the winning shot in an archery contest).
13   *come by … my chamber* This line is addressed to Feste (following on "bring me word") and not Maria, as some editors argue.

FESTE. [*Sings.*] "Hey, Robin, jolly Robin,[1]
              Tell me how thy lady does."   55

MALVOLIO. Fool!

FESTE.   "My lady is unkind, perdie."[2]

MALVOLIO. Fool!

FESTE.   "Alas, why is she so?"

MALVOLIO. Fool, I say!   60

FESTE.   "She loves another."
    Who calls, ha?

MALVOLIO. Good fool, as ever thou wilt deserve well at my hand, help me
to a candle, and pen, ink, and paper. As I am a gentleman, I will live to be
thankful to thee for't.   65

FESTE. Master[3] Malvolio?

MALVOLIO. Ay, good fool.

FESTE. Alas, sir, how fell you besides[4] your five wits?[5]

MALVOLIO. Fool, there was never man so notoriously[6] abused. I am as well in
my wits, fool, as thou art.   70

FESTE. But as well? Then you are mad indeed, if you be no better in your
wits than a fool.

MALVOLIO. They have here propertied me,[7] keep me in darkness, send ministers to me, asses, and do all they can to face[8] me out of my wits.

FESTE. Advise you[9] what you say, the minister is here. [*speaking as Sir To-*   75
paz] Malvolio, Malvolio, thy wits the heavens restore. Endeavour thyself
to sleep, and leave thy vain bibble-babble.[10]

MALVOLIO. Sir Topaz!

FESTE. [*as Sir Topaz*] Maintain no words with him, good fellow. [*as himself*]
Who, I, sir? Not I, sir. God buy you,[11] good Sir Topaz. [*as Sir Topaz*] Marry,   80
amen.[12] [*as himself*] I will sir, I will.

---

1   *Hey, Robin, jolly Robin* This song is probably traditional, but it may be based on the version by Sir Thomas Wyatt (1503–42) and music by William Cornish (1465–1523), both
contemporaries of King Henry VIII.

2   *perdie* By God, from French: *par dieu*.

3   *Master* The First Folio reads "M. Malvolio"; Maria earlier refers to him as "Monsieur,"
but "master" equally suggests Malvolio's social pretension (and winks at "Master Parson").

4   *besides* Out of.

5   *five wits* Medical texts variously named three principal wits—judgment, memory, and
imagination—while some added fantasy and common sense.

6   *notoriously* Outrageously.

7   *propertied me* Treated me as stage property (i.e., like furniture).

8   *face* Bully.

9   *Advise you* Be careful.

10   *bibble-babble* Common expression for empty talk.

11   *God buy you* God be with you.

12   *Marry, amen* Indeed, so be it (as if closing a prayer).

MALVOLIO. Fool, fool, fool, I say!

FESTE. Alas, sir, be patient. What say you, sir? I am shent[1] for speaking to
you.

85 MALVOLIO. Good fool, help me to some light and some paper. I tell thee I am
as well in my wits as any man in Illyria.

FESTE. Well-a-day[2] that you were, sir.

MALVOLIO. By this hand, I am. Good fool, some ink, paper, and light, and
convey what I will set down to my lady. It shall advantage thee more than
90 ever the bearing of letter did.

FESTE. I will help you to't. But tell me true, are you not mad indeed, or do
you but counterfeit?

MALVOLIO. Believe me, I am not. I tell thee true.

FESTE. Nay, I'll ne'er believe a madman till I see his brains.[3] I will fetch you
95 light and paper and ink.

MALVOLIO. Fool, I'll requite[4] it in the highest degree. I prithee be gone.

FESTE. [Sings.]

    I am gone, sir,[5]
    And anon,° sir,   *right away*
    I'll be with you again,
100   In a trice,
    Like to the old Vice[6]
    Your need to sustain,
    Who with dagger of lath,°   *wood*
    In his rage and his wrath,
105   Cries, "aha" to the devil,
    Like a mad lad,
    Pare thy nails, dad.
    Adieu, goodman devil.[7]

    (*Exit.*)

---

1   *shent* Rebuked.

2   *Well-a-day* Alas.

3   *till I see his brains* In fact, anatomists by this time knew there was no visible difference in
the brains of criminals or the insane.

4   *requite* Repay.

5   *I am gone, sir* It is uncertain whether this song is by Shakespeare; no contemporary music
survives.

6   *the old Vice* A comic character from the morality plays, typically associated with human
foibles and often cast as the son of the devil; the Vice typically wore a wooden stage-
dagger ("dagger of lath").

7   *goodman devil* Either the Vice's farewell to his father, the devil, or Feste's parting shot at
Malvolio; *goodman* Usually a title of respect, but here used ironically (in most performances, Feste delivers it with a sneer).

ACT 4, SCENE 3

(*Enter Sebastian.*)

SEBASTIAN. This is the air, that is the glorious sun,
    This pearl she gave me, I do feel't and see't,
    And though 'tis wonder that enwraps me thus,
    Yet 'tis not madness. Where's Antonio, then?
    I could not find him at the Elephant,   5
    Yet there he was,° and there I found this credit,°   *had been / report*
    That he did range° the town to seek me out.   *roam*
    His counsel now might do me golden° service.   *valuable*
    For though my soul disputes well with my sense[1]
    That this may be some error, but no madness,   10
    Yet doth this accident and flood of fortune
    So far exceed all instance, all discourse,
    That I am ready to distrust mine eyes
    And wrangle° with my reason, that persuades me   *argue*
    To any other trust° but that I am mad,   *conclusion* 15
    Or else the lady's mad. Yet if 'twere so,
    She could not sway° her house, command her followers,   *rule*
    Take and give back affairs and their dispatch[2]
    With such a smooth, discreet, and stable° bearing,   *poised*
    As I perceive she does.[3] There's something in't   20
    That is deceivable.° But here the lady comes.   *deceptive*

(*Enter Olivia and Priest.*)

OLIVIA. Blame not this haste of mine. If you mean well,
    Now go with me and with this holy man
    Into the chantry by.[4] There, before him
    And underneath that consecrated roof,   25
    Plight° me the full assurance of your faith,   *Pledge*
    That my most jealous° and too doubtful soul   *anxious*
    May live at peace. He shall conceal it

---

1   *disputes ... my sense* Agrees with the evidence of my senses, although "disputes" typically
    means "argue against," as in "wrangle with my reason" below.
2   *Take and give ... their dispatch* Ensure that her business affairs are carried out.
3   *I perceive she does* Sebastian has no knowledge of the misrule in her household during
    Acts 1–3.
4   *chantry by* Nearby chapel; ruling families endowed chapels where priests sang daily mass
    for the souls of its founders and their families (presumably, Olivia's chantry sang for her
    father and brother).

Whiles° you are willing it shall come to note,[1]   *Until*
30   What° time we will our celebration keep   *At which*
        According to my birth.° What do you say?   *rank*
SEBASTIAN. I'll follow this good man, and go with you,
        And having sworn truth, ever will be true.
OLIVIA. Then lead the way, good father, and heavens so shine
35   That they may fairly note this act of mine.

        (*Exeunt.*)

ACT 5, SCENE 1

(*Enter Feste and Fabian.*)

FABIAN. Now, as thou lov'st me, let me see his[2] letter.
FESTE. Good Master Fabian, grant me another request.
FABIAN. Anything.
FESTE. Do not desire to see this letter.
5 FABIAN. This is to give a dog, and in recompense desire my dog again.[3]

        (*Enter [Orsino], Viola, Curio, and Lords.*)

ORSINO. Belong you to the Lady Olivia, friends?
FESTE. Ay, sir, we are some of her trappings.[4]
ORSINO. I know thee well. How dost thou, my good fellow?[5]
FESTE. Truly, sir, the better for my foes and the worse for my friends.
10 ORSINO. Just the contrary: the better for thy friends.
FESTE. No, sir, the worse.
ORSINO. How can that be?
FESTE. Marry, sir, they praise me and make an ass of me. Now my foes tell
        me plainly I am an ass, so that by my foes, sir, I profit in the knowledge
15   of myself,[6] and by my friends I am abused.[7] So that, conclusions to be as

---

1   *conceal it ... come to note* A betrothal was as binding as marriage, but it could remain
     private until the publication of the marriage banns, the public declaration of an intention
     to marry.
2   *his* Malvolio's.
3   *give a dog ... my dog again* Fabian recalls an anecdote in which the Queen and her kins-
     man Dr. Boleyn discuss his beloved dog: asking that he grant her one request, she de-
     mands the dog, to which he replies, asking her for one request, and demands the dog back.
4   *trappings* Ornamental fittings on a horse's harness.
5   *I know thee ... good fellow* Orsino replies in verse, and uses the condescending "thee" and
     "thou."
6   *knowledge of myself* Feste plays on the fashionable Socratic dictum, *nosce teipsum*, "know
     thyself."
7   *abused* Deceived (by false praise).

kisses, if your four negatives make your two affirmatives,[1] why then, the
worse for my friends, and the better for my foes.

ORSINO. Why, this is excellent.

FESTE. By my troth, sir, no, though it please you to be one of my friends.

ORSINO. Thou shalt not be the worse for me. There's gold. [*Gives a coin.*]   20

FESTE. But that it would be double-dealing,[2] sir, I would you could make it
another.

ORSINO. O, you give me ill counsel.

FESTE. Put your grace in your pocket, sir, for this once, and let your flesh and
blood obey it.[3]   25

ORSINO. Well, I will be so much a sinner to be a double-dealer. There's another.

FESTE. *Primo, secundo, tertio*[4] is a good play; and the old saying is "the third
pays for all."[5] The triplex,[6] sir, is a good tripping measure, or the bells of
Saint Bennet,[7] sir, may put you in mind—one, two, three.   30

ORSINO. You can fool no more money out of me at this throw.[8] If you will
let your lady know I am here to speak with her, and bring her along with
you, it may awake my bounty[9] further.

FESTE. Marry, sir, lullaby[10] to your bounty till I come again. I go, sir, but I
would not have you to think that my desire of having is the sin of covet-   35
ousness.[11] But, as you say, sir, let your bounty take a nap. I will awake it
anon.[12] (*Exit.*)

(*Enter Antonio and Officers.*)

VIOLA. Here comes the man, sir, that did rescue me.

---

1   *conclusions to be ... two affirmatives* I.e., assuming that (as in grammar) a double-negative
is an affirmative, then logical conclusions are like kisses in that a woman who refuses a kiss
four times must be requesting one twice.

2   *But that ... double-dealing* Except for the fact that it would be double-tipping.

3   *Put your grace ... blood obey it* Set your sense of propriety (*grace*) aside and let your hand
obey your instinct (*ill counsel*).

4   *Primo, secundo, tertio* Latin: first, second, third; an allusion to a mathematical game for
children called *Primus secundus* in which, for example, 3 could be captured by 1 and 2.

5   *third pays for all* Proverbial, equivalent to the modern "three's a charm" or "third time
lucky."

6   *triplex* Triple time in music.

7   *Saint Bennet* Probably Saint Bennet (Benedict) Hithe, a church across the Thames from
the Globe theatre.

8   *at this throw* On this dice throw (i.e., on this occasion).

9   *bounty* Generosity.

10   *lullaby* Sing a lullaby (so it will "take a nap," below).

11   *sin of covetousness* Among the seven deadly sins, greed was considered the deadliest.

12   *anon* Soon.

ORSINO. That face of his I do remember well,
40   Yet when I saw it last it was besmeared°   *dirtied*
      As black as Vulcan[1] in the smoke of war.
      A baubling° vessel was he captain of,   *toy-like*
      For shallow draught and bulk unprizable,[2]
      With which such scathful grapple° did he make   *harmful attack*
45   With the most noble bottom[3] of our fleet
      That very envy and the tongue of loss
      Cried fame and honour on him.[4] What's the matter?
FIRST OFFICER. Orsino,[5] this is that Antonio
      That took the Phoenix and her fraught° from Candy.   *freight*
50   And this is he that did the Tiger board[6]
      When your young nephew Titus lost his leg.
      Here in the streets, desperate of shame and state,[7]
      In private brabble° did we apprehend° him.   *brawl / arrest*
VIOLA. He did me kindness, sir, drew on my side,[8]
55   But in conclusion put strange speech upon[9] me.
      I know not what 'twas but distraction.[10]
ORSINO. Notable° pirate, thou salt-water thief,   *Notorious*
      What foolish boldness brought thee to their mercies[11]
      Whom thou, in terms so bloody and so dear,[12]
60   Hast made thine enemies?
ANTONIO.   Orsino, noble sir,
      Be pleased that I shake off[13] these names you give me:
      Antonio never yet was thief or pirate,
      Though I confess, on base and ground enough,[14]

1   *Vulcan* Roman god of fire and metal-working.
2   *For shallow ... unprizeable* Of such small displacement and size (that it was not worth capturing).
3   *bottom* Hull (i.e., ship).
4   *very envy ... honour on him* Even envy and those he defeated declared his fame and honour.
5   *Orsino* The officer drops his title (perhaps to appear impartial and plainspoken).
6   *took the Phoenix ... Tiger board* The *Phoenix* and *Tiger* are ships in Orsino's navy; *Candy* Candia, a port town on the island of Crete.
7   *desperate of shame and state* Disregarding his guilt and the public order (contrasting with *private brabble*).
8   *drew on my side* Defended me with his sword.
9   *put strange speech upon* Spoke strangely to.
10 *but distraction* If not madness.
11 *their mercies* Put yourself at the mercy of those.
12 *terms so ... dear* Circumstances so violent and so grievous.
13 *Be pleased that I shake off* Please allow me to repudiate.
14 *base and ground enough* Sufficient grounds; *base* Foundation.

Orsino's enemy. A witchcraft° drew me hither: *spell*   65
That most ingrateful boy there by your side
From the rude° sea's enraged and foamy mouth   *rough*
Did I redeem. A wreck° past hope he was.   *shipwreck*
His life I gave him, and did thereto add
My love without retention° or restraint,   *reservation*   70
All his in dedication.[1] For his sake,
Did I expose myself, pure° for his love,   *solely*
Into the danger of this adverse° town,   *hostile*
Drew to defend him when he was beset,
Where being apprehended, his false cunning,   75
Not meaning to partake° with me in danger,   *share*
Taught him to face me out of his acquaintance,[2]
And grew a twenty years removèd thing
While one would wink,[3] denied me mine own purse,
Which I had recommended° to his use   *committed*   80
Not half an hour before.
VIOLA.   How can this be?
ORSINO. When came he to this town?
ANTONIO. Today, my lord, and for three months before,
    No int'rim,° not a minute's vacancy,°   *interim / interval*
    Both day and night did we keep company.[4]   85

(*Enter Olivia and Attendants.*)

ORSINO. Here comes the Countess; now heaven walks on earth.
    But for thee, fellow—fellow, thy words are madness.
    Three months this youth hath tended upon me.
    But more of that anon. Take him aside.
OLIVIA. What would my lord, but that he may not have,[5]   90
    Wherein Olivia may seem serviceable?°   *be of service*
    Cesario, you do not keep promise[6] with me.
VIOLA. Madam—

---

1   *All his in dedication* I.e., dedicated myself entirely to him.
2   *face me ... acquaintance* Deny he knew me.
3   *grew a twenty ... would wink* Became, in the blink of an eye, like someone who had not
     seen me in twenty years.
4   *for three months ... we keep company* This account establishes the play's dual-time scheme;
     in l. 88 below, Orsino now claims the same time has elapsed since he has known Cesario,
     while in 1.4.2 it was "but three days."
5   *but that he may not have* Except for that (i.e., my love) which I will not give.
6   *keep promise* Uphold your vow; Cesario's appearance in service to Orsino would seem to
     bring into question Sebastian's betrothal.

ORSINO. Gracious Olivia—

95 OLIVIA. What do you say, Cesario? Good my lord—

VIOLA. My lord would speak, my duty hushes me.

OLIVIA. If it be aught to the old tune,¹ my lord,
    It is as fat° and fulsome° to mine ear   *gross / revolting*
    As howling² after music.

100 ORSINO. Still so cruel?

OLIVIA. Still so constant,° lord.   *consistent*

ORSINO. What, to perverseness?° You uncivil lady,   *obstinacy*
    To whose ingrate and unauspicious³ altars
    My soul the faithfull'st off'rings⁴ hath breathed out

105   That e'er devotion tendered.° What shall I do?   *offered*

OLIVIA. Even what it please my lord that shall become him.⁵

ORSINO. Why should I not, had I the heart to do it,
    Like to the Egyptian thief at point of death,
    Kill what I love⁶—a savage jealousy

110   That sometime savours nobly.⁷ But hear me this:
    Since you to non-regardance° cast my faith,   *disregard*
    And that I partly know the instrument
    That screws⁸ me from my true place in your favour,
    Live you the marble-breasted tyrant⁹ still;

115   But this your minion,¹⁰ whom I know you love,
    And whom, by heaven I swear, I tender° dearly,   *care for*
    Him will I tear out of that cruel eye¹¹
    Where he sits crowned in his master's spite.¹²

---

1   *aught to the old tune* I.e., any of your usual romantic rhetoric.

2   *howling* Like a dog.

3   *ingrate and unauspicious* Ungrateful and unpromising.

4   *faithfull'st off'rings* Pledges of absolute fidelity.

5   *Even what ... become him* I.e., whatever suits you (equivalent to "what you will").

6   *the Egyptian thief ... what I love* Orsino compares himself to Thyamis, an Egyptian robber-chief in the Greek romance *Ethiopica* by Heliodorus (translated into English in 1569), who tries to kill his beloved Chariclea when his own life is threatened by rival robbers; critics debate the degree to which this is an implicit threat to Olivia or a melodramatic scenario that unwittingly reveals his love for Viola.

7   *savours nobly* I.e., tastes or smells of nobility.

8   *instrument that screws* Instrument of torture (i.e., Cesario) that wrenches.

9   *marble-breasted tyrant* I.e., the stereotypically cold, aloof object of unrequited courtly love.

10 *minion* Sexual favourite, as in Shakespeare's Sonnet 126.11–12: "Yet fear her, O thou minion of her pleasure: / She may detain, but not still keep, her treasure!"

11 *tear out of that cruel eye* I.e., forcibly remove him from your sight.

12 *in his master's spite* To spite his master (Orsino).

Come, boy, with me, my thoughts are ripe in mischief.[1]
I'll sacrifice the lamb that I do love[2]   120
To spite a raven's heart within a dove.[3]

VIOLA. And I, most jocund,° apt, and willingly,   *cheerfully*
  To do° you rest, a thousand deaths would die.   *give*

OLIVIA. Where goes Cesario?

VIOLA.   After him I love
  More than I love these eyes, more than my life,   125
  More, by all mores,[4] than e'er I shall love wife.
  If I do feign, you witnesses above,°   *in heaven*
  Punish my life for tainting of my love.

OLIVIA. Ay me, detested,° how am I beguiled!   *rejected*

VIOLA. Who does beguile you? Who does do you wrong?   130

OLIVIA. Hast thou forgot thyself? Is it so long?
  Call forth the holy father. [*Exit an Attendant.*]

ORSINO.   Come, away!

OLIVIA. Whither, my lord? Cesario, husband, stay.

ORSINO. Husband?

OLIVIA.   Ay, husband. Can he that deny?

ORSINO. Her husband, sirrah?   135

VIOLA.   No, my lord, not I.

OLIVIA. Alas, it is the baseness of thy fear
  That makes thee strangle thy propriety.[5]
  Fear not, Cesario, take thy fortunes up,[6]
  Be that thou know'st thou art, and then thou art
  As great as that thou fear'st.[7]   140

(*Enter Priest* [*and Attendant*].)

                              O, welcome, father!
  Father, I charge thee, by thy reverence
  Here to unfold—though lately we intended

---

1   *ripe in mischief* Prepared to do harm.
2   *sacrifice ... I do love* This probable allusion to Abraham's near-sacrifice of Isaac in Genesis
     22 recasts the story of Thyamis and Chariclea in Judeo-Christian terms.
3   *raven's heart within a dove* I.e., a raven (Olivia) that pretends to be a dove; "raven" may
     also be a slighting reference to Olivia's mourning (in some performances she is still wear-
     ing black at this point).
4   *mores* I.e., such comparisons.
5   *strangle thy propriety* I.e., deny your identity (as my betrothed).
6   *take thy fortunes up* I.e., accept your good fortune (in marrying a countess).
7   *As great as that thou fear'st* I.e., equal to whom you fear (Orsino); not technically true, as
     marriage to Olivia would bring Cesario into the nobility, but not elevate him to count.

To keep in darkness what occasion° now   *circumstance*
Reveals before 'tis ripe—what thou dost know
145 Hath newly passed between this youth and me.

PRIEST. A contract of eternal bond of love,
Confirmed by mutual joinder° of your hands,[1]   *joining*
Attested by the holy close° of lips,   *union*
Strengthened by interchangement° of your rings,   *exchange*
150 And all the ceremony of this compact°   *agreement*
Sealed in my function,[2] by my testimony;
Since when, my watch hath told me, toward my grave,
I have travelled but two hours.

ORSINO. (*to Viola*) O thou dissembling cub![3] What wilt thou be,
155 When time hath sowed a grizzle° on thy case?°   *grey hair / skin*
Or will not else thy craft° so quickly grow   *craftiness*
That thine own trip[4] shall be thine overthrow?
Farewell, and take her, but direct thy feet
Where thou and I henceforth may never meet.

160 VIOLA. My lord, I do protest.

OLIVIA.   O, do not swear!
Hold little° faith, though thou has too much fear.   *a little*

(*Enter Sir Andrew.*)

SIR ANDREW. For the love of God, a surgeon—send one presently to Sir Toby.

OLIVIA. What's the matter?

165 SIR ANDREW. Has broke[5] my head across, and has given Sir Toby a bloody coxcomb[6] too. For the love of God, your help! I had rather than forty pound I were at home.

OLIVIA. Who has done this, Sir Andrew?

SIR ANDREW. The Count's gentleman, one Cesario. We took him for a cow-
170 ard, but he's the very devil incardinate.[7]

ORSINO. My gentleman, Cesario?

---

1   *contract ... your hands* Betrothal was a pre-marital contract, in this case followed by the ceremony of hand fasting.
2   *Sealed in my function* Attested by my priestly authority.
3   *dissembling cub* Alluding to the proverb "as wily as a fox."
4   *trip* Leg movement used in wrestling to "overthrow" an opponent.
5   *Has broke* He has cut.
6   *bloody coxcomb* Synonymous with "head," deriving from a fool's cap shaped like a cock's comb.
7   *incardinate* To appoint as a cardinal; Andrew means "incarnate," in human form.

SIR ANDREW. 'Od's lifelings,[1] here he is! You broke my head for nothing, and
that that I did, I was set on to do't by Sir Toby.

VIOLA. Why do you speak to me? I never hurt you.

You drew your sword upon me without cause,   175
But I bespake you fair[2] and hurt you not.

(*Enter [Sir] Toby and Feste.*)

SIR ANDREW. If a bloody coxcomb be a hurt, you have hurt me. I think you
set nothing by[3] a bloody coxcomb. Here comes Sir Toby halting.[4] You shall
hear more, but if he had not been in drink, he would have tickled you
othergates[5] than he did.   180

ORSINO. How now, gentleman? How is't with you?

SIR TOBY. That's all one,[6] h'as hurt me, and there's th' end on't. Sot,[7] didst see
Dick Surgeon,[8] sot?

FESTE. O, he's drunk, Sir Toby, an hour agone. His eyes were set at eight i'
th' morning.[9]   185

SIR TOBY. Then he's a rogue and a passy measures pavin.[10] I hate a drunken
rogue.[11]

OLIVIA. Away with him! Who hath made this havoc with them?

SIR ANDREW. I'll help you, Sir Toby, because we'll be dressed[12] together.

SIR TOBY. Will *you* help—an ass-head and a coxcomb and a knave, a thin-   190
faced knave, a gull?[13]

OLIVIA. Get him to bed, and let his hurt be looked to.

[*Exeunt Sir Toby, Sir Andrew, Fabian, and Feste.*]

(*Enter Sebastian.*)

---

1   *'Od's lifelings* By God's little lives (a mild oath).
2   *bespake you fair* Addressed you courteously.
3   *set nothing by* Think nothing of.
4   *halting* Limping.
5   *tickled you othergates* Beat you otherwise.
6   *all one* No matter.
7   *Sot* Fool.
8   *Dick Surgeon* I.e., Dick the surgeon (a generic name).
9   *set at ... morning* I.e., fixed and unfocused like hands on a clock (not "closed by eight").
10 *passy measures pavin* Toby's tipsy attempt at "passing measures pavan," from Italian: *pas-samezzo pavana*, a slow dance in double time.
11 *I hate a drunken rogue* Toby is perhaps self-consciously comparing the movements of the dance to a swaying drunkard.
12 *dressed* Bandaged.
13 *Will you help ... a gull* In performance, Toby's sudden turn on Andrew usually registers in his complete shock; *you* Editor's emphasis; *gull* Dupe (of Toby).

SEBASTIAN. I am sorry, madam, I have hurt your kinsman,
But had it been the brother of my blood,[1]
195   I must have done no less with wit and safety.[2]
You throw a strange regard° upon me, and by that   *look*
I do perceive it hath offended you.
Pardon me, sweet one, even for[3] the vows
We made each other but so late ago.°   *recently*
200 ORSINO. One face, one voice, one habit,° and two persons!   *costume*
A natural perspective,[4] that is and is not.
SEBASTIAN. Antonio! O my dear Antonio,
How have the hours racked and tortured me
Since I have lost thee!
205 ANTONIO. Sebastian are you?
SEBASTIAN.   Fear'st thou[5] that, Antonio?
ANTONIO. How have you made division of[6] yourself?
An apple cleft in two is not more twin
Than these two creatures.[7] Which is Sebastian?
OLIVIA. Most wonderful!
210 SEBASTIAN. [*seeing Viola*] Do I stand there? I never had a brother,
Nor can there be that deity in my nature
Of here and everywhere.[8] I had a sister
Whom the blind waves and surges° have devoured.   *swells*
[*to Viola*] Of charity,[9] what kin are you to me?
215   What countryman, what name, what parentage?
VIOLA. Of Messaline. Sebastian was my father.
Such a Sebastian was my brother too.
So went he suited[10] to his watery tomb;
If spirits can assume both form and suit,°   *body and clothing*
220   You come to fright us.

---

1   *brother of my blood* My own brother.
2   *wit and safety* Sensible concern and self-protection.
3   *even for* Especially considering.
4   *natural perspective* I.e., an optical illusion produced by nature (not magic).
5   *Fear'st thou* Do you doubt.
6   *made division of* Split.
7   *An apple cleft ... two creatures* In Plato's *Symposium*, Aristophanes gives a theory of love: humans are female and male halves split (like an apple) by Zeus from an androgynous original; love draws every person to seek their "lost" half in lovers that are like or unlike themselves.
8   *that deity ... here and everywhere* I.e., divine power of omnipresence.
9   *Of charity* I.e., out of kindness (please tell me).
10   *suited* Dressed (as you are).

SEBASTIAN.   A spirit I am indeed,
But am in that dimension grossly clad[1]
Which from the womb I did participate.[2]
Were you a woman, as the rest goes even,[3]
I should my tears let fall upon your cheek,
And say "thrice welcome, drownèd Viola!"
VIOLA. My father had a mole upon his brow.   225
SEBASTIAN. And so had mine.
VIOLA. And died that day when Viola from her birth
Had numbered thirteen years.[4]
SEBASTIAN. O, that record is lively[5] in my soul!
He finishèd indeed his mortal act   230
That day that made my sister thirteen years.
VIOLA. If nothing lets° to make us happy both   *hinders*
But this my masculine usurped attire,
Do not embrace me[6] till each circumstance
Of place, time, fortune, do cohere and jump[7]   235
That I am Viola, which to confirm,
I'll bring you to a captain in this town
Where[8] lie my maiden weeds,° by whose gentle help   *clothes*
I was preserved to serve this noble Count.
All the occurrence of my fortune since   240
Hath been between this lady and this lord.
SEBASTIAN. [*to Olivia*] So comes it, lady, you have been mistook,°   *mistaken*
But nature to her bias drew in that.[9]
You would have been contracted° to a maid;   *married*

---

1   *A spirit ... grossly clad* I have a soul, but it is dressed in common flesh (echoing the
     Platonic and Christian idea of the immortal soul housed in an imperfect body); *dimen-
     sion* Physical (not spiritual).
2   *participate* Share with other humans.
3   *the rest goes even* Everything else suggests.
4   *numbered thirteen years* Placing herself in the third person, Viola offers her birthday as
     corroborating evidence that Sebastian can confirm (below), but without external confir-
     mation either can still be seen as impersonating the other.
5   *record is lively* Memory is vivid; *record* Pronounced "recòrd."
6   *Do not embrace me* Viola defers the celebration of their reunion until she has resumed her
     feminine identity.
7   *cohere and jump* Come together and agree.
8   *Where* I.e., at whose house.
9   *nature ... drew in that* I.e., nature drew you to me through your love for one disguised as
     me; *bias* The curve of a weighted ball in the game of bowls.

245   Nor are you therein, by my life, deceived:
       You are betrothed both to a maid and man.[1]
ORSINO. [*to Olivia*] Be not amazed. Right noble is his blood.
       If this be so, as yet the glass seems true,[2]
       I shall have share in this most happy wreck.°   *shipwreck*
250   [*to Viola*] Boy, thou hast said to me a thousand times
       Thou never shouldst love woman like to me.[3]
VIOLA. And all those sayings will I overswear,°   *swear again*
       And all those swearings° keep as true in soul   *oaths*
       As doth that orbèd continent[4] the fire
255   That severs day from night.
ORSINO.   Give me thy hand,
       And let me see thee in thy woman's weeds.
VIOLA. The captain that did bring me first on shore
       Hath my maid's garments. He upon some action°   *legal charge*
       Is now in durance,° at Malvolio's suit,[5]   *imprisoned*
260   A gentleman and follower of my lady's.
OLIVIA. He shall enlarge° him. Fetch Malvolio hither.   *free*
       And yet, alas, now I remember me,
       They say, poor gentleman, he's much distract.°   *distraught*

       (*Enter [Feste] with a letter, and Fabian.*)

       A most extracting° frenzy of mine own   *distracting*
265   From my remembrance clearly banished his.
       How does he, sirrah?
FESTE. Truly, madam, he holds Beelzebub at the stave's end[6] as well as a man
       in his case may do. H'as here writ a letter to you. I should have given you
       today morning, but as a madman's epistles are no gospels,[7] so it skills[8] not
270   much when they are delivered.

---

1   *both to a maid and man* I.e., to one (Sebastian) who is both a virgin and a man; "maid"
     or "maiden" was frequently used to indicate an innocent or virginal youth.
2   *the glass seems true* The "natural perspective" still appears to reflect truth (and not appear-
     ances).
3   *like to me* I.e., as well as (you love) me.
4   *orbèd continent* The sun; *orbèd* The planets and stars were thought to be fixed in crystal-
     line spheres (orbs); *continent* Container (of fire).
5   *at Malvolio's suit* The unexplained lawsuit serves to justify the captain's absence and to
     defer retrieving Viola's "woman's weeds" (and emphasizes Malvolio's arbitrary legalism).
6   *holds Beelzebub ... end* Proverbial: "keeps the devil at a distance"; *stave* Quarterstaff
     (used in fighting).
7   *epistles are no gospels* I.e., words convey no truth (playing on the New Testament Epistles
     and the first four Gospels).
8   *skills* Matters.

OLIVIA. Open't, and read it.

FESTE. Look then to be well edified when the fool delivers[1] the madman.
[*Reads madly.*] "By the Lord, madam"—

OLIVIA. How now, art thou mad?

FESTE. No, madam, I do but read madness. An your ladyship will have it as   275
it ought to be, you must allow *vox*.[2]

OLIVIA. Prithee read i'thy right wits.

FESTE. So I do, Madonna, but to read his right wits[3] is to read thus. Therefore
perpend,[4] my Princess, and give ear.

OLIVIA. [*to Fabian*] Read it you, sirrah.   280

FABIAN. (*Reads.*) "By the Lord, madam, you wrong me, and the world shall
know it. Though you have put me into darkness and given your drunken
cousin rule over me, yet have I the benefit of my senses as well as your
ladyship. I have your own letter that induced me to the semblance I put
on, with the which I doubt not but to do myself much right[5] or you much   285
shame. Think of me as you please. I leave my duty a little unthought of,[6]
and speak out of my injury.[7]

                                      The madly-used Malvolio."

OLIVIA. Did he write this?

FESTE. Ay, Madam.   290

ORSINO. This savours not much of distraction.

OLIVIA. See him delivered,[8] Fabian; bring him hither. [*Exit Fabian.*]
My lord, so please you, these things further thought on,
To think me as well a sister as a wife,[9]
One day shall crown th' alliance on't,[10] so please you,   295
Here at my house, and at my proper° cost.   *own*

ORSINO. Madam, I am most apt° t'embrace your offer.   *ready*
[*to Viola*] Your master quits° you, and for your service done him   *releases*
So much against the mettle° of your sex,   *temperament*
So far beneath your soft and tender breeding,   300
And since you called me master for so long,

---

1   *delivers* Speaks the words of.
2   *vox* Latin: voice (i.e., the appropriate voice).
3   *right wits* Mental state.
4   *perpend* Consider, attend.
5   *I doubt not ... much right* I intend to vindicate myself.
6   *unthought of* Neglected.
7   *injury* Sense of wrong.
8   *Delivered* Freed, the third sense of this word in this scene (see ll. 270 and 272).
9   *think me ... a wife* Think as well of me as a sister-in-law as you would have as a wife.
10   *crown th' alliance on't* I.e., celebrate our relationship with a double wedding.

Here is my hand. You shall from this time be
Your master's mistress.[1]
OLIVIA. [*to Viola*] A sister—you are she.

(*Enter Malvolio [with a letter, and Fabian]*.)

305 ORSINO. Is this the madman?
OLIVIA.   Ay, my lord, this same.
How now, Malvolio!
MALVOLIO.   Madam, you have done me wrong,
Notorious° wrong.   *Egregious*
OLIVIA.   Have I, Malvolio? No.
MALVOLIO. [*Shows the letter.*] Lady, you have, pray you peruse that letter.
You must not now deny it is your hand.
310 Write from it° if you can, in hand or phrase,   *differently*
Or say 'tis not your seal, not your invention.°   *composition*
You can say none of this. Well, grant it then,
And tell me, in the modesty of honour,[2]
Why you have given me such clear lights° of favour,   *signs*
315 Bade me come smiling and cross-gartered to you,
To put on yellow stockings, and to frown
Upon Sir Toby and the lighter° people,   *lesser*
And, acting° this in an obedient hope,   *doing*
Why have you suffered me to be imprisoned,
320 Kept in a dark house, visited by the priest,
And made the most notorious geck° and gull   *fool*
That e'er invention° played on? Tell me why.   *trickery*
OLIVIA. Alas, Malvolio, this is not my writing,
Though, I confess, much like the character,°   *style*
325 But out of question 'tis Maria's hand.
And now I do bethink me, it was she
First told me thou wast mad; then cam'st° in smiling,   *you came*
And in such forms which here were presupposed
Upon[3] thee in the letter. Prithee, be content;
330 This practice hath most shrewdly° passed upon thee,   *maliciously*
But, when we know the grounds° and authors of it,   *reasons*

---

1   *master's mistress* Compare with Shakespeare's Sonnet 20, l. 2, "the master-mistress of my passion."
2   *modesty of honour* Propriety of (your) honour.
3   *presupposed / Upon* Previously suggested.

Thou shalt be both the plaintiff and the judge
Of thine own cause.[1]

FABIAN. Good madam, hear me speak,
And let no quarrel nor no brawl to come   335
Taint the condition° of this present hour,   *Spoil the mood*
Which I have wondered° at. In hope it shall not,   *marvelled*
Most freely I confess myself and Toby
Set this device° against Malvolio here,   *trick*
Upon° some stubborn and uncourteous parts°   *Because of / behaviour*   340
We had conceived against° him. Maria writ   *attributed to*
The letter, at Sir Toby's great importance,°   *insistence*
In recompense whereof he hath married her.
How with a sportful malice it was followed°   *carried out*
May rather pluck on° laughter than revenge,   *induce*   345
If that the injuries° be justly weighed   *wrongs*
That have on both sides passed.

OLIVIA. [*to Malvolio*] Alas, poor fool, how have they baffled° thee!   *disgraced*

FESTE. Why, "some are born great, some achieve greatness, and some have
greatness thrown upon them." I was one, sir, in this interlude,[2] one Sir To-   350
paz, sir; but that's all one. "By the Lord, fool, I am not mad"—but do you
remember, "madam, why laugh you at such a barren rascal, an you smile
not, he's gagged"—and thus the whirligig of time brings in his revenges.[3]

MALVOLIO. I'll be revenged on the whole pack[4] of you. [*Exit.*]

OLIVIA. He hath most notoriously abused.   355

ORSINO. Pursue him, and entreat him to a peace.
He hath not told us of the captain yet. [*Exit Fabian.*]
When that[5] is known, and golden time[6] convents,°   *comes about*
A solemn combination shall be made
Of our dear° souls. Meantime, sweet sister,   *loving*   360

---

1   *the plaintiff ... own cause* This reverses the proverbial saying: "no man ought to be judge
     in his own cause."

2   *interlude* Play.

3   *whirligig of time ... revenges* Feste combines the images of a *whirligig*, a child's spinning-
     top, and the wheel of fortune (suggesting that Malvolio's treatment was less personal
     revenge than fate).

4   *pack* Of dogs (for hounding him).

5   *that* I.e., the motivation for Malvolio's lawsuit against the captain.

6   *golden time* A standard Renaissance allusion to the mythical, ideal world of the classical
     "Golden Age," typically a time of youth and hope such as in Shakespeare's Sonnet 3, "in
     this thy golden time" (but in the context of the imprisoned captain and Viola's missing
     weeds, this nostalgic image functions as another deferral of marriage).

We will not part from hence.[1] Cesario, come—
For so you shall be while you are a man;
But when in other habits you are seen,
Orsino's mistress, and his fancy's queen.[2]

   (*Exeunt [all but Feste]*.)

FESTE. (*Sings*.)
365   When that I was and a little tiny boy,[3]
          With hey, ho, the wind and the rain,
       A foolish thing was but a toy,
          For the rain it raineth every day.

       But when I came to man's estate,[4]
370   With hey, ho, the wind and the rain,
       'Gainst knaves and thieves men shut their gate,
          For the rain it raineth every day.

       But when I came, alas, to wive,°   *take a wife*
          With hey, ho, the wind and the rain,
375   By swaggering° could I never thrive,   *bullying*
          For the rain it raineth every day.

       But when I came unto my beds,[5]
          With hey, ho, the wind and the rain,
       With toss-pots° still had drunken heads,   *drunkards*
380   For the rain it raineth every day.

       A great while ago the world begun,
          With hey, ho, the wind and the rain,
       But that's all one, our play is done,
          And we'll strive to please you every day.

       [*Exit*.]

                                                                —c. 1601

---

1   *hence* I.e., Olivia's house.
2   *his fancy's queen* Ruler of his desire.
3   *When that ... tiny boy* It is unknown if Shakespeare wrote this song, but a variation on
     stanza 1 is sung in *King Lear* 3.2.73–77.
4   *when I ... man's estate* I.e., when I became a man.
5   *beds* I.e., the speaker sleeps where he can.

Richard Brinsley Sheridan

1751–1816

The Irish writer and politician Richard Brinsley Sheridan was one of the leading playwrights of the late eighteenth century. Writing in a style that had been pioneered a century before by Restoration playwrights (though without the overt sexual innuendo that permeates many of the plays of the earlier period), Sheridan created light yet pointed comedies of social and sexual politics. His plays were wildly popular with audiences of his time, and two of them—*The Rivals* (1775) and *The School for Scandal* (1777)—have remained popular ever since as the period's most successful exemplars of the comedy of manners.

As a playwright who also owned and managed London's Drury Lane Theatre for over 30 years, Sheridan took a pragmatic view of the stage as a means of supporting himself and financing his political ambitions; his desire to profit from his work ensured that he attended closely to the prevailing appetites of his audiences. His aptitude as a dramatist consisted not only of a talent for witty dialogue and intricate comic plots, but also in an ability to at once indulge and exceed popular expectations by infusing stock types and familiar devices with new vitality. As the critic William Hazlitt observed, Sheridan "could imitate with the spirit of an inventor," and "whatever he touched, he adorned with all the ease, grace, and brilliancy of his style."

Despite his talents, Sheridan died in poverty. He devoted the latter part of his life to the management of Drury Lane—which proved to be a financial sinkhole—and to a career as a member of the Whig opposition in Parliament, where he developed a reputation as a fine orator and a radical liberal. He was an incidental player on the political stage, but Sheridan's generation recognized his importance as a key figure in the history of English theatre, and he was buried with great pomp in Poet's Corner in Westminster Abbey.

The School for Scandal

PROLOGUE

Spoken by Mr. King[1]
Written by D. Garrick,[2]
Esq.

A School for Scandal! tell me, I beseech you,
Needs there a school this modish° art to teach you?   *fashionable*
No need of lessons now, the knowing think—
We might as well be taught to eat and drink.
5 Caused by a dearth of scandal, should the vapours[3]
Distress our fair ones—let 'em read the papers;
Their pow'rful mixtures such disorders hit;
Crave what they will, there's *quantum sufficit.*[4]
    "Lord!" cries my Lady Wormwood (who loves tattle,
10 And puts much salt and pepper in her prattle),
Just ris'n at noon, all night at cards when threshing
Strong tea and scandal—"Bless me, how refreshing!
Give me the papers, Lisp—how bold and free! (*sips*)
Last night Lord L— (sips) was caught with Lady D—
15 For aching heads what charming sal volatile![5] (*sips*)
If Mrs. B.— will still continue flirting,
We hope she'll DRAW, *or we'll* UNDRAW *the curtain.*
Fine satire, poz°—in public all abuse it,   *positively*
But, by ourselves (*sips*), our praise we can't refuse it.
20 Now, Lisp, *read you*—there, at that dash and star."[6]
    "Yes, ma'am.—*A certain Lord had best beware,*
Who lives not twenty miles from Grosv'nor Square;[7]
For should he Lady W— find willing,
WORMWOOD *is bitter*"—"Oh! that's me! the villain!

---

1   *Mr. King* Actor Thomas King (1730–1805), who appeared in the play's original cast as
     Peter Teazle.
2   *D. Garrick* Famous actor and theatre manager David Garrick (1717–79).
3   *the vapours* State of depression or ill health.
4   *quantum sufficit* Latin: sufficient quantity (i.e., enough to satisfy the readers).
5   *sal volatile* Substance used in smelling salts.
6   *dash and star* In eighteenth-century print media, dashes and asterisks marked places
     where a name or other identifying detail had been withheld.
7   *Grosv'nor Square* Grosvenor Square, site of aristocratic residences in London's West End.

Throw it behind the fire, and never more   25
Let that vile paper come within my door."—
    Thus at our friends we laugh, who feel the dart;
To reach our feelings, we ourselves must smart.
Is our young bard so young, to think that he
Can stop the full spring-tide of calumny?   30
Knows he the world so little, and its trade?
Alas! the devil is sooner raised than laid.
So strong, so swift, the monster there's no gagging:
Cut Scandal's head off—still the tongue is wagging.
Proud of your smiles once lavishly bestowed,   35
Again your young Don Quixote[1] takes the road:
To show his gratitude, he draws his pen,
And seeks this hydra,[2] Scandal, in his den.
For your applause all perils he would through— ⎫
He'll fight—that's *write*—a cavalliero[3] true, ⎬   40
Till every drop of blood—that's *ink*—is spilt for you. ⎭

DRAMATIS PERSONAE

[MEN]	[WOMEN]
Sir Peter Teazle	Lady Teazle
Sir Oliver Surface	Lady Sneerwell
Joseph Surface	Mrs. Candour
Charles Surface	Maria
Snake	
Rowley	
Moses	
Careless	
Sir Toby Bumper[4]	
Trip	
Sir Benjamin Backbite	
Crabtree	
[Servants]	

---

1   *Don Quixote* Title character of a Spanish comic romance (1605, 1615) by Miguel de Cervantes. The idealistic Quixote reads too many romances and believes himself to be a chivalric hero.

2   *hydra* Greek mythological monster that has multiple heads and grows two more whenever one is cut off.

3   *cavalliero* Spanish: knight or gentleman.

4   *Bumper* Full glass of alcohol used for a toast.

ACT 1, SCENE 1. [LADY SNEERWELL'S HOUSE.][1]

(Lady Sneerwell at the dressing table; Mr. Snake drinking chocolate.)

LADY SNEERWELL. The paragraphs you say, Mr. Snake, were all inserted?

SNAKE. They were, madam, and as I copied them myself in a feigned hand, there can be no suspicion whence they came.

LADY SNEERWELL. Did you circulate the report of Lady Brittle's intrigue with
5   Captain Boastall?

SNAKE. That is in as fine a train as your ladyship could wish; in the common course of things, I think it must reach Mrs. Clackit's ears within four-and-twenty hours, and then you know the business is as good as done.

LADY SNEERWELL. Why truly, Mrs. Clackit has a very pretty talent and a great
10   deal of industry.

SNAKE. True, madam, and has been tolerably successful in her day. To my knowledge she has been the cause of six matches being broken off and three sons being disinherited, of four forced elopements, as many close confinements,[2] nine separate maintenances,[3] and two divorces. Nay, I have
15   more than once traced her causing a tête-à-tête in the *Town and Country Magazine*[4] when the parties perhaps had never seen each others' faces before in the course of their lives.

LADY SNEERWELL. She certainly has talents, but her manner is gross.[5]

SNAKE. 'Tis very true: she generally designs well, has a free tongue and a bold
20   invention, but her colouring is too dark and her outline often extravagant. She wants[6] that delicacy of hint and mellowness of sneer which distinguishes your ladyship's scandal.

LADY SNEERWELL. Ah! You are partial, Snake.

SNAKE. Not in the least: everybody allows that Lady Sneerwell can do more
25   with a word or a look than many can with the most laboured detail, even when they happen to have a little truth on their side to support it.

LADY SNEERWELL. Yes, my dear Snake, and I am no hypocrite to deny the satisfaction I reap from the success of my efforts. Wounded myself in the early part of my life by the envenomed tongue of slander, I confess I have
30   since known no pleasure equal to the reducing others to the level of my own reputation.

---

1   *[LADY SNEERWELL'S HOUSE.]* Stage directions not appearing in the original play have been added in square brackets.
2   *close confinements* Secret childbirths.
3   *separate maintenances* Living allowance given by one member of a separated couple to the other; in the eighteenth century, a maintenance was provided by the husband.
4   *Town and Country Magazine* Gossip periodical publicizing high-society scandals.
5   *gross* Unrefined.
6   *wants* Lacks.

SNAKE. Nothing can be more natural. But Lady Sneerwell, there is one affair in which you have lately employed me wherein I confess I am at a loss to guess your motives.

LADY SNEERWELL. I conceive you mean with respect to my neighbour, Sir Peter Teazle, and his family? 35

SNAKE. I do. Here are two young men to whom Sir Peter has acted as a kind of guardian since their father's death: the eldest possessing the most amiable character and universally well spoken of; the youngest the most dissipated and extravagant young fellow in the kingdom, without friends 40 or character. The former an avowed admirer of your ladyship's and apparently your favourite; the latter attached to Maria, Sir Peter's ward, and confessedly beloved by her. Now on the face of these circumstances, it is utterly unaccountable to me why you, the widow of a City knight[1] with a good jointure,[2] should not close with the passion of a man of such char- 45 acter and expectation as Mr. Surface, and more so, why you should be so uncommonly earnest to destroy the mutual attachment between his brother Charles and Maria.

LADY SNEERWELL. Then at once to unravel this mystery, I must inform you that love has no share whatever in the intercourse between Mr. Surface 50 and me.

SNAKE. No!

LADY SNEERWELL. His real attachment is to Maria or her fortune, but finding in his brother a favoured rival, he has been obliged to mask his pretensions and profit by my assistance. 55

SNAKE. Yet still I am more puzzled why you should interest yourself in his success.

LADY SNEERWELL. Heavens, how dull you are! Cannot you surmise the weakness which I hitherto through shame have concealed even from you? Must I confess that Charles, that libertine, that extravagant, that bankrupt in 60 fortune and reputation, that he it is for whom I am thus anxious and malicious and to gain whom I would sacrifice everything?

SNAKE. Now, indeed your conduct appears consistent, but how came you and Mr.[3] Surface so confidential?

LADY SNEERWELL. For our mutual interest. I have found him out a long time 65 since. I know him to be artful, selfish, and malicious—in short, a sentimental knave[4]—while with Sir Peter, and indeed with all his acquaintance, he passes for a miracle of prudence, good sense, and benevolence.

---

1   *City knight* I.e., knighted London merchant; *City* City of London, the oldest area of London and the location of its business centres.

2   *jointure* Estate left to a widow by her husband to provide for her until the end of her life.

3   *Mr.* I.e., the older of the two Surface brothers.

4   *sentimental knave* I.e., a hypocrite who expresses respectably moral sentiments.

SNAKE. Nay, Sir Peter vows he has not his equal in England, and above all he
70   praises him as a Man of Sentiment.[1]

LADY SNEERWELL. True, and with the assistance of sentiments and hypocrisy, he has brought him entirely into his interest with regard to Maria, while poor Charles has no friend in the house, though I fear he has a powerful one in Maria's heart, against whom we must direct our schemes.

(*Enter servant.*)

75   SERVANT. Mr. Surface.

LADY SNEERWELL. Show him up.

(*Exit servant.*)

He generally calls about this time; I don't wonder at people's giving him to me for a lover.

(*Enter Joseph Surface.*)

JOSEPH SURFACE. My dear Lady Sneerwell, how do you do today? Mr. Snake,
80   your most obedient.

LADY SNEERWELL. Snake has just been arraigning me on our mutual attachment, but I have informed him of our real views. You know how useful he has been to us, and believe me, the confidence is not ill placed.

JOSEPH SURFACE. Madam, it is impossible for me to suspect a man of Mr.
85   Snake's sensibility and discernment.

LADY SNEERWELL. Well, well, no compliments now, but tell me when you saw your mistress, Maria, or what is more material to me, your brother.

JOSEPH SURFACE. I have not seen either since I left you, but I can inform you that they never meet. Some of your stories have taken a good effect
90   on Maria.

LADY SNEERWELL. Ah my dear Snake, the merit of this belongs to you.—But do your brother's distresses increase?

JOSEPH SURFACE. Every hour. I am told he has had another execution[2] in his house yesterday; in short, his dissipation and extravagance exceed every-
95   thing I ever heard of.

LADY SNEERWELL. Poor Charles!

JOSEPH SURFACE. True, madam, notwithstanding his vices, one cannot help feeling for him. Aye, poor Charles indeed. I am sure I wish it was in my power to be of any essential service to him. For the man who does not

---

1   *Man of Sentiment* Phrase with a double meaning; it could mean that Joseph Surface is "sentimental" in the sense used above, or that he is virtuously sympathetic.

2   *execution* Legal acquisition of a debtor's possessions in lieu of an unpaid debt.

share in the distresses of a brother, even though merited by his own mis- 100
conduct, deserves—

LADY SNEERWELL. Oh Lud![1] You are going to be moral and forget that you
are among friends.

JOSEPH SURFACE. Egad that's true. I'll keep that sentiment till I see Sir Peter.
However, it is certainly a charity to rescue Maria from such a libertine, 105
who, if he is to be reclaimed, can be so only by one of your ladyship's superior accomplishments and understanding.

SNAKE. I believe, Lady Sneerwell, here's company coming; I'll go and copy
the letter I mentioned to you.—Mr. Surface, your most obedient. (*Exit*.)

JOSEPH SURFACE. Sir, your very devoted—Lady Sneerwell, I am very sorry 110
you have put any further confidence in that fellow.

LADY SNEERWELL. Why so?

JOSEPH SURFACE. I have lately detected him in frequent conference with old
Rowley, who was formerly my father's steward and has never, you know,
been a friend of mine. 115

LADY SNEERWELL. And do you think he would betray us?

JOSEPH SURFACE. Nothing more likely, take my word for it, Lady Sneerwell,
that fellow has not virtue enough to be faithful or constant even to his own
villainy.—Hah, Maria!

   (*Enter Maria*.)

LADY SNEERWELL. Maria, my dear, how do you do? What's the matter? 120

MARIA. Oh, there's that disagreeable lover of mine, Sir Benjamin Backbite,
has just called at my guardian's with his odious uncle Crabtree, so I slipped
out and ran hither to avoid them.

LADY SNEERWELL. Is that all?

JOSEPH SURFACE. If my brother Charles had been of the party, madam, per- 125
haps you would not have been so much alarmed.

LADY SNEERWELL. Nay now, you are severe, for I dare swear the truth of the
matter is, Maria heard you were here.—But my dear, what has Sir Benjamin done that you should avoid him so?

MARIA. Oh, he has done nothing, but 'tis for what he has said. His conversa- 130
tion is a perpetual libel on all his acquaintance.

JOSEPH SURFACE. Aye, and the worst of it is, there is no advantage in not
knowing him, for he'll abuse a stranger just as soon as his best friend, and
his uncle is as bad.

LADY SNEERWELL. Nay, but we should make allowance: Sir Benjamin is a wit 135
and a poet.

---

1   *Lud* Swear word meaning "Lord."

MARIA. For my part I own, madam, wit loses its respect with me when I see it in company with malice.—What do you think, Mr. Surface?

JOSEPH SURFACE. Certainly, madam, to smile at the jest which plants a thorn
140 in another's breast is to become a principal in the mischief.

LADY SNEERWELL. Pshaw! There's no possibility of being witty without a little ill nature; malice of a good thing is the barb which makes it stick.—What's your opinion, Mr. Surface?

JOSEPH SURFACE. To be sure, madam, that conversation where the spirit of
145 railery[1] is suppressed will ever appear tedious and insipid.

MARIA. Well, I'll not debate how far scandal may be allowable, but in a man I am sure it is always contemptible. We have pride, envy, rivalship, and a thousand little motives to depreciate each other, but the male slanderer must have the cowardice of a woman before he can traduce one.

(*Enter servant.*)

150 SERVANT. Madam, Mrs. Candour is below and, if your ladyship's at leisure, will leave her carriage.

LADY SNEERWELL. Beg her to walk in.

(*Exit servant.*)

Now Maria, however, here is a character to your taste, for though Mrs. Candour is a little talkative, everybody allows her to be the best natured
155 and best sort of woman.

MARIA. Yet with a very gross affectation of good nature and benevolence, she does more mischief than the direct malice of old Crabtree.

JOSEPH SURFACE. I'faith, 'tis very true, Lady Sneerwell. Whenever I hear the current running against the characters of my friends, I never think them in
160 such danger as when Candour undertakes their defence.

LADY SNEERWELL. Hush! Here she is.

(*Enter Mrs. Candour.*)

MRS. CANDOUR. My dear Lady Sneerwell, how have you been this century? Mr. Surface, what news do you hear, though indeed it is no matter, for I think one hears nothing else but scandal.

165 JOSEPH SURFACE. Just so indeed, madam.

MRS. CANDOUR. Ah! Maria, child, is the whole affair off between you and Charles? His extravagance, I presume; the Town[2] talks of nothing else.

MARIA. I am very sorry, ma'am, the Town have so little to do.

---

1   *railery* Teasing.
2   *the Town* I.e., London high society.

MRS. CANDOUR. True, true, child, but there is no stopping people's tongues. I own I was hurt to hear it, as indeed I was to learn from the same quarter 170 that your guardian, Sir Peter, and Lady Teazle have not agreed lately so well as could be wished.

MARIA. 'Tis strangely impertinent for people to busy themselves so. I'm sure such reports are—

MRS. CANDOUR. Very true, child, but what's to be done? People will talk, 175 there's no preventing it. Why it was but yesterday I was told that Miss Gadabout had eloped with Sir Filagree Flirt—but Lord, there is no minding what one hears—though to be sure I had this from very good authority.

MARIA. Such reports are highly scandalous.

MRS. CANDOUR. So they are, child—shameful! shameful! But the world is 180 so censorious no character escapes. Lord now! Who would have suspected your friend Miss Prim of an indiscretion? Yet such is the ill nature of people that they say her uncle stopped her last week just as she was stepping into the York diligence[1] with her dancing master.

MARIA. I'll answer for it, there are no grounds for the report.   185

MRS. CANDOUR. Oh, no foundation in the world, I dare swear, no more probably than for the story circulated last month of Mrs. Festino's affair with Colonel Cassino,[2] though to be sure that matter was never rightly cleared up.

JOSEPH SURFACE. The license of invention some people take is monstrous 190 indeed!

MARIA. 'Tis so, but in my opinion those who report such things are equally culpable.

MRS. CANDOUR. To be sure they are: tale bearers are as bad as tale makers; 'tis an old observation and a very true one. But what's to be done, as I said 195 before? How will you prevent people from talking? Today Mrs. Clackit assured me Mr. and Mrs. Honeymoon were at last become mere man and wife like the rest of her acquaintance. She likewise hinted that a certain widow in the next street had got rid of her dropsy[3] and recovered her shape in a most surprising manner, and the same time Miss Tattle, who 200 was by, affirmed that Lord Buffalo had discovered his lady at a house of no extraordinary fame and that Sir Harry Bouquet and Tom Saunter were to measure swords on a similar provocation. But Lord, do you think I would report these things? No, no, tale-bearers, as I said before, are just as bad as tale-makers.

205

---

1   *York diligence* Public horse-drawn coach to York.

2   *Festino* Italian: party; *Cassino* Italian: dance hall; also the name of a card game.

3   *dropsy* Swelling caused by accumulation of fluid (here used as a cover for pregnancy).

JOSEPH SURFACE. Oh Mrs. Candour, if everybody had your forbearance and good nature!

MRS. CANDOUR. I confess, Mr. Surface, I cannot bear to hear people attacked behind their backs, and when ugly circumstances come out against one's acquaintances, I own I always love to think the best. By the bye, I hope 'tis not true that your brother is absolutely ruined.

JOSEPH SURFACE. I am afraid his circumstances are very bad indeed, madam.

MRS. CANDOUR. Ah, I heard so, but you must tell him to keep up his spirits: Sir Thomas Splint, Captain Quinzes, and Mr. Nickit, all up,[1] I hear, within this week, so if Charles is undone, he will find half his acquaintances ruined too, and that, you know, is a consolation.

JOSEPH SURFACE. Doubtless, ma'am, a very great one.

(*Enter servant.*)

SERVANT. Mr. Crabtree and Sir Benjamin Backbite. (*Exit.*)

LADY SNEERWELL. So Maria, you see your lover pursues you. Positively you shan't escape.

(*Enter Crabtree and Sir Benjamin Backbite.*)

CRABTREE. Lady Sneerwell, I kiss your hands.—Mrs. Candour, I don't believe you are acquainted with my nephew, Sir Benjamin Backbite. Egad ma'am, he has a pretty wit and is a pretty poet too.—Isn't he, Lady Sneerwell?

SIR BENJAMIN. Oh fie, Uncle!

CRABTREE. Nay, egad 'tis true: I'll back him at a rebus or a charade[2] against the best rhymer in the kingdom. Has your ladyship heard the epigram he wrote last week on Lady Frizzle's feather catching fire! Do, Benjamin, repeat it, or the charade you made last night extempore at Mrs. Drowzy's conversazione.[3] Come now, your first is the name of a fish, your second a great naval commander—and—

SIR BENJAMIN. Uncle—now—prithee!

CRABTREE. I'faith, madam, 'twould surprise you to hear how ready he is at these things.

LADY SNEERWELL. I wonder, Sir Benjamin, you never publish anything.

SIR BENJAMIN. To say truth, ma'am, 'tis very vulgar to print, and as my little productions are mostly satires and lampoons on particular people, I find they circulate more by giving copies in confidence to the friends of the

1   *Quinzes* French card game; *all up* Completely broke.
2   *rebus* Puzzle in which players must decode a message made up of pictures and letters; *charade* Riddle involving wordplay.
3   *conversazione* Small party intended for refined intellectual conversation.

parties; however, I have some love elegies which, when favoured with this lady's smiles, I mean to give to the public.

CRABTREE. 'Fore Heaven, ma'am, they'll immortalize you; you'll be handed down to posterity like Petrarch's Laura or Waller's Sacharissa.[1]

SIR BENJAMIN. Yes madam, I think you will like them when you shall see them on a beautiful quarto page,[2] where a neat rivulet of text shall murmur through a meadow of margin. 'Fore gad, they will be the most elegant things of their kind—

CRABTREE. But ladies, that's true. Have you heard the news?

MRS. CANDOUR. What, sir, do you mean the report of—

CRABTREE. No ma'am, that's not it. Miss Nicely is going to be married to her own footman.

MRS. CANDOUR. Impossible!

CRABTREE. Ask Sir Benjamin.

SIR BENJAMIN. 'Tis very true, ma'am: everything is fixed and the wedding livery bespoke.

CRABTREE. Yes, and they do say there were pressing reasons for it.

LADY SNEERWELL. Why, I have heard something of this before.

MRS. CANDOUR. It can't be, and I wonder anyone should believe such a story of so prudent a lady as Miss Nicely.

SIR BENJAMIN. Oh Lud ma'am, that's the very reason 'twas believed at once. She has always been so cautious and so reserved that everybody was sure there was some reason for it at bottom.

MRS. CANDOUR. Why, to be sure a tale of scandal is as fatal to the credit of a prudent lady of her stamp as a fever is generally to those of the strongest constitutions. But there is a sort of puny, sickly reputation that is always ailing yet will outlive the robuster character of a hundred prudes.

SIR BENJAMIN. True madam, there are valetudinarians[3] in reputation as well as constitution, who, being conscious of their weak part, avoid the least breath of air and supply their want of stamina by care and circumspection.

MRS. CANDOUR. Well, but this may be all a mistake. You know, Sir Benjamin, very trifling circumstances often give rise to the most injurious tales.

---

1   *Laura* Subject of the love sonnets of Francesco Petrarch (1304–74); *Waller's Sacharissa* In the 1630s Edmund Waller wrote a series of poems to Lady Dorothy Sidney (referred to in the poems as "Sacharissa"), which were extremely popular in the seventeenth and eighteenth centuries.

2   *on a ... quarto page* I.e., in print; quarto books are produced using large sheets of paper folded to produce four pages each.

3   *valetudinarians* Unhealthy people, or people who go to great lengths to preserve their health.

270 CRABTREE. That they do, I'll be sworn, ma'am. Did you ever hear how Miss
Piper came to lose her lover and her character last summer at Tunbridge?[1]
Sir Benjamin, you remember it?

SIR BENJAMIN. Oh, to be sure! The most whimsical circumstance—

LADY SNEERWELL. How was it pray?

275 CRABTREE. Why, one evening at Mrs. Ponto's assembly[2] the conversation
happened to turn on the difficulty of breeding Nova Scotia sheep in this
country; says a lady in company, "I have known instances of it, for Miss
Laetitia Piper, a first cousin of mine, had a Nova Scotia sheep that produced her twins." "What!" cries the Dowager Lady Dundizzy (who you
280 know is as deaf as a post) "has Miss Laetitia Piper had twins?" This mistake, as you may imagine, threw the whole company into a fit of laughter;
however, 'twas the next day reported, and in a few days believed by the
whole Town, that Miss Laetitia Piper had actually been brought to bed
of a fine boy and a girl, and in less than a week there were people who
285 could name the father and the farmhouse where the babies were put out
to nurse.[3]

LADY SNEERWELL. Strange indeed.

CRABTREE. Matter of fact, I assure you.—Oh Lud, Mr. Surface, pray is it true
that your Uncle Sir Oliver is coming home?

290 JOSEPH SURFACE. Not that I know of, indeed sir.

CRABTREE. He has been in the East Indies a long time; you can scarcely remember him, I believe. Sad comfort whenever he returns to hear how your
brother has gone on.

JOSEPH SURFACE. Charles has been imprudent, sir, to be sure, but I hope
295 no busy people have already prejudiced Sir Oliver against him; he may
reform.

SIR BENJAMIN. To be sure he may. For my part I never believed him so utterly
void of principle as people say, and though he has lost all his friends, I am
told nobody is better spoken of by the Jews.[4]

300 CRABTREE. That's true, egad Nephew. If the old Jewry was a ward,[5] I believe
Charles would be an alderman. No man more popular there. 'Fore gad, I

---

1   *Tunbridge* Tunbridge Wells, a fashionable resort town.

2   *assembly* I.e., party.

3   *put out to nurse* Sent to live in the country with a wet nurse.

4   *nobody ... Jews* Refers to the stereotypical association between Jews and moneylending.
Moneylending was a common profession for Jewish people, as social and legal discrimina-
tion prevented them from working in most professions, while religious doctrine forbade
Christians from making loans for profit (a prohibition not always obeyed in practice).

5   *old Jewry* Street in the City where many moneylenders' offices were located; *ward* Region of a city that elects an alderman as its representative in the city government.

hear he pays as many annuities as the Irish tontine[1] and that whenever he's sick they have prayers for the recovery of his health in the synagogue.

SIR BENJAMIN. Yet no man lives in greater splendour. They tell me when he entertains his friends, he can sit down to dinner with a dozen of his own securities, have a score of tradesman in the anti-chamber and an officer behind every guest's chair.

JOSEPH SURFACE. This may be entertainment to you, gentlemen, but you pay very little regard to the feelings of a brother.

MARIA. [*aside*] Their malice is intolerable.—Lady Sneerwell, I must wish you a good morning—I'm not very well. (*Exit.*)

MRS. CANDOUR. Oh dear, she changes colour very much.

LADY SNEERWELL. Do Mrs. Candour follow her, she may want assistance.

MRS. CANDOUR. That I will with all my soul, ma'am. Poor dear creature, who knows what her situation may be? (*Exit.*)

LADY SNEERWELL. 'Twas nothing but that she could not bear to hear Charles reflected on, notwithstanding their difference.

SIR BENJAMIN. The young lady's penchant is obvious.

CRABTREE. But Benjamin, you mustn't give up the pursuit for that. Follow her and put her into good humour, repeat her some of your verses. Come, I'll assist you.

SIR BENJAMIN. Mr. Surface, I did not mean to hurt you, but depend on't, your brother is utterly undone.[2]

CRABTREE. Oh Lud! Aye! undone as ever man was, can't raise a guinea.[3]

SIR BENJAMIN. Everything sold, I am told, that was moveable.[4]

CRABTREE. I have seen one that was at his house: not a thing left but some empty bottles that were overlooked and the family pictures, which I believe are framed in the wainscot.[5]

SIR BENJAMIN. And I am very sorry to hear also some bad stories against him. (*going*)

CRABTREE. Oh, he has done many mean[6] things, that's certain.

SIR BENJAMIN. But however, as he's your brother—(*going*)

CRABTREE. We'll tell you all another opportunity.

---

1   *tontine* Money-raising method in which a large group of participants contribute funds, for which they receive annuities (periodic payments) that increase as the other participants die. The Irish Parliament undertook several tontines in the latter half of the eighteenth century.

2   *utterly undone* Financially ruined.

3   *guinea* Coin worth slightly more than a pound.

4   *moveable* I.e., not land or buildings.

5   *framed in the wainscot* I.e., embedded in the wall panelling.

6   *mean* Base, contemptible.

(*Exeunt Sir Benjamin and Crabtree.*)

335   LADY SNEERWELL. Ha, ha, ha! 'tis very hard for them to leave a subject they have not quite run down.

JOSEPH SURFACE. And I believe their abuse was no more acceptable to your ladyship than Maria.

LADY SNEERWELL. I doubt[1] her affections are further engaged than we imag-
340   ined. But the family are to be here this evening, so you may as well dine where you are, and we shall have an opportunity of observing further; in the meantime, I'll go and plot mischief, and you shall study sentiments.

(*Exeunt.*)

ACT 1, SCENE 2. SIR PETER TEAZLE'S HOUSE.

(*Enter Sir Peter.*)

SIR PETER. When an old bachelor takes a young wife, what is he to expect? 'Tis now six months since Lady Teazle made me the happiest of men, and I have been the miserablest dog ever since. We tiffed a little going to church and came to a quarrel before the bells were done ringing. I was more than
5   once nearly choked with gall during the honeymoon and had lost all com-fort in life before my friends had done wishing me joy. Yet I chose with caution: a girl bred wholly in the country, who never knew luxury beyond one silk gown nor dissipation above the annual gala of a race ball. Yet now she plays her part in all the extravagant fopperies of the fashion and the
10   Town with as ready a grace as if she had never seen a bush nor a grass plot out of Grosvenor Square. I am sneered at by my old acquaintance, para-graphed in the newspapers; she dissipates my fortune and contradicts all humours. Yet the worst of it is, I doubt I love her, or I should never bear all this; however, I'll never be weak enough to own it.

(*Enter Rowley.*)

15   ROWLEY. Oh Sir Peter, your servant. How is it with you, sir?

SIR PETER. Very bad, Master Rowley, very bad. I meet with nothing but crosses and vexations.

ROWLEY. What can have happened to trouble you since yesterday?

SIR PETER. A good question to a married man.

20   ROWLEY. Nay, I'm sure Sir Peter, your lady can't be the cause of your uneasi-ness.

SIR PETER. Why, has anyone told you she was dead?

---

1   *doubt* Fear or suspect.

ROWLEY. Come, come, Sir Peter, you love her, notwithstanding your tempers don't exactly agree.

SIR PETER. But the fault is entirely hers, Master Rowley. I am myself the sweetest tempered man alive and hate a teasing temper, and so I tell her an hundred times a day.

ROWLEY. Indeed!

SIR PETER. Aye, and what is very extraordinary, in all our disputes she is always in the wrong. But Lady Sneerwell and the set she meets at her house encourage the perverseness of her disposition. Then to complete my vexations, Maria, my ward, whom I ought to have the power of a father over, is determined to turn rebel too and absolutely refuses the man whom I have long resolved on for her husband, meaning, I suppose, to bestow herself on his profligate brother.

ROWLEY. You know, Sir Peter, I have always taken the liberty to differ with you on the subject of these two young gentlemen. I only wish you may not be deceived in your opinion of the elder; for Charles, my life on't, he will retrieve his errors yet. Their worthy father, once my honoured master, was at his years nearly as wild a spark, but when he died, he did not leave a more benevolent heart to lament his loss.

SIR PETER. You are wrong, Master Rowley. On their father's death you know I acted as a kind of guardian to them both 'till their uncle Sir Oliver's eastern liberality[1] gave them an early independence. Of course, no person could have more opportunities of judging of their hearts, and I was never mistaken in my life. Joseph is indeed a model for the young men of the age: he is a man of sentiment and acts up to the sentiments he professes. But for the other, take my word for't, if he had any grains of virtue by descent, he has dissipated them with the rest of his inheritance. Ah, my old friend Sir Oliver will be deeply mortified when he finds how part of his bounty has been misapplied.

ROWLEY. I am sorry to find you so violent against the young man because this may be the most critical period of his fortune; I came hither with news that will surprise you.

SIR PETER. What? let me hear.

ROWLEY. Sir Oliver is arrived and at this moment in Town.

SIR PETER. How! You astonish me! I thought you did not expect him this month.

ROWLEY. I did not, but his passage has been remarkably quick.

SIR PETER. Egad, I shall rejoice to see my old friend; 'tis sixteen years since we met. We have had many a day together. But does he still enjoin us not to inform his nephews of his arrival?

---

1   *eastern liberality* I.e., generosity; Sir Oliver acquired his wealth in Southeast Asia.

ROWLEY. Most strictly. He means before it is known to make some trial of their dispositions.

SIR PETER. Ah, there needs no art to discover their merits; however, he shall
65 have his way. But pray, does he know I am married?

ROWLEY. Yes, and will soon wish you joy.

SIR PETER. What, as we drink health to a friend in a consumption?[1] Ah! Oliver will laugh at me. We used to rail at[2] matrimony together, but he has been steady to his text. Well, he must be at my house though. I'll instantly
70 give orders for his reception. But Master Rowley, don't drop a word that Lady Teazle and I disagree.

ROWLEY. By no means—

SIR PETER. For I should never be able to stand Noll's[3] jokes, so I'd have him think, Lord forgive me, that we are a very happy couple.

75 ROWLEY. I understand you. But then you must be very careful not to differ while he's in the house with you.

SIR PETER. Egad, and so we must—and that's impossible. Ah Master Rowley, when an old bachelor marries a young wife, he deserves—no, the crime carries the punishment along with it.

(*Exeunt.*)

ACT 2, SCENE 1. SIR PETER TEAZLE'S HOUSE.

(*Enter Sir Peter and Lady Teazle.*)

SIR PETER. Lady Teazle, Lady Teazle, I'll not bear it.

LADY TEAZLE. Sir Peter, Sir Peter, you may bear it or not, as you please, but I ought to have my own way in everything, and what's more, I will too. What, though I was educated in the country, I know very well that women
5 of fashion in London are accountable to nobody after they are married.

SIR PETER. Very well, ma'am, very well, so a husband is to have no influence, no authority?

LADY TEAZLE. Authority! No, to be sure. If you wanted authority over me, you should have adopted me and not married me; I am sure you were old
10 enough.

SIR PETER. Old enough! Aye, there it is, well, well, Lady Teazle, though my life may be made unhappy by your temper, I'll not be ruined by your extravagance.

---

1   *in a consumption* With a wasting disease such as tuberculosis.
2   *rail at* Make fun of.
3   *Noll* Contracted form of "Oliver."

LADY TEAZLE. My extravagance? I'm sure I'm not more extravagant than a woman of fashion ought to be.   15

SIR PETER. No, no, madam, you shall throw away no more sums on such unmeaning luxury. 'Slife,[1] to spend as much to furnish your dressing room with flowers in winter, as would suffice to turn the Pantheon into a greenhouse and give a fête champêtre[2] at Christmas.

LADY TEAZLE. Lord, Sir Peter, am I to blame because flowers are dear[3] in cold   20
weather; you should find fault with the climate and not with me. For my part I am sure I wish it were spring all the year round and that roses grew under our feet.

SIR PETER. 'Oons[4] madam! If you had been born to this, I should not wonder at your talking thus, but you forget what your situation was when I mar-   25
ried you.

LADY TEAZLE. No, no, I don't: 'twas a very disagreeable one, or I should never have married you.

SIR PETER. Yes, yes, madam, you were then somewhat in an humbler style: the daughter of a plain country squire. Recollect, Lady Teazle, when I first   30
saw you sitting at your tambour in a pretty figured[5] linen gown, with a bunch of keys by your side, your hair combed smoothly over a roll, and your apartment hung round with fruits in worsted of your own working.

LADY TEAZLE. Oh yes, I remember it very well, and a curious life I led! My daily occupation: to inspect the dairy, superintend the poultry, make ex-   35
tracts from the family receipt[6] book, and comb my aunt Deborah's lapdog.

SIR PETER. Yes, yes, madam, 'twas so indeed.

LADY TEAZLE. And then you know my evening amusements: to draw patterns for ruffles which I had not the materials to make, to play Pope Joan with the curate, read a sermon to my aunt, or be stuck down to an old spinet[7]   40
to strum my father to sleep after a fox chase.

SIR PETER. I am glad you have so good a memory. Yes madam, these were the recreations I took you from. But now you must have your coach, vis-à-vis, and three powdered footmen before your chair[8]—and in summer a pair

---

1   *'Slife* Swear word meaning "God's life."
2   *Pantheon* Neoclassical building of impressive size, constructed in London in the late eighteenth century as a site for fashionable entertainment; *fête champêtre* French: garden party.
3   *dear* Costly.
4   *'Oons* Contraction of "Zounds," a swear word meaning "God's wounds."
5   *tambour* Round frame used for embroidery; *pretty figured* With pretty designs.
6   *receipt* Recipe.
7   *Pope Joan* Card game for three players; *spinet* Small harpsichord.
8   *vis-à-vis* Two-person carriage in which the passengers sit facing each other; *chair* Sedan chair, carried on poles by servants as a mode of transport.

45   of white cats to draw you to Kensington Gardens.[1] No recollection I sup-
      pose when you were content to ride double behind the butler on a docked
      coach horse?[2]

LADY TEAZLE. No, I swear I never did that, I deny the butler and the coach
      horse.

50 SIR PETER. This, madam, was your situation, and what have I not done for
      you? I have made you a woman of fashion, of fortune, of rank; in short, I
      have made you *my wife*.

LADY TEAZLE. Well then, and there is but one thing more you can make me
      to add to the obligation—and that is—

55 SIR PETER. My widow, I suppose?

LADY TEAZLE. Hem, hem!

SIR PETER. Thank you, madam, but don't flatter yourself, for though your
      ill conduct may disturb my peace, it shall never break my heart, I promise
      you; however, I am equally obliged to you for the hint.

60 LADY TEAZLE. Then why will you endeavour to make yourself so disagreeable
      to me and thwart me in every little elegant expense?

SIR PETER. 'Slife madam, I say, had you any of these elegant expenses when
      you married me?

LADY TEAZLE. Lord, Sir Peter, would you have me be out of fashion?

65 SIR PETER. The fashion indeed! What had you to do with the fashion when
      you married me?

LADY TEAZLE. For my part I should think you would like to have your wife
      thought a woman of taste.

SIR PETER. Aye, there again—taste—Zounds, Madam! You had no taste
70   when you married me.

LADY TEAZLE. That's very true indeed, Sir Peter, and after having married
      you, I should never pretend to taste again, I allow. But now Sir Peter, if we
      have finished our daily jangle, I presume I may go to my engagement at
      Lady Sneerwell's?

75 SIR PETER. Aye, there's another precious circumstance, a charming set of
      acquaintance you have made there.

LADY TEAZLE. Nay Sir Peter, they are people of rank and fortune, and re-
      markably tenacious of reputation.

---

1   *cats* Presumably a slang term meaning "horses" or "ponies"; *Kensington Gardens* Fash-
    ionable London park. Members of high society travelled "the Ring," a path between
    Kensington Gardens and nearby Hyde Park, in order to display themselves and their
    carriages.

2   *docked coach horse* Large horse intended for heavy labour; working horses' tails were
    "docked" (cropped short) to keep them from getting caught in equipment.

SIR PETER. Yes, egad, they are tenacious of reputation with a vengeance! For they don't choose anybody should have a character but themselves. Such a crew! Ah! Many a wretch has rid on a hurdle[1] who has done less mischief than these utterers of forged tales, coiners of scandal, and clippers[2] of reputation.

LADY TEAZLE. What, would you restrain the freedom of speech?

SIR PETER. Oh, they have made you just as bad as any one of the society.

LADY TEAZLE. Why I believe I do bear a part with a tolerable grace, but I vow I have no malice against the people I abuse. When I say an ill-natured thing, 'tis out of pure good humour, and I take for granted they'll deal exactly in the same manner with me. But Sir Peter, you know you promised to come to Lady Sneerwell's too.

SIR PETER. Well, well, I'll call in just to look after my own character.

LADY TEAZLE. Then, indeed, you must make haste after me or you'll be too late. So goodbye to you. (*Exit.*)

SIR PETER. So! I have gained much by my intended expostulations. Yet with what a charming air she contradicts everything I say and how pleasingly she shows her contempt of my authority. Well, though I can't make her love me, there is great satisfaction in quarrelling with her, and I think she never appears to such advantage as when she's doing everything in her power to plague me.

(*Exit.*)

ACT 2, SCENE 2. LADY SNEERWELL'S HOUSE.

(*Lady Sneerwell, Mrs. Candour, Crabtree, Sir Benjamin Backbite, and Joseph Surface discovered;[3] servants attending with tea.*)

LADY SNEERWELL. Nay, positively we will have it.

JOSEPH SURFACE. Yes, yes, the epigram, by all means.

SIR BENJAMIN. Oh plague on't, Uncle, 'tis mere nonsense.

CRABTREE. No, no, 'fore gad, very clever for an extempore.

SIR BENJAMIN. But ladies, you should be acquainted with the circumstance. You must know that one day last week, as Lady Betty Curricle[4] was taking

---

1   *hurdle* Frame to which criminals were tied before being pulled by horse to their execution.

2   *clippers* Refers to the criminal practice of "clipping," devaluing a coin by shaving small amounts of precious metal from its edges. Like forgery, clipping was punishable by execution.

3   *discovered* Revealed.

4   *Curricle* Small carriage.

the dust in Hyde Park in a sort of duodecimo phaeton,[1] she desired me to write some verses on her ponies, upon which I took out my pocket book and in one moment produced the following:

10   Sure never were seen two such beautiful ponies,
        Other horses are clowns, and these macaronies;[2]
        Nay, to give them this title I'm sure is not wrong,
        Their legs are so slim, and their tails are so long.

CRABTREE.   There ladies, done in the smack of a whip and on horseback too.

15 JOSEPH SURFACE.   A very Phoebus[3] mounted indeed, Sir Benjamin.

SIR BENJAMIN.   Oh dear sir, trifles, trifles!

(*Enter Lady Teazle and Maria.*)

MRS. CANDOUR.   I must have a copy.

LADY SNEERWELL.   Lady Teazle, I hope we shall see Sir Peter.

LADY TEAZLE.   I believe he'll wait on your ladyship presently.

20 LADY SNEERWELL.   Maria my dear, you look grave. Come, you shall sit down to piquet[4] with Mr. Surface.

MARIA.   I take very little pleasure in cards; however, I'll do as your ladyship pleases.

LADY TEAZLE.   [*aside*] I am surprised Mr. Surface should sit down with her.
25 I thought he would have embraced this opportunity of speaking to me before Sir Peter came.

MRS. CANDOUR.   Now, I'll die but you are so scandalous, I'll foreswear your society.

LADY TEAZLE.   What's the matter, Mrs. Candour?

30 MRS. CANDOUR.   They'll not allow our friend, Miss Vermillion, to be handsome.

LADY SNEERWELL.   Oh surely, she's a pretty woman.

CRABTREE.   I'm very glad you think so, madam.

MRS. CANDOUR.   She has a charming, fresh colour.

35 LADY TEAZLE.   Yes, when it is fresh put on.

MRS. CANDOUR.   Oh fie! I'll swear her colour is natural. I have seen it come and go.

LADY TEAZLE.   I dare swear you have, ma'am; it goes off at night and comes again in the morning.

40 MRS. CANDOUR.   Ha, ha, ha! How I hate to hear you talk so. But surely now, her sister *is* or *was* very handsome.

---

1   *duodecimo phaeton* Very small open carriage pulled by two horses.
2   *macaronies* Flamboyantly fashionable men.
3   *Phoebus* Name applied to the Greek god Apollo in his role as sun god. He rides his chariot across the sky to bring sunlight to the earth.
4   *piquet* Two-player card game.

CRABTREE. Who, Mrs. Evergreen? Oh Lord! She's six-and-fifty if she's an hour.

MRS. CANDOUR. Now positively you wrong her, fifty-two or fifty-three is the utmost, and I don't think she looks more.   45

SIR BENJAMIN. Oh there's no judging by her looks, unless one could see her face.

LADY SNEERWELL. Well, well, if Mrs. Evergreen does take some pains to repair the ravages of time, you must allow she effects it with great ingenuity, and surely that's better than the careless manner in which the Widow   50
Ochre caulks her wrinkles.

SIR BENJAMIN. Nay now Lady Sneerwell, you are severe upon the widow. Come, come, it is not that the widow paints so ill, but when she has finished her face, she joins it on so badly to her neck that she looks like a mended statue in which the connoisseur discovers at once that the head is   55
modern though the trunk's antique.

CRABTREE. Ha, ha, ha! Well said, Nephew.

MRS. CANDOUR. Well, you make me laugh, but I vow I hate you for't. What do you think of Miss Simper?

SIR BENJAMIN. Why, she has very pretty teeth.   60

LADY TEAZLE. Yes, and on that account when she is neither speaking nor laughing, which very seldom happens, she never absolutely shuts her mouth but leaves it always on ajar as it were.

MRS. CANDOUR. How can you be so ill-natured?

LADY TEAZLE. I'll allow that's better than the pains Mrs. Prim takes to con-   65
ceal her losses in front. She draws her mouth till it positively resembles the aperture of a poor box,[1] and all her words appear to slide out edgeways.

LADY SNEERWELL. Very well, Lady Teazle, I see you can be a little severe.

LADY TEAZLE. In defence of a friend it is but justice.—But here comes Sir Peter to spoil our pleasantry.   70

    (*Enter Sir Peter.*)

SIR PETER. Ladies, your most obedient—Mercy on me, here is the whole set: a character dead at every word, I suppose.

MRS. CANDOUR. I am rejoiced you are come, Sir Peter; they have been so censorious, they'll allow good qualities to nobody, not even good nature to our friend, Mrs. Pursey.   75

LADY TEAZLE. What, the fat dowager who was at Mrs. Codille's[2] last night?

MRS. CANDOUR. Nay, her bulk is her misfortune, and when she takes such pains to get rid of it, you ought not to reflect on her.

---

1   *aperture of a poor box* Narrow slit in the top of a box used for charity collection.
2   *Codille* Term used in Ombre, a popular card game.

LADY SNEERWELL. That's very true, indeed.

80 LADY TEAZLE. Yes, I know she almost lives upon acids and small whey, laces herself by pulleys, and often in the hottest noon in summer you may see her on a little, squat pony with her hair plaited up behind like a drummer and puffing around the Ring in a full trot.

MRS. CANDOUR. I thank you, Lady Teazle, for defending her.

85 SIR PETER. Yes, a good defence, truly.

MRS. CANDOUR. But Sir Benjamin is as censorious as Miss Sallow.

CRABTREE. Yes, and she is a curious being to pretend to be censorious, an awkward gawky without any one good point under heaven.

MRS. CANDOUR. Positively you shall not be so severe. Miss Sallow is a rela-
90 tion of mine by marriage, and as for her person, great allowance is to be made, for let me tell you, a woman labours under many disadvantages who tries to pass for a girl at six-and-thirty.

LADY SNEERWELL. Though surely she *is* handsome still, and for the weakness in her eyes, considering how much she reads by candlelight, it is not to be
95 wondered at.

MRS. CANDOUR. True, and then as to her manner, upon my word I think it is particularly graceful, considering she never had the least education, for you know her mother was a Welsh milliner[1] and her father a sugar baker at Bristol.

100 SIR BENJAMIN. Ah, you are both of you too good-natured.

SIR PETER. Yes, damned good-natured—this is their own relation, mercy on me!

SIR BENJAMIN. And Mrs. Candour is of so moral a turn.

MRS. CANDOUR. Well, I will never join in ridiculing a friend. And so I con-
105 stantly tell my cousin Ogle, and you well know what pretensions she has to be critical in beauty.

CRABTREE. Oh, to be sure, she has herself the oddest countenance that ever was seen; 'tis a collection of features from all the different countries of the globe.

110 SIR BENJAMIN. She has indeed an Irish front.

CRABTREE. Caledonian[2] locks.

SIR BENJAMIN. Dutch nose.

CRABTREE. Austrian lip.[3]

SIR BENJAMIN. Complexion of a Spaniard.

---

1   *milliner* Hat-maker.
2   *Caledonian* Scottish.
3   *Austrian lip* Lip deformity also known as "Hapsburg lip" because of its prevalence among the Hapsburgs, an Austrian royal family that held power in several European nations.

CRABTREE. And teeth *à la chinoise*.[1]   115

SIR BENJAMIN. In short, her face resembles a table d'hôte at Spa,[2] where no two guests are of a nation.

CRABTREE. Or a congress at the close of a general war, where all the members, even to her eyes, appear to have a different interest, and her nose and chin are the only parties likely to join issue.   120

MRS. CANDOUR. Ha, ha, ha!

SIR PETER. Mercy on my life! A person they dine with twice a week.

MRS. CANDOUR. Nay, but I vow you shall not carry the laugh off so, for give me leave to say that Mrs. Ogle—

SIR PETER. Madam, madam, I beg your pardon, there is no stopping these good gentlemen's tongues, but when I tell you, Mrs. Candour, that the lady they are abusing is a particular friend of mine, I hope you'll not take her part.   125

LADY SNEERWELL. Well said, Sir Peter, but you are a cruel creature: too phlegmatic[3] yourself for a jest and too peevish to allow it in others.   130

SIR PETER. Ah madam, true wit is more nearly allied to good nature than your ladyship is aware of.

LADY TEAZLE. True, Sir Peter, I believe they are so near of kin they can never be united.

SIR BENJAMIN. Oh! Rather, ma'am, suppose them man and wife, because one so seldom sees them together.   135

LADY TEAZLE. But Sir Peter is such an enemy to scandal, I believe he would have it put down[4] by Parliament.

SIR PETER. 'Fore Heaven, madam, if they were to consider the sporting with reputation of as much importance as the poaching on manors[5] and pass an Act for the Preservation of Fame, I believe many would thank them for the bill.   140

LADY SNEERWELL. Oh Lud! Sir Peter, would you deprive us of our privileges?

SIR PETER. Aye madam, and then no person should be permitted to kill characters or run down reputations but qualified old maids and disappointed widows.   145

LADY SNEERWELL. Go, you monster!

---

1   *à la chinoise* French: in Chinese style. A tradition of coating teeth with black enamel was practiced in Japan and Vietnam, but not in China.

2   *table d'hôte at Spa* Table shared by tourists in the Belgian resort town of Spa.

3   *phlegmatic* Sluggish and apathetic.

4   *put down* I.e., made illegal.

5   *poaching on manors* Game preservation laws were severe, forbidding all but the most wealthy and propertied individuals to hunt.

MRS. CANDOUR. But sure you would not be quite so severe on those who only report what they hear?

150 SIR PETER. Yes madam, I would have law-merchant[1] for them too, and in all cases of slander currency, whenever the drawer of the lie was not to be found, the injured party should have a right to come on any of the endorsers.

CRABTREE. Well, for my part, I believe there never was a scandalous tale without some foundation.

155 LADY SNEERWELL. Come ladies, shall we sit down to cards in the next room?

(*Enter servant, who whispers to Sir Peter.*)

SIR PETER. I'll be with them directly.

[*Exit servant.*]

[*aside*] I'll get away unperceived. (*going*)

LADY SNEERWELL. Sir Peter, you are not leaving us?

SIR PETER. Your ladyship must excuse me; I'm called away by particular busi-
160 ness—but I'll leave my character behind me. (*Exit.*)

SIR BENJAMIN. Well certainly, Lady Teazle, that lord of yours is a strange being. I would tell you some stories of him that would make you laugh heartily, if he wasn't your husband.

LADY TEAZLE. Oh pray don't mind that, come, do, let's hear them.

(*They retire. Joseph Surface and Maria come forward.*)

165 JOSEPH SURFACE. Maria, I see you have no satisfaction in this society.

MARIA. How is it possible I should? If to raise malicious smiles at the infirmi-
ties and misfortunes of those who have never injured us be the province of wit or humour, Heaven grant me a double portion of dullness.

JOSEPH SURFACE. Yet they appear more ill-natured than they are; they have
170 no malice at heart.

MARIA. Then is their conduct more inexcusable, for in my opinion, nothing but a depravity of heart could tempt them to such practices.

JOSEPH SURFACE. But can you, Maria, feel thus for others and be unkind to me alone; is hope to be denied the tenderest passion?

175 MARIA. Why will you distress me by renewing the subject?

JOSEPH SURFACE. Ah Maria! You would not treat me thus and oppose your guardian's, Sir Peter's, will but that I see that profligate Charles is still a favoured rival.

MARIA. Ungenerously urged! But whatever my sentiments of that unfortu-
180 nate young man are, be assured I shall not feel more bound to give him up because his distresses have lost him the regard even of a brother.

---

1   *law-merchant* Assemblage of laws and customs governing mercantile transactions.

(*Lady Teazle returns.*)

JOSEPH SURFACE. [*kneeling*] Nay, but Maria, do not leave me with a frown.
By all that's honest, I swear—(*aside*) Gad's life, here is Lady Teazle.—You
must not, no, you shall not, for though I have the greatest regard for Lady
Teazle—   185

MARIA. Lady Teazle!

JOSEPH SURFACE. Yet were Sir Peter once to suspect—

LADY TEAZLE. [*aside*] What's this, pray? Does he take her for me?—Child,
you are wanted in the next room.

(*Exit Maria.*)

What's all this, pray?   190

JOSEPH SURFACE. Oh, the most unlucky circumstance in nature. Maria has
somehow suspected the tender concern which I have for your happiness
and threatened to acquaint Sir Peter with her suspicions, and I was just
endeavouring to reason with her when you came.

LADY TEAZLE. Indeed! But you seemed to adopt a very tender method of   195
reasoning: Do you usually argue on your knees?

JOSEPH SURFACE. Oh, she's a child, and I thought a little bombast—But
Lady Teazle, when are you to give me your judgment on my library[1] as
you promised?

LADY TEAZLE. No, no, I begin to think it would be imprudent, and you know   200
I admit you as a lover no further than fashion requires.

JOSEPH SURFACE. True, a mere platonic cicisbeo,[2] what every wife is entitled
to.

LADY TEAZLE. Certainly, one must not be out of the fashion; however, I have
so many of my country prejudices left that though Sir Peter's ill humour   205
may vex me ever so, it shall never provoke me to—

JOSEPH SURFACE. The only revenge in your power. Well, I applaud your
moderation.

LADY TEAZLE. Go, you are an insinuating wretch. But we shall be missed; let
us join the company.   210

JOSEPH SURFACE. But we had best not return together.

LADY TEAZLE. Well, don't stay, for Maria shan't come to hear any more of
your reasoning, I promise you. (*Exit.*)

JOSEPH SURFACE. A curious dilemma, truly, my politics have run me into: I
wanted at first only to ingratiate myself with Lady Teazle that she might   215
not be my enemy with Maria, and I have, I don't know how, become her

---

1   *give me ... my library* Literally, "examine the books in my library"; also a sexual innuendo.

2   *cicisbeo* Italian term for a married woman's male companion or escort.

serious lover! Sincerely, I begin to wish I had never made such a point of gaining so very good a character, for it has led me into so many rogueries that I doubt I shall be exposed at last.

(*Exit.*)

ACT 2, SCENE 3. SIR PETER TEAZLE'S HOUSE.

(*Enter Rowley and Sir Oliver.*)

SIR OLIVER. Ha, ha, ha! and so my old friend is married, hey! A young wife out of the country, ha, ha, ha! That he should have stood bluff[1] to old bachelor so long, and sink into husband at last.

ROWLEY. But you must not rally him on the subject, Sir Oliver; 'tis a tender
5   point I assure you, though he has been married only seven months.

SIR OLIVER. Then he has been just half a year on the stool of repentance. Poor Peter! But you say he has entirely given up Charles? Never sees him, hey?

ROWLEY. His prejudice against him is astonishing and, I'm sure, greatly increased by a jealousy of him with Lady Teazle, which he has been industri-
10   ously led into by a scandalous society in the neighbourhood, who have contributed not a little to Charles's ill name, whereas the truth is, I believe, if the lady is partial to either of them, his brother is the favourite.

SIR OLIVER. Aye, I know there is a set of malicious, prating, prudent gossips, both male and female, who murder characters to kill time and will rob a
15   young fellow of his good name before he has years to know the value of it. But I am not to be prejudiced against my nephew by such, I promise you; no, no, if Charles has done nothing false or mean, I shall compound for his extravagance.

ROWLEY. Then my life on't, you will reclaim him. Ah sir, it gives me new life
20   to find that your heart is not turned against him and that the son of my good old master has one friend, however, left.

SIR OLIVER. What, shall I forget, Master Rowley, when I was at his years myself? Egad, my brother and I were neither very prudent youths, and yet I believe you have not seen many better men than your old master was.

25 ROWLEY. Sir, 'tis this reflection gives me assurance that Charles may yet be a credit to his family.—But here comes Sir Peter.

SIR OLIVER. Egad, so he does. Mercy on me! he's greatly altered and seems to have a settled, married look! One may read husband in his face at this distance.

(*Enter Sir Peter.*)

---

1   *bluff* Unfalteringly.

SIR PETER. Hah! Sir Oliver, my old friend, welcome to England a thousand   30
times.

SIR OLIVER. Thank you, thank you, Sir Peter. And i'faith, I'm as glad to find
you well, believe me.

SIR PETER. Ah! 'Tis a long time since we met: sixteen years, I doubt, Sir Oliver, and many a cross accident in the time.   35

SIR OLIVER. Aye, I have had my share. But what, I find you are married, hey,
my old boy! Well, well, it can't be helped, and so I wish you joy with all
my heart.

SIR PETER. Thank you, thank you, Sir Oliver. Yes, I have entered into the
happy state—but we'll not talk of that now.   40

SIR OLIVER. True, true, Sir Peter, old friends should not begin on grievances
at first meeting, no, no, no.

ROWLEY. (*to Sir Oliver*) Take care, pray sir.

SIR OLIVER. So, one of my nephews I find is a wild, extravagant young rogue,
hey!   45

SIR PETER. Wild! Ah my old friend, I grieve for your disappointment there:
he's a lost young man indeed. However, his brother will make you amends;
Joseph is indeed what a youth should be. Everybody in the world speaks
well of him.

SIR OLIVER. I am sorry to hear it: he has too good a character to be an honest   50
fellow. Everybody speaks well of him! Pshaw! Then he has bowed as low to
knaves and fools as to the honest dignity of genius or virtue.

SIR PETER. What, Sir Oliver, do you blame him for not making enemies?

SIR OLIVER. Yes, if he has merit enough to deserve them.

SIR PETER. Well, well, you'll be convinced when you know him. 'Tis edifica-   55
tion to hear him converse. He possesses the noblest sentiments.

SIR OLIVER. Oh plague of his sentiments! If he salutes[1] me with a scrap of
morality in his mouth, I shall be sick directly. But, however, don't mistake
me, Sir Peter, I don't mean to defend Charles's errors, but before I form my
judgment of either of them, I intend to make a trial of their hearts, and my   60
friend Rowley and I have planned something for the purpose.

ROWLEY. And Sir Peter shall own he has been for once mistaken.

SIR PETER. Oh, my life on Joseph's honour.

SIR OLIVER. Well, come, give us a bottle of good wine, and we'll drink your
lady's good health and tell you all our scheme.   65

SIR PETER. Allons[2] then.

---

1   *salutes* Kisses in greeting.
2   *Allons* French: we shall go.

SIR OLIVER. And don't, Sir Peter, be so severe against your old friend's son. 'Odd's[1] my life! I'm not sorry that he has run out of the course a little. For my part, I hate to see prudence clinging to the green suckers of youth. 'Tis

70   like ivy round a sapling and spoils the growth of the tree.

(*Exeunt.*)

ACT 3, SCENE 1. SIR PETER TEAZLE'S HOUSE.

(*Enter Sir Peter, Sir Oliver, and Rowley.*)

SIR PETER. Well then, we will see this fellow first and have our wine afterwards. But how is this, Master Rowley? I don't see the gist of your scheme.

ROWLEY. Why sir, this Mr. Stanley, whom I was speaking of, is nearly related to them by their mother. He was once a merchant in Dublin but has been

5   ruined by a series of undeserved misfortunes. He has applied by letter since his confinement both to Mr. Surface and Charles. From the former he has received nothing but evasive promises of future service, while Charles has done all that his extravagance has left him power to do, and he is at this time endeavouring to raise a sum of money, part of which in the midst of

10   his own distresses, I know, he intends for the service of poor Stanley.

SIR OLIVER. Ah! He is my brother's son.

SIR PETER. Well, but how is Sir Oliver personally to—

ROWLEY. Why sir, I will inform Charles and his brother that Stanley has obtained permission to apply in person to his friends, and as they have

15   neither of them ever seen him, let Sir Oliver assume the character, and he will have a fair opportunity of judging at least of the benevolence of their dispositions. And believe me, sir, you will find in the youngest brother one, who in the midst of folly and dissipation, has still, as our immortal bard expresses it,

20   A tear for pity and a hand
          Open as day for melting charity.[2]

SIR PETER. Pshaw! What signifies his having an open hand or a purse either when he has nothing left to give? Well, well, make the trial if you please, but where is the fellow whom you brought for Sir Oliver to examine rela-

25   tive to Charles's affairs?

ROWLEY. Below, waiting his commands, and no one can give him better intelligence.—This, Sir Oliver, is a friendly Jew, who to do him justice, has done everything in his power to bring your nephew to a proper sense of his extravagance.

---

1   *'Odds* Swear word meaning "God's."

2   *A tear ... charity* From Shakespeare, *2 Henry IV* 4.4.31–32.

SIR PETER. Pray, let us have him in.   30

ROWLEY. Desire Mr. Moses to walk upstairs.

SIR PETER. But pray, why should you suppose he will speak the truth?

ROWLEY. Oh, I have convinced him he has no chance of recovering certain sums advanced to Charles but through the bounty of Sir Oliver, who he knows is arrived, so that you may depend on his fidelity to his own interest.   35
I have also another evidence[1] in my power, one Snake, whom I have detected in a matter little short of forgery, and shall shortly produce him to remove some of *your* prejudices, Sir Peter, relative to Charles and Lady Teazle.

SIR PETER. I have heard too much on that subject.

ROWLEY. Here comes the honest Israelite.   40

  (*Enter Moses.*)

ROWLEY. This is Sir Oliver.

SIR OLIVER. Sir, I understand you have lately had great dealings with my nephew, Charles?

MOSES. Yes, Sir Oliver. I done all my power for him, but he was ruined before he came to me for assistance.   45

SIR OLIVER. That was unlucky, truly, for you have had no opportunity of showing your talents.

MOSES. None at all. I had not the pleasure of knowing his distresses till he was some thousands worse than nothing.

SIR OLIVER. Unfortunate indeed! But I suppose you have done all in your   50
power for him, honest Moses?

MOSES. Yes, he knows that. This very evening I was to have brought him a gentleman from the City, who does not know him and will, I believe, advance him some money.

SIR PETER. What, one Charles never had money from before?   55

MOSES. Yes, Mr. Premium, of Crutched Friars,[2] formerly a broker.

SIR PETER. Egad, Sir Oliver, a thought strikes me.—Charles, you say, doesn't know Mr. Premium?

MOSES. Not at all.

SIR PETER. Now then, Sir Oliver, you may have an opportunity of satisfying   60
yourself better than by an old romancing tale of a poor relation.—Go with my friend, Moses, and present Mr. Premium.—And then I'll answer for't, you will see your nephew in all his glory.

SIR OLIVER. Egad, I like this idea better than the other, and I may visit Joseph afterwards as old Stanley.   65

SIR PETER. True, so you may.

---

1   *evidence* I.e., giver of evidence.
2   *Crutched Friars* Street in London.

ROWLEY. Well, this is taking Charles at a disadvantage to be sure; however, Moses, you understand Sir Peter and will be faithful.

MOSES. You may depend upon me. This is near the time I was to have gone.

70 SIR OLIVER. I'll accompany you as soon as you please, Moses, but hold, I forgot one thing: How the plague shall I be able to pass for a Jew?

MOSES. There is no need: the principal[1] is Christian.

SIR OLIVER. Is he? I am sorry to hear it. But then again, an't I too smartly dressed to look like a moneylender?

75 SIR PETER. Not at all. 'Twould not be out of character if you went in your own carriage, would it, Moses?

MOSES. Not in the least.

SIR OLIVER. Well, but how must I talk? There's certainly some cant of usury and mode of treating that I ought to know.

80 SIR PETER. Oh, there's not much to learn. The great point, as I take it, is to be exorbitant enough in your demands, hey Moses?

MOSES. Yes, that's a very great point.

SIR OLIVER. I'll answer for't; I'll not be wanting in that. I'll ask him eight, or ten percent, upon the loan, at least.

85 MOSES. If you ask him no more than that, you'll be discovered immediately.

SIR OLIVER. Hey, what a plague! How much then?

MOSES. That depends upon circumstances; if he appears not very anxious for the supply, you should require only forty or fifty percent, but if you find him in great distress and want the monies very bad, you may ask him
90 double.

SIR PETER. A good, honest trade you are learning, Sir Oliver.

SIR OLIVER. Truly, I think so, and not unprofitable.

MOSES. Then, you know, you haven't the monies yourself but are forced to borrow them for him of a friend.

95 SIR OLIVER. Oh! I borrow it of a friend, do I?

MOSES. Yes, and your friend is an unconscionable dog, but you can't help it.

SIR OLIVER. My friend is an unconscionable dog, is he?

MOSES. Yes, and he himself has not the monies by him but is forced to sell stock at a great loss.

100 SIR OLIVER. He's forced to sell stock at a great loss, is he? Well, that's very kind of him.

SIR PETER. I'faith, Sir Oliver, Mr. Premium I mean, you'll soon be master of the trade.

SIR OLIVER. Right, right! Well, Moses shall give me further instructions as
105 we go together.

---

1   *principal* I.e., the broker for whom Moses is acting as an agent.

SIR PETER. You will not have much time, for your nephew lives hard by.

SIR OLIVER. Oh, never fear, my tutor appears so able that, though Charles lived in the next street, it must be my own fault if I'm not a complete rogue before I turn the corner.

(*Exeunt Sir Oliver and Moses.*)

SIR PETER. So now I think Sir Oliver will be convinced you are partial, Row-   110
ley, and would have prepared Charles for the other plot.

ROWLEY. No, upon my word, Sir Peter.

SIR PETER. Well, go bring me this Snake, and I'll hear what he has to say presently.—I see Maria and want to speak with her.

(*Exit Rowley.*)

I should be glad to be convinced my suspicions of Lady Teazle and Charles   115
were unjust. I have never yet opened my mind on this subject to my friend Joseph; I am determined I will do it: he will give me his opinion sincerely.

(*Enter Maria.*)

SIR PETER. So child, has Mr. Surface returned with you?

MARIA. No sir, he was engaged.

SIR PETER. Well Maria, do you not reflect the more you converse with that   120
amiable young man what return his partiality for you deserves?

MARIA. Indeed, Sir Peter, your frequent importunity on this subject distresses me extremely; you compel me to declare that I know no man who has ever paid me a particular attention whom I would not prefer to Mr. Surface.

SIR PETER. So, here's perverseness! No, no, Maria, 'tis Charles only whom   125
you would prefer; 'tis evident his vices and follies have won your heart.

MARIA. This is unkind, sir. You know I have obeyed you in neither seeing nor corresponding with him. I have heard enough to convince me that he is unworthy my regard, yet I cannot think it culpable if, while my under-standing severely condemns his vices, my heart suggests some pity for his   130
distresses.

SIR PETER. Well, well, pity him as much as you please, but give your heart and hand to a worthier object.

MARIA. Never to his brother.

SIR PETER. Go, perverse and obstinate! But take care, madam, you have   135
never yet known what the authority of a guardian is; do not compel me to inform you of it.

MARIA. I can only say you shall not have just reason. 'Tis true, by my father's will I am for a short period bound to regard you as his substitute but must cease to think you so when you would compel me to be miserable. (*Exit.*)   140

SIR PETER. Was there ever man so crossed[1] as I am! Everything conspiring to fret me. I had not been involved in matrimony a fortnight[2] before her father, a hale and hearty man, died, on purpose, I believe, for the pleasure of plaguing me with the care of his daughter. But here comes my helpmate.
145 She appears in great good humour. How happy I should be if I could tease her into loving me, though but a little.

(*Enter Lady Teazle.*)

LADY TEAZLE. Lud! Sir Peter, I hope you haven't been quarrelling with Maria? It isn't using me well to be ill-humoured when I'm not by.
SIR PETER. Ah! Lady Teazle, you might have the power to make me good-
150 humoured at all times.
LADY TEAZLE. I am sure I wish I had, for I want you to be in a charming, sweet temper at this moment. Do be good-humoured now and let me have two hundred pounds, will you?
SIR PETER. Two hundred pounds! What, an't I to be in a good humour with-
155 out paying for it? But speak to me thus, and i'faith, there's nothing I would refuse you. You shall have it but seal me a bond[3] for the repayment.
LADY TEAZLE. Oh no! There's my note of hand[4] will do as well.
SIR PETER. And you shall no longer reproach me with not giving you an independent settlement—I mean shortly to surprise you—but shall we
160 always live thus, hey?
LADY TEAZLE. If you please. I'm sure I do not care how soon we leave off quarrelling, provided you'll own you were tired first.
SIR PETER. Well then, let our future contest be who shall be most obliging.
LADY TEAZLE. I assure you, Sir Peter, good nature becomes you; you look
165 now as you did before we were married! When you used to walk with me under the elms and tell me stories of what a gallant you were in your youth, and chuck me under the chin, you would, and ask me if I thought I could love an old fellow who would deny me nothing, didn't you?
SIR PETER. Yes, yes, and you were as kind and attentive—
170 LADY TEAZLE. Aye, so I was and would always take your part when my ac-quaintance used to abuse you and turn you into ridicule.
SIR PETER. Indeed!
LADY TEAZLE. Aye, and when my cousin Sophy called you a stiff, peevish old bachelor and laughed at me for thinking of marrying one who might be

---

1 *crossed* Unlucky in fate.
2 *a fortnight* Two weeks.
3 *bond* Formal promise of repayment on a loan; Sir Peter is playfully requesting a kiss.
4 *note of hand* Literally, a signed note; in performance, Lady Teazle would hold out her hand for Sir Peter to kiss.

my father, I have always defended you and said I didn't think you so ugly 175
by any means.

SIR PETER. Thank you!

LADY TEAZLE. And that I dared say you would make a very good sort of a
husband.

SIR PETER. And you prophesied right, and we shall certainly now be the 180
happiest couple—

LADY TEAZLE. And never differ again.

SIR PETER. No, never—though at the same time indeed, my dear Lady Teazle, you must watch your temper very narrowly, for in all our little quarrels,
my dear—if you recollect, my love, you always began first. 185

LADY TEAZLE. I beg pardon, my dear Sir Peter, indeed you always gave the
provocation.

SIR PETER. Now see my angel, contradicting isn't the way to keep friends.

LADY TEAZLE. Then don't you begin it, my love.

SIR PETER. There now—you—you are going on, you don't perceive, my life, 190
that you are just doing the very thing which you know always makes me
angry.

LADY TEAZLE. Nay, you know if you will be angry without any reason—

SIR PETER. There now, you want to quarrel again.

LADY TEAZLE. No, I'm sure I don't, but if you will be so peevish— 195

SIR PETER. There, *now* who begins first?

LADY TEAZLE. Why, you, to be sure. I said nothing, but there's no bearing
your temper.

SIR PETER. No, no, madam, the fault is in your own temper.

LADY TEAZLE. Aye, you are just what my cousin Sophy said you would be— 200

SIR PETER. Your cousin Sophy is a forward, impertinent Gypsy.

LADY TEAZLE. And you a great bear to abuse my relations.

SIR PETER. Now may all the plagues of marriage be doubled on me if ever I
try to be friends with you any more.

LADY TEAZLE. So much the better. 205

SIR PETER. No, no, madam, 'tis evident you never cared a pin for me, and I
was a madman to marry you: a pert, rural coquette[1] that had refused half
the honest squires in the neighbourhood.

LADY TEAZLE. And I am sure I was a fool to marry you: an old, dangling
bachelor, who was single at fifty only because he never could meet with 210
anyone who would have him.

SIR PETER. Aye, aye, madam, but you were pleased enough to listen to me:
you never had such an offer before.

---

1   *coquette* Flirt.

LADY TEAZLE. No! Didn't I refuse Sir Tivy Terrier, who everybody said would
215 have been a better match? For his estate is just as good as yours, and he has
broke his neck since we have been married.

SIR PETER. Oh, oh, oh! I have done with you, madam. You are unfeeling,
ungrateful—but there is an end of everything. I believe you capable of
anything that's bad. Yes madam, I now believe the report relative to you
220 and Charles, madam. Madam—yes, madam, you and Charles, not without grounds.

LADY TEAZLE. Take care, Sir Peter. You had better not insinuate any such
thing. I'll not be suspected without a cause, I promise you.

SIR PETER. Very well, madam, very well, a separate maintenance as soon as
225 you please—yes madam, or a divorce. I'll make an example of myself for
the benefit of all old bachelors. Let us separate, madam.

LADY TEAZLE. Agreed, agreed. And now my dear Sir Peter, we are of a mind
once more; we may be the happiest couple and never differ again, you
know, ha, ha! Well, you are going to be in a passion, I see, and I shall only
230 interrupt you, so bye bye. (*Exit.*)

SIR PETER. Plagues and tortures! Can't I make her angry either? Oh, I am the
miserablest fellow! But I'll not bear her presuming to keep her temper. No,
she may break my heart, but she shall not keep her temper.

(*Exit.*)

ACT 3, SCENE 2. A CHAMBER IN CHARLES'S HOUSE.

(*Enter Trip, Moses, and Sir Oliver.*)

TRIP. Here master, master, if you will stay a moment, I'll try whether—what's
the gentleman's name?

SIR OLIVER. [*aside*] Mr. Moses, what is my name?

MOSES. Mr. Premium.

5 TRIP. Premium—very well. (*Exit taking snuff.*)

SIR OLIVER. To judge by the servants, one would believe the master was ruined. But what! Sure this was my brother's house!

MOSES. Yes sir, Mr. Charles bought it of Mr. Joseph, with the furniture, pictures, etcetera, just as the old gentleman left it. Sir Peter thought it a great
10 piece of extravagance in him.

SIR OLIVER. In my mind the other's economy in selling it him was more
reprehensible by half.

(*Enter Trip.*)

TRIP. My master says you must wait, gentleman, he has company and can't
speak with you yet.

SIR OLIVER. If he knew who it was wanted to see him, perhaps he wouldn't   15
have sent such a message.

TRIP. Yes, yes, sir, he knows you are here; I didn't forget little Premium, no,
no, no.

SIR OLIVER. Very well, and I pray sir, what may be your name?

TRIP. Trip, sir, my name is Trip, at your service.   20

SIR OLIVER. Well then Mr. Trip, you have a pleasant sort of place here I guess?

TRIP. Why yes, here are three or four of us pass our time agreeably enough,
but then our wages are sometimes a little in arrear, and not very good either, but fifty pounds a year and find our own bags[1] and bouquets.

SIR OLIVER. Bags and bouquets! Halters and bastinadoes.[2]   25

TRIP. But apropos, Moses! Have you been able to get me that little bill
discounted?[3]

SIR OLIVER. [*aside*] Wants to raise money too—mercy on me—has his distresses, I warrant, like a lord, and affects creditors and duns.[4]

MOSES. 'Twas not to be done indeed, Mr. Trip.   30

TRIP. Good lack! You surprise me. My friend Brush has endorsed it, and I
thought, when he puts his mark to the back of the bill, 'twas as good as
cash.

MOSES. No, 'twouldn't do.

TRIP. A small sum—but twenty pounds. Harkee, Moses, do you think you   35
could get it me by way of annuity?[5]

SIR OLIVER. [*aside*] An annuity! Ha, ha, ha! A footman raise money by annuity! Well done, luxury, egad!

MOSES. But you must insure your place.

TRIP. Oh, with all my heart I'll insure my place—and my life too if you   40
please.

SIR OLIVER. [*aside*] It's more than I would your neck.

MOSES. But is there nothing you could deposit?

TRIP. Why nothing capital of my master's wardrobe has dropped lately,[6] but
I could give you a mortgage on some of his winter clothes, with equity   45

---

1   *bags* Wigs.
2   *Halters* Hangings; *bastinadoes* Canings of the feet.
3   *bill* I.e., bill of exchange, a document similar to a cheque in which one party promises to
     pay the holder at a specified date, usually some months in the future; *discounted* Sold for
     a reduced amount of immediate cash.
4   *duns* Debt collectors. Sir Oliver is suggesting that Trip is too low-class to have debt of this
     kind.
5   *annuity* Annual payment, usually obtained by way of an investment or insurance agree-
     ment.
6   *my master's ... dropped lately* As a senior servant, Trip would sometimes receive hand-me-
     down clothing from Charles Surface.

and redemption before November, or you shall have the reversion of the French velvet or a post-obit[1] on the blue and silver—these, I should think, Moses, with a few pair of point[2] ruffles, as a collateral security, hey my little fellow?

50 MOSES. Well, well—

(*Bell rings.*)

TRIP. Egad, I heard the bell. I believe, gentlemen, I can now introduce you.— Don't forget the annuity, little Moses.—This way, gentlemen.—Insure my place, you know!

SIR OLIVER. [*aside*] If the man be the shadow of the master, this is the temple
55   of dissipation indeed!

(*Exeunt.*)

ACT 3, SCENE 3.

5
(*Charles, Careless, Sir Toby Bumper, etc. discovered at a table drinking wine.*)

CHARLES. 'Fore Heaven 'tis true, there's the great degeneracy of the age: many of our acquaintance have taste, spirit, and politeness, but plague on't, they won't drink.

CARELESS. It is so indeed, Charles; they give into all the substantial luxuries of the table and abstain from nothing but wine and wit.

CHARLES. Oh certainly, society suffers by it intolerably, for now instead of the social spirit of raillery that used to mantle over a glass of bright burgundy, their conversation is become just like the spa-water[3] they drink, which has all the pertness and flatulence of champagne without its spirit or flavour.

10 FIRST GENTLEMAN. But what are they to do, who love play better than wine?

CARELESS. True, there's Harry diets himself for gaming and is now under a hazard[4] regimen.

CHARLES. Then he'll have the worst of it. What! You wouldn't train a horse for the course by keeping him from corn?[5] For my part, egad, I am now
15   never so successful as when I am a little merry; let me throw on a bottle of

---

1   *reversion* I.e., ownership rights after the current owner's death; *post-obit* Loan agreement in which repayment is postponed until the death of a person from whom the borrower expects to inherit.
2   *point* I.e., lace.
3   *spa-water* Water from a mineral spring.
4   *hazard* Complicated dice game.
5   *corn* Food grain, such as oats.

champagne, and I never lose, at least I never feel my losses, which is exactly the same thing.

SECOND GENTLEMAN. Aye, that I believe.

CHARLES. And then, what man can pretend to be a believer in love who is an abjurer of wine? 'Tis the test by which the lover knows his own heart. Fill 20
a dozen bumpers to a dozen beauties, and she that floats at top is the maid that has bewitched you.

CARELESS. Now then, Charles, be honest and give us your real favourite.

CHARLES. Why, I have withheld her only in compassion to you; if I toast her, you must give a round of her peers, which is impossible on earth. 25

CARELESS. Oh, then we'll find some canonized vestals[1] or heathen goddesses that will do, I warrant.

CHARLES. Here then, bumpers, you rogues, bumpers. Maria, Maria!

FIRST GENTLEMAN. Maria who?

CHARLES. Oh damn the surname, 'tis too formal to be registered in love's 30
calendar.—But now, Sir Toby, beware, we must have beauty's superlative.

CARELESS. Nay, never study, Sir Toby; we'll stand to the toast though your mistress should want an eye, and you know you have a song will excuse you.

SIR TOBY. Egad, so I have, and I'll give him the song instead of the lady. 35

[Song and Chorus.]
Here's to the maiden of bashful fifteen;
    Here's to the widow of fifty;
Here's to the flaunting, extravagant quean,°   *whore*
    And here's to the housewife that's thrifty.
            [Chorus.]
        Let the toast pass,   40
        Drink to the lass,
I'll warrant she'll prove an excuse for the glass.

Here's to the charmer whose dimples we prize;
    Now to the maid who has none, sir;
Here's to the girl with a pair of blue eyes,   45
    And here's to the nymph° with but one, sir.   *young woman*
        Let the toast pass, etc.

Here's to the maid with a bosom of snow;
    Now to her that's as brown as a berry;

---

1   *vestals* I.e., virgins.

50   Here's to the wife with her face full of woe,
     And now for the damsel that's merry.
          Let the toast pass, etc.

    For let them be clumsy or let them be slim,
     Young or ancient I care not a feather;
55   So fill a pint bumper quite up to the brim,
     And let us e'en toast them together.
          Let the toast pass, etc.

ALL. Bravo, Bravo!

(*Enter Trip, who whispers to Charles.*)

CHARLES. Gentlemen, you must excuse me a little.—Careless, take the chair,
60   will you?
CARELESS. Nay prithee Charles, what now? This is one of your peerless beau-
ties, I suppose, has dropped in by chance.
CHARLES. No, faith, to tell you the truth, 'tis a Jew and a broker who are
come by appointment.
65 CARELESS. Oh damn it, let's have the Jew in.
FIRST GENTLEMAN. Aye, and the broker too, by all means.
SECOND GENTLEMAN. Yes, yes, the Jew and the broker.
CHARLES. Egad, with all my heart.—Trip, bid the gentlemen walk in, (*Exit
Trip.*) though there's one of them a stranger, I can assure you.
70 CARELESS. Charles, let us give them some generous burgundy, and perhaps
they'll grow conscientious.
CHARLES. Oh hang 'em, no, wine does but draw forth the natural qualities
of a man, and to make them drink would only be to whet their knavery.

(*Enter Trip, Sir Oliver, and Moses.*)

75 CHARLES. So, honest Moses, walk in, walk in pray, Mr. Premium. That's the
gentleman's name, isn't it, Moses?
MOSES. Yes sir.
CHARLES. Set chairs, Trip.—Sit down, Mr. Premium.—Glasses, Trip.—Sit
down, Moses.—Come, Mr. Premium, I'll give you a sentiment: here's suc-
80   cess to usury.—Moses, fill the gentleman a bumper.
MOSES. Success to usury.
CARELESS. Right, Moses, usury is prudence and industry and deserves to
succeed.
SIR OLIVER. Then here's all the success it deserves.
85 CARELESS. No, no, that won't do, Mr. Premium. You have demurred to the
toast and must drink it in a pint-bumper.

FIRST GENTLEMAN. A pint bumper at least.

MOSES. Oh pray sir, consider Mr. Premium's a gentleman.

CARELESS. And therefore loves good wine.

SECOND GENTLEMAN. Give Moses a quart-glass; this is mutiny and a high   90
contempt of the chair.

CARELESS. Here now for't. I'll see justice done to the last drop of my bottle.

SIR OLIVER. Nay, pray gentlemen, I did not expect this usage.

CHARLES. No, hang it, Careless, you shan't. Mr. Premium's a stranger.

SIR OLIVER. [*aside*] 'Odd, I wish I was well out of their company.   95

CARELESS. Plague on them, then. If they won't drink, we'll not sit down with
them. Come Harry, the dice are in the next room. Charles, you'll join us
when you've finished your business with these gentlemen.

(*Exeunt Sir Toby and gentlemen.*)

CHARLES. I will, I will. Careless!

CARELESS. Well.   100

CHARLES. Perhaps I may want you.

CARELESS. Oh, you know I am always ready; word, note, or bond, 'tis all the
same to me. (*Exit.*)

MOSES. Sir, this is Mr. Premium, a gentleman of the strictest honour and
secrecy and always performs what he undertakes. Mr. Premium, this is—   105

CHARLES. Pshaw! Have done.—Sir, my friend Moses is a very honest fellow
but a little slow at expression; he'll be an hour giving us our titles. Mr.
Premium, the plain state of the matter is this: I am an extravagant young
fellow who wants money to borrow; you I take to be a prudent old fellow
who has got money to lend. I am blockhead enough to give fifty per cent[1]   110
sooner than not have it, and *you*, I presume, are rogue enough to take an
hundred if you can get it. Now sir, you see we are acquainted at once and
may proceed to business without any further ceremony.

SIR OLIVER. [*aside*] Exceeding frank, upon my word.—I see, sir, you are not
a man of many compliments.   115

CHARLES. Oh no, sir, plain dealing in business I always think best.

SIR OLIVER. Sir, I like you the better for't. However, you are mistaken in one
thing: I have no money to lend. But I believe I could procure some of a
friend, but then he's an unconscionable dog, isn't he, Moses? and must sell
stock to accommodate you, mustn't he, Moses?   120

MOSES. Yes indeed. You know I always speak the truth and scorn to tell a lie.

CHARLES. Right! People that speak the truth generally do.—But these are
trifles, Mr. Premium. What, I know money isn't to be bought without
paying for't.

---

1   *give fifty per cent* I.e., pay 50 per cent interest on the borrowed money.

125 SIR OLIVER. Well, but what security could you give? You have no land, I
    suppose?

CHARLES. Not a mole-hill nor a twig but what's in beau-pots[1] out at the
    window.

SIR OLIVER. Nor any stock, I presume?

130 CHARLES. Nothing but livestock, and that's only a few pointers and ponies.
    But pray, Mr. Premium, are you acquainted at all with any of my connec-
    tions?

SIR OLIVER. Why to say truth, I am.

CHARLES. Then you must know that I have a devilish rich uncle in the East
135   Indies, Sir Oliver Surface, from whom I have the greatest expectations.

SIR OLIVER. That you have a wealthy uncle, I have heard, but how your ex-
    pectations will turn out is more, I believe, than you can tell.

CHARLES. Oh no! There can be no doubt; they tell me I'm a prodigious fa-
    vourite and that he talks of leaving me everything.

140 SIR OLIVER. Indeed! This is the first I have heard of it.

CHARLES. Yes, yes, 'tis just so. Moses knows 'tis true, don't you, Moses?

MOSES. Oh yes, I'll swear to it.

SIR OLIVER. [aside] Egad, they'll persuade me presently I'm at Bengal.

CHARLES. Now I propose, Mr. Premium, if it is agreeable to you, to grant
145   you a post-obit on Sir Oliver's life, though at the same time the old fellow
    has been so liberal to me that I give you my word I should be very sorry to
    hear anything had happened to him.

SIR OLIVER. Not more than I should, I assure you. But the bond you men-
    tion happens to be just the worst security you could offer me, for I might
150   live to an hundred and never recover the principal.

CHARLES. Oh, yes you would, the moment Sir Oliver dies you know you
    would come on me for the money.

SIR OLIVER. Then I believe I should be the most unwelcome dun you ever
    had in your life.

155 CHARLES. What, I suppose you are afraid Sir Oliver is too good a life?

SIR OLIVER. No indeed, I am not though I have heard he is as hale and
    healthy as any man of his years in Christendom.

CHARLES. There again you are misinformed; no, no, the climate has hurt him
    considerably. Poor Uncle Oliver! Yes, he breaks apace, I am told, and so
160   much altered lately that his nearest relations would not know him.

SIR OLIVER. No? Ha, ha, ha! So much altered lately that his relations would
    not know him, ha, ha, ha! That's droll, egad, ha, ha, ha!

CHARLES. Ha, ha, ha! You're glad to hear that, little Premium?

---

1   *beau-pots* Containers of flowers.

SIR OLIVER. No, no, I am not.

CHARLES. Yes, yes, you are, ha, ha, ha! You know that mends your chance.   165

SIR OLIVER. But I'm told Sir Oliver is coming over; nay, some say he is actually arrived.

CHARLES. Pshaw! Sure I must know better than you whether he's coming
  or not; no, no, rely on't, he is at this moment at Calcutta, isn't he, Moses?

MOSES. Yes, certainly.   170

SIR OLIVER. Very true, as you say, you must know better than I, though I
  have it from pretty good authority, haven't I, Moses?

MOSES. Yes, most undoubted.

SIR OLIVER. But sir, as I understand you want a few hundreds immediately,
  is there nothing you would dispose of?   175

CHARLES. How do you mean?

SIR OLIVER. For instance, now, I have heard that your father left behind him
  a great quantity of massy old plate.[1]

CHARLES. Oh, Lud! That's gone long ago; Moses can tell you how better
  than I.   180

SIR OLIVER. [*aside*] Good lack! All the family race-cups and corporation
  bowls![2]—Then it was also supposed his library was one of the most valuable and complete.

CHARLES. Yes, yes, so it was, vastly too much so for a private gentleman; for
  my part I was always of a communicative disposition, so I thought it was a   185
  shame to keep so much knowledge to myself.

SIR OLIVER. [*aside*] Mercy on me! Learning that had run in the family like an
  heirloom.—Pray, what are become of the books?

CHARLES. You must inquire of the auctioneer, Master Premium, for I don't
  believe even Moses can direct you there.   190

MOSES. I know nothing of books.

SIR OLIVER. So, so, nothing of the family property left, I suppose?

CHARLES. Not much indeed, unless you have a mind to the family pictures. I
  have got a room full of ancestors above, and if you have taste for old paintings, egad, you shall have them a bargain.   195

SIR OLIVER. Hey, the devil! Sure you won't sell your forefathers, would you?

CHARLES. Every man of them to the best bidder.

SIR OLIVER. What, your great uncles and aunts?

CHARLES. Yes, and my grandfathers and grandmothers too.

---

1   *plate* Silver plate.

2   *race-cups* Trophies for horse racing; *corporation bowls* Bowls given by the city in recognition of service.

200 SIR OLIVER. [*aside*] Now I give him up.—What the plague, have you no bowels for your kindred? 'Odd's life! Do you take me for Shylock[1] in the play,
that you would raise money of me on your own flesh and blood?

CHARLES. Nay, my little broker, don't be angry. What need you care, if you
have your money's worth?

205 SIR OLIVER. Well, I'll be the purchaser; I think I can dispose of the family
canvas. [*aside*] Oh! I'll never forgive him this—never.

(*Enter Careless.*)

CARELESS. Come Charles, what keeps you?

CHARLES. I can't come yet, i'faith; we are going to have a sale above. Here's
little Premium will buy all my ancestors.

210 CARELESS. Oh, burn your ancestors!

CHARLES. No, he may do that afterwards, if he pleases. Stay, Careless, we
want you; egad, you shall be auctioneer, so come along with us.

CARELESS. Oh, have with you, if that's the case; I can handle a hammer as
well as a dice-box. A-going, a-going,[2] etcetera.

215 SIR OLIVER. [*aside*] Oh the profligates!

CHARLES. Come, Moses. You shall be appraiser, if we want one.—Gad's life,
little Premium, you don't seem to like the business?

SIR OLIVER. Oh, yes, I do vastly, ha, ha! Yes, yes, I think it a rare joke to sell
one's family by auction, ha, ha! (*aside*) Oh the prodigal!

220 CHARLES. To be sure! When a man wants money, where the plague should he
get assistance if he can't make free with his own relations?

SIR OLIVER. [*aside*] I'll never forgive him! Never, never!

(*Exeunt.*)

ACT 4, SCENE 1. PICTURE ROOM AT CHARLES'S HOUSE.

(*Enter Charles, Sir Oliver, Moses, and Careless.*)

CHARLES. Walk in, gentlemen, walk in pray. Here they are, the family of the
Surfaces up to the Conquest.[3]

SIR OLIVER. And in my opinion, a goodly collection.

---

1   *Shylock* Moneylender in Shakespeare's *The Merchant of Venice*. In Shakespeare's play, Shylock gives a loan on the condition that, if he is not repaid by a specified time, he is entitled
to a pound of flesh from the person who guaranteed the loan.

2   *A-going, a-going* Auctioneer's call.

3   *up to the Conquest* I.e., as far back as the eleventh century; the Norman Conquest was in
1066.

CHARLES. Aye, aye, they are done in the true spirit of portrait painting, no
volunteer grace or expression, not like the works of your modern Raphael,[1]   5
who gives you the strongest resemblance yet contrives to make your own
portrait independent of you, so that you may sink the original and not
hurt the pictures. No, no, the merit of these is the inveterate likeness:
all stiff and awkward as the originals and like nothing in human nature
beside.   10

SIR OLIVER. Ah! We shall never see such figures of men again.

CHARLES. I hope not. Well, you see, Master Premium, what a domestic character I am; here I sit of an evening surrounded by my family. But come, go
to your pulpit, Mr. Auctioneer. Here's an old gouty chair[2] of my grandfather's will answer the purpose.   15

CARELESS. Aye, aye, this will do, but Charles, I have ne'er a hammer, and
what's an auctioneer without his hammer?

CHARLES. Egad, that's true. What parchment do we have here? Richard, heir
to Thomas[3]—Oh, our genealogy in full.—Here Careless, you shall have no
common bit of mahogany; here's the family tree for you, you rogue. This   20
shall be your hammer, and now you may knock down my ancestors with
their own pedigree.

SIR OLIVER. [*aside*] What an unnatural rogue! An *ex post facto*[4] parricide!

CARELESS. Yes, yes, here's a list of your generation, indeed. 'Faith, Charles,
this is the most convenient thing you could have found for the business,   25
for 'twill serve not only as a hammer but a catalogue into the bargain. But
come, begin, a-going, a-going, a-going—

CHARLES. Bravo, Careless! Well, here's my great uncle, Sir Richard Raveline,[5]
a marvellous good general in his day, I assure you; he served in all the
Duke of Marlborough's wars and got that cut over his eye at the Battle of   30
Malplaquet.[6] What say you, Mr. Premium, look at him, there's a hero: not
cut out of his feathers as your modern clipped captains are but enveloped in
wig and regimentals as a general should be. What do you bid?

SIR OLIVER. (*aside to Moses*) Bid him speak.

MOSES. Mr. Premium would have you speak.   35

---

1   *modern Raphael* Phrase Sheridan used elsewhere to refer to his friend Sir Joshua Reynolds
(1723–92), an influential portrait painter. Raphael (1483–1520) was a major painter of
the Italian Renaissance.

2   *gouty chair* Chair made for someone with gout.

3   *Richard, heir to Thomas* Reference to the playwright's own family tree—Richard Brinsley
Sheridan's father was named Thomas.

4   *ex post facto* Latin: after the fact.

5   *Raveline* Suggestive of "ravelin," a form of fortification.

6   *Battle of Malplaquet* High-casualty battle (1709) in the War of the Spanish Succession
(1701–14).

CHARLES. Why, then he shall have him for ten pounds, and I'm sure that's not dear for a staff officer.

SIR OLIVER. [*aside*] Heaven deliver me! His famous uncle Richard for ten pounds!—Very well, sir, I take him at that.

40 CHARLES. Careless, knock down my Uncle Richard. Here now is a maiden sister of his, my great aunt Deborah, done by Kneller[1] in his best manner and esteemed a very formidable likeness; there she is, you see, a shepherdess feeding her flock. You shall have her at five pounds ten; the sheep are worth the money.

45 SIR OLIVER. [*aside*] Ah, poor Deborah! A woman who set such a value on herself.—Five pounds ten, she is mine.

CHARLES. Knock down my Aunt Deborah. This now is a grandfather of my mother's, a learned judge, well-known on the western circuit. What do you rate him at, Moses?

50 MOSES. Four guineas.

CHARLES. Four guineas! Gad's life, you don't bid me the price of his wig.— Mr. Premium, you have more respect for the woolsack.[2] Do let us knock his lordship down at fifteen.

SIR OLIVER. By all means.

55 CARELESS. Gone.

CHARLES. And there are two brothers of his, William and Walter Blunt, Esquires, both members of Parliament and noted speakers, and what's very extraordinary, I believe this is the first time they were ever bought and sold.

60 SIR OLIVER. That is very extraordinary indeed! I'll take them at your own price for the honour of Parliament.

CARELESS. Well said, little Premium; I'll knock them down at forty.

CHARLES. Here's a jolly fellow. I don't know what relation, but he was Mayor of Norwich. Take him at eight pounds.

65 SIR OLIVER. No, no, six will do for the mayor.

CHARLES. Come, make it guineas, and I'll throw you the two aldermen into the bargain.

SIR OLIVER. They are mine.

CHARLES. Careless, knock down the mayor and aldermen. But plague on't,
70 we shall be all day retailing in this manner. Do let us deal wholesale. What say you, Premium, give me three hundred pounds, and take all that remains on each side in the lump.

---

1   *Kneller* Sir Godfrey Kneller (1646–1723), a painter famous for his portraits of English nobility and prominent intellectuals.

2   *woolsack* I.e., the office of the Lord Chancellor in the House of Lords; his seat was made of a large sack of wool.

SIR OLIVER. Well, well, anything to accommodate you; they are mine. But there is one portrait which you have always passed over.

CARELESS. What! That little ill-looking fellow over the settee?   75

SIR OLIVER. Yes sir, I mean that, though I don't think him so ill-looking a little fellow by any means.

CHARLES. What, that! Oh, that's my Uncle Oliver; 'twas done before he went to India.

CARELESS. Your Uncle Oliver! Gad, then you'll never be friends, Charles.   80 That now to me is as stern a looking rogue as ever I saw: an unforgiving eye and a damned disinheriting countenance. An inveterate knave, depend on't. Don't you think so, little Premium?

SIR OLIVER. Upon my soul, sir, I do not. I think it as honest a looking face as any in the room, dead or alive.—But I suppose your Uncle Oliver goes   85 with the rest of the lumber.[1]

CHARLES. No, hang it, I'll not part with poor Noll; the old fellow has been very good to me, and egad, I'll keep his picture while I've a room to put it in.

SIR OLIVER. [*aside*] The rogue's my nephew after all!—But sir, I have some-how taken a fancy to that picture.   90

CHARLES. I'm sorry for't, for you certainly will not have it. 'Oons! Haven't you got enough of 'em?

SIR OLIVER. [*aside*] I forgive him everything!—But sir, when I take a whim in my head, I don't value money. I'll give you as much for that as for all the rest.   95

CHARLES. Don't tease me, Master Broker, I tell you I'll not part with it, and there's an end on't.

SIR OLIVER. [*aside*] How like his father the dog is. Well, well, I have done. I did perceive it before, but I never saw such a resemblance.—Well sir, here's a draft for the sum.   100

CHARLES. Why, 'tis for eight hundred pounds.

SIR OLIVER. You will not let Oliver go?

CHARLES. Zounds! No, I tell you once more.

SIR OLIVER. Then never mind the difference; we'll balance another time. But give me your hand on the bargain. You are an honest fellow, Charles. I beg   105 pardon for being so free.—Come, Moses.

CHARLES. [*aside*] Egad, this is a whimsical old fellow!—But harkee, Premium, you'll prepare lodgings for these gentlemen?

SIR OLIVER. Yes, yes, I'll send for them in a day or two.

CHARLES. But hold, do now send a genteel conveyance for them, for I assure   110 you they were most of them used to ride in their own carriages.

---

1   *lumber* Household clutter filling up storage space.

SIR OLIVER. I will, I will, for all but—Oliver.

CHARLES. Aye, all but the little nabob.[1]

SIR OLIVER. You're fixed!

115 CHARLES. Peremptorily.

SIR OLIVER. [*aside*] A dear extravagant rogue.—Good day. Come, Moses, let me hear now who dares call him profligate.

> (*Exeunt Sir Oliver and Moses.*)

CARELESS. Why this is the oddest genius of the sort I ever saw.

CHARLES. Egad, he's the prince of brokers, I think. I wonder how the devil

120 Moses got acquainted with so honest a fellow? But hark! Here's Rowley. Do, Careless, say that I'll join the company in a moment.

CARELESS. I will. But don't now let that old blockhead persuade you to squander any of that money on old musty debts or any such nonsense, for tradesmen, Charles, are the most exorbitant fellows.

125 CHARLES. Very true, and paying them is only encouraging them.

CARELESS. Nothing else.

CHARLES. Aye, aye, never fear.

> (*Exit Careless.*)

So, this was an odd fellow indeed—let me see—two thirds of this, five hundred and thirty odd pounds are mine by right. Fore Heaven, I find

130 one's ancestors are more valuable relations than I took them for! Ladies and gentlemen, your most obedient and very grateful humble servant.

> (*Enter Rowley.*)

Hah! Old Rowley, egad, you are just come in time to take leave of your old acquaintance.

ROWLEY. Yes, I heard they were going, but I wonder you can have such spirits

135 under so many distresses.

CHARLES. Why, there's the point: my distresses are so many that I can't afford to part with my spirits. But I shall be rich and splenetic[2] all in good time; however, I suppose that you are surprised that I am not more sorrowful at parting with so many near relations. To be sure, 'tis very affecting, but rot

140 'em, you see they never move a muscle, so why should I?

ROWLEY. There's no making you serious a moment.

---

1   *nabob* British person who became rich working for the East India Company, a powerful British trading company that dominated the government of India during the late eighteenth and early nineteenth centuries.

2   *splenetic* Ill-humoured.

CHARLES. Yes, faith I am so now. Here, my honest Rowley, here, get me this changed directly and take a hundred pounds of it immediately to old Stanley.

ROWLEY. A hundred pounds! Consider only—   145

CHARLES. Gad's life, don't talk about. Poor Stanley's wants are pressing, and if you don't make haste, we shall have someone call that has a better right to the money.

ROWLEY. Ah! there's the point. I never will cease dunning you with the old proverb—   150

CHARLES. "Be just before you're generous." Hey! Why, so I would if I could, but justice is an old, lame, hobbling beldam,[1] and I can't get her to keep pace with generosity for the soul of me.

ROWLEY. Yet Charles, believe me, one hour's reflection—

CHARLES. Aye, aye, it is very true, but harkee, Rowley, while I have, by   155 heaven I will give. So damn your economy and now for hazard.

(*Exeunt.*)

ACT 4, SCENE 2. THE PARLOUR.

(*Enter Sir Oliver and Moses.*)

MOSES. Well sir, I think, as Sir Peter said, you have seen Mr. Charles in high glory; 'tis great pity he's so extravagant.

SIR OLIVER. True, but he wouldn't sell my picture.

MOSES. And loves wine and women so much.

SIR OLIVER. But he wouldn't sell my picture.   5

MOSES. And game so deep.

SIR OLIVER. But he wouldn't sell my picture.—Oh, here's Rowley.

(*Enter Rowley.*)

ROWLEY. Oh Sir Oliver, I find you have made a purchase.

SIR OLIVER. Yes, yes, our young rake has parted with his ancestors like old tapestry.   10

ROWLEY. And here has he commissioned me to redeliver you a part of the purchase money, I mean, though, in your necessitous character of Old Stanley.

MOSES. Ah! There is the pity of all, he's so damned charitable.

ROWLEY. And I left a hosier and two tailors in the hall, who I'm sure won't be   15 paid, and this hundred would satisfy them.

---

1   *beldam* Elderly woman.

SIR OLIVER. Well, well, I'll pay his debts and his benevolence too. But now I'm no more a broker, and you shall introduce me to the brother as Old Stanley.

20 ROWLEY.   Not yet a while. Sir Peter, I know, means to call there about this time.

(*Enter Trip.*)

TRIP.   Oh gentlemen, I beg pardon for not showing you out. This way, gentlemen.—Moses, a word—

(*Exeunt Trip and Moses.*)

SIR OLIVER.   There's a fellow for you. Would you believe it, that puppy inter-
25   cepted the Jew on our coming and wanted to raise money before he got to his master.

ROWLEY.   Indeed!

SIR OLIVER.   Yes, they are now planning an annuity business. Ah Master Rowley, in my days servants were content with the follies of their masters
30   when they were worn a little threadbare, but now they have their vices like their birthday clothes,[1] with the gloss on.

(*Exeunt.*)

ACT 4, SCENE 3. A LIBRARY.

(*Enter Joseph Surface and servant.*)

JOSEPH SURFACE.   No letter from Lady Teazle?

SERVANT.   No sir.

JOSEPH SURFACE.   I am surprised she has not sent if she is prevented from coming. Sir Peter certainly does not suspect me, yet I wish I may not lose
5   the heiress through the scrape I have drawn myself in with the wife. However, Charles's imprudence and bad character are great points in my favour.

[*Knock within.*]

SERVANT.   Sir, I believe that must be Lady Teazle.

JOSEPH SURFACE.   Hold! See whether it is or not before you go to the door; I have a particular message for you if it should be my brother.

10 SERVANT.   'Tis her ladyship, sir, she always leaves her chair at the milliner's in the next street.

---

1   *birthday clothes* New, ornate clothing worn by those attending the king's birthday celebrations.

JOSEPH SURFACE. Stay, stay, draw that screen before the window; that will do. My opposite neighbour is a maiden lady of a curious temper.

(*Servant draws the screen, and exit.*)

I have a difficult hand to play in this affair. Lady Teazle has lately suspected my views on Maria, but she must by no means be let into that secret, at least till I have her more in my power.   15

(*Enter Lady Teazle.*)

LADY TEAZLE. What, sentiment in soliloquy! Have you been very impatient now? O Lud, don't pretend to look grave. I vow I couldn't come before.

JOSEPH SURFACE. Oh madam! Punctuality is a species of constancy—very unfashionable quality in a lady.   20

LADY TEAZLE. Upon my word, you ought to pity me. Do you know that Sir Peter is grown so ill-natured of late and so jealous of Charles too? That's the best of the story, isn't it?

JOSEPH SURFACE. (*aside*) I am glad my scandalous friends keep that up.

LADY TEAZLE. I'm sure I wish he would let Maria marry him, and then per-   25
haps he would be convinced. Don't you, Mr. Surface?

JOSEPH SURFACE. (*aside*) Indeed I do not.—Oh, certainly I do, for then my dear Lady Teazle would also be convinced how wrong her suspicions were of my having any design on the silly girl.

LADY TEAZLE. Well, well, I'm inclined to believe you, but isn't it provoking   30
to have the most ill-natured things said to one. There is my friend Lady Sneerwell has circulated I don't how many scandalous tales of me—and all without any foundation too. That's what vexes me.

JOSEPH SURFACE. Aye madam, that is the provoking circumstance—without foundation; yes, yes, there's the mortification indeed. For when a scandal-   35
ous story is believed against one, there certainly is no comfort like the consciousness of having deserved it.

LADY TEAZLE. No, to be sure. Then I'd forgive their malice. But to attack *me*, who am really so innocent and who never says an ill-natured thing of any-body, that is, of my friends—and then Sir Peter too to have him so peevish   40
and so suspicious—when I know the integrity of my own heart—indeed 'tis monstrous.

JOSEPH SURFACE. But my dear Lady Teazle, 'tis your own fault if you suffer it. When a husband entertains a groundless suspicion of his wife and with-draws his confidence from her, the original compact is broke, and she owes   45
it to the honour of her sex to endeavour to outwit him.

LADY TEAZLE. Indeed! So that if he suspects me without cause, it follows that the best way of curing his jealousy is to give him reason for't?

JOSEPH SURFACE. Undoubtedly, for your husband should never be deceived
50   in you, and in that case it becomes *you* to become frail in compliment to
his discernment.

LADY TEAZLE. To be sure what you say is very reasonable, and when the
consciousness of my own innocence—

JOSEPH SURFACE. Ah, my dear madam, there is the great mistake; 'tis this
55   very conscious innocence that is of the greatest prejudice to you. What
is it makes you negligent of forms and careless of the world's opinion?
Why, the consciousness of your innocence. What makes you thoughtless
in your conduct and apt to run into a thousand little imprudences? Why,
the consciousness of your innocence. What makes you impatient of Sir
60   Peter's temper, and outrageous at his suspicions? Why, the consciousness
of your own innocence.

LADY TEAZLE. 'Tis very true.

JOSEPH SURFACE. Now my dear Lady Teazle, if you would but once make
a trifling faux-pas, you can't conceive how cautious you would grow and
65   how ready to humour and agree with your husband.

LADY TEAZLE. Do you think so?

JOSEPH SURFACE. Oh, I'm sure on't. And then you'd find all scandal would
cease at once, for in short, your character at present is like a person in a
plethora:[1] absolutely dying of too much health.

70 LADY TEAZLE. Why, if my understanding were once convinced—

JOSEPH SURFACE. Oh certainly, madam. Your understanding *should* be convinced—yes, yes. Heaven forbid I should persuade you to do anything you
thought wrong—no, no. I have too much honour to desire it.

LADY TEAZLE. Don't you think we may as well leave honour out of the argu-
75   ment.

JOSEPH SURFACE. Ah! The ill effects of your country education I see still remain with you.

LADY TEAZLE. I doubt they do, indeed, and I will fairly own to you that, if
I could be persuaded to do wrong, it would be Sir Peter's ill usage sooner
80   than your honourable logic after all.

JOSEPH SURFACE. Then by this hand which he is unworthy of—

(*Enter Servant.*)

'Sdeath,[2] you blockhead, what do you want?

SERVANT. I beg pardon, sir, but I thought you wouldn't choose Sir Peter's
coming upstairs without announcing him.

1   *plethora* Sickness thought to be caused by an overabundance of blood.
2   *'Sdeath* Swear word meaning "God's death."

JOSEPH SURFACE. Sir Peter, 'oons, and the devil!   85

LADY TEAZLE. Sir Peter! Oh Lud, I'm ruined! I'm ruined!

SERVANT. Sir, 'twasn't I let him in.

LADY TEAZLE. Oh! I'm undone. What will become of me now, Mr. Logic? Oh
mercy, he's on the stairs! I'll get behind here, and if ever I'm so imprudent
again! (*Goes behind the screen.*)   90

JOSEPH SURFACE. Give me a book.

    (*Enter Sir Peter.*)

SIR PETER. Aye, ever improving himself.—Mr. Surface! Mr. Surface!

JOSEPH SURFACE. Oh my dear Sir Peter, I beg your pardon, (*gaping and
throwing away the book*) I have been dozing over a stupid book. Well, I
am much obliged to you for this call. You have not been here, I believe,   95
since I fitted up this room. Books, you know, are the only things I am a
coxcomb[1] in.

SIR PETER. 'Tis very neat indeed. Well, well, that's proper, and you make even
your screen a source of knowledge: hung, I perceive, with maps.

JOSEPH SURFACE. Oh yes, I find great use in that screen.   100

SIR PETER. I dare say you must, certainly, when you want to find anything
in a hurry.

JOSEPH SURFACE. (*aside*) Aye, or to hide anything in a hurry either.

SIR PETER. Well, I have a little private business.

JOSEPH SURFACE. You needn't stay.   105

SERVANT. No sir. (*Exit.*)

JOSEPH SURFACE. Here's a chair, Sir Peter. I beg—

SIR PETER. Well now we are alone, there is a subject, my dear friend, on
which I wish to unburden my mind to you, a point of greatest moment
to my peace—in short, my good friend, Lady Teazle's conduct of late has 110
made me very unhappy.

JOSEPH SURFACE. Indeed, I am sorry to hear it.

SIR PETER. Yes, 'tis but too plain she has not the least regard for me, but
what's worse, I have pretty good authority to suppose that she must have
formed an attachment to another.   115

JOSEPH SURFACE. Indeed! You astonish me!

SIR PETER. Yes, and between ourselves, I think I have discovered the person.

JOSEPH SURFACE. How! You alarm me exceedingly!

SIR PETER. Ah my dear friend, I knew you would sympathize with me!

JOSEPH SURFACE. Yes, believe me, Sir Peter, such a discovery would distress me 120
just as much as it would you.

---

1   *coxcomb* Dandy; excessively showy man.

SIR PETER. I am convinced of it. Ah, it is a happiness to have a friend whom one can trust even with one's family secrets. But have you no guess who I mean?

125 JOSEPH SURFACE. I haven't the most distant idea. It can't be Sir Benjamin Backbite?

SIR PETER. Oh, no. What say you to Charles?

JOSEPH SURFACE. My brother! Impossible!

SIR PETER. It's very true.

130 JOSEPH SURFACE. Oh no, Sir Peter, you must not credit the scandalous insinuation you hear. No, no, Charles, to be sure, has been charged many things of this kind, but I can never think he could meditate[1] so gross an injury.

SIR PETER. Ah, my dear friend! The goodness of your own heart misleads you; you judge of others by yourself.

135 JOSEPH SURFACE. Certainly, Sir Peter, the heart that is conscious of its own integrity is ever slow to credit another's baseness.

SIR PETER. True, but your brother has no sentiment; you never hear him talk so.

JOSEPH SURFACE. Yet I can't but think that Lady Teazle herself has too much
140   principle.

SIR PETER. Aye, but what's her principle against the flattery of a handsome, lively, young fellow.

JOSEPH SURFACE. That's very true.

SIR PETER. And then you know the difference of our ages makes it highly
145   improbable that she should have any violent affection for me, and if she were to be frail, and I were to make it public, why the Town would only laugh at me, the foolish old bachelor who had married a girl.

JOSEPH SURFACE. That's true. To be sure, they would laugh.

SIR PETER. Laugh, aye, and make ballads and paragraphs and the devil knows
150   what of me.

JOSEPH SURFACE. No, you must never make it public.

SIR PETER. But then again, that the nephew of my old friend, Sir Oliver, should be the person to do such a wrong hurts one more nearly.

JOSEPH SURFACE. Aye, there's the point: When ingratitude barbs the dart of
155   injury, the wound has double danger in it.

SIR PETER. Aye, I that was in a manner left his guardian, in whose house he has been so often entertained, who never in my life denied him my advice.

JOSEPH SURFACE. Oh 'tis not to be credited. There may be a man capable of such baseness to be sure, but for my part, till you can give me positive
160   proofs, I cannot but doubt it; however, if this should be proved on him, he

---

1   *meditate* Consider.

is no longer a brother of mine. I disclaim kindred with him. For the man who can break through the laws of hospitality and attempt the wife of his friend deserves to be branded as the pest of society.

SIR PETER. What a difference there is between you! What noble sentiments!

JOSEPH SURFACE. Yet I cannot suspect Lady Teazle's honour.   165

SIR PETER. I am sure I wish to think well of her and to remove all ground of quarrel between us. She has lately reproached me more than once with having made no settlement on her, and in our last quarrel she almost hint- ed that she would not break her heart if I was dead. Now as we seem to differ in our ideas of expense, I have resolved she shall be her own mistress 170 in that respect for the future, and if I were to die, she shall find that I have not been inattentive to her interests while living. Here, my friend, are the drafts of two deeds which I wish to have your opinion on: by one, she will enjoy eight hundred a year, independent, while I live, and by the other, the bulk of my fortune after my death.   175

JOSEPH SURFACE. This conduct, Sir Peter, is indeed truly generous! (*aside*) I wish it may not corrupt my pupil.

SIR PETER. Yes, I am determined she shall have no cause to complain, though I would not have her acquainted with the latter instance of my affection yet awhile.   180

JOSEPH SURFACE. [*aside*] Nor I, if I could help it.

SIR PETER. And now, my dear friend, if you please, we will talk over the situ- ation of your hopes with Maria.

JOSEPH SURFACE. [*softly*] No, no, Sir Peter, another time if you please.

SIR PETER. I am sensibly chagrined at the little progress you seem to make in 185 her affections—

JOSEPH SURFACE. (*softly*) I beg you will not mention it, sir. What are my disappointments when your happiness is in debate. [*aside*] 'Sdeath, I shall be ruined every way.

SIR PETER. And though you are so averse to my acquainting Lady Teazle with 190 your passion, I am sure she is not your enemy in the affair.

JOSEPH SURFACE. Pray Sir Peter, oblige me—I am really too much affected by the subject we have been talking to bestow a thought on my own concerns. The man who is entrusted with his friend's distresses—can never—Well, sir—   195

(*Enter Servant.*)

SERVANT. Your brother, sir, is speaking to a gentleman in the street and says he knows you are within.

JOSEPH SURFACE. 'Sdeath! Blockhead, I am not within; I am out for the day.

SIR PETER. Stay, hold, a thought has struck me: you shall be at home.

200 JOSEPH SURFACE. Well, well, let him up. (*Exit Servant.*)

(*aside*) He'll interrupt Sir Peter, however.

SIR PETER. Now my good friend, oblige me, I entreat you: before Charles comes, let me conceal myself some-where; then do you tax him on the point we have been talking on, and his answers may satisfy me at once.

205 JOSEPH SURFACE. Oh fie, Sir Peter! Would you have me join in so mean a trick—to trepan[1] my brother too—

SIR PETER. Nay, you tell me you are sure he's innocent; if so, you do him the greatest service in giving him an opportunity to clear himself, and you will set my heart at rest. Come, you shall not refuse me. Here behind

210 this screen will be—Hey! What the devil! There seems to be one listener already. I'll swear I saw a petticoat.

JOSEPH SURFACE. Ha, ha, ha! Well, this is ridiculous enough. I'll tell you, Sir Peter, though I hold a man of intrigue to be a most despicable character, yet you know it does not follow that one is to be an absolute Joseph[2] either.

215 Harkee, 'tis a little French milliner, a silly[3] rogue that plagues me, and having some character, on your coming in she ran behind the screen.

SIR PETER. Ah, you rogue. But egad, she has overheard all I have been saying of my wife.

JOSEPH SURFACE. Oh, 'twill never go any farther, you may depend on't.

220 SIR PETER. No! Then i'faith, let her hear it out. Here's a closet will do as well.

JOSEPH SURFACE. Well, go in then.

SIR PETER. Sly rogue, sly rogue! (*Goes into the closet.*)

JOSEPH SURFACE. A narrow escape indeed, and a curious situation I am in, to part man and wife in this manner.

225 LADY TEAZLE. (*peeping out*) Couldn't I steal off?

JOSEPH SURFACE. Keep close, my angel.

SIR PETER. (*peeping out*) Joseph, tax him home.

JOSEPH SURFACE. Back, my dear friend.

LADY TEAZLE. Couldn't you lock Sir Peter in?

230 JOSEPH SURFACE. Lie still, my life.

SIR PETER. You are sure the little milliner won't blab?

JOSEPH SURFACE. In, in, my dear Sir Peter. Foregad, I wish I had a key to the door.

(*Enter Charles.*)

---

1 *trepan* I.e., trick into confessing his behaviour.
2 *Joseph* Biblical figure who is propositioned by his master's wife and refuses her.
3 *silly* Simple, insignificant.

CHARLES. Holla, brother! What has been the matter? Your fellow wouldn't let me up at first. What, have you had a Jew or a wench with you?   235

JOSEPH SURFACE. Neither brother, I assure you.

CHARLES. And what has made Sir Peter steal off? I thought he had been with you.

JOSEPH SURFACE. He was, brother, but hearing you were coming, he did not choose to stay.   240

CHARLES. What! Was the old gentleman afraid I wanted to borrow money of him?

JOSEPH SURFACE. No, sir. But I am sorry to find, Charles, that you have lately given that worthy man grounds for great uneasiness.

CHARLES. Yes, yes, they tell me I do that to a great many worthy men, but   245 how so pray?

JOSEPH SURFACE. To be plain with you, brother, he thinks you are endeavouring to gain Lady Teazle's affections from him.

CHARLES. Who I? Oh Lud! Not I, upon my word. Ha, ha, ha! So the old fellow has found out that he has got a young wife, has he?   250

JOSEPH SURFACE. This is no subject to jest upon, brother. He who can laugh—

CHARLES. True, true, as you were going to say—then seriously, I never had the least idea of what you charge me with, upon my honour.

JOSEPH SURFACE. Well, well, it will give Sir Peter great satisfaction to hear it.

CHARLES. To be sure, I once thought the lady seemed to have taken a fancy   255 to me, but upon my soul, I never gave the least encouragement; besides, you know my attachment to Maria.

JOSEPH SURFACE. But sure brother, if Lady Teazle had betrayed the fondest partiality for you—

CHARLES. Why, look ye Joseph, I hope I shall never deliberately do a dishon-   260 ourable action—but if a pretty woman were purposely to throw herself in my way—and that pretty woman married to a man old enough to be her father—

JOSEPH SURFACE. Well!

CHARLES. Why, I believe I should be obliged to borrow a little of your moral-   265 ity, that's all. But brother, do you know now that you surprise me exceedingly by naming me with Lady Teazle, for 'faith, I always understood *you* were her favourite.

JOSEPH SURFACE. For shame, Charles, this retort is foolish.

CHARLES. Nay, I swear I have seen you exchange such significant glances.   270

JOSEPH SURFACE. Nay, nay sir, this is no jest.

CHARLES. Egad, I'm serious, don't you remember one day when I called here—

JOSEPH SURFACE. Nay prithee Charles—

275 CHARLES. And found you together—

JOSEPH SURFACE. Zounds sir! I insist—

CHARLES. And another time when your servant—

JOSEPH SURFACE. Brother, brother, a word with you. (*aside*) Gad I must stop him.

280 CHARLES. Informed me, I say, that—

JOSEPH SURFACE. Hush! I beg your pardon, but Sir Peter has overheard all we have been saying; I knew you would clear yourself, or I should not have consented.

CHARLES. How! Sir Peter! Where is he?

285 JOSEPH SURFACE. Softly—there. (*Points to the closet.*)

CHARLES. Oh! 'Fore Heaven, I'll have him out.—Sir Peter, come forth.

JOSEPH SURFACE. No, no.

CHARLES. I say, Sir Peter, come into court. (*Pulls in Sir Peter.*) What, my old guardian! What! Turned inquisitor, and taking evidence incog?[1]

290 SIR PETER. Give me your hand, Charles, I believe I have suspected you wrongfully. But you mustn't be angry with Joseph—'twas my plan.

CHARLES. Indeed!

SIR PETER. But I acquit you. I promise you, I don't think near so ill of you as I did. What I have heard has given me great satisfaction.

295 CHARLES. Egad then! 'twas lucky you didn't hear any more.—Wasn't it, Joseph?

SIR PETER. Ah! You would have retorted on him.

CHARLES. Aye, aye, that was a joke.

SIR PETER. Yes, yes, I know his honour too well.

300 CHARLES. But you might as well have suspected *him* as me in this matter for all that.—Mightn't he, Joseph?

SIR PETER. Well, well, I believe you.

JOSEPH SURFACE. (*aside*) I wish they were both well out of the room.

SIR PETER. And in future perhaps we may not be such strangers.

(*Enter servant who speaks to Joseph Surface.*)

305 SERVANT. Sir, Lady Sneerwell is below and says she will come up.

JOSEPH SURFACE. (*to the servant*) Lady Sneerwell—Gad's life! She mustn't come here.—Gentlemen, I beg pardon—I must wait on you downstairs— here is a person come on particular business.

CHARLES. Well, well, you can see him in another room; Sir Peter and I have

310 not met for a long time, and I have something to say to him.

---

1   *incog* Incognito.

JOSEPH SURFACE. [*aside*] They must not be left together. I'll send Lady Sneerwell away directly.—Sir Peter, not a word of the French milliner.
SIR PETER. Oh not for the world!

(*Exit Joseph Surface* [*and servant*].)

Ah Charles, if you associated more with your brother, one might indeed
hope for your reformation. He is a man of sentiment. Well, there's nothing   315
so noble as a man of sentiment.
CHARLES. Pshaw, he is too moral by half and so apprehensive of his good
name, as he calls it, that I suppose he would as soon let a priest into his
house as a wench.
SIR PETER. No, no, come, come, you wrong him. No, no, Joseph is no rake,   320
but he is no such saint in that respect either. (*aside*) I have a great mind to
tell him; we should have such a laugh.
CHARLES. Oh, hang him! He's a very anchorite—a young hermit!
SIR PETER. Hark ye, you must not abuse him; he may chance to hear of it
again, I promise.   325
CHARLES. Why, you won't tell him?
SIR PETER. No—but—this way—[*aside*] Egad, I'll tell him.—Hark ye, have
you a mind to have a good laugh against Joseph?
CHARLES. I should like it of all things.
SIR PETER. Then, faith, we will. [*aside*] I'll be quit with him for discovering[1]   330
me. (*whispers*) He had a girl with him when I called.
CHARLES. What, Joseph! You jest.
SIR PETER. Hush! A little French milliner—and the best of the jest is—she's
in the room now.
CHARLES. The devil she is! (*looking at the closet*)   335
SIR PETER. Hush I tell you! (*Points to the screen.*)
CHARLES. Behind the screen? 'Odd's life! Let us unveil her.
SIR PETER. No, no, he's coming, you shan't indeed.
CHARLES. Oh egad, we'll have a peep at the little milliner!
SIR PETER. No, not for the world—Joseph will never forgive me.   350
CHARLES. I'll stand by you.
SIR PETER. 'Odd's life! Here he is.

(*Joseph enters as Charles throws down the screen.*)

CHARLES. Lady Teazle, by all that's wonderful!
SIR PETER. Lady Teazle, by all that's damnable!

---

1   *discovering* Revealing.

355   CHARLES. Sir Peter, this is one of the smartest French milliners I ever saw.
        Egad, you seem all to have been diverting yourselves at hide and seek. And
        I don't see who is out of the secret.—Shall I beg your ladyship to inform
        me? Not a word!—Brother, will you please to explain this matter? What, is
        morality dumb too?—Sir Peter, though I found you in the dark, perhaps
360   you are not so now. All mute! Well, though I can make nothing of this af-
        fair, I suppose you perfectly understand one another, so I shall leave you to
        yourselves. (*going*) Brother, I am sorry to find you have given that worthy
        man grounds for so much uneasiness.—Sir Peter, there's nothing in the
        world so noble as a man of sentiment! (*Exit.*)
365   JOSEPH SURFACE. Sir Peter, notwithstanding I confess that appearances are
        against me, if you will afford me your patience, I make no doubt but I shall
        explain everything to your satisfaction.
        SIR PETER. If you please, sir.
        JOSEPH SURFACE. The fact is, sir—that Lady Teazle, knowing my pretensions
370   to your ward, Maria—I say, sir, Lady Teazle being apprehensive of the

James Roberts, Act 4, Scene 3 of The School for Scandal, *1777. This painting shows the
actors who appeared in the first production of* The School for Scandal, *staged at Drury
Lane Theatre in 1777. The subject is a well-known portion of the play that is often referred to as the "screen scene"; in front of Lady Teazle is the fallen screen, which Charles
has thrown down to reveal her.*

jealousy of your temper and knowing my friendship to the family—she, sir, I say, called here, in order that I might explain those pretensions—but on your coming, being apprehensive as I said of your jealousy—she withdrew—and this, you may depend on't, is the whole truth of the matter.

SIR PETER. A very clear account upon my word, and I dare swear the lady will 375 vouch for every article of it.

LADY TEAZLE. For not one word of it, Sir Peter.

SIR PETER. How! Don't you think it worthwhile to agree in the lie?

LADY TEAZLE. There is not one syllable of truth in what that gentleman has told you.   380

SIR PETER. I believe you, upon my soul, madam.

JOSEPH SURFACE. 'Sdeath, madam, will you betray me?

LADY TEAZLE. Good Mr. Hypocrite, by your leave, I will speak for myself.

SIR PETER. Aye, let her alone, sir; you'll find she'll make a better story than you without prompting.   385

LADY TEAZLE. Hear me, Sir Peter, I came hither on no matter relating to your ward and even ignorant of this gentleman's pretensions to her. But I came here seduced by his insidious arguments, at least to listen to his pretended passion, if not to sacrifice your honour to his baseness.

SIR PETER. Now I believe the truth is coming indeed.   390

JOSEPH SURFACE. The woman's mad.

LADY TEAZLE. No sir, she has recovered her senses, and your own arts have furnished her with the means.—Sir Peter, I do not expect you to credit me, but the tenderness you expressed for me, when I'm sure you could not think I was a witness to it, has penetrated so to my heart that, had I 395 left the place without the shame of the discovery, my future life should have spoken the sincerity of my gratitude. As for that smoothed-tongue hypocrite, who would have seduced the wife of his too credulous friend while he affected honourable addresses to his ward, I behold him now in a light so truly despicable that I never again shall respect myself for having 400 listened to him. (*Exit.*)

JOSEPH SURFACE. Notwithstanding all this, Sir Peter, Heaven knows—

SIR PETER. That you are a villain, and so I leave you to your conscience.

JOSEPH SURFACE. You are too rash, Sir Peter—you shall hear me—the man who shuts out conviction by refusing to—   405

SIR PETER. Oh, damn your sentiment!

(*Exeunt.*)

ACT 5, SCENE 1. A LIBRARY.

(*Enter Joseph Surface and servant.*)

JOSEPH SURFACE. Mr. Stanley! and why should you think I would see him? You must know he comes to ask something.

SERVANT. Sir, I should not have let him in, but that Mr. Rowley came to the door with him.

5 JOSEPH SURFACE. Pshaw! Blockhead! To suppose that I should now be in a temper to receive visits from poor relations! Well, why don't you show the fellow up?

SERVANT. I will, sir. Why sir, it wasn't my fault that Sir Peter discovered my lady. (*Exit.*)

10 JOSEPH SURFACE. Go, fool. Sure, Fortune never played a man of my policy such a trick before. My character with Sir Peter, my hopes with Maria, destroyed in a moment! I am in a rare humour to listen to other people's distresses! I shan't be able to bestow even a benevolent sentiment on Stanley.—Oh, here he comes, and Rowley with him. I must try to recover
15 myself and put a little charity into my face, however. (*Exit.*)

(*Enter Sir Oliver and Rowley.*)

SIR OLIVER. What, does he avoid us? That was he, was it not?

ROWLEY. It was, sir, but I doubt you are come a little too abruptly. His nerves are so weak that the sight of a poor relation may be too much for him. I should have gone first to break you to him.

20 SIR OLIVER. A plague of his nerves! Yet this is he whom Sir Peter extols as a man of the most benevolent way of thinking.

ROWLEY. As to his way of thinking, I cannot pretend to decide, for to do him justice, he appears to have as much speculative benevolence as any private gentleman in the kingdom, though he is seldom so sensual as to indulge
25 himself in the exercise of it.

SIR OLIVER. Yet has a string of charitable sentiments, I suppose, at his fingers' ends.

ROWLEY. Or rather at his tongue's end, Sir Oliver, for I believe there is no sentiment he has more faith in than that "Charity begins at home."

30 SIR OLIVER. And his, I presume, is of that domestic sort, it never stirs abroad at all.

ROWLEY. I doubt you'll find it so. But he's coming. I must not seem to interrupt you, and you know, immediately as you leave him, I come in to announce your arrival in your real character.

35 SIR OLIVER. True, and afterwards you'll meet me at Sir Peter's.

ROWLEY. Without losing a moment. (*Exit.*)

SIR OLIVER. So! I don't like the complaisance of his features.

(*Enter Joseph Surface.*)

JOSEPH SURFACE. Sir, I beg you ten thousand pardons for keeping you a moment waiting. Mr. Stanley, I presume?

SIR OLIVER. At your service, sir.   40

JOSEPH SURFACE. Sir, I beg you will do me the honour to sit down. I entreat you, sir.

SIR OLIVER. Dear sir, there's no occasion. (*aside*) Too civil by half.

JOSEPH SURFACE. I have not the pleasure of knowing you, Mr. Stanley, but I am extremely happy to see you look so well. You were nearly related to my   45
mother, Mr. Stanley, I think?

SIR OLIVER. I was, sir, so nearly that my present poverty, I fear, may do discredit to her wealthy children, else I should not have presumed to trouble you.

JOSEPH SURFACE. Dear sir, there needs no apology. He that is in distress,   50
though a stranger, has a right to claim kindred with the wealthy. I'm sure I wish I was of that class and had it in my power to offer you even a small relief.

SIR OLIVER. If your uncle Sir Oliver was here, I should have a friend.

JOSEPH SURFACE. I wish he was, sir, with all my heart. You should not want   55
an advocate with him, believe me Sir.

SIR OLIVER. I should not need one; my distresses would recommend me. But I imagined his bounty had enabled you to become the agent of his charity.

JOSEPH SURFACE. My dear sir, you are strangely misinformed. Sir Oliver is a worthy man, a very worthy sort of a man, but avarice, Mr. Stanley, is the   60
vice of the age. I will tell you, my good sir, in confidence, what he has done for me has been a mere nothing, though people, I know, have thought otherwise, and for my part, I never chose to contradict the report.

SIR OLIVER. What! Has he never transmitted you bullion, rupees, pagodas?[1]

JOSEPH SURFACE. Oh dear sir! Nothing of the kind. No, no, a few presents   65
now and then, china, shawls, congou tea, avadavats, and India crackers,[2] little more, believe me.

SIR OLIVER. [*aside*] Here's gratitude for twelve thousand pounds! Avadavats and India crackers!

JOSEPH SURFACE. Then, my dear sir, you have heard, I doubt not, of the ex-   70
travagance of my brother; there are very few would credit what I have done for that unfortunate young man.

---

1   *bullion* Unminted gold or silver; *rupees, pagodas* Indian money.
2   *congou tea* Chinese black tea; *avadavats* South Asian birds often kept as pets; *India crackers* I.e., firecrackers.

SIR OLIVER. (*aside*) Not I, for one.

JOSEPH SURFACE. The sums I have lent him—Indeed I have been exceedingly
75   to blame. It was an amiable weakness; however, I don't pretend to defend
it, and now I feel it doubly culpable since it has deprived me of the power
of serving you, Mr. Stanley, as my heart directs.

SIR OLIVER. [*aside*] Dissembler!—Then, sir, you cannot assist me.

JOSEPH SURFACE. At present it grieves me to say I cannot, but whenever I
80   have the ability, you may depend upon hearing from me.

SIR OLIVER. I am extremely sorry—

JOSEPH SURFACE. Not more than I am, believe me; to pity without the power
to relieve is still more painful than to ask and be denied.

SIR OLIVER. Kind sir, your most obedient humble servant.

85   JOSEPH SURFACE. You leave me deeply affected, Mr. Stanley—William, be
ready to open the door.

SIR OLIVER. Oh dear sir, no ceremony!

JOSEPH SURFACE. Your very obedient.

SIR OLIVER. Sir, your most obsequious.

90   JOSEPH SURFACE. You may depend upon hearing from me, whenever I can
be of service.

SIR OLIVER. Sweet sir, you are too good.

JOSEPH SURFACE. In the meantime, I wish you health and spirits.

SIR OLIVER. Your ever grateful and perpetual humble servant.

95   JOSEPH SURFACE. Sir, yours as sincerely.

SIR OLIVER. Now I'm satisfied. (*Exit.*)

JOSEPH SURFACE. This is one of the bad effects of a good character. It invites
application from the unfortunate, and there needs no small degree of address to gain the reputation of benevolence without incurring the expense.
100   The silver ore of pure charity is an expensive article in the catalogue of a
man's good qualities, whereas the sentimental French plate I use instead of
it makes just as good a show and pays no tax.

(*Enter Rowley.*)

ROWLEY. Mr. Surface, your servant. I was apprehensive of interrupting you,
though my business demands immediate action, as this note will inform
105   you.

JOSEPH SURFACE. Always happy to see Mr. Rowley. (*aside*) A rascal!—How!
Sir Oliver Surface, my uncle, arrived!

ROWLEY. He is indeed—we have just parted—quite well after a speedy voyage, and impatient to embrace his worthy nephew.

110   JOSEPH SURFACE. I am astonished!—William, stop Mr. Stanley if he's not
gone.

ROWLEY. Oh he's out of reach, I believe.

JOSEPH SURFACE. Why didn't you let me know this when you came in together?

ROWLEY. I thought you had particular business, but I must be gone to inform   115
your brother and appoint him here to meet his uncle. He will be with you
in a quarter of an hour.

JOSEPH SURFACE. So he says. Well, I'm strangely overjoyed at his coming.
(*aside*) Never was anything, to be sure, so damned unlucky.

ROWLEY. You will be delighted to see how well he looks.   120

JOSEPH SURFACE. Oh, I am rejoiced to hear it. (*aside*) Just at this time.

ROWLEY. I will tell him how impatient you expect him. (*Exit.*)

JOSEPH SURFACE. Do, do, pray give my best duty and affection.—Indeed, I
cannot express the sensations I feel at the thought of seeing him. Certainly
his coming just at this time is the cruellest piece of ill fortune.   125

(*Exit.*)

ACT 5, SCENE 2. SIR PETER TEAZLE'S HOUSE.

(*Enter Mrs. Candour and maid.*)

MAID. Indeed, ma'am, my lady will see nobody at present.

MRS. CANDOUR. Did you tell her it was her friend, Mrs. Candour?

MAID. Yes ma'am, but she begs you will excuse her.

MRS. CANDOUR. Do go again. I shall be glad to see her only for a moment,
for I'm sure she must be in great distress. (*Exit maid.*) Dear heart, how pro-   5
voking! I'm not mistress of half the circumstances. We shall have the whole
affair in the newspapers with the names of the parties at full length before
I have dropped the story at a dozen houses. (*Enter Sir Benjamin Backbite.*)
Oh dear, Sir Benjamin! You have heard I suppose—

SIR BENJAMIN. Of Lady Teazle and Mr. Surface.   10

MRS. CANDOUR. And Sir Peter's discovery.

SIR BENJAMIN. Oh, the strangest piece of business, to be sure!

MRS. CANDOUR. Well, I never was so surprised in my life. I am sorry for all
parties indeed!

SIR BENJAMIN. Now, I don't pity Sir Peter at all; he was so extravagantly   15
partial to Mr. Surface.

MRS. CANDOUR. Mr. Surface! Why, 'twas with Charles Lady Teazle was detected.

SIR BENJAMIN. No such thing. Mr. Surface is the gallant.

MRS. CANDOUR. No, no, Charles is the man. 'Twas Mr. Surface brought Sir   20
Peter on purpose to discover them.

SIR BENJAMIN. I tell you I have it from one—

MRS. CANDOUR. And I have it from one—

SIR BENJAMIN. Who had it from one—who had it—

25 MRS. CANDOUR. From one immediately—but here's Lady Sneerwell; perhaps she knows the whole affair.

(*Enter Lady Sneerwell.*)

LADY SNEERWELL. So my dear Mrs. Candour, here's a sad affair of our friend Teazle.

MRS. CANDOUR. Aye, my dear friend, who could have thought it.

30 LADY SNEERWELL. Well, there's no trusting to appearances, though indeed she was always too lively for me.

MRS. CANDOUR. To be sure, her manners were a little too free, but she was very young.

LADY SNEERWELL. And had indeed some good qualities.

35 MRS. CANDOUR. She had indeed—but have you heard the particulars?

LADY SNEERWELL. No, but everybody says that Mr. Surface—

SIR BENJAMIN. Aye, there I told you, Mr. Surface was the man.

MRS. CANDOUR. No, no indeed, the assignation was with Charles.

LADY SNEERWELL. With Charles! You alarm me, Mrs. Candour.

40 MRS. CANDOUR. Yes, yes, he was the lover; Mr. Surface, to do him justice, was only the informer.

SIR BENJAMIN. Well, I'll not dispute with you, Mrs. Candour. Be it which it may, I hope that Sir Peter's wound will not—

MRS. CANDOUR. Sir Peter's wound! Oh mercy, I did not hear a word of their
45   fighting.

LADY SNEERWELL. Nor I a syllable.

SIR BENJAMIN. No! What, no mention of the duel!

MRS. CANDOUR. Not a word.

SIR BENJAMIN. Oh Lord! Yes, yes, they fought before they left the room.

50 LADY SNEERWELL. Pray, let us hear.

MRS. CANDOUR. Aye, do oblige us with the duel.

SIR BENJAMIN. "Sir," says Sir Peter, immediately after the discovery, "you are a most ungrateful fellow"—

MRS. CANDOUR. Aye, to Charles.

55 SIR BENJAMIN. No, no, to Mr. Surface—"a most ungrateful fellow, and old as I am, sir," says he, "I insist on immediate satisfaction."

MRS. CANDOUR. Aye, that must have been to Charles, for 'tis very unlikely Mr. Surface should go fight in his own house.

SIR BENJAMIN. Gad's life, madam, not at all—"giving me immediate satis-
60   faction"—on this, madam, Lady Teazle, seeing Sir Peter in such danger,

ran out of the room in strong hysterics and Charles after her, calling for hartshorn[1] and water; then madam, they began to fight with swords—

(*Enter Crabtree.*)

CRABTREE. With pistols, Nephew, I have it from undoubted authority.

MRS. CANDOUR. Oh Mr. Crabtree, then it's all true.

CRABTREE. Too true indeed, ma'am, and Sir Peter is dangerously wounded.   65

SIR BENJAMIN. By a thrust in segoon,[2] quite through his left side.

CRABTREE. By a bullet lodged in the thorax.

MRS. CANDOUR. Mercy on me, poor Sir Peter!

CRABTREE. Yes ma'am, though Charles would have avoided the matter if he could.   70

MRS. CANDOUR. I knew Charles was the person.

SIR BENJAMIN. My uncle, I see, knows nothing of the matter.

CRABTREE. But Sir Peter taxed him with the basest ingratitude.

SIR BENJAMIN. That I told you, you know.

CRABTREE. Do, Nephew, let me speak—and insisted on immediate satisfac-   75
tion.

SIR BENJAMIN. Just as I said.

CRABTREE. 'Odd's life! Nephew, allow others to know something too—a pair of pistols lay on the bureau (for Mr. Surface, it seems, had come the night before late from Salt Hill where he had been to see the Montem[3] with a   80 friend who has a son at Eton), so unluckily the pistols were left charged.

SIR BENJAMIN. I heard nothing of this.

CRABTREE. Sir Peter forced Charles to take one, and they fired, it seems, pretty nearly together; Charles's shot took place as I tell you, and Sir Peter's missed. But what is very extraordinary, the ball struck against a little   85 bronze Shakespeare that stood over the chimneypiece, grazed out of the window at a right angle, and wounded the postman, who was just coming to the door with a double letter[4] from Northamptonshire.

SIR BENJAMIN. My uncle's account is more circumstantial,[5] I must confess—but I believe mine is the true one for all that.   90

LADY SNEERWELL. [*aside*] I am more interested in this affair than they imagine and must have better information. (*Exit.*)

SIR BENJAMIN. Ah! Lady Sneerwell's alarm is very easily accounted for.

---

1   *hartshorn* Smelling salt made from a deer's (hart's) horn.
2   *segoon* Seconde, a position in fencing.
3   *Montem* Customary trek in which the students at Eton boys' school walked to Salt Hill, two miles away, requesting money from the people they passed.
4   *double letter* Two-page letter.
5   *circumstantial* Detailed.

CRABTREE. Yes, yes, they certainly *do* say—but that's neither here nor there.

95 MRS. CANDOUR. But pray, where is Sir Peter at present?

CRABTREE. Oh, they brought him home, and he is now in the house, though the servants are ordered to deny it.

MRS. CANDOUR. I believe so, and Lady Teazle, I suppose, attending him.

CRABTREE. Yes, yes, I saw one of the Faculty[1] enter just before me.

100 SIR BENJAMIN. Hey! Who comes here?

CRABTREE. Oh this is he! Physician, depend on't.

MRS. CANDOUR. Oh certainly, it must be the physician—and now we shall know.

(*Enter Sir Oliver.*)

CRABTREE. Well, Doctor, what hopes?

MRS. CANDOUR. Aye Doctor, how's your patient?

105 SIR BENJAMIN. Now Doctor, isn't it a wound with a small sword?

CRABTREE. A bullet lodged in the thorax, for a hundred.

SIR OLIVER. Doctor! A wound with a small sword and a bullet in the thorax! What, are you mad, good people?

SIR BENJAMIN. Perhaps, sir, you are not a doctor?

110 SIR OLIVER. Truly, I am to thank you for my degrees if I am.

CRABTREE. Only a friend of Sir Peter's then, I presume. But sir, you must have heard of his accident?

SIR OLIVER. Not a word.

CRABTREE. Not of his being dangerously wounded?

115 SIR OLIVER. The devil he is!

SIR BENJAMIN. Run through the body!

CRABTREE. Shot in the breast.

SIR BENJAMIN. By one Mr. Surface.

CRABTREE. Aye, by the younger.

120 SIR OLIVER. Hey! What the plague! You seem to differ strangely in your accounts. However, you agree that Sir Peter is dangerously wounded?

SIR BENJAMIN. Oh yes, we agree in that.

CRABTREE. Yes, yes, I believe there can be no doubt of that.

SIR OLIVER. Then upon my word, for a person in that situation, he is the

125 most imprudent man alive, for here he comes walking as if nothing at all was the matter.

(*Enter Sir Peter.*)

'Odd's heart! Sir Peter, you are come in good time, I promise you, for we had just given you over.

---

1   *one of the Faculty* I.e., a medical doctor.

SIR BENJAMIN. Egad Uncle, this is the most sudden recovery—

SIR OLIVER. Why man, what do you do out of your bed, with a small sword 130
through your body and a bullet lodged in your thorax?

SIR PETER. A small sword and a bullet?

SIR OLIVER. Aye, these gentlemen would have killed you without law or
physic and wanted to dub me a doctor to make me an accomplice.

SIR PETER. Why, what is all this? 135

SIR BENJAMIN. We rejoice, Sir Peter, that the story of the duel is not true and
are sincerely sorry for your other misfortunes.

SIR PETER. [*aside*] So, it's all over the Town already.

CRABTREE. Though, Sir Peter, you were certainly vastly to blame to marry at
all at your years. 140

SIR PETER. What business is that of yours, sir?

MRS. CANDOUR. Though indeed, as Sir Peter made so good a husband, he's
very much to be pitied.

SIR PETER. Plague on your pity, ma'am, I desire none of it.

SIR BENJAMIN. However, Sir Peter, you mustn't mind the laughing and jests 145
you will meet with on the occasion.

SIR PETER. Sir, I desire to be master of my own house.

CRABTREE. 'Tis no uncommon case—that's one comfort.

SIR PETER. I insist on being left to myself; without ceremony, I insist on your
leaving my house directly. 150

MRS. CANDOUR. Well, well, we are going—and depend on't, we'll make the
best report of you we can.

SIR PETER. Leave my house.

CRABTREE. And tell how hard you have been treated.

SIR PETER. Leave my house. 155

SIR BENJAMIN. And how patiently you bear it.

SIR PETER. Leave my house—

(*Exeunt Mrs. Candour, Sir Benjamin, and Crabtree.*)

Fiends! Vipers! Furies! Oh that their own venom would choke them.

SIR OLIVER. They are very provoking indeed, Sir Peter.

(*Enter Rowley.*)

ROWLEY. I heard high words. What has ruffled you, Sir Peter? 160

SIR PETER. Pshaw! What signifies asking? Do I ever pass a day without my
vexations?

SIR OLIVER. Well, I'm not inquisitive. I come only to tell you that I have seen
both my nephews in the manner we proposed.

SIR PETER. A precious couple they are! 165

ROWLEY. Yes, and Sir Oliver is convinced that your judgement was right, Sir
    Peter.

SIR OLIVER. Yes, I find Joseph is indeed the man after all.

ROWLEY. Aye, as Sir Peter says, he's a man of sentiment.

170 SIR OLIVER. And acts up to the sentiments he professes.

ROWLEY. It's certainly edification to hear him talk!

SIR OLIVER. Oh, he's a model for the young men of the age! But how's this,
    Sir Peter? You don't join in your friend Joseph's praise, as I expected.

SIR PETER. Sir Oliver, we live in a damned, wicked world, and the fewer we

175   praise, the better.

ROWLEY. What, do you say so, Sir Peter, who never were mistaken in your
    life?

SIR PETER. Pshaw! Plague on you both. I see by your sneering you have heard
    the whole affair. I shall go mad among you.

180 ROWLEY. Then, to fret you no longer, Sir Peter, we are indeed acquainted
    with it all. I met Lady Teazle coming from Mr. Surface's so humbled that
    she deigned to request me to be her advocate with you.

SIR PETER. And does Sir Oliver know all too?

SIR OLIVER. Every circumstance.

185 SIR PETER. What, of the closet—and the screen, hey?

SIR OLIVER. Yes, yes, and the little French milliner! Oh, I have been vastly
    diverted with the story—ha, ha!

SIR PETER. 'Twas very pleasant.

SIR OLIVER. I never laughed more in my life, I assure you, ha, ha, ha!

190 SIR PETER. Oh, vastly diverting, ha, ha, ha!

ROWLEY. To be sure, Joseph with his sentiments—ha, ha, ha!

SIR PETER. Yes, yes, his sentiments—ha, ha, ha! A hypocritical villain!

SIR OLIVER. Aye, and that rogue Charles to pull Sir Peter out of the closet—
    ha, ha, ha!

195 SIR PETER. Ha, ha!—'twas devilish entertaining, to be sure.

SIR OLIVER. Ha, ha! Egad, Sir Peter, I should like to have seen your face when
    the screen was thrown down—ha, ha, ha!

SIR PETER. Yes, yes, my face when the screen was thrown down—ha, ha! Oh,
    I must never show my head again.

200 SIR OLIVER. But come, come, it isn't fair to laugh at you neither, my old
    friend, though upon my soul I can't help it.

SIR PETER. Oh pray, don't restrain your mirth on my account; it doesn't
    hurt me at all. I laugh at the whole affair myself. Yes, yes, I think being
    a standing jest for all one's acquaintances a very happy situation. Oh yes,

205   and then of a morning to read the paragraphs about Lady T. and Sir P. will

be so entertaining. I shall certainly leave town tomorrow and never look mankind in the face again.

ROWLEY. Without affectation, Sir Peter, you may despise the ridicule of fools. But I see Lady Teazle going towards the next room; I am sure you must desire a reconciliation as much as she does.   210

SIR OLIVER. Perhaps my being here prevents her coming to you. Well, I'll leave honest Rowley to mediate between you—but he must bring you all presently to Mr. Surface's, where I am now returning, if not to reclaim a libertine, at least to expose hypocrisy. (*Exit.*)

SIR PETER. Ah! I'll be present at your discovering yourself there with all my   215
heart, though 'tis a vile, unlucky place for discoveries.

ROWLEY. We'll follow.

SIR PETER. She's not coming here, you see, Rowley.

ROWLEY. No. But she has left the door of that room open, you perceive. She's in tears.   220

SIR PETER. Certainly a little mortification appears very becoming in a wife. Don't you think 'twill do her good to let her pine a little?

ROWLEY. Oh! This is ungenerous in you.

SIR PETER. Well, I know not what to think. You remember, Rowley, the letter I found of hers evidently intended for Charles.   225

ROWLEY. Oh mere forgery, Sir Peter, laid in your way on purpose; this is one of the points I intend Snake shall give you conviction on.

SIR PETER. I wish I was once satisfied of that.—She looks this way. What a remarkably elegant turn of the head she has.—Rowley, I'll go to her.

ROWLEY. Certainly.   230

SIR PETER. Though when 'tis known we are reconciled, people will laugh at me ten times more.

ROWLEY. Let them laugh, and retort their malice only by showing you are happy in spite of it.

SIR PETER. I'faith, so I will, and if I am not mistaken we may be the happiest   235
couple in the country.

ROWLEY. Nay Sir Peter, he who once lays aside suspicion—

SIR PETER. Hold, Master Rowley! If you have any regard for me, never let me hear you utter anything like a sentiment. I have had enough of *them* to serve me the rest of my life.   240

(*Exeunt.*)

ACT 5, SCENE 3. THE LIBRARY.

(*Enter Joseph Surface and Lady Sneerwell.*)

LADY SNEERWELL.   Impossible! Will not Sir Peter immediately be reconciled to Charles and of consequence no longer oppose his union with Maria? The thought is distraction to me.

JOSEPH SURFACE.   Can passion furnish a remedy?

5   LADY SNEERWELL.   No, nor cunning either. Oh, I was a fool! an idiot! to league with such a blunderer.

JOSEPH SURFACE.   Sure Lady Sneerwell, I am the greatest sufferer, yet you see I bear the accident with calmness.

LADY SNEERWELL.   Because the disappointment doesn't reach your heart; your
10   interest only attached you to Maria. Had you felt for her what I have felt for that ungrateful libertine, neither your temper nor hypocrisy could prevent your showing the sharpness of your vexation.

JOSEPH SURFACE.   But why should your reproaches fall on me for this disappointment?

15   LADY SNEERWELL.   Are you not the cause of it? What had you to do to bate in your pursuit of Maria, to pervert Lady Teazle by the way? Had you not a sufficient field for your roguery in blinding Sir Peter and supplanting your brother? I hate such an avarice of crimes; 'tis an unfair monopoly and never prospers.

20   JOSEPH SURFACE.   Well, I admit I have been to blame. I confess I have deviated from the direct road of wrong, but I don't think we are so totally defeated either.

LADY SNEERWELL.   No?

JOSEPH SURFACE.   You tell me you have made a trial of Snake since we met
25   and that you still believe him faithful to us?

LADY SNEERWELL.   I do believe so.

JOSEPH SURFACE.   And that he has undertaken, should it be necessary, to swear and prove that Charles is at this time contracted by vows and honour to your ladyship, which some of his former letters to you will serve to
30   support.

LADY SNEERWELL.   This indeed might have assisted.

JOSEPH SURFACE.   Come, come, it is not too late yet.

(*Knocking.*)

But hark! This is probably my uncle, Sir Oliver. Retire to that room and we'll consult farther when he's gone.

35   LADY SNEERWELL.   I have no diffidence of your abilities, only to be constant to one roguery at a time. (*Exit.*)

JOSEPH SURFACE. I will, I will—So, 'tis confounded hard after such bad fortune to be baited by one's confederate in evil. Well, at all events my character is so much better than Charles's that I certainly—Hey! What! This is
not Sir Oliver but old Stanley again. Plague on't that he should return to   40
tease me just now. We shall have Sir Oliver come and find him here and—

    (*Enter Sir Oliver.*)

Gad's life, Mr. Stanley, you have come back to plague me at this time? You
must not stay, upon my word.

SIR OLIVER. Sir, I hear your uncle Sir Oliver is expected here, and though he
has been so penurious to you, I'll try what he will do for me.   45

JOSEPH SURFACE. Sir, 'tis impossible for you to stay now. So I must beg you,
come any other time, and I promise you, you shall be assisted.

SIR OLIVER. No. Sir Oliver and I must be acquainted.

JOSEPH SURFACE. Zounds sir, then I insist on your quitting the room directly.

SIR OLIVER. Nay sir—   50

JOSEPH SURFACE. Sir, I insist on't.—Here William, show this gentleman out.—
Since you compel me, sir—not one moment—this is such insolence—

    (*Enter Charles.*)

CHARLES. Heyday! What's the matter? What the devil, have you got hold of
my little broker here? Zounds, don't hurt little Premium! What's the matter, my little fellow?   55

JOSEPH SURFACE. So he has been with you too, has he?

CHARLES. To be sure he has. Why, 'tis as honest a little—But sure, Joseph,
you have not been borrowing money too, have you?

JOSEPH SURFACE. Borrowing! No. But Brother, you know here we expect Sir
Oliver every—   60

CHARLES. Oh gad! That's true. Noll mustn't find the little broker here, to be
sure.

JOSEPH SURFACE. Yet Mr. Stanley insists—

CHARLES. Stanley! Why, his name is Premium.

JOSEPH SURFACE. No, no, Stanley.   65

CHARLES. No, no, Premium.

JOSEPH SURFACE. Well, no matter which—but—

CHARLES. Aye, aye, Stanley or Premium, 'tis the same thing, as you say, for I
suppose he goes by half an hundred names, besides A and B at the coffee
house.[1]   70

    (*Knocking.*)

---

1   *A and ... coffee house* Anonymous newspaper advertisements sometimes gave the adver-
tiser's initials as "A.B." and directed readers to a coffee house where they could respond to
the posting.

JOSEPH SURFACE. 'Sdeath! Here's Sir Oliver at the door. Now I beg, Mr. Stanley—

CHARLES. Aye, aye, and I beg, Mr. Premium—

SIR OLIVER. Gentlemen—

75 JOSEPH SURFACE. Sir, by Heaven you shall go.

CHARLES. Aye, out with him certainly.

SIR OLIVER. This violence—

JOSEPH SURFACE. 'Tis your own fault.

CHARLES. Out with him to be sure.

> (*Both forcing Sir Oliver out. Enter Sir Peter, Lady Teazle, Maria and Rowley.*)

80 SIR PETER. My old friend, Sir Oliver, hey! What in the name of wonder! Here are dutiful nephews! assault their uncle at the first visit.

LADY TEAZLE. Indeed, Sir Oliver, 'twas well we came in to rescue you.

ROWLEY. Truly it was, for I perceive, Sir Oliver, the character of Old Stanley was not a protection to you.

85 SIR OLIVER. No, nor of Premium either: the necessities of the former couldn't extort a shilling from that benevolent gentleman, and with the other I stood a chance of faring worse than my ancestors and being knocked down without being bid for.

JOSEPH SURFACE. Charles!

90 CHARLES. Joseph!

JOSEPH SURFACE. 'Tis now complete.

CHARLES. Very.

SIR OLIVER. Sir Peter, my friend, and Rowley too, look on that elder nephew of mine. You know what he has already received from my bounty, and

95 you know also how gladly I would have regarded half my fortune as held in trust for him. Judge then my disappointment in discovering him to be destitute of truth, charity, and gratitude.

SIR PETER. Sir Oliver, I should be more surprised at this declaration if I had not myself found him to be selfish, treacherous, and hypocritical.

100 LADY TEAZLE. And if the gentleman pleads not guilty to these, pray let him call me to his character.

SIR PETER. Then I believe we need add no more. If he knows himself, he will consider it as the most perfect punishment that he is known by the world.

CHARLES. [*aside*] If they talk this way to honesty, what will they say to me

105 by and by?

SIR OLIVER. As for that prodigal his brother there—

CHARLES. [*aside*] Aye, now comes my turn—the damned family pictures will ruin me.

JOSEPH SURFACE. Sir Oliver! Uncle! If you will honour me with a hearing.

SIR OLIVER. (*Turns from him with contempt.*) Pshaw!   110

CHARLES. (*aside*) Now if Joseph would make one of his long speeches, I might recollect myself a little.

SIR OLIVER. I suppose you would undertake to justify yourself entirely.

JOSEPH SURFACE. I trust I could.

SIR OLIVER. Pshaw. Nay, if you desert your roguery in its distress and try   115
to be justified, you have even less principle than I thought you had. (*to Charles*) Well sir, and you could justify yourself too, I suppose.

CHARLES. Not that I know of, Sir.

SIR OLIVER. What, little Premium has been let too much into the secret, I presume.   120

CHARLES. True, sir, but they were family secrets and should never be mentioned again, you know.

ROWLEY. Come, Sir Oliver, I know you cannot speak of Charles's follies with anger.

SIR OLIVER. 'Odd's heart! No more I can, nor with gravity either.—Sir Pe-   125
ter, do you know the rogue bargained with me for all his ancestors: sold me judges and generals by the foot, and maiden aunts as cheap as broken china.

CHARLES. To be sure, Sir Oliver, I did make free with the family canvas, that's the truth on't; my ancestors may certainly rise in evidence against   130
me, there's no denying. But believe me sincere when I tell you, and upon my soul I would not say it if it was not, that, if I do not appear mortified at the exposure of my follies, it is because I feel at this moment the warmest satisfaction in seeing *you*, my liberal benefactor.

SIR OLIVER. Charles, I believe you, give me your hand: the ill-looking little   135
fellow over the settee has made your peace.

CHARLES. Then sir, my gratitude to the original is still increased.

LADY TEAZLE. Yet I believe, Sir Oliver, there is one whom Charles is still more anxious to be reconciled to.

SIR OLIVER. Oh, I have heard of his attachment there, and with the young   140
lady's pardon, if I construe right that blush—

SIR PETER. Well, child, speak your sentiments.

MARIA. Sir, I have little to say but that I shall rejoice to hear that he is happy; for me, whatever claim I had to his attention, I willingly resign it to one who has a better title.   145

CHARLES. How Maria!

SIR PETER. Heyday! What's the mystery now? While he appeared an incorrigible rake, you would give your hand to no one else, and now that he's likely to reform, I warrant you won't have him.

150 MARIA. His own heart and Lady Sneerwell's knows the cause.

CHARLES. Lady Sneerwell!

JOSEPH SURFACE. Brother, it is with great concern I am obliged to speak on this point, but my regard to justice obliges me, and Lady Sneerwell's injuries can no longer be concealed. (*Goes to the door.*)

(*Enter Lady Sneerwell.*)

155 ALL. Lady Sneerwell!!!

SIR PETER. So! Another French milliner. Egad, he has one in every room in the house, I suppose.

LADY SNEERWELL. Ungrateful Charles! Well may you be surprised and feel for the indelicate situation which your perfidy has forced me into.

160 CHARLES. Pray, Uncle, is this another plot of yours, for as I have life, I don't understand it.

JOSEPH SURFACE. I believe, sir, there is but the evidence of one person more necessary to make it extremely clear.

SIR PETER. And that person, I imagine, is Mr. Snake.—Rowley, you were
165 perfectly right to bring him with us, and pray let him appear.

ROWLEY. Walk in, Mr. Snake.

(*Enter Snake.*)

I thought his testimony might be wanted; however, it happens unluckily that he comes to confront Lady Sneerwell and not to support her.

LADY SNEERWELL. A villain! treacherous to me at last. Speak fellow, have you
170 conspired against me?

SNAKE. I beg your ladyship ten thousand pardons: You paid me extremely liberally for the lie in question, but I have unfortunately been offered double the sum to speak the truth.

SIR PETER. Plot and counterplot.

175 LADY SNEERWELL. The torments of shame and disappointment on you all.

LADY TEAZLE. Hold, Lady Sneerwell, before you go, let me thank you for the trouble you and that gentleman have taken in writing letters to me from Charles and answering them yourself. And let me also request you to make my respects to the Scandalous College, of which you are president, and
180 inform them that Lady Teazle, licentiate, begs leave to return the diploma they granted her—as she leaves off practice and kills characters no longer.

LADY SNEERWELL. You too, madam—provoking—insolent—may your husband live these fifty years. (*Exit.*)

LADY TEAZLE. What a malicious creature it is!

185 SIR PETER. Hey! What, not for her last wish?

LADY TEAZLE. Oh, no.

SIR OLIVER. Well sir, what have you to say now?

JOSEPH SURFACE. Sir, I am so confounded that Lady Sneerwell could be guilty of suborning Mr. Snake in this manner to impose on us all that I know not what to say; however, lest her revengeful spirit should prompt 190 her to injure my brother, I had certainly better follow her directly. (*Exit.*)

SIR PETER. Moral to the last drop.

SIR OLIVER. Aye, and marry her, Joseph, if you can, oil and vinegar, egad you'll do very well together.

ROWLEY. I believe we have no more occasion for Mr. Snake at present.   195

SNAKE. Before I go, I beg pardon once for all for whatever uneasiness I have been the humble instrument of causing to the parties present.

SIR PETER. Well, well, you have made atonement by a good deed at last.

SNAKE. But I must request of the company that it shall never be known.

SIR PETER. Hey! What the plague, are you ashamed of having done a right 200 thing once in your life.

SNAKE. Ah sir, consider I live by the badness of my character. I have nothing but my infamy to depend on, and if it were once known that I had been betrayed into an honest action, I should lose every friend I have in the world. (*Exit.*)   205

SIR PETER. Here's a precious rogue.

SIR OLIVER. Well, well, we'll not traduce you by saying any thing to your praise, never fear.

LADY TEAZLE. See, Sir Oliver, there needs no persuasion now to reconcile your nephew and Maria.   210

SIR OLIVER. Aye, aye, that's as it should be, and egad, we'll have the wedding tomorrow morning.

CHARLES. Thank you, my dear uncle.

SIR PETER. What, you rogue! Don't you ask the girl's consent first?

CHARLES. I have done that a long time—a minute—ago, and she looked— 215 yes.

MARIA. For shame, Charles.—I protest, Sir Peter, there has not been a word.

SIR OLIVER. Well then, the fewer the better. May your love for each other never know abatement.

SIR PETER. And may you live as happily together as Lady Teazle and I—in- 220 tend to do.

CHARLES. Rowley, my old friend, I am sure you congratulate me, and I suspect that I owe you much.

SIR OLIVER. You do indeed, Charles.

ROWLEY. If my efforts to serve you had not succeeded, you would have been 225 in my debt for the attempt, but deserve to be happy, and you overpay me.

SIR PETER. Aye! Honest Rowley always said you would reform.

CHARLES. Why as to reforming, Sir Peter, I'll make no promises—and that I
take to be a proof that I intend to set about it. But here shall be my moni-
230   tor, my gentle guide. Ah! can I leave the virtuous path those eyes illumine?
(*to the audience*)
For thou, dear maid, shouldst waive thy beauty's sway.
Thou still must rule because I will obey.
An humbled fugitive from folly view—
No sanctuary near but love and you.
235   You can indeed each anxious fear remove,
For even scandal dies if you approve.

[*Exeunt.*]

THE END.

EPILOGUE
Written by G. Colman,[1] *Esq.*
Spoken by Mrs. Abington[2]

I, who was late so volatile and gay,
Like a trade-wind must now blow all one way,
Bend all my cares, my studies, and my vows,
To one old rusty weathercock—my spouse!
5   So wills our virtuous bard—the motley Bayes[3]
Of crying epilogues and laughing plays!
Old bachelors, who marry smart young wives,
Learn from our play to regulate your lives:
Each bring his dear to town, all faults upon her—
10   London will prove the very source of honour.
Plunged fairly in, like a cold bath it serves,
When principles relax, to brace the nerves.
Such is my case—and yet I might deplore
That the gay dream of dissipation's o'er;
15   And say, ye fair, was ever lively wife,
Born with a genius for the highest life,
Like me untimely blasted in her bloom,
Like me condemned to such a dismal doom?

---

1   *G. Colman* George Colman the Elder (1732–99), English theatre manager and playwright.
2   *Mrs. Abington* Actress Frances Abington (1737–1815), who appeared in the play's original cast as Lady Teazle.
3   *Bayes* Playwright. "Bayes" is the name of the playwright character mocked in the Duke of Buckingham's *The Rehearsal* (1671).

Save money—when I just knew how to waste it!
Leave London—just as I began to taste it!   20
Must I then watch the early crowing cock,
The melancholy ticking of a clock;
In the lone rustic hall for ever pounded,
With dogs, cats, rats, and squalling brats surrounded?
With humble curates can I now retire,   25
(While good Sir Peter boozes with the squire)
And at backgammon mortify my soul,
That pants for loo,[1] or flutters at a vole?[2]
Seven's the main![3] Dear sound!—that must expire,
Lost at hot cockles,[4] round a Christmas fire!   30
The transient hour of fashion too soon spent,
Farewell the tranquil mind, farewell content!
Farewell the plumèd head, the cushioned tête,[5]
That takes the cushion from its proper seat!
That spirit-stirring drum!—card drums° I mean,   *parties*   35
Spadille—odd trick—pam—basto—king and queen![6]
And you, ye knockers, that, with brazen throat,
The welcome visitors' approach denote;
Farewell! all quality of high renown,
Pride, pomp, and circumstance of glorious town!   40
Farewell! your revels I partake no more,
And Lady Teazle's occupation's o'er!
All this I told our bard°—he smiled, and said 'twas clear,   *playwright*
I ought to play deep tragedy next year.
Meanwhile he drew wise morals from his play,   45
And in these solemn periods stalked away:—
"Blest were the fair like you; her faults who stopped,
And closed her follies when the curtain dropped!
No more in vice or error to engage,
Or play the fool at large on life's great stage."   50

—1777

---

1   *loo* Gambling card game.
2   *vole* Round of cards in which the same player wins every trick.
3   *Seven's the main* Phrase that might be spoken by a player of hazard; the choice of main
    affects what dice rolls win and lose during the caster's turn.
4   *hot cockles* Unsophisticated game, often played by families at Christmas, in which a play-
    er is blindfolded and hit from behind, and must then guess who did it.
5   *cushioned tête* Padded head; padding was used to add volume to elaborate hairstyles.
6   *Spadille ... king and queen* Terms from popular card games.

Henrik Ibsen
1828–1906

Henrik Ibsen's plays, which sought to be true to life and tackled serious moral issues, shocked audiences far more used to the light, diverting works of drama that were common during his era. His influence reached far beyond his native Norway, helping to shape such major English-language playwrights as Bernard Shaw and Arthur Miller.

Ibsen was born to prosperous parents, but the dissolution of his father's business led to the family's exile from the bourgeois circles they had comfortably moved within. After some time working as a director and theatre manager in Norway, Ibsen exiled himself in 1864; thereafter he lived in Italy and then in Germany, where he composed many of his most famous plays. These plays—among them *A Doll's House* (1879), *Ghosts* (1881), and *Hedda Gabler* (1890)—present unflattering portraits of the hypocrisies and expectations of late nineteenth-century society. Ibsen's work from this period often concerns a central character placed under pressure by societal forces such as religion, marriage, or middle-class norms; moreover, we frequently see these characters brought to a moment of crisis by the burden of their own dark secrets or moral failings. Toward the end of his career, Ibsen's emphasis gradually shifted from the examination of social problems to the exploration of psychological complexity in his characters.

Ibsen returned to Norway in 1891, by which time his international reputation as an important, if controversial, playwright was firmly established; Shaw would publish an essay expounding the concept of "Ibsenism" that same year. Writing in 1905, the British theatre critic William Archer observed that "Ibsen sees one side of a case intensely at one moment, and the other side at another moment, with no less intensity." That intensity, whether focused on social or on psychological forces, continues to engage audiences more than a century after Ibsen's death.

A Doll's House[1]

CHARACTERS

Torvald Helmer
Nora, his wife
Dr. Rank
Mrs. Linden[2]
Nils Krogstad
Anna[3] ⎫
Ellen ⎭ *Servants*
Ivar ⎫
Emmy ⎬ *The Helmers' children*
Bob ⎭
A porter.

Scene: Sitting-room in Helmer's house (a flat) in Christiania.[4]
Time: The present day;[5] *Christmastime.*
The action takes place on three consecutive days.

ACT 1

A room furnished comfortably and tastefully, but not expensively. In the background, on the right, a door leads to the hall; to the left another door leads to Helmer's study. Between the two doors a piano. In the middle of the left wall, a door, and nearer the front a window. Near the window a round table with armchairs and a small sofa. In the right wall, somewhat to the back, a door; and against the same wall, further forward, a porcelain stove; in front of it a couple of armchairs and a rocking chair. Between the stove and the side door a small table. Engravings on the walls. A display cabinet with china and small decorative items. A small bookcase filled with showily bound books. Carpet. A fire in the stove. A winter day.

---

1 *A Doll's House* Translated by William Archer, from the Walter H. Baker edition prepared by Edmund Gosse. The translation has been lightly modernized for this anthology by Broadview Press.
2 *Mrs. Linden* Called Linde in Ibsen's original.
3 *Anna* Called Anne-Marie in Ibsen's original.
4 *Christiania* Freetown Christiania, a small, partially autonomous neighbourhood in Copenhagen, Denmark.
5 *present day* I.e., around 1879.

A bell rings in the hall outside. Presently the outer door is heard to open. Then Nora enters, humming contentedly. She is wearing outdoor clothes, and carries several parcels, which she lays on the right-hand table. She leaves the door into the hall open behind her, and a porter is seen outside, carrying a Christmas tree and a basket, which he gives to the maidservant who has opened the door.

NORA. Hide the Christmas tree carefully, Ellen; the children mustn't see it before this evening, when it's lit up. (*To the porter, taking out her purse.*) How much?

PORTER. Fifty øre.[1]

5 NORA. There's a crown. No, keep the change.

(*The porter thanks her and goes. Nora shuts the door. She continues smiling in quiet glee as she takes off her cloak and hat. Then she takes from her pocket a bag of macaroons, and eats one or two. As she does so, she goes on tip-toe to her husband's door and listens.*)

10 NORA. Yes; he is at home. (*She begins humming again, going to the table on the right.*)

HELMER. (*In his room.*) Is that my lark twittering there?

NORA. (*Busy opening some of her parcels.*) Yes, it is.

HELMER. Is it the squirrel skipping about?

NORA. Yes!

15 HELMER. When did the squirrel get home?

NORA. Just this minute. (*Hides the bag of macaroons in her pocket and wipes her mouth.*) Come here, Torvald, and see what I've bought.

HELMER. Don't disturb me. (*A little later he opens the door and looks in, pen in hand.*) "Bought," did you say? What! All that? Has my little spendthrift

20 been making the money fly again?

NORA. Why, Torvald, surely we can afford to launch out a little now! It's the first Christmas we haven't had to pinch.

HELMER. Come, come; we can't afford to squander money.

NORA. Oh yes, Torvald, do let us squander a little—just the least little bit,

25 won't you? You know you'll soon be earning heaps of money.

HELMER. Yes, from New Year's Day. But there's a whole quarter before my first salary is due.

NORA. Never mind; we can borrow in the meantime.

HELMER. Nora! (*He goes up to her and takes her playfully by the ear.*) Thought-

30 less as ever! Supposing I borrowed a thousand crowns today, and you spent

---

1   *øre* Danish currency; one hundred *øre* equals one *krone* (crown).

it during Christmas week, and that on New Year's Eve a tile blew off the roof and knocked my brains out—

NORA. (*Laying her hand on his mouth.*) Hush! How can you talk so horridly?

HELMER. But supposing it were to happen—what then?

NORA. If anything so dreadful happened, I shouldn't care whether I was in debt or not.

HELMER. But what about the creditors?

NORA. They! Who cares for them? They're only strangers.

HELMER. Nora, Nora! What a woman you are! But seriously, Nora, you know my ideas on these points. No debts! No credit! Home life ceases to be free and beautiful as soon as it is founded on borrowing and debt. We two have held out bravely till now, and we won't give in at the last.

NORA. (*Going to the fireplace.*) Very well—as you like, Torvald.

HELMER. (*Following her.*) Come come; my little lark mustn't let her wings droop like that. What? Is the squirrel pouting there? (*Takes out his purse.*) Nora, what do you think I've got here?

NORA. (*Turning round quickly.*) Money!

HELMER. There! (*Gives her some notes.*) Of course I know all sorts of things are wanted at Christmas.

NORA. (*Counting.*) Ten, twenty, thirty, forty. Oh! Thank you, thank you, Torvald. This will go a long way.

HELMER. I should hope so.

NORA. Yes, indeed, a long way! But come here, and see all I've been buying. And so cheap! Look, here is a new suit for Ivar, and a little sword. Here are a horse and a trumpet for Bob. And here are a doll and a cradle for Emmy. They're only simple; but she'll soon pull them all to pieces. And dresses and neckties for the servants; only I should have got something better for dear old Anna.

HELMER. And what's in that other parcel?

NORA. (*Crying out.*) No, Torvald, you're not to see that until this evening.

HELMER. Oh! Ah! But now tell me, you little rogue, what have you got for yourself?

NORA. For myself? Oh, I don't want anything.

HELMER. Nonsense. Just tell me something sensible you would like to have.

NORA. No. Really I want nothing … Well, listen, Torvald—

HELMER. Well?

NORA. (*Playing with his coat buttons, without looking him in the face.*) If you really want to give me something, you might, you know, you might—

HELMER. Well, well? Out with it!

NORA. (*Quickly.*) You might give me money, Torvald. Only just what you think you can spare; then I can buy something with it later.

HELMER. But, Nora—

NORA. Oh, please do, dear Torvald, please do! Then I would hang the money in lovely gilt paper on the Christmas tree. Wouldn't that be fun?

75 HELMER. What do they call the birds that are always making the money fly?

NORA. Yes, I know—spendthrifts, of course. But please do as I say, Torvald. Then I shall have time to think what I want most. Isn't that very sensible, now?

HELMER. (*Smiling.*) Certainly; that is to say, if you really kept the money
80 I gave you, and really bought yourself something with it. But it all goes toward housekeeping, and for all sorts of useless things, and then I have to find more.

NORA. But, Torvald—

HELMER. Can you deny it, Nora dear? (*He puts his arm round her.*) It's a sweet
85 little lark; but it gets through a lot of money. No one would believe how much it costs a man to keep such a little bird as you.

NORA. For shame! How can you say so? Why, I really save as much as I can.

HELMER. (*Laughing.*) Very true—as much as you can—but you can't.

NORA. (*Hums and smiles in quiet satisfaction.*) H'm! You should just know,
90 Torvald, what expenses we larks and squirrels have.

HELMER. You're a strange little being! Just like your father—always eager to get hold of money; but the moment you have it, it seems to slip through your fingers; you never know what becomes of it. Well, one must take you as you are. It's in the blood. Yes, Nora, that sort of thing
95 is inherited.

NORA. I wish I had inherited many of my father's qualities.

HELMER. And I don't wish you to be anything but just what you are—my own, sweet little songbird. But I say—it strikes me you look so—so—what can I call it? So suspicious today—

100 NORA. Do I?

HELMER. You do, indeed. Look me full in the face.

NORA. (*Looking at him.*) Well?

HELMER. (*Threatening with his finger.*) Hasn't the little sweet-tooth been breaking the rules today?

105 NORA. No! How can you think of such a thing!

HELMER. Didn't she just look in at the confectioner's?

NORA. No, Torvald, really—

HELMER. Not to sip a little jelly?

NORA. No, certainly not.

110 HELMER. Hasn't she even nibbled a macaroon or two?

NORA. No, Torvald, indeed, indeed!

HELMER. Well, well, well; of course I'm only joking.

NORA. (*Goes to the table on the right.*) I shouldn't think of doing what you disapprove of.

HELMER. No, I'm sure of that; and, besides, you've given me your word. (*Going towards her.*) Well, keep your little Christmas secrets to yourself, Nora darling. The Christmas tree will bring them all to light, I daresay.

NORA. Have you remembered to ask Doctor Rank?

HELMER. No. But it's not necessary; he'll come as a matter of course. Besides, I shall invite him when he looks in today. I've ordered some fine wine. Nora, you can't think how I look forward to this evening.

NORA. And I too. How the children will enjoy themselves, Torvald!

HELMER. Ah! It's glorious to feel that one has an assured position and ample means. Isn't it delightful to think of?

NORA. Oh, it's wonderful!

HELMER. Do you remember last Christmas? For three whole weeks beforehand you shut yourself up every evening till long past midnight to make flowers for the Christmas tree, and all sorts of other marvels that were to have astonished us. I was never so bored in my life.

NORA. I did not bore myself at all.

HELMER. (*Smiling.*) And it came to so little after all, Nora.

NORA. Oh! Are you going to tease me about that again? How could I help the cat getting in and spoiling it all?

HELMER. To be sure you couldn't, my poor little Nora. You did your best to amuse us all, and that's the main thing. But, all the same, it's a good thing the hard times are over.

NORA. Oh, isn't it wonderful?

HELMER. Now I needn't sit here boring myself all alone; and you needn't tire your dear eyes and your delicate little fingers—

NORA. (*Clapping her hands.*) No, I needn't, need I, Torvald? Oh! It's wonderful to think of! (*Takes his arm.*) And now I'll tell you how I think we ought to manage, Torvald. As soon as Christmas is over—(*The hall doorbell rings.*) Oh, there's a ring! (*Arranging the room.*) That's somebody come to call. How vexing!

HELMER. I am not at home to callers; remember that.

ELLEN. (*In the doorway.*) A lady to see you, ma'am.

NORA. Show her in.

ELLEN. (*To Helmer.*) And the doctor is just come, sir.

HELMER. Has he gone into my study?

ELLEN. Yes, sir.

(*Helmer goes into his study. Ellen ushers in Mrs. Linden, in travelling clothes, and shuts the door behind her.*)

MRS. LINDEN. (*Timidly and with hesitation.*) How do you do, Nora?

NORA. (*Doubtfully.*) How do you do?

MRS. LINDEN. I daresay you don't recognize me?

NORA. No, I don't think—oh yes!—I believe—(*Effusively.*) What! Christina!
155　Is it really you?

MRS. LINDEN. Yes, really I!

NORA. Christina! And to think I didn't know you! But how could I—(*More softly.*) How changed you are, Christina!

MRS. LINDEN. Yes, no doubt. In nine or ten years—

160　NORA. Is it really so long since we met? Yes, so it is. Oh! The last eight years have been a happy time, I can tell you. And now you have come to town? All that long journey in midwinter! How brave of you!

MRS. LINDEN. I arrived by this morning's steamer.

NORA. To keep Christmas, of course. Oh, how delightful! What fun we shall
165　have! Take your things off. Aren't you frozen? (*Helping her.*) There, now we'll sit down here cosily by the fire. No, you take the armchair; I'll sit in this rocking chair. (*Seizes her hand.*) Yes, now I can see your dear old face again. It was only at first glance—But you're a little paler, Christina, and perhaps a little thinner.

170　MRS. LINDEN. And much, much older, Nora.

NORA. Yes, perhaps a little older—not much—ever so little. (*She suddenly stops; seriously.*) Oh! What a thoughtless wretch I am! Here I sit chattering on, and—Dear, dear Christina, can you forgive me!

MRS. LINDEN. What do you mean, Nora?

175　NORA. (*Softly.*) Poor Christina! I forgot, you are a widow?

MRS. LINDEN. Yes, my husband died three years ago.

NORA. I know, I know, I saw it in the papers. Oh! Believe me, Christina, I did mean to write to you; but I kept putting it off, and something always came in the way.

180　MRS. LINDEN. I can quite understand that, Nora dear.

NORA. No, Christina; it was horrid of me. Oh, you poor darling! How much you must have gone through! And he left you nothing?

MRS. LINDEN. Nothing.

NORA. And no children?

185　MRS. LINDEN. None.

NORA. Nothing, nothing at all?

MRS. LINDEN. Not even a sorrow or a longing to dwell upon.

NORA. (*Looking at her incredulously.*) My dear Christina, how is that possible?

MRS. LINDEN. (*Smiling sadly and stroking her hair.*) Oh, it happens so some-
190　times, Nora.

NORA. So utterly alone. How dreadful that must be! I have three of the loveliest children. I can't show them to you just now; they're out with their nurse. But now you must tell me everything.

MRS. LINDEN. No, no, I want you to tell me—

NORA. No, you must begin; I won't be egotistical today. Today, I will think of you only. Oh! I must tell you one thing; but perhaps you've heard of our great stroke of fortune? 195

MRS. LINDEN. No. What is it?

NORA. Only think! My husband has been made manager of the Joint Stock Bank. 200

MRS. LINDEN. Your husband! Oh, how fortunate!

NORA. Yes, isn't it? A lawyer's position is so uncertain, you see, especially when he won't touch any business that's the least bit … shady, as of course Torvald won't; and in that I quite agree with him. Oh! You can imagine how glad we are. He is to enter on his new position at the New Year, and then he will have a large salary, and percentages. In future we shall be able to live quite differently—just as we please, in fact. Oh, Christina, I feel so light and happy! It's splendid to have lots of money, and no need to worry about things, isn't it? 205

MRS. LINDEN. Yes, it must be delightful to have what you need. 210

NORA. No, not only what you need, but heaps of money—heaps!

MRS. LINDEN. (*Smiling.*) Nora, Nora, haven't you learnt reason yet? In our school days you were a shocking little spendthrift!

NORA. (*Quietly smiling.*) Yes, Torvald says I am still. (*Threatens with her finger.*) But "Nora, Nora," is not so silly as you all think. Oh! I haven't had the chance to be much of a spendthrift. We have both had to work. 215

MRS. LINDEN. You too?

NORA. Yes, light needlework—crochet, and embroidery, and things of that sort, (*significantly*) and other work too. You know, of course, that Torvald left the Government service when we were married. He had little chance of promotion, and of course he needed to make more money. But in the first year of our marriage he overworked himself terribly. He had to undertake all sorts of odd jobs, you know, and to work early and late. He couldn't stand it, and fell dangerously ill. Then the doctors declared he must go to the South. 220 225

MRS. LINDEN. Yes, you spent a whole year in Italy, didn't you?

NORA. We did. It wasn't easy to manage, I can tell you. It was just after Ivar's birth. But of course we had to go. Oh, it was a delicious journey! And it saved Torvald's life. But it cost a frightful lot of money, Christina.

MRS. LINDEN. So I should think. 230

NORA. Twelve hundred dollars! Four thousand eight hundred crowns! Isn't that a lot of money?

MRS. LINDEN. How lucky you had the money to spend!

NORA. I must tell you we got it from father.

235 MRS. LINDEN. Ah, I see. He died just about that time, didn't he?

NORA. Yes, Christina, just then. And only think! I couldn't go and nurse him! I was expecting little Ivar's birth daily. And then I had my Torvald to attend to. Dear, kind old father! I never saw him again, Christina. Oh! That's the hardest thing I have had to bear since my marriage.

240 MRS. LINDEN. I know how fond you were of him. And then you went to Italy?

NORA. Yes; we had the money, and the doctors insisted. We started a month later.

MRS. LINDEN. And your husband returned completely cured?

245 NORA. Sound as a bell.

MRS. LINDEN. But—the doctor?

NORA. What about him?

MRS. LINDEN. I thought as I came in your servant announced the doctor—

NORA. Oh, yes, Doctor Rank. But he doesn't come as a doctor. He's our best
250 friend, and never lets a day pass without looking in. No, Torvald hasn't had an hour's illness since that time. And the children are so healthy and well, and so am I. (*Jumps up and claps her hands.*) Oh, Christina, Christina, it's so lovely to live and to be happy! Oh! But it's really too horrid of me! Here am I talking about nothing but my own concerns. (*Sits down upon
255 a footstool close to her and lays her arms on Christina's lap.*) Oh! Don't be angry with me! Now just tell me, is it really true that you didn't love your husband? What made you take him?

MRS. LINDEN. My mother was alive then, bedridden and helpless; and I had my two younger brothers to think of. I thought it my duty to accept him.

260 NORA. Perhaps it was. I suppose he was rich then?

MRS. LINDEN. Very well off, I believe. But his business was uncertain. It fell to pieces at his death, and there was nothing left.

NORA. And then—?

MRS. LINDEN. Then I had to fight my way by keeping a shop, a little school,
265 anything I could turn my hand to. The last three years have been one long struggle for me. But now it's over, Nora. My poor mother no longer needs me; she is at rest. And the boys are in business, and can look after themselves.

NORA. How free your life must feel!

270 MRS. LINDEN. No, Nora, only inexpressibly empty. No one to live for. (*Stands up restlessly.*) That is why I couldn't bear to stay any longer in that out-of-

the-way corner. Here it must be easier to find something really worth do-ing—something to occupy one's thoughts. If I could only get some settled employment—some office work.

NORA. But, Christina, that's so tiring, and you look worn out already. You 275 should rather go to some health resort and rest.

MRS. LINDEN. (*Going to the window.*) I have no father to give me the money, Nora.

NORA. (*Rising.*) Oh! Don't be angry with me.

MRS. LINDEN. (*Going toward her.*) My dear Nora, don't you be angry with 280 me. The worst of a position like mine is that it makes one bitter. You have no one to work for, yet you have to strain yourself constantly. You must live; and so you become selfish. When I heard of the happy change in your circumstances—can you believe it?—I rejoiced more on my own account than on yours. 285

NORA. How do you mean? Ah! I see. You mean Torvald could perhaps do something for you.

MRS. LINDEN. Yes, I thought so.

NORA. And so he shall, Christina. Just you leave it all to me. I shall lead up to it beautifully, and think of something pleasant to put him in a good 290 humour! Oh! I should so love to do something for you.

MRS. LINDEN. How good of you, Nora! And doubly good in you, who know so little of the troubles of life.

NORA. I? I know so little of—?

MRS. LINDEN. (*Smiling.*) Ah, well! A little needlework, and so forth. You're 295 a mere child, Nora.

NORA. (*Tosses her head and paces the room.*) Oh, come, you mustn't be so patronizing!

MRS. LINDEN. No?

NORA. You're like the rest. You all think I'm fit for nothing really serious— 300

MRS. LINDEN. Well—

NORA. You think I've had no troubles in this weary world.

MRS. LINDEN. My dear Nora, you've just told me all your troubles.

NORA. Pooh—these trifles! (*Softly.*) I haven't told you the great thing.

MRS. LINDEN. The great thing? What do you mean? 305

NORA. I know you look down upon me, Christina; but you've no right to. You are proud of having worked so hard and so long for your mother?

MRS. LINDEN. I'm sure I don't look down upon anyone, but it's true I'm both proud and glad when I remember that I was able to make my mother's last days free from care. 310

NORA. And you're proud to think of what you have done for your brothers, too.

MRS. LINDEN. Don't I have the right to be?

NORA. Yes, surely. But now let me tell you, Christina—I, too, have some-
315   thing to be proud and glad of.

MRS. LINDEN. I don't doubt it. But what do you mean?

NORA. Hush! Not so loud. Only think, if Torvald were to hear! He mustn't—
not for anything in the world! No one must know about it, Christina—no
one but you.

320 MRS. LINDEN. What can it be?

NORA. Come over here. (*Draws her beside her on the sofa.*) Yes—I, too, have
something to be proud and glad of. *I* saved Torvald's life.

MRS. LINDEN. Saved his life? How?

NORA. I told you about our going to Italy. Torvald would have died but for that.

325 MRS. LINDEN. Yes—and your father gave you the money.

NORA. (*Smiling.*) Yes, so Torvald and everyone believes, but—

MRS. LINDEN. But—?

NORA. Father didn't give us one penny. *I* found the money.

MRS. LINDEN. You? All that money?

330 NORA. Twelve hundred dollars. Four thousand eight hundred crowns. What
do you say to that?

MRS. LINDEN. My dear Nora, how did you manage it? Did you win it in the
lottery?

NORA. (*Contemptuously.*) In the lottery? Pooh! Any fool could have done
335   that!

MRS. LINDEN. Then wherever did you get it from?

NORA. (*Hums and smiles mysteriously.*) H'm; tra-la-la-la!

MRS. LINDEN. Of course you couldn't borrow it.

NORA. No? Why not?

340 MRS. LINDEN. Why, a wife can't borrow without her husband's consent.

NORA. (*Tossing her head.*) Oh! When the wife knows a little of business, and
how to set about things, then—

MRS. LINDEN. But, Nora, I don't understand—

NORA. Well you needn't. I never said I borrowed the money. Perhaps I got it
345   another way. (*Throws herself back on the sofa.*) I may have got it from some
admirer. When one is so—attractive as I am—

MRS. LINDEN. You're too silly, Nora.

NORA. Now I'm sure you're dying of curiosity, Christina—

MRS. LINDEN. Listen to me, Nora dear. Haven't you been a little rash?

350 NORA. (*Sitting upright again.*) Is it rash to save one's husband's life?

MRS. LINDEN. I think it was rash of you, without his knowledge—

NORA. But it would have been fatal for him to know! Can't you understand
that? He was never to suspect how ill he was. The doctors came to me

privately and told me that his life was in danger—that nothing could save him but a trip to the South. Do you think I didn't try diplomacy first? I 355 told him how I longed to have a trip abroad, like other young wives; I wept and prayed; I said he ought to think of my condition, and indulge me; and then I hinted that he could borrow the money. But then, Christina, he almost got angry. He said I was frivolous, and that it was his duty as a husband not to yield to my whims and fancies—so he called them. Very 360 well, I thought, but saved you must be; and then I found the way to do it.

MRS. LINDEN. And did your husband never learn from your father that the money was not from him?

NORA. No, never. Father died at that very time. I meant to have told him all about it, and begged him to say nothing. But he was so ill—sadly, it was 365 not necessary.

MRS. LINDEN. And you have never confessed to your husband?

NORA. Good heavens! What can you be thinking? Tell him, when he has such a loathing of debt? And besides—how painful and humiliating it would be for Torvald, with his manly self-reliance, to know that he owed anything 370 to me! It would utterly upset the relation between us; our beautiful, happy home would never again be what it is.

MRS. LINDEN. Will you never tell him?

NORA. (*Thoughtfully, half-smiling.*) Yes, sometime perhaps—after many years, when I'm—not so pretty. You mustn't laugh at me. Of course I mean when 375 Torvald is not so much in love with me as he is now; when it doesn't amuse him any longer to see me skipping about, and dressing up and acting. Then it might be good to have something in reserve. (*Breaking off.*) Nonsense! Nonsense! That time will never come. Now, what do you say to my grand secret, Christina? Am I fit for nothing now? You may believe it has cost me 380 a lot of anxiety. It has not been easy to meet my commitments on time. You must know, Christina, that in business there are things called installments, and quarterly interest, that are terribly hard to meet. So I had to pinch a little here and there, wherever I could. I could not save anything out of the housekeeping, for of course Torvald had to live well. And I 385 couldn't let the children go about badly dressed; all I got for them, I spent on them, the darlings.

MRS. LINDEN. Poor Nora! So it had to come out of your own necessities.

NORA. Yes, of course. After all, the whole thing was my doing. When Torvald gave me money for clothes, and so on, I never spent more than half of it; I 390 always bought the simplest things. It's a mercy everything suits me so well; Torvald never noticed anything. But it was often very hard, Christina dear. For it's nice to be beautifully dressed. Now, isn't it?

MRS. LINDEN. Indeed it is.

395 NORA. Well, and besides that, I made money in other ways. Last winter I was so lucky—I got a heap of copying to do. I shut myself up every evening and wrote far on into the night. Oh, sometimes I was so tired, so tired. And yet it was splendid to work like that and earn money. I almost felt as if I was a man.

400 MRS. LINDEN. Then how much have you been able to pay off?

NORA. Well, I can't precisely say. It's difficult to keep that sort of business clear. I only know that I paid everything I could scrape together. Sometimes I really didn't know where to turn. (*Smiles.*) Then I used to imagine that a rich old gentleman was in love with me—

405 MRS. LINDEN. What! What gentleman?

NORA. Oh! Nobody—that he was now dead, and that when his will was opened, there stood in large letters: Pay over at once everything I possess to that charming person, Mrs. Nora Helmer.

MRS. LINDEN. But, dear Nora, what gentleman do you mean?

410 NORA. Dear, dear, can't you understand? There wasn't any old gentleman: it was only what I used to dream and dream when I was at my wits' end for money. But it's all over now—the tiresome old creature may stay where he is for me; I care nothing for him or his will; for now my troubles are over. (*Springing up.*) Oh, Christina, how glorious it is to think of! Free from all
415 cares! Free, quite free. To be able to play and romp about with the children; to have things tasteful and pretty in the house, exactly as Torvald likes it! And then the spring is coming, with the great blue sky. Perhaps then we shall have a short holiday. Perhaps I shall see the sea again. Oh, what a wonderful thing it is to live and to be happy! (*The hall doorbell
420 rings.*)

MRS. LINDEN. (*Rising.*) There's a ring. Perhaps I had better go.

NORA. No, do stay. No one will come here. It's sure to be someone for Torvald.

ELLEN. (*In the doorway.*) If you please, ma'am, there's a gentleman to speak to Mr. Helmer.

425 NORA. Who is the gentleman?

KROGSTAD. (*In the doorway.*) It is I, Mrs. Helmer. (*Ellen goes. Mrs. Linden starts and turns away to the window.*)

NORA. (*Goes a step towards him, anxiously, half aloud.*) You? What is it? What do you want with my husband?

KROGSTAD. Bank business—in a way. I hold a small post in the Joint Stock
430 Bank, and your husband is to be our new chief, I hear.

NORA. Then it is—?

KROGSTAD. Only tiresome business, Mrs. Helmer; nothing more.

NORA. Then will you please go to his study. (*Krogstad goes. She bows indifferently while she closes the door into the hall. Then she goes to the stove and looks to the fire.*)

MRS. LINDEN. Nora—who was that man?   435

NORA. A Mr. Krogstad. Do you know him?

MRS. LINDEN. I used to know him—many years ago. He was in a lawyer's office in our town.

NORA. Yes, so he was.

MRS. LINDEN. How he has changed!   440

NORA. I believe his marriage was unhappy.

MRS. LINDEN. And he is a widower now?

NORA. With a lot of children. There! Now it'll burn up. (*She closes the stove, and pushes the rocking chair a little aside.*)

MRS. LINDEN. His business is not of the most creditable, they say?

NORA. Isn't it? I daresay not. I don't know—But don't let us think of busi- 445
ness—it's so tiresome.

(*Dr. Rank comes out of Helmer's room.*)

RANK. (*Still in the doorway.*) No, no, I won't keep you. I'll just go and have a chat with your wife. (*Shuts the door and sees Mrs. Linden.*) Oh, I beg your pardon. I am in the way here too.

NORA. No, not in the least. (*Introduces them.*) Doctor Rank—Mrs. Linden.   450

RANK. Oh, indeed; I've often heard Mrs. Linden's name; I think I passed you on the stairs as we came up.

MRS. LINDEN. Yes, I go so very slowly. Stairs try me so much.

RANK. You're not very strong?

MRS. LINDEN. Only overworked.   455

RANK. Ah! Then you have come to town to find rest in recreation.

MRS. LINDEN. I have come to look for employment.

RANK. Is that an approved remedy for overwork?

MRS. LINDEN. One must live, Doctor Rank.

RANK. Yes, that seems to be the general opinion.   460

NORA. Come, Doctor Rank, you know you want to live yourself.

RANK. To be sure I do. However wretched I may be, I want to drag on as long as possible. And my patients all have the same mania. And it's the same with people whose complaint is moral. At this very moment Helmer is talking to such a wreck as I mean.   465

MRS. LINDEN. (*Softly.*) Ah!

NORA. Whom do you mean?

RANK. Oh, a fellow named Krogstad, a man you know nothing about—corrupt to the very core of his character. But even he began by announcing solemnly that he must live.   470

NORA. Indeed? And what did he want with Torvald?

RANK. I have no idea; I only gathered that it was some bank business.

NORA. I didn't know that Krog—that this Mr. Krogstad had anything to do with the bank?

475 RANK. He has some sort of place there. (*To Mrs. Linden.*) I don't know whether, in your part of the country, you have people who go wriggling and snuffing around in search of moral rottenness—whose policy it is to fill good places with men of tainted character whom they can keep under their eye and in their power? The honest men they leave out in the cold.

480 MRS. LINDEN. Well, I suppose the—delicate characters require most care.

RANK. (*Shrugs his shoulders.*) There we have it! It's that notion that makes society a hospital. (*Nora, deep in her own thoughts, breaks into half-stifled laughter and claps her hands.*) What are you laughing at? Have you any idea what society is?

485 NORA. What do I care for your tiresome society. I was laughing at something else—something awfully amusing. Tell me, Doctor Rank, are all the employees at the bank dependent on Torvald now?

RANK. Is that what strikes you as awfully amusing?

NORA. (*Smiles and hums.*) Never mind, never mind! (*Walks about the room.*)

490 Yes, it *is* amusing to think that we—that Torvald has such power over so many people. (*Takes the bag from her pocket.*) Doctor Rank, will you have a macaroon?

RANK. Oh dear, dear—macaroons! I thought they were contraband here.

NORA. Yes, but Christina brought me these.

495 MRS. LINDEN. What! I?

NORA. Oh, well! Don't be frightened. You couldn't possibly know that Torvald had forbidden them. The fact is, he is afraid of me spoiling my teeth. But, oh bother, just for once! That's for you, Doctor Rank! (*Puts a macaroon into his mouth.*) And you, too, Christina. And I will have one at the

500 same time—only a tiny one, or at most two. (*Walks about again.*) Oh dear, I *am* happy! There is only one thing in the world I really want.

RANK. Well; what's that?

NORA. There's something I should so like to say—in Torvald's hearing.

RANK. Then why don't you say it?

505 NORA. Because I daren't, it's so ugly.

MRS. LINDEN. Ugly?

RANK. In that case you'd better not. But to us you might. What is it you would so like to say in Helmer's hearing?

NORA. I should so love to say—"Damn!"[1]

---

1   [Archer's note] "Död og pine," literally "death and torture"; but by usage a comparatively mild oath.

RANK. Are you out of your mind?   510

MRS. LINDEN. Good gracious, Nora!

RANK. Say it. There he is!

NORA. (*Hides the macaroons.*) Hush, hush, hush!

(*Helmer comes out of his room, hat in hand, with his overcoat on his arm.*)

NORA. (*Going toward him.*) Well, Torvald, dear, have you got rid of him?   515

HELMER. Yes, he's just gone.

NORA. May I introduce you? This is Christina, who has come to town—

HELMER. Christina? Pardon me, but I don't know—

NORA. Mrs. Linden, Torvald dear—Christina Linden.

HELMER. (*To Mrs. Linden.*) A school-friend of my wife's, no doubt?   520

MRS. LINDEN. Yes, we knew each other as girls.

NORA. And only think! She has taken this long journey to speak to you.

HELMER. To speak to me!

MRS. LINDEN. Well, not quite—

NORA. You see Christina is tremendously clever at accounts, and she is so   525
anxious to work under a first-rate man of business in order to learn still
more—

HELMER. (*To Mrs. Linden.*) Very sensible indeed.

NORA. And when she heard you were appointed manager—it was tele-
graphed, you know—she started off at once, and—Torvald dear, for my   530
sake, you must do something for Christina. Now can't you?

HELMER. It's not impossible. I presume Mrs. Linden is a widow?

MRS. LINDEN. Yes.

HELMER. And you have already had some experience in office work?

MRS. LINDEN. A good deal.   535

HELMER. Well then, it is very likely I may be able to find a place for you.

NORA. (*Clapping her hands.*) There now! There now!

HELMER. You have come at a lucky moment, Mrs. Linden.

MRS. LINDEN. Oh! How can I thank you—?

HELMER. (*Smiling.*) There's no need. (*Puts his overcoat on.*) But for the present   540
you must excuse me.

RANK. Wait; I'll go with you. (*Fetches his fur coat from the hall and warms it
at the fire.*)

NORA. Don't be long, dear Torvald.

HELMER. Only an hour; not more.

NORA. Are you going too, Christina?   545

MRS. LINDEN. (*Putting on her cloak and hat.*) Yes, I must start looking for
lodgings.

HELMER. Then perhaps we can go together?

NORA. (*Helping her.*) What a pity we haven't a spare room for you, but I'm
afraid—

MRS. LINDEN. I shouldn't think of troubling you. Goodbye, dear Nora, and
thank you for all your kindness.

NORA. Goodbye for a little while. Of course you'll come back this evening.
And you, too, Doctor Rank. What! If you're well enough? Of course you'll
be well enough. Only wrap up warmly. (*They go out into the hall, talking.
Outside on the stairs are heard children's voices.*) There they are! There they
are! (*She runs to the door and opens it. The nurse Anna enters with the children.*) Come in! Come in! (*Bends down and kisses the children.*) Oh! my
sweet darlings! Do you see them, Christina? Aren't they lovely?

RANK. Don't let's stand here chattering in the draught.

HELMER. Come, Mrs. Linden; only mothers can stand such a temperature.
(*Dr. Rank, Helmer, and Mrs. Linden go down the stairs; Anna enters the room
with the children; Nora also, shutting the door.*)

NORA. How fresh and bright you look! And what red cheeks you have! Like
apples and roses. (*The children talk low to her during the following.*) Have
you had great fun? That's splendid! Oh, really! You've been giving Emmy
and Bob a ride on your sledge! Both at once, only think! Why you're quite
a man, Ivar. Oh, give her to me a little, Anna. My sweet little dolly! (*Takes
the smallest from the nurse and dances with her.*) Yes, yes, mother will dance
with Bob too. What! Did you have a game of snowballs? Oh! I wish I'd
been there. No, leave them, Anna; I'll take their things off. Oh, yes, let me
do it; it's such fun. Go to the nursery; you look frozen. You'll find some hot
coffee on the stove. (*The nurse goes into the room on the left. Nora takes off
the children's things, and throws them down anywhere, while the children talk
to each other and to her.*) Really! A big dog ran after you all the way home?
But he didn't bite you? No, dogs don't bite dear little dolly children. Don't
peep into those parcels, Ivar. What is it? Wouldn't you like to know? Take
care—it'll bite! What! Shall we have a game? What shall we play at? Hide-
and-seek? Yes, let's play hide-and-seek. Bob shall hide first. Should I? Yes,
let me hide first. (*She and the children play, with laughter and shouting, in
the room and the adjacent one to the right. At last Nora hides under the table;
the children come rushing in, look for her, but cannot find her, hear her half-
choked laughter, rush to the table, lift up the cover and see her. Loud shouts.
She creeps out, as though to frighten them. Fresh shouts. Meanwhile there has
been a knock at the door leading into the hall. No one has heard it. Now the
door is half opened and Krogstad is seen. He waits a little; the game is renewed.*)

KROGSTAD. I beg your pardon, Mrs. Helmer—

NORA. (*With a suppressed cry, turns round and half jumps up.*) Ah! What do
you want?

KROGSTAD. Excuse me; the outer door was ajar—somebody must have forgotten to shut it—

NORA. (*Standing up.*) My husband is not at home, Mr. Krogstad.

KROGSTAD. I know it.   585

NORA. Then—what do you want here?

KROGSTAD. To say a few words to you.

NORA. To me? (*To the children, softly.*) Go in to Anna. What? No, the strange man won't hurt mamma. When he's gone we'll go on playing. (*She leads the children into the left-hand room, and shuts the door behind them. Uneasy,*   590 *with suspense.*) It's with me you wish to speak?

KROGSTAD. Yes.

NORA. Today? But it's not the first yet—

KROGSTAD. No, today is Christmas Eve. It will depend upon yourself whether you have a merry Christmas.   595

NORA. What do you want? I certainly can't today—

KROGSTAD. Never mind that just now. It's about another matter. You have a minute to spare?

NORA. Oh, yes, I suppose so, although—

KROGSTAD. Good. I was sitting in the restaurant opposite, and I saw your   600 husband go down the street.

NORA. Well!

KROGSTAD. With a lady.

NORA. What then?

KROGSTAD. May I ask if the lady was a Mrs. Linden?   605

NORA. Yes.

KROGSTAD. Who has just come to town?

NORA. Yes. Today.

KROGSTAD. I believe she's an intimate friend of yours?

NORA. Certainly. But I don't understand—   610

KROGSTAD. I used to know her too.

NORA. I know you did.

KROGSTAD. Ah! You know all about it. I thought as much. Now, frankly, is Mrs. Linden to have a place at the bank?

NORA. How dare you interrogate me in this way, Mr. Krogstad, you, a sub-   615 ordinate of my husband's? But since you ask you shall know. Yes, Mrs. Linden is to be employed. And it's I who recommended her, Mr. Krogstad. Now you know.

KROGSTAD. Then my guess was right.

NORA. (*Walking up and down.*) You see one has a little wee bit of influence. It   620 doesn't follow because one's only a woman that—When one is in a subordinate position, Mr. Krogstad, one ought really to take care not to offend anybody who—h'm—

KROGSTAD. Who has influence?

625 NORA. Exactly!

KROGSTAD. (*Taking another tone.*) Mrs. Helmer, will you have the kindness to employ your influence on my behalf?

NORA. What? How do you mean?

KROGSTAD. Will you be so good as to see that I retain my subordinate position at the bank?

630 NORA. What do you mean? Who wants to take it from you?

KROGSTAD. Oh, you needn't pretend ignorance. I can very well understand that it cannot be pleasant for your friend to meet me; and I can also understand now for whose sake I am to be hounded out.

635 NORA. But I assure you—

KROGSTAD. Come now, once for all: there is time yet, and I advise you to use your influence to prevent it.

NORA. But, Mr. Krogstad, I have absolutely no influence.

KROGSTAD. None? I thought you just said—

640 NORA. Of course not in that sense! I! How should I have such influence over my husband?

KROGSTAD. Oh! I know your husband from our college days. I don't think he's firmer than other husbands.

NORA. If you talk disrespectfully of my husband, I must ask you to go.

645 KROGSTAD. You are bold, madam.

NORA. I am afraid of you no longer. When New Year's Day is over, I shall soon be out of the whole business.

KROGSTAD. (*Controlling himself.*) Listen to me, Mrs. Helmer. If need be, I shall fight as though for my life to keep my little place at the bank.

650 NORA. Yes, so it seems.

KROGSTAD. It's not only for the money; that matters least to me. It's something else. Well, I'd better make a clean breast of it. Of course you know, like everyone else, that some years ago I—got into trouble.

NORA. I think I've heard something of the sort.

655 KROGSTAD. The matter never came into court, but from that moment all paths were barred to me. Then I took up the business you know about. I was obliged to grasp at something, and I don't think I've been one of the worst. But now I must clear out of it all. My sons are growing up; for their sake I must try to win back as much respectability as I can. This place in

660 the bank was the first step, and now your husband wants to kick me off the ladder, back into the mire.

NORA. But I assure you, Mr. Krogstad, I haven't the power to help you.

KROGSTAD. You have not the will; but I can compel you.

NORA. You won't tell my husband that I owe you money!

KROGSTAD. H'm; suppose I were to? 665

NORA. It would be shameful of you! (*With tears in her voice.*) This secret which is my joy and my pride—that he should learn it in such an ugly, coarse way—and from you! It would involve me in all sorts of unpleasant-ness.

KROGSTAD. Only unpleasantness? 670

NORA. (*Hotly.*) But just do it. It will be worst for you, for then my husband will see what a bad man you are, and then you certainly won't keep your place.

KROGSTAD. I asked if it was only domestic unpleasantness you feared?

NORA. If my husband gets to know about it, he will of course pay you off at 675 once, and then we'll have nothing more to do with you.

KROGSTAD. (*Stepping a pace nearer.*) Listen, Mrs. Helmer. Either you have a weak memory, or you don't know much about business. I must make your position clearer to you.

NORA. How so? 680

KROGSTAD. When your husband was ill, you came to me to borrow twelve hundred dollars.

NORA. I knew nobody else.

KROGSTAD. I promised to find you the money—

NORA. And you did find it. 685

KROGSTAD. I promised to find you the money under certain conditions. You were then so much taken up with your husband's illness, and so eager to have the money for your journey, that you probably did not give much thought to the details. Let me to remind you of them. I promised to find you the amount in exchange for a promissory note which I drew up. 690

NORA. Yes, and I signed it.

KROGSTAD. Quite right. But then I added a few lines, making your father a security for the debt. Your father was to sign this.

NORA. Was to? He did sign it!

KROGSTAD. I had left the date blank. That is to say, your father was himself 695 to date his signature. Do you recollect that?

NORA. Yes, I believe—

KROGSTAD. Then I gave you the paper to send to your father. Is not that so?

NORA. Yes.

KROGSTAD. And of course you did so at once? For within five or six days 700 you brought me back the paper, signed by your father, and I gave you the money.

NORA. Well! Haven't I made my payments punctually?

KROGSTAD. Fairly—yes. But to return to the point. You were in great trouble at the time, Mrs. Helmer. 705

NORA. I was indeed!

KROGSTAD. Your father was very ill, I believe?

NORA. He was on his deathbed.

KROGSTAD. And died soon after?

710 NORA. Yes.

KROGSTAD. Tell me, Mrs. Helmer, do you happen to recollect the day of his death? The day of the month, I mean?

NORA. Father died on the 29th of September.

KROGSTAD. Quite correct. I have made inquiries, and here comes in the re-
715 markable point—(*produces a paper*) which I cannot explain.

NORA. What remarkable point? I don't know—

KROGSTAD. The remarkable point, madam, that your father signed this paper three days after his death!

NORA. What! I don't understand—

720 KROGSTAD. Your father died on the 29th of September. But look here, he has dated his signature October 2nd! Isn't that remarkable, Mrs. Helmer? (*Nora is silent.*) Can you explain it? (*Nora continues to be silent.*) It is note-worthy too that the words "October 2nd" and the year are not in your father's handwriting, but in one which I believe I know. Well, this may be
725 explained; your father may have forgotten to date his signature, and some-body may have added the date at random before the fact of your father's death was known. There is nothing wrong in that. Everything depends on the signature. Of course it is genuine, Mrs. Helmer? It was really your father who with his own hand wrote his name here?

730 NORA. (*After a short silence throws her head back and looks defiantly at him.*) No. I wrote father's name there.

KROGSTAD. Ah! Are you aware, madam, that that is a dangerous admission?

NORA. Why? You'll soon get your money.

KROGSTAD. May I ask you one more question? Why did you not send the
735 paper to your father?

NORA. It was impossible. Father was ill. If I had asked him for his signature, I should have had to tell him why I wanted the money; but he was so ill I really could not tell him that my husband's life was in danger. It was impossible.

740 KROGSTAD. Then it would have been better to have given up your tour.

NORA. No, I couldn't do that; my husband's life depended on that journey. I couldn't give it up.

KROGSTAD. And did you not consider that you were playing me false?

NORA. That was nothing to me. I didn't care in the least about you. I couldn't
745 endure you for all the cruel difficulties you made, although you knew how ill my husband was.

KROGSTAD. Mrs. Helmer, you have evidently no clear idea what you have really done. But I can assure you it was nothing more and nothing worse that made me an outcast from society.

NORA. You! You want me to believe that you did a brave thing to save your wife's life?   750

KROGSTAD. The law takes no account of motives.

NORA. Then it must be a very bad law.

KROGSTAD. Bad or not, if I lay this document before a court of law you will be condemned according to law.   755

NORA. I don't believe that. Do you mean to tell me that a daughter has no right to spare her dying father anxiety? That a wife has no right to save her husband's life? I don't know much about the law, but I'm sure that, somewhere or another, *that* is allowed. And you don't know that—you, a lawyer! You must be a bad one, Mr. Krogstad.   760

KROGSTAD. Possibly. But business—such business as ours—I do understand. You believe that? Very well; now do as you please. But this I can tell you, that if I am flung into the gutter a second time, you shall keep me company. (*Bows and goes out through hall.*)

NORA. (*Stands a while thinking, then throws her head back.*) Never! He wants to frighten me. I'm not so foolish as that. (*Begins folding the children's clothes. Pauses.*) But—? No, it's impossible. I did it for love!   765

CHILDREN. (*At the door, left.*) Mamma, the strange man is gone now.

NORA. Yes, yes, I know. But don't tell anyone about the strange man. Do you hear? Not even papa!   770

CHILDREN. No, mamma; and now will you play with us again?

NORA. No, no, not now.

CHILDREN. Oh, do, mamma; you know you promised.

NORA. Yes, but I can't just now. Run to the nursery; I've so much to do. Run along, run along, and be good, my darlings! (*She pushes them gently into the inner room, and closes the door behind them. Sits on the sofa, embroiders a few stitches, but soon pauses.*) No! (*Throws down the work, rises, goes to the hall door and calls out.*) Ellen, bring in the Christmas tree! (*Goes to table, left, and opens the drawer; again pauses.*) No, it's quite impossible!   775

ELLEN. (*With Christmas tree.*) Where shall I stand it, ma'am?   780

NORA. There, in the middle of the room.

ELLEN. Shall I bring in anything else?

NORA. No, thank you, I have all I want.

(*Ellen, having put down the tree, goes out.*)

NORA. (*Busy dressing the tree.*) There must be a candle here, and flowers there.—The horrid man! Nonsense, nonsense! There's nothing in it. The   785

Christmas tree shall be beautiful. I will do everything to please you, Torvald; I'll sing and dance, and—

(*Enter Helmer by the hall door, with bundle of documents.*)

NORA. Oh! You're back already?

HELMER. Yes. Has anybody been here?

790 NORA. Here? No.

HELMER. Curious! I saw Krogstad come out of the house.

NORA. Did you? Oh, yes, by the bye, he was here for a minute.

HELMER. Nora, I can see by your manner that he has been asking you to put in a good word for him.

795 NORA. Yes.

HELMER. And you were to do it as if of your own accord? You were to say nothing to me of his having been here! Didn't he suggest that too?

NORA. Yes, Torvald, but—

HELMER. Nora, Nora! And you could condescend to that! To speak to such

800   a man, to make him a promise! And then to tell me an untruth about it!

NORA. An untruth!

HELMER. Didn't you say nobody had been here? (*Threatens with his finger.*) My little bird must never do that again. A songbird must never sing false notes. (*Puts his arm round her.*) That's so, isn't it? Yes, I was sure of it. (*Lets*

805   *her go.*) And now we'll say no more about it. (*Sits down before the fire.*) Oh, how cosy and quiet it is here. (*Glances into his documents.*)

NORA. (*Busy with the tree, after a short silence.*) Torvald.

HELMER. Yes.

NORA. I'm looking forward so much to the Stenborgs' fancy ball the day after

810   tomorrow.

HELMER. And I'm incredibly curious to see what surprise you have in store for me.

NORA. Oh, it's too tiresome!

HELMER. What is?

815 NORA. I can't think of anything good. Everything seems so foolish and meaningless.

HELMER. Has little Nora made that discovery?

NORA. (*Behind his chair, with her arms on the back.*) Are you very busy, Torvald?

820 HELMER. Well—

NORA. What papers are those?

HELMER. Bank business.

NORA. Already?

HELMER. I got the retiring manager to let me make some necessary changes

in the staff, and so forth. This will occupy Christmas week. Everything will   825
be straight by the New Year.

NORA.   Then that's why that poor Krogstad—

HELMER.   H'm.

NORA.   (*Still leaning over the chair back, and slowly stroking his hair.*) If you
hadn't been so very busy I should have asked you a great, great favour,   830
Torvald.

HELMER.   What can it be? Let's hear it.

NORA.   Nobody has such exquisite taste as you. Now, I should so love to look
nice at the fancy ball. Torvald dear, couldn't you take me in hand, and
settle what I'm to be, and arrange my costume for me?   835

HELMER.   Aha! So my wilful little woman's at a loss, and making signals of
distress.

NORA.   Yes *please*, Torvald. I can't get on without you.

HELMER.   Well, well, I'll think it over, and we'll soon hit upon something.

NORA.   Oh, how good that is of you! (*Goes to the tree again; pause.*) How well   840
the red flowers show. Tell me, was it anything so very dreadful this Krogstad got into trouble about?

HELMER.   Forgery, that's all. Don't you know what that means?

NORA.   Mayn't he have been driven to it by need?

HELMER.   Yes, or like so many others, done it out of heedlessness. I'm not so   845
hard-hearted as to condemn a man absolutely for a single fault.

NORA.   No, surely not, Torvald!

HELMER.   Many a man can retrieve his character if he owns his crime and
takes the punishment.

NORA.   Crime?   850

HELMER.   But Krogstad didn't do that; he resorted to tricks and dodges; and
it's that that has corrupted him.

NORA.   Do you think that—?

HELMER.   Just think how a man with that on his conscience must be always
lying and shamming. Think of the mask he must wear even toward his own   855
wife and children. It's worst for the children, Nora!

NORA.   Why?

HELMER.   Because such a dust cloud of lies poisons and contaminates the whole
air of a home. Every breath the children draw contains some germ of evil.

NORA.   (*Closer behind him.*) Are you sure of that!   860

HELMER.   As a lawyer, my dear, I've seen it often enough. Nearly all cases of
early corruption may be traced to lying mothers.

NORA.   Why—mothers?

HELMER.   It generally comes from the mother's side, but of course the father's
influence may act in the same way. And this Krogstad has been poison-   865

ing his own children for years with his life of lies and hypocrisy—that's why I say he is morally ruined. (*Stretches out his hands toward her.*) So my sweet little Nora must promise not to plead his cause. Shake hands upon it. Come, come, what's this? Give me your hand. That's right. Then it's a bargain. I assure you it would have been impossible for me to work with him. It gives me a positive sense of physical discomfort to come in contact with such people. (*Nora snatches her hand away, and moves to the other side of the Christmas tree.*)

NORA. How warm it is here; and I have so much to do.

HELMER. Yes, and I must try to get some of these papers looked through before dinner; and I'll think over your costume, too. And perhaps I may even find something to hang in gilt paper on the Christmas tree! (*Lays his hand on her head.*) My precious little songbird. (*He goes into his room and shuts the door behind him.*)

NORA. (*Softly, after a pause.*) It can't be—It's impossible. It must be impossible!

ANNA. (*At the door, left.*) The little ones are begging so prettily to come to mamma.

NORA. No, no, don't let them come to me! Keep them with you, Anna.

ANNA. Very well, ma'am. (*Shuts the door.*)

NORA. (*Pale with terror.*) Corrupt my children! Poison my home! (*Short pause. She raises her head.*) It's not true. It can never, never be true.

ACT 2

The same room. In the corner, beside the piano, stands the Christmas tree, stripped, and the candles burnt out. Nora's cloak and hat lie on the sofa. Nora discovered walking about restlessly. She stops by the sofa, and takes up cloak, then lays it down again.

NORA. There's somebody coming. (*Goes to hall door; listens.*) Nobody; nobody is likely to come today, Christmas day; nor tomorrow either. But perhaps—(*Opens the door and looks out.*) No, nothing in the letter box; quite empty. (*Comes forward.*) Stuff and nonsense! Of course he only meant to frighten me. There's no fear of any such thing. It's impossible! Why, I have three little children.

(*Enter Anna, from the left with a large cardboard box.*)

ANNA. At last I've found the box with the fancy dress.

NORA. Thanks; put it down on the table.

ANNA. (*Does so.*) But I'm afraid it's in terrible disarray.

NORA. Oh, I wish I could tear it into a hundred thousand pieces.

ANNA. Oh, no. It can easily be put to rights—just a little patience.

NORA. I'll go and get Mrs. Linden to help me.

ANNA. Going out again! In such weather as this! You'll catch cold, ma'am, and be ill.

NORA. Worse things might happen—What are the children doing?   15

ANNA. They're playing with their Christmas presents, poor little dears; but—

NORA. Do they often ask for me?

ANNA. You see they've been so used to having their mamma with them.

NORA. Yes, but, Anna, in future I can't have them so much with me.

ANNA. Well, little children get used to anything.   20

NORA. Do you think they do? Do you believe they would forget their mother if she went quite away?

ANNA. Gracious me! Quite away?

NORA. Tell me, Anna—I've so often wondered about it—how could you bring yourself to give your child up to strangers?   25

ANNA. I had to when I came as nurse to my little Miss Nora.

NORA. But how could you make up your mind to it?

ANNA. When I had the chance of such a good place? A poor girl who's been in trouble must take what comes. That wicked man did nothing for me.

NORA. But your daughter must have forgotten you.   30

ANNA. Oh, no, ma'am, that she hasn't. She wrote to me both when she was confirmed[1] and when she was married.

NORA. (*Embracing her.*) Dear old Anna—you were a good mother to me when I was little.

ANNA. My poor little Nora had no mother but me.   35

NORA. And if my little ones had nobody else, I'm sure you would—nonsense, nonsense! (*Opens the box.*) Go in to the children. Now I must—Tomorrow you shall see how beautiful I'll be.

ANNA. I'm sure there will be no one at the ball so beautiful as my Miss Nora. (*She goes into the room on the left.*)   40

NORA. (*Takes the costume out of the box, but soon throws it down again.*) Oh, if I dared go out. If only nobody would come. If only nothing would happen here in the meantime. Rubbish; nobody will come. Only not to think. What a delicious muff! Beautiful gloves, beautiful gloves! Away with it all—away with it all! One, two, three, four, five, six—(*With a scream.*) Ah, there they come—(*Goes toward the door, then stands undecidedly.*)   45

(*Mrs. Linden enters from hall where she has taken off her things.*)

---

1   *confirmed* Fully admitted into the Christian church after affirming religious faith; confirmation ceremonies are most often held for older children or teenagers.

NORA. Oh, it's you, Christina. There's nobody else there? How delightful of you to come.

MRS. LINDEN. I hear you called at my lodgings.

50 NORA. Yes, I was just passing. I do so want you to help me. Let us sit here on the sofa—like so. Tomorrow evening there's to be a fancy ball at Consul Stenborg's, who lives upstairs, and Torvald wants me to appear as a Neapolitan fisher girl, and dance the tarantella; I learnt it at Capri.[1]

MRS. LINDEN. I see—quite a performance!

55 NORA. Yes, Torvald wishes me to. Look, this is the costume; Torvald had it made for me in Italy. But now it is all so torn, I don't know—

MRS. LINDEN. Oh! We'll soon set that to rights. It's only the trimming that's got loose here and there. Have you a needle and thread? Ah! Here's the very thing.

60 NORA. Oh, how kind of you.

MRS. LINDEN. So you're to be in costume tomorrow, Nora? I'll tell you what—I shall come in for a moment to see you in all your glory. But I've quite forgotten to thank you for the pleasant evening yesterday.

NORA. (*Rises and walks across the room.*) Oh! Yesterday, it didn't seem so 65 pleasant as usual. You should have come a little sooner, Christina. Torvald certainly has the art of making a home bright and beautiful.

MRS. LINDEN. You, too, I should think, or you wouldn't be your father's daughter. But tell me—is Doctor Rank always as depressed as he was yesterday?

70 NORA. No, yesterday it was particularly striking. You see he has a terrible illness. He has spinal consumption,[2] poor fellow. They say his father led a terrible life—kept mistresses and all sorts of things—so the son has been sickly from his childhood, you understand.

MRS. LINDEN. (*Lets her sewing fall into her lap.*) Why, my darling Nora, how 75 do you learn such things?

NORA. (*Walking.*) Oh! When one has three children one has visits from women who know something about medicine—and they talk of this and that.

MRS. LINDEN. (*Goes on sewing—a short pause.*) Does Doctor Rank come here every day?

80 NORA. Every day. He's been Torvald's friend from boyhood, and he's a good friend of mine too. Doctor Rank is quite one of the family.

---

1   *tarantella* Italian folkdance. It was thought that the bite of a tarantula caused "tarantism," an irrepressible urge to dance, which an afflicted person could supposedly cure by dancing the tarantella until he or she was too tired to continue; *Capri* Italian island near Naples.

2   *spinal consumption* Pott's disease, a form of tuberculosis that can cause severe curvature of the spine and other health problems.

MRS. LINDEN. But tell me—is he quite sincere? I mean, doesn't he like to say
flattering things to people?

NORA. On the contrary. Why should you think so?

MRS. LINDEN. When you introduced us yesterday he declared he had often   85
heard my name, but I noticed your husband had no notion who I was.
How could Doctor Rank—?

NORA. Yes, he was quite right, Christina. You see, Torvald loves me so indescribably, he wants to have me all to himself, as he says. When we were
first married he was almost jealous if I even mentioned one of the people   90
at home, so naturally I let it alone. But I often talk to Doctor Rank about
the old times, for he likes to hear about them.

MRS. LINDEN. Listen to me, Nora! You're still a child in many ways. I am
older than you, and have had more experience. I'll tell you something: you
ought to get clear of all the whole affair with Dr. Rank.

NORA. What affair?   95

MRS. LINDEN. You were talking yesterday of a rich admirer who was to find
you money—

NORA. Yes, one who never existed, worse luck. What then?

MRS. LINDEN. Has Doctor Rank money?

NORA. Yes, he has.   100

MRS. LINDEN. And nobody to provide for?

NORA. Nobody. But—?

MRS. LINDEN. And he comes here every day?

NORA. Yes, every day.

MRS. LINDEN. I should have thought he'd have acted in better taste.   105

NORA. I don't understand you.

MRS. LINDEN. Don't pretend, Nora. Do you suppose I don't guess who lent
you the twelve hundred dollars?

NORA. Are you out of your senses? You think *that*! A friend who comes here
every day! How painful that would be!   110

MRS. LINDEN. Then it really is not him?

NORA. No, I assure you. It never for a moment occurred to me. Besides, at
that time he had nothing to lend; he came into his property afterward.

MRS. LINDEN. Well, I believe that was lucky for you, Nora dear.

NORA. No, really, it would never have struck me to ask Dr. Rank. But I'm   115
certain that if I did—

MRS. LINDEN. But of course you never would?

NORA. Of course not. It's inconceivable that it should ever be necessary. But
I'm quite sure that if I spoke to Doctor Rank—

MRS. LINDEN. Behind your husband's back?   120

NORA. I must get out of the other thing; that's behind his back too. I must
get out of that.

MRS. LINDEN. Yes, yes, I told you so yesterday; but—

NORA. (*Walking up and down.*) A man can manage these things much better
125   than a woman.

MRS. LINDEN. One's own husband, yes.

NORA. Nonsense. (*Stands still.*) When everything is paid, one gets back the
paper?

MRS. LINDEN. Of course.

130   NORA. And can tear it into a hundred thousand pieces, and burn it, the nasty,
filthy thing!

MRS. LINDEN. (*Looks at her fixedly, lays down her work, and rises slowly.*) Nora,
you're hiding something from me.

NORA. Can you see that in my face?

135   MRS. LINDEN. Something has happened since yesterday morning. Nora,
what is it?

NORA. (*Going toward her.*) Christina (*listens*)—Hush! There's Torvald coming
home. Here, go into the nursery. Torvald cannot bear to see dressmaking.
Let Anna help you.

140   MRS. LINDEN. (*Gathers some of the things together.*) Very well, but I shan't go
away until you've told me all about it. (*She goes out to the left as Helmer
enters from the hall.*)

NORA. (*Runs to meet him.*) Oh! How I've been longing for you to come,
Torvald dear.

HELMER. Was the dressmaker here?

145   NORA. No, Christina. She is helping me with my costume. You'll see how
nice I shall look.

HELMER. Yes, wasn't that a lucky thought of mine?

NORA. Splendid. But isn't it good of me, too, to have given in to you?

HELMER. (*Takes her under the chin.*) Good of you! To give in to your own
150   husband? Well, well, you little madcap, I know you don't mean it. But I
won't disturb you. I daresay you want to try on your dress.

NORA. And you are going to work, I suppose?

HELMER. Yes. (*Shows her bundle of papers.*) Look here. (*Goes toward his room.*)
I've just come from the bank.

155   NORA. Torvald.

HELMER. (*Stopping.*) Yes?

NORA. If your little squirrel were to beg you for something so prettily—

HELMER. Well?

NORA. Would you do it?

160   HELMER. I must know first what it is.

NORA. The squirrel would jump about and play all sorts of tricks if you
would only be nice and kind.

HELMER. Come, then, out with it.

NORA. Your lark would twitter from morning till night—

HELMER. Oh, that she does in any case.   165

NORA. I'll be an elf and dance in the moonlight for you, Torvald.

HELMER. Nora—you can't mean what you were hinting at this morning?

NORA. (*Coming nearer.*) Yes, Torvald, I beg and implore you.

HELMER. Have you really the courage to begin that again?

NORA. Yes, yes, for my sake, you must let Krogstad keep his place at the bank.   170

HELMER. My dear Nora, it's his place I intend for Mrs. Linden.

NORA. Yes, that's so good of you. But instead of Krogstad, you could dismiss some other clerk.

HELMER. Why, this is incredible obstinacy! Because you thoughtlessly promised to put in a word for him, I am to—   175

NORA. It's not that, Torvald. It's for your own sake. This man writes for the most slanderous newspapers; you said so yourself. He can do you such a lot of harm. I'm terribly afraid of him.

HELMER. Oh, I understand; it's old recollections that are frightening you.

NORA. What do you mean?   180

HELMER. Of course you're thinking of your father.

NORA. Yes, of course. Only think of the shameful things wicked people used to write about father. I believe they'd have got him dismissed if you hadn't been sent to look into the thing and been kind to him and helped him.

HELMER. My dear Nora, between your father and me there is all the differ-   185 ence in the world. Your father was not altogether unimpeachable. I am; and I hope to remain so.

NORA. Oh, no one knows what wicked men can hit upon. We could live so happily now, in our cosy, quiet home, you and I and the children, Torvald! That's why I beg and implore you—   190

HELMER. And it's just by pleading his cause that you make it impossible for me to keep him. It's already known at the bank that I intend to dismiss Krogstad. If it were now reported that the new manager let himself be turned round his wife's little finger—

NORA. What then?   195

HELMER. Oh, nothing! So long as a wilful woman can have her way I am to make myself the laughingstock of everyone, and make people think I depend on all kinds of outside influence? Take my word for it, I should soon feel the consequences. And besides, there's one thing that makes Krogstad impossible for me to work with.   200

NORA. What thing?

HELMER. I could perhaps have overlooked his shady character in a pinch—

NORA. Yes, couldn't you, Torvald?

HELMER. And I hear he is good at his work. But the fact is, he was a college
205   chum of mine—there was one of those rash friendships between us that
one so often repents of later. I don't mind confessing it—he calls me by
my first name, and he insists on doing it even when others are present. He
delights in putting on airs of familiarity—Torvald here, Torvald there! I assure you it's most painful to me. He would make my position at the bank
210   perfectly unendurable.

NORA. Torvald, you're not serious?

HELMER. No? Why not?

NORA. That's such a petty reason.

HELMER. What! Petty! Do you consider me petty?

215 NORA. No, on the contrary, Torvald dear and that's just why—

HELMER. Never mind; you call my motives petty; then I must be petty too.
Petty! Very well. Now we'll put an end to this once for all. (*Goes to the door
into the hall and calls.*) Ellen!

NORA. What do you want?

220 HELMER. (*Searching among his papers.*) To settle the thing. (*Ellen enters.*)
There, take this letter, give it to a messenger. See that he takes it at once.
The address is on it. Here is the money.

ELLEN. Very well. (*Goes with the letter.*)

HELMER. (*Arranging papers.*) There, Madam Obstinacy!

225 NORA. (*Breathless.*) Torvald—what was in that letter?

HELMER. Krogstad's dismissal.

NORA. Call it back again, Torvald! There is still time. Oh, Torvald, get it back
again! For my sake, for your own, for the children's sake! Do you hear,
Torvald? Do it. You don't know what that letter may bring upon us all.

230 HELMER. Too late.

NORA. Yes, too late.

HELMER. My dear Nora, I forgive your anxiety, though it's anything but
flattering to me. Why should I be afraid of a lowlife scribbler's spite? But
I forgive you all the same, for it's a proof of your great love for me. (*Takes
235   her in his arms.*) That's how it should be, my own dear Nora. Let what
will happen—when the time comes, I shall have strength and courage
enough. You shall see, my shoulders are broad enough to bear the whole
burden.

NORA. (*Terror-struck.*) What do you mean by that?

240 HELMER. The whole burden, I say.

NORA. (*With decision.*) That you shall never, never do.

HELMER. Very well, then we'll share it, Nora, as man and wife. (*Petting her.*)
Are you satisfied now? Come, come, come, don't look like a scared dove. It
is all nothing—just fancy. Now you must play the tarantella through, and

practise the tambourine. I shall sit in my inner room and shut both doors, 245
so that I shall hear nothing. You can make as much noise as you please.
(*Turns round in doorway.*) And when Rank comes, just tell him where I'm
to be found. (*He nods to her, and goes with his papers into his room, closing
the door.*)

NORA. (*Bewildered with terror, stands as though rooted to the ground, and whispers.*) He would do it. Yes, he would do it. He would do it, in spite of all 250
the world. No, never that, never, never! Anything rather than that! Oh, for
some way of escape! What to do! (*Hall bell rings.*) Anything rather than
that—anything, anything! (*Nora draws her hands over her face, pulls herself
together, goes to the door and opens it. Rank stands outside hanging up his
overcoat. During the following, it grows dark.*)

NORA.   Good afternoon, Doctor Rank, I knew you by your ring. But you
mustn't go to Torvald now. I believe he's busy.   255

RANK. And you?

NORA. Oh, you know very well I've always time for you.

RANK. Thank you. I shall avail myself of your kindness as long as I can!

NORA. What do you mean? As long as you can?

RANK. Yes. Does that frighten you?   260

NORA. I think it's an odd expression. Do you expect anything to happen?

RANK. Something I've long been prepared for, but I didn't think it would
come so soon.

NORA. (*Seizing his arm.*) What is it, Doctor Rank? You must tell me.

RANK. (*Sitting down by the stove.*) I am running downhill. There's no help 265
for it.

NORA. (*Draws a long breath of relief.*) It's *you*?

RANK. Who else should it be? Why lie to oneself? I'm the most wretched
of all my patients, Mrs. Helmer. I have been auditing my life-account—
bankrupt! Before a month is over I shall lie rotting in the churchyard. 270

NORA. Oh! What an ugly way to talk.

RANK. The thing itself is so confoundedly ugly, you see. But the worst of it is,
so many other ugly things have to be gone through first. There is only one
last investigation to be made, and when that is over I shall know exactly
when the breakdown will begin. There's one thing I want to say to you: 275
Helmer's delicate nature shrinks with such disgust from all that is horrible;
I will not have him in my sickroom.

NORA. But, Doctor Rank—

RANK. I won't have him, I say—not on any account! I shall lock my door
against him. As soon as I have ascertained the worst, I shall send you my 280
visiting card with a black cross on it, and then you will know that the final
horror has begun.

NORA. Why, you're perfectly unreasonable today. And I did so want you to be in a really good humour.

285 RANK. With death staring me in the face? And to suffer thus for another's sin! Where's the justice of it? And in every family you can see some such inexorable retribution—

NORA. (*Stopping her ears.*) Nonsense, nonsense; now cheer up.

RANK. Well, after all, the whole thing's only worth laughing at. My poor in-
290   nocent spine must do penance for my father's wild oats.

NORA. (*At table, left.*) I suppose he was too fond of asparagus and Strasbourg paté, wasn't he?

RANK. Yes; and truffles.

NORA. Yes, truffles, to be sure. And oysters,[1] I believe?

295 RANK. Yes, oysters; oysters, of course.

NORA. And then all the port and champagne. It's sad that all these good things should attack the spine.

RANK. Especially when the luckless spine attacked never had the good of them.

300 NORA. Yes, that's the worst of it.

RANK. (*Looks at her searchingly.*) H'm—

NORA. (*A moment later.*) Why did you smile?

RANK. No; it was you that laughed.

NORA. No; it was you that smiled, Doctor Rank.

305 RANK. (*Standing up.*) You're more of a rogue than I thought.

NORA. I'm in such a crazy mood today.

RANK. So it seems.

NORA. (*With her hands on his shoulders.*) Dear, dear Doctor Rank, death shall not take you away from Torvald and me.

310 RANK. Oh, you'll easily get over the loss. The absent are soon forgotten.

NORA. (*Looks at him anxiously.*) Do you think so?

RANK. People make fresh ties, and then—

NORA. Who make fresh ties?

RANK. You and Helmer will, when I'm gone. You yourself are already on your
315   way to it, it seems to me. What was that Mrs. Linden doing here yesterday?

NORA. Oh! You're surely not jealous of Christina?

RANK. Yes, I am. She will be my successor in this house. When I'm gone, this woman will perhaps—

NORA. Hush! Not so loud; she is in there.

320 RANK. Today as well? You see!

---

1   *I suppose ... oysters* Asparagus, Strasbourg paté, truffles, and oysters are all foods commonly thought to be aphrodisiacs.

NORA. Only to put my costume in order—how unreasonable you are! (*Sits on sofa.*) Now do be good, Doctor Rank. Tomorrow you shall see how beautifully I dance; and then you may fancy that I am doing it all to please you—and of course Torvald as well. (*Takes various things out of box.*) Doctor Rank, sit here, and I'll show you something. 325

RANK. (*Sitting.*) What is it?

NORA. Look here. Look!

RANK. Silk stockings.

NORA. Flesh-coloured. Aren't they lovely? Oh, it's so dark here now, but tomorrow—No, no, no, you must only look at the feet. Oh, well, I suppose 330 you may look at the rest too.

RANK. H'm—

NORA. What are you looking so critical about? Do you think they won't fit me?

RANK. I can't possibly have any valid opinion on that point.

NORA. (*Looking at him a moment.*) For shame! (*Hits him lightly on the ear* 335 *with the stockings.*) Take that. (*Rolls them up again.*)

RANK. And what other wonders am I to see?

NORA. You shan't see any more, for you don't behave nicely. (*She hums a little and searches among the things.*)

RANK. (*After a short silence.*) When I sit here gossiping with you, I simply can't imagine what would have become of me if I had never entered this 340 house.

NORA. (*Smiling.*) Yes, I think you do feel at home with us.

RANK. (*More softly—looking straight before him.*) And now to have to leave it all—

NORA. Nonsense. You shan't leave us. 345

RANK. (*In the same tone.*) And not to be able to leave behind the slightest token of gratitude; scarcely even a passing regret—nothing but an empty place, that can be filled by the first comer.

NORA. And if I were to ask for—? No—

RANK. For what? 350

NORA. For a great proof of your friendship.

RANK. Yes? Yes?

NORA. No, I mean—for a very, very great service.

RANK. Would you really for once make me so happy?

NORA. Oh! You don't know what it is. 355

RANK. Then tell me.

NORA. No, I really can't; it's far, far too much—not only a service, but help and advice besides—

RANK. So much the better. I can't think what you can mean. But go on. Don't you trust me? 360

NORA. As I trust no one else. I know you are my best and truest friend. So I will tell you. Well then, Doctor Rank, you must help me to prevent something. You know how deeply, how wonderfully Torvald loves me; he would not hesitate a moment to give his very life for my sake.

365 RANK. (*Bending towards her.*) Nora, do you think he is the only one who—

NORA. (*With a slight start.*) Who—?

RANK. Who would gladly give his life for you?

NORA. (*Sadly.*) Oh!

RANK. I have sworn that you shall know it before I—go. I should never find a
370 better opportunity—Yes, Nora, now you know it; and now you know too that you can trust me as you can no one else.

NORA. (*Standing up, simply and calmly.*) Let me pass, please.

RANK. (*Makes way for her, but remains sitting.*) Nora—

NORA. (*In the doorway.*) Ellen, bring the lamp. (*Crosses to the stove.*) Oh, dear,
375 Doctor Rank, that was too bad of you.

RANK. (*Rising.*) That I have loved you as deeply as—anyone else? Was that too bad of me?

NORA. No, but that you should tell me so. It was so unnecessary—

RANK. What do you mean? Did you know—?

(*Ellen enters with the lamp; sets it on the table and goes out again.*)

380 RANK. Nora—Mrs. Helmer—I ask you, did you know?

NORA. Oh, how can I tell what I knew or didn't know. I really can't say— How could you be so clumsy, Doctor Rank? It was all so nice!

RANK. Well, at any rate, you know now that I am at your service, soul and body. And now, go on.

385 NORA. (*Looking at him.*) Go on—now?

RANK. I beg you to tell me what you want.

NORA. I can tell you nothing now.

RANK. Yes, yes! You mustn't punish me in that way. Let me do for you whatever a man can.

390 NORA. You can really do nothing for me now. Besides, I really want no help. You'll see it was only my fancy. Yes, it must be so. Of course! (*Sits in the rocking chair smiling at him.*) You're a nice person, Doctor Rank. Aren't you ashamed of yourself now that the lamp's on the table?

RANK. No, not exactly. But perhaps I ought to go—forever.

395 NORA. No, indeed you mustn't. Of course you must come and go as you've always done. You know very well that Torvald can't do without you.

RANK. Yes, but you?

NORA. Oh, you know I always like to have you here.

RANK. That's just what led me astray. You're a riddle to me. It has often

seemed to me as if you liked being with me almost as much as being with   400
Helmer.

NORA. Yes, don't you see? There are people one loves, and others one likes
to talk to.

RANK. Yes—there's something in that.

NORA. When I was a girl I naturally loved papa best. But it always delighted   405
me to steal into the servants' room. In the first place they never lectured
me, and in the second it was such fun to hear them talk.

RANK. Oh, I see; then it's their place I have taken?

NORA. (*Jumps up and hurries towards him.*) Oh, my dear Doctor Rank, I don't
mean that. But you understand, with Torvald it's the same as with papa—   410

(*Ellen enters from the hall.*)

ELLEN. Please, ma'am—(*Whispers to Nora, and gives her a card.*)

NORA. (*Glances at the card.*) Ah! (*Puts it in her pocket.*)

RANK. Anything wrong?

NORA. No, not in the least. It's only—it's my new costume—

RANK. Why, it's there.   415

NORA. Oh, that one, yes. But it's another that—I ordered it—Torvald
mustn't know—

RANK. Aha! So that's the great secret.

NORA. Yes, of course. Do just go to him; he's in the inner room; do keep him
as long as you can.   420

RANK. Make yourself easy; he shan't escape. (*Goes into Helmer's room.*)

NORA. (*To Ellen.*) Is he waiting in the kitchen?

ELLEN. Yes, he came up the back stair—

NORA. Didn't you tell him I was engaged?

ELLEN. Yes, but it was no use.   425

NORA. He won't go away?

ELLEN. No, ma'am, not until he has spoken to you.

NORA. Then let him come in, but quietly. And, Ellen—say nothing about it;
it's a surprise for my husband.

ELLEN. Oh, yes, ma'am, I understand—(*She goes out.*)   430

NORA. It's coming! It's coming after all. No, no, no, it can never be; it shall
not! (*She goes to Helmer's door and slips the bolt. Ellen opens the hall door for
Krogstad, and shuts it after him. He wears a travelling coat, high boots, and
a fur cap.*)

NORA. Speak quietly; my husband is at home.

KROGSTAD. All right. I don't care.

NORA. What do you want.   435

KROGSTAD. A little information.

NORA. Be quick, then. What is it?

KROGSTAD. You know I've got my dismissal.

NORA. I could not prevent it, Mr. Krogstad. I fought for you to the last, but
440   it was no good.

KROGSTAD. Does your husband care for you so little? He knows what I can
bring upon you, and yet he dares—

NORA. How can you think I would tell him?

KROGSTAD. I knew very well you hadn't. It wasn't like my friend Torvald
445   Helmer to show so much courage—

NORA. Mr. Krogstad, be good enough to speak respectfully of my husband.

KROGSTAD. Certainly, with all due respect. But since you're so anxious to
keep the matter secret, I suppose you're a little clearer than yesterday as to
what you have done.

450   NORA. Clearer than you could ever make me.

KROGSTAD. Yes, such a bad lawyer as I—

NORA. What is it you want?

KROGSTAD. Only to see how you're getting on, Mrs. Helmer. I've been thinking about you all day. Even a mere moneylender, a newspaper hack, a—in
455   short, a creature like me—has a little bit of what people call "heart."

NORA. Then show it; think of my little children.

KROGSTAD. Did you and your husband think of mine? But enough of that.
I only wanted to tell you that you needn't take this matter too seriously. I
shall not prosecute you for the present.

460   NORA. No, surely not. I knew you would not.

KROGSTAD. The whole thing can be settled quite quietly. Nobody need know.
It can remain among us three.

NORA. My husband must never know.

KROGSTAD. How can you prevent it? Can you pay off the debt?

465   NORA. No, not at once.

KROGSTAD. Or have you any means of raising the money in the next few
days?

NORA. None that I will make use of.

KROGSTAD. And if you had it would be no good to you now. If you offered
470   me ever so much ready money, you should not get back your IOU.

NORA. Tell me what you want to do with it.

KROGSTAD. I only want to keep it, to have it in my possession. No outsider
shall hear anything of it. So, if you've got any desperate scheme in your
head—

475   NORA. What if I have?

KROGSTAD. If you should think of leaving your husband and children—

NORA. What if I do?

KROGSTAD. Or if you should think of—something worse—

NORA. How do you know that?

KROGSTAD. Put all that out of your head.   480

NORA. How did you know what I had in my mind?

KROGSTAD. Most of us think of *that* at first. I thought of it, too; but I had
not the courage—

NORA. (*Voicelessly.*) Nor I.

KROGSTAD. (*Relieved.*) No, you don't, you haven't the courage either, have   485
you?

NORA. I haven't, I haven't.

KROGSTAD. Besides, it would be very silly—once the first storm is over—I
have a letter in my pocket for your husband—

NORA. Telling him everything?   490

KROGSTAD. Sparing you as much as possible.

NORA. (*Quickly.*) He must never have that letter. Tear it up. I will get the
money somehow.

KROGSTAD. Pardon me, Mrs. Helmer, but I believe I told you—

NORA. Oh, I'm not talking about the money I owe you. Tell me how much   495
you demand from my husband—I'll get it.

KROGSTAD. I demand no money from your husband.

NORA. What *do* you demand then?

KROGSTAD. I'll tell you. I want to regain my footing in the world. I want to
rise, and your husband shall help me to do it. For the last eighteen months   500
my record has been spotless; I've been in bitter need all the time, but I was
content to fight my way up, step by step. Now, I've been thrust down, and
I won't be satisfied with merely being allowed to sneak back again. I want
to rise, I tell you. I must get into the bank again, in a higher position than
before. Your husband shall create a place for me—   505

NORA. He will never do that!

KROGSTAD. He will do it; I know him—he won't dare to refuse! And when
I'm in, you'll soon see! I shall be the manager's right hand. It won't be Torvald Helmer, but Nils Krogstad, that manages the Joint Stock Bank.

NORA. That will never be.   510

KROGSTAD. Perhaps you'll—?

NORA. *Now* I have the courage for it.

KROGSTAD. Oh, you don't frighten me! A sensitive, petted creature like you—

NORA. You shall see, you shall see!

KROGSTAD. Under the ice, perhaps? Down in the cold, black water? And next   515
spring to come up again, ugly, hairless, unrecognizable—

NORA. You can't frighten me.

KROGSTAD. Nor you me. People don't do that sort of thing, Mrs. Helmer. And, after all, what good would it be? I have your husband in my pocket all the same.

NORA. Afterward? When I am no longer—

KROGSTAD. You forget, your reputation remains in my hands! (*Nora stands speechless and looks at him.*) Well, now you are prepared. Do nothing foolish. As soon as Helmer has received my letter I shall expect to hear from him. And remember that it is your husband himself who has forced me back again onto such paths. That I will never forgive him. Goodbye, Mrs. Helmer. (*Goes through hall. Nora hurries to the door, opens it a little, and listens.*)

NORA. He's going. He is not putting the letter into the box. No, no, it would be impossible. (*Opens the door farther and farther.*) What's that? He's standing still, not going downstairs. Is he changing his mind? Is he—? (*A letter falls into the box. Krogstad's footsteps are heard gradually receding down the stair. Nora utters a suppressed shriek; pause.*) In the letterbox! (*Slips shrinkingly up to the hall door.*) There it lies—Torvald, Torvald—now we are lost!

(*Mrs. Linden enters from the left with the costume.*)

MRS. LINDEN. There, I think it's all right now. Shall we just try it on?

NORA. (*Hoarsely and softly.*) Christina, come here.

MRS. LINDEN. (*Throws dress on sofa.*) What's the matter? You look quite aghast.

NORA. Come here. Do you see that letter? There, see—through the glass of the letterbox.

MRS. LINDEN. Yes, yes, I see it.

NORA. That letter is from Krogstad—

MRS. LINDEN. Nora—it was Krogstad who lent you the money!

NORA. Yes, and now Torvald will know everything.

MRS. LINDEN. Believe me, Nora, it's the best thing for both of you.

NORA. You don't know all yet. I have forged a name—

MRS. LINDEN. Good heavens!

NORA. Now, listen to me, Christina; you shall bear me witness.

MRS. LINDEN. What do you mean? Witness? What am I to—?

NORA. If I should go out of my mind—it might easily happen—

MRS. LINDEN. Nora!

NORA. Or if anything else should happen to me—so that I couldn't be here myself—!

MRS. LINDEN. Now, Nora, you're quite beside yourself!

NORA. In case anyone wanted to take it all upon himself—the whole blame— you understand—

MRS. LINDEN. Yes, but how can you think—

NORA. You shall bear witness that it's not true, Christina. I'm not out of my mind at all; I know quite well what I'm saying; and I tell you nobody else knew anything about it; I did the whole thing, I myself. Don't forget that.

MRS. LINDEN. I won't forget. But I don't understand what you mean—   560

NORA. Oh, how should you? It's the miracle coming to pass.

MRS. LINDEN. The miracle?

NORA. Yes, the miracle. But it's so terrible, Christina; it mustn't happen for anything in the world.

MRS. LINDEN. I will go straight to Krogstad and talk to him.   565

NORA. Don't; he will do you some harm.

MRS. LINDEN. Once he would have done anything for me.

NORA. He?

MRS. LINDEN. Where does he live?

NORA. Oh, how should I know—? Yes; (*feels in her pocket*) here's his card. But   570 the letter, the letter!

HELMER. (*Knocking outside.*) Nora!

NORA. (*Shrieks in terror.*) What is it? What do you want?

HELMER. Don't be frightened, we're not coming in; you've bolted the door. Are you trying on your dress?   575

NORA. Yes, yes, I'm trying it on. It suits me so well, Torvald.

MRS. LINDEN. (*Who has read the card.*) Then he lives close by here?

NORA. Yes, but it's no use now. The letter is actually in the box.

MRS. LINDEN. And your husband has the key?

NORA. Always.   580

MRS. LINDEN. Krogstad must demand his letter back, unread. He must make some excuse—

NORA. But this is the very time when Torvald generally—

MRS. LINDEN. Prevent him. Keep him occupied. I'll come back as quickly as I can. (*She goes out quickly through the hall door.*)   585

NORA. (*Opens Helmer's door and peeps in.*) Torvald!

HELMER. Well, now may one come back into one's own room? Come, Rank, we'll have a look—(*In the doorway.*) But how's this?

NORA. What, Torvald dear?

HELMER. Rank led me to expect a grand dressing-up.   590

RANK. (*In the doorway.*) So I understood. I suppose I was mistaken.

NORA. No, no one shall see me in my glory till tomorrow evening.

HELMER. Why, Nora dear, you look so tired. Have you been practising too hard?

NORA. No, I haven't practised at all yet.   595

HELMER. But you'll have to—

NORA. Yes, it's absolutely necessary. But, Torvald, I can't get on without your help. I've forgotten everything.

HELMER. Oh, we shall soon freshen it up again.

600 NORA. Yes, do help me, Torvald. You must promise me—Oh, I'm so nervous about it. Before so many people—this evening you must give yourself up entirely to me. You mustn't do a stroke of work! Now promise, Torvald dear!

HELMER. I promise. All this evening I will be your slave. Little helpless thing!

605   But, by the bye, I must first—(*Going to hall door.*)

NORA. What do you want there?

HELMER. Only to see if there are any letters.

NORA. No, no, don't do that, Torvald.

HELMER. Why not?

610 NORA. Torvald, I beg you not to. There are none there.

HELMER. Let me just see. (*Is going. Nora, at the piano, plays the first bars of the tarantella.*)

HELMER. (*At the door, stops.*) Aha!

NORA. I can't dance tomorrow if I don't rehearse with you first.

HELMER. (*Going to her.*) Are you really so nervous, dear Nora?

615 NORA. Yes, dreadfully! Let me rehearse at once. We have time before dinner. Oh! Do sit down and accompany me, Torvald dear; direct me, as you usually do.

HELMER. With all the pleasure in life, if you wish it. (*Sits at piano. Nora snatches the tambourine out of the box, and hurriedly drapes herself in a long multi-coloured shawl; then, with a bound, stands in the middle of the floor.*)

NORA. Now play for me! Now I'll dance! (*Helmer plays and Nora dances. Rank stands at the piano behind Helmer and looks on.*)

620 HELMER. (*Playing.*) Slower! Slower!

NORA. Can't do it slower.

HELMER. Not so violently, Nora.

NORA. I must! I must!

HELMER. (*Stops.*) Nora—that'll never do.

625 NORA. (*Laughs and swings her tambourine.*) Didn't I tell you so?

RANK. Let me accompany her.

HELMER. (*Rising.*) Yes, do—then I can direct her better. (*Rank sits down to the piano and plays. Nora dances more and more wildly. Helmer stands by the stove and addresses frequent corrections to her. She seems not to hear. Her hair breaks loose, and falls over her shoulders. She does not notice it, but goes on dancing. Mrs. Linden enters and stands spellbound in the doorway.*)

MRS. LINDEN. Ah!

NORA. (*Dancing.*) We're having such fun here, Christina!

HELMER. Why, Nora dear, you're dancing as if it were a matter of life and   630
death.

NORA. So it is.

HELMER. Rank, stop! This is absolute madness. Stop, I say! (*Rank stops play-ing, and Nora comes to a sudden standstill. Helmer going toward her.*) I couldn't have believed it. You've positively forgotten all I taught you.   635

NORA. (*Throws tambourine away.*) You see for yourself.

HELMER. You really do need teaching.

NORA. Yes, you see how much I need it. You must practise with me up to the last moment. Will you promise me, Torvald?

HELMER. Certainly, certainly.   640

NORA. Neither today nor tomorrow must you think of anything but me. You mustn't open a single letter—mustn't look at the letterbox!

HELMER. Ah, you're still afraid of that man—

NORA. Oh yes, yes, I am.

HELMER. Nora, I can see it in your face—there's a letter from him in the box.   645

NORA. I don't know, I believe so. But you're not to read anything now; noth-ing ugly must come between us until it's all over.

RANK. (*Softly to Helmer.*) You mustn't contradict her.

HELMER. (*Putting his arm around her.*) The child shall have her own way. But tomorrow night, when the dance is over—   650

NORA. Then you will be free.

(*Ellen appears in doorway, right.*)

ELLEN. Dinner is ready, ma'am.

NORA. We'll have some champagne, Ellen!

ELLEN. Yes, ma'am. (*Goes out.*)

HELMER. Dear me! Quite a feast.   655

NORA. Yes, and we'll keep it up till morning. (*Calling out.*) And macaroons, Ellen—plenty—just this once.

HELMER. (*Seizing her hands.*) Come, come, don't let us have this wild excite-ment! Be my own little lark again.

NORA. Oh, yes I will. But now go into the dining room; and you too, Doctor   660
Rank. Christina, you must help me to do up my hair.

RANK. (*Softly, as they go.*) There is nothing going on? Nothing—I mean—

HELMER. Oh no, nothing of the kind. It's merely this babyish anxiety I was telling you about. (*They go out to the right.*)

NORA. Well?   665

MRS. LINDEN. He's gone out of town.

NORA. I saw it in your face.

MRS. LINDEN. He comes back tomorrow evening. I left a note for him.

NORA. You shouldn't have done that. Things must take their course. After all,
there's something glorious in waiting for the miracle.

MRS. LINDEN. What are you waiting for?

NORA. Oh, you can't understand. Go to them in the dining room; I'll come in a moment. (*Mrs. Linden goes into the dining room; Nora stands for a moment as though collecting her thoughts; then looks at her watch.*) Five. Seven hours till midnight. Then twenty-four hours till the next midnight. Then the tarantella will be over. Twenty-four and seven? Thirty-one hours to live.

(*Helmer appears at the door, right.*)

HELMER. What's become of my little lark?

NORA. (*Runs to him with open arms.*) Here she is!

ACT 3

The same room. The table with the chairs around it is in the middle. A lamp lit on the table. The door to the hall stands open. Dance music is heard from the floor above. Mrs. Linden sits by the table, and turns the pages of a book absently. She tries to read, but seems unable to fix her attention; she frequently listens and looks anxiously toward the hall door.

MRS. LINDEN. (*Looks at her watch.*) Still not here; and the time's nearly up. If only he hasn't—(*Listens again.*) Ah, there he is—(*She goes into the hall and opens the outer door; soft footsteps are heard on the stairs; she whispers:*) Come in; there's no one here.

KROGSTAD. (*In the doorway.*) I found a note from you at my house. What does it mean?

MRS. LINDEN. I must speak with you.

KROGSTAD. Indeed? And in this house?

MRS. LINDEN. I could not see you at my rooms. They have no separate entrance. Come in; we are quite alone. The servants are asleep and the Helmers are at the ball upstairs.

KROGSTAD. (*Coming into room.*) Ah! So the Helmers are dancing this evening? Really?

MRS. LINDEN. Yes. Why not?

KROGSTAD. Quite right. Why not?

MRS. LINDEN. And now let us talk a little.

KROGSTAD. Have we anything to say to each other?

MRS. LINDEN. A great deal.

KROGSTAD. I should not have thought so.

MRS. LINDEN. Because you have never really understood me.

KROGSTAD. What was there to understand? The most natural thing in the world—a heartless woman throws a man over when a better match offers itself.

MRS. LINDEN. Do you really think me so heartless? Do you think I broke with you lightly?   25

KROGSTAD. Did you not?

MRS. LINDEN. Do you really think so?

KROGSTAD. If not, why did you write me that letter?

MRS. LINDEN. Was it not best? Since I had to break with you, was it not right that I should try to put an end to your love for me?   30

KROGSTAD. (*Pressing his hands together.*) So that was it? And all this—for the sake of money!

MRS. LINDEN. You ought not to forget that I had a helpless mother and two little brothers. We could not wait for you, Nils, as your prospects then stood.   35

KROGSTAD. Did that give you the right to discard me for another?

MRS. LINDEN. I don't know. I've often asked myself whether I did right.

KROGSTAD. (*More softly.*) When I had lost you the very ground seemed to sink from under my feet. Look at me now. I am a shipwrecked man cling-ing to a wreck.   40

MRS. LINDEN. Rescue may be at hand.

KROGSTAD. It was at hand, but then you stood in the way.

MRS. LINDEN. Without my knowledge, Nils. I did not know till today that it was you I was to replace at the bank.

KROGSTAD. Well, I take your word for it. But now you do know, do you   45
mean to give way?

MRS. LINDEN. No, for that would not help you.

KROGSTAD. Oh, help, help! I should do it whether it helped or not.

MRS. LINDEN. I have learnt prudence. Life and bitter necessity have schooled me.   50

KROGSTAD. And life has taught me not to trust fine speeches.

MRS. LINDEN. Then life has taught you a very sensible thing. But deeds you will trust?

KROGSTAD. What do you mean?

MRS. LINDEN. You said you were a shipwrecked man, clinging to a wreck.   55

KROGSTAD. I have good reason to say so.

MRS. LINDEN. I am a shipwrecked woman clinging to a wreck. I have no one to care for.

KROGSTAD. You made your own choice.

MRS. LINDEN. I had no choice.   60

KROGSTAD. Well, what then?

Mrs. Linden. Nils, what if we two shipwrecked people could join hands?

Krogstad. What!

Mrs. Linden. Suppose we lashed the wrecks together?

65 Krogstad. Christina!

Mrs. Linden. What do you think brought me to town?

Krogstad. Had you any thought of me?

Mrs. Linden. I must have work, or I can't live. All my life, as long as I can remember, I have worked; work has been my one great joy. Now I stand

70 quite alone in the world, so terribly aimless and forsaken. There is no happiness in working for oneself. Nils, give me somebody and something to work for.

Krogstad. No, no, that can never be. It's simply a woman's romantic notion of self-sacrifice.

75 Mrs. Linden. Have you ever found me romantic?

Krogstad. Would you really—? Tell me, do you know my past?

Mrs. Linden. Yes.

Krogstad. And do you know what people say of me?

Mrs. Linden. Did you not say just now that with me you would have been

80 another man?

Krogstad. I am sure of it.

Mrs. Linden. Is it too late?

Krogstad. Christina, do you know what you are doing? Yes, you do; I see it in your face. Have you the courage?

85 Mrs. Linden. I need someone to tend, and your children need a mother. You need me, and I—I need you. Nils, I believe in your better self. With you I fear nothing.

Krogstad. (*Seizing her hands.*) Thank you—thank you, Christina. Now I shall make others see me as you do. Ah, I forgot—

90 Mrs. Linden. (*Listening.*) Hush! The tarantella! Go, go!

Krogstad. Why? What is it?

Mrs. Linden. Don't you hear the dancing overhead? As soon as that is over they will be here.

Krogstad. Oh yes, I'll go. But it's too late now. Of course you don't know

95 the step I have taken against the Helmers?

Mrs. Linden. Yes, Nils, I do know.

Krogstad. And yet you have the courage to—

Mrs. Linden. I know what lengths despair can drive a man to.

Krogstad. Oh, if I could only undo it!

100 Mrs. Linden. You can. Your letter is still in the box.

Krogstad. Are you sure?

Mrs. Linden. Yes, but—

KROGSTAD. (*Looking to her searchingly.*) Ah, now I understand. You want to save your friend at any price. Say it outright—is that your idea?

MRS. LINDEN. Nils, a woman who has once sold herself for the sake of others 105 does not do so again.

KROGSTAD. I will demand my letter back again.

MRS. LINDEN. No, no.

KROGSTAD. Yes, of course. I'll wait till Helmer comes; I'll tell him to give it back to me—that it's only about my dismissal—that I don't want it read. 110

MRS. LINDEN. No, Nils, you must not recall the letter.

KROGSTAD. But tell me, wasn't that just why you got me to come here?

MRS. LINDEN. Yes, in my first terror. But a day has passed since then, and in that day I have seen incredible things in this house. Helmer must know everything; there must be an end to this unhappy secret. These two must 115 come to a full understanding. They can't possibly go on with all these shifts and concealments.

KROGSTAD. Very well, if you want to risk it. But one thing I can do, and at once—

MRS. LINDEN. (*Listening.*) Make haste! Go, go! The dance is over; we are not 120 safe another moment.

KROGSTAD. I'll wait for you in the street.

MRS. LINDEN. Yes, do; you must see me home.

KROGSTAD. I never was so happy in all my life! (*Krogstad goes, by the outer door. The door between the room and the hall remains open.*)

MRS. LINDEN. (*Setting furniture straight and getting her outdoor things to-* 125 *gether.*) What a change! What a change! To have someone to work for; a home to make happy. I shall have to set to work in earnest. I wish they would come. (*Listens.*) Ah, here they are! I must get my things on. (*Takes bonnet and cloak. Helmer's and Nora's voices are heard outside; a key is turned in the lock, and Helmer drags Nora almost by force into the hall. She wears the Italian costume with a large black shawl over it. He is in evening dress and wears a black domino.*[1])

NORA. (*Still struggling with him in the doorway.*) No, no, no; I won't go in! I want to go upstairs again; I don't want to leave so early! 130

HELMER. But, my dearest girl—

NORA. Oh, please, please, Torvald, only one hour more.

HELMER. Not one minute more, Nora dear; you know what we agreed! Come, come in; you are catching cold here. (*He leads her gently into the room in spite of her resistance.*)

MRS. LINDEN. Good evening. 135

---

1   *domino* Hooded cloak worn with a mask during masquerades.

NORA. Christina!

HELMER. What, Mrs. Linden, you here so late!

MRS. LINDEN. Yes, pardon me! I did so want to see Nora in her costume!

NORA. Have you been sitting here waiting for me?

140 MRS. LINDEN. Yes; unfortunately I came too late. You had already gone upstairs, and I couldn't go away without seeing you.

HELMER. (*Taking Nora's shawl off.*) Well then, just look at her! I think she's worth looking at. Isn't she lovely, Mrs. Linden?

MRS. LINDEN. Yes, I must say—

145 HELMER. Isn't she exquisite? Everyone said so. But she is dreadfully obstinate, dear little creature. What's to be done with her? Just think, I almost had to force her away.

NORA. Oh, Torvald, you'll be sorry someday you didn't let me stay, if only for one half hour.

150 HELMER. There! You hear her, Mrs. Linden? She dances her tarantella with wild applause, and well she deserved it, I must say—though there was, perhaps, a little too much nature in her rendering of the idea—more than was, strictly speaking, artistic. But never mind—she was a great success, and that's the main thing. Ought I to let her stay after that—to weaken the
155 impression? Not in the least. I took my sweet little Capri girl—my capricious little Capri girl, I might say—under my arm; a rapid turn round the room, a curtsey to all sides, and—as they say in novels—the lovely apparition vanished! An exit should always be effective, Mrs. Linden, but I can't get Nora to see it. By Jove, it's warm here. (*Throws his domino on a chair
160 and opens the door to his room.*) What! No light here? Oh, of course. Excuse me—(*Goes in and lights candles.*)

NORA. (*Whispers breathlessly.*) Well?

MRS. LINDEN. (*Softly.*) I have spoken to him.

NORA. And—?

165 MRS. LINDEN. Nora—you must tell your husband everything—

NORA. (*Almost voiceless.*) I knew it!

MRS. LINDEN. You have nothing to fear from Krogstad, but you must speak out.

NORA. I shall not speak!

170 MRS. LINDEN. Then the letter will.

NORA. Thank you, Christina. Now I know what I have to do. Hush!

HELMER. (*Coming back.*) Well, Mrs. Linden, have you admired her?

MRS. LINDEN. Yes, and now I'll say goodnight.

HELMER. What, already? Does this knitting belong to you?

175 MRS. LINDEN. (*Takes it.*) Yes, thanks; I was nearly forgetting it.

HELMER. Then you do knit?

MRS. LINDEN. Yes.

HELMER. Do you know, you ought to embroider instead?

MRS. LINDEN. Indeed! Why?

HELMER. Because it's so much prettier. Look now! You hold the embroidery 180 in the left hand so, and then work the needle with the right hand, in a long, easy curve, don't you?

MRS. LINDEN. Yes, I suppose so.

HELMER. But knitting is always ugly. Look now, your arms close to your sides, and the needles going up and down—there's something Chinese 185 about it—They really gave us splendid champagne tonight.

MRS. LINDEN. Well, goodnight, Nora, and don't be obstinate any more.

HELMER. Well said, Mrs. Linden!

MRS. LINDEN. Goodnight, Mr. Helmer.

HELMER. (*Going with her to the door.*) Goodnight, goodnight; I hope you'll 190 get safely home. I should be glad to—but really you haven't far to go. Goodnight, goodnight! (*She goes; Helmer shuts the door after her and comes down again.*) At last we've got rid of her: she's an awful bore.

NORA. Aren't you very tired, Torvald?

HELMER. No, not in the least. 195

NORA. Nor sleepy?

HELMER. Not a bit. I feel particularly lively. But you? You do look tired and sleepy.

NORA. Yes, very tired. I shall soon sleep now.

HELMER. There, you see. I was right after all not to let you stay longer. 200

NORA. Oh, everything you do is right.

HELMER. (*Kissing her forehead.*) Now my lark is speaking like a reasonable being. Did you notice how jolly Rank was this evening?

NORA. Was he? I had no chance to speak to him.

HELMER. Nor I, much; but, I haven't seen him in such good spirits for a long 205 time. (*Looks at Nora a little, then comes nearer to her.*) It's splendid to be back in our own home, to be quite alone together! Oh, you enchanting creature!

NORA. Don't look at me that way, Torvald.

HELMER. I am not to look at my dearest treasure? At the loveliness that is 210 mine, mine only, wholly and entirely mine?

NORA. (*Goes to the other side of the table.*) You mustn't say these things to me this evening.

HELMER. (*Following.*) I see you have the tarantella still in your blood—and that makes you all the more enticing. Listen! the other people are going 215 now. (*More softly.*) Nora—soon the whole house will be still.

NORA. I hope so.

HELMER. Yes, don't you, Nora darling? When we're among strangers do you
know why I speak so little to you, and keep so far away, and only steal a
220   glance at you now and then—do you know why I do it? Because I am fancying that we love each other in secret, that I am secretly betrothed to you,
and that no one dreams there is anything between us.

NORA. Yes, yes, yes. I know all your thoughts are with me.

HELMER. And then, when we have to go, and I put the shawl about your
225   smooth, soft shoulders, and this glorious neck of yours, I imagine you are
my bride, that our wedding is just over, that I am bringing you for the first
time to my home, and that I am alone with you for the first time, quite
alone with you, in your quivering loveliness! All this evening I was longing
for you, and you only. When I watched you swaying and whirling in the
230   tarantella—my blood boiled—I could endure it no longer, and that's why
I made you come home with me so early.

NORA. Go now, Torvald. Go away from me. I won't have all this.

HELMER. What do you mean? Ah! I see you're teasing me! "Won't! Won't!"
Am I not your husband? (*A knock at the outer door.*)

235   NORA. (*Starts.*) Did you hear?

HELMER. (*Going toward the hall.*) Who's there?

RANK. (*Outside.*) It's I; may I come in for a moment?

HELMER. (*In a low tone, annoyed.*) Oh! What can he want? (*Aloud.*) Wait a
moment. (*Opens door.*) Come, it's nice of you to give us a look in.

240   RANK. I thought I heard your voice, and that put it into my head. (*Looks
round.*) Ah! This dear old place! How cosy you two are here!

HELMER. You seemed to find it pleasant enough upstairs, too.

RANK. Exceedingly. Why not? Why shouldn't one get all one can out of the
world? All one can for as long as one can. The wine was splendid—

245   HELMER. Especially the champagne.

RANK. Did you notice it? It's incredible the quantity I managed to get down.

NORA. Torvald drank plenty of champagne too.

RANK. Did he?

NORA. Yes, and it always puts him in such spirits.

250   RANK. Well, why shouldn't one have a jolly evening after a well-spent day?

HELMER. Well-spent! Well, I haven't much to boast of.

RANK. (*Slapping him on the shoulder.*) But I have, don't you see?

NORA. I suppose you have been engaged in a scientific investigation, Doctor
Rank?

255   RANK. Quite right.

HELMER. Bless me! Little Nora talking about scientific investigations!

NORA. Am I to congratulate you on the result?

RANK. By all means.

Nora. It was good then?

Rank. The best possible, both for doctor and patient—certainty.   260

Nora. (*Quickly and searchingly.*) Certainty?

Rank. Absolute certainty. Wasn't I right to enjoy myself after it?

Nora. Yes, quite right, Doctor Rank.

Helmer. And so say I, provided you don't have to pay for it tomorrow.

Rank. Well, in this life nothing's to be had for nothing.   265

Nora. Doctor Rank, aren't you very fond of masquerades?

Rank. Yes, when there are plenty of comical disguises.

Nora. Tell me, what shall we two be at our next masquerade?

Helmer. Little insatiable! Thinking of your next already!

Rank. We two? I'll tell you. You must go as a good fairy.   270

Helmer. Oh, but what costume would indicate that?

Rank. She has simply to wear her everyday dress.

Helmer. Splendid! But don't you know what you yourself will be?

Rank. Yes, my dear friend, I am perfectly clear upon that point.

Helmer. Well?   275

Rank. At the next masquerade I shall be invisible.

Helmer. What a comical idea!

Rank. There's a big black hat—haven't you heard of the invisible hat? It comes down all over you, and then no one can see you.

Helmer. (*With a suppressed smile.*) No, you're right there.   280

Rank. But I'm quite forgetting what I came for. Helmer, give me a cigar, one of the dark Havanas.

Helmer. With the greatest pleasure. (*Hands case.*)

Rank. (*Takes one and cuts the end off.*) Thanks.

Nora. (*Striking a wax match.*) Let me give you a light.   285

Rank. A thousand thanks. (*She holds match. He lights his cigar at it.*) And now, goodbye.

Helmer. Goodbye, goodbye, my dear fellow.

Nora. Sleep well, Doctor Rank.

Rank. Thanks for the wish.   290

Nora. Wish me the same.

Rank. You? Very well, since you ask me—Sleep well. And thanks for the light. (*He nods to them both and goes out.*)

Helmer. (*In an undertone.*) He's been drinking a good deal.

Nora. (*Absently.*) I daresay. (*Helmer takes his bunch of keys from his pocket and*   295 *goes into the hall.*) Torvald, what are you doing there?

Helmer. I must empty the letterbox, it's quite full; there will be no room for the newspapers tomorrow morning.

Nora. Are you going to work tonight?

300 HELMER. Not very likely! Why, what's this? Someone has been at the lock.

NORA. The lock—?

HELMER. I'm sure of it. What does it mean? I can't think that the servants—? Here's a broken hairpin. Nora, it's one of yours.

NORA. (*Quickly.*) It must have been the children.

305 HELMER. Then you must break them of such tricks. H'm, h'm! There! At last I've got it open. (*Takes contents out and calls into the kitchen.*) Ellen! Ellen, just put the hall door lamp out. (*He returns with letters in his hand, and shuts the inner door.*) Just see how they've accumulated. (*Turning them over.*) Why, what's this?

310 NORA. (*At the window.*) The letter! Oh, no, no, Torvald!

HELMER. Two visiting cards—from Rank.

NORA. From Doctor Rank?

HELMER. (*Looking at them.*) Doctor Rank. They were on the top. He must just have put them in.

315 NORA. Is there anything on them?

HELMER. There's a black cross over the name. Look at it. What a horrid idea! It looks just as if he were announcing his own death.

NORA. So he is.

HELMER. What! Do you know anything? Has he told you anything?

320 NORA. Yes. These cards mean that he has taken his last leave of us. He intends to shut himself up and die.

HELMER. Poor fellow! Of course I knew we couldn't hope to keep him long. But so soon—and to go and creep into his lair like a wounded animal—

NORA. What must be, must be, and the fewer words the better. Don't you

325 think so, Torvald?

HELMER. (*Walking up and down.*) He had so grown into our lives, I can't realize that he's gone. He and his sufferings and his loneliness formed a sort of cloudy background to the sunshine of our happiness. Well, perhaps it's best so—at any rate for him. (*Stands still.*) And perhaps for us, too, Nora.

330 Now we two are thrown entirely upon each other. (*Puts his arm round her.*) My darling wife! I feel as if I could never hold you close enough. Do you know, Nora, I often wish some danger might threaten you, that I might risk body and soul, and everything, everything, for your dear sake.

NORA. (*Tears herself from him and says firmly.*) Now you shall read your let-

335 ters, Torvald.

HELMER. No, no, not tonight. I want to be with you, sweet wife.

NORA. With the thought of your dying friend?

HELMER. You are right. This has shaken us both. Unloveliness has come between us—thoughts of death and decay. We must seek to cast them off.

340 Till then we will remain apart.

NORA. (*Her arms round his neck.*) Torvald! Goodnight, goodnight.

HELMER. (*Kissing her forehead.*) Goodnight, my little songbird. Sleep well, Nora. Now I'll go and read my letters. (*He goes into his room and shuts the door.*)

NORA. (*With wild eyes, gropes about her, seizes Helmer's domino, throws it round her, and whispers quickly, hoarsely, and brokenly.*) Never to see him 345 again. Never, never, never. (*Throws her shawl over her head.*) Never to see the children again. Never, never. Oh that black, icy water! Oh that bottomless—If it were only over! Now he has it; he's reading it. Oh, no, no, no, not yet. Torvald, goodbye. Goodbye, my little ones! (*She is rushing out by the hall; at the same moment Helmer tears his door open, and stands with an open letter in his hand.*)

HELMER. Nora!   350

NORA. (*Shrieking.*) Ah—!

HELMER. What is this? Do you know what is in this letter?

NORA. Yes, I know. Let me go! Let me pass!

HELMER. (*Holds her back.*) Where do you want to go?

NORA. (*Tries to get free.*) You shan't save me, Torvald.   355

HELMER. (*Falling back.*) True! Is it true what he writes? No, no, it cannot be.

NORA. It is true. I have loved you beyond all else in the world.

HELMER. Pshaw—no silly evasions.

NORA. (*A step nearer him.*) Torvald—

HELMER. Wretched woman! What have you done?   360

NORA. Let me go—you shall not save me. You shall not take my guilt upon yourself.

HELMER. I don't want any melodramatic games. (*Locks the door.*) Here you shall stay and give an account of yourself. Do you understand what you have done? Answer. Do you understand it?   365

NORA. (*Looks at him fixedly, and says with a stiffening expression.*) Yes, now I begin fully to understand it.

HELMER. (*Walking up and down.*) Oh, what an awful awakening! During all these eight years—she who was my pride and my joy—a hypocrite, a liar—worse, worse—a criminal. Oh! The hideousness of it! Ugh! Ugh!   370 (*Nora is silent, and continues to look fixedly at him.*) I ought to have foreseen something of the kind. All your father's dishonesty—be silent! I say all your father's dishonesty you have inherited—no religion, no morality, no sense of duty. How I am punished for shielding him! I did it for your sake, and you reward me like this.   375

NORA. Yes—like this!

HELMER. You have destroyed my whole happiness. You have ruined my future. Oh! It's frightful to think of! I am in the power of a scoundrel; he

380 can do whatever he pleases with me, demand whatever he chooses, and I must submit. And all this disaster is brought upon me by an unprincipled woman!

NORA. When I am gone, you will be free.

HELMER. Oh, no fine phrases. Your father, too, was always ready with them. What good would it do to me, if you were "gone," as you say? No good in
385 the world! He can publish the story all the same; I might even be suspected of collusion. People will think I was at the bottom of it all and egged you on. And for all this I have you to thank—you whom I have done nothing but pet and spoil during our whole married life. Do you understand now what you have done to me?

390 NORA. (*With cold calmness.*) Yes.

HELMER. It's incredible. I can't grasp it. But we must come to an under-standing. Take that shawl off. Take it off, I say. I must try to pacify him in one way or another—the secret must be kept, cost what it may. As for ourselves, we must live as we have always done, but of course only in
395 the eyes of the world. Of course you will continue to live here. But the children cannot be left in your care. I dare not trust them to you—Oh, to have to say this to one I have loved so tenderly—whom I still—but that must be a thing of the past. Henceforward there can be no question of happiness, but merely of saving the ruins, the shreds, the show of it (*A*
400 *ring; Helmer starts.*) What's that? So late! Can it be the worst? Can he—? Hide yourself, Nora; say you are ill. (*Nora stands motionless. Helmer goes to the door and opens it.*)

ELLEN. (*Half dressed, in the hall.*) Here is a letter for you, ma'am.

HELMER. Give it to me. (*Seizes the letter and shuts the door.*) Yes, from him. You shall not have it. I shall read it.

405 NORA. Read it!

HELMER. (*By the lamp.*) I have hardly the courage to. We may be lost, both you and I. Ah! I must know. (*Tears the letter hastily open; reads a few lines, looks at an enclosure; a cry of joy.*) Nora! (*Nora looks interrogatively at him.*) Nora! Oh! I must read it again. Yes, yes, it is so. I am saved! Nora, I am
410 saved!

NORA. And I?

HELMER. You too, of course; we are both saved, both of us. Look here, he sends you back your promissory note. He writes that he regrets and apolo-gizes—that a happy turn in his life—Oh, what matter what he writes. We
415 are saved, Nora! No one can harm you. Oh! Nora, Nora—No, first to get rid of this hateful thing. I'll just see—(*Glances at the IOU*) No, I won't look at it; the whole thing shall be nothing but a dream to me. (*Tears the IOU and both letters in pieces. Throws them into the fire and watches*

them burn.) There, it's gone. He wrote that ever since Christmas Eve—Oh, Nora, they must have been three awful days for you!   420

NORA. I have fought a hard fight for the last three days.

HELMER. And in your agony you saw no other outlet but—no; we won't think of that horror. We will only rejoice and repeat—it's over, all over. Don't you hear, Nora? You don't seem able to grasp it. Yes, it's over. What is this set look on your face? Oh, my poor Nora, I understand; you can't be-   425 lieve that I have forgiven you. But I have, Nora; I swear it. I have forgiven everything. I know that what you did was all for love of me.

NORA. That's true.

HELMER. You loved me as a wife should love her husband. It was only the means you misjudged. But do you think I love you the less for your help-   430 lessness? No, no. Only lean on me. I will counsel and guide you. I should be no true man if this very womanly helplessness did not make you doubly dear in my eyes. You mustn't think of the hard things I said in my first moment of terror, when the world seemed to be tumbling about my ears. I have forgiven you, Nora—I swear I have forgiven you.   435

NORA. I thank you for your forgiveness. (*Goes out, right.*)

HELMER. No, stay. (*Looks in.*) What are you going to do?

NORA. (*Inside.*) To take off my doll's dress.

HELMER. (*In doorway.*) Yes, do, dear. Try to calm down, and recover your balance, my scared little songbird. You may rest secure. I have broad wings   440 to shield you. (*Walking up and down near the door.*) Oh, how lovely—how cosy our home is, Nora. Here you are safe; here I can shelter you like a hunted dove, whom I have saved from the claws of the hawk. I shall soon bring your poor beating heart to rest; believe me, Nora, I will. Tomorrow all this will seem quite different—everything will be as before. I shall not   445 need to tell you again that I forgive you; you will feel for yourself that it is true. How could you think I could find it in my heart to drive you away, or even so much as to reproach you? Oh, you don't know a true man's heart, Nora. There is something indescribably sweet and soothing to a man in having forgiven his wife—honestly forgiven her from the bottom of his   450 heart. She becomes his property in a double sense. She is as though born again; she has become, so to speak, at once his wife and his child. That is what you shall henceforth be to me, my bewildered, helpless darling. Don't be troubled about anything, Nora; only open your heart to me, and I will be both will and conscience to you. (*Nora enters, crossing to table in*   455 *everyday dress.*) Why, what's this? Not gone to bed? You have changed your dress.

NORA. Yes, Torvald; now I have changed my dress.

HELMER. But why now so late?

460 NORA. I shall not sleep tonight.

HELMER. But, Nora dear—

NORA. (*Looking at her watch.*) It's not so late yet. Sit down, Torvald; you and I have much to say to each other. (*She sits on one side of the table.*)

HELMER. Nora, what does this mean? Your cold, set face—

465 NORA. Sit down. It will take some time; I have much to talk over with you. (*Helmer sits at the other side of the table.*)

HELMER. You alarm me; I don't understand you.

NORA. No, that's just it. You don't understand me; and I have never understood you—till tonight. No, don't interrupt. Only listen to what I say. We

470 must come to a final settlement, Torvald!

HELMER. How do you mean?

NORA. (*After a short silence.*) Does not one thing strike you as we sit here?

HELMER. What should strike me?

NORA. We have been married eight years. Does it not strike you that this is

475 the first time we two, you and I, man and wife, have talked together seriously?

HELMER. Seriously! Well, what do you call seriously?

NORA. During eight whole years, and more—ever since the day we first met—we have never exchanged one serious word about serious things.

480 HELMER. Was I always to trouble you with the cares you could not help me to bear?

NORA. I am not talking of cares. I say that we have never yet set ourselves seriously to get to the bottom of anything.

HELMER. Why, my dear Nora, what have you to do with serious things?

485 NORA. There we have it! You have never understood me. I have had great injustice done me, Torvald; first by my father and then by you.

HELMER. What! By your father and me? By us who have loved you more than all the world?

NORA. (*Shaking her head.*) You have never loved me. You only thought it

490 amusing to be in love with me.

HELMER. Why, Nora, what a thing to say!

NORA. Yes, it is so, Torvald. While I was at home with father, he used to tell me all his opinions, and I held the same opinions. If I had others I concealed them, because he would not have liked it. He used to call me his

495 doll child, and play with me as I played with my dolls. Then I came to live in your house—

HELMER. What an expression to use about our marriage!

NORA. (*Undisturbed.*) I mean I passed from father's hands into yours. You settled everything according to your taste; and I got the same tastes as you;

500 or I pretended to—I don't know which—both ways, perhaps. When I look

back on it now, I seem to have been living here like a beggar, from hand to mouth. I lived by performing tricks for you, Torvald. But you would have it so. You and father have done me a great wrong. It's your fault that my life has been wasted.

HELMER. Why, Nora, how unreasonable and ungrateful you are. Haven't you been happy here? 505

NORA. No, never; I thought I was, but I never was.

HELMER. Not—not happy?

NORA. No; only merry. And you have always been so kind to me. But our house has been nothing but a playroom. Here I have been your doll-wife, 510 just as at home I used to be papa's doll-child. And the children in their turn have been my dolls. I thought it fun when you played with me, just as the children did when I played with them. That has been our marriage, Torvald.

HELMER. There is some truth in what you say, exaggerated and overstrained 515 though it is. But henceforth it shall be different. Playtime is over; now comes the time for education.

NORA. Whose education? Mine, or the children's.

HELMER. Both, my dear Nora.

NORA. Oh, Torvald, you are not the man to teach me to be a fit wife for you. 520

HELMER. And you say that?

NORA. And I—am I fit to educate the children?

HELMER. Nora!

NORA. Did you not say yourself a few minutes ago you dared not trust them to me? 525

HELMER. In the excitement of the moment! Why should you dwell upon that?

NORA. No—you are perfectly right. That problem is beyond me. There's another to be solved first—I must try to educate myself. You are not the man to help me in that. I must set about it alone. And that is why I am 530 leaving you!

HELMER. (*Jumping up.*) What—do you mean to say—?

NORA. I must stand quite alone to know myself and my surroundings; so I cannot stay with you.

HELMER. Nora! Nora! 535

NORA. I am going at once. Christina will take me in for tonight—

HELMER. You are mad. I shall not allow it. I forbid it.

NORA. It's no use your forbidding me anything now. I shall take with me what belongs to me. From you I will accept nothing, either now or afterward. 540

HELMER. What madness!

NORA. Tomorrow I shall go home.

HELMER. Home!

NORA. I mean to what was my home. It will be easier for me to find some
545   opening there.

HELMER. Oh, in your blind inexperience—

NORA. I must try to gain experience, Torvald.

HELMER. To forsake your home, your husband, and your children! You don't
consider what the world will say.

550 NORA. I can pay no heed to that! I only know that I must do it.

HELMER. It's exasperating! Can you forsake your holiest duties in this way?

NORA. What do you call my holiest duties?

HELMER. Do you ask me that? Your duties to your husband and your children.

555 NORA. I have other duties equally sacred.

HELMER. Impossible! What duties do you mean?

NORA. My duties toward myself.

HELMER. Before all else you are a wife and a mother.

NORA. That I no longer believe. I believe that before all else I am a human
560   being, just as much as you are—or at least that I will try to become one.
I know that most people agree with you, Torvald, and that they say so in
books. But henceforth I can't be satisfied with what most people say, and
what is in books. I must think things out for myself, and try to get clear
about them.

565 HELMER. Are you not clear about your place in your own home? Have you
not an infallible guide in questions like these? Have you not religion?

NORA. Oh, Torvald, I don't know properly what religion is.

HELMER. What do you mean?

NORA. I know nothing but what our clergyman told me when I was con-
570   firmed. He explained that religion was this and that. When I get away from
here and stand alone I will look into that matter too. I will see whether
what he taught me is true, or, at any rate, whether it is true for me.

HELMER. Oh, this is unheard of! But if religion cannot keep you right, let me
appeal to your conscience—I suppose you have some moral feeling? Or,
575   answer me, perhaps you have none?

NORA. Well, Torvald, it's not easy to say. I really don't know—I am all at sea
about these things. I only know that I think quite differently from you
about them. I hear, too, that the laws are different from what I thought;
but I can't believe that they are right. It appears that a woman has no right
580   to spare her dying father, or to save her husband's life. I don't believe that.

HELMER. You talk like a child. You don't understand the society in which
you live.

NORA. No, I don't. But now I shall try to. I must make up my mind which is right—society or I.

HELMER. Nora, you are ill, you are feverish. I almost think you are out of your senses. 585

NORA. I have never felt so much clearness and certainty as tonight.

HELMER. You are clear and certain enough to forsake husband and children?

NORA. Yes, I am.

HELMER. Then there is only one explanation possible. 590

NORA. What is that?

HELMER. You no longer love me.

NORA. No, that is just it.

HELMER. Nora! Can you say so!

NORA. Oh, I'm so sorry, Torvald, for you've always been so kind to me. But 595
I can't help it. I do not love you any longer.

HELMER. (*Keeping his composure with difficulty.*) Are you clear and certain on this point too?

NORA. Yes, quite. That is why I won't stay here any longer.

HELMER. And can you also make clear to me, how I have forfeited your love? 600

NORA. Yes, I can. It was this evening, when the miracle did not happen. For then I saw you were not the man I had taken you for.

HELMER. Explain yourself more clearly; I don't understand

NORA. I have waited so patiently all these eight years, for, of course, I saw clearly enough that miracles do not happen every day. When this crushing 605
blow threatened me, I said to myself, confidently, "Now comes the miracle!" When Krogstad's letter lay in the box, it never for a moment occurred to me that you would think of submitting to that man's conditions. I was convinced that you would say to him, "Make it known to all the world," and that then— 610

HELMER. Well? When I had given my own wife's name up to disgrace and shame?

NORA. Then I firmly believed that you would come forward, take everything upon yourself, and say, "I am the guilty one."

HELMER. Nora! 615

NORA. You mean I would never have accepted such a sacrifice? No, certainly not. But what would my assertions have been worth in opposition to yours? That was the miracle that I hoped for and dreaded. And it was to hinder that that I wanted to die.

HELMER. I would gladly work for you day and night, Nora—bear sorrow 620
and want for your sake—but no man sacrifices his honour, even for one he loves.

NORA. Millions of women have done so.

HELMER. Oh, you think and talk like a silly child.

625 NORA. Very likely. But you neither think nor talk like the man I can share my life with. When your terror was over—not for me, but for yourself—when there was nothing more to fear—then it was to you as though nothing had happened. I was your lark again, your doll—whom you would take twice as much care of in future, because she was so weak and fragile. (*Stands up.*)

630 Torvald, in that moment it burst upon me that I had been living here these eight years with a strange man, and had borne him three children—Oh, I can't bear to think of it—I could tear myself to pieces!

HELMER. (*Sadly.*) I see it, I see it; an abyss has opened between us—But, Nora, can it never be filled up?

635 NORA. As I now am, I am no wife for you.

HELMER. I have strength to become another man.

NORA. Perhaps—when your doll is taken away from you.

HELMER. To part—to part from you! No, Nora, no; I can't grasp the thought.

NORA. (*Going into room, right.*) The more reason for the thing to happen. (*She comes back with a cloak, hat, and small travelling bag, which she puts on a chair.*)

640 HELMER. Nora, Nora, not now! Wait till tomorrow.

NORA. (*Putting on cloak.*) I can't spend the night in a strange man's house.

HELMER. But can't we live here as brother and sister?

NORA. (*Fastening her hat.*) You know very well that would not last long. Goodbye, Torvald. No, I won't go to the children. I know they are in better

645 hands than mine. As I now am, I can be nothing to them.

HELMER. But some time, Nora—some time—

NORA. How can I tell? I have no idea what will become of me.

HELMER. But you are my wife, now and always!

NORA. Listen, Torvald—when a wife leaves her husband's house, as I am do-

650 ing, I have heard that in the eyes of the law he is free from all duties toward her. At any rate I release you from all duties. You must not feel yourself bound any more than I shall. There must be perfect freedom on both sides. There, there is your ring back. Give me mine.

HELMER. That too?

655 NORA. That too.

HELMER. Here it is.

NORA. Very well. Now it is all over. Here are the keys. The servants know about everything in the house, better than I do. Tomorrow, when I have started, Christina will come to pack up my things. I will have them sent

660 after me.

HELMER. All over! All over! Nora, will you never think of me again?

NORA. Oh, I shall often think of you, and the children—and this house.

HELMER. May I write to you, Nora?

NORA. No, never. You must not.

HELMER. But I must send you—   665

NORA. Nothing, nothing.

HELMER. I must help you if you need it.

NORA. No, I say. I take nothing from strangers.

HELMER. Nora, can I never be more than a stranger to you?

NORA. (*Taking her travelling bag.*) Oh, Torvald, then the miracle of miracles   670
would have to happen.

HELMER. What is the miracle of miracles?

NORA. Both of us would have to change so that—Oh, Torvald, I no longer
believe in miracles.

HELMER. But I will believe. We must so change that—?   675

NORA. That our lives together could be a marriage. Goodbye. (*She goes out.*)

HELMER. (*Sinks in a chair by the door with his face in his hands.*) Nora! Nora!
(*He looks around and stands up.*) Empty. She's gone! (*A hope inspires him.*)
Ah! The miracle of miracles—?! (*From below is heard the reverberation of a
heavy door closing.*)

—1879[1]

---

1   *1879* Shortly after the play's first performance, Ibsen wrote an alternative ending to *A
Doll's House* in an attempt to prevent unauthorized, less controversial adaptations from
appearing in Germany. In the alternative ending, after Nora says goodbye, Helmer takes
her by the arm and leads her to the room where their children are sleeping. Unable to
leave her children, Nora is overcome and falls to the floor. Ibsen made the change in an
attempt to maintain control of his play, but publicly stated his dislike of the altered ending, and said that whoever performed it did so against his wishes.

Betty Hennings in the role of Nora, 1880. A Doll's House *was first performed at the Royal Danish Theatre in Copenhagen, Denmark; Hennings originated the role in this production.*

Samuel Beckett
1906–1989

Samuel Beckett was a prolific writer of poetry, fiction, and criticism, but he remains best known for plays such as *Waiting for Godot* (1952) and *Endgame* (1957). Fragmented, filled with absences and silences, and sparing of plot, characterization, and setting, Beckett's drama attempts to dispense with elements previously thought to be essential to dramatic productions. His plays were defined by Martin Esslin as exemplars of the "Theatre of the Absurd"—they present the absurdity and futility of the human condition as a given. In such plays, Esslin suggests, "everything that happens seems to be beyond rational motivation, happening at random or through the demented caprice of an unaccountable idiot fate."

Beckett was born in Ireland and attended Trinity College in Dublin. Upon attaining his Bachelor of Arts he left to teach in France, where he became close friends with the writer James Joyce; this friendship strongly influenced Beckett's early work. He spent much of World War II as an active member of the French Resistance. In the four years following the war he was extraordinarily productive, composing four novellas, two plays, and four novels. During this period, which he referred to as "the siege in the room," he decided to write entirely in French, translating his work back into English once it was completed. This process enhanced the distinctive sparseness of his writing style.

Disregarding convention, Beckett experimented with new ideas, new media, and even new technology—such as the reel-to-reel tape recorder, which soon after its invention played a central role in his groundbreaking short play *Krapp's Last Tape* (1958). The importance of his work was acknowledged in 1969, when Beckett was awarded the Nobel Prize for Literature. He continued to direct many of his plays and to assist in their production for television, retiring only a few years before his death in 1989.

Krapp's Last Tape

A late evening in the future.

Krapp's den.

Front centre a small table, the two drawers of which open towards audience.

Sitting at the table, facing front, i.e. across from the drawers, a wearish old man: Krapp.

Rusty black narrow trousers too short for him. Rusty black sleeveless waistcoat, four capacious pockets. Heavy silver watch and chain. Grimy white shirt open at neck, no collar. Surprising pair of dirty white boots, size ten at least, very narrow and pointed.

White face. Purple nose. Disordered grey hair. Unshaven.

Very near-sighted (but unspectacled). Hard of hearing.

Cracked voice. Distinctive intonation.

Laborious walk.

On the table a tape-recorder with microphone and a number of cardboard boxes containing reels of recorded tapes.

Table and immediately adjacent area in strong white light. Rest of stage in darkness.

Krapp remains a moment motionless, heaves a great sigh, looks at his watch, fumbles in his pockets, takes out an envelope, puts it back, fumbles, takes out a small bunch of keys, raises it to his eyes, chooses a key, gets up and moves to front of table. He stoops, unlocks first drawer, peers into it, feels about inside it, takes out a reel of tape, peers at it, puts it back, locks drawer, unlocks second drawer, peers into it, feels about inside it, takes out a large banana, peers at it, locks drawer, puts keys back in his pocket. He turns, advances to edge of stage, halts, strokes banana, peels it, drops skin at his feet, puts end of banana in his mouth and remains motionless, staring vacuously before him. Finally he bites off the end, turns aside and begins pacing to and fro at edge of stage, in the light, i.e. not more than four or five paces either way, meditatively eating banana. He treads on skin, slips, nearly falls, recovers himself, stoops and peers at skin and finally pushes it, still stooping, with his foot over the edge of stage into pit. He resumes his pacing, finishes banana, returns to table, sits down, remains a moment motionless, heaves a great sigh, takes keys from his pockets, raises them to his eyes, chooses key, gets up and moves to front of table, unlocks second drawer, takes out a second large banana, peers at it, locks drawer, puts back keys in his pocket, turns, advances to edge of stage, halts, strokes banana, peels it, tosses skin into pit, puts end of banana in his mouth and remains motionless, staring vacuously before him. Finally he has an idea, puts banana in his waistcoat pocket, the end emerging, and goes with all the speed he can muster backstage into darkness. Ten seconds. Loud pop of cork. Fifteen seconds. He comes back into light carrying an old ledger and sits down at table. He lays ledger on table, wipes his mouth, wipes his hands on the front of his waistcoat, brings them smartly together and rubs them.

KRAPP.   (*Briskly.*) Ah! (*He bends over ledger, turns the pages, finds the entry he wants, reads.*) Box … thrree … spool … five. (*He raises his head and stares front. With relish.*) Spool! (*Pause.*) Spooool! (*Happy smile. Pause. He bends over table, starts peering and poking at the boxes.*) Box … thrree … thrree …

four ... two ... (*with surprise*) nine! good God! ... seven ... ah! the little   5
rascal! (*He takes up box, peers at it.*) Box thrree. (*He lays it on table, opens it
and peers at spools inside.*) Spool ... (*he peers at ledger*) ... five ... (*he peers
at spools*) ... five ... five ... ah! the little scoundrel! (*He takes out a spool,
peers at it.*) Spool five. (*He lays it on table, closes box three, puts it back with
the others, takes up the spool.*) Box thrree, spool five. (*He bends over the ma-*   10
chine, looks up. With relish.) Spooool! (*Happy smile. He bends, loads spool on
machine, rubs his hands.*) Ah! (*He peers at ledger, reads entry at foot of page.*)
Mother at rest at last ... Hm ... The black ball ... (*He raises his head, stares
blankly front. Puzzled.*) Black ball? ... (*He peers again at ledger, reads.*) The
dark nurse ... (*He raises his head, broods, peers again at ledger, reads.*) Slight   15
improvement in bowel condition ... Hm ... Memorable ... what? (*He
peers closer.*) Equinox, memorable equinox. (*He raises his head, stares blankly
front. Puzzled.*) Memorable equinox? ... (*Pause. He shrugs his shoulders,
peers again at ledger, reads.*) Farewell to—(*he turns the page*)—love.

> (*He raises his head, broods, bends over machine, switches on and assumes
> listening posture, i.e., leaning forward, elbows on table, hand cupping ear
> towards machine, face front.*)

TAPE. (*Strong voice, rather pompous, clearly Krapp's at a much earlier time.*)   20
Thirty-nine today, sound as a—(*Settling himself more comfortably he knocks
one of the boxes off the table, curses, switches off, sweeps boxes and ledger
violently to the ground, winds tape back to beginning, switches on, resumes
posture.*) Thirty-nine today, sound as a bell, apart from my old weakness,
and intellectually I have now every reason to suspect at the ... (*hesitates*)   25
... crest of the wave—or thereabouts. Celebrated the awful occasion, as
in recent years, quietly at the Winehouse. Not a soul. Sat before the fire
with closed eyes, separating the grain from the husks. Jotted down a few
notes, on the back of an envelope. Good to be back in my den, in my
old rags. Have just eaten I regret to say three bananas and only with dif-   30
ficulty refrained from a fourth. Fatal things for a man with my condition.
(*Vehemently.*) Cut 'em out! (*Pause.*) The new light above my table is a great
improvement. With all this darkness round me I feel less alone. (*Pause.*) In
a way. (*Pause.*) I love to get up and move about in it, then back here to ...
(*hesitates*) ... me. (*Pause.*) Krapp.   35

> (*Pause.*)

The grain, now what I wonder do I mean by that, I mean ... (*hesitates*) ...
I suppose I mean those things worth having when all the dust has—when
all *my* dust has settled. I close my eyes and try and imagine them.

> (*Pause. Krapp closes his eyes briefly.*)

40 Extraordinary silence this evening, I strain my ears and do not hear a sound. Old Miss McGlome always sings at this hour. But not tonight. Songs of her girlhood, she says. Hard to think of her as a girl. Wonderful woman though. Connaught,[1] I fancy. (*Pause.*) Shall I sing when I am her age, if I ever am? No. (*Pause.*) Did I sing as a boy? No. (*Pause.*) Did I ever sing? No.

(*Pause.*)

45 Just been listening to an old year, passages at random. I did not check in the book, but it must be at least ten or twelve years ago. At that time I think I was still living on and off with Bianca in Kedar Street. Well out of that, Jesus yes! Hopeless business. (*Pause.*) Not much about her, apart from a tribute to her eyes. Very warm. I suddenly saw them again. (*Pause.*)
50 Incomparable! (*Pause.*) Ah well ... (*Pause.*) These old P.M.s are gruesome, but I often find them—(*Krapp switches off, broods, switches on.*)—a help before embarking on a new ... (*hesitates*) ... retrospect. Hard to believe I was ever that young whelp. The voice! Jesus! And the aspirations! (*Brief laugh in which Krapp joins.*) And the resolutions! (*Brief laugh in which*
55 *Krapp joins.*) To drink less, in particular. (*Brief laugh of Krapp alone.*) Statistics. Seventeen hundred hours, out of the preceding eight thousand odd, consumed on licensed premises alone. More than 20%, say 40% of his waking life. (*Pause.*) Plans for a less ... (*hesitates*) ... engrossing sexual life. Last illness of his father. Flagging pursuit of happiness. Unattainable
60 laxation.[2] Sneers at what he calls his youth and thanks to God that it's over. (*Pause.*) False ring there. (*Pause.*) Shadows of the opus ... magnum. Closing with a—(*brief laugh*)—yelp to Providence. (*Prolonged laugh in which Krapp joins.*) What remains of all that misery? A girl in a shabby green coat, on a railway-station platform? No?

(*Pause.*)

65 When I look—

(*Krapp switches off, broods, looks at his watch, gets up, goes backstage into darkness. Ten seconds. Pop of cork. Ten seconds. Second cork. Ten seconds. Third cork. Ten seconds. Brief burst of quavering song.*)

KRAPP. (*Sings.*)   Now the day is over,
    Night is drawing nigh-igh,
    Shadows—[3]

---

1   *Connaught* Western province of Ireland.
2   *laxation* Relaxed state; also defecation.
3   *Now ... Shadows* From an old hymn, words by Sabine Baring-Gould (1865).

(*Fit of coughing. He comes back into light, sits down, wipes his mouth, switches on, resumes his listening posture.*)

TAPE. —back on the year that is gone, with what I hope is perhaps a glint of 70 the old eye to come, there is of course the house on the canal where mother lay a-dying, in the late autumn, after her long viduity (*Krapp gives a start*), and the—(*Krapp switches off, winds back tape a little, bends his ear closer to machine, switches on*)—a-dying, after her long viduity, and the—

(*Krapp switches off, raises his head, stares blankly before him. His lips move in the syllables of "viduity." No sound. He gets up, goes backstage into darkness, comes back with an enormous dictionary, lays it on table, sits down and looks up the word.*)

KRAPP. (*Reading from dictionary.*) State—or condition of being—or remain- 75 ing—a widow—or widower. (*Looks up. Puzzled.*) Being—or remaining? ... (*Pause. He peers again at dictionary. Reading.*) "Deep weeds of viduity" ... Also of an animal, especially a bird ... the vidua or weaver-bird ... Black plumage of male ... (*He looks up. With relish.*) The vidua-bird!

(*Pause. He closes dictionary, switches on, resumes listening posture.*)

TAPE. —bench by the weir from where I could see her window. There I sat, 80 in the biting wind, wishing she were gone. (*Pause.*) Hardly a soul, just a few regulars, nursemaids, infants, old men, dogs. I got to know them quite well—oh by appearance of course I mean! One dark young beauty I recollect particularly, all white and starch, incomparable bosom, with a big black hooded perambulator, most funereal thing. Whenever I looked 85 in her direction she had her eyes on me. And yet when I was bold enough to speak to her—not having been introduced—she threatened to call a po- liceman. As if I had designs on her virtue! (*Laugh. Pause.*) The face she had! The eyes! Like ... (*hesitates*) ... chrysolite![1] (*Pause.*) Ah well ... (*Pause.*) I was there when—(*Krapp switches off, broods, switches on again*)—the blind 90 went down, one of those dirty brown roller affairs, throwing a ball for a little white dog, as chance would have it. I happened to look up and there it was. All over and done with, at last. I sat on for a few moments with the ball in my hand and the dog yelping and pawing at me. (*Pause.*) Mo- ments. Her moments, my moments. (*Pause.*) The dog's moments. (*Pause.*) 95 In the end I held it out to him and he took it in his mouth, gently, gently. A small, old, black, hard, solid rubber ball. (*Pause.*) I shall feel it, in my hand, until my dying day. (*Pause.*) I might have kept it. (*Pause.*) But I gave it to the dog.

---

1   *chrysolite* Green gem.

(*Pause.*)

100   Ah well …

(*Pause.*)

Spiritually a year of profound gloom and indigence until that memorable night in March, at the end of the jetty, in the howling wind, never to be forgotten, when suddenly I saw the whole thing. The vision, at last. This I fancy is what I have chiefly to record this evening, against the day when
105   my work will be done and perhaps no place left in my memory, warm or cold, for the miracle that … (*hesitates*) … for the fire that set it alight. What I suddenly saw then was this, that the belief I had been going on all my life, namely—(*Krapp switches off impatiently, winds tape forward, switches on again*)—great granite rocks the foam flying up in the light of
110   the lighthouse and the wind-gauge spinning like a propeller, clear to me at last that the dark I have always struggled to keep under is in reality my most—(*Krapp curses, switches off, winds tape forward, switches on again*)— unshatterable association until my dissolution of storm and night with the light of the understanding and the fire—(*Krapp curses louder, switches*
115   *off, winds tape forward, switches on again*)—my face in her breasts and my hand on her. We lay there without moving. But under us all moved, and moved us, gently, up and down, and from side to side.

(*Pause.*)

Past midnight. Never knew such silence. The earth might be uninhabited.

(*Pause.*)

Here I end—

(*Krapp switches off, winds tape back, switches on again.*)

120   —upper lake, with the punt,[1] bathed off the bank, then pushed out into the stream and drifted. She lay stretched out on the floorboards with her hands under her head and her eyes closed. Sun blazing down, bit of a breeze, water nice and lively. I noticed a scratch on her thigh and asked her how she came by it. Picking gooseberries, she said. I said again I thought
125   it was hopeless and no good going on, and she agreed, without opening her eyes. (*Pause.*) I asked her to look at me and after a few moments— (*Pause.*)—after a few moments she did, but the eyes just slits, because of the glare. I bent over her to get them in the shadow and they opened.

---

1   *punt* Shallow, flat-bottomed boat.

(*Pause. Low.*) Let me in. (*Pause.*) We drifted in among the flags[1] and stuck. The way they went down, sighing, before the stem! (*Pause.*) I lay down across her with my face in her breasts and my hand on her. We lay there without moving. But under us all moved, and moved us, gently, up and down, and from side to side. 130

(*Pause.*)

Past midnight. Never knew—

(*Krapp switches off, broods. Finally he fumbles in his pockets, encounters the banana, takes it out, peers at it, puts it back, fumbles, brings out the envelope, fumbles, puts back envelope, looks at his watch, gets up and goes backstage into darkness. Ten seconds. Sound of bottle against glass, then brief siphon. Ten seconds. Bottle against glass alone. Ten seconds. He comes back a little unsteadily into light, goes to front of table, takes out keys, raises them to his eyes, chooses key, unlocks first drawer, peers into it, feels about inside, takes out reel, peers at it, locks drawer, puts keys back in his pocket, goes and sits down, takes reel off machine, lays it on dictionary, loads virgin reel on machine, takes envelope from his pocket, consults back of it, lays it on table, switches on, clears his throat and begins to record.*)

KRAPP. Just been listening to that stupid bastard I took myself for thirty 135 years ago, hard to believe I was ever as bad as that. Thank God that's all done with anyway. (*Pause.*) The eyes she had! (*Broods, realizes he is recording silence, switches off, broods. Finally.*) Everything there, everything, all the—(*Realizes this is not being recorded, switches on.*) Everything there, everything on this old muckball, all the light and dark and famine and feast- 140 ing of ... (*hesitates*) ... the ages! (*In a shout.*) Yes! (*Pause.*) Let that go! Jesus! Take his mind off his homework! Jesus! (*Pause. Weary.*) Ah well, maybe he was right. (*Pause.*) Maybe he was right. (*Broods. Realizes. Switches off. Consults envelope.*) Pah! (*Crumples it and throws it away. Broods. Switches on.*) Nothing to say, not a squeak. What's a year now? The sour cud and 145 the iron stool. (*Pause.*) Revelled in the word spool. (*With relish.*) Spoool! Happiest moment of the past half million. (*Pause.*) Seventeen copies sold, of which eleven at trade price to free circulating libraries beyond the seas. Getting known. (*Pause.*) One pound six and something, eight I have little doubt. (*Pause.*) Crawled out once or twice, before the summer was cold. 150 Sat shivering in the park, drowned in dreams and burning to be gone. Not a soul. (*Pause.*) Last fancies. (*Vehemently.*) Keep 'em under! (*Pause.*) Scalded

1   *flags* Irises.

the eyes out of me reading *Effie*[1] again, a page a day, with tears again. Effie … (*Pause.*) Could have been happy with her, up there on the Baltic,
155 and the pines, and the dunes. (*Pause.*) Could I? (*Pause.*) And she? (*Pause.*)
Pah! (*Pause.*) Fanny came in a couple of times. Bony old ghost of a whore.
Couldn't do much, but I suppose better than a kick in the crutch. The last
time wasn't so bad. How do you manage it, she said, at your age? I told her
I'd been saving up for her all my life. (*Pause.*) Went to Vespers[2] once, like
160 when I was in short trousers. (*Pause. Sings.*)

> Now the day is over,
> Night is drawing nigh-igh,
> Shadows—(*coughing, then almost inaudible*)—of the evening
> Steal across the sky.

165 (*Gasping.*) Went to sleep and fell off the pew. (*Pause.*) Sometimes wondered in the night if a last effort mightn't—(*Pause.*) Ah finish your booze
now and get to your bed. Go on with this drivel in the morning. Or leave
it at that. (*Pause.*) Leave it at that. (*Pause.*) Lie propped up in the dark—
and wander. Be again in the dingle[3] on a Christmas Eve, gathering holly,
170 the red-berried. (*Pause.*) Be again on Croghan[4] on a Sunday morning, in
the haze, with the bitch, stop and listen to the bells. (*Pause.*) And so on.
(*Pause.*) Be again, be again. (*Pause.*) All that old misery. (*Pause.*) Once
wasn't enough for you. (*Pause.*) Lie down across her.

(*Long pause. He suddenly bends over machine, switches off, wrenches off
tape, throws it away, puts on the other, winds it forward to the passage he
wants, switches on, listens staring front.*)

TAPE. —gooseberries, she said. I said again I thought it was hopeless and no
175 good going on, and she agreed, without opening her eyes. (*Pause.*) I asked
her to look at me and after a few moments—(*Pause.*)—after a few moments she did, but the eyes just slits, because of the glare. I bent over her to
get them in the shadow and they opened. (*Pause. Low.*) Let me in. (*Pause.*)
We drifted in among the flags and stuck. The way they went down, sigh-
180 ing, before the stem! (*Pause.*) I lay down across her with my face in her
breasts and my hand on her. We lay there without moving. But under us
all moved, and moved us, gently, up and down, and from side to side.

(*Pause. Krapp's lips move. No sound.*)

---

1   *Effie* The novel *Effi Briest* (1895), a sentimental work by Theodor Fontane about a
failed love affair.
2   *Vespers* Evening prayer service.
3   *dingle* Valley.
4   *Croghan* Croghan Hill in County Wicklow, Ireland.

Past midnight. Never knew such silence. The earth might be uninhabited.

(*Pause.*)

Here I end this reel. Box—(*Pause.*)—three, spool—(*Pause.*)—five. (*Pause.*) Perhaps my best years are gone. When there was a chance of happiness. But I wouldn't want them back. Not with the fire in me now. No, I wouldn't want them back. 185

(*Krapp motionless staring before him. The tape runs on in silence.*)

CURTAIN

—1958

Tennessee Williams

1911–1983

Tennessee Williams helped define American postwar theatre, bringing 18 plays to Broadway and winning the Pulitzer Prize twice—for *A Streetcar Named Desire* (1947) and *Cat on a Hot Tin Roof* (1955). He is best known for memorable characters who, in his words, are often "trapped by circumstance"; for dialogue that combines realism with poetic sensitivity; and for his explicit treatment of sexuality and violence. In response to audiences that were shocked by the content of his plays, he said, "I don't think that anything that occurs in life should be omitted from art, though the artist should present it in a fashion that is artistic and not ugly."

Williams was born Thomas Lanier Williams III in Columbus, Mississippi; his father was a travelling salesman and his mother was the daughter of an Episcopal minister. He had a troubled family life and would find inspiration for his plays in his parents' unstable marriage, as well as in the mental illness of his beloved sister Rose, who was lobotomized in 1943.

Williams had already produced some plays as a student at the University of Iowa when *The Glass Menagerie* (1944), a veiled autobiographical drama, propelled him out of obscurity into sudden fame. His reputation grew with *A Streetcar Named Desire*, the 1951 film version of which won four Academy Awards. Williams's next major success, *Cat on a Hot Tin Roof*, was also transformed into a successful film (1958).

After his partner Frank Merlo died of cancer in 1963, Williams's use of drugs and alcohol became a serious problem, and his work from the last two decades of his life was not as popular or critically acclaimed as his previous work. It is primarily on the strength of his earlier plays that he is considered one of the most important writers in the history of American theatre.

Cat on a Hot Tin Roof

CHARACTERS

Margaret
Brick
Mae, *sometimes called*
    Sister Woman
Big Mama
Dixie, *a little girl*
Big Daddy

Reverend Tooker
Gooper, *sometimes called*
    Brother Man
Doctor Baugh, *pronounced "Baw"*
Lacey, *a Negro servant*
Sookey, *another*
Children

NOTES FOR THE DESIGNER

The set is the bed-sitting-room of a plantation home in the Mississippi Delta.[1] It is along an upstairs gallery which probably runs around the entire house; it has two pairs of very wide doors opening onto the gallery, showing white balustrades against a fair summer sky that fades into dusk and night during the course of the play, which occupies precisely the time of its performance, excepting, of course, the fifteen minutes of intermission.

Perhaps the style of the room is not what you would expect in the home of the Delta's biggest cotton-planter. It is Victorian with a touch of the Far East. It hasn't changed much since it was occupied by the original owners of the place, Jack Straw and Peter Ochello, a pair of old bachelors who shared this room all their lives together. In other words, the room must evoke some ghosts; it is gently and poetically haunted by a relationship that must have involved a tenderness which was uncommon. This may be irrelevant or unnecessary, but I once saw a reproduction of a faded photograph of the verandah of Robert Louis Stevenson's home on that Samoan Island[2] where he spent his last years, and there was a quality of tender light on weathered wood, such as porch furniture made of bamboo and wicker, exposed to tropical suns and tropical rains, which came to mind when I thought about the set for this play, bringing also to mind the grace and comfort of light, the reassurance it gives, on a late and fair afternoon in summer, the way that no matter what, even dread of death, is gently touched and soothed by it. For the set is the background for a play that deals with human extremities of emotion, and it needs that softness behind it.

The bathroom door, showing only pale-blue tile and silver towel racks, is in one side wall; the hall door in the opposite wall. Two articles of furniture need mention: a big double bed which staging should make a functional part of the set as often as suitable, the surface of which should be slightly raked to make figures on it seen more easily; and against the wall space between the two huge double doors upstage: a monumental monstrosity peculiar to our times, a huge console combination of radio-phonograph (hi-fi with three speakers) TV set and liquor cabinet, bearing and containing many glasses and bottles, all in one piece, which is a composition of muted silver tones, and the opalescent tones of reflecting glass, a chromatic link, this thing, between the sepia (tawny gold) tones of the interior and the cool (white and blue) tones of the gallery and sky. This piece of furniture (?!), this monument, is a very complete and

---

1   *Mississippi Delta* Area in the state of Mississippi between the Mississippi and Yazoo rivers.
2   *Robert ... Island* Scottish novelist and poet Robert Louis Stevenson (1850–94) lived on the Samoan island Upolu during the final years of his life.

compact little shrine to virtually all the comforts and illusions behind which we hide from such things as the characters in the play are faced with ...

The set should be far less realistic than I have so far implied in this description of it. I think the walls below the ceiling should dissolve mysteriously into air; the set should be roofed by the sky; stars and moon suggested by traces of milky pallor, as if they were observed through a telescope lens out of focus. Anything else I can think of? Oh, yes, fanlights (transoms shaped like an open glass fan) above all the doors in the set, with panes of blue and amber, and above all, the designer should take as many pains to give the actors room to move about freely (to show their restlessness, their passion for breaking out) as if it were a set for a ballet.

An evening in summer. The action is continuous, with two intermissions.

ACT 1

At the rise of the curtain someone is taking a shower in the bathroom, the door of which is half open. A pretty young woman, with anxious lines in her face, enters the bedroom and crosses to the bathroom door.

MARGARET. (*shouting above roar of water*) One of those no-neck monsters hit me with a hot buttered biscuit so I have t' change!

(*Margaret's voice is both rapid and drawling. In her long speeches she has the vocal tricks of a priest delivering a liturgical chant,*[1] *the lines are almost sung, always continuing a little beyond her breath so she has to gasp for another. Sometimes she intersperses the lines with a little wordless singing, such as "Da-da-daaaa!"*

Water turns off and Brick calls out to her, but is still unseen. A tone of politely feigned interest, masking indifference, or worse, is characteristic of his speech with Margaret.)

BRICK. Wha'd you say, Maggie? Water was on s' loud I couldn't hearya....
MARGARET. Well, I!—just remarked that!—one of th' no-neck monsters
5   messed up m' lovely lace dress so I got t'—cha-a-ange....

(*She opens and kicks shut drawers of the dresser.*)

BRICK. Why d'ya call Gooper's kiddies no-neck monsters?
MARGARET. Because they've got no necks! Isn't that a good enough reason?
BRICK. Don't they have any necks?

---

1   *liturgical chant* Song or spoken passage recited during religious ceremonies.

MARGARET. None visible. Their fat little heads are set on their fat little bodies   10
    without a bit of connection.

BRICK. That's too bad.

MARGARET. Yes, it's too bad because you can't wring their necks if they've got
    no necks to wring! Isn't that right, honey?

(*She steps out of her dress, stands in a slip of ivory satin and lace.*)

Yep, they're no-neck monsters, all no-neck people are monsters ...

(*Children shriek downstairs.*)

Hear them? Hear them screaming? I don't know where their voice boxes   15
are located since they don't have necks. I tell you I got so nervous at that
table tonight I thought I would throw back my head and utter a scream
you could hear across the Arkansas border an' parts of Louisiana an' Tennessee. I said to your charming sister-in-law, Mae, honey, couldn't you feed
those precious little things at a separate table with an oilcloth[1] cover? They   20
make such a mess an' the lace cloth looks so pretty! She made enormous
eyes at me and said, "Ohhh, noooooo! On Big Daddy's birthday? Why,
he would never forgive me!" Well, I want you to know, Big Daddy hadn't
been at the table two minutes with those five no-neck monsters slobbering
and drooling over their food before he threw down his fork an' shouted,   25
"Fo' God's sake, Gooper, why don't you put them pigs at a trough in th'
kitchen?"—Well, I swear, I simply could have di-ieed!

   Think of it, Brick, they've got five of them and number six is coming.
They've brought the whole bunch down here like animals to display at a
county fair. Why, they have those children doin' tricks all the time! "Junior,   30
show Big Daddy how you do this, show Big Daddy how you do that, say
your little piece fo' Big Daddy, Sister. Show your dimples, Sugar. Brother,
show Big Daddy how you stand on your head!"—It goes on all the time,
along with constant little remarks and innuendos about the fact that you
and I have not produced any children, are totally childless and therefore   35
totally useless!—Of course it's comical but it's also disgusting since it's so
obvious what they're up to!

BRICK. (*without interest*) What are they up to, Maggie?

MARGARET. Why, you know what they're up to!

BRICK. (*appearing*) No, I don't know what they're up to.   40

(*He stands there in the bathroom doorway drying his hair with a towel
and hanging onto the towel rack because one ankle is broken, plastered
and bound. He is still slim and firm as a boy. His liquor hasn't started*

---

1   *oilcloth* Fabric treated with oil to increase water resistance.

tearing him down outside. He has the additional charm of that cool air of detachment that people have who have given up the struggle. But now and then, when disturbed, something flashes behind it, like lightning in a fair sky, which shows that at some deeper level he is far from peaceful. Perhaps in a stronger light he would show some signs of deliquescence, but the fading, still warm, light from the gallery treats him gently.)

MARGARET. I'll tell you what they're up to, boy of mine!—They're up to cutting you out of your father's estate, and—

(*She freezes momentarily before her next remark. Her voice drops as if it were somehow a personally embarrassing admission.*)

—Now we know that Big Daddy's dyin' of—cancer....

(*There are voices on the lawn below: long-drawn calls across distance. Margaret raises her lovely bare arms and powders her armpits with a light sigh. She adjusts the angle of a magnifying mirror to straighten an eyelash, then rises fretfully saying:*)

There's so much light in the room it—

45 BRICK. (*softly but sharply*) Do we?
MARGARET. Do we what?
BRICK. Know Big Daddy's dyin' of cancer?
MARGARET. Got the report today.
BRICK. Oh ...
50 MARGARET. (*letting down bamboo blinds which cast long, gold-fretted shadows over the room*) Yep, got th' report just now ... it didn't surprise me, Baby....

(*Her voice has range, and music; sometimes it drops low as a boy's and you have a sudden image of her playing boy's games as a child.*)

I recognized the symptoms soon's we got here last spring and I'm willin' to bet you that Brother Man and his wife were pretty sure of it, too. That more than likely explains why their usual summer migration to the coolness of the Great Smokies[1] was passed up this summer in favour of—hustlin' down here ev'ry whipstitch[2] with their whole screamin' tribe! And why so many allusions have been made to Rainbow Hill lately. You know what Rainbow Hill is? Place that's famous for treatin' alcoholics an dope fiends in the movies!
60 BRICK. I'm not in the movies.

---

1   *Great Smokies* Mountain range in the southeastern United States.
2   *ev'ry whipstitch* I.e., every moment.

MARGARET. No, and you don't take dope. Otherwise you're a perfect candidate for Rainbow Hill, Baby, and that's where they aim to ship you—over my dead body! Yep, over my dead body they'll ship you there, but nothing would please them better. Then Brother Man could get a-hold of the purse strings and dole out remittances[1] to us, maybe get power of attorney and sign checks for us and cut off our credit wherever, whenever he wanted! Son-of-a-bitch!—How'd you like that, Baby?—Well, you've been doin' just about ev'rything in your power to bring it about, you've just been doin' ev'rything you can think of to aid and abet them in this scheme of theirs! Quittin' work, devoting yourself to the occupation of drinkin'!—Breakin' your ankle last night on the high school athletic field: doin' what? Jumpin' hurdles? At two or three in the morning? Just fantastic! Got in the paper. Clarksdale Register carried a nice little item about it, human interest story about a well-known former athlete stagin' a one-man track meet on the Glorious Hill High School athletic field last night, but was slightly out of condition and didn't clear the first hurdle! Brother Man Gooper claims he exercised his influence t' keep it from goin' out over AP or UP[2] or every goddam "P."

But, Brick? You still have one big advantage! 65 70 75

(*During the above swift flood of words, Brick has reclined with contrapuntal[3] leisure on the snowy surface of the bed and has rolled over carefully on his side or belly.*)

BRICK. (*wryly*) Did you say something, Maggie? 80

MARGARET. Big Daddy dotes on you, honey. And he can't stand Brother Man and Brother Man's wife, that monster of fertility, Mae. Know how I know? By little expressions that flicker over his face when that woman is holding fo'th on one of her choice topics such as—how she refused twilight sleep![4]—when the twins were delivered! Because she feels motherhood's an experience that a woman ought to experience fully!—in order to fully appreciate the wonder and beauty of it! HAH!—and how she made Brother Man come in an' stand beside her in the delivery room so he would not miss out on the "wonder and beauty" of it either!—producin' those no-neck monsters.... 85 90

---

1   *remittances* Monetary allowances.
2   *AP or UP* Associated Press or United Press International, large American news agencies.
3   *contrapuntal* I.e., in contrast or counterpoint to her energy.
4   *twilight sleep* Semi-anaesthetized state induced with the injection of scopolamine and morphine. These drugs were administered to women to prevent pain during childbirth.

(*A speech of this kind would be antipathetic from almost anybody but Margaret; she makes it oddly funny, because her eyes constantly twinkle and her voice shakes with laughter which is basically indulgent.*)

—Big Daddy shares my attitude toward those two! As for me, well—I give him a laugh now and then and he tolerates me. In fact!—I sometimes suspect that Big Daddy harbours a little unconscious "lech" fo' me....

BRICK. What makes you think that Big Daddy has a lech for you, Maggie?

95 MARGARET. Way he always drops his eyes down my body when I'm talkin' to him, drops his eyes to my boobs an' licks his old chops! Ha ha!

BRICK. That kind of talk is disgusting.

MARGARET. Did anyone ever tell you that you're an ass-aching Puritan,[1] Brick?

100 I think it's mighty fine that that ole fellow, on the doorstep of death, still takes in my shape with what I think is deserved appreciation!

And you wanta know something else? Big Daddy didn't know how many little Maes and Goopers had been produced! "How many kids have you got?" he asked at the table, just like Brother Man and his wife were

105 new acquaintances to him! Big Mama said he was jokin', but that ole boy wasn't jokin', Lord, no!

And when they infawmed him that they had five already and were turning out number six!—the news seemed to come as a sort of unpleasant surprise ...

(*Children yell below.*)

110 Scream, monsters!

(*Turns to Brick with a sudden, gay, charming smile which fades as she notices that he is not looking at her but into fading gold space with a troubled expression. It is constant rejection that makes her humour "bitchy."*)

Yes, you should of been at that supper-table, Baby.

(*Whenever she calls him "baby" the word is a soft caress.*)

Y'know, Big Daddy, bless his ole sweet soul, he's the dearest ole thing in the world, but he does hunch over his food as if he preferred not to notice anything else. Well, Mae an' Gooper were side by side at the table, direckly

115 across from Big Daddy, watchin' his face like hawks while they jawed an' jabbered about the cuteness an' brilliance of th' no-neck monsters!

---

1 *Puritan* I.e., morally uptight person. Puritanism was a sixteenth- and seventeenth-century branch of Christianity known for its severe beliefs surrounding morality, luxury, and self-indulgence.

(She giggles with a hand fluttering at her throat and her breast and her long throat arched. She comes downstage and recreates the scene with voice and gesture.)

And the no-neck monsters were ranged around the table, some in high chairs and some on th' Books of Knowledge,[1] all in fancy little paper caps in honor of Big Daddy's birthday, and all through dinner, well, I want you to know that Brother Man an' his partner never once, for one moment, stopped exchanging pokes an' pinches an' kicks an' signs an' signals!— 120 Why, they were like a couple of cardsharps[2] fleecing a sucker.—Even Big Mama, bless her ole sweet soul, she isn't th' quickest an' brightest thing in the world, she finally noticed, at last, an' said to Gooper, "Gooper, what are you an' Mae makin' all these signs at each other about?"—I swear t' goodness, I nearly choked on my chicken!   125

(Margaret, back at the dressing table, still doesn't see Brick. He is watching her with a look that is not quite definable—Amused? shocked? contemptuous?—part of those and part of something else.)

Y'know—your brother Gooper still cherishes the illusion he took a giant step up on the social ladder when he married Miss Mae Flynn of the Memphis Flynns.

But I have a piece of Spanish news[3] for Gooper. The Flynns never had a thing in this world but money and they lost that, they were nothing at 130 all but fairly successful climbers. Of course, Mae Flynn came out in Memphis eight years before I made my debut in Nashville, but I had friends at Ward-Belmont[4] who came from Memphis and they used to come to see me and I used to go to see them for Christmas and spring vacations, and so I know who rates an' who doesn't rate in Memphis society. Why, y'know 135 ole Papa Flynn, he barely escaped doing time in the Federal pen for shady manipulations on th' stock market when his chain stores crashed, and as for Mae having been a cotton carnival queen,[5] as they remind us so often, lest we forget, well, that's one honour that I don't envy her for!—Sit on a brass throne on a tacky float an' ride down Main Street, smilin', bowin', 140 and blowin' kisses to all the trash on the street—

1   *Books of Knowledge* Volumes of *The Book of Knowledge*, a well-known general knowledge encyclopedia.
2   *cardsharps* Players who cheat or hide their superior skill to win at card games.
3   *Spanish news* I.e., bad news.
4   *debut* Extravagant dance held to mark an upper-class girl's coming-of-age; *Ward-Belmont* Ward-Belmont College, a former woman's college in Nashville, Tennessee.
5   *cotton carnival queen* College girl chosen as "queen" for the annual Carnival Memphis, formerly known as the Memphis Cotton Carnival.

(She picks out a pair of jewelled sandals and rushes to the dressing table.)

Why, year before last, when Susan McPheeters was singled out fo' that
honour, y' know what happened to her? Y'know what happened to poor
little Susie McPheeters?

BRICK. *(absently)* No. What happened to little Susie McPheeters?

145 MARGARET. Somebody spit tobacco juice in her face.

BRICK. *(dreamily)* Somebody spit tobacco juice in her face?

MARGARET. That's right, some old drunk leaned out of a window in the
Hotel Gayoso[1] and yelled, "Hey, Queen, hey, hey, there, Queenie!" Poor
Susie looked up and flashed him a radiant smile and he shot out a squirt of
150 tobacco juice right in poor Susie's face.

BRICK. Well, what d'you know about that.

MARGARET. *(gaily)* What do I know about it? I was there, I saw it!

BRICK. *(absently)* Must have been kind of funny.

MARGARET. Susie didn't think so. Had hysterics. Screamed like a banshee.
155 They had to stop th' parade an' remove her from her throne an' go on
with—

*(She catches sight of him in the mirror, gasps slightly, wheels about to face
him. Count ten.)*

—Why are you looking at me like that?

BRICK. *(whistling softly, now)* Like what, Maggie?

MARGARET. *(intensely, fearfully)* The way y' were lookin' at me just now, befo'
160 I caught your eye in the mirror and you started t' whistle! I don't know
how t' describe it but it froze my blood!—I've caught you lookin' at me
like that so often lately. What are you thinkin' of when you look at me like
that?

BRICK. I wasn't conscious of lookin' at you, Maggie.

165 MARGARET. Well, I was conscious of it! What were you thinkin'?

BRICK. I don't remember thinking of anything, Maggie.

MARGARET. Don't you think I know that—? Don't you—?—Think I know
that—?

BRICK. *(coolly)* Know what, Maggie?

170 MARGARET. *(struggling for expression)* That I've gone through this—hideous!—transformation, become—hard! Frantic!

(Then she adds, almost tenderly:)

—cruel!!

---

1   *Hotel Gayoso* Historic hotel in Memphis, Tennessee.

That's what you've been observing in me lately. How could y' help but observe it? That's all right. I'm not—thin-skinned any more, can't afford t' be thin-skinned any more.   175

(*She is now recovering her power.*)

—But Brick? Brick?

BRICK. Did you say something?

MARGARET. I was *goin'* t' say something: that I get—lonely. Very!

BRICK. Ev'rybody gets that ...

MARGARET. Living with someone you love can be lonelier—than living en-   180
tirely alone!—if the one that y'love doesn't love you ....

(*There is a pause. Brick hobbles downstage and asks, without looking at her:*)

BRICK. Would you like to live alone, Maggie?

(*Another pause: then—after she has caught a quick, hurt breath:*)

MARGARET. *No!—God!—God!—I wouldn't!*

(*Another gasping breath. She forcibly controls what must have been an impulse to cry out. We see her deliberately, very forcibly, going all the way back to the world in which you can talk about ordinary matters.*)

Did you have a nice shower?

BRICK. Uh-huh.   185

MARGARET. Was the water cool?

BRICK. No.

MARGARET. But it made y' feel fresh, huh?

BRICK. Fresher ...

MARGARET. I know something would make y' feel *much* fresher!   190

BRICK. What?

MARGARET. An alcohol rub. Or cologne, a rub with cologne!

BRICK. That's good after a workout but I haven't been workin' out, Maggie.

MARGARET. You've kept in good shape, though.

BRICK. (*indifferently*) You think so, Maggie?   195

MARGARET. I always thought drinkin' men lost their looks, but I was plainly mistaken.

BRICK. (*wryly*) Why, thanks, Maggie.

MARGARET. You're the only drinkin' man I know that it never seems t' put fat on.   200

BRICK. I'm gettin' softer, Maggie.

MARGARET. Well, sooner or later it's bound to soften you up. It was just beginning to soften up Skipper when—

(*She stops short.*)

205 I'm sorry. I never could keep my fingers off a sore—I wish you *would* lose your looks. If you did it would make the martyrdom of Saint Maggie a little more bearable. But no such goddam luck. I actually believe you've gotten better looking since you've gone on the bottle. Yeah, a person who didn't know you would think you'd never had a tense nerve in your body or a strained muscle.

(*There are sounds of croquet*[1] *on the lawn below: the click of mallets, light voices, near and distant.*)

210 Of course, you always had that detached quality as if you were playing a game without much concern over whether you won or lost, and now that you've lost the game, not lost but just quit playing, you have that rare sort of charm that usually only happens in very old or hopelessly sick people, the charm of the defeated.—You look so cool, so cool, so enviably cool.

215 REVEREND TOOKER. (*off stage right*) Now looka here, boy, lemme show you how to get outa that!

MARGARET. They're playing croquet. The moon has appeared and it's white, just beginning to turn a little bit yellow....

You were a wonderful lover....

220 Such a wonderful person to go to bed with, and I think mostly because you were really indifferent to it. Isn't that right? Never had any anxiety about it, did it naturally, easily, slowly, with absolute confidence and per- fect calm, more like opening a door for a lady or seating her at a table than giving expression to any longing for her. Your indifference made you

225 wonderful at lovemaking—*strange?*—but true....

REVEREND TOOKER. Oh! That's a beauty.

DOCTOR BAUGH. Yeah. I got you boxed.[2]

MARGARET. You know, if I thought you would never, never, *never*, make love to me again—I would go downstairs to the kitchen and pick out the

230 longest and sharpest knife I could find and stick it straight into my heart, I swear that I would!

REVEREND TOOKER. Watch out, you're gonna miss it.

DOCTOR BAUGH. You just don't know me, boy!

MARGARET. But one thing I don't have is the charm of the defeated, my hat

235 is still in the ring, and I am determined to win!

---

1   *croquet* Lawn game in which wooden mallets are used to knock wooden balls through a series of wickets.
2   *boxed* I.e., trapped.

(There is the sound of croquet mallets hitting croquet balls.)

REVEREND TOOKER. Mmm—You're too slippery for me.

MARGARET. —What is the victory of a cat on a hot tin roof?—I wish I knew....

Just staying on it, I guess, as long as she can....

DOCTOR BAUGH. Jus' like an eel, boy, jus' like an eel!   240

(More croquet sounds.)

MARGARET. Later tonight I'm going to tell you I love you an' maybe by that time you'll be drunk enough to believe me. Yes, they're playing croquet....

Big Daddy is dying of cancer....   245

What were you thinking of when I caught you looking at me like that? Were you thinking of Skipper?

(Brick takes up his crutch, rises.)

Oh, excuse me, forgive me, but laws of silence don't work! No, laws of silence don't work....

(Brick crosses to the bar, takes a quick drink, and rubs his head with a towel.)

Laws of silence don't work....   250

When something is festering in your memory or your imagination, laws of silence don't work, it's just like shutting a door and locking it on a house on fire in hope of forgetting that the house is burning. But not facing a fire doesn't put it out. Silence about a thing just magnifies it. It grows and festers in silence, becomes malignant....   255

(He drops his crutch.)

BRICK. Give me my crutch.

(He has stopped rubbing his hair dry but still stands hanging onto the towel rack in a white towel-cloth robe.)

MARGARET. Lean on me.

BRICK. No, just give me my crutch.

MARGARET. Lean on my shoulder.

BRICK. *I don't want to lean on your shoulder, I want my crutch!*   260

(This is spoken like sudden lightning.)

Are you going to give me my crutch or do I have to get down on my knees on the floor and—

MARGARET. *Here, here, take it, take it!*

(*She has thrust the crutch at him.*)

BRICK. (*hobbling out*) Thanks ...

265 MARGARET. We mustn't scream at each other, the walls in this house have ears....

(*He hobbles directly to liquor cabinet to get a new drink.*)

—but that's the first time I've heard you raise your voice in a long time,
270 Brick. A crack in the wall?—Of composure?
—I think that's a good sign....
A sign of nerves in a player on the defensive!

(*Brick turns and smiles at her coolly over his fresh drink.*)

BRICK. It just hasn't happened yet, Maggie.

MARGARET. What?

275 BRICK. The click I get in my head when I've had enough of this stuff to make me peaceful....
Will you do me a favour?

MARGARET. Maybe I will. What favour?

BRICK. Just, just keep your voice down!

280 MARGARET. (*in a hoarse whisper*) I'll do you that favour, I'll speak in a whisper, if not shut up completely, if *you* will do *me* a favour and make that drink your last one till after the party.

BRICK. What party?

MARGARET. Big Daddy's birthday party.

285 BRICK. Is this Big Daddy's birthday?

MARGARET. You know this is Big Daddy's birthday!

BRICK. No, I don't, I forgot it.

MARGARET. Well, I remembered it for you....

(*They are both speaking as breathlessly as a pair of kids after a fight, drawing deep exhausted breaths and looking at each other with faraway eyes, shaking and panting together as if they had broken apart from a violent struggle.*)

BRICK. Good for you, Maggie.

290 MARGARET. You just have to scribble a few lines on this card.

BRICK. You scribble something, Maggie.

MARGARET. It's got to be your handwriting; it's your present, I've given him my present; it's got to be your handwriting!

(*The tension between them is building again, the voices becoming shrill once more.*)

BRICK. I didn't get him a present.

MARGARET. I got one for you.   295

BRICK. All right. You write the card, then.

MARGARET. And have him know you didn't remember his birthday?

BRICK. I didn't remember his birthday.

MARGARET. You don't have to prove you didn't!

BRICK. I don't want to fool him about it.   300

MARGARET. Just write "Love, Brick!" for God's—

BRICK. No.

MARGARET. You've *got* to!

BRICK. I don't have to do anything I don't want to do. You keep forgetting the conditions on which I agreed to stay on living with you.   305

MARGARET. (*out before she knows it*) I'm not living with you. We occupy the same cage.

BRICK. You've got to remember the conditions agreed on.

SONNY. (*off stage*) Mommy, give it to me. I had it first.

MAE. Hush.   310

MARGARET. They're impossible conditions!

BRICK. Then why don't you—?

SONNY. I want it, I want it!

MAE. Get away!

MARGARET. HUSH! Who is out there? Is somebody at the door?   315

(*There are footsteps in hall.*)

MAE. (*outside*) May I enter a moment?

MARGARET. Oh, *you!* Sure. Come in, Mae.

(*Mae enters bearing aloft the bow of a young lady's archery set.*)

MAE. Brick, is this thing yours?

MARGARET. Why, Sister Woman—that's my Diana[1] Trophy. Won it at the intercollegiate archery contest on the Ole Miss campus.[2]   320

MAE. It's a mighty dangerous thing to leave exposed round a house full of nawmal rid-blooded children attracted t'weapons.

MARGARET. "Nawmal rid-blooded children attracted t'weapons" ought t'be taught to keep their hands off things that don't belong to them.

MAE. Maggie, honey, if you had children of your own you'd know how funny   325 that is. Will you please lock this up and put the key out of reach?

---

1   *Diana* In Roman mythology, the goddess of the hunt who is often depicted with a bow and arrows.

2   *Ole Miss* University of Mississippi.

MARGARET. Sister Woman, nobody is plotting the destruction of your kiddies.—Brick and I still have our special archers' licence. We're goin' deer-
huntin' on Moon Lake as soon as the season starts. I love to run with dogs
330   through chilly woods, run, run leap over obstructions—

(*She goes into the closet carrying the bow.*)

MAE. How's the injured ankle, Brick?

BRICK. Doesn't hurt. Just itches.

MAE. Oh, my! Brick—Brick, you should've been downstairs after supper!
Kiddies put on a show. Polly played the piano, Buster an' Sonny drums, an'
335   then they turned out the lights an' Dixie an' Trixie puhfawmed a toe dance
in fairy costume with *spahkluhs!* Big Daddy just beamed! He just beamed!

MARGARET. (*from the closet with a sharp laugh*) Oh, I bet. It breaks my heart
that we missed it!

(*She reenters.*)

But Mae? Why did y'give dawgs' names to all your kiddies?

340   MAE. *Dogs'* names?

MARGARET. (*sweetly*) Dixie, Trixie, Buster, Sonny, Polly!—Sounds like four
dogs and a parrot ...

MAE. Maggie?

(*Margaret turns with a smile.*)

Why are you so catty?

345   MARGARET. Cause I'm a cat! But why can't *you* take a joke, Sister Woman?

MAE. Nothin' pleases me more than a joke that's funny. You know the real
names of our kiddies. Buster's real name is Robert. Sonny's real name is
Saunders. Trixie's real name is Marlene and Dixie's—

(*Gooper downstairs calls for her.* "Hey, Mae! Sister Woman, intermission
is over!"—*She rushes to door, saying:*)

Intermission is over! See ya later!

350   MARGARET. I wonder what Dixie's real name is?

BRICK. Maggie, being catty doesn't help things any ...

MARGARET. I know! *WHY!*—Am I so catty?—Cause I'm consumed with envy
an' eaten up with longing?—Brick, I'm going to lay out your beautiful
Shantung silk[1] suit from Rome and one of your monogrammed silk shirts.
355   I'll put your cuff links in it, those lovely star sapphires I get you to wear
so rarely....

---

1   *Shantung silk* Silk originally from the province of Shandong in eastern China.

BRICK. I can't get trousers on over this plaster cast.

MARGARET. Yes, you can, I'll help you.

BRICK. I'm not going to get dressed, Maggie.

MARGARET. Will you just put on a pair of white silk pajamas? 360

BRICK. Yes, I'll do that, Maggie.

MARGARET. *Thank* you, thank you so *much!*

BRICK. Don't mention it.

MARGARET. *Oh, Brick!* How long does it have t' go on? This punishment? Haven't I done time enough, haven't I served my term, can't I apply for 365 a—pardon?

BRICK. Maggie, you're spoiling my liquor. Lately your voice always sounds like you'd been running upstairs to warn somebody that the house was on fire!

MARGARET. Well, no wonder, no wonder. Y'know what I feel like, Brick? 370

(*Children's and grown-ups' voices are blended, below, in a loud but uncertain rendition of "My Wild Irish Rose."*[1])

I feel all the time like a cat on a hot tin roof!

BRICK. Then jump off the roof, jump off it, cats can jump off roofs and land on their four feet uninjured.

MARGARET. Oh, yes!

BRICK. Do it!—fo' God's sake, do it ... 375

MARGARET. Do what?

BRICK. Take a lover!

MARGARET. I can't see a man but you! Even with my eyes closed, I just see you! Why don't you get ugly, Brick, why don't you please get fat or ugly or something so I could stand it? 380

(*She rushes to hall door, opens it, listens.*)

The concert is still going on. Bravo, no-necks, bravo!

(*She slams and locks door fiercely.*)

BRICK. What did you lock the door for?

MARGARET. To give us a little privacy for a while.

BRICK. You know better, Maggie.

MARGARET. No, I don't know better.... 385

(*She rushes to gallery doors, draws the rose-silk drapes across them.*)

BRICK. Don't make a fool of yourself.

---

1   *My Wild Irish Rose* Popular 1899 song by Chancellor Olcott.

MARGARET. I don't mind makin' a fool of myself over you!

BRICK. I mind, Maggie. I feel embarrassed for you.

MARGARET. Feel embarrassed! But don't continue my torture. I can't live on
390   and on under these circumstances.

BRICK. You agreed to—

MARGARET. I know but—

BRICK. —Accept that condition!

MARGARET. I CAN'T! CAN'T! CAN'T

(*She seizes his shoulder.*)

395   BRICK. Let go!

(*He breaks away from her and seizes the small boudoir chair and raises
it like a lion-tamer facing a big circus cat. Count five. She stares at him
with her fist pressed to her mouth, then bursts into shrill, almost hysterical
laughter. He remains grave for a moment, then grins and puts the chair
down.*)

(*Big Mama calls through closed door.*)

400   BIG MAMA. Son? Son? Son?

BRICK. What is it, Big Mama?

BIG MAMA. (*outside*) Oh, son! We got the most wonderful news about Big
Daddy. I just had t'run up an' tell you right this—

(*She rattles the knob.*)

—What's this door doin', locked, faw? You all think there's robbers in the
405   house?

MARGARET. Big Mama, Brick is dressin', he's not dressed yet.

BIG MAMA. That's all right, it won't be the first time I've seen Brick not
dressed. Come on, open this door!

(*Margaret, with a grimace, goes to unlock and open the hall door, as Brick
hobbles rapidly to the bathroom and kicks the door shut. Big Mama has
disappeared from the hall.*)

MARGARET. Big Mama?

(*Big Mama appears through the opposite gallery doors behind Margaret,
huffing and puffing like an old bulldog. She is a short, stout woman; her
sixty years and 170 pounds have left her somewhat breathless most of the
time; she's always tensed like a boxer, or rather, a Japanese wrestler. Her
"family" was maybe a little superior to Big Daddy's, but not much. She
wears a black or silver lace dress and at least half a million in flashy gems.
She is very sincere.*)

BIG MAMA. (*loudly, startling Margaret*) Here—I come through Gooper's and   410
Mae's gall'ry door. Where's Brick? *Brick*—Hurry on out of there, son, I just
have a second and want to give you the news about Big Daddy.—I hate
locked doors in a house....

MARGARET. (*with affected lightness*) I've noticed you do, Big Mama, but people have got to have *some* moments of privacy, don't they?   415

BIG MAMA. No, ma'am, not in *my* house. (*without pause*) Whacha took off
you' dress faw? I thought that little lace dress was so sweet on yuh, honey.

MARGARET. I thought it looked sweet on me, too, but one of m' cute little
table-partners used it for a napkin so—!

BIG MAMA. (*picking up stockings on floor*) What?   420

MARGARET. You know, Big Mama, Mae and Gooper's so touchy about those
children—thanks, Big Mama ...

(*Big Mama has thrust the picked-up stockings in Margaret's hand with a
grunt.*)

—that you just don't dare to suggest there's any room for improvement in
their—

BIG MAMA. Brick, hurry out!—Shoot, Maggie, you just don't like children.   425

MARGARET. I do so like children! Adore them!—well brought up!

BIG MAMA. (*gentle—loving*) Well, why don't you have some and bring them
up well, then, instead of all the time pickin' on Gooper's an' Mae's?

GOOPER. (*shouting up the stairs*) Hey, hey, Big Mama, Betsy an' Hugh got to
go, waitin' t' tell yuh g'by!   430

BIG MAMA. Tell 'em to hold their hawses, I'll be right down in a jiffy!

GOOPER. Yes ma'am!

(*She turns to the bathroom door and calls out.*)

BIG MAMA. Son? Can you hear me in there?

(*There is a muffled answer.*)

We just got the full report from the laboratory at the Ochsner Clinic,[1]
completely negative, son, ev'rything negative, right on down the line!   435
Nothin' a-tall's wrong with him but some little functional thing called a
spastic colon.[2] Can you hear me, son?

MARGARET. He can hear you, Big Mama.

---

1   *Ochsner Clinic* Ochsner Medical Center, renowned clinic founded in 1942 and especially
    known for its cancer facilities.
2   *spastic colon* Irritable bowel syndrome.

BIG MAMA. Then why don't he say something? God Almighty, a piece of
440   news like that should make him shout. It made *me* shout, I can tell you. I
shouted and sobbed and fell right down on my knees!—Look!

    (*She pulls up her skirt.*)

See the bruises where I hit my kneecaps? Took both doctors to haul me
back on my feet!

    (*She laughs—she always laughs like hell at herself.*)

Big Daddy was furious with me! But ain't that wonderful news?

    (*Facing bathroom again, she continues:*)

445   After all the anxiety we been through to git a report like that on Big Daddy's birthday? Big Daddy tried to hide how much of a load that news took
off his mind, but didn't fool *me*. He was mighty close to crying about it
himself!

    (*Goodbyes are shouted downstairs, and she rushes to door.*)

GOOPER. Big Mama!
450 BIG MAMA. *Hold those people down there, don't let them go!*—Now, git dressed,
    we're all comin' up to this room fo' Big Daddy's birthday party because of
    your ankle.—How's his ankle, Maggie?
MARGARET. Well, he broke it, Big Mama.
BIG MAMA. I know he broke it.

    (*A phone is ringing in hall. A Negro voice answers: "Mistuh Polly's
res'dence."*)

455   I mean does it hurt him much still.
MARGARET. I'm afraid I can't give you that information, Big Mama. You'll
    have to ask Brick if it hurts much still or not.
SOOKEY. (*in the hall*) It's Memphis, Mizz Polly, it's Miss Sally in Memphis.
BIG MAMA. Awright, Sookey.

    (*Big Mama rushes into the hall and is heard shouting on the phone:*)

460   Hello, Miss Sally. How are you, Miss Sally?—Yes, well, I was just gonna
    call you about it. *Shoot!*—
MARGARET. Brick, don't!

    (*Big Mama raises her voice to a bellow.*)

BIG MAMA. *Miss Sally? Don't ever call me from the Gayoso Lobby, too much talk*
465   *goes on in that hotel lobby, no wonder you can't hear me!* Now listen, Miss Sally.

They's nothin' serious wrong with Big Daddy. We got the report just now, they's nothin' wrong but a thing called a—spastic! *SPASTIC!*—colon ...

(*She appears at the hall door and calls to Margaret.*)

—Maggie, come out here and talk to that fool on the phone. I'm shouted breathless!

MARGARET. (*goes out and is heard sweetly at phone*) Miss Sally? This is Brick's   470
wife, Maggie. So nice to hear your voice. Can you hear *mine?* Well, *good!*—
Big Mama just wanted you to know that they've got the report from the Ochsner Clinic and what Big Daddy has is a spastic colon. Yes. Spastic colon, Miss Sally. That's right, spastic colon. *G'bye, Miss Sally, hope I'll see you real soon!*   475

(*Hangs up a little before Miss Sally was probably ready to terminate the talk. She returns through the hall door.*)

She heard me perfectly. I've discovered with deaf people the thing to do is not shout at them but just enunciate clearly. My rich old Aunt Cornelia was deaf as the dead but I could make her hear me just by sayin' each word slowly, distinctly, close to her ear. I read her the *Commercial Appeal*[1] ev'ry night, read her the classified ads in it, even, she never missed a word of it.   480
But was she a mean ole thing! Know what I got when she died? Her un-expired subscriptions to five magazines and the Book-of-the-Month Club and a LIBRARY full of ev'ry dull book ever written! All else went to her hellcat of a sister ... meaner than she was, even!

(*Big Mama has been straightening things up in the room during this speech.*)

BIG MAMA. (*closing closet door on discarded clothes*) Miss Sally sure is a case! Big   485
Daddy says she's always got her hand out fo' something. He's not mistaken. That poor ole thing always has her hand out fo' somethin'. I don't think Big Daddy gives her as much as he should.
GOOPER. Big Mama! Come on now! Betsy and Hugh can't wait no longer!
BIG MAMA. (*shouting*) I'm comin'!   490

(*She starts out. At the hall door, turns and jerks a forefinger, first toward the bathroom door, then toward the liquor cabinet, meaning: "Has Brick been drinking?" Margaret pretends not to understand, cocks her head and raises her brows as if the pantomimic performance was completely mystifying to her. Big Mama rushes back to Margaret:*)

Shoot! Stop playin' so dumb!—I mean has he been drinkin' that stuff much yet?

---

1   *Commercial Appeal* Popular Memphis daily newspaper.

MARGARET. (*with a little laugh*) Oh! I think he had a highball[1] after supper.

BIG MAMA. Don't laugh about it!—Some single men stop drinkin' when they git married and others start! Brick never touched liquor before he—!

495 MARGARET. (*crying out*) THAT'S NOT FAIR!

BIG MAMA. Fair or not fair I want to ask you a question, one question: D'you make Brick happy in bed?

MARGARET. Why don't you ask if he makes *me* happy in bed?

BIG MAMA. Because I know that—

500 MARGARET. *It works both ways!*

BIG MAMA. Something's not right! You're childless and my son drinks!

GOOPER. Come on, Big Mama!

(*Gooper has called her downstairs and she has rushed to the door on the line above. She turns at the door and points at the bed.*)

BIG MAMA. —When a marriage goes on the rocks, the rocks are *there*, right there!

505 MARGARET. *That's*—

(*Big Mama has swept out of the room and slammed the door.*)

—not—*fair* ...

(*Margaret is alone, completely alone, and she feels it. She draws in, hunches her shoulders, raises her arms with fists clenched, shuts her eyes tight as a child about to be stabbed with a vaccination needle. When she opens her eyes again, what she sees is the long oval mirror and she rushes straight to it, stares into it with a grimace and says: "Who are you?"—Then she crouches a little and answers herself in a different voice which is high, thin, mocking: "I am Maggie the Cat!"—Straightens quickly as bathroom door opens a little and Brick calls out to her.*)

BRICK. Has Big Mama gone?

MARGARET. She's gone.

(*He opens the bathroom door and hobbles out, with his liquor glass now empty, straight to the liquor cabinet. He is whistling softly. Margaret's head pivots on her long, slender throat to watch him. She raises a hand uncertainly to the base of her throat, as if it was difficult for her to swallow, before she speaks:*)

You know, our sex life didn't just peter out in the usual way, it was cut off
510 short, long before the natural time for it to, and it's going to revive again,

---

1   *highball* Type of drink that combines liquor with a non-alcoholic beverage.

just as sudden as that. I'm confident of it. That's what I'm keeping myself attractive for. For the time when you'll see me again like other men see me. Yes, like other men see me. They still see me, Brick, and they like what they see. Uh-huh. Some of them would give their—Look, Brick!

(*She stands before the long oval mirror, touches her breast and then her hips with her two hands.*)

How high my body stays on me!—Nothing has fallen on me—not a frac-   515
tion....

(*Her voice is soft and trembling: a pleading child's. At this moment as he turns to glance at her—a look which is like a player passing a ball to another player, third down and goal to go—she has to capture the audience in a grip so tight that she can hold it till the first intermission without any lapse of attention.*)

Other men still want me. My face looks strained, sometimes, but I've kept my figure as well as you've kept yours, and men admire it. I still turn heads on the street. Why, last week in Memphis everywhere that I went men's eyes burned holes in my clothes, at the country club and in restaurants and   520
department stores, there wasn't a man I met or walked by that didn't just eat me up with his eyes and turn around when I passed him and look back at me. Why, at Alice's party for her New York cousins, the best-lookin' man in the crowd—followed me upstairs and tried to force his way in the powder room[1] with me, followed me to the door and tried to force his way   525
in!

BRICK. Why didn't you let him, Maggie?

MARGARET. Because I'm not that common, for one thing. Not that I wasn't almost tempted to. You like to know who it was? It was Sonny Boy Maxwell, that's who!   530

BRICK. Oh, yeah, Sonny Boy Maxwell, he was a good end-runner but had a little injury to his back and had to quit.

MARGARET. He has no injury now and has no wife and still has a lech for me!

BRICK. I see no reason to lock him out of a powder room in that case.

MARGARET. And have someone catch me at it? I'm not that stupid. Oh, I   535
might sometime cheat on you with someone, since you're so insultingly eager to have me do it!—But if I do, you can be damned sure it will be in a place and a time where no one but me and the man could possibly know. Because I'm not going to give you any excuse to divorce me for being unfaithful or anything else....   540

---

1   *powder room* Bathroom.

BRICK. Maggie, I wouldn't divorce you for being unfaithful or anything else.
Don't you know that? Hell. I'd be relieved to know that you'd found yourself a lover.

MARGARET. Well, I'm taking no chances. No, I'd rather stay on this hot tin
545   roof.

BRICK. A hot tin roof's 'n uncomfo'table place t' stay on....

(*He starts to whistle softly.*)

MARGARET. (*through his whistle*) Yeah, but I can stay on it just as long as I
have to.

BRICK. You could leave me, Maggie.

(*He resumes his whistle. She wheels about to glare at him.*)

550   MARGARET. *Don't want to and will not!* Besides if I did, you don't have a cent
to pay for it but what you get from Big Daddy and he's dying of cancer!

(*For the first time a realization of Big Daddy's doom seems to penetrate to
Brick's consciousness, visibly, and he looks at Margaret.*)

BRICK. Big Mama just said he *wasn't*, that the report was okay.

MARGARET. That's what she thinks because she got the same story that they
gave Big Daddy. And was just as taken in by it as he was, poor ole things....
555   But tonight they're going to tell her the truth about it. When Big Daddy
goes to bed, they're going to tell her that he is dying of cancer.

(*She slams the dresser drawer.*)

—It's malignant and it's terminal.

BRICK. Does Big Daddy know it?

MARGARET. Hell, do they *ever* know it? Nobody says, "You're dying." You
560   have to fool them. They have to fool *themselves.*

BRICK. Why?

MARGARET. *Why?* Because human beings dream of life everlasting, that's the
reason! But most of them want it on earth and not in heaven.

(*He gives a short, hard laugh at her touch of humour.*)

Well.... (*She touches up her mascara.*) That's how it is, anyhow.... (*She looks
565   about.*) Where did I put down my cigarette? Don't want to burn up the
home-place, at least not with Mae and Gooper and their five monsters in
it!

(*She has found it and sucks at it greedily. Blows out smoke and continues:*)

So this is Big Daddy's last birthday. And Mae and Gooper, they know it,
oh, *they* know it, all right. They got the first information from the Ochsner

Clinic. That's why they rushed down here with their no-neck monsters. 570
Because. Do you know something? Big Daddy's made no will? Big Daddy's
never made out any will in his life, and so this campaign's afoot to impress
him, forcibly as possible, with the fact that you drink and I've borne no
children!

(*He continues to stare at her a moment, then mutters something sharp but
not audible and hobbles rather rapidly out onto the long gallery in the
fading, much faded, gold light.*)

MARGARET. (*continuing her liturgical chant*) Y'know, I'm *fond* of Big Daddy, 575
I am genuinely fond of that old man, I really *am*, you know....
BRICK. (*faintly, vaguely*) Yes, I know you are....
MARGARET. I've always sort of admired him in spite of his coarseness, his
four-letter words and so forth. Because Big Daddy *is* what he *is*, and he
makes no bones about it. He hasn't turned gentleman farmer, he's still a 580
Mississippi redneck, as much of a redneck as he must have been when he
was just overseer here on the old Jack Straw and Peter Ochello place. But
he got hold of it an' built it into th' biggest an' finest plantation in the
Delta.—I've always *liked* Big Daddy....

(*She crosses to the proscenium.*[1])

Well, this is Big Daddy's last birthday. I'm sorry about it. But I'm facing 585
the facts. It takes money to take care of a drinker and that's the office that
I've been elected to lately.
BRICK. You don't have to take care of me.
MARGARET. Yes, I do. Two people in the same boat have got to take care of
each other. At least you want money to buy more Echo Spring[2] when this 590
supply is exhausted, or will you be satisfied with a ten-cent beer?
    Mae an' Gooper are plannin' to freeze us out of Big Daddy's estate be-
cause you drink and I'm childless. But we can defeat that plan. We're *going*
to defeat that plan!
    Brick, y'know, I've been so God damn disgustingly poor all my life!—That's 595
the *truth*, Brick!
BRICK. I'm not sayin' it isn't.
MARGARET. Always had to suck up to people I couldn't stand because they
had money and I was poor as Job's turkey.[3] You don't know what that's

1   *proscenium* In this context, the arched doorway to the gallery.
2   *Echo Spring* Brand of bourbon whiskey.
3   *poor ... turkey* Reference to the biblical Job, who lost all his wealth while his loyalty was
    being tested by God.

600 like. Well, I'll tell you, it's like you would feel a thousand miles away from Echo Spring!—And had to get back to it on that broken ankle ... without a crutch!

That's how it feels to be as poor as Job's turkey and have to suck up to relatives that you hated because they had money and all you had was a 605 bunch of hand-me-down clothes and a few old mouldy three-per-cent government bonds. My daddy loved his liquor, he fell in love with his liquor the way you've fallen in love with Echo Spring!—And my poor Mama, having to maintain some semblance of social position, to keep appearances up, on an income of one hundred and fifty dollars a month on those old 610 government bonds!

When I came out, the year that I made my debut, I had just two evening dresses! One Mother made me from a pattern in *Vogue*, the other a hand-me-down from a snotty rich cousin I hated!

—The dress that I married you in was my grandmother's weddin' 615 gown....

So that's why I'm like a cat on a hot tin roof!

(*Brick is still on the gallery. Someone below calls up to him in a warm Negro voice,* "Hiya, Mistuh Brick, how yuh feelin'?" *Brick raises his liquor glass as if that answered the question.*)

MARGARET.   You can be young without money, but you can't be old without it. You've got to be old *with* money because to be old without it is just too awful, you've got to be one or the other, either *young* or *with money*, you 620 can't be old and *without* it.—That's the *truth*, Brick....

(*Brick whistles softly, vaguely.*)

Well, now I'm dressed, I'm all dressed, there's nothing else for me to do.

(*Forlornly, almost fearfully.*)

I'm dressed, all dressed, nothing else for me to do....

(*She moves about restlessly, aimlessly, and speaks, as if to herself.*)

What am I—? Oh!—my bracelets....

(*She starts working a collection of bracelets over her hands onto her wrists, about six on each, as she talks.*)

I've thought a whole lot about it and now I know when I made my mis-625 take. Yes, I made my mistake when I told you the truth about that thing with Skipper. Never should have confessed it, a fatal error, tellin' you about that thing with Skipper.

BRICK. Maggie, shut up about Skipper. I mean it, Maggie; you got to shut
up about Skipper.

MARGARET. You ought to understand that Skipper and I—   630

BRICK. You don't think I'm serious, Maggie? You're fooled by the fact that
I am saying this quiet? Look, Maggie. What you're doing is a dangerous
thing to do. You're—you're—you're—foolin' with something that—nobody ought to fool with.

MARGARET. This time I'm going to finish what I have to say to you. Skipper   635
and I made love, if love you could call it, because it made both of us feel a
little bit closer to you. You see, you son of a bitch, you asked too much of
people, of me, of him, of all the unlucky poor damned sons of bitches that
happen to love you, and there was a whole pack of them, yes, there was
a pack of them besides me and Skipper, you asked too goddam much of   640
people that loved you, you—superior creature!—you godlike being!—And
so we made love to each other to dream it was you, both of us! Yes, yes, yes!
Truth, truth! What's so awful about it? I like it, I think the truth is—yeah!
I shouldn't have told you....

BRICK. (*holding his head unnaturally still and uptilted a bit*) It was Skipper   645
that told me about it. Not you, Maggie.

MARGARET. I told you!

BRICK. After he told me!

MARGARET. What does it matter who—?

DIXIE. I got your mallet, I got your mallet.   650

TRIXIE. Give it to me, give it to me. It's mine.

(*Brick turns suddenly out upon the gallery and calls:*)

BRICK. Little girl! Hey, little girl!

LITTLE GIRL. (*at a distance*) What, Uncle Brick?

BRICK. Tell the folks to come up!—Bring everybody upstairs!

TRIXIE. It's mine, it's mine.   655

MARGARET. I can't stop myself! I'd go on telling you this in front of them all,
if I had to!

BRICK. Little girl! Go on, go on, will you? Do what I told you, call them!

DIXIE. Okay.

MARGARET. Because it's got to be told and you, you!—you never let me!   660

(*She sobs, then controls herself, and continues almost calmly.*)

It was one of those beautiful, ideal things they tell about in the Greek leg-
ends, it couldn't be anything else, you being you, and that's what made it
so sad, that's what made it so awful, because it was love that never could be
carried through to anything satisfying or even talked about plainly.

665 BRICK. Maggie, you gotta stop this.

MARGARET. Brick, I tell you, you got to believe me, Brick, I *do* understand all about it! I—I think it was—*noble!* Can't you tell I'm sincere when I say I respect it? My only point, the only point that I'm making, is life has got to be allowed to continue even after the *dream* of life is—all—over....

(*Brick is without his crutch. Leaning on furniture, he crosses to pick it up as she continues as if possessed by a will outside herself.*)

670 Why, I remember when we double-dated at college, Gladys Fitzgerald and I and you and Skipper, it was more like a date between you and Skipper. Gladys and I were just sort of tagging along as if it was necessary to chaperone you!—to make a good public impression—

BRICK. (*turns to face her, half lifting his crutch*) Maggie, you want me to hit

675 you with this crutch? Don't you know I could kill you with this crutch?

MARGARET. Good Lord, man, d'you think I'd care if you did?

BRICK. One man has one great good true thing in his life. One great good thing which is true!—I had friendship with Skipper.—You are naming it dirty!

680 MARGARET. I'm not naming it dirty! I am naming it clean.

BRICK. Not love with you, Maggie, but friendship with Skipper was that one great true thing, and you are naming it dirty!

MARGARET. Then you haven't been listenin', not understood what I'm saying! I'm naming it so damn clean that it killed poor Skipper!—You two had

685 something that had to be kept on ice, yes, incorruptible, yes!—and death was the only icebox where you could keep it....

BRICK. I married you, Maggie. Why would I marry you, Maggie, if I was—?

MARGARET. Brick, let me finish!—I know, believe me I know, that it was only Skipper that harboured even any *unconscious* desire for anything not

690 perfectly pure between you two!—Now let me skip a little. You married me early that summer we graduated out of Ole Miss, and we were happy, weren't we, we were blissful, yes, hit heaven together ev'ry time that we loved! But that fall you an' Skipper turned down wonderful offers of jobs in order to keep on bein' football heroes—pro-football heroes. You or-

695 ganized the Dixie Stars that fall, so you could keep on bein' teammates forever! But somethin' was not right with it!—*Me included!*—between you. Skipper began hittin' the bottle ... you got a spinal injury—couldn't play the Thanksgivin' game in Chicago, watched it on TV from a traction bed in Toledo. I joined Skipper. The Dixie Stars lost because poor Skipper was

700 drunk. We drank together that night all night in the bar of the Blackstone[1]

---

1   *Blackstone* Historic hotel in Chicago, Illinois.

and when cold day was comin' up over the Lake an' we were comin' out drunk to take a dizzy look at it, I said, *"SKIPPER! STOP LOVIN' MY HUSBAND OR TELL HIM HE'S GOT TO LET YOU ADMIT IT TO HIM!"*—one way or another!

HE SLAPPED ME HARD ON THE MOUTH! —then turned and ran without   705
stopping once, I am sure, all the way back into his room at the Blackstone....

—When I came to his room that night, with a little scratch like a shy little mouse at his door, he made that pitiful, ineffectual little attempt to prove that what I had said wasn't true....   710

> (*Brick strikes at her with crutch, a blow that shatters the gem-like lamp on the table.*)

—In this way, I destroyed him, by telling him truth that he and his world which he was born and raised in, yours and his world, had told him could not be told?

—From then on Skipper was nothing at all but a receptacle for liquor and drugs....   715
—*Who shot cock robin? I with my*—

> (*She throws back her head with tight shut eyes.*)

—*merciful arrow!* [1]

> (*Brick strikes at her; misses.*)

Missed me!—Sorry,—I'm not tryin' to whitewash my behaviour, Christ, no! Brick, I'm not good. I don't know why people have to pretend to be good, nobody's good. The rich or the well-to-do can afford to respect mor-   720
al patterns, conventional moral patterns, but I could never afford to, yeah, but—I'm honest! Give me credit for just that, will you *please?*—Born poor, raised poor, expect to die poor unless I manage to get us something out of what Big Daddy leaves when he dies of cancer! But Brick?!—*Skipper is dead! I'm alive!* Maggie the cat is—   725

> (*Brick hops awkwardly forward and strikes at her again with his crutch.*)

—alive! I am alive, alive! I am ...

> (*He hurls the crutch at her, across the bed she took refuge behind, and pitches forward on the floor as she completes her speech.*)

—alive!

---

1   *Who ... arrow* Reference to the popular children's rhyme "Who Killed Cock Robin?"

(*A little girl, Dixie, bursts into the room, wearing an Indian war bonnet and firing a cap pistol at Margaret and shouting: "Bang, bang, bang!" Laughter downstairs floats through the open hall door. Margaret had crouched gasping to bed at child's entrance. She now rises and says with cool fury:*)

Little girl, your mother or someone should teach you—(*gasping*)—to knock at a door before you come into a room. Otherwise people might
730   think that you—lack—good breeding....

DIXIE.   Yanh, yanh, yanh, what is Uncle Brick doin' on th' floor?

BRICK.   I tried to kill your Aunt Maggie, but I failed—and I fell. Little girl, give me my crutch so I can get up off th' floor.

MARGARET.   Yes, give your uncle his crutch, he's a cripple, honey, he broke his
735   ankle last night jumping hurdles on the high school athletic field!

DIXIE.   What were you jumping hurdles for, Uncle Brick?

BRICK.   Because I used to jump them, and people like to do what they used to do, even after they've stopped being able to do it....

MARGARET.   That's right, that's your answer, now go away, little girl.

(*Dixie fires cap pistol at Margaret three times.*)

740   *Stop, you stop that, monster! You little no-neck monster!*

(*She seizes the cap pistol and hurls it through gallery doors.*)

DIXIE.   (*with a precocious instinct for the cruelest thing*) You're *jealous!*—You're just jealous because you can't have babies!

(*She sticks out her tongue at Margaret as she sashays past her with her stomach stuck out, to the gallery. Margaret slams the gallery doors and leans panting against them. There is a pause. Brick has replaced his spilt drink and sits, faraway, on the great four-poster bed.*)

MARGARET.   You see?—they gloat over us being childless, even in front of their five little no-neck monsters!

(*Pause. Voices approach on the stairs.*)

745   Brick?—I've been to a doctor in Memphis, a—a gynecologist....
I've been completely examined, and there is no reason why we can't have a child whenever we want one. And this is my time by the calendar to conceive. Are you listening to me? Are you? Are you LISTENING TO ME!

BRICK.   Yes. I hear you, Maggie.

750   (*His attention returns to her inflamed face.*)

—But how in hell on earth do you imagine—that you're going to have a child by a man that can't stand you?

MARGARET. That's a problem that I will have to work out.

(*She wheels about to face the hall door.*)

MAE. (*off stage left*) Come on, Big Daddy. We're all goin' up to Brick's room.

(*From off stage left, voices: Reverend Tooker, Doctor Baugh, Mae.*)

MARGARET. *Here they come!*

(*The lights dim.*)

ACT 2

There is no lapse of time. Margaret and Brick are in the same positions they held at the end of Act 1.

MARGARET. (*at door*) *Here they come!*

(*Big Daddy appears first, a tall man with a fierce, anxious look, moving carefully not to betray his weakness even, or especially, to himself.*)

GOOPER. I read in the *Register* that you're getting a new memorial window.

(*Some of the people are approaching through the hall, others along the gallery: voices from both directions. Gooper and Reverend Tooker become visible outside gallery doors, and their voices come in clearly. They pause outside as Gooper lights a cigar.*)

REVEREND TOOKER. (*vivaciously*) Oh, but St. Paul's in Grenada has three memorial windows, and the latest one is a Tiffany[1] stained-glass window that cost twenty-five hundred dollars, a picture of Christ the Good Shepherd with a Lamb in His arms.

MARGARET. Big Daddy.

BIG DADDY. Well, Brick.

BRICK. Hello Big Daddy.—Congratulations!

BIG DADDY. —Crap....

GOOPER. Who give that window, Preach?

REVEREND TOOKER. Clyde Fletcher's widow. Also presented St. Paul's with a baptismal font.[2]

---

1   *Tiffany* Louis Comfort Tiffany (1848–1933), American artist and founder of Tiffany Studios, a design company known for its innovative and highly sought-after stained-glass windows, mosaics, and lamps.

2   *baptismal font* Basin or tank found in church sanctuaries and used to hold the holy water in baptism ceremonies.

GOOPER. Y'know what somebody ought t' give your church is a *coolin'* sys-
15 tem, Preach.
REVEREND TOOKER. Yes, siree, Bob! And y'know what Gus Hamma's family
gave in his memory to the church at Two Rivers? A complete new stone
parish-house with a basketball court in the basement and a—
BIG DADDY. (*uttering a loud barking laugh which is far from truly mirthful*)
20 Hey, Preach! What's all this talk about memorials, Preach? Y' think somebody's about t' kick off around here? 'S that it?

(*Startled by this interjection, Reverend Tooker decides to laugh at the
question almost as loud as he can. How he would answer the question we'll
never know, as he's spared that embarrassment by the voice of Gooper's wife,
Mae, rising high and clear as she appears with "Doc" Baugh, the family
doctor, through the hall door.*)

MAE. (*almost religiously*)—Let's see now, they've had their tyyy-phoid shots,
and their tetanus shots, their diphtheria shots and their hepatitis shots
and their polio shots, they got *those* shots every month from May through
25 September, and—Gooper? Hey! Gooper!—What all have the kiddies been
shot faw?
MARGARET. (*overlapping a bit*) Turn on the hi-fi,[1] Brick! Let's have some music t' start off th' party with!
BRICK. You turn it on, Maggie.

(*The talk becomes so general that the room sounds like a great aviary of
chattering birds. Only Brick remains unengaged, leaning upon the liquor
cabinet with his faraway smile, an ice cube in a paper napkin with which he
now and then rubs his forehead. He doesn't respond to Margaret's command.
She bounds forward and stoops over the instrument panel of the console.*)

30 GOOPER. We gave 'em that thing for a third anniversary present, got three
speakers in it.

(*The room is suddenly blasted by the climax of a Wagnerian opera or a
Beethoven symphony.[2]*)

BIG DADDY. *Turn that dam thing off!*

(*Almost instant silence, almost instantly broken by the shouting charge of
Big Mama, entering through hall door like a charging rhino.*)

BIG MAMA. *Wha's my Brick, wha's mah precious baby!!*

---

1   *hi-fi* "High fidelity" sound system.
2   *Wagnerian* Intense and theatrical; characteristic of the German composer Richard Wag-
ner (1813–83); *Beethoven* German composer Ludwig van Beethoven (1770–1827).

BIG DADDY.   *Sorry! Turn it back on!*

> (*Everyone laughs very loud. Big Daddy is famous for his jokes at Big Mama's expense, and nobody laughs louder at these jokes than Big Mama herself, though sometimes they're pretty cruel and Big Mama has to pick up or fuss with something to cover the hurt that the loud laugh doesn't quite cover. On this occasion, a happy occasion because the dread in her heart has also been lifted by the false report on Big Daddy's condition, she giggles, grotesquely, coyly, in Big Daddy's direction and bears down upon Brick, all very quick and alive.*)

BIG MAMA.   Here he is, here's my precious baby! What's that you've got in   35
your hand? You put that liquor down, son, your hand was made fo' holdin'
somethin' better than that!

GOOPER.   Look at Brick put it down!

> (*Brick has obeyed Big Mama by draining the glass and handing it to her. Again everyone laughs, some high, some low.*)

BIG MAMA.   Oh, you bad boy, you, you're my bad little boy. Give Big Mama
a kiss, you bad boy, you!—Look at him shy away, will you? Brick never   40
liked bein' kissed or made a fuss over, I guess because he's always had too
much of it!

Son, you turn that thing off!

> (*Brick has switched on the TV set.*)

I can't stand TV, radio was bad enough but TV has gone it one better, I
mean—(*plops wheezing in chair*) —one worse, ha, ha! Now what'm I sittin'   45
down here faw? I want t' sit next to my sweetheart on the sofa, hold hands
with him and love him up a little!

> (*Big Mama has on a black and white figured chiffon. The large irregular patterns, like the markings of some massive animal, the lustre of her great diamonds and many pearls, the brilliants set in the silver frames of her glasses, her riotous voice, booming laugh, have dominated the room since she entered. Big Daddy has been regarding her with a steady grimace of chronic annoyance.*)

BIG MAMA.   (*still louder*) Preacher, Preacher, hey, Preach! Give me you' hand
an' help me up from this chair!

REVEREND TOOKER.   None of your tricks, Big Mama!   50

BIG MAMA.   What tricks? You give me you' hand so I can get up an'—

> (*Reverend Tooker extends her his hand. She grabs it and pulls him into her lap with a shrill laugh that spans an octave in two notes.*)

Ever seen a preacher in a fat lady's lap? Hey, hey, folks! Ever seen a preacher in a fat lady's lap?

(*Big Mama is notorious throughout the Delta for this sort of inelegant horseplay. Margaret looks on with indulgent humour, sipping Dubonnet*[1] *"on the rocks" and watching Brick, but Mae and Gooper exchange signs of humourless anxiety over these antics, the sort of behaviour which Mae thinks may account for their failure to quite get in with the smartest young married set in Memphis, despite all.*

One of the Negroes, Lacy or Sookey, peeks in, cackling. They are waiting for a sign to bring in the cake and champagne. But Big Daddy's not amused. He doesn't understand why, in spite of the infinite mental relief he's received from the doctor's report, he still has these same old fox teeth in his guts. "This spastic condition is something else," he says to himself, but aloud he roars at Big Mama:)

BIG DADDY.   *BIG MAMA, WILL YOU QUIT HORSIN'?*—You're too old an' too fat
55   fo' that sort of crazy kid stuff an' besides a woman with your blood pres-
        sure—she had two hundred last spring!—is riskin' a stroke when you mess
        around like that....

(*Mae blows on a pitch pipe.*)

60 BIG MAMA.   *Here comes Big Daddy's birthday!*

(*Negroes in white jackets enter with an enormous birthday cake ablaze with candles and carrying buckets of champagne with satin ribbons about the bottle necks. Mae and Gooper strike up song, and everybody, including the Negroes and Children, joins in. Only Brick remains aloof.*)

EVERYONE.
        Happy birthday to you.
        Happy birthday to you.
        Happy birthday, Big Daddy—

(*Some sing:* "Dear, Big Daddy!")

        Happy birthday to you.

(*Some sing:* "How old are you?"

Mae has come down centre and is organizing her children like a chorus. She gives them a barely audible: "One, two, three!" *and they are off in the new tune.*)

---

1   *Dubonnet* Sweet alcoholic drink traditionally consumed before a meal.

CHILDREN.

> Skinamarinka—dinka—dink   65
> Skinamarinka—do
> We love you.
> Skinamarinka—dinka—dink
> Skinamarinka—do.

> (*All together, they turn to Big Daddy.*)

> Big Daddy, you!   70

> (*They turn back front, like a musical comedy chorus.*)

> We love you in the morning;
> We love you in the night.
> We love you when we're with you,
> And we love you out of sight.
> Skinamarinka—dinka—dink   75
> Skinamarinka—do.

> (*Mae turns to Big Mama.*)

> Big Mama, too!

> (*Big Mama bursts into tears. The Negroes leave.*)

BIG DADDY. Now Ida, what the hell is the matter with you?
MAE. She's just so happy.
BIG MAMA. I'm just so happy, Big Daddy, I have to cry or something.   80

> (*Sudden and loud in the hush:*)

Brick, do you know the wonderful news that Doc Baugh got from the clinic about Big Daddy? Big Daddy's one hundred per cent!
MARGARET. Isn't that wonderful?
BIG MAMA. He's just one hundred per cent. Passed the examination with flying colours. Now that we know there's nothing wrong with Big Daddy but   85
a spastic colon, I can tell you something. I was worried sick, half out of my mind, for fear that Big Daddy might have a thing like—

> (*Margaret cuts through this speech, jumping up and exclaiming shrilly:*)

MARGARET. Brick, honey, aren't you going to give Big Daddy his birthday present?

> (*Passing by him, she snatches his liquor glass from him. She picks up a fancily wrapped package.*)

> Here it is, Big Daddy, this is from Brick!   90

BIG MAMA. This is the biggest birthday Big Daddy's ever had, a hundred
   presents and bushels of telegrams from—

MAE. (*at the same time*) What is it, Brick?

GOOPER. I bet 500 to 50 that Brick don't *know* what it is.

95 BIG MAMA. The fun of presents is not knowing what they are till you open
   the package. Open your present, Big Daddy.

BIG DADDY. Open it you'self. I want to ask Brick somethin! Come here,
   Brick.

MARGARET. Big Daddy's callin' you, Brick.

(*She is opening the package.*)

100 BRICK. Tell Big Daddy I'm crippled.

BIG DADDY. I see you're crippled. I want to know how you got crippled.

MARGARET. (*making diversionary tactics*) Oh, look, oh, look, why, it's a cashmere
   robe!

(*She holds the robe up for all to see.*)

MAE. You sound surprised, Maggie.

105 MARGARET. I never saw one before.

MAE. That's funny.—*Hah!*

MARGARET. (*turning on her fiercely, with a brilliant smile*) Why is it funny?
   All my family ever had was family—and luxuries such as cashmere robes
   still surprise me!

110 BIG DADDY. (*ominously*) Quiet!

MAE. (*heedless in her fury*) I don't see how you could be so surprised when you
   bought it yourself at Loewenstein's[1] in Memphis last Saturday. You know
   how I know?

BIG DADDY. I said, Quiet!

115 MAE. —I know because the salesgirl that sold it to you waited on me and
   said, Oh, Mrs. Pollitt, your sister-in-law just bought a cashmere robe for
   your husband's father!

MARGARET. Sister Woman! Your talents are wasted as a housewife and mother, you really ought to be with the FBI or—

120 BIG DADDY. QUIET!

(*Reverend Tooker's reflexes are slower than the others'. He finishes a sentence
   after the bellow.*)

REVEREND TOOKER. (*to Doc Baugh*)—the Stork and the Reaper are running
   neck and neck!

---

1   *Loewenstein's* Lowenstein and Bros., a Memphis-based department store that operated
    until the 1980s.

(*He starts to laugh gaily when he notices the silence and Big Daddy's glare. His laugh dies falsely.*)

BIG DADDY. Preacher, I hope I'm not butting in on more talk about memorial stained-glass windows, am I, Preacher?

(*Reverend Tooker laughs feebly, then coughs dryly in the embarrassed silence.*)

Preacher?   125

BIG MAMA. Now, Big Daddy, don't you pick on Preacher!

BIG DADDY. (*raising his voice*) You ever hear that expression all hawk and no spit? You bring that expression to mind with that little dry cough of yours, all hawk an' no spit....

(*The pause is broken only by a short startled laugh from Margaret, the only one there who is conscious of and amused by the grotesque.*)

MAE. (*raising her arms and jangling her bracelets*) I wonder if the mosquitoes   130
are active tonight?

BIG DADDY. What's that, Little Mama? Did you make some remark?

MAE. Yes, I said I wondered if the mosquitoes would eat us alive if we went out on the gallery for a while.

BIG DADDY. Well, if they do, I'll have your bones pulverized for fertilizer!   135

BIG MAMA. (*quickly*) Last week we had an airplane spraying the place and I think it done some good, at least I haven't had a —

BIG DADDY. (*cutting her speech*) Brick, they tell me, if what they tell me is true, that you done some jumping last night on the high school athletic field?   140

BIG MAMA. Brick, Big Daddy is talking to you, son.

BRICK. (*smiling vaguely over his drink*) What was that, Big Daddy?

BIG DADDY. They said you done some jumping on the high school track field last night.

BRICK. That's what they told me, too.   145

BIG DADDY. Was it jumping or humping that you were doing out there? What were you doing out there at three A.M., layin' a woman on that cinder track?

BIG MAMA. Big Daddy, you are off the sick-list, now, and I'm not going to excuse you for talkin' so—   150

BIG DADDY. Quiet!

BIG MAMA. —*nasty* in front of Preacher and—

BIG DADDY. *QUIET!*—I ast you, Brick, if you was cuttin' you'self a piece o' poon-tang last night on that cinder track? I thought maybe you were chasin' poon-tang on that track an' tripped over something in the heat of the   155
chase—'sthat it?

(*Gooper laughs, loud and false, others nervously following suit. Big Mama stamps her foot, and purses her lips, crossing to Mae and whispering something to her as Brick meets his father's hard, intent, grinning stare with a slow, vague smile that he offers all situations from behind the screen of his liquor.*)

BRICK. No, sir, I don't think so....

MAE. (*at the same time, sweetly*) Reverend Tooker, let's you and I take a stroll on the widow's walk.[1]

(*She and the preacher go out on the gallery as Big Daddy says:*)

160 BIG DADDY. Then what the hell were you doing out there at three o'clock in the morning?

BRICK. Jumping the hurdles, Big Daddy, runnin' and jumpin' the hurdles, but those high hurdles have gotten too high for me, now.

BIG DADDY. Cause you was drunk?

165 BRICK. (*his vague smile fading a little*) Sober I wouldn't have tried to jump the *low* ones....

BIG MAMA. (*quickly*) Big Daddy, blow out the candles on your birthday cake!

MARGARET. (*at the same time*) I want to propose a toast to Big Daddy Pollitt on his sixty-fifth birthday, the biggest cotton planter in—

170 BIG DADDY. (*bellowing with fury and disgust*) *I told you to stop it, now stop it, quit this—!*

BIG MAMA. (*coming in front of Big Daddy with the cake*) Big Daddy, I will not allow you to talk that way, not even on your birthday, I—

BIG DADDY. I'll talk like I want to on my birthday, Ida, or any other goddam
175 day of the year and anybody here that don't like it knows what they can do!

BIG MAMA. You don't mean that!

BIG DADDY. What makes you think I don't mean it?

(*Meanwhile various discreet signals have been exchanged and Gooper has also gone out on the gallery.*)

BIG MAMA. I just know you don't mean it.

BIG DADDY. You don't know a goddam thing and you never did!

180 BIG MAMA. Big Daddy, you don't mean that.

BIG DADDY. Oh, yes, I do, oh, yes, I do, I mean it! I put up with a whole lot of crap around here because I thought I was dying. And you thought I was dying and you started taking over, well, you can stop taking over now, Ida, because I'm not gonna die, you can just stop now this business of taking
185 over because you're not taking over because I'm not dying, I went through

1   *widow's walk* Walkway or lookout on a rooftop.

the laboratory and the goddam exploratory operation and there's nothing wrong with me but a spastic colon. And I'm not dying of cancer which you thought I was dying of. Ain't that so? Didn't you think that I was dying of cancer, Ida?

(*Almost everybody is out on the gallery but the two old people glaring at each other across the blazing cake. Big Mama's chest heaves and she presses a fat fist to her mouth. Big Daddy continues, hoarsely:*)

Ain't that so, Ida? Didn't you have an idea I was dying of cancer and now you could take control of this place and everything on it? I got that impression, I seemed to get that impression. Your loud voice everywhere, your fat old body butting in here and there!

BIG MAMA. Hush! The Preacher!

BIG DADDY. Fuck the goddam preacher!

(*Big Mama gasps loudly and sits down on the sofa which is almost too small for her.*)

Did you hear what I said? I said fuck the goddam preacher!

(*Somebody closes the gallery doors from outside just as there is a burst of fireworks and excited cries from the children.*)

BIG MAMA. I never seen you act like this before and I can't think what's got in you!

BIG DADDY. I went through all that laboratory and operation and all just so I would know if you or me was the boss here! Well, now it turns out that I am and you ain't—and that's my birthday present—and my cake and champagne!—because for three years now you been gradually taking over. Bossing. Talking. Sashaying your fat old body around the place I made! I made this place! I was overseer on it! I was the overseer on the old Straw and Ochello plantation. I quit school at ten! I quit school at ten years old and went to work like a nigger in the fields. And I rose to be overseer of the Straw and Ochello plantation. And old Straw died and I was Ochello's partner and the place got bigger and bigger and bigger and bigger and bigger! I did all that myself with no goddam help from you, and now you think you're just about to take over. Well, I am just about to tell you that you are not just about to take over, you are not just about to take over a God damn thing. Is that clear to you, Ida? Is that very plain to you, now? Is that understood completely? I been through the laboratory from A to Z. I've had the goddam exploratory operation, and nothing is wrong with me but a spastic colon—made spastic, I guess, by *disgust!* By all the goddam lies and liars that I have had to put up with, and all the goddam hypocrisy that I lived with all these forty years that we been livin' together!

Hey! Ida!! Blow out the candles on the birthday cake! Purse up your lips and draw a deep breath and blow out the goddam candles on the cake!

220

BIG MAMA. Oh, Big Daddy, oh, oh, oh, Big Daddy!

BIG DADDY. What's the matter with you?

BIG MAMA. *In all these years you never believed that I loved you??*

BIG DADDY. Huh?

225 BIG MAMA. *And I did, I did so much, I did love you!*—I even loved your hate and your hardness, Big Daddy!

(*She sobs and rushes awkwardly out onto the gallery.*)

BIG DADDY. (*to himself*) *Wouldn't it be funny if that was true....*

(*A pause is followed by a burst of light in the sky from the fireworks.*)

BRICK! HEY, BRICK!

(*He stands over his blazing birthday cake. After some moments, Brick hobbles in on his crutch, holding his glass. Margaret follows him with a bright, anxious smile.*)

MARGARET. I'm just delivering him to you.

(*She kisses Brick on the mouth which he immediately wipes with the back of his hand. She flies girlishly back out. Brick and his father are alone.*)

230 BIG DADDY. Why did you do that?

BRICK. Do what, Big Daddy?

BIG DADDY. Wipe her kiss off your mouth like she'd spit on you.

BRICK. I don't know. I wasn't conscious of it.

BIG DADDY. That woman of yours has a better shape on her than Gooper's

235 but somehow or other they got the same look about them.

BRICK. What sort of look is that, Big Daddy?

BIG DADDY. I don't know how to describe it but it's the same look.

BRICK. They don't look peaceful, do they?

BIG DADDY. No, they sure in hell don't.

240 BRICK. They look nervous as cats?

BIG DADDY. That's right, they look nervous as cats.

BRICK. Nervous as a couple of cats on a hot tin roof?

BIG DADDY. That's right, boy, they look like a couple of cats on a hot tin roof. It's funny that you and Gooper being so different would pick out the same

245 type of woman.

BRICK. Both of us married into society, Big Daddy.

BIG DADDY. Crap ... I wonder what gives them both that look?

BRICK. Well. They're sittin' in the middle of a big piece of land, Big Daddy, twenty-eight thousand acres is a pretty big piece of land and so they're squaring off on it, each determined to knock off a bigger piece of it than 250 the other whenever you let it go.

BIG DADDY. I got a surprise for those women. I'm not gonna let it go for a long time yet if that's what they're waiting for.

BRICK. That's right, Big Daddy. You just sit tight and let them scratch each other's eyes out....   255

BIG DADDY. You bet your life I'm going to sit tight on it and let those sons of bitches scratch their eyes out, ha ha ha....

But Gooper's wife's a good breeder, you got to admit she's fertile. Hell, at supper tonight she had them all at the table and they had to put a couple of extra leafs in the table to make room for them, she's got five head of 260 them, now, and another one's comin'.

BRICK. Yep, number six is comin'....

BIG DADDY. Six hell, she'll probably drop a litter next time. Brick, you know, I swear to God, I don't know the way it happens?

BRICK. The way what happens, Big Daddy?   265

BIG DADDY. You git you a piece of land, by hook or crook, an' things start growin' on it, things accumulate on it, and the first thing you know it's completely out of hand, completely out of hand!

BRICK. Well, they say nature hates a vacuum, Big Daddy.

BIG DADDY. That's what they say, but sometimes I think that a vacuum is a 270 hell of a lot better than some of the stuff that nature replaces it with.

Is someone out there by that door?

GOOPER. Hey Mae.

BRICK. Yep.

BIG DADDY. Who?   275

(*He has lowered his voice.*)

BRICK. Someone int'rested in what we say to each other.

BIG DADDY. Gooper?—*GOOPER!*

(*After a discreet pause, Mae appears in the gallery door.*)

MAE. Did you call Gooper, Big Daddy?

BIG DADDY. Aw, it was you.

MAE. Do you want Gooper, Big Daddy?   280

BIG DADDY. No, and I don't want you. I want some privacy here, while I'm having a confidential talk with my son Brick. Now it's too hot in here to close them doors, but if I have to close those fuckin' doors in order to

have a private talk with my son Brick, just let me know and I'll close 'em.
285 Because I hate eavesdroppers, I don't like any kind of sneakin' an' spyin'.

MAE. Why, Big Daddy—

BIG DADDY. You stood on the wrong side of the moon, it threw your shadow!

MAE. I was just—

BIG DADDY. You was just nothing but *spyin'* an' you *know* it!

290 MAE. (*begins to sniff and sob*) Oh, Big Daddy, you're so unkind for some reason to those that really love you!

BIG DADDY. Shut up, shut up, shut up! I'm going to move you and Gooper out of that room next to this! It's none of your goddam business what goes on in here at night between Brick an' Maggie. You listen at night like a
295 couple of rutten peekhole spies and go and give a report on what you hear to Big Mama an' she comes to me and says they say such and such and so and so about what they heard goin' on between Brick an' Maggie, and Jesus, it makes me sick. I'm goin' to move you an' Gooper out of that room, I can't stand sneakin' an' spyin', it makes me puke....

(*Mae throws back her head and rolls her eyes heavenward and extends her arms as if invoking God's pity for this unjust martyrdom; then she presses a handkerchief to her nose and flies from the room with a loud swish of skirts.*)

300 BRICK. (*now at the liquor cabinet*) They listen, do they?

BIG DADDY. Yeah. They listen and give reports to Big Mama on what goes on in here between you and Maggie. They say that—

(*He stops as if embarrassed.*)

—You won't sleep with her, that you sleep on the sofa. Is that true or not true? If you don't like Maggie, get rid of Maggie!—What are you doin'
305 there now?

BRICK. Fresh'nin' up my drink.

BIG DADDY. Son, you know you got a real liquor problem?

BRICK. Yes, sir, yes, I know.

BIG DADDY. Is that why you quit sports-announcing, because of this liquor
310 problem?

BRICK. Yes, sir, yes, sir, I guess so.

(*He smiles vaguely and amiably at his father across his replenished drink.*)

BIG DADDY. Son, don't guess about it, it's too important.

BRICK. (*vaguely*) Yes, sir.

BIG DADDY. And listen to me, don't look at the damn chandelier....

(*Pause. Big Daddy's voice is husky.*)

—Somethin' else we picked up at th' big fire sale[1] in Europe.   315

    (*Another pause.*)

Life is important. There's nothing else to hold onto. A man that drinks is throwing his life away. Don't do it, hold onto your life. There's nothing else to hold onto....

    Sit down over here so we don't have to raise our voices, the walls have ears in this place.   320

BRICK. (*hobbling over to sit on the sofa beside him*) All right, Big Daddy.

BIG DADDY. Quit!—how'd that come about? Some disappointment?

BRICK. I don't know. Do you?

BIG DADDY. I'm askin' you, God damn it! How in hell would I know if you don't?   325

BRICK. I just got out there and found that I had a mouth full of cotton. I was always two or three beats behind what was goin' on on the field and so I—

BIG DADDY. Quit!

BRICK. (*amiably*) Yes, quit.

BIG DADDY. Son?   330

BRICK. Huh?

BIG DADDY. (*inhales loudly and deeply from his cigar; then bends suddenly a little forward, exhaling loudly and raising his forehead*) —Whew!—ha ha!— I took in too much smoke, it made me a little lightheaded....

    (*The mantel clock chimes.*)

Why is it so damn hard for people to talk?   335

BRICK. Yeah....

    (*The clock goes on sweetly chiming till it has completed the stroke of ten.*)

—Nice peaceful-soundin' clock, I like to hear it all night....

    (*He slides low and comfortable on the sofa; Big Daddy sits up straight and rigid with some unspoken anxiety. All his gestures are tense and jerky as he talks. He wheezes and pants and sniffs through his nervous speech, glancing quickly, shyly, from time to time, at his son.*)

BIG DADDY. We got that clock the summer we wint to Europe, me an' Big Mama on that damn Cook's Tour, never had such an awful time in my life, I'm tellin' you, son, those gooks[2] over there, they gouge your eyeballs 340

---

1   *fire sale* Sale with extremely discounted prices; the term implies that the goods are damaged or the seller is near bankruptcy.

2   *Cook's Tour* Tour offered by the travel company Thomas Cook and Son; *gooks* Offensive slang: foreigners.

out in their grand hotels. And Big Mama bought more stuff than you could haul in a couple of boxcars, that's no crap. Everywhere she wint on this whirlwind tour, she bought, bought, bought. Why, half that stuff she bought is still crated up in the cellar, under water last spring!

345   That Europe is nothin' on earth but a great big auction, that's all it is, that bunch of old wornout places, it's just a big fire sale, the whole fuckin' thing, an' Big Mama wint wild in it, why, you couldn't hold that woman with a mule's harness! Bought, bought, bought!—lucky I'm a rich man, yes siree, Bob, an' half that stuff is mildewin' in th' basement. It's lucky I'm

350   a rich man, it sure is lucky, well, I'm a rich man, Brick, yep, I'm a mighty rich man.

(*His eyes light up for a moment.*)

Y'know how much I'm worth? Guess, Brick! Guess how much I'm worth!

(*Brick smiles vaguely over his drink.*)

Close on ten million in cash an' blue-chip stocks,[1] outside, mind you, of twenty-eight thousand acres of the richest land this side of the valley Nile.

355   But a man can't buy his life with it, he can't buy back his life with it when his life has been spent, that's one thing not offered in the Europe fire-sale or in the American markets or any markets on earth, a man can't buy his life with it, he can't buy back his life when his life is finished....

That's a sobering thought, a very sobering thought, and that's a thought

360   that I was turning over in my head, over and over and over—until today....

I'm wiser and sadder, Brick, for this experience which I just gone through. They's one thing else that I remember in Europe.

BRICK. What is that, Big Daddy?

BIG DADDY. The hills around Barcelona in the country of Spain and the chil-

365   dren running over those bare hills in their bare skins beggin' like starvin' dogs with howls and screeches, and how fat the priests are on the streets of Barcelona, so many of them and so fat and so pleasant, ha ha!—Y'know I could feed that country? I got money enough to feed that goddam country, but the human animal is a selfish beast and I don't reckon the money

370   I passed out there to those howling children in the hills around Barcelona would more than upholster the chairs in this room, I mean pay to put a new cover on this chair!

Hell, I threw them money like you'd scatter feed corn for chickens, I threw money at them just to get rid of them long enough to climb back

375   into th' car and—drive away....

---

1   *blue-chip stocks* High-priced stocks that pay reliable dividends.

And then in Morocco, them Arabs, why, I remember one day in Marrakech,[1] that old walled Arab city, I set on a broken-down wall to have a cigar, it was fearful hot there and this Arab woman stood in the road and looked at me till I was embarrassed, she stood stock still in the dusty hot road and looked at me till I was embarrassed. But listen to this. She had a naked child with her, a little naked girl with her, barely able to toddle, and after a while she set this child on the ground and give her a push and whispered something to her.

The child come toward me, barely able t' walk, come toddling up to me and—

Jesus, it makes you sick t' remember a thing like this!

It stuck out its hand and tried to unbutton my trousers!

That child was not yet five! Can you believe me? Or do you think that I am making this up? I wint back to the hotel and said to Big Mama, Git packed! We're clearing out of this country....

BRICK. Big Daddy, you're on a talkin' jag tonight.

BIG DADDY. (*ignoring this remark*) Yes, sir, that's how it is, the human animal is a beast that dies but the fact that he's dying don't give him pity for others, no, sir, it—

—Did you say something?

BRICK. Yes.

BIG DADDY. What?

BRICK. Hand me over that crutch so I can get up.

BIG DADDY. Where you goin'?

BRICK. I'm takin' a little short trip to Echo Spring.

BIG DADDY. To where?

BRICK. Liquor cabinet....

BIG DADDY. Yes, sir, boy—

(*He hands Brick the crutch.*)

—the human animal is a beast that dies and if he's got money he buys and buys and buys and I think the reason he buys everything he can buy is that in the back of his mind he has the crazy hope that one of his purchases will be life everlasting!—Which it never can be.... The human animal is a beast that—

BRICK. (*at the liquor cabinet*) Big Daddy, you sure are shootin' th' breeze here tonight.

(*There is a pause and voices are heard outside.*)

1   *Marrakech* City in western Morocco.

BIG DADDY. I been quiet here lately, spoke not a word, just sat and stared into space. I had something heavy weighing on my mind but tonight that load was took off me. That's why I'm talking.—The sky looks diff'rent to me....

BRICK. You know what I like to hear most?

415 BIG DADDY. What?

BRICK. Solid quiet. Perfect unbroken quiet.

BIG DADDY. Why?

BRICK. Because it's more peaceful.

BIG DADDY. Man, you'll hear a lot of that in the grave.

(*He chuckles agreeably.*)

420 BRICK. Are you through talkin' to me?

BIG DADDY. Why are you so anxious to shut me up?

BRICK. Well, sir, ever so often you say to me, Brick, I want to have a talk with you, but when we talk, it never materializes. Nothing is said. You sit in a chair and gas about this and that and I look like I listen. I try to look like

425 I listen, but I don't listen, not much. Communication is—awful hard between people an'—somehow between you and me, it just don't—happen.

BIG DADDY. Have you ever been scared? I mean have you ever felt downright terror of something?

(*He gets up.*)

Just one moment.

(*He looks off as if he were going to tell an important secret.*)

430 BIG DADDY. Brick?

BRICK. What?

BIG DADDY. Son, I thought I had it!

BRICK. Had what? Had what, Big Daddy?

BIG DADDY. Cancer!

435 BRICK. Oh ...

BIG DADDY. I thought the old man made out of bones had laid his cold and heavy hand on my shoulder!

BRICK. Well, Big Daddy, you kept a tight mouth about it.

BIG DADDY. A pig squeals. A man keeps a tight mouth about it, in spite of a

440 man not having a pig's advantage.

BRICK. What advantage is that?

BIG DADDY. Ignorance—of mortality—is a comfort. A man don't have that comfort, he's the only living thing that conceives of death, that knows what it is. The others go without knowing which is the way that anything

445 living should go, go without knowing, without any knowledge of it, and

yet a pig squeals, but a man sometimes, he can keep a tight mouth about it. Sometimes he—

(*There is a deep, smouldering ferocity in the old man.*)

—can keep a tight mouth about it. I wonder if—
BRICK. What, Big Daddy?
BIG DADDY. A whiskey highball would injure this spastic condition?   450
BRICK. No, sir, it might do it good.
BIG DADDY. (*grins suddenly, wolfishly*) Jesus, I can't tell you! The sky is open! Christ, it's open again! It's open, boy, it's open!

(*Brick looks down at his drink.*)

BRICK. You feel better, Big Daddy?
BIG DADDY. Better? Hell! I can breathe!—All of my life I been like a doubled   455
up fist....

(*He pours a drink.*)

—Poundin', smashin', drivin'!—now I'm going to loosen these doubled-up hands and touch things *easy* with them....

(*He spreads his hands as if caressing the air.*)

You know what I'm contemplating?
BRICK. (*vaguely*) No, sir. What are you contemplating?   460
BIG DADDY. Ha ha!—*Pleasure!*—pleasure with *women!*

(*Brick's smile fades a little but lingers.*)

—Yes, boy. I'll tell you something that you might not guess. I still have desire for women and this is my sixty-fifth birthday.
BRICK. I think that's mighty remarkable, Big Daddy.
BIG DADDY. Remarkable?   465
BRICK. *Admirable*, Big Daddy.
BIG DADDY. You're damn right it is, remarkable and admirable both. I realize now that I never had me enough. I let many chances slip by because of scruples about it, scruples, convention—crap.... All that stuff is bull, bull, bull!—It took the shadow of death to make me see it. Now that shadow's   470
lifted, I'm going to cut loose and have, what is it they call it, have me a—ball!
BRICK. A ball, huh?
BIG DADDY. That's right, a ball, a ball! Hell!—I slept with Big Mama till, let's see, five years ago, till I was sixty and she was fifty-eight, and never even   475
liked her, never did!

(The phone has been ringing down the hall. Big Mama enters, exclaiming:)

BIG MAMA. Don't you men hear that phone ring? I heard it way out on the gall'ry.

BIG DADDY. There's five rooms off this front gall'ry that you could go through. Why do you go through this one?

(Big Mama makes a playful face as she bustles out the hall door.)

480   Hunh!—Why, when Big Mama goes out of a room, I can't remember what that woman looks like—

BIG MAMA. Hello.

BIG DADDY. —But when Big Mama comes back into the room, boy, then I see what she looks like, and I wish I didn't!

(Bends over laughing at this joke till it hurts his guts and he straightens with a grimace. The laugh subsides to a chuckle as he puts the liquor glass a little distrustfully down on the table.)

485   BIG MAMA. Hello, Miss Sally.

(Brick has risen and hobbled to the gallery doors.)

BIG DADDY. Hey! Where you goin'?

BRICK. Out for a breather.

BIG DADDY. Not yet you ain't. Stay here till this talk is finished, young fellow.

BRICK. I thought it was finished, Big Daddy.

490   BIG DADDY. It ain't even begun.

BRICK. My mistake. Excuse me. I just wanted to feel that river breeze.

BIG DADDY. Set back down in that chair.

(Big Mama's voice rises, carrying down the hall.)

BIG MAMA. Miss Sally, you're a case! You're a caution, Miss Sally.

BIG DADDY. Jesus, she's talking to my old maid sister again.

495   BIG MAMA. Why didn't you give me a chance to explain it to you?

BIG DADDY. Brick, this stuff burns me.

BIG MAMA. Well, goodbye, now, Miss Sally. You come down real soon. Big Daddy's dying to see you.

BIG DADDY. Crap!

500   BIG MAMA. Yaiss, goodbye, Miss Sally....

(She hangs up and bellows with mirth. Big Daddy groans and covers his ears as she approaches. Bursting in:)

Big Daddy, that was Miss Sally callin' from Memphis again! You know what she done, Big Daddy? She called her doctor in Memphis to git him to tell her what that spastic thing is! Ha-*HAAAA*!—! And called back to tell me how relieved she was that—Hey! Let me in!

(*Big Daddy has been holding the door half closed against her.*)

BIG DADDY. Naw I ain't. I told you not to come and go through this room. 505
You just back out and go through those five other rooms.

BIG MAMA. Big Daddy? Big Daddy? Oh, Big Daddy!—You didn't mean
those things you said to me, did you? (*He shuts door firmly against her but
she still calls.*) Sweetheart? Sweetheart? Big Daddy? You didn't mean those
awful things you said to me?—I know you didn't. I know you didn't mean 510
those things in your heart....

(*The childlike voice fades with a sob and her heavy footsteps retreat down
the hall. Brick has risen once more on his crutches and starts for the gallery
again.*)

BIG DADDY. All I ask of that woman is that she leave me alone. But she can't
admit to herself that she makes me sick. That comes of having slept with
her too many years. Should of quit much sooner but that old woman she
never got enough of it—and I was good in bed ... I never should of wasted 515
so much of it on her.... They say you got just so many and each one is
numbered. Well, I got a few left in me, a few, and I'm going to pick me a
good one to spend 'em on! I'm going to pick me a choice one, I don't care
how much she costs, I'll smother her in—minks! Ha ha! I'll strip her naked
and smother her in minks and choke her with diamonds! Ha ha! I'll strip 520
her naked and choke her with diamonds and smother her with minks and
hump her from hell to breakfast. *Ha aha ha ha ha!*

MAE. (*gaily at door*) Who's that laughin' in there?

GOOPER. Is Big Daddy laughin' in there?

BIG DADDY. Crap!—them two—*drips*....   525

(*He goes over and touches Brick's shoulder.*)

Yes, son, Brick, boy.—I'm—*happy!* I'm happy, son, I'm happy!

(*He chokes a little and bites his under lip, pressing his head quickly,
shyly against his son's head and then, coughing with embarrassment, goes
uncertainly back to the table where he set down the glass. He drinks and
makes a grimace as it burns his guts. Brick sighs and rises with effort.*)

What makes you so restless? Have you got ants in your britches?

BRICK. Yes, sir ...

BIG DADDY. Why?

BRICK. —Something—hasn't—happened....   530

BIG DADDY. Yeah? What is that!

BRICK. (*sadly*) —the click....

BIG DADDY. Did you say click?

BRICK. Yes, click.

535 BIG DADDY. What click?

BRICK. A click that I get in my head that makes me peaceful.

BIG DADDY. I sure in hell don't know what you're talking about, but it disturbs me.

BRICK. It's just a mechanical thing.

540 BIG DADDY. What is a mechanical thing?

BRICK. This click that I get in my head that makes me peaceful. I got to drink till I get it. It's just a mechanical thing, something like a—like a—like a—

BIG DADDY. Like a—

BRICK. Switch clicking off in my head, turning the hot light off and the cool

545 night on and—

(*He looks up, smiling sadly.*)

—all of a sudden there's—peace!

BIG DADDY. (*whistles long and soft with astonishment; he goes back to Brick and clasps his son's two shoulders*) Jesus! I didn't know it had gotten that bad with you. Why, boy, you're—*alcoholic!*

550 BRICK. That's the truth, Big Daddy. I'm alcoholic.

BIG DADDY. This shows how I—let things go!

BRICK. I have to hear that little click in my head that makes me peaceful. Usually I hear it sooner than this, sometimes as early as—noon, but—
—Today it's—dilatory....

555 —I just haven't got the right level of alcohol in my bloodstream yet!

(*This last statement is made with energy as he freshens his drink.*)

BIG DADDY. Uh—huh. Expecting death made me blind. I didn't have no idea that a son of mine was turning into a drunkard under my nose.

BRICK. (*gently*) Well, now you do, Big Daddy, the news has penetrated.

BIG DADDY. UH-huh, yes, now I do, the news has—penetrated....

560 BRICK. And so if you'll excuse me—

BIG DADDY. No, I won't excuse you.

BRICK. —I'd better sit by myself till I hear that click in my head, it's just a mechanical thing but it don't happen except when I'm alone or talking to no one....

565 BIG DADDY. You got a long, long time to sit still, boy, and talk to no one, but now you're talkin' to me. At least I'm talking to you. And you set there and listen until I tell you the conversation is over!

BRICK. But this talk is like all the others we've ever had together in our lives! It's nowhere, nowhere!—it's—it's *painful*, Big Daddy....

BIG DADDY. All right, then let it be painful, but don't you move from that 570 chair!—I'm going to remove that crutch....

(*He seizes the crutch and tosses it across the room.*)

BRICK. I can hop on one foot, and if I fall, I can crawl!

BIG DADDY. If you ain't careful you're gonna crawl off this plantation and then, by Jesus, you'll have to hustle your drinks along Skid Row!

BRICK. That'll come, Big Daddy.   575

BIG DADDY. Naw, it won't. You're my son and I'm going to straighten you out; now that *I'm* straightened out, I'm going to straighten out you!

BRICK. Yeah?

BIG DADDY. Today the report came in from Ochsner Clinic. Y'know what they told me?   580

(*His face glows with triumph.*)

The only thing that they could detect with all the instruments of science in that great hospital is a little spastic condition of the colon! And nerves torn to pieces by all that worry about it.

(*A little girl bursts into room with a sparkler clutched in each fist, hops and shrieks like a monkey gone mad and rushes back out again as Big Daddy strikes at her. Silence. The two men stare at each other. A woman laughs gaily outside.*)

I want you to know I breathed a sigh of relief almost as powerful as the Vicksburg tornado![1]   585

(*There is laughter outside, running footsteps, the soft, plushy sound and light of exploding rockets. Brick stares at him soberly for a long moment; then makes a sort of startled sound in his nostrils and springs up on one foot and hops across the room to grab his crutch, swinging on the furniture for support. He gets the crutch and flees as if in horror for the gallery. His father seizes him by the sleeve of his white silk pajamas.*)

Stay here, you son of a bitch!—till I say go!

BRICK. I can't.

BIG DADDY. You sure in hell will, God damn it.

---

1   *Vicksburg tornado* 1953 tornado that passed through the city of Vicksburg, Mississippi; it was one of the worst tornadoes in the history of the state.

BRICK. No, I can't. We talk, you talk, in—circles! We get no where, no where!
590   It's always the same, you say you want to talk to me and don't have a
fuckin' thing to say to me!

BIG DADDY. Nothin' to say when I'm tellin' you I'm going to live when I
thought I was dying?!

BRICK. Oh—*that!*—Is that what you have to say to me?

595 BIG DADDY. Why, you son of a bitch! Ain't that, ain't that—*important?!*

BRICK. Well, you said that, that's said, and now I—

BIG DADDY. Now you set back down.

BRICK. You're all balled up, you—

BIG DADDY. I ain't balled up!

600 BRICK. You are, you're all balled up!

BIG DADDY. Don't tell me what I am, you drunken whelp! I'm going to tear
this coat sleeve off if you don't set down!

BRICK. Big Daddy—

BIG DADDY. Do what I tell you! I'm the boss here, now! I want you to know
605   I'm back in the driver's seat now!

(*Big Mama rushes in, clutching her great heaving bosom.*)

BIG MAMA. Big Daddy!

BIG DADDY. What in hell do you want in here, Big Mama?

BIG MAMA. Oh, Big Daddy! Why are you shouting like that? I just cain't
stainnnnnnnd—it....

610 BIG DADDY. (*raising the back of his hand above his head*) GIT!—outa here.

(*She rushes back out, sobbing.*)

BRICK. (*softly, sadly*) Christ....

BIG DADDY. (*fiercely*) Yeah! Christ!—is right ...

(*Brick breaks loose and hobbles toward the gallery. Big Daddy jerks his
crutch from under Brick so he steps with the injured ankle. He utters a
hissing cry of anguish, clutches a chair and pulls it over on top of him on
the floor.*)

Son of a—tub of—hog fat....

BRICK. Big Daddy! Give me my crutch.

(*Big Daddy throws the crutch out of reach.*)

615   Give me that crutch, Big Daddy.

BIG DADDY. Why do you drink?

BRICK. Don't know, give me my crutch!

BIG DADDY. You better think why you drink or give up drinking!

BRICK. Will you please give me my crutch so I can get up off this floor?

BIG DADDY. First you answer my question. Why do you drink? Why are you 620
throwing your life away, boy, like somethin' disgusting you picked up on
the street?

BRICK. (*getting onto his knees*) Big Daddy, I'm in pain, I stepped on that foot.

BIG DADDY. Good! I'm glad you're not too numb with the liquor in you to
feel some pain!   625

BRICK. You—spilled my—drink ...

BIG DADDY. I'll make a bargain with you. You tell me why you drink and I'll
hand you one. I'll pour you the liquor myself and hand it to you.

BRICK. Why do I drink?

BIG DADDY. Yea! Why?   630

BRICK. Give me a drink and I'll tell you.

BIG DADDY. Tell me first!

BRICK. I'll tell you in one word.

BIG DADDY. What word?

BRICK. DISGUST!   635

(*The clock chimes softly, sweetly. Big Daddy gives it a short, outraged glance.*)

Now how about that drink?

BIG DADDY. What are you disgusted with? You got to tell me that, first. Otherwise being disgusted don't make no sense!

BRICK. Give me my crutch.

BIG DADDY. You heard me, you got to tell me what I asked you first.   640

BRICK. I told you, I said to kill my disgust.

BIG DADDY. DISGUST WITH WHAT!

BRICK. You strike a hard bargain.

BIG DADDY. What are you disgusted with?—an' I'll pass you the liquor.

BRICK. I can hop on one foot, and if I fall, I can crawl.   645

BIG DADDY. You want liquor that bad?

BRICK. (*dragging himself up, clinging to bedstead*) Yeah, I want it that bad.

BIG DADDY. If I give you a drink, will you tell me what it is you're disgusted
with, Brick?

BRICK. Yes, sir, I will try to.   650

(*The old man pours him a drink and solemnly passes it to him. There is
silence as Brick drinks.*)

Have you ever heard the word "mendacity?"

BIG DADDY. Sure. Mendacity is one of them five dollar words that cheap
politicians throw back and forth at each other.

BRICK. You know what it means?

655   BIG DADDY. Don't it mean lying and liars?
      BRICK. Yes, sir, lying and liars.
      BIG DADDY. Has someone been lying to you?
      CHILDREN. (*chanting in chorus offstage*)
        We want Big Dad-dee!
660   We want Big Dad-dee!

      (*Gooper appears in the gallery door.*)

      GOOPER. Big Daddy, the kiddies are shouting for you out there.
      BIG DADDY. (*fiercely*) Keep out, Gooper!
      GOOPER. 'Scuse *me!*

      (*Big Daddy slams the doors after Gooper.*)

      BIG DADDY. Who's been lying to you, has Margaret been lying to you, has
665   your wife been lying to you about something, Brick?
      BRICK. Not her. That wouldn't matter.
      BIG DADDY. Then who's been lying to you, and what about?
      BRICK. No one single person, and no one lie....
      BIG DADDY. Then what, what then, for Christ's sake?
670   BRICK. —The whole, the whole—thing....
      BIG DADDY. Why are you rubbing your head? You got a headache?
      BRICK. No, I'm tryin' to—
      BIG DADDY. —Concentrate, but you can't because your brain's all soaked
      with liquor, is that the trouble? Wet brain!

      (*He snatches the glass from Brick's hand.*)

675   What do you know about this mendacity thing? Hell! I could write a book
     on it! Don't you know that? I could write a book on it and still not cover
     the subject? Well, I could, I could write a goddam book on it and still not
     cover the subject anywhere near enough!!—Think of all the lies I got to
     put up with!—Pretenses! Ain't that mendacity? Having to pretend stuff
680   you don't think or feel or have any idea of? Having for instance to act like I
     care for Big Mama!—I haven't been able to stand the sight, sound, or smell
     of that woman for forty years now!—even when I *laid* her!—regular as a
     piston....
        Pretend to love that son of a bitch of a Gooper and his wife Mae and
685   those five same screechers out there like parrots in a jungle? Jesus! Can't
     stand to look at 'em!
        Church!—it bores the bejesus out of me but I go!—I go an' sit there and
     listen to the fool preacher! Clubs!—Elks! Masons! Rotary!—*crap!*

(A spasm of pain makes him clutch his belly. He sinks into a chair and his voice is softer and hoarser.)

You I *do* like for some reason, did always have some kind of real feeling for—affection—respect—yes, always....   690

You and being a success as a planter is all I ever had any devotion to in my whole life!—and that's the truth....

I don't know why, but it is!

I've lived with mendacity!—Why can't *you* live with it? Hell, you *got* to live with it, there's nothing *else* to *live* with except mendacity, is there?   695

BRICK. Yes, sir. Yes, sir there is something else that you can live with!

BIG DADDY. What?

BRICK. *(lifting his glass)* This!—Liquor....

BIG DADDY. That's not living, that's dodging away from life.

BRICK. I want to dodge away from it.   700

BIG DADDY. Then why don't you kill yourself, man?

BRICK. I like to drink....

BIG DADDY. Oh, God, I can't talk to you....

BRICK. I'm sorry, Big Daddy.

BIG DADDY. Not as sorry as I am. I'll tell you something. A little while back   705
when I thought my number was up—

(This speech should have torrential pace and fury.)

—before I found out it was just this—spastic—colon. I thought about you. Should I or should I not, if the jig was up, give you this place when I go— since I hate Gooper an' Mae an' know that they hate me, and since all five same monkeys are little Maes an' Goopers.—And I thought, No!—Then I   710 thought, Yes!—I couldn't make up my mind. I hate Gooper and his five same monkeys and that bitch Mae! Why should I turn over twenty-eight thousand acres of the richest land this side of the valley Nile to not my kind?— But why in hell, on the other hand, Brick—should I subsidize a goddam fool on the bottle?—Liked or not liked, well, maybe even—*loved!*—Why   715 should I do that?—Subsidize worthless behaviour? Rot? Corruption?

BRICK. *(smiling)* I understand.

BIG DADDY. Well, if you do, you're smarter than I am, God damn it, because I don't understand. And this I will tell you frankly. I didn't make up my mind at all on that question and still to this day I ain't made out no will!—   720 Well, now I don't *have* to. The pressure is gone. I can just wait and see if you pull yourself together or if you don't.

BRICK. That's right, Big Daddy.

BIG DADDY. You sound like you thought I was kidding.

725 BRICK. (*rising*) No, sir, I know you're not kidding.

BIG DADDY. But you don't care—?

BRICK. (*hobbling toward the gallery door*) No, sir, I don't care....

> (*He stands in the gallery doorway as the night sky turns pink and green and gold with successive flashes of light.*)

BIG DADDY. *WAIT!*—Brick....

> (*His voice drops. Suddenly there is something shy, almost tender, in his restraining gesture.*)

730 Don't let's—leave it like this, like them other talks we've had, we've always—talked around things, we've—just talked around things for some fuckin' reason, I don't know what, it's always like something was left not spoken, something avoided because neither of us was honest enough with the—other....

735 BRICK. I never lied to you, Big Daddy.

BIG DADDY. Did I ever to *you?*

BRICK. No, sir....

BIG DADDY. Then there is at least two people that never lied to each other.

BRICK. But we've never *talked* to each other.

740 BIG DADDY. We can *now.*

BRICK. Big Daddy, there don't seem to be anything much to say.

BIG DADDY. You say that you drink to kill your disgust with lying.

BRICK. You said to give you a reason.

BIG DADDY. Is liquor the only thing that'll kill this disgust?

745 BRICK. Now. Yes.

BIG DADDY. But not once, huh?

BRICK. Not when I was still young an' believing. A drinking man's someone who wants to forget he isn't still young an' believing.

BIG DADDY. Believing what?

750 BRICK. Believing....

BIG DADDY. Believing *what?*

BRICK. (*stubbornly evasive*) Believing....

BIG DADDY. I don't know what the hell you mean by believing and I don't think you know what you mean by believing, but if you still got sports in

755 your blood, go back to sports announcing and—

BRICK. Sit in a glass box watching games I can't play? Describing what I can't do while players do it? Sweating out their disgust and confusion in contests I'm not fit for? Drinkin' a coke, half bourbon, so I can stand it? That's no goddam good any more, no help—time just outran me, Big Daddy—got

760 there first ...

BIG DADDY. I think you're passing the buck.

BRICK. You know many drinkin' men?

BIG DADDY. (*with a slight, charming smile*) I have known a fair number of that species.

BRICK. Could any of them tell you why he drank?   765

BIG DADDY. Yep, you're passin' the buck to things like time and disgust with "mendacity" and—crap!—if you got to use that kind of language about a thing, it's ninety-proof[1] bull, and I'm not buying any.

BRICK. I had to give you a reason to get a drink!

BIG DADDY. You started drinkin' when your friend Skipper died.   770

(*Silence for five beats. Then Brick makes a startled movement, reaching for his crutch.*)

BRICK. What are you suggesting?

BIG DADDY. I'm suggesting nothing.

(*The shuffle and clop of Brick's rapid hobble away from his father's steady, grave attention.*)

—But Gooper an' Mae suggested that there was something not right exactly in your—

BRICK. (*stopping short downstage as if backed to a wall*) "Not right"?   775

BIG DADDY. Not, well, exactly *normal* in your friendship with—

BRICK. They suggested that, too? I thought that was Maggie's suggestion.

(*Brick's detachment is at last broken through. His heart is accelerated; his forehead sweat-beaded; his breath becomes more rapid and his voice hoarse. The thing they're discussing, timidly and painfully on the side of Big Daddy, fiercely, violently on Brick's side, is the inadmissible thing that Skipper died to disavow between them. The fact that if it existed it had to be disavowed to "keep face" in the world they lived in, may be at the heart of the "mendacity" that Brick drinks to kill his disgust with. It may be the root of his collapse. Or maybe it is only a single manifestation of it, not even the most important. The bird that I hope to catch in the net of this play is not the solution of one man's psychological problem. I'm trying to catch the true quality of experience in a group of people, that cloudy, flickering, evanescent—fiercely charged!—interplay of live human beings in the thundercloud of a common crisis. Some mystery should be left in the revelation of character in a play, just as a great deal of mystery is always left in the revelation of character in life, even in one's own character to*

---

1   *ninety-proof* I.e., concentrated; a ninety-proof alcoholic drink contains forty-five per cent pure alcohol.

himself. This does not absolve the playwright of his duty to observe and probe as clearly and deeply as he legitimately can: but it should steer him away from "pat" conclusions, facile definitions which make a play just a play, not a snare for the truth of human experience. The following scene should be played with great concentration, with most of the power leashed but palpable in what is left unspoken.)

Who else's suggestion is it, is it *yours?* How many others thought that Skipper and I were—

780 BIG DADDY. *(gently)* Now, hold on, hold on a minute, son.—I knocked around in my time.

BRICK. What's that got to do with—

BIG DADDY. I said "Hold on!"—I bummed, I bummed this country till I was—

785 BRICK. Whose suggestion, who else's suggestion is it?

BIG DADDY. Slept in hobo jungles and railroad Y's[1] and flophouses in all cities before I—

BRICK. Oh, *you* think so, too, you call me your son and a queer. Oh! Maybe that's why you put Maggie and me in this room that was Jack Straw's and
790 Peter Ochello's, in which that pair of old sisters slept in a double bed where both of 'em died!

BIG DADDY. *Now just don't go throwing rocks at—*

(Suddenly Reverend Tooker appears in the gallery doors, his head slightly, playfully, fatuously cocked, with a practised clergyman's smile, sincere as a bird call blown on a hunter's whistle, the living embodiment of the pious, conventional lie. Big Daddy gasps a little at this perfectly timed, but incongruous, apparition.)

—What're you lookin' for, Preacher?

REVEREND TOOKER. The gentleman's lavoratory, ha ha!—heh, heh ...

795 BIG DADDY. *(with strained courtesy)*—Go back out and walk down to the other end of the gallery, Reverend Tooker, and use the bathroom connected with my bedroom, and if you can't find it, ask them where it is!

REVEREND TOOKER. Ah, thanks.

(He goes out with a deprecatory chuckle.)

BIG DADDY. It's hard to talk in this place ...

---

1   *hobo jungles* Camps or communities created near railroads by jobless people who travelled as stowaways on freight trains; *Y's* YMCA (Young Men's Christian Association) facilities, which offered cheap accommodation for young men. They were sometimes built near railway stations for the benefit of rail workers.

BRICK. Son of a—!   800

BIG DADDY. (*leaving a lot unspoken*)—I seen all things and understood a lot of them, till 1910. Christ, the year that—I had worn my shoes through, hocked my—I hopped off a yellow dog freight car half a mile down the road, slept in a wagon of cotton outside the gin—Jack Straw an' Peter Ochello took me in. Hired me to manage this place which grew into this   805 one.—When Jack Straw died—why, old Peter Ochello quit eatin' like a dog does when its master's dead, and died, too!

BRICK. Christ!

BIG DADDY. I'm just saying I understand such—

BRICK. (*violently*) Skipper is dead. I have not quit eating!   810

BIG DADDY. No, but you started drinking.

(*Brick wheels on his crutch and hurls his glass across the room shouting.*)

BRICK. YOU THINK SO, TOO?

(*Footsteps run on the gallery. There are women's calls. Big Daddy goes toward the door. Brick is transformed, as if a quiet mountain blew suddenly up in volcanic flame.*)

BRICK. You think so, too? You think so, too? You think me an' Skipper did, did, did!—*sodomy!* —together?

BIG DADDY. Hold—!   815

BRICK. That what you—

BIG DADDY. —ON—a minute!

BRICK. You think we did dirty things between us, Skipper an'—

BIG DADDY. Why are you shouting like that? Why are you—

BRICK. —Me, is that what you think of Skipper, is that—   820

BIG DADDY. —so excited? I don't think nothing. I don't know nothing. I'm simply telling you what—

BRICK. You think that Skipper and me were a pair of dirty old men?

BIG DADDY. Now that's—

BRICK. Straw? Ochello? A couple of—   825

BIG DADDY. Now just—

BRICK. —fucking sissies? Queers? Is that what you—

BIG DADDY. Shhh.

BRICK. —think?

(*He loses his balance and pitches to his knees without noticing the pain. He grabs the bed and drags himself up.*)

BIG DADDY. Jesus!—Whew.... Grab my hand!   830

BRICK. Naw, I don't want your hand....

BIG DADDY. Well, I want yours. Git up! (*He draws him up, keeps an arm about him with concern and affection.*) You broken out in sweat! You're panting like you'd run a race with—

835 BRICK. (*freeing himself from his father's hold*) Big Daddy, you shock me, Big Daddy, you, you—*shock* me! Talkin' so—

(*He turns away from his father.*)

—casually!—about a—thing like that ...

—Don't you know how people *feel* about things like that? How, how *disgusted* they are by things like that? Why, at Ole Miss when it was discov-
840 ered a pledge to our fraternity, Skipper's and mine, did a, *attempted* to do a, unnatural thing with—

We not only dropped him like a hot rock!—We told him to git off the campus, and he did, he got!—All the way to—

(*He halts, breathless.*)

BIG DADDY. —Where?

845 BRICK. —North Africa, last I heard!

BIG DADDY. Well, I have come back from further away than that, I have just now returned from the other side of the moon, death's country, son, and I'm not easy to shock by anything here.

(*He comes downstage and faces out.*)

Always, anyhow, lived with too much space around me to be infected by
850 ideas of other people. One thing you can grow on a big place more important than cotton!—is *tolerance!*—I grown it. (*He returns toward Brick.*)

BRICK. Why can't exceptional friendship, *real, real, deep, deep friendship!* between two men be respected as something clean and decent without being thought of as—

855 BIG DADDY. It can, it is, for God's sake.

BRICK. —*Fairies....*

(*In his utterance of this word, we gauge the wide and profound reach of the conventional mores he got from the world that crowned him with early laurel.*[1])

BIG DADDY. I told Mae an' Gooper—

BRICK. Frig Mae and Gooper, frig all dirty lies and liars!—Skipper and me had a clean, true thing between us!—had a clean friendship, practically all
860 our lives, till Maggie got the idea you're talking about. Normal? No!—It

---

1   *crowned ... laurel* In classical times a crown of laurels was worn to denote victory.

was too rare to be normal, any true thing between two people is too rare to be normal. Oh, once in a while he put his hand on my shoulder or I'd put mine on his, oh, maybe even, when we were touring the country in pro-football an' shared hotel-rooms we'd reach across the space between the two beds and shake hands to say goodnight, yeah, one or two times we— 865

BIG DADDY. Brick, nobody thinks that that's not normal!

BRICK. Well, they're mistaken, it was! It was a pure an' true thing an' that's not normal.

MAE. (*off stage*) Big Daddy, they're startin' the fireworks.

(*They both stare straight at each other for a long moment. The tension breaks and both turn away as if tired.*)

BIG DADDY. Yeah, it's—hard t'—talk.... 870

BRICK. All right, then, let's—let it go....

BIG DADDY. Why did Skipper crack up? Why have you?

(*Brick looks back at his father again. He has already decided, without knowing that he has made this decision, that he is going to tell his father that he is dying of cancer. Only this could even the score between them: one inadmissible thing in return for another.*)

BRICK. (*ominously*) All right. You're asking for it, Big Daddy. We're finally going to have that real true talk you wanted. It's too late to stop it, now, we got to carry it through and cover every subject. 875

(*He hobbles back to the liquor cabinet.*)

Uh-huh.

(*He opens the ice bucket and picks up the silver tongs with slow admiration of their frosty brightness.*)

Maggie declares that Skipper and I went into pro-football after we left "Ole Miss" because we were scared to grow up ...

(*He moves downstage with the shuffle and clop of a cripple on a crutch. As Margaret did when her speech became "recitative," he looks out into the house, commanding its attention by his direct, concentrated gaze—a broken, "tragically elegant" figure telling simply as much as he knows of "the Truth":*)

—Wanted to—keep on tossing—those long, long!—high, high!—passes that—couldn't be intercepted except by time, the aerial attack that made 880 us famous! And so we did, we did, we kept it up for one season, that aerial attack, we held it high!—Yeah, but—

—that summer, Maggie, she laid the law down to me, said, Now or never, and so I married Maggie....

885 BIG DADDY. How was Maggie in bed?

BRICK. (*wryly*) Great! the greatest!

(*Big Daddy nods as if he thought so.*)

She went on the road that fall with the Dixie Stars. Oh, she made a great show of being the world's best sport. She wore a—wore a—tall bearskin cap! A shako, they call it, a dyed moleskin coat, a moleskin coat dyed

890 red!—Cut up crazy! Rented hotel ballrooms for victory celebrations, wouldn't cancel them when it—turned out—defeat....

MAGGIE THE CAT! Ha ha!

(*Big Daddy nods.*)

—But Skipper, he had some fever which came back on him which doctors couldn't explain and I got that injury—turned out to be just a shadow on

895 the X-ray plate—and a touch of bursitis.[1]...

I lay in a hospital bed, watched our games on TV, saw Maggie on the bench next to Skipper when he was hauled out of a game for stumbles, fumbles!—Burned me up the way she hung on his arm!—Y'know, I think that Maggie had always felt sort of left out because she and me never got

900 any closer together than two people just get in bed, which is not much closer than two cats on a—fence humping....

So! She took this time to work on poor dumb Skipper. He was a less than average student at Ole Miss, you know that, don't you?!—Poured in his mind the dirty, false idea that what we were, him and me, was a frus-

905 trated case of that ole pair of sisters that lived in this room, Jack Straw and Peter Ochello!—He, poor Skipper, went to bed with Maggie to prove it wasn't true, and when it didn't work out, he thought it *was* true!—Skipper broke in two like a rotten stick—nobody ever turned so fast to a lush—or died of it so quick....

910 —Now are you satisfied?

(*Big Daddy has listened to this story, dividing the grain from the chaff. Now he looks at his son.*)

BIG DADDY. Are *you* satisfied?

BRICK. With what?

BIG DADDY. That half-ass story!

BRICK. What's half-ass about it?

---

1 *bursitis* Inflammation of the joints.

BIG DADDY. Something's left out of that story. What did you leave out?   915

> (*The phone has started ringing in the hall.*)

GOOPER. (*off stage*) Hello.

> (*As if it reminded him of something, Brick glances suddenly toward the sound and says:*)

BRICK. Yes!—I left out a long-distance call which I had from Skipper—
GOOPER. Speaking, go ahead.
BRICK. —In which he made a drunken confession to me and on which I hung up!   920
GOOPER. No.
BRICK. —Last time we spoke to each other in our lives ...
GOOPER. No, sir.
BIG DADDY. You musta said something to him before you hung up.
BRICK. What could I say to him?   925
BIG DADDY. Anything. Something.
BRICK. Nothing.
BIG DADDY. Just hung up?
BRICK. Just hung up.
BIG DADDY. Uh-huh. Anyhow now!—we have tracked down the lie with   930 which you're disgusted and which you are drinking to kill your disgust with, Brick. You been passing the buck. This disgust with mendacity is disgust with yourself.

> *You!*—dug the grave of your friend and kicked him in it!—before you'd face truth with him!   935

BRICK. *His* truth, not *mine!*
BIG DADDY. His truth, okay! But you wouldn't face it with him!
BRICK. Who *can* face truth? Can *you?*
BIG DADDY. Now don't start passin' the rotten buck again, boy!
BRICK. How about these birthday congratulations, these many, many happy   940 returns of the day, when ev'rybody knows there won't be any except you!

> (*Gooper, who has answered the hall phone, lets out a high, shrill laugh; the voice becomes audible saying: "No, no, you got it all wrong! Upside down! Are you crazy?"*
>
> *Brick suddenly catches his breath as he realizes that he has made a shocking disclosure. He hobbles a few paces, then freezes, and without looking at this father's shocked face, says:*)

Let's, let's—go out, now, and—watch the fireworks. Come on, Big Daddy.

(*Big Daddy moves suddenly forward and grabs hold of the boy's crutch like it was a weapon for which they were fighting for possession.*)

945 BIG DADDY. Oh, no, no! No one's going out! What did you start to say?
BRICK. I don't remember.
BIG DADDY. "Many happy returns when they know there won't be any"?
BRICK. Aw, hell, Big Daddy, forget it. Come on out on the gallery and look at the fireworks they're shooting off for your birthday....
950 BIG DADDY. First you finish that remark you were makin' before you cut off. "Many happy returns when they know there won't be any"?—Ain't that what you just said?
BRICK. Look, now. I can get around without that crutch if I have to but it would be a lot easier on the furniture an' glassware if I didn' have to go
955 swinging along like Tarzan of th'—
BIG DADDY. *FINISH! WHAT YOU WAS SAYIN'!*

(*An eerie green glow shows in sky behind him.*)

BRICK. (*sucking the ice in his glass, speech becoming thick*). Leave th' place to Gooper and Mae an' their five little same little monkeys. All I want is—
BIG DADDY. "LEAVE TH' PLACE," did you say?
960 BRICK. (*vaguely*) All twenty-eight thousand acres of the richest land this side of the valley Nile.
BIG DADDY. Who said I was "leaving the place" to Gooper or anybody? This is my sixty-fifth birthday! I got fifteen years or twenty years left in me! I'll outlive *you!* I'll bury you an' have to pay for your coffin!
965 BRICK. Sure. Many happy returns. Now let's go watch the fireworks, come on, let's—
BIG DADDY. Lying, have they been lying? About the report from th'—clinic? Did they, did they—find something?—*Cancer.* Maybe?
BRICK. Mendacity is a system that we live in. Liquor is the one way out an'
970 death's the other....

(*He takes the crutch from Big Daddy's loose grip and swings out on the gallery leaving the doors open. A song, "Pick a Bale of Cotton,"[1] is heard.*)

MAE. (*appearing in door*) Oh, Big Daddy, the field hands are singin' fo' you!
BRICK. I'm sorry, Big Daddy. My head don't work any more and it's hard for me to understand how anybody could care if he lived or died or was dying or cared about anything but whether or not there was liquor left in the bot-
975 tle and so I said what I said without thinking. In some ways I'm no better than the others, in some ways worse because I'm less alive. Maybe it's be-

1   *"Pick a Bale of Cotton"* Traditional Southern folk song.

ing alive that makes them lie, and being almost *not* alive makes me sort of accidentally truthful—I don't know but—anyway—we've been friends ...
—And being friends is telling each other the truth....

(*There is a pause.*)

You told *me!* I told *you!*   980
BIG DADDY. (*slowly and passionately*) CHRIST—DAMN—
GOOPER. (*off stage*) Let her go!

(*Fireworks off stage right.*)

BIG DADDY. —ALL—LYING SONS OF—LYING BITCHES!

(*He straightens at last and crosses to the inside door. At the door he turns and looks back as if he had some desperate question he couldn't put into words. Then he nods reflectively and says in a hoarse voice:*)

Yes, all liars, all liars, all lying dying liars!

(*This is said slowly, slowly, with a fierce revulsion. He goes on out.*)

—Lying! Dying! Liars!   985

(*Brick remains motionless as the lights dim out and the curtain falls.*)

CURTAIN

ACT 3

There is no lapse of time. Big Daddy is seen leaving as at the end of Act II.

BIG DADDY. ALL LYIN'—DYIN'!—LIARS! LIARS!—LIARS!

(*Margaret enters.*)

MARGARET. Brick, what in the name of God was goin' on in this room?

(*Dixie and Trixie enter through the doors and circle around Margaret shouting. Mae enters from the lower gallery window.*)

MAE. Dixie, Trixie, you quit that!

(*Gooper enters through the doors.*)

Gooper, will y' please get these kiddies to bed right now!
GOOPER. Mae, you seen Big Mama?   5
MAE. Not yet.

(*Gooper and kids exit through the doors. Reverend Tooker enters through the windows.*)

REVEREND TOOKER. Those kiddies are so full of vitality. I think I'll have to be starting back to town.

MAE. Not yet, Preacher. You know we regard you as a member of this family,
10   one of our closest an' dearest, so you just got t' be with us when Doc Baugh gives Big Mama th'actual truth about th' report from the clinic.

MARGARET. Where do you think you're going?

BRICK. Out for some air.

MARGARET. Why'd Big Daddy shout "Liars?"

15   MAE. Has Big Daddy gone to bed, Brick?

GOOPER. (*entering*) Now where is that old lady?

REVEREND TOOKER. I'll look for her.

(*He exits to the gallery.*)

MAE. Cain'tcha find her, Gooper?

GOOPER. She's avoidin' this talk.

20   MAE. I think she senses somethin'.

MARGARET. (*going out on the gallery to Brick*) Brick, they're goin' to tell Big Mama the truth about Big Daddy and she's goin' to need you.

DOCTOR BAUGH. This is going to be painful.

MAE. Painful things caint always be avoided.

25   REVEREND TOOKER. I see Big Mama.

GOOPER. Hey, Big Mama, come here.

MAE. Hush, Gooper, don't holler.

BIG MAMA. (*entering*) Too much smell of burnt fireworks makes me feel a little bit sick at my stomach.—Where is Big Daddy?

30   MAE. That's what I want to know, where has Big Daddy gone?

BIG MAMA. He must have turned in, I reckon he went to baid ...

GOOPER. Well, then, now we can talk.

BIG MAMA. What *is* this talk, *what* talk?

(*Margaret appears on the gallery, talking to Doctor Baugh.*)

MARGARET. (*musically*) My family freed their slaves ten years before aboli-
35   tion.[1] My great-great-grandfather gave his slaves their freedom five years before the War between the States[2] started!

MAE. Oh, for God's sake! Maggie's climbed back up in her family tree!

MARGARET. (*sweetly*) What, Mae?

---

1   *abolition* In the United States, slavery was officially abolished in 1865.
2   *War between the States* I.e., the American Civil War (1861–65).

(*The pace must be very quick: great Southern animation.*)

BIG MAMA. (*addressing them all*) I think Big Daddy was just worn out. He
loves his family, he loves to have them around him, but it's a strain on his   40
nerves. He wasn't himself tonight, Big Daddy wasn't himself, I could tell
he was all worked up.

REVEREND TOOKER. I think he's remarkable.

BIG MAMA. Yaisss! Just remarkable. Did you all notice the food he ate at that
table? Did you all notice the supper he put away? Why he ate like a hawss!   45

GOOPER. I hope he doesn't regret it.

BIG MAMA. What? Why that man—ate a huge piece of cawn bread with
molasses on it! Helped himself twice to hoppin' John.[1]

MARGARET. Big Daddy loves hoppin' John.—We had a real country dinner.

BIG MAMA. (*overlapping Margaret*) Yaiss, he simply adores it! an' candied   50
yams? Son? That man put away enough food at that table to stuff a *field*
hand!

GOOPER. (*with grim relish*) I hope he don't have to pay for it later on ...

BIG MAMA. (*fiercely*) What's *that*, Gooper?

MAE. Gooper says he hopes Big Daddy doesn't suffer tonight.   55

BIG MAMA. Oh, shoot, Gooper says, Gooper says! Why should Big Daddy
suffer for satisfying a normal appetite? There's nothin' wrong with that
man but nerves, he's sound as a dollar! And now he knows he is an' that's
why he ate such a supper. He had a big load off his mind, knowin' he
wasn't doomed t'—what he thought he was doomed to ...   60

MARGARET. (*sadly and sweetly*) Bless his old sweet soul ...

BIG MAMA. (*vaguely*) Yais, bless his heart, where's Brick?

MAE. Outside.

GOOPER. —Drinkin' ...

BIG MAMA. I know he's drinkin'. Cain't I see he's drinkin' without you con-   65
tinually tellin' me that boy's drinkin'?

MARGARET. Good for you, Big Mama!

(*She applauds.*)

BIG MAMA. Other people *drink* and *have* drunk an' will *drink*, as long as they
make that stuff an' put it in bottles.

MARGARET. That's the truth. I never trusted a man that didn't drink.   70

BIG MAMA. *Brick? Brick!*

MARGARET. He's still on the gall'ry. I'll go bring him in so we can talk.

BIG MAMA. (*worriedly*) I don't know what this mysterious family conference
is about.

---

1   *hoppin' John* Southern dish made with black-eyed peas, rice, bacon, and onions.

(*Awkward silence. Big Mama looks from face to face, then belches slightly and mutters, "Excuse me ..." She opens an ornamental fan suspended about her throat. A black lace fan to go with her black lace gown, and fans her wilting corsage, sniffing nervously and looking from face to face in the uncomfortable silence as Margaret calls "Brick?" and Brick sings to the moon on the gallery.*)

75 MARGARET. Brick, they're gonna tell Big Mama the truth an' she's gonna need you.

BIG MAMA. I don't know what's wrong here, you all have such long faces! Open that door on the hall and let some air circulate through here, will you please, Gooper?

80 MAE. I think we'd better leave that door closed, Big Mama, till after the talk.

MARGARET. Brick!

BIG MAMA. Reveren' Tooker, will *you* please open that door?

REVEREND TOOKER. I sure will, Big Mama.

MAE. I just didn't think we ought t' take any chance of Big Daddy hearin' a
85 word of this discussion.

BIG MAMA. *I swan!*[1] Nothing's going to be said in Big Daddy's house that he caint hear if he wants to!

GOOPER. Well, Big Mama, it's—

(*Mae gives him a quick, hard poke to shut him up. He glares at her fiercely as she circles before him like a burlesque[2] ballerina, raising her skinny bare arms over her head, jangling her bracelets, exclaiming:*)

MAE. *A breeze! A breeze!*

90 REVEREND TOOKER. I think this house is the coolest house in the Delta.— Did you all know that Halsey Banks's widow put air-conditioning units in the church and rectory at Friar's Point in memory of Halsey?

(*General conversation has resumed; everybody is chatting so that the stage sounds like a bird cage.*)

GOOPER. Too bad nobody cools your church off for you. I bet you sweat in that pulpit these hot Sundays, Reverend Tooker.

95 REVEREND TOOKER. Yes, my vestments[3] are drenched. Last Sunday the gold in my chasuble[4] faded into the purple.

GOOPER. Reveren', you musta been preachin' hell's fire last Sunday.

---

1   *I swan* I.e., I swear.
2   *burlesque* Exaggerated for comedic effect.
3   *vestments* Garments worn by religious officials during public ceremonies.
4   *chasuble* Outer vestment worn by Catholic and Anglican priests during Mass.

MAE. (*at the same time to Doctor Baugh*) You reckon those vitamin B12 injections are what they're cracked up t' be, Doc Baugh?

DOCTOR BAUGH. Well, if you want to be stuck with something I guess they're as good to be stuck with as anything else. 100

BIG MAMA. (*at the gallery door*) Maggie, Maggie, aren't you comin' with Brick?

MAE. (*suddenly and loudly, creating a silence*) I have a strange feeling, I have a peculiar feeling!

BIG MAMA. (*turning from the gallery*) What feeling? 105

MAE. That Brick said somethin' he shouldn't of said t' Big Daddy.

BIG MAMA. Now what on earth could Brick of said t' Big Daddy that he shouldn't say?

GOOPER. Big Mama, there's somethin'—

MAE. NOW, WAIT! 110

(*She rushes up to Big Mama and gives her a quick hug and kiss. Big Mama pushes her impatiently off.*)

DOCTOR BAUGH. In my day they had what they call the Keeley cure[1] for heavy drinkers.

BIG MAMA. Shoot!

DOCTOR BAUGH. But now I understand they just take some kind of tablets.

GOOPER. They call them "Annie Bust" tablets.[2] 115

BIG MAMA. *Brick* don't need to take *nothin'*.

(*Brick and Margaret appear in gallery doors, Big Mama unaware of his presence behind her.*)

That boy is just broken up over Skipper's death. You know how poor Skipper died. They gave him a big, big dose of that sodium amytal[3] stuff at his home and then they called the ambulance and give him another big, big dose of it at the hospital and that and all of the alcohol in his system fo' 120 months an' months just proved too much for his heart ... I'm scared of needles! I'm more scared of a needle than the knife ... I think more people have been needled out of this world than—

(*She stops short and wheels about.*)

Oh—here's Brick! My precious baby—

---

1   *Keeley cure* Treatment for alcoholism from the Keeley Institute. Especially popular in the 1890s, the Keeley cure utilized ineffective secret tonics and injections of "gold chloride."

2   *"Annie Bust" tablets* Tablets of Antabuse, the trade name of the drug disulfiram, which causes unpleasant reactions after the consumption of alcohol.

3   *sodium amytal* Sedative not recommended for people with histories of alcoholism or impaired liver function.

(*She turns upon Brick with short, fat arms extended, at the same time uttering a loud, short sob, which is both comic and touching. Brick smiles and bows slightly, making a burlesque gesture of gallantry for Margaret to pass before him into the room. Then he hobbles on his crutch directly to the liquor cabinet and there is absolute silence, with everybody looking at Brick as everybody has always looked at Brick when he spoke or moved or appeared. One by one he drops ice cubes in his glass, then suddenly, but not quickly, looks back over his shoulder with a wry, charming smile, and says:*)

125 BRICK. I'm sorry! Anyone else?

BIG MAMA. (*sadly*) No, son, I *wish* you wouldn't!

BRICK. I wish I didn't have to, Big Mama, but I'm still waiting for that click in my head which makes it all smooth out!

BIG MAMA. Ow, Brick, you—BREAK MY HEART!

130 MARGARET. (*at the same time*) Brick, go sit with Big Mama!

BIG MAMA. I just cain't staiiiiii-nnnnnnnd-it ...

(*She sobs.*)

MAE. Now that we're all assembled—

GOOPER. We kin talk ...

BIG MAMA. Breaks my heart ...

135 MARGARET. Sit with Big Mama, Brick, and hold her hand.

(*Big Mama sniffs very loudly three times, almost like three drumbeats in the pocket of silence.*)

BRICK. You do that, Maggie. I'm a restless cripple. I got to stay on my crutch.

(*Brick hobbles to the gallery door; leans there as if waiting. Mae sits beside Big Mama, while Gooper moves in front and sits on the end of the couch, facing her. Reverend Tooker moves nervously into the space between them; on the other side, Doctor Baugh stands looking at nothing in particular and lights a cigar. Margaret turns away.*)

BIG MAMA. Why're you all *surroundin'* me—like this? Why're you all starin' at me like this an' makin' signs at each other?

(*Reverend Tooker steps back startled.*)

MAE. Calm yourself, Big Mama.

140 BIG MAMA. Calm you'self, *you'self*, Sister Woman. How could I calm myself with everyone starin' at me as if big drops of blood had broken out on m'face? What's this all about, annh! What?

(*Gooper coughs and takes a centre position.*)

GOOPER. Now, Doc Baugh.

MAE. Doc Baugh?

GOOPER. Big Mama wants to know the complete truth about the report we 145
got from the Ochsner Clinic.

MAE. (*eagerly*)—on Big Daddy's condition!

GOOPER. Yais, on Big Daddy's condition, we got to face it.

DOCTOR BAUGH. Well ...

BIG MAMA. (*terrified, rising*) Is there? Something? Something that I? Don't— 150
know?

> (*In these few words, this startled, very soft, question, Big Mama reviews
> the history of her forty-five years with Big Daddy, her great, almost
> embarrassingly true-hearted and simple-minded devotion to Big Daddy,
> who must have had something Brick has, who made himself loved so much
> by the "simple expedient" of not loving enough to disturb his charming
> detachment, also once coupled, like Brick, with virile beauty. Big Mama
> has a dignity at this moment; she almost stops being fat.*)

DOCTOR BAUGH. (*after a pause, uncomfortably*) Yes?—Well—

BIG MAMA. I!!!—want to—*knowwwwww* ...

> (*Immediately she thrusts her fist to her mouth as if to deny that statement.
> Then for some curious reason, she snatches the withered corsage from her
> breast and hurls it on the floor and steps on it with her short, fat feet.*)

> *Somebody must be lyin'!—I want to know!*

MAE. Sit down, Big Mama, sit down on this sofa. 155

MARGARET. Brick, go sit with Big Mama.

BIG MAMA. *What is it, what is it?*

DOCTOR BAUGH. I never have seen a more thorough examination than Big
Daddy Pollitt was given in all my experience with the Ochsner Clinic.

GOOPER. It's one of the best in the country. 160

MAE. It's THE best in the country—bar *none!*

> (*For some reason she gives Gooper a violent poke as she goes past him. He
> slaps at her hand without removing his eyes from his mother's face.*)

DOCTOR BAUGH. Of course they were ninety-nine and nine-tenths per cent
sure before they even started.

BIG MAMA. Sure of what, sure of what, sure of—*what?—what?*

> (*She catches her breath in a startled sob. Mae kisses her quickly. She thrusts
> Mae fiercely away from her, staring at the Doctor.*)

MAE. Mommy, be a brave girl! 165

BRICK. (*in the doorway, singing softly*) "By the light, by the light, Of the sil-
ve-ry mo-oo-n ..."[1]

GOOPER. Shut up!—Brick.

BRICK. Sorry ...

(*He wanders out on the gallery.*)

170 DOCTOR BAUGH. But now, you see, Big Mama, they cut a piece off this
growth, a specimen of the tissue and—

BIG MAMA. Growth? You told Big Daddy—

DOCTOR BAUGH. Now wait.

BIG MAMA. (*fiercely*) You told me and Big Daddy there wasn't a thing wrong
175 with him but—

MAE. Big Mama, they always—

GOOPER. Let Doc Baugh talk, will yuh?

BIG MAMA. —little spastic condition of—

(*Her breath gives out in a sob.*)

DOCTOR BAUGH. Yes, that's what we told Big Daddy. But we had this bit of
180 tissue run through the laboratory and I'm sorry to say the test was positive
on it. It's—well—malignant ...

(*Pause*)

BIG MAMA. —Cancer?! Cancer?!

(*Doctor Baugh nods gravely. Big Mama gives a long gasping cry.*)

MAE AND GOOPER. Now, now, now, Big Mama, you had to know ...

BIG MAMA. WHY DIDN'T THEY CUT IT OUT OF HIM? HANH? HANH?

185 DOCTOR BAUGH. Involved too much, Big Mama, too many organs affected.

MAE. Big Mama, the liver's affected and so's the kidneys, both! It's gone way
past what they call a—

GOOPER. A surgical risk.

MAE. —Uh-huh ...

190 (*Big Mama draws a breath like a dying gasp.*)

REVEREND TOOKER. Tch, tch, tch, tch, tch!

DOCTOR BAUGH. Yes it's gone past the knife.

MAE. *That's why he's turned yellow, Mommy!*

---

1   *By the light ... mo-oo-on* Line from "By the Light of the Silvery Moon" (1909), a popular
song by Gus Edwards and Edward Madden.

BIG MAMA. *Git away from me, git away from me, Mae!*

(*She rises abruptly.*)

I want Brick! Where's Brick? Where is my only son?   195

MAE. Mama! Did she say "*only* son"?

GOOPER. What does that make *me*?

MAE. A sober responsible man with five precious children!—*Six!*

BIG MAMA. I want Brick to tell me! Brick! Brick!

MARGARET. (*rising from her reflections in a corner*) Brick was so upset he went   200
back out.

BIG MAMA. *Brick!*

MARGARET. Mama, let *me* tell you!

BIG MAMA. No, no, leave me alone, you're not my blood!

GOOPER. *Mama, I'm your son!* Listen to *me!*   205

MAE. Gooper's your son, he's your first-born!

BIG MAMA. Gooper never liked Daddy.

MAE. (*as if terribly shocked*) That's not TRUE!

(*There is a pause. The minister coughs and rises.*)

REVEREND TOOKER. (*to Mae*) I think I'd better slip away at this point.

(*Discreetly*)

Good night, good night, everybody, and God bless you all ... on this   210
place ...

(*He slips out. Mae coughs and points at Big Mama.*)

GOOPER. Well, Big Mama ...

(*He sighs.*)

BIG MAMA. It's all a mistake, I know it's just a bad dream.

DOCTOR BAUGH. We're gonna keep Big Daddy as comfortable as we can.

BIG MAMA. Yes, it's just a bad dream, that's all it is, it's just an awful dream.   215

GOOPER. In my opinion Big Daddy is having some pain but won't admit
that he has it.

BIG MAMA. Just a dream, a bad dream.

DOCTOR BAUGH. That's what lots of them do, they think if they don't admit
they're having the pain they can sort of escape the fact of it.   220

GOOPER. (*with relish*) Yes, they get sly about it, they get real sly about it.

MAE. Gooper and I think—

GOOPER. Shut up, Mae! Big Mama, I think—Big Daddy ought to be started
on morphine.

225 BIG MAMA. Nobody's going to give Big Daddy morphine.

DOCTOR BAUGH. Now, Big Mama, when that pain strikes it's going to strike mighty hard and Big Daddy's going to need the needle to bear it.

BIG MAMA. I tell you, nobody's going to give him morphine.

MAE. Big Mama, you don't want to see Big Daddy suffer, you know you—

(*Gooper, standing beside her, gives her a savage poke.*)

230 DOCTOR BAUGH. (*placing a package on the table*) I'm leaving this stuff here, so if there's a sudden attack you all won't have to send out for it.

MAE. I know how to give a hypo.

BIG MAMA. Nobody's gonna give Big Daddy morphine.

GOOPER. Mae took a course in nursing during the war.

235 MARGARET. Somehow I don't think Big Daddy would want Mae to give him a hypo.

MAE. You think he'd want *you* to do it?

DOCTOR BAUGH. Well ...

(*Doctor Baugh rises.*)

GOOPER. Doctor Baugh is goin'.

240 DOCTOR BAUGH. Yes, I got to be goin'. Well, keep you chin up, Big Mama.

GOOPER. (*with jocularity*) She's gonna keep *both* chins up, aren't you, Big Mama?

(*Big Mama sobs.*)

Now stop that, Big Mama.

GOOPER. (*at the door with Doctor Baugh*) Well, Doc, we sure do appreciate all
245 you done. I'm telling you, we're surely obligated to you for—

(*Doctor Baugh has gone out without a glance at him.*)

—I guess that doctor has got a lot on his mind but it wouldn't hurt him to act a little more human ... (*Big Mama sobs.*)
Now be a brave girl, Mommy.

BIG MAMA. It's not true, I know that it's just not true!

250 GOOPER. Mama, those tests are infallible!

BIG MAMA. Why are you so determined to see your father daid?

MAE. Big Mama!

MARGARET. (*gently*) I know what Big Mama means.

MAE. (*fiercely*) Oh, do you?

255 MARGARET. (*quietly and very sadly*) Yes, I think I do.

MAE. For a newcomer in the family you sure do show a lot of understanding.

MARGARET. Understanding is needed on this place.

MAE. I guess you must have needed a lot of it in your family, Maggie, with your father's liquor problem and now you've got Brick with his!

MARGARET. Brick does not have a liquor problem at all. Brick is devoted to Big Daddy. This thing is a terrible strain on him. 260

BIG MAMA. Brick is Big Daddy's boy, but he drinks too much and it worries me and Big Daddy, and, Margaret, you've got to co-operate with us, you've got to co-operate with Big Daddy and me in getting Brick straightened out. Because it will break Big Daddy's heart if Brick don't pull himself 265 together and take hold of things.

MAE. Take hold of *what* things, Big Mama?

BIG MAMA. The place.

(*There is a quick and violent look between Mae and Gooper.*)

GOOPER. Big Mama, you've had a shock.

MAE. Yais, we've all had a shock, but ... 270

GOOPER. Let's be realistic—

MAE. —Big Daddy would never, would *never*, be foolish enough to—

GOOPER. —put this place in irresponsible hands!

BIG MAMA. Big Daddy ain't going to leave the place in anybody's hands; Big Daddy is *not* going to die. I want you to get that in your heads, all of you! 275

MAE. Mommy, Mommy, Big Mama, we're just as hopeful an' optimistic as you are about Big Daddy's prospects, we have faith in *prayer*—but nevertheless there are certain matters that have to be discussed an' dealt with, because otherwise—

GOOPER. Eventualities have to be considered and now's the time ... Mae, will 280 you please get my brief case out of our room?

MAE. Yes, honey.

(*She rises and goes out through the hall door.*)

GOOPER. (*standing over Big Mama*) Now, Big Mom. What you said just now was not at all true and you know it. I've always loved Big Daddy in my own quiet way. I never made a show of it, and I know that Big Daddy has 285 always been fond of me in a quiet way, too, and he never made a show of it neither.

(*Mae returns with Gooper's brief case.*)

MAE. Here's your brief case, Gooper, honey.

GOOPER. (*handing the brief case back to her*) Thank you ... Of cou'se, my relationship with Big Daddy is different from Brick's. 290

MAE. You're eight years older'n Brick an' always had t' carry a bigger load of th' responsibilities than Brick ever had t' carry. He never carried a thing in his life but a football or a highball.

GOOPER. Mae, will y' let me talk, please?

295 MAE. Yes, honey.

GOOPER. Now, a twenty-eight-thousand-acre plantation's a mighty big thing t' run.

MAE. Almost singlehanded.

(*Margaret has gone out onto the gallery and can be heard calling softly to Brick.*)

BIG MAMA. You never had to run this place! What are you talking about? As
300 if Big Daddy was dead and in his grave, you had to run it? Why, you just helped him out with a few business details and had your law practice at the same time in Memphis!

MAE. Oh, Mommy, Mommy, Big Mommy! Let's be fair!

MARGARET. Brick!

305 MAE. Why, Gooper has given himself body and soul to keeping this place up for the past five years since Big Daddy's health started failing.

MARGARET. Brick!

MAE. Gooper won't say it, Gooper never thought of it as a duty, he just did it. And what did Brick do? Brick kept living in his past glory at college! Still
310 a football player at twenty-seven!

MARGARET. (*returning alone*) Who are you talking about now? Brick? A football player? He isn't a football player and you know it. Brick is a sports announcer on T.V. and one of the best-known ones in the country!

MAE. I'm talking about what he was.

315 MARGARET. Well, I wish you would just stop talking about my husband.

GOOPER. I've got a right to discuss my brother with other members of MY OWN family, which don't include *you*. Why don't you go out there and drink with Brick?

MARGARET. I've never seen such malice toward a brother.

320 GOOPER. How about his for me? Why, he can't stand to be in the same room with me!

MARGARET. This is a deliberate campaign of vilification for the most disgusting and sordid reason on earth, and I know what it is! It's *avarice, avarice, greed, greed!*

325 BIG MAMA. *Oh, I'll scream! I will scream in a moment unless this stops!*

(*Gooper has stalked up to Margaret with clenched fists at his sides as if he would strike her. Mae distorts her face again into a hideous grimace behind Margaret's back.*)

BIG MAMA. (*sobs*) Margaret. Child. Come here. Sit next to Big Mama.

MARGARET. Precious Mommy. I'm sorry, I'm sorry, I—!

(*She bends her long graceful neck to press her forehead to Big Mama's bulging shoulder under its black chiffon.*)

MAE. How beautiful, how touching, this display of devotion! Do you know why she's childless? She's childless because that big, beautiful athlete husband of hers won't go to bed with her!   330

GOOPER. You jest won't let me do this in a nice way, will yah? Aw right—I don't give a goddam if Big Daddy likes me or don't like me or did or never did or will or will never! I'm just appealing to a sense of common decency and fair play. I'll tell you the truth. I've resented Big Daddy's partiality to Brick ever since Brick was born, and the way I've been treated like I was   335 just barely good enough to spit on and sometimes not even good enough for that. Big Daddy is dying of cancer, and it's spread all through him and it's attacked all his vital organs including the kidneys and right now he is sinking into uremia, and you all know what uremia is, it's poisoning of the whole system due to the failure of the body to eliminate its poisons.   340

MARGARET. (*to herself, downstage, hissingly*) Poisons, poisons! Venomous thoughts and words! In hearts and minds!—That's poisons!

GOOPER. (*overlapping her*) I am asking for a square deal, and, by God, I expect to get one. But if I don't get one, if there's any peculiar shenanigans going on around here behind my back, well, I'm not a corporation lawyer   345 for nothing, I know how to protect my own interests.

(*Brick enters from the gallery with a tranquil, blurred smile, carrying an empty glass with him.*)

BRICK. Storm coming up.

GOOPER. Oh! A late arrival!

MAE. Behold the conquering hero comes!

GOOPER. The fabulous Brick Pollitt! Remember him?—Who could forget   350 him!

MAE. He looks like he's been injured in a game!

GOOPER. Yep, I'm afraid you'll have to warm the bench at the Sugar Bowl[1] this year, Brick!

(*Mae laughs shrilly.*)

Or was it the Rose Bowl[2] that he made that famous run in?—   355

(*Thunder*)

---

1   *Sugar Bowl* Popular American college football game played annually in New Orleans, Louisiana.

2   *Rose Bowl* Popular American college football game played annually in Pasadena, California.

MAE. The punch bowl, honey. It was in the punch bowl, the cut-glass punch bowl!

GOOPER. Oh, that's right, I'm getting the bowls mixed up!

MARGARET. Why don't you stop venting your malice and envy on a sick boy?

360 BIG MAMA. *Now you two hush, I mean it, hush, all of you, hush!*

DAISY, SOOKEY. Storm! Storm comin'! Storm! Storm!

LACEY. Brightie, close them shutters.

GOOPER. Lacey, put the top up on my Cadillac, will yuh?

LACEY. Yes, suh, Mistah Pollitt!

365 GOOPER. (*at the same time*) Big Mama, you know it's necessary for me t' go back to Memphis in th' mornin' t' represent the Parker estate in a lawsuit.

(*Mae sits on the bed and arranges papers she has taken from the brief case.*)

BIG MAMA. Is it, Gooper?

MAE. Yaiss.

GOOPER. That's why I'm forced to—to bring up a problem that—

370 MAE. Somethin' that's too important t' be put off!

GOOPER. If Brick was sober, he ought to be in on this.

MARGARET. Brick is present; we're present.

GOOPER. Well, good. I will now give you this outline my partner, Tom Bullitt, an' me have drawn up—a sort of dummy—trusteeship.

375 MARGARET. Oh, that's it! You'll be in charge an' dole out remittances, will you?

GOOPER. This we did as soon as we got the report on Big Daddy from th' Ochsner Laboratories. We did this thing, I mean we drew up this dummy outline with the advice and assistance of the Chairman of the Boa'd of Directors of th' Southern Plantahs Bank and Trust Company in Memphis,

380 C.C. Bellowes, a man who handles estates for all th' prominent fam'lies in West Tennessee and th' Delta.

BIG MAMA. Gooper?

GOOPER. (*crouching in front of Big Mama*) Now this is not—not final, or anything like it. This is just a preliminary outline. But it does provide a

385 basis—a design—a—possible, feasible—*plan!*

MARGARET. Yes, I'll bet it's a plan.

(*Thunder*)

MAE. It's a plan to protect the biggest estate in the Delta from irresponsibility an'—

390 BIG MAMA. Now you listen to me, all of you, you listen here! They's not goin' to be any more catty talk in my house! And Gooper, you put that away before I grab it out of your hand and tear it right up! I don't know what the

hell's in it, and I don't want to know what the hell's in it. I'm talkin' in Big
Daddy's language now; I'm his *wife*, not his *widow*, I'm still his *wife!* And
I'm talkin' to you in his language an'—   395

GOOPER. Big Mama, what I have here is—

MAE. (*at the same time*) Gooper explained that it's just a plan ...

BIG MAMA. I don't care what you got there. Just put it back where it came
from, an' don't let me see it again, not even the outside of the envelope of
it! Is that understood? Basis! Plan! Preliminary! Design! I say—what is it   400
Big Daddy always says when he's disgusted?

BRICK. (*from the bar*) Big Daddy says "crap" when he's disgusted.

BIG MAMA. (*rising*) That's right—CRAP! I say CRAP too, like Big Daddy!

    (*Thunder rolls.*)

MAE. Coarse language doesn't seem called for in this—

GOOPER. Somethin' in me is *deeply outraged* by hearin' you talk like this.   405

BIG MAMA. *Nobody's goin' to take nothin'!*—till Big Daddy lets go of it—maybe, just possibly, not—not even then! No, not even then!

    (*Thunder.*)

MAE. Sookey, hurry up an' git that po'ch furniture covahed; want th' paint
to come off?

GOOPER. Lacey, put mah car away!   410

LACEY. Caint, Mistah Pollitt, you got the keys!

GOOPER. Naw, you got 'em, man. (*Calls to Mae.*) *Where* th' keys to th' car,
honey?

MAE. You got 'em in your pocket!

    (*Gooper exits R.*)

BRICK. (*singing*) "You can always hear me singin' this song, Show me the way   415
to go home."[1]

    (*Thunder distantly*)

BIG MAMA. Brick! Come here, Brick, I need you. Tonight Brick looks like he
used to look when he was a little boy, just like he did when he played wild
games and used to come home when I hollered myself hoarse for him, all
sweaty and pink cheeked and sleepy, with his—red curls shining ...   420

    (*She comes over to him and runs her fat, shaky hand through his hair. Brick
    draws aside as he does from all physical contact and continues the song in*

---

1   *You can ... go home* From "Show Me the Way to Go Home" (1925), a popular song writ-
    ten by Irvine King (pseudonym of Jimmy Campbell and Reg Connelly).

a whisper, opening the ice bucket and dropping in the ice cubes one by one as if he were mixing some important chemical formula. Distant thunder.)

Time goes by so fast. Nothin' can outrun it. Death commences too early—almost before you're half acquainted with life—you meet the other ... Oh, you know we just got to love each other an' stay together, all of us, just as close as we can, especially now that such a *black* thing has come and moved into this place without invitation.

425

(*Awkwardly embracing Brick, she presses her head to his shoulder. A dog howls off stage.*)

Oh, Brick, son of Big Daddy, Big Daddy does so love you. Y'know what would be his fondest dream come true? If before he passed on, if Big Daddy has to pass on ...

(*A dog howls.*)

... you give him a child of yours, a grandson as much like his son as his son is like Big Daddy.

430

MARGARET. I know that's Big Daddy's dream.

BIG MAMA. That's his dream.

MAE. Such a pity that Maggie and Brick can't oblige.

BIG DADDY. (*off down stage right on the gallery*) Looks like the wind was takin' liberties with this place.

435

SERVANT. (*off stage*) Yes, sir, Mr. Pollitt.

MARGARET. (*crossing to the right door*) Big Daddy's on the gall'ry.

(*Big Mama has turned toward the hall door at the sound of Big Daddy's voice on the gallery.*)

BIG MAMA. I can't stay here. He'll see somethin' in my eyes.

(*Big Daddy enters the room from up stage right.*)

BIG DADDY. Can I come in?

(*He puts his cigar in an ash tray.*)

440

MARGARET. Did the storm wake you up, Big Daddy?

BIG DADDY. Which stawm are you talkin' about—th' one outside or th' hullaballoo in here?

(*Gooper squeezes past Big Daddy.*)

GOOPER. 'Scuse me:

(*Mae tries to squeeze past Big Daddy to join Gooper, but Big Daddy puts his arm firmly around her.*)

BIG DADDY. I heard some mighty loud talk. Sounded like somethin' impor-   445
tant was bein' discussed. What was the powwow about?

MAE. (*flustered*) Why—nothin', Big Daddy ...

BIG DADDY. (*crossing to extreme left centre, taking Mae with him*) What is that
pregnant-lookin' envelope you're puttin' back in your brief case, Gooper?

GOOPER. (*at the foot of the bed, caught, as he stuffs papers into envelope*) That?   450
Nothin', suh—nothin' much of anythin' at all ...

BIG DADDY. Nothin'? It looks like a whole lot of nothin'!

(*He turns up stage to the group.*)

You all know th' story about th' young married couple—

GOOPER. Yes, sir!

BIG DADDY. Hello, Brick—

BRICK. Hello, Big Daddy.   455

(*The group is arranged in a semicircle above Big Daddy, Margaret at the
extreme right, then Mae and Gooper, then Big Mama, with Brick at the
left.*)

BIG DADDY. Young married couple took Junior out to th' zoo one Sunday,
inspected all of God's creatures in their cages, with satisfaction.

GOOPER. Satisfaction.

BIG DADDY. (*crossing to up stage centre, facing front*) This afternoon was a
warm afternoon in spring an' that ole elephant had somethin' else on his   460
mind which was bigger'n peanuts. You know this story, Brick?

(*Gooper nods.*)

BRICK. No, sir, I don't know it.

BIG DADDY. Y'see, in th' cage adjoinin' they was a young female elephant in
heat!

BIG MAMA. (*at Big Daddy's shoulder*) Oh, Big Daddy!   465

BIG DADDY. What's the matter, preacher's gone, ain't he? All right. That female elephant in the next cage was permeatin' the atmosphere about her
with a powerful and excitin' odour of female fertility! Huh! Ain't that a nice
way to put it, Brick?

BRICK. Yes, sir, nothin' wrong with it.   470

BIG DADDY. Brick says th's nothin' wrong with it!

BIG MAMA. Oh, Big Daddy!

BIG DADDY. (*crossing to down stage centre*) So this ole bull elephant still had a
couple of fornications left in him. He reared back his trunk an' got a whiff
of that elephant lady next door!—began to paw at the dirt in his cage an'   475
butt his head against the separatin' partition and, first thing y'know, there

was a conspicuous change in his *profile*—very *conspicuous!* Ain't I tellin' this
story in decent language, Brick?

BRICK. Yes, sir, too fuckin' decent!

480 BIG DADDY. So, the little boy pointed at it and said, "What's that?" His
mama said, "Oh, that's—nothin'!"—His papa said, "She's spoiled!"

(*Big Daddy crosses to Brick at left.*)

You didn't laugh at that story, Brick.

(*Big Mama crosses to down stage right crying. Margaret goes to her. Mae
and Gooper hold up stage right centre.*)

BRICK. No, sir, I didn't laugh at that story.

BIG DADDY. What is the smell in this room? Don't you notice it, Brick? Don't
485   you notice a powerful and obnoxious odour of mendacity in this room?

BRICK. Yes, sir, I think I do, sir.

GOOPER. Mae, Mae ...

BIG DADDY. There is nothing more powerful. Is there, Brick?

BRICK. No, sir. No, sir, there isn't, an' nothin' more obnoxious.

490 BIG DADDY. Brick agrees with me. The odour of mendacity is a powerful and
obnoxious odour an' the stawm hasn't blown it away from this room yet.
You notice it, Gooper?

GOOPER. What, sir?

BIG DADDY. How about you, Sister Woman? You notice the unpleasant
495   odour of mendacity in this room?

MAE. Why, Big Daddy, I don't even know what that is.

BIG DADDY. You can smell it. Hell it smells like death!

(*Big Mama sobs. Big Daddy looks toward her.*)

What is wrong with that fat woman over there, loaded with diamonds?
Hey, what's-you-name, what's the matter with you?

500 MARGARET. (*crossing toward Big Daddy*) She had a slight dizzy spell, Big
Daddy.

BIG DADDY. You better watch that, Big Mama. A stroke is a bad way to go.

MARGARET. (*crossing to Big Daddy at centre*) Oh, Brick, Big Daddy has on
your birthday present to him, Brick, he has on your cashmere robe, the
505   softest material I have ever felt.

BIG DADDY. Yeah, this is my soft birthday, Maggie ... Not my gold or my
silver birthday, but my soft birthday, everything's got to be soft for Big
Daddy on this soft birthday.

(*Maggie kneels before Big Daddy at centre.*)

MARGARET. Big Daddy's got on his Chinese slippers that I gave him, Brick. Big Daddy, I haven't given you my big present yet, but now I will, now's 510 the time for me to present it to you! I have an announcement to make!

MAE. What? What kind of announcement?

GOOPER. A sports announcement, Maggie?

MARGARET. Announcement of life beginning! A child is coming, sired by Brick, and out of Maggie the Cat! I have Brick's child in my body, an' that's 515 my birthday present to Big Daddy on this birthday!

> (*Big Daddy looks at Brick who crosses behind Big Daddy to down stage portal, left.*)

BIG DADDY. Get up, girl, get up off your knees, girl.

> (*Big Daddy helps Margaret to rise. He crosses above her, to her right, bites off the end of a fresh cigar, taken from his bathrobe pocket, as he studies Margaret.*)

Uh-huh, this girl has life in her body, that's no lie!

BIG MAMA. BIG DADDY'S DREAM COME TRUE!

BRICK. JESUS! 520

BIG DADDY. (*crossing right below wicker stand*) Gooper, I want my lawyer in the morning'.

BRICK. Where are you goin', Big Daddy?

BIG DADDY. Son, I'm goin' up on the roof, to the belvedere[1] on th' roof to look over my kingdom before I give up my kingdom—twenty-eight thou- 525 sand acres of th' richest land this side of the valley Nile!

> (*He exits through right doors, and down right on the gallery.*)

BIG MAMA. (*following*) Sweetheart, sweetheart, sweetheart—can I come with you?

> (*She exits down stage right. Margaret is down stage centre in the mirror area. Mae has joined Gooper and she gives him a fierce poke, making a low hissing sound and a grimace of fury.*)

GOOPER. (*pushing her aside*) Brick, could you possibly spare me one small shot of that liquor? 530

BRICK. Why, help yourself, Gooper boy.

GOOPER. I will.

MAE. (*shrilly*) Of course we know that this is—a lie.

GOOPER. *Be still, Mae.*

---

1   *belvedere* Gallery with a view.

535 MAE. I won't be still! I know she's made this up!

GOOPER. Goddam it, I said shut up!

MARGARET. Gracious! I didn't know that my little announcement was going to provoke such a storm!

MAE. *That* woman isn't *pregnant!*

540 GOOPER. Who said she was?

MAE. *She* did.

GOOPER. The doctor didn't. Doc Baugh didn't.

MARGARET. I haven't gone to Doc Baugh.

GOOPER. Then who'd you go to, Maggie?

545 MARGARET. One of the best gynecologists in the South.

GOOPER. Uh huh, uh huh!—I see ...

(*He takes out a pencil and notebook.*)

—May we have his name, please?

MARGARET. No, you may not, Mister Prosecuting Attorney!

MAE. He doesn't have any name, he doesn't exist!

550 MARGARET. Oh, he exists all right, and so does my child, Brick's baby!

MAE. You can't conceive a child by a man that won't sleep with you unless you think you're—

(*Brick has turned on the phonograph. A scat¹ song cuts Mae's speech.*)

GOOPER. *Turn that off!*

MAE. We know it's a lie because we hear you in here; he won't sleep with you,
555 we hear you! So don't imagine you're going to put a trick over on us, to fool a dying man with a—

(*A long drawn cry of agony and rage fills the house. Margaret turns the phonograph down to a whisper. The cry is repeated.*)

MAE. Did you hear that, Gooper, did you hear that?

GOOPER. Sounds like the pain has struck.

Come along and leave these lovebirds together in their nest!

(*He goes out first. Mae follows but turns at the door, contorting her face and hissing at Margaret.*)

560 MAE. *Liar!*

(*She slams the door. Margaret exhales with relief and moves a little unsteadily to catch hold of Brick's arm.*)

---

1   *scat* Type of jazz music in which singers improvise long vocal runs using nonsense words.

MARGARET.   Thank you for—keeping still ...
BRICK.   O.K., Maggie.
MARGARET.   It was gallant of you to save my face!

(*He now pours down three shots in quick succession and stands waiting, silent. All at once he turns with a smile and says:*)

BRICK.   *There!*
MARGARET.   What?   565
BRICK.   The *click* ...

(*His gratitude seems almost infinite as he hobbles out on the gallery with a drink. We hear his crutch as he swings out of sight. Then, at some distance, he begins singing to himself a peaceful song. Margaret holds the big pillow forlornly as if it were her only companion, for a few moments, then throws it on the bed. She rushes to the liquor cabinet, gathers all the bottles in her arms, turns about undecidedly, then runs out of the room with them, leaving the door ajar on the dim yellow hall. Brick is heard hobbling back along the gallery, singing his peaceful song. He comes back in, sees the pillow on the bed, laughs lightly, sadly, picks it up. He has it under his arm as Margaret returns to the room. Margaret softly shuts the door and leans against it, smiling softly at Brick.*)

MARGARET.   Brick, I used to think that you were stronger than me and I didn't want to be overpowered by you. But now, since you've taken to liquor—you know what?—I guess it's bad, but now I'm stronger than you and I can love you more truly! Don't move that pillow. I'll move it right   570
back if you do!—Brick?

(*She turns out all the lamps but a single rose-silk-shaded one by the bed.*)

I really have been to a doctor and I know what to do and—Brick?—this is my time by the calendar to conceive?
BRICK.   Yes, I understand, Maggie. But how are you going to conceive a child by a man in love with his liquor?   575
MARGARET.   By locking his liquor up and making him satisfy my desire before I unlock it!
BRICK.   Is that what you've done, Maggie?
MARGARET.   Look and see. The cabinet's mighty empty compared to before!
BRICK.   Well, I'll be a son of a—   580

(*He reaches for his crutch but she beats him to it and rushes out on the gallery, hurls the crutch over the rail and comes back in, panting.*)

MARGARET. And so tonight we're going to make the lie true, and when that's done, I'll bring the liquor back here and we'll get drunk together, here, tonight, in this place that death has come into ...—What do you say?

BRICK. I don't say anything. I guess there's nothing to say.

585 MARGARET. Oh, you weak people, you weak, beautiful people!—who give up with such grace. What you want is someone to—

(*She turns out the rose-silk lamp.*)

—take hold of you.—Gently, gently with love hand your life back to you, like somethin' gold you let go of. I do love you, Brick, I do!

BRICK. (*smiling with charming sadness*) Wouldn't it be funny if that was

590   true?

THE END

—1954, 1974[1]

---

1   *1954, 1974* Tennessee Williams wrote three different versions of *Cat on a Hot Tin Roof*'s third act. Initially the final act of the play (published for the first time in 1955) did not include Big Daddy at all and was much bleaker than the version that ultimately debuted on Broadway in 1954. For the Broadway debut, stage director Elia Kazan requested three major changes: a final appearance by Big Daddy; a visible change in Brick's demeanour as a result of the conversation in Act 2; and a more likeable version of Maggie. Williams approved of making Maggie more sympathetic but was not satisfied with the other changes, especially Brick's transformation. In 1974, Williams's final rewrite of the play was performed. This rewrite—the text presented here—combines elements from both earlier versions.

Sharon Pollock
b. 1936

Sharon Pollock is known for stage and radio plays with politically charged ideas at their centre. Her daring choice of subject matter is matched by an experimental approach to playwriting; as critic Anne Nothof observes, in Pollock's work "scenes intersect or blend, time inhabits a simultaneous present and past, [and] characters are divided into multiple selves who interact with and observe each other."

Pollock was born in New Brunswick in 1936. Her young adult life was marked by a series of personal hardships, including her mother's suicide and an abusive marriage. Pollock moved to Calgary in 1966, and a few years later she won the Alberta Culture playwriting competition with her first work, *A Compulsory Option* (1972).

Especially in her early plays, Pollock often incorporates events from Canadian history; *Walsh* (1973), for example, addresses the relationship between a Mounted Police superintendent and the Sioux chief Sitting Bull, while *The Komagata Maru Incident* (1976) is based on a 1914 confrontation that resulted from Canada's racist immigration policies. Such plays use the past to comment on present-day issues while also correcting, Pollock says, Canadians' false "view of themselves as nice civilized people who have never participated in historical crimes and atrocities."

With works such as *Generations* (1981) and the semi-autobiographical *Doc* (1986), Pollock shifted her focus from major events to the ways in which family dynamics and individual psychology are shaped by political or historical circumstances. Her sources range from the Lizzie Borden murder trial in 1890s Massachusetts—the subject of *Blood Relations* (1980)—to the treatment of suspected terrorists held by the American military in *Man Out of Joint* (2007).

As well as a prolific playwright, Pollock is an award-winning actor and has been artistic director at several theatres. She received Governor General's Awards for *Doc* and for *Blood Relations*, and in 2012 she was awarded the Order of Canada.

Blood Relations

CHARACTERS

Miss Lizzie, *who will play* Bridget, *the Irish maid*
The Actress, *who will play* Lizzie Borden[1]
Harry, *Mrs. Borden's brother*
Emma, *Lizzie's older sister*
Andrew, *Lizzie's father*
Abigail, *Lizzie's step-mother*
Dr. Patrick, *the Irish doctor; sometimes* The Defence

SETTING

The time proper is late Sunday afternoon and evening, late fall, in Fall River, 1902; the year of the "dream thesis," if one might call it that, is 1892.

The playing areas include (a) within the Borden house: the dining room from which there is an exit to the kitchen; the parlour; a flight of stairs leading to the second floor; and (b) in the Borden yard: the walk outside the house; the area in which the birds are kept.

PRODUCTION NOTE

Action must be free-flowing. There can be no division of the script into scenes by blackout, movement of furniture, or sets. There may be freezes of some characters while other scenes are being played. There is no necessity to "get people off" and "on" again for, with the exception of The Actress and Miss Lizzie (and Emma in the final scene), all characters are imaginary, and all action in reality would be taking place between Miss Lizzie and The Actress in the dining room and parlour of her home.

The defence may actually be seen, may be a shadow, or a figure behind a scrim.[2]

While Miss Lizzie exits and enters with her Bridget business, she is a presence, often observing unobtrusively when as Bridget she takes no part in the action.

---

1   *Lizzie Borden* American murder suspect (1860–1927) who in 1892 allegedly killed her father and stepmother with a hatchet. She was tried for the crime but acquitted, and she continued to live in her hometown of Fall River, Massachussetts, until her death. The case was never solved, and many remained convinced that she was guilty.
2   *scrim* Screen that is opaque when lit from the front and translucent when lit from behind.

ACT 1

Lights up on the figure of a woman standing centre stage. It is a somewhat formal pose. A pause. She speaks:

"Since what I am about to say must be but that
Which contradicts my accusation, and
The testimony on my part no other
But what comes from myself, it shall scarce boot me
To say 'Not Guilty.'   5
But, if Powers Divine
Behold our human action as they do,
I doubt not then but innocence shall make
False accusation blush and tyranny
Tremble at ... at ..."[1]   10

(She wriggles the fingers of an outstretched hand searching for the word.)

"Aaaat" ... Bollocks!!

(She raises her script, takes a bite of chocolate.)

"Tremble at Patience," patience patience! ...

(Miss Lizzie enters from the kitchen with tea service. The actress's attention drifts to Miss Lizzie. The actress watches Miss Lizzie sit in the parlour and proceed to pour two cups of tea. The actress sucks her teeth a bit to clear the chocolate as she speaks:)

THE ACTRESS. Which ... is proper, Lizzie?

MISS LIZZIE. Proper?

THE ACTRESS. To pour first the cream, and add the tea—or first tea and add   15
cream. One is proper. Is the way you do the proper way, the way it's done
in circles where it counts?

MISS LIZZIE. Sugar?

THE ACTRESS. Well, is it?

MISS LIZZIE. I don't know, sugar?   20

THE ACTRESS. Mmmn. *(Miss Lizzie adds sugar.)* I suppose if we had Mrs.
Beeton's *Book of Etiquette*,[2] we could look it up.

MISS LIZZIE. I do have it, shall I get it?

---

1   *Since what ... at ...* See Shakespeare's *The Winter's Tale* 3.2.22–32; the actress is rehears-
    ing Hermione's speech, delivered when the character is falsely accused of adultery and
    attempted poisoning; *boot* Benefit.

2   *Mrs. Beeton's ... Etiquette* First published in 1861, *Mrs. Beeton's Book of Household Man-
    agement*, a wide-ranging book of recipes and domestic advice, remained popular until
    well into the twentieth century.

THE ACTRESS. No.... You could ask your sister, she might know.

25 MISS LIZZIE. Do you want this tea or not?

THE ACTRESS. I hate tea.

MISS LIZZIE. You drink it every Sunday.

THE ACTRESS. I drink it because you like to serve it.

MISS LIZZIE. Pppu.

30 THE ACTRESS. It's true. You've no idea how I suffer from this toast and tea ritual. I really do. The tea upsets my stomach and the toast makes me fat because I eat so much of it.

MISS LIZZIE. Practice some restraint then.

THE ACTRESS. Mmmm ... Why don't we ask your sister which is proper?

35 MISS LIZZIE. You ask her.

THE ACTRESS. How can I? She doesn't speak to me. I don't think she even sees me. She gives no indication of it. (*She looks up the stairs.*) What do you suppose she does up there every Sunday afternoon?

MISS LIZZIE. She sulks.

40 THE ACTRESS. And reads the Bible I suppose, and Mrs. Beeton's *Book of Etiquette.* Oh Lizzie.... What a long day. The absolutely longest day.... When does that come anyway, the longest day?

MISS LIZZIE. June.

THE ACTRESS. Ah yes, June. (*She looks at Miss Lizzie.*) June?

45 MISS LIZZIE. June.

THE ACTRESS. Mmmmmm....

MISS LIZZIE. I know what you're thinking.

THE ACTRESS. Of course you do.... I'm thinking ... shall I pour the sherry— or will you.

50 MISS LIZZIE. No.

THE ACTRESS. I'm thinking ... June ... in Fall River.

MISS LIZZIE. No.

THE ACTRESS. August in Fall River? (*She smiles. Pause.*)

MISS LIZZIE. We could have met in Boston.

55 THE ACTRESS. I prefer it here.

MISS LIZZIE. You don't find it ... a trifle boring?

THE ACTRESS. Au contraire.

(*Miss Lizzie gives a small laugh at the affectation.*)

THE ACTRESS. What?

MISS LIZZIE. I find it a trifle boring ... I know what you're doing. You're soak-

60 ing up the ambience.

THE ACTRESS. Nonsense, Lizzie. I come to see you.

MISS LIZZIE. Why?

THE ACTRESS. Because ... of us. (*Pause.*)

MISS LIZZIE. You were a late arrival last night. Later than usual.

THE ACTRESS. Don't be silly.   65

MISS LIZZIE. I wonder why.

THE ACTRESS. The show was late, late starting, late coming down.

MISS LIZZIE. And?

THE ACTRESS. And—then we all went out for drinks.

MISS LIZZIE. We?   70

THE ACTRESS. The other members of the cast.

MISS LIZZIE. Oh yes.

THE ACTRESS. And then I caught a cab ... all the way from Boston.... Do you know what it cost?

MISS LIZZIE. I should. I paid the bill, remember?   75

THE ACTRESS. (*Laughs.*) Of course. What a jumble all my thoughts are. There're too many words running round inside my head today. It's terrible.

MISS LIZZIE. It sounds it.

(*Pause.*)

THE ACTRESS. ... You know ... you do this thing ... you stare at me ... You look directly at my eyes. I think ... you think ... that if I'm lying ... it will come   80
up, like lemons on a slot machine. (*She makes a gesture at her eyes.*) Tick. Tick ... (*Pause.*) In the alley, behind the theatre the other day, there were some kids. You know what they were doing?

MISS LIZZIE. How could I?

THE ACTRESS. They were playing skip rope, and you know what they were   85
singing? (*She sings, and claps her hands arhythmically to:*)
"Lizzie Borden took an ax,
Gave her Mother forty whacks,
When the job was nicely done,
She gave her father forty-one."   90

MISS LIZZIE. Did you stop them?

THE ACTRESS. No.

MISS LIZZIE. Did you tell them I was acquitted?

THE ACTRESS. No.

MISS LIZZIE. What did you do?   95

THE ACTRESS. I shut the window.

MISS LIZZIE. A noble gesture on my behalf.

THE ACTRESS. We were doing lines—the noise they make is dreadful. Some-times they play ball, ka-thunk, ka-thunk, ka-thunk against the wall. Once I saw them with a cat and—   100

MISS LIZZIE. And you didn't stop them?

THE ACTRESS. That time I stopped them.

(*The actress crosses to table where there is a gramophone. She prepares to play a record. She stops.*)

THE ACTRESS. Should I?
MISS LIZZIE. Why not?
105   THE ACTRESS. Your sister, the noise upsets her.
MISS LIZZIE. And she upsets me. On numerous occasions.
THE ACTRESS. You're incorrigible, Lizzie.

(*The actress holds out her arms to Miss Lizzie. They dance the latest "in" dance, a Scott Joplin[1] composition. It requires some concentration, but they chat while dancing rather formally in contrast to the music.*)

THE ACTRESS. ... Do you think your jawline's heavy?
MISS LIZZIE. Why do you ask?
110   THE ACTRESS. They said you had jowls.
MISS LIZZIE. Did they.
THE ACTRESS. The reports of the day said you were definitely jowly.
MISS LIZZIE. That was ten years ago.
THE ACTRESS. Imagine. You were only thirty-four.
115   MISS LIZZIE. Yes.
THE ACTRESS. It happened here, this house.
MISS LIZZIE. You're leading.
THE ACTRESS. I know.
MISS LIZZIE. ... I don't think I'm jowly. Then or now. Do you?
120   THE ACTRESS. Lizzie? Lizzie.
MISS LIZZIE. What?
THE ACTRESS. ... did you?
MISS LIZZIE. Did I what?

(*Pause.*)

THE ACTRESS. You never tell *me* anything. (*She turns off the music.*)
125   MISS LIZZIE. I tell you everything.
THE ACTRESS. No you don't!
MISS LIZZIE. Oh yes, I tell you the most personal things about myself, my thoughts, my dreams, my—
THE ACTRESS. But never that one thing.... (*She lights a cigarette.*)
130   MISS LIZZIE. And don't smoke those—they stink.

(*The actress ignores her, inhales, exhales a volume of smoke in Miss Lizzie's direction.*)

---

1   *Scott Joplin* Ragtime composer and pianist (1868–1917).

MISS LIZZIE. Do you suppose ... people buy you drinks ... or cast you even ... because you have a "liaison" with Lizzie Borden? Do you suppose they do that?

THE ACTRESS. They cast me because I'm good at what I do.

MISS LIZZIE. They never pry? They never ask? What's she really like? Is she 135 really jowly? Did she? Didn't she?

THE ACTRESS. What could I tell them? You never tell me anything.

MISS LIZZIE. I tell you everything.

THE ACTRESS. But that! (*Pause.*) You think everybody talks about you—they don't. 140

MISS LIZZIE. Here they do.

THE ACTRESS. You think they talk about you.

MISS LIZZIE. But never to me.

THE ACTRESS. Well ... you give them lots to talk about.

MISS LIZZIE. You know you're right, your mind is a jumble. 145

THE ACTRESS. I told you so.

(*Pause.*)

MISS LIZZIE. You remind me of my sister.

THE ACTRESS. Oh God, in what way?

MISS LIZZIE. Day in, day out, ten years now, sometimes at breakfast as she 150 rolls little crumbs of bread in little balls, sometimes at noon, or late at night ... "Did you, Lizzie?" "Lizzie, did you?"

THE ACTRESS. Ten years, day in, day out?

MISS LIZZIE. Oh yes. She sits there where Papa used to sit and I sit there, where I have always sat. She looks at me and at her plate, then at me, and 155 at her plate, then at me and then she says "Did you Lizzie?" "Lizzie, did you?"

THE ACTRESS. (*A nasal imitation of Emma's voice.*) "Did-you-Lizzie—Lizzie-did-you." (*Laughs.*)

MISS LIZZIE. Did I what? 160

THE ACTRESS. (*Continues her imitation of Emma.*) "You know."

MISS LIZZIE. Well, what do you think?

THE ACTRESS. "Oh, I believe you didn't, in fact I know you didn't, what a thought! After all, you were acquitted."

MISS LIZZIE. Yes, I was. 165

THE ACTRESS. "But sometimes when I'm on the street ... or shopping ... or at the church even, I catch somebody's eye, they look away ... and I think to myself 'Did-you-Lizzie—Lizzie-did-you.'"

MISS LIZZIE. (*Laughs.*) Ah, poor Emma.

THE ACTRESS. (*Dropping her Emma imitation.*) Well, did you? 170

MISS LIZZIE. Is it important?

THE ACTRESS. Yes.

MISS LIZZIE. Why?

THE ACTRESS. I have ... a compulsion to know the truth.

175 MISS LIZZIE. The truth?

THE ACTRESS. Yes.

MISS LIZZIE. ... Sometimes I think you look like me, and you're not jowly.

THE ACTRESS. No.

MISS LIZZIE. You look like me, or how I think I look, or how I ought to look

180   ... sometimes you think like me ... do you feel that?

THE ACTRESS. Sometimes.

MISS LIZZIE. (*Triumphant.*) You shouldn't have to ask then. You should know. "Did I, didn't I." You tell me.

THE ACTRESS. I'll tell you what I think.... I think ... that you're aware there is

185   a certain fascination in the ambiguity.... You always paint the background but leave the rest to my imagination. Did Lizzie Borden take an axe? ... If you didn't I should be disappointed ... and if you did I should be horrified.

MISS LIZZIE. And which is worse?

THE ACTRESS. To have murdered one's parents, or to be a pretentious small-

190   town spinster? I don't know.

MISS LIZZIE. Why're you so cruel to me?

THE ACTRESS. I'm teasing, Lizzie, I'm only teasing. Come on, paint the background again.

MISS LIZZIE. Why?

195 THE ACTRESS. Perhaps you'll give something away.

MISS LIZZIE. Which you'll dine out on.

THE ACTRESS. Of course. (*Laughs.*) Come on, Lizzie. Come on.

MISS LIZZIE. A game.

THE ACTRESS. What?

200 MISS LIZZIE. A game? ... And you'll play me.

THE ACTRESS. Oh—

MISS LIZZIE. It's your stock in trade, my love.

THE ACTRESS. Alright.... A game!

MISS LIZZIE. Let me think ... Bridget ... Brrridget. We had a maid then. And

205   her name was Bridget. Oh, she was a great one for stories, stood like this, very straight back, and her hair ... and there she was in the courtroom in her new dress on the stand. "Do you swear to tell the truth, the whole truth, and nothing but the truth, so help you God?" (*Imitates Irish accent.*) "I do sir," she said.

210   "Would you give the court your name."

   "Bridget O'Sullivan, sir."

(*Very faint echo of the voice of the defence under Miss Lizzie's next line.*)

"And occupation."

"I'm like what you'd call a maid, sir. I do a bit of everything, cleanin' and cookin'."

(*The actual voice of the defence is heard alone; he may also be seen.*)

THE DEFENCE. You've been in Fall River how long?   215

MISS LIZZIE. (*Who continues as Bridget, while the actress [who will play Lizzie] observes.*) Well now, about five years sir, ever since I came over. I worked up on the hill for a while but it didn't—well, you could say, suit me, too lah-de-dah—so I—

THE DEFENCE. Your employer in June of 1892 was?   220

BRIDGET. Yes sir. Mr. Borden, sir. Well, more rightly, Mrs. Borden for she was the one who—

THE DEFENCE. Your impression of the household?

BRIDGET. Well ... the man of the house, Mr. Borden, was a bit of a ... tight-wad, and Mrs. B. could nag you into the grave, still she helped with the   225
dishes and things which not everyone does when they hire a maid. (*Harry appears on the stairs; approaches Bridget stealthily. She is unaware of him.*) Then there was the daughters, Miss Emma and Lizzie, and that day, Mr. Wingate, Mrs. B.'s brother who'd stayed for the night and was—(*He grabs her ass with both hands. She screams.*)   230

BRIDGET. Get off with you!

HARRY. Come on, Bridget, give me a kiss!

BRIDGET. I'll give you a good poke in the nose if you don't keep your hands to yourself.

HARRY. Ohhh-hh-hh Bridget!   235

BRIDGET. Get away you old sod!

HARRY. Haven't you missed me?

BRIDGET. I have not! I was pinched black and blue last time—and I'll be suf-ferin' the same before I see the end of you this time.

HARRY. (*Tilts his ass at her.*) You want to see my end?   240

BRIDGET. You're a dirty old man.

HARRY. If Mr. Borden hears that, you'll be out on the street. (*Grabs her.*) Where's my kiss!

BRIDGET. (*Dumps glass of water on his head.*) There! (*Harry splutters.*) Would you like another? You silly thing you—and leave me towels alone!   245

HARRY. You've soaked my shirt.

BRIDGET. Shut up and pour yourself a cup of coffee.

HARRY. You got no sense of fun, Bridget.

BRIDGET. Well now, if you tried actin' like the gentleman farmer you're sup-
250   posed to be, Mr. Wingate—

HARRY. I'm tellin' you you can't take a joke.

BRIDGET. If Mr. Borden sees you jokin', it's not his maid he'll be throwin' out
on the street, but his brother-in-law, and that's the truth.

HARRY. What's between you and me's between you and me, eh?

255   BRIDGET. There ain't nothin' between you and me.

HARRY. ... Finest cup of coffee in Fall River.

BRIDGET. There's no gettin' on the good side of me now, it's too late for
that.

HARRY. ... Bridget? ... You know what tickles my fancy?

260   BRIDGET. No and I don't want to hear.

HARRY. It's your Irish temper.

BRIDGET. It is, is it? ... Can I ask you something?

HARRY. Ooohhh—anything.

BRIDGET. (*Innocently.*) Does Miss Lizzie know you're here? ... I say does Miss
265   Lizzie—

HARRY. Why do you bring her up?

BRIDGET. She don't then, eh? (*Teasing.*) It's a surprise visit?

HARRY. No surprise to her father.

BRIDGET. Oh?

270   HARRY. We got business.

BRIDGET. I'd of thought the last bit of business was enough.

HARRY. It's not for—[*you to say*]

BRIDGET. You don't learn a thing, from me or Lizzie, do you?

HARRY. Listen here—

275   BRIDGET. You mean you've forgotten how mad she was when you got her
father to sign the rent from the mill house over to your sister? Oh my.

HARRY. She's his wife, isn't she?

BRIDGET. (*Lightly.*) Second wife.

HARRY. She's still got her rights.

280   BRIDGET. Who am I to say who's got a right? But I can tell you this—Miss
Lizzie don't see it that way.

HARRY. It don't matter how Miss Lizzie sees it.

BRIDGET. Oh it matters enough—she had you thrown out last time, didn't
she? By jasus that was a laugh!

285   HARRY. You mind your tongue.

BRIDGET. And after you left, you know what happened?

HARRY. Get away.

BRIDGET. She and sister Emma got her father's rent money from the other
mill house to make it all even-steven—and now, here you are back again?

What kind of business you up to this time? (*Whispers in his ear.*) Mind   290
Lizzie doesn't catch you.

HARRY. Get away!

BRIDGET. (*Laughs.*) Ohhhh—would you like some more coffee, sir? It's the
finest coffee in all Fall River! (*She pours it.*) Thank you sir. You're welcome,
sir. (*She exits to the kitchen.*)   295

HARRY. There'll be no trouble this time!! Do you hear me!

BRIDGET. (*Off.*) Yes sir.

HARRY. There'll be no trouble. (*Sees a basket of crusts.*) What the hell's this? I
said is this for breakfast!

BRIDGET. (*Entering.*) Is what for—oh no—Mr. Borden's not economizin' to   300
that degree yet, it's the crusts for Miss Lizzie's birds.

HARRY. What birds?

BRIDGET. Some kind of pet pigeons she's raisin' out in the shed. Miss Lizzie
loves her pigeons.

HARRY. Miss Lizzie loves kittens and cats and horses and dogs. What Miss   305
Lizzie doesn't love is people.

BRIDGET. Some people. (*She looks past Harry to the actress/Lizzie. Harry turns
to follow Bridget's gaze. Bridget speaks, encouraging an invitation for the actress to join her.*) Good mornin' Lizzie.

THE ACTRESS. (*She is a trifle tentative in the role of Lizzie.*) Is the coffee on?   310

BRIDGET. Yes ma'am.

LIZZIE. I'll have some then.

BRIDGET. Yes ma'am. (*She makes no move to get it, but watches as Lizzie stares
at Harry.*)

HARRY. Well ... I think ... maybe I'll ... just split a bit of that kindling out   315
back. (*He exits. Lizzie turns to Bridget.*)

LIZZIE. Silly ass.

BRIDGET. Oh Lizzie. (*She laughs. She enjoys the actress/Lizzie's comments as she
guides her into her role by "painting the background."*)

LIZZIE. Well, he is. He's a silly ass.   320

BRIDGET. Can you remember him last time with your Papa? Oh, I can still
hear him: "Now Andrew, I've spent my life raisin' horses and I'm gonna tell
you somethin'—a *woman* is just like a *horse!* You keep her on a tight rein,
or she'll take the bit in her teeth and next thing you know, road, destination, and purpose is all behind you, and you'll be damn lucky if she don't   325
pitch you right in a sewer ditch!"

LIZZIE. Stupid bugger.

BRIDGET. Oh Lizzie, what language! What would your father say if he heard
you?

LIZZIE. Well ... I've never used a word I didn't hear from him first.   330

BRIDGET. Do you think he'd be congratulatin' you?

LIZZIE. Possibly. (*Bridget gives a subtle shake of her head.*) Not.

BRIDGET. Possibly not is right.... And what if *Mrs.* B. should hear you?

LIZZIE. I hope and pray that she does.... Do you know what I think, Bridget?

335   I think there's nothing wrong with Mrs. B.... that losing 80 pounds and tripling her intellect wouldn't cure.

BRIDGET. (*Loving it.*) You ought to be ashamed.

LIZZIE. It's the truth, isn't it?

BRIDGET. Still, what a way to talk of your Mother.

340   LIZZIE. Step-mother.

BRIDGET. Still you don't mean it, do you?

LIZZIE. Don't I? (*Louder.*) She's a *silly ass* too!

BRIDGET. Shhhh.

LIZZIE. It's alright, she's deaf as a picket fence when she wants to be.... What's

345   he here for?

BRIDGET. Never said.

LIZZIE. He's come to worm more money out of Papa I bet.

BRIDGET. Lizzie.

LIZZIE. What.

350   BRIDGET. Your sister, Lizzie. (*Bridget indicates Emma, Lizzie turns to see her on the stairs.*)

EMMA. You want to be quiet, Lizzie, a body can't sleep for the racket upstairs.

LIZZIE. Oh?

EMMA. You've been makin' too much noise.

355   LIZZIE. It must have been Bridget, she dropped a pot, didn't you, Bridget.

EMMA. A number of pots from the sound of it.

BRIDGET. I'm all thumbs this mornin', ma'am.

EMMA. You know it didn't sound like pots.

LIZZIE. Oh.

360   EMMA. Sounded more like voices.

LIZZIE. Oh?

EMMA. Sounded like your voice, Lizzie.

LIZZIE. Maybe you dreamt it.

EMMA. I wish I had, for someone was using words no lady would use.

365   LIZZIE. When Bridget dropped the pot, she did say "pshaw!" didn't you, Bridget.

BRIDGET. Pshaw! That's what I said.

EMMA. That's not what I heard.

   (*Bridget will withdraw.*)

LIZZIE. Pshaw?

EMMA. If Mother heard you, you know what she'd say.   370

LIZZIE. She's not my mother or yours.

EMMA. Well she married our father twenty-seven years ago, if that doesn't make her our mother—

LIZZIE. It doesn't.

EMMA. Don't talk like that.   375

LIZZIE. I'll talk as I like.

EMMA. We're not going to fight, Lizzie. We're going to be quiet and have our breakfast!

LIZZIE. Is that what we're going to do?

EMMA. Yes.   380

LIZZIE. Oh.

EMMA. At least—that's what I'm going to do.

LIZZIE. Bridget, Emma wants her breakfast!

EMMA. I could have yelled myself.

LIZZIE. You could, but you never do.   385

(*Bridget serves Emma, Emma is reluctant to argue in front of Bridget.*)

EMMA. Thank you, Bridget.

LIZZIE. Did you know Harry Wingate's back for a visit? ... He must have snuck in late last night so I wouldn't hear him. Did you?

(*Emma shakes her head. Lizzie studies her.*)

LIZZIE. Did you know he was coming?

EMMA. No.   390

LIZZIE. No?

EMMA. But I do know he wouldn't be here unless Papa asked him.

LIZZIE. That's not the point. You know what happened last time he was here. Papa was signing property over to her.

EMMA. Oh Lizzie.   395

LIZZIE. Oh Lizzie nothing. It's bad enough Papa's worth thousands of dollars, and here we are, stuck in this tiny bit of a house on Second Street, when we should be up on the hill—and that's her doing. Or hers and Harry's.

EMMA. Shush.

LIZZIE. I won't shush. They cater to Papa's worst instincts.   400

EMMA. They'll hear you.

LIZZIE. I don't care if they do. It's true, isn't it? Papa tends to be miserly, he probably has the first penny he ever earned—or more likely *she* has it.

EMMA. You talk rubbish.

LIZZIE. Papa *can* be very warm-hearted and generous *but he needs encourage-* 405
ment.

EMMA. If Papa didn't save his money, Papa wouldn't have any money.

LIZZIE. And neither will we if he keeps signing things over to her.

EMMA. I'm not going to listen.

410 LIZZIE. Well try thinking.

EMMA. Stop it.

LIZZIE. (*Not a threat, a simple statement of fact.*) Someday Papa will die—

EMMA. Don't say that.

LIZZIE. Someday Papa will die. And I don't intend to spend the rest of my life

415   licking Harry Wingate's boots, or toadying to his sister.

MRS. BORDEN. (*From the stairs.*) What's that?

LIZZIE. Nothing.

MRS. BORDEN. (*Making her way downstairs.*) Eh?

LIZZIE. I said, nothing!

420 BRIDGET. (*Holds out basket of crusts. Lizzie looks at it.*) For your birds, Miss
       Lizzie.

LIZZIE. (*She takes the basket.*) You want to know what I think? I think she's a
       fat cow and I hate her. (*She exits.*)

EMMA. ... Morning, Mother.

425 MRS. BORDEN. Morning Emma.

EMMA. ... Did you have a good sleep?

       (*Bridget will serve breakfast.*)

MRS. BORDEN. So so.... It's the heat you know. It never cools off proper at
       night. It's too hot for a good sleep.

EMMA. ... Is Papa up?

430 MRS. BORDEN. He'll be down in a minute ... sooo.... What's wrong with
       Lizzie this morning?

EMMA. Nothing.

MRS. BORDEN. ... Has Harry come down?

EMMA. I'm not sure.

435 MRS. BORDEN. Bridget. Has Harry come down?

BRIDGET. Yes ma'am.

MRS. BORDEN. And?

BRIDGET. And he's gone out back for a bit.

MRS. BORDEN. Lizzie see him?

440 BRIDGET. Yes ma'am. (*Beats it back to the kitchen.*)

       (*Emma concentrates on her plate.*)

MRS. BORDEN. ... You should have said so.... She have words with him?

EMMA. Lizzie has more manners than that.

MRS. BORDEN. She's incapable of disciplining herself like a lady and we all know it.

EMMA. Well she doesn't make a habit of picking fights with people.   445

MRS. BORDEN. That's just it. She does.

EMMA. Well—she may—

MRS. BORDEN. And you can't deny that.

EMMA. (*Louder.*) Well this morning she may have been a bit upset because no one told her he was coming and when she came down he was here. But   450 that's all there was to it.

MRS. BORDEN. If your father wants my brother in for a stay, he's to ask Lizzie's permission I suppose.

EMMA. No.

MRS. BORDEN. You know, Emma—   455

EMMA. She didn't argue with him or anything like that.

MRS. BORDEN. You spoiled her. You may have had the best of intentions, but you spoiled her.

(*Miss Lizzie/Bridget is speaking to Actress/Lizzie.*)

MISS LIZZIE/BRIDGET. I was thirty-four years old, and I still daydreamed.... I did ... I daydreamed ... I dreamt that my name was Lisbeth ... and I lived   460 up on the hill in a corner house ... and my hair wasn't red. I hate red hair. When I was little, everyone teased me.... When I was little, we never stayed in this house for the summer, we'd go to the farm.... I remember ... my knees were always covered with scabs, god knows how I got them, but you know what I'd do? I'd sit in the field, and haul up my skirts, and my pet-   465 ticoat and my bloomers and roll down my stockings and I'd *pick* the scabs on my knees! And Emma would catch me! You know what she'd say? "Nice little girls don't have scabs on their knees!"

(*They laugh.*)

LIZZIE. Poor Emma.

MISS LIZZIE/BRIDGET. I dreamt ... someday I'm going to live ... in a corner   470 house on the hill.... I'll have parties, grand parties. I'll be ... witty, not bit-ing, but witty. Everyone will be witty. Everyone who is *any*one will want to come to my parties ... and if ... I can't ... live in a corner house on the hill ... I'll live on the farm, all by myself on the farm! There was a barn there, with barn cats and barn kittens and two horses and barn swallows that lived in   475 the eaves.... The birds I kept here were pigeons, not swallows.... They were grey, a dull grey ... but ... when the sun struck their feathers, I'd see blue, a steel blue with a sheen, and when they'd move in the sun they were bright blue and maroon and over it all, an odd sparkle as if you'd ... grated a new

480   silver dollar and the gratings caught in their feathers.... Most of the time
      they were dull ... and stupid perhaps ... but they weren't really. They were
      ... hiding I think.... They knew me.... They liked me.... The truth ... is ...

ACTRESS/LIZZIE.   The truth is ... thirty-four is too old to daydream....

MRS. BORDEN.   The truth is she's spoilt rotten. (*Mr. Borden will come down*
485   *stairs and take his place at the table. Mrs. Borden continues for his benefit.*
      Mr. Borden ignores her. He has learned the fine art of tuning her out. He is not
      intimidated or henpecked.) And we're paying the piper for that. In most of
      the places I've been the people who pay the piper call the tune. Of course I
      haven't had the advantage of a trip to Europe with a bunch of lady friends
490   like our Lizzie had three years ago, all expenses paid by her father.

EMMA.   Morning Papa.

MR. BORDEN.   Mornin'.

MRS. BORDEN.   I haven't had the benefit of that experience.... Did you know
      Lizzie's seen Harry?

495 MR. BORDEN.   Has she.

MRS. BORDEN.   You should have met him down town. You should never have
      asked him to stay over.

MR. BORDEN.   Why not?

MRS. BORDEN.   You know as well as I do why not. I don't want a repeat of last
500   time. She didn't speak civil for months.

MR. BORDEN.   There's no reason for Harry to pay for a room when we've got
      a spare one.... Where's Lizzie?

EMMA.   Out back feeding the birds.

MR. BORDEN.   She's always out at those birds.

505 EMMA.   Yes Papa.

MR. BORDEN.   And tell her to get a new lock for the shed. There's been some-
      one in it again.

EMMA.   Alright.

MR. BORDEN.   It's those little hellions from next door. We had no trouble with
510   them playin' in that shed before, they always played in their own yard before.

EMMA.   ... Papa?

MR. BORDEN.   It's those damn birds, that's what brings them into the yard.

EMMA.   ... About Harry ...

MR. BORDEN.   What about Harry?

515 EMMA.   Well ... I was just wondering why ... [*he's here*]

MR. BORDEN.   You never mind Harry—did you speak to Lizzie about Johnny
      MacLeod?

EMMA.   I ah—

MR. BORDEN.   Eh?

520 EMMA.   I said I tried to—

MR. BORDEN. What do you mean, you tried to.

EMMA. Well, I was working my way round to it but—

MR. BORDEN. What's so difficult about telling Lizzie Johnny MacLeod wants to call?

EMMA. Then why don't you tell her? I'm always the one that has to go run- 525
ning to Lizzie telling her this and telling her that, and taking the abuse for
it!

MRS. BORDEN. We all know why that is, she can wrap her father round her
little finger, always has, always could. If everything else fails, she throws a
tantrum and her father buys her off, trip to Europe, rent to the mill house, 530
it's all the same.

EMMA. Papa, what's Harry here for?

MR. BORDEN. None of your business.

MRS. BORDEN. And don't you go runnin' to Lizzie stirring things up.

EMMA. You know I've never done that! 535

MR. BORDEN. What she means—

EMMA. (*With anger but little fatigue.*) I'm tired, do you hear? Tired! (*She gets
up from the table and leaves for upstairs.*)

MR. BORDEN. Emma!

EMMA. You ask Harry here, you know there'll be trouble, and when I try to 540
find out what's going on, so once again good old Emma can stand between
you and Lizzie, all you've got to say is "none of your business"! Well then,
it's *your* business, you look after it, because I'm not! (*She exits.*)

MRS. BORDEN. ... She's right.

MR. BORDEN. That's enough. I've had enough. I don't want to hear from you 545
too.

MRS. BORDEN. I'm only saying she's right. You have to talk straight and plain
to Lizzie and tell her things she don't want to hear.

MR. BORDEN. About the farm?

MRS. BORDEN. About Johnny MacLeod! Keep your mouth shut about the 550
farm and she won't know the difference.

MR. BORDEN. Alright.

MRS. BORDEN. Speak to her about Johnny MacLeod.

MR. BORDEN. Alright!

MRS. BORDEN. You know what they're sayin' in town. About her and that 555
doctor.

(*Miss Lizzie/Bridget is speaking to the actress/Lizzie.*)

MISS LIZZIE/BRIDGET. They're saying if you live on Second Street and you
need a house call, and you don't mind the Irish, call Dr. Patrick. Dr. Patrick is very prompt with his Second Street house calls.

560 ACTRESS/LIZZIE. Do they really say that?

MISS LIZZIE/BRIDGET. No they don't. I'm telling a lie. But he is very prompt with a Second Street call, do you know why that is?

ACTRESS/LIZZIE. Why?

MISS LIZZIE/BRIDGET. Well—he's hoping to see someone who lives on Sec-
565 ond Street—someone who's yanking up her skirt and showing her ankle— so she can take a decent-sized step—and forgetting everything she was ever taught in Miss Cornelia's School for Girls, and talking to the Irish as if she never heard of the Pope! Oh yes, he's very prompt getting to Second Street ... getting away is something else....

570 DR. PATRICK. Good morning, Miss Borden!

LIZZIE. I haven't decided ... if it is ... or it isn't ...

DR. PATRICK. No, you've got it all wrong. The proper phrase is "good morn-ing, Dr. Patrick," and then you smile, discreetly of course, and lower the eyes just a titch, twirl the parasol—

575 LIZZIE. The parasol?

DR. PATRICK. The parasol, but not too fast; and then you murmur in a voice that was ever sweet and low, "And how are you doin' this morning, Dr. Patrick?" Your education's been sadly neglected, Miss Borden.

LIZZIE. You're forgetting something. You're married—and Irish besides—I'm
580 supposed to ignore you.

DR. PATRICK. No.

LIZZIE. Yes. Don't you realize Papa and Emma have fits every time we engage in "illicit conversation." They're having fits right now.

DR. PATRICK. Well, does Mrs. Borden approve?

585 LIZZIE. Ahhh. She's the real reason I keep stopping and talking. Mrs. Borden is easily shocked. I'm hoping she dies from the shock.

DR. PATRICK. (Laughs.) Why don't you ... run away from home, Lizzie?

LIZZIE. Why don't you "run away" with me?

DR. PATRICK. Where'll we go?

590 LIZZIE. Boston.

DR. PATRICK. Boston?

LIZZIE. For a start.

DR. PATRICK. And when will we go?

LIZZIE. Tonight.

595 DR. PATRICK. But you don't really mean it, you're havin' me on.

LIZZIE. I do mean it.

DR. PATRICK. How can you joke—and look so serious?

LIZZIE. It's a gift.

DR. PATRICK. (Laughs.) Oh Lizzie—

600 LIZZIE. Look!

DR. PATRICK. What is it?

LIZZIE. It's those little beggars next door. Hey! Hey get away! Get away there! ... They break into the shed to get at my birds and Papa gets angry.

DR. PATRICK. It's a natural thing.

LIZZIE. Well, Papa doesn't like it.   605

DR. PATRICK. They just want to look at them.

LIZZIE. Papa says what's his is his own—you need a formal invitation to get into our yard.... (*Pause.*) How's your wife?

DR. PATRICK. My wife.

LIZZIE. Shouldn't I ask that? I thought nice polite ladies always inquired after   610 the wives of their friends or acquaintances or ... whatever.

(*Harry observes them.*)

DR. PATRICK. You've met my wife, my wife is always the same.

LIZZIE. How boring for you.

DR. PATRICK. Uh-huh.

LIZZIE. And for her—   615

DR. PATRICK. Yes indeed.

LIZZIE. And for me.

DR. PATRICK. Do you know what they say, Lizzie? They say if you live on Second Street, and you need a house call, and you don't mind the Irish, call Dr. Patrick. Dr. Patrick is very prompt with his Second Street house calls.   620

LIZZIE. I'll tell you what I've heard them say—Second Street is a nice place to visit, but you wouldn't want to live there. I certainly don't.

HARRY. Lizzie.

LIZZIE. Well, look who's here. Have you had the pleasure of meeting my uncle, Mr. Wingate.   625

DR. PATRICK. No, Miss Borden, that pleasure has never been mine.

LIZZIE. That's exactly how I feel.

DR. PATRICK. Mr. Wingate, sir.

HARRY. Dr.... Patrick is it?

DR. PATRICK. Yes it is, sir.   630

HARRY. Who's sick? (*In other words, "What the hell are you doing here?"*)

LIZZIE. No one. He just dropped by for a visit; you see Dr. Patrick and I are very old, very dear friends, isn't that so?

(*Harry stares at Dr. Patrick.*)

DR. PATRICK. Well ... (*Lizzie jabs him in the ribs.*) Ouch! ... It's her sense of humour, sir ... a rare trait in a woman....   635

HARRY. You best get in, Lizzie, it's gettin' on for lunch.

LIZZIE. Don't be silly, we just had breakfast.

HARRY. You best get in!

LIZZIE. ... Would you give me your arm, Dr. Patrick? (*She moves away with Dr. Patrick, ignoring Harry.*)

640 DR. PATRICK. Now see what you've done?

LIZZIE. What?

DR. PATRICK. You've broken two of my ribs and ruined my reputation all in one blow.

LIZZIE. It's impossible to ruin an Irishman's reputation.

645 DR. PATRICK. (*Smiles.*) ... I'll be seeing you, Lizzie....

MISS LIZZIE/BRIDGET. They're sayin' it's time you were married.

LIZZIE. What time is that?

MISS LIZZIE/BRIDGET. You need a place of your own.

LIZZIE. How would getting married get me that?

650 MISS LIZZIE/BRIDGET. Though I don't know what man would put up with your moods!

LIZZIE. What about me putting up with his!

MISS LIZZIE/BRIDGET. Oh Lizzie!

LIZZIE. What's the matter, don't men have moods?

655 HARRY. I'm tellin' you, as God is my witness, she's out in the walk talkin' to that Irish doctor, and he's fallin' all over her.

MRS. BORDEN. What's the matter with you? For her own sake you should speak to her.

MR. BORDEN. I will.

660 HARRY. The talk around town can't be doin' you any good.

MRS. BORDEN. Harry's right.

HARRY. Yes sir.

MRS. BORDEN. He's tellin' you what you should know.

HARRY. If a man can't manage his own daughter, how the hell can he manage

665 a business—that's what people say, and it don't matter a damn whether there's any sense in it or not.

MR. BORDEN. I know that.

MRS. BORDEN. Knowin' is one thing, doin' something about it is another. What're you goin' to do about it?

670 MR. BORDEN. God damn it! I said I was goin' to speak to her and I am!

MRS. BORDEN. Well speak good and plain this time!

MR. BORDEN. Jesus christ woman!

MRS. BORDEN. Your "speakin' to Lizzie" is a ritual around here.

MR. BORDEN. Abbie—

675 MRS. BORDEN. She talks, you listen, and nothin' changes!

MR. BORDEN. That's enough!

MRS. BORDEN. Emma isn't the only one that's fed to the teeth!

MR. BORDEN. Shut up!

MRS. BORDEN. You're gettin' old, Andrew! You're gettin' old! (*She exits.*)

> (*An air of embarrassment from Mr. Borden at having words in front of Harry. Mr. Borden fumbles with his pipe.*)

HARRY. (*Offers his pouch of tobacco.*) Here ... have some of mine.   680

MR. BORDEN. Don't mind if I do.... Nice mix.

HARRY. It is.

MR. BORDEN. ... I used to think ... by my seventies ... I'd be bouncin' a grand-son on my knee....

HARRY. Not too late for that.   685

MR. BORDEN. Nope ... never had any boys ... and girls ... don't seem to have the same sense of family.... You know it's all well and good to talk about speakin' plain to Lizzie, but the truth of the matter is, if Lizzie puts her mind to a thing, she does it, and if she don't, she don't.

HARRY. It's up to you to see she does.   690

MR. BORDEN. It's like Abigail says, knowin' is one thing, doin' is another.... You're lucky you never brought any children into the world, Harry, you don't have to deal with them.

HARRY. Now that's no way to be talkin'.

MR. BORDEN. There's Emma ... Emma's a good girl ... when Abbie and I get   695
on, there'll always be Emma.... Well! You're not sittin' here to listen to me and my girls, are you, you didn't come here for that. Business, eh, Harry?

> (*Harry whips out a sheet of figures.*)

MISS LIZZIE/BRIDGET. I can remember distinctly ... that moment I was un-dressing for bed, and I looked at my knees—and there were no scabs! At last! I thought I'm the nice little girl Emma wants me to be! ... But it wasn't   700
that at all. I was just growing up. I didn't fall down so often.... (*She smiles.*) Do you suppose ... do you suppose there's a formula, a magic formula for being "a woman"? Do you suppose every girl baby receives it at birth, it's the last thing that happens just before birth, the magic formula is stamped indelibly on the brain—Ka Thud!! (*Her mood of amusement changes.*) ...   705
and ... through some terrible oversight ... perhaps the death of my Mother ... I didn't get that Ka Thud!! I was born ... defective.... (*She looks at the actress.*)

LIZZIE. (*Low.*) No.

MISS LIZZIE/BRIDGET. Not defective?

LIZZIE. Just ... born.   710

THE DEFENCE. Gentlemen of the Jury!! I ask you to look at the defendant, Miss Lizzie Borden. I ask you to recall the nature of the crime of which

she is accused. I ask you—do you believe Miss Lizzie Borden, the youngest daughter of a scion of our community, a recipient of the fullest amenities
715 our society can bestow upon its most fortunate members, do you believe Miss Lizzie Borden capable of wielding the murder weapon—thirty-two blows, gentlemen, thirty-two blows—fracturing Abigail Borden's skull, leaving her bloody and broken body in an upstairs bedroom, then, Miss Borden, with no hint of frenzy, hysteria, or trace of blood upon her person,
720 engages in casual conversation with the maid, Bridget O'Sullivan, while awaiting her father's return home, upon which, after sending Bridget to her attic room, Miss Borden deals thirteen blows to the head of her father, and minutes later—in a state utterly compatible with that of a loving daughter upon discovery of murder most foul—Miss Borden calls for aid!
725 Is this the aid we give her? Accusation of the most heinous and infamous of crimes? Do you believe Miss Lizzie Borden capable of these acts? I can tell you I do not!! I can tell you these acts of violence are acts of madness!! Gentlemen! If this gentlewoman is capable of such an act—I say to you—look to your daughters—if this gentlewoman is capable of such an
730 act, which of us can lie abed at night, hear a step upon the stairs, a rustle in the hall, a creak outside the door.... Which of you can plump your pillow, nudge your wife, close your eyes, and sleep? Gentlemen, Lizzie Borden is not mad. Gentlemen, Lizzie Borden is not guilty.

MR. BORDEN. Lizzie?

735 LIZZIE. Papa ... have you and Harry got business?

HARRY. 'lo Lizzie. I'll ah ... finish up later. (*He exits with the figures. Lizzie watches him go.*)

MR. BORDEN. Lizzie?

LIZZIE. What?

740 MR. BORDEN. Could you sit down a minute?

LIZZIE. If it's about Dr. Patrick again, I—

MR. BORDEN. It isn't.

LIZZIE. Good.

MR. BORDEN. But we could start there.

745 LIZZIE. Oh Papa.

MR. BORDEN. Sit down Lizzie.

LIZZIE. But I've heard it all before, another chat for a wayward girl.

MR. BORDEN. (*Gently.*) Bite your tongue, Lizzie.

(*She smiles at him, there is affection between them. She has the qualities he would like in a son but deplores in a daughter.*)

MR. BORDEN. Now ... first off ... I want you to know that I ... understand
750 about you and the doctor.

LIZZIE. What do you understand?

MR. BORDEN. I understand ... that it's a natural thing.

LIZZIE. What is?

MR. BORDEN. I'm saying there's nothing unnatural about an attraction between a man and a woman. That's a natural thing.   755

LIZZIE. I find Dr. Patrick ... amusing and entertaining ... if that's what you
mean ... is that what you mean?

MR. BORDEN. This attraction ... points something up—you're a woman of
thirty-four years—

LIZZIE. I know that.   760

MR. BORDEN. Just listen to me, Lizzie.... I'm choosing my words, and I want
you to listen. Now ... in most circumstances ... a woman of your age would
be married, eh? have children, be running her own house, that's the natural
thing, eh? (*Pause.*) Eh, Lizzie?

LIZZIE. I don't know.   765

MR. BORDEN. Of course you know.

LIZZIE. You're saying I'm unnatural ... am I supposed to agree, is that what
you want?

MR. BORDEN. No, I'm not saying that! I'm saying the opposite to that! ... I'm
saying the feelings you have towards Dr. Patrick—   770

LIZZIE. What feelings?

MR. BORDEN. What's ... what's happening there, I can understand, but what
you have to understand is that he's a married man, and there's nothing for
you there.

LIZZIE. If he weren't married, Papa, I wouldn't be bothered talking to him!   775
It's just a game, Papa, it's a game.

MR. BORDEN. A game.

LIZZIE. You have no idea how boring it is looking eligible, interested, and
alluring, when I feel none of the three. So I play games. And it's a blessed
relief to talk to a married man.   780

MR. BORDEN. What're his feelings for you?

LIZZIE. I don't know, I don't care. Can I go now?

MR. BORDEN. I'm not finished yet! ... You know Mr. MacLeod, Johnny Mac-
Leod?

LIZZIE. I know his three little monsters.   785

MR. BORDEN. He's trying to raise three boys with no mother!

LIZZIE. That's not my problem! I'm going.

MR. BORDEN. Lizzie!

LIZZIE. What!

MR. BORDEN. Mr. MacLeod's asked to come over next Tuesday.   790

LIZZIE. I'll be out that night.

MR. BORDEN. No you won't!

LIZZIE. Yes I will! ... Whose idea was this?

MR. BORDEN. No one's.

795 LIZZIE. That's a lie. She wants to get rid of me.

MR. BORDEN. I want what's best for you!

LIZZIE. No you don't! 'Cause you don't care what I want!

MR. BORDEN. You don't know what you want!

LIZZIE. But I know what you want! You want me living my life by the Farm-
800 ers' Almanac; having everyone over for Christmas dinner; waiting up for
my husband; and *serving at socials!*

MR. BORDEN. It's good enough for your mother!

LIZZIE. She is *not* my *mother!*

MR. BORDEN. ... John MacLeod is looking for a wife.

805 LIZZIE. No, god damn it, he isn't!

MR. BORDEN. Lizzie!

LIZZIE. He's looking for a housekeeper and it isn't going to be me!

MR. BORDEN. You've a filthy mouth!

LIZZIE. Is that why you hate me?

810 MR. BORDEN. You don't make sense.

LIZZIE. Why is it when I pretend things I don't feel, that's when you like me?

MR. BORDEN. You talk foolish.

LIZZIE. I'm supposed to be a mirror. I'm supposed to reflect what you want to
see, but everyone wants something different. If no one looks in the mirror,
815 I'm not even there, I don't exist!

MR. BORDEN. Lizzie, you talk foolish!

LIZZIE. No, I don't, that isn't true.

MR. BORDEN. About Mr. MacLeod—

LIZZIE. You can't make me get married!

820 MR. BORDEN. Lizzie, do you want to spend the rest of your life in this house?

LIZZIE. No ... No ... I want out of it, but I won't get married to do it.

MRS. BORDEN. (*On her way through to the kitchen.*) You've never been asked.

LIZZIE. Oh listen to her! I must be some sort of failure, then, eh? You had no
son and a daughter that failed! What does that make you, Papa!

825 MR. BORDEN. I want you to think about Johnny MacLeod!

LIZZIE. To hell with him!!!

(*Mr. Borden appears defeated. After a moment, Lizzie goes to him, she holds
his hand, strokes his hair.*)

LIZZIE. Papa? ... Papa, I love you, I try to be what you want, really I do try, I
try ... but ... I don't want to get married. I wouldn't be a good mother, I—

MR. BORDEN. How do you know—

LIZZIE. I know it! ... I want out of all this ... I hate this house, I hate ... I want   830
out. Try to understand how I feel ... Why can't I do something? ... Eh? I
mean ... I could ... I could go into your office ... I could ... learn how to
keep books?

MR. BORDEN. Lizzie.

LIZZIE. Why can't I do something like that?   835

MR. BORDEN. For god's sake, talk sensible.

LIZZIE. Alright then! Why can't we move up on the hill to a house where we
aren't in each other's laps!

MRS. BORDEN. (*Returning from kitchen.*) Why don't you move out!

LIZZIE. Give me the money and I'll go!   840

MRS. BORDEN. Money.

LIZZIE. And give me enough that I won't ever have to come back!

MRS. BORDEN. She always gets round to money!

LIZZIE. You drive me to it!

MRS. BORDEN. She's crazy!   845

LIZZIE. You drive me to it!

MRS. BORDEN. She should be locked up!

LIZZIE. (*Begins to smash the plates in the dining room.*) There!! There!!

MR. BORDEN. Lizzie!

MRS. BORDEN. Stop her!   850

LIZZIE. There!

(*Mr. Borden attempts to restrain her.*)

MRS. BORDEN. For god's sake, Andrew!

LIZZIE. Lock me up! Lock me up!

MR. BORDEN. Stop it! Lizzie!

(*She collapses against him, crying.*)

LIZZIE. Oh, Papa, I can't stand it.   855

MR. BORDEN. There, there, come on now, it's alright, listen to me, Lizzie, it's
alright.

MRS. BORDEN. You may as well get down on your knees.

LIZZIE. Look at her. She's jealous of me. She can't stand it whenever you're
nice to me.   860

MR. BORDEN. There now.

MRS. BORDEN. Ask her about Dr. Patrick.

MR. BORDEN. I'll handle this my way.

LIZZIE. He's an entertaining person, there're very few around!

MRS. BORDEN. Fall River ain't Paris and ain't that a shame for our Lizzie!   865

LIZZIE. One trip three years ago and you're still harping on it; it's true, Papa, an elephant never forgets!

MR. BORDEN. Show some respect!

LIZZIE. She's a fat cow and I hate her!

(*Mr. Borden slaps Lizzie. There is a pause as he regains control of himself.*)

870 MR. BORDEN. Now ... now ... you'll see Mr. MacLeod Tuesday night.

LIZZIE. No.

MR. BORDEN. God damn it!! I said you'll see Johnny MacLeod Tuesday night!!

LIZZIE. No.

875 MR. BORDEN. Get the hell upstairs to your room!

LIZZIE. No.

MR. BORDEN. I'm telling you to go upstairs to your room!!

LIZZIE. I'll go when I'm ready.

MR. BORDEN. I said, Go!

(*He grabs her arm to move her forcibly, she hits his arm away.*)

880 LIZZIE. No! ... There's something you don't understand, Papa. You can't make me do one thing that I don't want to do. I'm going to keep on doing just what I want just when I want—like always!

MR. BORDEN. (*Shoves her to the floor to gain a clear exit from the room. He stops on the stairs, looks back to her on the floor.*) ... I'm ... (*He continues off.*)

885 MRS. BORDEN. (*Without animosity.*) You know, Lizzie, your father keeps you. You know you got nothing but what he gives you. And that's a fact of life. You got to come to deal with facts. I did.

LIZZIE. And married Papa.

MRS. BORDEN. And married your father. You never made it easy for me. I
890 took on a man with two little ones, and Emma was your mother.

LIZZIE. You got stuck so I should too, is that it?

MRS. BORDEN. What?

LIZZIE. The reason I should marry Johnny MacLeod.

MRS. BORDEN. I just know, this time, in the end, you'll do what your Papa
895 says, you'll see.

LIZZIE. No, I won't. I have a right. A right that frees me from all that.

MRS. BORDEN. No, Lizzie, you got no rights.

LIZZIE. I've a legal right to one-third because I am his flesh and blood.

MRS. BORDEN. What you don't understand is your father's not dead yet, your
900 father's got many good years ahead of him, and when his time comes, well, we'll see what his will says then.... Your father's no fool, Lizzie.... Only a fool would leave money to you. (*She exits.*)

(*After a moment, Bridget enters from the kitchen.*)

BRIDGET. Ah Lizzie ... you outdid yourself that time. (*She is comforting Lizzie.*) ... Yes you did ... an elephant never forgets!

LIZZIE. Oh Bridget.   905

BRIDGET. Come on now.

LIZZIE. I can't help it.

BRIDGET. Sure you can ... sure you can ... stop your cryin' and come and sit down ... you want me to tell you a story?

LIZZIE. No.   910

BRIDGET. Sure, a story. I'll tell you a story. Come on now ... now ... before I worked here I worked up on the hill and the lady of the house ... are you listenin'? Well, she swore by her cook, finest cook in creation, yes, always bowin' and scrapin' and smilin' and givin' up her day off if company arrived. Oh the lady of the house she loved that cook—and I'll tell you   915 her name! It was Mary! Now listen! Do you know what Mary was doin'? (*Lizzie shakes her head.*) Before eatin' the master'd serve drinks in the parlour—and out in the kitchen, Mary'd be spittin' in the soup!

LIZZIE. What?

BRIDGET. She'd spit in the soup! And she'd smile when they served it!   920

LIZZIE. No.

BRIDGET. Yes. I've seen her cut up hair for an omelette.

LIZZIE. You're lying.

BRIDGET. Cross me heart.... They thought it was pepper!

LIZZIE. Oh, Bridget!   925

BRIDGET. These two eyes have seen her season up mutton stew when it's off and gone bad.

LIZZIE. Gone bad?

BRIDGET. Oh and they et it, every bit, and the next day they was hit with ... *stomach flu!* So cook called it. By jasus Lizzie, I daren't tell you what she   930 served up in their food, for fear you'd be sick!

LIZZIE. That's funny.... (*A fact—Lizzie does not appear amused.*)

BRIDGET. (*Starts to clear up the dishes.*) Yes, well, I'm tellin' you I kept on the good side of cook.

(*Lizzie watches her for a moment.*)

LIZZIE. ... Do you ... like me?   935

BRIDGET. Sure I do ... You should try bein' more like cook, Lizzie. Smile and get round them. You can do it.

LIZZIE. It's not ... *fair* that I have to.

BRIDGET. There ain't nothin' fair in this world.

940 LIZZIE. Well then ... well then, I don't want to!

BRIDGET. You dream, Lizzie ... you dream dreams ... Work. Be sensible. What could you do?

LIZZIE. I could ...

MISS LIZZIE/BRIDGET. No.

945 LIZZIE. I could ...

MISS LIZZIE/BRIDGET. No.

LIZZIE. I could ...

MISS LIZZIE/BRIDGET. No!

LIZZIE. I ... dream.

950 MISS LIZZIE/BRIDGET. You dream ... of a carousel ... you see a carousel ... you see lights that go on and go off ... you see yourself on a carousel horse, a red-painted horse with its head in the air, and green staring eyes, and a white flowing mane, it looks wild! ... It goes up and comes down, and the carousel whirls round with the music and lights, on and off ... and you
955 watch ... watch yourself on the horse. You're wearing a mask, a white mask like the mane of the horse, it looks like your face except that it's rigid and white ... and it changes! With each flick of the lights, the expression, it changes, but always so rigid and hard, like the flesh of the horse that is red that you ride. You ride with no hands! No hands on this petrified horse,
960 its head flung in the air, its wide staring eyes like those of a doe run down by the dogs! ... And each time you go round, your hands rise a fraction nearer the mask ... and the music and the carousel and the horse ... they all three slow down, and they stop.... You can reach out and touch ... you ... you on the horse ... with your hands so at the eyes.... You look into the
965 eyes! (*A sound from Lizzie, she is horrified and frightened. She covers her eyes.*) There are none! None! Just black holes in a white mask.... (*Pause.*) Only a dream.... The eyes of your birds ... are round ... and bright ... a light shines from inside ... they ... can see into your heart ... they're pretty ... they love you....

970 MR. BORDEN. I want this settled, Harry, I want it settled while Lizzie's out back.

(*Miss Lizzie/Bridget draws Lizzie's attention to the Mr. Borden/Harry scene. Lizzie listens, will move closer.*)

HARRY. You know I'm for that.

MR. BORDEN. I want it all done but the signin' of the papers tomorrow, that's if I decide to—

975 HARRY. You can't lose, Andrew. That farm's just lyin' fallow.

MR. BORDEN. Well, let's see what you got.

HARRY. (*Gets out his papers.*) Look at this ... I'll run horse auctions and a buggy rental—now I'll pay no rent for the house or pasturage but you get twenty percent, eh? That figure there—

MR. BORDEN. Mmmn. 980

HARRY. From my horse auctions last year, it'll go up on the farm and you'll get twenty percent off the top.... My buggy rental won't do so well ... that's that figure there, approximate ... but it all adds up, eh? Adds up for you.

MR. BORDEN. It's a good deal, Harry, but ...

HARRY. Now I know why you're worried—but the farm will still be in the 985 family, 'cause aren't I family? and whenever you or the girls want to come over for a visit, why I'll send a buggy from the rental, no need for you to have the expense of a horse, eh?

MR. BORDEN. It looks good on paper.

HARRY. There's ... ah ... something else, it's a bit awkward but I got to men- 990 tion it; I'll be severin' a lot of my present connections, and what I figure I've a right to, is some kind of guarantee....

MR. BORDEN. You mean a renewable lease for the farm?

HARRY. Well—what I'm wondering is ... No offence, but you're an older man, Andrew ... now if something should happen to you, where would the 995 farm stand in regards to your will? That's what I'm wondering.

MR. BORDEN. I've not made a will.

HARRY. You know best—but I wouldn't want to be in a position where Lizzie would be havin' anything to do with that farm. The less she knows now the better, but she's bound to find out—I don't feel I'm steppin' out of line 1000 by bringin' this up.

(*Lizzie is within earshot. She is staring at Harry and Mr. Borden. They do not see her.*)

MR. BORDEN. No.

HARRY. If you mind you come right out and say so.

MR. BORDEN. That's alright.

HARRY. Now ... if you ... put the farm—in Abbie's name, what do you think? 1005

MR. BORDEN. I don't know, Harry.

HARRY. I don't want to push.

MR. BORDEN. ... I should make a will ... I want the girls looked after, it don't seem like they'll marry ... and Abbie, she's younger than me, I know Emma will see to her, still ... money-wise I got to consider these things ... it makes 1010 a difference no men in the family.

HARRY. You know you can count on me for whatever.

MR. BORDEN. If ... *If* I changed title to the farm, Abbie'd have to come down to the bank, I wouldn't want Lizzie to know.

1015 HARRY. You can send a note for her when you get to the bank; she can say it's a note from a friend, and come down and meet you. Simple as that.

MR. BORDEN. I'll give it some thought.

HARRY. You see, Abbie owns the farm, it's no difference to you, but it gives me protection.

1020 MR. BORDEN. Who's there?

HARRY. It's Lizzie.

MR. BORDEN. What do you want? ... Did you lock the shed? ... Is the shed locked? (*Lizzie makes a slow motion which Mr. Borden takes for assent.*) Well you make sure it stays locked! I don't want any more of those god

1025 damned.... I ... ah ... I think we about covered everything, Harry, we'll ... ah ... we'll let it go till tomorrow.

HARRY. Good enough ... well ... I'll just finish choppin' that kindlin', give a shout when it's lunchtime. (*He exits.*)

(*Lizzie and Mr. Borden stare at each other for a moment.*)

LIZZIE. (*Very low.*) What are you doing with the farm?

(*Mr. Borden slowly picks up the papers, places them in his pocket.*)

1030 LIZZIE. Papa! ... Papa. I want you to show me what you put in your pocket.

MR. BORDEN. It's none of your business.

LIZZIE. The farm is my business.

MR. BORDEN. It's nothing.

LIZZIE. Show me!

1035 MR. BORDEN. I said it's nothing!

(*Lizzie makes a quick move towards her father to seize the paper from his pocket. Even more quickly and smartly he slaps her face. It is all very quick and clean. A pause as they stand frozen.*)

HARRY. (*Off.*) Andrew, there's a bunch of kids broken into the shed!

MR. BORDEN. Jesus christ.

LIZZIE. (*Whispers.*) What about the farm.

MR. BORDEN. You! You and those god damn birds! I've told you! I've told

1040 you time and again!

LIZZIE. What about the farm!

MR. BORDEN. Jesus christ ... You never listen! Never!

HARRY. (*Enters carrying the hand hatchet.*) Andrew!!

MR. BORDEN. (*Grabs the hand hatchet from Harry, turns to Lizzie.*) There'll be

1045 no more of your god damn birds in this yard!!

LIZZIE. No!

(*Mr. Borden raises the hatchet and smashes it into the table as Lizzie screams.*)

LIZZIE. No Papa!! Nooo!!

(*The hatchet is embedded in the table. Mr. Borden and Harry assume a soft freeze as the actress/Lizzie whirls to see Miss Lizzie/Bridget observing the scene.*)

LIZZIE. Nooo!
MISS LIZZIE. I loved them.

(*Blackout.*)

ACT 2

Lights come up on the actress/Lizzie sitting at the dining-room table. She is very still, her hands clasped in her lap. Miss Lizzie/Bridget is near her. She too is very still. A pause.

ACTRESS/LIZZIE. (*Very low.*) Talk to me.
MISS LIZZIE/BRIDGET. I remember ...
ACTRESS/LIZZIE. (*Very low.*) No.
MISS LIZZIE/BRIDGET. On the farm, Papa's farm, Harry's farm, when I was little and thought it was my farm and I loved it, we had some puppies, 5 the farm dog had puppies, brown soft little puppies with brown ey ... (*She does not complete the word "eyes."*) And one of the puppies got sick. I didn't know it was sick, it seemed like the others, but the mother, she knew. It would lie at the back of the box, she would lie in front of it while she nursed all the others. They ignored it, that puppy didn't exist for the oth- 10 ers.... I think inside it was different, and the mother thought the difference she sensed was a sickness ... and after a while ... anyone could tell it was sick. It had nothing to eat! ... And Papa took it and drowned it. That's what you do on a farm with things that are different.
ACTRESS/LIZZIE. Am I different? 15
MISS LIZZIE/BRIDGET. You kill them.

(*Actress/Lizzie looks at Miss Lizzie/Bridget. Miss Lizzie/Bridget looks towards the top of the stairs. Bridget gets up and exits to the kitchen. Emma appears at the top of the stairs. She is dressed for travel and carries a small suitcase and her gloves. She stares down at Lizzie still sitting at the table. After several moments Lizzie becomes aware of that gaze and turns to look at Emma. Emma then descends the stairs. She puts down her suitcase. She is not overjoyed at seeing Lizzie, having hoped to get away before Lizzie arose, nevertheless she begins with an excess of enthusiasm to cover the implications of her departure.*)

EMMA. Well! You're up early ... Bridget down? ... did you put the coffee on? (*She puts her gloves on the table.*) My goodness, Lizzie, cat got your tongue? (*She exits to the kitchen. Lizzie picks up the gloves. Emma returns.*)

20 Bridget's down, she's in the kitchen.... Well ... looks like a real scorcher today, doesn't it? ...

LIZZIE. What's the bag for?

EMMA. I ... decided I might go for a little trip, a day or two, get away from the heat.... The girls've rented a place out beach way and I thought ... with

25 the weather and all ...

LIZZIE. How can you do that?

EMMA. Do what? ... Anyway, I thought I might stay with them a few days.... Why don't you come with me?

LIZZIE. No.

30 EMMA. Just for a few days, come with me.

LIZZIE. No.

EMMA. You know you like the water.

LIZZIE. I said no!

EMMA. Oh, Lizzie.

(*Pause.*)

35 LIZZIE. I don't see how you can leave me like this.

EMMA. I asked you to come with me.

LIZZIE. You know I can't do that.

EMMA. Why not?

LIZZIE. Someone has to *do* something, you just run away from things.

(*Pause.*)

40 EMMA. ... Lizzie ... I'm sorry about the—[*birds*]

LIZZIE. No!

EMMA. Papa was angry.

LIZZIE. I don't want to talk about it.

EMMA. He's sorry now.

45 LIZZIE. Nobody *listens* to me, can't you hear me? I said *don't* talk about it. I don't want to talk about it. Stop talking about it!!

(*Bridget enters with the coffee.*)

EMMA. Thank you, Bridget.

(*Bridget withdraws.*)

EMMA. Well! ... I certainly can use this this morning.... Your coffee's there.

LIZZIE. I don't want it.

EMMA. You're going to ruin those gloves.   50

LIZZIE. I don't care.

EMMA. Since they're not yours.

> (*Lizzie bangs the gloves down on the table. A pause. Then Emma picks them up and smooths them out.*)

LIZZIE. Why are you leaving me?

EMMA. I feel like a visit with the girls. Is there something wrong with that?

LIZZIE. How can you go now?   50

EMMA. I don't know what you're getting at.

LIZZIE. I heard them. I heard them talking yesterday. Do you know what they're saying?

EMMA. How could I?

LIZZIE. "How could I?" What do you mean "How could I?" Did you know?   55

EMMA. No, Lizzie, I did not.

LIZZIE. *Did-not-what.*

EMMA. Know.

LIZZIE. But you know now. How do you know now?

EMMA. I've put two and two together and I'm going over to the girls for a   60
visit!

LIZZIE. Please Emma!

EMMA. It's too hot.

LIZZIE. I need you, don't go.

EMMA. I've been talking about this trip.   65

LIZZIE. That's a lie.

EMMA. They're expecting me.

LIZZIE. You're lying to me!

EMMA. I'm going to the girls' place. You can come if you want, you can stay if you want. I planned this trip and I'm taking it!   70

LIZZIE. Stop lying!

EMMA. If I want to tell a little white lie to avoid an altercation in this house, I'll do so. Other people have been doing it for years!

LIZZIE. You don't understand, you don't understand anything.

EMMA. Oh, I understand enough.   75

LIZZIE. You don't! Let me explain it to you. You listen carefully, you listen.... Harry's getting the farm, can you understand that? Harry is here and he's moving on the farm and he's going to be there, on the farm, living on the farm. *Our farm.* Do you understand that? ... Do you understand that!

EMMA. Yes.   80

LIZZIE. Harry's going to be on the farm. That's the first thing.... No ... no it isn't.... The first thing ... was the mill house, that was the first thing! And *now* the farm. You see there's a pattern, Emma, you can see that, can't you?

EMMA. I don't—

85 LIZZIE. You can see it! The mill house, then the farm, and the next thing is the papers for the farm—do you know what he's doing, Papa's doing? He's signing the farm over to her. It will never be ours, we will never have it, not ever. It's ours by rights, don't you feel that?

EMMA. The farm—has always meant a great deal to me, yes.

90 LIZZIE. Then what are you doing about it! You can't leave me now ... but that's not all. Papa's going to make a will, and you can see the pattern, can't you, and if the pattern keeps on, what do you suppose his will will say. What do you suppose, answer me!

EMMA. I don't know.

95 LIZZIE. Say it!

EMMA. He'll see we're looked after.

LIZZIE. I don't want to be looked after! What's the matter with you? Do you really want to spend the rest of your life with that cow, listening to her drone on and on for years! That's just what they think you'll do. Papa'll

100 leave you a monthly allowance, just like he'll leave me, just enough to keep us all living together. We'll be worth millions on paper, and be stuck in this house and by and by Papa will die and Harry will move in and you will wait on that cow while she gets fatter and fatter and I—will—sit in my room.

105 EMMA. Lizzie.

LIZZIE. We have to do something, you can see that. We have to do something!

EMMA. There's nothing we can do.

LIZZIE. Don't say that!

110 EMMA. Alright, then, what can we do?

LIZZIE. I ... I ... don't know. But we have to do something, you have to help me, you can't go away and leave me alone, you can't do that.

EMMA. Then—

LIZZIE. You know what I thought? I thought you could talk to him, really

115 talk to him, make him understand that we're people. *Individual people*, and we have to live separate lives, and his will should make it possible for us to do that. And the farm can't go to Harry.

EMMA. You know it's no use.

LIZZIE. I can't talk to him anymore. Every time I talk to him I make every-

120 thing worse. I hate him, no. No I don't. I hate her.

(*Emma looks at her brooch watch.*)

LIZZIE. Don't look at the time.

EMMA. I'll miss my connections.

LIZZIE. No!

EMMA. (*Puts on her gloves.*) Lizzie. There's certain things we have to face. One of them is, we can't change a thing.   125

LIZZIE. I won't let you go!

EMMA. I'll be back on the weekend.

LIZZIE. He killed my birds! He took the axe and he killed them! Emma, I ran out and held them in my hands, I felt their hearts throbbing and pumping and the blood gushed out of their necks, it was all over my hands, don't   130
you care about that?

EMMA. I ... I ... have a train to catch.

LIZZIE. He didn't care how much he hurt me and you don't care either. Nobody cares.

EMMA. I ... have to go now.   135

LIZZIE. That's right. Go away. I don't even like you, Emma. Go away! (*Emma leaves, Lizzie runs after her calling.*) I'm sorry for all the things I told you! Things I really felt! You pretended to me, and I don't like you!! Go away!! (*Lizzie runs to the window and looks out after Emma's departing figure. After a moment she slowly turns back into the room. Miss Lizzie/Bridget is there.*)   140

LIZZIE. I want to die ... I want to die, but something inside won't let me ... inside something says *no.* (*She shuts her eyes.*) I can do anything.

DEFENCE. Miss Borden.

(*Both Lizzies turn.*)

DEFENCE. Could you describe the sequence of events upon your father's arrival home?   145

LIZZIE. (*With no animation.*) Papa came in ... we exchanged a few words ... Bridget and I spoke of the yard goods sale downtown, whether she would buy some. She went up to her room....

DEFENCE. And then?

LIZZIE. I went out back ... through the yard ... I picked up several pears from   150
the ground beneath the trees ... I went into the shed ... I stood looking out the window and ate the pears ...

DEFENCE. How many?

LIZZIE. Four.

DEFENCE. It wasn't warm, stifling in the shed?   155

LIZZIE. No, it was cool.

DEFENCE. What were you doing, apart from eating the pears?

LIZZIE. I suppose I was thinking. I just stood there, looking out the window, thinking, and eating the pears I'd picked up.

DEFENCE. You're fond of pears?   160

LIZZIE. Otherwise, I wouldn't eat them.

DEFENCE. Go on.

LIZZIE. I returned to the house. I found—Papa. I called for Bridget.

(*Mrs. Borden descends the stairs. Lizzie and Bridget turn to look at her. Mrs. Borden is only aware of Lizzie's stare. Pause.*)

MRS. BORDEN. ... What're you staring at? ... I said what're you staring at?

165 LIZZIE. (*Continuing to stare at Mrs. Borden.*) Bridget.

BRIDGET. Yes ma'am.

(*Pause.*)

MRS. BORDEN. Just coffee and a biscuit this morning, Bridget, it's too hot for a decent breakfast.

BRIDGET. Yes ma'am.

(*She exits for the biscuit and coffee. Lizzie continues to stare at Mrs. Borden.*)

170 MRS. BORDEN. ... Tell Bridget I'll have it in the parlour.

(*Lizzie is making an effort to be pleasant, to be "good." Mrs. Borden is more aware of this as unusual behaviour from Lizzie than were she to be rude, biting, or threatening. Lizzie, at the same time, feels caught in a dimension other than the one in which the people around her are operating. For Lizzie, a bell-jar[1] effect. Simple acts seem filled with significance. Lizzie is trying to fulfill other people's expectations of "normal.")*

LIZZIE. It's not me, is it?

MRS. BORDEN. What?

LIZZIE. You're not moving into the parlour because of me, are you?

MRS. BORDEN. What?

175 LIZZIE. I'd hate to think I'd driven you out of your own dining room.

MRS. BORDEN. No.

LIZZIE. Oh good, because I'd hate to think that was so.

MRS. BORDEN. It's cooler in the parlour.

LIZZIE. You know, you're right.

180 MRS. BORDEN. Eh?

LIZZIE. It is cooler....

(*Bridget enters with the coffee and biscuit.*)

LIZZIE. I will, Bridget.

---

1   *bell-jar* Bell-shaped glass lid placed over objects to isolate, protect, or contain them.

(*She takes the coffee and biscuit, gives it to Mrs. Borden. Lizzie watches her eat and drink. Mrs. Borden eats the biscuit delicately. Lizzie's attention is caught by it.*)

LIZZIE. Do you like that biscuit?

MRS. BORDEN. It could be lighter.

LIZZIE. You're right.   185

(*Mr. Borden enters, makes his way into the kitchen, Lizzie watches him pass.*)

LIZZIE. You know, Papa doesn't look well, Papa doesn't look well at all. Papa looks sick.

MRS. BORDEN. He had a bad night.

LIZZIE. Oh?

MRS. BORDEN. Too hot.   190

LIZZIE. But it's cooler in here, isn't it ... (*Not trusting her own evaluation of the degree of heat.*) Isn't it?

MRS. BORDEN. Yes, yes, it's cooler in here.

(*Mr. Borden enters with his coffee. Lizzie goes to him.*)

LIZZIE. Papa? You should go in the parlour. It's much cooler in there, really it is.   195

(*He goes into the parlour. Lizzie remains in the dining room. She sits at the table, folds her hands in her lap. Mr. Borden begins to read the paper.*)

MRS. BORDEN. ... I think I'll have Bridget do the windows today ... they need doing ... get them out of the way first thing.... Anything in the paper, Andrew?

MR. BORDEN. (*As he continues to read.*) Nope.

MRS. BORDEN. There never is ... I don't know why we buy it.   200

MR. BORDEN. (*Reading.*) Yup.

MRS. BORDEN. You going out this morning?

MR. BORDEN. Business.

MRS. BORDEN. ... Harry must be having a bit of a sleep-in.

MR. BORDEN. Yup.   205

MRS. BORDEN. He's always up by—(*Harry starts down the stairs.*) Well, speak of the devil—coffee and biscuits?

HARRY. Sounds good to me.

(*Mrs. Borden starts off to get it. Lizzie looks at her, catching her eye. Mrs. Borden stops abruptly.*)

LIZZIE. (*Her voice seems too loud.*) Emma's gone over to visit at the girls' place.
210   (*Mr. Borden lowers his paper to look at her. Harry looks at her. Suddenly aware of the loudness of her voice, she continues softly, too softly.*) ... Till the weekend.
MR. BORDEN.   She didn't say she was going, when'd she decide that?

>   (*Lizzie looks down at her hands, doesn't answer. A pause. Then Mrs. Borden continues out to the kitchen.*)

HARRY.   Will you be ah ... going down town today?
MR. BORDEN.   This mornin'. I got ... business at the bank.

>   (*A look between them. They are very aware of Lizzie's presence in the dining room.*)

215   HARRY.   This mornin' eh? Well now ... that works out just fine for me. I can ... I got a bill to settle in town myself.

>   (*Lizzie turns her head to look at them.*)

HARRY.   I'll be on my way after that.
MR. BORDEN.   Abbie'll be disappointed you're not stayin' for lunch.
HARRY.   'Nother time.
220   MR. BORDEN.   (*Aware of Lizzie's gaze.*) I ... I don't know where she is with that coffee. I'll—
HARRY.   Never you mind, you sit right there, I'll get it. (*He exits.*)

>   (*Lizzie and Mr. Borden look at each other. The bell-jar effect is lessened.*)

LIZZIE.   (*Softly.*) Good mornin' Papa.
MR. BORDEN.   Mornin' Lizzie.
225   LIZZIE.   Did you have a good sleep?
MR. BORDEN.   Not bad.
LIZZIE.   Papa?
MR. BORDEN.   Yes Lizzie.
LIZZIE.   You're a very strong-minded person, Papa, do you think I'm like you?
230   MR. BORDEN.   In some ways ... perhaps.
LIZZIE.   I must be like someone.
MR. BORDEN.   You resemble your mother.
LIZZIE.   I look like my mother?
MR. BORDEN.   A bit like your mother.
235   LIZZIE.   But my mother's dead.
MR. BORDEN.   Lizzie—
LIZZIE.   I remember you told me she died because she was sick ... I was born and she died.... Did you love her?
MR. BORDEN.   I married her.

LIZZIE. Can't you say if you loved her?   240

MR. BORDEN. Of course I did, Lizzie.

LIZZIE. Did you hate me for killing her?

MR. BORDEN. You don't think of it that way, it was just something that happened.

LIZZIE. Perhaps she just got tired and died. She didn't want to go on, and the   245
chance came up and she took it. I could understand that.... Perhaps she
was like a bird, she could see all the blue sky and she wanted to fly away
but she couldn't. She was caught, Papa, she was caught in a horrible snare,
and she saw a way out and she took it.... Perhaps it was a very brave thing
to do, Papa, perhaps it was the only way, and she hated to leave us because   250
she loved us so much, but she couldn't breathe all caught in the snare....
(*Long pause.*) Some people have very small wrists, have you noticed? Mine
aren't ...

> (*There is a murmur from the kitchen, then muted laughter. Mr. Borden
> looks towards it.*)

LIZZIE. Papa! ... I'm a very strong person.

MRS. BORDEN. (*Off, laughing.*) You're tellin' tales out of school, Harry!   255

HARRY. (*Off.*) God's truth. You should have seen the buggy when they
brought it back.

MRS. BORDEN. (*Off.*) You've got to tell Andrew. (*Pokes her head in.*) Andrew,
come on out here, Harry's got a story. (*Off.*) Now you'll have to start at the
beginning again. Oh my goodness.   260

> (*Mr. Borden starts for the kitchen. He stops, and looks back at Lizzie.*)

LIZZIE. Is there anything you want to tell me, Papa?

MRS. BORDEN. (*Off.*) Andrew!

LIZZIE. (*Softly, an echo.*) Andrew.

MR. BORDEN. What is it, Lizzie?

LIZZIE. If I promised to be a good girl forever and ever, would anything   265
change?

MR. BORDEN. I don't know what you're talking about.

LIZZIE. I would be lying ... Papa! ... Don't do any business today. Don't go
out. Stay home.

MR. BORDEN. What for?   270

LIZZIE. Everyone's leaving. Going away. Everyone's left.

MRS. BORDEN. (*Off.*) Andrew!

LIZZIE. (*Softly, an echo.*) Andrew.

MR. BORDEN. What is it?

LIZZIE. I'm calling you.   275

(Mr. Borden looks at her for a moment, then leaves for the kitchen. Dr. Patrick is heard whistling very softly. Lizzie listens.)

LIZZIE. Listen ... can you hear it ... can you?
MISS LIZZIE/BRIDGET. I can hear it.... It's stopped.

(Dr. Patrick can't be seen. Only his voice is heard.)

DR. PATRICK. *(Very low.)* Lizzie?
LIZZIE. *(Realization.)* I could hear it before [*you*]. *(Pause.)* It sounded so sad
280   I wanted to cry.
MISS LIZZIE/BRIDGET. You mustn't cry.
LIZZIE. I mustn't cry.
DR. PATRICK. I bet you know this one. *(He whistles an Irish jig.)*
LIZZIE. I know that! *(She begins to dance. Dr. Patrick enters. He claps in time to the dance. Lizzie finishes the jig.)*

(Dr. Patrick applauds.)

285   DR. PATRICK. Bravo! Bravo!!
LIZZIE. You didn't know I could do that, did you?
DR. PATRICK. You're a woman of many talents, Miss Borden.
LIZZIE. You're not making fun of me?
DR. PATRICK. I would never do that.
290   LIZZIE. I can do anything I want.
DR. PATRICK. I'm sure you can.
LIZZIE. If I wanted to die—I could even do that, couldn't I?
DR. PATRICK. Well now, I don't think so.
LIZZIE. Yes, I could!
295   DR. PATRICK. Lizzie—
LIZZIE. You wouldn't know—you can't see into my heart.
DR. PATRICK. I think I can.
LIZZIE. Well you can't.
DR. PATRICK. ... It's only a game.
300   LIZZIE. I never play games.
DR. PATRICK. Sure you do.
LIZZIE. I hate games.
DR. PATRICK. You're playin' one now.
LIZZIE. You don't even know me!
305   DR. PATRICK. Come on Lizzie, we don't want to fight. I know what we'll do ... we'll start all over.... Shut your eyes, Lizzie. *(She does so.)* Good mornin' Miss Borden.... Good mornin' Miss Borden....
LIZZIE. ... I haven't decided.... *(She slowly opens her eyes.)* ... if it is or it isn't.

DR. PATRICK. Much better ... and now ... would you take my arm, Miss Borden? How about a wee promenade?   310
LIZZIE. There's nowhere to go.
DR. PATRICK. That isn't so.... What about Boston? ... Do you think it's too
far for a stroll? ... I know what we'll do, we'll walk 'round to the side and
you'll show me your birds. (*They walk.*) ... I waited last night but you never
showed up ... there I was, travellin' bag and all, and you never appeared.... I 315
know what went wrong! We forgot to agree on an hour! Next time, Lizzie,
you must set the hour.... Is this where they're kept?

   (*Lizzie nods, she opens the cage and looks in it.*)

DR. PATRICK. It's empty. (*He laughs.*) And you say you never play games?
LIZZIE. They're gone.
DR. PATRICK. You've been havin' me on again, yes you have.   320
LIZZIE. They've run away.
DR. PATRICK. Did they really exist?
LIZZIE. I had blood on my hands.
DR. PATRICK. What do you say?
LIZZIE. You can't see it now, I washed it off, see?   325
DR. PATRICK. (*Takes her hands.*) Ah Lizzie....
LIZZIE. Would you ... help someone die?
DR. PATRICK. Why do you ask that?
LIZZIE. Some people are better off dead. I might be better off dead.
DR. PATRICK. You're a precious and unique person, Lizzie, and you shouldn't 330
think things like that.
LIZZIE. Precious and unique?
DR. PATRICK. All life is precious and unique.
LIZZIE. I am precious and unique? ... I *am* precious and unique. You said
that.   335
DR. PATRICK. Oh, I believe it.
LIZZIE. And I am. I know it. People mix things up on you, you have to be
careful. I am a person of worth.
DR. PATRICK. Sure you are.
LIZZIE. Not like that fat cow in there.   340
DR. PATRICK. Her life too is—
LIZZIE. No!
DR. PATRICK. Liz—
LIZZIE. Do you know her!
DR. PATRICK. That doesn't matter.   345
LIZZIE. Yes it does, it does matter.
DR. PATRICK. You can't be—

LIZZIE. You're a doctor, isn't that right?

DR. PATRICK. Right enough there.

350 LIZZIE. So, tell me, tell me, if a dreadful accident occurred ... and two people were dying ... but you could only save one.... Which would you save?

DR. PATRICK. You can't ask questions like that.

LIZZIE. Yes I can, come on, it's a game. How does a doctor determine? If one were old and the other were young—would you save the younger one first?

355 DR. PATRICK. Lizzie.

LIZZIE. You said you liked games! If one were a bad person and the other was good, was trying to be good, would you save the one who was good and let the bad person die?

DR. PATRICK. I don't know.

360 LIZZIE. Listen! If you could go back in time ... what would you do if you met a person who was evil and wicked?

DR. PATRICK. Who?

LIZZIE. I don't know, Attila the Hun!

DR. PATRICK. (*Laughs.*) Oh my.

365 LIZZIE. Listen, if you met Attila the Hun, and you were in a position to kill him, would you do it?

DR. PATRICK. I don't know.

LIZZIE. Think of the suffering he caused, the unhappiness.

DR. PATRICK. Yes, but I'm a doctor, not an assassin.

370 LIZZIE. I think you're a coward.

(*Pause.*)

DR. PATRICK. What I do is try to save lives ...

LIZZIE. But you put poison out for the slugs in your garden.

DR. PATRICK. You got something mixed up.

LIZZIE. I've never been clearer. Everything's clear. I've lived all of my life for
375 this one moment of absolute clarity! If war were declared, would you serve?

DR. PATRICK. I would fight in a war.

LIZZIE. You wouldn't fight, you would kill—you'd take a gun and shoot people, people who'd done nothing to you, people who were trying to be good, you'd kill them! And you say you wouldn't kill Attila the Hun, or
380 that that stupid cow's life is precious—*My life is precious!!*

DR. PATRICK. To you.

LIZZIE. Yes to me, are you stupid!?

DR. PATRICK. And hers is to her.

LIZZIE. I don't care about her! (*Pause.*) I'm glad you're not my doctor, you
385 can't make decisions, can you? You are a coward.

(*Dr. Patrick starts off.*)

LIZZIE. You're afraid of your wife ... you can *only* play games.... If I really wanted to go to Boston, you wouldn't come with me because you're a coward! *I'm not a coward!!*

(*Lizzie turns to watch Mrs. Borden sit with needlework. After a moment Mrs. Borden looks at Lizzie, aware of her scrutiny.*)

LIZZIE. ... Where's Papa?

MRS. BORDEN. Out.   390

LIZZIE. And Mr. Wingate?

MRS. BORDEN. He's out too.

LIZZIE. So what are you going to do ... Mrs. Borden?

MRS. BORDEN. I'm going to finish this up.

LIZZIE. You do that.... (*Pause.*) Where's Bridget?   395

MRS. BORDEN. Out back washing windows.... You got clean clothes to go upstairs, they're in the kitchen.

(*Pause.*)

LIZZIE. Did you know Papa killed my birds with the axe? He chopped off their heads. (*Mrs. Borden is uneasy.*) ... It's alright. At first I felt bad, but I feel better now. I feel much better now.... I am a woman of decision, Mrs.   400
Borden. When I decide to do things, I do them, yes, I do. (*Smiles.*) How many times has Papa said—when Lizzie puts her mind to a thing, she does it—and I do.... It's always me who puts the slug poison out because they eat all the flowers and you don't like that, do you? They're bad things, they must die. You see, not all life is precious, is it?   405

(*After a moment Mrs. Borden makes an attempt casually to gather together her things, to go upstairs. She does not want to be in the room with Lizzie.*)

LIZZIE. Where're you going?

MRS. BORDEN. Upstairs.... (*An excuse.*) The spare room needs changing.

(*A knock at the back door.... A second knock.*)

LIZZIE. Someone's at the door.... (*A third knock.*) I'll get it.

(*She exits to the kitchen. Mrs. Borden waits. Lizzie returns. She's a bit out of breath. She carries a pile of clean clothes which she puts on the table. She looks at Mrs. Borden.*)

LIZZIE. Did you want something?

MRS. BORDEN. Who was it?—the door?   410

LIZZIE. Oh yes. I forgot. I had to step out back for a moment and—it's a note. A message for you.

MRS. BORDEN. Oh.

LIZZIE. Shall I open it?

415 MRS. BORDEN. That's alright. (*She holds out her hand.*)

LIZZIE. Looks like Papa's handwriting…. (*She passes over the note.*) Aren't you going to open it?

MRS. BORDEN. I'll read it upstairs.

LIZZIE. Mrs. Borden! … Would you mind … putting my clothes in my room?

420 (*She gets some clothes from the table, Mrs. Borden takes them, something she would never normally do. Before she can move away, Lizzie grabs her arm.*) Just a minute … I would like you to look into my eyes. What's the matter? Nothing's wrong. It's an experiment…. Look right into them. Tell me … what do you see … can you see anything?

425 MRS. BORDEN. … Myself.

LIZZIE. Yes. When a person dies, retained on her eye is the image of the last thing she saw. Isn't that interesting? (*Pause.*)

(*Mrs. Borden slowly starts upstairs. Lizzie picks up remaining clothes on table. The hand hatchet is concealed beneath them. She follows Mrs. Borden up the stairs.*)

LIZZIE. Do you know something? If I were to kill someone, I would come up behind them very slowly and quietly. They would never even hear me, they

430 would never turn around. (*Mrs. Borden stops on the stairs. She turns around to look at Lizzie who is behind her.*) They would be too frightened to turn around even if they heard me. They would be so afraid they'd see what they feared. (*Mrs. Borden makes a move which might be an effort to go past Lizzie back down the stairs. Lizzie stops her.*) Careful. Don't fall. (*Mrs. Borden turns

435 and slowly continues up the stairs with Lizzie behind her.*) And then, I would strike them down. With them not turning around, they would retain no image of me on their eye. It would be better that way.

(*Lizzie and Mrs. Borden disappear at the top of the stairs. The stage is empty for a moment. Bridget enters. She carries the pail for washing the windows. She sets the pail down, wipes her forehead. She stands for a moment looking towards the stairs as if she might have heard a sound. She picks up the pail and exits to the kitchen. Lizzie appears on the stairs. She is carrying the pile of clothes she carried upstairs. The hand hatchet is concealed under the clothes. Lizzie descends the stairs, she seems calm, self-possessed. She places the clothes on the table. She pauses, then she slowly turns to look at Mrs. Borden's chair at the table. After a moment she moves to it, pauses a moment, then sits down in it. She sits there at ease, relaxed, thinking. Bridget enters from the kitchen, she sees Lizzie, she stops, she takes in Lizzie*) *sitting in Mrs. Borden's chair. Bridget glances towards the stairs, back to Lizzie. Lizzie looks, for the first time, at Bridget.*)

LIZZIE. We must hurry before Papa gets home.

BRIDGET. Lizzie?

LIZZIE. I have it all figured out, but you have to help me, Bridget, you have   440
to help me.

BRIDGET. What have you done?

LIZZIE. He would never leave me the farm, not with her on his back, but
now (*She gets up from the chair*) I will have the farm, and I will have the
money, yes, to do what I please! And you too Bridget, I'll give you some of   445
my money but you've got to help me. (*She moves towards Bridget who backs
away a step.*) Don't be afraid, it's me, it's Lizzie, you like me!

BRIDGET. What have you done! (*Pause. Bridget moves towards the stairs.*)

LIZZIE. Don't go up there!

BRIDGET. You killed her!   450

LIZZIE. Someone broke in and they killed her.

BRIDGET. They'll know!

LIZZIE. Not if you help me.

BRIDGET. I can't Miss Lizzie, I can't!

LIZZIE. (*Grabs Bridget's arm.*) Do you want them to hang me! Is that what   455
you want! Oh Bridget, look! Look! (*She falls to her knees.*) I'm begging for
my life, I'm begging. Deny me, and they will kill me. Help me, Bridget,
please help me.

BRIDGET. But ... what ... could we do?

LIZZIE. (*Up off her knees.*) Oh I have it all figured out. I'll go down town as   460
quick as I can and you leave the doors open and go back outside and work
on the windows.

BRIDGET. I've finished them, Lizzie.

LIZZIE. Then do them again! Remember last year when the burglar broke in?
Today someone broke in and she caught them.   465

BRIDGET. They'll never believe us.

LIZZIE. Have coffee with Lucy next door, stay with her till Papa gets home
and he'll find her, and then each of us swears she was fine when we left, she
was alright when we left!—it's going to work, Bridget, I know it!

BRIDGET. Your papa will guess.   470

LIZZIE. (*Getting ready to leave for down town.*) If he found me here he might
guess, but he won't.

BRIDGET. Your papa will know!

LIZZIE. Papa loves me, if he has another story to believe, he'll believe it. He'd
want to believe it, he'd have to believe it.   475

BRIDGET. Your papa will know.

LIZZIE. Why aren't you happy? I'm happy. We both should be happy! (*Lizzie embraces Bridget. Lizzie steps back a pace.*) Now—how do I look?

(*Mr. Borden enters. Bridget sees him. Lizzie slowly turns to see what Bridget is looking at.*)

LIZZIE. Papa?

480 MR. BORDEN. What is it? Where's Mrs. Borden?

BRIDGET. I ... don't know ... sir ... I ... just came in, sir.

MR. BORDEN. Did she leave the house?

BRIDGET. Well, sir ...

LIZZIE. She went out. Someone delivered a message and she left.

(*Lizzie takes off her hat and looks at her father.*)

485 LIZZIE. ... You're home early, Papa.

MR. BORDEN. I wanted to see Abbie. She's gone out, has she? Which way did she go? (*Lizzie shrugs, he continues, more thinking aloud.*) Well ... I ... I ... best wait for her here. I don't want to miss her again.

LIZZIE. Help Papa off with his coat, Bridget.... I hear there's a sale of dress
490 goods on down-town. Why don't you go buy yourself a yard?

BRIDGET. Oh ... I don't know, ma'am.

LIZZIE. You don't want any?

BRIDGET. I don't know.

LIZZIE. Then ... why don't you go upstairs and lie down. Have a rest before
495 lunch.

BRIDGET. I don't think I should.

LIZZIE. Nonsense.

BRIDGET. Lizzie, I—

LIZZIE. You go up and lie down. I'll look after things here.

(*Lizzie smiles at Bridget. Bridget starts up the stairs, suddenly stops. She looks back at Lizzie.*)

500 LIZZIE. It's alright ... go on ... it's alright. (*Bridget continues up the stairs. For the last bit of interchange, Mr. Borden has lowered the paper he's reading. Lizzie looks at him.*) Hello Papa. You look so tired.... I make you unhappy.... I don't like to make you unhappy. I love you.

MR. BORDEN. (*Smiles and takes her hand.*) I'm just getting old, Lizzie.

505 LIZZIE. You've got on my ring.... Do you remember when I gave you that? ... When I left Miss Cornelia's—it was in a little blue velvet box, you hid it behind your back, and you said, "guess which hand, Lizzie!" And I guessed. And you gave it to me and you said, "it's real gold, Lizzie, it's for

you because you are very precious to me." Do you remember, Papa? (*Mr. Borden nods.*) And I took it out of the little blue velvet box, and I took your 510 hand, and I put my ring on your finger and I said "thank you, Papa, I love you." ... You've never taken it off ... see how it bites into the flesh of your finger. (*She presses his hand to her face.*) I forgive you, Papa, I forgive you for killing my birds.... You look so tired, why don't you lie down and rest, put your feet up, I'll undo your shoes for you. (*She kneels and undoes his shoes.*) 515

MR. BORDEN. You're a good girl.

LIZZIE. I could never stand to have you hate me, Papa. Never. I would do anything rather than have you hate me.

MR. BORDEN. I don't hate you, Lizzie.

LIZZIE. I would not want you to find out anything that would make you hate 520 me. Because I love you.

MR. BORDEN. And I love you, Lizzie, you'll always be precious to me.

LIZZIE. (*Looks at him, and then smiles.*) Was I—when I had scabs on my knees?

MR. BORDEN. (*Laughs.*) Oh yes. Even then. 525

LIZZIE. (*Laughs.*) Oh Papa! ... Kiss me! (*He kisses her on the forehead.*) Thank you, Papa.

MR. BORDEN. Why're you crying?

LIZZIE. Because I'm so happy. Now ... put your feet up and get to sleep ... that's right ... shut your eyes ... go to sleep ... go to sleep.... 530

(*She starts to hum, continues humming as Mr. Borden falls asleep. Miss Lizzie/Bridget appears on the stairs unobtrusively. Lizzie still humming, moves to the table, slips her hand under the clothes, withdraws the hatchet. She approaches her father with the hatchet behind her back. She stops humming. A pause, then she slowly raises the hatchet very high to strike him. Just as the hatchet is about to start its descent, there is a blackout. Children's voices are heard singing:*)

"Lizzie Borden took an axe,
Gave her Mother forty whacks,
When the job was nicely done,
She gave her father forty-one!
Forty-one! 535
Forty-one!"

(*The singing increases in volume and in distortion as it nears the end of the verse till the last words are very loud but discernible, just. Silence. Then the sound of slow measured heavy breathing which is growing into a wordless sound of hysteria. Light returns to the stage, dim light from late in the day.*)

The actress stands with the hatchet raised in the same position in which we saw her before the blackout, but the couch is empty. Her eyes are shut. The sound comes from her. Miss Lizzie is at the foot of the stairs. She moves to the actress, reaches up to take the hatchet from her. When Miss Lizzie's hand touches the actress's, the actress releases the hatchet and whirls around to face Miss Lizzie who is left holding the hatchet. The actress backs away from Miss Lizzie. There is a flickering of light at the top of the stairs.)

EMMA. (*From upstairs.*) Lizzie! Lizzie! You're making too much noise!

(*Emma descends the stairs carrying an oil lamp. The actress backs away from Lizzie, turns and runs into the kitchen. Miss Lizzie turns to see Emma. The hand hatchet is behind Miss Lizzie's back concealed from Emma. Emma pauses for a moment.*)

EMMA. Where is she?

MISS LIZZIE. Who?

540 EMMA. (*A pause then Emma moves to the window and glances out.*) It's raining.

MISS LIZZIE. I know.

EMMA. (*Puts the lamp down, sits, lowers her voice.*) Lizzie.

MISS LIZZIE. Yes?

EMMA. I want to speak to you, Lizzie.

545 MISS LIZZIE. Yes Emma.

EMMA. That ... actress who's come up from Boston.

MISS LIZZIE. What about her?

EMMA. People talk.

MISS LIZZIE. You needn't listen.

550 EMMA. In your position you should do nothing to *inspire talk*.

MISS LIZZIE. People need so little in the way of inspiration. And Miss Cornelia's classes didn't cover "Etiquette for Acquitted Persons."

EMMA. Common sense should tell you what you ought or ought not do.

MISS LIZZIE. Common sense is repugnant to me. I prefer uncommon sense.

555 EMMA. I forbid her in this house, Lizzie!

(*Pause.*)

MISS LIZZIE. Do you?

EMMA. (*Backing down, softly.*) It's ... disgraceful.

MISS LIZZIE. I see.

(*Miss Lizzie turns away from Emma a few steps.*)

EMMA. I simply cannot—

560 MISS LIZZIE. You could always leave.

EMMA. Leave?

MISS LIZZIE. Move. Away. Why don't you?

EMMA. I—

MISS LIZZIE. You could never, could you?

EMMA. If I only—   565

MISS LIZZIE. Knew.

EMMA. Lizzie, did you?

MISS LIZZIE. Oh Emma, do you intend asking me that question from now
     till death us do part?

EMMA. It's just—   570

MISS LIZZIE. For if you do, I may well take something sharp to you.

EMMA. Why do you joke like that!

MISS LIZZIE. (*Turning back to Emma who sees the hatchet for the first time.
     Emma's reaction is not any verbal or untoward movement. She freezes as Miss
     Lizzie advances on her.*) Did you never stop and think that if I did, then 575
     you were guilty too?

EMMA. What?

> (*The actress will enter unobtrusively on the periphery. We are virtually
> unaware of her entrance until she speaks and moves forward.*)

MISS LIZZIE. It was you who brought me up, like a mother to me. Almost
     like a mother. Did you ever stop and think that I was like a puppet, your
     puppet. My head your hand, yes, your hand working my mouth, me say-   580
     ing all the things you felt like saying, me doing all the things you felt like
     doing, me spewing forth, me hitting out, and you, you—!

THE ACTRESS. (*Quietly.*) Lizzie.

> (*Miss Lizzie is immediately in control of herself.*)

EMMA. (*Whispers.*) I wasn't even here that day.

MISS LIZZIE. I can swear to that.   585

EMMA. Do you want to drive me mad?

MISS LIZZIE. Oh yes.

EMMA. You didn't ... did you?

MISS LIZZIE. Poor ... Emma.

THE ACTRESS. Lizzie. (*She takes the hatchet from Miss Lizzie.*) Lizzie you did. 590

MISS LIZZIE. I didn't. (*The actress looks to the hatchet—then to the audience.*)
     You did.

> (*Blackout.*)

—1980

Tom Stoppard
b. 1937

Tom Stoppard is a British dramatist who writes prolifically for radio, stage, and screen. His plays have been as distinctive as they have been popular. Typically they bring together improbable story elements in ways that open up possibilities for both sophisticated wordplay and farcical humour; typically too they touch on genuinely serious philosophical themes.

Stoppard's early years were tumultuous. In 1939 his family was displaced from Zlín, Czechoslovakia (Stoppard's birthplace), to Singapore by the invasion of the Nazis. World War II eventually forced them to Australia, then to India. Stoppard's father died during the war, and after his mother was re-married to a British army officer, the family moved to England.

Stoppard dropped out of grammar school to work as a newspaper reporter, and then spent a year as a drama critic while building his career as a playwright. He made his name with clever, absurdist dramas in which theatricality itself becomes a central thematic concern. His first major success was the Tony Award-winning *Rosencrantz and Guildenstern Are Dead* (1966), in which two minor characters from Shakespeare's *Hamlet* are controlled by narrative forces beyond their understanding. In the late 1970s Stoppard's Czech roots led him toward issues of censorship and brutality in the Soviet Union, addressed in plays such as *Every Good Boy Deserves Favour* (1977). Intellectual inquiry remains an important engine for his writing; *Arcadia* (1993), for example, incorporates concepts from mathematics, science, and history, juxtaposing events taking place in 1809 with their interpretation by academics in 1989. Stoppard's 2002 trilogy of plays *The Coast of Utopia* concerns a series of philosophical debates between literary and political characters in pre-revolutionary Russia.

Stoppard has found an even wider audience with his original screenplays and screen adaptations. In 1990, he adapted and directed a successful film version of *Rosencrantz and Guildenstern Are Dead*. He also wrote the screenplay for Terry Gilliam's influential film *Brazil* (1985), and in 1998 he won an Academy Award as co-author of the screenplay for *Shakespeare in Love*.

Arcadia[1]

CHARACTERS

(*In order of appearance*)
Thomasina Coverly, *aged thirteen, later sixteen*
Septimus Hodge, *her tutor, aged twenty-two, later twenty-five*
Jellaby, *a butler, middle-aged*
Ezra Chater, *a poet, aged thirty-one*
Richard Noakes, *a landscape architect, middle-aged*
Lady Croom, *middle thirties*
Capt. Brice, RN,[2] *middle thirties*
Hannah Jarvis, *an author, late thirties*
Chloë Coverly, *aged eighteen*
Bernard Nightingale, *a don,*[3] *late thirties*
Valentine Coverly, *aged twenty-five to thirty*
Gus Coverly, *aged fifteen*
Augustus Coverly, *aged fifteen*

ACT 1, SCENE 1

A room on the garden front of a very large country house in Derbyshire[4] in April 1809. Nowadays, the house would be called a stately home. The upstage wall is mainly tall, shapely, uncurtained windows, one or more of which work as doors. Nothing much need be said or seen of the exterior beyond. We come to learn that the house stands in the typical English park of the time. Perhaps we see an indication of this, perhaps only light and air and sky.

The room looks bare despite the large table which occupies the centre of it. The table, the straight-backed chairs and, the only other item of furniture, the architect's stand or reading stand, would all be collectable pieces now but here, on an uncarpeted wood floor, they have no more pretension than a schoolroom, which is indeed the main use of this room at this time. What elegance there is, is architectural, and nothing is impressive but the scale. There is a door in each of the side walls. These are closed, but one of the french windows[5] is open to a bright but sunless morning.

---

1   *Arcadia* Figuratively, an ideal pastoral paradise; literally, a real region of Greece that was often depicted as a paradise in classical literature.
2   *RN* Royal Navy.
3   *don* University instructor.
4   *Derbyshire* County in the East Midlands of England.
5   *french windows* Windows that also function as doors.

There are two people, each busy with books and paper and pen and ink, separately occupied. The pupil is Thomasina Coverly, aged 13. The tutor is Septimus Hodge, aged 22. Each has an open book. Hers is a slim mathematics primer. His is a handsome thick quarto,[1] brand new, a vanity production, with little tapes to tie when the book is closed. His loose papers, etc, are kept in a stiff-backed portfolio which also ties up with tapes.

Septimus has a tortoise which is sleepy enough to serve as a paperweight.

Elsewhere on the table there is an old-fashioned theodolite[2] and also some other books stacked up.

THOMASINA. Septimus, what is carnal embrace?

SEPTIMUS. Carnal embrace is the practice of throwing one's arms around a side of beef.

THOMASINA. Is that all?

SEPTIMUS. No ... a shoulder of mutton, a haunch of venison well hugged, an
5   embrace of grouse ... *caro, carnis;*[3] feminine; flesh.

THOMASINA. Is it a sin?

SEPTIMUS. Not necessarily, my lady, but when carnal embrace is sinful it is a sin of the flesh, QED. We had *caro* in our Gallic Wars—"The Britons live on milk and meat"—"*lacte et carne vivunt.*" I am sorry that the seed fell
10   on stony ground.[4]

THOMASINA. That was the sin of Onan,[5] wasn't it, Septimus?

SEPTIMUS. Yes. He was giving his brother's wife a Latin lesson and she was hardly the wiser after it than before. I thought you were finding a proof for Fermat's last theorem.[6]

15

---

1   *quarto* Large book composed of quarto pages, which are created when a printer folds a large sheet of paper twice to make four leaves.

2   *theodolite* Surveying tool used to measure angles.

3   *caro, carnis* Latin: flesh or meat.

4   *QED* Abbreviation of the Latin term *quod erat demonstrandum*—meaning "which was to be shown"—used to indicate the end of a logical argument or mathematical proof; *Gallic Wars* Roman campaigns led by Julius Ceasar in 58–51 BCE, during which Britain was invaded twice; *lacte ... vivunt* From Julius Caesar, *Commentarii de Bello Gallico* (*Commentaries on the Gallic War*). Septimus provides a translation; *seed ... stony ground* See Mark 4.5.

5   *Onan* Biblical figure who was struck down by God. When his brother died, Onan was instructed by God to give his childless sister-in-law Tamar an heir. Onan slept with Tamar but ejaculated onto the floor instead of impregnating her. See Genesis 38.8–10.

6   *Fermat's last theorem* 1637 conjecture made by French mathematician Pierre de Fermat and recorded without an accompanying proof. It states that, when n has a value higher than 2 in the equation $x^n + y^n = z^n$, there are no three positive integers that can be successfully substituted for x, y, and z. The theorem remained unverified until the first successful proof was published in the 1990s.

THOMASINA. It is very difficult, Septimus. You will have to show me how.

SEPTIMUS. If I knew how, there would be no need to ask *you*. Fermat's last theorem has kept people busy for a hundred and fifty years, and I hoped it would keep *you* busy long enough for me to read Mr. Chater's poem in praise of love with only the distraction of its own absurdities.   20

THOMASINA. Our Mr. Chater has written a poem?

SEPTIMUS. He believes he has written a poem, yes. I can see that there might be more carnality in your algebra than in Mr. Chater's "Couch of Eros."[1]

THOMASINA. Oh, it was not my algebra. I heard Jellaby telling cook that Mrs. Chater was discovered in carnal embrace in the gazebo.   25

SEPTIMUS. (*Pause*) Really? With whom, did Jellaby happen to say?

(*Thomasina considers this with a puzzled frown.*)

THOMASINA. What do you mean, with whom?

SEPTIMUS. With what? Exactly so. The idea is absurd. Where did this story come from?

THOMASINA. Mr. Noakes.   30

SEPTIMUS. Mr. Noakes!

THOMASINA. Papa's landskip[2] gardener. He was taking bearings in the garden when he saw—through his spyglass—Mrs. Chater in the gazebo in carnal embrace.

SEPTIMUS. And do you mean to tell me that Mr. Noakes told the butler?   35

THOMASINA. No. Mr. Noakes told Mr. Chater. *Jellaby* was told by the groom, who overheard Mr. Noakes telling Mr. Chater, in the stable yard.

SEPTIMUS. Mr. Chater being engaged in closing the stable door.

THOMASINA. What do you mean, Septimus?

SEPTIMUS. So, thus far, the only people who know about this are Mr. Noakes   40
the landskip gardener, the groom, the butler, the cook and, of course, Mrs. Chater's husband, the poet.

THOMASINA. And Arthur who was cleaning the silver, and the bootboy. And now you.

SEPTIMUS. Of course. What else did he say?   45

THOMASINA. Mr. Noakes?

SEPTIMUS. No, not Mr. Noakes. Jellaby. You heard Jellaby telling the cook.

THOMASINA. Cook hushed him almost as soon as he started. Jellaby did not see that I was being allowed to finish yesterday's upstairs' rabbit pie[3] before

---

1   *Eros* Greek god of love.

2   *landskip* Landscape.

3   *upstairs' rabbit pie* I.e., the rabbit pie made for the upper-class inhabitants of the house (as opposed to the servants).

50   I came to my lesson. I think you have not been candid with me, Septimus. A gazebo is not, after all, a meat larder.[1]

SEPTIMUS. I never said my definition was complete.

THOMASINA. Is carnal embrace kissing?

SEPTIMUS. Yes.

55 THOMASINA. And throwing one's arms around Mrs. Chater?

SEPTIMUS. Yes. Now, Fermat's last theorem—

THOMASINA. I thought as much. I hope you are ashamed.

SEPTIMUS. I, my lady?

THOMASINA. If *you* do not teach me the true meaning of things, who will?

60 SEPTIMUS. Ah. Yes, I am ashamed. Carnal embrace is sexual congress, which is the insertion of the male genital organ into the female genital organ for purposes of procreation and pleasure. Fermat's last theorem, by contrast, asserts that when x, y and z are whole numbers each raised to power of n, the sum of the first two can never equal the third when n is greater than 2.

   (*Pause.*)

65 THOMASINA. Eurghhh!

SEPTIMUS. Nevertheless, that is the theorem.

THOMASINA. It is disgusting and incomprehensible. Now when I am grown to practise it myself I shall never do so without thinking of you.

SEPTIMUS. Thank you very much, my lady. Was Mrs. Chater down this
70 morning?

THOMASINA. No. Tell me more about sexual congress.

SEPTIMUS. There is nothing more to be said about sexual congress.

THOMASINA. Is it the same as love?

SEPTIMUS. Oh no, it is much nicer than that.

   (*One of the side doors leads to the music room. It is the other side door which now opens to admit Jellaby, the butler.*)

75   I am teaching, Jellaby.

JELLABY. Beg your pardon, Mr. Hodge, Mr. Chater said it was urgent you receive his letter.

SEPTIMUS. Oh, very well. (*Septimus takes the letter.*) Thank you. (*And to dismiss Jellaby.*) Thank you.

80 JELLABY. (*Holding his ground*) Mr. Chater asked me to bring him your answer.

SEPTIMUS. My answer?

   (*He opens the letter. There is no envelope as such, but there is a "cover" which, folded and sealed, does the same service. Septimus tosses the cover negligently aside and reads.*)

---

1   *larder* Cool room used to store perishable foods.

Well, my answer is that as is my custom and my duty to his lordship I am engaged until a quarter to twelve in the education of his daughter. When I am done, and if Mr. Chater is still there, I will be happy to wait upon him   85
in—(*he checks the letter*)—in the gunroom.

JELLABY. I will tell him so, thank you, sir.

> (*Septimus folds the letter and places it between the pages of "The Couch of Eros."*)

THOMASINA. What is for dinner, Jellaby?

JELLABY. Boiled ham and cabbages, my lady, and a rice pudding.

THOMASINA. Oh, goody.   90

> (*Jellaby leaves.*)

SEPTIMUS. Well, so much for Mr. Noakes. He puts himself forward as a gentleman, a philosopher of the picturesque, a visionary who can move mountains and cause lakes, but in the scheme of the garden he is as the serpent.[1]

THOMASINA. When you stir your rice pudding, Septimus, the spoonful of   95
jam spreads itself round making red trails like the picture of a meteor in my astronomical atlas. But if you stir backward, the jam will not come together again. Indeed, the pudding does not notice and continues to turn pink just as before. Do you think this is odd?

SEPTIMUS. No.   100

THOMASINA. Well, I do. You cannot stir things apart.

SEPTIMUS. No more you can, time must needs run backward, and since it will not, we must stir our way onward mixing as we go, disorder out of disorder into disorder until pink is complete, unchanging and unchangeable, and we are done with it for ever. This is known as free will or self-   105
determination.

> (*He picks up the tortoise and moves it a few inches as though it had strayed, on top of some loose papers, and admonishes it.*)

Sit!

---

1   *picturesque* Aesthetic principle bridging the gap between the awe-inspiring qualities of untamed nature and the beauty of harmonious, deliberate composition; picturesque gar-
dens look much rougher and less manicured than the gardens of the preceding period. The concept of the picturesque is also applied to art and literature, and is associated with Romanticism, a major social and cultural movement that began in the late eighteenth century and valued individualism, humans' relationship to nature, and emotion over reason; *serpent* Reference to Genesis 3.1–20, in which a serpent persuades Adam and Eve to eat the fruit forbidden them by God in the Garden of Eden.

THOMASINA. Septimus, do you think God is a Newtonian?[1]

SEPTIMUS. An Etonian?[2] Almost certainly, I'm afraid. We must ask your
brother to make it his first enquiry.

THOMASINA. No, Septimus, a Newtonian. Septimus! Am I the first person to
have thought of this?

SEPTIMUS. No.

THOMASINA. I have not said yet.

SEPTIMUS. "If everything from the furthest planet to the smallest atom of
our brain acts according to Newton's law of motion, what becomes of free
will?"

THOMASINA. No.

SEPTIMUS. God's will.

THOMASINA. No.

SEPTIMUS. Sin.

THOMASINA. (*Derisively*) No!

SEPTIMUS. Very well.

THOMASINA. If you could stop every atom in its position and direction, and
if your mind could comprehend all the actions thus suspended, then if you
were really, *really* good at algebra you could write the formula for all the
future; and although nobody can be so clever as to do it, the formula must
exist just as if one could.

SEPTIMUS. (*Pause*) Yes. (*Pause*) Yes, as far as I know, you are the first person
to have thought of this. (*Pause. With an effort.*) In the margin of his copy
of *Arithmetica*,[3] Fermat wrote that he had discovered a wonderful proof
of his theorem but, the margin being too narrow for his purpose, did not
have room to write it down. The note was found after his death, and from
that day to this—

THOMASINA. Oh! I see now! The answer is perfectly obvious.

SEPTIMUS. This time you may have overreached yourself.

(*The door is opened, somewhat violently. Chater enters.*)

Mr. Chater! Perhaps my message miscarried. I will be at liberty at a quarter
to twelve, if that is convenient.

1   *Newtonian* Follower of the English mathematician and physicist Isaac Newton (1642–
1727); more specifically, a follower of Newtonian mechanics, a subfield of physics based
on Newton's laws describing the motion of objects. Until the late nineteenth century, it
was thought that Newtonian mechanics could be extended to explain all physical phenomena in the universe.

2   *Etonian* Student or alumnus of Eton, a prestigious British boarding school founded in
1440.

3   *Arithmetica* Algebra text of the third century CE composed by the ancient Greek mathematician Diophantus.

CHATER. It is not convenient, sir. My business will not wait.

SEPTIMUS. Then I suppose you have Lord Croom's opinion that your busi-   140
ness is more important than his daughter's lesson.

CHATER. I do not, but, if you like, I will ask his lordship to settle the point.

SEPTIMUS. (*Pause*) My lady, take Fermat into the music room. There will be
an extra spoonful of jam if you find his proof.

THOMASINA. There is no proof, Septimus. The thing that is perfectly obvious   145
is that the note in the margin was a joke to make you all mad.

(*Thomasina leaves.*)

SEPTIMUS. Now, sir, what is this business that cannot wait?

CHATER. I think you know it, sir. You have insulted my wife.

SEPTIMUS. Insulted her? That would deny my nature, my conduct, and the
admiration in which I hold Mrs. Chater.   150

CHATER. I have heard of your admiration, sir! You insulted my wife in the
gazebo yesterday evening!

SEPTIMUS. You are mistaken. I made love to your wife in the gazebo. She
asked me to meet her there, I have her note somewhere, I dare say I could
find it for you, and if someone is putting it about that I did not turn up,   155
by God, sir, it is a slander.

CHATER. You damned lecher! You would drag down a lady's reputation to
make a refuge for your cowardice. It will not do! I am calling you out!

SEPTIMUS. Chater! Chater, Chater, Chater! My dear friend!

CHATER. You dare to call me that. I demand satisfaction!   160

SEPTIMUS. Mrs. Chater demanded satisfaction and now you are demanding
satisfaction. I cannot spend my time day and night satisfying the demands
of the Chater family. As for your wife's reputation, it stands where it ever
stood.

CHATER. You blackguard![1]   165

SEPTIMUS. I assure you. Mrs. Chater is charming and spirited, with a pleasing voice and a dainty step, she is the epitome of all the qualities society
applauds in her sex—and yet her chief renown is for a readiness that keeps
her in a state of tropical humidity as would grow orchids in her drawers
in January.   170

CHATER. Damn you, Hodge, I will not listen to this! Will you fight or not?

SEPTIMUS. (*Definitively*) Not! There are no more than two or three poets of
the first rank now living, and I will not shoot one of them dead over a per-
pendicular poke in a gazebo with a woman whose reputation could not be
adequately defended with a platoon of musketry deployed by rota.[2]   175

1   *blackguard* Dishonourable person.
2   *rota* Schedule.

CHATER. Ha! You say so! Who are the others? In your opinion?—no—
no—!—this goes very ill, Hodge. I will not be flattered out of my course.
You say so, do you?

SEPTIMUS. I do. And I would say the same to Milton[1] were he not already
180   dead. Not the part about his wife, of course—

CHATER. But among the living? Mr. Southey?[2]

SEPTIMUS. Southey I would have shot on sight.

CHATER. (*Shaking his head sadly*) Yes, he has fallen off. I admired "Thalaba" *quite*, but "Madoc,"[3] (*he chuckles*) oh dear me!—but we are straying
185   from the business here—you took advantage of Mrs. Chater, and if that
were not bad enough, it appears every stableboy and scullery maid on the
strength—

SEPTIMUS. Damn me! Have you not listened to a word I said?

CHATER. I have heard you, sir, and I will not deny I welcome your regard,
190   God knows one is little appreciated if one stands outside the coterie of
hacks and placemen who surround Jeffrey and the *Edinburgh*[4]—

SEPTIMUS. My dear Chater, they judge a poet by the seating plan of Lord
Holland's[5] table!

CHATER. By heaven, you are right! And I would very much like to know the
195   name of the scoundrel who slandered my verse drama "The Maid of Turkey" in the *Piccadilly Recreation*, too!

SEPTIMUS. "The Maid of Turkey!" I have it by my bedside! When I cannot
sleep I take up "The Maid of Turkey" like an old friend!

CHATER. (*Gratified*) There you are! And the scoundrel wrote he would not
200   give it to his dog for dinner were it covered in bread sauce and stuffed with
chestnuts. When Mrs. Chater read that, she wept, sir, and would not give
herself to me for a fortnight—which recalls me to my purpose—

SEPTIMUS. The new poem, however, will make your name perpetual—

CHATER. Whether it do or not—

205   SEPTIMUS. It is not a question, sir. No coterie can oppose the acclamation of
the reading public. "The Couch of Eros" will take the town.

CHATER. Is that your estimation?

SEPTIMUS. It is my intent.

---

1   *Milton* English poet John Milton (1608–74).

2   *Southey* English poet Robert Southey (1774–1843).

3   *"Thalaba" quite, but "Madoc"* "Thalaba the Destroyer" (1801) and "Madoc" (1805) are
two epic poems by Southey.

4   *coterie* Exclusive group of people with shared tastes; *Jeffrey and the Edinburgh* Scottish
literary critic Francis Jeffrey (1773–1850) was the editor of the *Edinburgh Review* (1802–
1929).

5   *Lord Holland* Henry Richard Vassall-Fox (1773–1840), English politician.

CHATER. Is it, is it? Well, well! I do not understand you.

SEPTIMUS. You see I have an early copy—sent to me for review. I say review,   210
but I speak of an extensive appreciation of your gifts and your rightful
place in English literature.

CHATER. Well, I must say. That is certainly ... You have written it?

SEPTIMUS. (*Crisply*) Not yet.

CHATER. Ah. And how long does ...?   215

SEPTIMUS. To be done right, it first requires a careful re-reading of your
book, of both books, several readings, together with outlying works
for an exhibition of deference or disdain as the case merits. I make notes,
of course, I order my thoughts, and finally, when all is ready and I am *calm
in my mind* ...   220

CHATER. (*Shrewdly*) Did Mrs. Chater know of this before she—before you—

SEPTIMUS. I think she very likely did.

CHATER. (*Triumphantly*) There is nothing that woman would not do for me!
Now you have an insight to her character. Yes, by God, she is a wife to me,
sir!   225

SEPTIMUS. For that alone, I would not make her a widow.

CHATER. Captain Brice once made the same observation!

SEPTIMUS. Captain Brice did?

CHATER. Mr. Hodge, allow me to inscribe your copy in happy anticipation.
Lady Thomasina's pen will serve us.   230

SEPTIMUS. Your connection with Lord and Lady Croom you owe to your
fighting her ladyship's brother?

CHATER. No! It was all nonsense, sir—a canard![1] But a fortunate mistake, sir.
It brought me the patronage of a captain of His Majesty's Navy and the
brother of a countess. I do not think Mr. Walter Scott[2] can say as much,   235
and here I am, a respected guest at Sidley Park.

SEPTIMUS. Well, sir, you can say you have received satisfaction.

(*Chater is already inscribing the book, using the pen and ink-pot on the
table. Noakes enters through the door used by Chater. He carries rolled-up
plans. Chater, inscribing, ignores Noakes. Noakes on seeing the occupants,
panics.*)

NOAKES. Oh!

SEPTIMUS. Ah, Mr. Noakes!—my muddy-mettled rascal! Where's your spyglass?   240

NOAKES. I beg your leave—I thought her ladyship—excuse me—

---

1   *canard* Misleading report.

2   *Walter Scott* Sir Walter Scott (1771–1832), Scottish poet and novelist.

(*He is beating an embarrassed retreat when he becomes rooted by Chater's voice. Chater reads his inscription in ringing tones.*)

CHATER. "To my friend Septimus Hodge, who stood up and gave his best on behalf of the Author—Ezra Chater, at Sidley Park, Derbyshire, April 10th, 1809." (*Giving the book to Septimus.*) There, sir—something to show your
245   grandchildren!
SEPTIMUS. This is more than I deserve, this is handsome, what do you say, Noakes?

(*They are interrupted by the appearance, outside the windows, of Lady Croom and Captain Edward Brice, RN. Her first words arrive through the open door.*)

LADY CROOM. Oh, no! Not the gazebo!

(*She enters, followed by Brice who carries a leatherbound sketch book.*)

Mr. Noakes! What is this I hear?
250 BRICE. Not only the gazebo, but the boat-house, the Chinese bridge, the shrubbery—
CHATER. By God, sir! Not possible!
BRICE. Mr. Noakes will have it so.
SEPTIMUS. Mr. Noakes, this is monstrous!
255 LADY CROOM. I am glad to hear it from *you*, Mr. Hodge.
THOMASINA. (*Opening the door from the music room*) May I return now?
SEPTIMUS. (*Attempting to close the door*) Not just yet—
LADY CROOM. Yes, let her stay. A lesson in folly is worth two in wisdom.

(*Brice takes the sketch book to the reading stand, where he lays it open. The sketch book is the work of Mr. Noakes, who is obviously an admirer of Humphry Repton's "Red Books."[1] The pages, drawn in watercolours, show "before" and "after" views of the landscape, and the pages are cunningly cut to allow the latter to be superimposed over portions of the former, though Repton did it the other way round.*)

BRICE. Is Sidley Park to be an Englishman's garden or the haunt of Corsican
260   brigands?[2]
SEPTIMUS. Let us not hyperbolize, sir.

---

1   *Humphry Repton's "Red Books"* English landscape designer Humphry Repton (1752–1818) kept a series of watercolours in bound books in order to be able to show before-and-after pictures of his projects.
2   *Corsican brigands* Highway robbers from Corsica, a French island in the Mediterranean Sea. Corsicans were often stereotyped as highwaymen and bandits.

BRICE. It is rape, sir!

NOAKES. (*Defending himself.*) It is the modern style.

CHATER. (*Under the same misapprehension as Septimus*) Regrettable, of course, but so it is.   265

(*Thomasina has gone to examine the sketch book.*)

LADY CROOM. Mr. Chater, you show too much submission. Mr. Hodge, I appeal to you.

SEPTIMUS. Madam, I regret the gazebo, I sincerely regret the gazebo—and the boat-house up to a point—but the Chinese bridge, fantasy!—and the shrubbery I reject with contempt! Mr. Chater!—would you take the word   270
of a jumped-up jobbing[1] gardener who sees carnal embrace in every nook and cranny of the landskip!

THOMASINA. Septimus, they are not speaking of carnal embrace, are you, Mama?

LADY CROOM. Certainly not. What do you know of carnal embrace?   275

THOMASINA. Everything, thanks to Septimus. In my opinion, Mr. Noakes's scheme for the garden is perfect. It is a Salvator!

LADY CROOM. What does she mean?

NOAKES. (*Answering the wrong question*) Salvator Rosa,[2] your ladyship, the painter. He is indeed the very exemplar of the picturesque style.   280

BRICE. Hodge, what is this?

SEPTIMUS. She speaks from innocence not from experience.

BRICE. You call it innocence? Has he ruined you, child?

(*Pause.*)

SEPTIMUS. Answer your uncle!

THOMASINA. (*To Septimus.*) How is a ruined child different from a ruined   285
castle?

SEPTIMUS. On such questions I defer to Mr. Noakes.

NOAKES. (*Out of his depth*) A ruined castle is picturesque, certainly.

SEPTIMUS. That is the main difference. (*To Brice*) I teach the classical authors. If I do not elucidate their meaning, who will?   290

BRICE. As her tutor you have a duty to keep her in ignorance.

LADY CROOM. Do not dabble in paradox, Edward, it puts you in danger of fortuitous wit. Thomasina, wait in your bedroom.

THOMASINA. (*Retiring*) Yes, mama. I did not intend to get you into trouble, Septimus. I am very sorry for it. It is plain that there are some things a girl   295

---

1   *jobbing* Working odd jobs.

2   *Salvator Rosa* Italian poet and painter (1615–73) known for his landscape paintings, which frequently feature ruins and bandits.

is allowed to understand, and these include the whole of algebra, but there are others, such as embracing a side of beef, that must be kept from her until she is old enough to have a carcass of her own.

LADY CROOM. One moment.

300 BRICE. What is she talking about?

LADY CROOM. Meat.

BRICE. Meat?

LADY CROOM. Thomasina, you had better remain. Your knowledge of the picturesque obviously exceeds anything the rest of us can offer. Mr. Hodge,

305 ignorance should be like an empty vessel waiting to be filled at the well of truth—not a cabinet of vulgar curios. Mr. Noakes—now at last it is your turn.

NOAKES. Thank you, your ladyship—

LADY CROOM. Your drawing is a very wonderful transformation. I would

310 not have recognized my own garden but for your ingenious book—is it not?—look! Here is the Park as it appears to us now, and here as it might be when Mr. Noakes has done with it. Where there is the familiar pastoral refinement of an Englishman's garden, here is an eruption of gloomy forest and towering crag, of ruins where there was never a house, of water dash-

315 ing against rocks where there was neither spring nor a stone I could not throw the length of a cricket pitch. My hyacinth dell is become a haunt for hobgoblins, my Chinese bridge, which I am assured is superior to the one at Kew, and for all I know at Peking, is usurped by a fallen obelisk[1] overgrown with briars—

320 NOAKES. (*Bleating*) Lord Little has one very similar—

LADY CROOM. I cannot relieve Lord Little's misfortunes by adding to my own. Pray, what is this rustic hovel that presumes to superpose itself on my gazebo?

NOAKES. That is the hermitage,[2] madam.

325 LADY CROOM. The hermitage? I am bewildered.

BRICE. It is all irregular, Mr. Noakes.

NOAKES. It is, sir. Irregularity is one of the chiefest principles of the picturesque style—

LADY CROOM. But Sidley Park is already a picture, and a most amiable pic-

330 ture too. The slopes are green and gentle. The trees are companionably

---

1   *crag* Steep cliff; *cricket pitch* In the sport of cricket, a 20-metre strip at the centre of the field; *hobgoblins* Pesky or bothersome sprites from folklore; *Kew* I.e., London's Royal Botanic Gardens, also known as Kew Gardens; *Peking* Beijing, capital city of China; *obelisk* Large tapering stone pillar. Picturesque gardens often incorporated artificial ruins.

2   *hermitage* Sanctuary and retreat of a hermit, usually quite small and isolated.

grouped at intervals that show them to advantage. The rill is a serpentine ribbon unwound from the lake peaceably contained by meadows on which the right amount of sheep are tastefully arranged—in short, it is nature as God intended, and I can say with the painter, "*Et in Arcadia ego!*"[1] "Here I am in Arcadia," Thomasina.

THOMASINA. Yes, mama, if you would have it so.

LADY CROOM. Is she correcting my taste or my translation?

THOMASINA. Neither are beyond correction, mama, but it was your geography caused the doubt.

LADY CROOM. Something has occurred with the girl since I saw her last, and surely that was yesterday. How old are you this morning?

THOMASINA. Thirteen years and ten months, mama.

LADY CROOM. Thirteen years and ten months. She is not due to be pert for six months at the earliest, or to have notions of taste for much longer. Mr. Hodge, I hold you accountable. Mr. Noakes, back to you—

NOAKES. Thank you, my—

LADY CROOM. You have been reading too many novels by Mrs. Radcliffe, that is my opinion. This is a garden for *The Castle of Otranto*[2] or *The Mysteries of Udolpho*—

CHATER. *The Castle of Otranto*, my lady, is by Horace Walpole.

NOAKES. (*Thrilled*) Mr. Walpole the gardener?![3]

LADY CROOM. Mr. Chater, you are a welcome guest at Sidley Park but while you are one, *The Castle of Otranto* was written by whomsoever I say it was, otherwise what is the point of being a guest or having one?

(*The distant popping of guns heard.*)

Well, the guns have reached the brow—I will speak to his lordship on the subject, and we will see by and by—(*She stands looking out.*) Ah!—your friend has got down a pigeon, Mr. Hodge. (*Calls out.*) Bravo, sir!

SEPTIMUS. The pigeon, I am sure, fell to your husband or to your son, your ladyship—my schoolfriend was never a sportsman.

---

1   *rill* Stream; *Et in Arcadia ego* Title given to two paintings by the French artist Nicolas Poussin (1594–1665), both of which depict classical shepherds gathered around a tomb inscribed with the title phrase. Lady Croom mistranslates the Latin; a more accurate translation would be "Even in Arcadia, I (am)." The "I" in the expression is understood to be death.

2   *Mrs. Radcliffe* Anne Radcliffe (1764–1823), English Gothic novelist and the author of *The Mysteries of Udolpho*; *The Castle of Otranto* Written in 1765 by Horace Walpole and generally considered the first English-language Gothic novel.

3   *Mr. Walpole the gardener* Although he was better known as a writer and politician, Walpole also designed his personal home, a tourist attraction noted for its Gothic architecture and landscape. His "Essay on Modern Gardening" (1780) was influential.

360 BRICE. (*Looking out*) Yes, to Augustus!—bravo, lad!

LADY CROOM. (*Outside*) Well, come along! Where are my troops?

(*Brice, Noakes and Chater obediently follow her, Chater making a detour to shake Septimus's hand fervently.*)

CHATER. My dear Mr. Hodge!

(*Chater leaves also. The guns are heard again, a little closer.*)

THOMASINA. Pop, pop, pop ... I have grown up in the sound of guns like the
365 child of a siege. Pigeons and rooks in the close season, grouse on the heights
from August, and the pheasants to follow—partridge, snipe, woodcock,
and teal—pop—pop—pop, and the culling of the herd. Papa has no need
of the recording angel, his life is written in the game book.[1]

SEPTIMUS. A calendar of slaughter. "Even in Arcadia, there am I!"

370 THOMASINA. Oh, phooey to Death!

(*She dips a pen and takes it to the reading stand.*)

I will put in a hermit, for what is a hermitage without a hermit? Are you in
love with my mother, Septimus?

SEPTIMUS. You must not be cleverer than your elders. It is not polite.

THOMASINA. Am I cleverer?

375 SEPTIMUS. Yes. Much.

THOMASINA. Well, I am sorry, Septimus. (*She pauses in her drawing and produces a small envelope from her pocket.*) Mrs. Chater came to the music
room with a note for you. She said it was of scant importance, and that
therefore I should carry it to you with the utmost safety, urgency and dis-
380 cretion. Does carnal embrace addle the brain?

SEPTIMUS. (*Taking the letter*) Invariably. Thank you. That is enough education for today.

THOMASINA. There. I have made him like the Baptist in the wilderness.[2]

SEPTIMUS. How picturesque.

(*Lady Croom is heard calling distantly for Thomasina who runs off into
the garden, cheerfully, an uncomplicated girl. Septimus opens Mrs. Chater's
note. He crumples the envelope and throws it away. He reads the note, folds
it and inserts it into the pages of "The Couch of Eros."*)

---

1   *recording angel* Angel who writes down all the events and deeds of a person's life; *game
book* Record of the gaming (i.e., hunting) occurring on an estate.

2   *the Baptist in the wilderness* Biblical prophet John the Baptist, who preached in the wilderness. See Matthew 3.

ACT 1, SCENE 2

The lights come up on the same room, on the same sort of morning, in the present day, as is instantly clear from the appearance of Hannah Jarvis; and from nothing else.

Something needs to be said about this. The action of the play shuttles back and forth between the early nineteenth century and the present day, always in this same room. Both periods must share the state of the room, without the additions and subtractions which would normally be expected. The general appearance of the room should offend neither period. In the case of props—books, paper, flowers, etc., there is no absolute need to remove the evidence of one period to make way for another. However, books, etc., used in both periods should exist in both old and new versions. The landscape outside, we are told, has undergone changes. Again, what we see should neither change nor contradict.

On the above principle, the ink and pens etc., of the first scene can remain. Books and papers associated with Hannah's research, in Scene Two, can have been on the table from the beginning of the play. And so on. During the course of the play the table collects this and that, and where an object from one scene would be an anachronism in another (say a coffee mug) it is simply deemed to have become invisible. By the end of the play the table has collected an inventory of objects.

Hannah is leafing through the pages of Mr. Noakes's sketch book. Also to hand, opened and closed, are a number of small volumes like diaries (these turn out to be Lady Croom's "garden books"). After a few moments, Hannah takes the sketch book to the windows, comparing the view with what has been drawn, and then she replaces the sketch book on the reading stand.

She wears nothing frivolous. Her shoes are suitable for the garden, which is where she goes now after picking up the theodolite from the table. The room is empty for a few moments.

One of the other doors opens to admit Chloë and Bernard. She is the daughter of the house and is dressed casually. Bernard, the visitor, wears a suit and a tie. His tendency is to dress flamboyantly, but he has damped it down for the occasion, slightly. A peacock-coloured display handkerchief boils over in his breast pocket. He carries a capacious leather bag which serves as a briefcase.

CHLOË. Oh! Well, she *was* here ...
BERNARD. Ah ... the french window ...
CHLOË. Yes. Hang on.

(*Chloë steps out through the garden door and disappears from view. Bernard hangs on. The second door opens and Valentine looks in.*)

VALENTINE. Sod.[1]

(*Valentine goes out again, closing the door. Chloë returns, carrying a pair of rubber boots. She comes in and sits down and starts exchanging her shoes for the boots, while she talks.*)

5 CHLOË. The best thing is, you wait here, save you tramping around. She spends a good deal of time in the garden, as you may imagine.
BERNARD. Yes. Why?
CHLOË. Well, she's writing a history of the garden, didn't you know?
BERNARD. No, I knew she was working on the Croom papers but ...
10 CHLOË. Well, it's not exactly a history of the garden either. I'll let Hannah explain it. The trench you nearly drove into is all to do with it. I was going to say make yourself comfortable but that's hardly possible, everything's been cleared out, it's en route to the nearest lavatory.[2]
BERNARD. Everything is?
15 CHLOË. No, this room is. They drew the line at chemical "Ladies'."[3]
BERNARD. Yes, I see. Did you say Hannah?
CHLOË. Hannah, yes. Will you be all right?

(*She stands up wearing the boots.*)

I won't be ... (*But she has lost him.*) Mr. Nightingale?
BERNARD. (*Waking up*) Yes. Thank you. Miss Jarvis is Hannah Jarvis the
20 author?
CHLOË. Yes. Have you read her book?
BERNARD. Oh, yes. Yes.
CHLOË. I bet she's in the hermitage, can't see from here with the marquee[4] ...
BERNARD. Are you having a garden party?
25 CHLOË. A dance for the district, our annual dressing up and general drunkenness. The wrinklies[5] won't have it in the house, there was a teapot we once had to bag back from Christie's in the nick of time, so anything that can be destroyed, stolen or vomited on has been tactfully removed; tactlessly, I should say—

1 *Sod* Mild British swear word.
2 *lavatory* Bathroom.
3 *chemical "Ladies'"* Ladies' portable toilets.
4 *marquee* Tent used for outdoor events.
5 *wrinklies* Older members of the household.

(*She is about to leave.*)

BERNARD. Um—look—would you tell her—would you mind not mention-   30
ing my name just yet?

CHLOË. Oh. All right.

BERNARD. (*Smiling*) More fun to surprise her. Would you mind?

CHLOË. No. But she's bound to ask ... Should I give you another name, just
for the moment?   35

BERNARD. Yes, why not?

CHLOË. Perhaps another bird, you're not really a Nightingale.

(*She leaves again. Bernard glances over the books on the table. He puts his
briefcase down. There is the distant pop-pop of a shotgun. It takes Bernard
vaguely to the window. He looks out. The door he entered by now opens and
Gus looks into the room. Bernard turns and sees him.*)

BERNARD. Hello.

(*Gus doesn't speak. He never speaks. Perhaps he cannot speak. He has no
composure, and faced with a stranger, he caves in and leaves again. A
moment later the other door opens again and Valentine crosses the room,
not exactly ignoring Bernard and yet ignoring him.*)

VALENTINE. Sod, sod, sod, sod, sod, sod ... (*As many times as it takes him to
leave by the opposite door, which he closes behind him. Beyond it, he can be
heard shouting. "Chlo! Chlo!" Bernard's discomfort increases. The same door
opens and Valentine returns. He looks at Bernard.*)

BERNARD. She's in the garden looking for Miss Jarvis.   40

VALENTINE. Where is everything?

BERNARD. It's been removed for the, er ...

VALENTINE. The dance is all in the tent, isn't it?

BERNARD. Yes, but this is the way to the nearest toilet.

VALENTINE. I need the commode.   45

BERNARD. Oh. Can't you use the toilet?[1]

VALENTINE. It's got all the game books in it.

BERNARD. Ah. The toilet has or the commode has?

VALENTINE. Is anyone looking after you?

BERNARD. Yes. Thank you. I'm Bernard Nigh—I've come to see Miss Jarvis.   50
I wrote to Lord Croom but unfortunately I never received a reply, so I—

VALENTINE. Did you type it?

BERNARD. Type it?

---

1   *commode ... toilet* Play on the word "commode," which can mean either a chest of drawers, a toilet, or, more traditionally, a piece of furniture that disguises a chamber pot.

VALENTINE. Was your letter typewritten?
55 BERNARD. Yes.
VALENTINE. My father never replies to typewritten letters.

(*He spots a tortoise which has been half-hidden on the table.*)

Oh! Where have you been hiding, Lightning? (*He picks up the tortoise.*)
BERNARD. So I telephoned yesterday and I think I spoke to you—
VALENTINE. To me? Ah! Yes! Sorry! You're doing a talk about—someone—
60 and you wanted to ask Hannah—something—
BERNARD. Yes. As it turns out. I'm hoping Miss Jarvis will look kindly on me.
VALENTINE. I doubt it.
BERNARD. Ah, you know about research?
VALENTINE. I know Hannah.
65 BERNARD. Has she been here long?
VALENTINE. Well in possession, I'm afraid. My mother had read her book, you see. Have you?
BERNARD. No. Yes. Her book. Indeed.
VALENTINE. She's terrifically pleased with herself.
70 BERNARD. Well, I dare say if I wrote a bestseller—
VALENTINE. No, for reading it. My mother basically reads gardening books.
BERNARD. She must be delighted to have Hannah Jarvis writing a book about her garden.
VALENTINE. Actually it's about hermits.

(*Gus returns through the same door, and turns to leave again.*)

75 It's all right, Gus—what do you want?—

(*But Gus has gone again.*)

Well ... I'll take Lightning for his run.
BERNARD. Actually, we've met before. At Sussex, a couple of years ago, a seminar ...
VALENTINE. Oh. Was I there?
80 BERNARD. Yes. One of my colleagues believed he had found an unattributed short story by D.H. Lawrence,[1] and he analyzed it on his home computer, most interesting, perhaps you remember the paper?
VALENTINE. Not really. But I often sit with my eyes closed and it doesn't necessarily mean I'm awake.
85 BERNARD. Well, by comparing sentence structures and so forth, this chap showed that there was a ninety per cent chance that the story had indeed

---

1   *D.H. Lawrence* English writer (1885–1930).

been written by the same person as *Women in Love*. To my inexpressible
joy, one of your maths mob was able to show that on the same statistical
basis there was a ninety per cent chance that Lawrence also wrote the *Just
William* books and much of the previous day's *Brighton and Hove Argus*.[1]   90

VALENTINE. (*Pause*) Oh, Brighton. Yes. I was there. (*And looking out.*) Oh—
here she comes, I'll leave you to talk. By the way, is yours the red Mazda?

BERNARD. Yes.

VALENTINE. If you want a tip I'd put it out of sight through the stable arch
before my father comes in. He won't have anyone in the house with a Japa-   95
nese car. Are you queer?

BERNARD. No, actually.

VALENTINE. Well, even so.

(*Valentine leaves, closing the door. Bernard keeps staring at the closed door.
Behind him, Hannah comes to the garden door.*)

HANNAH. Mr. Peacock?

(*Bernard looks round vaguely then checks over his shoulder for the missing
Peacock, then recovers himself and turns on the Nightingale bonhomie.*)

BERNARD. Oh ... hello! Hello. Miss Jarvis, of course. Such a pleasure. I was   100
thrown for a moment—the photograph doesn't do you justice.

HANNAH. Photograph?

(*Her shoes have got muddy and she is taking them off.*)

BERNARD. On the book. I'm sorry to have brought you indoors, but Lady
Chloë kindly insisted she—

HANNAH. No matter—you would have muddied your shoes.   105

BERNARD. How thoughtful. And how kind of you to spare me a little of your
time.

(*He is overdoing it. She shoots him a glance.*)

HANNAH. Are you a journalist?

BERNARD. (*Shocked*) No!

HANNAH. (*Resuming*) I've been in the ha-ha,[2] very squelchy.   110

BERNARD. (*Unexpectedly*) Ha-*hah*!

---

1   *Women in Love* 1921 novel by D.H. Lawrence; *Just William books* Children's book series by English writer Richmal Crompton (1890–1969); *Brighton and Hove Argus* Local
newspaper out of Brighton and Hove, East Sussex.

2   *ha-ha* Ditch with one sloped side and one straight side. A ha-ha cannot be seen from a
distance and is used to create a boundary, especially for livestock, without altering the
view.

HANNAH. What?

BERNARD. A theory of mine. Ha-hah, not ha-ha. If you were strolling down the garden and all of a sudden the ground gave way at your feet, you're not going to go "ha-ha," you're going to jump back and go "ha-hah!," or more probably, "Bloody 'ell!" ... though personally I think old Murray was up the pole[1] on that one—in France, you know, "ha-ha" is used to denote a strikingly ugly woman, a much more likely bet for something that keeps the cows off the lawn.

(*This is not going well for Bernard but he seems blithely unaware. Hannah stares at him for a moment.*)

HANNAH. Mr. Peacock, what can I do for you?

BERNARD. Well, to begin with, you can call me Bernard, which is my name.

HANNAH. Thank you.

(*She goes to the garden door to bang her shoes together and scrape off the worst of the mud.*)

BERNARD.   The book!—the book is a revelation! To see Caroline Lamb[2] through your eyes is really like seeing her for the first time. I'm ashamed to say I never read her fiction, and how right you are, it's extraordinary stuff—Early Nineteenth is my period as much as anything is.

HANNAH. You teach?

BERNARD. Yes. And write, like you, like we all, though I've never done anything which has sold like *Caro*.[3]

HANNAH. I don't teach.

BERNARD. No. All the more credit to you. To rehabilitate a forgotten writer, I suppose you could say that's the main reason for an English don.

HANNAH. Not to teach?

BERNARD. Good God, no, let the brats sort it out for themselves. Anyway, many congratulations. I expect someone will be bringing out Caroline Lamb's oeuvre[4] now?

HANNAH. Yes, I expect so.

BERNARD. How wonderful! Bravo! Simply as a document shedding reflected light on the character of Lord Byron,[5] it's bound to be—

---

1   *old Murray* Sir James Murray (1837–1915), Scottish lexicographer and main editor of the *Oxford English Dictionary; up the pole* I.e., crazy, incorrect, off the mark.

2   *Caroline Lamb* Lady Caroline Lamb (1725–1828), English writer.

3   *Caro* Diminutive form of Caroline, adopted as a nickname by Lady Lamb.

4   *oeuvre* Body of work.

5   *Lord Byron* George Gordon Byron (1788–1824), English poet and satirist. One of the most influential figures of the British Romantic movement, Byron was notorious for his frequent love affairs, including one with Lady Caroline Lamb.

HANNAH. Bernard. You did say Bernard, didn't you?   140

BERNARD. I did.

HANNAH. I'm putting my shoes on again.

BERNARD. Oh. You're not going to go out?

HANNAH. No, I'm going to kick you in the balls.

BERNARD. Right. Point taken. Ezra Chater.   145

HANNAH. Ezra Chater.

BERNARD. Born Twickenham, Middlesex,[1] 1778, author of two verse narratives, "The Maid of Turkey," 1808, and "The Couch of Eros," 1809. Nothing known after 1809, disappears from view.

HANNAH. I see. And?   150

BERNARD. (*Reaching for his bag*) There is a Sidley Park connection.

  (*He produces "The Couch of Eros" from the bag. He reads the inscription.*)

  To my friend Septimus Hodge, who stood up and gave his best on behalf of the Author—Ezra Chater, at Sidley Park, Derbyshire, April 10th,
  1809."

  (*He gives her the book.*)

  I am in your hands.   155

HANNAH. "The Couch of Eros." Is it any good?

BERNARD. Quite surprising.

HANNAH. You think there's a book in him?

BERNARD. No, no—a monograph[2] perhaps for the *Journal of English Studies*.
  There's almost nothing on Chater, not a word in the *DNB*,[3] of course—by   160
  that time he'd been completely forgotten.

HANNAH. Family?

BERNARD. Zilch. There's only one other Chater in the British Library data-
  base.

HANNAH. Same period?   165

BERNARD. Yes, but he wasn't a poet like our Ezra, he was a botanist who
  described a dwarf dahlia in Martinique[4] and died there after being bitten
  by a monkey.

HANNAH. And Ezra Chater?

BERNARD. He gets two references in the Periodical index, one for each book,   170

---

1 *Twickenham, Middlesex* English town that became a part of Greater London in the twentieth century.

2 *monograph* Academic essay or book on a single subject, intended for a specialist audience.

3 *DNB* Abbreviated title of the *Dictionary of National Biography*, originally published in
   1885. It provides a regularly updated listing of notable British historical figures.

4 *Martinique* French island in the Caribbean Sea.

in both cases a substantial review in the *Piccadilly Recreation*, a thrice weekly folio sheet,[1] but giving no personal details.

HANNAH.   And where was this (*the book*)?

BERNARD.   Private collection. I've got a talk to give next week, in London, and
I think Chater is interesting, so anything on him, or this Septimus Hodge,
Sidley Park, any leads at all ... I'd be most grateful.

(*Pause.*)

HANNAH.   Well! This is a new experience for me. A grovelling academic.

BERNARD.   Oh, I say.

HANNAH.   Oh, but it is. All the academics who reviewed my book patronized
it.

BERNARD.   Surely not.

HANNAH.   Surely yes. The Byron gang unzipped their flies and patronized all
over it. Where is it you don't bother to teach, by the way?

BERNARD.   Oh, well, Sussex, actually.

HANNAH.   Sussex. (*She thinks a moment.*) Nightingale. Yes; a thousand words
in the *Observer*[2] to see me off the premises with a pat on the bottom. You
must know him.

BERNARD.   As I say, I'm in your hands.

HANNAH.   Quite. Say please, then.

BERNARD.   Please.

HANNAH.   Sit down, do.

BERNARD.   Thank you.

(*He takes a chair. She remains standing. Possibly she smokes; if so, perhaps
now. A short cigarette-holder sounds right, too. Or brown-paper cigarillos.*[3])

HANNAH.   How did you know I was here?

BERNARD.   Oh, I didn't. I spoke to the son on the phone but he didn't mention you by name ... and then he forgot to mention me.

HANNAH.   Valentine. He's at Oxford, technically.

BERNARD.   Yes, I met him. Brideshead Regurgitated.[4]

HANNAH.   My fiancé.

(*She holds his look.*)

BERNARD.   (*Pause*) I'll take a chance. You're lying.

---

1   *folio sheet* Single large page.
2   *Observer* Major British newspaper.
3   *cigarillos* Small, thin cigars.
4   *Brideshead Regurgitated* Reference to *Brideshead Revisited* (1945), a novel by English
    writer Evelyn Waugh in which the primary characters meet as students at Oxford Univer-
    sity.

HANNAH. (*Pause*) Well done, Bernard.   200

BERNARD. Christ.

HANNAH. He calls me his fiancée.

BERNARD. Why?

HANNAH. It's a joke.

BERNARD. You turned him down?   205

HANNAH. Don't be silly, do I look like the next Countess of—

BERNARD. No, no—a freebie. The joke that consoles. My tortoise Lightning,
my fiancée Hannah.

HANNAH. Oh. Yes. You have a way with you, Bernard. I'm not sure I like it.

BERNARD. What's he doing, Valentine?   210

HANNAH. He's a postgrad. Biology.

BERNARD. No, he's a mathematician.

HANNAH. Well, he's doing grouse.

BERNARD. Grouse?

HANNAH. Not actual grouse. Computer grouse.   215

BERNARD. Who's the one who doesn't speak?

HANNAH. Gus.

BERNARD. What's the matter with him?

HANNAH. I didn't ask.

BERNARD. And the father sounds like a lot of fun.   220

HANNAH. Ah yes.

BERNARD. And the mother is the gardener. What's going on here?

HANNAH. What do you mean?

BERNARD. I nearly took her head off—she was standing in a trench at the
time.   225

HANNAH. Archaeology. The house had a formal Italian garden until about
1740. Lady Croom is interested in garden history. I sent her my book—it
contains, as you know if you've read it—which I'm not assuming, by the
way—a rather good description of Caroline's garden at Brocket Hall.[1] I'm
here now helping Hermione.   230

BERNARD. (*Impressed*) Hermione.

HANNAH. The records are unusually complete and they have never been
worked on.

BERNARD. I'm beginning to admire you.

HANNAH. Before was bullshit?   235

BERNARD. Completely. Your photograph does you justice, I'm not sure the
book does.

(*She considers him. He waits, confident.*)

---

1   *Brocket Hall* Country house in Hertfordshire, England, owned by the Lamb family.

HANNAH. Septimus Hodge was the tutor.

BERNARD. (*Quietly*) Attagirl.

240 HANNAH. His pupil was the Croom daughter. There was a son at Eton. Septimus lived in the house: the pay book specifies allowances for wine and candles. So, not quite a guest but rather more than a steward.[1] His letter of self-recommendation is preserved among the papers. I'll dig it out for you. As far as I remember he studied mathematics and natural philosophy

245   at Cambridge. A scientist, therefore, as much as anything.

BERNARD. I'm impressed. Thank you. And Chater?

HANNAH. Nothing.

BERNARD. Oh. Nothing at all?

HANNAH. I'm afraid not.

250 BERNARD. How about the library?

HANNAH. The catalogue was done in the 1880s. I've been through the lot.

BERNARD. Books or catalogue?

HANNAH. Catalogue.

BERNARD. Ah. Pity.

255 HANNAH. I'm sorry.

BERNARD. What about the letters? No mention?

HANNAH. I'm afraid not. I've been very thorough in your period because, of course, it's my period too.

BERNARD. Is it? Actually, I don't quite know what it is you're ...

260 HANNAH. The Sidley hermit.

BERNARD. Ah. Who's he?

HANNAH. He's my peg for the nervous breakdown of the Romantic Imagination. I'm doing landscape and literature 1750 to 1834.

BERNARD. What happened in 1834?

265 HANNAH. My hermit died.

BERNARD. Of course.

HANNAH. What do you mean, of course?

BERNARD. Nothing.

HANNAH. Yes, you do.

270 BERNARD. No, no ... However, Coleridge[2] also died in 1834.

HANNAH. So he did. What a stroke of luck. (*Softening.*) Thank you, Bernard.

(*She goes to the reading stand and opens Noakes's sketch book.*)

Look—there he is.

---

1   *steward* Primary servant in charge of fellow servants and household affairs.

2   *Coleridge* English poet Samuel Taylor Coleridge (1772–1834); he was a central figure of the Romantic movement.

(*Bernard goes to look.*)

BERNARD. Mmm.

HANNAH. The only known likeness of the Sidley hermit.

BERNARD. Very biblical.   275

HANNAH. Drawn in by a later hand, of course. The hermitage didn't yet exist when Noakes did the drawings.

BERNARD. Noakes ... the painter?

HANNAH. Landscape gardener. He'd do these books for his clients, as a sort of prospectus. (*She demonstrates.*) Before and after, you see. This is how it   280 all looked until, say, 1810—smooth, undulating, serpentine—open water, clumps of trees, classical boat-house—

BERNARD. Lovely. The real England.

HANNAH. You can stop being silly now, Bernard. English landscape was invented by gardeners imitating foreign painters who were evoking classical   285 authors. The whole thing was brought home in the luggage from the grand tour. Here, look—Capability Brown doing Claude, who was doing Virgil.[1] Arcadia! And here, superimposed by Richard Noakes, untamed nature in the style of Salvator Rosa. It's the Gothic novel expressed in landscape. Everything but vampires. There's an account of my hermit in a letter by   290 your illustrious namesake.

BERNARD. Florence?

HANNAH. What?

BERNARD. No. You go on.

HANNAH. Thomas Love Peacock.[2]   295

BERNARD. Ah yes.

HANNAH. I found it in an essay on hermits and anchorites published in the *Cornhill Magazine*[3] in the 1860s ... (*She fishes for the magazine itself among the books on the table, and finds it.*) ... 1862 ... Peacock calls him (*She quotes from memory.*) "Not one of your village simpletons to frighten the ladies,   300 but a savant among idiots, a sage of lunacy."

BERNARD. An oxy-moron, so to speak.

HANNAH. (*Busy*) Yes. What?

BERNARD. Nothing.

---

1   *Capability Brown* Lancelot Brown (1716–83), English landscaper who popularized English gardens that were designed to look undomesticated and wild; *Claude* Claude Lorrain (1600–82), French painter known for his landscape paintings; *Virgil* Roman poet (70–19 BCE); some of his works depict country life.

2   *Thomas Love Peacock* English novelist and satirist (1785–1866).

3   *anchorites* Religious recluses; *Cornhill Magazine* Literary journal (1859–1975) once edited by English novelist and satirist William Makepeace Thackeray (1811–63).

305 HANNAH. (*Having found the place*) Here we are. "A letter we have seen, written by the author of *Headlong Hall*[1] nearly thirty years ago, tells of a visit to the Earl of Croom's estate, Sidley Park—"

BERNARD. Was the letter to Thackeray?

HANNAH. (*Brought up short*) I don't know. Does it matter?

310 BERNARD. No. Sorry.

   (*But the gaps he leaves for her are false promises—and she is not quick enough. That's how it goes.*)

Only, Thackeray edited the *Cornhill* until '63 when, as you know, he died. His father had been with the East India Company[2] where Peacock, of course, had held the position of Examiner, so it's quite possible that if the essay were by Thackeray, the *letter* ... Sorry. Go on. Of course, the East

315 India Library in Blackfriars[3] has most of Peacock's letters, so it would be quite easy to ... Sorry. Can I look?

   (*Silently she hands him the Cornhill.*)

Yes, it's been topped and tailed,[4] of course. It might be worth ... Go on. I'm listening ...

(*Leafing through the essay, he suddenly chuckles.*) Oh yes, it's Thackeray all

320 right ...

(*He slaps the book shut.*) Unbearable ...

(*He hands it back to her.*) What were you saying?

HANNAH. Are you always like this?

BERNARD. Like what?

325 HANNAH. The point is, the Crooms, of course, had the hermit under their noses for twenty years so hardly thought him worth remarking. As I'm finding out. The Peacock letter is still the main source, unfortunately. When I read this (*the magazine in her hand*) well, it was one of those moments that tell you what your next book is going to be. The hermit of

330 Sidley Park was my ...

BERNARD. Peg.

HANNAH. Epiphany.

BERNARD. Epiphany, that's it.

HANNAH. The hermit was *placed* in the landscape exactly as one might place

335 a pottery gnome. And there he lived out his life as a garden ornament.

---

1   *the author of Headlong Hall* Peacock.

2   *East India Company* Powerful British trading company (1600–1873) that dominated the government of India during the late eighteenth and early nineteenth centuries.

3   *Blackfriars* Area of central London.

4   *topped and tailed* I.e., with the beginning and end removed (and therefore with the name of the recipient omitted).

BERNARD. Did he do anything?

HANNAH. Oh, he was very busy. When he died, the cottage was stacked solid with paper. Hundreds of pages. Thousands. Peacock says he was suspected of genius. It turned out, of course, he was off his head. He'd covered every sheet with cabalistic[1] proofs that the world was coming to an end. It's per- 340 fect, isn't it? A perfect symbol, I mean.

BERNARD. Oh, yes. Of what?

HANNAH. The whole Romantic sham, Bernard! It's what happened to the Enlightenment,[2] isn't it? A century of intellectual rigour turned in on itself. A mind in chaos suspected of genius. In a setting of cheap thrills and 345 false emotion. The history of the garden says it all, beautifully. There's an engraving of Sidley Park in 1730 that makes you want to weep. Paradise in the age of reason. By 1760 everything had gone—the topiary, pools and terraces, fountains, an avenue of limes—the whole sublime geometry was ploughed under by Capability Brown. The grass went from the doorstep to 350 the horizon and the best box hedge in Derbyshire was dug up for the ha-ha so that the fools could pretend they were living in God's countryside. And then Richard Noakes came in to bring God up to date. By the time he'd finished it looked like this (*the sketch book*). The decline from thinking to feeling, you see. 355

BERNARD. (*A judgement*) That's awfully good.

(*Hannah looks at him in case of irony but he is professional.*)

No, that'll stand up.

HANNAH. Thank you.

BERNARD. Personally I like the ha-ha. Do you like hedges?

HANNAH. I don't like sentimentality. 360

BERNARD. Yes, I see. Are you sure? You seem quite sentimental over geometry. But the hermit is very very good. The genius of the place.

HANNAH. (*Pleased*) That's my title!

BERNARD. Of course.

HANNAH. (*Less pleased*) Of course? 365

BERNARD. Of course. Who was he when he wasn't being a symbol?

HANNAH. I don't know.

BERNARD. Ah.

HANNAH. I mean, yet.

BERNARD. Absolutely. What did they do with all the paper? Does Peacock say? 370

---

1   *cabalistic* Mystical, esoteric.

2   *Enlightenment* Movement of the seventeenth and eighteenth centuries that placed importance on reason and scientific thought. The Romantic period followed the Enlightenment and is often seen as a reaction to it.

HANNAH. Made a bonfire.

BERNARD. Ah, well.

HANNAH. I've still got Lady Croom's garden books to go through.

BERNARD. Account books or journals?

375 HANNAH. A bit of both. They're gappy but they span the period.

BERNARD. Really? Have you come across Byron at all? As a matter of interest.

HANNAH. A first edition of "Childe Harold" in the library, and *English Bards*,[1] I think.

BERNARD. Inscribed?

380 HANNAH. No.

BERNARD. And he doesn't pop up in the letters at all?

HANNAH. Why should he? The Crooms don't pop up in his.

BERNARD. (*Casually*) That's true, of course. But Newstead[2] isn't so far away. Would you mind terribly if I poked about a bit? Only in the papers you've
385 done with, of course.

(*Hannah twigs[3] something.*)

HANNAH. Are you looking into Byron or Chater?

(*Chloë enters in stockinged feet through one of the side doors, laden with an armful of generally similar leather-covered ledgers. She detours to collect her shoes.*)

CHLOË. Sorry—just cutting through—there's tea in the pantry if you don't mind mugs—

BERNARD. How kind.

390 CHLOË. Hannah will show you.

BERNARD. Let me help you.

CHLOË. No, it's all right—

(*Bernard opens the opposite door for her.*)

Thank you—I've been saving Val's game books. Thanks.

(*Bernard closes the door.*)

BERNARD. Sweet girl.

395 HANNAH. Mmm.

BERNARD. Oh, really?

---

1   *"Childe Harold"… English Bards* Hannah mentions two long poems by Byron: the semi-autobiographical *Childe Harold's Pilgrimage* (1812–16) and *English Bards and Scotch Reviewers* (1809), a satire.

2   *Newstead* Newstead Abbey, Lord Byron's home.

3   *twigs* I.e., realizes.

HANNAH. Oh really what?

(*Chloë's door opens again and she puts her head round it.*)

CHLOË. Meant to say, don't worry if father makes remarks about your car, Mr. Nightingale, he's got a thing about—(*and the Nightingale now being out of the bag*) ooh—ah, how was the surprise?—not yet, eh? Oh, well—   400
sorry—tea, anyway—so sorry if I—(*Embarrassed, she leaves again, closing the door. Pause.*)

HANNAH. You absolute shit.

(*She heads off to leave.*)

BERNARD. The thing is, there's a Byron connection too.

(*Hannah stops and faces him.*)

HANNAH. I don't care.   405

BERNARD. You should. The Byron gang are going to get their dicks caught in their zip.

HANNAH. (*Pause*) Oh really?

BERNARD. If we collaborate.

HANNAH. On what?   410

BERNARD. Sit down, I'll tell you.

HANNAH. I'll stand for the moment.

BERNARD. This copy of "The Couch of Eros" belonged to Lord Byron.

HANNAH. It belonged to Septimus Hodge.

BERNARD. Originally, yes. But it was in Byron's library which was sold to pay   415
his debts when he left England for good in 1816. The sales catalogue is in the British Library. "Eros" was lot 74A and was bought by the bookseller and publisher John Nightingale of Opera Court, Pall Mall[1] ... whose name survives in the firm of Nightingale and Matlock, the present Nightingale being my cousin.   420

(*He pauses. Hannah hesitates and then sits down at the table.*)

I'll just give you the headlines. 1939, stock removed to Nightingale country house in Kent.[2] 1945, stock returned to bookshop. Meanwhile, overlooked box of early nineteenth-century books languish in country house cellar until house sold to make way for the Channel Tunnel[3] rail-link. "Eros" discovered with sales slip from 1816 attached—photocopy avail-   425
able for inspection.

---

1   *Pall Mall* Famous street in London.
2   *Kent* County in Southeast England.
3   *Channel Tunnel* Tunnel that runs under the English Channel to connect Folkestone, Kent, to Coquelles, Pas-de-Calais, in France. It was completed in 1994.

(*He brings this from his bag and gives it to Hannah who inspects it.*)

HANNAH. All right. It was in Byron's library.

BERNARD. A number of passages have been underlined.

(*Hannah picks up the book and leafs through it.*)

430 All of them, and only them—no, no, look at me, not at the book—all the underlined passages, word for word, were used as quotations in the review of "The Couch of Eros" in the *Piccadilly Recreation* of April 30th 1809. The reviewer begins by drawing attention to his previous notice in the same periodical of "The Maid of Turkey."

HANNAH. The reviewer is obviously Hodge. "My friend Septimus Hodge

435 who stood up and gave his best on behalf of the Author."

BERNARD. That's the point. The *Piccadilly* ridiculed both books.

HANNAH. (*Pause.*) Do the reviews read like Byron?

BERNARD. (*Producing two photocopies from his case*) They read a damn sight more like Byron than Byron's review of Wordsworth[1] the previous year.

(*Hannah glances over the photocopies.*)

440 HANNAH. I see. Well, congratulations. Possibly. Two previously unknown book reviews by the young Byron. Is that it?

BERNARD. No. Because of the tapes, three documents survived undisturbed in the book.

(*He has been carefully opening a package produced from his bag. He has the originals. He holds them carefully one by one.*)

"Sir—we have a matter to settle. I wait on you in the gun room. E. Chater,

445 Esq."

"My husband has sent to town for pistols. Deny what cannot be proven— for Charity's sake—I keep my room this day." Unsigned.

"Sidley Park, April 11th 1809. Sir—I call you a liar, a lecher, a slanderer in the press and a thief of my honour. I wait upon your arrangements for

450 giving me satisfaction as a man and a poet. E. Chater, Esq."

(*Pause.*)

HANNAH. Superb. But inconclusive. The book had seven years to find its way into Byron's possession. It doesn't connect Byron with Chater, or with Sidley Park. Or with Hodge for that matter. Furthermore, there isn't a hint in Byron's letters and this kind of scrape is the last thing he would have

455 kept quiet about.

---

1   *Wordsworth* William Wordsworth (1770–1850), English poet.

BERNARD. *Scrape?*

HANNAH. He would have made a comic turn out of it.

BERNARD. Comic turn, fiddlesticks! (*He pauses for effect.*) He killed Chater!

HANNAH. (*A raspberry*) Oh, really!

BERNARD. Chater was thirty-one years old. The author of two books. Noth-   460
ing more is heard from him after "Eros." He disappears completely after
April 1809. And Byron—Byron had just published his satire, *English Bards
and Scotch Reviewers*, in March. He was just getting a name. Yet he sailed
for Lisbon as soon as he could find a ship, and stayed abroad for two
years. Hannah, *this is fame*. Somewhere in the Croom papers there will be   465
something—

HANNAH. There isn't, I've looked.

BERNARD. But you were looking for something else! It's not going to jump
out at you like "Lord Byron remarked wittily at breakfast!"

HANNAH. Nevertheless his presence would be unlikely to have gone unre-   470
marked. But there is nothing to suggest that Byron was here, and I don't
believe he ever was.

BERNARD. All right, but let me have a look.

HANNAH. You'll queer my pitch.[1]

BERNARD. Dear girl, I know how to handle myself—   475

HANNAH. And don't call me dear girl. If I find anything on Byron, or Chater,
or Hodge, I'll pass it on. Nightingale, Sussex.

>   (*Pause. She stands up.*)

BERNARD. Thank you. I'm sorry about that business with my name.

HANNAH. Don't mention it ...

BERNARD. What was Hodge's college, by the way?   480

HANNAH. Trinity.[2]

BERNARD. Trinity?

HANNAH. Yes. (*She hesitates.*) Yes. Byron's old college.

BERNARD. How old was Hodge?

HANNAH. I'd have to look it up but a year or two older than Byron. Twenty-   485
two ...

BERNARD. Contemporaries at Trinity?

HANNAH. (*Wearily*) Yes, Bernard, and no doubt they were both in the cricket
eleven when Harrow played Eton at Lords![3]

---

1   *queer my pitch* I.e., spoil my work.

2   *Trinity* Trinity College, a college of Cambridge University.

3   *cricket eleven* Cricket teams are made up of eleven players; *Harrow* Harrow School,
English school for boys; *Lords* Lord's Cricket Ground in London, which has held the
Eton vs. Harrow cricket match annually since the early 1800s.

(*Bernard approaches her and stands close to her.*)

490 BERNARD. (*Evenly*) Do you mean that Septimus Hodge was at school with Byron?

HANNAH. (*Falters slightly*) Yes ... he must have been ... as a matter of fact.

BERNARD. Well, you silly cow.

(*With a large gesture of pure happiness, Bernard throws his arms around Hannah and gives her a great smacking kiss on the cheek. Chloë enters to witness the end of this.*)

CHLOË. Oh—erm ... I thought I'd bring it to you.

(*She is carrying a small tray with two mugs on it.*)

495 BERNARD. I have to go and see about my car.

HANNAH. Going to hide it?

BERNARD. Hide it? I'm going to sell it! Is there a pub I can put up at in the village?

(*He turns back to them as he is about to leave through the garden.*)

Aren't you glad I'm here?

(*He leaves.*)

500 CHLOË. He said he knew you.

HANNAH. He couldn't have.

CHLOË. No, perhaps not. He said he wanted to be a surprise, but I suppose that's different. I thought there was a lot of sexual energy there, didn't you?

HANNAH. What?

505 CHLOË. Bouncy on his feet, you see, a sure sign. Should I invite him for you?

HANNAH. To what? No.

CHLOË. You can invite him—that's better. He can come as your partner.

HANNAH. Stop it. Thank you for the tea.

CHLOË. If you don't want him, I'll have him. Is he married?

510 HANNAH. I haven't the slightest idea. Aren't you supposed to have a pony?

CHLOË. I'm just trying to fix you up, Hannah.

HANNAH. Believe me, it gets less important.

CHLOË. I mean for the dancing. He can come as Beau Brummell.[1]

HANNAH. I don't want to dress up and I don't want a dancing partner, least
515 of all Mr. Nightingale. I don't dance.

CHLOË. Don't be such a prune. You were kissing him, anyway.

HANNAH. He was kissing me, and only out of general enthusiasm.

---

1   *Beau Brummell* George Bryan "Beau" Brummell (1778–1840), a trendsetter in men's fashion often credited with popularizing the British dandy look.

CHLOË. Well, don't say I didn't give you first chance. My genius brother will be much relieved. He's in love with you, I suppose you know.

HANNAH. (*Angry*) That's a joke!   520

CHLOË. It's not a joke to him.

HANNAH. Of course it is—not even a joke—how can you be so ridiculous?

(*Gus enters from the garden, in his customary silent awkwardness.*)

CHLOË. Hello, Gus, what have you got?

(*Gus has an apple, just picked, with a leaf or two still attached. He offers the apple to Hannah.*)

HANNAH. (*Surprised*) Oh! ... Thank you!

CHLOË. (*Leaving*) Told you.   525

(*Chloë closes the door on herself.*)

HANNAH. Thank you. Oh dear.

(*Hannah puts the apple on the table.*)

ACT 1, SCENE 3

The schoolroom. The next morning. Present are: Thomasina, Septimus, Jellaby. We have seen this composition before: Thomasina at her place at the table; Septimus reading a letter which has just arrived; Jellaby waiting, having just delivered the letter.

"The Couch of Eros" is in front of Septimus, open, together with sheets of paper on which he has been writing. His portfolio is on the table. Plautus[1] (the tortoise) is the paperweight. There is also an apple on the table now.

SEPTIMUS. (*With his eyes on the letter*) Why have you stopped?

(*Thomasina is studying a sheet of paper, a "Latin unseen" lesson.[2] She is having some difficulty.*)

THOMASINA. *Solio insessa ... in igne* ... seated on a throne ... in the fire ... and also on a ship ... *sedebat regina* ... sat the queen ...

SEPTIMUS. There is no reply, Jellaby. Thank you.

(*He folds the letter up and places it between the leaves of "The Couch of Eros."*)

---

1   *Plautus* After Roman comic playwright Titus Maccius Plautus (c. 254–184 BCE).

2   *"Latin unseen" lesson* Unfamiliar passage given to a student as a translation test.

5 JELLABY. I will say so, sir.

THOMASINA. ... the wind smelling sweetly ... *purpureis velis* ... by, with or from purple sails—

SEPTIMUS. (*To Jellaby*) I will have something for the post, if you would be so kind.

10 JELLABY. (*Leaving*) Yes, sir.

THOMASINA. ... was like as to—something—by, with or from lovers—oh, Septimus!—*musica tibiarum imperabat* ... music of pipes commanded ...

SEPTIMUS. "Ruled" is better.

THOMASINA. ... the silver oars—exciting the ocean—as if—as if—amorous—

15 SEPTIMUS. That is very good.

(*He picks up the apple. He picks off the twig and leaves, placing these on the table. With a pocket knife he cuts a slice of apple, and while he eats it, cuts another slice which he offers to Plautus.*)

THOMASINA. *Regina reclinabat* ... the queen—was reclining—*praeter descriptionem*—indescribably—in a golden tent ... like Venus and yet more—

SEPTIMUS. Try to put some poetry into it.

THOMASINA. How can I if there is none in the Latin?

20 SEPTIMUS. Oh, a critic!

THOMASINA. Is it Queen Dido?[1]

SEPTIMUS. No.

THOMASINA. Who is the poet?

SEPTIMUS. Known to you.

25 THOMASINA. Known to me?

SEPTIMUS. Not a Roman.

THOMASINA. Mr. Chater?

SEPTIMUS. Your translation is quite like Chater.

(*Septimus picks up his pen and continues with his own writing.*)

THOMASINA. I know who it is, it is your friend Byron.

30 SEPTIMUS. Lord Byron, if you please.

THOMASINA. Mama is in love with Lord Byron.

SEPTIMUS. (*Absorbed*) Yes. Nonsense.

THOMASINA. It is not nonsense. I saw them together in the gazebo.

(*Septimus's pen stops moving, he raises his eyes to her at last.*)

Lord Byron was reading to her from his satire, and mama was laughing, 35 with her head in her best position.

---

1   *Queen Dido* Legendary founder and first queen of Carthage; she appears in Virgil's *Aeneid*.

SEPTIMUS. She did not understand the satire, and was showing politeness to
a guest.

THOMASINA. She is vexed with papa for his determination to alter the park,
but that alone cannot account for her politeness to a guest. She came
downstairs hours before her custom. Lord Byron was amusing at breakfast.   40
He paid you a tribute, Septimus.

SEPTIMUS. Did he?

THOMASINA. He said you were a witty fellow, and he had almost by heart
an article you wrote about—well, I forget what, but it concerned a book
called "The Maid of Turkey" and how you would not give it to your dog   45
for dinner.

SEPTIMUS. Ah. Mr. Chater was at breakfast, of course.

THOMASINA. He was, not like certain lazybones.

SEPTIMUS. He does not have Latin to set and mathematics to correct.

(*He takes Thomasina's lesson book from underneath Plautus and tosses it
down the table to her.*)

THOMASINA. Correct? What was incorrect in it? (*She looks into the book.*)   50
Alpha minus? Pooh! What is the minus for?

SEPTIMUS. For doing more than was asked.

THOMASINA. You did not like my discovery?

SEPTIMUS. A fancy is not a discovery.

THOMASINA. A gibe is not a rebuttal.   55

(*Septimus finishes what he is writing. He folds the pages into a letter. He
has sealing wax and the means to melt it. He seals the letter and writes on
the cover. Meanwhile—*)

You are churlish with me because mama is paying attention to your friend.
Well, let them elope, they cannot turn back the advancement of knowledge. I think it is an excellent discovery. Each week I plot your equations
dot for dot, xs against ys in all manner of algebraical relation, and every
week they draw themselves as commonplace geometry, as if the world of   60
forms were nothing but arcs and angles. God's truth, Septimus, if there is
an equation for a curve like a bell, there must be an equation for one like a
bluebell, and if a bluebell, why not a rose? Do we believe nature is written
in numbers?

SEPTIMUS. We do.   65

THOMASINA. Then why do your equations only describe the shapes of manufacture?

SEPTIMUS. I do not know.

THOMASINA. Armed thus, God could only make a cabinet.

70 SEPTIMUS. He has mastery of equations which lead into infinities where we
    cannot follow.

THOMASINA. What a faint-heart! We must work outward from the middle of
    the maze. We will start with something simple. (*She picks up the apple leaf.*)
    I will plot this leaf and deduce its equation. You will be famous for being
75 my tutor when Lord Byron is dead and forgotten.

    (*Septimus completes the business with his letter. He puts the letter in his
    pocket.*)

SEPTIMUS. (*Firmly*) Back to Cleopatra.[1]

THOMASINA. Is it Cleopatra?—I hate Cleopatra!

SEPTIMUS. You hate her? Why?

THOMASINA. Everything is turned to love with her. New love, absent love,
80 lost love—I never knew a heroine that makes such noodles of our sex. It
    only needs a Roman general to drop anchor outside the window and away
    goes the empire like a christening mug into a pawn shop. If Queen Eliza-
    beth had been a Ptolemy[2] history would have been quite different—we
    would be admiring the pyramids of Rome and the great Sphinx of Verona.

85 SEPTIMUS. God save us.

THOMASINA. But instead, the Egyptian noodle made carnal embrace with the
    enemy who burned the great library of Alexandria[3] without so much as a
    fine for all that is overdue. Oh, Septimus!—can you bear it? All the lost
    plays of the Athenians! Two hundred at least by Aeschylus, Sophocles, Eu-
90 ripides—thousands of poems—Aristotle's[4] own library brought to Egypt
    by the noodle's ancestors! How can we sleep for grief?

---

1   *Cleopatra* Cleopatra VII Philopator (c. 69–30 BCE), Egyptian pharaoh often remembered
    for her political alliances and romantic relationships with Julius Caesar and later Marc
    Antony. When it became clear that Egypt would fall to Roman rule, Cleopatra commit-
    ted suicide.

2   *Queen Elizabeth* Elizabeth I (1533–1603), queen of England, a very successful ruler. She
    never married and was known as "The Virgin Queen"; *Ptolemy* Member of the Ptol-
    emaic dynasty, which ruled Egypt from 323 BCE until the death of Cleopatra, who was
    the last Ptolemaic pharaoh.

3   *great library of Alexandria* One of the most important libraries of the ancient world until
    its destruction by fire. It is not known exactly when the fire occurred, but a popular story
    is that Julius Caesar caused it accidentally as he was destroying a fleet of his own ships in
    48 BCE. The last existing copies of many ancient works are thought to have been lost in
    the fire.

4   *Aeschylus, Sophocles, Euripides* Considered to be the three greatest tragedians of ancient
    Greece. Only a fraction of their work survives in complete form; *Aristotle* Greek phi-
    losopher (384–322 BCE) considered one of the most important figures in the history of
    Western thought.

SEPTIMUS. By counting our stock. Seven plays from Aeschylus, seven from
Sophocles, *nineteen* from Euripides, my lady! You should no more grieve
for the rest than for a buckle lost from your first shoe, or for your lesson
book which will be lost when you are old. We shed as we pick up, like   95
travellers who must carry everything in their arms, and what we let fall
will be picked up by those behind. The procession is very long and life is
very short. We die on the march. But there is nothing outside the march
so nothing can be lost to it. The missing plays of Sophocles will turn up
piece by piece, or be written again in another language. Ancient cures   100
for diseases will reveal themselves once more. Mathematical discoveries
glimpsed and lost to view will have their time again. You do not suppose,
my lady, that if all of Archimedes[1] had been hiding in the great library of
Alexandria, we would be at a loss for a corkscrew? I have no doubt that the
improved steam-driven heat-engine which puts Mr. Noakes into an ecstasy   105
that he and it and the modern age should all coincide, was described on
papyrus.[2] Steam and brass were not invented in Glasgow. Now, where are
we? Let me see if I can attempt a free translation for you. At Harrow I was
better at this than Lord Byron.

> (*He takes the piece of paper from her and scrutinizes it, testing one or two
> Latin phrases speculatively before committing himself.*)

Yes—"The barge she sat in, like a burnished throne ... burned on the water   110
... the—something—the poop was beaten gold, purple the sails, and—
what's this?—oh yes,—so perfumed that[3]—"
THOMASINA. (*Catching on and furious*) Cheat!
SEPTIMUS. (*Imperturbably*) "—the winds were lovesick with them ..."
THOMASINA. Cheat!   115
SEPTIMUS. "... the oars were silver which to the tune of flutes kept stroke ..."
THOMASINA. (*Jumping to her feet*) Cheat! Cheat! Cheat!
SEPTIMUS. (*As though it were too easy to make the effort worthwhile*) "... and
made the water which they beat to follow faster, as *amorous* of their strokes.
For her own person, it beggared all description—she did lie in her pavil-   120
ion—"

> (*Thomasina, in tears of rage, is hurrying out through the garden.*)

---

1   *Archimedes* Ancient Greek mathematician and physicist (287–212 BCE); one of his surviving works is titled *On Spirals*.
2   *papyrus* Material similar to paper; it was used for writing by the ancient Egyptians.
3   *The barge ...perfumed that* From Shakespeare's *Antony and Cleopatra* 2.2.902–11. Septimus has translated the passage into Latin and given it to Thomasina to translate back into
English; his supposed "free translation" is actually a memorized quotation.

THOMASINA. I hope you die!

> (*She nearly bumps into Brice who is entering. She runs out of sight. Brice enters.*)

BRICE. Good God, man, what have you told her?

SEPTIMUS. Told her? Told her what?

125 BRICE. Hodge!

> (*Septimus looks outside the door, slightly contrite about Thomasina, and sees that Chater is skulking out of view.*)

SEPTIMUS. Chater! My dear fellow! Don't hang back—come in, sir!

> (*Chater allows himself to be drawn sheepishly into the room, where Brice stands on his dignity.*)

CHATER. Captain Brice does me the honour—I mean to say, sir, whatever you have to say to me, sir, address yourself to Captain Brice.

SEPTIMUS. How unusual. (*To Brice*) Your wife did not appear yesterday, sir. I

130 trust she is not sick?

BRICE. My wife? I have no wife. What the devil do you mean, sir?

> (*Septimus makes to reply, but hesitates, puzzled. He turns back to Chater.*)

SEPTIMUS. I do not understand the scheme, Chater. Whom do I address when I want to speak to Captain Brice?

BRICE. Oh, slippery, Hodge—slippery!

135 SEPTIMUS. (*To Chater*) By the way, Chater—(*he interrupts himself and turns back to Brice, and continues as before*) by the way, Chater, I have amazing news to tell you. Someone has taken to writing wild and whirling letters in your name. I received one not half an hour ago.

BRICE. (*Angrily*) Mr. Hodge! Look to your honour, sir! If you cannot attend

140 to me without this foolery, nominate your second[1] who might settle the business as between gentlemen. No doubt your friend Byron would do you the service.

> (*Septimus gives up the game.*)

SEPTIMUS. Oh yes, he would do me the service. (*His mood changes, he turns to Chater.*) Sir—I repent your injury. You are an honest fellow with no more

145 malice in you than poetry.

CHATER. (*Happily*) Ah well!—that is more like the thing! (*Overtaken by doubt.*) Is he apologizing?

---

1   *second* Person who assists the primary fighter in a duel.

BRICE. There is still the injury to his conjugal property, Mrs. Chater's—

CHATER. Tush,[1] sir!

BRICE. As you will—her tush. Nevertheless—   150

> (*But they are interrupted by Lady Croom, also entering from the garden.*)

LADY CROOM. Oh—excellently found! Mr. Chater, this will please you very
   much. Lord Byron begs a copy of your new book. He dies to read it and
   intends to include your name in the second edition of his *English Bards
   and Scotch Reviewers.*

CHATER. *English Bards and Scotch Reviewers*, your ladyship, is a doggerel[2]   155
   aimed at Lord Byron's seniors and betters. If he intends to include me, he
   intends to insult me.

LADY CROOM. Well, of course he does, Mr. Chater. Would you rather be
   thought not worth insulting? You should be proud to be in the company
   of Rogers and Moore[3] and Wordsworth—ah! "The Couch of Eros!" (*For*   160
   she has spotted Septimus's copy of the book on the table.)

SEPTIMUS. That is my copy, madam.

LADY CROOM. So much the better—what are a friend's books for if not to
   be borrowed?

> (*Note: "The Couch of Eros" now contains the three letters, and it must do so
> without advertising the fact. This is why the volume has been described as
> a substantial quarto.*)

Mr. Hodge, you must speak to your friend and put him out of his affecta-   165
tion of pretending to quit us. I will not have it. He says he is determined
on the Malta packet sailing out of Falmouth! His head is full of Lisbon and
Lesbos, and his portmanteau[4] of pistols, and I have told him it is not to be
thought of. The whole of Europe is in a Napoleonic[5] fit, all the best ruins
will be closed, the roads entirely occupied with the movement of armies,   170
the lodgings turned to billets and the fashion for godless republicanism not

---

1   *Tush* Slang expression of disapproval; its alternative meaning of "rear end" is punningly
     suggested in the next line.

2   *doggerel* Poorly written verse.

3   *Rogers* English poet Samuel Rogers (1763–1855); *Moore* Thomas Moore (1779–1852),
     Irish poet and musician.

4   *Malta* European island country located in the Mediterranean Sea; *packet* Ship that runs
     a pre-determined route with scheduled stops; *Falmouth* Falmouth harbour in Cornwall,
     England; *Lisbon* Capital city of Portugal; *Lesbos* Greek island; *portmanteau* Luggage
     bag.

5   *Napoleonic* Reference to the Napoleonic Wars (1803–15) in which the French Empire,
     under the leadership of Napoleon Bonaparte, conquered much of Europe and then lost
     it.

yet arrived at its natural reversion. He says his aim is poetry. One does not aim at poetry with pistols. At poets, perhaps. I charge you to take command of his pistols, Mr. Hodge! He is not safe with them. His lameness,[1] he confessed to me, is entirely the result of his habit from boyhood of shooting himself in the foot. What is that *noise*?

(*The noise is a badly played piano in the next room. It has been going on for some time since Thomasina left.*)

SEPTIMUS. The new Broadwood pianoforte,[2] madam. Our music lessons are at an early stage.

LADY CROOM. Well, restrict your lessons to the *piano* side of the instrument and let her loose on the *forte*[3] when she has learned something.

(*Lady Croom, holding the book, sails out back into the garden.*)

BRICE. Now! If that was not God speaking through Lady Croom, he never spoke through anyone!

CHATER. (*Awed*) Take command of Lord Byron's pistols!

BRICE. You hear Mr. Chater, sir—how will you answer him?

(*Septimus has been watching Lady Croom's progress up the garden. He turns back.*)

SEPTIMUS. By killing him. I am tired of him.

CHATER. (*Startled*) Eh?

BRICE. (*Pleased*) Ah!

SEPTIMUS. Oh, damn your soul, Chater! Ovid would have stayed a lawyer and Virgil a farmer if they had known the bathos to which love would descend in your sportive satyrs and noodle nymphs![4] I am at your service with a half-ounce ball[5] in your brain. May it satisfy you—behind the boathouse at daybreak—shall we say five o'clock? My compliments to Mrs. Chater—have no fear for her, she will not want for protection while Captain Brice has a guinea[6] in his pocket, he told her so himself.

BRICE. You lie, sir!

---

1   *His lameness* Byron suffered from a club foot.

2   *Broadwood pianoforte* Piano made by well-known manufacturer Broadwood and Sons.

3   *piano ... forte* The word "*pianoforte*" comes from the musical terms "*piano*" and "*forte*," directives to play softly and loudly, respectively.

4   *Ovid* Roman poet (43 BCE–c. 17 CE) famous for *Metamorphoses*. He studied law before becoming a writer; *bathos* Ridiculousness caused by a writer's unintentional descent from an elevated subject or tone to a trivial one; *satyrs* Greek mythological goat-men. In classical art and literature, they are often depicted in the lustful pursuit of nymphs; *nymphs* In Greek mythology, beautiful female nature spirits.

5   *half-ounce ball* Musket ball used as ammunition in duelling pistols.

6   *guinea* Gold coin worth about 21 shillings.

SEPTIMUS. No, sir. Mrs. Chater, perhaps.

BRICE. You lie, or you will answer to me!

SEPTIMUS. (*Wearily*) Oh, very well—I can fit you in at five minutes after five. And then it's off to the Malta packet out of Falmouth. You two will be dead, my penurious[1] schoolfriend will remain to tutor Lady Thomasina,   200 and I trust everybody including Lady Croom will be satisfied!

(*Septimus slams the door behind him.*)

BRICE. He is all bluster and bladder. Rest assured, Chater, I will let the air out of him.

(*Brice leaves by the other door. Chater's assurance lasts only a moment. When he spots the flaw ...*)

CHATER. Oh! But ... Captain Brice ...!

(*He hurries out after Brice.*)

ACT 1, SCENE 4

Hannah and Valentine. She is reading aloud. He is listening. Lightning, the tortoise, is on the table and is not readily distinguishable from Plautus. In front of Valentine is Septimus's portfolio, recognizably so but naturally somewhat faded. It is open. Principally associated with the portfolio (although it may contain sheets of blank paper also) are three items: a slim maths primer; a sheet of drawing paper on which there is a scrawled diagram and some mathematical notations, arrow marks, etc.; and Thomasina's mathematics lesson book, i.e., the one she writes in, which Valentine is leafing through as he listens to Hannah reading from the primer.

HANNAH. "I, Thomasina Coverly, have found a truly wonderful method whereby all the forms of nature must give up their numerical secrets and draw themselves through number alone. This margin being too mean for my purpose, the reader must look elsewhere for the New Geometry of Irregular Forms discovered by Thomasina Coverly."   5

(*Pause. She hands Valentine the text book. Valentine looks at what she has been reading.*
From the next room, a piano is heard, beginning to play quietly, unintrusively, improvisationally.)

Does it mean anything?

---

1   *penurious* Very poor.

VALENTINE. I don't know. I don't know what it means, except mathematically.

HANNAH. I meant mathematically.

VALENTINE. (*Now with the lesson book again*) It's an iterated algorithm.

10 HANNAH. What's that?

VALENTINE. Well, it's ... Jesus ... it's an algorithm that's been ... iterated. How'm I supposed to ...? (*He makes an effort.*) The left-hand pages are graphs of what the numbers are doing on the right-hand pages. But all on different scales. Each graph is a small section of the previous one, blown

15 up. Like you'd blow up a detail of a photograph, and then a detail of the detail, and soon, forever. Or in her case, till she ran out of pages.

HANNAH. Is it difficult?

VALENTINE. The maths isn't difficult. It's what you did at school. You have some *x*-and-*y* equation. Any value for *x* gives you a value for *y*. So you

20 put a dot where it's right for both *x* and *y*. Then you take the next value for *x* which gives you another value for *y*, and when you've done that a few times you join up the dots and that's your graph of whatever the equation is.

HANNAH. And is that what she's doing?

25 VALENTINE. No. Not exactly. Not at all. What she's doing is, every time she works out a value for *y*, she's using *that* as her next value for *x*. And so on. Like a feedback. She's feeding the solution back into the equation, and then solving it again. Iteration, you see.

HANNAH. And that's surprising, is it?

30 VALENTINE. Well, it is a bit. It's the technique I'm using on my grouse numbers, and it hasn't been around for much longer than, well, call it twenty years.

(*Pause.*)

HANNAH. Why would she be doing it?

VALENTINE. I have no idea.

(*Pause.*)

35 I thought you were doing the hermit.

HANNAH. I am. I still am. But Bernard, damn him ... Thomasina's tutor turns out to have interesting connections. Bernard is going through the library like a bloodhound. The portfolio was in a cupboard.

VALENTINE. There's a lot of stuff around. Gus loves going through it. No old

40 masters or anything ...

HANNAH. The maths primer she was using belonged to him—the tutor; he wrote his name in it.

VALENTINE. (*Reading*) "Septimus Hodge."

HANNAH. Why were these things saved, do you think?

VALENTINE. Why should there be a reason?   45

HANNAH. And the diagram, what's it of?

VALENTINE. How would I know?

HANNAH. Why are you cross?

VALENTINE. I'm not cross. (*Pause.*) When your Thomasina was doing maths it had been the same maths for a couple of thousand years. Classical. And   50 for a century after Thomasina. Then maths left the real world behind, just like modern art, really. Nature was classical, maths was suddenly Picassos.[1] But now nature is having the last laugh. The freaky stuff is turning out to be the mathematics of the natural world.

HANNAH. This feedback thing?   55

VALENTINE. For example.

HANNAH. Well, could Thomasina have—

VALENTINE. (*Snaps*) No, of course she bloody couldn't!

HANNAH. All right, you're not cross. What did you mean you were doing the same thing she was doing? (*Pause.*) What *are* you doing?   60

VALENTINE. Actually I'm doing it from the other end. She started with an equation and turned it into a graph. I've got a graph—real data—and I'm trying to find the equation which would give you the graph if you used it the way she's used hers. Iterated it.

HANNAH. What for?   65

VALENTINE. It's how you look at population changes in biology. Goldfish in a pond, say. This year there are x goldfish. Next year there'll be y goldfish. Some get born, some get eaten by herons, whatever. Nature manipulates the x and turns it into y. Then y goldfish is your starting population for the following year. Just like Thomasina. Your value for y becomes your next   70 value for x. The question is: what is being done to x? What is the manipulation? Whatever it is, it can be written down as mathematics. It's called an algorithm.

HANNAH. It can't be the same every year.

VALENTINE. The details change, you can't keep tabs on everything, it's not   75 nature in a box. But it isn't necessary to know the details. When they are all put together, it turns out the population is obeying a mathematical rule.

HANNAH. The goldfish are?

VALENTINE. Yes. No. The numbers. It's not about the behaviour of fish. It's about the behaviour of numbers. This thing works for any phenomenon   80

---

1   *Picassos* Reference to the Spanish painter Pablo Picasso (1881–1973), best known for his work in Cubism, a movement in which artists attempted to portray objects as though seen from multiple perspectives at once.

which eats its own numbers—measles, epidemics, rainfall averages, cotton prices, it's a natural phenomenon in itself. Spooky.

HANNAH. Does it work for grouse?

VALENTINE. I don't know yet. I mean, it does undoubtedly, but it's hard to show. There's more noise with grouse.

HANNAH. Noise?

VALENTINE. Distortions. Interference. Real data is messy. There's a thousand acres of moorland that had grouse on it, always did till about 1930. But nobody counted the grouse. They shot them. So you count the grouse they shot. But burning the heather interferes, it improves the food supply. A good year for foxes interferes the other way, they eat the chicks. And then there's the weather. It's all very, very noisy out there. Very hard to spot the tune. Like a piano in the next room, it's playing your song, but unfortunately it's out of whack, some of the strings are missing, and the pianist is tone deaf and drunk—I mean, the *noise*! Impossible!

HANNAH. What do you do?

VALENTINE. You start guessing what the tune might be. You try to pick it out of the noise. You try this, you try that, you start to get something—it's half-baked but you start putting in notes which are missing or not quite the right notes ... and bit by bit ... (*He starts to dumdi-da to the tune of "Happy Birthday."*) Dumdi-dum-dum, dear Val-en-tine, dumdi-dum-dum to you—the lost algorithm!

HANNAH. (*Soberly*) Yes, I see. And then what?

VALENTINE. I publish.

HANNAH. Of course. Sorry. Jolly good.

VALENTINE. That's the theory. Grouse are bastards compared to goldfish.

HANNAH. Why did you choose them?

VALENTINE. The game books. My true inheritance. Two hundred years of real data on a plate.

HANNAH. Somebody wrote down everything that's shot?

VALENTINE. Well, that's what a game book is. I'm only using from 1870, when butts and beaters[1] came in.

HANNAH. You mean the game books go back to Thomasina's time?

VALENTINE. Oh yes. Further. (*And then getting ahead of her thought.*) No— really. I promise you. I *promise* you. Not a schoolgirl living in a country house in Derbyshire in eighteen-something!

HANNAH. Well, what was she doing?

---

1   *butts* Camouflaged bird blinds used in grouse hunting; *beaters* Workers who drive game out of sheltered areas toward a blind by making noise by or swinging sticks.

VALENTINE. She was just playing with the numbers. The truth is, she wasn't
    doing anything.

HANNAH. She must have been doing something.   120

VALENTINE. Doodling. Nothing she understood.

HANNAH. A monkey at a typewriter?[1]

VALENTINE. Yes. Well, a piano.

> (*Hannah picks up the algebra book and reads from it.*)

HANNAH. "... a method whereby all the forms of nature must give up their
    numerical secrets and draw themselves through number alone." This feed-   125
    back, is it a way of making pictures of forms in nature? Just tell me if it is
    or it isn't.

VALENTINE. (*Irritated*) To *me* it is. Pictures of turbulence—growth—
    change—creation—it's not a way of drawing an elephant, for God's sake!

HANNAH. I'm sorry.   130

> (*She picks up an apple leaf from the table. She is timid about pushing the
> point.*)

So you couldn't make a picture of this leaf by iterating a whatsit?

VALENTINE. (*Off-hand*) Oh yes, you could do that.

HANNAH. (*Furiously*) Well, tell me! Honestly, I could kill you!

VALENTINE. If you knew the algorithm and fed it back say ten thousand
    times, each time there'd be a dot somewhere on the screen. You'd never   135
    know where to expect the next dot. But gradually you'd start to see this
    shape, because every dot will be inside the shape of this leaf. It wouldn't *be*
    a leaf, it would be a mathematical object. But yes. The unpredictable and
    the predetermined unfold together to make everything the way it is. It's
    how nature creates itself, on every scale, the snowflake and the snowstorm.   140
    It makes me so happy. To be at the beginning again, knowing almost noth-
    ing. People were talking about the end of physics. Relativity and quan-
    tum[2] looked as if they were going to clean out the whole problem between
    them. A theory of everything. But they only explained the very big and
    the very small. The universe, the elementary particles. The ordinary-sized   145
    stuff which is our lives, the things people write poetry about—clouds—

---

1   *monkey ... typewriter* Refers to the popular idea that, given infinite time, a monkey ran-
     domly hitting keys on a typewriter would eventually hit the right combinations to repro-
     duce the works of Shakespeare.

2   *Relativity and quantum* Twentieth-century advances in physics that address phenomena
     Newtonian physics does not. The theory of relativity describes the motion of objects at
     extreme speeds and levels of gravity, while quantum mechanics applies to the behaviour
     of particles at the atomic level.

daffodils—waterfalls—and what happens in a cup of coffee when the cream goes in—these things are full of mystery, as mysterious to us as the heavens were to the Greeks. We're better at predicting events at the edge

150 of the galaxy or inside the nucleus of an atom than whether it'll rain on auntie's garden party three Sundays from now. Because the problem turns out to be different. We can't even predict the next drip from a dripping tap when it gets irregular. Each drip sets up the conditions for the next, the smallest variation blows prediction apart, and the weather is unpredictable

155 the same way, will always be unpredictable. When you push the numbers through the computer you can see it on the screen. The future is disorder. A door like this has cracked open five or six times since we got up on our hind legs. It's the best possible time to be alive, when almost everything you thought you knew is wrong.

(*Pause.*)

160 HANNAH. The weather is fairly predictable in the Sahara.[1]
VALENTINE. The scale is different but the graph goes up and down the same way. Six thousand years in the Sahara looks like six months in Manchester, I bet you.
HANNAH. How much?
165 VALENTINE. Everything you have to lose.
HANNAH. (*Pause*) No.
VALENTINE. Quite right. That's why there was corn in Egypt.[2]

(*Hiatus. The piano is heard again.*)

HANNAH. What is he playing?
VALENTINE. I don't know. He makes it up.
170 HANNAH. Chloë called him "genius."
VALENTINE. It's what my mother calls him—only *she* means it. Last year some expert had her digging in the wrong place for months to find something or other—the foundations of Capability Brown's boat-house—and Gus put her right first go.
175 HANNAH. Did he ever speak?
VALENTINE. Oh yes. Until he was five. You've never asked about him. You get high marks here for good breeding.
HANNAH. Yes, I know. I've always been given credit for my unconcern.

(*Bernard enters in high excitement and triumph.*)

---

1   *Sahara* Largest desert in the world, located in Northern Africa.
2   *corn in Egypt* See Genesis 42.1. In Genesis 41, Joseph predicts seven years of abundance followed by seven years of famine.

BERNARD.   *English Bards and Scotch Reviewers.* A pencilled superscription.
Listen and kiss my cycle-clips!   180

(*He is carrying the book. He reads from it.*)

"O harbinger of Sleep, who missed the press
And hoped his drone might thus escape redress!
The wretched Chater, bard of Eros' Couch,
For his narcotic let my pencil vouch!"

You see, *you have to turn over every page.*   185
HANNAH.   Is it his handwriting?
BERNARD.   Oh, come *on.*
HANNAH.   Obviously not.
BERNARD.   Christ, what do you want?
HANNAH.   Proof.   190
VALENTINE.   Quite right. Who are you talking about?
BERNARD.   Proof? *Proof?* You'd have to be there, you silly bitch!
VALENTINE.   (*Mildly*) I say, you're speaking of my fiancée.
HANNAH.   Especially when I have a present for you. Guess what I found.
(*Producing the present for Bernard.*) Lady Croom writing from London to 195
her husband. Her brother, Captain Brice, married a Mrs. Chater. In other
words, one might assume, a widow.

(*Bernard looks at the letter.*)

BERNARD.   I *said* he was dead. What year? 1810! Oh my God, 1810! Well
done, Hannah! Are you going to tell me it's a different Mrs. Chater?
HANNAH.   Oh no. It's her all right. Note her Christian name.   200
BERNARD.   Charity. Charity ... "Deny what cannot be proven for Charity's sake!"
HANNAH.   Don't kiss me!
VALENTINE.   She won't let anyone kiss her.
BERNARD.   You see! They wrote—they scribbled—they put it on paper. It was
their employment. Their diversion. Paper is what they had. And there'll be 205
more. There is always more. We can find it!
HANNAH.   Such passion. First Valentine, now you. It's moving.
BERNARD.   The aristocratic friend of the tutor—under the same roof as the
poor sod whose book he savaged—the first thing he does is seduce Chater's
wife. All is discovered. There is a duel. Chater dead, Byron fled! P.S. guess 210
what?, the widow married her ladyship's brother! Do you honestly think
no one wrote a word? How could they not! It dropped from sight but we
will write it again!
HANNAH.   You can, Bernard. I'm not going to take any credit, I haven't done
anything.   215

(*The same thought has clearly occurred to Bernard. He becomes instantly po-faced.*[1])

BERNARD. Well, that's—very fair—generous—
HANNAH. Prudent. Chater could have died of anything, anywhere.

(*The po-face is forgotten.*)

BERNARD. But he fought a duel with Byron!
HANNAH. You haven't established it was fought. You haven't established it
220   was Byron. For God's sake, Bernard, you haven't established Byron was
even here!
BERNARD. I'll tell you your problem. No guts.
HANNAH. Really?
BERNARD. By which I mean a visceral belief in yourself. Gut instinct. The
225   part of you which doesn't reason. The certainty for which there is no back-
reference. Because time is reversed. Tock, tick goes the universe and then
recovers itself, but it was enough, you were in there and you bloody *know.*
VALENTINE. Are you talking about Lord Byron, the poet?
BERNARD. No, you fucking idiot, we're talking about Lord Byron the char-
230   tered accountant.
VALENTINE. (*Unoffended*) Oh well, *he* was here all right, the poet.

(*Silence.*)

HANNAH. How do you know?
VALENTINE. He's in the game book. I think he shot a hare. I read through
the whole lot once when I had mumps—some quite interesting people—
235 HANNAH. Where's the book?
VALENTINE. It's not one I'm using—too early, of course—
HANNAH. 1809.
VALENTINE. They've always been in the commode. Ask Chloë.

(*Hannah looks to Bernard. Bernard has been silent because he has been incapable of speech. He seems to have gone into a trance, in which only his mouth tries to work. Hannah steps over to him and gives him a demure kiss on the cheek. It works. Bernard lurches out into the garden and can be heard croaking for "Chloë ... Chloë!"*)

VALENTINE. My mother's lent him her bicycle. Lending one's bicycle is a form
240   of safe sex, possibly the safest there is. My mother is in a flutter about Bernard, and he's no fool. He gave her a first edition of Horace Walpole, and
now she's lent him her bicycle.

1   *po-faced* I.e., with a disapproving expression.

(*He gathers up the three items* [*the primer, the lesson book and the diagram*] *and puts them into the portfolio.*)

Can I keep these for a while?

HANNAH. Yes, of course.

(*The piano stops. Gus enters hesitantly from the music room.*)

VALENTINE. (*To Gus*) Yes, finished ... coming now. (*To Hannah*) I'm trying to   245
work out the diagram.

(*Gus nods and smiles, at Hannah too, but she is preoccupied.*)

HANNAH. What I don't understand is ... why nobody did this feedback thing
before—it's not like relativity, you don't have to be Einstein.[1]
VALENTINE. You couldn't see to look before. The electronic calculator was
what the telescope was for Galileo.[2]   250
HANNAH. Calculator?
VALENTINE. There wasn't enough time before. There weren't enough *pencils*!
(*He flourishes Thomasina's lesson book.*) This took her I don't know how
many days and she hasn't scratched the paintwork. Now she'd only have to
press a button, the same button over and over. Iteration. A few minutes.   255
And what I've done in a couple of months, with only a *pencil* the calculations would take me the rest of my life to do again—thousands of pages—
tens of thousands! And so boring!
HANNAH. Do you mean—?

(*She stops because Gus is plucking Valentine's sleeve.*)

Do you mean—?   260
VALENTINE. All right, Gus, I'm coming.
HANNAH. Do you mean that was the only problem? Enough time? And pa-
per? And the boredom?
VALENTINE. We're going to get out the dressing-up box.
HANNAH. (*Driven to raising her voice*) Val! Is that what you're saying?   265
VALENTINE. (*Surprised by her. Mildly*) No, I'm saying you'd have to have a
reason for doing it.

(*Gus runs out of the room, upset.*)

(*Apologetically*) He hates people shouting.

---

1 *Einstein* Albert Einstein (1876–1955), German-born physicist responsible for the theory
of relativity.
2 *Galileo* Galileo Galilei (1564–1642), Italian physicist and astronomer; the discoveries he
made using early telescopes transformed the study of astronomy.

HANNAH. I'm sorry.

(*Valentine starts to follow Gus.*)

270   But anything else?

VALENTINE. Well, the other thing is, you'd have to be insane.

(*Valentine leaves.*

Hannah stays, thoughtful. After a moment, she turns to the table and picks up the Cornhill Magazine. She looks into it briefly, then closes it, and, after going to look at the open page showing Noake's hermitage on the reading stand, she leaves the room, taking the magazine with her.

The empty room.

The light changes to early morning. From a long way off, there is a pistol shot. A moment later there is the cry of dozens of crows disturbed from the unseen trees.)

ACT 2, SCENE 5[1]

Bernard is pacing around, reading aloud from a handful of typed sheets. Valentine, Chloë and Gus are his audience. Gus sits somewhat apart, perhaps less attentive. Valentine has his tortoise and is eating a sandwich from which he extracts shreds of lettuce to offer the tortoise.

BERNARD. "Did it happen? Could it happen?

"Undoubtedly it could. Only three years earlier the Irish poet Tom Moore appeared on the field of combat to avenge a review by Jeffrey of the *Edinburgh*. These affairs were seldom fatal and sometimes farcical but,
5   potentially, the duellist stood in respect to the law no differently from a murderer. As for the murderee, a minor poet like Ezra Chater could go to his death in a Derbyshire glade as unmissed and unremembered as his contemporary and namesake, the minor botanist who died in the forests of the West Indies, lost to history like the monkey that bit him. On April
10   16th 1809, a few days after he left Sidley Park, Byron wrote to his solicitor John Hanson: 'If the consequences of my leaving England were ten times as ruinous as you describe, I have no alternative; there are circumstances which render it absolutely indispensable, and quit the country I must immediately.' To which, the editor's note in the Collected Letters reads as
15   follows: 'What Byron's urgent reasons for leaving England were at this time has never been revealed.' The letter was written from the family seat, Newstead Abbey, Nottinghamshire. A long day's ride to the north-west

---

1   ACT 2, Scene 5 As in the 1993 published version of *Arcadia*, scene numbers for this play do not restart at the beginning of the second act.

lay Sidley Park, the estate of the Coverlys—a far grander family, raised by
Charles II[1] to the Earldom of Croom ...”

(*Hannah enters briskly, a piece of paper in her hand.*)

HANNAH. Bernard ...! Val ...   20
BERNARD. Do you mind?

(*Hannah puts her piece of paper down in front of Valentine.*)

CHLOË. (*Angrily*) *Hannah*!
HANNAH. What?
CHLOË. She's so *rude*!
HANNAH. (*Taken aback*) What? Am I?   25
VALENTINE. Bernard's reading us his lecture.
HANNAH. Yes, I know. (*Then recollecting herself.*) Yes—yes—that *was* rude.
  I'm sorry, Bernard.
VALENTINE. (*With the piece of paper*) What is this?
HANNAH. (*To Bernard*) Spot on—the India Office Library. (*To Valentine*) 30
  Peacock's letter in holograph, I got a copy sent—
CHLOË. *Hannah*! Shut up!
HANNAH. (*Sitting down*) Yes, sorry.
BERNARD. It's all right, I'll read it to myself.
CHLOË. *No.*   35

(*Hannah reaches for the Peacock letter and takes it back.*)

HANNAH. Go on, Bernard. Have I missed anything? Sorry.

(*Bernard stares at her balefully but then continues to read.*)

BERNARD. “The Byrons of Newstead in 1809 comprised an eccentric widow
  and her undistinguished son, the 'lame brat,' who until the age of ten
  when he came into the title, had been carted about the country from lodging to lodging by his vulgar hectoring monster of a mother—” (*Hannah's* 40
  hand has gone up)—overruled—“and who four months past his twenty-
  first birthday was master of nothing but his debts and his genius. Between
  the Byrons and the Coverlys there was no social equality and none to be
  expected. The connection, undisclosed to posterity until now, was with
  Septimus Hodge, Byron's friend at Harrow and Trinity College—” (*Han-* 45
  nah's hand goes up again)—sustained—(*He makes an instant correction with*
  a silver pencil.) “Byron's contemporary at Harrow and Trinity College,
  and now tutor in residence to the Croom daughter, Thomasina Coverly.

---

1   *Charles II* King of England, Scotland, and Ireland from 1660–85.

50   Byron's letters tell us where he was on April 8th and on April 12th. He was at Newstead. But on the 10th he was at Sidley Park, as attested by the game book preserved there: 'April 10th 1809—forenoon. High cloud, dry, and sun between times, wind southeasterly. Self—Augustus—Lord Byron. Fourteen pigeon, one hare (Lord B.).' But, as we know now, the drama of life and death at Sidley Park was not about pigeons but about sex and
55   literature."

VALENTINE.   Unless you were the pigeon.

BERNARD.   I don't have to do this. I'm paying you a compliment.

CHLOË.   Ignore him, Bernard—go on, get to the duel.

BERNARD.   Hannah's not even paying attention.

60   HANNAH.   Yes I am, it's all going in. I often work with the radio on.

BERNARD.   Oh thanks!

HANNAH.   Is there much more?

CHLOË.   *Hannah!*

HANNAH.   No, it's fascinating. I just wondered how much more there was. I
65   need to ask Valentine about this (*letter*)—sorry, Bernard, go on, this will keep.

VALENTINE.   Yes—sorry, Bernard.

CHLOË.   Please, Bernard!

BERNARD.   Where was I?

70   VALENTINE.   Pigeons.

CHLOË.   Sex.

HANNAH.   Literature.

BERNARD.   Life and death. Right. "Nothing could be more eloquent of that than the three documents I have quoted: the terse demand to settle a mat-
75   ter in private; the desperate scribble of 'my husband has sent for pistols'; and on April 11th, the gauntlet thrown down by the aggrieved and cuck-olded author Ezra Chater. The covers have not survived. What is certain is that all three letters were in Byron's possession when his books were sold in 1816—preserved in the pages of 'The Couch of Eros' which seven years
80   earlier at Sidley Park Byron had borrowed from Septimus Hodge."

HANNAH.   Borrowed?

BERNARD.   I will be taking questions at the end. Constructive comments will be welcome. Which is indeed my reason for trying out in the provinces before my London opening under the auspices of the Byron Society prior
85   to publication. By the way, Valentine, do you want a credit?—"the game book recently discovered by"?

VALENTINE.   It was never lost, Bernard.

BERNARD.   "As recently pointed out by." I don't normally like giving credit where it's due, but with scholarly articles as with divorce, there is a certain

cachet in citing a member of the aristocracy. I'll pop it in ad lib for the 90
lecture, and give you a mention in the press release. How's that?

VALENTINE. Very kind.

HANNAH. Press release? What happened to the *Journal of English Studies*?

BERNARD. That comes later with the apparatus, and in the recognized tone—
very dry, very modest, absolutely gloat-free, and yet unmistakably "Eat 95
your heart out, you dozy bastards." But first, it's "Media Don, book early
to avoid disappointment." Where was I?

VALENTINE. Game book.

CHLOË. Eros.

HANNAH. Borrowed. 100

BERNARD. Right. "—borrowed from Septimus Hodge. Is it conceivable that
the letters were already in the book when Byron borrowed it?"

VALENTINE. Yes.

CHLOË. Shut up, Val.

VALENTINE. Well, it's conceivable. 105

BERNARD. "Is it *likely* that Hodge would have lent Byron the book without
first removing the three private letters?"

VALENTINE. Look, sorry—I only meant, Byron could have borrowed the
book without asking.

HANNAH. That's true. 110

BERNARD. Then why wouldn't Hodge get them back?

HANNAH. I don't know, I wasn't there.

BERNARD. That's right, you bloody weren't.

CHLOË. Go on, Bernard.

BERNARD. "It is the third document, the challenge itself, that convinces. 115
Chater 'as a man and a poet,' points the finger at his 'slanderer in the press.'
Neither as a man nor a poet did Ezra Chater cut such a figure as to be habitually slandered or even mentioned in the press. It is surely indisputable
that the slander was the review of 'The Maid of Turkey' in the *Piccadilly
Recreation*. Did Septimus Hodge have any connection with the London 120
periodicals? No. Did Byron? Yes! He had reviewed Wordsworth two years
earlier, he was to review Spencer[1] two years later. And do we have any clue
as to Byron's opinion of Chater the poet? Yes! Who but Byron could have
written the four lines pencilled into Lady Croom's copy of *English Bards
and Scotch Reviewers*—" 125

HANNAH. Almost anybody.

BERNARD. Darling—

HANNAH. Don't call me darling.

---

1 *Spencer* English poet William Spencer (1770–1834).

BERNARD. Dickhead, then, is it likely that the man Chater calls his friend
130   Septimus Hodge is the same man who screwed his wife and kicked the shit
       out of his last book?

HANNAH. Put it like that, almost certain.

CHLOË. (*Earnestly*) You've been deeply wounded in the past, haven't you,
       Hannah?

135 HANNAH. Nothing compared to listening to this. Why is there nothing in
       Byron's letters about the *Piccadilly* reviews?

BERNARD. Exactly. Because he killed the author.

HANNAH. But the first one, "The Maid of Turkey," was the year before. Was
       he clairvoyant?

140 CHLOË. Letters get lost.

BERNARD. Thank you! Exactly! There is a platonic letter which confirms ev-
       erything—lost but ineradicable, like radio voices rippling through the uni-
       verse for all eternity. "My dear Hodge—here I am in Albania and you're the
       only person in the whole world who knows why. Poor C! I never wished
145   him any harm—except in the *Piccadilly*, of course—it was the woman who
       bade me eat, dear Hodge!—what a tragic business, but thank God it ended
       well for poetry. Yours ever, B.—PS. Burn this."

VALENTINE. How did Chater find out the reviewer was Byron?

BERNARD. (*Irritated*) I don't know, I wasn't there, was I? (*Pause. To Hannah*)
150   You wish to say something?

HANNAH. Moi?

CHLOË. I know. Byron told Mrs. Chater in bed. Next day he dumped her so
       she grassed[1] on him, and pleaded date rape.

BERNARD. (*Fastidiously*) Date rape? What do you mean, date rape?

155 HANNAH. April the tenth.

       (*Bernard cracks. Everything becomes loud and overlapped as Bernard
       threatens to walk out and is cajoled into continuing.*)

BERNARD. Right!—forget it!

HANNAH. Sorry—

BERNARD. No—I've had nothing but sarcasm and childish interruptions—

VALENTINE. What did I do?

160 BERNARD. No credit for probably the most sensational literary discovery of
       the century—

CHLOË. I think you're jolly unfair—they're jealous, Bernard—

HANNAH. I won't say another word—

---

1   *grassed* Told.

VALENTINE. Yes, go on, Bernard—we promise.

BERNARD. (*Finally*) Well, only if you stop *feeding tortoises*!   165

VALENTINE. Well, it's his lunch time.

BERNARD. And on condition that I am afforded the common courtesy of a scholar among scholars—

HANNAH. Absolutely mum till you're finished—

BERNARD. After which, any comments are to be couched in terms of accepted   170 academic—

HANNAH. Dignity—you're right, Bernard.

BERNARD. —respect.

HANNAH. Respect. Absolutely. The language of scholars. Count on it.

(*Having made a great show of putting his pages away, Bernard reassembles them and finds his place, glancing suspiciously at the other three for signs of levity.*)

BERNARD. Last paragraph. "Without question, Ezra Chater issued a chal-   175 lenge to *somebody*. If a duel was fought in the dawn mist of Sidley Park in April 1809, his opponent, on the evidence, was a critic with a gift for ridi-cule and a taste for seduction. Do we need to look far? Without question, Mrs. Chater was a widow by 1810. If we seek the occasion of Ezra Chater's early and unrecorded death, do we need to look far? Without question,   180 Lord Byron, in the very season of his emergence as a literary figure, quit the country in a cloud of panic and mystery, and stayed abroad for two years at a time when Continental travel was unusual and dangerous. If we seek his reason, *do we need to look far?*"

(*No mean performer, he is pleased with the effect of his peroration. There is a significant silence.*)

HANNAH. Bollocks.   185

CHLOË. Well, I think it's true.

HANNAH. You've left out everything which doesn't fit. Byron had been bang-ing on for months about leaving England—there's a letter in *February*—

BERNARD. But he didn't go, did he?

HANNAH. And then he didn't sail until the beginning of July!   190

BERNARD. Everything moved more slowly then. Time was different. He was two weeks in Falmouth waiting for wind or something—

HANNAH. Bernard, I don't know why I'm bothering—you're arrogant, greedy and reckless. You've gone from a glint in your eye to a sure thing in a hop, skip and a jump. You deserve what you get and I think you're mad. But I   195 can't help myself, you're like some exasperating child pedalling its tricycle towards the edge of a cliff, and I have to do something. So listen to me. If Byron killed Chater in a duel I'm Marie of Romania.[1] You'll end up with so much *fame* you won't leave the house without a paper bag over your head.

200 VALENTINE. Actually, Bernard, as a scientist, your theory is incomplete.

BERNARD. But I'm not a scientist.

VALENTINE. (*Patiently*) No, *as a scientist*—

BERNARD. (*Beginning to shout*) I have yet to hear a proper argument.

HANNAH. Nobody would kill a man and then pan his book. I mean, not in

205 that order. So he must have borrowed the book, written the review, *posted it*, seduced Mrs. Chater, fought a duel and departed, all in the space of two or three days. Who would do that?

BERNARD. Byron.

HANNAH. It's hopeless.

210 BERNARD. You've never understood him, as you've shown in your novelette.

HANNAH. In my what?

BERNARD. Oh, sorry—did you think it was a work of historical revisionism? Byron the spoilt child promoted beyond his gifts by the spirit of the age! And Caroline the closet intellectual shafted by a male society!

215 VALENTINE. I read that somewhere—

HANNAH. It's his review.

BERNARD. And bloody well said, too!

(*Things are turning a little ugly and Bernard seems in a mood to push them that way.*)

You got them backwards, darling. Caroline was Romantic waffle on wheels with no talent, and Byron was an eighteenth-century Rationalist[2] touched

220 by genius. And he killed Chater.

HANNAH. (*Pause*) If it's not too late to change my mind, I'd like you to go ahead.

BERNARD. I intend to. Look to the mote in your own eye![3]—you even had the wrong bloke on the dust-jacket!

225 HANNAH. Dust-jacket?

VALENTINE. What about my computer model? Aren't you going to mention it?

BERNARD. It's inconclusive.

VALENTINE. (*To Hannah*) The *Piccadilly* reviews aren't a very good fit with

230 Byron's other reviews, you see.

---

1   *Marie of Romania* Queen of Romania from 1914–27.

2   *Rationalist* Someone who believes that reason is the basis for all knowledge.

3   *mote … eye* See Matthew 7.5: "Thou hypocrite, first cast out the beam out of thine own eye; and then shalt thou see clearly to cast out the mote out of thy brother's eye."

HANNAH. (*To Bernard*) What do you mean, the wrong bloke?

BERNARD. (*Ignoring her*) The other reviews aren't a very good fit for each other, are they?

VALENTINE. No, but differently. The parameters—

BERNARD. (*Jeering*) Parameters! You can't stick Byron's head in your laptop! 235
Genius isn't like your average grouse.

VALENTINE. (*Casually*) Well, it's all trivial anyway.

BERNARD. What is?

VALENTINE. Who wrote what when ...

BERNARD. Trivial?   240

VALENTINE. Personalities.

BERNARD. I'm sorry—did you say trivial?

VALENTINE. It's a technical term.

BERNARD. Not where I come from, it isn't.

VALENTINE. The questions you're asking don't matter, you see. It's like argu- 245
ing who got there first with the calculus. The English say Newton, the
Germans say Leibniz.[1] But it doesn't *matter*. Personalities. What matters is
the calculus. Scientific progress. Knowledge.

BERNARD. Really? Why?

VALENTINE. Why what?   250

BERNARD. Why does scientific progress matter more than personalities?

VALENTINE. Is he serious?

HANNAH. No, he's trivial. Bernard—

VALENTINE. (*Interrupting, to Bernard*) Do yourself a favour, you're on a loser.

BERNARD. Oh, you're going to zap me with penicillin and pesticides. Spare 255
me that and I'll spare you the bomb and aerosols. But don't confuse progress with perfectibility. A great poet is always timely. A great philosopher is an urgent need. There's no rush for Isaac Newton. We were quite
happy with Aristotle's cosmos.[2] Personally, I preferred it. Fifty-five crystal
spheres geared to God's crankshaft is my idea of a satisfying universe. I 260
can't think of anything more trivial than the speed of light. Quarks, quasars[3]—big bangs, black holes—who gives a shit? How did you people con

---

1   *Leibniz* Gottfried Wilhelm Leibniz (1646–1716), German philosopher and mathematician. Liebniz and Newton were contemporaries and each invented calculus independently.

2   *Aristotle's cosmos* Aristotle proposed that the universe was composed of nested, rotating
spheres with planets and stars fixed inside them.

3   *Quarks* In quantum physics, fundamental particles that join to form composite particles, such as protons and neutrons; *quasars* Distant, extremely bright celestial objects
that resemble stars but are thought to be the result of a black hole in the centre of a
galaxy.

us out of all that status? All that money? And why are you so pleased with
yourselves?

265 CHLOË. Are you against penicillin, Bernard?

BERNARD. Don't feed the animals. (*Back to Valentine*) I'd push the lot of you
over a cliff myself. Except the one in the wheelchair,[1] I think I'd lose the
sympathy vote before people had time to think it through.

HANNAH. (*Loudly*) What the hell do you mean, the dust-jacket?

270 BERNARD.   (*Ignoring her*) If knowledge isn't self-knowledge it isn't doing
much, mate. Is the universe expanding? Is it contracting? Is it standing on
one leg and singing "When Father Painted the Parlour"?[2] Leave me out. I
can expand my universe without you. "She walks in beauty, like the night
of cloudless climes and starry skies, and all that's best of dark and bright

275   meet in her aspect and her eyes."[3] There you are, he wrote it after coming
home from a party. (*With offensive politeness.*) What is it that you're doing
with grouse, Valentine, I'd love to know?

   (*Valentine stands up and it is suddenly apparent that he is shaking and close
   to tears.*)

VALENTINE. (*To Chloë*) He's not against penicillin, and he knows I'm not
against poetry. (*To Bernard*) I've given up on the grouse.

280 HANNAH. You haven't, Valentine!

VALENTINE. (*Leaving*) I can't do it.

HANNAH. *Why?*

VALENTINE. Too much noise. There's just too much *bloody noise*!

   (*On which, Valentine leaves the room. Chloë, upset and in tears, jumps up
   and briefly pummels Bernard ineffectually with her fists.*)

CHLOË. You bastard, Bernard!

   (*She follows Valentine out and is followed at a run by Gus. Pause.*)

285 HANNAH. Well, I think that's everybody. You can leave now, give Lightning
a kick on your way out.

BERNARD. Yes, I'm sorry about that. It's no fun when it's not among pros, is
it?

HANNAH. No.

---

1   *the one on the wheelchair* I.e., Stephen Hawking (b. 1942), an important theoretical
    physicist who has a severe physical disability.
2   *When Father Painted the Parlour* Reference to the 1910 comic song "When Father Pa-
    pered the Parlour."
3   *She walks ... her eyes* Opening lines of Byron's poem "She Walks in Beauty" (1815).

BERNARD. Oh, well ... (*he begins to put his lecture sheets away in his briefcase,* 290
and is thus reminded ...) do you want to know about your book jacket?
"Lord Byron and Caroline Lamb at the Royal Academy?" Ink study by
Henry Fuseli?[1]

HANNAH. What about it?

BERNARD. It's not them.   295

HANNAH. (*She explodes*) Who says!?

(*Bernard brings the* Byron Society Journal *from his briefcase.*)

BERNARD. This Fuseli expert in the *Byron Society Journal*. They sent me the
latest ... as a distinguished guest speaker.

HANNAH. But of course it's them! Everyone knows—

BERNARD. Popular tradition only. (*He is finding the place in the journal.*) Here 300
we are. "No earlier than 1820." He's analyzed it. (*Offers it to her.*) Read at
your leisure.

HANNAH. (*She sounds like Bernard jeering*) Analyzed it?

BERNARD. Charming sketch, of course, but Byron was in Italy ...

HANNAH. But, Bernard—I *know* it's them.   305

BERNARD. How?

HANNAH. How? It just *is*. "Analyzed it," my big toe!

BERNARD. Language!

HANNAH. He's wrong.

BERNARD. Oh, gut instinct, you mean?   310

HANNAH. (*Flatly*) He's wrong.

(*Bernard snaps shut his briefcase.*)

BERNARD. Well, it's all trivial, isn't it? Why don't you come?

HANNAH. Where?

BERNARD. With me.

HANNAH. To London? What for?   315

BERNARD. What for.

HANNAH. Oh, your lecture.

BERNARD. No, no, bugger that. Sex.

HANNAH. Oh ... No. Thanks ... (*then, protesting*) Bernard!

BERNARD. You should try it. It's very underrated.   320

HANNAH. Nothing against it.

BERNARD. Yes, you have. You should let yourself go a bit. You might have
written a better book. Or at any rate the right book.

---

1   *Henry Fuseli* Swiss painter (1741–1825), a notable figure in the Romantic movement.

HANNAH. Sex and literature. Literature and sex. Your conversation, left to
325   itself, doesn't have many places to go. Like two marbles rolling around a
pudding basin. One of them is always sex.

BERNARD. Ah well, yes. Men all over.

HANNAH. No doubt. Einstein—relativity and sex. Chippendale[1]—sex and
furniture. Galileo—"Did the earth move?" What the hell is it with you
330   people? Chaps sometimes wanted to marry me, and I don't know a worse
bargain. Available sex against not being allowed to fart in bed. What do
you mean the right book?

BERNARD. It takes a romantic to make a heroine of Caroline Lamb. You were
cut out for Byron.

(*Pause.*)

335   HANNAH. So, cheerio.

BERNARD. Oh, I'm coming back for the dance, you know. Chloë asked me.

HANNAH. She meant well, but I don't dance.

BERNARD. No, no—I'm going with her.

HANNAH. Oh, I see. I don't, actually.

340   BERNARD. I'm her date. Sub rosa.[2] Don't tell Mother.

HANNAH. She doesn't want her mother to know?

BERNARD. No—*I* don't want her mother to know. This is my first experience
of the landed aristocracy. I tell you, I'm boggle-eyed.

HANNAH. Bernard!—you haven't seduced that girl?

345   BERNARD. Seduced her? Every time I turned round she was up a library ladder. In the end I gave in. That reminds me—I spotted something between
her legs that made me think of you.

(*He instantly receives a sharp stinging slap on the face but manages to
remain completely unperturbed by it. He is already producing from his
pocket a small book. His voice has hardly hesitated.*)

The Peaks Traveller and Gazetteer—James Godolphin 1832—unillustrated,
I'm afraid. (*He has opened the book to a marked place.*) "Sidley Park in Der-
350   byshire, property of the Earl of Croom ..."

HANNAH. (*Numbly*) The world is going to hell in a handcart.

BERNARD. "Five hundred acres including forty of lake—the Park by Brown
and Noakes has pleasing features in the horrid style—viaduct, grotto,[3]

---

1   *Chippendale* Thomas Chippendale (1718–79), influential English furniture-maker; also
refers to Chippendales, a well-known dance troupe of male strippers.

2   *Sub rosa* Latin: under the rose; i.e., secretly.

3   *viaduct* Bridge supported by a series of small arches; *grotto* Small cave, often built artificially as a garden feature.

etc—a hermitage occupied by a lunatic since twenty years without discourse or companion save for a pet tortoise, Plautus by name, which he   355
suffers children to touch on request." (*He holds out the book for her.*) A
tortoise. They must be a feature.

(*After a moment Hannah takes the book.*)

HANNAH. Thank you.

(*Valentine comes to the door.*)

VALENTINE. The station taxi is at the front ...
BERNARD. Yes ... thanks ... Oh—did Peacock come up trumps?   360
HANNAH. For some.
BERNARD. Hermit's name and CV?[1]

(*He picks up and glances at the Peacock letter.*)

"My dear Thackeray ..." God, I'm good.

(*He puts the letter down.*)

Well, wish me luck—(*Vaguely to Valentine*) Sorry about ... you know ...
(*and to Hannah*) and about your ...   365
VALENTINE. Piss off, Bernard.
BERNARD. Right.

(*Bernard goes.*)

HANNAH. Don't let Bernard get to you. It's only performance art, you know.
Rhetoric. They used to teach it in ancient times, like PT.[2] It's not about
being right, they had philosophy for that. Rhetoric was their talk show.   370
Bernard's indignation is a sort of aerobics for when he gets on television.
VALENTINE. I don't care to be rubbished by the dustbin man. (*He has been
looking at the letter.*) The what of the lunatic?

(*Hannah reclaims the letter and reads it for him.*)

HANNAH. "The testament of the lunatic serves as a caution against French
fashion ... for it was Frenchified mathematick that brought him to the   375
melancholy certitude of a world without light or life ... as a wooden stove
that must consume itself until ash and stove are as one, and heat is gone
from the earth."
VALENTINE. (*Amused, surprised*) Huh!

---

1   *CV* Curriculum vitae; a résumé.
2   *PT* Physical training, also called "physical education" or "gym class."

380 HANNAH. "He died aged two score years and seven, hoary as Job[1] and meagre as a cabbage-stalk, the proof of his prediction even yet unyielding to his labours for the restitution of hope through good English algebra."

VALENTINE. That's it?

HANNAH. (*Nods*) Is there anything in it?

385 VALENTINE. In what? We are all doomed? (*Casually.*) Oh yes, sure—it's called the second law of thermodynamics.[2]

HANNAH. Was it known about?

VALENTINE. By poets and lunatics from time immemorial.

HANNAH. Seriously.

390 VALENTINE. No.

HANNAH. Is it anything to do with ... you know, Thomasina's discovery?

VALENTINE. She didn't discover anything.

HANNAH. Her lesson book.

VALENTINE. No.

395 HANNAH. A coincidence, then?

VALENTINE. What is?

HANNAH. (*Reading*) "He died aged two score years and seven." That was in 1834. So he was born in 1787. So was the tutor. He says so in his letter to Lord Croom when he recommended himself for the job: "Date of

400 birth—1787." The hermit was born in the same year as Septimus Hodge.

VALENTINE. (*Pause*) Did Bernard bite you in the leg?

HANNAH. Don't you see? I thought my hermit was a perfect symbol. An idiot in the landscape. But this is better. The Age of Enlightenment banished into the Romantic wilderness! The genius of Sidley Park living on in a

405 hermit's hut!

VALENTINE. You don't *know* that.

HANNAH. Oh, but I do. I do. Somewhere there will be *something* ... if only I can find it.

---

1   *hoary* Grey-haired, old; *Job* Biblical figure who lived a long and blessed life after being tested by God.

2   *second law of thermodynamics* Physical law formulated in 1850. According to this law, heat can only move from warmer objects to colder ones—never from colder objects to warmer ones—so the amount of available energy in a closed system can never increase. A possible implication of this law is that eventually all matter in the universe will be of equal temperature, no energy will be available, and nothing will ever change again. The effect of the second law of thermodynamics on the universe is sometimes also interpreted as an irreversible increase in disorder, meaning that all matter in the universe will eventually blend together until everything is completely uniform.

ACT 2, SCENE 6

The room is empty.

A reprise: early morning—a distant pistol shot—the sound of the crows.
Jellaby enters the dawn-dark room with a lamp. He goes to the windows
and looks out. He sees something. He returns to put the lamp on the table,
and then opens one of the french windows and steps outside.

JELLABY. (*Outside*) Mr. Hodge!

(*Septimus comes in, followed by Jellaby, who closes the garden door. Septimus*
is wearing a greatcoat.)

SEPTIMUS. Thank you, Jellaby. I was expecting to be locked out. What time
is it?

JELLABY. Half past five.

SEPTIMUS. That is what I have. Well!—what a bracing experience!   5

(*He produces two pistols from inside his coat and places them on the table.*)

The dawn, you know. Unexpectedly lively. Fishes, birds, frogs ... rabbits ...
(*he produces a dead rabbit from inside his coat*) and very beautiful. If only it
did not occur so early in the day. I have brought Lady Thomasina a rabbit.
Will you take it?

JELLABY. It's dead.   10

SEPTIMUS. Yes. Lady Thomasina loves a rabbit pie.

(*Jellaby takes the rabbit without enthusiasm. There is a little blood on it.*)

JELLABY. You were missed, Mr. Hodge.

SEPTIMUS. I decided to sleep last night in the boat-house. Did I see a carriage
leaving the Park?

JELLABY. Captain Brice's carriage, with Mr. and Mrs. Chater also.   15

SEPTIMUS. Gone?!

JELLABY. Yes, sir. And Lord Byron's horse was brought round at four o'clock.

SEPTIMUS. Lord Byron too!

JELLABY. Yes, sir. The house has been up and hopping.

SEPTIMUS. But I have his rabbit pistols! What am I to do with his rabbit   20
pistols?

JELLABY. You were looked for in your room.

SEPTIMUS. By whom?

JELLABY. By her ladyship.

SEPTIMUS. In my room?   25

JELLABY. I will tell her ladyship you are returned.

(*He starts to leave.*)

SEPTIMUS. Jellaby! Did Lord Byron leave a book for me?

JELLABY. A book?

SEPTIMUS. He had the loan of a book from me.

30 JELLABY. His lordship left nothing in his room, sir, not a coin.

SEPTIMUS. Oh. Well, I'm sure he would have left a coin if he'd had one. Jellaby—here is a half-guinea for you.

JELLABY. Thank you very much, sir.

SEPTIMUS. What has occurred?

35 JELLABY. The servants are told nothing, sir.

SEPTIMUS. Come, come, does a half-guinea buy nothing any more?

JELLABY. (*Sighs*) Her ladyship encountered Mrs. Chater during the night.

SEPTIMUS. Where?

JELLABY. On the threshold of Lord Byron's room.

40 SEPTIMUS. Ah. Which one was leaving and which entering?

JELLABY. Mrs. Chater was leaving Lord Byron's room.

SEPTIMUS. And where was Mr. Chater?

JELLABY. Mr. Chater and Captain Brice were drinking cherry brandy. They
had the footman to keep the fire up until three o'clock. There was a loud

45 altercation upstairs, and—

(*Lady Croom enters the room.*)

LADY CROOM. Well, Mr. Hodge.

SEPTIMUS. My lady.

LADY CROOM. All this to shoot a hare?

SEPTIMUS. A rabbit. (*She gives him one of her looks.*) No, indeed, a hare,

50 though very rabbit-like—

(*Jellaby is about to leave.*)

LADY CROOM. My infusion.[1]

JELLABY. Yes, my lady.

(*He leaves. Lady Croom is carrying two letters. We have not seen them
before. Each has an envelope which has been opened. She flings them on
the table.*)

LADY CROOM. How dare you!

SEPTIMUS. I cannot be called to account for what was written in private and

55 read without regard to propriety.

LADY CROOM. Addressed to me!

---

1   *infusion* Steeped tea.

SEPTIMUS. Left in my room, in the event of my death—

LADY CROOM. Pah!—what earthly use is a love letter from beyond the grave?

SEPTIMUS. As much, surely, as from this side of it. The second letter, however, was not addressed to your ladyship.   60

LADY CROOM. I have a mother's right to open a letter addressed by you to my daughter, whether in the event of your life, your death, or your imbecility. What do you mean by writing to her of rice pudding when she has just suffered the shock of violent death in our midst?

SEPTIMUS. Whose death?   65

LADY CROOM. Yours, you wretch!

SEPTIMUS. Yes, I see.

LADY CROOM. I do not know which is the madder of your ravings. One envelope full of rice pudding, the other of the most insolent familiarities regarding several parts of my body, but have no doubt which is the more   70 intolerable to me.

SEPTIMUS. Which?

LADY CROOM. Oh, aren't we saucy when our bags are packed! Your friend has gone before you, and I have despatched the harlot Chater and her husband—and also my brother for bringing them here. Such is the sentence,   75 you see, for choosing unwisely in your acquaintance. Banishment. Lord Byron is a rake and a hypocrite, and the sooner he sails for the Levant[1] the sooner he will find society congenial to his character.

SEPTIMUS. It has been a night of reckoning.

LADY CROOM. Indeed I wish it had passed uneventfully with you and Mr.   80 Chater shooting each other with the decorum due to a civilized house. You have no secrets left, Mr. Hodge. They spilled out between shrieks and oaths and tears. It is fortunate that a lifetime's devotion to the sporting gun has halved my husband's hearing to the ear he sleeps on.

SEPTIMUS. I'm afraid I have no knowledge of what has occurred.   85

LADY CROOM. Your trollop was discovered in Lord Byron's room.

SEPTIMUS. Ah. Discovered by Mr. Chater?

LADY CROOM. Who else?

SEPTIMUS. I am very sorry, madam, for having used your kindness to bring my unworthy friend to your notice. He will have to give an account of   90 himself to me, you may be sure.

(Before Lady Croom can respond to this threat, Jellaby enters the room with her "infusion." This is quite an elaborate affair: a pewter tray on small feet on which there is a kettle suspended over a spirit lamp.[2] There

---

1   *Levant* Land bordering the eastern side of the Mediterranean Sea.
2   *spirit lamp* Lamp that burns spirits or another solution.

is a cup and saucer and the silver "basket" containing the dry leaves for the tea. Jellaby places the tray on the table and is about to offer further assistance with it.)

LADY CROOM. I will do it.

JELLABY. Yes, my lady. (*To Septimus*) Lord Byron left a letter for you with the valet, sir.

95   SEPTIMUS. Thank you.

(*Septimus takes the letter off the tray. Jellaby prepares to leave. Lady Croom eyes the letter.*)

LADY CROOM. When did he do so?

JELLABY. As he was leaving, your ladyship.

(*Jellaby leaves. Septimus puts the letter into his pocket.*)

SEPTIMUS. Allow me.

(*Since she does not object, he pours a cup of tea for her. She accepts it.*)

LADY CROOM. I do not know if it is proper for you to receive a letter written

100   in my house from someone not welcome in it.

SEPTIMUS. Very improper, I agree. Lord Byron's want of delicacy is a grief to his friends, among whom I no longer count myself. I will not read his letter until I have followed him through the gates.

(*She considers that for a moment.*)

LADY CROOM. That may excuse the reading but not the writing.

105   SEPTIMUS. Your ladyship should have lived in the Athens of Pericles![1] The philosophers would have fought the sculptors for your idle hour!

LADY CROOM. (*Protesting*) Oh, really! ... (*Protesting less.*) Oh really ...

(*Septimus has taken Byron's letter from his pocket and is now setting fire to a corner of it using the little flame from the spirit lamp.*)

Oh ... really ...

(*The paper blazes in Septimus's hand and he drops it and lets it burn out on the metal tray.*)

SEPTIMUS. Now there's a thing—a letter from Lord Byron never to be read by

110   a living soul. I will take my leave, madam, at the time of your desiring it.

LADY CROOM. To the Indies?

---

1   *Pericles* Greek general and statesman (c. 495–429 BCE) known for fostering Athenian cultural and political prominence.

SEPTIMUS. The Indies! Why?

LADY CROOM. To follow the Chater, of course. She did not tell you?

SEPTIMUS. She did not exchange half-a-dozen words with me.

LADY CROOM. I expect she did not like to waste the time. The Chater sails 115
with Captain Brice.

SEPTIMUS. Ah. As a member of the crew?

LADY CROOM. No, as wife to Mr. Chater, plant-gatherer to my brother's
expedition.

SEPTIMUS. I knew he was no poet. I did not know it was botany under the 120
false colours.

LADY CROOM. He is no more a botanist. My brother paid fifty pounds to
have him published, and he will pay a hundred and fifty to have Mr. Chater picking flowers in the Indies for a year while the wife plays mistress of
the Captain's quarters. Captain Brice has fixed his passion on Mrs. Chater, 125
and to take her on voyage he has not scrupled to deceive the Admiralty, the
Linnean Society and Sir Joseph Banks,[1] botanist to His Majesty at Kew.

SEPTIMUS. Her passion is not as fixed as his.

LADY CROOM. It is a defect of God's humour that he directs our hearts everywhere but to those who have a right to them.   130

SEPTIMUS. Indeed, madam. (*Pause.*) But is Mr. Chater deceived?

LADY CROOM. He insists on it, and finds the proof of his wife's virtue in his
eagerness to defend it. Captain Brice is *not* deceived but cannot help himself. He would die for her.

SEPTIMUS. I think, my lady, he would have Mr. Chater die for her.   135

LADY CROOM. Indeed, I never knew a woman worth the duel, or the other
way about. Your letter to me goes very ill with your conduct to Mrs. Chater, Mr. Hodge. I have had experience of being betrayed before the ink is
dry, but to be betrayed before the pen is even dipped, and with the village
noticeboard, what am I to think of such a performance?   140

SEPTIMUS. My lady, I was alone with my thoughts in the gazebo, when Mrs.
Chater ran me to ground, and I being in such a passion, in an agony of
unrelieved desire—

LADY CROOM. Oh ...!

SEPTIMUS. —I thought in my madness that the Chater with her skirts over 145
her head would give me the momentary illusion of the happiness to which
I dared not put a face.

(*Pause.*)

---

1   *Linnean Society* Long-standing scientific society with a specific focus on natural history; *Sir Joseph Banks* English naturalist and botanist (1743–1820).

LADY CROOM. I do not know when I have received a more unusual compliment, Mr. Hodge. I hope I am more than a match for Mrs. Chater with her head in a bucket. Does she wear drawers?

SEPTIMUS. She does.

LADY CROOM. Yes, I have heard that drawers are being worn now. It is unnatural for women to be got up like jockeys. I cannot approve.

(*She turns with a whirl of skirts and moves to leave.*)

I know nothing of Pericles or the Athenian philosophers. I can spare them an hour, in my sitting room when I have bathed. Seven o'clock. Bring a book.

(*She goes out. Septimus picks up the two letters, the ones he wrote, and starts to burn them in the flame of the spirit lamp.*)

ACT 2, SCENE 7

Valentine and Chloë are at the table. Gus is in the room.

Chloë is reading from two Saturday newspapers. She is wearing workaday period clothes, a Regency[1] dress, no hat.

Valentine is pecking at a portable computer. He is wearing unkempt Regency clothes, too.

The clothes have evidently come from a large wicker laundry hamper, from which Gus is producing more clothes to try on himself. He finds a Regency coat and starts putting it on.

The objects on the table now include two geometrical solids, pyramid and cone, about twenty inches high, of the type used in a drawing lesson; and a pot of dwarf dahlias (which do not look like modern dahlias).

CHLOË. "Even in Arcadia—Sex, Literature and Death at Sidley Park." Picture of Byron.

VALENTINE. Not of Bernard?

CHLOË. "Byron Fought Fatal Duel, Says Don" ... Valentine, do you think I'm the first person to think of this?

VALENTINE. No.

CHLOË. I haven't said yet. The future is all programmed like a computer—that's a proper theory, isn't it?

VALENTINE. The deterministic universe,[2] yes.

---

1   *Regency* I.e., in the style of early nineteenth-century England.

2   *deterministic universe* Theoretical system in which all events are already determined by the universe's physical laws; the concept precludes free will.

CHLOË. Right. Because everything including us is just a lot of atoms bouncing off each other like billiard balls. 10

VALENTINE. Yes. There was someone, forget his name, 1820s, who pointed out that from Newton's laws you could predict everything to come—I mean, you'd need a computer as big as the universe but the formula would exist.

CHLOË. But it doesn't work, does it? 15

VALENTINE. No. It turns out the maths is different.

CHLOË. No, it's all because of sex.

VALENTINE. Really?

CHLOË. That's what I think. The universe is deterministic all right, just like Newton said, I mean it's trying to be, but the only thing going wrong is 20 people fancying people who aren't supposed to be in that part of the plan.

VALENTINE. Ah. The attraction that Newton left out. All the way back to the apple in the garden. Yes. (*Pause.*) Yes, I think you're the first person to think of this.

(*Hannah enters, carrying a tabloid paper, and a mug of tea.*)

HANNAH. Have you seen this? "Byron Bangs Wife, Shoots Hubby." 25

CHLOË. (*Pleased*) Let's see.

(*Hannah gives her the paper, smiles at Gus.*)

VALENTINE. He's done awfully well, hasn't he? How did they all know?

HANNAH. Don't be ridiculous. (*To Chloë*) Your father wants it back.

CHLOË. All right.

HANNAH. What a fool. 30

CHLOË. Jealous. I think it's brilliant. (*She gets up to go. To Gus*) Yes, that's perfect, but not with trainers. Come on, I'll lend you a pair of flatties, they'll look period on you—

HANNAH. Hello, Gus. You all look so romantic.

(*Gus following Chloë out, hesitates, smiles at her.*)

CHLOË. (*Pointedly*) Are you coming? 35

(*She holds the door for Gus and follows him out, leaving a sense of her disapproval behind her.*)

HANNAH. The important thing is not to give two monkeys for what young people think about you.

(*She goes to look at the other newspapers.*)

VALENTINE. (*Anxiously*) You don't think she's getting a thing about Bernard, do you?

40 HANNAH. I wouldn't worry about Chloë, she's old enough to vote on her back. "Byron Fought Fatal Duel, Says Don." Or rather—(*skeptically*) "Says Don!"

VALENTINE. It may all prove to be true.

HANNAH. It can't prove to be true, it can only not prove to be false yet.

45 VALENTINE. (*Pleased*) Just like science.

HANNAH. If Bernard can stay ahead of getting the rug pulled till he's dead, he'll be a success.

VALENTINE. *Just* like science ... The ultimate fear is of posterity ...

HANNAH. Personally I don't think it'll take that long.

50 VALENTINE. ... and then there's the afterlife. An afterlife would be a mixed blessing. "Ah—Bernard Nightingale, I don't believe you know Lord Byron." It must be heaven up there.

HANNAH. You can't believe in an afterlife, Valentine.

VALENTINE. Oh, you're going to disappoint me at last.

55 HANNAH. Am I? Why?

VALENTINE. Science and religion.

HANNAH. No, no, been there, done that, boring.

VALENTINE. Oh, Hannah. Fiancée. Have pity. Can't we have a trial marriage and I'll call it off in the morning?

60 HANNAH. (*Amused*) I don't know when I've received a more unusual proposal.

VALENTINE. (*Interested*) Have you had many?

HANNAH. That would be telling.

VALENTINE. Well, why not? Your classical reserve is only a mannerism; and
65   neurotic.

HANNAH. Do you want the room?

VALENTINE. You get nothing if you give nothing.

HANNAH. I ask nothing.

VALENTINE. No, stay.

(*Valentine resumes work at his computer. Hannah establishes herself among her references at "her" end of the table. She has a stack of pocket-sized volumes, Lady Croom's "garden books."*)

70 HANNAH. What are you doing? Valentine?

VALENTINE. The set of points on a complex plane made by—

HANNAH. Is it the grouse?

VALENTINE. Oh, the grouse. The damned grouse.

HANNAH. You mustn't give up.

75 VALENTINE. Why? Didn't you agree with Bernard?

HANNAH. Oh, that. It's *all* trivial—your grouse, my hermit, Bernard's Byron.

Comparing what we're looking for misses the point. It's wanting to know that makes us matter. Otherwise we're going out the way we came in. That's why you can't believe in the afterlife, Valentine. Believe in the after, by all means, but not the life. Believe in God, the soul, the spirit, the infi-   80
nite, believe in angels if you like, but not in the great celestial get-together for an exchange of views. If the answers are in the back of the book I can wait, but what a drag. Better to struggle on knowing that failure is final. (*She looks over Valentine's shoulder at the computer screen. Reacting*) Oh!, but ... how beautiful!   85

VALENTINE. The Coverly set.

HANNAH. The Coverly set! My goodness, Valentine!

VALENTINE. Lend me a finger.

(*He takes her finger and presses one of the computer keys several times.*)

See? In an ocean of ashes, islands of order. Patterns making themselves out of nothing. I can't show you how deep it goes. Each picture is a detail of   90
the previous one, blown up. And so on. For ever. Pretty nice, eh?

HANNAH. Is it important?

VALENTINE. Interesting. Publishable.

HANNAH. Well done!

VALENTINE. Not me. It's Thomasina's. I just pushed her equation through   95
the computer a few million times further than she managed to do with her pencil.

(*From the old portfolio he takes Thomasina's lesson book and gives it to Hannah. The piano starts to be heard.*)

You can have it back now.

HANNAH. What does it mean?

VALENTINE. Not what you'd like it to.   100

HANNAH. Why not?

VALENTINE. Well, for one thing, she'd be famous.

HANNAH. No, she wouldn't. She was dead before she had time to be famous ...

VALENTINE. She died?   105

HANNAH. ... burned to death.

VALENTINE. (*Realizing*) Oh ... the girl who died in the fire!

HANNAH. The night before her seventeenth birthday. You can see where the dormer[1] doesn't match. That was her bedroom under the roof. There's a memorial in the Park.   110

---

1   *dormer* Protruding, usually windowed, section of a sloped roof.

VALENTINE. (*Irritated*) I know—it's my house.

(*Valentine turns his attention back to his computer. Hannah goes back to her chair. She looks through the lesson book.*)

HANNAH. Val, Septimus was her tutor—he and Thomasina would have—
VALENTINE. You do yours.

(*Pause. Two researchers.*

Lord Augustus, fifteen years old, wearing clothes of 1812, bursts in through the non-music room door. He is laughing. He dives under the table. He is chased into the room by Thomasina, aged sixteen and furious. She spots Augustus immediately.)

THOMASINA. You swore! You crossed your heart!

(*Augustus scampers out from under the table and Thomasina chases him around it.*)

115 AUGUSTUS. I'll tell mama! I'll tell mama!
THOMASINA. You beast!

(*She catches Augustus as Septimus enters from the other door, carrying a book, a decanter and a glass, and his portfolio.*)

SEPTIMUS. Hush! What is this? My lord! Order, order!

(*Thomasina and Augustus separate.*)

I am obliged.

(*Septimus goes to his place at the table. He pours himself a glass of wine.*)

AUGUSTUS. Well, good day to you, Mr. Hodge!

(*He is smirking about something.*
Thomasina dutifully picks up a drawing book and settles down to draw the geometrical solids.
Septimus opens his portfolio.)

120 SEPTIMUS. Will you join us this morning, Lord Augustus? We have our drawing lesson.
AUGUSTUS. I am a master of it at Eton, Mr. Hodge, but we only draw naked women.
SEPTIMUS. You may work from memory.
125 THOMASINA. Disgusting!
SEPTIMUS. We will have silence now, if you please.

(*From the portfolio Septimus takes Thomasina's lesson book and tosses it to her; returning homework. She snatches it and opens it.*)

THOMASINA. No marks?! Did you not like my rabbit equation?

SEPTIMUS. I saw no resemblance to a rabbit.

THOMASINA. It eats its own progeny.

SEPTIMUS. (*Pause*) I did not see that.   130

(*He extends his hand for the lesson book. She returns it to him.*)

THOMASINA. I have not room to extend it.

(*Septimus and Hannah turn the pages doubled by time. Augustus indolently starts to draw the models.*)

HANNAH. Do you mean the world is saved after all?

VALENTINE. No, it's still doomed. But if this is how it started, perhaps it's how the next one will come.

HANNAH. From good English algebra?   135

SEPTIMUS. It will go to infinity or zero, or nonsense.

THOMASINA. No, if you set apart the minus roots they square back to sense.

(*Septimus turns the pages.*
    Thomasina starts drawing the models.

Hannah closes the lesson book and turns her attention to her stack of "garden books.")

VALENTINE. Listen—you know your tea's getting cold.

HANNAH. I like it cold.

VALENTINE. (*Ignoring that*) I'm telling you something. Your tea gets cold by   140
itself, it doesn't get hot by itself. Do you think that's odd?

HANNAH. No.

VALENTINE. Well, it is odd. Heat goes to cold. It's a one-way street. Your tea will end up at room temperature. What's happening to your tea is happening to everything everywhere. The sun and the stars. It'll take a while   145
but we're all going to end up at room temperature. When your hermit set up shop nobody understood this. But let's say you're right, in 18-whatever nobody knew more about heat than this scribbling nutter living in a hovel in Derbyshire.

HANNAH. He was at Cambridge—a scientist.   150

VALENTINE. Say he was. I'm not arguing. And the girl was his pupil, she had a genius for her tutor.

HANNAH. Or the other way round.

VALENTINE. Anything you like. But not *this*! Whatever he thought he was
155   doing to save the world with good English algebra it wasn't this!
HANNAH. Why? Because they didn't have calculators?
VALENTINE. No. Yes. Because there's an order things can't happen in. You
    can't open a door till there's a house.
HANNAH. I thought that's what genius was.
160 VALENTINE. Only for lunatics and poets.

> (*Pause.*)

HANNAH. "I had a dream which was not all a dream.
    The bright sun was extinguished, and the stars
    Did wander darkling in the eternal space,
    Rayless, and pathless, and the icy earth
165   Swung blind and blackening in the moonless air ..."[1]
VALENTINE. Your own?
HANNAH. Byron.

> (*Pause. Two researchers again.*)

THOMASINA. Septimus, do you think that I will marry Lord Byron?
AUGUSTUS. Who is he?
170 THOMASINA. He is the author of "Childe Harold's Pilgrimage," the most
    poetical and pathetic and bravest hero of any book I ever read before, and
    the most modern and the handsomest, for Harold is Lord Byron himself to
    those who know him, like myself and Septimus. Well, Septimus?
SEPTIMUS. (*Absorbed*) No.

> (*Then he puts her lesson book away into the portfolio and picks up his own
> book to read.*)

175 THOMASINA. Why not?
SEPTIMUS. For one thing, he is not aware of your existence.
THOMASINA. We exchanged many significant glances when he was at Sidley
    Park. I do wonder that he has been home almost a year from his adventures
    and has not written to me once.
180 SEPTIMUS. It is indeed improbable, my lady.
AUGUSTUS. Lord Byron?!—he claimed my hare, although my shot was the
    earlier! He said I missed by a hare's breadth. His conversation was very
    facetious. But I think Lord Byron will not marry you, Thom, for he was
    only lame and not blind.

---

1   *I had a dream ... air* Opening lines of Bryon's poem "Darkness" (1816).

SEPTIMUS. Peace! Peace until a quarter to twelve. It is intolerable for a tutor   185
to have his thoughts interrupted by his pupils.

AUGUSTUS. You are not *my* tutor, sir. I am visiting your lesson by my free will.

SEPTIMUS. If you are so determined, my lord.

(*Thomasina laughs at that, the joke is for her. Augustus, not included, becomes angry.*)

AUGUSTUS. Your peace is nothing to me, sir. You do not rule over me.

THOMASINA. (*Admonishing*) Augustus!   190

SEPTIMUS. I do not rule here, my lord. I inspire by reverence for learning and
the exaltation of knowledge whereby man may approach God. There will
be a shilling for the best cone and pyramid drawn in silence by a quarter
to twelve *at the earliest*.

AUGUSTUS. You will not buy my silence for a shilling, sir. What I know to tell   195
is worth much more than that.

(*And throwing down his drawing book and pencil, he leaves the room on
his dignity, closing the door sharply. Pause. Septimus looks enquiringly at
Thomasina.*)

THOMASINA. I told him you kissed me. But he will not tell.

SEPTIMUS. When did I kiss you?

THOMASINA. What! Yesterday!

SEPTIMUS. Where?   200

THOMASINA. On the lips!

SEPTIMUS. In which county?

THOMASINA. In the hermitage, Septimus!

SEPTIMUS. On the lips in the hermitage! That? That was not a shilling kiss!
I would not give sixpence to have it back. I had almost forgot it already.   205

THOMASINA. Oh, cruel! Have you forgotten our compact?

SEPTIMUS. God save me! Our compact?

THOMASINA. To teach me to waltz! Sealed with a kiss, and a second kiss due
when I can dance like mama!

SEPTIMUS. Ah yes. Indeed. We were all waltzing like mice in London.   210

THOMASINA. I must waltz, Septimus! I will be despised if I do not waltz! It
is the most fashionable and gayest and boldest invention conceivable—
started in Germany!

SEPTIMUS. Let them have the waltz, they cannot have the calculus.

THOMASINA. Mama has brought from town a whole book of waltzes for the   215
Broadwood, to play with Count Zelinsky.

SEPTIMUS. I need not be told what I cannot but suffer. Count Zelinsky banging on the Broadwood without relief has me reading in waltz time.

THOMASINA. Oh, stuff! What is your book?

220 SEPTIMUS. A prize essay of the Scientific Academy in Paris.[1] The author deserves your indulgence, my lady, for you are his prophet.

THOMASINA. I? What does he write about? The waltz?

SEPTIMUS. Yes. He demonstrates the equation of the propagation of heat in a solid body. But in doing so he has discovered heresy—a natural contradiction of Sir Isaac Newton.

225

THOMASINA. Oh!—he contradicts determinism?

SEPTIMUS. No! ... Well, perhaps. He shows that the atoms do not go according to Newton.[2]

(*Her interest has switched in the mercurial way characteristic of her—she has crossed to take the book.*)

THOMASINA. Let me see—oh! In French?

230 SEPTIMUS. Yes. Paris is the capital of France.

THOMASINA. Show me where to read.

(*He takes the book back from her and finds the page for her. Meanwhile, the piano music from the next room has doubled its notes and its emotion.*)

THOMASINA. Four-handed now! Mama is in love with the Count.

SEPTIMUS. He is a Count in Poland. In Derbyshire he is a piano tuner.

(*She has taken the book and is already immersed in it. The piano music becomes rapidly more passionate, and then breaks off suddenly in midphrase. There is an expressive silence next door which makes Septimus raise his eyes. It does not register with Thomasina. The silence allows us to hear the distant regular thump of the steam engine which is to be a topic. A few moments later Lady Croom enters from the music room, seeming surprised and slightly flustered to find the schoolroom occupied. She collects herself, closing the door behind her. And remains watching, aimless and discreet, as though not wanting to interrupt the lesson. Septimus has stood, and she nods him back into his chair.*

Chloë, in Regency dress, enters from the door opposite the music room. She takes in Valentine and Hannah but crosses without pausing to the music room door.)

---

1   *prize essay ... in Paris* Septimus is reading "On the Propagation of Heat in Solid Bodies" (1812), an essay by the French physicist Joseph Fourier.

2   *the atoms ... to Newton* Newton's laws do not distinguish a temporal direction—theoretically, the processes they describe could happen either backwards or forwards in time—but processes involving the transfer of heat cannot be reversed. Fourier did not show this, but his work constituted a step toward the formulation of the second law of thermodynamics, which would.

CHLOË. Oh!—where's Gus?

VALENTINE. Dunno.   235

    (*Chloë goes into the music room.*)

LADY CROOM. (*Annoyed*) Oh!—Mr. Noakes's engine!

    (*She goes to the garden door and steps outside.*

    Chloë re-enters.)

CHLOË. Damn.

LADY CROOM. (*Calls out*) Mr. Noakes!

VALENTINE. He was there not long ago ...

LADY CROOM. Halo!?   240

CHLOË. Well, he has to be in the photograph—is he dressed?

HANNAH. Is Bernard back?

CHLOË. No—he's late!

    (*The piano is heard again, under the noise of the steam engine.*
    Lady Croom steps back into the room.

    Chloë steps outside the garden door. Shouts.)

Gus!

LADY CROOM. I wonder you can teach against such a disturbance and I am   245
sorry for it, Mr. Hodge.

    (*Chloë comes back inside.*)

VALENTINE. (*Getting up*) Stop ordering everybody about.

LADY CROOM. It is an unendurable noise.

VALENTINE. The photographer will wait.

    (*But, grumbling, he follows Chloë out of the door she came in by, and closes*
    the door behind them. Hannah remains absorbed.
      In the silence, the rhythmic thump can be heard again.)

LADY CROOM. The ceaseless dull overbearing monotony of it! It will drive me   250
distracted. I may have to return to town to escape it.

SEPTIMUS. Your ladyship could remain in the country and let Count Zelinsky return to town where you would not hear him.

LADY CROOM. I mean Mr. Noakes's engine! (*Semi-aside to Septimus.*) Would
you sulk? I will not have my daughter study sulking.   255

THOMASINA. (*Not listening*) What, mama?

(*Thomasina remains lost in her book. Lady Croom returns to close the garden door and the noise of the steam engine subsides.*

Hannah closes one of the "garden books," and opens the next. She is making occasional notes.

The piano ceases.)

LADY CROOM. (*To Thomasina*) What are we learning today? (*Pause.*) Well, not manners.

SEPTIMUS. We are drawing today.

(*Lady Croom negligently examines what Thomasina had started to draw.*)

260   LADY CROOM. Geometry. I approve of geometry.

SEPTIMUS. Your ladyship's approval is my constant object.

LADY CROOM. Well, do not despair of it. (*Returning to the window impatiently.*) Where is "Culpability" Noakes? (*She looks out and is annoyed.*) Oh!—he has gone for his hat so that he may remove it.

(*She returns to the table and touches the bowl of dahlias.*

Hannah sits back in her chair, caught by what she is reading.)

265   For the widow's dowry of dahlias I can almost forgive my brother's marriage. We must be thankful the monkey bit Mr. Chater. If it had bit Mrs. Chater the monkey would be dead and we would not be first in the kingdom to show a dahlia. (*Hannah, still reading the garden book, stands up.*) I sent one potted to Chatsworth. The Duchess was most satisfactorily put

270   out by it when I called at Devonshire House. Your friend was there lording it as a poet.

(*Hannah leaves through the door, following Valentine and Chloë.*

Meanwhile, Thomasina thumps the book down on the table.)

THOMASINA. Well! Just as I said! Newton's machine which would knock our atoms from cradle to grave by the laws of motion is incomplete! Determinism leaves the road at every corner, as I knew all along, and the cause is very

275   likely hidden in this gentleman's observation.

LADY CROOM. Of what?

THOMASINA. The action of bodies in heat.

LADY CROOM. Is this geometry?

THOMASINA. This? No, I despise geometry!

280   LADY CROOM. (*Touching the dahlias she adds, almost to herself.*) The Chater would overthrow the Newtonian system in a weekend.

SEPTIMUS. Geometry, Hobbes[1] assures us in the *Leviathan*, is the only science God has been pleased to bestow on mankind.

LADY CROOM. And what does he mean by it?

SEPTIMUS. Mr. Hobbes or God?   285

LADY CROOM. I am sure I do not know what either means by it.

THOMASINA. Oh, pooh to Hobbes! Mountains are not pyramids and trees are not cones. God must love gunnery and architecture if Euclid[2] is his only geometry. There is another geometry which I am engaged in discovering by trial and error, am I not, Septimus?   290

SEPTIMUS. Trial and error perfectly describes your enthusiasm, my lady.

LADY CROOM. How old are you today?

THOMASINA. Sixteen years and eleven months, mama, and three weeks.

LADY CROOM. Sixteen years and eleven months. We must have you married before you are educated beyond eligibility.   300

THOMASINA. I am going to marry Lord Byron.

LADY CROOM. Are you? He did not have the manners to mention it.

THOMASINA. You have spoken to him?!

LADY CROOM. Certainly not.

THOMASINA. Where did you see him?   305

LADY CROOM. (*With some bitterness*) Everywhere.

THOMASINA. Did you, Septimus?

SEPTIMUS. At the Royal Academy where I had the honour to accompany your mother and Count Zelinsky.

THOMASINA. What was Lord Byron doing?   310

LADY CROOM. Posing.

SEPTIMUS. (*Tactfully*) He was being sketched during his visit ... by the Professor of Painting ... Mr. Fuseli.

LADY CROOM. There was more posing *at* the pictures than *in* them. His companion likewise reversed the custom of the Academy that the ladies view- 315 ing wear more than the ladies viewed—well, enough! Let him be hanged there for a Lamb. I have enough with Mr. Noakes, who is to a garden what a bull is to a china shop.

(*This as Noakes enters.*)

---

1   *Hobbes* Thomas Hobbes, English philosopher best known for his book *Leviathan* (1651), in which he argues that without a powerful government to keep its natural tendencies in check, humankind would revert to lawlessness and violence.

2   *Euclid* Greek mathematician (fl. 300 BCE) whose work provided the foundation for all geometry for the next two millennia; the first work to explicitly contradict Euclid's geometry was published in the 1820s. Euclidean geometry is still used for most practical applications, such as architecture, but more complex forms of geometry also have applications in the physical world.

THOMASINA. The Emperor of Irregularity!

(*She settles down to drawing the diagram which is to be the third item in the surviving portfolio.*)

320 LADY CROOM. Mr. Noakes!

NOAKES. Your ladyship—

LADY CROOM. What have you done to me!

NOAKES. Everything is satisfactory, I assure you. A little behind, to be sure, but my dam will be repaired within the month—

325 LADY CROOM. (*Banging the table*) Hush!

(*In the silence, the steam engine thumps in the distance.*)

Can you hear, Mr. Noakes?

NOAKES. (*Pleased and proud*) The Improved Newcomen steam pump[1]—the only one in England!

LADY CROOM. That is what I object to. If everybody had his own I would

330 bear my portion of the agony without complaint. But to have been singled out by the only Improved Newcomen steam pump in England, this is hard, sir, this is not to be borne.

NOAKES. Your lady—

LADY CROOM. And for what? My lake is drained to a ditch for no purpose

335 I can understand, unless it be that snipe and curlew[2] have deserted three counties so that they may be shot in our swamp. What you painted as forest is a mean plantation, your greenery is mud, your waterfall is wet mud, and your mount is an opencast mine for the mud that was lacking in the dell. (*Pointing through the window.*) What is that cowshed?

340 NOAKES. The hermitage, my lady?

LADY CROOM. It is a cowshed.

NOAKES. Madam, it is, I assure you, a very habitable cottage, properly founded and drained, two rooms and a closet under a slate roof and a stone chimney—

345 LADY CROOM. And who is to live in it?

NOAKES. Why, the hermit.

LADY CROOM. Where is he?

NOAKES. Madam?

LADY CROOM. You surely do not supply a hermitage without a hermit?

350 NOAKES. Indeed, madam—

---

1   *Newcomen steam pump* The first steam engine to convert steam into practical mechanical energy; it was created in 1712 by the English inventor Thomas Newcomen.

2   *snipe and curlew* Two different types of long-legged birds, found in marshes and wetlands.

LADY CROOM. Come, come, Mr. Noakes. If I am promised a fountain I expect it to come with water. What hermits do you have?

NOAKES. I have no hermits, my lady.

LADY CROOM. Not one? I am speechless.

NOAKES. I am sure a hermit can be found. One could advertise.   355

LADY CROOM. Advertise?

NOAKES. In the newspapers.

LADY CROOM. But surely a hermit who takes a newspaper is not a hermit in whom one can have complete confidence.

NOAKES. I do not know what to suggest, my lady.   360

SEPTIMUS. Is there room for a piano?

NOAKES. (*Baffled*) A piano?

LADY CROOM. We are intruding here—this will not do, Mr. Hodge. Evidently, nothing is being learned. (*To Noakes*) Come along, sir!

THOMASINA. Mr. Noakes—bad news from Paris!   365

NOAKES. Is it the Emperor Napoleon?

THOMASINA. No. (*She tears the page off her drawing block, with her "diagram" on it.*) It concerns your heat engine. Improve it as you will, you can never get out of it what you put in. It repays eleven pence in the shilling[1] at most. The penny is for this author's thoughts.   370

(*She gives the diagram to Septimus who looks at it.*)

NOAKES. (*Baffled again*) Thank you, my lady.

(*Noakes goes out into the garden.*)

LADY CROOM. (*To Septimus*) Do you understand her?

SEPTIMUS. No.

LADY CROOM. Then this business is over. I was married at seventeen. *Ce soir il faut qu'on parle français, je te demande,*[2] Thomasina, as a courtesy to the   375
Count. Wear your green velvet, please, I will send Briggs to do your hair. Sixteen and eleven months ...!

(*She follows Noakes out of view.*)

THOMASINA. Lord Byron was with a lady?

SEPTIMUS. Yes.

THOMASINA. Huh!   380

(*Now Septimus retrieves his book from Thomasina. He turns the pages, and also continues to study Thomasina's diagram. He strokes the tortoise*

---

1   *shilling* Twelve pence.
2   *Ce soir ... demande* French: I ask that tonight we speak French.

absently as he reads. Thomasina takes up pencil and paper and starts to draw Septimus with Plautus.)

SEPTIMUS. Why does it mean Mr. Noakes's engine pays eleven pence in the shilling? Where does he say it?

THOMASINA. Nowhere. I noticed it by the way. I cannot remember now.

SEPTIMUS. Nor is he interested by determinism—

385 THOMASINA. Oh ... yes. Newton's equations go forwards and backwards, they do not care which way. But the heat equation cares very much, it goes only one way. That is the reason Mr. Noakes's engine cannot give the power to drive Mr. Noakes's engine.

SEPTIMUS. Everybody knows that.

390 THOMASINA. Yes, Septimus, they know it about engines!

SEPTIMUS. (*Pause. He looks at his watch.*) A quarter to twelve. For your essay this week, explicate your diagram.

THOMASINA. I cannot. I do not know the mathematics.

SEPTIMUS. Without mathematics, then.

(*Thomasina has continued to draw. She tears the top page from her drawing pad and gives it to Septimus.*)

395 THOMASINA. There. I have made a drawing of you and Plautus.

SEPTIMUS. (*Looking at it*) Excellent likeness. Not so good of me.

(*Thomasina laughs, and leaves the room.*
Augustus appears at the garden door. His manner cautious and diffident. Septimus does not notice him for a moment.
Septimus gathers his papers together.)

AUGUSTUS. Sir ...

SEPTIMUS. My lord ...?

AUGUSTUS. I gave you offence, sir, and I am sorry for it.

400 SEPTIMUS. I took none, my lord, but you are kind to mention it.

AUGUSTUS. I would like to ask you a question, Mr. Hodge. (*Pause.*) You have an elder brother, I dare say, being a Septimus?[1]

SEPTIMUS. Yes, my lord. He lives in London. He is the editor of a newspaper, the *Piccadilly Recreation*. (*Pause.*) Was that your question?

(*Augustus, evidently embarrassed about something, picks up the drawing of Septimus.*)

405 AUGUSTUS. No. Oh ... it is you? ... I would like to keep it. (*Septimus inclines his head in assent.*) There are things a fellow cannot ask his friends. Carnal

---

1   *Septimus* In Latin, "*septimus*" means "seventh."

things. My sister has told me ... my sister believes such things as I cannot, I assure you, bring myself to repeat.

SEPTIMUS. You must not repeat them, then. The walk between here and dinner will suffice to put us straight, if we stroll by the garden. It is an   410 easy business. And then I must rely on you to correct your sister's state of ignorance.

(*A commotion is heard outside—Bernard's loud voice in a sort of agony.*)

BERNARD. (*outside the door*) Oh no—no—no—oh, bloody hell!—

AUGUSTUS. Thank you, Mr. Hodge, I will.

(*Taking the drawing with him, Augustus allows himself to be shown out through the garden door, and Septimus follows him.*

Bernard enters the room, through the door Hannah left by. Valentine comes in with him, leaving the door open and they are followed by Hannah who is holding the "garden book.")

BERNARD. Oh, no—no—   415

HANNAH. I'm sorry, Bernard.

BERNARD. Fucked by a dahlia! Do you think? Is it open and shut? Am I fucked? What does it really amount to? When all's said and done? Am I fucked? What do you think, Valentine? Tell me the truth.

VALENTINE. You're fucked.   420

BERNARD. Oh God! Does it mean that?

HANNAH. Yes, Bernard, it does.

BERNARD. I'm not sure. Show me where it says. I want to see it. No—read it—no, wait ...

(*Bernard sits at the table. He prepares to listen as though listening were an oriental art.*)

Right.   425

HANNAH. (*Reading*) "October 1st, 1810. Today under the direction of Mr. Noakes, a parterre[1] was dug on the south lawn and will be a handsome show next year, a consolation for the picturesque catastrophe of the second and third distances. The dahlia having propagated under glass with no ill effect from the sea voyage, is named by Captain Brice 'Charity' for his   430 bride, though the honour properly belongs to the husband who exchanged beds with my dahlia, and an English summer for everlasting night in the Indies."

---

1   *parterre* Type of level garden with carefully arranged flowerbeds and pathways.

(*Pause.*)

BERNARD. Well it's so round the houses, isn't it? Who's to say what it means?

435 HANNAH. (*Patiently*) It means that Ezra Chater of the Sidley Park connection is the same Chater who described a dwarf dahlia in Martinique in 1810 and died there, of a monkey bite.

BERNARD. (*Wildly*) Ezra wasn't a botanist! He was a poet!

HANNAH. He was not much of either, but he was both.

440 VALENTINE. It's not a disaster.

BERNARD. Of course it's a disaster! I was on "The Breakfast Hour!"

VALENTINE. It doesn't mean Byron didn't fight a duel, it only means Chater wasn't killed in it.

BERNARD. Oh, pull yourself together!—do you think I'd have been on "The
445 Breakfast Hour" if Byron had *missed*!

HANNAH. Calm down, Bernard. Valentine's right.

BERNARD. (*Grasping at straws*) Do you think so? You mean the *Piccadilly* reviews? Yes, two completely unknown Byron essays—*and* my discovery of the lines he added to 'English Bards'. That counts for something.

450 HANNAH. (*Tactfully*) Very possible—persuasive, indeed.

BERNARD. Oh, bugger persuasive! I've proved Byron was here and as far as I'm concerned he wrote those lines as sure as he shot that hare. If only I hadn't somehow ... made it all about *killing Chater*. Why didn't you stop me?! It's bound to get out, you know—I mean this—this *gloss* on my discovery—I
455 mean how long do you think it'll be before some botanical pedant blows the whistle on me?

HANNAH. The day after tomorrow. A letter in *The Times*.

BERNARD. You wouldn't.

HANNAH. It's a dirty job but somebody—

460 BERNARD. Darling. Sorry. Hannah—

HANNAH. —and, after all, it is my discovery.

BERNARD. Hannah.

HANNAH. Bernard.

BERNARD. Hannah.

465 HANNAH. Oh, shut up. It'll be very short, very dry, absolutely gloat-free. Would you rather it were one of your friends?

BERNARD. (*Fervently*) Oh God, no!

HANNAH. And then in *your* letter to *The Times*—

BERNARD. Mine?

470 HANNAH. Well, of course. Dignified congratulations to a colleague, in the language of scholars, I trust.

BERNARD. Oh, eat shit, you mean?

HANNAH. Think of it as a breakthrough in dahlia studies.

(*Chloë hurries in from the garden.*)

CHLOË. Why aren't you coming?!—Bernard! And you're not dressed! How
long have you been back?   475

(*Bernard looks at her and then at Valentine and realizes for the first time
that Valentine is unusually dressed.*)

BERNARD. Why are you wearing those clothes?
CHLOË. Do be quick!

(*She is already digging into the basket and producing odd garments for
Bernard.*)

Just put anything on. We're all being photographed. Except Hannah.
HANNAH. I'll come and watch.

(*Valentine and Chloë help Bernard into a decorative coat and fix a lace
collar round his neck.*)

CHLOË. (*To Hannah*) Mummy says have you got the theodolite?   480
VALENTINE. What are you supposed to be, Chloë? Bo-Peep?
CHLOË. Jane Austen![1]
VALENTINE. Of course.
HANNAH. (*To Chloë*) Oh—it's in the hermitage! Sorry.
BERNARD. I thought it wasn't till this evening. What photograph?   485
CHLOË. The local paper of course—they always come before we start. We
want a good crowd of us—Gus looks gorgeous—
BERNARD. (*Aghast*) The newspaper!

(*He grabs something like a bishop's mitre[2] from the basket and pulls it down
completely over his face.*)

(*Muffled*) I'm ready!

(*And he staggers out with Valentine and Chloë, followed by Hannah.*
A light change to evening. The paper lanterns outside begin to glow.
Piano music from the next room.

Septimus enters with an oil lamp. He carries Thomasina's algebra primer,
and also her essay on loose sheets. He settles down to read at the table. It is
nearly dark outside, despite the lanterns.)

---

1   *Jane Austen* English author (1775–1817).
2   *mitre* Tall, pointed hat.

Thomasina enters, in a nightgown and barefoot, holding a candlestick. Her manner is secretive and excited.)

490 SEPTIMUS. My lady! What is it?
THOMASINA. Septimus! Shush!

(*She closes the door quietly.*)

Now is our chance!
SEPTIMUS. For what, dear God?

(*She blows out the candle and puts the candlestick on the table.*)

THOMASINA. Do not act the innocent! Tomorrow I will be seventeen!

(*She kisses Septimus full on the mouth.*)

495 There!
SEPTIMUS. Dear Christ!
THOMASINA. Now you must show me, you are paid in advance.
SEPTIMUS. (*Understanding*) Oh!
THOMASINA. The Count plays for us, it is God-given! I cannot be seventeen
500 and not waltz.
SEPTIMUS. But your mother—
THOMASINA. While she swoons, we can dance. The house is all abed. I heard
the Broadwood. Oh, Septimus, teach me now!
SEPTIMUS. Hush! I cannot now!
505 THOMASINA. Indeed you can, and I am come barefoot so mind my toes.
SEPTIMUS. I cannot because it is not a waltz.
THOMASINA. It is not?
SEPTIMUS. No, it is too slow for waltzing.
THOMASINA. Oh! Then we will wait for him to play quickly.
510 SEPTIMUS. My lady—
THOMASINA. Mr. Hodge!

(*She takes a chair next to him and looks at his work.*)

Are you reading my essay? Why do you work here so late?
SEPTIMUS. To save my candles.
THOMASINA. You have my old primer.
515 SEPTIMUS. It is mine again. You should not have written in it.

(*She takes it, looks at the open page.*)

THOMASINA. It was a joke.
SEPTIMUS. It will make me mad as you promised. Sit over there. You will have
us in disgrace.

(Thomasina gets up and goes to the furthest chair.)

THOMASINA. If mama comes I will tell her we only met to kiss, not to waltz.

SEPTIMUS. Silence or bed. 520

THOMASINA. Silence!

(Septimus pours himself some more wine. He continues to read her essay.

The music changes to party music from the marquee. And there are fireworks—small against the sky, distant flares of light like exploding meteors.

Hannah enters. She has dressed for the party. The difference is not, however, dramatic. She closes the door and crosses to leave by the garden door. But as she gets there, Valentine is entering. He has a glass of wine in his hand.)

HANNAH. Oh ...

(But Valentine merely brushes past her, intent on something, and half-drunk.)

VALENTINE. *(To her)* Got it!

(He goes straight to the table and roots about in what is now a considerable mess of papers, books and objects. Hannah turns back, puzzled by his manner. He finds what he has been looking for—the "diagram."

Meanwhile, Septimus reading Thomasina's essay, also studies the diagram. Septimus and Valentine study the diagram doubled by time.)

VALENTINE. It's heat.

HANNAH. Are you tight,[1] Val? 525

VALENTINE. It's a diagram of heat exchange.

SEPTIMUS. So, we are all doomed!

THOMASINA. *(Cheerfully)* Yes.

VALENTINE. Like a steam engine, you see—

(Hannah fills Septimus's glass from the same decanter, and sips from it.)

She didn't have the maths, not remotely. She saw what things meant, way 530 ahead, like seeing a picture.

SEPTIMUS. This is not science. This is story-telling.

THOMASINA. Is it a waltz now?

SEPTIMUS. No.

(The music is still modern.)

---

1   *tight* Drunk.

535 VALENTINE. Like a film.

HANNAH. What did she see?

VALENTINE. That you can't run the film backwards. Heat was the first thing which didn't work that way. Not like Newton. A film of a pendulum, or a ball falling through the air—backwards, it looks the same.

540 HANNAH. The ball would be going the wrong way.

VALENTINE. You'd have to know that. But with heat—friction—a ball breaking a window—

HANNAH. Yes.

VALENTINE. It won't work backwards.

545 HANNAH. Who thought it did?

VALENTINE. She saw why. You can put back the bits of glass but you can't collect up the heat of the smash. It's gone.

SEPTIMUS. So the Improved Newtonian Universe must cease and grow cold. Dear me.

550 VALENTINE. The heat goes into the mix.

(*He gestures to indicate the air in the room, in the universe.*)

THOMASINA. Yes, we must hurry if we are going to dance.

VALENTINE. And everything is mixing the same way, all the time, irreversibly ...

SEPTIMUS. Oh, we have time, I think.

555 VALENTINE. ... till there's no time left. That's what time means.

SEPTIMUS. When we have found all the mysteries and lost all the meaning, we will be alone, on an empty shore.

THOMASINA. Then we will dance. Is this a waltz?

SEPTIMUS. It will serve.

(*He stands up.*)

560 THOMASINA. (*Jumping up*) Goody!

(*Septimus takes her in his arms carefully and the waltz lesson, to the music from the marquee, begins.*

Bernard, in unconvincing Regency dress, enters carrying a bottle.)

BERNARD. Don't mind me, I left my jacket ...

(*He heads for the area of the wicker basket.*)

VALENTINE. Are you leaving?

(*Bernard is stripping off his period coat. He is wearing his own trousers, tucked into knee socks and his own shirt.*)

BERNARD. Yes, I'm afraid so.

HANNAH. What's up, Bernard?

BERNARD. Nothing I can go into—   565

VALENTINE. Should I go?

BERNARD. No, *I'm* going!

(*Valentine and Hannah watch Bernard struggling into his jacket and adjusting his clothes.*

Septimus, holding Thomasina, kisses her on the mouth. The waltz lesson pauses. She looks at him. He kisses her again, in earnest. She puts her arms round him.)

THOMASINA. Septimus ...

(*Septimus hushes her. They start to dance again, with the slight awkwardness of a lesson.*

Chloë bursts in from the garden.)

CHLOË. I'll kill her! I'll *kill* her!

BERNARD. Oh dear.   570

VALENTINE. What the hell is it, Chlo?

CHLOË. (*Venomously*) Mummy!

BERNARD. (*To Valentine*) Your mother caught us in that cottage.

CHLOË. She snooped!

BERNARD. I don't think so. She was rescuing a theodolite.   575

CHLOË. I'll come with you, Bernard.

BERNARD. No, you bloody won't.

CHLOË. Don't you want me to?

BERNARD. Of course not. What for? (*To Valentine*) I'm sorry.

CHLOË. (*In furious tears*) What are you saying sorry to *him* for?   580

BERNARD. Sorry to you too. Sorry one and all. Sorry, Hannah—sorry, Hermione—sorry, Byron—sorry, sorry, sorry, now can I go?

(*Chloë stands stiffly, tearfully.*)

CHLOË. Well ...

(*Thomasina and Septimus dance.*)

HANNAH. What a bastard you are, Bernard.

(*Chloë rounds on her.*)

CHLOË. And you mind your own business! What do you know about any- 585
thing?

HANNAH. Nothing.

CHLOË. (*to Bernard*) It *was* worth it, though, wasn't it?

BERNARD. It was wonderful.

(*Chloë goes out, through the garden door, towards the party.*)

590 HANNAH. (*An echo*) Nothing.

VALENTINE. Well, you shit. I'd drive you but I'm a bit sloshed.

(*Valentine follows Chloë out and can be heard outside calling "Chlo! Chlo!"*)

BERNARD. A scrape.

HANNAH. Oh ... (*she gives up*) Bernard!

BERNARD. I look forward to *The Genius of the Place*. I hope you find your
595   hermit. I think out front is the safest.

(*He opens the door cautiously and looks out.*)

HANNAH. Actually, I've got a good idea who he was, but I can't prove it.

BERNARD. (*With a carefree expansive gesture*) Publish!

(*He goes out closing the door.*

*Septimus and Thomasina are now waltzing freely. She is delighted with
herself.*)

THOMASINA. Am I waltzing?

SEPTIMUS. Yes, my lady.

(*He gives her a final twirl, bringing them to the table where he bows to her.
He lights her candlestick.*

*Hannah goes to sit at the table, playing truant from the party. She pours
herself more wine. The table contains the geometrical solids, the computer,
decanter, glasses, tea mug, Hannah's research books, Septimus's books, the
two portfolios, Thomasina's candlestick, the oil lamp, the dahlia, the Sunday
papers ...*

    *Gus appears in the doorway. It takes a moment to realize that he is not
Lord Augustus; perhaps not until Hannah sees him.*)

600 SEPTIMUS. Take your essay, I have given it an alpha in blind faith. Be careful
   with the flame.

THOMASINA. I will wait for you to come.

SEPTIMUS. I cannot.

THOMASINA. You may.

605 SEPTIMUS. I may not.

THOMASINA. You must.

SEPTIMUS. I will not.

(*She puts the candlestick and the essay on the table.*)

THOMASINA. Then I will not go. Once more, for my birthday.

(*Septimus and Thomasina start to waltz together.*

Gus comes forward, startling Hannah.)

HANNAH. Oh!—you made me jump.

(*Gus looks resplendent. He is carrying an old and somewhat tattered stiff-backed folio fastened with a tape tied in a bow. He comes to Hannah and thrusts this present at her.*)

Oh ...   610

(*She lays the folio down on the table and starts to open it. It consists only of two boards hinged, containing Thomasina's drawing.*)

"Septimus holding Plautus." (*To Gus*) I was looking for that. Thank you.

(*Gus nods several times. Then, rather awkwardly, he bows to her. A Regency bow, an invitation to dance.*)

Oh, dear, I don't really ...

(*After a moment's hesitation, she gets up and they hold each other, keeping a decorous distance between them, and start to dance, rather awkwardly.*

Septimus and Thomasina continue to dance, fluently, to the piano.)

END

—1993

Hannah Moscovitch
b. 1978

Toronto-based playwright Hannah Moscovitch, called "the wunderkind of Canadian theatre" by CBC radio, achieved national success early in her career. She made her name by addressing difficult subjects—in her words, finding "unusual slants on old topics, complex stories, and unheard voices"—in a style that often blends satire and dark humour with emotional sensitivity. "The darker the story gets, the funnier it gets," she has said; "that's what life seems like to me."

Moscovitch was born in Ottawa and grew up in a left-leaning, academic environment; her father was a professor of social policy and her mother a labour researcher and writer of feminist non-fiction. After graduating from the National Theatre School of Canada in the acting stream, Moscovitch studied literature at the University of Toronto. She worked as a waitress at an upscale Toronto restaurant for several years before her successes enabled her to write full-time.

Moscovitch first gained widespread acclaim with the debut of her short plays *Essay* (2005) and *The Russian Play* (2006) at Toronto's SummerWorks festival; *Essay* won the Contra Guys Award for Best New Play, and *The Russian Play* was awarded Jury Prize for Best New Production. She is still perhaps best known for these works—together with *East of Berlin* (2007), which won the Dora Mavor Moore Award and was nominated for a Governor General's Award in 2009.

The content of Moscovitch's work is often challenging or controversial: *Essay* confronts issues of gender and power in academia, *East of Berlin* addresses the legacy of the Holocaust, and *This Is War* (2013) is based on a true story involving Canadian soldiers in 2008 Afghanistan. Regarding the social and political complexity of her plays, she says, "I want to ask the audience questions. I get excited by the idea of a character being forced to confront a hostile audience. There's something so fascinating about watching those dynamics play out."

Essay

CHARACTERS

Jeffrey: thirty
Pixie: eighteen
Professor Galbraith: early sixties

SCENE 1

A small office on campus. An open laptop sits on a desk amidst piles of papers, files and books. The greenish hue of fluorescent lighting fills the room. Lights up on Jeffrey, behind the desk, and Pixie, in front of it.

JEFFREY. Just, uh, please take a seat while I finish this paragraph and then I'll leave off.
PIXIE. Am I early ...? Or ...?
JEFFREY. No, no, just finishing up, just finishing up.

(*Jeffrey closes his laptop.*)

Now. Essay proposal, is that right? Essay due on the eighteenth?   5
PIXIE. Thank you for letting me come and—
JEFFREY. No, please. Just remind me. I rejected your proposal, is that ...?
PIXIE. Uh, yes, you did, but—
JEFFREY. Right. Good. Well, my notes are vague sometimes, and my handwriting is very bad, so before you raze the field, we might as well take a   10
closer look at it.
PIXIE. (*getting out her essay proposal*) Okay, great, um, well what I wanted to—
JEFFREY. It's usually just a question of coming up with an alteration that will render it—   15
PIXIE. —um, okay—
JEFFREY. —more precise, more scholarly.
PIXIE. Okay. That's what I wanted to talk to you about.
JEFFREY. Good. Yes. Let's talk!
PIXIE. Your objections, because I—I think I can make an argument for this   20
essay proposal.
JEFFREY. This one?
PIXIE. Yeah.
JEFFREY. This essay proposal?
PIXIE. Yes?   25

(*Beat.*)

JEFFREY. Ah. I see. You've come to contest.

PIXIE. Or at least I just wanted to—

JEFFREY. To make your case, is that it?

PIXIE. I—I just think that—that it's possible—that it's possible to argue, I
30   mean if the problem is just sourcing.

JEFFREY. Let me take a look at it, can I?

> (*Pixie hands him the essay proposal.*)

Let's just see what we've got here before we ... (*laughs*) ... have it out.

> (*Beat.*)

PIXIE. (*waiting, shifting*) If—if you read the notes you made ...

> (*Jeffrey holds out his hand to indicate to Pixie that she should give him a minute to finish reading.*)

> (*Beat.*)

JEFFREY. (*scanning*) Elizabeth Farnese.[1] Strategies of, important contributions
35   to. Summary, summary, more summary. Look. What you've got here is
very interesting. A very interesting historical figure—

PIXIE. Yeah, well I thought—

JEFFREY. —who no doubt deserves more.... An argument could be made
that this is an oversight. The historical record has failed to illuminate this
40   neglected but highly engaging corner of European history.

PIXIE. Unhunh, well—

JEFFREY. Hoards of insensitive historians have obscured a very important
character, as it were.

PIXIE. Yeah, well—

45 JEFFREY. And she is worthy, entitled to, a second glance, now, in our modern
era. However, that said—

PIXIE. Unhunh.

JEFFREY. —that said, I'm not sure that for the purposes of this first year
course it's—it's—if there would be enough material to support a ten-page
50   essay on the topic.

PIXIE. Yeah, but—

JEFFREY. Ten pages. You'll need more than a cursory—

PIXIE. Yeah.

---

1   *Elizabeth Farnese* Italian noblewoman (1692–1766) and queen consort of Spain.
Through her influence over her husband Philip V, she orchestrated Spain's foreign policy,
including the country's involvement in several wars. Because Philip already had children
by his first wife, Elizabeth's primary ambition was to secure Italian thrones for her sons.

JEFFREY. —more than a brief mention in a larger—

PIXIE. Yeah, I have. I have plenty of material. And also, there's one listed at   55
the bottom of the supplementary readings, on page twenty-one.

JEFFREY. One what?

PIXIE. An article on her.

(*Beat.*)

JEFFREY. That's very possible, all right.

PIXIE. And I found ample sources in the stacks.   60

JEFFREY. That's very possible.

PIXIE. And the article was on the list—

JEFFREY. Right, right I see the—now we're getting to the bottom of the—

PIXIE. —and so—

JEFFREY. This is progress!   65

PIXIE. And so, I thought—

JEFFREY. You thought it was on the list, it must be—

PIXIE. Yeah.

JEFFREY. And I want to stress that your idea is not invalid, by any means, all
right?   70

PIXIE. Unhunh.

JEFFREY. At least not in general terms, all right?

PIXIE. Unhunh?

(*Beat.*)

JEFFREY. I'm not the—I don't want to be the big bad—

PIXIE. Yeah?   75

JEFFREY. —the big bad—

PIXIE. Yeah?

JEFFREY. Is that ...? Is it Pixie? Is that your ...?

PIXIE. Yeah. Pixie.

JEFFREY. Look, Pixie—   80

PIXIE. Yeah?

JEFFREY. I understand you feel very passionately about this. Here you are in
my office, overflowing with passion ... (*laughs*) ...

(*Pixie shifts away from Jeffrey.*)

No, no, what I mean is you've made the effort to come here, to defend
your proposal to me, the topic you've chosen indicates that you're trying to   85
avoid the banal and revitalize history, as it were, and so—

PIXIE. Yeah?

JEFFREY. I want to stress that I appreciate your passion.

(*Beat.*)

PIXIE. But—

90 JEFFREY. Your topic is frankly.... You see, this is a history course that—

PIXIE. And this is history.

JEFFREY. Yes, yes it's history, but Pixie, this course deals with war and state-craft. In the eighteenth and early nineteenth century.

PIXIE. Yeah?

95 JEFFREY. Eighteenth and early nineteenth century. Now I'm not saying that women haven't, in more recent times, made very valuable contributions to war efforts. But, in the eighteenth century, women didn't yet—

PIXIE. —unhuhn—

JEFFREY. —possess the freedom of movement, the—the wherewithal to—

100 PIXIE. —unhuhn—

JEFFREY. —and so women couldn't as yet be classified as "military leaders," per se.

PIXIE. Okay, but—

JEFFREY. And—just a minute—and that is why I can't allow you to write a

105 paper on a woman who, while she may be very compelling from a social history perspective—

PIXIE. Yeah, but she—

JEFFREY. —is not an appropriate subject given the requirements of this particular writing assignment. Now I commend you for finding source mate-

110 rial. Good work there! But the thing is you're simply not on topic.

(*Jeffrey hands back Pixie's essay proposal.*)

If you need to hear this from a higher source, by all means, take it up with the professor, he is the final word—

PIXIE. No, it's fine, I'm just—I don't know, a little—

JEFFREY. Disappointed, I see that.

115 PIXIE. No, I'm confused.

JEFFREY. Yes. Confused, disappointed, and believe me, I understand. European history is a ... bewildering series of men who prance about, waging war, and making a nuisance of themselves. And so, you light on Elizabeth Farnese because you'd like to champion her, establish her worth, she is one

120 of the unacknowledged greats of history, and that's a very understandable response given the material—

PIXIE. Wait.

JEFFREY. —the time period—

PIXIE. You—wait—you think I picked her because she's a girl? You think I

125 picked Elizabeth Farnese because she's a girl?

(*Beat.*)

JEFFREY. Well, what I was suggesting wasn't quite so simplistic—

PIXIE. I didn't. I really—I'm not a feminist. It said war and strategy and she was a great strategist, really, if you read the material I found.

JEFFREY. I—Pixie, I'm sure she was, but—

PIXIE. She was.   130

JEFFREY. I'm sure she was, but—

PIXIE. She was. She was a great strategist, she played everyone. The French, the Austrians—

JEFFREY. Yes, Pixie, that's the history.

PIXIE. Well, that's why I picked her. 'Cause I thought that was on topic.   135

JEFFREY. I—let's back up here for a moment—

PIXIE. I thought I was on topic.

JEFFREY. Pixie, let's—please, let's back up for a moment—

PIXIE. If I'm not on topic, then—

JEFFREY. Pixie! Please. I want to—we must address a statement you made a   140
moment ago. Did I, or am I mistaken, hear you say you're not a feminist?

PIXIE. No, I'm not, I was just doing the assignment.

JEFFREY. Yes, yes, but—

PIXIE. I thought it was just a question of sources. That's what you wrote on my sheet, that's why I came here.   145

JEFFREY. Yes, but Pixie. Feminism—

PIXIE. I'm not a feminist.

JEFFREY. But you ... (*laughs uncomfortably*) ... I don't think you—

PIXIE. I'm not. I took this course. I wanted to take the history of war, I didn't take a women's studies course—   150

JEFFREY. —but—

PIXIE. —I took this course.

JEFFREY. But, Pixie, women's studies is a very valuable body of knowledge, and you are a feminist.

PIXIE. No I'm not.   155

JEFFREY. Yes you ...! Perhaps you don't realize—

PIXIE. I'm not a feminist—

JEFFREY. —because the very fact that you're standing here, before me, in this institution—a hundred years ago, fifty, that would not have been possible, and you would not have received adequate education to be able to argue to   160
me that Elizabeth Farnese is a military leader—

PIXIE. No, this is the point. I didn't pick her because she's a girl.

JEFFREY. But Pixie—

PIXIE. I didn't go looking for some girl so I could pick her, so I could make some big point to you to vindicate women or whatever you're thinking—   165

JEFFREY. Why did you pick her, then?

(*Beat.*)

Why pick her?

(*Beat.*)

PIXIE. Okay. Fine. I picked a girl. But the point I was trying to make about not being a feminist was—

170 JEFFREY. You are a feminist.

PIXIE. No I'm not.

JEFFREY. Yes you ...! Pixie, look—

PIXIE. I'm not.

JEFFREY. Look. Take you and I, you and I, Pixie. You believe yourself to be

175 equal to me, don't you?

PIXIE. I'm your student.

JEFFREY. Yes, but, aside from our status as—as—I'm a bad example. Take any of your fellow students, the male members of your classes, you believe yourself to be equal to them, don't you?

(*Beat.*)

180 That's feminism. That is feminism. And so you are, by definition—

PIXIE. Fine. Fine. I'm a feminist.

JEFFREY. Now, all right—

PIXIE. I'm a fucking feminist.

JEFFREY. All right. Let's not—let's please—

185 PIXIE. All I was trying to say was I thought Elizabeth Farnese was really effective and interesting, but I don't care, okay? I'll write on Napoleon.

JEFFREY. Yes, all right.

PIXIE. I'll write on Napoleon like everyone else.

JEFFREY. Pixie. Please, just slow down. Let's not raise our voices please.

(*Beat.*)

190 PIXIE. (*more confused than sorry*) Sorry.

JEFFREY. That's all right.

(*Beat.*)

Napoleon would be a highly appropriate choice, in the context of this ...

(*Pixie has walked out.*)

Pixie, where are you going?

(*Jeffrey walks after her.*)

Can you—can we please finish our ...?

(*Beat.*)

Pixie?   195

(*Pixie is gone. Jeffrey shakes his head, and goes back over to his desk. He crosses off his meeting with Pixie in his date book. Lights out.*)

SCENE 2

Jeffrey's office, a week and a half later. There is a pile of essays on his desk. Jeffrey is marking. Professor Galbraith enters and looks at the office.

GALBRAITH. This is a dismal little office, Jeffrey.

JEFFREY. (*standing*) Professor Galbraith!

GALBRAITH. I haven't been down here since, well, the seventies, and I don't think it's changed.

JEFFREY. Thank you for ... stopping by.   5

GALBRAITH. Who are you sharing it with, some social science ...?

JEFFREY. She's, yes, an anthropology Ph.D., but she's on a very different schedule, opposite hours—

GALBRAITH. Good.

JEFFREY. It's worked out well. I barely ever see her.   10

(*Beat.*)

And I keep meaning to say thank you for finding me this office—

GALBRAITH. So what's the matter, Jeffrey? Hm? Your email, your phone call? I'm sorry I've been unresponsive, the conference—

JEFFREY. Yes, I know, the timing—

GALBRAITH. I agreed to moderate a couple of panels, deliver a keynote, and   15
suddenly when the coffee machine breaks down, they all come to me.

JEFFREY. Yes, I can see how that would happen.

GALBRAITH. This is the downside of heading the department. There are up-sides! There are upsides!

JEFFREY. I'm sure there are.   20

(*Beat.*)

So, Professor—

GALBRAITH. So what is it, Jeffrey? Hm? You need to consult? You need to be supervised? Someone to hold your hand?

JEFFREY. Well—

GALBRAITH. It's difficult, this juncture in the dissertation-writing process.   25

The tunnel, they call it.

JEFFREY. Uh, no—

GALBRAITH. Which is apt because you're pretty much hunting down your own asshole at this point, excuse the.... Because, once the research is done
30 and you're writing—

JEFFREY. Yes, no, I—

GALBRAITH. —there it is, looming on the horizon, your own anus. That's what a Ph.D. is. An heroic-apocalyptic confrontation with the self.

JEFFREY. Professor, that's very ... funny, and sometimes it does feel as though
35 I'm peering into my own ... but no, it's not my dissertation.

GALBRAITH. Dissertation is going well, is it?

JEFFREY. Yes, it's going, but I've been trying to grade the essays for History 103?

(*Galbraith picks up a pile of essays.*)

GALBRAITH. This them?
40 JEFFREY. Yes, and what I need to ask you is—

GALBRAITH. Lots of little comments. Good point. This is awkward.

JEFFREY. (*laughs*) Yes.

GALBRAITH. Where's your thesis?

JEFFREY. Yes ... (*laughs*) ... and, uh, Professor, what I wanted to ask you is—
45 GALBRAITH. I haven't seen you at the conference, by the way.

(*Beat.*)

JEFFREY. No. I haven't been attending. I've been so intent on getting through these—

GALBRAITH. I chaired what turned out to be a very energetic panel on inter- pretations of Napoleonic law.
50 JEFFREY. Well, I'm sorry I missed it.

GALBRAITH. Also a lecture on problems of coalition warfare. Quite compel- ling. A Chicago University professor, Sheila Newbery. Right up your alley, research wise. I hope you weren't grading undergraduate essays rather than attending the conference?
55 JEFFREY. I—well—I—

GALBRAITH. I hope you were at least chasing—or—what's the euphemism these days for female companionship? The conference falls a little short there. One look at the participants and.... (*laughs*) Don't expect to find love in the history department, Jeffrey.
60 JEFFREY. I ... won't hold my breath. (*trying to joke*) Perhaps the English de- partment.

GALBRAITH. There's a good hunting ground. The English department!

(*Professor Galbraith and Jeffrey share a laugh. Beat.*)

JEFFREY. Professor, I wanted to ask you—
GALBRAITH. Oh, right, yes, ask me the—
JEFFREY. A student of mine, an essay—   65
GALBRAITH. Right.

(*Jeffrey begins looking through the pile for Pixie's essay.*)

JEFFREY. I'm trying to grade this one paper, but it's very difficult. I rejected
    this student's essay proposal when she submitted it two weeks ago. We   70
    discussed it, I thought she'd resolved to write on a more appropriate topic,
    but, as it turns out, she hasn't. She's written on the original.
GALBRAITH. Ah.
JEFFREY. And, yes, and now I'm not sure whether to fail her, or what's the
    procedure? I told her to come by my office this afternoon, thinking I'd   75
    have a chance to confer with you first—

(*Jeffrey finds the essay and hands it to Professor Galbraith.*)

The title should give you a good sense of the type of—
GALBRAITH. Cock-up?
JEFFREY. Yes.

(*Beat. Professor Galbraith and Jeffrey look at the title.*)

GALBRAITH. Hmmm, yes! Quite the—   80
JEFFREY. You see the ...

(*Beat.*)

GALBRAITH. (*reading*) Elizabeth Farnese and Napoleon Bonaparte: A Critical
    Comparison of their Wartime Strategies.
JEFFREY. You see the difficulty. And, for grading, it reads like an English
    paper, all conjecture and—   85
GALBRAITH. Yes.

(*Beat.*)

JEFFREY. The sources are fine, but—
GALBRAITH. Yes.

(*Beat.*)

Yes, this certainly isn't what I discussed with her. I didn't approve a comparison. Although, I suppose she was trying to appease you and write on   90
her topic. Servant of two masters.

(*Professor Galbraith looks through the essay.*)

JEFFREY. I'm ... sorry. I'm sorry, Professor. You—did she—

GALBRAITH. Didn't I tell you, Jeffrey? This girl came to see me a week, a week
and a half ago, asked if she could write on Elizabeth Farnese, Philip the
95   fifth's second wife?

JEFFREY. (*to confirm that he knows who she is*) Yes.

GALBRAITH. How Elizabeth Farnese is a military leader ... (*laughs*) ... I'm
interested to know.

(*Professor Galbraith flips through the essay.*)

JEFFREY. Yes, but, she's not. I'm sorry, she's not, at least not considered to
100   be—

GALBRAITH. Elizabeth Farnese?

JEFFREY. She's not generally considered to be a military leader—

GALBRAITH. No, no, of course not. But, she seemed.... This girl—the girl ...?

JEFFREY. Pixie Findley?

105 GALBRAITH. She seemed very—I'm probably looking for attractive, but let's
say determined for the sake of decorum. I thought, why not let her have a
go, she's likely going to argue something preposterous. Has she?

JEFFREY. I—I don't know.

GALBRAITH. I was hoping for something a little risqué, at least euphemisti-
110   cally, as in Elizabeth Farnese's victories were won not on the battlefield but
in the bedroom, or Frederick the Great favoured the oblique attack while
Elizabeth perfected the horizontal one, something to that effect.

(*Professor Galbraith reads through the essay.*)

JEFFREY. But the guidelines for this essay were very specific—

GALBRAITH. I let the leash out a little.

(*Beat.*)

115 JEFFREY. I—yes—I can see why you might. I hesitated, uh, briefly before I
rejected her proposal. It's sensitive, of course, and highly charged, but the
reason why I ultimately did turn her down was—

GALBRAITH. (*referring to Pixie's essay*) This is quite good, this opening.

(*Beat.*)

JEFFREY. The reason, Professor, why I didn't allow Pixie to write on Elizabeth
120   Farnese is that I felt fairly certain that, given the parameters of the assignment that you set, military leader, it would result in her producing a very
weak essay.

(*Beat.*)

And she has produced a very weak essay. Professor.

GALBRAITH. Ah, now, here we have it! (reading from Pixie's essay) "While Napoleon engaged in warfare to resolve international strife," very nice, "Elizabeth relied on her feminine wiles." 125

JEFFREY. Professor.

GALBRAITH. Very nice phrasing. Wiles. Where do you suppose her wiles were located?

JEFFREY. Look, I— 130

GALBRAITH. Adjacent to her thighs, presumably.

JEFFREY. I—Professor—this is a student's essay!

(*Galbraith stops reading Pixie's essay and looks at Jeffrey.*)

I realize some of it's laughable, but ...

(*Beat.*)

I'm sorry, I'm just a little surprised you allowed a student to write on Elizabeth Farnese. 135

GALBRAITH. What are you concerned about, Jeffrey? Her grade?

JEFFREY. Well, yes, her grade, but also—

GALBRAITH. Pass her, write a few comments on it. Good effort. Fails to convince.

JEFFREY. I suppose I can do that. This essay certainly doesn't deserve a passing 140 grade. I don't feel all that comfortable with—

GALBRAITH. Jeffrey—

JEFFREY. —arbitrarily assigning it one.

(*Beat.*)

GALBRAITH. B minus.

(*Beat.*)

JEFFREY. No—you—no, the point is, I'm forced to arbitrarily assign her a 145 grade because she was allowed to write on a, I think, inappropriate ... B minus. That's at least a firm hold on the material. Look, I—I really don't like being put in this position at all, I feel very—

GALBRAITH. Jeffrey.

JEFFREY. B minus? Based on what criteria? 150

GALBRAITH. Well, no doubt she learned something while writing it.

JEFFREY. She learned. She learned something. That's your criterion?

GALBRAITH. You don't like my criterion?

JEFFREY. This is a very unconvincing essay!

155 GALBRAITH. How bad can it be?

JEFFREY. It's a terrible essay! It's ridiculous.

GALBRAITH. Jeffrey.

JEFFREY. A short story would be more convincing. A finger-painting!

GALBRAITH. Oh, for Christ's sake, Jeffrey, she wrote a bad essay! The girl is

160 seventeen. Eighteen. Let her go skip off and neck in the quad.

(*Beat.*)

JEFFREY. Neck in the ...!

GALBRAITH. Or what do they say, make out?

(*Beat.*)

JEFFREY. Professor, this is the student who argued that Elizabeth Farnese is a military leader, and now you're trivializing—

165 GALBRAITH. All right—

JEFFREY. —and—and ridiculing her very earnest attempt—

GALBRAITH. All right!

JEFFREY. —to include women in the history of—

GALBRAITH. Yes, I know, Jeffrey, because I'm the one who let her. I approved

170 her essay topic. I said yes. Write on Elizabeth Farnese. Prove she's on par with Nelson,[1] Napoleon. Set us all straight, us men.

(*Beat.*)

(*smiling*) We have to let the girls have their day, Jeffrey.

(*Beat.*)

JEFFREY. We have to ... let the girls ...?

(*Beat.*)

I'm sorry?

175 GALBRAITH. In my experience, it's best to just let them, well, have their day.

(*Beat.*)

JEFFREY. What do you mean?

GALBRAITH. It may make for weak scholarship, but I think it's best to allow for it, at the moment, despite its weaknesses.

(*Beat.*)

---

1   *Nelson* Viscount Horatio Nelson (1758–1805), famous English admiral responsible for British victories in the important naval battles of several wars.

JEFFREY. I—I'm sorry. What—what makes for weak scholarship?

GALBRAITH. There's a great deal of so-called research in circulation these days   180
that's entirely based on resentment.

JEFFREY. What are you talking about?

GALBRAITH. Gendered revisionism,[1] Jeffrey. Biographies of Napoleon's lover,
James Joyce's wife,[2] the unsung women of history, herstory, all very fashionable, but at a certain point ... (*laughs*) ... it fails to convince.   185

(*Beat.*)

JEFFREY. It—it fails to ... are you joking? Professor?

GALBRAITH. You said it yourself. Pixie's essay is a failure. Why? Because Elizabeth Farnese is, at best, a second-rate figure who cannot yield any important historical insight.

JEFFREY. Yes, perhaps in the context of this assignment—   190

GALBRAITH. And the result, an unscholarly, as you said, paper—

JEFFREY. But not as a general—

GALBRAITH. That you deemed weak—

JEFFREY. I—I wouldn't make that kind of a sweeping—

GALBRAITH. That you rejected—   195

JEFFREY. Yes! I—yes—I rejected her essay proposal, not the whole field of
inquiry!

(*Beat.*)

GALBRAITH. All right, Jeffrey, what is history? What is it?

(*Beat.*)

JEFFREY. What is ... history?

GALBRAITH. Too broad? What isn't history?   200

(*Beat.*)

JEFFREY. What is not—

GALBRAITH. What can we say is not history?

(*Beat.*)

Seventeenth, eighteenth century. What are men doing?

---

1   *revisionism* I.e., reinterpretation of history in opposition to conventional approaches; although the term can be value-neutral, it is sometimes used disparagingly to suggest an
intellectually unjustified denial of accepted facts.

2   *Napoleon's lover* Napoleon's several lovers included a countess, a queen, and a famous
actress; *James Joyce's wife* The Irish novelist James Joyce was married to Nora Barnacle
(1884–1951), who inspired the character of Molly Bloom in his novel *Ulysses* (1922).

(*Beat.*)

Revolutionizing warfare. And what are women doing?

205 JEFFREY. Well, they're—

GALBRAITH. Curling their hair, boiling potatoes, et cetera, et cetera. They are not central to the major events. They are—it's unfortunate, it's unlikeable—marginal to them. If we want to include women, we have to reorient history to the mundane, and frankly—

210 JEFFREY. —uh, Professor—

GALBRAITH. —frankly—

JEFFREY. —Professor—

GALBRAITH. —then it's no longer history, is it? It's sociology, anthropology, women's studies-ology.

(*Beat.*)

215 JEFFREY. Look, Professor, that is all ... very controversial and I—

GALBRAITH. What?

JEFFREY. I—I—

GALBRAITH. What?

JEFFREY. —disagree. I think we should be privileging a female discourse, 220 given how excluded and sidelined—

GALBRAITH. So Elizabeth Farnese is a military leader.

JEFFREY. No, that's not—that's a bad example.

GALBRAITH. Which is it?

JEFFREY. I don't think it's an either-or—

225 GALBRAITH. So she is?

JEFFREY. Well, one could argue, I mean, as it stands, no.

GALBRAITH. So she isn't.

JEFFREY. No—she—I just—no, I don't think it's that simple. Because—

GALBRAITH. Jeffrey.

230 JEFFREY. No! Because one could argue, one could radically redefine the term military leader—

GALBRAITH. Yes, and one could write an essay about how Napoleon's horse influenced his decisions. If a horse came to you and asked if it could write that essay, you would probably say, let the horse have its day. Call it 235 horsestory. And it may be true, to a certain extent, that Napoleon's horse did influence his decisions, but who really gives a damn?

(*Beat.*)

JEFFREY. Professor, I'm sorry, are you actually not joking? Because I—I can't believe I'm hearing this.

GALBRAITH. Jeffrey, relax, all right?

JEFFREY. I can't believe you just said horsestory.   240

GALBRAITH. Jeffrey.

JEFFREY. Horsestory? Professor? Horsestory? That's a very pejorative, uh, derisive, misogynist—

GALBRAITH. Misogynist?

JEFFREY. I, yes, I think, misogynist—   245

GALBRAITH. All right, all right, relax, I'm ... what? Toying with your liberal sensibilities? I'm not rejecting all revisionism, per se. However, one gets tired, worn down. The relentless onslaught of victimology. The history department's awash in it. We're being strangled to death by cultural studies. They've got their own fucking department, why do they want mine? 250 What is wrong with Napoleon? Personally, I love the guy. You love the guy!

    (*Beat.*)

JEFFREY. Well, yes, but—

GALBRAITH. That's history, Jeffrey. That's history. A love affair with Napoleon.

JEFFREY. I—no, you see—no—I don't agree.

    (*Beat.*)

  I disagree!   255

GALBRAITH. You're researching Napoleon—

JEFFREY. Yes, fine, I am, but I don't think Napoleon Bonaparte is the only valid ...! I think this whole argument only highlights the fact that we've constructed a false notion of history as male, as centred on male events, male figures, in which case, we should be trying to update, and redress— 260

GALBRAITH. —yes, fine—

JEFFREY. —to try and right the balance.

GALBRAITH. Yes. You're right.

JEFFREY. And broaden the scope of ...

    (*Beat.*)

  I'm right.   265

GALBRAITH. Yes, I agree. I agree with you, as in Pixie's case. Pixie got to write her essay. Write on a female figure, have her say—

JEFFREY. No, but, no —

GALBRAITH. Right the balance, redress the what-have-you—

JEFFREY. But, no—that's not—no—you think her say has no merit.   270

    (*Beat.*)

  You think it's merit-less.

GALBRAITH. So do you.

JEFFREY. But, no, look, that's patronizing.

GALBRAITH. No Jeffrey.

275 JEFFREY. That's—yes it is. You're humouring her, you're cynically appeasing
her—

GALBRAITH. Pixie is happy.

(*Beat.*)

JEFFREY. That's ...! You're patronizing her!

GALBRAITH. I am allowing her to have her say.

280 JEFFREY. You don't value her say!

GALBRAITH. She can't tell the difference. If she can't tell the difference, then—

JEFFREY. What? Then it's not patronizing?

GALBRAITH. Then, no, it's not patronizing, largely because she doesn't feel
patronized.

285 JEFFREY. Yes, but that's only because—

GALBRAITH. Or are you claiming to be better qualified to determine what's
patronizing for Pixie than Pixie is herself?

JEFFREY. No, no I'm not. Except, yes, at this moment, yes, I'm the one who's—

GALBRAITH. What?

290 JEFFREY. Here! Listening to—privy to—

GALBRAITH. What?

JEFFREY. To ... your—

GALBRAITH. What? Jeffrey?

JEFFREY. —sexism!

(*Long beat.*)

295 GALBRAITH. Hm.

(*Beat.*)

Do you think you might be a little worn down?

JEFFREY. Uh, no, I think I'm fine.

GALBRAITH. (*considering*) Three, four years into your Ph.D. Middle of your
thesis, three tutorials, this little office, working until all hours, you haven't
300 been attending the conference, leaving me a series of phone and email
messages about one undergraduate paper.

(*Beat.*)

JEFFREY. If you're suggesting that—

GALBRAITH. Because it's inadvisable to throw around words like sexist, all
right Jeffrey? Given the current climate in campus politics. And, once

you've been in the department a little longer, then you'll start to— 305

JEFFREY. What? Then I'll what? I'll start referring to my female students as girls and allowing the attractive ones to write personal responses instead of essays. "How do you feel about Napoleon, Pixie?" "Oh, I really like him." B minus!

GALBRAITH. (*laughs*) No, but, over time, you will come to realize that stu- 310 dents such as Pixie float through here every year on their way to the cultural studies department. Next year she'll switch to commerce, business admin. Why? Because she likes their building better. And then, when you've seen enough Pixies come and go, you'll realize it's best to just let them have their little say. 315

(*A momentary standoff between the men. Pixie enters at the doorway.*)

PIXIE. Hi! Sorry to interrupt. (*to Galbraith*) Hi Professor. (*to Jeffrey*) I just wanted to let you know I'm here. If you're—uh—in the middle of something, I'll just wait in the hallway until you're—

GALBRAITH. No, Pixie, please, come in.

PIXIE. I can just wait in the hallway. 320

GALBRAITH. No, no, please, come in. Jeffrey and I were just discussing, but please.

JEFFREY. Uh, yes. Come in Pixie.

(*Pixie enters.*)

PIXIE. Am I in trouble ... or ...?

JEFFREY. Uh no, no Pixie, I'm sorry, please sit down— 325

PIXIE. Okay, just with the two of you standing there ...

JEFFREY. Yes, I'm sorry, we were just finishing up. (*to Professor Galbraith*) Professor, I asked Pixie here to talk about her essay.

GALBRAITH. Right, right.

JEFFREY. And so I think I should, uh— 330

GALBRAITH. Right. Well, I'm off. I'll leave you to it.

(*Beat.*)

Jeffrey, the conference resumes at ten tomorrow morning, should you choose to grace us. (*to Pixie*) Pixie. Nice to see you again so soon.

PIXIE. Yeah.

GALBRAITH. And the assignment we discussed ...? When was it, a week, a 335 week and a half ago?

PIXIE. Yeah.

GALBRAITH. How did it go? Hm? Did you enjoy writing it?

PIXIE. (*with a quick glance at Jeffrey*) I, yes, I really enjoyed—I learned a lot.

340   GALBRAITH. That's good. That's good. That's very good.

(*Galbraith looks at Jeffrey. So does Pixie, causing Jeffrey to turn away. Beat.*)

There are sources, Pixie, that suggest Elizabeth Farnese may have led the Spanish Army against the French in 1717,[1] not long after her accession.

PIXIE. Yeah, I came across that.

GALBRAITH. (*picturing it*) On horseback, at the head of the Spanish Army, as
345   the formidable Louis XV crossed the Pyrenees.[2]

PIXIE. Yes.

GALBRAITH. Quite the—quite the—

PIXIE. Yeah—

GALBRAITH. —feat! For a young ...!

350   PIXIE. (*with a quick glance at Jeffrey*) Unhunh, yeah, I thought so too.

GALBRAITH. A very ambitious young person. Shared a number of qualities with Napoleon Bonaparte.

PIXIE. Uh, yeah! The comparison is kind of a stretch, of course. Napoleon conquered Europe, and Elizabeth got her sons thrones through her diplo-
355   macy, but, um, I think it holds.

GALBRAITH. (*considering her*) Elizabeth Farnese! It's a shame she wasn't al-lowed to cultivate her talents more fully. But, in the eighteenth century—

PIXIE. Yeah! I, uh—it's weird. There's not a lot of, um, women in this history we're covering—

360   GALBRAITH. No.

PIXIE. No, and the funny thing is, all term I've had this feeling of being left out. Like, it's all been very interesting, but it doesn't feel like it's about me, or for me, if that makes any sense?

(*Galbraith smiles at her.*)

I thought it might just be because I'm in first year, and everything is a little
365   ...! But I think it's actually the content of the course. (*to Jeffrey*) And I was thinking about, uh, what you asked. Why—why I chose Elizabeth, why I wanted to write on her, and I think that probably, without realizing it, I chose her because—I don't know.

(*Beat.*)

---

1   *Spanish Army ... in 1717* In 1717, Spain briefly conquered Sardinia, initiating the War of the Quadruple Alliance (1718–20), in which France, Britain, the Netherlands, and the Holy Roman Empire united against Spain.

2   *Louis XV* King Louis XV of France (1710–74) was still a child when the French army invaded Spain as part of the War of the Quadruple Alliance; *Pyrenees* Mountain range separating France and Spain.

(*to Jeffrey*) Because I wanted to be in it, you know?

(*Beat.*)

GALBRAITH. Well, that's very nice, Pixie. That's a very nice sentiment.   370
PIXIE. Uh, yeah.

(*Beat.*)

JEFFREY. And Pixie, now that you've written on Elizabeth Farnese, do you feel there is a place for women in history? Or, are they just left out?

(*Beat.*)

PIXIE. Uh, um—
GALBRAITH. I'm sorry, Pixie. We're interrogating you. (*to Jeffrey*) Jeffrey, we're   375
interrogating her, I think we should stop.
PIXIE. No, I just didn't, uh, come prepared to—
GALBRAITH. No, of course you didn't—
JEFFREY. I—I'm sorry Pixie, just the one last question, if you don't mind, and then we'll talk about your essay.   380

(*Beat.*)

PIXIE. What was the question?
GALBRAITH. Jeffrey, this is getting a little heavy-handed—
JEFFREY. The question was, is there a place for women in history?

(*Beat.*)

PIXIE. Well, from the lectures and the textbooks, I would say women don't have a place in history. But I don't know if I believe that.   385
JEFFREY. What do you believe?

(*Beat.*)

PIXIE. Is this about my essay?
GALBRAITH. All right, we've asked our questions. I think we should stop now before Pixie begins to feel put upon—
JEFFREY. (*a little too vehement*) She—no—she wants to answer!   390

(*Beat.*)

I—I'm sorry, is there some reason why Pixie shouldn't be allowed to offer a response?

(*Beat.*)

GALBRAITH. Pixie, would you please wait in the hallway for a moment—

PIXIE. Uh, okay—

395 JEFFREY. (*motioning for Pixie to wait*) Uh, no, Pixie. (*to Galbraith*) Professor, why? Is there some reason why Pixie can't answer?

GALBRAITH. She can answer, Jeffrey, it's not a question of whether or not she can answer—

JEFFREY. Then—

400 GALBRAITH. I have no objections to hearing Pixie's response—

JEFFREY. Then, good! Let's—

GALBRAITH. —but I'm afraid we're overburdening her—

JEFFREY. With one question?

(*Beat.*)

GALBRAITH. (*to Pixie*) Pixie, I'm sorry, if you could please wait in the hallway
405   for one moment—

PIXIE. Uh, okay—

JEFFREY. I don't see why Pixie should wait in the hallway—

GALBRAITH. (*to Pixie*) Jeffrey and I are ... (*laughs*)—

JEFFREY. (*to Galbraith*)—while we—

410 GALBRAITH. (*to Pixie*)—in the midst of a.... Your essay raised a number of questions—

JEFFREY. (*to Pixie*)—about women and their under-representation in the historical record, and, Pixie, your essay interests us in that—

GALBRAITH. (*low, to Jeffrey*) Jeffrey—

415 JEFFREY. (*to Pixie*)—in that it speaks to the deficit of female figures—

GALBRAITH. (*low, to Jeffrey*) I'd really prefer if you didn't—

JEFFREY. (*to Pixie*)—as well as history departments' traditional unwillingness to—

GALBRAITH. (*to Jeffrey*)—extend our argument into student affairs!

420 JEFFREY. (*to Galbraith*) Extend it into ...! It's about her. Her essay is the subject of the argument!

(*Beat.*)

GALBRAITH. (*to Pixie*) Thank you, Pixie, it will just be one minute.

PIXIE. Okay—

JEFFREY. (*to Galbraith*) Just now, Professor, Pixie very clearly expressed feel-
425   ings of exclusion. She's been left out. The subject matter doesn't seem to be addressed to her—

GALBRAITH. Yes, I heard her—

JEFFREY. —the history excludes her.

GALBRAITH. I heard her.

430 JEFFREY. I'd like to—can we hear her out? Because I don't see how she can be included in the discourse if she's sitting in the hallway.

(*Beat.*)

GALBRAITH. Fine, go ahead.

(*Jeffrey stares at Galbraith.*)

Go ahead.

(*Galbraith indicates that Jeffrey can ask his question.*)

JEFFREY. Pixie, I'm sorry, the question, should women have a place in history? I would very much like to hear your response.   435

(*Beat.*)

PIXIE. Look, I—I don't know, okay? You're the experts. Why don't you tell me. I came here to learn, to be taught, so I really don't know.

(*Beat.*)

JEFFREY. Yes—
PIXIE. You're the experts.
JEFFREY. Yes, we are, but, we're asking you because you wrote on Elizabeth   440
Farnese, and, arguably, that makes you an expert. An Elizabeth Farnese expert.
PIXIE. Okay, but that's a pretty limited, um, field, Elizabeth Farnese. And you asked me if women should be in history?
JEFFREY. Yes.   445
PIXIE. I think Elizabeth Farnese should be in history, is that what you're ask-ing me?

(*Beat.*)

JEFFREY. Well, Pixie, yes, okay, that's—yes, Elizabeth Farnese is part of this because you appealed your essay topic to Professor Galbraith, and that was a very strong gesture on your part, and it indicates to me that you are em- 450
bracing feminist—but I'd like to broaden our discussion from—and talk about what you said a moment ago—that while taking this course history seemed closed to, or seemed to leave out, women.

(*Beat.*)

PIXIE. Yeah?
JEFFREY. And you said, I don't know if I believe that.   455

(*Beat.*)

PIXIE. Yeah?

JEFFREY. And you meant ... what?

(*Beat. Pixie shifts, thinks.*)

All right. Pixie, look, the essay topic, military leader, Elizabeth Farnese is not a military leader.

460　PIXIE. Well—

JEFFREY. Yes! Exactly! You questioned that! And I think this is important, because what you hit upon, Pixie, is that there's a certain amount of exclusivity, a certain sexism built into the terminology, into the wording of the essay questions, which are, of course, formulated by Professor Galbraith.

(*Jeffrey looks at Professor Galbraith, who looks away.*)

465　And I think this relates to what you said a moment ago, about the textbooks, and the lectures—

PIXIE. —okay—

JEFFREY. —about your growing awareness of the emphasis on male figures—

PIXIE. —okay—

470　JEFFREY. (*half to Galbraith*)—and of the almost complete absence of female figures—

'PIXIE. Yeah, okay—

JEFFREY. —and of the feelings of exclusion generated by what is a pronounced bias in the course material—

475　PIXIE. —unhunh—

JEFFREY. —as well as your skepticism. Your sense that women are a part of history—

PIXIE. (*soft*)—unhunh—

JEFFREY. —and that—that they would be a part of history if they weren't

480　being under-represented in Professor Galbraith's lectures and on Professor Galbraith's course lists, and that, Pixie, that is what I'd like to hear about!

(*Beat.*)

PIXIE. Why are you yelling at me?

JEFFREY. I'm not ...! (*dropping the intensity level*) I'm not yelling, I'm trying to—

485　PIXIE. I, no, I don't want to answer this anymore.

(*Beat.*)

JEFFREY. No, Pixie, I'm sorry, let's—please, let's—

PIXIE. I feel uncomfortable answering this.

JEFFREY. But, but, Pixie—

GALBRAITH. Jeffrey—

JEFFREY. (*to Galbraith*) No. (*to Pixie*) Pixie—   490
PIXIE. No. I don't want to—
JEFFREY. But ...! Listen, let's just—
PIXIE. No.
GALBRAITH. Jeffrey—
JEFFREY. Look Pixie, let's just—   495
PIXIE. No.
JEFFREY. But, but Pixie!
PIXIE. You're yelling at me!
JEFFREY. I'm not—I'm not ...! Pixie, just listen for one—
PIXIE. No.   500
JEFFREY. Just for one—
PIXIE. No.
JEFFREY. Please! Pixie! Just for one—
PIXIE. No, I—no. I don't care. I don't care about women in history, okay?
   This is my fucking elective. I have no idea!   505

> (*Beat.*)

JEFFREY. You don't care.

> (*Beat.*)

Doesn't it, for one second, occur to you that I am trying to defend you?
GALBRAITH. Jeffrey, I think we should stop now—
JEFFREY. That more is at stake than just your essay, and your grades—
GALBRAITH. Jeffrey, let's stop this right now.   510
JEFFREY. But, you know what, Pixie? Why don't you just glaze over—
GALBRAITH. —Jeffrey!—
JEFFREY. —while we determine that women and horses have equal historic
   significance! Or—or apply your fucking lip gloss one more time—
GALBRAITH. All right, Jeffrey!   515
JEFFREY. —while Professor Galbraith eliminates women from the historical
   record!
GALBRAITH. That's enough!
JEFFREY. You are being degraded and—and patronized—
GALBRAITH. That's enough, Jeffrey!   520
JEFFREY. —and you are sitting there like a lobotomized ...! Like a lobotomy
   in a ... skirt!

> (*Long beat. Long enough for Jeffrey to contemplate the possible ramifications of his outburst. Very little motion occurs on stage. Pixie begins to cry and covers her face.*)

I—shit.

(*Beat.*)

I—Pixie—I didn't—I didn't mean to—fuck.

(*Beat.*)

525   I—I—fuck.
GALBRAITH. Hm, yes. Jeffrey? Would you please wait in the hallway for a
     moment?
JEFFREY. (*half to Galbraith, half to Pixie*) I—no, look, I—I'm sorry—
GALBRAITH. Yes, I know you are—
530 JEFFREY. I just got—I got—
GALBRAITH. Yes, I know. But now I would prefer if you went out into the
     hallway.
JEFFREY. But—I—Professor, I—
GALBRAITH. Because, as you can see, Pixie is crying, and I think it would be
535   best to give her a chance to collect herself.

     (*Jeffrey doesn't go.*)

Jeffrey?
JEFFREY. I—yes, I just—I don't feel all that comfortable leaving her ... with ...
GALBRAITH. The head of the department?

     (*A standoff between the two men. Beat. Pixie's crying is audible.*)

All right, Jeffrey. Can we please offer Pixie some Kleenex?

     (*Jeffrey gets a box of tissues off the bookshelf. Galbraith takes the box of
     tissues from Jeffrey, and goes over to Pixie. She takes a couple of tissues
     without looking up. Long beat of crying.*)

540 PIXIE. I'm just trying to ... (*gestures*) ...
GALBRAITH. Please. I think it would be very strange if you weren't crying. I
     would cry if the dean yelled at me.

     (*Galbraith smiles at Pixie. Pixie tries to pull it together again. Another beat
     of crying.*)

     (*with sympathy*) You're upset.

     (*Pixie nods.*)

PIXIE. (*quiet*) Yeah.
545 GALBRAITH. (*with sympathy*) Hm.

(*Beat.*)

I'm very sorry about this, Pixie. I shouldn't have let Jeffrey yell at you, I should have ... stepped in. (*for Jeffrey's benefit*) This is not how we encourage our TAs to behave.

(*Beat.*)

Jeffrey hasn't been raising his voice in tutorial, has he?

(*Pixie shakes her head no.*)

PIXIE. No.   550
GALBRAITH. No. Hm.

(*Beat.*)

You should know that we do have a formal complaints procedure at the university, Pixie. There is a women's coordinator. Or, rather, what is the current ...?

(*Beat.*)

Jeffrey?   555
JEFFREY. Yes?
GALBRAITH. What's the new title for the women's coordinator?
JEFFREY. The equity officer?
GALBRAITH. The equity officer. (*to Pixie*) She's in the Office of the Dean of Students. She's a very approachable person, and I'm sure she would help 560 you make your case.

(*Beat.*)

One of the avenues of appeal, when incidents of this type occur, is to come and talk with me. We've bypassed that step, as I witnessed the incident. And, in my experience, handling these types of incidents in the department, I've found that it's important for the student to hear from the pro- 565 fessor, or, in this case, TA, themselves. What's important for the student is to hear the faculty member acknowledge that their behaviour was not ... appropriate. Then, hopefully, a teaching relationship can be re-established.

(*Beat.*)

I know Jeffrey would like to apologize to you. And I will be here supervising, so if anything makes you feel uncomfortable, then we'll stop, and I'll 570 ask Jeffrey to leave.

(*Beat.*)

Hm? Pixie? Is that ...?

(*Pixie shrugs—sure. Galbraith smiles at her.*)

Jeffrey.

(*Galbraith indicates to Jeffrey that he should speak to Pixie.*)

JEFFREY. (*half to Galbraith*) I—I—yes. I'm very sorry. I lost my—I uh—I
575 shouldn't have used that language to—
GALBRAITH. (*sharp*) Are you apologizing to Pixie, Jeffrey?
JEFFREY. (*confused*) Yes?

(*Galbraith indicates that Pixie is over there.*)

(*to Pixie*) Pixie, I shouldn't have used—I was frustrated, and I chose the
wrong words to express that—
580 PIXIE. You yelled at me!
JEFFREY. Yes. I—yes. I'm sorry.
PIXIE. I came here to get my essay. I came here to pick up my essay, so can I
have it please, or are you all on crack?
JEFFREY. Yes, I—I know that this must seem—
585 PIXIE. You wanted to talk to me about my essay, that's what you said, that's
why I came here, to talk about my essay! And then—
JEFFREY. Yes, I know, I see that—
PIXIE. —and then you YELL AT ME!!!
JEFFREY. I—yes, I appreciate that this isn't what you were expecting. You were
590 expecting a formal discussion of your essay and your grade, but Pixie, we
were, in fact, talking about your essay—
PIXIE. No we weren't. You were arguing with Professor Galbraith.

(*Beat.*)

JEFFREY. (*quiet*) But ... (*laughs*) ... Pixie, yes, but—
PIXIE. You were arguing.
595 JEFFREY. Yes, but, what you don't understand is, I was trying to—I was advo-
cating for you, because, you see—
PIXIE. You were in the middle of an argument! You and the Professor were
arguing!
JEFFREY. But—yes—I—yes, but you see, the argument was ... about you.
600 PIXIE. No it wasn't!
JEFFREY. But you don't ...! (*laughs*) It—it—yes, it was about ... you—
PIXIE. No.

(*Beat.*)

JEFFREY. But it—yes—

PIXIE. It wasn't about me!

(*Beat.*)

JEFFREY. But—but, okay, Pixie—   605

PIXIE. This wasn't about me.

JEFFREY. But I was—I was advocating for you. I was trying to advocate for you. You—what do you want? I was trying to—what do you women fucking want!

GALBRAITH. Jeffrey!   610

JEFFREY. I was putting my—I was—fuck—I was advocating for women!

PIXIE. You were arguing with Professor Galbraith! You were arguing with him about women in history. I was just ... in the room!

(*Beat.*)

Which is so funny, because in the textbook—the reason—the reason why I wrote the essay is because in the textbook, at the bottom of one of the   615
pages, there's a footnote. Elizabeth Farnese, second wife of Philip the Fifth of Spain, secured her sons the thrones of Parma and Tuscany. She got her sons thrones. How? It doesn't say. There's just the footnote. So I wrote the essay. And I was sitting here, looking at you, and I could tell you wanted me to say certain things for the sake of your argument, and I was thinking,   620
my history TA is yelling at me for no reason and I am pissed off because I am kind of like a footnote here!

(*Beat.*)

"Professor Galbraith and Jeffrey had an argument about whether or not women should be included in history. And by the way, they were arguing because of Pixie Findley." "Pixie Findley? Who's she?" "Let's check the   625
footnote." And somehow, even though you think it's about me, it's not. It's about you. And your argument. I'm just the excuse for you to argue with each other. So I don't care which one of you wins because it's not about me.

(*Beat.*)

So ... yeah.   630

(*Long beat.*)

JEFFREY. I see what you're ... saying, but, Pixie, I didn't mean to.... It's—yes—you're talking about—yes, I see what you're pointing out, and I didn't mean to—to—I—you're right. I shouldn't have—I didn't, uh—I never,

635   uh, asked you if you wanted me to—but my intention—my intention wasn't to appropriate, to—uh ... yeah.

(*Beat.*)

I'm—Pixie, I'm sorry.

(*Beat.*)

I'm ... sorry.
PIXIE. That's okay.
JEFFREY. I'm sorry. You're right, I—yes. I was—yes.
640   PIXIE. That's okay.
GALBRAITH. Have we, perhaps, resolved this? Pixie?

(*Pixie shrugs, nods.*)

PIXIE. Yeah.
GALBRAITH. Good, good. Good. Then perhaps we can leave this for now?
PIXIE. Yeah.

(*Pixie picks up her bag and Professor Galbraith ushers her to the doorway over the course of his speech.*)

645   GALBRAITH. We have a lot to offer here in the history department, Pixie. Perhaps not as much as the business school—that's the large architectural tribute to Fort Knox and the Playboy Mansion up that way—but we have a lot to offer. And Pixie? Please come to me if you feel uncomfortable, or if you would like to discuss this further.
650   PIXIE. Okay. Thanks.

(*Pixie exits. The men look after her for a moment. Beat.*)

GALBRAITH. Off she goes.

(*Long beat.*)

If you were tenured, Jeffrey, I would say, by all means, go ahead and yell gendered slurs at the female undergraduates. But, at this juncture in your career ... (*laughs*).

(*Beat.*)

655   I appreciate that you wanted to argue your point to me. But we're the— you're a Ph.D. candidate, I'm a professor; distinguished, books published, summa cum laude, et cetera, et cetera. What could Pixie Findley possibly have contributed to our discussion? Hm?

(*Beat.*)

Connect up the dots for me.

JEFFREY. It started off with me trying to defend her—   660

GALBRAITH. (*sharp*) From?

JEFFREY. Yes, I—I—yes, I'm the one who insulted her, who verbally ... insulted her, in a gendered—in a language that was—I don't know where I—how I—what made me—

GALBRAITH. Oh, for Christ's sake, the girl's name is Pixie! Her name is Pixie! 665 She's asking to be patronized.

(*Beat.*)

If you were to crack her skull open, butterflies would flutter out. Or, what did you say? Lobotomy in a skirt?

(*Galbraith laughs, regards Jeffrey, laughs again. Jeffrey stares at Galbraith.*)

Lucky for you. Let's just pray she doesn't pick up Simone de Beauvoir over the weekend, hm?   670

(*Beat.*)

Let's just pray she sticks to *Cosmopolitan*, or what is it my wife reads? *Vanity Fair.*

(*Beat.*)

And Jeffrey? Give her a B minus.

(*Galbraith hands Jeffrey the essay and exits. Jeffrey holds it for a moment, then he opens it and begins to read. Lights out.*)

—2005

Poetry

Why poetry? Why, when we hear so much of the value of making one's meaning plain to others, of striving for clarity, of avoiding ambiguity, should we pay attention to writing that much of the time seems to willfully ignore all of that? Is poetry important? Is poetry meaningless? What *is* it, anyway! And why should we study it?

If the human animal were so constructed as to always think without feeling, and feel without thinking, the human world would have no place for poetry. In the twenty-first century, what poetry may do best is to explore through words the places where reason and the emotions and senses meet. When we "think" of death, of loss, or of love, our powers of reasoning are unlikely to be untouched by our emotions—or by our senses. And much the same is often true when we think of morning, or of light, or of the sea. Poetry at its best can give full expression to the ways in which our thoughts and feelings come together with our sense impressions—and can itself give rise to powerful sense impressions. Not infrequently, indeed, poetry has been defined by the physical reactions it is capable of producing. "If I read a book and it makes my whole body so cold no fire can ever warm me," wrote the American poet Emily Dickinson, "I know that is poetry." "If I feel physically as if the top of my head were taken off, I know *that* is poetry," she added.

It seems safe to conclude that few lose their heads to poetry in the way Dickinson describes—but a great many others find there is a natural association between poetry and intensity of feeling. Carol Ann Duffy tells us that poems, above all, "are a series of intense moments." Of her own poetry she writes, "I'm not dealing with facts. I'm dealing with emotions." The Australian poet Les Murray suggests that "a true poem is dreamed and danced as well as thought."

Murray knows perfectly well that a poem cannot be danced—not in any literal sense. Like Dickinson, in attempting to describe poetry he has resorted to the language of poetry: language that suggests and likens and associates as it moves toward meaning. Even more than in prose fiction or in drama, language is central to the ways in which poems work. In a poem the connotations of a word or phrase—the things that it is capable of suggesting—are often at least as important as the word's denotative meaning. Poetry works above all through association. Associations of thought and emotion and sense impressions; associations of sound and of sense; associations between physical images; and associations between what we see on a printed page and what goes on in our minds. Let's turn to that last one first.

The Look of Poetry

The layers of an onion have frequently been a metaphorical reference point when people talk about trying to get to the centre of something. Let's begin this section by looking at a few lines from a poem about the real thing—"Onions," by Lorna Crozier:

> If Eve had bitten it
> Instead of the apple
> How different
> Paradise

Compare that with how the same words would look on the page written as prose:

> If Eve had bitten it instead of the apple how different paradise.

Why do these words work better set out in the way that Crozier has chosen? Does setting them out this way on the page make them more easily intelligible? In prose, arguably, one would have to add not only punctuation but also extra words to convey the same meaning:

> If Eve had bitten it instead of the apple, how different paradise would have been.

As is often the case, poetry is here a means of expression more concise than prose. It also gives the words different emphases; giving "Paradise" a line on its own draws attention to the notion of paradise itself.

Laying out words in the way that Crozier has done may also encourage the reader to feel suggestions of a variety of meanings; ambiguity, which we generally take to be a fault if it occurs in essay writing, can add interest and richness to poetry. A poem's presence as words and lines upon a page can open up a rich world of suggestion for the reader—and open up too the possibility of surprise. Let's turn to another example. The following lines are taken from a poem by Al Purdy about the experience of pioneers trying to farm in early Ontario, "The Country North of Belleville":

> a lean land
>   not like the fat south
> with inches of black soil on
>   earth's round belly —

And where the farms are
        it's as if a man stuck
both thumbs in the stony earth and pulled
        it apart
        to make room
enough between the trees
for a wife
        and maybe some cows and
        room for some
of the more easily kept illusions

Which are the lines here that end in ways that open up different possible meanings? Where are we surprised? Does that surprise happen differently because the words and lines are laid out in verse? Perhaps the most notable thing about the layout of these lines is the way in which the lines "it apart" and "to make room" are set with plenty of space to each side, suggesting through the look of the words on the page their literal meaning. Do the lines "for a wife" and "of the more easily kept illusions" also surprise? Surely they strike the reader in a slightly different way than they would if they were set out as prose.

Laying the words of a poem out on the page in irregular lines in this way (as **free verse**) has become commonplace—so much so that many now think of it as the primary form in which poetry is written. But until the late nineteenth century in France, and until well into the twentieth century in the English-speaking world, such poetry was unheard of. Before the **imagist** verse of Ezra Pound and of H.D. and, even more influentially, the early poetry of T.S. Eliot, the layout of a poem on the page was typically governed by formal metrical patterns (and also, often, by rhyme)—governed, in short, by structures of sound.

Poetry and Sound

There are many ways in which poetry can be organized according to sound. In a language such as Shona (a Bantu language), tonal patterns may provide the structure; much of Shona poetry is characterized by a drifting downwards in pitch from the beginning to the end of each line. In ancient Greece and Rome the organizing principle was the lengths of the sounds, with each line organized into patterns of alternating long and short sounds. The length of a sound is also referred to as its **quantity**, and poetry based on a system of alternating lengths of sound as **quantitative verse**. The Greeks developed a set of terms to describe sound combinations with this system—terms we still use today (albeit with a twist, as discussed below). A pattern in which short sounds were followed by long sounds was called iambic, and a single grouping of a short sound followed by a long sound was called an **iamb**. Other possible patterns of long and short sounds were similarly categorized. A long sound followed by a short sound was called a **trochee**; a long sound followed by two short sounds was called a **dactyl**; two short sounds followed by a long sound was called an **anapest**; a group of two long sounds together was called a **spondee**, and so on. Each group of sounds was termed a **foot**, and lines of poetry would be formed with a set number of poetic feet. If each line in a poem comprised five iambs in a row, then the **metre**, or pattern of poetic rhythm, was called **iambic pentameter**—the most common metre in ancient Greek and Roman poetry.

The Anglo-Saxon (or Old English) language was organized according to very different structures of sound. What mattered was not which syllables were long and which were short, but which were **stressed** (or **accented**) and which were not. A line of poetry in Old English is typically divided into two halves, in each of which there are two stressed syllables. Here, for example, are two lines from the most famous poem in Old English, *Beowulf*:

Swa sceal geong guma   gode gewyrcean
Fromum feohgiftum   on faeder bearme

So shall [a] young man   good make-happen
[with] pious gifts   from [his] father's coffers

In the first of these lines the syllables "geong" and "gu-" are stressed, as are the syllables "gode" and "wyrc"; in the next line the syllables "From-" and "gift" are stressed, as are the syllables "fae-" and "bear-." It is a structure of sound that does not take into account the *total* number of sounds or syllables in each line; what matters is the number of *stressed* syllables in each line.

Even without any knowledge of Old English, it's easy to notice that another organizing principle is operating in the sounds of these lines: **alliteration**. In Old English poetry there is typically alliteration between one or both of the stressed syllables in the first half-line and the first stressed syllable of the second half-line. (There is often also a good deal of alliteration beyond that—as there is here.)

A third way of structuring a poem according to sounds may also be found in Old English poetry, but it appears in only a single poem that has survived. It is a poem known as "The Rhyming Poem," and **rhyme** is indeed its organizing principle, with lines organized into rhyming pairs, or **couplets**. Aside from that one example, rhyme is nowhere present in the Anglo-Saxon literature that has come down to us; rhyme evidently never took hold in Anglo-Saxon poetry. It became a staple of later English poetry due to the influence of French poetry on English—specifically, songs of love and chivalry of the twelfth- and thirteenth-century French poets known as troubadours. Rhyme is a strong presence in the poetry of Geoffrey Chaucer (most of whose work comprises lines of 10 syllables with no clear pattern of stressed and unstressed syllables but with a rhyme at the end of every line). But there is no uniformity in the sound structures of medieval English poetry; some of the most important medieval poems (notably *Sir Gawain and the Green Knight*) use alliterative structures of sounds very similar to those found in Old English poetry.

Metre and Rhythm

The English Renaissance of the sixteenth century breathed new life into the ideas and the literary works of ancient Greece and Rome. It also picked up on the literary work and intellectual currents of the Italian Renaissance that had begun more than a century earlier. By the late sixteenth century the metrical patterns of ancient Greek and Latin poetry had become dominant in English poetry as well. But where the ancient Greeks and Romans had structured poetic metre on the basis of *long* and *short* syllables, English substituted a system based on *stressed* and *unstressed* syllables. In ancient Greece a line of iambic pentameter was a line in which a short syllable was followed by a long syllable five times in a row; in Renaissance England it became a line in which an unstressed syllable is followed by a stressed syllable five times in a row. Because it is based on counting the syllables in each line (and in each group of sounds, or poetic foot, within that line), this system of metre is syllabic; because it is also based on stress, or accent, it is accentual. The system, then, is known as **accentual-syllabic verse**.

Given that spoken English tends toward substantial variation in levels of stress (far more so than Greek or Latin or French or Italian), it is perhaps not very surprising that English would emphasize alternation between stressed and unstressed syllables rather than between longer and shorter syllables. But the degree to which the new accentual-syllabic approach to structuring the sounds of poetry came to dominate—and the speed with which it came to dominate—is remarkable. At the beginning of the sixteenth century accentual-syllabic poetry was still a rarity in England; by the end of the century virtually all poetry written in English used some form of accentual-syllabic metre.

Where accentual-syllabic metre is strictly adhered to, the alternation of stressed and unstressed syllables follows an absolutely regular pattern. Such is the case, for example, in these lines from Sir Walter Ralegh's "The Nymph's Reply to the Shepherd":

> If all the world and love were young,
> And truth in ev'ry shepherd's tongue,
> These pretty pleasures might me move
> To live with thee and be thy love.

These lines are written in iambic tetrameter—an accentual-syllabic metre in which each line is composed of four iambic feet; that is to say, each group of syllables (or foot) is made up of an unstressed syllable followed by a stressed syllable, with four such groups in every line. Here are the lines again with the feet and the stressed syllables marked:

    /   /   /   /

If all / the world / and love / were young,

        /   /   /   /

And truth / in ev'- / ry shep- / herd's tongue,

       /   /   /   /

These pret- / ty pleas- / ures might / me move

    /   /   /   /

To live / with thee / and be / thy love.

Iambic tetrameter is one common accentual-syllabic metre; more common still is iambic pentameter—in which each line has five feet rather than four. A metre in which the lines have three feet is call **trimeter**; a metre in which the lines have six feet is called **hexameter**.

Together with an accentual-syllabic metre, Ralegh employs rhyme as a second structure of sound in the poem; the lines are in couplets, with the last words in each couplet rhyming (*young* and *tongue*) or almost rhyming (*move* and *love*[1]).

It is worth noticing here that in the interests of maintaining the regular pattern of metre and of rhyme, the ordering of the words has been made (to modern ears at least) less regular; Ralegh writes "might me move" instead of using the more common syntactical arrangement "might move me." Such alterations of word order are called **syntactical inversions**.

Rhyme is very commonly used in poems that follow an accentual-syllabic metrical structure, but there is no necessary connection between the two. Indeed, some of the best-known poetry in English is written in **blank verse**— lines in iambic pentameter that do not rhyme. Such verse is found frequently in William Shakespeare's plays and is used throughout John Milton's epic poem *Paradise Lost*. Here are the final four lines of that poem:

The world was all before them, where to choose
Their place of rest, and Providence their guide.
They, hand in hand, with wand'ring steps and slow
Through Eden took their solitary way.

---

1   It is entirely possible that "move" and "love" may have rhymed fully in England in Ralegh's time.

The syllables at the ends of these lines (*choose, guide, slow, way*) do not rhyme—but the lines do follow a regular pattern of unstressed and stressed syllables. Here are the lines again, this time with the feet and the stressed syllables[1] marked:

> /   /   /   /   /
> The world / was all / be-fore / them, where / to choose
>   /   /   /   /   /
> Their place / of rest, / and Pro- /vi- dence / their guide.
>   /   /   /   /   /
> They, hand / in hand, / with wand'- / ring steps / and slow
>   /   /   /   /   /
> Through E- /den took / their sol- / i-tar- / y way.

The lines have a very different feel to them than do the lines from the Ralegh poem—and that's more than a matter of their being unrhymed, or than their having five feet in each line rather than four. Three of the four lines from the Ralegh poem are **end stopped**—that is, they end with punctuation such as a comma or period that brings a marked pause in the verse. And none of the Ralegh lines is written with a significant pause in the middle of the line. In contrast, there are significant pauses in the middle of three of the four lines from *Paradise Lost*—and only two of the four are end stopped. Both these features have names. The practice of carrying sense and grammatical construction past the end of a line in poetry is called **enjambment**; a pause in the middle of a line of poetry is called a **caesura**. By using enjambment and caesura, poets can vary the rhythm of a poem while the underlying metre—the arrangement of stressed and unstressed syllables—remains the same.

Enjambment and caesura are two of several aspects of rhythm that do not depend on metre. Another is the *degree* to which the sounds of syllables may be stressed or unstressed. A widely unappreciated aspect of rhythm is that not all accented syllables are stressed to the same degree. Compare for example the lines from the Ralegh poem quoted above with the first two lines of Philip Larkin's "This Be the Verse":

> If all the world and love were young,
> And truth in ev'ry shepherd's tongue,
>
> They fuck you up, your mum and dad.
> They may not mean to, but they do.

---

1 To some degree the accenting of syllables is subjective, of course. One might, for example, read these lines with a stress placed on *They* at the beginning of the third line.

Here are the Larkin lines again, with the stressed syllables and the poetic feet marked:

    /   /   /   /

They fuck / you up, / your mum / and dad.

    /   /   /   /

They may / not mean / to, but / they do.

The pattern of stressed and unstressed syllables in these lines is exactly the same as with the Ralegh lines (or, to put it another way, the lines **scan** identically). Yet the rhythm is very different. The reader naturally places a stronger stress on the second syllable of the first line here ("they *fuck* you up") than on the second syllable of the first line from Ralegh ("if *all* the world ...").

What about the levels of stress on other syllables? Overall, the first two lines of the Larkin poem read far less smoothly than do the first lines of Ralegh's; that has something to do with the caesuras in both the Larkin lines. But just as important are the levels of emphasis that we naturally put on the syllables, which vary far more widely in the Larkin lines. In the lines from Ralegh the stressed syllables are stressed to roughly the same degree, and the unstressed syllables are unstressed to roughly the same degree. That consistency imparts a good deal of smoothness to the sound of the lines—a smoothness entirely appropriate to the sense of the lines. In the Larkin the wider variation in levels of stress, together with the caesuras, creates an aural sense of disorder that is entirely appropriate to the sense of those lines.

If variation in levels of stress is one underappreciated element of poetic rhythm, another is variation in quantity—in the length of time it takes to say different syllables. Of course everyone speaks at a different rate; no two people are likely to take exactly the same time to say the same group of syllables or the same poetic line, any more than any two people are likely to place exactly the same level of stress on a particular group of syllables. But no one is likely to put as much emphasis on the stressed syllables of "level sands" as on the stressed syllables of "break, blow, burn." By the same token, no one is likely to take as long to say the three syllables "bit of it" as to say the three syllables "lengths of sound," or take as long to say the two syllables "so-so" as to say the two syllables "skunks cringe." Everyone has long accepted that an entire system based on quantity—such as that of the ancient Greeks and Romans—would not work in English. But that should not be taken as evidence that the local effects of quantity in a poem are unimportant. To get a sense of how greatly such things can affect the rhythm of a line of poetry, let's compare another pair of lines: the final line of Thomas Hardy's "During Wind and Rain" and the final line of Larkin's "This Be the Verse." Each has eight syllables:

Down their carved names the rain drop ploughs.

And don't have any kids yourself.

Larkin's eight quick, no-nonsense syllables bring the poem skidding to a close. The eight syllables that end the Hardy poem, in contrast, move as slowly as a plough—the sound entirely suggestive of the sense of the line.

The idea that a poem works most effectively when its sounds suggest its sense is an old one; the eighteenth-century poet Alexander Pope gave memorable expression to it in *An Essay on Criticism*, asserting that in poetry, "the sound must seem an echo to the sense." Poets have in many cases continued to strive for these aural effects. The effect they are striving for might perhaps be termed broad onomatopoeia. In an individual word or phrase, **onomatopoeia** occurs when the sounds of the words in themselves seem to imitate the sound they are naming—as do, for example, the words *burst* or *scrape*. A broader sort of imitation is involved in phrases such as Tennyson's "as moving seems asleep," Milton's "with wandering steps and slow," or Hardy's "the rain drop ploughs." And perhaps something that might be called onomatopoeia may operate more broadly still. Arguably, some form of onomatopoeia—of the sounds of a poem imitating its sense—can operate throughout entire poems, such as Robert Herrick's "Delight in Disorder" and Theodore Roethke's "My Papa's Waltz."

Rhyme

The examples of patterns of rhyme we have touched on thus far have been rhyming couplets. That is only one way of rhyming; many possible **rhyme schemes** may be used as part of the organizing principle of a poem: rhyming every other line; carrying on patterns of rhyme from one stanza to another; returning at the end of a poem to rhymes used at the beginning.

Ever since the dramatic break with the past that modernism ushered in early in the twentieth century, poets in the English-speaking world have generally chosen not to rhyme. In North America, rhyme is thought of as appropriate to certain forms of music—from folk music to hip-hop. But the thought of rhyming in *poetry* often conjures up images of verse that is childish or sentimental or hopelessly old fashioned, or all of the above. Those who disparage rhyme as an adult activity think of a conventional rhyme scheme operating in conjunction with a highly regular metre—and of rhymed verse where it seems the poet has been entirely willing to meddle with normal grammar and syntax for no better purpose than to achieve rhymes at the end of each line. A few lines from Letitia Landon's "The Improvisatrice" may be enough to convey the idea:

And fondly round his neck she clung;
Her long black tresses round him flung,
Love-chains, which would not let him part;
And he could feel her beating heart,
The pulses of her small white hand,
The tears she could no more command.

It was no doubt with this sort of poetry in the back of her mind that the modern Irish poet Eavan Boland wrote "Against Love Poetry"—as a prose poem, without lines, without stanzas, without metre, without rhyme. But rhyme has no necessary connection to particular sentiments or poetic traditions, and it may be used quite independently of any accentual-syllabic metrical system. It may be used loosely in free verse—as T.S. Eliot does in these lines from *The Waste Land*:

> The river sweats
> Oil and tar
> The barges drift
> With the turning tide
> Red sails
> Wide
> To leeward, swing on the heavy spar.

It may also be used to provide a structure of sound through an entire poem that lacks any strict pattern of metre—as is the case in Larkin's "The Old Fools." It may be used within the framework of a traditional form such as a sonnet, but in ways that are entirely varied and fresh. Such is the case, for example, in Alice Oswald's "Wedding," in which **slant rhymes** and other imperfect rhymes help to create a sense of exuberant abandon:

> And this, my love, when millions come and go
> Beyond the need of us, is like a trick;
> And when the trick begins, it's like a toe
> Tip-toeing on a rope, which is like luck;
> And when this luck begins, it's like a wedding,
> Which is like love, which is like everything.

As every child senses intuitively, rhyme gives the human ear an opportunity to recognize and confirm a regular pattern—something the mind delights in. Because it has served this purpose for so long, it's sometimes used by modern and contemporary poets to suggest the very idea of regularity and order—or to suggest a sense of delight. An excellent example of this is Dorothy Livesay's "The Three Emilys," which begins with a regular rhyme scheme of three rhyming couplets (aabbcc). Then, as the speaker's thought processes become more complex and confused, the rhyme scheme falls away, and the poem's form becomes increasingly disordered, its sounds suggesting the speaker's mental state.

A more contemporary, and equally inventive, use of rhyme to convey meaning is found in Kim Addonizio's "First Poem for You," which uses the rhyme scheme of the Shakespearian sonnet to perfection, but makes such extensive use of enjambment that the human ear has to strain to actually detect the rhyme. Here's how the poem begins:

> I like to touch your tattoos in complete
> darkness, when I can't see them. I'm sure of
> where they are, know by heart the neat
> lines of lightning pulsing just above
> your nipple,

We may sometimes think of rhyme as being an inherently intrusive aural element in a poem—something that will inevitably draw attention to itself rather than to the meaning of the lines. But if the rhyming syllables are only lightly stressed, as is the case here, rhyme can operate quite unobtrusively. And that is all the more true if, again as here, the poet employs enjambment and caesura, so that the reader never stops and lingers at the rhymes.

"First Poem for You" continues in the same vein for 12 of its 14 lines. Not until the final two lines are there any end-stopped lines. And that creates an ongoing gentle tension. The quiet regularity with which the rhyme scheme operates pulls in one direction, the thoughts running past the ends of the lines in another. Is there a similar tension in the speaker's mind? She is attracted to the tattoo, but at the same time terrified by its permanence. Are her feelings toward the tattoo suggestive of her feelings toward her lover and the possibility of a commitment that might be permanent?

In the Shakespearian sonnet form the final two lines are a rhymed couplet—and here too Addonizio holds to the form. But now the poem abandons enjambment; both these final lines are end-stopped, thus giving strong emphasis to each line's final word.

> ... whatever persists
> or turns to pain between us, they will still
> be there. Such permanence is terrifying.
> So I touch them in the dark; but touch them, trying.

In a poem that seems in large part to be about trying to deal with the terror of permanence in a relationship, it is wonderfully appropriate to have the two words "trying" and "terrifying" rhymed in a couplet at the poem's end. There are many tensions and harmonies in "First Poem for You"—and throughout the poem, sound echoes sense. To observe such unity is to be reminded that rhyme isn't just a sound effect; it can be a lovely "aha!" shared by mind and ear together.

• • •

It is sometimes imagined that sound is only an important element of poetry when some sound-related organizing principle is involved—metre, or rhyme, or some wholly different aural principle (such as that involved in Christian Bök's *Eunoia*, in which each section uses one vowel only). But even poets who tend not to organize their poems according to aural principles are often highly attuned to sound. Margaret Atwood is a good example. She remains a poet better known for the striking ways in which her poems lay words out on a page than she is for the sounds of her poems. Yet here is how she responded in 1984 to an interviewer's question about "words on the page":

> First of all, a poem is not words on a page. A poem is words in the air; or I should say words in the ear, because a poem is heard. And the words on the page are a notation like a musical score. We would not say that Beethoven was a bunch of black marks on a page; you would say that Beethoven is what we hear when we transcribe those black marks. And it's the same with a poem; when you are reading a poem the words are in your ear.

Is she right? Interestingly, when Atwood reads her own poems, her voice is quite flat. That is to say, it does not vary much in pitch; there are no "high notes" or "low notes" as there are in most pieces of music. The effect is to focus one's ears more strongly on the aural elements that *do* vary in any poem in English—levels of stress and lengths of sound chief among them.

Imagery, Metaphor and Simile, Symbol

If poetry is very largely about the power of suggestion, the **images** that a poem conjures up are often central to that power. When readers think of imagery, they often think first of imagist poets such as Ezra Pound, H.D., and William Carlos Williams—poets who use the spacing of the words on the page (and the sounds those words convey) in ways that draw attention to the physical images the words name. This is what Williams does in poems such as "The Red Wheelbarrow" and "This Is Just to Say," poems that offer the reader fragments of experience.

I have eaten
the plums

that were in
the icebox

and which
you were probably
saving
for breakfast

Forgive me
they were delicious
so sweet
and so cold

It is often imagined that what gives an image specificity must be purely a matter of physical description. But an image may also be made specific by human circumstance; what gives the plums specificity here is not only the physical attributes of sweetness and coldness but also their "history"—the small part they play in the relationship between the speaker and the one he is addressing.

It is useful in discussing poetic imagery to distinguish between the two axes concrete/abstract and specific/general. Whereas the opposite of concrete is abstract, the opposite of specific is general. The terms "concrete" and "specific" are often used almost interchangeably in discussing imagery, and certainly there is an overlap between the two. Yet they are in fact distinct from each other. The word "fruit" expresses something concrete but general; the word "nourishment" expresses a far more abstract concept. To speak of "plums" is to be both more specific and more concrete than to speak of "fruit." To speak of "ripe plums" is again both more concrete and more specific. "The plums that were in the icebox," though, is not a more concrete image than "the plums"; it adds a degree of specificity to the image without adding to the concreteness of it.

It is sometimes implied when attention is drawn to the specificity of images in such poems as these, that it is inherently better poetically if particular plums are referenced. Is there in fact anything inherently poetic about specificity? Certainly specificity helps to make William Carlos Williams's images memorable. But it is also true that many of the best loved and most admired poems are remembered at least as much for images that convey a very general sense of the physical—even a sense of vagueness. Would not the door in Atwood's "The Door," to choose one recent example, lose much of its suggestive power if it were made more specific, located more clearly in a specific place or time?

Even in poems inspired by very specific things or places, the images in the resulting poetry may often appeal to us through images that are far from specific—that are quite general or even vague. "Tintern Abbey" is a good example. Inspired by a specific place familiar to him, William Wordsworth appeals to us through images that have a high degree of generality, as he speaks of how he has been affected by his experiences:

> ... changed, no doubt, from what I was when first
> I came among these hills; when like a roe
> I bounded o'er the mountains, by the sides
> Of the deep rivers, and the lonely streams,
> Wherever nature led.

Much as specificity in images can be of value, it may also be the case that imagery with a certain vagueness or generality to it can be particularly effective in allowing the imagination of the reader to enter the poem.

Imagery in poetry is sometimes imagined to consist almost entirely of metaphor or simile—of using figures of speech to liken one thing to another. We will get to those in a moment. But the pure description found in poems such as the ones referenced above by Williams and Wordsworth may help to remind us that metaphor is not everything when it comes to imagery. Another example of how powerful imagery can be without metaphor or simile is Douglas LePan's "The Haystack." In that poem there are likenesses drawn between the still-alive soldier writing the poem, with his sunburn, and the soldier immolated by the haystack—but they are simple comparisons, not figures of speech.

If metaphor and simile are not everything when it comes to imagery, they are nevertheless central to a very great deal of what poetry does. In essence, **metaphor** is a way of likening one thing to another thing through language. In its simplest form, the **simile**, the likeness is made explicit through the use of words such as *like* or *as if.* "Like a roe I bounded o'er the mountains" is a simile in which Wordsworth is likening himself to an animal. That example—like the line so often used as the paradigm of a simile, Robert Burns's "My love is like a red, red rose"—offers a likeness that is easy for almost any reader to comprehend. Many similes, though, draw connections that are far more tenuous. Such is the case, for example, with the simile in the last line of Dylan Thomas's "Fern Hill" ("I sang in my chains like the sea"), or this simile from John Ashbery's "The Improvement": "the leopard is transparent, like iced tea." Such is the case also with the famous simile at the opening of "The Love Song of J. Alfred Prufrock":

> Let us go then, you and I,
> When the evening is spread out against the sky
> Like a patient etherized upon a table

The suggestive power of a simile can often be arresting in ways that are surprising or puzzling or disturbing; the same is true of other forms of metaphorical language. Sometimes such metaphors may be compressed into a powerful phrase, as is the case when Karen Solie writes of a sturgeon landed on the water's edge being unable to contain

> the old current he had for a mind, its pull
> and his body a muscle called river, called spawn.

Using highly concentrated metaphorical language, Solie likens the fish's body to the river that is its natural home, the fish's mind to the current of the river—and then ends by drawing a further likeness.

In a longer poem patterns of imagery and metaphor may appear and reappear, taking on different shadings each time. In *Maud*, for example—Alfred, Lord Tennyson's long 1856 poem about love and war—the first part ends with the protagonist imagining flowers blooming over the grave of the woman he loves: "blossom in purple and red." Much later in the poem, the final section of Tennyson's original version ends with the protagonist, having lost all hope of love, leaving for the Crimean War, where he imagines that from the

> … deathful-grinning mouths of the fortress flames
> The blood-red blossom of war with a heart of fire.

The suggestiveness of such contrasting images as these takes us about as far as could be imagined from the simplicity of "like a red, red rose."

The rose appears and reappears in different contexts in *Maud*, but at no point does the poet dwell on it in extended or elaborate fashion. Some poems, however, do precisely that: elaborate on a single metaphor in a sustained way over several stanzas. Such is the case with the comparison between two souls and the twin feet of a compass in the final stanzas of John Donne's "A Valediction: Forbidding Mourning." An elaborate and sustained metaphor such as Donne's twin feet is often referred to as a **conceit** or a Petrarchan conceit; many of the poems of Petrarch include this sort of extended metaphor. Indeed, a metaphor may be extended throughout an entire poem—as it is, for example, when Lady Mary Wroth compares love to a child in "Love, a Child, is Ever Crying."

When a comparison (metaphorical or otherwise) is made or implied between something non-human and human qualities, it is often referred to as **personification**. Thus Sir Philip Sidney personifies the moon in this opening to one of his sonnets:

> With how sad steps, O Moon, thou climb'st the skies!
> How silently, and with how wan a face!

And thus Allen Ginsberg personifies his country in his poem "America":

> America, when will you be angelic?
> When will you take off your clothes?

A figure of speech that is sometimes grouped with metaphor and simile is **metonymy**. Like metaphors and similes, metonyms do bring together different things. But whereas with metaphor and simile the connection is a matter of comparison, with metonymy it is a matter of association. The following sentences may clarify the distinction:

> Numerous scientists have criticized Ottawa's plan to close the environmental research centre.

> What dish are you cooking tonight?

In the first of these examples the word "Ottawa" is standing for "the federal government of Canada"; as the capital, Ottawa is the home of the federal government and is thus naturally associated with it, but it is not being compared to the federal government. Nor, in the second example, is the dish being compared to the food; it is associated with the food rather than likened to it. When T.S. Eliot writes in "The Love Song of J. Alfred Prufrock" of "sawdust restaurants" he is employing metonymy; the restaurants are not being likened to sawdust but rather associated with one particular characteristic: the sawdust on the floor.

A related literary device is **synecdoche**—the practice of referring to a part of something in a way that stands for the whole. If someone asks "Have you got wheels?" the rhetorical device of synecdoche is being used—as it is in a number of vulgar expressions in which a person's sexual organs are named as a way of referring to an entire person ("The prick followed me all the way home"). Synecdoche may be thought of as one form of metonymy: wheels are part of a car and that is one way of being associated with a car. But (unlike with metaphor and simile) they are not being *likened* to a car. Eliot's "The Love Song of J. Alfred Prufrock" may again provide a poetic example; he employs synecdoche when he writes "after the teacups" rather than saying "after we had finished with the tea and the teacups and the sandwiches...." It is useful to be aware of devices such as metonymy and synecdoche—but it is also useful to be aware that they occur far less frequently in poetry than do metaphor, simile, and personification.

One other concept that is important to the understanding of poetic imagery—and of poetry generally—is **symbol**. This is a term used more loosely than most of the terms discussed above—it is one that may overlap with many of them (a metaphor may act as a symbol, but so may a metonym). In Christian tradition a cross evokes the crucifix but may also symbolize Christianity or Christ's body. The beaver and the maple leaf are symbols of Canada, as the bald eagle is a symbol of the United States. But not all symbols are entrenched in tradition as are these—and not all are cast in stone. A bird is often in poetry a symbol of freedom, but in Ted Hughes's poem "Heptonstall Old Church," a bird is a symbol for Christian religion. The rose is traditionally a symbol of love, but it may also carry other associations. As Atwood's "The Door" illustrates, a door may be a symbol of possibilities opening up—but it may also symbolize their final closing.

Meaning

In every age there have been poets and poems whose meanings are more difficult to discern than others. There have also been significant shifts over time in the ways in which poets strive to express meaning—or, in some cases, to problematize the very idea that a poem should have a meaning. One such shift began in France in the second half of the nineteenth century. The young poet Arthur Rimbaud was one who rejected the conventions both of Western poetry and of Western society altogether. Here is how he put it in his 1871 collection *Une Saison en Enfer* (*A Season in Hell*):

> Un soir, j'ai assis la Beauté sur mes genoux—et je l'ai trouvée amère— et je l'ai injuriée. (One night I set Beauty down on my lap—and I found her bitter—and I gave her a rough time.)

When Edgar Allan Poe, writing in 1849, described the poetry of words as "the rhythmical creation of beauty," he was giving memorable expression to an idea that for centuries had been generally assumed to be central to the art of poetry. Rimbaud turned all that on its head: the rejection of any idea that the poet should be creating something beautiful is a consistent theme in his work, with images of vomit and of mucus jostling together with images of children and of the sea. What is the reader to make of such poetry? How are we to construct meaning out of it?

The modernist revolution in English poetry that poets such as Ezra Pound and T.S. Eliot ushered in early in the twentieth century has deep roots in the work of nineteenth-century French poets such as Rimbaud, Jules Laforgue, and Stéphane Mallarmé. Both Pound and Eliot rejected the conventionally beautiful, and both rejected conventional order in poetry. No longer was it felt that incidents or images should connect clearly and coherently with meaning, or that the images and meanings of one line should follow from that of the previous one in ways that could be clearly understood. "What branches grow Out of this stony rubbish?" Eliot asked in *The Waste Land*—

and answered, "You cannot say, or guess, for you know only A heap of broken images."

Modernism forged its own traditions, which have remained strong through the twentieth century and on into the twenty-first. The disconnectedness of the images in John Ashbery's poems is striking, but so too is the *sense* that there is meaning here, even if it may be impossible to express in words other than those used by the poet himself. What meaning is there in the sort of suggestive "heap of images" that we find in a poem such as Ashbery's "Civilization and Its Discontents"?

> ... What is agreeable
> Is to hold your hand. The gravel
> Underfoot. The time is for coming close. Useless
> Verbs shooting the other words far away.
> I had already swallowed the poison
> And could only gaze into the distance at my life
> Like a saint's with each day distinct.
> No heaviness in the upland pastures. Nothing
> In the forest. Only life under the huge trees
> Like a coat that has grown too big, moving far away,
> Cutting swamps for men like lapdogs, holding its own,
> Performing once again, for you and for me.

That some sense of meaning can emerge out of apparently disconnected images may be psychologically less strange than it might seem, given what is now being discovered about the human brain. "What is the sound of the gravel underfoot?" seems a question that asks for unsurprising associations to be made. But research conducted by scientists such as Anne-Sylvie Crisinel and Charles Spence of the University of Oxford suggests that associations that cross sense barriers may operate far more widely than has been suspected. It's not only that loud sounds suggest brightness, or that high-pitched sounds suggest smallness. Experiments have shown, for example, that the smell of blackberries evokes the sound of a piano in many people's minds, and that bitter tastes suggest lower pitched sounds to most people. Such research is still in its infancy, but it may be far from ludicrous to ask, in responding to lines such as Ashbery's, such questions as these: Do the sounds he gives us lead us to smell the upland pastures? Does it feel right to have the distance low-pitched, a saint high-pitched? What colour is heaviness? Though this introduction has for convenience treated sound and sense and visual image as largely separate phenomena, it has recognized that they are inter-related. How deeply and broadly the connections extend—and how far they may take the suggestiveness of images in the direction of poetic meaning—is something we are still finding out.

In the medieval period and through the Renaissance the accepted view was that poetry should have both a clear meaning and a clear moral purpose. One way of conveying a moral message was simply to tell a story, and have the good characters end up rewarded and the bad characters punished—though to put it so crudely is to grossly oversimplify the poetic theory of the time. Even when poetry was not telling a story, it was felt that moral improvement was a natural accompaniment to the art of poetry. Poetry should imitate the world—but in doing so should always make plain the world as it *should* be. As Sir Philip Sidney put it in the late sixteenth century, poetry is "an art of imitation, a speaking picture with this end, to teach and delight."

The consensus that instruction and delight were twin purposes of poetry (and indeed of all literature) remained powerful through to the late eighteenth century, when the French Revolution and the birth of Romanticism brought a shift; the idea that poetry should provide moral instruction began to lose favour, while the idea that poetry should give expression to the truths of nature, and to unbridled human feeling (including feelings of romantic love, certainly, but including as well strong political feeling) came to the fore. It was during this era that Wordsworth defined poetry as "the spontaneous overflow of powerful feelings: it takes its origin from emotion recollected in tranquility." It was in this era too that Percy Shelley argued that poetry had to it "something divine," but that it also could and should be used to further political causes. He wrote with equal passion of the spiritual force of nature and of the oppressive force of the wealthy landlords and heartless manufacturers of the era. Here, for example, is how he addresses the labouring classes in "Song to the Men of England," a poem widely taken up by the British labour movement:

> Men of England, wherefore plough
> For the lords who lay ye low?
> Wherefore weave with toil and care
> The rich robes your tyrants wear?

The notion that conveying a political message can be as appropriate to poetry as conveying thoughts of nature or of love did not begin with Shelley, nor did it end with him; it remained a powerful sub-current in nineteenth-century aesthetics. The modernism of the early twentieth century, however, was antithetical not only to the notion that poetry should try to teach, but also to the idea that it should have any clear meaning. Perhaps the most extreme expression of this view (on the face of it, at least) appears in "Ars Poetica," a poem by the American modernist Archibald MacLeish, which concludes as follows:

> A poem should be equal to:
> Not true.

For all the history of grief
An empty doorway and a maple leaf.

For love
the leaning grasses and two lights above the sea—

A poem should not mean
But be.

Does MacLeish really mean that a poem should be without meaning? Or is he simply trying to argue that what comes naturally to poetry is suggestion and association—that poetry does not naturally convey meaning in any fixed or conventional sense?

Eliot, the most important figure of modernism, did not go so far as to suggest that a poem should be without meaning. But he did feel that it was natural to the spirit of the age for poetry to be difficult. Here is how he put it in his 1926 essay "The Metaphysical Poets":

> ... it appears likely that poets in our civilization, must be *difficult*.... The poet must become more and more comprehensive, more allusive, more indirect, in order to force, to dislocate if necessary, language into his meaning.

The idea that meanings in poetry should be allusive and indirect—perhaps even by their very nature inexpressible in words other than those chosen by the poet—remained strong through the twentieth century and into the twenty-first. It is the governing idea in Les Murray's "The Meaning of Existence":

> Everything except language
> knows the meaning of existence.
> Trees, planets, rivers, time
> know nothing else. They express it
> moment by moment as the universe.
>
> Even this fool of a body
> lives it in part, and would
> have full dignity within it
> but for the ignorant freedom
> of my talking mind.

Does language truly get in the way of meaning, as Murray suggests? It is one irony of the poem that, even as it suggests that the meaning of existence is inexpressible through language, it conveys that thought in a wonderfully clear and coherent fashion, through language.

A great many poems from the past hundred years are less paradoxical than this, but also less clear in the ways that they convey meaning. To appreciate them we have to be open to the ways in which meanings can be suggested even when they are not stated clearly. And we must be able to recognize a central truth about poetry: the fact that meaning is not always plain does not mean it is absent.

None of the above should be taken to imply that all twentieth- and twenty-first-century poets eschew plain speaking. Some strive quite consistently for clarity of meaning in writing about a wide range of topics, while remaining attuned to the ways in which their poems can suggest meanings above and beyond those stated. Others write with a clear ethical or political stance, and have wanted for those reasons to make their meanings plain. Perhaps not surprisingly, strong political poetry in the twentieth and twenty-first centuries has come disproportionately from poets belonging to groups who have been in one way or another disadvantaged, or have been lacking in power—women, the colonized, visible minorities, Native North Americans, gays and lesbians. No reader is likely to be unclear about what W.H. Auden is driving at in "Unknown Citizen," or Langston Hughes in "Let America Be America Again":

> From those who live like leeches on the people's lives,
> We must take back our land again,
> America!

It is important not to presume, however, that once one has acknowledged the most transparent meaning of a poem which makes a clear point, nothing is left to be said. Even in a poem that aims to convey a clear political message there may be layered or multiple meanings.

Point of View

One of the most important ways in which the genres of literature differ one from another is in the way that they present human characters. Whereas the presentation of different human characters is central to prose fiction and to drama, it is often much less important to poetry. If one wishes to give direct expression to one's feelings or thoughts about nature, or death, or love, poetry is the natural medium to write in. But it is not always that simple.

As readers, how do we know who is behind a poem? If it is an "I" or a "we"—if it is written in the first person, in other words, how do we know who that "I" or "we" is? Sometimes we may need to bring historical or biographical information to bear. If we read the late nineteenth-century African American poet Paul Laurence Dunbar's "We Wear the Mask" without knowing the identity of "we," we will be missing a detail that greatly affects our reading of the poem. And sometimes the poem will say "I" or "we" but we cannot and should not be confident that the poet means what she says.

To say that poetry is often the most personal of the genres is not to say that we should read all poems as being direct expressions of the poet's thoughts or feelings. When we read a work of prose fiction in which a narrator tells a story, we should never assume that narrator to be the author; very frequently the author narrates a story through a *persona*, in order to provide a particular perspective on the events being narrated. The character of that persona may be very different indeed from that of the author. Much the same can be true in poetry. In some cases the poet may adopt a persona radically different from herself—as Margaret Atwood does, for example, in "Death of a Young Son by Drowning" and the other poems in her book *The Journals of Susanna Moodie*, in which she writes from the point of view of a woman who emigrated to Canada in the nineteenth century.

In *The Journals of Susanna Moodie* it is usually quite obvious who the "I" in the poems is. In other cases it may be much less clear whether the "I" in a poem is a persona. To what extent is the "I" in a love poem by John Donne the poet speaking directly? Or a sonnet by Shakespeare? Or, for that matter, any one of the thousands of love poems written in the first person, with an "I" addressing a "you"? In the case of a poem such as "Tintern Abbey," where there is external evidence that Wordsworth saw the proper function of poetry as being the direct expression of personal feeling, we may be reasonably confident that the "I" of the poem is indeed the poet himself, though even with such a seemingly direct poem, one must refer to the "speaker" in the poem, not the author. Further, poetry that reads as "personal" may be expressing a point of view quite independent from that of the poet. Such may be the case even with poetry that is highly intimate, even confessional (as the poetry of Sylvia Plath is often described as being).

With some poems written in the first person (or the first and second person), we may gradually come to realize as we read the poem not only that the "I" behind the poem is someone other than the poet, but also that this "I" is someone we should not trust. In a dramatic monologue such as Robert Browning's "My Last Duchess," we need to pay attention to character in much the same way as we do when trying to respond to a work of prose fiction in which we recognize that the narrator is unreliable. In a poem such as that one, the point of view is maintained consistently throughout the poem. Such is the case as well with dramatic monologues such as Tennyson's "Ulysses." A poem such as "The Love Song of J. Alfred Prufrock," however, begins very much like a dramatic monologue, but then seems to shift from time to time in its point of view. Is the "we" of "We have lingered in the chambers of the sea" near the poem's end written from the same point of view as that of the "I" with which the poem begins—or the "I" of "Do I dare to eat a peach?" a few lines earlier? Or is the viewpoint unstable in a poem such as this one?

The dramatic monologue is not the only form poets use to adopt an entirely different persona. Ted Hughes's "Hawk Roosting" and Les Murray's "Pig" are examples of poems in which traditional forms are used to give expression to the imagined point of view of a non-human animal.

One often unappreciated aspect of point of view in poetry is the degree to which a wide range of poems may be written very largely in the second person. This is true of a great deal of love poetry, certainly, and also of many dramatic monologues. It is true as well of a poem such as Tom Wayman's "Did I Miss Anything?"—a poem consisting entirely of a professor's answers to the question posed by a student in the title of the poem. And it is true of Carol Ann Duffy's "The Good Teachers," a very different sort of poem about education, in which "you" is used not in the way we usually use the second person, but in the way we use "one" when speaking in the third person.

Another interesting aspect of point of view is how subtle shifts in grammatical person may help to signal shifts in tone. Such is the case with the Larkin poems "Church Going" and "The Old Fools." In "Church Going," a poem written in the first person through its first six stanzas shifts in the final stanza to the third person: "someone will forever be surprising / A hunger in himself to be more serious." And in "The Old Fools" the sudden appearance in the final line of the first person plural—"We shall find out"—at the end of a poem that until then has been written entirely in the third person brings us up short. It is worth asking how these shifts tie in with the sense of the lines, and contribute to the feelings we are left with at the end of each poem.

Form

This introduction has already touched on a number of aspects of the formal properties a poem may exhibit. It may follow a particular metrical form, for example, and it may have a set rhyme scheme. The **stanza** is another aspect to the form a poem may take. Stanzas are groups of lines into which a poem may be divided; each stanza follows a pattern in its metre and/or in its rhyme scheme. Conventional stanza forms include **tercets** (stanzas of three lines, often linked by an interlocking rhyme scheme) and **quatrains** (stanzas of four lines, also usually rhymed).

There are also various forms in which complete poems may be written. The most common of these by far in English poetry is the **sonnet**—a poem of 14 lines, usually written in iambic pentameter, and generally following a strict rhyme scheme. Details concerning several of the main types of sonnet (including the **Petrarchan**, the **Spenserian**, the **Shakespearian**, and the **Miltonic**), as well as many more technical aspects of poetry than are dealt with in this introduction, will be found in the glossary of this anthology.

The sonnet is itself only one of several different complete poem forms. The **villanelle**, for example, is a poem generally consisting of 19 lines, with 5 tercets rhyming aba followed by a quatrain rhyming abaa. Dylan Thomas's "Do Not Go Gentle Into That Good Night" is one example of a villanelle included in these pages; Elizabeth Bishop's "One Art" is another.

Many other poetic forms—including the **ballad**, the **ghazal**, the **rondelle**, and the **sestina**—are also described in the glossary. So too are various categories of poem—the **elegy**, for example—that are defined less by such characteristics as metre or rhyme scheme than by subject matter and tone. The reader will also find in the glossary far more detail than is provided in this introduction on such things as the various forms of accentual-syllabic metre, the various forms of rhyme, and the various figures of speech commonly used in poetry.

Almost all of the above applies to **lyric** poetry, the sort of poetry that has been dominant in Western culture since the Renaissance. A lyric is a relatively short poem expressive of an individual's thoughts or feelings, and often appreciated for its aural qualities. Sonnets, elegies, dramatic monologues—all these are different sorts of lyric, as are poems as diverse as Andrew Marvell's "To His Coy Mistress," Emily Dickinson's "[Tell all the Truth, but tell it slant]," E.E. Cummings's "anyone lived in a pretty how town," Margaret Atwood's "[you fit into me]," George Elliott Clarke's "blank sonnet," and Alice Oswald's "Woods etc." But in other cultures and in other eras poetry has taken very different shapes. Nowadays Carol Ann Duffy speaks for a great many poets (and a great many readers of poetry too) in her belief that "poetry's power is not in narrative." To the ancient Greeks, however, the **epic** poem—a long poem telling a story, or a series of stories—was considered the most important form of poetry. The ancient Greeks also wrote plays in verse, and most plays in English-speaking cultures were also written largely or entirely in verse until the eighteenth century. In other times and other cultures even science and philosophy have been thought fit matter for poetry. *De Rerum Natura*, a long Latin poem about the nature of physical things and of life and death by the first century BCE writer Lucretius, is written entirely in verse—some 7,400 lines in total, all in dactylic hexameter. What poet today could even imagine writing such a work? Yet Stephen Greenblatt, a prominent critic and scholar of our time, has written a series of recent books and articles on Lucretius that have helped to bring *On The Nature of Things* (as the poem's title translates into English) to the admiring attention of fresh generations of readers, two millennia after it was written. When a poet writes with intensity and feeling of life and of death and of nature, there seem to be few limits to how widely read or how long lasting the resulting work may turn out to be.

—D.L.

The Exeter Book

C. 970–1000 CE

"Saga hwæt ic hatte (Say what I am called)": thus do many of the riddles compiled in the Exeter Book challenge the reader to identify their true subjects. Named for the cathedral in which it has resided for nearly a millennium, the Exeter Book is one of just four extant manuscripts consisting entirely of Anglo-Saxon writing. On its calfskin pages are preserved some 200 anonymous poems—roughly half of them riddles—written predominantly in the West Saxon vernacular and traditional four-stress line of Old English alliterative metre.

In some respects, the group of "elegies," serious meditative poems that constitute a portion of the Exeter Book, are as ambiguous as the riddles they accompany. Most, such as *The Wanderer* and *The Wife's Lament*, are monologues spoken by an unidentified character whose situation is unclear but who seems to be cut off from human society and the comforts of home and friendship. The meaning of individual lines is sometimes difficult to unravel because, in Old English poetic language, sentence boundaries and relationships between clauses are often uncertain. And yet despite these interpretive challenges, the Exeter Book elegies are among the most moving and powerful poems in Old English; their vision of life as both infinitely precious and inevitably transitory still resonates with many readers.

That the riddles were transcribed alongside these elegies and other serious works suggests that, though probably intended primarily as entertainments, the riddles were also esteemed for their poetry. Undoubtedly they are much more than cunning descriptions of objects in terms intended to suggest something else: their elaborate extended metaphors prompt the reader to consider even the most mundane articles in a different light, challenging fixed habits of mind and perception and revealing unlooked-for connections between things apparently unlike.

Many riddles rely on *prosopopoeia*, a device whereby a creature or object cryptically addresses itself to the reader in the first person. Others draw on double meanings to lure the reader astray and playfully expose misguided assumptions. Still others juxtapose contrasting states of being to present a single subject as fundamentally double in nature.

The Wife's Lament[1]

I make this song of myself, deeply sorrowing,
my own life's journey. I am able to tell
all the hardships I've suffered since I grew up,
but new or old, never worse than now—
5   ever I suffer the torment of my exile.
        First my lord left his people
over the tumbling waves; I worried at dawn
where on earth my leader of men might be.
When I set out myself in my sorrow,
10   a friendless exile, to find his retainers,
that man's kinsmen began to think
in secret that they would separate us,
so we would live far apart in the world,
most miserably, and longing seized me.
15   My lord commanded me to live here;[2]
I had few loved ones or loyal friends
in this country, which causes me grief.
Then I found that my most fitting man
was unfortunate, filled with grief,
20   concealing his mind, plotting murder
with a smiling face. So often we swore
that only death could ever divide us,
nothing else—all that is changed now;
it is now as if it had never been,
25   our friendship. Far and near, I must
endure the hatred of my dearest one.
        They forced me to live in a forest grove,
under an oak tree in an earthen cave.[3]
This earth-hall is old, and I ache with longing;
30   the dales are dark, the hills too high,
harsh hedges overhung with briars,
a home without joy. Here my lord's leaving
often fiercely seized me. There are friends on earth,
lovers living who lie in their bed,

---

1   *The Wife's Lament* Translation by R.M. Liuzza, copyright Broadview Press.
2   *live here* Or, "take up a dwelling in a grove" or "live in a (pagan) shrine." The precise
     meaning of the line, like the general meaning of the poem, is a matter of dispute and
     conjecture.
3   *earthen cave* Or "an earthen grave" or barrow.

while I walk alone in the first light of dawn   35
under the oak-tree and through this earth-cave,
where I must sit the summer-long day;
there I can weep for all my exiles,
my many troubles; and so I can never
escape from the cares of my sorrowful mind,   40
nor all the longings that seize me in this life.
     May the young man always be sad-minded
with hard heart-thoughts, yet let him have
a smiling face along with his heartache,
a crowd of constant sorrows. Let to himself   45
all his worldly joys belong! let him be outlawed
in a far distant land, so my friend sits
under stone cliffs chilled by storms,
weary-minded, surrounded by water
in a sad dreary hall! My beloved will suffer   50
the cares of a sorrowful mind; he will remember
too often a happier home. Woe to the one
who must wait with longing for a loved one.[1]

—10th century

Exeter Book Riddles[2]

Riddle 23

I am a wondrous thing, a joy to women,
Of use to close companions; no one
Do I harm, except the one who slays me.
High up I stand above the bed;
Underneath I am shaggy. Sometimes   5
Will come to me the lovely daughter
Of a peasant—will grab me, eager girl, rushing to grip
My red skin, holding me fast,
Taking my head. Soon she feels
What happens when you meet me,   10
She with curly hair. Wet will be her eye.

---

1   *May the young man ... loved one* These difficult lines have been read as a particular reflection, imagining the mental state of her distant beloved, or as a general reflection on
the double-faced nature of the world; here, following the reading of some critics, they
are taken as a kind of curse.

2   *Exeter Book Riddles* Translations by R.M. Liuzza, copyright Broadview Press.

Riddle 33

Creature came through waves, sailed strangely
As if a ship's stem, shouting at land,
Sounding loudly. Its laughter horrible,
Chilling to all. Sharp were her sides.
5   She was spiteful, sluggish in battle,
Biting in her bad works, smashing any ship's shield wall.
Hard in her taking, binding with spells
Spoke with cunning of her own creation:
"My mother is of the dearest race of women,
10 And my mother is my daughter too,
Grown big, pregnant. It is known to men of old
And to all people that she stands
In beauty in all lands of the world."

Riddle 81

Not silent is my house; I am quiet.
We are two together, moving
As our Maker meant. I am faster than he is,
Sometimes stronger; he runs harder, lasts longer.
5   Sometimes I rest; he must run on.
He is my house all my life long
If we are parted death is my destiny.

—10th century

Solutions to the Exeter Book Riddles are provided with the Permissions Acknowledgements on page 1519.

Geoffrey Chaucer

c. 1343–1400

Geoffrey Chaucer is generally considered the father of English poetry, a title bestowed by John Dryden, who held his forebear "in the same degree of veneration as the Grecians held Homer, or the Romans Virgil." Together with William Langland and the anonymous author of *Sir Gawain and the Green Knight*, Chaucer was among the first poets to craft sophisticated literary expressions in a Middle English vernacular. But whereas Langland and the *Gawain* poet wrote in an unrhymed alliterative style characteristic of Old English verse, Chaucer's poetry reflects the fashions and influences of the Continent and is written in a dialect more closely related to modern English.

Chaucer was born at a time that saw the beginnings of a breakdown in strict divisions between the aristocracy, the Church, and the commoners. Born into the newly expanding mercantile class, he was able to transcend the restrictions of the old social order to procure a variety of high positions— including Controller of Customs and Justice of the Peace—and to marry a lady-in-waiting to the queen. It is speculated that he began his literary career as a translator when, in 1359, he took part in the war in France, where he was captured and held until the king paid his ransom in 1360. Most of his best work, however, was composed after a 1372 diplomatic trip to Italy, where he probably acquired his knowledge of the Italian literary masters, who strongly influenced his later work.

Though Chaucer wrote some short poems (such as "To Rosemounde"), he is best known for his longer works, most notably *The Parliament of Fowls* (1380), an early dream vision; *Troilus and Criseyde* (c. 1385), a masterly romance of great psychological complexity; and *The Canterbury Tales*, generally considered his masterpiece. Frequently hilarious, sometimes bawdy, and often revealing, *The Canterbury Tales* presents itself as a series of stories told by a group of pilgrims on their way from London to Canterbury. Chaucer worked on *The Canterbury Tales* during the last decades of his life, producing 24 tales totalling over 17,000 lines, but leaving the work unfinished when he died.

To Rosemounde

A Balade

Madame, ye ben of al beaute shryne°   *shrine*
As fer as cercled° is the mapamounde,°1   *rounded / map of the world*

---

1   *ye ben of al … mapamounde* You are the shrine of all beauty throughout the world.

For as the cristal glorious ye shyne,
And lyke ruby ben your chekes rounde.
5   Therwith ye ben so mery and so jocounde°   *pleasant, joyful*
That at a revel° whan that I see you daunce,   *festival*
It is an oynement° unto my wounde,   *ointment*
Thogh ye to me ne do no daliaunce.[1]

For thogh I wepe of teres ful a tyne,°   *barrel*
10 Yet may that wo myn herte nat confounde;°   *destroy*
Your semy° voys that ye so smal out twyne°   *small, high / twist out*
Maketh my thoght in joy and blis habounde.°   *abound, be full of*
So curtaysly I go with love bounde
That to myself I sey in my penaunce,
15 "Suffyseth me to love you, Rosemounde,
Thogh ye to me ne do no daliaunce."[2]

Nas never pyk walwed° in galauntyne[3]   *immersed*
As I in love am walwed and ywounde,°   *wound*
For which ful ofte I of myself devyne°   *discover, understand*
20 That I am trewe Tristam[4] the secounde.
My love may not refreyde° nor affounde,°   *grow cold / founder, grow numb*
I brenne° ay in an amorous plesaunce.°   *burn / desire*
Do what you lyst,° I wyl your thral be founde,[5]   *wish*
Thogh ye to me ne do no daliaunce.

tregentil————————//————————chaucer[6]

—c. 1477

---

1   *Thogh … daliaunce* Even though you give me no encouragement.
2   *daliaunce* Sociable interaction, or more explicitly amorous or sexual exchange.
3   *Nas … galauntyne* No pike was ever steeped in galantine sauce.
4   *Tristam* Tristan, lover of Isolde, often presented as the ideal lover in medieval romance.
5   *I … founde* I will remain your servant.
6   *tregentil … chaucer* Although the words appear joined (or separated) by a line or flourish
    in the manuscript, the status of *tregentil* is uncertain. It may be an epithet (French: very
    gentle) or a proper name.

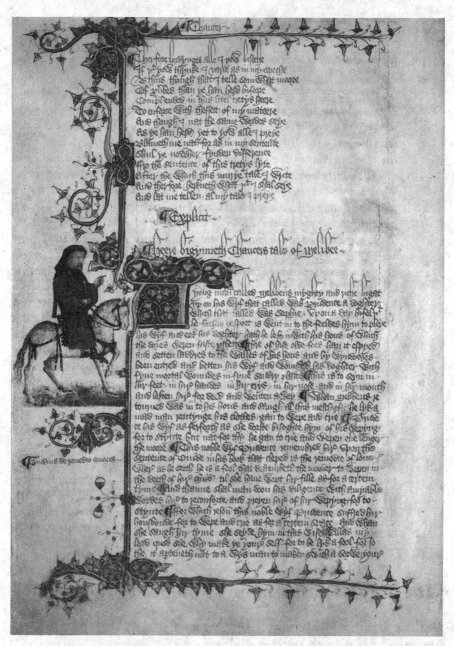

The first page of Chaucer's Tale of Melibee, *from the Ellesmere manuscript of* The Canterbury Tales, *1400–05. The figure on horseback is generally taken to be a representation of Chaucer. The actual size of pages in the Ellesmere manuscript is approximately 15¾ × 11⅛".*

Sir Thomas Wyatt

c. 1503–1542

Thomas Wyatt lived his entire adult life amidst the political intrigue and turmoil that accompanied the reign of King Henry VIII, and was twice imprisoned in the Tower of London. Even his poems on subjects far from the machinations of the king and his courtiers—subjects such as love and idyllic country life—can carry a subtext about the court's political dramas. Wyatt wrote in many poetic forms, but is best known for the artistry of his satires and songs and, along with Henry Howard, Earl of Surrey (1517–47), for introducing the Italian sonnet to England.

Wyatt was born into a family of wealth and status. He was a man of many accomplishments, adept at music and poetry as well as politics, and he soon became a valued member of King Henry VIII's court. He began a diplomatic career in 1526 with missions to France, Rome, and Venice, where he may have acquired his knowledge of Italian sonnets. He was knighted in 1536 but soon afterward had his first falling out with the king and was imprisoned in the Tower of London—possibly because of a past relationship with the queen, Anne Boleyn, who would be executed that year. Wyatt temporarily regained the king's favour, but in 1541 he was imprisoned again, this time on trumped-up charges of treason. He was spared and returned to favour a second time, but died the next year, succumbing to fever in 1542.

Few of Wyatt's poems were printed in his lifetime, but many appeared in Richard Tottel's 1557 volume *Songes and Sonettes* (later to become known as *Tottel's Miscellany*). Some years later, the Elizabethan critic George Puttenham summarized Sir Thomas Wyatt's importance to the English literary tradition in terms that remain broadly accepted today: "[Wyatt and Surrey] travailed into Italie, and there tasted the sweet and stately measures and stile of the Italian Poesie.... They greatly pollished our rude & homely maner of vulgar Poesie, from that it had been before, and for that cause may justly be said the first reformers of our English meetre and stile."

[The long love that in my thought doth harbour]¹

The long love that in my thought doth harbour
And in mine heart doth keep his residence
Into my face presseth with bold pretence
And therein campeth, spreading his banner.
5   She that me learneth° to love and suffer   *teaches*

---

1   [*The long love ... doth harbour*] This poem is an adaptation of Sonnet 140 from the
     Italian poet Petrarch's *Rime sparse* (*Scattered Rhymes*).

And will° that my trust and lust's negligence — *wishes*
Be reined by reason, shame,° and reverence, — *modesty*
With his hardiness° taketh displeasure. — *daring*
Wherewithal unto the heart's forest he fleeth,
Leaving his enterprise with pain and cry, — 10
And there him hideth and not appeareth.
What may I do when my master feareth,
But in the field with him to live and die?
For good is the life ending faithfully.

—1557

[They flee from me that sometime did me seek]

They flee from me that sometime did me seek
With naked foot stalking° in my chamber. — *treading softly*
I have seen them gentle, tame, and meek
That now are wild and do not remember
That sometime they put themself in danger — 5
To take bread at my hand; and now they range,
Busily seeking with a continual change.

Thanked be fortune it hath been otherwise
Twenty times better; but once in special,
In thin array after° a pleasant guise,° — *in accordance with / style* 10
When her loose gown from her shoulders did fall
And she me caught in her arms long and small,
Therewithal sweetly did me kiss
And softly said, "Dear heart, how like you this?"

It was no dream; I lay broad waking.° — *wide awake* 15
But all is turned, through my gentleness,
Into a strange fashion of forsaking.
And I have leave to go of her goodness,[1]
And she also to use newfangleness.° — *inconstancy*
But since that I so kindly[2] am served, — 20
I would fain° know what she hath deserved. — *gladly*
—1557

---

1   *I have ... goodness* I have her permission to go from her.
2   *kindly* Naturally, according to natural laws (i.e., that women are fickle). The word also ironically suggests the modern "with kindness." In the original printing after Wyatt's death, the text was amended to "unkindly," removing the irony.

[Whoso list to hunt, I know where is an hind]¹

Whoso list° to hunt, I know where is an hind,°   *likes / female deer*
But as for me, alas, I may no more:
The vain travail hath wearied me so sore.
I am of them that farthest cometh behind;
5 Yet may I by no means my wearied mind
Draw from the deer: but as she fleeth afore,
Fainting I follow. I leave off therefore,
Since in a net I seek to hold the wind.
Who list her hunt, I put him out of doubt,
10 As well as I may spend his time in vain:
And, graven with diamonds, in letters plain
There is written her fair neck round about:
"*Noli me tangere*, for Caesar's I am,²
And wild for to hold, though I seem tame."

—1557

---

1   *[Whoso list ... an hind]* This poem is an adaptation of Sonnet 190 from Petrarch's *Rime sparse* (*Scattered Rhymes*).
2   *Noli me tangere* Latin: Touch me not; words spoken by Christ after his resurrection; *for Caesar's I am* It was thought that Caesar's deer wore collars with this inscription to ensure they would not be hunted. Wyatt's readers who identified the deer with Anne Boleyn (whom Wyatt knew and perhaps loved) would have read the lines as suggesting that the "hind" belongs to Henry VIII.

Edmund Spenser

1552?–1599

Best known for his epic poem *The Faerie Queene* (1590–96), Edmund Spenser was an extraordinarily accomplished poet in other forms as well. Born to parents of modest means, he nevertheless earned two degrees from Cambridge and embarked on a career as a servant of the Crown. It was a successful career—though nowhere near as successful as Spenser's poetic work turned out to be. He was a secretary to the Earl of Leicester, then to the Lord Deputy of Ireland, and served briefly as Sheriff of Cork.

In 1579 Spenser used the pseudonym "Immerito" on his first significant publication, *The Shepheardes Calender*, a set of illustrated pastoral poems for each month of the year. He spent the following decade working on the first three books of *The Faerie Queene* (1590), an allegorical examination of the virtues set in a magical romance world. This work was politically as well as poetically motivated: the poem was a bid for more direct royal patronage from Queen Elizabeth. Its central if often absent figure is Prince Arthur, the future British king, who is seeking the always absent heroine, the "Faerie Queene" Gloriana—an allegorical "mirror" of Queen Elizabeth in her public role as ruler. Spenser had hoped to write twelve books, but completed only six, the second set of three books being published in a 1596 edition. Spenser won a pension from the queen, but Elizabeth's patronage seems to have gone no further, perhaps because his satirical "Mother Hubberds Tale," included in his *Complaints* (1591), angered the authorities.

In between the two installments of *The Faerie Queene*, Spenser wrote several other volumes, including *Colin Clouts Come Home Againe* (1595), a sometimes satirical anti-court pastoral; and *Astrophel* (1596), an elegy for fellow poet Philip Sidney. During this time he also completed his *Amoretti* (1595), a series of sonnets commemorating his courtship of Elizabeth Boyle, issued with *Epithalamion*, a marriage hymn celebrating their union. Spenser died early in 1599 and is buried in Westminster Abbey, next to Chaucer.

from *Amoretti*[1]

1

Happy ye leaves° when as those lilly hands,   *pages*
   which hold my life in their dead doing° might,   *death-dealing*
   shall handle you and hold in loves soft bands,°   *bonds*
   lyke captives trembling at the victors sight.

---

1   *Amoretti* Italian: Little Loves.

5 And happy lines, on which with starry light,
  those lamping° eyes will deigne sometimes to look   *blazing*
  and reade the sorrowes of my dying spright,°   *spirit*
  written with teares in harts close bleeding book.
And happy rymes bath'd in the sacred brooke,
10   of *Helicon*[1] whence she derivèd is,
  when ye behold that Angels blessèd looke,
  my soules long lackèd foode, my heavens blis.
Leaves, lines, and rymes, seeke her to please alone,
  whom if ye please, I care for other none.

75

One day I wrote her name upon the strand,°   *shore*
  but came the waves and washèd it away:
  agayne I wrote it with a second hand,
  but came the tyde, and made my paynes his pray.°   *prey*
5 Vayne man, sayd she, that doest in vaine assay,°   *attempt*
  a mortall thing so to immortalize.
  for I my selve shall lyke to this decay,
  and eek° my name bee wypèd out lykewize.   *also*
Not so, (quod° I) let baser things devize   *said*
10   to dy in dust, but you shall live by fame:
  my verse your vertues rare shall eternize,
  and in the hevens wryte your glorious name.
Where whenas° death shall all the world subdew,   *whenever*
  our love shall live, and later life renew.

                —1595

---

1 *Helicon* One of the mountains sacred to the Nine Muses, the goddesses of the arts and sciences. The sacred spring that flows from Helicon is the Hippocrene.

Sir Walter Ralegh
c. 1554–1618

Known as an explorer, courtier, writer, and adventurer—and as a knight and captain of the Queen's Guard who was later accused of treason—Sir Walter Ralegh was a controversial figure. A great portion of his writing has been lost over the centuries, but the remaining works reveal a dynamic voice imaginatively relaying his experiences and boldly critiquing the social and political climate in which he lived.

Born in Hayes Barton, Devonshire, Ralegh was a student at Oxford and a soldier in France and Ireland before becoming a favourite of Elizabeth I in the early 1580s. A secret marriage to one of Elizabeth's ladies-in-waiting caused him to fall out of favour, and in 1592 he was imprisoned for several months in the Tower of London—the occasion of his long poem *The Ocean to Cynthia*, lamenting Elizabeth's displeasure. Before and after his imprisonment Ralegh made attempts to establish colonies in what is now Virginia and the Carolinas, and he undertook several expeditions to the New World, including a 1595 voyage to Guiana in search of the legendary golden city of El Dorado. In 1596 he wrote *The Discovery of Guiana*, a vivid and partly fantastical account of his travels that influenced the popular European conception of South America as an exotic locale.

After his tumultuous relationship with Elizabeth I, Ralegh found a less sympathetic ruler in James I, who had him condemned under dubious charges of treason and imprisoned in the Tower from 1603 to 1616. Upon his release Ralegh embarked on another failed search for El Dorado. During this expedition, his crew attacked a Spanish settlement in contradiction of James's diplomatic policy, and when Ralegh returned home he was executed for his defiance.

Ralegh's poetry is characterized by an intensely personal treatment of such conventional themes as love, loss, beauty, and time. The majority of his poems are short lyrics—many of them occasional, written in response to particular events. Although he wrote throughout his eventful life, he was most prolific during the period of his imprisonment, producing poetry, political treatises, and an unfinished *History of the World* intended to chronicle life on Earth from the time of creation to Ralegh's own era.

The Nymph's Reply to the Shepherd[1]

If all the world and love were young,
And truth in every shepherd's tongue,
These pretty pleasures might me move
To live with thee and be thy love.

Time drives the flocks from field to fold
When rivers rage and rocks grow cold,
And Philomel becometh dumb;[2]
The rest complains of cares to come.

The flowers do fade, and wanton° fields   *unrestrained, unruly*
To wayward winter reckoning yields;
A honey tongue, a heart of gall,°   *bitterness, rancour*
Is fancy's spring, but sorrow's fall.

Thy gowns, thy shoes, thy beds of roses,
Thy cap, thy kirtle,° and thy posies   *tunic or skirt*
Soon break, soon wither, soon forgotten—
In folly ripe, in reason rotten.

Thy belt of straw and ivy buds,
Thy coral clasps and amber studs,
All these in me no means can move
To come to thee and be thy love.

But could youth last and love still breed,
Had joys no date nor age no need,[3]
Then these delights my mind might move
To live with thee and be thy love.

—1600

---

1   *The Nymph's … Shepherd* Response to Christopher Marlowe's "The Passionate Shepherd
    to His Love" (1599), also included in this anthology.
2   *Philomel becometh dumb* I.e., the nightingale does not sing. In classical mythology,
    Philomela, the daughter of the King of Athens, was transformed into a nightingale after
    being pursued and raped by her brother-in-law, Tereus, who tore out her tongue.
3   *Had joys … no need* If joys had no ending and aging did not bring with it its own needs.

Christopher Marlowe

1564–1593

As Tennyson wrote, "if Shakespeare is the dazzling sun" of the English Renaissance, then his fellow poet-playwright Christopher Marlowe "is certainly the morning star." Marlowe's plays heralded a new dawn for English drama in their use of blank verse (unrhymed iambic pentameter): by demonstrating its potential to capture the dynamic cadence of natural speech in plays such as *Tamburlaine the Great* (1587) and *Doctor Faustus* (1592?), he helped to make blank verse a standard form for playwrights of the period. Marlowe's facility with language extended to poetry, and he was known for his translations of Latin poets as well as for his original work. "The Passionate Shepherd to His Love," based in part on Virgil's Second Eclogue, is perhaps his most famous English poem.

Despite his success as a writer, Marlowe was dogged by controversy throughout his career. Not only was he a party to a homicide (of which he was acquitted on grounds of self-defence), he was also arrested for coining money and arraigned before the Privy Council on charges of blasphemy and heresy, both serious transgressions in Elizabethan England.

Marlowe's troubles came to a brutal head when at 29 he was fatally stabbed in what may have been a planned assassination connected with his apparent service to the Crown as a government agent. The enigmatic circumstances of his life and death have contributed to Marlowe's reputation as a man who—as Thomas Kyd attested—was "intemperate and of a cruel heart," skeptical of religion, scornful of decorum, and bold unto recklessness. Whatever the truth may be, Marlowe produced an extraordinary body of work that emits what William Hazlitt described as "a glow of the imagination, unhallowed by anything but its own energies."

The Passionate Shepherd to His Love

Come live with me and be my love,
And we will all the pleasures prove°   try
That valleys, groves, hills, and fields,
Woods, or steepy mountain yields.

And we will sit upon the rocks,   5
Seeing the shepherds feed their flocks,
By shallow rivers to whose falls
Melodious birds sing madrigals.[1]

---

1   *madrigals* Part-songs for several voices, often with pastoral or amatory associations.

And I will make thee beds of roses
10　And a thousand fragrant posies,
　　A cap of flowers, and a kirtle°　　　　　　　　　　　　　　*tunic or skirt*
　　Embroidered all with leaves of myrtle;

　　A gown made of the finest wool
　　Which from our pretty lambs we pull;
15　Fair linèd slippers for the cold,
　　With buckles of the purest gold;

　　A belt of straw and ivy buds,
　　With coral clasps and amber studs:
　　And if these pleasures may thee move,
20　Come live with me, and be my love.

　　The shepherd swains° shall dance and sing　　　　　　　*rustic lovers*
　　For thy delight each May morning:
　　If these delights thy mind may move,
　　Then live with me and be my love.

　　　　　　　　　　　　　　　　　　　　　　　　　　　　　—1599

William Shakespeare
1564–1616

As his fellow poet-playwright Ben Jonson declared, William Shakespeare "was not of an age, but for all time." Without doubt, the "Bard of Avon" has proved worthy of this monumental phrase: nearly four centuries after his death, Shakespeare's histories, comedies, tragedies, and romances continue to be staged the world over.

Today, Shakespeare's name is connected less with a flesh-and-blood human being—the son of a glover, born in the small town of Stratford-on-Avon, who left for London to pursue a career in the theatre after fathering three children—than with an extraordinary body of work. Shakespeare's oeuvre includes as many as 38 plays, many of them masterpieces; two narrative poems, *Venus and Adonis* (1593) and *The Rape of Lucrece* (1594), both much admired in Shakespeare's lifetime; and 154 sonnets, which were not necessarily conceived as a sequence but were published as one in 1609, perhaps without Shakespeare's consent.

In the sonnets the chief object of the poet's desire is not a chaste fair-haired lady but an idealized young man who prefers the praises of a rival poet and who occupies the centre of a psychologically complex love triangle in which the poet-speaker and a promiscuous "dark lady" are entangled. Because of their intensely intimate expression of love, lust, jealousy, and shame, the sonnets have been the subject of endless biographical speculation, yet it is by no means certain whether the poet-speaker is Shakespeare himself or a persona constructed for dramatic effect.

The enduring power of the sonnets resides not merely in what they mean but in how they produce meaning, that is, in the emotional and intellectual tensions and continuities between their several interworking parts.

Sonnets

18

Shall I compare thee to a summer's day?
Thou art more lovely and more temperate:
Rough winds do shake the darling buds of May,
And summer's lease hath all too short a date:
Sometime too hot the eye of heaven shines,
And often is his gold complexion dimmed;
And every fair° from fair sometime declines,   *beauty*
By chance, or nature's changing course, untrimmed:
But thy eternal summer shall not fade,

5

10 Nor lose possession of that fair thou ow'st,°   *own*
   Nor shall death brag thou wander'st in his shade
   When in eternal lines to time thou grow'st:
        So long as men can breathe or eyes can see,
        So long lives this, and this gives life to thee.

29

   When in disgrace with fortune and men's eyes
   I all alone beweep my outcast state,
   And trouble deaf heav'n with my bootless° cries,   *unavailing*
   And look upon myself, and curse my fate,
5 Wishing me like to one more rich in hope,
   Featured like him,[1] like him with friends possessed,
   Desiring this man's art° and that man's scope,   *skill*
   With what I most enjoy contented least;
   Yet in these thoughts myself almost despising,
10 Haply° I think on thee, and then my state,   *by chance*
   Like to the lark at break of day arising,
   From sullen° earth sings hymns at heaven's gate;   *dark, gloomy*
        For thy sweet love remembered such wealth brings
        That then I scorn to change my state with kings.

73

   That time of year thou mayst in me behold,
   When yellow leaves, or none, or few do hang
   Upon those boughs which shake against the cold,
   Bare ruined choirs[2] where late the sweet birds sang;
5 In me thou seest the twilight of such day
   As after sunset fadeth in the west,
   Which by and by black night doth take away,
   Death's second self[3] that seals up all in rest;
   In me thou seest the glowing of such fire
10 That on the ashes of his youth doth lie,
   As the deathbed, whereon it must expire,
   Consumed with that which it was nourished by;
        This thou perceiv'st, which makes thy love more strong,
        To love that well, which thou must leave° ere long.   *lose*

---

1 *Featured like him* With physical attractions like his.
2 *choirs* Parts of churches designated for singers.
3 *Death's second self* Sleep.

116

Let me not to the marriage of true minds
Admit impediments;[1] love is not love
Which alters when it alteration finds,
Or bends with the remover[2] to remove.
O no, it is an ever-fixèd mark,   5
That looks on tempests and is never shaken;
It is the star to every wand'ring bark,°   *boat*
Whose worth's unknown, although his height be taken.[3]
Love's not Time's fool, though rosy lips and cheeks
Within his bending sickle's compass° come;   *sweep* 10
Love alters not with his brief hours and weeks,
But bears it out even to the edge of doom.
    If this be error and upon me proved,
    I never writ, nor no man ever loved.

130

My mistress' eyes are nothing like the sun;
Coral is far more red than her lips' red;
If snow be white, why then her breasts are dun;°   *greyish-brown*
If hairs be wires, black wires grow on her head;
I have seen roses damasked,° red and white,   *parti-coloured* 5
But no such roses see I in her cheeks;
And in some perfumes is there more delight
Than in the breath that from my mistress reeks.
I love to hear her speak, yet well I know
That music hath a far more pleasing sound;   10
I grant I never saw a goddess go;°   *walk*
My mistress when she walks treads on the ground.
    And yet, by heaven, I think my love as rare
    As any she[4] belied with false compare.

—1609

---

1   *impediments* Cf. the marriage service in the Book of Common Prayer (c. 1552): "If any
    of you know cause, or just impediment, why these two persons should not be joined
    together in holy Matrimony, ye are to declare it."
2   *remover* One who changes, i.e., ceases to love.
3   *Whose ... taken* Referring to the "star" of the previous line, most likely the North Star,
    whose altitude can be reckoned for navigation purposes using a sextant, but whose es-
    sence remains unknown.
4   *any she* Any woman.

Thomas Campion
1567–1620

Thomas Campion was both a poet and a composer who, as he wrote in the introduction to one of his volumes of lyric poems, "chiefly aymed to couple [his] Words and Notes louingly together."

Campion was born in London and attended the University of Cambridge and Gray's Inn, one of England's four Inns of Court for the study of law. While he never did take up a legal profession, he had an active social life at the Inns of Court and formed many friendships with musicians and poets. His first collection, *Poemata* (1595), was a volume of Latin verse, but it was *A Booke of Ayres* (1601), his first book in English, that cemented his reputation as a lyric poet. Written in collaboration with the lutist Philip Rosseter, *A Booke of Ayres* was the first of several volumes of lyrics with lute accompaniment that Campion would produce. He followed it with the manifesto *Observations in the Art of English Poesie* (1602), in which he championed the use of classical metres and deplored the "vulgar and unarteficiall custome of riming"—although he frequently disregarded this philosophy and used traditional English rhyme and metre in much of his own work.

In 1605, Campion completed a medical degree at Caen University in France. He practised medicine for the rest of his life, but he continued to write songs and poetry, as well as the libretti for several elaborate masques that were performed at important court weddings. His last book, *Third and Fourth Booke of Ayres*, was published in 1617, three years before his death.

[There is a garden in her face]

There is a garden in her face,
Where roses and white lilies grow;
    A heav'nly paradise is that place,
Wherein all pleasant fruits do flow.
    There cherries grow, which none may buy
5   Till cherry ripe[1] themselves do cry.

Those cherries fairly do enclose
Of orient pearl[2] a double row,
    Which when her lovely laughter shows,
10 They look like rosebuds filled with snow.

---

1   *cherry ripe* The cry of a London street seller.
2   *orient pearl* High-quality pearl.

Yet them nor peer nor prince can buy,
Till cherry ripe themselves do cry.

Her eyes like angels watch them still;
Her brows like bended bows do stand,
  Threat'ning with piercing frowns to kill
All that attempt with eye or hand
  Those sacred cherries to come nigh,
  Till cherry ripe themselves do cry.

—1617

John Donne

1572–1631

John Donne was an innovator who set out to startle readers with his disdain for convention, writing poems that challenged expectations about what was appropriate in poetic subject matter, form, tone, language, and imagery.

As with the speaker of his "Holy Sonnet 19," in Donne "contraries meet in one." Some critics and readers try to resolve these "contraries" by separating Donne's career in two: in early life, a witty man-about-London whose love poems combine erotic energy with high-minded argument; in later life, a learned minister famous for his religious verse and his sermons. But Donne frequently blurs the differences between the sacred and the secular, sometimes presenting erotic love as a form of religious experience, and sometimes portraying religious devotion as an erotic experience. His poetic voice, moreover, ranges across a multitude of roles and postures, from misogynist cynicism to tender idealism and devout religious passion.

Donne was the son of a prosperous ironmonger, and his family was Catholic at a time when the government viewed all Catholics with suspicion. Donne studied at both Oxford and Cambridge but took no degree—perhaps because graduation required accepting the Church of England's 39 "articles of religion." In 1592 he began legal studies in London, and over the next few years wrote many of the love lyrics for which he later became famous; like most of his poems, these were circulated in manuscript but not published during his lifetime.

Donne eventually converted to Anglicanism, and in 1615 he became a clergyman. In 1621, he was appointed Dean of St. Paul's Cathedral in London, where he attracted large audiences for his intellectually challenging and emotionally stirring sermons. His *Poems* first appeared in 1633, two years after his death.

The Flea

Mark but this flea, and mark in this,
How little that which thou deny'st me is;
It sucked me first, and now sucks thee,
And in this flea, our two bloods mingled be;[1]
5   Thou know'st that this cannot be said
A sin, nor shame, nor loss of maidenhead,
        Yet this enjoys before it woo,

---

1   *mingled be* The speaker's subsequent argument hinges on the traditional belief that blood mixed during sexual intercourse.

And pampered swells with one blood made of two
And this, alas, is more than we would do.

Oh stay, three lives in one flea spare,   10
Where we almost, yea more than married are.
This flea is you and I, and this
Our marriage bed, and marriage temple is;
Though parents grudge, and you, we're met,
And cloistered in these living walls of jet.   15
    Though use° make you apt to kill me,   *habit*
    Let not to that, self murder added be,
    And sacrilege, three sins in killing three.

Cruel and sudden, hast thou since
Purpled thy nail, in blood of innocence?   20
Wherein could this flea guilty be,
Except in that drop which it sucked from thee?
Yet thou triumph'st, and sayest that thou
Find'st not thy self, nor me the weaker now;
    'Tis true, then learn how false, fears be;   25
    Just so much honour, when thou yield'st to me,
    Will waste, as this flea's death took life from thee.

—1633

from *Holy Sonnets*

10

Death be not proud, though some have called thee
Mighty and dreadful, for thou art not so,
For, those, whom thou think'st thou dost overthrow
Die not, poor death, nor yet canst thou kill me.
From rest and sleep, which but thy pictures be,   5
Much pleasure, then from thee, much more must flow,
And soonest our best men with thee do go,
Rest of their bones, and soul's delivery.
Thou art slave to Fate, Chance, kings, and desperate men,
And dost with poison, war, and sickness dwell,   10
And poppy, or charms, can make us sleep as well,
And better than thy stroke; why swell'st thou then?
One short sleep past, we wake eternally,
And death shall be no more; death, thou shalt die.

14

Batter my heart, three personed God; for you
As yet but knock, breathe, shine, and seek to mend;
That I may rise and stand, o'erthrow me, and bend
Your force, to break, blow, burn and make me new.
5 I, like an usurped town, to another due,
Labour to admit You, but oh, to no end,
Reason Your viceroy in me, me should defend,
But is captived, and proves weak or untrue.
Yet dearly I love You, and would be loved fain,
10 But am betrothed unto Your enemy:
Divorce me, untie, or break that knot again,
Take me to you, imprison me, for I
Except you enthrall me, never shall be free,
Nor ever chaste, except you ravish me.

—1633

A Valediction: Forbidding Mourning

As virtuous men pass mildly away,
    And whisper to their souls to go,
Whilst some of their sad friends do say,
    The breath goes now, and some say, no:

5 So let us melt, and make no noise,
    No tear-floods, nor sigh-tempests move,
'Twere profanation of our joys
    To tell the laity our love.

Moving of th'earth° brings harms and fears,   *earthquake*
10   Men reckon what it did and meant,
But trepidation of the spheres,[1]
    Though greater far, is innocent.

---

1   *the spheres* According to Ptolemaic theory, a concentric series of spheres revolved around
the earth; the heavenly bodies were set into these spheres. Enveloping all the rest was an
outer sphere known as the "*Primum Mobile*" ("First Mover"), thought to give motion to
the other spheres, and to introduce variations into the times of the equinoxes.

Dull sublunary[1] lovers' love
    (Whose soul is sense) cannot admit
Absence, because it doth remove   15
    Those things which elemented it.

But we by a love, so much refined,
    That our selves know not what it is,
Inter-assured of the mind,
    Care less, eyes, lips, and hands to miss.   20

Our two souls therefore, which are one,
    Though I must go, endure not yet
A breach, but an expansion,
    Like gold to airy thinness beat.

If they be two, they are two so   25
    As stiff twin compasses[2] are two,
Thy soul, the fixed foot, makes no show
    To move, but doth, if th'other do.

And though it in the centre sit,
    Yet when the other far doth roam,   30
It leans, and hearkens after it,
    And grows erect, as that comes home.

Such wilt thou be to me, who must
    Like th'other foot, obliquely run;
Thy firmness draws my circle just,   35
    And makes me end, where I begun.

—1633

---

1   *sublunary* Beneath the moon, hence earthly (as opposed to heavenly) and therefore cor-
ruptible and subject to change.
2   *twin compasses* Single drawing compass (with twin "feet").

Lady Mary Wroth
1587–1653?

Lady Mary Wroth wrote the first work of prose romance and the first amatory sonnet sequence published by a woman in English. Her work was admired by a number of poets of her day—Ben Jonson proclaimed that her verse had made him "a better lover, and much better poet"—and although her reputation faded during the ensuing centuries, today she is recognized as a significant Jacobean writer and pioneer.

Born Mary Sidney, Wroth was a member of an illustrious political and literary family. She was educated by tutors and was already an accomplished scholar and musician by the time of her arranged marriage in 1604. The marriage was unhappy; when her husband died in 1614, Wroth was left with crushing debts, but was also free to pursue more openly a long-time illicit affair with her cousin, William Herbert. This affair, and financial constraints, may have limited Wroth's access to court and spurred her to write more seriously.

Wroth published a court romance, *The Countess of Montgomery's Urania*, in 1621. A groundbreaking work, *Urania* exploits a genre traditionally written by men—pastoral romance—in untraditional ways to examine the social situation of women in actual court society. Appended to *Urania* was a sequence of 83 sonnets and 20 songs entitled *Pamphilia to Amphilanthus*. These poems highlight love's tensions and contradictions with great poetic skill; the climax of *Pamphilia to Amphilanthus* is a technical *tour de force*, a "corona" or "crown" of 14 sonnets in which the last line of each poem becomes the first line of the next.

from *Pamphilia to Amphilanthus*

Song [Love, a child, is ever crying]

Love, a child, is ever crying,
    Please him, and he straight is flying;
    Give him, he the more is craving,
    Never satisfied with having.

5 His desires have no measure,
    Endless folly is his treasure;
    What he promiseth he breaketh;
    Trust not one word that he speaketh.

He vows nothing but false matter,
    And to cozen° you he'll flatter;   *deceive*   10
    Let him gain the hand, he'll leave you,
    And still glory to deceive you.

He will triumph in your wailing,
    And yet cause be of your failing:
    These his virtues are, and slighter   15
    Are his gifts, his favours lighter.

Feathers are as firm in staying,
    Wolves no fiercer in their preying.
    As a child then leave him crying,
    Nor seek him, so giv'n to flying.   20

77[1]

In this strange labyrinth how shall I turn?
    Ways° are on all sides while the way I miss: *paths*
    If to the right hand, there in love I burn;
    Let me go forward, therein danger is;
If to the left, suspicion hinders bliss;   5
    Let me turn back, shame cries I ought return,
    Nor faint, though crosses° with my fortunes kiss;   *troubles*
    Stand still is harder, although sure to mourn.[2]
Thus let me take the right, or left-hand way,
    Go forward, or stand still, or back retire: 10
    I must these doubts endure without allay°   *relief*
    Or help, but travail[3] find for my best hire.
Yet that which most my troubled sense doth move,
Is to leave all, and take the thread of Love.[4]

                                                       —1621

---

1   *77* The first sonnet in the 14-poem sequence *A Crown of Sonnets Dedicated to Love*, part of the larger sequence of *Pamphilia to Amphilanthus*.

2   *sure to mourn* Sure to make me mourn.

3   *travail* Take pains to; possibly meant as a pun on "travel," which was the word used in an early edition of the poem.

4   *thread of Love* Referring to the myth of Ariadne, who gave her beloved Theseus a spool of thread to unwind behind him as he travelled through the labyrinth of the Minotaur; by following the thread he could find his way back out.

Robert Herrick
1591–1674

Of the "sons of Ben" who basked in the genius of poet and playwright Ben Jonson in 1620s London, Robert Herrick is the poet most familiar to modern readers—more so, to many readers, than Jonson himself. "Gather ye rosebuds while ye may," the opening line of Herrick's "To the Virgins, to Make Much of Time," is the most famous version of a classical refrain, while poems such as "Delight in Disorder" are fixtures in anthologies. That Herrick's fame rests on a few crystalline lyrics obscures the fact that he possessed a fairly varied repertoire. His major collection, *Hesperides* (1648), containing over 1,400 poems, includes epigrams, epistles, odes, eclogues, and other lyric forms. The introduction to *Hesperides* genially invites the reader to enjoy the book in a spirit of "cleanly wantonness," to share the poet's delight in such things as good food, drink, and company; female beauty; and love of the countryside. Whether playful or earnest, many of Herrick's poems are exhortations in the *carpe diem* tradition: since all things are subject to "Time's trans-shifting," we must seize every fleeting chance for happiness, but we must do so with due regard for the classical virtue of moderation.

Although *Hesperides* was published during the English Civil Wars (1642–51), Herrick, a staunch Royalist, often seems insensible of the political upheaval that is embraced by his more rebellious contemporaries, such as Milton. Partly because its light bucolic tone did not match the seriousness of the time, *Hesperides* achieved little notice during Herrick's life; in the nineteenth century, however, the Romantic attraction to pastoral and rural themes made Herrick popular with anthologists. More recent critics, appreciating his cunning and delicate artistry, have accorded him a high status among seventeenth-century poets.

Delight in Disorder

A sweet disorder in the dress
Kindles in clothes a wantonness:
A lawn[1] about the shoulders thrown
Into a fine distractiòn;
5   An erring lace, which here and there
Enthralls the crimson stomacher:[2]
A cuff neglectful, and thereby
Ribbons to flow confusedly:

---

1   *lawn* Shawl or scarf of finely woven cotton or linen.
2   *stomacher* Decorative garment worn over the breast and stomach and secured by lacing.

A winning wave, deserving note,
In the tempestuous petticoat;   10
A careless shoestring, in whose tie
I see a wild civility:
Do more bewitch me than when art
Is too precise in every part.

                                                        —1648

To the Virgins, to Make Much of Time

Gather ye rosebuds while ye may,
    Old time is still a-flying;[1]
And this same flower that smiles today,
    Tomorrow will be dying.

The glorious lamp of heaven, the sun,   5
    The higher he's a-getting;
The sooner will his race be run,[2]
    And nearer he's to setting.

That age is best, which is the first,
    When youth and blood are warmer;   10
But being spent, the worse, and worst
    Times still succeed the former.

Then be not coy, but use your time,
    And while ye may, go marry;
For having lost but once your prime,   15
    You may for ever tarry.

                                                        —1648

Upon Julia's Clothes

Whenas° in silks my Julia goes,   *Whenever*
Then, then, methinks, how sweetly flows
That liquefaction of her clothes.

Next, when I cast mine eyes and see
That brave° vibration each way free,   *beautiful*   5
Oh, how that glittering taketh me!

                                                        —1648

---

1   *Old ... a-flying* Paraphrase of the Latin *tempus fugit* ("time flies").
2   *his race be run* The sun's movement was pictured in Greek mythology as the chariot of
     Phoebus Apollo racing across the sky.

George Herbert
1593–1633

George Herbert was born in Wales to a well-connected family and was educated at Trinity College in Cambridge, becoming a university orator, a member of Parliament, and later an Anglican priest. Deeply religious, he bemoaned the number of "love poems that are daily writ and consecrated to Venus" and the much smaller number of poems that "look toward God and Heaven." His own work opposed this trend: Herbert is known for devotion poetry that employs varied metre, unusual figurative language, and visual effects in the expression of faith.

Herbert experimented with poetic form: the words of his poem "Easter Wings," for example, are assembled on the page to depict two pairs of wings, while the text of "The Altar" takes the shape of an altar. Such typographical pattern poems influenced nineteenth- and twentieth-century poets such as Lewis Carroll, E.E. Cummings, and bpNichol, among others, and his work is considered a precursor to the "concrete poetry" movement of the 1950s. *The Temple* (1633), Herbert's major collection of poetry, was published in the year of his death.

Herbert had immense influence on the devotional poets of the 1600s, but by the nineteenth century his reputation had waned. In the twentieth century he rejoined the poetic mainstream when T.S. Eliot praised his fusion of emotion and intellect. Herbert was, Eliot wrote, "an anatomist of feeling and a trained theologian too; his mind is working continually both on the mysteries of faith and the motives of the heart."

The Altar

A broken A L T A R, Lord, thy servant rears,
Made of a heart, and cemented with tears:[1]
    Whose parts are as thy hand did frame;
    No workman's tool hath touched the same.[2]
           A H E A R T alone   5
           Is such a stone,
           As nothing but
           Thy pow'r doth cut.
           Wherefore° each part   *accordingly*
           Of my hard heart   10
           Meets in this frame,
           To praise thy name.
    That, if I chance to hold my peace,
    These stones to praise thee may not cease.[3]
O let thy blessed S A C R I F I C E be mine,   15
And sanctify this A L T A R to be thine.

—1633

---

1   *A broken ... tears* See Psalms 51.17: "The sacrifices of God are a broken spirit: a broken and a contrite heart, O God, thou wilt not despise."

2   *No ... same* See Exodus 20.25: "And if thou wilt make me an altar of stone, thou shalt not build it of hewn stone: for if thou lift up thy tool upon it, thou hast polluted it."

3   *That ... cease* In Luke 19.40, Jesus says of his disciples, "if these should hold their peace, the stones would immediately cry out."

Easter Wings

Lord, who createdst man in wealth and store,
Though foolishly he lost the same,
Decaying more and more,
Till he became
Most poor:
With thee
O let me rise
As larks, harmoniously,
And sing this day thy victories:
Then shall the fall further the flight in me.

My tender age in sorrow did begin:
And still with sicknesses and shame
Thou didst so punish sin,
That I became
Most thin.
With thee
Let me combine,
And feel this day thy victory:
For, if I imp¹ my wing on thine,
Affliction shall advance the flight in me.

—1633

---

1   *imp* Graft feathers from one falcon onto the wing of another, a technique used in falconry to mend damaged wings and improve flight.

John Milton
1608–1674

███████ Missionary poet, Puritan sage, and radical champion of religious, domestic, and civil liberties, John Milton is among the most influential figures in English literature, a writer who, as the critic Matthew Arnold wrote, was "of the highest rank in the great style." In *Paradise Lost* (1667), his culminating achievement, Milton at once works within and transforms the epic tradition of Homer, Virgil, and Dante, casting off "the troublesome and modern bondage of rhyming" for majestic blank verse (unrhymed lines of iambic pentameter).

Milton was a Puritan, a Protestant who wanted to "purify" and simplify English religion, and, like other Puritans during the English Civil Wars (1642–51), he supported rebellion against the king—a support he expressed in an array of tracts and polemics. However, his religious opinions diverged from Puritanism to become increasingly heretical in his later years. Denounced for his pamphlets advocating divorce, which were prompted by his troubled marriage, Milton wrote the *Areopagitica* (1644), one of history's most rousing defences of a free press. He later reconciled with his wife only to lose her in childbirth, the first in a series of personal crises that saw the death of his son, his second wife, and their infant daughter, as well as the complete loss of his sight. Despite these blows, Milton continued late into his life to produce poetry of vast ambition.

On Shakespeare

What needs my Shakespeare for his honoured bones
The labour of an age in pilèd stones,
Or that his hallowed relics should be hid
Under a star-ypointing pyramid?
Dear son of memory,[1] great heir of Fame,   5
What need'st thou such weak witness of thy name?
Thou in our wonder and astonishment
Hast built thyself a livelong monument.
For whilst to th'shame of slow-endeavouring art,
Thy easy numbers flow, and that each heart   10
Hath from the leaves of thy unvalued° Book   *invaluable*
Those Delphic[2] lines with deep impression took,

---

1   *memory* Mnemosyne, mother of the muses.
2   *Delphic* Apollo, god of poetry, had his temple at Delphi.

Then thou our fancy of itself bereaving,
Dost make us marble with too much conceiving;
15 And so sepùlchered in such pomp dost lie,
That kings for such a tomb would wish to die.

—1632

[When I consider how my light is spent]¹

When I consider how my light is spent,
    Ere half my days, in this dark world and wide,
    And that one talent² which is death to hide,
    Lodged with me useless, though my soul more bent
5 To serve therewith my maker, and present
    My true account, lest he returning chide,
    Doth God exact day-labour, light denied,
    I fondly° ask; but patience to prevent   *foolishly*
That murmur, soon replies, God doth not need
10   Either man's work or his own gifts; who best
    Bear his mild yoke, they serve him best, his state
Is kingly. Thousands at his bidding speed
    And post° o'er land and ocean without rest: *ride*
    They also serve who only stand and wait.

—1673 (written c. 1652–55)

---

1   *[When ... spent]* Milton became blind in 1651.
2   *talent* Reference to the biblical parable of the talents; see Matthew 25.14–30. In this parable, a master gives varying amounts of money to three servants: five talents, two talents, and one talent, respectively. The servants that received larger sums invest the money, double it, and are celebrated, while the servant with one talent buries it for safekeeping and is punished for his failure to collect interest.

Anne Bradstreet
1612–1672

A member of an affluent and well-connected English family, Anne Bradstreet was well read and well learned in languages and literatures. At 18, she left England with her husband and parents aboard the *Arbella*, a ship headed for Massachusetts. Twenty years later, Bradstreet would become the first published female writer in the new colonies with her poetry collection *The Tenth Muse Lately Sprung Up in America* (1650).

Bradstreet's early writing bears the impress of her education, but her later poetry was also deeply influenced by her new life in America. Initially, she wrote, her "heart rose up" in protest at the "new world and new manners" that she found there. However, she continued to write under the difficult conditions of colonial life, while also raising eight children in the country so different from her birthplace. Her poetry conveyed familial devotion toward her husband and children as well as documenting the hardships endured by early settlers. Much of Bradstreet's poetry expressed strong Puritan faith, and the ornate diction and forms of her earlier work gave way to mature work distinguished by a lyrical voice, biblical themes, and biblical language.

The Tenth Muse was admired upon its publication, and Bradstreet has long been counted among the early literary lights of American poetry.

The Author to Her Book[1]

Thou ill-formed offspring of my feeble brain,
Who after birth didst by my side remain,
Till snatched from thence by friends, less wise than true
Who thee abroad, exposed to public view,
Made thee in rags, halting to th' press to trudge,   5
Where errors were not lessened (all may judge).
At thy return my blushing was not small,
My rambling brat (in print) should mother call,
I cast thee by as one unfit for light,
Thy visage° was so irksome in my sight;   *face*   10
Yet being mine own, at length affection would
Thy blemishes amend, if so I could:

---

1   *The Author to Her Book* These lines are thought to be a preface intended for a new edition of Bradstreet's collection *The Tenth Muse*, which was first published without her permission.

I washed thy face, but more defects I saw,
And rubbing off a spot still made a flaw.
15 I stretched thy joints to make thee even feet,
Yet still thou run'st more hobbling than is meet;°   *appropriate*
In better dress to trim thee was my mind,
But nought save homespun cloth i' th' house I find.
In this array 'mongst vulgars may'st thou roam.
20 In critic's hands beware thou dost not come,
And take thy way where yet thou art not known;
If for thy father asked, say thou hadst none;
And for thy mother, she alas is poor,
Which caused her thus to send thee out of door.

—1678

Andrew Marvell
1621–1678

▰▰▰ Andrew Marvell's poems are complex, full of paradox and irony, and frequently employ naïve or ambivalent personae who present debates or balance competing claims. His poem "An Horation Ode upon Cromwell's Return from Ireland" (1650), for example, oscillates between admiration for King Charles I and praise for (and veiled criticism of) Oliver Cromwell, who choreographed the abolition of the monarchy through the English Civil Wars (1642–51), executing Charles I in the process. Marvell was known primarily as a politician and satirist during his lifetime, and his reputation as one of the best lyric poets of his era was not fully established until the twentieth century.

The son of a clergyman, Marvell grew up in Hull in northeast England. At age 12 he was admitted to the University of Cambridge, where he studied for seven years and where he published his first poems, written in Latin and Greek. Instead of completing his degree, Marvell left England in 1642 for four years of travel in continental Europe, perhaps to wait out the period of the English Civil Wars. In 1650, he began working as a tutor to the 12-year-old daughter of Thomas, Lord Fairfax, the recently retired Commander-in-Chief of Cromwell's army. It was likely during his two years on the Fairfax estate that Marvell composed many of his most famous works, including the sensuous and witty "To His Coy Mistress."

Marvell served in Cromwell's government as Latin Secretary and was elected in 1659 as Member of Parliament for Hull, a seat he would maintain until his death. He was highly critical of Charles II (who was restored to the monarchy in 1660 after the collapse of Cromwell's Commonwealth), but Marvell's harshest criticisms were published anonymously. When he died in 1678, there was still an outstanding government reward offered for the name of the man who had written "An Account of the Growth of Popery and Arbitrary Government in England" a year earlier.

The Garden

1

How vainly men themselves amaze
To win the palm, the oak, or bays,[1]
And their uncessant labours see
Crowned from some single herb or tree,

---

1   *the palm, the oak, or bays* Wreaths or garlands; the traditional rewards signifying military (palm leaves), civic or political (oak leaves), or poetic (bay laurel leaves) achievement.

5 Whose short and narrow vergèd shade
Does prudently their toils upbraid,
While all flow'rs and all trees do close
To weave the garlands of repose.

2

Fair Quiet, have I found thee here,
10 And Innocence, thy sister dear!
Mistaken long, I sought you then
In busy companies of men.
Your sacred plants, if here below,
Only among the plants will grow.
15 Society is all but rude,°   *ignorant*
To this delicious solitude.

3

No white nor red¹ was ever seen
So am'rous as this lovely green.
Fond lovers, cruel as their flame,
20 Cut in these trees their mistress' name.
Little, alas, they know, or heed,
How far these beauties hers exceed!
Fair trees! wheres'e'er your barks I wound,
No name shall but your own be found.

4

25 When we have run our passions' heat,
Love hither makes his best retreat.
The gods, that mortal beauty chase,
Still in a tree did end their race.
Apollo hunted Daphne so,
30 Only that she might laurel grow.
And Pan did after Syrinx speed,
Not as a nymph, but for a reed.²

---

1   *white nor red* Colours traditionally associated with female beauty.
2   *Apollo ... reed* Reference to two classical myths associated with erotic pursuit and transformation. While being chased by Apollo, the god of poetry, Daphne was transformed into the laurel tree that became Apollo's sacred emblem. Syrinx, chased by Pan, god of flocks and shepherds, was transformed into a reed, the basis of the pan-pipe, emblem of pastoral poetry.

5

What wondrous life is this I lead!
Ripe apples drop about my head;
The luscious clusters of the vine   35
Upon my mouth do crush their wine;
The nectarine, and curious peach,
Into my hands themselves do reach;
Stumbling on melons, as I pass,
Ensnared with flow'rs, I fall on grass.   40

6

Meanwhile the mind, from pleasures less,
Withdraws into its happiness:
The mind, that ocean where each kind
Does straight its own resemblance find;[1]
Yet it creates, transcending these,   45
Far other worlds, and other seas,
Annihilating all that's made
To a green thought in a green shade.

7

Here at the fountain's sliding foot,
Or at some fruit-tree's mossy root,   50
Casting the body's vest aside,
My soul into the boughs does glide:
There like a bird it sits, and sings,
Then whets,° and combs its silver wings;   *preens*
And, till prepared for longer flight,   55
Waves in its plumes the various light.

8

Such was that happy garden-state,
While man there walked without a mate:
After a place so pure, and sweet,
What other help could yet be meet?[2]   60

---

1   *that ocean ... own resemblance find* Alluding to the Renaissance belief that the ocean
    contains a counterpart for every plant and animal on land.
2   *help ... meet* See Genesis 2.18: "And the Lord God said, It is not good that the man
    should be alone; I will make him an help meet for him."

But 'twas beyond a mortal's share
To wander solitary there:
Two Paradises 'twere in one
To live in Paradise alone.

9

65 How well the skilful gardener drew
Of flowers and herbs this dial[1] new,
Where from above the milder sun
Does through a fragrant zodiac run;
And, as it works, the industrious bee
70 Computes its time as well as we.
How could such sweet and wholesome hours
Be reckoned but with herbs and flowers!

—1681 (probably written in the early 1650s)

To His Coy Mistress

Had we but world enough, and time,
This coyness Lady were no crime.
We would sit down, and think which way
To walk, and pass our long love's day.
5 Thou by the Indian Ganges' side
Should'st rubies find: I by the tide
Of Humber[2] would complain. I would
Love you ten years before the Flood:
And you should, if you please, refuse
10 Till the conversion of the Jews.[3]
My vegetable love should grow[4]
Vaster than empires, and more slow.
An hundred years should go to praise
Thine eyes, and on thy forehead gaze.
15 Two hundred to adore each breast:
But thirty thousand to the rest.

---

1   *dial* Floral sundial.
2   *Humber* River in northern England; it flows alongside Hull, Marvell's home town.
3   *conversion of the Jews* Event supposed to usher in the final millennium leading to the end of time.
4   *vegetable love should grow* His love (or its physical manifestation) would grow slowly and steadily: Aristotle (384-322 BCE) defined the vegetative part of the soul as that characterized only by growth.

An age at least to every part,
And the last age should show your heart.
For Lady you deserve this state;
Nor would I love at lower rate.   20
But at my back I always hear,
Time's wingèd chariot hurrying near:
And yonder all before us lie
Deserts of vast eternity.
Thy beauty shall no more be found;   25
Nor, in thy marble vault, shall sound
My echoing song; then worms shall try
That long preserved virginity:
And your quaint honour turn to dust;
And into ashes all my lust.   30
The grave's a fine and private place,
But none I think do there embrace.
Now therefore, while the youthful glew
Sits on thy skin like morning dew,[1]
And while thy willing soul transpires   35
At every pore with instant fires,
Now let us sport us while we may;
And now, like am'rous birds of prey,
Rather at once our time devour,
Than languish in his slow-chapt[2] pow'r.   40
Let us roll all our strength, and all
Our sweetness, up into one ball:
And tear our pleasures with rough strife,
Thorough° the iron gates[3] of life.   *through*
Thus, though we cannot make our sun   45
Stand still,[4] yet we will make him run.

—1681

---

1   *youthful glew … morning dew* This wording is as it appears in Marvell's original manu-
    script, but there are many early variants on the final words in each line of this couplet.
    Most of these changes occurred in printer's attempts to correct "glew" (which may mean
    "sweat," or be a variant spelling of "glow").
2   *slow-chapt* Slowly devouring; "chaps" are jaws.
3   *gates* "Grates" in the 1681 printed edition with manuscript corrections, but many editors
    see "gates of life" as a typically Marvellian inversion of the biblical "gates of death" (see
    Psalm 9.13).
4   *sun / Stand still* Refers both to the love poetry convention in which lovers ask for time to
    stop when they are together, and to Joshua 10.12–14, in which Joshua made the sun and
    moon stand still while his army slaughtered the Amorites.

Anne Finch, Countess of Winchilsea

1661–1720

One of very few women to publish poetry in the early part of the eighteenth century, Anne Finch was a versatile poet who wrote in all of the traditional neoclassical forms and addressed a broad range of subjects including gender politics, art, nature, and religion. Her best-known poem during her lifetime was "The Spleen," which concerns what today we would categorize as depression—an affliction from which Finch herself suffered.

Finch began writing poetry in the 1680s, and she first circulated her work in manuscript form in the 1690s, but it was not until 1713 that she openly published a book, *Miscellany Poems on Several Occasions*. She had become a countess the year before, but publishing poetry was nonetheless a bold move for a woman, as Finch acknowledges in "The Introduction": "a woman that attempts the pen, / Such an intruder on the rights of men, / Such a presumptuous creature is esteemed, / The fault can by no virtue be redeemed." *Miscellany Poems*, however, was well-received and praised by her friends in London's literary circles, among them Jonathan Swift and Alexander Pope, who included seven of her poems in a 1717 anthology.

After her death, Finch's work fell into obscurity until the nineteenth century, when William Wordsworth commended her poem "Nocturnal Reverie" for its nature imagery. In the early twentieth century, her unpublished "Wellesley manuscript" came to light, adding more than 50 poems to her known oeuvre.

There's No Tomorrow

A fable imitated from Sir Roger L'Estrange[1]

Two long had loved, and now the nymph[2] desired,
The cloak of wedlock, as the case required;
Urged that, the day he wrought her to this sorrow,
He vowed, that he would marry her tomorrow.
5 Again he swears, to shun the present storm,
That he, tomorrow, will that vow perform.

---

1   *Sir Roger L'Estrange* English translator and political writer; Finch's poem retells a fable included in his translation *Fables of Aesop and Other Eminent Mythologists, with Morals and Reflections* (1692).

2   *nymph* Beautiful young woman.

The morrows in their due successions came;
Impatient still on each, the pregnant dame
Urged him to keep his word, and still he swore the same.
When tired at length, and meaning no redress,   10
But yet the lie not caring to confess,
He for his oath this salvo° chose to borrow,   *excuse*
That he was free, since there was no tomorrow;
For when it comes in place to be employed,
'Tis then today; tomorrow's ne'er enjoyed.   15
The tale's a jest, the moral is a truth;
Tomorrow and tomorrow, cheat our youth:
In riper age, tomorrow still we cry,
Not thinking, that the present day we die;
Unpractised all the good we had designed;   20
There's no tomorrow to a willing mind.

—1713

Alexander Pope
1688–1744

■■■■■ "The proper study of mankind is man," declared Alexander Pope, who based his enormously successful literary career on social commentary and the documentation of contemporary experience. Almost all of his work is composed in closed heroic couplets (a popular verse form consisting of self-contained pairs of rhymed ten-syllable lines), but Pope adapted this form to an astonishing range of poetic modes—among them pastoral, lyric, and mock-epic—and to approaches ranging from the viciously satiric to the earnestly philosophical.

Disabled as a boy by tuberculosis of the spine, Pope was scarcely four and a half feet tall when fully grown. But this was merely one among many disadvantages he overcame in his career: as a Roman Catholic, Pope was forbidden to vote, hold public office, own land, or live within ten miles of London. As he once bitterly observed, "The life of a wit is a warfare upon the earth," and his religion, Tory political leanings, and disability made him the frequent subject of savage critical attack. Pope got the better of his critics in his *The Dunciad* (1728–43), an ironic epic of praise to hack writers; it ranges far beyond personal insult to expose pettiness, mediocrity, and dullness as forces capable of destroying culture.

The number of Pope's enemies only increased with the release of *The Dunciad*, but Pope is much better remembered for his circle of friends—especially the fellow members of the Scriblerus Club, which he formed in 1714 with Jonathan Swift, Lord Bolingbroke, and other influential intellectuals of the day. The club was named for a character of their own invention, Martinus Scriblerus, a learned fool to whom they attributed all that was tedious, narrow-minded, and pedantic in contemporary scholarship.

In addition to his satire, Pope was famous for his ambitious verse essays, such as *An Essay on Criticism* (1711), a sweeping overview of literary history and literary criticism; and *Essay on Man* (1733–34), which analyzes aspects of human nature and discusses humanity's place in the universe.

from *An Essay on Criticism*

True ease in writing comes from art, not chance,
As those move easiest who have learned to dance.
'Tis not enough no harshness gives offence,
The sound must seem an echo to the sense:
5 Soft is the strain when Zephyr° gently blows,   *the west wind*
And the smooth stream in smoother numbers flows;

But when loud surges lash the sounding shore,
The hoarse, rough verse should like the torrent roar.
When Ajax[1] strives some rock's vast weight to throw,
The line too labours, and the words move slow;   10
Not so when swift Camilla[2] scours the plain,
Flies o'er th'unbending corn, and skims along the main.°   sea
Hear how Timotheus'[3] varied lays surprise,
And bid alternate passions fall and rise!

—1711

The Rape of the Lock

An Heroi-Comical Poem in Five Cantos

To Mrs. Arabella Fermor[4]

Madam,
It will be in vain to deny that I have some regard for this piece, since I dedicate it to you. Yet you may bear me witness, it was intended only to divert a few young ladies, who have good sense and good humour enough, to laugh not only at their sex's little unguarded follies, but at their own. But, as it was communicated with the air of a secret, it soon found its way into the world. An imperfect copy having been offered to a bookseller,[5] you had the good nature for my sake to consent to the publication of one more correct; this I was forced to before I had executed half my design, for the machinery was entirely wanting to complete it.

The machinery, Madam, is a term invented by the critics to signify that part which the deities, angels, or demons are made to act in a poem; for the ancient poets are in one respect like many modern ladies: let an action be never so trivial in itself, they always make it appear of the utmost importance.

---

1   *Ajax* Greek mythological figure who is proverbially strong; in Homer's *Iliad* he throws a large rock at his opponent Hector during a duel.
2   *Camilla* In classical mythology, a warrior virgin; she appears in Book 7 of Virgil's *Aeneid*, where the poet describes her as so swift that she "Flew o'er the fields, nor hurt the bearded grain. / She swept the seas."
3   *Timotheus* Accomplished Greek poet and musician (4th century BCE).
4   *Mrs. Arabella Fermor* Arabella Fermor, the daughter of a prominent Catholic family, was celebrated for her beauty. Lord Robert Petre snipped off a lock of her hair, occasioning Pope's poem. Mrs. was a title of respect for married or unmarried women.
5   *bookseller* Publisher.

These machines I determined to raise on a very new and odd foundation, the Rosicrucian[1] doctrine of spirits.

I know how disagreeable it is to make use of hard words before a lady, but 'tis so much the concern of a poet to have his works understood, and particularly by your sex, that you must give me leave to explain two or three difficult terms.

The Rosicrucians are a people I must bring you acquainted with. The best account I know of them is in a French book called *Le Comte de Gabalis*,[2] which both in its title and size is so like a novel that many of the fair sex have read it for one by mistake. According to these gentlemen, the four elements are inhabited by spirits, which they call Sylphs, Gnomes, Nymphs, and Salamanders.[3] The Gnomes, or demons of earth, delight in mischief, but the Sylphs, whose habitation is in the air, are the best-conditioned creatures imaginable. For they say any mortals may enjoy the most intimate familiarities with these gentle spirits, upon a condition very easy to all true adepts, an inviolate preservation of chastity.

As to the following Cantos, all the passages of them are as fabulous[4] as the vision at the beginning, or the transformation at the end (except the loss of your hair, which I always mention with reverence). The human persons are as fictitious as the airy ones, and the character of Belinda, as it is now managed, resembles you in nothing but in beauty.

If this poem had as many graces as there are in your person, or in your mind, yet I could never hope it should pass through the world half so uncensured as you have done. But let its fortune be what it will, mine is happy enough, to have given me this occasion of assuring you that I am, with the truest esteem,

Madam,

Your most obedient humble servant.

A. POPE

---

1   *Rosicrucian* Religious sect, originating in Germany, which existed in the seventeenth and eighteenth centuries. Its members were devoted to the study of arcane philosophy and mystical doctrines.
2   *Le Comte de Gabalis* Written by Abbé de Monfaucon de Villars and published in 1670, this was a lighthearted exploration of Rosicrucian philosophy. It was printed in duodecimo (about five by eight inches), a common size for novels and other inexpensive books.
3   *Salamanders* Salamanders were believed to be able to withstand, and live in, fire.
4   *fabulous* Mythical, fictional.

CANTO 1

What dire offence from am'rous causes springs,
What mighty contests rise from trivial things,
I sing—This verse to Caryll,[1] Muse! is due;
This, ev'n Belinda may vouchsafe to view:
Slight is the subject, but not so the praise,   5
If she inspire, and he approve my lays.°   *verses*

     Say what strange motive, Goddess! could compel
A well-bred lord t' assault a gentle belle?
Oh say what stranger cause, yet unexplored,°   *undiscovered*
Could make a gentle belle reject a lord?   10
In tasks so bold can little men engage,
And in soft bosoms dwells such mighty rage?

     Sol° through white curtains shot a tim'rous ray,   *sun*
And oped those eyes that must eclipse the day;
Now lapdogs give themselves the rousing shake,   15
And sleepless lovers, just at twelve, awake:
Thrice rung the bell, the slipper knocked the ground,[2]
And the pressed watch[3] returned a silver sound.
Belinda still her downy pillow pressed,
Her guardian Sylph prolonged the balmy rest.   20
'Twas he had summoned to her silent bed
The morning dream[4] that hovered o'er her head.
A youth more glitt'ring than a birthnight beau[5]
(That ev'n in slumber caused her cheek to glow)
Seemed to her ear his winning lips to lay,   25
And thus in whispers said, or seemed to say:

     "Fairest of mortals, thou distinguished care
Of thousand bright inhabitants of air!
If e'er one vision touched thy infant thought,
Of all the nurse and all the priest have taught,   30
Of airy elves by moonlight shadows seen,

---

1   *Caryll* Pope's friend John Caryll (c. 1666–1736), who requested the poem.
2   *slipper ... ground* She bangs her slipper on the floor to summon the maid.
3   *pressed watch* "Repeater" watches would chime the time, to the nearest quarter hour, when the stem was pressed.
4   *morning dream* Morning dreams were believed to be particularly portentous.
5   *birthnight beau* On the birthday of the sovereign, members of the court dressed in their most lavish attire.

The silver token, and the circled green,[1]
Or virgins visited by angel pow'rs,
With golden crowns and wreaths of heav'nly flow'rs,
35 Hear and believe! thy own importance know,
Nor bound thy narrow views to things below.
Some secret truths, from learned pride concealed,
To maids alone and children are revealed.
What though no credit doubting wits may give?
40 The fair and innocent shall still believe.
Know then, unnumbered spirits round thee fly,
The light militia of the lower sky;
These, though unseen, are ever on the wing,
Hang o'er the box, and hover round the Ring.[2]
45 Think what an equipage thou hast in air,
And view with scorn two pages and a chair.°   *sedan chair*
As now your own, our beings were of old,
And once enclosed in woman's beauteous mould;
Thence, by a soft transition, we repair
50 From earthly vehicles to these of air.
Think not, when woman's transient breath is fled,
That all her vanities at once are dead:
Succeeding vanities she still regards,
And though she plays no more, o'erlooks the cards.
55 Her joy in gilded chariots, when alive,
And love of ombre,[3] after death survive.
For when the fair in all their pride expire,
To their first elements[4] their souls retire:
The sprites° of fiery termagants[5] in flame   *spirits*
60 Mount up, and take a Salamander's name.
Soft yielding minds to water glide away,
And sip, with Nymphs, their elemental tea.

---

1   *silver token* Fairies were said to skim the cream from the top of jugs of milk left over-
    night, leaving a silver coin in exchange; *circled green* Rings in the grass were said to be
    produced by dancing fairies.
2   *box* Private compartment in a theatre; *the Ring* Circular drive that divides Hyde
    Park from Kensington Gardens. The most fashionable members of society would drive
    around the Ring, displaying themselves and their equipages (coaches with attendants).
3   *ombre* Popular card game.
4   *first elements* All things on earth had been thought to be made from the four elements
    (earth, air, fire, and water), with one of these elements predominant in the tempera-
    ment of each person.
5   *termagants* Quarrelsome, turbulent, or hot-tempered women.

The graver prude sinks downward to a Gnome,
In search of mischief still on earth to roam.
The light coquettes in Sylphs aloft repair,   65
And sport and flutter in the fields of air.
    "Know further yet, whoever fair and chaste
Rejects mankind, is by some Sylph embraced:
For spirits, freed from mortal laws, with ease
Assume what sexes and what shapes they please.[1]   70
What guards the purity of melting maids
In courtly balls, and midnight masquerades,
Safe from the treach'rous friend, the daring spark,°   *suitor*
The glance by day, the whisper in the dark,
When kind occasion prompts their warm desires,   75
When music softens, and when dancing fires?
'Tis but their Sylph, the wise celestials know,
Though *honour* is the word with men below.
    "Some nymphs° there are, too conscious of their face,   *maidens*
For life predestined to the Gnomes' embrace.   80
These swell their prospects and exalt their pride
When offers are disdained, and love denied.
Then gay ideas° crowd the vacant brain,   *images*
While peers° and dukes, and all their sweeping train,   *nobles*
And garters, stars, and coronets[2] appear,   85
And in soft sounds, 'your Grace' salutes their ear.
'Tis these that early taint the female soul,
Instruct the eyes of young coquettes to roll,
Teach infant cheeks a bidden blush to know,
And little hearts to flutter at a beau.   90
    "Oft, when the world imagine women stray,
The Sylphs through mystic mazes guide their way,
Through all the giddy circle they pursue,
And old impertinence expel by new.
What tender maid but must a victim fall   95
To one man's treat,° but for another's ball?   *feast*
When Florio speaks, what virgin could withstand,
If gentle Damon did not squeeze her hand?
With varying vanities, from ev'ry part,

---

1   *spirits ... please* See Milton's *Paradise Lost* 1.423–24: "For spirits when they please /
     Can either sex assume, or both." This is one of many allusions to Milton's epic poem.
2   *garters, stars, and coronets* Emblems of noble ranks.

100 They shift the moving toyshop[1] of their heart;
    Where wigs with wigs, with sword-knots[2] sword-knots strive,
    Beaux banish beaux, and coaches coaches drive.
    This erring mortals levity may call,
    Oh blind to truth! the sylphs contrive it all.
105   "Of these am I, who thy protection claim,
    A watchful sprite, and Ariel is my name.
    Late, as I ranged the crystal wilds of air,
    In the clear mirror of thy ruling star
    I saw, alas! some dread event impend,
110 Ere to the main° this morning sun descend;   sea
    But Heav'n reveals not what, or how, or where:
    Warned by thy Sylph, oh pious maid beware!
    This to disclose is all thy guardian can:
    Beware of all, but most beware of man!"
115   He said; when Shock,[3] who thought she slept too long,
    Leaped up, and waked his mistress with his tongue.
    'Twas then, Belinda, if report say true,
    Thy eyes first opened on a billet-doux;°   love letter
    Wounds, charms, and ardours were no sooner read,
120 But all the vision vanished from thy head.
            And now, unveiled, the toilet° stands displayed,   dressing table
    Each silver vase in mystic order laid.
    First, robed in white, the nymph intent adores,
    With head uncovered, the cosmetic pow'rs.
125 A heav'nly image in the glass appears,
    To that she bends, to that her eyes she rears.°   lifts
    Th' inferior priestess,[4] at her altar's side,
    Trembling begins the sacred rites of pride.
    Unnumbered treasures ope at once, and here
130 The various off'rings of the world appear;
    From each she nicely culls with curious toil,
    And decks the goddess with the glitt'ring spoil.
    This casket India's glowing gems unlocks,
    And all Arabia breathes from yonder box.

---

1   *toyshop* Store that sold not only toys but various trinkets, accessories, and ornaments.
2   *sword-knots* Fashionable men of society wore ribbons knotted around the hilts of their
     swords. They also wore wigs.
3   *Shock* Belinda's lapdog, named after a popular breed of long-haired, Icelandic toy poo-
     dle called the "shough," or "shock."
4   *Th' inferior priestess* Betty, Belinda's maid.

The tortoise here and elephant unite,   135
Transformed to combs, the speckled and the white.
Here files of pins extend their shining rows,
Puffs, powders, patches,[1] Bibles, billet-doux.
Now awful° beauty puts on all its arms;   *awe-inspiring*
The fair each moment rises in her charms,   140
Repairs her smiles, awakens ev'ry grace,
And calls forth all the wonders of her face;
Sees by degrees a purer blush arise,
And keener lightnings quicken in her eyes.[2]
The busy Sylphs surround their darling care,   145
These set the head, and those divide the hair,
Some fold the sleeve, whilst others plait the gown;
And Betty's praised for labours not her own.

CANTO 2

Not with more glories, in th' ethereal plain,
The sun first rises o'er the purpled main,   150
Than issuing forth, the rival of his beams
Launched on the bosom of the silver Thames.[3]
Fair nymphs and well-dressed youths around her shone,
But every eye was fixed on her alone.
On her white breast a sparkling cross she wore,   155
Which Jews might kiss, and infidels adore.
Her lively looks a sprightly mind disclose,
Quick as her eyes, and as unfixed as those:
Favours to none, to all she smiles extends;
Oft she rejects, but never once offends.   160
Bright as the sun, her eyes the gazers strike,
And, like the sun, they shine on all alike.
Yet graceful ease, and sweetness void of pride,
Might hide her faults, if belles had faults to hide:
If to her share some female errors fall,   165
Look on her face, and you'll forget 'em all.
        This nymph, to the destruction of mankind,

---

1   *patches* Artificial beauty marks made of silk or plaster cut into various shapes and
     placed on the face, either for decoration or to hide imperfections.
2   *keener ... eyes* As a result of drops of belladonna, or deadly nightshade, which enlarges
     the pupils.
3   *Launched ... Thames* Belinda voyages upstream to Hampton Court for the day. By tak-
     ing a boat she avoids the crowds and filth in the streets.

Nourished two locks, which graceful hung behind
In equal curls, and well conspired to deck
170 With shining ringlets the smooth iv'ry neck.
Love in these labyrinths his slaves detains,
And mighty hearts are held in slender chains;
With hairy springes° we the birds betray;   *snares*
Slight lines of hair surprise the finny prey;
175 Fair tresses man's imperial race ensnare,
And beauty draws us with a single hair.
      Th' adventurous Baron the bright locks admired;
He saw, he wished, and to the prize aspired.
Resolved to win, he meditates the way,
180 By force to ravish, or by fraud betray;
For when success a lover's toil attends,
Few ask if fraud or force attained his ends.
      For this, ere Phoebus[1] rose, he had implored
Propitious Heav'n, and every pow'r adored,°   *worshipped*
185 But chiefly Love—to Love an altar built,
Of twelve vast French romances, neatly gilt.
There lay three garters, half a pair of gloves,
And all the trophies of his former loves.
With tender billet-doux he lights the pyre,
190 And breathes three am'rous sighs to raise the fire.
Then prostrate falls, and begs with ardent eyes
Soon to obtain, and long possess the prize:
The pow'rs gave ear, and granted half his prayer;
The rest the winds dispersed in empty air.
195   But now secure the painted vessel glides,
The sunbeams trembling on the floating tides,
While melting music steals upon the sky,
And softened sounds along the waters die.
Smooth flow the waves, the zephyrs gently play,
200 Belinda smiled, and all the world was gay.
All but the Sylph—with careful thoughts oppressed,
Th' impending woe sat heavy on his breast.
He summons strait his denizens of air;
The lucid squadrons round the sails repair:
205 Soft o'er the shrouds[2] aerial whispers breathe

---

1   *Phoebus* One of the names of Apollo, god of the sun.
2   *shrouds* Ropes that brace the mast of the ship.

That seemed but zephyrs° to the train beneath.   *mild breezes*
Some to the sun their insect-wings unfold,
Waft on the breeze, or sink in clouds of gold.
Transparent forms, too fine for mortal sight,
Their fluid bodies half dissolved in light,   210
Loose to the wind their airy garments flew,
Thin glitt'ring textures of the filmy dew,
Dipped in the richest tincture of the skies,
Where light disports in ever-mingling dyes,
While every beam new transient colours flings,   215
Colours that change whene'er they wave their wings.
Amid the circle, on the gilded mast,
Superior by the head, was Ariel placed;
His purple pinions° op'ning to the sun,   *wings*
He raised his azure wand, and thus begun: 220
    "Ye Sylphs and Sylphids, to your chief give ear!
Fays, Fairies, Genii, Elves, and Demons, hear!
Ye know the spheres and various tasks assigned,
By laws eternal, to th' aerial kind.
Some in the fields of purest ether[1] play,   225
And bask and whiten in the blaze of day.
Some guide the course of wand'ring orbs on high,
Or roll the planets through the boundless sky.
Some, less refined, beneath the moon's pale light
Pursue the stars that shoot athwart the night,   230
Or suck the mists in grosser[2] air below,
Or dip their pinions in the painted bow,
Or brew fierce tempests on the wintry main,
Or o'er the glebe° distill the kindly rain.   *fields*
Others on earth o'er human race preside,   235
Watch all their ways, and all their actions guide:
Of these the chief the care of nations own,
And guard with arms divine the British Throne.
    "Our humbler province is to tend the fair,
Not a less pleasing, though less glorious care: 240
To save the powder from too rude a gale,
Nor let th' imprisoned essences° exhale;   *perfumes*
To draw fresh colours from the vernal flow'rs;

---

1   *fields of purest ether* Clear regions above the moon.
2   *grosser* Material, as opposed to ethereal.

To steal from rainbows ere they drop in show'rs
245 A brighter wash;° to curl their waving hairs,   *liquid cosmetic*
Assist their blushes, and inspire their airs;
Nay, oft in dreams invention we bestow,
To change a flounce, or add a furbelo.°   *pleated trim*
     "This day, black omens threat the brightest fair
250 That e'er deserved a watchful spirit's care;
Some dire disaster, or by force or slight,
But what, or where, the Fates have wrapped in night.
Whether the nymph shall break Diana's law,[1]
Or some frail China jar receive a flaw,
255 Or stain her honour, or her new brocade,
Forget her prayers, or miss a masquerade,
Or lose her heart, or necklace, at a ball;
Or whether Heav'n has doomed that Shock must fall.
Haste then, ye spirits! To your charge repair:
260 The flutt'ring fan be Zephyretta's care;
The drops° to thee, Brillante, we consign;   *diamond earrings*
And, Momentilla, let the watch be thine;
Do thou, Crispissa,[2] tend her fav'rite lock;
Ariel himself shall be the guard of Shock.
265   "To fifty chosen Sylphs, of special note,
We trust th' important charge, the petticoat:
Oft have we known that sev'nfold fence[3] to fail,
Though stiff with hoops, and armed with ribs of whale.
Form a strong line about the silver bound,
270 And guard the wide circumference around.
     "Whatever spirit, careless of his charge,
His post neglects, or leaves the fair at large,
Shall feel sharp vengeance soon o'ertake his sins,
Be stopped in vials, or transfixed with pins,
275 Or plunged in lakes of bitter washes lie,
Or wedged whole ages in a bodkin's[4] eye;
Gums and pomatums° shall his flight restrain,   *hair ointments*
While clogged he beats his silken wings in vain,

---

1   *break Diana's law* Lose her virginity (Diana was the Roman goddess of chastity).
2   *Crispissa* From the Latin verb *crispere*, meaning "to curl."
3   *sev'nfold fence* Allusion to Achilles's "sevenfold shield" in the *Iliad*.
4   *bodkin* Blunt needle with both a large and a small eye, used to draw ribbon through a hem.

Or alum styptics[1] with contracting pow'r
Shrink his thin essence like a riveled° flow'r.   *shriveled* 280
Or, as Ixion[2] fixed, the wretch shall feel
The giddy motion of the whirling mill,
In fumes of burning chocolate shall glow,
And tremble at the sea that froths below!"
     He spoke; the spirits from the sails descend;   285
Some, orb in orb, around the nymph extend;
Some thread the mazy° ringlets of her hair;   *maze-like*
Some hang upon the pendants of her ear.
With beating hearts the dire event they wait,
Anxious, and trembling for the birth of fate.   290

CANTO 3

Close by those meads° forever crowned with flow'rs,   *meadows*
Where Thames with pride surveys his rising tow'rs,
There stands a structure of majestic frame,[3]
Which from the neighb'ring Hampton takes its name.
Here Britain's statesmen oft the fall foredoom   295
Of foreign tyrants, and of nymphs at home;
Here thou, great Anna! whom three realms obey,
Dost sometimes counsel take—and sometimes tea.
     Hither the heroes and the nymphs resort,
To taste awhile the pleasures of a court;   300
In various talk th' instructive hours they passed,
Who gave the ball, or paid the visit last;
One speaks the glory of the British Queen,
And one describes a charming Indian screen;
A third interprets motions, looks, and eyes;   305
At every word a reputation dies.
Snuff, or the fan, supply each pause of chat,
With singing, laughing, ogling, and all that.
     Meanwhile, declining from the noon of day,
The sun obliquely shoots his burning ray;   310
The hungry judges soon the sentence sign,

---

1   *alum styptics* Astringent substances applied to cuts to contract tissue and stop bleeding.
2   *Ixion* Zeus punished Ixion, who had attempted to seduce Hera, by tying him to a continuously revolving wheel in Hades. Here the wheel would be that of a machine that beats hot chocolate to a froth.
3   *structure ... majestic frame* Hampton Court, the largest of Queen Anne's residences, located about 12 miles up the Thames from London.

And wretches hang that jurymen may dine;
The merchant from th' Exchange[1] returns in peace,
And the long labours of the toilette cease.
315 Belinda now, whom thirst of fame invites,
Burns to encounter two adventurous knights
At ombre,[2] singly to decide their doom,
And swells her breast with conquests yet to come.
Straight the three bands prepare in arms to join,
320 Each band the number of the sacred nine.[3]
Soon as she spreads her hand, th' aerial guard
Descend, and sit on each important card:
First Ariel perched upon a Matadore,[4]
Then each according to the rank they bore;
325 For Sylphs, yet mindful of their ancient race,
Are, as when women, wondrous fond of place.°   *social status*
    Behold, four Kings in majesty revered,
With hoary whiskers and a forky beard;
And four fair Queens whose hands sustain a flow'r,
330 Th' expressive emblem of their softer pow'r;
Four Knaves in garbs succinct,[5] a trusty band,
Caps on their heads, and halberds[6] in their hand;
And parti-coloured troops, a shining train,
Draw forth to combat on the velvet plain.
335   The skilful nymph reviews her force with care;
"Let Spades be trumps!" she said, and trumps they were.
    Now move to war her sable Matadores,
In show like leaders of the swarthy Moors.

---

1   *th' Exchange* The Royal Exchange, located in the commercial centre of London, was
    the principal market where merchants traded and where bankers and brokers met to do
    business.
2   *ombre* In the game of ombre that Belinda plays against the two men, Pope conveys an
    accurate sense of the game, the rules of which are similar to those of bridge. Each of the
    three players receives 9 cards from the 40 that are used (8s, 9s, and 10s are discarded).
    Belinda, as the challenger, or "ombre" (from the Spanish *hombre*, "man"), names the
    trumps. To win, she must make more tricks than either of the other two. For a complete
    description of the game, see Geoffrey Tillotson's Twickenham edition of Pope's poems,
    volume 2.
3   *sacred nine* Muses.
4   *Matadore* Matadores are the three highest cards of the game. When spades are trump,
    as they are here, the highest card is the ace of spades ("Spadillio"), followed by the two
    of spades ("Manillio"), and then the ace of clubs ("Basto").
5   *succinct* Brief, short. The knaves are wearing short tunics.
6   *halberds* Weapons that combine the spear and battle axe.

Spadillio first, unconquerable lord!
Led off two captive trumps, and swept the board.   340
As many more Manillio forced to yield,
And marched a victor from the verdant field.
Him Basto followed, but, his fate more hard,
Gained but one trump and one plebeian card.
With his broad sabre next, a chief in years,   345
The hoary Majesty of Spades appears,
Puts forth one manly leg, to sight revealed,
The rest his many-coloured robe concealed.
The rebel Knave, who dares his prince engage,
Proves the just victim of his royal rage.   350
Ev'n mighty Pam,[1] that kings and queens o'erthrew,
And mowed down armies in the fights of Loo,
Sad chance of war! now, destitute of aid,
Falls undistinguished by the victor Spade!
    Thus far both armies to Belinda yield;   355
Now to the Baron fate inclines the field.
His warlike Amazon[2] her host invades,
Th' imperial consort of the crown of Spades.
The Club's black tyrant first her victim died,
Spite of his haughty mien° and barb'rous pride.   *look*   360
What boots the regal circle on his head,
His giant limbs in state unwieldy spread?
That long behind he trails his pompous robe,
And of all monarchs only grasps the globe?
    The Baron now his Diamonds pours apace;   365
Th' embroidered King, who shows but half his face,
And his refulgent Queen, with pow'rs combined,
Of broken troops an easy conquest find.
Clubs, Diamonds, Hearts, in wild disorder seen,
With throngs promiscuous strew the level green.   370
Thus when dispersed a routed army runs,
Of Asia's troops, and Afric's sable sons,
With like confusion diff'rent nations fly,
Of various habit, and of various dye,
The pierced battalions disunited fall   375
In heaps on heaps; one fate o'erwhelms them all.

---

1   *Pam* Jack (knave) of clubs, the highest card in Loo, another popular card game.
2   *Amazon* Female warrior; here, the Queen of Spades.

The Knave of Diamonds tries his wily arts,
And wins (oh, shameful chance!) the Queen of Hearts.
At this, the blood the virgin's cheek forsook,
380 A livid paleness spreads o'er all her look;
She sees, and trembles at th' approaching ill,
Just in the jaws of ruin, and Codille.[1]
And now (as oft in some distempered state)
On one nice trick depends the gen'ral fate.
385 An Ace of Hearts steps forth: the King unseen
Lurked in her hand, and mourned his captive Queen.
He springs to vengeance with an eager pace,
And falls like thunder on the prostrate Ace.
The nymph, exulting, fills with shouts the sky;
390 The walls, the woods, and long canals reply.
    O thoughtless mortals! ever blind to fate,
Too soon dejected, and too soon elate!
Sudden these honours shall be snatched away,
And cursed forever this victorious day.
395 For lo! the board with cups and spoons is crowned,
The berries crackle, and the mill turns round.[2]
On shining altars of Japan[3] they raise
The silver lamp; the fiery spirits blaze.
From silver spouts the grateful liquors glide,
400 While China's earth[4] receives the smoking tide.
At once they gratify their scent and taste,
And frequent cups prolong the rich repast.
Straight hover round the fair her airy band;
Some, as she sipped, the fuming liquor fanned,
405 Some o'er her lap their careful plumes displayed,
Trembling, and conscious of the rich brocade.
Coffee (which makes the politician wise,
And see through all things with his half-shut eyes)
Sent up in vapours to the Baron's brain
410 New stratagems, the radiant lock to gain.
Ah, cease, rash youth! desist ere 'tis too late,

---

1   *Codille* Defeat of the ombre.
2   *berries ... round* Coffee beans ("berries") roasted and then ground.
3   *altars of Japan* I.e., lacquered, or "japanned" tables, highly decorated and varnished.
    The style originated in Japan.
4   *China's earth* China cups.

Fear the just gods, and think of Scylla's[1] fate!
Changed to a bird, and sent to flit in air,
She dearly pays for Nisus' injured hair!
    But when to mischief mortals bend their will,   415
How soon they find fit instruments of ill!
Just then, Clarissa drew with tempting grace
A two-edged weapon° from her shining case;   *pair of scissors*
So ladies in romance assist their knight,
Present the spear, and arm him for the fight.   420
He takes the gift with rev'rence, and extends
The little engine° on his fingers' ends;   *instrument*
This just behind Belinda's neck he spread,
As o'er the fragrant steams she bends her head.
Swift to the lock a thousand sprites repair,   425
A thousand wings, by turns, blow back the hair,
And thrice they twitched the diamond in her ear;
Thrice she looked back, and thrice the foe drew near.
Just in that instant, anxious Ariel sought
The close recesses of the virgin's thought;   430
As on the nosegay in her breast reclined,
He watched th' ideas rising in her mind.
Sudden he viewed, in spite of all her art,
An earthly lover lurking at her heart.
Amazed, confused, he found his pow'r expired,   435
Resigned to fate, and with a sigh retired.
    The Peer now spreads the glitt'ring forfex° wide,   *scissors*
T' enclose the lock; now joins it, to divide.
Ev'n then, before the fatal engine closed,
A wretched Sylph too fondly interposed;   440
Fate urged the sheers, and cut the Sylph in twain
(But airy substance soon unites again).
The meeting points the sacred hair dissever
From the fair head, forever and forever!
    Then flashed the living lightning from her eyes,   445
And screams of horror rend th' affrighted skies.
Not louder shrieks to pitying heav'n are cast,
When husbands or when lapdogs breathe their last,

---

1   *Scylla* According to Ovid's *Metamorphoses*, Scylla was turned into a seabird by her fa-
    ther, King Nisus, after she cut off his purple lock of hair (on which the kingdom's safety
    depended) to please her lover, Minos, who was besieging the city.

Or when rich china vessels, fall'n from high,
450 In glitt'ring dust and painted fragments lie!
    "Let wreaths of triumph now my temples twine,"
The victor cried, "the glorious prize is mine!
While fish in streams, or birds delight in air,
Or in a coach and six the British fair,
455 As long as *Atalantis*[1] shall be read,
Or the small pillow grace a lady's bed,
While visits shall be paid on solemn days,
When num'rous wax-lights in bright order blaze,
While nymphs take treats, or assignations give,
460 So long my honour, name, and praise shall live!
    "What time would spare, from steel receives its date,
And monuments, like men, submit to fate!
Steel could the labour of the Gods destroy,
And strike to dust th' imperial towers of Troy;
465 Steel could the works of mortal pride confound,
And hew triumphal arches to the ground.
What wonder then, fair nymph! thy hairs should feel
The conqu'ring force of unresisted steel?"

Canto 4

But anxious cares the pensive nymph oppressed,
470 And secret passions laboured in her breast.
Not youthful kings in battle seized alive,
Not scornful virgins who their charms survive,
Not ardent lovers robbed of all their bliss,
Not ancient ladies when refused a kiss,
475 Not tyrants fierce that unrepenting die,
Not Cynthia when her manteau's pinned awry,
Ev'r felt such rage, resentment, and despair,
As thou, sad virgin! for thy ravished hair.
    For, that sad moment when the sylphs withdrew,
480 And Ariel weeping from Belinda flew,
Umbriel, a dusky, melancholy sprite
As ever sullied the fair face of light,
Down to the central earth, his proper scene,

---

1   *Atalantis* Delarivier Manley's *New Atalantis* was an enormously creative rendering of the latest political scandals and social intrigues, which she recreated as fiction.

Repaired to search the gloomy Cave of Spleen.[1]

    Swift on his sooty pinions flits the Gnome,   485
And in a vapour reached the dismal dome.
No cheerful breeze this sullen region knows,
The dreaded east[2] is all the wind that blows.
Here, in a grotto, sheltered close from air,
And screened in shades from day's detested glare,   490
She sighs forever on her pensive bed,
Pain at her side, and megrim° at her head.   *migraine*

    Two handmaids wait the throne: alike in place,
But diff'ring far in figure and in face.
Here stood Ill-Nature like an ancient maid,   495
Her wrinkled form in black and white arrayed;
With store of prayers for mornings, nights, and noons
Her hand is filled; her bosom with lampoons.

    There Affectation, with a sickly mien,
Shows in her cheek the roses of eighteen,   500
Practised to lisp, and hang the head aside,
Faints into airs, and languishes with pride;
On the rich quilt sinks with becoming woe,
Wrapped in a gown, for sickness and for show.
The fair ones feel such maladies as these,   505
When each new nightdress gives a new disease.

    A constant vapour o'er the palace flies,
Strange phantoms rising as the mists arise;
Dreadful as hermit's dreams in haunted shades,
Or bright as visions of expiring maids.   510
Now glaring fiends and snakes on rolling spires,°   *coils*
Pale spectres, gaping tombs, and purple fires;
Now lakes of liquid gold, Elysian° scenes,   *of paradise*
And crystal domes, and angels in machines.°   *vehicles*

    Unnumbered throngs on every side are seen   515
Of bodies changed to various forms by spleen.
Here living teapots stand, one arm held out,
One bent; the handle this, and that the spout.

---

1   *Cave of Spleen* The spleen was thought to be the seat of melancholy or morose feelings, and "spleen" became a term used to cover any number of complaints including headaches, depression, irritability, hallucinations, or hypochondria.

2   *dreaded east* An east wind was thought to bring on attacks of spleen (also called "the vapours").

A pipkin° there like Homer's tripod[1] walks; *small earthen pot*
520 Here sighs a jar, and there a goose pie[2] talks;
Men prove with child, as pow'rful fancy works,
And maids turned bottles call aloud for corks.
    Safe passed the Gnome through this fantastic band,
A branch of healing spleenwort[3] in his hand.
525 Then thus addressed the pow'r: "Hail, wayward Queen!
Who rule the sex to fifty from fifteen,
Parent of vapours and of female wit,
Who give th' hysteric or poetic fit,
On various tempers act by various ways,
530 Make some take physic,° others scribble plays; *medicine*
Who cause the proud their visits to delay,
And send the godly in a pet,[4] to pray.
A nymph there is that all thy pow'r disdains,
And thousands more in equal mirth maintains.
535 But oh! if e'er thy Gnome could spoil a grace,
Or raise a pimple on a beauteous face,
Like citron-waters[5] matrons' cheeks inflame,
Or change complexions at a losing game;
If e'er with airy horns[6] I planted heads,
540 Or rumpled petticoats, or tumbled beds,
Or caused suspicion when no soul was rude,
Or discomposed the headdress of a prude,
Or e'er to costive lapdog gave disease,
Which not the tears of brightest eyes could ease—
545 Hear me, and touch Belinda with chagrin;
That single act gives half the world the spleen."
    The Goddess with a discontented air
Seems to reject him, though she grants his prayer.
A wondrous bag with both her hands she binds,

---

1 *Homer's tripod* In Homer's *Iliad* (Book 18), the god Vulcan makes three-legged stools
   that move by themselves.
2 [Pope's note] Alludes to a real fact, a Lady of distinction imagined herself in this condition.
3 *spleenwort* Herb said to cure ailments of the spleen. Here it is reminiscent of the golden
   bough that Aeneas carries for protection on his journey to the underworld (*Aeneid*,
   Book 6).
4 *pet* Fit of ill-humour.
5 *citron-waters* Lemon-flavoured brandy-based liquor.
6 *horns* Sign of a cuckold. The horns here are "airy" because the wife's infidelity is only
   imagined by her jealous husband.

Like that where once Ulysses held the winds;[1]   550
There she collects the force of female lungs:
Sighs, sobs, and passions, and the war of tongues.
A vial next she fills with fainting fears,
Soft sorrows, melting griefs, and flowing tears.
The Gnome rejoicing bears her gifts away,   555
Spreads his black wings, and slowly mounts to day.
    Sunk in Thalestris'[2] arms the nymph he found,
Her eyes dejected and her hair unbound.
Full o'er their heads the swelling bag he rent,
And all the Furies issued at the vent.   560
Belinda burns with more than mortal ire,
And fierce Thalestris fans the rising fire.
"O wretched maid!" she spread her hands, and cried
(While Hampton's echoes, "Wretched maid!" replied),
"Was it for this you took such constant care   565
The bodkin, comb, and essence to prepare?
For this your locks in paper durance[3] bound,
For this with tort'ring irons wreathed around?
For this with fillets strained your tender head,
And bravely bore the double loads of lead?   570
Gods! shall the ravisher display your hair,
While the fops envy, and the ladies stare!
Honour forbid! at whose unrivaled shrine
Ease, pleasure, virtue, all, our sex resign.
Methinks already I your tears survey,   575
Already hear the horrid things they say,
Already see you a degraded toast,[4]
And all your honour in a whisper lost!
How shall I, then, your helpless fame defend?
'Twill then be infamy to seem your friend!   580
And shall this prize, th' inestimable prize,
Exposed through crystal to the gazing eyes,

---

1   *Ulysses ... winds* In Homer's *Odyssey*, Aeolus, keeper of the winds, gives Ulysses a bag
    filled with all the winds that, if they blew, would hinder his journey home.
2   *Thalestris* Queen of the Amazons; here, suggesting a fierce, pugnacious woman.
3   *paper durance* Curling papers, which were fastened to the hair with strips of hot lead.
    The head was then encircled by a fillet, or thin crown.
4   *toast* Woman whose health is drunk. Since toasting a woman implied familiarity with
    her, it was detrimental to a lady's reputation if it was done too frequently, or by too
    many men.

And heightened by the diamond's circling rays,
On that rapacious hand forever blaze?[1]
585 Sooner shall grass in Hyde Park Circus[2] grow,
And wits take lodgings in the sound of Bow;[3]
Sooner let earth, air, sea, to chaos fall,
Men, monkeys, lapdogs, parrots, perish all!"
        She said; then raging to Sir Plume repairs,
590 And bids her beau demand the precious hairs
(Sir Plume, of amber snuffbox justly vain,
And the nice conduct of a clouded° cane).   *marbled*
With earnest eyes and round unthinking face,
He first the snuffbox opened, then the case,
595 And thus broke out—"My Lord, why, what the devil?
Z—ds!° damn the lock! 'fore Gad, you must be civil!   *zounds*
Plague on't! 'tis past a jest—nay prithee, pox!
Give her the hair"—he spoke, and rapped his box.
        "It grieves me much," replied the Peer again,
600 "Who speaks so well should ever speak in vain.
But by this lock, this sacred lock I swear
(Which never more shall join its parted hair;
Which never more its honours shall renew,
Clipped from the lovely head where late it grew)
605 That while my nostrils draw the vital air,
This hand, which won it, shall forever wear."
He spoke, and, speaking, in proud triumph spread
The long-contended honours of her head.
        But Umbriel, hateful Gnome! forbears not so;
610 He breaks the vial whence the sorrows flow.
Then see! the nymph in beauteous grief appears,
Her eyes half languishing, half drowned in tears;
On her heaved bosom hung her drooping head,
Which with a sigh she raised, and thus she said:
615   "Forever cursed be this detested day,
Which snatched my best, my fav'rite curl away!
Happy! ah ten times happy had I been,
If Hampton Court these eyes had never seen!

---

1   *Exposed ... blaze* I.e., the Baron will set the hair in a ring.
2   *Hyde Park Circus* Another name for the Ring road in Hyde Park.
3   *in the sound of Bow* Within the sound of the church bells of St. Mary-le-Bow in Cheap-
     side, an unfashionable part of town.

Yet am not I the first mistaken maid
By love of courts to num'rous ills betrayed.   620
Oh, had I rather unadmired remained
In some lone isle, or distant northern land;
Where the gilt chariot never marks the way,
Where none learn ombre, none e'er taste bohea![1]
There kept my charms concealed from mortal eye,   625
Like roses that in deserts bloom and die.
What moved my mind with youthful lords to roam?
Oh, had I stayed and said my prayers at home!
'Twas this the morning omens seemed to tell;
Thrice from my trembling hand the patch box fell;   630
The tott'ring china shook without a wind,
Nay, Poll[2] sat mute, and Shock was most unkind!
A Sylph too warned me of the threats of fate,
In mystic visions, now believed too late!
See the poor remnants of these slighted hairs!   635
My hands shall rend what ev'n thy rapine spares.
These, in two sable ringlets taught to break,
Once gave new beauties to the snowy neck.
The sister lock now sits uncouth, alone,
And in its fellow's fate foresees its own;   640
Uncurled it hangs, the fatal shears demands,
And tempts once more thy sacrilegious hands.
Oh, hadst thou, cruel! been content to seize
Hairs less in sight, or any hairs but these!"

CANTO 5

She said; the pitying audience melt in tears,   645
But Fate and Jove[3] had stopped the Baron's ears.
In vain Thalestris with reproach assails,
For who can move when fair Belinda fails?
Not half so fixed the Trojan could remain,
While Anna begged and Dido raged in vain.[4]   650

---

1   *bohea* Expensive Chinese black tea.
2   *Poll* Belinda's parrot.
3   *Jove* King of the Roman gods.
4   *the Trojan ... vain* Commanded by the gods, Aeneas left his distraught lover, Dido, to
     found the city of Rome. Dido's sister Anna begged him to return, but he refused.

Canto 5, illustration from the 1714 edition of The Rape of the Lock.

Then grave Clarissa[1] graceful waved her fan;
Silence ensued, and thus the nymph began:
    "Say, why are beauties praised and honoured most,
The wise man's passion, and the vain man's toast?
Why decked with all that land and sea afford,   655
Why angels called, and angel-like adored?
Why round our coaches crowd the white-gloved beaux,
Why bows the side box from its inmost rows?
How vain are all these glories, all our pains,
Unless good sense preserve what beauty gains;   660
That men may say, when we the front box grace,
'Behold the first in virtue, as in face!'
Oh! if to dance all night, and dress all day,
Charmed the smallpox, or chased old age away,
Who would not scorn what housewife's cares produce,   665
Or who would learn one earthly thing of use?
To patch, nay ogle, might become a saint,
Nor could it sure be such a sin to paint.
But since, alas! frail beauty must decay,
Curled or uncurled, since locks will turn to grey;   670
Since painted, or not painted, all shall fade,
And she who scorns a man must die a maid;
What then remains but well our pow'r to use,
And keep good humour still, whate'er we lose?
And trust me, dear! good humour can prevail,   675
When airs and flights and screams and scolding fail.
Beauties in vain their pretty eyes may roll;
Charms strike the sight, but merit wins the soul."
    So spoke the dame, but no applause ensued;[2]
Belinda frowned, Thalestris called her prude.   680
"To arms, to arms!" the fierce virago[3] cries,
And swift as lightning to the combat flies.
All side in parties, and begin th' attack;
Fans clap, silks rustle, and tough whalebones crack;

---

1   [Pope's note] A new character introduced in the subsequent editions to open more
    clearly the moral of the poem, in a parody of the speech of Sarpedon to Glaucus in
    Homer. [See Homer's *Iliad* 12, in which Sarpedon reflects on glory and urges Glaucus
    to join the attack on Troy.]
2   [Pope's note] It is a verse frequently repeated in Homer after any speech, "So spoke
    ———, and all the heroes applauded."
3   *virago* Female warrior.

685 Heroes' and heroines' shouts confus'dly rise,
And base and treble voices strike the skies.
No common weapons in their hands are found;
Like Gods they fight, nor dread a mortal wound.
        So when bold Homer makes the Gods engage,
690 And heav'nly breasts with human passions rage;
'Gainst Pallas, Mars; Latona, Hermes[1] arms;
And all Olympus rings with loud alarms.
Jove's thunder roars, heav'n trembles all around;
Blue Neptune[2] storms, the bellowing deeps resound;
695 Earth shakes her nodding tow'rs, the ground gives way,
And the pale ghosts start at the flash of day!
        Triumphant Umbriel on a sconce's[3] height
Clapped his glad wings, and sat to view the fight.
Propped on their bodkin spears, the sprites survey
700 The growing combat, or assist the fray.
        While through the press enraged Thalestris flies,
And scatters deaths around from both her eyes,
A beau and witling° perished in the throng—   *inferior wit*
One died in metaphor, and one in song.
705 "O cruel nymph! a living death I bear,"
Cried Dapperwit, and sunk beside his chair.
A mournful glance Sir Fopling upwards cast,
"Those eyes are made so killing"—was his last.
Thus on Maeander's flow'ry margin lies
710 Th' expiring swan, and as he sings he dies.[4]
        When bold Sir Plume had drawn Clarissa down,
Chloe stepped in, and killed him with a frown;
She smiled to see the doughty° hero slain,   *valiant*
But at her smile the beau revived again.
715   Now Jove suspends his golden scales[5] in air,
Weighs the men's wits against the lady's hair;
The doubtful beam long nods from side to side;
At length the wits mount up, the hairs subside.

---

1   *Pallas* Athena, goddess of wisdom; *Mars* God of war; *Latona* Goddess of light;
    Hermes Among other attributions, god of deceit.
2   *Neptune* Roman god of the sea.
3   *sconce* Wall bracket for holding a candle; also a small fort or earthwork.
4   *Maeander ... dies* River in Phrygia (present-day Turkey). Swans were said to sing before
    their deaths.
5   *golden scales* Used by the god to weigh the fates of mortals, particularly in battle.

See, fierce Belinda on the Baron flies
With more than usual lightning in her eyes;   720
Nor feared the chief th' unequal fight to try,
Who sought no more than on his foe to die.[1]
But this bold lord, with manly strength endued,
She with one finger and a thumb subdued:
Just where the breath of life his nostrils drew,   725
A charge of snuff the wily virgin threw;
The Gnomes direct, to every atom just,
The pungent grains of titillating dust.
Sudden, with starting tears each eye o'erflows,
And the high dome re-echoes to his nose.   730
    "Now meet thy fate," incensed Belinda cried,
And drew a deadly bodkin from her side.
(The same, his ancient personage to deck,
Her great-great-grandsire wore about his neck
In three seal rings;[2] which after, melted down,   735
Formed a vast buckle for his widow's gown.
Her infant grandame's whistle next it grew,
The bells she jingled, and the whistle blew;
Then in a bodkin graced her mother's hairs,
Which long she wore, and now Belinda wears.)   740
    "Boast not my fall," he cried, "insulting foe!
Thou by some other shalt be laid as low.
Nor think to die dejects my lofty mind;
All that I dread is leaving you behind!
Rather than so, ah let me still survive,   745
And burn in Cupid's flames—but burn alive."
    "Restore the lock!" she cries, and all around,
"Restore the lock!" the vaulted roofs rebound.
Not fierce Othello in so loud a strain
Roared for the handkerchief that caused his pain.[3]   750
But see how oft ambitious aims are crossed,
And chiefs contend 'till all the prize is lost!
The lock, obtained with guilt and kept with pain,
In every place is sought, but sought in vain;
With such a prize no mortal must be blessed,   755

---

1   *to die* Metaphorically, to experience an orgasm.
2   *seal rings* Rings used to imprint the wax that seals an envelope.
3   *fierce Othello ... pain* See Shakespeare's *Othello* 3.4.

So Heav'n decrees! with Heav'n who can contest?
    Some thought it mounted to the lunar sphere,
Since all things lost on earth are treasured there.
There heroes' wits are kept in pond'rous vases,
760 And beaux' in snuffboxes and tweezer cases.
There broken vows and deathbed alms are found,
And lovers' hearts with ends of ribbon bound;
The courtier's promises, and sick man's prayers,
The smiles of harlots, and the tears of heirs,
765 Cages for gnats, and chains to yoke a flea,
Dried butterflies, and tomes of casuistry.[1]
    But trust the Muse—she saw it upward rise,
Though marked by none but quick poetic eyes
(So Rome's great founder[2] to the heav'ns withdrew,
770 To Proculus alone confessed in view);
A sudden star, it shot through liquid° air,   *transparent*
And drew behind a radiant trail of hair.
Not Berenice's[3] locks first rose so bright,
The heav'ns bespangling with dishevelled light.
775 The Sylphs behold it kindling as it flies,
And, pleased, pursue its progress through the skies.
    This the beau monde shall from the Mall[4] survey,
And hail with music its propitious ray.
This the blessed lover shall for Venus take,
780 And send up vows from Rosamonda's Lake.[5]
This Partridge[6] soon shall view in cloudless skies
When next he looks through Galileo's eyes;[7]

---

1   *casuistry* The application of general rules of ethics or morality to specific matters of conscience (often through minutely detailed, yet ultimately false or evasive reasoning).

2   *Rome's great founder* Romulus, who was apparently transported from earth in a storm cloud, never to be seen again except by Proculus, who claimed Romulus came to him in a vision from heaven.

3   *Berenice* Berenice dedicated a lock of her hair to Aphrodite to ensure her husband's safe return from war. She placed the lock in Aphrodite's temple, but it disappeared the next day, and was reputed to have ascended to the heavens, where it became a new constellation.

4   *the Mall* Walk in St. James's Park.

5   *Rosamonda's Lake* Pond in St. James's Park that is associated with unhappy lovers. (According to legend, Rosamond was Henry II's mistress and was murdered by his queen.)

6   [Pope's note] John Partridge was a ridiculous star-gazer who, in his almanacs every year, never failed to predict the downfall of the Pope, and the King of France, then at war with the English.

7   *Galileo's eyes* Telescope.

And hence th' egregious wizard shall foredoom
The fate of Louis, and the fall of Rome.
    Then cease, bright nymph! to mourn thy ravished hair,   785
Which adds new glory to the shining sphere!
Not all the tresses that fair head can boast
Shall draw such envy as the lock you lost.
For, after all the murders of your eye,
When, after millions slain, yourself shall die;   790
When those fair suns shall set, as set they must,
And all those tresses shall be laid in dust;
This lock the Muse shall consecrate to fame,
And 'midst the stars inscribe Belinda's name!
           —1717 (original, two-canto version published 1712)

Thomas Gray

1716–1771

A scholar and a recluse who produced only a handful of poems, Thomas Gray nevertheless occupies a pivotal position in the history of English literature. His reputation is secured by his "Elegy Written in a Country Churchyard" (1751), which brought him immediate (and unwelcomed) fame. The poem represents an important moment in the gradual transition from the Neoclassical to the Romantic period: its style embodies neoclassical restraint while its themes echo the sentiments of sensibility, the mid-century movement toward the expression of "universal feelings."

Gray had published only a few poems—all anonymously—before the "Elegy." The poem, which draws on traditions that included landscape poetry, the funeral elegy, and graveyard poetry, received immediate and widespread praise from both critics and readers. It went through twelve editions by 1763, appeared in several periodicals, was imitated, parodied, and translated into numerous languages, and became arguably the most quoted poem in English.

After the success of the "Elegy" six of Gray's poems were published in an illustrated collection (1753), and he turned to writing more elaborate poetry. In 1757, he was offered the Poet Laureateship, which he declined, and he published two odes, "The Progress of Poesy" and "The Bard"—complex, allusive poems that puzzled many readers (and were parodied in two odes to "Oblivion" and "Obscurity"). In later years he travelled, studied more and wrote less, and, in 1768, accepted a professorship of modern history at Cambridge, but never delivered a lecture. In temperament, he described himself as melancholic and others described him as socially withdrawn, but his letters reveal a lively wit and superior intellect.

Elegy Written in a Country Churchyard

The curfew tolls the knell of parting day,
The lowing herd wind slowly o'er the lea,[1]
The plowman homeward plods his weary way,
And leaves the world to darkness and to me.

5 Now fades the glimm'ring landscape on the sight,
And all the air a solemn stillness holds,
Save where the beetle wheels his droning flight,
And drowsy tinklings lull the distant folds;

---

1   *lea* Meadow or area of grassland.

Save that from yonder ivy-mantled tow'r
The moping owl does to the moon complain   10
Of such as, wand'ring near her secret bow'r,
Molest her ancient solitary reign.

Beneath those rugged elms, that yew-tree's shade,
Where heaves the turf in many a mould'ring heap,
Each in his narrow cell for ever laid,   15
The rude° forefathers of the hamlet sleep.   *unlearned*

The breezy call of incense-breathing morn,
The swallow twitt'ring from the straw-built shed,
The cock's shrill clarion or the echoing horn,
No more shall rouse them from their lowly bed.   20

For them no more the blazing hearth shall burn,
Or busy housewife ply her evening care:
No children run to lisp their sire's return,
Or climb his knees the envied kiss to share.

Oft did the harvest to their sickle yield,   25
Their furrow oft the stubborn glebe° has broke;   *soil*
How jocund° did they drive their team afield!   *merrily*
How bowed the woods beneath their sturdy stroke!

Let not Ambition mock their useful toil,
Their homely joys, and destiny obscure;   30
Nor Grandeur hear, with a disdainful smile,
The short and simple annals of the poor.

The boast of heraldry, the pomp of pow'r,
And all that beauty, all that wealth e'er gave,
Awaits alike th' inevitable hour.   35
The paths of glory lead but to the grave.

Nor you, ye Proud, impute to these the fault,
If Mem'ry o'er their tomb no trophies raise,
Where through the long-drawn aisle and fretted[1] vault
The pealing anthem swells the note of praise.   40

---

1   *fretted* Carved with decorative patterns.

Can storied urn or animated bust
Back to its mansion call the fleeting breath?
Can Honour's voice provoke the silent dust,
Or Flatt'ry soothe the dull cold ear of Death?

45 Perhaps in this neglected spot is laid
Some heart once pregnant with celestial fire;
Hands that the rod of empire might have swayed,
Or waked to ecstasy the living lyre.

But Knowledge to their eyes her ample page
50 Rich with the spoils of time did ne'er unroll;
Chill Penury repressed their noble rage,[1]
And froze the genial current of the soul.

Full many a gem of purest ray serene
The dark unfathomed caves of ocean bear:
55 Full many a flow'r is born to blush unseen
And waste its sweetness on the desert air.

Some village-Hampden[2] that with dauntless breast
The little tyrant of his fields withstood;
Some mute inglorious Milton[3] here may rest,
60 Some Cromwell[4] guiltless of his country's blood.

Th' applause of list'ning senates to command,
The threats of pain and ruin to despise,
To scatter plenty o'er a smiling land,
And read their hist'ry in a nation's eyes,

65 Their lot forbade: nor circumscribed alone
Their growing virtues, but their crimes confined;
Forbade to wade through slaughter to a throne,
And shut the gates of mercy on mankind,

---

1   *rage* Ardour, enthusiasm.
2   *Hampden* John Hampden (1594–1643), member of Parliament who defied Charles I
    and died early in the ensuing civil war.
3   *Milton* John Milton (1608–74), English poet and dramatist.
4   *Cromwell* Oliver Cromwell, military and political leader during the English Civil Wars
    (1642–51) and Lord Protector of England (1653–58).

The struggling pangs of conscious truth to hide,
To quench the blushes of ingenuous shame,   70
Or heap the shrine of Luxury and Pride
With incense kindled at the Muse's flame.[1]

Far from the madding crowd's ignoble strife,
Their sober wishes never learned to stray;
Along the cool sequestered vale of life   75
They kept the noiseless tenor of their way.

Yet ev'n these bones from insult to protect
Some frail memorial still erected nigh,
With uncouth rhymes and shapeless sculpture decked,
Implores the passing tribute of a sigh.   80

Their name, their years, spelt by th' unlettered muse,
The place of fame and elegy supply:
And many a holy text around she strews,
That teach the rustic moralist to die.

For who to dumb Forgetfulness a prey,   85
This pleasing anxious being e'er resigned,

---

1   *With ... flame* After this line, the earliest extant draft of the poem contains four stanzas
    that appear to be an earlier ending to the poem:

> The thoughtless World to Majesty may bow
> Exalt the brave, and idolize Success
> But more to Innocence their Safety owe
> Than Power and Genius e'er conspired to bless
>
> And thou, who mindful of the unhonoured Dead
> Dost in these Notes their artless Tale relate
> By Night and lonely Contemplation led
> To linger in the gloomy Walks of Fate
>
> Hark how the sacred Calm, that broods around
> Bids ev'ry fierce tumultuous Passion cease
> In still small Accents whisp'ring from the Ground
> A grateful Earnest of eternal Peace
>
> No more with Reason and thyself at strife;
> Give anxious Cares and endless Wishes room
> But thro' the cool sequestred Vale of Life
> Pursue the silent Tenor of thy Doom.

Left the warm precincts of the cheerful day,
Nor cast one longing ling'ring look behind?

On some fond breast the parting soul relies,
90 Some pious drops the closing eye requires;
Ev'n from the tomb the voice of nature cries,
Ev'n in our ashes live their wonted fires.

For thee who, mindful of th' unhonoured dead,
Dost in these lines their artless tale relate;
95 If chance, by lonely Contemplation led,
Some kindred spirit shall inquire thy fate,

Haply some hoary-headed swain[1] may say,
"Oft have we seen him at the peep of dawn
Brushing with hasty steps the dews away
100 To meet the sun upon the upland lawn.

"There at the foot of yonder nodding beech
That wreathes its old fantastic roots so high,
His listless length at noontide would he stretch,
And pore upon the brook that babbles by.

105 "Hard by yon wood, now smiling as in scorn,
Mutt'ring his wayward fancies he would rove,
Now drooping, woeful wan, like one forlorn,
Or crazed with care, or crossed in hopeless love.

"One morn I missed him on the customed hill,
110 Along the heath and near his fav'rite tree;
Another came; nor yet beside the rill,
Nor up the lawn, nor at the wood was he;

"The next with dirges due in sad array
Slow through the church-way path we saw him borne.
115 Approach and read (for thou can'st read) the lay,
Graved on the stone beneath yon aged thorn."

---

1   *hoary-headed swain* I.e., white-haired farmer.

THE EPITAPH

Here rests his head upon the lap of earth
A youth to fortune and to fame unknown.
Fair Science° frowned not on his humble birth,   learning
And Melancholy marked him for her own.

Large was his bounty and his soul sincere,   5
Heav'n did a recompense as largely send:
He gave to Mis'ry all he had, a tear,
He gained from Heav'n ('twas all he wished) a friend.

No farther seek his merits to disclose,
Or draw his frailties from their dread abode,   10
(There they alike in trembling hope repose)
The bosom of his Father and his God.

—1751

Anna Laetitia Barbauld
1743–1825

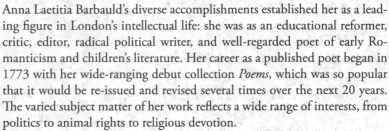

Anna Laetitia Barbauld's diverse accomplishments established her as a leading figure in London's intellectual life: she was as an educational reformer, critic, editor, radical political writer, and well-regarded poet of early Romanticism and children's literature. Her career as a published poet began in 1773 with her wide-ranging debut collection *Poems*, which was so popular that it would be re-issued and revised several times over the next 20 years. The varied subject matter of her work reflects a wide range of interests, from politics to animal rights to religious devotion.

Barbauld's father superintended one of the Protestant alternatives to England's exclusive Anglican schools; from him she learned languages such as Greek and Latin and received an education in literary classics. She followed in her father's footsteps when she and her husband co-founded their own boarding school for boys. Her work there inspired her *Lessons for Children* (1778–79) and *Hymns in Prose for Children* (1781), primers with literacy and faith as their respective goals. The large type in these small texts was an innovation that popularized children's books, and *Lessons* and *Hymns* were influential in both England and the newly formed United States.

Barbauld was also a political writer whose essays, pamphlets, and persuasive verse addressed topics such as freedom of religion, the abolition of slavery, and Britain's engagement in the Napoleonic Wars.

The Caterpillar

No, helpless thing, I cannot harm thee now;
Depart in peace, thy little life is safe,
For I have scanned thy form with curious eye,
Noted the silver line that streaks thy back,
5   The azure and the orange that divide
Thy velvet sides; thee, houseless wanderer,
My garment has enfolded, and my arm
Felt the light pressure of thy hairy feet;
Thou hast curled round my finger; from its tip,
10   Precipitous descent! with stretched out neck,
Bending thy head in airy vacancy,
This way and that, inquiring, thou hast seemed
To ask protection; now, I cannot kill thee.
Yet I have sworn perdition° to thy race,   *damnation, destruction*

And recent from the slaughter am I come   15
Of tribes and embryo nations: I have sought
With sharpened eye and persecuting zeal,
Where, folded in their silken webs they lay
Thriving and happy; swept them from the tree
And crushed whole families beneath my foot;   20
Or, sudden, poured on their devoted heads
The vials of destruction.[1]—This I've done,
Nor felt the touch of pity: but when thou—
A single wretch, escaped the general doom,
Making me feel and clearly recognize   25
Thine individual existence, life,
And fellowship of sense with all that breathes—
Present'st thyself before me, I relent,
And cannot hurt thy weakness.—So the storm
Of horrid war, o'erwhelming cities, fields,   30
And peaceful villages, rolls dreadful on:
The victor shouts triumphant; he enjoys
The roar of cannon and the clang of arms,
And urges, by no soft relentings stopped,
The work of death and carnage. Yet should one,   35
A single sufferer from the field escaped,
Panting and pale, and bleeding at his feet,
Lift his imploring eyes—the hero weeps;
He is grown human, and capricious Pity,
Which would not stir for thousands, melts for one   40
With sympathy spontaneous: 'Tis not Virtue,
Yet 'tis the weakness of a virtuous mind.

—1825

---

1   *vials of destruction* I.e., pesticides.

Phillis Wheatley

1753–1784

■■■■■■ The first black person of African heritage to have a book published, Phillis Wheatley gained an international readership for her poetry, yet died impoverished and largely forgotten. During her lifetime, she published some 50 poems in American newspapers, an exceptional number for the time, and had a collection of poetry, *Poems on Various Subjects, Religious and Moral* (1773), published in London.

Born in Africa, Wheatley was transported to the British colonies in America on the slave ship *Phillis* in 1761. She was purchased as a slave-servant by a businessman and his wife, John and Susannah Wheatley, who gave her an education in English, Latin, classics, and the Bible. Her first published poem appeared in a Rhode Island newspaper when she was only 14 years old.

The 38 *Poems on Various Subjects* include several on nature and morality, a number of poems written to mark specific occasions (called occasional poems), and a racially self-conscious poem on religious transformation, "On Being Brought from Africa to America." Many of the poems are elegies for the dead, which display a reluctance to mourn and instead celebrate the passage of the departed to a happier and better life.

Wheatley gained her freedom in 1778, and in the same year she married a free black man. They lived in extreme poverty, which contributed to the death of all three of her children in infancy—and to Wheatley's own premature death at age 31.

On Being Brought from Africa to America

'Twas mercy brought me from my Pagan land,
Taught my benighted soul to understand
That there's a God, that there's a Saviour too:
Once I redemption neither sought nor knew.
5 Some view our sable race with scornful eye—
"Their colour is a diabolic dye."
Remember, Christians, Negroes, black as Cain,[1]
May be refined, and join th' angelic train.

—1773

---

1   *Cain* In Genesis 4.1–15, the son of Adam and Eve, who murdered his brother Abel and was cursed and marked by God as punishment. A popular interpretation of this story was that the mark of Cain turned his skin dark.

William Blake
1757–1827

"I labour upwards into futurity," wrote William Blake on the back of one of the "tablets" of his visionary art. Blake's genius was largely unrecognized during his own lifetime, but the mysterious and powerful poetry that he crafted—perhaps most memorably in *Songs of Innocence and Experience* (1789, 1794)—would eventually be recognized as having revolutionary significance.

As a child living above his parents' hosiery shop in London, Blake once received a thrashing for declaring he had seen the face of God. Apprenticed at 14 to a highly respected engraver, he spent seven years learning the trade that would earn him his keep. As an adult, Blake claimed to communicate daily with the spirit of his brother Robert, who had died of tuberculosis; the unique style of "illuminated printing" that Blake later devised came to him in a visitation from Robert. Etching words backwards into copper plates so that they would reverse to normal upon printing, Blake in 1788 created his first illuminated texts. Over the next 20 years he would produce an extraordinary series of works in which he used both words and images to express his artistic vision.

The Bible was a tremendous imaginative reserve upon which Blake drew all of his life, and one vision to which he often returns is that of an earthly Eden triumphing over forces of repression. He also had associations with decidedly non-mystical movements calling for political reforms, although he never fully participated in any organization, religious or political.

Blake found his soul mate in Catherine Boucher, a market gardener's daughter whom he taught to read and trained in the printing business. Catherine was evidently a submissive, devoted wife, and some have denigrated Blake's approach to marriage, citing his pronouncement that "the female ... lives from the light of the male." But at the same time, Blake abjured sexual domination and celebrated "the moment of desire!" as a portal to the divine.

Against the grain of the times—he lived during the Industrial Revolution—Blake continued producing labour-intensive, elaborately illustrated books, none of which was commercially successful. Only 20 copies of *Songs of Experience* had been sold at the time of his death.

from *Songs of Innocence*

The Lamb

Little lamb, who made thee?
    Dost thou know who made thee,
Gave thee life & bid thee feed
By the stream & o'er the mead—

William Blake, "The Lamb," Songs of Innocence, *1789. Blake produced his illuminated books, including* Songs of Innocence *and* Songs of Experience, *by etching both text and illustrations onto copper plates, which he then used for printing. Often, he coloured the printed images by hand.*

5   Gave thee clothing of delight,
     Softest clothing, woolly bright,
     Gave thee such a tender voice,
     Making all the vales rejoice?
         Little lamb, who made thee,
10   Dost thou know who made thee?

     Little lamb, I'll tell thee,
     Little lamb, I'll tell thee!

He is called by thy name,
For he calls himself a Lamb;
He is meek & he is mild,[1]   15
He became a little child:
I a child, & thou a lamb,
We are called by his name.
    Little lamb, God bless thee,
    Little lamb, God bless thee!   20

The Chimney Sweeper[2]

When my mother died I was very young,
And my father sold me while yet my tongue
Could scarcely cry 'weep! 'weep! 'weep! 'weep![3]
So your chimneys I sweep, & in soot I sleep.[4]

There's little Tom Dacre, who cried when his head,   5
That curl'd like a lamb's back, was shav'd; so I said,
"Hush Tom! never mind it, for when your head's bare,
You know that the soot cannot spoil your white hair."

And so he was quiet, & that very night,
As Tom was a-sleeping he had such a sight!   10
That thousands of sweepers, Dick, Joe, Ned, & Jack,
Were all of them lock'd up in coffins of black;

And by came an Angel who had a bright key,
And he open'd the coffins & set them all free;
Then down a green plain leaping, laughing they run,   15
And wash in a river and shine in the Sun.

Then naked & white, all their bags left behind,
They rise upon clouds and sport in the wind.
And the Angel told Tom, if he'd be a good boy,
He'd have God for his father & never want joy.   20

---

1   *He is ... is mild* See Charles Wesley's hymn "Gentle Jesus, Meek and Mild" (1742).
2   *The Chimney Sweeper* Children were often forced to climb up chimneys to clean them—a filthy, dangerous, and unhealthy job. A law ameliorating their working conditions was passed in 1788, but it was rarely enforced.
3   *'weep ... 'weep* The child is attempting to say "sweep," the chimney-sweeper's street cry. The act of 1788 should have prevented the apprenticing of children younger than eight.
4   *in soot I sleep* The sweeps used their bags of soot as blankets.

And so Tom awoke; and we rose in the dark,
And got with our bags & our brushes to work.
Tho' the morning was cold, Tom was happy & warm;
So if all do their duty, they need not fear harm.

—1789

from *Songs of Experience*

The Chimney Sweeper

A little black thing among the snow
Crying 'weep! 'weep! in notes of woe!
"Where are thy father & mother, say?"
"They are both gone up to the church to pray.

5   "Because I was happy upon the heath
And smil'd among the winter's snow,
They clothed me in the clothes of death
And taught me to sing the notes of woe.

"And because I am happy & dance & sing,
10   They think they have done me no injury,
And are gone to praise God & his Priest & King,
Who make up a heaven of our misery."

The Sick Rose

O Rose, thou art sick:
The invisible worm,
That flies in the night,
In the howling storm,

5   Has found out thy bed
Of crimson joy;
And his dark secret love
Does thy life destroy.

The Tyger

Tyger! Tyger! burning bright
In the forests of the night,
What immortal hand or eye
Could frame thy fearful symmetry?

In what distant deeps or skies 5
Burnt the fire of thine eyes?
On what wings dare he aspire?[1]
What the hand dare seize the fire?[2]

And what shoulder, & what art,
Could twist the sinews of thy heart? 10
And when thy heart began to beat,
What dread hand? & what dread feet?

William Blake, "The Tyger," Songs of Experience,
1794.

---

1   *wings … aspire* In Greek mythology, Icarus flew using wings made of wax and feathers;
    these melted when he attempted to fly too close to the sun.
2   *hand … fire* In Greek mythology, Prometheus stole fire from heaven to give to humans.

What the hammer? What the chain?
In what furnace was thy brain?
15 What the anvil? what dread grasp
Dare its deadly terrors clasp?

When the stars threw down their spears
And water'd heaven with their tears,
Did he smile his work to see?
20 Did he who made the Lamb make thee?

Tyger! Tyger! burning bright
In the forests of the night,
What immortal hand or eye
Dare frame thy fearful symmetry?

London

I wander thro' each charter'd[1] street
Near where the charter'd Thames does flow,
And mark in every face I meet
Marks of weakness, marks of woe.

5 In every cry of every Man,
In every Infant's cry of fear,
In every voice, in every ban,
The mind-forg'd manacles I hear.

How the Chimney-sweeper's cry
10 Every black'ning Church appalls,
And the hapless Soldier's sigh
Runs in blood down Palace walls.

But most thro' midnight streets I hear
How the youthful Harlot's curse[2]
15 Blasts the new-born Infant's tear,[3]
And blights with plagues the marriage hearse.

—1794

---

1   *charter'd* Licensed. Charters grant freedoms, often for a select minority (such as merchants).
2   *Harlot's curse* Referring to both the oaths she utters and the venereal diseases she spreads.
3   *Blasts … tear* Reference to the blindness caused in infants if they contract certain venereal diseases (such as gonorrhea) from their mother.

William Wordsworth

1770–1850

William Wordsworth is often credited with initiating the shifts in poetic form and content that characterized the Romantic era in British poetry. The most frequent subjects of his poems are nature, the sublime, and the lives of ordinary country people—of interest because, according to Wordsworth, in "low and rustic life ... the essential passions of the heart find a better soil in which they can attain their maturity, are less under restraint, and speak a plainer and more emphatic language." Wordsworth himself viewed poetry as a divine gift and, in addition to celebrating "rustic living" and nature, many of his poems celebrate the imaginative capacity of the author.

Wordsworth was born in the English Lake District. His parents were both dead by the time he was 13, and he was sent by relatives to be educated at a boarding school, later completing his degree at Cambridge. He spent parts of his young adulthood walking throughout Europe, an experience which deepened his interest in politics as well as in nature; his time spent in Revolutionary France had an especially profound impact on his poetry. After these travels were concluded, Wordsworth would spend much of the rest of his life sharing a home with his "beloved sister" Dorothy, whom he described as one of "the two beings to whom my intellect is most indcbtcd" (the other was his friend and fellow poet Samuel Taylor Coleridge).

Lyrical Ballads (1798), which Wordsworth co-authored with Coleridge, is often considered the most important single volume of poetry of the period. Wordsworth's self-stated ambition to write about "incidents and situations from common life" in "language really used by men" was a shift from the impersonal, formulaic poetry of the eighteenth century. This deviation stirred up a great deal of criticism, but by the last decades of his life, Wordsworth's skill and mastery as a poet were widely acknowledged. He was awarded the title of Poet Laureate at the age of 73. In the year after his death, his long poem *The Prelude* was published; originally written in 1798–99, and expanded then revised over the next 40 years, it is often regarded as Wordsworth's crowning achievement.

Lines Written a Few Miles above Tintern Abbey

On Revisiting the Banks of the Wye during a Tour, July 13, 1798 [1]

Five years have passed; five summers, with the length
Of five long winters! and again I hear
These waters, rolling from their mountain-springs
With a sweet inland murmur.[2] Once again
5   Do I behold these steep and lofty cliffs,
Which on a wild secluded scene impress
Thoughts of more deep seclusion; and connect
The landscape with the quiet of the sky.
The day is come when I again repose
10   Here, under this dark sycamore, and view
These plots of cottage-ground, these orchard-tufts,
Which, at this season, with their unripe fruits,
Among the woods and copses lose themselves,
Nor, with their green and simple hue, disturb
15   The wild green landscape. Once again I see
These hedge-rows, hardly hedge-rows, little lines
Of sportive wood run wild; these pastoral farms
Green to the very door; and wreaths of smoke
Sent up, in silence, from among the trees,
20   With some uncertain notice, as might seem,
Of vagrant dwellers in the houseless woods,
Or of some hermit's cave, where by his fire
The hermit sits alone.

                Though absent long,
25   These forms of beauty have not been to me,
As is a landscape to a blind man's eye:
But oft, in lonely rooms, and 'mid the din
Of towns and cities, I have owed to them,
In hours of weariness, sensations sweet,
30   Felt in the blood, and felt along the heart,

---

1   [Wordsworth's note] No poem of mine was composed under circumstances more
pleasant for me to remember than this. I began it upon leaving Tintern, after crossing
the Wye, and concluded it just as I was entering Bristol in the evening, after a ramble
of 4 or 5 days, with my sister. Not a line of it was altered, and not any part of it was
written down till I reached Bristol.

2   [Wordsworth's note] The river is not affected by the tides a few miles above Tintern.

And passing even into my purer mind
With tranquil restoration—feelings too
Of unremembered pleasure; such, perhaps,
As may have had no trivial influence
On that best portion of a good man's life;   35
His little, nameless, unremembered acts
Of kindness and of love. Nor less, I trust,
To them I may have owed another gift,
Of aspect more sublime; that blessed mood,
In which the burthen of the mystery,   40
In which the heavy and the weary weight
Of all this unintelligible world
Is lighten'd—that serene and blessed mood,
In which the affections gently lead us on,
Until, the breath of this corporeal frame,   45
And even the motion of our human blood
Almost suspended, we are laid asleep
In body, and become a living soul:
While with an eye made quiet by the power
Of harmony, and the deep power of joy,   50
We see into the life of things.

                        If this
Be but a vain belief, yet, oh! how oft,
In darkness, and amid the many shapes
Of joyless day-light; when the fretful stir   55
Unprofitable, and the fever of the world,
Have hung upon the beatings of my heart,
How oft, in spirit, have I turned to thee
O sylvan° Wye! Thou wanderer through the woods,   *wooded*
How often has my spirit turned to thee!   60

And now, with gleams of half-extinguish'd thought,
With many recognitions dim and faint,
And somewhat of a sad perplexity,
The picture of the mind revives again:
While here I stand, not only with the sense   65
Of present pleasure, but with pleasing thoughts
That in this moment there is life and food
For future years. And so I dare to hope
Though changed, no doubt, from what I was, when first

70 I came among these hills; when like a roe°   *deer*
   I bounded o'er the mountains, by the sides
   Of the deep rivers, and the lonely streams,
   Wherever nature led; more like a man
   Flying from something that he dreads, than one
75 Who sought the thing he loved. For nature then
   (The coarser pleasures of my boyish days,
   And their glad animal movements all gone by)
   To me was all in all. I cannot paint
   What then I was. The sounding cataract
80 Haunted me like a passion: the tall rock,
   The mountain, and the deep and gloomy wood,
   Their colours and their forms, were then to me
   An appetite: a feeling and a love,
   That had no need of a remoter charm,
85 By thought supplied, or any interest
   Unborrowed from the eye. That time is past,
   And all its aching joys are now no more,
   And all its dizzy raptures. Not for this
   Faint[1] I, nor mourn nor murmur: other gifts
90 Have followed, for such loss, I would believe,
   Abundant recompense. For I have learned
   To look on nature, not as in the hour
   Of thoughtless youth, but hearing oftentimes
   The still, sad music of humanity,
95 Not harsh nor grating, though of ample power
   To chasten and subdue. And I have felt
   A presence that disturbs me with the joy
   Of elevated thoughts; a sense sublime
   Of something far more deeply interfused,
100 Whose dwelling is the light of setting suns,
    And the round ocean, and the living air,
    And the blue sky, and in the mind of man,
    A motion and a spirit, that impels
    All thinking things, all objects of all thought,
105 And rolls through all things. Therefore am I still
    A lover of the meadows and the woods,
    And mountains; and of all that we behold
    From this green earth; of all the mighty world

---

1   *Faint* Lose heart; grow weak.

Of eye and ear, both what they half create,
And what perceive; well pleased to recognize   110
In nature and the language of the sense,
The anchor of my purest thoughts, the nurse,
The guide, the guardian of my heart, and soul
Of all my moral being.

           Nor, perchance,   115
If I were not thus taught, should I the more
Suffer my genial° spirits to decay: *creative*
For thou art with me, here, upon the banks
Of this fair river; thou, my dearest Friend,[1]
My dear, dear Friend, and in thy voice I catch   120
The language of my former heart, and read
My former pleasures in the shooting lights
Of thy wild eyes. Oh! yet a little while
May I behold in thee what I was once,
My dear, dear Sister! And this prayer I make,   125
Knowing that Nature never did betray
The heart that loved her; 'tis her privilege,
Through all the years of this our life, to lead
From joy to joy: for she can so inform
The mind that is within us, so impress   130
With quietness and beauty, and so feed
With lofty thoughts, that neither evil tongues,
Rash judgments, nor the sneers of selfish men,
Nor greetings where no kindness is, nor all
The dreary intercourse of daily life,   135
Shall e'er prevail against us, or disturb
Our cheerful faith that all which we behold
Is full of blessings. Therefore let the moon
Shine on thee in thy solitary walk;
And let the misty mountain winds be free   140
To blow against thee: and in after years,
When these wild ecstasies shall be matured
Into a sober pleasure, when thy mind
Shall be a mansion for all lovely forms,
Thy memory be as a dwelling-place   145
For all sweet sounds and harmonies; Oh! then,

---

1   *my dearest Friend* I.e., Dorothy Wordsworth, the poet's sister.

If solitude, or fear, or pain, or grief,
Should be thy portion, with what healing thoughts
Of tender joy wilt thou remember me,
150 And these my exhortations! Nor, perchance,
If I should be, where I no more can hear
Thy voice, nor catch from thy wild eyes these gleams
Of past existence, wilt thou then forget
That on the banks of this delightful stream
155 We stood together; and that I, so long
A worshipper of Nature, hither came,
Unwearied in that service: rather say
With warmer love, oh! with far deeper zeal
Of holier love. Nor wilt thou then forget,
160 That after many wanderings, many years
Of absence, these steep woods and lofty cliffs,
And this green pastoral landscape, were to me
More dear, both for themselves, and for thy sake.

—1798

[The world is too much with us]

The world is too much with us; late and soon,
Getting and spending, we lay waste our powers:
Little we see in nature that is ours;
We have given our hearts away, a sordid boon!°   *gift*
5 The Sea that bares her bosom to the moon;
The Winds that will be howling at all hours
And are up-gathered now like sleeping flowers;
For this, for every thing, we are out of tune;
It moves us not. Great God! I'd rather be
10 A Pagan suckled in a creed outworn;
So might I, standing on this pleasant lea,
Have glimpses that would make me less forlorn;
Have sight of Proteus[1] coming from the sea;
Or hear old Triton[2] blow his wreathed horn.

—1807

---

1 *Proteus* Shape-changing sea god.
2 *Triton* Sea god with the head and torso of a man and the tail of a fish. He was frequently depicted blowing on a conch shell.

Samuel Taylor Coleridge
1772–1834

Coleridge wrote in a 1796 letter, "I am, and ever have been, a great reader, and have read almost everything—a library-cormorant." His own work was similarly wide-ranging and prolific; Coleridge's collected writings comprise 50 volumes and reveal his interest in a myriad of subjects from history and politics to science and literary criticism. He is chiefly remembered, however, for his significant contribution to English Romantic poetry: poems such as "The Rime of the Ancient Mariner" and "Kubla Khan" that have remained fresh and affecting for generations of readers.

The son of a school headmaster, Coleridge received a robust classical education and later briefly attended Cambridge, although he left without taking a degree. After several false starts—he joined the army, and upon his release concocted an ill-fated plan to move to America to found a communal society—he began to publish his writing. His second book of poetry was *Lyrical Ballads* (1798), a collaboration with his friend William Wordsworth; it opened with "The Rime of the Ancient Mariner," which remains Coleridge's most critically lauded single poem.

Coleridge composed little poetry during the last 35 years of his life. His most important writing from this period is the two-volume *Biographia Literaria* (1817), a work of autobiography and literary criticism in which he anatomizes both poetry and poetic production, considering not only formal elements but also the psychology of the creative process.

Frost at Midnight

The Frost performs its secret ministry,
Unhelped by any wind. The owlet's cry
Came loud—and hark, again! loud as before.
The inmates of my cottage, all at rest,
Have left me to that solitude, which suits   5
Abstruser musings: save that at my side
My cradled infant slumbers peacefully.
'Tis calm indeed! so calm, that it disturbs
And vexes meditation with its strange
And extreme silentness. Sea, hill, and wood,   10
This populous village! Sea, and hill, and wood,
With all the numberless goings-on of life,
Inaudible as dreams! the thin blue flame
Lies on my low-burnt fire, and quivers not;

15 Only that film,¹ which fluttered on the grate,
   Still flutters there, the sole unquiet thing.
   Methinks, its motion in this hush of nature
   Gives it dim sympathies with me who live,
   Making it a companionable form,
20 Whose puny flaps and freaks the idling Spirit
   By its own moods interprets, every where
   Echo or mirror seeking of itself,
   And makes a toy of Thought.

                          But O! how oft,
25 How oft, at school, with most believing mind,
   Presageful, have I gazed upon the bars,
   To watch that fluttering *stranger*! and as oft
   With unclosed lids, already had I dreamt
   Of my sweet birth-place, and the old church-tower,
30 Whose bells, the poor man's only music, rang
   From morn to evening, all the hot Fair-day,
   So sweetly, that they stirred and haunted me
   With a wild pleasure, falling on mine ear
   Most like articulate sounds of things to come!
35 So gazed I, till the soothing things, I dreamt,
   Lulled me to sleep, and sleep prolonged my dreams!
   And so I brooded all the following morn,
   Awed by the stern preceptor's° face, mine eye   *teacher's*
   Fixed with mock study on my swimming book:
40 Save if the door half opened, and I snatched
   A hasty glance, and still my heart leaped up,
   For still I hoped to see the *stranger's* face,
   Townsman, or aunt, or sister more beloved,
   My play-mate when we both were clothed alike!

45   Dear Babe, that sleepest cradled by my side,
   Whose gentle breathings, heard in this deep calm,
   Fill up the interspersèd vacancies
   And momentary pauses of the thought!
   My babe so beautiful! it thrills my heart
50 With tender gladness, thus to look at thee,
   And think that thou shalt learn far other lore,

---

1   [Coleridge's note] In all parts of the kingdom these films are called *strangers* and sup-
     posed to portend the arrival of some absent friend.

And in far other scenes! For I was reared
In the great city, pent 'mid cloisters dim,
And saw nought lovely but the sky and stars.
But *thou*, my babe! shalt wander like a breeze   55
By lakes and sandy shores, beneath the crags
Of ancient mountain, and beneath the clouds,
Which image in their bulk both lakes and shores
And mountain crags: so shalt thou see and hear
The lovely shapes and sounds intelligible   60
Of that eternal language, which thy God
Utters, who from eternity doth teach
Himself in all, and all things in himself.
Great universal Teacher! he shall mould
Thy spirit, and by giving make it ask.   65

　　　Therefore all seasons shall be sweet to thee,
Whether the summer clothe the general earth
With greenness, or the redbreast sit and sing
Betwixt the tufts of snow on the bare branch
Of mossy apple-tree, while the nigh thatch   70
Smokes in the sun-thaw; whether the eave-drops fall
Heard only in the trances of the blast,
Or if the secret ministry of frost
Shall hang them up in silent icicles,
Quietly shining to the quiet Moon.   75

　　　　　　　　　　　　　　　　　　—1798

Kubla Khan

Or, A Vision in a Dream. A Fragment[1]

In Xanadu did Kubla Khan
A stately pleasure-dome decree:
Where Alph, the sacred river, ran
Through caverns measureless to man
　　　Down to a sunless sea.   5

1　[Coleridge's note] The following fragment is here published at the request of a poet
[Lord Byron] of great and deserved celebrity, and as far as the Author's own opinions
are concerned, rather as a psychological curiosity, than on the ground of any supposed
poetic merits.
　　In the summer of the year 1797, the Author, then in ill health, had retired to a lonely farmhouse between Porlock and Linton, on the Exmoor confines of Somerset and

So twice five miles of fertile ground
With walls and towers were girdled round:
And there were gardens bright with sinuous rills,°   brooks
Where blossomed many an incense-bearing tree;
10 And here were forests ancient as the hills,
Enfolding sunny spots of greenery.

But oh! that deep romantic chasm which slanted
Down the green hill athwart a cedarn cover!
A savage place! as holy and enchanted
15 As e'er beneath a waning moon was haunted

Devonshire. In consequence of a slight indisposition [dysentery], an anodyne [opium] had been prescribed, from the effects of which he fell asleep in his chair at the moment that he was reading the following sentence, or words of the same substance, in *Purchas's Pilgrimage*: "Here the Khan Kubla commanded a palace to be built, and a stately garden thereunto. And thus ten miles of fertile ground were inclosed with a wall." The author continued for about three hours in a profound sleep, at least of the external senses, during which time he has the most vivid confidence, that he could not have composed less than from two to three hundred lines, if that indeed can be called composition in which all the images rose up before him as things, with a parallel production of the correspondent expressions, without any sensation or consciousness of effort. On awaking he appeared to himself to have a distinct recollection of the whole, and taking his pen, ink, and paper, instantly and eagerly wrote down the lines that are here preserved. At this moment he was unfortunately called out by a person on business from Porlock, and detained by him above an hour, and on his return to his room, found to his no small surprise and mortification, that though he still retained some vague and dim recollection of the general purpose of the vision, yet, with the exception of some eight or ten scattered lines and images, all the rest had passed away like the images on the surface of a stream into which a stone has been cast, but, alas! without the after restoration of the latter!

> Then all the charm
> Is broken—all that phantom-world so fair
> Vanishes, and a thousand circlets spread,
> And each mis-shape the other. Stay awhile,
> Poor youth! who scarcely dar'st lift up thine eyes—
> The stream will soon renew its smoothness, soon
> The visions will return! And lo, he stays,
> And soon the fragments dim of lovely forms
> Come trembling back, unite, and now once more
> The pool becomes a mirror.

[from Coleridge's "The Picture, or the Lover's Resolution" (1802), 69–78]

Yet from the still surviving recollections in his mind, the Author has frequently purposed to finish for himself what had been originally, as it were, given to him. Σαμερον αδιον ασω [from Theocritus's *Idyll* 1.145]: but the tomorrow is yet to come.

As a contrast to this vision, I have annexed a fragment of a very different character [Coleridge's poem "The Pains of Sleep," not included in this anthology], describing with equal fidelity the dream of pain and disease.

By woman wailing for her demon-lover!
And from this chasm, with ceaseless turmoil seething,
As if this earth in fast thick pants were breathing,
A mighty fountain momently was forced:
Amid whose swift half-intermitted burst   20
Huge fragments vaulted like rebounding hail,
Or chaffy grain beneath the thresher's flail:
And 'mid these dancing rocks at once and ever
It flung up momently the sacred river.
Five miles meandering with a mazy° motion   *labyrinthine* 25
Through wood and dale the sacred river ran,
Then reached the caverns measureless to man,
And sank in tumult to a lifeless ocean:
And 'mid this tumult Kubla heard from far
Ancestral voices prophesying war!   30
    The shadow of the dome of pleasure
    Floated midway on the waves;
    Where was heard the mingled measure
    From the fountain and the caves.
It was a miracle of rare device,   35
A sunny pleasure-dome with caves of ice!
    A damsel with a dulcimer
    In a vision once I saw:
    It was an Abyssinian maid,
    And on her dulcimer she played,   40
    Singing of Mount Abora.
    Could I revive within me
    Her symphony and song,
    To such a deep delight 'twould win me,
That with music loud and long,   45
I would build that dome in air,
That sunny dome! those caves of ice!
And all who heard should see them there,
And all should cry, Beware! Beware!
His flashing eyes, his floating hair!   50
Weave a circle round him thrice,
And close your eyes with holy dread,
For he on honey-dew hath fed,
And drunk the milk of Paradise.

—1816 (written 1798)

Percy Bysshe Shelley
1792–1822

Although he was born into wealth and privilege, Percy Bysshe Shelley opposed the powerful, especially the Tory government and press whom he believed were responsible for the oppression of the working classes. He was called "Mad Shelley" at Oxford not only for his political radicalism but also for his vocal atheism and his intense interest in science. These intellectual passions underwrite a body of remarkable visionary poetry characterized by an elegance and complexity that is at once very wonderful and very difficult.

Shelley, heir to the estate and title of his baronet father and grandfather, attended Eton College, and was still a student there when he published *Zastrozzi* (1810), a Gothic romance novel. He continued to publish during his short stint at the University of Oxford, from which he and a friend were expelled for co-authoring a pamphlet entitled *The Necessity of Atheism* (1811). In 1813 Shelley published his first important work: *Queen Mab*, a poetic utopian dream-vision that vilified conventional morality and institutional religion.

In 1819–20 Shelley wrote his greatest utopian fantasy, *Prometheus Unbound*, which imagined a world grown young again as human beings unlearn historically acquired fear and hatred in favour of love, which Shelley called "the great secret" of all morality. A year later, he penned perhaps his best-known prose work, *A Defence of Poetry* (1821), which famously ends with the bold claim, "Poets are the unacknowledged legislators of the world."

Shelley's reputation was marred by personal as well as political scandal, not least because he abandoned his wife for Mary Godwin (later Mary Shelley, the author of *Frankenstein*), whom he married when his first wife committed suicide. Although he enjoyed scant fame or immediate influence during his lifetime, he has long been recognized as one of the most important poets of the Romantic era.

Ozymandias[1]

I met a traveller from an antique land
Who said: Two vast and trunkless legs of stone
Stand in the desert ... Near them, on the sand,
Half sunk, a shattered visage lies, whose frown,

---

1   *Ozymandias*   Greek name for King Ramses II of Egypt (1304–1237 BCE). First century BCE Greek historian Diodorus Siculus records the story of this monument (Ozymandias's tomb was in the shape of a male sphinx) and its inscription, which Diodorus says reads: "King of Kings am I, Ozymandias. If anyone would know how great I am and where I lie, let him surpass one of my exploits."

And wrinkled lip, and sneer of cold command,   5
Tell that its sculptor well those passions read
Which yet survive, stamped on these lifeless things,
The hand that mocked them, and the heart that fed:
And on the pedestal these words appear:
"My name is Ozymandias, king of kings: 10
Look on my works, ye Mighty, and despair!"
Nothing beside remains. Round the decay
Of that colossal wreck, boundless and bare
The lone and level sands stretch far away.

—1818

Ode to the West Wind[1]

1

O Wild West Wind, thou breath of Autumn's being,
Thou, from whose unseen presence the leaves dead
Are driven, like ghosts from an enchanter fleeing,

Yellow, and black, and pale, and hectic° red,   *feverish*
Pestilence-stricken multitudes: O thou,   5
Who chariotest to their dark wintry bed

The wingèd seeds, where they lie cold and low,
Each like a corpse within its grave, until
Thine azure sister of the Spring shall blow

Her clarion[2] o'er the dreaming earth, and fill   10
(Driving sweet buds like flocks to feed in air)
With living hues and odours plain and hill:

Wild Spirit, which art moving everywhere;
Destroyer and Preserver; hear, oh, hear!

---

1   [Shelley's note] This poem was conceived and chiefly written in a wood that skirts the
    Arno, near Florence, and on a day when that tempestuous wind, whose temperature is
    at once mild and animating, was collecting the vapours which pour down the autumnal
    rains. They began, as I foresaw, at sunset with a violent tempest of hail and rain, at-
    tended by that magnificent thunder and lightning peculiar to the Cispaline regions.
2   *clarion* High-pitched trumpet.

2

15 Thou on whose stream, 'mid the steep sky's commotion,
Loose clouds like earth's decaying leaves are shed,
Shook from the tangled boughs of Heaven and Ocean,

Angels° of rain and lightning: there are spread   *harbingers*
On the blue surface of thine aëry surge,
20 Like the bright hair uplifted from the head

Of some fierce Mænad,[1] even from the dim verge
Of the horizon to the zenith's height,
The locks of the approaching storm. Thou dirge

Of the dying year, to which this closing night
25 Will be the dome of a vast sepulchre,
Vaulted with all thy congregated might

Of vapours,° from whose solid atmosphere   *clouds*
Black rain, and fire, and hail will burst: oh, hear!

3

Thou who didst waken from his summer dreams
30 The blue Mediterranean, where he lay,
Lulled by the coil of his chrystàlline streams,[2]

Beside a pumice isle in Baiae's bay,[3]
And saw in sleep old palaces and towers
Quivering within the wave's intenser day,

35 All overgrown with azure moss and flowers
So sweet, the sense faints picturing them! Thou
For whose path the Atlantic's level powers

---

1   *Mænad* Female attendant of Bacchus, the Greek god of wine.
2   *coil ... streams* Currents of the Mediterranean, the colours of which are often different
    from the surrounding water.
3   *pumice* Porous stone made from cooled lava; *Baiae's bay* Bay west of Naples that con-
    tains the ruins of several imperial villas.

Cleave themselves into chasms, while far below
The sea-blooms and the oozy woods which wear
The sapless foliage of the ocean, know   40

Thy voice, and suddenly grow grey with fear,
And tremble and despoil themselves:[1] oh, hear!

4

If I were a dead leaf thou mightest bear;
If I were a swift cloud to fly with thee;
A wave to pant beneath thy power, and share   45

The impulse of thy strength, only less free
Than thou, O uncontrollable! If even
I were as in my boyhood, and could be

The comrade of thy wanderings over Heaven,
As then, when to outstrip thy skiey° speed   *lofty*   50
Scarce seemed a vision; I would ne'er have striven

As thus with thee in prayer in my sore need.
Oh! lift me as a wave, a leaf, a cloud!
I fall upon the thorns of life! I bleed!

A heavy weight of hours has chained and bowed   55
One too like thee: tameless, and swift, and proud.

5

Make me thy lyre,[2] even as the forest is:
What if my leaves are falling like its own!
The tumult of thy mighty harmonies

---

1   [Shelley's note] The phenomenon alluded to at the conclusion of the third stanza is
     well known to naturalists. The vegetation at the bottom of the sea, of rivers, and of
     lakes, sympathizes with that of the land in the change of seasons, and is consequently
     influenced by the winds which announce it.
2   *lyre* Aeolian harp, a stringed instrument that produces music when exposed to wind.

60 Will take from both a deep, autumnal tone,
Sweet though in sadness. Be thou, Spirit fierce,
My spirit! Be thou me, impetuous one!

Drive my dead thoughts over the universe
Like withered leaves to quicken a new birth!
65 And, by the incantation of this verse,

Scatter, as from an unextinguished hearth
Ashes and sparks, my words among mankind!
Be through my lips to unawakened Earth

The trumpet of a prophecy! O, Wind,
70 If Winter comes, can Spring be far behind?

—1820

John Keats
1795–1821

John Keats has come to epitomize the popular conception of the Romantic poet as a passionate dreamer whose intense, sensuous poetry celebrates the world of the imagination over that of everyday life. Keats published only 54 poems in his short lifetime, but his work ranges across a number of poetic genres, including sonnets, odes, romances, and epics. His poetry often seeks a beauty and truth that will transcend the world of suffering, and often questions its own process of interpretation.

Keats, who died of tuberculosis at 25, often despaired of achieving the immortality he wanted for his work. In a note to his beloved, Fanny Brawne, he expresses regret that, "if I should die ... I have left no immortal work behind me—nothing to make my friends proud of my memory—but I have loved the principle of beauty in all things, and if I had had time I would have made myself remembered." Keats had scarcely a year to live when he wrote these words, but already he had completed, in an extraordinary surge of creativity, almost all the poetry on which his reputation rests, including "The Eve of St. Agnes," "La Belle Dame sans Merci," "Lamia," and his "great Odes," which remain among the highest expressions of the form in English.

Keats was also a highly skilled letter-writer, and his extensive correspondence, in which he reflects on aesthetics, the social role of the poet, and his own sense of poetic mission, reveals a nature acutely alive to the extremes of joy and heartbreak.

When I Have Fears that I May Cease to Be

When I have fears that I may cease to be
    Before my pen has glean'd my teeming brain,
Before high piled books, in charact'ry,[1]
    Hold like rich garners° the full-ripen'd grain;   *granaries*
When I behold, upon the night's starr'd face,   5
    Huge cloudy symbols of a high romance,
And think that I may never live to trace
    Their shadows, with the magic hand of chance;
And when I feel, fair creature of an hour!
    That I shall never look upon thee more,   10
Never have relish in the fairy power
    Of unreflecting love;—then on the shore

---

1   *charact'ry* Symbols or letters.

Of the wide world I stand alone, and think
    Till love and fame to nothingness do sink.

                    —1848 (written 1818)

La Belle Dame sans Merci: A Ballad[1]

O what can ail thee, knight-at-arms,
    Alone and palely loitering?
The sedge[2] has wither'd from the lake,
    And no birds sing.

5 O what can ail thee, knight-at-arms,
    So haggard and so woe-begone?
The squirrel's granary is full,
    And the harvest's done.

I see a lily[3] on thy brow
10   With anguish moist and fever dew,
And on thy cheeks a fading rose
    Fast withereth too.

I met a lady in the meads,°   *meadows*
    Full beautiful, a fairy's child;
15 Her hair was long, her foot was light,
    And her eyes were wild.

I made a garland for her head,
    And bracelets too, and fragrant zone;°   *belt, girdle*
She look'd at me as she did love,
20   And made sweet moan.

I set her on my pacing steed,
    And nothing else saw all day long,
For sidelong would she bend, and sing
    A faery's song.

---

1   *La Belle Dame sans Merci* French: The Beautiful Lady without Pity. This original version
    of the poem, found in a journal letter to George and Georgiana Keats, was first published
    in 1848. Keats's revised version was published in 1820.
2   *sedge* Rush-like grass.
3   *lily* Flower traditionally associated with death.

She found me roots of relish sweet,   25
    And honey wild, and manna dew,[1]
And sure in language strange she said
    "I love thee true."

She took me to her elfin grot,°   *grotto*
    And there she wept, and sigh'd full sore,   30
And there I shut her wild wild eyes
    With kisses four.

And there she lulled me asleep,
    And there I dream'd—Ah! woe betide!
The latest° dream I ever dream'd   *last*   35
    On the cold hill side.

I saw pale kings, and princes too,
    Pale warriors, death pale were they all;
They cried, "La belle dame sans merci
    Hath thee in thrall!"   40

I saw their starv'd lips in the gloom°   *gloaming, twilight*
    With horrid warning gaped wide,
And I awoke and found me here
    On the cold hill's side.

And this is why I sojourn here,   45
    Alone and palely loitering,
Though the sedge is wither'd from the lake,
    And no birds sing.

—1848 (written 1819)

---

1   *manna dew* See Exodus 16, in which God provides the Israelites with a food that falls
from heaven, called manna.

Ode to a Nightingale

1

My heart aches, and a drowsy numbness pains
    My sense, as though of hemlock° I had drunk,   *poison*
    Or emptied some dull opiate to the drains
    One minute past, and Lethe-wards[1] had sunk:
5 'Tis not through envy of thy happy lot,
    But being too happy in thine happiness—
        That thou, light-winged Dryad° of the trees,   *wood-nymph*
           In some melodious plot
Of beechen green, and shadows numberless,
10   Singest of summer in full-throated ease.

2

O, for a draught of vintage! that hath been
    Cool'd a long age in the deep-delved earth,
Tasting of Flora[2] and the country green,
    Dance, and Provençal[3] song, and sunburnt mirth!
15 O for a beaker full of the warm South,
    Full of the true, the blushful Hippocrene,[4]
        With beaded bubbles winking at the brim,
          And purple-stained mouth;
That I might drink, and leave the world unseen,
20   And with thee fade away into the forest dim:

3

Fade far away, dissolve, and quite forget
    What thou among the leaves hast never known,
The weariness, the fever, and the fret
    Here, where men sit and hear each other groan;
25 Where palsy shakes a few, sad, last grey hairs,
    Where youth grows pale, and spectre-thin, and dies;
        Where but to think is to be full of sorrow
          And leaden-eyed despairs,

---

1   *Lethe-wards* In classical myth, Lethe was a river in Hades, the waters of which brought
    forgetfulness.
2   *Flora* Roman goddess of flowers.
3   *Provençal* From Provence, the region in France associated with troubadours.
4   *Hippocrene* Water from the spring on Mount Helicon, sacred to the Muses.

Where Beauty cannot keep her lustrous eyes,
    Or new Love pine at them beyond to-morrow.   30

4

Away! away! for I will fly to thee,
    Not charioted by Bacchus and his pards,[1]
But on the viewless wings of Poesy,
    Though the dull brain perplexes and retards:
Already with thee! tender is the night,   35
    And haply° the Queen-Moon is on her throne,   *perhaps*
        Cluster'd around by all her starry Fays;°   *fairies*
            But here there is no light,
Save what from heaven is with the breezes blown
    Through verdurous glooms and winding mossy ways.   40

5

I cannot see what flowers are at my feet,
    Nor what soft incense hangs upon the boughs,
But, in embalmed° darkness, guess each sweet   *fragrant, perfumed*
    Wherewith the seasonable month endows
The grass, the thicket, and the fruit-tree wild;   45
    White hawthorn, and the pastoral eglantine;
        Fast fading violets cover'd up in leaves;
        And mid-May's eldest child,
The coming musk-rose, full of dewy wine,
    The murmurous haunt of flies on summer eves.   50

6

Darkling[2] I listen; and, for many a time
    I have been half in love with easeful Death,
Call'd him soft names in many a mused rhyme,
    To take into the air my quiet breath;
Now more than ever seems it rich to die,   55
    To cease upon the midnight with no pain,
        While thou art pouring forth thy soul abroad
        In such an ecstasy!

---

1   *Bacchus and his pards* Bacchus, the Roman god of wine, rides a chariot drawn by leopards.
2   *Darkling* In the dark.

Still wouldst thou sing, and I have ears in vain—
60   To thy high requiem become a sod.

7

Thou wast not born for death, immortal Bird!
      No hungry generations tread thee down;
The voice I hear this passing night was heard
      In ancient days by emperor and clown:°   *rustic*
65 Perhaps the self-same song that found a path
      Through the sad heart of Ruth,[1] when, sick for home,
            She stood in tears amid the alien corn;
            The same that oft-times hath
Charm'd magic casements, opening on the foam
70   Of perilous seas, in faery lands forlorn.

8

Forlorn! the very word is like a bell
      To toll me back from thee to my sole self!
Adieu! the fancy cannot cheat so well
      As she is fam'd to do, deceiving elf.
75 Adieu! adieu! thy plaintive anthem fades
      Past the near meadows, over the still stream,
            Up the hill-side; and now 'tis buried deep
            In the next valley-glades:
Was it a vision, or a waking dream?
80   Fled is that music—Do I wake or sleep?

—1819

Ode on a Grecian Urn

1

Thou still unravish'd bride of quietness,
      Thou foster-child of silence and slow time,
Sylvan° historian, who canst thus express   *woodland*
      A flowery tale more sweetly than our rhyme:
5 What leaf-fring'd legend haunts about thy shape
      Of deities or mortals, or of both,

---

1   *Ruth* In the biblical story the widowed Ruth leaves her native Moab for Judah, there
     helping her mother-in-law by working in the fields at harvest time.

In Tempe or the dales of Arcady?[1]
What men or gods are these? What maidens loth?°   *reluctant*
What mad pursuit? What struggle to escape?
What pipes and timbrels?° What wild ecstasy?[2]   *tambourines* 10

2

Heard melodies are sweet, but those unheard
Are sweeter; therefore, ye soft pipes, play on;
Not to the sensual ear, but, more endear'd,
Pipe to the spirit ditties of no tone:
Fair youth, beneath the trees, thou canst not leave   15
Thy song, nor ever can those trees be bare;
Bold lover, never, never canst thou kiss,
Though winning near the goal—yet, do not grieve;
She cannot fade, though thou hast not thy bliss,
For ever wilt thou love, and she be fair!   20

3

Ah, happy, happy boughs! that cannot shed
Your leaves, nor ever bid the Spring adieu;
And, happy melodist, unwearied,
For ever piping songs for ever new;
More happy love! more happy, happy love!   25
For ever warm and still to be enjoy'd,
For ever panting, and for ever young;
All breathing human passion far above,
That leaves a heart high-sorrowful and cloy'd,
A burning forehead, and a parching tongue.   30

4

Who are these coming to the sacrifice?
To what green altar, O mysterious priest,
Lead'st thou that heifer lowing at the skies,
And all her silken flanks with garlands drest?
What little town by river or sea shore,   35
Or mountain-built with peaceful citadel,
Is emptied of this folk, this pious morn?

---

1   *Tempe* Valley in ancient Greece renowned for its beauty; *Arcady* Ideal region of rural
life, named for a mountainous district in Greece.

2   *What pipes ... ecstasy* This side of the vase seems to depict a Dionysian ritual, in which
participants sometimes attained a state of frenzy.

And, little town, thy streets for evermore
    Will silent be, and not a soul to tell
40   Why thou art desolate, can e'er return.

5

O Attic[1] shape! Fair attitude! with brede°   *interwoven design*
    Of marble men and maidens overwrought,°   *overlaid*
With forest branches and the trodden weed;
    Thou, silent form, dost tease us out of thought
45 As doth eternity: Cold Pastoral!
    When old age shall this generation waste,
        Thou shalt remain, in midst of other woe
Than ours, a friend to man, to whom thou say'st,
    "Beauty is truth, truth beauty,"—that is all
50   Ye know on earth, and all ye need to know.

—1820

To Autumn

1

Season of mists and mellow fruitfulness,
    Close bosom-friend of the maturing sun;
Conspiring with him how to load and bless
    With fruit the vines that round the thatch-eves run;
5 To bend with apples the moss'd cottage-trees,
    And fill all fruit with ripeness to the core;
        To swell the gourd, and plump the hazel shells
With a sweet kernel; to set budding more,
And still more, later flowers for the bees,
10 Until they think warm days will never cease,
        For Summer has o'er-brimm'd their clammy cells.

2

Who hath not seen thee oft amid thy store?
    Sometimes whoever seeks abroad may find
Thee sitting careless on a granary floor,
15   Thy hair soft-lifted by the winnowing wind;
Or on a half-reap'd furrow sound asleep,

---

1   *Attic* From Attica, the region around Athens.

Drows'd with the fume of poppies, while thy hook°   *scythe*
 Spares the next swath and all its twined flowers:
And sometimes like a gleaner thou dost keep
 Steady thy laden head across a brook;   20
 Or by a cyder-press, with patient look,
  Thou watchest the last oozings hours by hours.

3

Where are the songs of Spring? Ay, where are they?
 Think not of them, thou hast thy music too—
While barred clouds bloom the soft-dying day,   25
 And touch the stubble-plains with rosy hue;
Then in a wailful choir the small gnats mourn
 Among the river sallows,° borne aloft   *willows*
  Or sinking as the light wind lives or dies;
And full-grown lambs loud bleat from hilly bourn;° *realm* 30
 Hedge-crickets sing; and now with treble soft
 The red-breast whistles from a garden-croft;° *enclosed garden*
  And gathering swallows twitter in the skies.

—1820

Elizabeth Barrett Browning
1806–1861

Once considered for the position of Poet Laureate of England, Elizabeth Barrett Browning was a writer of tremendous versatility. Best known for her sonorous love poetry, she was also one of the foremost political poets of the nineteenth century.

When she was a child in Herefordshire, England, Barrett Browning's love of reading and writing was fostered by her parents. As an adolescent, she developed an unknown illness and became dependent on the opium she was prescribed, but in 1826 she published her first collection, *An Essay on Mind and Other Poems*. By the time she published her next book, *The Seraphim and Other Poems* (1838), she had begun to suffer from either bronchiectasis or tuberculosis. However, she continued to write prolifically and to maintain an active correspondence with other writers and critics; the scholar Marjorie Stone claims that "she literally wrote herself back to life."

Barrett Browning gained international recognition for her *Poems* (1844), admiration for which motivated her future husband, the poet Robert Browning, to write to her. The love poems published as *Sonnets from the Portuguese* (1850) were written during their courtship; though they were relatively unnoticed at first, before long they became her most famous work.

Barrett Browning also published several long poems, the most significant of which was the "verse-novel" *Aurora Leigh* (1856). An epic poem focused on the character of a woman writer, it encompasses Barrett Browning's convictions on desire, power, art, love, romance, race, class structures, and the subjugation of women. Although it was her most controversial work, the poem's many admirers included George Eliot and the critic John Ruskin, who called it the "greatest poem" of the century.

from *Sonnets from the Portuguese*

Sonnet 22

When our two souls stand up erect and strong,
Face to face, silent, drawing nigh and nigher,
Until the lengthening wings break into fire
At either curvèd point—what bitter wrong
5 Can the earth do to us, that we should not long
Be here contented? Think. In mounting higher,
The angels would press on us and aspire
To drop some golden orb of perfect song
Into our deep, dear silence. Let us stay

Rather on earth, Belovèd—where the unfit   10
Contrarious moods of men recoil away
And isolate pure spirits, and permit
A place to stand and love in for a day,
With darkness and the death-hour rounding it.

Sonnet 24

Let the world's sharpness like a clasping knife
Shut in upon itself and do no harm
In this close hand of Love, now soft and warm,
And let us hear no sound of human strife
After the click of the shutting. Life to life—   5
I lean upon thee, Dear, without alarm,
And feel as safe as guarded by a charm
Against the stab of worldlings, who if rife
Are weak to injure. Very whitely still
The lilies of our lives may reassure   10
Their blossoms from their roots, accessible
Alone to heavenly dews that drop not fewer;
Growing straight, out of man's reach, on the hill.
God only, who made us rich, can make us poor.

Sonnet 43

How do I love thee? Let me count the ways.
I love thee to the depth and breadth and height
My soul can reach, when feeling out of sight
For the ends of Being and ideal Grace.
I love thee to the level of everyday's   5
Most quiet need, by sun and candlelight.
I love thee freely, as men strive for Right;
I love thee purely, as they turn from Praise.
I love thee with the passion put to use
In my old griefs, and with my childhood's faith.   10
I love thee with a love I seemed to lose
With my lost saints—I love thee with the breath,
Smiles, tears, of all my life!—and, if God choose,
I shall but love thee better after death.

—1850

Edgar Allan Poe
1809–1849

Edgar Allan Poe is one of antebellum America's most famous and controversial literary figures. Dubbed "the Leader of the Cult of the Unusual" by Jules Verne, Poe continues to be regarded as a haunted and enigmatic outcast, a public image he himself cultivated following his childhood hero, the poet Lord Byron.

Contemporary reviewers often identified Poe with the manic, mentally unhinged narrators of stories such as "The Tell-Tale Heart" (1843) and "The Black Cat" (1843), attributing his preoccupation with the perverse impulses and abysmal depths of the mind to a moral defect in his character. A notorious obituary by his literary executor, which depicted him as a mad and melancholy lost soul, his "heart gnawed by anguish," his "face shrouded in gloom," did much to establish the legend of Poe as an erratic and disturbed outsider. More recently, psychoanalytic critics—not least Freud himself—have made prooftexts of his poems and tales, speculating that Poe, who famously declared the death of a beautiful woman "the most poetical topic in the world," never overcame the loss of his mother, foster mother, and young wife, whose ghosts return in works such as "Ligeia" (1838), "The Raven" (1845), and "Annabel Lee" (1849).

Of all Poe's poetic creations, "The Raven" remains the best known and most beloved. Widely reprinted and parodied in his lifetime, the poem made him famous but did little to relieve his near constant poverty. Poe offered a meticulous, if at times tongue-in-cheek, account of the poem's construction in "The Philosophy of Composition," an essay in which he rejects the Romantic notion that poetry is born of a "fine frenzy" of spontaneous creativity. The burnished formalism of "The Raven"—its incantatory metre, sonorous diction, tightly controlled rhyme scheme, and famous refrain—is a testament to Poe's belief in the primacy of method and craft over "ecstatic intuition."

The Raven

Once upon a midnight dreary, while I pondered, weak and weary,
Over many a quaint and curious volume of forgotten lore—
While I nodded, nearly napping, suddenly there came a tapping,
As of some one gently rapping, rapping at my chamber door.
5   "'Tis some visitor," I muttered, "tapping at my chamber door—
                              Only this and nothing more."

Ah, distinctly I remember it was in the bleak December,
And each separate dying ember wrought its ghost upon the floor.

Eagerly I wished the morrow;—vainly I had sought to borrow
From my books surcease of sorrow—sorrow for the lost Lenore[1]—   10
For the rare and radiant maiden whom the angels name Lenore—
                Nameless here for evermore.

And the silken sad uncertain rustling of each purple curtain
Thrilled me—filled me with fantastic terrors never felt before;
So that now, to still the beating of my heart, I stood repeating   15
"'Tis some visitor entreating entrance at my chamber door—
Some late visitor entreating entrance at my chamber door;—
                This it is and nothing more."

Presently my soul grew stronger; hesitating then no longer;
"Sir," said I, "or Madam, truly your forgiveness I implore;   20
But the fact is I was napping, and so gently you came rapping,
And so faintly you came tapping, tapping at my chamber door,
That I scarce was sure I heard you"—here I opened wide the door;—
                Darkness there and nothing more.

Deep into that darkness peering, long I stood there wondering, fearing,   25
Doubting, dreaming dreams no mortal ever dared to dream before;
But the silence was unbroken, and the stillness gave no token,
And the only word there spoken was the whispered word, "Lenore!"
This *I* whispered, and an echo murmured back the word "Lenore!"
                Merely this and nothing more.   30

Back into the chamber turning, all my soul within me burning,
Soon again I heard a tapping somewhat louder than before.
"Surely," said I, "surely that is something at my window lattice;
Let me see, then, what thereat is, and this mystery explore—
Let my heart be still a moment and this mystery explore;—   35
                'Tis the wind and nothing more!"

Open here I flung the shutter, when, with many a flirt and flutter,
In there stepped a stately raven of the saintly days of yore;
Not the least obeisance made he; not a minute stopped or stayed he;
But, with mien of lord or lady, perched above my chamber door—   40
Perched upon a bust of Pallas[2] just above my chamber door—
                Perched, and sat, and nothing more.

---

1   *Lenore* Poe's poem "Lenore" (1831) dramatizes the death of a young woman mourned by
    her lover.
2   *Pallas* Pallas Athena, Greek goddess of wisdom.

Then this ebony bird beguiling my sad fancy into smiling,
By the grave and stern decorum of the countenance it wore,
45 "Though thy crest be shorn and shaven, thou," I said, "art sure no craven,
Ghastly grim and ancient raven wandering from the Nightly shore—
Tell me what thy lordly name is on the Night's Plutonian[1] shore!"
                                   Quoth the raven "Nevermore."

Much I marvelled this ungainly fowl to hear discourse so plainly,
50 Though its answer little meaning—little relevancy bore;
For we cannot help agreeing that no living human being
Ever yet was blessed with seeing bird above his chamber door—
Bird or beast upon the sculptured bust above his chamber door,
                                   With such name as "Nevermore."

55 But the raven, sitting lonely on the placid bust, spoke only
That one word, as if his soul in that one word he did outpour.
Nothing farther then he uttered—not a feather then he fluttered—
Till I scarcely more than muttered "Other friends have flown before—
On the morrow *he* will leave me, as my hopes have flown before."
60   Then the bird said "Nevermore."

Startled at the stillness broken by reply so aptly spoken,
"Doubtless," said I, "what it utters is its only stock and store
Caught from some unhappy master whom unmerciful Disaster
Followed fast and followed faster till his songs one burden[2] bore—
65 Till the dirges of his Hope that melancholy burden bore
                                   Of 'Never—nevermore.'"

But the raven still beguiling all my sad soul into smiling.
Straight I wheeled a cushioned seat in front of bird, and bust and door;
Then, upon the velvet sinking, I betook myself to linking
70 Fancy unto fancy, thinking what this ominous bird of yore—
What this grim, ungainly, ghastly, gaunt, and ominous bird of yore
                                   Meant in croaking "Nevermore."

This I sat engaged in guessing, but no syllable expressing
To the fowl whose fiery eyes now burned into my bosom's core;
75 This and more I sat divining, with my head at ease reclining
On the cushion's velvet lining that the lamplight gloated° o'er,   *refracted*
But whose velvet violet lining with the lamplight gloating o'er,
                                   She shall press, ah, nevermore!

---

1   *Plutonian* In Roman mythology, Pluto is god of the underworld.
2   *burden* Theme; in a poem or song, chorus or refrain.

Then, methought, the air grew denser, perfumed from an unseen censer
Swung by angels whose faint foot-falls tinkled on the tufted¹ floor.   80
"Wretch," I cried, "thy God hath lent thee—by these angels he hath
    sent thee
Respite—respite and nepenthe² from thy memories of Lenore!
Quaff, oh quaff this kind nepenthe and forget this lost Lenore!"
                  Quoth the raven "Nevermore."

"Prophet!" said I, "thing of evil!—prophet still, if bird or devil!—   85
Whether Tempter sent, or whether tempest tossed thee here ashore,
Desolate yet all undaunted, on this desert land enchanted—
On this home by Horror haunted—tell me truly, I implore—
Is there—*is* there balm in Gilead?³—tell me—tell me, I implore!"
                  Quoth the raven "Nevermore."   90

"Prophet!" said I, "thing of evil!—prophet still, if bird or devil!
By that Heaven that bends above us—by that God we both adore—
Tell this soul with sorrow laden if, within the distant Aidenn,°   *Eden*
It shall clasp a sainted maiden whom the angels name Lenore—
Clasp a rare and radiant maiden whom the angels name Lenore."   95
                  Quoth the raven "Nevermore."

"Be that word our sign of parting, bird or fiend!" I shrieked, upstarting—
"Get thee back into the tempest and the Night's Plutonian shore!
Leave no black plume as a token of that lie thy soul hath spoken!
Leave my loneliness unbroken!—quit the bust above my door!   100
Take thy beak from out my heart, and take thy form from off my door!"
                  Quoth the raven "Nevermore."

And the raven, never flitting, still is sitting, *still* is sitting
On the pallid bust of Pallas just above my chamber door;
And his eyes have all the seeming of a demon's that is dreaming,   105
And the lamp-light o'er him streaming throws his shadow on the floor;
And my soul from out that shadow that lies floating on the floor
                  Shall be lifted—nevermore!

                        —1845

---

1   *tufted* I.e., carpeted.
2   *nepenthe* Drink supposed to banish sorrow by inducing forgetfulness.
3   *Is there … Gilead* See Jeremiah 8.22: "Is there no balm in Gilead?"; *balm* Soothing oint-
    ment; *Gilead* In the Bible, the land east of the River Jordan.

Alfred, Lord Tennyson
1809–1892

More than any other poet, Alfred, Lord Tennyson gave voice to the ambitions, anxieties, and myths of the Victorian era; he was Poet Laureate for 42 years.

Born in 1809 to a privileged, somewhat eccentric family, Tennyson decided early on that poetry was his true vocation. He left the University of Cambridge without taking a degree and devoted himself to writing in a variety of poetic forms, among them dramatic monologues (such as "Ulysses," 1842), short lyrics (such as "Tears, Idle Tears," 1847), and retellings of Arthurian narratives (such as "The Lady of Shalott," 1832). The year 1850 was trebly significant for Tennyson: after a 14-year courtship, he married Emily Sellwood; he was named Poet Laureate; and he published *In Memoriam A.H.H.*, a long, reflective poem in memory of his friend Arthur Hallam that was immediately recognized as his most important work.

Tennyson's appearance conveyed a solemn sense of respectability, and his poetry often deals with issues such as the individual's responsibility to society. But both his personality and his poetry are multi-dimensional; in much of his work, anxieties over sexuality, violence, and death lie close to the surface. Perhaps because of his engagement with such concepts, Tennyson was no stranger to controversy. For example, his long poem *Maud* (1855), which ends with the tormented protagonist departing for Crimea and "the blood-red blossom of war," was attacked by several reviewers (the writer George Eliot notable among them) for allegedly expressing a "hatred of peace."

Tennyson's verse has often been praised for its "verbal music," although his reading voice was an urgent rattle. His voice may still be heard: not long before he died, he was recorded by Thomas Edison reading "The Charge of the Light Brigade" and a few other poems.

The Lady of Shalott[1]

PART 1

On either side the river lie
Long fields of barley and of rye,
That clothe the wold° and meet the sky;   *plain*
And through the field the road runs by

---

1   *The Lady of Shalott* Elaine of the Arthurian romances, who dies of love for Lancelot; she is called "the lily maid of Astolat" in Malory's *Morte Darthur* (1485). Tennyson first encountered the story, however, in a medieval Italian romance called "La Donna di Scalotta" and changed the name to Shalott for a softer sound.

To many-towered Camelot;   5
And up and down the people go,
Gazing where the lilies blow
Round an island there below,
    The island of Shalott.

Willows whiten,[1] aspens quiver,   10
Little breezes dusk° and shiver   *darken*
Through the wave that runs for ever
By the island in the river
    Flowing down to Camelot.
Four grey walls, and four grey towers,   15
Overlook a space of flowers,
And the silent isle imbowers°   *encloses*
    The Lady of Shalott.

By the margin, willow-veiled,
Slide the heavy barges trailed   20
By slow horses; and unhailed
The shallop[2] flitteth silken-sailed
    Skimming down to Camelot:
But who hath seen her wave her hand?
Or at the casement seen her stand?   25
Or is she known in all the land,
    The Lady of Shalott?

Only reapers, reaping early
In among the bearded barley,
Hear a song that echoes cheerly   30
From the river winding clearly,
    Down to towered Camelot:
And by the moon the reaper weary,
Piling sheaves in uplands airy,
Listening, whispers "'Tis the fairy   35
    Lady of Shalott."

---

1   *Willows whiten* I.e., the wind exposes the white undersides of the leaves.
2   *shallop* Light open boat for use in shallow water.

PART 2

There she weaves by night and day
A magic web with colours gay.
She has heard a whisper say,
40   A curse is on her if she stay
     To look down to Camelot.
She knows not what the curse may be,
And so she weaveth steadily,
And little other care hath she,
45   The Lady of Shalott.

And moving through a mirror clear
That hangs before her all the year,
Shadows of the world appear.
There she sees the highway near
50   Winding down to Camelot:
There the river eddy whirls,
And there the surly village-churls,
And the red cloaks of market girls,
     Pass onward from Shalott.

55   Sometimes a troop of damsels glad,
An abbot on an ambling pad,°   *horse*
Sometimes a curly shepherd-lad,
Or long-haired page in crimson clad,
     Goes by to towered Camelot;
60   And sometimes through the mirror blue
The knights come riding two and two:
She hath no loyal knight and true,
     The Lady of Shalott.

But in her web she still delights
65   To weave the mirror's magic sights,
For often through the silent nights
A funeral, with plumes and lights
     And music, went to Camelot:
Or when the moon was overhead,
70   Came two young lovers lately wed;
"I am half sick of shadows," said
     The Lady of Shalott.

PART 3

A bow-shot from her bower-eaves,
He rode between the barley-sheaves,
The sun came dazzling through the leaves, 75
And flamed upon the brazen greaves[1]
    Of bold Sir Lancelot.
A red-cross knight for ever kneeled
To a lady in his shield,
That sparkled on the yellow field, 80
    Beside remote Shalott.

The gemmy° bridle glittered free,   *brilliant*
Like to some branch of stars we see
Hung in the golden Galaxy.
The bridle bells rang merrily 85
    As he rode down to Camelot:
And from his blazoned baldric° slung   *shoulder-strap*
A mighty silver bugle hung,
And as he rode his armour rung,
    Beside remote Shalott. 90

All in the blue unclouded weather
Thick-jewelled shone the saddle-leather,
The helmet and the helmet-feather
Burned like one burning flame together,
    As he rode down to Camelot. 95
As often through the purple night,
Below the starry clusters bright,
Some bearded meteor, trailing light,
    Moves over still Shalott.

His broad clear brow in sunlight glowed; 100
On burnished hooves his war-horse trode;
From underneath his helmet flowed
His coal-black curls as on he rode,
    As he rode down to Camelot.
From the bank and from the river 105
He flashed into the crystal mirror,
"Tirra lirra," by the river
    Sang Sir Lancelot.

---

1   *greaves* Armour worn below the knee.

She left the web, she left the loom,
110 She made three paces through the room,
She saw the water-lily bloom,
She saw the helmet and the plume,
    She looked down to Camelot.
Out flew the web and floated wide;
115 The mirror cracked from side to side;
"The curse is come upon me," cried
    The Lady of Shalott.

PART 4

In the stormy east-wind straining,
The pale yellow woods were waning,
120 The broad stream in his banks complaining,
Heavily the low sky raining
    Over towered Camelot;
Down she came and found a boat
Beneath a willow left afloat,
125 And round about the prow she wrote
    The Lady of Shalott.

And down the river's dim expanse
Like some bold seer in a trance,
Seeing all his own mischance—
130 With a glassy countenance
    Did she look to Camelot.
And at the closing of the day
She loosed the chain, and down she lay;
The broad stream bore her far away,
135   The Lady of Shalott.

Lying, robed in snowy white
That loosely flew to left and right—
The leaves upon her falling light—
Through the noises of the night
140   She floated down to Camelot:
And as the boat-head wound along
The willowy hills and fields among,
They heard her singing her last song,
    The Lady of Shalott.

Heard a carol, mournful, holy,   145
Chanted loudly, chanted lowly,
Till her blood was frozen slowly,
And her eyes were darkened wholly,
    Turned to towered Camelot.
For ere she reached upon the tide   150
The first house by the water-side,
Singing in her song she died,
    The Lady of Shalott.

Under tower and balcony,
By garden-wall and gallery,   155
A gleaming shape she floated by,
Dead-pale between the houses high,
    Silent into Camelot.
Out upon the wharfs they came,
Knight and burgher, lord and dame,   160
And round the prow they read her name,
    The Lady of Shalott.

Who is this? and what is here?
And in the lighted palace near
Died the sound of royal cheer;   165
And they crossed themselves for fear,
    All the knights at Camelot:
But Lancelot mused a little space;
He said, "She has a lovely face;
God in his mercy lend her grace,   170
    The Lady of Shalott."

          —1832 (revised 1842)

John William Waterhouse, The Lady of Shalott, *1888. The Lady of Shalott was a frequent subject for art in the nineteenth century; perhaps the most famous example is Waterhouse's painting.*

The Lotos-Eaters[1]

"Courage!" he said, and pointed toward the land,
"This mounting wave will roll us shoreward soon."
In the afternoon they came unto a land
In which it seemed always afternoon.
5   All round the coast the languid air did swoon,
Breathing like one that hath a weary dream.
Full-faced above the valley stood the moon;
And like a downward smoke, the slender stream
Along the cliff to fall and pause and fall did seem.

10 A land of streams! some, like a downward smoke,
Slow-dropping veils of thinnest lawn,° did go;   *fine fabric*

---

1   *Lotos-Eaters* In Greek mythology, the Lotus Eaters (or Lotophagi) were a race of people who inhabited an island near north Africa. They existed in peaceful apathy because of the narcotic effects of the lotus plants they ate. When Odysseus landed on the island, some of his men ate the lotus plants and wanted to stay on the island, rather than return home to their families. The incident is described in Homer's *Odyssey* 9.2.

And some through wavering lights and shadows broke,
Rolling a slumbrous sheet of foam below.
They saw the gleaming river seaward flow
From the inner land: far off, three mountain-tops,   15
Three silent pinnacles of agèd snow,
Stood sunset-flushed: and, dewed with showery drops,
Up-clomb the shadowy pine above the woven copse.°   *thicket*

The charmèd sunset lingered low adown
In the red West: through mountain clefts the dale   20
Was seen far inland, and the yellow down
Bordered with palm, and many a winding vale
And meadow, set with slender galingale;[1]
A land where all things always seemed the same!
And round about the keel with faces pale,   25
Dark faces pale against that rosy flame,
The mild-eyed melancholy Lotos-eaters came.

Branches they bore of that enchanted stem,
Laden with flower and fruit, whereof they gave
To each, but whoso did receive of them,   30
And taste, to him the gushing of the wave
Far far away did seem to mourn and rave
On alien shores; and if his fellow spake,
His voice was thin, as voices from the grave;
And deep-asleep he seemed, yet all awake,   35
And music in his ears his beating heart did make.

They sat them down upon the yellow sand,
Between the sun and moon upon the shore;
And sweet it was to dream of Fatherland,
Of child, and wife, and slave; but evermore   40
Most weary seemed the sea, weary the oar,
Weary the wandering fields of barren foam.
Then some one said, "We will return no more";
And all at once they sang, "Our island home
Is far beyond the wave; we will no longer roam."   45

---

1   *galingale* Species of sedge; rush-like grass.

CHORIC SONG[1]

1

There is sweet music here that softer falls
Than petals from blown roses on the grass,
Or night-dews on still waters between walls
Of shadowy granite, in a gleaming pass;
5 Music that gentlier on the spirit lies,
Than tired eyelids upon tired eyes;
Music that brings sweet sleep down from the blissful skies.
Here are cool mosses deep,
And through the moss the ivies creep,
10 And in the stream the long-leaved flowers weep,
And from the craggy ledge the poppy hangs in sleep.

2

Why are we weighed upon with heaviness,
And utterly consumed with sharp distress,
While all things else have rest from weariness?
15 All things have rest: why should we toil alone,
We only toil, who are the first of things,
And make perpetual moan,
Still from one sorrow to another thrown:
Nor ever fold our wings,
20 And cease from wanderings,
Nor steep our brows in slumber's holy balm;
Nor harken what the inner spirit sings,
"There is no joy but calm!"
Why should we only toil, the roof and crown of things?

3

25 Lo! in the middle of the wood,
The folded leaf is wooed from out the bud
With winds upon the branch, and there
Grows green and broad, and takes no care,
Sun-steeped at noon, and in the moon
30 Nightly dew-fed; and turning yellow
Falls, and floats adown the air.
Lo! sweetened with the summer light,
The full-juiced apple, waxing over-mellow,

---

1   *Choric Song* As performed by the Chorus in an ancient Greek play.

Drops in a silent autumn night.
All its allotted length of days,   35
The flower ripens in its place,
Ripens and fades, and falls, and hath no toil,
Fast-rooted in the fruitful soil.

4

Hateful is the dark-blue sky,
Vaulted o'er the dark-blue sea.   40
Death is the end of life; ah, why
Should life all labour be?
Let us alone. Time driveth onward fast,
And in a little while our lips are dumb.
Let us alone. What is it that will last?   45
All things are taken from us, and become
Portions and parcels of the dreadful Past.
Let us alone. What pleasure can we have
To war with evil? Is there any peace
In ever climbing up the climbing wave?   50
All things have rest, and ripen toward the grave
In silence; ripen, fall and cease:
Give us long rest or death, dark death, or dreamful ease.

5

How sweet it were, hearing the downward stream,
With half-shut eyes ever to seem   55
Falling asleep in a half-dream!
To dream and dream, like yonder amber light,
Which will not leave the myrrh-bush on the height;
To hear each other's whispered speech;
Eating the Lotos day by day,   60
To watch the crisping ripples on the beach,
And tender curving lines of creamy spray;
To lend our hearts and spirits wholly
To the influence of mild-minded melancholy;
To muse and brood and live again in memory,   65
With those old faces of our infancy
Heaped over with a mound of grass,
Two handfuls of white dust,¹ shut in an urn of brass!

---

1   *white dust* I.e., cremated remains.

6

Dear is the memory of our wedded lives,
70 And dear the last embraces of our wives
And their warm tears: but all hath suffered change:
For surely now our household hearths are cold:
Our sons inherit us: our looks are strange:
And we should come like ghosts to trouble joy.
75 Or else the island princes over-bold
Have eat our substance, and the minstrel sings
Before them of the ten years' war in Troy,
And our great deeds, as half-forgotten things.
Is there confusion in the little isle?
80 Let what is broken so remain.
The Gods are hard to reconcile:
'Tis hard to settle order once again.
There *is* confusion worse than death,
Trouble on trouble, pain on pain,
85 Long labour unto agèd breath,
Sore task to hearts worn out by many wars
And eyes grown dim with gazing on the pilot-stars.

7

But, propped on beds of amaranth and moly,[1]
How sweet (while warm airs lull us, blowing lowly)
90 With half-dropped eyelid still,
Beneath a heaven dark and holy,
To watch the long bright river drawing slowly
His waters from the purple hill—
To hear the dewy echoes calling
95 From cave to cave through the thick-twinèd vine—
To watch the emerald-coloured water falling
Through many a woven acanthus[2]-wreath divine!
Only to hear and see the far-off sparkling brine,
Only to hear were sweet, stretched out beneath the pine.

---

1   *amaranth* Mythical flowers that never wilt; also a plant with medicinal and culinary
     uses; *moly* Herb with magical protective powers.
2   *acanthus* Plant native to Mediterranean shores. The Greeks and Romans esteemed the
     plant for the elegance of its leaves.

8

The Lotos blooms below the barren peak: 100
The Lotos blows by every winding creek:
All day the wind breathes low with mellower tone:
Through every hollow cave and alley lone
Round and round the spicy downs the yellow Lotos-dust is blown.
We have had enough of action, and of motion we,   105
Rolled to starboard, rolled to larboard,° when the surge was   *port*
    seething free,
Where the wallowing monster spouted his foam-fountains in the sea.
Let us swear an oath, and keep it with an equal mind,
In the hollow Lotos-land to live and lie reclined
On the hills like Gods together, careless of mankind.   110
For they lie beside their nectar, and the bolts are hurled
Far below them in the valleys, and the clouds are lightly curled
Round their golden houses, girdled with the gleaming world:
Where they smile in secret, looking over wasted lands,
Blight and famine, plague and earthquake, roaring deeps and fiery   115
    sands,
Clanging fights, and flaming towns, and sinking ships, and praying
    hands.
But they smile, they find a music centred in a doleful song
Steaming up, a lamentation and an ancient tale of wrong,
Like a tale of little meaning though the words are strong;
Chanted from an ill-used race of men that cleave the soil,   120
Sow the seed, and reap the harvest with enduring toil,
Storing yearly little dues of wheat, and wine and oil;
Till they perish and they suffer—some, 'tis whispered—down in hell
Suffer endless anguish, others in Elysian[1] valleys dwell,
Resting weary limbs at last on beds of asphodel.[2]   125
Surely, surely, slumber is more sweet than toil, the shore
Than labour in the deep mid-ocean, wind and wave and oar;
Oh rest ye, brother mariners, we will not wander more.

                          —1842 (written 1833)

---

1   *Elysian* Heavenly. According to the ancient Greeks, Elysium was the dwelling place of
    the blessed after death.
2   *asphodel* Plant said to cover the Elysian fields.

Ulysses[1]

It little profits that an idle king,
By this still hearth, among these barren crags,
Matched with an agèd wife, I mete and dole
Unequal laws unto a savage race,
5   That hoard, and sleep, and feed, and know not me.
I cannot rest from travel: I will drink
Life to the lees:° all times I have enjoyed   *dregs*
Greatly, have suffered greatly, both with those
That loved me, and alone; on shore, and when
10 Thro' scudding drifts the rainy Hyades[2]
Vexed the dim sea: I am become a name;
For always roaming with a hungry heart
Much have I seen and known; cities of men
And manners, climates, councils, governments,
15 Myself not least, but honoured of them all;
And drunk delight of battle with my peers,
Far on the ringing plains of windy Troy.
I am a part of all that I have met;
Yet all experience is an arch wherethrough
20 Gleams that untravelled world, whose margin° fades   *horizon*
For ever and for ever when I move.
How dull it is to pause, to make an end,
To rust unburnished, not to shine in use!
As though to breathe were life. Life piled on life
25 Were all too little, and of one to me
Little remains: but every hour is saved
From that eternal silence, something more,
A bringer of new things; and vile it were
For some three suns to store and hoard myself,
30 And this grey spirit yearning in desire
To follow knowledge like a sinking star,
Beyond the utmost bound of human thought.

This is my son, mine own Telemachus,
To whom I leave the sceptre and the isle—

---

1   *Ulysses* Latin name for Odysseus, the protagonist of Homer's *Odyssey*. Here, long after
     the adventures recounted in that poem, the aged, yet restless Ulysses prepares to em-
     bark on one last voyage.
2   *Hyades* Group of stars near the constellation Taurus and associated with rainstorms.

Well-loved of me, discerning to fulfil   35
This labour, by slow prudence to make mild
A rugged people, and through soft degrees
Subdue them to the useful and the good.
Most blameless is he, centred in the sphere
Of common duties, decent not to fail   40
In offices of tenderness, and pay
Meet° adoration to my household gods,   appropriate
When I am gone. He works his work, I mine.

     There lies the port; the vessel puffs her sail:
There gloom the dark broad seas. My mariners,   45
Souls that have toiled, and wrought, and thought with me—
That ever with a frolic welcome took
The thunder and the sunshine, and opposed
Free hearts, free foreheads—you and I are old;
Old age hath yet his honour and his toil;   50
Death closes all: but something ere the end,
Some work of noble note, may yet be done,
Not unbecoming men that strove with Gods.
The lights begin to twinkle from the rocks:
The long day wanes: the slow moon climbs: the deep   55
Moans round with many voices. Come, my friends,
'Tis not too late to seek a newer world.
Push off, and sitting well in order smite
The sounding furrows; for my purpose holds
To sail beyond the sunset, and the baths   60
Of all the western stars, until I die.
It may be that the gulfs will wash us down:
It may be we shall touch the Happy Isles,[1]
And see the great Achilles,[2] whom we knew.
Though much is taken, much abides; and though   65
We are not now that strength which in old days
Moved earth and heaven; that which we are, we are;
One equal temper of heroic hearts,
Made weak by time and fate, but strong in will
To strive, to seek, to find, and not to yield.   70

                 —1842 (written 1833)

---

1   *Happy Isles* Elysium, or Isles of the Blessed, where heroes enjoyed the afterlife.
2   *Achilles* Hero from Greek mythology, also the central character of Homer's *Iliad*.

The Charge of the Light Brigade[1]

1

Half a league,[2] half a league,
Half a league onward,
All in the valley of Death
    Rode the six hundred.[3]
5 "Forward, the Light Brigade!
Charge for the guns!" he said:
Into the valley of Death
    Rode the six hundred.

2

"Forward, the Light Brigade!"
10 Was there a man dismayed?
Not though the soldier knew
    Some one had blundered:
Theirs not to make reply,
Theirs not to reason why,
15 Theirs but to do and die:
Into the valley of Death
    Rode the six hundred.

3

Cannon to right of them,
Cannon to left of them,
20 Cannon in front of them
    Volleyed and thundered;
Stormed at with shot and shell,
Boldly they rode and well,

---

1   *The Charge … Brigade* Written some weeks after a disastrous engagement during the Crimean War. At the Battle of Balaclava on 25 October 1854, the 700 cavalrymen of the Light Brigade, acting on a misinterpreted order, directly charged the Russian artillery.

2   *league* About three miles.

3   *six hundred* The initial newspaper account read by Tennyson mentioned "607 sabres," and he retained the number even when the correct number was discovered to be considerably higher because "six is much better than seven hundred … metrically" (*Letters* 2.101).

Into the jaws of Death,
Into the mouth of Hell 25
    Rode the six hundred.

4

Flashed all their sabres bare,
Flashed as they turned in air
Sabring the gunners there,
Charging an army, while 30
    All the world wondered:
Plunged in the battery-smoke
Right through the line they broke;
Cossack and Russian
Reeled from the sabre-stroke 35
    Shattered and sundered.
Then they rode back, but not
    Not the six hundred.

5

Cannon to right of them,
Cannon to left of them, 40
Cannon behind them
    Volleyed and thundered;
Stormed at with shot and shell,
While horse and hero fell,
They that had fought so well 45
Came through the jaws of Death,
Back from the mouth of Hell,
All that was left of them,[1]
    Left of six hundred.

6

When can their glory fade? 50
O the wild charge they made!
    All the world wondered.
Honour the charge they made!
Honour the Light Brigade,
    Noble six hundred! 55

—1854

---

1   *All ... them* 118 men were killed and 127 wounded; after the charge, only 195 men
were still with their horses.

Roger Fenton, Cookhouse of the 8th Hussars, *1855. In the Crimean War (1853–56), waged primarily on the Crimean Peninsula in Eastern Europe, the Russian Empire fought a group of allies that included the French, British, and Ottoman Empires. The Crimean War was the first to be photographed extensively, but both the technology of the time and the demands of Victorian taste prevented photographers from shooting scenes of battle directly. This photograph depicts the 8th Hussars, a regiment of Irish cavalry, preparing a meal.*

Roger Fenton, Valley of the Shadow of Death, *1855. This image, one of the most famous photographs of the Crimean War, came to be closely associated with Tennyson's famous 1854 poem "The Charge of the Light Brigade." The valley in the photograph is not the place where the charge occurred but another valley in the vicinity—one that soldiers had begun to call "the valley of the shadow of death" (in an echo both of Tennyson's poem and of the Bible) because of the frequency with which the Russians shelled it.*

Robert Browning
1812–1889

Robert Browning was not a popular poet for much of his lifetime. His poetry, in the eyes of many of his contemporaries, was far too obscure, littered as it was with recondite historical and literary references and with dubious subject matter—husbands murdering their wives, artists frolicking with prostitutes. Fame did come, however, and scholars now credit Browning for having realized new possibilities in the dramatic monologue, a form of poetry that, like a monologue in a dramatic production, showcases the speech of a character to an implied or imaginary audience.

Browning was born to a relatively wealthy family, and his father provided him with a rich home education, an extensive personal library, and financial support that allowed him to dedicate himself to writing. He gained moderate critical attention with the dramatic poem *Paracelsus* (1835), but most found his next long narrative poem, *Sordello* (1840), to be incomprehensible. His next volume, *Dramatic Lyrics* (1842), was more successful; it included now-famous shorter poems such as "My Last Duchess" and "Porphyria's Lover."

In 1845 Browning began corresponding with the poet Elizabeth Barrett, and the following year they eloped to Italy. Although their marriage was a happy and intensely devoted one, Browning wrote little during this time, with the notable exception of the short collection *Men and Women* (1855).

After his wife's death in 1861, Browning returned to London society, where he produced several volumes that would at last make him popular among British readers. These works included his 12-part epic "murder-poem" (as Browning called it), *The Ring and the Book* (1868–69), which told the story of a 1698 Italian murder trial in the voices of multiple characters. The 1879–80 volumes of *Dramatic Idyls* brought the poet even greater fame, both in England and internationally. Browning was at the peak of his popularity during the last decade of his life.

Porphyria's Lover[1]

The rain set early in tonight,
    The sullen wind was soon awake,
It tore the elm-tops down for spite,
    And did its worst to vex the lake:
    I listened with heart fit to break.   5
When glided in Porphyria; straight

---

1   *Porphyria's Lover* The heroine's name is derived from the Greek word meaning "purple" (the word "porphyria" was not used as a label for a group of genetically based disorders until much later in the nineteenth century).

She shut the cold out and the storm,
And kneeled and made the cheerless grate
    Blaze up, and all the cottage warm;
10   Which done, she rose, and from her form
Withdrew the dripping cloak and shawl,
    And laid her soiled gloves by, untied
Her hat and let the damp hair fall,
    And, last, she sat down by my side
15   And called me. When no voice replied,
She put my arm about her waist,
    And made her smooth white shoulder bare,
And all her yellow hair displaced,
    And, stooping, made my cheek lie there
20   And spread, o'er all, her yellow hair,
Murmuring how she loved me—she
    Too weak, for all her heart's endeavour,
To set its struggling passion free
    From pride, and vainer ties dissever,
25   And give herself to me forever.
But passion sometimes would prevail,
    Nor could tonight's gay feast restrain
A sudden thought of one so pale
    For love of her, and all in vain:
30   So, she was come through wind and rain.
Be sure I looked up at her eyes
    Happy and proud; at last I knew
Porphyria worshipped me; surprise
    Made my heart swell, and still it grew
35   While I debated what to do.
That moment she was mine, mine, fair,
    Perfectly pure and good: I found
A thing to do, and all her hair
    In one long yellow string I wound
40   Three times her little throat around
And strangled her. No pain felt she;
    I am quite sure she felt no pain.
As a shut bud that holds a bee,
    I warily oped her lids: again
45   Laughed the blue eyes without a stain.
And I untightened next the tress
    About her neck, her cheek once more
Blushed bright beneath my burning kiss:

I propped her head up as before
    Only, this time my shoulder bore,   50
Her head, which droops upon it still:
    The smiling rosy little head,
So glad it has its utmost will,
    That all it scorned at once is fled,
    And I, its love, am gained instead!   55
Porphyria's love: she guessed not how
    Her darling one wish would be heard.
And thus we sit together now,
    And all night long we have not stirred,
    And yet God has not said a word!   60

—1836

My Last Duchess[1]

Ferrara

That's my last Duchess painted on the wall,
Looking as if she were alive. I call
That piece a wonder, now: Fra Pandolf 's[2] hands
Worked busily a day, and there she stands.
Will't please you sit and look at her? I said   5
"Fra Pandolf " by design, for never read
Strangers like you that pictured countenance,
The depth and passion of its earnest glance,
But to myself they turned (since none puts by
The curtain I have drawn for you, but I)   10
And seemed as they would ask me, if they durst,
How such a glance came there; so, not the first
Are you to turn and ask thus. Sir, 'twas not
Her husband's presence only, called that spot
Of joy into the Duchess' cheek: perhaps   15
Fra Pandolf chanced to say "Her mantle laps
Over my lady's wrist too much," or "Paint
Must never hope to reproduce the faint
Half-flush that dies along her throat": such stuff

---

1   *My Last Duchess* Based on events in the life of Alfonso II, first Duke of Ferrara, Italy, whose first wife died in 1561 under suspicious circumstances after three years of marriage. Upon her death, the Duke entered into negotiations with an agent of Count Ferdinand I of Tyrol, whose daughter he married in 1565.

2   *Fra Pandolf* Brother Pandolf, an imaginary painter, just as "Claus of Innsbruck" (line 56) is an imaginary sculptor.

20 Was courtesy, she thought, and cause enough
For calling up that spot of joy. She had
A heart—how shall I say?—too soon made glad,
Too easily impressed; she liked whate'er
She looked on, and her looks went everywhere.
25 Sir, 'twas all one! My favour at her breast,[1]
The dropping of the daylight in the West,
The bough of cherries some officious fool
Broke in the orchard for her, the white mule
She rode with round the terrace—all and each
30 Would draw from her alike the approving speech,
Or blush, at least. She thanked men—good! but thanked
Somehow—I know not how—as if she ranked
My gift of a nine-hundred-years-old name
With anybody's gift. Who'd stoop to blame
35 This sort of trifling? Even had you skill
In speech—(which I have not)—to make your will
Quite clear to such an one, and say, "Just this
Or that in you disgusts me; here you miss,
Or there exceed the mark"—and if she let
40 Herself be lessoned so, nor plainly set
Her wits to yours, forsooth, and made excuse,
—E'en then would be some stooping; and I choose
Never to stoop. Oh sir, she smiled, no doubt,
Whene'er I passed her; but who passed without
45 Much the same smile? This grew; I gave commands;
Then all smiles stopped together. There she stands
As if alive. Will't please you rise? We'll meet
The company below, then. I repeat,
The Count your master's known munificence
50 Is ample warrant that no just pretence
Of mine for dowry will be disallowed;
Though his fair daughter's self, as I avowed
At starting, is my object. Nay, we'll go
Together down, sir. Notice Neptune,[2] though,
55 Taming a sea-horse, thought a rarity,
Which Claus of Innsbruck cast in bronze for me!

—1842

---

1   *My favour at her breast* I.e., a scarf or ribbon decorated with the Duke's heraldic colours
    or armorial bearings.
2   *Neptune* Roman god of the sea, who rides in a chariot pulled by seahorses.

Emily Brontë
1818–1848

It would seem that there were two Emily Brontës: one a shy, introverted, and unremarkable young woman, and the other the strong-willed, brilliant, and legendary woman who became almost a mythic figure after her death at the age of 30. Both versions develop from the impressions her sister Charlotte gave of her in the preface to the 1850 edition of Emily's only novel, *Wuthering Heights*. For many years it was this work for which she was best known; it was not until the start of the twentieth century that her poetry began to receive serious critical attention.

The fifth of six children born to a literary-minded Anglican clergyman, Brontë grew up in a village in the moors of West Yorkshire—a landscape that is frequently reflected in her poetic imagery. Her literary talent flourished in a house of creative writers that included her sisters Charlotte (author of *Jane Eyre*) and Anne (author of *The Tenant of Wildfell Hall*). As adults, the three sisters collaborated on a volume of poetry, which they published pseudonymously as *The Poems of Currer, Ellis, and Acton Bell* (1846); though its significance is recognized today, the edition published by the sisters sold only two copies.

Wuthering Heights and much of Brontë's poetry share a bleak tone and a preoccupation with passion, loss, and death, yet her poems exhibit a degree of tenderness not evident in her novel. Many explore an existence free of the restraints of everyday life, though attainable only through imagination—a tendency that connects Brontë to her Romantic predecessors more than to her Victorian contemporaries.

Brontë died of tuberculosis in December 1848, only one year after the publication of *Wuthering Heights*. Charlotte Brontë championed her sister's poetic reputation after Emily's death, arguing that the poems evoke the stirrings of the "heart like the sound of a trumpet."

[No coward soul is mine]

No coward soul is mine
No trembler in the world's storm-troubled sphere
I see Heaven's glories shine
And Faith shines equal arming me from Fear

O God within my breast
Almighty ever-present Deity
Life, that in me hast rest
As I Undying Life, have power in Thee

5

Vain are the thousand creeds
10 That move men's hearts, unutterably vain,
Worthless as withered weeds
Or idlest froth amid the boundless main°   *sea*

To waken doubt in one
Holding so fast by thy infinity
15 So surely anchored on
The steadfast rock of Immortality.

With wide-embracing love
Thy spirit animates eternal years
Pervades and broods above,
20 Changes, sustains, dissolves, creates and rears

Though Earth and moon were gone
And suns and universes ceased to be
And thou wert left alone
Every Existence would exist in thee

25 There is not room for Death
Nor atom that his might could render void
Since thou art Being and Breath
And what thou art may never be destroyed.

—1850 (written 1846)

[Often rebuked, yet always back returning][1]

Often rebuked, yet always back returning
       To those first feelings that were born with me,
And leaving busy chase of wealth and learning
       For idle dreams of things which cannot be:

5 Today, I will seek not the shadowy region;
       Its unsustaining vastness waxes drear;
And visions rising, legion after legion,
       Bring the unreal world too strangely near.

---

1   *[Often ... returning]* The authorship of this poem has been variously credited to Emily,
     Charlotte, and Anne Brontë; when the poem was first printed, under the title "Stanzas,"
     it was recorded as having been written by Emily.

I'll walk, but not in old heroic traces,
    And not in paths of high morality,   10
And not among the half-distinguished faces,
    The clouded forms of long-past history.

I'll walk where my own nature would be leading:
    It vexes me to choose another guide:
Where the grey flocks in ferny glens are feeding;   15
    Where the wild wind blows on the mountain side.

What have those lonely mountains worth revealing?
    More glory and more grief than I can tell:
The earth that wakes *one* human heart to feeling
    Can centre both the worlds of Heaven and Hell.   20

                        —1850

[I'll come when thou art saddest]

I'll come when thou art saddest,
Laid alone in the darkened room;
When the mad day's mirth has vanished
And the smile of joy is banished
From evening's chilly gloom.   5

I'll come when the heart's real feeling
Has entire, unbiased sway,
And my influence o'er thee stealing,
Grief deepening, joy congealing,
Shall bear thy soul away.   10

Listen! 'tis just the hour,
The awful time for thee:
Dost thou not feel upon thy soul
A flood of strange sensations roll,
Forerunners of a sterner power,   15
Heralds of me?

                    —1902 (written 1837)

Walt Whitman
1819–1892

An essayist, journalist, school teacher, nurse, wanderer, and lover of the natural world, Walt Whitman is best known for his ground-breaking and influential work of poetry, *Leaves of Grass* (1855–92). Although it addresses universal subjects such as selfhood, nature, and the body, Whitman intended his work primarily as a contribution to the establishment of a uniquely American literature "with neither foreign spirit, nor imagery nor form, but adapted to our case, ... strengthening and intensifying the national soul."

Whitman was born to working-class parents near Hempstead, Long Island, and the family moved to Brooklyn when he was still a child. He received six years of public school education before providing himself with an informal education in a variety of subjects using publicly available resources in New York City. As a young man, he worked as a journalist and editor and became involved with the Democratic Party; this background is reflected in the frequent political focus of *Leaves of Grass*.

A provocative work in its time, *Leaves of Grass* was criticized for its informal diction, nontraditional metre, and overt references to sex and the body, but it was also recognized by a few as a literary masterwork. Whitman sent copies of the first edition to well-known writers of the day, including John Greenleaf Whittier, who is said to have thrown his copy in the fire. Ralph Waldo Emerson, however, wrote Whitman in praise of the book.

Leaves of Grass remained an amorphous work in progress, published in a sequence of editions with Whitman's own substantial changes and additions; the first edition contained 12 poems, while the last contained more than 350.

from *Song of Myself*

1

I celebrate myself, and sing myself,
And what I assume you shall assume,
For every atom belonging to me as good belongs to you.

I loafe and invite my soul,
I lean and loafe at my ease observing a spear of summer grass.

My tongue, every atom of my blood, form'd from this soil, this air,
Born here of parents born here from parents the same, and their
    parents the same,
I, now thirty-seven years old in perfect health begin,

Hoping to cease not till death.
Creeds and schools in abeyance,
Retiring back a while sufficed at what they are, but never forgotten,
I harbour for good or bad, I permit to speak at every hazard,
Nature without check with original energy.

—1855, 1881

I Hear America Singing

I hear America singing, the varied carols I hear;
Those of mechanics, each one singing his as it should be blithe and strong,
The carpenter singing his as he measures his plank or beam,
The mason singing his as he makes ready for work, or leaves off work.
The boatman singing what belongs to him in his boat, the deckhand
    singing on the steamboat deck,
The shoemaker singing as he sits on his bench, the hatter singing as he
    stands,
The wood-cutter's song, the ploughboy's on his way in the morning, or
    at noon intermission or at sundown,
The delicious singing of the mother, or of the young wife at work, or of
    the girl sewing or washing,
Each singing what belongs to him or her and to none else,
The day what belongs to the day—at night the party of young fellows,
    robust, friendly,
Singing with open mouths their strong melodious songs.

—1860

When I Heard the Learn'd Astronomer

When I heard the learn'd astronomer,
When the proofs, the figures, were ranged in columns before me,
When I was shown the charts and diagrams, to add, divide, and
    measure them,
When I sitting heard the astronomer where he lectured with much
    applause in the lecture-room,
How soon unaccountable I became tired and sick,
Till rising and gliding out I wander'd off by myself,
In the mystical moist night-air, and from time to time,
Look'd up in perfect silence at the stars.

—1865

Matthew Arnold
1822–1888

■■■■■ Though Matthew Arnold did not compose a large body of poetry, a great deal of the poetry he did write has proved to be lasting. So too has his larger legacy of edifying and intriguing prose; Arnold's influence as a leading Victorian literary and social critic continues to be felt in current scholarly debates.

As a youth Matthew Arnold was educated at Rugby School under the direct supervision of his father, Thomas Arnold, the most famous English educator of his time. Matthew won a scholarship to Balliol College, Oxford, where he would win the prestigious Newdigate Prize for poetry three years later. His experience at Oxford made a lasting impression on the young man—one of his most celebrated poems, "The Scholar Gipsy" (1853), commemorates the spiritual beauty and elevated culture that Arnold came to associate with this educational institution.

Arnold's first book of poems, *The Strayed Reveller, and Other Poems* (1849), was published under the pseudonym "A," and displayed the aloofness and nonchalance for which he had developed a reputation at Oxford. *Poems by Matthew Arnold* (1853)—the first collection to be published under his name—exhibits a distinctive combination of angst and whimsy. But by the time that book was published Arnold was already writing poetry in a deeper, more melancholic vein; his "Dover Beach," often described as the quintessential poem of the Victorian era, was not published until 1867, but dates from c. 1851. Arnold's most important long poem, *Empedocles on Etna* (1852), dramatizes the reflections of an ancient philosopher in the hours before he commits suicide.

Arnold was elected professor of poetry at Oxford in 1857. By this time, however, he was becoming successful as a literary and social critic, and was writing very little poetry. His most important critical work is *Culture and Anarchy* (1869), which is still widely considered to be a masterpiece of social analysis; in it, he argues that the middle class should be given an education in high culture.

Dover Beach

The sea is calm tonight.
The tide is full, the moon lies fair
Upon the straits—on the French coast the light
Gleams and is gone; the cliffs of England stand,
5 Glimmering and vast, out in the tranquil bay.
Come to the window, sweet is the night-air!

Only, from the long line of spray
Where the sea meets the moon-blanched land,
Listen! you hear the grating roar
Of pebbles which the waves draw back, and fling,   10
At their return, up the high strand,°   *shore*
Begin, and cease, and then again begin,
With tremulous cadence slow, and bring
The eternal note of sadness in.

Sophocles long ago   15
Heard it on the Aegaean, and it brought
Into his mind the turbid ebb and flow
Of human misery;[1] we
Find also in the sound a thought,
Hearing it by this distant northern sea.   20

The Sea of Faith
Was once, too, at the full, and round earth's shore
Lay like the folds of a bright girdle furled.
But now I only hear
Its melancholy, long, withdrawing roar,   25
Retreating, to the breath
Of the night-wind, down the vast edges drear
And naked shingles[2] of the world.

Ah, love, let us be true
To one another! for the world, which seems   30
To lie before us like a land of dreams,
So various, so beautiful, so new,
Hath really neither joy, nor love, nor light,
Nor certitude, nor peace, nor help for pain;
And we are here as on a darkling plain   35
Swept with confused alarms of struggle and flight,
Where ignorant armies clash by night.[3]

                                                   —1867

---

1   *Sophocles ... misery* See Sophocles's *Antigone* 583–91: "Blest are those whose days have
not tasted of evil. For when a house has once been shaken by the gods, no form of ruin is
lacking, but it spreads over the bulk of the race, just as, when the surge is driven over the
darkness of the deep by the fierce breath of Thracian sea-winds, it rolls up the black sand
from the depths, and the wind-beaten headlands that front the blows of the storm give
out a mournful roar"; *Aegaean* Arm of the Mediterranean Sea near Greece.
2   *shingles* Water-worn pebbles.
3   *ignorant ... by night* Reference to Thucydides's *History of the Peloponnesian War*, in which
the invading Athenians became confused as night fell on the battle at Epipolae. Combat-
ants could not tell friend from foe in the moonlight.

Emily Dickinson
1830–1886

Emily Dickinson is often compared to Walt Whitman; they are the leading figures of mid-nineteenth-century American literature, and both exerted enormous influence on the writing of later generations. But whereas Whitman was an exuberantly public figure, Dickinson was intensely private. Whitman strove continually to make a mark; Dickinson remained all but unknown until after her death.

Dickinson was one of three children of Emily and Edward Norcross of Amherst, Massachusetts; her father was an officer of Amherst College and a representative in Congress. She was educated at Amherst Academy and, briefly, at nearby Mount Holyoke College; after one year at Mount Holyoke, however, she returned to Amherst, and from the age of 18 onward she again lived with her family, allowing very few people to visit her. After reaching 30, she became a recluse. Although she acknowledged the appeal of fame and public recognition, she criticized it often in her poems; in one it was "a bright but tragic thing," in another "a fickle food / Upon a shifting plate."

Dickinson's work has a deeply personal flavour to it, but her subject matter is wide-ranging—as was her knowledge of classical and English literature. Her poems often engage with religious themes, yet they also at times suggest a profound religious skepticism. The voice we hear in her poetry is often forceful and direct—yet the poems are filled with ambiguities of syntax and of punctuation.

Dickinson wrote more than 1,700 poems, but most of these did not circulate while she was alive, even in manuscript; only a handful were published during her lifetime. The majority were discovered in a trunk in her bedroom after her death. They were first published in edited versions that regularized and "corrected" many of the eccentricities of Dickinson's punctuation; only in recent decades have readers been able to read the poems as Dickinson wrote them.

249

Wild Nights—Wild Nights!
Were I with thee
Wild Nights should be
Our luxury!

5 Futile—the Winds—
To a Heart in port—

Done with the Compass—
Done with the Chart!

Rowing in Eden—
Ah, the Sea!
Might I but moor—Tonight—
In Thee!

10

—1891 (written c. 1861)

288

I'm Nobody! Who are you?
Are you—Nobody—Too?
Then there's a pair of us!
Don't tell! they'd advertise—you know!

How dreary—to be—Somebody!
How public—like a Frog—
To tell one's name—the livelong June—
To an admiring Bog!

5

—1891 (written c. 1861)

341

After great pain, a formal feeling comes—
The Nerves sit ceremonious, like Tombs—
The stiff Heart questions was it He, that bore,
And Yesterday, or Centuries before?

The Feet, mechanical, go round—
Of Ground, or Air, or Ought—
A Wooden way
Regardless grown,
A Quartz contentment, like a stone—

5

This is the Hour of Lead—
Remembered, if outlived,
As Freezing persons, recollect the Snow—
First—Chill—then Stupor—then the letting go—

10

—1929 (written c. 1862)

465

I heard a Fly buzz—when I died—
The Stillness in the Room
Was like the Stillness in the Air—
Between the Heaves of Storm—

5   The Eyes around—had wrung them dry—
And Breaths were gathering firm
For that last Onset—when the King
Be witnessed—in the Room—

I willed my Keepsakes—Signed away
10   What portion of me be
Assignable—and then it was
There interposed a Fly—

With Blue—uncertain stumbling Buzz—
Between the light—and me—
15   And then the Windows failed—and then
I could not see to see—

—1896 (written c. 1862)

712

Because I could not stop for Death—
He kindly stopped for me—
The Carriage held but just Ourselves—
And Immortality.

5   We slowly drove—He knew no haste
And I had put away
My labour and my leisure too,
For His Civility—

We passed the School, where Children strove
10   At Recess—in the Ring—
We passed the Fields of Gazing Grain—
We passed the Setting Sun—

Or rather—He passed Us—
The Dews drew quivering and chill—
For only Gossamer,[1] my Gown—   15
My Tippet°—only Tulle—   *shawl*

We paused before a House that seemed
A Swelling of the Ground—
The Roof was scarcely visible—
The Cornice[2]—in the Ground—   20

Since then—'tis Centuries—and yet
Feels shorter than the Day
I first surmised the Horses' Heads
Were toward Eternity—

—1890 (written c. 1863)

754

My Life had stood—a Loaded Gun—
In Corners—till a Day
The Owner passed—identified—
And carried Me away—

And now We roam in Sovereign Woods—   5
And now We hunt the Doe—
And every time I speak for Him—
The Mountains straight reply—

And do I smile, such cordial light
Upon the Valley glow—   10
It is as a Vesuvian[3] face
Had let its pleasure through—

And when at Night—Our good Day done—
I guard My Master's Head—

---

1   *Gossamer* Fine, sheer fabric.
2   *Cornice* Decorative moulding that runs along the top of a building's exterior wall where
     it meets the roof.
3   *Vesuvian* Refers to Mount Vesuvius, a volcano in Italy.

15 'Tis better than the Eider-Duck's[1]
   Deep Pillow—to have shared—

   To foe of His—I'm deadly foe—
   None stir the second time—
   On whom I lay a Yellow Eye—
20 Or an emphatic Thumb—

   Though I than He—may longer live
   He longer must—than I—
   For I have but the power to kill,
   Without—the power to die—

                              —1929 (written c. 1863)

1129

   Tell all the Truth but tell it slant—
   Success in Circuit lies
   Too bright for our infirm Delight
   The Truth's superb surprise

5 As Lightning to the Children eased
   With explanation kind
   The Truth must dazzle gradually
   Or every man be blind—

                              —1945 (written c. 1868)

---

1   *Eider-Duck* Duck whose down feathers are used to stuff pillows.

Christina Rossetti

1830–1894

To the late-Victorian critic Edmund Gosse, Christina Rossetti was "one of the most perfect poets of the age." Her melding of sensuous imagery and stringent form earned her the admiration and devotion of many nineteenth-century readers, and the ease of her lyric voice remains apparent in works as diverse as the sensual "Goblin Market" and the subtle religious hymns she penned throughout her career.

Rossetti was born in London in 1830. Her father, a scholar and Italian expatriate, and her mother, who had been a governess before her marriage, inculcated in each of their four children a love of language, literature, and the arts. In 1850 several of her poems were published in *The Germ*, the journal of the Pre-Raphaelite Brotherhood founded in part by her two brothers, Dante Gabriel and William Michael. Although Rossetti was not formally a member of the Brotherhood, her aesthetic sense—and especially her attention to colour and detail—link her to the movement. Other Pre-Raphaelite values were also central to Rossetti's poetic vision, including a devotion to the faithful representation of nature and, at the same time, a penchant for symbols.

Rossetti first gained attention in the literary world with her 1862 publication of *Goblin Market and Other Poems*. The vast majority of her Victorian critics praised the volume for what one reviewer called its "very decided character and originality, both in theme and treatment," and "Goblin Market" remains among her most discussed works. Few readers have believed William Michael Rossetti's insistence that his sister "did not mean anything profound" by "Goblin Market," but many have found the precise nature of its deep suggestiveness elusive.

In 1871, Rossetti was stricken with Graves's disease, a thyroid problem, which led her to retreat even further into an already quiet life. She continued, however, to publish poetry, including *Sing-Song* (1872), a children's collection; *A Pageant and Other Poems* (1881); and *Verses* (1893). In 1892 she was among those mentioned as a possible successor to Tennyson as England's Poet Laureate. She died in 1894 as a result of breast cancer.

Goblin Market

Morning and evening
Maids heard the goblins cry:
"Come buy our orchard fruits,
Come buy, come buy:

5 Apples and quinces,
 Lemons and oranges,
 Plump unpecked cherries,
 Melons and raspberries,
 Bloom-down-cheeked peaches,
10 Swart°-headed mulberries,   *dark*
 Wild free-born cranberries,
 Crabapples, dewberries,
 Pine-apples, blackberries,
 Apricots, strawberries;—
15 All ripe together
 In summer weather,—
 Morns that pass by,
 Fair eves that fly;
 Come buy, come buy:
20 Our grapes fresh from the vine,
 Pomegranates full and fine,
 Dates and sharp bullaces,
 Rare pears and greengages,
 Damsons[1] and bilberries
25 Taste them and try:
 Currants and gooseberries,
 Bright-fire-like barberries,
 Figs to fill your mouth,
 Citrons from the South,
30 Sweet to tongue and sound to eye;
 Come buy, come buy."

 Evening by evening
 Among the brookside rushes,
 Laura bowed her head to hear,
35 Lizzie veiled her blushes:
 Crouching close together
 In the cooling weather,
 With clasping arms and cautioning lips,
 With tingling cheeks and finger tips.
40 "Lie close," Laura said,
 Pricking up her golden head:
 "We must not look at goblin men,

---

1 *bullaces … Damsons* Bullaces, greengages, and damsons are all varieties of plums.

We must not buy their fruits:
Who knows upon what soil they fed
Their hungry thirsty roots?"
"Come buy," call the goblins   45
Hobbling down the glen.
"Oh," cried Lizzie, "Laura, Laura,
You should not peep at goblin men."
Lizzie covered up her eyes,   50
Covered close lest they should look;
Laura reared her glossy head,
And whispered like the restless brook:
"Look, Lizzie, look, Lizzie,
Down the glen tramp little men.   55
One hauls a basket,
One bears a plate,
One lugs a golden dish
Of many pounds weight.
How fair the vine must grow   60
Whose grapes are so luscious;
How warm the wind must blow
Through those fruit bushes."
"No," said Lizzie: "No, no, no;
Their offers should not charm us,   65
Their evil gifts would harm us."
She thrust a dimpled finger
In each ear, shut eyes and ran:
Curious Laura chose to linger
Wondering at each merchant man.   70
One had a cat's face,
One whisked a tail,
One tramped at a rat's pace,
One crawled like a snail,
One like a wombat prowled obtuse and furry,   75
One like a ratel° tumbled hurry skurry.   *badger*
She heard a voice like voice of doves
Cooing all together:
They sounded kind and full of loves
In the pleasant weather.   80

Laura stretched her gleaming neck
Like a rush-imbedded swan,

Like a lily from the beck,°   *stream*
Like a moonlit poplar branch,
85 Like a vessel at the launch
When its last restraint is gone.

Backwards up the mossy glen
Turned and trooped the goblin men,
With their shrill repeated cry,
90 "Come buy, come buy."
When they reached where Laura was
They stood stock still upon the moss,
Leering at each other,
Brother with queer brother;
95 Signalling each other,
Brother with sly brother.
One set his basket down,
One reared his plate;
One began to weave a crown
100 Of tendrils, leaves, and rough nuts brown
(Men sell not such in any town);
One heaved the golden weight
Of dish and fruit to offer her:
"Come buy, come buy," was still their cry.
105 Laura stared but did not stir,
Longed but had no money:
The whisk-tailed merchant bade her taste
In tones as smooth as honey,
The cat-faced purr'd,
110 The rat-paced spoke a word
Of welcome, and the snail-paced even was heard;
One parrot-voiced and jolly
Cried "Pretty Goblin" still for "Pretty Polly";—
One whistled like a bird.

115 But sweet-tooth Laura spoke in haste:
"Good Folk, I have no coin;
To take were to purloin:
I have no copper in my purse,
I have no silver either,
120 And all my gold is on the furze°   *evergreen shrub*
That shakes in windy weather

Above the rusty heather."
"You have much gold upon your head,"
They answered all together:
"Buy from us with a golden curl." 125
She clipped a precious golden lock,
She dropped a tear more rare than pearl,
Then sucked their fruit globes fair or red.
Sweeter than honey from the rock,[1]
Stronger than man-rejoicing wine, 130
Clearer than water flowed that juice;
She never tasted such before,
How should it cloy with length of use?
She sucked and sucked and sucked the more
Fruits which that unknown orchard bore; 135
She sucked until her lips were sore;
Then flung the emptied rinds away
But gathered up one kernel-stone,
And knew not was it night or day
As she turned home alone. 140

Lizzie met her at the gate
Full of wise upbraidings:
"Dear, you should not stay so late,
Twilight is not good for maidens;
Should not loiter in the glen 145
In the haunts of goblin men.
Do you not remember Jeanie,
How she met them in the moonlight,
Took their gifts both choice and many,
Ate their fruits and wore their flowers 150
Plucked from bowers
Where summer ripens at all hours?
But ever in the moonlight
She pined and pined away;
Sought them by night and day, 155
Found them no more but dwindled and grew grey;
Then fell with the first snow,
While to this day no grass will grow
Where she lies low:

---

1   *honey from the rock* See Deuteronomy 32.13.

160 I planted daisies there a year ago
That never blow.
You should not loiter so."
"Nay, hush," said Laura:
"Nay, hush, my sister:
165 I ate and ate my fill,
Yet my mouth waters still;
Tomorrow night I will
Buy more": and kissed her:
"Have done with sorrow;
170 I'll bring you plums tomorrow
Fresh on their mother twigs,
Cherries worth getting;
You cannot think what figs
My teeth have met in,
175 What melons icy cold
Piled on a dish of gold
Too huge for me to hold,
What peaches with a velvet nap,
Pellucid° grapes without one seed: *translucent*
180 Odorous indeed must be the mead°   *meadow*
Whereon they grow, and pure the wave they drink
With lilies at the brink,
And sugar-sweet their sap."

Golden head by golden head,
185 Like two pigeons in one nest
Folded in each other's wings,
They lay down in their curtained bed:
Like two blossoms on one stem,
Like two flakes of new-fall'n snow,
190 Like two wands of ivory
Tipped with gold for awful° kings.   *awe-inspiring*
Moon and stars gazed in at them,
Wind sang to them lullaby,
Lumbering owls forbore to fly,
195 Not a bat flapped to and fro
Round their rest:
Cheek to cheek and breast to breast
Locked together in one nest.

Early in the morning
When the first cock crowed his warning,   200
Neat like bees, as sweet and busy,
Laura rose with Lizzie:
Fetched in honey, milked the cows,
Aired and set to rights the house,
Kneaded cakes of whitest wheat,   205
Cakes for dainty mouths to eat,
Next churned butter, whipped up cream,
Fed their poultry, sat and sewed;
Talked as modest maidens should:
Lizzie with an open heart,   210
Laura in an absent dream,
One content, one sick in part;
One warbling for the mere bright day's delight,
One longing for the night.

At length slow evening came: 215
They went with pitchers to the reedy brooks;
Lizzie most placid in her look,
Laura most like a leaping flame.
They drew the gurgling water from its deep.
Lizzie plucked purple and rich golden flags,   220
Then turning homeward said: "The sunset flushes
Those furthest loftiest crags;
Come Laura, not another maiden lags.
No wilful squirrel wags,
The beasts and birds are fast asleep."   225
But Laura loitered still among the rushes,
And said the bank was steep.

And said the hour was early still,
The dew not fall'n, the wind not chill;
Listening ever, but not catching   230
The customary cry,
"Come buy, come buy,"
With its iterated jingle
Of sugar-baited words:
Not for all her watching   235
Once discerning even one goblin
Racing, whisking, tumbling, hobbling—

Let alone the herds
That used to tramp along the glen,
240 In groups or single,
Of brisk fruit-merchant men.
Till Lizzie urged, "O Laura, come;
I hear the fruit-call, but I dare not look:
You should not loiter longer at this brook:
245 Come with me home.
The stars rise, the moon bends her arc,
Each glowworm winks her spark,
Let us get home before the night grows dark:
For clouds may gather
250 Though this is summer weather,
Put out the lights and drench us thro';
Then if we lost our way what should we do?"

Laura turned cold as stone
To find her sister heard that cry alone,
255 That goblin cry,
"Come buy our fruits, come buy."
Must she then buy no more such dainty fruit?
Must she no more such succous° pasture find,   *juicy*
Gone deaf and blind?
260 Her tree of life drooped from the root:
She said not one word in her heart's sore ache;
But peering through the dimness, nought discerning,
Trudged home, her pitcher dripping all the way;
So crept to bed, and lay
265 Silent till Lizzie slept;
Then sat up in a passionate yearning,
And gnashed her teeth for baulked desire, and wept
As if her heart would break.

Day after day, night after night,
270 Laura kept watch in vain
In sullen silence of exceeding pain.
She never caught again the goblin cry,
"Come buy, come buy"—
She never spied the goblin men
275 Hawking their fruits along the glen:
But when the noon waxed bright

Her hair grew thin and grey;
She dwindled, as the fair full moon doth turn
To swift decay and burn
Her fire away.   280

One day remembering her kernel-stone
She set it by a wall that faced the south;
Dewed it with tears, hoped for a root,
Watched for a waxing shoot,
But there came none.   285
It never saw the sun,
It never felt the trickling moisture run:
While with sunk eyes and faded mouth
She dreamed of melons, as a traveller sees
False waves in desert drouth°   *drought* 290
With shade of leaf-crowned trees,
And burns the thirstier in the sandful breeze.

She no more swept the house,
Tended the fowl or cows,
Fetched honey, kneaded cakes of wheat,   295
Brought water from the brook:
But sat down listless in the chimney-nook
And would not eat.

Tender Lizzie could not bear
To watch her sister's cankerous care,   300
Yet not to share.
She night and morning
Caught the goblins' cry:
"Come buy our orchard fruits,
Come buy, come buy:"—   305
Beside the brook, along the glen,
She heard the tramp of goblin men,
The voice and stir
Poor Laura could not hear;
Longed to buy fruit to comfort her,   310
But feared to pay too dear.
She thought of Jeanie in her grave,
Who should have been a bride;
But who for joys brides hope to have

315 Fell sick and died
In her gay prime,
In earliest winter time,
With the first glazing rime,°   *hoar frost*
With the first snow-fall of crisp Winter time.

320 Till Laura dwindling
Seemed knocking at Death's door.
Then Lizzie weighed no more
Better and worse;
But put a silver penny in her purse,
325 Kissed Laura, crossed the heath with clumps of furze
At twilight, halted by the brook:
And for the first time in her life
Began to listen and look.

Laughed every goblin
330 When they spied her peeping:
Came towards her hobbling,
Flying, running, leaping,
Puffing and blowing,
Chuckling, clapping, crowing.
335 Clucking and gobbling,
Mopping and mowing,
Full of airs and graces,
Pulling wry faces,
Demure grimaces,
340 Cat-like and rat-like,
Ratel- and wombat-like,
Snail-paced in a hurry,
Parrot-voiced and whistler,
Helter skelter, hurry skurry,
345 Chattering like magpies,
Fluttering like pigeons,
Gliding like fishes,—
Hugged her and kissed her:
Squeezed and caressed her:
350 Stretched up their dishes,
Panniers, and plates:
"Look at our apples
Russet and dun,°   *dark*

Bob at our cherries,
Bite at our peaches,
Citrons and dates,
Grapes for the asking,
Pears red with basking
Out in the sun,
Plums on their twigs;
Pluck them and suck them,—
Pomegranates, figs."

355

360

Dante Gabriel Rossetti, frontispiece to Goblin Market and Other Poems,
1862. The first edition of Goblin Market *appeared with illustrations by
Christina Rossetti's brother, the Pre-Raphaelite painter and poet Dante
Gabriel Rossetti. In this frontispiece, the round inset above the drawing of
sisters Laura and Lizzie depicts the goblins carrying their fruits to market.*

"Good folk," said Lizzie,
Mindful of Jeanie:
365   "Give me much and many"—
Held out her apron,
Tossed them her penny.
"Nay, take a seat with us,
Honour and eat with us,"
370   They answered grinning:
"Our feast is but beginning.
Night yet is early,
Warm and dew-pearly,
Wakeful and starry:
375   Such fruits as these
No man can carry;
Half their bloom would fly,
Half their dew would dry,
Half their flavour would pass by.
380   Sit down and feast with us,
Be welcome guest with us,
Cheer you and rest with us."—
"Thank you," said Lizzie: "But one waits
At home alone for me:
385   So without further parleying,°   *discussion*
If you will not sell me any
Of your fruits though much and many,
Give me back my silver penny
I tossed you for a fee."—
390   They began to scratch their pates,°   *heads*
No longer wagging, purring,
But visibly demurring,
Grunting and snarling.
One called her proud,
395   Cross-grained, uncivil;
Their tones waxed loud,
Their looks were evil.
Lashing their tails
They trod and hustled her,
400   Elbowed and jostled her,
Clawed with their nails,
Barking, mewing, hissing, mocking,
Tore her gown and soiled her stocking,

Twitched her hair out by the roots,
Stamped upon her tender feet,   405
Held her hands and squeezed their fruits
Against her mouth to make her eat.

White and golden Lizzie stood,
Like a lily in a flood,—
Like a rock of blue-veined stone   410
Lashed by tides obstreperously,—
Like a beacon left alone
In a hoary roaring sea,
Sending up a golden fire,—
Like a fruit-crowned orange tree   415
White with blossoms honey-sweet
Sore beset by wasp and bee,—
Like a royal virgin town
Topped with gilded dome and spire
Close beleaguered by a fleet   420
Mad to tug her standard down.

One may lead a horse to water,
Twenty cannot make him drink.
Though the goblins cuffed and caught her,
Coaxed and fought her,   425
Bullied and besought her,
Scratched her, pinched her black as ink,
Kicked and knocked her,
Mauled and mocked her,
Lizzie uttered not a word;   430
Would not open lip from lip
Lest they should cram a mouthful in:
But laughed in heart to feel the drip
Of juice that syruped all her face,
And lodged in dimples of her chin,   435
And streaked her neck which quaked like curd.
At last the evil people,
Worn out by her resistance,
Flung back her penny, kicked their fruit
Along whichever road they took,   440
Not leaving root or stone or shoot;
Some writhed into the ground,

Some dived into the brook
With ring and ripple,
445 Some scudded on the gale without a sound,
Some vanished in the distance.

In a smart, ache, tingle,
Lizzie went her way;
Knew not was it night or day;
Sprang up the bank, tore through the furze,
450 Threaded copse and dingle,°   dell
And heard her penny jingle
Bouncing in her purse,—
Its bounce was music to her ear.
She ran and ran
455 As if she feared some goblin man
Dogged her with gibe or curse
Or something worse:
But not one goblin skurried after,
Nor was she pricked by fear;
460 The kind heart made her windy-paced
That urged her home quite out of breath with haste
And inward laughter.

She cried, "Laura," up the garden,
"Did you miss me?
465 Come and kiss me.
Never mind my bruises,
Hug me, kiss me, suck my juices
Squeezed from goblin fruits for you,
Goblin pulp and goblin dew.
470 Eat me, drink me, love me;
Laura, make much of me;
For your sake I have braved the glen
And had to do with goblin merchant men."

Laura started from her chair,
475 Flung her arms up in the air,
Clutched her hair:
"Lizzie, Lizzie, have you tasted
For my sake the fruit forbidden?
Must your light like mine be hidden,

Your young life like mine be wasted,   480
Undone in mine undoing,
And ruined in my ruin,
Thirsty, cankered, goblin-ridden?"—
She clung about her sister,
Kissed and kissed and kissed her: 485
Tears once again
Refreshed her shrunken eyes,
Dropping like rain
After long sultry drouth;
Shaking with aguish° fear, and pain,   *feverish* 490
She kissed and kissed her with a hungry mouth.

Her lips began to scorch,
That juice was wormwood to her tongue,
She loathed the feast:
Writhing as one possessed she leaped and sung,   495
Rent all her robe, and wrung
Her hands in lamentable haste,
And beat her breast.
Her locks streamed like the torch
Borne by a racer at full speed,   500
Or like the mane of horses in their flight,
Or like an eagle when she stems the light
Straight toward the sun,
Or like a caged thing freed,
Or like a flying flag when armies run.   505

Swift fire spread through her veins, knocked at her heart,
Met the fire smouldering there
And overbore its lesser flame;
She gorged on bitterness without a name:
Ah! fool, to choose such part   510
Of soul-consuming care!
Sense failed in the mortal strife:
Like the watchtower of a town
Which an earthquake shatters down,
Like a lightning-stricken mast,   515
Like a wind-uprooted tree
Spun about,
Like a foam-topped waterspout

Cast down headlong in the sea,
520 She fell at last;
Pleasure past and anguish past,
Is it death or is it life?

Life out of death.
That night long Lizzie watched by her,
525 Counted her pulse's flagging stir,
Felt for her breath,
Held water to her lips, and cooled her face
With tears and fanning leaves.
But when the first birds chirped about their eaves,
530 And early reapers plodded to the place
Of golden sheaves,
And dew-wet grass
Bowed in the morning winds so brisk to pass,
And new buds with new day
535 Opened of cup-like lilies on the stream,
Laura awoke as from a dream,
Laughed in the innocent old way,
Hugged Lizzie but not twice or thrice;
Her gleaming locks showed not one thread of grey,
540 Her breath was sweet as May,
And light danced in her eyes.

Days, weeks, months, years
Afterwards, when both were wives
With children of their own;
545 Their mother-hearts beset with fears,
Their lives bound up in tender lives;
Laura would call the little ones
And tell them of her early prime,
Those pleasant days long gone
550 Of not-returning time:
Would talk about the haunted glen,
The wicked quaint fruit-merchant men,
Their fruits like honey to the throat
But poison in the blood;
555 (Men sell not such in any town):
Would tell them how her sister stood
In deadly peril to do her good,

And win the fiery antidote:
Then joining hands to little hands
Would bid them cling together,— 560
"For there is no friend like a sister
In calm or stormy weather;
To cheer one on the tedious way,
To fetch one if one goes astray,
To lift one if one totters down, 565
To strengthen whilst one stands."

—1862 (written 1859)

Laurence Housman, illustration from Goblin Market, *1893. A very popular edition of* Goblin Market, *released about three decades after the poem was first published, featured art nouveau illustrations by the writer and artist Laurence Housman.*

Cobwebs

It is a land with neither night nor day,
 Nor heat nor cold, nor any wind, nor rain,
 Nor hills nor valleys; but one even plain
Stretches thro' long unbroken miles away:
5 While thro' the sluggish air a twilight grey
 Broodeth; no moons or seasons wax and wane,
 No ebb and flow are there along the main,°   *open ocean*
 No bud-time no leaf-falling there for aye:°—   *forever*
 No ripple on the sea, no shifting sand,
10 No beat of wings to stir the stagnant space,
 No pulse of life thro' all the loveless land:
And loveless sea; no trace of days before,
 No guarded home, no toil-won resting place
 No future hope, no fear for evermore.

           —1896 (written 1855)

In an Artist's Studio

One face looks out from all his canvasses,
 One selfsame figure sits or walks or leans;
 We found her hidden just behind those screens,
That mirror gave back all her loveliness.
5 A queen in opal or in ruby dress,
 A nameless girl in freshest summer greens,
 A saint, an angel—every canvass means
The same one meaning, neither more nor less.
He feeds upon her face by day and night,
10 And she with true kind eyes looks back on him
Fair as the moon and joyful as the light:
Not wan with waiting, not with sorrow dim;
Not as she is, but was when hope shone bright;
Not as she is, but as she fills his dream.

           —1896 (written 1856)

Thomas Hardy
1840–1928

Novelist, dramatist, essayist, and poet, Thomas Hardy produced a prodigious body of work in the course of his long life. His writing—highly original and yet intimately connected with centuries-old traditions—is as important to the history of the novel in English as it is to that of English poetry, and as central to early twentieth-century literature as it is to that of the Victorian era.

Hardy was born outside Dorchester, surrounded by the south English landscape that would figure prominently in many of his works. Though he began a career as an architect, he left the profession in order to write. In 22 years, he produced 11 novels and 3 collections of short stories, but he turned his energies to poetry in 1895 after his novel *Jude the Obscure* was attacked by critics for its overt sexual content. (The controversy around the novel, ironically, ensured its large readership.)

Hardy's poetic work is rooted in the physical details of place—especially of natural settings—and often contemplates human suffering, disappointment, and the loss of love. He frequently returns to traditional poetic forms, such as the ballad, approaching rhythm and rhyme with precision and sensitivity. In later years, Hardy's critics judged him a superlative writer in both prose and poetry, and he was awarded honorary doctorates, fellowships, and the gold medal of the Royal Society of Literature.

After his death, Hardy's heart was removed and placed in the grave of his first wife, close to the land of his youth. His remains were then buried in Poets' Corner of Westminster Abbey where he was mourned by contemporaries including Rudyard Kipling, W.B. Yeats, and George Bernard Shaw. He was described by the British intellectual Leonard Woolf as "one of the few people who have left upon me the personal impression of greatness."

The Darkling[1] Thrush

I leant upon a coppice gate[2]
    When Frost was spectre-grey,
And Winter's dregs made desolate
    The weakening eye of day.
The tangled bine[3]-stems scored the sky
    Like strings of broken lyres,

5

---

1   *Darkling* In the dark.
2   *coppice gate* Gate leading to a thicket or small forest.
3   *bine* Hop, a climbing plant.

And all mankind that haunted nigh
    Had sought their household fires.

The land's sharp features seemed to be
10   The Century's corpse outleant,[1]
His crypt the cloudy canopy,
    The wind his death-lament.
The ancient pulse of germ and birth
    Was shrunken hard and dry,
15 And every spirit upon earth
    Seemed fervourless as I.

At once a voice arose among
    The bleak twigs overhead
In a full-hearted evensong
20   Of joy illimited;
An aged thrush, frail, gaunt, and small,
    In blast-beruffled plume,
Had chosen thus to fling his soul
    Upon the growing gloom.

25 So little cause for carolings
    Of such ecstatic sound
Was written on terrestrial things
    Afar or nigh around,
That I could think there trembled through
30   His happy good-night air
Some blessed Hope, whereof he knew
    And I was unaware.

—1901 (written 31 December 1900)

---

1   *The Century's corpse outleant* I.e., as if the century were leaning out of its coffin.

The Convergence of the Twain

(Lines on the Loss of the "Titanic"[1])

1

    In a solitude of the sea
    Deep from human vanity,
And the Pride of Life that planned her, stilly couches she.

2

    Steel chambers, late the pyres
    Of her salamandrine fires,[2]
Cold currents thrid,° and turn to rhythmic tidal lyres.   *thread* 5

3

    Over the mirrors meant
    To glass the opulent
The sea-worm crawls—grotesque, slimed, dumb, indifferent.

4

    Jewels in joy designed   10
    To ravish the sensuous mind
Lie lightless, all their sparkles bleared and black and blind.

5

    Dim moon-eyed fishes near
    Gaze at the gilded gear
And query: "What does this vaingloriousness down here?" ...   15

6

    Well: while was fashioning
    This creature of cleaving wing,
The Immanent Will[3] that stirs and urges everything

---

1   *the "Titanic"* At the time the largest ship ever built, the ocean liner *Titanic* had been
    described as unsinkable, but on its maiden voyage in 1912 it collided with an iceberg;
    over 1,400 people drowned when it sank.
2   *salamandrine fires* According to mythology, salamanders are able to survive any heat.
3   *The Immanent Will* The force that pervades and determines human existence.

7

Prepared a sinister mate
20   For her—so gaily great—
A Shape of Ice, for the time far and dissociate.

8

And as the smart ship grew
In stature, grace, and hue,
In shadowy silent distance grew the Iceberg too.

9

25   Alien they seemed to be:
No mortal eye could see
The intimate welding of their later history,

10

Or sign that they were bent
By paths coincident
30 On being anon twin halves of one august event,

11

Till the Spinner of the Years
Said "Now!" And each one hears,
And consummation comes, and jars two hemispheres.

—1914

During Wind and Rain

They sing their dearest songs—
He, she, all of them—yea,
Treble and tenor and bass,
        And one to play;
5   With the candles mooning each face....
        Ah, no; the years O!
How the sick leaves reel down in throngs!

They clear the creeping moss—
Elders and juniors—aye,
10 Making the pathways neat
        And the garden gay;

And they build a shady seat....
    Ah, no; the years, the years;
See, the white storm-birds wing across.

    They are blithely breakfasting all—   15
    Men and maidens—yea,
    Under the summer tree,
        With a glimpse of the bay,
    While pet fowl come to the knee....
        Ah, no; the years O!   20
And the rotten rose is ript from the wall.

    They change to a high new house,
    He, she, all of them—aye,
    Clocks and carpets and chairs
        On the lawn all day,   25
    And brightest things that are theirs....
        Ah, no; the years, the years;
Down their carved names the rain-drop ploughs.

                                    —1917

Gerard Manley Hopkins
1844–1889

Although Gerard Manley Hopkins lived and worked during the Victorian period, his poems were not published until 1919, when they were released by his literary executor and gained him posthumous fame. That some critics treated Hopkins as a modernist poet is not only a matter of this timing; indeed, the close observations and fine descriptions found in his poetry do resemble the singular sensory images of modernist literature. As the reviewer Arthur Clutton-Brock wrote in 1919, Hopkins's "poems are crowded with objects sharply cut, and with sounds no less sharp and clashing."

Hopkins was educated at Oxford, where the poet and cultural critic Matthew Arnold (1822–88) was one of his teachers. In 1866, Hopkins entered the Roman Catholic Church, eventually becoming a Jesuit priest and, later, a professor of classics at University College in Dublin. He burned his early efforts at poetry (imitations of Keats written during the 1860s), but went on to write poems in his own distinctive style—syntactically disjunctive, highly alliterative, and densely rhyming—that often aim to celebrate the spiritual and the divine. His few poetry submissions to journals were rejected; uncertain about the quality of his work, and struggling with the fear that a religious life was incompatible with any attempt at artistic fame, he soon stopped trying to publish his poems.

Much of Hopkins's historical importance as a poet comes from his experimentation with metre and form. He devised a precursor to free verse that he called "sprung rhythm," a style of metre in which only the number of stressed syllables in each line is fixed, while the number of unstressed syllables can vary; Hopkins included frequent stress marks in his own verse to clarify the intended rhythm. He also used invented compound words (such as "piece-bright" and "blue-bleak") to link an object's striking characteristics. Such compounds represent an attempt to convey "inscape," a term Hopkins coined to refer to the dynamic, individual design or essence specific to each object in the world.

God's Grandeur

The world is charged with the grándeur of God.
    It will flame out, like shining from shook foil;[1]

---

1   [Hopkins's note] I mean foil in its sense of leaf or tinsel…. Shaken goldfoil gives off broad glares like sheet lightning and also, and this is true of nothing else, owing to its zigzag dints and creasings and network of small many cornered facets, a sort of fork lightning too.

It gathers to a greatness, like the ooze of oil
Crushed.[1] Why do men then now not reck° his rod?   *regard*
Génerátions have trod, have trod, have trod;   5
   And all is seared with trade; bleared, smeared, with toil;
   And wears man's smudge and shares man's smell: the soil
Is bare now, nor can foot feel, being shod.

Ánd, for° all this, náture is never spent;   *despite*
   There lives the dearest freshness deep down things;   10
And though the last lights off the black West went
   Oh, morning, at the brown brink eastward, springs—
Because the Holy Ghost óver the bent
   World broods with warm breast and with ah! bright wings.

                              —1918 (written 1877)

The Windhover[2]

To Christ Our Lord

I caught this morning morning's minion, king-
   dom of daylight's dauphin,[3] dapple-dáwn-drawn Falcon,
      in his riding
   Of the rólling level úndernéath him steady air, and striding
High there, how he rung upon the rein of a wimpling° wing   *rippling*
In his écstasy! then off, off forth on swing,   5
   As a skate's heel sweeps smooth on a bow-bend: the hurl and gliding
   Rebuffed the bíg wind. My heart in hiding
Stírred for a bird,—the achieve of, the mástery of the thing!

Brute beauty and valour and act, oh, air, pride, plŭme, here
   Buckle! AND the fire that breaks from thee then, a billion   10
Tímes told lovelier, more dangerous, O my chevalier!°   *horseman*

   No wŏnder of it: shéer plód makes plóugh down síllion°   *furrows*
Shíne, and blue-bleak embers, ah my dear,
   Fall, gáll themsélves, and gásh gŏld-vermílion.

                              —1918 (written 1877)

---

1   *oil / Crushed* I.e., as olive oil.
2   *Windhover* Another name for a kestrel, a small falcon that appears to hover in the
    wind.
3   *dauphin* Title of the eldest son of the king of France—the heir.

A.E. Housman
1859–1936

Although he is best remembered as a poet, most of Alfred Edward Housman's life was dedicated to his scholarly work, the translation of classical texts. His definitive edition of Manilius's *Astronomica* represents his greatest achievement in translation, although he also worked on Propertius, Ovid, Juvenal, and other classical authors. Poetry, for Housman, served as an emotional outlet and was something he worked at sporadically. As he once said: "I have seldom written poetry unless I was rather out of health, and the experience, though pleasurable, was generally agitating and exhausting."

Housman published his major poetic work at his own expense in 1896; originally written under the title *The Poems of Terence Hearsay* for the character of a young man that appears in the poems, it was published as *A Shropshire Lad*. The volume, which displays the influence of both English ballads and classical poetry, exhibits nostalgia for earlier times. Although *A Shropshire Lad* did not generate much immediate interest, it became increasingly popular during World War I, perhaps because its themes of loss and early death resonated more strongly in that era. Housman also published *Last Poems* in 1922, and a final collection, *More Poems*, was published posthumously in 1936.

Terence, This Is Stupid Stuff

"Terence, this is stupid stuff:
You eat your victuals fast enough;
There can't be much amiss, 'tis clear,
5   To see the rate you drink your beer.
But oh, good Lord, the verse you make,
It gives a chap the belly-ache.
The cow, the old cow, she is dead;
It sleeps well, the hornèd head:
10   We poor lads, 'tis our turn now
To hear such tunes as killed the cow.
Pretty friendship 'tis to rhyme
Your friends to death before their time
Moping melancholy mad:
15   Come, pipe a tune to dance to, lad."

Why, if 'tis dancing you would be,
There's brisker pipes than poetry.

Say, for what were hop-yards[1] meant,
Or why was Burton built on Trent?[2]
Oh many a peer[3] of England brews   20
Livelier liquor than the Muse,[4]
And malt does more than Milton can
To justify God's ways to man.[5]
Ale, man, ale's the stuff to drink
For fellows whom it hurts to think: 25
Look into the pewter pot°   *mug*
To see the world as the world's not.
And faith, 'tis pleasant till 'tis past:
The mischief is that 'twill not last.
Oh I have been to Ludlow[6] fair   30
And left my necktie God knows where,
And carried half-way home, or near,
Pints and quarts of Ludlow beer:
Then the world seemed none so bad,
And I myself a sterling lad;   35
And down in lovely muck I've lain,
Happy till I woke again.
Then I saw the morning sky:
Heigho, the tale was all a lie;
The world, it was the old world yet,   40
I was I, my things were wet,
And nothing now remained to do
But begin the game anew.

    Therefore, since the world has still
Much good, but much less good than ill,   45
And while the sun and moon endure
Luck's a chance, but trouble's sure,
I'd face it as a wise man would,

---

1   *hop-yards* Areas of land upon which hops are grown.
2   *Burton … Trent* Burton-on-Trent, a town in East Staffordshire, is the historical centre of the British brewing industry. Brewing was first begun there by Benedictine monks in the eleventh century.
3   *peer* Member of the British nobility. Brewers were among those raised to the peerage, and were thus referred to as "beer barons."
4   *Muse* One of nine Greek goddesses of arts and learning; here, the source of poetic inspiration.
5   *Milton … man* See John Milton's *Paradise Lost* (1667), 1.26.
6   *Ludlow* Market town in Shropshire.

And train for ill and not for good.
50 'Tis true the stuff I bring for sale
Is not so brisk a brew as ale:
Out of a stem that scored the hand
I wrung it in a weary land.
But take it: if the smack is sour,
55 The better for the embittered hour;
It should do good to heart and head
When your soul is in my soul's stead;
And I will friend you, if I may,
In the dark and cloudy day.

60   There was a king reigned in the East:
There, when kings will sit to feast,
They get their fill before they think
With poisoned meat and poisoned drink.
He gathered all that springs to birth
65 From the many-venomed earth;
First a little, thence to more,
He sampled all her killing store;
And easy, smiling, seasoned sound,
Sate the king when healths went round.
70 They put arsenic in his meat
And stared aghast to watch him eat;
They poured strychnine in his cup
And shook to see him drink it up:
They shook, they stared as white's their shirt:
75 Them it was their poison hurt.
—I tell the tale that I heard told.
Mithridates, he died old.[1]

—1896

---

1   *There was ... died old* According to Pliny's *Natural History*, Mithridates, king of Pontus
     from approximately 114 to 63 BCE, gradually built up a tolerance to all known poisons
     by ingesting a small amount of each daily, starting in childhood.

W.B. Yeats
1865–1939

William Butler Yeats was born in Sandymount, Dublin, of Anglo-Irish parentage. He spent his early years moving between London and Sligo, a small town in the west of Ireland where his maternal grandparents lived. In London, the family moved in artistic circles that included William Morris, Bernard Shaw, and Oscar Wilde.

His early work is imbued with what he saw as the mystery and beauty of Irish myth and landscape. When Yeats's father saw his son's first poem, he declared that Yeats had "given tongue to the sea-cliffs." The early poems also contain some of the most memorable love poetry in English. In 1899, Yeats was involved in the foundation of the Irish National Theatre; he would become its director and write more than 20 plays that were performed there. But he also continued to write poetry, developing a more dramatic, colloquial, and compact voice. Beginning with the volume *Responsibilities* (1914), he began to explore increasingly complex themes and poetic forms as he sought to give voice to the "blood-dimmed tide" of modern experience.

Yeats was deeply interested in the occult and explored the symbolic worlds of astrology, Theosophism, the tarot, and alchemy. He developed his own system of symbols and conception of history; the poems "Leda and the Swan" and "The Second Coming" are both, for example, influenced by his idea that civilizations are born cyclically, through violent, mystical, and sexual encounters.

Yeats was a formative influence on modern poetry and on the cultural and political history of Ireland; T.S. Eliot described him as "part of the consciousness of an age which cannot be understood without him." Yeats worked all his life to foster an Irish national literature, and in 1923 he was the first writer from Ireland to receive the Nobel Prize.

Easter 1916[1]

I have met them at close of day
Coming with vivid faces
From counter or desk among grey
Eighteenth-century houses.
I have passed with a nod of the head   5
Or polite meaningless words,

---

1   *Easter 1916* On Easter Monday, 24 April 1916, Irish nationalists instigated an unsuccessful rebellion against the British government (which was then at war with Germany); the Easter Rebellion lasted until 29 April. Many of the Irish nationalist leaders were executed that May.

Or have lingered awhile and said
Polite meaningless words,
And thought before I had done
10 Of a mocking tale or a gibe
To please a companion
Around the fire at the club,
Being certain that they and I
But lived where motley° is worn: *jester's costume*
15 All changed, changed utterly:
A terrible beauty is born.

That woman's days were spent
In ignorant good-will,
Her nights in argument
20 Until her voice grew shrill.[1]
What voice more sweet than hers
When, young and beautiful,
She rode to harriers?[2]
This man had kept a school
25 And rode our wingèd horse;[3]
This other his helper and friend[4]
Was coming into his force;
He might have won fame in the end,
So sensitive his nature seemed,
30 So daring and sweet his thought.
This other man I had dreamed
A drunken, vainglorious lout.[5]
He had done most bitter wrong
To some who are near my heart,

1   *That woman's ... shrill*   Countess Markiewicz, née Constance Gore-Booth (1868–1927), played a central role in the Easter Rebellion; she was arrested and sentenced to death (though the death sentence was later commuted). Yeats later wrote a poem about her and her Irish-nationalist sister, "In Memory of Eva Gore-Booth and Con Markiewicz" (1929).

2   *rode to harriers*   Went hunting with hounds.

3   *This man ... wingèd horse*   Pádraic Pearse (1879–1916) founded St. Enda's School near Dublin. He was a leader in the effort to revive the Gaelic language, and wrote both Irish and English poetry; *wingèd horse* Refers to Pegasus, the horse of the Muses.

4   *This other his helper and friend*   Thomas MacDonagh (1878–1916), an Irish poet and playwright who also taught school.

5   *vainglorious lout*   Major John MacBride (1865–1916), estranged husband of Irish nationalist Maud Gonne; their separation just two years after marriage was due in part to his drinking bouts.

Yet I number him in the song;   35
He, too, has resigned his part
In the casual comedy;
He, too, has been changed in his turn,
Transformed utterly:
A terrible beauty is born.   40

Hearts with one purpose alone
Through summer and winter seem
Enchanted to a stone
To trouble the living stream.
The horse that comes from the road,   45
The rider, the birds that range
From cloud to tumbling cloud,
Minute by minute they change;
A shadow of cloud on the stream
Changes minute by minute;   50
A horse-hoof slides on the brim,
And a horse plashes within it;
The long-legged moor-hens dive,
And hens to moor-cocks call;
Minute by minute they live: 55
The stone's in the midst of all.

Too long a sacrifice
Can make a stone of the heart.
O when may it suffice?
That is Heaven's part, our part   60
To murmur name upon name,
As a mother names her child
When sleep at last has come
On limbs that had run wild.
What is it but nightfall?   65
No, no, not night but death;
Was it needless death after all?
For England may keep faith
For all that is done and said.[1]
We know their dream; enough   70
To know they dreamed and are dead;

---

1   *For England … said* England had originally granted Ireland Home Rule in 1913, but
    then postponed it due to World War I, promising to institute it after the war.

And what if excess of love
Bewildered them till they died?
I write it out in a verse—
75 MacDonagh and MacBride
And Connolly and Pearse[1]
Now and in time to be,
Wherever green is worn,
Are changed, changed utterly:
80 A terrible beauty is born.

—1916

The Second Coming[2]

Turning and turning in the widening gyre[3]
The falcon cannot hear the falconer;
Things fall apart; the centre cannot hold;
Mere anarchy is loosed upon the world,
5 The blood-dimmed tide is loosed, and everywhere
The ceremony of innocence is drowned;
The best lack all conviction, while the worst
Are full of passionate intensity.

Surely some revelation is at hand;
10 Surely the Second Coming is at hand.
The Second Coming! Hardly are those words out
When a vast image out of *Spiritus Mundi*[4]
Troubles my sight: somewhere in sands of the desert
A shape with lion body and the head of a man,[5]
15 A gaze blank and pitiless as the sun,
Is moving its slow thighs, while all about it
Reel shadows of the indignant desert birds.
The darkness drops again; but now I know
That twenty centuries of stony sleep

1   *Connolly* James Connolly (1868–1916), Irish socialist; *MacDonagh ... Pearse* All four
    men were executed for their involvement in the Easter Rebellion of 1916.
2   *The Second Coming* The return of Christ, as predicted in the New Testament. See Reve-
    lation 1.7: "Behold, he cometh with clouds; and every eye shall see him."
3   *gyre* Spiral formed from concentric circles.
4   *Spiritus Mundi* Latin: Spirit of the World; universal spirit that houses the images of
    civilization's past memories and provides divine inspiration for the poet. The human
    race is a connected whole in the *spiritus mundi*.
5   *shape ... man* The Egyptian Sphinx.

Were vexed to nightmare by a rocking cradle,[1]   20
And what rough beast, its hour come round at last,
Slouches towards Bethlehem to be born?

—1920

Leda and the Swan[2]

A sudden blow: the great wings beating still
Above the staggering girl, her thighs caressed
By the dark webs, her nape caught in his bill,
He holds her helpless breast upon his breast.

How can those terrified vague fingers push   5
The feathered glory from her loosening thighs?
And how can body, laid in that white rush,
But feel the strange heart beating where it lies?

A shudder in the loins engenders there
The broken wall, the burning roof and tower   10
And Agamemnon dead.[3]
                              Being so caught up,
So mastered by the brute blood of the air,
Did she put on his knowledge with his power
Before the indifferent beak could let her drop?   15

—1924

Sailing to Byzantium[4]

1

That is no country for old men. The young
In one another's arms, birds in the trees

---

1   *rocking cradle* Cradle of the Christ Child.
2   *Leda and the Swan* In Greek mythology, Leda was visited by Zeus in the form of a swan,
    who in some versions of the story seduced her and in other versions raped her. From this
    union she bore two eggs, one becoming the twins Castor and Pollux, the other Helen
    (whose abduction later initiated the Trojan War).
3   *broken wall ... Agamemnon dead* Events of the Trojan War.
4   *Byzantium* Ancient city eventually renamed Constantinople (now Istanbul), capital
    of the Eastern Roman Empire. In *A Vision*, Yeats envisioned Byzantium as a centre for
    artists: "The painter, the mosaic worker, the worker in gold and silver, the illuminator
    of sacred books were almost impersonal, almost perhaps without the consciousness
    of individual design, absorbed in their subject matter and that the vision of a whole
    people."

—Those dying generations—at their song,
The salmon-falls, the mackerel-crowded seas,
5 Fish, flesh, or fowl, commend all summer long
Whatever is begotten, born, and dies.
Caught in that sensual music all neglect
Monuments of unageing intellect.

2

An aged man is but a paltry thing,
10 A tattered coat upon a stick, unless
Soul clap its hands and sing, and louder sing
For every tatter in its mortal dress,
Nor is there singing school but studying
Monuments of its own magnificence;
15 And therefore I have sailed the seas and come
To the holy city of Byzantium.

3

O sages standing in God's holy fire
As in the gold mosaic of a wall,
Come from the holy fire, perne in a gyre,[1]
20 And be the singing-masters of my soul.
Consume my heart away; sick with desire
And fastened to a dying animal
It knows not what it is; and gather me
Into the artifice of eternity.

4

25 Once out of nature I shall never take
My bodily form from any natural thing,
But such a form as Grecian goldsmiths make
Of hammered gold and gold enamelling
To keep a drowsy Emperor awake;
30 Or set upon a golden bough to sing[2]
To lords and ladies of Byzantium
Of what is past, or passing, or to come.

—1927

---

1   *perne in a gyre* Rotate in a spiral; the literal definition of "perne" is "bobbin."
2   [Yeats's note] I have read somewhere that in the Emperor's palace at Byzantium was a
     tree made of gold and silver, and artificial birds that sang.

Paul Laurence Dunbar
1872–1906

Born in Dayton, Ohio, to parents who had both been slaves in the American South, Paul Laurence Dunbar is considered the first African American poet to have been read widely in both white and African American communities. His second book of poetry, *Majors and Minors* (1896), brought him to national attention, particularly because of that collection's "minors," poems composed in African American dialect. (The "majors" were more traditional poems influenced by the Romantic tradition and by Dunbar's contemporaries.) Though Dunbar's traditional poetic works were more numerous, it was the dialect poems that caught the public's imagination—to a degree that troubled both Dunbar and some of his critics.

Though known primarily as a poet, Dunbar worked in a wide variety of genres. In addition to poetry, he founded a newspaper and wrote short stories, novels, song lyrics, a libretto for an operetta, and the lyrics to the first all-black musical on Broadway, *In Dahomey* (1902). Gavin Jones has characterized Dunbar as "a wily manipulator of the conventions, a subtle overturner of racist stereotypes, a sensitive renderer of the multiple facets of Black consciousness at the turn of the twentieth century."

We Wear the Mask

We wear the mask that grins and lies,
It hides our cheeks and shades our eyes,—
This debt we pay to human guile;
With torn and bleeding hearts we smile,
And mouth with myriad subtleties.   5

Why should the world be over-wise,
In counting all our tears and sighs?
Nay, let them only see us, while
    We wear the mask.

We smile, but, O great Christ, our cries   10
To thee from tortured souls arise.
We sing, but oh the clay is vile
Beneath our feet, and long the mile;
But let the world dream otherwise,
    We wear the mask!   15

—1895

Robert Frost

1874–1963

Though Robert Frost's career spanned the modernist period and displays modernist influences, his work is not so easily categorized. Unlike many of his contemporaries, Frost insisted on observing rules of traditional verse—he relied on regular metre and rhyme in crafting his work—and famously said that "writing free verse is like playing tennis with the net down." A merging of traditional form with colloquial speech is the hallmark of Frost's style.

Born in San Francisco in 1874, Frost moved to New England at the age of 11. He began writing poetry while still in high school; he attended both Dartmouth College and Harvard University but never completed a degree. In 1912, Frost and his family relocated to England, a move that would prove to be a turning point in his career. While in London, he published *A Boy's Will* (1913) and *North of Boston* (1914), two full-length collections that earned Frost critical acclaim and attracted the attention of well-known poets such as Ezra Pound. By the time of Frost's return to the United States in 1915, he was established as a serious poet. Over the following decades, his reputation would grow even further with the publication of four Pulitzer Prize-winning collections: *New Hampshire: A Poem with Notes and Grace Notes* (1924), *Collected Poems* (1931), *A Further Range* (1937), and *A Witness Tree* (1943).

When Frost died in 1963, President John F. Kennedy said that the poet's death left "a vacancy in the American spirit." His epitaph reads: "I Had A Lover's Quarrel With The World."

The Road Not Taken

Two roads diverged in a yellow wood,
And sorry I could not travel both
And be one traveller, long I stood
And looked down one as far as I could
5 To where it bent in the undergrowth;

Then took the other, as just as fair,
And having perhaps the better claim,
Because it was grassy and wanted wear;
Though as for that, the passing there
10 Had worn them really about the same,

And both that morning equally lay
In leaves no step had trodden black.
Oh, I kept the first for another day!
Yet knowing how way leads on to way,
I doubted if I should ever come back.   15

I shall be telling this with a sigh
Somewhere ages and ages hence:
Two roads diverged in a wood, and I—
I took the one less travelled by,
And that has made all the difference.   20

—1916

Stopping by Woods on a Snowy Evening

Whose woods these are I think I know.
His house is in the village, though;
He will not see me stopping here
To watch his woods fill up with snow.

My little horse must think it queer   5
To stop without a farmhouse near
Between the woods and frozen lake
The darkest evening of the year.

He gives his harness bells a shake
To ask if there is some mistake.   10
The only other sound's the sweep
Of easy wind and downy flake.

The woods are lovely, dark, and deep,
But I have promises to keep,
And miles to go before I sleep,   15
And miles to go before I sleep.

—1923

Design

I found a dimpled spider, fat and white,
On a white heal-all,[1] holding up a moth
Like a white piece of rigid satin cloth—
Assorted characters of death and blight
5   Mixed ready to begin the morning right,
Like the ingredients of a witches' broth—
A snow-drop spider, a flower like a froth,
And dead wings carried like a paper kite.

What had that flower to do with being white,
10 The wayside blue and innocent heal-all?
What brought the kindred spider to that height,
Then steered the white moth thither in the night?
What but design of darkness to appall?—
If design govern in a thing so small.

—1936

---

1   *heal-all* Wildflower that is usually purple or blue; completely white ones are rare.

Wallace Stevens
1879–1955

■■■■■ "Life," Wallace Stevens wrote, "consists of propositions about life." His work reflects this idea insofar as it examines the relationship between the human understanding of reality—an ever-shifting product of perception and imagination—and reality itself. Although he was strongly influenced by Romanticism's emphases on nature and poetic imagination, Stevens was modernist in his concern with the role of poetry in the spiritually disillusioned world of the twentieth century.

Stevens was born in Pennsylvania and attended Harvard, where he edited the *Harvard Monthly* but left before completing a degree. After a brief and unsatisfying period as a journalist, Stevens became a lawyer. He would spend the rest of his life working in insurance firms, eventually becoming vice president of the Hartford Accident and Indemnity Company. But he also continued to write, and in his thirties he began to publish plays and some of the individual poems that would appear in his first collection, *Harmonium* (1923).

Harmonium contains some of what would become Stevens's best-known work, though its initial critical reception was lukewarm. With later volumes such as *Ideas of Order* (1935) and *The Man with the Blue Guitar* (1937), he attracted more attention, but some critics found his work too abstract and difficult, and he was disparaged for not engaging directly with the political concerns of his time. Stevens received much more profound and favourable recognition, however, toward the end of his career, when he won two National Book Awards: one for *The Auroras of Autumn* (1951), and another for his *Collected Poems* (1954), which was also awarded the Pulitzer Prize.

Thirteen Ways of Looking at a Blackbird

I

Among twenty snowy mountains,
The only moving thing
Was the eye of the blackbird.

II

I was of three minds,
Like a tree
In which there are three blackbirds.

5

III

The blackbird whirled in the autumn winds.
It was a small part of the pantomime.

IV

A man and a woman
10   Are one.
A man and a woman and a blackbird
Are one.

V

I do not know which to prefer,
The beauty of inflections
15   Or the beauty of innuendoes,
The blackbird whistling
Or just after.

VI

Icicles filled the long window
With barbaric glass.
20   The shadow of the blackbird
Crossed it, to and fro.
The mood
Traced in the shadow
An indecipherable cause.

VII

25   O thin men of Haddam,[1]
Why do you imagine golden birds?
Do you not see how the blackbird
Walks around the feet
Of the women about you?

VIII

30   I know noble accents
And lucid, inescapable rhythms;
But I know, too,
That the blackbird is involved
In what I know.

---

1   *Haddam* Town in Connecticut.

IX

When the blackbird flew out of sight,   35
It marked the edge
Of one of many circles.

X

At the sight of blackbirds
Flying in a green light,
Even the bawds° of euphony°   *brothel operators / pleasant sound*   40
Would cry out sharply.

XI

He rode over Connecticut
In a glass coach.
Once, a fear pierced him,
In that he mistook   45
The shadow of his equipage[1]
For blackbirds.

XII

The river is moving.
The blackbird must be flying.

XIII

It was evening all afternoon.   50
It was snowing
And it was going to snow.
The blackbird sat
In the cedar-limbs.

—1917

---

1   *equipage* Horses and carriage.

Anecdote of the Jar

I placed a jar in Tennessee,
And round it was, upon a hill.
It made the slovenly wilderness
Surround that hill.

5   The wilderness rose up to it,
And sprawled around, no longer wild.
The jar was round upon the ground
And tall and of a port in air.

It took dominion everywhere.
10 The jar was grey and bare.
It did not give of bird or bush,
Like nothing else in Tennessee.

—1917

William Carlos Williams
1883–1963

A major poet of the twentieth century, William Carlos Williams was also a working medical doctor who spent most of his life in his birthplace, Rutherford, New Jersey. As a poet, his primary allegiance was to American culture, and he strove to capture quintessentially American ideas and experiences in colloquial language: "not the speech of English country people ... but language modified by ... the American environment." Although he is most remembered for his poetry, it comprised only half of his more than 40 published works, which also included critical prose, short stories, novels, plays, and letters.

Of Williams's many friends in the artistic and literary avant-gardes of New York and Europe, the most significant to his career was undoubtedly fellow poet Ezra Pound, a leader in the imagist movement in which Williams became a major participant. Williams's early style was profoundly shaped by imagism's quest to capture impressions through precise, concentrated language, and this influence remains in the direct and unornamented spirit of his later work. However, he also continued to evolve as a poet, experimenting with form and idiom throughout his career.

Perhaps because of his work's deceptively easy style, critics did not begin to count Williams among the best poets of his era until the last decades of his life. The rise of his reputation began with the publication of the first book of *Paterson* (1946–63), a long poem that explores the city of Paterson (near Rutherford) from diverse angles, in both poetry and prose. Despite failing health, Williams continued writing until his death in 1963, and was posthumously awarded the Pulitzer Prize for his final collection, *Pictures from Brueghel and Other Poems* (1962).

The Red Wheelbarrow

so much depends
upon

a red wheel
barrow

glazed with rain
water

5

beside the white
chickens

—1923

Spring and All

By the road to the contagious hospital
under the surge of the blue
mottled clouds driven from the
northeast—a cold wind. Beyond, the
5 waste of broad, muddy fields
brown with dried weeds, standing and fallen

patches of standing water
the scattering of tall trees

All along the road the reddish
10 purplish, forked, upstanding, twiggy
stuff of bushes and small trees
with dead, brown leaves under them
leafless vines—

Lifeless in appearance, sluggish
15 dazed spring approaches—

They enter the new world naked,
cold, uncertain of all
save that they enter. All about them
the cold, familiar wind—

20 Now the grass, tomorrow
the stiff curl of wildcarrot leaf

One by one objects are defined—
It quickens: clarity, outline of leaf

But now the stark dignity of
25 entrance—Still, the profound change
has come upon them: rooted they
grip down and begin to awaken

—1923

This Is Just to Say

I have eaten
the plums
that were in
the icebox

and which
you were probably   5
saving
for breakfast

Forgive me
they were delicious   10
so sweet
and so cold
                                                        —1934

Landscape with the Fall of Icarus[1]

According to Brueghel
when Icarus fell
it was spring

a farmer was ploughing
his field   5
the whole pageantry

of the year was
awake tingling
near

the edge of the sea   10
concerned
with itself

sweating in the sun
that melted
the wings' wax   15

unsignificantly
off the coast
there was

a splash quite unnoticed
this was   20
Icarus drowning
                                                        —1962

---

1   *Landscape ... of Icarus* Painting (c. 1555) by Pieter Brueghel the Elder based on an ancient Greek story. Wearing wings made by his father Daedalus, Icarus flew too close to the
sun; the wax on the wings melted, and Icarus fell to his death. In Brueghel's painting, an
ordinary farmer ploughing on a hill dominates the foreground, while Icarus's drowning
body appears very small in the ocean below, next to a much larger ship.

Ezra Pound
1885–1972

A modernist poet, editor, and critic, Ezra Pound promoted novelty and formal experimentation in poetry, contributing to the rise of free verse and strongly influencing the development of the twentieth-century literary avant-garde. Pound's early views were unequivocal: "no good poetry is ever written in a manner twenty years old, for to write in such a manner shows conclusively that the writer thinks from books, convention and cliché, and not from life."

Born in Indiana, in 1908 Pound moved to Europe, where he became the centre of a literary circle that included established writers such as W.B. Yeats, as well as talented new writers such as T.S. Eliot and James Joyce, whose work Pound promoted. His first collection of poetry, *Personae* (1909), a mix of traditional and newer forms of expression, was well-received by critics; his next books, however, lost critical favour due to their non-traditional nature.

In 1924 Pound moved to Italy, where he became involved in fascist politics and, during World War II, broadcast fascist and anti-Semitic propaganda for the Italian government. During the American occupation of Italy, he was arrested for treason and imprisoned in a US military camp, where he suffered a mental breakdown; declared unfit for trial, he spent the following decade in an American psychiatric hospital. Despite the controversy surrounding his politics, Pound was awarded the Bollingen Prize in 1948 for his *Pisan Cantos* (1924–48), a self-contained section of his major work, the unfinished long poem *The Cantos* (1917–69).

Pound was a leading force behind the poetic movement known as imagism. Partly drawn from tenets of classical Chinese and Japanese poetry—of which Pound was a translator—imagism departs from the elaborate style and regular metre of Victorian poetry, instead advocating the clear, precise, and economical use of language for what Pound called "the direct treatment of the 'thing'."

The River-Merchant's Wife: A Letter[1]

While my hair was still cut straight across my forehead
I played about the front gate, pulling flowers.
You came by on bamboo stilts, playing horse,
You walked about my seat, playing with blue plums.
5   And we went on living in the village of Chōkan:[2]
Two small people, without dislike or suspicion.

---

1   *The River-Merchant's ... Letter* Pound's adaptation of a poem by the Chinese poet Li Po (701–62 CE), whose name is given in its Japanese form ("Rihaku") at the end of the poem.
2   *Chōkan* Suburb of Nanking.

At fourteen I married My Lord you.
I never laughed, being bashful.
Lowering my head, I looked at the wall.
Called to, a thousand times, I never looked back.   10

At fifteen I stopped scowling,
I desired my dust to be mingled with yours
Forever and forever and forever.
Why should I climb the look out?

At sixteen you departed,   15
You went into far Ku-tō-en,[1] by the river of swirling eddies,
And you have been gone five months.
The monkeys make sorrowful noise overhead.

You dragged your feet when you went out.
By the gate now, the moss is grown, the different mosses,   20
Too deep to clear them away!
The leaves fall early this autumn, in wind.
The paired butterflies are already yellow with August
Over the grass in the West garden;
They hurt me. I grow older.   25
If you are coming down through the narrows of the river Kiang,
Please let me know beforehand,
And I will come out to meet you
          As far as Chō-fū-Sa.[2]

                                        Rihaku
                                        —1915

In a Station of the Metro

The apparition of these faces in the crowd;
Petals on a wet, black bough.

                    —1916 (earlier version published 1913)

---

1   *Ku-tō-en* Chang Jiang, a Chinese river, also called the Yangtze Kiang in Japanese.
2   *Chō-fū-Sa* Chang-feng Sha, a beach located in Anhui several hundred miles upriver.

Marianne Moore

1887–1972

Born in Kirkwood, Missouri, Marianne Moore was raised by her mother in the home of her grandfather, a Presbyterian pastor. Her family moved to Pennsylvania, where she received her BA from Bryn Mawr College and subsequently became a teacher at a boarding school for Native American children. In 1918, she moved with her mother to New York City, where she was soon noticed in literary circles. Some of her work was published in the journal *Dial*, which she eventually edited from 1925 until 1929.

Moore is known for poems grounded in the observation of nature, and for her deft experimentation with form and metre. She is also famous for revising her work long after publication; for instance, "Poetry," 29 lines long in 1921, is reduced to three lines in the final version published in 1967. Moore's revisions have not always been well-received, but her modest attitude toward writing suggests her rationale for revisiting works: "I'm a happy hack as a writer.... I never knew anyone with a passion for words who had as much difficulty in saying things as I do. I seldom say them in a manner I like."

Moore's *Collected Poems* (1951) was awarded the National Book Award, the Pulitzer Prize, and the Bollingen Prize. The poet James Dickey has written in praise of her style that "every poem of hers lifts us towards our own discovery-prone lives. It does not state, in effect, that I am more intelligent than you, more creative because I found this item and used it and you didn't. It seems to say, rather, I found this, and what did you find? Or, a better, what can you find?"

Poetry

I, too, dislike it: there are things that are important beyond all this fiddle.
    Reading it, however, with a perfect contempt for it, one discovers in
    it after all, a place for the genuine.
        Hands that can grasp, eyes
5   that can dilate, hair that can rise
            if it must, these things are important not because a

high-sounding interpretation can be put upon them but because they are
    useful. When they become so derivative as to become unintelligible,
    the same thing may be said for all of us, that we
10   do not admire what
        we cannot understand: the bat
            holding on upside down or in quest of something to

eat, elephants pushing, a wild horse taking a roll, a tireless wolf under
   a tree, the immovable critic twitching his skin like a horse that feels
      a flea, the base-
    ball fan, the statistician—   15
      nor is it valid
         to discriminate against "business documents and

schoolbooks":[1] all these phenomena are important. One must make
    a distinction
   however: when dragged into prominence by half poets, the result
      is not poetry,
  nor till the poets among us can be   20
    "literalists of
    the imagination"[2]—above
      insolence and triviality and can present

for inspection, "imaginary gardens with real toads in them,"[3] shall we have
   it. In the meantime, if you demand on the one hand,   25
  the raw material of poetry in
    all its rawness and
    that which is on the other hand
      genuine, then you are interested in poetry.

                                —1921

Poetry (Revised version)

I, too, dislike it.
   Reading it, however, with a perfect contempt for it, one discovers in
   it, after all, a place for the genuine.

                                —1967

---

1   *business documents and schoolbooks* Moore's note quotes from the *Diaries of Tolstoy* (1917), in which Tolstoy considers the boundary between poetry and prose: "Poetry is verse: prose is not verse. Or else poetry is everything with the exception of business documents and schoolbooks."
2   *literalists of the imagination* In *Ideas of Good and Evil* (1903), W.B. Yeats calls William Blake "a too literal realist of imagination as others are of nature."
3   *imaginary gardens ... in them* No source has been found for this phrase; despite the quotation marks, it is generally thought to be Moore's.

T.S. Eliot
1888–1965

No twentieth-century writer did more to shape the direction of modern poetry and criticism than T.S. Eliot. In poems such as "The Love Song of J. Alfred Prufrock" (1915) and *The Waste Land* (1922), Eliot founded a radical new poetical idiom to express the alienation and the "chaotic, irregular, fragmentary" experience of the modern mind, which he considered disconnected from any meaningful sense of tradition. Eliot's many essays and reviews, notably "Tradition and the Individual Talent" (1919) and "The Metaphysical Poets" (1921), were scarcely less influential. Such writings not only provided a theoretical foundation for New Criticism, one of the most prominent critical schools of the early to mid-twentieth century; they also introduced new terms and concepts—"objective correlative," "the dissociation of sensibility," the ideal development of the poet as a "continual extinction of personality"—that have enriched the study of modern literature, not least by illuminating Eliot's own complex poetics.

Eliot's poetry is challenging, but in his reckoning it could hardly be otherwise, for he believed that "poets in our civilization, as it exists at present, must be *difficult*. Our civilization comprehends great variety and complexity, and this variety and complexity, playing upon a refined sensibility, must produce various and complex results." Among the most striking of these results is the absence—particularly in his early poetry—of fluid transitions: images are precise but often jarring and incongruous, arrestingly juxtaposed to suggest broader patterns of meaning. At once colloquial and erudite, fragmentary and unified, much of Eliot's poetry relies on ironies, tensions, and paradoxes. These qualities are ideally suited to the rigorous methodology of close reading championed by the New Critics, who focused not on the mind of the poet or the external conditions of the text's creation but on the details of the text itself.

Eliot's thought and technique evolved over his career, particularly following his conversion to Anglo-Catholicism, when—as in "Journey of the Magi" (1927) and *Four Quartets* (1943)—he began to explore more religious themes. Although his poetic output was relatively modest, his body of work occupies the very centre of literary modernism. As Northrop Frye remarked, "a thorough knowledge of Eliot is compulsory for anyone interested in contemporary literature. Whether he is liked or disliked is of no importance, but he must be read."

The Love Song of J. Alfred Prufrock[1]

S'io credesse che mia risposta fosse
A persona che mai tornasse al mondo,
Questa fiamma staria senza piu scosse.
Ma perciocche giammai di questo fondo
Non torno viva alcun, s'i'odo il vero,   5
Senza tema d'infamia ti rispondo.[2]

Let us go then, you and I,
When the evening is spread out against the sky
Like a patient etherized upon a table;
Let us go, through certain half-deserted streets,   10
The muttering retreats
Of restless nights in one-night cheap hotels
And sawdust restaurants with oyster-shells:
Streets that follow like a tedious argument
Of insidious intent   15
To lead you to an overwhelming question …
Oh, do not ask, "What is it?"
Let us go and make our visit.

In the room the women come and go
Talking of Michelangelo.   20

The yellow fog that rubs its back upon the window-panes,
The yellow smoke that rubs its muzzle on the window-panes
Licked its tongue into the corners of the evening,
Lingered upon the pools that stand in drains,
Let fall upon its back the soot that falls from chimneys,   25
Slipped by the terrace, made a sudden leap,
And seeing that it was a soft October night,
Curled once about the house, and fell asleep.

And indeed there will be time
For the yellow smoke that slides along the street,   30

---

1   *J. Alfred Prufrock* The name is likely taken from the The Prufrock-Littau Company, a
     furniture dealer located in St. Louis, Eliot's birthplace.
2   *S'io credesse … ti rispondo* Italian: "If I thought that my reply were given to anyone who
     might return to the world, this flame would stand forever still; but since never from this
     deep place has anyone ever returned alive, if what I hear is true, without fear of infamy
     I answer thee," Dante's *Inferno* 27.61–66; Guido da Montefeltro's speech as he burns in
     Hell.

Rubbing its back upon the window panes;
There will be time, there will be time[1]
To prepare a face to meet the faces that you meet
There will be time to murder and create,
35 And time for all the works and days[2] of hands
That lift and drop a question on your plate;
Time for you and time for me,
And time yet for a hundred indecisions,
And for a hundred visions and revisions,
40 Before the taking of a toast and tea.

In the room the women come and go
Talking of Michelangelo.

And indeed there will be time
To wonder, "Do I dare?" and, "Do I dare?"
45 Time to turn back and descend the stair,
With a bald spot in the middle of my hair—
(They will say: "How his hair is growing thin!")
My morning coat,[3] my collar mounting firmly to the chin,
My necktie rich and modest, but asserted by a simple pin—
50 (They will say: "But how his arms and legs are thin!")
Do I dare
Disturb the universe?
In a minute there is time
For decisions and revisions which a minute will reverse.

55 For I have known them all already, known them all—
Have known the evenings, mornings, afternoons,
I have measured out my life with coffee spoons;
I know the voices dying with a dying fall[4]
Beneath the music from a farther room.
60   So how should I presume?

And I have known the eyes already, known them all—
The eyes that fix you in a formulated phrase,

1   *there will be time* See Ecclesiastes 3.1–8. "To everything there is a season, and a time to
     every purpose under heaven: A time to be born, and a time to die; a time to plant, and
     a time to pluck up that which is planted; a time to kill, and a time to heal...."
2   *works and days* Title of a poem by eighth-century BCE Greek poet Hesiod.
3   *morning coat* Formal coat with tails.
4   *with a dying fall* In Shakespeare's *Twelfth Night* 1.1.1–15 Duke Orsino commands,
     "That strain again, it had a dying fall."

And when I am formulated, sprawling on a pin,
When I am pinned and wriggling on the wall,
Then how should I begin   65
To spit out all the butt-ends of my days and ways?
    And how should I presume?

And I have known the arms already, known them all—
Arms that are braceleted and white and bare
(But in the lamplight, downed with light brown hair!)   70
Is it perfume from a dress
That makes me so digress?
Arms that lie along a table, or wrap about a shawl.
    And should I then presume?
    And how should I begin?   75

      *   *   *

Shall I say, I have gone at dusk through narrow streets
And watched the smoke that rises from the pipes
Of lonely men in shirt-sleeves, leaning out of windows? ...[1]

I should have been a pair of ragged claws
Scuttling across the floors of silent seas.[2]   80

      *   *   *

And the afternoon, the evening, sleeps so peacefully!
Smoothed by long fingers,
Asleep ... tired ... or it malingers,
Stretched on the floor, here beside you and me.
Should I, after tea and cakes and ices,   85
Have the strength to force the moment to its crisis?
But though I have wept and fasted, wept and prayed,
Though I have seen my head (grown slightly bald) brought in
    upon a platter,[3]
I am no prophet[4]—and here's no great matter;

---

1   ... The ellipsis here makes note of a 38 line insertion written by Eliot, entitled *Pru-frock's Pervigilium*. The subtitle and 33 of the lines were later removed.

2   *I should ... seas* See Shakespeare's *Hamlet* 2.2, in which Hamlet tells Polonius, "for you yourself, sir, should be old as I am, if like a crab you could go backwards."

3   *brought in upon a platter* Reference to Matthew 14.1–12, in which the prophet John the Baptist is beheaded at the command of Herod, and his head presented to Salomé upon a platter.

4   *I am no prophet* See Amos 7.14. When commanded by King Amiziah not to proph-esize, the Judean Amos answered; "I was no prophet, neither was I a prophet's son; but I was a herdsman, and a farmer of sycamore fruit."

90 I have seen the moment of my greatness flicker,
And I have seen the eternal Footman hold my coat, and snicker,
And in short, I was afraid.

And would it have been worth it, after all,
After the cups, the marmalade, the tea,
95 Among the porcelain, among some talk of you and me,
Would it have been worth while,
To have bitten off the matter with a smile,
To have squeezed the universe into a ball[1]
To roll it toward some overwhelming question,
100 To say: "I am Lazarus,[2] come from the dead,
Come back to tell you all, I shall tell you all"—
If one, settling a pillow by her head,
    Should say: "That is not what I meant at all;
    That is not it, at all."

105 And would it have been worth it, after all,
Would it have been worth while,
After the sunsets and the dooryards and the sprinkled streets,[3]
After the novels, after the teacups, after the skirts that trail along
    the floor—
And this, and so much more?—
110 It is impossible to say just what I mean!
But as if a magic lantern[4] threw the nerves in patterns on a screen:
Would it have been worth while
If one, settling a pillow or throwing off a shawl,
And turning toward the window, should say:
115   "That is not it at all,
    That is not what I meant, at all."

    *   *   *

No! I am not Prince Hamlet, nor was meant to be;
Am an attendant lord, one that will do
To swell a progress,[5] start a scene or two,
120 Advise the prince; no doubt, an easy tool,

---

1   *squeezed … ball* See Andrew Marvell's "To His Coy Mistress," 41–42: "Let us roll our strength and all / Our sweetness up into one ball."
2   *Lazarus* Raised from the dead by Jesus in John 11.1–44.
3   *sprinkled streets* Streets sprayed with water to keep dust down.
4   *magic lantern* In Victorian times, a device used to project images painted on glass onto a blank screen or wall.
5   *progress* Journey made by royalty through the country.

Deferential, glad to be of use,
Politic, cautious, and meticulous;
Full of high sentence,[1] but a bit obtuse;
At times, indeed, almost ridiculous—
Almost, at times, the Fool.   125

I grow old ... I grow old ...
I shall wear the bottoms of my trousers rolled.

Shall I part my hair behind? Do I dare to eat a peach?
I shall wear white flannel trousers, and walk upon the beach.
I have heard the mermaids singing,[2] each to each.   130

I do not think that they will sing to me.

I have seen them riding seaward on the waves
Combing the white hair of the waves blown back
When the wind blows the water white and black.

We have lingered in the chambers of the sea   135
By sea-girls wreathed with seaweed red and brown
Till human voices wake us, and we drown.

—1915, 1917

Journey of the Magi[3]

"A cold coming we had of it,
Just the worst time of the year
For a journey, and such a long journey:
The ways deep and the weather sharp,
The very dead of winter."[4]   5
And the camels galled, sore-footed, refractory,
Lying down in the melting snow.
There were times we regretted
The summer palaces on slopes, the terraces,
And the silken girls bringing sherbet.   10

---

1   *high sentence* Serious, elevated sentiments or opinions.
2   *I have ... singing* See John Donne's "Song": "Teach me to hear the mermaids singing."
3   *Magi* Three wise men who journeyed to Bethlehem to honour Jesus at his birth (see
     Matthew 2.1–12).
4   *A cold ... winter* Adapted from a sermon given by Anglican preacher Lancelot Andrews
     on Christmas Day, 1622.

Then the camel men cursing and grumbling
And running away, and wanting their liquor and women,
And the night-fires going out, and the lack of shelters,
And the cities hostile and the towns unfriendly
15 And the villages dirty and charging high prices:
A hard time we had of it.
At the end we preferred to travel all night,
Sleeping in snatches,
With the voices singing in our ears, saying
20 That this was all folly.

Then at dawn we came down to a temperate valley,
Wet, below the snow line, smelling of vegetation;
With a running stream and a water-mill beating the darkness,
And three trees[1] on the low sky,
25 And an old white horse[2] galloped away in the meadow.
Then we came to a tavern with vine-leaves over the lintel,°   *doorframe*
Six hands at an open door dicing for pieces of silver,[3]
And feet kicking the empty wine-skins.
But there was no information, and so we continued
30 And arrived at evening, not a moment too soon
Finding the place; it was (you may say) satisfactory.

All this was a long time ago, I remember,
And I would do it again, but set down
This set down
35 This: were we led all that way for
Birth or Death? There was a Birth, certainly,
We had evidence and no doubt. I had seen birth and death,
But had thought they were different; this Birth was
Hard and bitter agony for us, like Death, our death.
40 We returned to our places, these Kingdoms,
But no longer at ease here, in the old dispensation,
With an alien people clutching their gods.
I should be glad of another death.

—1927

---

1   *three trees* Suggests the three crosses on Calvary, on which Christ and two criminals
     were crucified (see Luke 23.32–43).
2   *white horse* Ridden by Christ in Revelation 6.2 and 19.11–14.
3   *dicing … silver* Allusion to Judas's betrayal of Jesus for 30 pieces of silver, and to the
     soldiers who played dice for the robes of Christ at his crucifixion (Matthew 26.14 and
     27.35).

Edna St. Vincent Millay

1892–1950

Edna St. Vincent Millay wrote the iconic line "My candle burns at both ends" in her poem "First Fig" (1920)—a poem that inspired the imaginations of an emerging generation of sexually liberated American women. This American poet and playwright embodied the spirit of romantic rebellion characteristic of the 1920s and, throughout her career, remained a powerful presence in American public consciousness.

Millay demonstrated a talent for writing poetry at an early age, her first published poem appearing in a children's magazine when she was 14. Following her graduation from Vassar College, Millay published her first book, *Renascence and Other Poems* (1917), and moved to Greenwich Village in New York. Over the next few years her growing reputation as a poet was matched by her reputation as a freethinker in the realm of sexual politics. Two of her most significant verse collections date from this period: *A Few Figs from Thistles* (1920) and *The Harp-Weaver and Other Poems* (1923), which won the Pulitzer Prize for poetry.

Although Millay's fame was earned primarily during the early years of her career, she remained active and innovative well into the 1940s, and her work became more politically and emotionally intense. The 52 sonnets in her collection *Fatal Interview* (1931) were widely admired for their mastery of the form; the sequence draws on centuries of poetic tradition, but was reviewed as expressing "the thoughts of a new age."

[I, being born a woman and distressed]

I, being born a woman and distressed
By all the needs and notions of my kind,
Am urged by your propinquity° to find   *proximity*
Your person fair, and feel a certain zest
To bear your body's weight upon my breast: 5
So subtly is the fume of life designed,
To clarify the pulse and cloud the mind,
And leave me once again undone, possessed.
Think not for this, however, the poor treason
Of my stout blood against my staggering brain,   10
I shall remember you with love, or season
My scorn with pity,—let me make it plain:
I find this frenzy insufficient reason
For conversation when we meet again.

—1923

[What lips my lips have kissed, and where, and why]

What lips my lips have kissed, and where, and why,
I have forgotten, and what arms have lain
Under my head till morning; but the rain
Is full of ghosts tonight, that tap and sigh
5 Upon the glass and listen for reply,
And in my heart there stirs a quiet pain
For unremembered lads that not again
Will turn to me at midnight with a cry.
Thus in winter stands the lonely tree,
10 Nor knows what birds have vanished one by one,
Yet knows its boughs more silent than before:
I cannot say what loves have come and gone;
I only know that summer sang in me
A little while, that in me sings no more.

—1923

Wilfred Owen
1893–1918

One of 16 World War I poets commemorated in Westminster Abbey's Poet's Corner, Wilfred Owen is best remembered for poems such as "Anthem for Doomed Youth" and "Dulce et Decorum Est" (1920), in which he offers searing indictments of those who would send young men to war.

Owen began to experiment with poetry as a teenager. He spent the years prior to the war working as a lay assistant to the vicar of Dunsden, and later as a private tutor in Bordeaux, France. In 1915, he enlisted in the army and was commissioned as second lieutenant in the Manchester Regiment. The trauma he experienced on the front haunted Owen, who once spent days trapped in a dugout with the remains of a fellow officer. Diagnosed with shell shock in 1917, the poet was sent to recuperate at Craiglockhart War Hospital near Edinburgh. His biographer Jon Stallworthy suggests that the nightmares that are a symptom of shellshock were "a principal factor in the liberation and organization of [Owen's work....] The realities of battle, banished from his waking mind, [...] erupt into his dreams and into his poems."

At the War Hospital, he met fellow patient and recently published poet Siegfried Sassoon, who became a mentor to Owen. Up to this point, Owen's style had reflected his admiration of Romantic poets such as John Keats and Percy Shelley, but with Sassoon's encouragement, he abandoned Romantic poetics for a colloquial style similar to Sassoon's. Almost all of his best-known work was composed in the year before he was discharged from the War Hospital and sent back to France in August 1918.

Owen was killed in action one week before the end of the war.

Anthem for Doomed Youth

What passing-bells for these who die as cattle?
Only the monstrous anger of the guns.
Only the stuttering rifles' rapid rattle
Can patter out their hasty orisons.°   *prayers*
No mockeries for them from prayers or bells,   5
Nor any voice of mourning save the choirs,—
The shrill, demented choirs of wailing shells;
And bugles calling for them from sad shires.

What candles may be held to speed them all?
Not in the hands of boys, but in their eyes   10
Shall shine the holy glimmers of good-byes.

The pallor of girls' brows shall be their pall;[1]
Their flowers the tenderness of silent minds,
And each slow dusk a drawing-down of blinds.

—1920

Dulce et Decorum Est[2]

Bent double, like old beggars under sacks,
Knock-kneed, coughing like hags, we cursed through sludge,
Till on the haunting flares we turned our backs,
And towards our distant rest began to trudge.
5 Men marched asleep. Many had lost their boots,
But limped on, blood-shod. All went lame, all blind;
Drunk with fatigue; deaf even to the hoots
Of gas-shells dropping softly behind.
Gas! GAS! Quick, boys!—An ecstasy of fumbling,
10 Fitting the clumsy helmets just in time,
But someone still was yelling out and stumbling
And flound'ring like a man in fire or lime—
Dim, through the misty panes[3] and thick green light,
As under a green sea, I saw him drowning.

15 In all my dreams before my helpless sight
He plunges at me, guttering, choking, drowning.

If in some smothering dreams, you too could pace
Behind the wagon that we flung him in,
And watch the white eyes writhing in his face,
20 His hanging face, like a devil's sick of sin;
If you could hear, at every jolt, the blood
Come gargling from the froth-corrupted lungs,
Bitter as the cud
Of vile, incurable sores on innocent tongues,—
25 My friend, you would not tell with such high zest
To children ardent for some desperate glory,
The old Lie: Dulce et decorum est
Pro patria mori.

—1920

---

1   *pall* Cloth spread over a coffin, hearse, or tomb.
2   *Dulce et Decorum Est* Owen's poem takes its title from a famous line from the Roman
     poet Horace's *Odes* (3.2): "*Dulce et decorum est pro patria mori*" (Latin: "Sweet and fitting
     it is to die for one's country").
3   *panes* Visors of gas masks.

E.E. Cummings
1894–1962

Edward Estlin Cummings is best known for his avant-garde poetry, in which he experiments with syntax, grammar, and punctuation. Cummings's work found an unusually large popular audience; according to poet and critic Randall Jarrell, "No one else has ever made avant-garde, experimental poems so attractive to the general and the specific reader."

Cummings grew up in an intellectual home in Cambridge, Massachusetts, and attended Harvard University, where several of his poems were published in the anthology *Eight Harvard Poets* (1917). Upon graduating from university during World War I, Cummings went to France to be an ambulance driver, but instead was put into an internment camp for "suspicious" foreigners. He fictionalized this experience in the prose work *The Enormous Room* (1922), which was much admired by other young writers.

This was followed in 1923 by his first book of poetry, *Tulips and Chimneys*, showcasing his facility with typographical experimentation and invented language. The characteristic poem "[In Just-]," for example, describes a children's world using vibrant and playful terms such as "mud- / luscious," "balloonMan," and "puddle-wonderful." Cummings continued to write prolifically for the next several decades, producing 15 books of poems ranging from lyrical love poetry to cynical criticism of the modern world.

In 1931, Cummings visited the Soviet Union. He had been hoping to find that communism had created an ideal society, but was disillusioned by his experience, and wrote a travelogue, *Eimi* (1933), strongly critical of the Soviet regime.

[in Just-]

in Just-
spring   when the world is mud-
luscious the little
lame balloonman

whistles   far   and wee

and eddieandbill come
running from marbles and
piracies and it's
spring

5

10   when the world is puddle-wonderful

the queer
old balloonman whistles
far   and   wee
and bettyandisbel come dancing

15   from hop-scotch and jump-rope and

it's
spring
and

          the

20   goat-footed

balloonMan   whistles
far
and
wee

—1923

[(ponder,darling,these busted statues]

(ponder,darling,these busted statues
of yon motheaten forum[1] be aware
notice what hath remained
—the stone cringes
5   clinging to the stone,how obsolete

lips utter their extant smile . . . .
remark

a few deleted of texture
or meaning monuments and dolls

10   resist Them Greediest Paws of careful
time all of which is extremely
unimportant)whereas Life

matters if or

when the your-and my-
15   idle vertical worthless

---

1   *forum* Public space in an ancient Roman city.

self unite in a peculiarly
momentary

partnership(to instigate
constructive
              Horizontal   20
business . . . . even so,let us make haste
—consider well this ruined aqueduct

lady,
which used to lead something into somewhere)

                                      —1926

[somewhere i have never travelled,gladly beyond]

somewhere i have never travelled,gladly beyond
any experience,your eyes have their silence:
in your most frail gesture are things which enclose me,
or which i cannot touch because they are too near

your slightest look easily will unclose me   5
though i have closed myself as fingers,
you open always petal by petal myself as Spring opens
(touching skilfully,mysteriously)her first rose

or if your wish be to close me,i and
my life will shut very beautifully,suddenly,   10
as when the heart of this flower imagines
the snow carefully everywhere descending;

nothing which we are to perceive in this world equals
the power of your intense fragility:whose texture
compels me with the colour of its countries,   15
rendering death and forever with each breathing

(i do not know what it is about you that closes
and opens;only something in me understands
the voice of your eyes is deeper than all roses)
nobody,not even the rain,has such small hands   20

                                      —1931

anyone lived in a pretty how town

anyone lived in a pretty how town
(with up so floating many bells down)
spring summer autumn winter
he sang his didn't he danced his did.

5 Women and men(both little and small)
cared for anyone not at all
they sowed their isn't they reaped their same
sun moon stars rain

children guessed(but only a few
10 and down they forgot as up they grew
autumn winter spring summer)
that noone loved him more by more

when by now and tree by leaf
she laughed his joy she cried his grief
15 bird by snow and stir by still
anyone's any was all to her

someones married their everyones
laughed their cryings and did their dance
(sleep wake hope and then)they
20 said their nevers they slept their dream

stars rain sun moon
(and only the snow can begin to explain
how children are apt to forget to remember
with up so floating many bells down)

25 one day anyone died i guess
(and noone stooped to kiss his face)
busy folk buried them side by side
little by little and was by was

all by all and deep by deep
30 and more by more they dream their sleep
noone and anyone earth by april
wish by spirit and if by yes.

Women and men(both dong and ding)
summer autumn winter spring
reaped their sowing and went their came   35
sun moon stars rain

                                                                —1940

[l(a]

l(a

le
af
fa

ll   5

s)
one
l

iness

                                                                —1958

Langston Hughes
1902–1967

In his first autobiography, *The Big Sea* (1940), Langston Hughes wrote, "my best poems were all written when I felt the worst. When I was happy, I didn't write anything." His career produced many lyric poems that have the sadness but also the vitality of jazz, blues, and bebop, and that participate in an African American tradition of struggle for positive social change. Hughes contributed to American letters not only as a poet but also as a playwright, journalist, short story writer, novelist, historian, and translator.

In the early 1920s Hughes worked odd jobs—including a stint on an American freighter travelling the African coastline—as he began to publish his work in magazines. His first poetry collection, *Weary Blues* (1926), established him as a major figure in the Harlem Renaissance, a movement of African American writers, artists, and musicians that flourished in the 1920s and 1930s. Even more than some of his Harlem Renaissance contemporaries, Hughes celebrated black working-class culture and experience in his writing.

Hughes became a Marxist in the 1930s, and he spent time in Haiti, Cuba, and the USSR learning about alternatives to American politics and economics. He also began to address contemporary urban politics more directly in his work, pronouncing his faith in Marxism in poems such as "Goodbye Christ" (1932): "And nobody's gonna sell ME / To a king, or a general, / Or a millionaire." Hughes abandoned communism after World War II but continued to write on political themes; his last work, for example, *The Panther and the Lash* (1967), was a collection of poetry focused on the civil rights movement.

The Negro Speaks of Rivers

(To W.E.B. Du Bois)[1]

I've known rivers:
I've known rivers ancient as the world and older than the flow of human
    blood in human veins.
My soul has grown deep like the rivers.

---

1   *W.E.B. Du Bois* American activist (1868–1963) and one of the founders of the NAACP
    (National Association for the Advancement of Colored People).

I bathed in the Euphrates when dawns were young. 5
I built my hut near the Congo and it lulled me to sleep.
I looked upon the Nile and raised the pyramids above it.
I heard the singing of the Mississippi when Abe Lincoln went down
     to New Orleans,[1] and I've seen its muddy bosom turn all golden
     in the sunset.

I've known rivers:
Ancient, dusky rivers. 10

My soul has grown deep like the rivers.

                             —1926

Harlem (2)

What happens to a dream deferred?

    Does it dry up
    like a raisin in the sun?
    Or fester like a sore—
    And then run?
    Does it stink like rotten meat? 5
    Or crust and sugar over—
    like a syrupy sweet?
    Maybe it just sags
    like a heavy load. 10

    Or does it explode?

                             —1951

---

1   *when Abe … New Orleans* In 1831, Lincoln travelled down the Mississippi to New Orleans, where he witnessed the brutality of the slave market there. Some biographers suggest that this experience consolidated his opinion against slavery.

Stevie Smith

1902–1971

Stevie Smith's poetry is deceptively simple. Its plain language, playful rhymes, odd syntax, and repetitive, singsong rhythms convey a child-like sensibility—one accentuated by the bizarre "doodles" of men, women, and animals that she included with her writing. Beneath her poetry's light-hearted and humorous surface, however, is a serious engagement with such concepts as loneliness, religion, suicide, and death. As poet Peter Porter suggests, Smith was not the "naive writer" she appeared to be; on the contrary, "her unshockable eye and brilliant ear enabled her to cover almost all the unmentionable topics."

Smith lived most of her life in London, where she worked as a secretary. Her first published work was a novel entitled *Novel on Yellow Paper* (1936); its commercial success enabled her to publish her first volume of poems, *A Good Time Was Had By All* (1937). Smith would go on to write seven more poetry collections, as well as short stories, essays, literary reviews, and two more novels.

Skilled at performing her own verse, Smith was a popular figure at poetry readings in the 1960s. Although she had a large and admiring readership, for most of her career she did not receive a great deal of approval from critics, who were put off by the atypical, apparently frivolous tone of her work. However, she had gained respect as a serious poet by the time her *Selected Poems* was published in 1962, and in the last years of her life she received the Queen's Gold Medal for Poetry (1969).

Not Waving but Drowning

Nobody heard him, the dead man,
But still he lay moaning:
I was much further out than you thought
And not waving but drowning.

5 Poor chap, he always loved larking
And now he's dead
It must have been too cold for him his heart gave way,
They said.

Oh, no no no, it was too cold always
10 (Still the dead one lay moaning)
I was much too far out all my life
And not waving but drowning.

—1957

Earle Birney

1904–1995

A mountain climber, travel writer, and political activist as well as an important Canadian poet, Earle Birney was as adventurous in his work as he was in his life. He experimented with compound nouns (e.g., "seajet"), syntax and sound, and unconventional punctuation, and he frequently changed his style during his long career. As the critic George Woodcock writes, Birney possessed an "openness to the new and the unorthodox" that enabled him to create "the special voice and form appropriate to each situation."

Raised in Alberta and British Columbia, Birney attended university in Vancouver and Toronto; he lived for brief periods in England and in Utah before returning to Canada to teach at the University of British Columbia—and to publish poetry. He was an immediate success: his first collection, *David and Other Poems* (1942), won a Governor General's Award. He spent the next several decades writing prolifically and teaching, and in 1965 established Canada's first Creative Writing program.

Birney addressed many topics and adopted many different poetic styles over his long career. His work often engages with the issues of the day—Birney was a Marxist when young, and always remained strongly on the left politically—and it engages experimentally with several poetic movements, including sound poetry and concrete poetry.

Vancouver Lights

About me the night   moonless   wimples¹ the mountains
wraps ocean   land   air   and mounting
sucks at the stars   The city   throbbing below
webs the sable peninsula   The golden
strands overleap the seajet   by bridge and buoy
vault the shears of the inlet   climb the woods   5
toward me   falter   and halt   Across to the firefly
haze of a ship on the gulf's erased horizon
roll the lambent° spokes of a lighthouse   *radiant*

Through the feckless years we have come to the time
when to look on this quilt of lamps is a troubling delight   10
Welling from Europe's bog   through Africa flowing

---

1   *wimples* I.e., covers; a wimple is the head covering traditionally worn by nuns.

and Asia   drowning the lonely lumes[1] on the oceans
tiding up over Halifax   now to this winking
15 outpost comes flooding the primal ink

On this mountain's brutish forehead with terror of space
I stir   of the changeless night and the stark ranges
of nothing   pulsing down from beyond and between
the fragile planets   We are a spark beleaguered
20 by darkness   this twinkle we make in a corner of emptiness
how shall we utter our fear that the black Experimentress
will never in the range of her microscope find it?   Our Phoebus[2]
himself is a bubble that dries on Her slide   while the Nubian[3]
wears for an evening's whim a necklace of nebulae

25 Yet we must speak   we the unique glowworms
Out of the waters and rocks of our little world
we conjured these flames   hooped these sparks
by our will   From blankness and cold we fashioned stars
to our size   and signalled Aldebaran[4]
30 This must we say   whoever may be to hear us
if murk devour   and none weave again in gossamer:

These rays were ours
we made and unmade them   Not the shudder of continents
doused us   the moon's passion   nor crash of comets
35 In the fathomless heat of our dwarfdom   our dream's combustion
we contrived the power   the blast that snuffed us
No one bound Prometheus[5]   Himself he chained
and consumed his own bright liver   O stranger
Plutonian   descendant   or beast in the stretching night—
40 there was light.

—1948

---

1   *lumes* Variant form of "leams," meaning lights or rays.
2   *Phoebus* Epithet of Apollo, god of the sun; here, the sun itself.
3   *Nubian* Inhabitant of the African region of Nubia.
4   *Aldebaran* Red star of the first magnitude, in the constellation of Taurus.
5   *Prometheus* In Greek myth, the Titan who stole fire from Heaven to give to humankind;
    for this, his punishment was to be chained to a rock while an eagle devoured his liver each
    day.

The Bear on the Delhi Road

Unreal   tall as a myth
by the road the Himalayan bear
is beating the brilliant air
with his crooked arms
About him two men   bare   5
spindly as locusts   leap

One pulls on a ring
in the great soft nose   His mate
flicks   flicks with a stick
up at the rolling eyes   10

They have not led him here
down from the fabulous hills
to this bald alien plain
and the clamorous world   to kill
but simply to teach him to dance   15

They are peaceful both   these spare
men of Kashmir   and the bear
alive is their living   too
If   far on the Delhi way
around him galvanic they dance   20
it is merely to wear   wear
from his shaggy body the tranced
wish forever to stay
only an ambling bear
four-footed in berries   25

It is no more joyous for them
in this hot dust to prance
out of reach of the praying claws
sharpened to paw for ants
in the shadows of deodars[1]   30
It is not easy to free
myth from reality
or rear this fellow up
to lurch   lurch with them
in the tranced dancing of men   35

—1973

---

1   *deodars* Indian cedars.

John Betjeman
1906–1984

Poet Laureate of England from 1972 until his death, Sir John Betjeman was a public figure who frequently appeared on radio and television programs and regularly published articles in books and magazines. Known for using light verse with serious purpose, he approached his work with a sense of humour. As he once said, "I don't think I am any good. If I thought I was any good, I wouldn't be."

Born in London, Betjeman published his first book of poems in 1931. During the early thirties he also worked as the assistant editor of *The Architectural Review*, where he developed a lifelong passion for architecture that would provide the subject matter for some of his poems as well as several prose books and documentaries. He continued to write and publish poetry while working for the British Representative in Dublin as a Press Officer, for the Ministry of Information on film propaganda during World War II, and for various newspapers and magazines as a freelance journalist.

Betjeman's *Collected Poems* (1958) was well-received by the public and critics alike, and with its publication he became what literary critic Ralph J. Mills describes as "a phenomenon in contemporary English literature, a truly popular poet." Betjeman was awarded the Queen's Gold Medal for poetry in 1960, and was knighted in 1969.

In Westminster Abbey[1]

Let me take this other glove off
    As the *vox humana*[2] swells,
And the beauteous fields of Eden
    Bask beneath the Abbey bells.
5 Here, where England's statesmen lie,
Listen to a lady's cry.

Gracious Lord, oh bomb the Germans.[3]
    Spare their women for Thy Sake,
And if that is not too easy
10   We will pardon Thy Mistake.

---

1   *Westminster Abbey* Important central London church where coronations are held and where many influential political figures, scientists, and intellectuals are buried.

2   *vox humana* Set of pipes in a pipe organ, so named because their sound resembles that of a human voice.

3   *bomb the Germans* This poem was published during World War II (1939–45).

But, gracious Lord, whate'er shall be,
Don't let anyone bomb me.

Keep our Empire undismembered
    Guide our Forces by Thy Hand,
Gallant blacks from far Jamaica, 15
    Honduras and Togoland;[1]
Protect them Lord in all their fights,
And, even more, protect the whites.

Think of what our Nation stands for,
    Books from Boots[2] and country lanes, 20
Free speech, free passes, class distinction,
    Democracy and proper drains.
Lord, put beneath Thy special care
One-eighty-nine Cadogan Square.

Although dear Lord I am a sinner, 25
    I have done no major crime;
Now I'll come to Evening Service
    Whensoever I have the time.
So, Lord, reserve for me a crown,
And do not let my shares go down. 30

I will labour for Thy Kingdom,
    Help our lads to win the war,
Send white feathers to the cowards[3]
    Join the Women's Army Corps,
Then wash the Steps around Thy Throne 35
In the Eternal Safety Zone.

Now I feel a little better,
    What a treat to hear Thy Word
Where the bones of leading statesmen,
    Have so often been interred. 40
And now, dear Lord, I cannot wait
Because I have a luncheon date.

—1940

---

1   *Togoland* Area of western Africa once divided into French Togoland (now the Republic
    of Togo) and British Togoland (now part of Ghana).
2   *Boots* British chain of for-profit libraries that rented books to customers.
3   *Send white ... cowards* Reference to the practice of giving out white feathers (symbolizing
    cowardice) to men not in military uniform as a means of shaming them into enlisting.
    This occurred during both world wars.

W.H. Auden

1907–1973

W.H. Auden's poetry documents the changing political, social, and psychological landscape of his time, describing society's material troubles and seeking a clear understanding of human existence. His work often couples contemporary speech with more traditional, structured verse forms.

Born in York, England, Wystan Hugh Auden spent his childhood in Birmingham. He won a scholarship to study natural science at Oxford, but a developing passion for poetry soon led him to transfer to English. At university, he became the central member of a cohort of writers known as the "Oxford Group," and soon after graduation he published his first major volume, *Poems* (1930).

In the thirties, Auden travelled extensively and worked variously as a schoolmaster, a university lecturer, a writer of nonfiction and experimental drama, and a verse commentator on documentary films. Though he was gay, in 1935 he entered into a marriage of convenience with Erika Mann, daughter of the German novelist Thomas Mann, to enable her escape from Nazi Germany. During the Spanish Civil War (1936–39), Auden volunteered as a propaganda writer on the side of the left—an experience that left him somewhat disillusioned with socialist politics.

In 1939, Auden moved to New York, where he settled for most of his later life. A year later he published *Another Time* (1940), which includes some of his best-known poems, such as "Musée des Beaux Arts" and "September 1, 1939." From then on, his work began to take on more subjective overtones, often with religious themes (he had abandoned Anglicanism as a youth, but returned to it in 1941). While his earlier poetry had examined concrete social ills, his later poetry developed a more complex worldview, often casting social problems in terms of personal responsibility.

With *The Collected Poetry* (1945), Auden began revising his earlier work, a task that included rewriting and even suppressing some of his most left-wing poems. When he was awarded the National Medal for Literature in 1967, the committee declared that Auden's work, "branded by the moral and ideological fires of our age, breathes with eloquence, perception, and intellectual power."

Funeral Blues[1]

Stop all the clocks, cut off the telephone,
Prevent the dog from barking with a juicy bone,
Silence the pianos and with muffled drum
Bring out the coffin, let the mourners come.

Let aeroplanes circle moaning overhead   5
Scribbling on the sky the message He is Dead,
Put crêpe bows[2] round the white necks of the public doves,
Let the traffic policemen wear black cotton gloves.

He was my North, my South, my East and West,
My working week and my Sunday rest,   10
My noon, my midnight, my talk, my song;
I thought that love would last forever: I was wrong.

The stars are not wanted now; put out every one;
Pack up the moon and dismantle the sun;
Pour away the ocean and sweep up the wood;   15
For nothing now can ever come to any good.

—1936, 1940

Musée des Beaux Arts

About suffering they were never wrong,
The Old Masters: how well they understood
Its human position; how it takes place
While someone else is eating or opening a window or just walking
    dully along;
How, when the aged are reverently, passionately waiting   5
For the miraculous birth, there always must be
Children who did not specially want it to happen, skating
On a pond at the edge of the wood:

---

1   *Funeral Blues* This poem first appeared in *The Ascent of F6* (1936), a play co-written by
     Auden and Christopher Isherwood. A revised version with the present title later appeared
     in Auden's 1940 collection *Another Time*. The original 1936 version has five stanzas and
     is considerably more satirical.
2   *crêpe bows* Black crêpe, a woven fabric with a wrinkled surface, is often associated with
     mourning.

They never forgot
10   That even the dreadful martyrdom must run its course
Anyhow in a corner, some untidy spot
Where the dogs go on with their doggy life and the torturer's horse
Scratches its innocent behind on a tree.

In Brueghel's *Icarus*[1] for instance: how everything turns away
15   Quite leisurely from the disaster; the ploughman may
Have heard the splash, the forsaken cry,
But for him it was not an important failure; the sun shone
As it had to on the white legs disappearing into the green
Water; and the expensive delicate ship that must have seen
20   Something amazing, a boy falling out of the sky,
Had somewhere to get to and sailed calmly on.

—1940

September 1, 1939[2]

I sit in one of the dives
On Fifty-second Street
Uncertain and afraid
As the clever hopes expire
5   Of a low dishonest decade:
Waves of anger and fear
Circulate over the bright
And darkened lands of the earth,
Obsessing our private lives;
10   The unmentionable odour of death
Offends the September night.

Accurate scholarship can
Unearth the whole offence

---

1   *Brueghel's Icarus* The reference is to *Landscape with the Fall of Icarus* (c. 1555), a painting
    by Pieter Brueghel the Elder. It references an ancient Greek story in which Daedalus and
    his son Icarus tried to escape from Crete, where they were imprisoned, using wings of
    feathers and wax. Icarus flew too high, the wax melted, and he drowned. In Brueghel's
    painting, an ordinary farmer ploughing on a hill dominates the foreground, while Icarus's
    drowning body appears very small in the ocean below, next to a much larger ship.
2   *September 1, 1939* Date of Hitler's invasion of Poland; France and Britain declared war
    on Germany two days later. Auden had left England to take up residence in the United
    States the previous January.

From Luther[1] until now
That has driven a culture mad,   15

Find what occurred at Linz,[2]
What huge imago[3] made
A psychopathic god:
I and the public know
What all schoolchildren learn,   20
Those to whom evil is done
Do evil in return.

Exiled Thucydides[4] knew
All that a speech can say
About Democracy,   25
And what dictators do,
The elderly rubbish they talk
To an apathetic grave;
Analysed all in his book,
The enlightenment driven away,   30
The habit-forming pain,
Mismanagement and grief:
We must suffer them all again.

Into this neutral air
Where blind skyscrapers use   35
Their full height to proclaim
The strength of Collective Man,
Each language pours its vain
Competitive excuse:

---

1   *Luther* Martin Luther (1483–1546), the German religious leader whose attacks on eccle-
     siastical corruption began the Protestant Reformation in Europe. Luther's writings grew
     markedly more anti-Semitic as he aged; in his book *Mein Kampf,* Hitler ranks Martin
     Luther as a great German cultural hero.
2   *Linz* Capital of upper Austria where Hitler grew up.
3   *imago* Psychoanalytic term for an idealized image of a person; imagos are formed in
     childhood and influence adult behaviour.
4   *Thucydides* Athenian historian (c. 460–c. 395 BCE) whose failure as a naval commander
     led to his 20-year exile, during which time he wrote *The History of the Peloponnesian
     War.* In his *History,* Thucydides records Pericles's funeral oration for the dead Athenian
     soldiers, which outlines the dangers and benefits of democracy. Elected 16 times to the
     position of general, Pericles instituted many democratic reforms while retaining a signifi-
     cant degree of personal power.

40 But who can live for long
   In an euphoric dream;
   Out of the mirror they stare,
   Imperialism's face
   And the international wrong.

45 Faces along the bar
   Cling to their average day:
   The lights must never go out,
   The music must always play,
   All the conventions conspire
50 To make this fort assume
   The furniture of home;
   Lest we should see where we are,
   Lost in a haunted wood,
   Children afraid of the night
55 Who have never been happy or good.

   The windiest militant trash
   Important Persons shout
   Is not so crude as our wish:
   What mad Nijinsky[1] wrote
60 About Diaghilev
   Is true of the normal heart;
   For the error bred in the bone
   Of each woman and each man
   Craves what it cannot have,
65 Not universal love
   But to be loved alone.

   From the conservative dark
   Into the ethical life
   The dense commuters come,
70 Repeating their morning vow;
   "I *will* be true to the wife,
   I'll concentrate more on my work,"

---

1   *Nijinsky* Vaslav Nijinsky (1890–1950), Russian ballet dancer and choreographer, worked
    with the Russian ballet producer Sergei Diaghilev (1872–1929) until their falling out in
    1913. In 1917 Nijinsky's mental instability forced him into permanent retirement. In his
    diary, published in 1937, Nijinsky wrote: "Some politicians are hypocrites like Diaghilev,
    who does not want universal love, but to be loved alone. I want universal love."

And helpless governors wake
To resume their compulsory game:
Who can release them now,   75
Who can reach the deaf,
Who can speak for the dumb?

Defenceless under the night
Our world in stupor lies;
Yet, dotted everywhere,   80
Ironic points of light
Flash out wherever the Just
Exchange their messages:
May I, composed like them
Of Eros[1] and of dust,   85
Beleaguered by the same
Negation and despair,
Show an affirming flame.

—1940

The Unknown Citizen

(To JS/07/M/378
This Marble Monument
Is Erected by the State)

He was found by the Bureau of Statistics to be
One against whom there was no official complaint,
And all the reports on his conduct agree
That, in the modern sense of an old-fashioned word, he was a saint,
For in everything he did he served the Greater Community.   5
Except for the War till the day he retired
He worked in a factory and never got fired,
But satisfied his employers, Fudge Motors Inc.
Yet he wasn't a scab[2] or odd in his views,
For his Union reports that he paid his dues,   10
(Our report on his Union shows it was sound)
And our Social Psychology workers found

---

1   *Eros* In contrast to the New Testament *agape*, or Christian love, *eros* represents earthly, or
    sexual love. In Greek myth, the winged Eros, son of Aphrodite, is the god of love.
2   *scab* Someone who works during a strike or refuses to join a union.

That he was popular with his mates and liked a drink.
The Press are convinced that he bought a paper every day
15 And that his reactions to advertisements were normal in every way.
Policies taken out in his name prove that he was fully insured,
And his Health-card shows he was once in hospital but left it cured.
Both Producers Research and High-Grade Living declare
He was fully sensible to the advantages of the Instalment Plan
20 And had everything necessary to the Modern Man,
A phonograph, a radio, a car and a frigidaire.
Our researchers into Public Opinion are content
That he held the proper opinions for the time of year;
When there was peace, he was for peace; when there was war, he
    went.
25 He was married and added five children to the population,
Which our Eugenist[1] says was the right number for a parent of his
    generation.
And our teachers report that he never interfered with their education.
Was he free? Was he happy? The question is absurd:
Had anything been wrong, we should certainly have heard.

—1940

---

1   *Eugenist* Scientist who studies the development of physically or mentally improved human beings through selective breeding. Eugenics has played a key role in legitimizing racist ideologies such as Nazism.

George Oppen
1908–1984

George Oppen contributed to literary and political spheres not only as a poet but also as an activist, publisher, and mentor. A deeply philosophical poet, he explored ethical questions, the nature of truth, and his own humanity through his exacting words.

Oppen was born in New Rochelle, New York, and raised in affluence. After being expelled from a military academy, he attended Oregon State University at Corvallis, where he met his wife, Mary Colby. While travelling the country, the couple befriended Louis Zukofsky and other poets who became Oppen's writing peers; they dedicated their "objectivist" poetry to communicating clear, impartial perceptions of the actual world. The Oppens began to publish their colleagues' poems, co-founding first To Publishers in France in 1931 and then Objectivist Press in the United States, which printed Oppen's first collection, *Discrete Series* (1934).

After 1934 Oppen and his wife turned their attention to activism, helping those struggling through the Great Depression, and both joined the Communist Party. Oppen eventually distanced himself from the Party, and he fought in Europe during World War II, for which service he received a Purple Heart. However, the Oppens still fell under scrutiny during the anti-Communist fervour following the war, and in 1950 they went into exile in Mexico City.

In 1958 Oppen returned to the United States and resumed writing, publishing first *The Materials* (1962) then *This in Which* (1965). He received lifetime achievement awards from the American Academy and Institute of Arts and Letters and the National Endowment for the Arts, as well as the Pulitzer Prize for the celebrated collection *Of Being Numerous* (1968). He was later diagnosed with Alzheimer's disease and, with the help of Mary, he published one last collection, *Primitive* (1978), before his death.

Psalm

Veritas sequitur ...[1]

In the small beauty of the forest
The wild deer bedding down—
That they are there!

---

1   *Veritas sequitur* Latin: truth follows. The complete expression is *"veritas sequitur esse"* ("truth follows the existence of things").

<blockquote>

        Their eyes
5   Effortless, the soft lips
    Nuzzle and the alien small teeth
    Tear at the grass

        The roots of it
    Dangle from their mouths
10   Scattering earth in the strange woods.
    They who are there.

        Their paths
    Nibbled thru the fields, the leaves that shade them
    Hang in the distances
15   Of sun

        The small nouns
    Crying faith
    In this in which the wild deer
    Startle, and stare out.
</blockquote>

—1963

The Forms of Love

Parked in the fields
All night
So many years ago,
We saw
5 A lake beside us
When the moon rose.
I remember

Leaving that ancient car
Together. I remember
10 Standing in the white grass
Beside it. We groped
Our way together
Downhill in the bright
Incredible light

Beginning to wonder   15
Whether it could be lake
Or fog
We saw, our heads
Ringing under the stars we walked
To where it would have wet our feet   20
Had it been water

                                                           —1964

Latitude, Longitude

      climbed from the road and found
over the flowers at the mountain's
rough top a bee yellow
and heavy as

      pollen in the mountainous   5
air thin legs crookedly
a-dangle if we could

find all
the gale's evidence what message
is there for us in these   10
glassy bottles the Encyclopedist

was wrong was wrong many things
too foolish
to sing
may be said this matter-   15
of-fact defines

poetry

                                                           —1975

Theodore Roethke

1908–1963

Known for his introspective verse, Theodore Roethke was both praised and criticized for his focus on the self. Some critics saw his personal exploration as a means to valuable insight into the human body and the unconscious mind, but others considered his scope too limited and irrelevant to the political and social concerns of the day. Despite the inward focus of his poetry, Roethke read widely, and his style was strongly influenced by the poets he admired, such as William Blake, T.S. Eliot, and W.B. Yeats. He also formed literary friendships with fellow poets W.H. Auden, Dylan Thomas, and William Carlos Williams.

Born in Michigan into a German-American family, Roethke had ambivalent childhood memories of his horticulturalist father that centred on the family's extensive greenhouses. Images of growth, decay, and death recur in his poetry, especially in what he referred to as the "greenhouse poems" included in *The Lost Son and Other Poems* (1948). By contrast, joyful love is the subject of "I Knew a Woman" from *Words for the Wind* (1958), published after his marriage to Beatrice O'Connell. *Words for the Wind* marked a new direction for Roethke, who frequently returned to love poetry in his later work.

Roethke taught at Michigan State College and was very dedicated to his teaching; however, he was dismissed after the first of what became a series of mental breakdowns and psychiatric hospitalizations. He then taught at the University of Washington where, although he was often unwell, he was valued for both his teaching and his writing. Roethke's honours include the Pulitzer Prize, two National Book Awards, and the Shelley Memorial Award.

My Papa's Waltz

The whiskey on your breath
Could make a small boy dizzy;
But I hung on like death:
Such waltzing was not easy.

5 We romped until the pans
Slid from the kitchen shelf;
My mother's countenance
Could not unfrown itself.

The hand that held my wrist
Was battered on one knuckle;   10
At every step you missed
My right ear scraped a buckle.

You beat time on my head
With a palm caked hard by dirt,
Then waltzed me off to bed   15
Still clinging to your shirt.

—1948

Root Cellar

Nothing would sleep in that cellar, dank as a ditch,
Bulbs broke out of boxes hunting for chinks in the dark,
Shoots dangled and drooped,
Lolling obscenely from mildewed crates,
Hung down long yellow evil necks, like tropical snakes.   5
And what a congress of stinks!—
Roots ripe as old bait,
Pulpy stems, rank, silo-rich,
Leaf-mould, manure, lime, piled against slippery planks.
Nothing would give up life: 10
Even the dirt kept breathing a small breath.

—1948

I Knew a Woman

I knew a woman, lovely in her bones,
When small birds sighed, she would sigh back at them;
Ah, when she moved, she moved more ways than one:
The shapes a bright container can contain!
Of her choice virtues only gods should speak,   5
Or English poets who grew up on Greek
(I'd have them sing in chorus, cheek to cheek).

How well her wishes went! She stroked my chin,
She taught me Turn, and Counter-turn, and Stand;[1]
10 She taught me Touch, that undulant white skin;
I nibbled meekly from her proffered hand;
She was the sickle; I, poor I, the rake,
Coming behind her for her pretty sake
(But what prodigious mowing we did make).

15 Love likes a gander, and adores a goose:
Her full lips pursed, the errant note to seize;
She played it quick, she played it light and loose;
My eyes, they dazzled at her flowing knees;
Her several parts could keep a pure repose,
20 Or one hip quiver with a mobile nose
(She moved in circles, and those circles moved).

Let seed be grass, and grass turn into hay:
I'm martyr to a motion not my own;
What's freedom for? To know eternity.
25 I swear she cast a shadow white as stone.
But who would count eternity in days?
These old bones live to learn her wanton ways:
(I measure time by how a body sways).

—1958

---

1   *Turn, and Counter-turn, and Stand* Allusion to *strophe, antistrophe,* and *epode,* the three
    parts of a typical Greek ode.

Dorothy Livesay
1909–1996

In a career spanning six decades, Dorothy Livesay produced an extensive body of work that is remarkable not only for its diversity but also for its commitment to her aesthetic and ethical ideals. Chief among these was the conviction that a poem should not be an esoteric literary artifact frozen on the page but rather an accessible expression of "living speech," a popular, vital form of communication. Regardless of her subject—which included life in rural Ontario, her experience living and teaching in Africa, social injustice, class struggle, and women's rights—Livesay's poetry retains its characteristic clarity of image, forthrightness of language, and musicality.

Over the course of her writing life, Livesay experimented with an array of poetic forms, from imagist love lyrics and Georgian pastorals to socially conscious "documentary poetry" that bears witness to historical events. Although certain critics have looked askance on her more politically motivated, polemical work, Livesay rejected the notion that art should be wholly separate from activism or ideological causes. Having seen police brutality, labour unrest, and civil disobedience as a student in Europe, as well as the effects of the Depression on the working poor as a social worker in North America, Livesay felt obligated to distance herself from what she came to regard as the "decadence in modern bourgeois poetry." Many of the resulting poems were published in the Governor General's Award-winning collections *Day and Night* (1944) and *Poems for People* (1947), which together established Livesay as one of the most important Canadian poets of her generation.

Green Rain

I remember long veils of green rain
Feathered like the shawl of my grandmother—
Green from the half-green of the spring trees
Waving in the valley.

I remember the road   5
Like the one which leads to my grandmother's house,
A warm house, with green carpets,
Geraniums, a trilling canary
And shining horse-hair chairs;
And the silence, full of the rain's falling   10
Was like my grandmother's parlour

Alive with herself and her voice, rising and falling—
Rain and wind intermingled.

I remember on that day
15   I was thinking only of my love
And of my love's house.
But now I remember the day
As I remember my grandmother.
I remember the rain as the feathery fringe of her shawl.

—1932

The Three Emilys[1]

These women crying in my head
Walk alone, uncomforted:
The Emilys, these three
Cry to be set free—
5   And others whom I will not name
Each different, each the same.

Yet they had liberty!
Their kingdom was the sky:
They batted clouds with easy hand,
10   Found a mountain for their stand;
From wandering lonely they could catch
The inner magic of a heath—
A lake their palette, any tree
Their brush could be.

15   And still they cry to me
As in reproach—
I, born to hear their inner storm
Of separate man in woman's form,
I yet possess another kingdom, barred
20   To them, these three, this Emily.
I move as mother in a frame,

1   *The Three Emilys* Emily Brontë (1818–48), English poet and novelist; Emily Dickinson
(1830–86), American poet; and Emily Carr (1871–1945), Canadian artist and writer.

My arteries
Flow the immemorial way
Towards the child, the man;
And only for brief span   25
Am I an Emily on mountain snows
And one of these.

And so the whole that I possess
Is still much less—
They move triumphant through my head: 30
I am the one
Uncomforted.

—1953

Elizabeth Bishop
1911–1979

Although respected by her contemporaries and honoured with a host of prestigious appointments, prizes, awards, and fellowships, Elizabeth Bishop came to be recognized only posthumously as a major American poet on the strength of a small but scrupulously crafted body of work. That she published just 101 poems in a cluster of slender volumes is a testament to the pains she took with her art. According to the poet Robert Lowell, with whom she shared a close friendship, she was "an unerring Muse" who made "the casual perfect."

Born in Massachusetts, Bishop was raised there and in Nova Scotia, and during her adult life she travelled extensively. She lived in Brazil from 1951 to 1966, for most of that time with architect Lota de Macedo Soares. In 1956 she received the Pulitzer Prize for a collection of poetry, *Poems: North & South/A Cold Spring*; thereafter she was frequently a recipient of honours and awards.

As one who spent much of her life roving from country to country, Bishop explained her "passion for accuracy" in the following terms: "since we do float on an unknown sea I think we should examine the floating things that come our way very carefully; who knows what might depend on it?" Some of Bishop's poems, such as "First Death in Nova Scotia," draw on elements of her personal life. But she remained wary of confessional poetry, believing that a poem that luxuriates in the feelings of the poet must be of diminished significance to other readers. She made a discipline of reticence and discretion, striving never to fall into sentimental self-pity or intrude too much of herself in order that the particular might serve to illuminate and bear the weight of the universal.

First Death in Nova Scotia

In the cold, cold parlour
my mother laid out Arthur
beneath the chromographs:
Edward, Prince of Wales,
5   with Princess Alexandra,
and King George with Queen Mary.[1]

---

1   *chromographs* Coloured prints; *Edward, Prince ... Queen Mary* Members of the British royal family. Edward VII was Prince of Wales when he married Alexandra of Denmark in 1863. They became king and queen consort in 1901 and were succeeded by King George V and Mary of Teck in 1910.

Below them on the table
stood a stuffed loon
shot and stuffed by Uncle
Arthur, Arthur's father.   10

Since Uncle Arthur fired
a bullet into him,
he hadn't said a word.
He kept his own counsel
on his white, frozen lake,   15
the marble-topped table.
His breast was deep and white,
cold and caressable;
his eyes were red glass,
much to be desired.   20

"Come," said my mother,
"Come and say good-bye
to your little cousin Arthur."
I was lifted up and given
one lily of the valley   25
to put in Arthur's hand.
Arthur's coffin was
a little frosted cake,
and the red-eyed loon eyed it
from his white, frozen lake.   30

Arthur was very small.
He was all white, like a doll
that hadn't been painted yet.
Jack Frost had started to paint him
the way he always painted   35
the Maple Leaf (Forever).[1]
He had just begun on his hair,
a few red strokes, and then
Jack Frost had dropped the brush
and left him white, forever.   40

---

1   *the Maple Leaf (Forever)* Reference to "The Maple Leaf Forever" (1867), an unofficial
     Canadian anthem.

The gracious royal couples
were warm in red and ermine;
their feet were well wrapped up
in the ladies' ermine trains.
45 They invited Arthur to be
the smallest page at court.
But how could Arthur go,
clutching his tiny lily,
with his eyes shut up so tight
50 and the roads deep in snow?

—1962

One Art

The art of losing isn't hard to master;
so many things seem filled with the intent
to be lost that their loss is no disaster.

Lose something every day. Accept the fluster
5 of lost door keys, the hour badly spent.
The art of losing isn't hard to master.

Then practice losing farther, losing faster:
places, and names, and where it was you meant
to travel. None of these will bring disaster.

10 I lost my mother's watch. And look! my last, or
next-to-last, of three loved houses went.
The art of losing isn't hard to master.

I lost two cities, lovely ones. And, vaster,
some realms I owned, two rivers, a continent.
15 I miss them, but it wasn't a disaster.

—Even losing you (the joking voice, a gesture
I love) I shan't have lied. It's evident
the art of losing's not too hard to master
though it may look like (*Write* it!) like disaster.

—1976

Douglas LePan
1914–1998

Over the course of his long career, Douglas LePan was a soldier, diplomat, economist, civil servant, administrator, professor of English, and college principal. He is, however, chiefly remembered for the small yet distinguished body of literature that he produced as one of just a handful of Canadian writers to have been honoured with the Governor General's Award for fiction as well as poetry. The Toronto-born LePan was regarded during much of his life as a quintessentially Canadian writer; many of his poems ruminate on the Canadian landscape and its formative influence on the national psyche. But LePan also aspired to a borderless writing in his fiction and poetry, which is rich in allusions to classical and European writers. Though he believed that there would "always be a place for books that are redolent of a particular region or a particular aspect of Canadian life and experience," he also argued that there would likewise be a place "for writing which is more stripped and bare and absolute, for writing marked by little or nothing on the surface to distinguish it as Canadian and which will ultimately reveal its origin by imparting a spirit that is both adventurous and responsible and by being able to pass everywhere as true."

The poetry of *The Net and the Sword* (1953) is based primarily on LePan's experiences as a gunner in Italy during World War II—as is his one novel, *The Deserter* (1964). Though he published a volume of gay love poems in the 1990s (*Far Voyages*), it was not until after his death that critics began to appreciate the degree to which his earlier work is also infused with strong homoerotic elements.

LePan's early poetry is characteristically measured, decorous, and studded with self-consciously ornate language. Much of his later work is quite different in style—less formal, less elevated in its diction, and more direct.

A Country without a Mythology

No monuments or landmarks guide the stranger
Going among this savage people, masks
Taciturn or babbling out an alien jargon
And moody as barbaric skies are moody.

Berries must be his food. Hurriedly
He shakes the bushes, plucks pickerel from the river,
Forgetting every grace and ceremony,
Feeds like an Indian, and is on his way.   5

And yet, for all his haste, time is worth nothing.
10   The abbey clock, the dial in the garden,
Fade like saint's days and festivals.
Months, years, are here unbroken virgin forests.

There is no law—even no atmosphere
To smooth the anger of the flagrant sun.
15   November skies sting, sting like icicles.
The land is open to all violent weathers.

Passion is not more quick. Lightnings in August
Stagger, rocks split, tongues in the forest hiss,
As fire drinks up the lovely sea-dream coolness.
20   This is the land the passionate man must travel.

Sometimes—perhaps at the tentative fall of twilight—
A belief will settle that waiting around the bend
Are sanctities of childhood, that melting birds
Will sing him into a limpid gracious Presence.

25   The hills will fall in folds, the wilderness
Will be a garment innocent and lustrous
To wear upon a birthday, under a light
That curls and smiles, a golden-haired Archangel.

And now the channel opens. But nothing alters,
30   Mile after mile of tangled struggling roots,
Wild-rice, stumps, weeds, that clutch at the canoe,
Wild birds hysterical in tangled trees.

And not a sign, no emblem in the sky
Or boughs to friend him as he goes; for who
35   Will stop where, clumsily constructed, daubed
With war-paint, teeters some lust-red manitou?[1]

—1948

---

1   *manitou* Algonquin term for a spirit, deity, or other manifestation of the supernatural.

Aubade[1]

Your name on my lips. Every night
as my eyes close. And the sweetness
of your body, as though you were with me.

Your name on my lips. Every morning,
waking, that one word on my lips.   5
I remember everything, everything.

But this morning there was nothing.
Then before I could think how strange it was
I was murmuring other words,

"Deeper than death or the dark,"   10
as though your mouth were on mine.
I love you that deeply, that deeply.

—1982

The Haystack

It doesn't take a Hiroshima[2] to burn a man to a crisp.
A haystack will do. And what could be more bucolic
than that? And you get tired of sleeping in cellars or slit-trenches,
so why not behind a haystack that has simmered all day
in the warmth of an Italian September sun? But at night   5
the jackals are ready to spring, the German eighty-eights,
with their high muzzle-velocities and their low trajectories,
so that the haystack ignites like a torch and a gunner is burnt
to a crisp. How far back was that? thirty years? forty years?
He doesn't remember. He only remembers the stench   10
of fear, his own fear, and a grey army blanket, and a young
sunburned back alive on the banks of the Volturno,[3]
then burning, burning. By dire subtleties such as these
he was being prepared for the carbonization of cities.

—1987

---

1   *Aubade* Poem or song about lovers parting at dawn.
2   *Hiroshima* Japanese city that was the first city ever subjected to a nuclear attack. The
    United States dropped an atomic bomb on Hiroshima on 6 August 1945, killing ap-
    proximately 130,000 people and levelling 90 per cent of the city.
3   *Volturno* River in south-central Italy, the bank of which formed the Volturno line, a Ger-
    man defensive position in World War II .

Randall Jarrell
1914–1965

Randall Jarrell was a literary critic with exacting standards, and his entertaining and perceptive writing on twentieth-century American poetry was extremely influential. He was also an important poet in his own right, addressing subjects such as childhood and women's domestic lives—and, most famously, World War II—with simultaneous tenderness and unflinching honesty. In addition to criticism and poetry, Jarrell also authored a novel, children's books, translations, essays, and reviews.

Jarrell earned his BA (1935) and MA (1937) from Vanderbilt University in his hometown of Nashville, Tennessee. His first book of poems, *Blood for a Stranger*, was published in 1942, the same year that he enlisted in the military. His next two books, *Little Friend, Little Friend* (1945) and *Losses* (1948), drew on his experiences of the Second World War as a navigation tower operator. Together, these texts established his reputation as a skilled and sensitive poet—a reputation that grew with the publication of *The Woman at the Washington Zoo* (1960), which received the National Book Award. Jarrell also taught English and Creative Writing at a number of American universities and served as American Poet Laureate from 1956 to 1958.

The Death of the Ball Turret Gunner[1]

From my mother's sleep I fell into the State,
And I hunched in its belly till my wet fur froze.
Six miles from earth, loosed from its dream of life,
I woke to black flak° and the nightmare fighters.   *anti-aircraft fire*
5 When I died they washed me out of the turret with a hose.

—1945

---

1   *Ball Turret Gunner* Mounted on B-17 or B-24 planes, the Sperry ball turret was a one-person gun turret that required a short crew member to curl into the fetal position in order to aim and shoot.

Dylan Thomas
1914–1953

Dylan Thomas was a raucous fixture in the taverns of London's Soho-Fitzrovia district, and he haunted the rural hills and seashores of Wales. Influenced by a romantic sensibility, he sought to articulate his sense that life and death were rolled together in nature's driving "green fuse."

Thomas was born in Swansea, Wales, and his youth and childhood there would be a recurring subject in his poetry. His father was a teacher at Swansea Grammar School, which Thomas attended and where he was far from a prize pupil; as a teenager, he regularly cut classes to work on his own poetry. His first published work, "And Death Shall Have No Dominion" (1933), was printed in a literary magazine when he was only 18.

When Thomas's *18 Poems* was published the following year, the strange and disturbing power of his verse woke up London's literary establishment. The cool, controlled style of T.S. Eliot, which conditioned poetic attitudes well into the 1950s, appeared subdued next to what one critic called Thomas's "belligerent syntax." While fresh and vital, Thomas's poems are also complex, built of dense interlocking images, and tightly structured: "Do Not Go Gentle into That Good Night" (1951), for example, adopts the restrictive form of a villanelle.

Despite his heavy drinking and a turbulent marriage, Thomas continued to publish poems—as well as short stories and radio plays—until the end of his life. Constant money troubles were lessened when he began making recordings of his poetry and touring to give public readings, which were enormously popular in Europe, and even more so in the United States. He was 39 when he died in New York of problems related to alcoholism.

The Force That Through the Green Fuse Drives the Flower

The force that through the green fuse drives the flower
Drives my green age; that blasts the roots of trees
Is my destroyer.
And I am dumb to tell the crooked rose
My youth is bent by the same wintry fever.

5

The force that drives the water through the rocks
Drives my red blood; that dries the mouthing streams
Turns mine to wax.

And I am dumb to mouth unto my veins
10   How at the mountain spring the same mouth sucks.

The hand that whirls the water in the pool[1]
Stirs the quicksand; that ropes the blowing wind
Hauls my shroud sail.
And I am dumb to tell the hanging man
15   How of my clay is made the hangman's lime.[2]

The lips of time leech to the fountain head;
Love drips and gathers, but the fallen blood
Shall calm her sores.
And I am dumb to tell a weather's wind
20   How time has ticked a heaven round the stars.

And I am dumb to tell the lover's tomb
How at my sheet goes the same crooked worm.

—1933

Fern Hill

Now as I was young and easy under the apple boughs
About the lilting house and happy as the grass was green,
    The night above the dingle° starry,   *wooded dell*
        Time let me hail and climb
5   Golden in the heydays of his eyes,
And honoured among wagons I was prince of the apple towns
And once below a time I lordly had the trees and leaves
        Trail with daisies and barley
    Down the rivers of the windfall light.

10 And as I was green and carefree, famous among the barns
About the happy yard and singing as the farm was home,
    In the sun that is young once only,
        Time let me play and be
      Golden in the mercy of his means,

---

1   *The hand ... the pool* In John 5.4, an angel goes to a pool in Bethesda and imbues it
    with healing properties by stirring the water.
2   *lime* Mineral used to speed up decomposition.

And green and golden I was huntsman and herdsman, the calves 15
Sang to my horn, the foxes on the hills barked clear and cold,
     And the sabbath rang slowly
    In the pebbles of the holy streams.

All the sun long it was running, it was lovely, the hay
Fields high as the house, the tunes from the chimneys, it was air 20
    And playing, lovely and watery
      And fire green as grass.
    And nightly under the simple stars
As I rode to sleep the owls were bearing the farm away,
All the moon long I heard, blessed among stables, the 25
     nightjars°   *nocturnal birds*
    Flying with the ricks° and the horses   *haystacks*
      Flashing into the dark.

And then to awake, and the farm, like a wanderer white
With the dew, come back, the cock on his shoulder: it was all
    Shining, it was Adam and maiden,   30
      The sky gathered again
    And the sun grew round that very day.
So it must have been after the birth of the simple light
In the first, spinning place, the spellbound horses walking warm
    Out of the whinnying green stable   35
      On to the fields of praise.

And honoured among foxes and pheasants by the gay house
Under the new made clouds and happy as the heart was long,
    In the sun born over and over,
      I ran my heedless ways,   40
    My wishes raced through the house high hay
And nothing I cared, at my sky blue trades,° that time   *occupations*
    allows
In all his tuneful turning so few and such morning songs
    Before the children green and golden
      Follow him out of grace,   45

Nothing I cared, in the lamb white days, that time would take me
Up to the swallow thronged loft by the shadow of my hand,
    In the moon that is always rising,
      Nor that riding to sleep

50   I should hear him fly with the high fields
And wake to the farm forever fled from the childless land.
Oh as I was young and easy in the mercy of his means,
        Time held me green and dying
        Though I sang in my chains like the sea.

—1946

Do Not Go Gentle into That Good Night

Do not go gentle into that good night,
Old age should burn and rave at close of day;
Rage, rage against the dying of the light.

Though wise men at their end know dark is right,
5   Because their words had forked no lightning they
Do not go gentle into that good night.

Good men, the last wave by, crying how bright
Their frail deeds might have danced in a green bay,
Rage, rage against the dying of the light.

10 Wild men who caught and sang the sun in flight,
And learn, too late, they grieved it on its way,
Do not go gentle into that good night.

Grave men, near death, who see with blinding sight
Blind eyes could blaze like meteors and be gay,
15 Rage, rage against the dying of the light.

And you, my father, there on the sad height,
Curse, bless, me now with your fierce tears, I pray.
Do not go gentle into that good night.
Rage, rage against the dying of the light.

—1951

P.K. Page
1916–2010

Although she was also a visual artist of no small talent and an accomplished writer of fiction and non-fiction, P.K. Page is best known as a visionary poet with a gift for fusing the physical and the metaphysical through an elaborate system of evocative imagery.

After emigrating from her native England at a young age, Page grew up on the Canadian prairies, eventually settling in Montreal. Over the course of her long career, she explored a vast intellectual terrain, from ancient philosophy and mysticism to modern psychology and neuroscience, in a style that became increasingly spare and transparent. For this reason, and because Page was a significant part of the movement to modernize Canadian poetry, she is known as a modernist poet, though her frequent use of densely patterned imagery also affiliates her with Symbolism.

Following the publication of her Governor General's Award-winning collection *The Metal and the Flower* (1954), Page lapsed into a 13-year poetic silence while accompanying her husband to Australia, Brazil, Mexico, and Guatemala on his political and diplomatic appointments. Whereas the early poems have been described as aloof portraits that observe and ruminate in a spirit of analytical detachment, the work she wrote after her return to Canada is often regarded as an attempt to move beyond aesthetic portraiture, to transcend what she called the "tyranny of subjectivity" for a more compassionate, expansive, even mystical vision of the world.

Page continued to write until her death at the age of 93. In 1998 she was made a Companion of the Order of Canada, and in 2003 her collection *Planet Earth: Poems Selected and New* was shortlisted for the Griffin Prize.

The Stenographers

After the brief bivouac[1] of Sunday,
their eyes, in the forced march of Monday to Saturday,
hoist the white flag, flutter in the snow-storm of paper,
haul it down and crack in the mid-sun of temper.

In the pause between the first draft and the carbon
they glimpse the smooth hours when they were children—
the ride in the ice-cart, the ice-man's name,
the end of the route and the long walk home;

5

---

1   *bivouac* Military camp made without covered shelters.

remember the sea where floats at high tide
10 were sea marrows growing on the scatter-green vine
or spools of grey toffee, or wasps' nests on water;
remember the sand and the leaves of the country.

Bell rings and they go and the voice draws their pencil
like a sled across snow; when its runners are frozen
15 rope snaps and the voice then is pulling no burden
but runs like a dog on the winter of paper.

Their climates are winter and summer—no wind
for the kites of their hearts—no wind for a flight;
a breeze at the most, to tumble them over
20 and leave them like rubbish—the boy-friends of blood.

In the inch of the noon as they move they are stagnant.
The terrible calm of the noon is their anguish;
the lip of the counter, the shapes of the straws
like icicles breaking their tongues, are invaders.

25 Their beds are their oceans—salt water of weeping
the waves that they know—the tide before sleep;
and fighting to drown they assemble their sheep
in columns and watch them leap desks for their fences
and stare at them with their own mirror-worn faces.

30 In the felt of the morning the calico-minded,
sufficiently starched, insert papers, hit keys,
efficient and sure as their adding machines;
yet they weep in the vault, they are taut as net curtains
stretched upon frames. In their eyes I have seen
35 the pin men of madness in marathon trim
race round the track of the stadium pupil.

—1946

Stories of Snow

Those in the vegetable rain retain
an area behind their sprouting eyes
held soft and rounded with the dream of snow
precious and reminiscent as those globes—
souvenir of some never nether land—
which hold their snowstorms circular, complete,
high in a tall and teakwood cabinet.

In countries where the leaves are large as hands
where flowers protrude their fleshy chins
and call their colours
an imaginary snowstorm sometimes falls
among the lilies.
And in the early morning one will waken
to think the glowing linen of his pillow
a northern drift, will find himself mistaken
and lie back weeping.
And there the story shifts from head to head,
of how, in Holland, from their feather beds
hunters arise and part the flakes and go
forth to the frozen lakes in search of swans—
the snow light falling white along their guns,
their breath in plumes.
While tethered in the wind like sleeping gulls
ice boats await the raising of their wings
to skim the electric ice at such a speed
they leap jet strips of naked water,
and how these flying, sailing hunters feel
air in their mouths as terrible as ether.
And on the story runs that even drinks
in that white landscape dare to be no colour;
how, flasked and water clear, the liquor slips
silver against the hunters' moving hips.
And of the swan in death these dreamers tell
of its last flight and how it falls, a plummet,
pierced by the freezing bullet
and how three feathers, loosened by the shot,
descend like snow upon it.

5

10

15

20

25

30

35

While hunters plunge their fingers in its down
deep as a drift, and dive their hands
40   up to the neck of the wrist
in that warm metamorphosis of snow
as gentle as the sort that woodsmen know
who, lost in the white circle, fall at last
and dream their way to death.

45   And stories of this kind are often told
in countries where great flowers bar the roads
with reds and blues which seal the route to snow
as if, in telling, raconteurs unlock
the colour with its complement and go
50   through to the area behind the eyes
where silent, unrefractive whiteness lies.

—1946

Al Purdy

1918–2000

Al Purdy was a staunch Canadian nationalist whose love of country was an overwhelming presence in his poetic works. Purdy wrote realistically about Canada's geography and regional history, drawing on material ranging from the lives of the long-dead Dorset Inuit to his own formative experiences train-hopping across the country, to his great love for the rock-strewn, formidable landscape of Eastern Ontario where he spent much of his life. His rough, sometimes self-deprecating poetic persona is distinctly Canadian, too, as is the colloquial style he evolved over the course of his career to reflect everyday Canadian speech. Of his writing, Purdy's friend and collaborator Doug Beardsley said, "He spoke to us, for us, he gave articulation to our lives as Canadians. He consciously set out to map this country with poetry and he did that."

Born in 1918, Purdy dropped out of school and, during his youth, spent time travelling across the country. He served in the Royal Canadian Air Force during World War II, and went on to become a cab driver and a mattress factory employee. In 1944 he published his first collection of poetry, *The Enchanted Echo*; he would later decry his early works, claiming that it was not until 1965 that he was truly a poet. That year he won his first Governor General's Award for *The Cariboo Horses*, and in 1986 he would receive another for *The Collected Poems of Al Purdy, 1956–1986*. Over the course of his career, Purdy published over 30 volumes of poetry and championed the work of other Canadian poets in his work as an editor and anthologist.

Trees at the Arctic Circle

(*Salix Cordifolia*—Ground Willow)

They are 18 inches long
or even less
crawling under rocks
grovelling among the lichens
bending and curling to escape   5
making themselves small
finding new ways to hide
Coward trees
I am angry to see them
like this   10
not proud of what they are

bowing to weather instead
careful of themselves
worried about the sky
15 afraid of exposing their limbs
like a Victorian married couple

I call to mind great Douglas Firs
I see tall maples waving green
and oaks like gods in autumn gold
20 the whole horizon jungle dark
and I crouched under that continual night
But these
even the dwarf shrubs of Ontario
mock them
25 Coward trees

And yet—and yet—
their seed pods glow
like delicate grey earrings
their leaves are veined and intricate
30 like tiny parkas
They have about three months
to ensure the species does not die
and that's how they spend their time
unbothered by any human opinion
35 just digging in here and now
sending their roots down down down
And you know it occurs to me
        about 2 feet under
those roots must touch permafrost
40 ice that remains ice forever
and they use it for their nourishment
they use death to remain alive

I see that I've been carried away
in my scorn of the dwarf trees
45 most foolish in my judgments
To take away the dignity
        of any living thing
even tho it cannot understand
        the scornful words

is to make life itself trivial   50
and yourself the Pontifex Maximus°   *High Priest*
   of nullity
I have been stupid in a poem
I will not alter the poem
but let the stupidity remain permanent   55
as the trees are
in a poem
the dwarf trees of Baffin Island

Pangnirtung[1]

—1967

Lament for the Dorsets[2]

(Eskimos extinct in the 14th century AD)

Animal bones and some mossy tent rings
scrapers and spearheads carved ivory swans
all that remains of the Dorset giants
who drove the Vikings back to their long ships[3]
talked to spirits of earth and water   5
—a picture of terrifying old men
so large they broke the backs of bears
so small they lurk behind bone rafters
in the brain of modern hunters
among good thoughts and warm things   10
and come out at night
to spit on the stars

The big men with clever fingers
who had no dogs and hauled their sleds
over the frozen northern oceans   15
awkward giants
        killers of seal
they couldn't compete with little men

---

1   *Pangnirtung* Hamlet on Baffin Island.
2   *Dorsets* Dorset people lived in the central and eastern Canadian Arctic until about 500
    years ago.
3   *drove the ... long ships* In the late tenth century, Norse people briefly established tempo-
    rary settlements in North America.

who came from the west with dogs
20 Or else in a warm climatic cycle
the seals went back to cold waters
and the puzzled Dorsets scratched their heads
with hairy thumbs around 1350 A.D.
—couldn't figure it out
25 went around saying to each other plaintively
        "What's wrong? What happened?
          Where are the seals gone?"
And died

Twentieth-century people
30 apartment dwellers
executives of neon death
warmakers with things that explode
—they have never imagined us in their future
how could we imagine them in the past
35 squatting among the moving glaciers
six hundred years ago
with glowing lamps?
As remote or nearly
as the trilobites and swamps
40 when coal became
or the last great reptile hissed
at a mammal the size of a mouse
that squeaked and fled

Did they ever realize at all
45 what was happening to them?
Some old hunter with one lame leg
a bear had chewed
sitting in a caribou-skin tent
—the last Dorset?
50 Let's say his name was Kudluk
and watch him sitting there
carving 2-inch ivory swans
for a dead grand-daughter
taking them out of his mind
55 the places in his mind
where pictures are
He selects a sharp stone tool

to gouge a parallel pattern of lines
on both sides of the swan
holding it with his left hand   60
bearing down and transmitting
his body's weight
from brain to arm and right hand
and one of his thoughts
turns to ivory   65
The carving is laid aside
in beginning darkness
at the end of hunger
and after a while wind
blows down the tent and snow   70
begins to cover him

After 600 years
the ivory thought
is still warm

                                                                —1968

Gwen Harwood

1920–1995

Gwen Harwood spent her childhood in Brisbane and most of her adult life in Tasmania, where she moved with her husband in 1945. In addition to publishing under her own name, Harwood is known for publishing in a series of fictional personae—a means not only of getting more work published more quickly, but also, in the case of her male personae, of garnering more serious critical attention from a literary establishment that she felt dismissed her as a "poet-housewife." Despite the sexism she encountered, Harwood earned a reputation as one of the best Australian poets of her generation and received numerous honours during her lifetime, including the Robert Frost Medallion (1977), the Patrick White Literary Award (1978), and the Order of Australia.

Before Harwood became a poet, she had considered a career in music, and she continued to develop both talents as a librettist; her poetry, too, often addresses music as a theme and displays the influence of contemporary composers in its experimentation with syntax and metre. Her work was also shaped by another passion, philosophy; Harwood's poetic preoccupation with the limits of language is informed by this interest. While much of her work explores universal themes such as growth, aging, memory, and death, some of her best-known poems address women's experiences of motherhood and domesticity through a feminist lens.

In the Park

She sits in the park. Her clothes are out of date.
Two children whine and bicker, tug her skirt.
A third draws aimless patterns in the dirt.
Someone she loved once passes by—too late

5   to feign indifference to that casual nod.
"How nice," et cetera. "Time holds great surprises."
From his neat head unquestionably rises
a small balloon ... "but for the grace of God ..."

They stand a while in flickering light, rehearsing
10 the children's names and birthdays. "It's so sweet
to hear their chatter, watch them grow and thrive,"
she says to his departing smile. Then, nursing
the youngest child, sits staring at her feet.
To the wind she says, "They have eaten me alive."

—1963

Howard Nemerov

1920–1991

Howard Nemerov combined a distinguished academic career with a writing career in both poetry and prose. His prose works—including three novels written early in his life, as well as short stories and several collections of essays—were praised, but he was best known for his 13 volumes of poetry. In these volumes he approached subjects such as death, morality, spirituality, and the importance of language in a style that is sometimes witty and sometimes serious. He often made use of traditional metrical structures and of rhyme, but strove for, as he phrased it, "simplicity and the appearance of ease" even when employing technically challenging and restrictive forms.

After graduating from Harvard University, Nemerov spent World War II as a fighter pilot. Upon his return to the United States, he began a university teaching career and published his first book of poems, *The Image and the Law* (1947). In his early work, critics noted the influence of modernist poets such as T.S. Eliot and W.H. Auden; beginning with the publication of *The Salt Garden* (1955), Nemerov's growing interest in nature and landscape led to comparisons with the poet Robert Frost (1874–1963).

In 1978, Nemerov was awarded both the Pulitzer Prize and the National Book Award for *The Collected Poems of Howard Nemerov* (1977). Ten years later, he served as Poet Laureate for the United States (1988–90). James Billington, in his announcement of the appointment, praised the range of Nemerov's writing, which, in Billington's words, extended "from the profound to the poignant to the comic."

The Vacuum

The house is so quiet now
The vacuum cleaner sulks in the corner closet,
Its bag limp as a stopped lung, its mouth
Grinning into the floor, maybe at my
Slovenly life, my dog-dead youth.   5

I've lived this way long enough,
But when my old woman died her soul
Went into that vacuum cleaner, and I can't bear
To see the bag swell like a belly, eating the dust
And the woolen mice, and begin to howl   10

Because there is old filth everywhere
She used to crawl, in the corner and under the stair.
I know now how life is cheap as dirt,
And still the hungry, angry heart
15 Hangs on and howls, biting at air.

—1955

A Way of Life

It's been going on a long time.
For instance, these two guys, not saying much, who slog
Through sun and sand, fleeing the scene of their crime,
Till one turns, without a word, and smacks
5   His buddy flat with the flat of an axe,
Which cuts down on the dialogue
Some, but it is viewed rather as normal than sad
By me, as I wait for the next ad.

It seems to me it's been quite a while
10 Since the last vision of blonde loveliness
Vanished, her shampoo and shower and general style
Replaced by this lean young lunk-
head parading along with a gun in his back to confess
How yestereve, being drunk
15 And in a state of existential despair,
He beat up his grandma and pawned her invalid chair.

But here at last is a pale beauty
Smoking a filter beside a mountain stream,
Brief interlude, before the conflict of love and duty
20 Gets moving again, as sheriff and posse expound,
Between jail and saloon, the American Dream
Where Justice, after considerable horsing around,
Turns out to be Mercy; when the villain is knocked off,
A kindly uncle offers syrup for my cough.

25 And now these clean-cut athletic types
In global hats are having a nervous debate
As they stand between their individual rocket ships
Which have landed, appropriately, on some rocks

Somewhere in Space, in an atmosphere of hate
Where one tells the other to pull up his socks   30
And get going, he doesn't say where; they fade,
And an angel food cake flutters in the void.

I used to leave now and again;
No more. A lot of violence in American life
These days, mobsters and cops all over the scene.   35
But there's a lot of love, too, mixed with the strife,
And kitchen-kindness, like a bedtime story
With rich food and a more kissable depilatory.
Still, I keep my weapons handy, sitting here
Smoking and shaving and drinking the dry beer.   40

—1967

Philip Larkin

1922–1985

Holding fast to the principle that poetry is to be read rather than studied, the British poet Philip Larkin rejected what he considered the modernist critical dogma that a poem's complexity is a measure of its worthiness. In his hostility toward the poetic avant-garde, Larkin is often identified with "the Movement," a group of British writers who shunned "the aberration of modernism" and the ostentatious "culture-mongering" of poets such as T.S. Eliot and Ezra Pound, whom Larkin believed had made a virtue of obscurity and perverted a native English tradition of plain-style lyric poetry.

"There's not much to say about my work," he once observed. "When you've read a poem, that's it, it's all quite clear what it means." In stark and deliberate contrast to the modernist pursuit of impersonality, Larkin typically adopts an intimate, lucidly colloquial tone in which—in the guise of his poetic persona—he often addresses the reader directly.

Three slender volumes—*The Less Deceived* (1955), *The Whitsun Weddings* (1964), and *High Windows* (1974)—established Larkin as one of the foremost poets of his generation. Many of the poems in these collections examine the experiences of loneliness, disappointment, and despair. But while Larkin's work often suggests the futility of struggle against time's "endless extinction," many of the poems also poignantly register the momentary beauties of the world. As Larkin phrased it, echoing Keats, "One of the jobs of the poem is to make the beautiful seem true and the true beautiful," even if "the disguise can usually be penetrated."

Church Going

Once I am sure there's nothing going on
I step inside, letting the door thud shut.
Another church: matting, seats, and stone,
And little books; sprawlings of flowers, cut
5 For Sunday, brownish now; some brass and stuff
Up at the holy end; the small neat organ;
And a tense, musty, unignorable silence,
Brewed God knows how long. Hatless, I take off
My cycle-clips in awkward reverence,

10 Move forward, run my hand around the font.[1]
From where I stand, the roof looks almost new—

---

1   *font* Baptismal receptacle.

Cleaned, or restored? Someone would know: I don't.
Mounting the lectern, I peruse a few
Hectoring large-scale verses, and pronounce
"Here endeth" much more loudly than I'd meant.   15
The echoes snigger briefly. Back at the door
I sign the book, donate an Irish sixpence,
Reflect the place was not worth stopping for.

Yet stop I did: in fact I often do,
And always end much at a loss like this,   20
Wondering what to look for; wondering, too,
When churches fall completely out of use
What we shall turn them into, if we shall keep
A few cathedrals chronically on show,
Their parchment, plate and pyx[1] in locked cases,   25
And let the rest rent-free to rain and sheep.
Shall we avoid them as unlucky places?

Or, after dark, will dubious women come
To make their children touch a particular stone;
Pick simples° for a cancer; or on some   *medicinal herbs*   30
Advised night see walking a dead one?
Power of some sort or other will go on
In games, in riddles, seemingly at random;
But superstition, like belief, must die,
And what remains when disbelief has gone?   35
Grass, weedy pavement, brambles, buttress, sky,

A shape less recognisable each week,
A purpose more obscure. I wonder who
Will be the last, the very last, to seek
This place for what it was; one of the crew   40
That tap and jot and know what rood-lofts° were?   *church galleries*
Some ruin-bibber,[2] randy for antique,
Or Christmas-addict, counting on a whiff
Of gown-and-bands and organ-pipes and myrrh?
Or will he be my representative,   45

---

1   *pyx* Vessel in which the bread of the Eucharist is kept.
2   *bibber* Someone who compulsively drinks a specific drink.

Bored, uninformed, knowing the ghostly silt
Dispersed, yet tending to this cross of ground
Through suburb scrub because it held unspilt
So long and equably what since is found
50 Only in separation—marriage, and birth,
And death, and thoughts of these—for which was built
This special shell? For, though I've no idea
What this accoutred frowsty° barn is worth,   *stuffy*
It pleases me to stand in silence here;

55 A serious house on serious earth it is,
In whose blent air all our compulsions meet,
Are recognised, and robed as destinies.
And that much never can be obsolete,
Since someone will forever be surprising
60 A hunger in himself to be more serious,
And gravitating with it to this ground,
Which, he once heard, was proper to grow wise in,
If only that so many dead lie round.

—1954

Talking in Bed

Talking in bed ought to be easiest,
Lying together there goes back so far,
An emblem of two people being honest.

Yet more and more time passes silently.
5 Outside, the wind's incomplete unrest
Builds and disperses clouds about the sky,

And dark towns heap up on the horizon.
None of this cares for us. Nothing shows why
At this unique distance from isolation

10 It becomes still more difficult to find
Words at once true and kind,
Or not untrue and not unkind.

—1960

This Be the Verse

They fuck you up, your mum and dad.
    They may not mean to, but they do.
They fill you with the faults they had
    And add some extra, just for you.

But they were fucked up in their turn   5
    By fools in old-style hats and coats,
Who half the time were soppy-stern
    And half at one another's throats.

Man hands on misery to man.
    It deepens like a coastal shelf.   10
Get out as early as you can,
    And don't have any kids yourself.

                            —1971

The Old Fools

What do they think has happened, the old fools,
To make them like this? Do they somehow suppose
It's more grown-up when your mouth hangs open and drools
And you keep on pissing yourself, and can't remember
Who called this morning? Or that, if they only chose,   5
They could alter things back to when they danced all night,
Or went to their wedding, or sloped arms some September?
Or do they fancy there's really been no change,
And they've always behaved as if they were crippled or tight,
Or sat through days of thin continuous dreaming   10
Watching light move? If they don't (and they can't), it's strange;
            Why aren't they screaming?

At death, you break up: the bits that were you
Start speeding away from each other for ever
With no one to see. It's only oblivion, true: 15
We had it before, but then it was going to end,
And was all the time merging with a unique endeavour
To bring to bloom the million-petalled flower
Of being here. Next time you can't pretend

20 There'll be anything else. And these are the first signs:
   Not knowing how, not hearing who, the power
   Of choosing gone. Their looks show that they're for it:
   Ash hair, toad hands, prune face dried into lines—
                    How can they ignore it?

25 Perhaps being old is having lighted rooms
   Inside your head, and people in them, acting.
   People you know, yet can't quite name; each looms
   Like a deep loss restored, from known doors turning,
   Setting down a lamp, smiling from a stair, extracting
30 A known book from the shelves; or sometimes only
   The rooms themselves, chairs and a fire burning,
   The blown bush at the window, or the sun's
   Faint friendliness on the wall some lonely
   Rain-ceased midsummer evening. That is where they live:
35 Not here and now, but where all happened once.
                    This is why they give

   An air of baffled absence, trying to be there
   Yet being here. For the rooms grow farther, leaving
   Incompetent cold, the constant wear and tear
40 Of taken breath, and them crouching below
   Extinction's alp, the old fools, never perceiving
   How near it is. This must be what keeps them quiet:
   The peak that stays in view wherever we go
   For them is rising ground. Can they never tell
45 What is dragging them back, and how it will end?
   Not at night? Not when the strangers come? Never, throughout
   The whole hideous inverted childhood? Well,
                    We shall find out.

                                        —1973

Allen Ginsberg
1926–1997

Along with writers Jack Kerouac and William S. Burroughs, Allen Ginsberg was one of the most prominent writers of the 1950s "Beat Generation," remembered for their literary rebellion against middle-class values and formalist poetry.

Ginsberg is perhaps best known for his poem "Howl," first delivered at a poetry reading in San Francisco in 1955 and published the following year. Drawing on influences from Jewish liturgy to William Blake, the long poem condemns American society's repressive attitudes toward homosexuality, drug use, and mental illness, presenting the demonic god Moloch as an embodiment of America's obsession with money and order. Because the poem makes explicit references to drug use and homosexuality at a time when both were illegal, the publishers of "Howl" were charged with distributing obscene literature, and Ginsberg's poem became the centrepiece of a landmark obscenity trial in the United States. The publishers and the poem ultimately triumphed.

After the Beat era, Ginsberg continued to write until his death, publishing letters and essays as well as poetry. His interest in religion and philosophy, especially Hindu and Buddhist thought, provided an increasingly important focus in his later work. Like "Howl," his post-Beat poems are often politically motivated; *Wichita Vortex Sutra* (1966), for example, censures the Vietnam War, against which Ginsberg was an effective and dedicated activist.

A Supermarket in California

What thoughts I have of you tonight, Walt Whitman,[1] for I walked down the sidestreets under the trees with a headache self-conscious looking at the full moon.

In my hungry fatigue, and shopping for images, I went into the neon fruit supermarket, dreaming of your enumerations!

What peaches and what penumbras![2] Whole families shopping at night! Aisles full of husbands! Wives in the avocados, babies in the tomatoes!—and you, García Lorca,[3] what were you doing down by the watermelons?

---

1   *Walt Whitman* American poet (1819–92), one of Ginsberg's major influences. "A Supermarket in California" was written in 1955, 100 years after Whitman published the first edition of his collection *Leaves of Grass*.
2   *penumbras* Partially shaded regions at the edges of a shadow.
3   *García Lorca* Federico García Lorca (1899–1936), Spanish poet and dramatist.

I saw you, Walt Whitman, childless, lonely old grubber, poking among
10 the meats in the refrigerator and eyeing the grocery boys.[1]

I heard you asking questions of each: Who killed the pork chops? What
price bananas? Are you my Angel?

I wandered in and out of the brilliant stacks of cans following you, and
followed in my imagination by the store detective. We strode down the
15 open corridors together in our solitary fancy tasting artichokes, possessing
every frozen delicacy, and never passing the cashier.

Where are we going, Walt Whitman? The doors close in an hour.
Which way does your beard point tonight?

(I touch your book and dream of our odyssey in the supermarket and
20 feel absurd.)

Will we walk all night through solitary streets? The trees add shade to
shade, lights out in the houses, we'll both be lonely.

Will we stroll dreaming of the lost America of love past blue
automobiles in driveways, home to our silent cottage?

25 Ah, dear father, greybeard, lonely old courage-teacher, what America
did you have when Charon[2] quit poling his ferry and you got out on a
smoking bank and stood watching the boat disappear on the black waters of
Lethe?[3]

—1956 (written 1955)

---

1   *I saw you ... grocery boys* Although the full nature of his sexuality is still debated, most
    scholars believe that Whitman was gay.
2   *Charon* In Greek mythology, the boatman who ferried the souls of the dead across the
    river Styx to Hades.
3   *Lethe* River in Hades, the waters of which brought forgetfulness.

John Ashbery
b. 1927

John Ashbery's admiration for avant-garde music, surrealism, and American abstract expressionist painting has strongly influenced his poetry. The resulting style is experimental, complex, and often difficult. "My poetry imitates or reproduces the way knowledge or awareness come to me, which is by fits and starts and by indirection…," Ashbery has said; "[m]y poetry is disjunct, but then so is life." Ashbery is considered a leading figure in the "New York School" of poets whose work shared affinities with the city's avant-garde art scene during the 1950s and 1960s.

Ashbery was born in Rochester, New York, and attended Harvard and Columbia Universities. He then spent a decade in Paris working as a newspaper editor and art critic while also composing poetry. The collection *Some Trees* (1956) first brought him critical attention; it was followed by the experimental *The Tennis Court Oath* (1962). His reputation grew steadily after this point, and Ashbery has since become widely acknowledged as one of the most important American poets of his era. Of his more than 20 volumes of poetry, the most highly regarded is perhaps *Self-Portrait in a Convex Mirror* (1975), which won three major American literary awards, including the Pulitzer Prize.

As critical admiration for Ashbery has increased, a minority of critics have continued to find fault with the inaccessibility of his approach. For Ashbery, however, difficulty of interpretation is a sign that a poem has something new and profound to show its audience; as he says, "a poem that communicates something that's already known by the reader is not really communicating anything to him, and in fact shows a lack of respect for him."

Civilization and Its Discontents

A people chained to aurora[1]
I alone disarming you

Millions of facts of distributed light

Helping myself with some big boxes
Up the steps, then turning to no neighbourhood: 5
The child's psalm, slightly sung
In the hall rushing into the small room.

---

1   *aurora* Roman goddess personifying the dawn; also another name for the Northern and Southern Lights.

Such fire! leading away from destruction.
Somewhere in the outer ether I glimpsed you
10 Coming at me, the solo barrier did it this time,
Guessing us staying, true to be at the blue mark
Of the threshold. Tired of planning it again and again,
The cool boy distant, and the soaked-up
Afterthought, like so much rain, or roof.

15 The miracle took you in beside him.
Leaves rushed the window, there was clear water and the sound of a lock.
Now I never see you much any more.
The summers are much colder than they used to be
In that other time, when you and I were young.
20 I miss the human truth of your smile,
The halfhearted gaze of your palms,
And all things together, but there is no comic reign
Only the facts you put to me. You must not, then,
Be very surprised if I am alone: it is all for you,
25 The night, and the stars, and the way we used to be.

There is no longer any use in harping on
The incredible principle of daylong silence, the dark sunlight
As only the grass is beginning to know it,

The wreath of the north pole,
30 Festoons for the late return, the shy pensioners
Agasp on the lamplit air. What is agreeable
Is to hold your hand. The gravel
Underfoot. The time is for coming close. Useless
Verbs shooting the other words far away.

35 I had already swallowed the poison
And could only gaze into the distance at my life
Like a saint's with each day distinct.
No heaviness in the upland pastures. Nothing
In the forest. Only life under the huge trees
40 Like a coat that has grown too big, moving far away,
Cutting swamps for men like lapdogs, holding its own,
Performing once again, for you and for me.

—1963

The Improvement

Is that where it happens?
Only yesterday when I came back, I had this
diaphanous disaffection for this room, for spaces,
for the whole sky and whatever lies beyond.
I felt the eggplant, then the rhubarb.
Nothing seems strong enough for
this life to manage, that sees beyond
into particles forming some kind of entity—
so we get dressed kindly, crazy at the moment.
A life of afterwords begins.

We never live long enough in our lives
to know what today is like.
Shards, smiling beaches,
abandon us somehow even as we converse with them.
And the leopard is transparent, like iced tea.

I wake up, my face pressed
in the dewy mess of a dream. It mattered,
because of the dream, and because dreams are by nature sad
even when there's a lot of exclaiming and beating
as there was in this one. I want the openness
of the dream turned inside out, exploded
into pieces of meaning by its own unasked questions,
beyond the calculations of heaven. Then the larkspur[1]
would don its own disproportionate weight,
and trees return to the starting gate.
See, our lips bend.

—1994

---

1   *larkspur* Plant with spikes of flowers.

Thom Gunn

1929–2004

As diverse in subject matter as in style, the poetry of Thom Gunn is difficult to classify. His friend and fellow poet Clive Wilmer described it as "contained energy," an attempt to reconcile passion and intellect, lyricism and argument, by harnessing the flow of experience through traditional verse forms.

The son of London journalists, Gunn spent much of his life in California, where he studied at Stanford and later taught at Berkeley. Gunn is often identified with "the Movement," a group of British poets who turned away from avant-gardism in favour of a more "native English" tradition of plain-style lyric poetry. Yet he always preferred to be understood as an Anglo-American writer, and his influences ranged from seventeenth-century English poets such as John Donne to the American modernist verse of Wallace Stevens and William Carlos Williams.

From his first collection, *Fighting Words* (1954), to his last, *Boss Cupid* (2000), Gunn experimented with styles and techniques. His early poetry, much of it concerned with the existential struggle for self-definition, is characterized by tightly controlled schemes of rhyme and metre. He later experimented with free verse and with varying degrees of formal regularity in the attempt to represent his liberating experiences with LSD and the utopian counterculture in 1960s San Francisco, where he lived until his death. Gunn changed tone again with *The Man with Night Sweats* (1992), which established him as a poet-chronicler and elegist of the AIDS epidemic that claimed many of his friends in the 1980s.

While many have seen Gunn's as a poetry of "tensions," Gunn himself preferred the word "continuities." His life and work, he said, "insists on continuities—between America and England, between free verse and metre, between vision and everyday consciousness."

Tamer and Hawk

I thought I was so tough,
But gentled at your hands,
Cannot be quick enough
To fly for you and show
That when I go I go
At your commands.

Even in flight above
I am no longer free:

You seeled[1] me with your love,
I am blind to other birds—   10
The habit of your words
Has hooded me.

As formerly, I wheel
I hover and I twist,
But only want the feel,   15
In my possessive thought,
Of catcher and of caught
Upon your wrist.

You but half civilize,
Taming me in this way.   20
Through having only eyes
For you I fear to lose,
I lose to keep, and choose
Tamer as prey.

                                                        —1953

To His Cynical Mistress

And love is then no more than a compromise?
An impermanent treaty waiting to be signed
                    By the two enemies?
—While the calculating Cupid feigning impartial blind
Drafts it, promising peace, both leaders wise   5
To his antics sign but secretly double their spies.

On each side is the ignorant animal nation
Jostling friendly in streets, enjoying in good faith
                    This celebration
Forgetting their enmity with cheers and drunken breath   10
But for them there has not been yet amalgamation:
The leaders calmly plot assassination.

                                                        —1958

---

1   *seeled* Part of the taming process in falconry, seeling requires the tamer to stitch up the
    eyes of the hawk.

The Hug

It was your birthday, we had drunk and dined
        Half of the night with our old friend
                Who'd showed us in the end
        To a bed I reached in one drunk stride.
5   Already I lay snug,
        And drowsy with the wine dozed on one side.

I dozed, I slept. My sleep broke on a hug,
                Suddenly, from behind,
In which the full lengths of our bodies pressed:
10   Your instep to my heel,
        My shoulder-blades against your chest.
        It was not sex, but I could feel
        The whole strength of your body set,
                Or braced, to mine,
15   And locking me to you
        As if we were still twenty-two
        When our grand passion had not yet
                Become familial.
        My quick sleep had deleted all
20   Of intervening time and place.
                I only knew
The stay of your secure firm dry embrace.

                                        —1992

Adrienne Rich

1929–2012

Adrienne Rich was born in Baltimore, Maryland. Over her long career, she published more than sixteen volumes of poetry and five volumes of critical prose, most recently *Tonight No Poetry Will Serve: Poems 2007-2010, A Human Eye: Essays on Art in Society,* and *Later Poems: Selected and New 1971-2012,* published posthumously. She edited Muriel Rukeyser's *Selected Poems* for the Library of America. Among numerous other recognitions, Rich was the 2006 recipient of the National Book Foundation's Medal for Distinguished Contribution to American Letters. Her poetry and essays have been widely translated and published internationally.[1]

Aunt Jennifer's Tigers

Aunt Jennifer's tigers prance across a screen,
Bright topaz denizens of a world of green.
They do not fear the men beneath the tree;
They pace in sleek chivalric certainty.

Aunt Jennifer's fingers fluttering through her wool   5
Find even the ivory needle hard to pull.
The massive weight of Uncle's wedding band
Sits heavily upon Aunt Jennifer's hand.

When Aunt is dead, her terrified hands will lie
Still ringed with ordeals she was mastered by.   10
The tigers in the panel that she made
Will go on prancing, proud and unafraid.

—1951

---

1   Editors' note: This author biography was provided by the rights holders of Adrienne Rich's poetry, and is included at their request. Its relative brevity in no way reflects the editors' views as to the importance of Rich's work.

Living in Sin

She had thought the studio would keep itself;
no dust upon the furniture of love.
Half heresy, to wish the taps less vocal,
the panes relieved of grime. A plate of pears,
5 a piano with a Persian shawl, a cat
stalking the picturesque amusing mouse
had risen at his urging.
Not that at five each separate stair would writhe
under the milkman's tramp; that morning light
10 so coldly would delineate the scraps
of last night's cheese and three sepulchral bottles;
that on the kitchen shelf among the saucers
a pair of beetle-eyes would fix her own—
envoy from some black village in the mouldings ...
15 Meanwhile, he, with a yawn,
sounded a dozen notes upon the keyboard,
declared it out of tune, shrugged at the mirror,
rubbed at his beard, went out for cigarettes;
while she, jeered by the minor demons,
20 pulled back the sheets and made the bed and found
a towel to dust the table-top,
and let the coffee-pot boil over on the stove.
By evening she was back in love again,
though not so wholly but throughout the night
25 she woke sometimes to feel the daylight coming
like a relentless milkman up the stairs.

—1955

Diving into the Wreck

First having read the book of myths,
and loaded the camera,
and checked the edge of the knife-blade,
I put on
5 the body-armour of black rubber
the absurd slippers
the grave and awkward mask.
I am having to do this

not like Cousteau[1] with his
assiduous team   10
aboard the sun-flooded schooner
but here alone.

There is a ladder.
The ladder is always there
hanging innocently   15
close to the side of the schooner.
We know what it is for,
we who have used it.
Otherwise
it's a piece of maritime floss   20
some sundry equipment.

I go down.
Rung after rung and still
the oxygen immerses me
the blue light   25
the clear atoms
of our human air.
I go down.
My flippers cripple me,
I crawl like an insect down the ladder   30
and there is no one
to tell me when the ocean
will begin.

First the air is blue and then
it is bluer and then green and then   35
black I am blacking out and yet
my mask is powerful
it pumps my blood with power
the sea is another story
the sea is not a question of power   40
I have to learn alone
to turn my body without force
in the deep element.

---

1   *Cousteau* Jacques Cousteau (1910–97), well-known oceanographer and undersea ex-
     plorer.

And now: it is easy to forget
45 what I came for
among so many who have always
lived here
swaying their crenellated fans
between the reefs
50 and besides
you breathe differently down here.

I came to explore the wreck.
The words are purposes.
The words are maps.
55 I came to see the damage that was done
and the treasures that prevail.
I stroke the beam of my lamp
slowly along the flank
of something more permanent
60 than fish or weed

the thing I came for:
the wreck and not the story of the wreck
the thing itself and not the myth
the drowned face always staring
65 toward the sun
the evidence of damage
worn by salt and sway into this threadbare beauty
the ribs of the disaster
curving their assertion
70 among the tentative haunters.

This is the place.
And I am here, the mermaid whose dark hair
streams black, the merman in his armoured body
We circle silently
75 about the wreck
we dive into the hold.
I am she: I am he

whose drowned face sleeps with open eyes
whose breasts still bear the stress

whose silver, copper, vermeil[1] cargo lies   80
obscurely inside barrels
half-wedged and left to rot
we are the half-destroyed instruments
that once held to a course
the water-eaten log   85
the fouled compass

We are, I am, you are
by cowardice or courage
the one who find our way
back to this scene   90
carrying a knife, a camera
a book of myths
in which
our names do not appear.

—1973

---

1   *vermeil* Gold plate over silver.

Ted Hughes
1930–1998

With bold metaphors and forceful rhythms, poet Ted Hughes paints grim, often violent, visions of human existence. At the same time, he celebrates the power of nature and attempts to reunite humanity with the natural world. Hughes's first volume of poetry, *The Hawk in the Rain* (1957), received critical praise for its strong, earthy language and intense natural imagery. He further established his reputation as a major new poet with his second book, *Lupercal* (1960), and he continued to write prolifically, producing many volumes of poetry as well as verse for children, radio plays, and translations.

In 1956 Hughes married the American poet Sylvia Plath (1932–63); the couple separated in 1962, and Plath committed suicide less than a year later. Hughes put his own poetry on hold to focus on editing and publishing his wife's poems and journals, and the editorial decisions he made as her executor received intense criticism from some of her admirers. Hughes would say very little regarding his relationship with Plath until his 1998 publication of *Birthday Letters*, a series of poems addressed to her.

Wodwo (1967), Hughes's return to poetry after Plath's death, signalled a change in direction from his earlier work. A marked interest in anthropology—and especially in occult, mythic, and folktale sources—began to colour his writing. Several of his volumes were produced in collaboration with visual artists, such as photographer Fay Godwin, with whom he created *Remains of Elmet* (1979), an exploration of the history and landscape of his native West Yorkshire from ancient to industrial times.

Hughes was Britain's Poet Laureate from 1984 until his death in 1998. British poet and critic Dick Davis has offered this explanation for the continuing appeal of Hughes's poetry: "He brings back to our suburban, centrally-heated and, above all, *safe* lives reports from an authentic frontier of reality and the imagination."

The Thought-Fox

I imagine this midnight moment's forest:
Something else is alive
Beside the clock's loneliness
And this blank page where my fingers move.

5 Through the window I see no star:
Something more near
Though deeper within darkness
Is entering the loneliness:

Cold, delicately as the dark snow
A fox's nose touches twig, leaf;   10
Two eyes serve a movement, that now
And again now, and now, and now

Sets neat prints into the snow
Between trees, and warily a lame
Shadow lags by stump and in hollow   15
Of a body that is bold to come

Across clearings, an eye,
A widening deepening greenness,
Brilliantly, concentratedly,
Coming about its own business   20

Till, with a sudden sharp hot stink of fox,
It enters the dark hole of the head.
The window is starless still; the clock ticks,
The page is printed.

—1957

Pike[1]

Pike, three inches long, perfect
Pike in all parts, green tigering the gold.
Killers from the egg: the malevolent aged grin.
They dance on the surface among the flies.

Or move, stunned by their own grandeur,   5
Over a bed of emerald, silhouette
Of submarine delicacy and horror.
A hundred feet long in their world.

In ponds, under the heat-struck lily pads—
Gloom of their stillness: 10
Logged on last year's black leaves, watching upwards.
Or hung in an amber cavern of weeds

---

1   *Pike* Family of freshwater fish, some species of which can grow longer than two metres.
     Considered unusually aggressive predators, they eat other fish, amphibians, small mam-
     mals, birds, and sometimes each other.

The jaws' hooked clamp and fangs
Not to be changed at this date;
15 A life subdued to its instrument;
The gills kneading quietly, and the pectorals.

Three we kept behind glass,
Jungled in weed: three inches, four,
And four and a half: fed fry to them—
20 Suddenly there were two. Finally one.

With a sag belly and the grin it was born with.
And indeed they spare nobody.
Two, six pounds each, over two feet long,
High and dry and dead in the willow-herb—

25 One jammed past its gills down the other's gullet:
The outside eye stared: as a vice locks—
The same iron in this eye
Though its film shrank in death.

A pond I fished, fifty yards across,
30 Whose lilies and muscular tench[1]
Had outlasted every visible stone
Of the monastery that planted them—

Stilled legendary depth:
It was as deep as England. It held
35 Pike too immense to stir, so immense and old
That past nightfall I dared not cast

But silently cast and fished
With the hair frozen on my head
For what might move, for what eye might move.
40 The still splashes on the dark pond,

Owls hushing the floating woods
Frail on my ear against the dream
Darkness beneath night's darkness had freed,
That rose slowly towards me, watching.

—1959

---

1   *tench* Fish similar to carp.

Hawk Roosting

I sit in the top of the wood, my eyes closed.
Inaction, no falsifying dream
Between my hooked head and hooked feet:
Or in sleep rehearse perfect kills and eat.

The convenience of the high trees!   5
The air's buoyancy and the sun's ray
Are of advantage to me;
And the earth's face upward for my inspection.

My feet are locked upon the rough bark.
It took the whole of Creation   10
To produce my foot, my each feather:
Now I hold Creation in my foot

Or fly up, and revolve it all slowly—
I kill where I please because it is all mine.
There is no sophistry in my body: 15
My manners are tearing off heads—

The allotment of death.
For the one path of my flight is direct
Through the bones of the living.
No arguments assert my right: 20

The sun is behind me.
Nothing has changed since I began.
My eye has permitted no change.
I am going to keep things like this.

—1960

Heptonstall Old Church[1]

A great bird landed here.

Its song drew men out of rock,
Living men out of bog and heather.

---

1   *Heptonstall Old Church* The town of Heptonstall was three miles from Hughes's childhood home of Mytholmroyd, in West Yorkshire. The ruins of the "old church" (dating from the thirteenth century) stand beside the present church, constructed in 1854. The bodies of Sylvia Plath (1932–63) and of Hughes's parents are buried in its churchyard.

Its song put a light in the valleys
5   And harness on the long moors.

Its song brought a crystal from space
And set it in men's heads.

Then the bird died.

Its giant bones
10   Blackened and became a mystery.

The crystal in men's heads
Blackened and fell to pieces.

The valleys went out.
The moorland broke loose.

—1979

Heptonstall Old Church, 1970s.

Derek Walcott
b. 1930

In 1992, Derek Walcott became the first Caribbean writer to receive the Nobel Prize in Literature. Throughout his career, he has grappled with the central issues of twentieth- and twenty-first-century Caribbean writing: the use of the English language versus that of Creole; the effects of a history of slavery and colonization on the region; and the deep-seated ambivalence toward English culture that results from that history.

Walcott's personal background reflects the cultural complexities of the Caribbean. A descendant both of Europeans and of former slaves, he was born into an English-speaking family on the predominantly French Creole-speaking island of St. Lucia, and has lived there or in Trinidad for most of his life. In his Nobel acceptance speech he expressed his wish that the people of the Caribbean would move beyond their painful history, claiming that "[we] make too much of that long groan which underlines the past." He proffered instead a vision of Caribbean poetry as a route to rebuilding and celebrating Caribbean culture: "the fate of poetry is to fall in love with the world, in spite of History."

Some Caribbean intellectuals have criticized Walcott's attitude toward the colonial past, arguing for an unequivocal return to African traditions or for a turning away from the English language in favour of Creole. In response to criticism of his decision to write in English, Walcott has argued that the language is shaped by those who use it.

Walcott's more than 20 books of poetry include the epic *Omeros* (1990), which merges Homer's *Odyssey* with the history of St. Lucia, and the T.S. Eliot Prize-winning collection *White Egrets* (2011). Walcott is also a prolific playwright whose work has been instrumental to the development of indigenous theatre in Trinidad.

A Far Cry from Africa

A wind is ruffling the tawny pelt
Of Africa. Kikuyu,[1] quick as flies,
Batten upon[2] the bloodstreams of the veldt.°   open country
Corpses are scattered through a paradise.
Only the worm, colonel of carrion, cries: 5
"Waste no compassion on these separate dead!"

---

1   *Kikuyu* Bantu-speaking people of Kenya who fought against British colonial settlers as part of the eight-year Mau Mau uprising of the 1950s.
2   *Batten upon* Thrive on; revel in.

Statistics justify and scholars seize
The salients of colonial policy.
What is that to the white child hacked in bed?
10 To savages, expendable as Jews?

Threshed out by beaters, the long rushes break
In a white dust of ibises[1] whose cries
Have wheeled since civilization's dawn
From the parched river or beast-teeming plain.
15 The violence of beast on beast is read
As natural law, but upright man
Seeks his divinity by inflicting pain.
Delirious as these worried beasts, his wars
Dance to the tightened carcass of a drum,
20 While he calls courage still that native dread
Of the white peace contracted by the dead.

Again brutish necessity wipes its hands
Upon the napkin of a dirty cause, again
A waste of our compassion, as with Spain,[2]
25 The gorilla wrestles with the superman.
I who am poisoned with the blood of both,
Where shall I turn, divided to the vein?
I who have cursed
The drunken officer of British rule, how choose
30 Between this Africa and the English tongue I love?
Betray them both, or give back what they give?
How can I face such slaughter and be cool?
How can I turn from Africa and live?

—1962

---

1   *ibises* Long-legged, stork-like birds that inhabit lakes and swamps.
2   *Spain* I.e., the Spanish Civil War (1936–39). Many foreign volunteers participated in
the Civil War, perceiving it as a way to resist the international rise of fascism. After brutality on both sides, the war ended with the establishment of a dictatorship supported
by the German Nazis and the Italian Fascists.

Ruins of a Great House

though our longest sun sets at right declensions and makes but winter
arches, it cannot be long before we lie down in darkness, and have our
light in ashes ...[1]

—BROWNE, *Urn Burial*

Stones only, the disjecta membra[2] of this Great House,
Whose moth-like girls are mixed with candledust,
Remain to file the lizard's dragonish claws.
The mouths of those gate cherubs shriek with stain;
Axle and coach wheel silted under the muck   5
Of cattle droppings.
                Three crows flap for the trees
And settle, creaking the eucalyptus boughs.
A smell of dead limes quickens in the nose
The leprosy of empire.   10
            "Farewell, green fields,
              Farewell, ye happy groves!"[3]
Marble like Greece, like Faulkner's South[4] in stone,
Deciduous beauty prospered and is gone,
But where the lawn breaks in a rash of trees   15
A spade below dead leaves will ring the bone
Of some dead animal or human thing
Fallen from evil days, from evil times.

It seems that the original crops were limes
Grown in the silt that clogs the river's skirt;   20
The imperious rakes[5] are gone, their bright girls gone,
The river flows, obliterating hurt.
I climbed a wall with the grille ironwork
Of exiled craftsmen protecting that great house
From guilt, perhaps, but not from the worm's rent   25
Nor from the padded cavalry of the mouse.

---

1   *though our ... ashes* From English essayist Thomas Browne's *Hydriotaphia: Urne Buriall*
     (1658).
2   *disjecta membra* Latin: scattered remains.
3   *"Farewell, green ... happy groves!"* See William Blake's poem "Night" (1789): "Farewell,
     green fields and happy groves."
4   *Faulkner's South* The American South as depicted in the fiction of William Faulkner
     (1897–1962).
5   *rakes* Wild young noblemen.

And when a wind shook in the limes I heard
What Kipling[1] heard, the death of a great empire, the abuse
Of ignorance by Bible and by sword.

30 A green lawn, broken by low walls of stone,
Dipped to the rivulet, and pacing, I thought next
Of men like Hawkins, Walter Raleigh, Drake,[2]
Ancestral murderers and poets, more perplexed
In memory now by every ulcerous crime.
35 The world's green age then was a rotting lime
Whose stench became the charnel° galleon's text.   *mortuary*
The rot remains with us, the men are gone.
But, as dead ash is lifted in a wind
That fans the blackening ember of the mind,
40 My eyes burned from the ashen prose of Donne.[3]

Ablaze with rage I thought,
Some slave is rotting in this manorial lake,
But still the coal of my compassion fought
That Albion° too was once   *England*
45 A colony like ours, "part of the continent, piece of the main,"[4]
Nook-shotten, rook o'erblown, deranged
By foaming channels and the vain expense
Of bitter faction.
                All in compassion ends
50 So differently from what the heart arranged:
"as well as if a manor of thy friend's …"

                                    —1962

1   *Kipling* Rudyard Kipling (1865–1936), English novelist and short story writer whose works often interrogated British imperialism.
2   *Hawkins* John Hawkins, sixteenth-century British slave trader who brought slaves from Africa to West Indian plantations; *Walter Raleigh* English explorer and poet (1552–1618); *Drake* Sir Francis Drake (1543–96), British explorer and military commander who became the first Englishman to sail around the world.
3   *Donne* English poet and minister John Donne (1572–1631).
4   *part of … main* From John Donne's *Devotions upon Emergent Occasions*, Meditation 17 (1624): "No man is an island, entire of itself; every man is a piece of the continent, a part of the main. If a clod be washed away by the sea, Europe is the less, as well as if a promontory were, as well as if a manor of thy friend's or of thine own were…."

from *Midsummer*

52

I heard them marching the leaf-wet roads of my head,
the sucked vowels of a syntax trampled to mud,
a division of dictions, one troop black, barefooted,
the other in redcoats bright as their sovereign's blood;
their feet scuffled like rain, the bare soles with the shod.   5
One fought for a queen, the other was chained in her service,
but both, in bitterness, travelled the same road.
Our occupation and the Army of Occupation
are born enemies, but what mortar can size
the broken stones of the barracks of Brimstone Hill[1]   10
to the gaping brick of Belfast? Have we changed sides
to the mustached sergeants and the horsy gentry
because we serve English, like a two-headed sentry
guarding its borders? No language is neutral;
the green oak of English is a murmurous cathedral   15
where some took umbrage, some peace, but every shade, all,
helped widen its shadow. I used to haunt the arches
of the British barracks of Vigie.[2] There were leaves there,
bright, rotting like revers or epaulettes,[3] and the stenches
of history and piss. Leaves piled like the dropped aitches   20
of soldiers from rival shires, from the brimstone trenches
of Agincourt to the gas of the Somme.[4] On Poppy Day[5]
our schools bought red paper flowers. They were for Flanders.

---

1   *Brimstone Hill* Eighteenth-century fortress built by slaves on the island of Saint Kitts,
    in the Caribbean. First settled by the British in the early seventeenth century, Saint Kitts
    became a British colony in 1783 and gained independence as part of the Federation of
    Saint Kitts and Nevis in 1983.
2   *barracks of Vigie* On the island of St. Lucia in the Caribbean.
3   *revers* Reversed edges of a coat, vest, etc.; *epaulettes* Ornamental shoulder pieces on
    military uniforms.
4   *Agincourt* Site of Henry V's famous victory over the French in 1415; *Somme* Site of a
    World War I battle in France, which began on 1 July 1916 and lasted five months.
5   *Poppy Day* Remembrance Day (in Britain and the Commonwealth) or Veteran's Day
    (in the US), when poppies are worn to commemorate those killed in World Wars I and
    II. (See John McCrae's 1915 poem "In Flanders Fields.")

I saw Hotspur[1] cursing the smoke through which a popinjay
25 minced from the battle. Those raging commanders from
Thersites[2] to Percy, their rant is our model.
I pinned the poppy to my blazer. It bled like a vowel.

—1984

Central America

Helicopters are cutlassing the wild bananas.
Between a nicotine thumb and forefinger
brittle faces crumble like tobacco leaves.
Children waddle in vests, their legs bowed,
5 little shrimps curled under their navels.
The old men's teeth are stumps in a charred forest.
Their skins grate like the iguana's.
Their gaze like slate stones.
Women squat by the river's consolations
10 where children wade up to their knees,
and a stick stirs up a twinkling of butterflies.
Up there, in the blue acres
of forest, flies circle their fathers.
In spring, in the upper provinces
15 of the Empire, yellow tanagers
float up through the bare branches.
There is no distinction in these distances.

—1987

---

1   *Hotspur* Nickname of Sir Henry Percy (1366–1403), an English nobleman who led an
    uprising against King Henry IV and who figures as the hot-headed rival to Prince Hal
    in Shakespeare's *I Henry IV*. In a speech in *I Henry IV* 1.3.28–68, he expresses anger
    about a "popinjay" (frivolous, foppish man) making disrespectful small talk as bodies
    are carried off the battlefield.
2   *Thersites* Cowardly soldier of Greek legend who appears in Homer's *Iliad* and Shake-
    speare's *Troilus and Cressida*. In the *Iliad*, he complains about the incompetence of his
    rulers; in Shakespeare's play, he delivers cynical commentary about the foolishness of
    war.

I could hardly speak.
I thought every German was you.
And the language obscene   30

An engine, an engine
Chuffing me off like a Jew.
A Jew to Dachau, Auschwitz, Belsen.[1]
I began to talk like a Jew.
I think I may well be a Jew.   35

The snows of the Tyrol,[2] the clear beer of Vienna
Are not very pure or true.
With my gypsy ancestress and my weird luck
And my Taroc° pack and my Taroc pack   *Tarot*
I may be a bit of a Jew.   40

I have always been scared of *you*,
With your Luftwaffe,[3] your gobbledygoo.
And your neat moustache
And your Aryan eye, bright blue.
Panzer-man,[4] panzer-man, O You—   45

Not God but a swastika
So black no sky could squeak through.
Every woman adores a Fascist,
The boot in the face, the brute
Brute heart of a brute like you.   50

You stand at the blackboard,[5] daddy,
In the picture I have of you,
A cleft in your chin instead of your foot
But no less a devil for that, no not
Any less the black man who   55

---

1 *Dachau, Auschwitz, Belsen* Sites of Nazi concentration camps during World War II.
2 *Tyrol* State in Austria.
3 *Luftwaffe* German air force during World War II.
4 *Panzer-man* "Panzers" were German armoured divisions, notably those equipped with tanks.
5 *You ... blackboard* Otto Plath taught biology and German at Boston University.

Bit my pretty red heart in two.
I was ten when they buried you.
At twenty I tried to die
And get back, back, back to you.
60 I thought even the bones would do.

But they pulled me out of the sack,
And they stuck me together with glue.
And then I knew what to do.
I made a model of you,
65 A man in black with a Meinkampf[1] look

And a love of the rack and the screw.
And I said I do, I do.
So daddy, I'm finally through.
The black telephone's off at the root,
70 The voices just can't worm through.

If I've killed one man, I've killed two—
The vampire who said he was you
And drank my blood for a year,
Seven years, if you want to know.
75 Daddy, you can lie back now.

There's a stake in your fat black heart
And the villagers never liked you.
They are dancing and stamping on you.
They always *knew* it was you.
80 Daddy, daddy, you bastard, I'm through.

—1965 (written 1962)

Lady Lazarus[2]

I have done it again.
One year in every ten
I manage it—

---

1   *Meinkampf* Adolf Hitler's book *Mein Kampf* (1924) outlines his political philosophy.
2   *Lazarus* Man brought back to life by Jesus after being dead for four days. See John 11.1–44.

A sort of walking miracle, my skin
Bright as a Nazi lampshade,[1]   5
My right foot

A paperweight,
My featureless, fine
Jew linen.

Peel off the napkin   10
O my enemy.
Do I terrify?—

The nose, the eye pits, the full set of teeth?
The sour breath
Will vanish in a day.   15

Soon, soon the flesh
The grave cave ate will be
At home on me

And I a smiling woman.
I am only thirty.   20
And like the cat I have nine times to die.

This is Number Three.
What a trash
To annihilate each decade.

What a million filaments.   25
The peanut-crunching crowd
Shoves in to see

Them unwrap me hand and foot—
The big strip tease.
Gentlemen, ladies   30

---

1   *Nazi lampshade* Some Nazi officials allegedly created leather souvenirs, such as lamp-
     shades, using the skin of concentration camp victims.

These are my hands
My knees.
I may be skin and bone,

Nevertheless, I am the same, identical woman.
35 The first time it happened I was ten.
It was an accident.

The second time I meant
To last it out and not come back at all.
I rocked shut

40 As a seashell.
They had to call and call
And pick the worms off me like sticky pearls.

Dying
Is an art, like everything else.
45 I do it exceptionally well.

I do it so it feels like hell.
I do it so it feels real.
I guess you could say I've a call.

It's easy enough to do it in a cell.
50 It's easy enough to do it and stay put.
It's the theatrical

Comeback in broad day
To the same place, the same face, the same brute
Amused shout:

55 "A miracle!"
That knocks me out.
There is a charge

For the eyeing of my scars, there is a charge
For the hearing of my heart—
60 It really goes.

And there is a charge, a very large charge
For a word or a touch
Or a bit of blood

Or a piece of my hair or my clothes.
So, so, Herr[1] Doktor.   65
So, Herr Enemy.

I am your opus,
I am your valuable,
The pure gold baby

That melts to a shriek.   70
I turn and burn.
Do not think I underestimate your great concern.

Ash, ash—
You poke and stir.
Flesh, bone, there is nothing there—   75

A cake of soap,[2]
A wedding ring,
A gold filling.

Herr God, Herr Lucifer
Beware   80
Beware.

Out of the ash
I rise with my red hair
And I eat men like air.

—1965 (written 1962)

---

1   *Herr* German: Sir, Lord, Mister.
2   *cake of soap* During and after the war, it was widely believed that the bodies of the dead
     from concentration camps were used to mass produce soap; historians have not found
     evidence to substantiate this rumour.

Adrian Henri

1932–2000

An artist, poet, teacher, and musician, Adrian Henri rose to prominence as one of the "Liverpool Poets" in the 1960s. Known for making poetry accessible to young and working-class audiences, this group of popular poets frequently performed their works to music before crowds of people in busy cafés and other bohemian haunts.

In 1967 Henri and fellow Liverpool Poets Roger McGough and Brian Patten were published together in the anthology *The Mersey Sound*—a collection named after the local music movement that produced The Beatles and spurred the "British invasion" of American popular music. Since its publication, *The Mersey Sound* has sold more than half a million copies, making it one of the best selling anthologies of poetry in the UK.

Henri's involvement in performance poetry eventually led to the founding of The Liverpool Scene, a poetry rock group. Henri was also a prolific painter, a passion that fellow band member Mike Evans notes was apparent in his poetry: "He wrote what he saw, as much as what he felt, though what he described was often expressed with such passion that even the most simplistic listings of people or places were lit with an emotional glow."

Mrs. Albion You've Got a Lovely Daughter[1]

(for Allen Ginsberg)[2]

Albion's most lovely daughter sat on the banks of the
    Mersey[3] dangling her landing stage in the water.

The daughters of Albion
    arriving by underground at Central Station
5   eating hot ecclescakes at the Pierhead[4]
    writing "Billy Blake is fab" on a wall in Mathew St.[5]

---

1   *Mrs. Albion ... Lovely Daughter* Reference to the song "Mrs. Brown, You've Got a Lovely Daughter," popularized by the British pop band Herman's Hermits in 1963; *Albion* Ancient name for the island of Britain.
2   *Allen Ginsberg* American beat poet (1926–97).
3   *Mersey* River that runs through North West England.
4   *ecclescakes* Small flat pastries filled with currants, named after the English town Eccles; *Pierhead* Located by the riverside in Liverpool.
5   *Billy Blake* English poet William Blake (1757–1827); *Mathew St.* Street in Liverpool famous for the Cavern Club, where the Beatles frequently played.

taking off their navyblue schooldrawers and
putting on nylon panties ready for the night

The daughters of Albion
    see the moonlight beating down on them in Bebington[1]   10
    throw away their chewinggum ready for the goodnight kiss
sleep in the dinnertime sunlight with old men
    looking up their skirts in St. Johns Gardens
comb their darkblonde hair in suburban bedrooms
powder their delicate little nipples/wondering if tonight will be the night   15
their bodies pressed into dresses or sweaters
lavender at The Cavern or pink at The Sink[2]

The daughters of Albion
    wondering how to explain why they didn't go home

The daughters of Albion   20
    taking the dawn ferry to tomorrow
    worrying about what happened
    worrying about what hasn't happened
    lacing up blue sneakers over brown ankles
    fastening up brown stockings to blue suspenderbelts°   *garter belts* 25

Beautiful boys with bright red guitars
in the spaces between the stars

Reelin' an' a-rockin'
Wishin' an' a-hopin'
Kissin' an' a-prayin'   30
Lovin' an' a-layin'

Mrs. Albion you've got a lovely daughter.

—1967

---

1   *Bebington* Small town close to Liverpool.
2   *The Sink* Popular Liverpool nightclub that opened in the 1960s.

Lucille Clifton
1936–2010

Lucille Clifton consciously broke from poetic conventions in her work, which celebrates family life, the female body, biblical characters (often envisioned as Caribbean or African), and African American history, including the history of her own family. She addressed these subjects in personal, evocative, and straightforward language. Clifton tidily expressed her impatience with conventional images of the poet with a few comments in her final interview: "There's a way you're supposed to look if you're an American poet. There's a way you're supposed to sound.... And I think it's hogwash."

Born Thelma Lucille Sayles, Clifton grew up in Buffalo, New York; her working-class parents exposed their large family to an abundance of literature. She attended university and teacher's college, but dropped out to work on her writing. A few years later, she gave birth to the first of her six children; although she claimed that at home she was "wife and mama mostly," she also said that her experience as a mother was an important source of poetic inspiration. When Clifton published her first poetry collection, *Good Times*, in 1969, it was named by *The New York Times* as one of the year's ten best books.

Clifton received the National Book Award for *Blessing the Boats: New and Selected Poems, 1988–2000* (2000), and was posthumously awarded the Frost Medal in 2010. In addition to writing more than ten poetry books for adults, Clifton was also a prolific author of children's literature that often addressed difficult subjects such as death, history, and abuse.

Miss Rosie

when i watch you
wrapped up like garbage
sitting, surrounded by the smell
of too old potato peels
5 or
when i watch you
in your old man's shoes
with the little toe cut out
sitting, waiting for your mind
10 like next week's grocery
i say
when i watch you
you wet brown bag of a woman

who used to be the best looking gal in georgia
used to be called the Georgia Rose   15
i stand up
through your destruction
i stand up

—1969

The Lost Baby Poem

the time i dropped your almost body down
down to meet the waters under the city
and run one with the sewage to the sea
what did i know about waters rushing back
what did i know about drowning   5
or being drowned

you would have been born into winter
in the year of the disconnected gas
and no car   we would have made the thin
walk over genesee hill into the canada wind   10
to watch you slip like ice into strangers' hands
you would have fallen naked as snow into winter
if you were here i could tell you these
and some other things

if i am ever less than a mountain   15
for your definite brothers and sisters
let the rivers pour over my head
let the sea take me for a spiller
of seas   let black men call me stranger
always   for your never named sake   20

—1987

Roger McGough
b. 1937

High-spirited and conversational in tone, the work of British contemporary poet Roger McGough has earned international praise. A prolific writer with more than 50 books to his credit, he has twice won the Signal Award for excellence in children's poetry, and is a Fellow of the Royal Society of Literature.

McGough began publishing poetry together with Adrian Henri and Brian Patten in the 1960s. The three became known as the "Liverpool Poets"; their work is anthologized in the popular collection *The Mersey Sound* (1967), which has sold over half a million copies. The Liverpool Poets were credited with making poetry accessible to middle- and working-class audiences, challenging the perception that this form of expression belonged exclusively to the educated and the wealthy. McGough has said that he wrote with a popular audience in mind: "If I'd written a serious poem I'd always end up making it funny, to prove to this imagined reader or listener, which would have been a fellow Liverpudlian, that I'm not better than you."

McGough is known for his comedic edge and his playful approach to language. Though his work is often lighthearted, it can also be ambiguous and melancholy. He comments: "People always seem to say I'm whimsical and anti-establishment. Sarcastic. I don't think I'm any of these things really. A bit of whimsy, maybe; sentimental, yes, I'd own up to that."

Comeclose and Sleepnow

it is afterwards
and you talk on tiptoe
happy to be part
of the darkness
5   lips becoming limp
a prelude to tiredness.
Comeclose and Sleepnow
for in the morning
when a policeman
10   disguised as the sun
creeps into the room
and your mother
disguised as birds
calls from the trees
15   you will put on a dress of guilt

and shoes with broken high ideals
and refusing coffee
run
alltheway
home.   20

—1967

Les Murray
b. 1938

Les Murray's humble upbringing as the son of a dairy farmer in rural New South Wales has long been a point of pride and a source of inspiration for him. In recognition both of his contribution to Australia's literary landscape and of the central part he has played in various cultural debates, Murray is today widely recognized not only as "the Bard of Bunyah"—the bush territory of his childhood—but also as Australia's national poet.

Although pointedly local in its celebration of Australia's rural heartland, Murray's poetry seeks more broadly to give, he says, "utterance and form to hitherto unexpressed elements of Australian mind and character." As he conceives it, Australia's essential nature abides in the outback: it is fundamentally pastoral, tribal, traditional, hardy, and uncompromised by the elitism and affectation of urban culture. This is the Australia—"part imaginary and part historical"—that Murray summons in collections such as *Poems against Economics* (1972) and the verse novel *The Boys Who Stole the Funeral* (1980). For Murray, despite the degrading legacy of colonialism, the rise of machine culture, and the sterility of modern city life, this indigenous Australia may be sought and recovered; to do so he looks to aboriginal history, to folklore, to pioneer and wartime experiences, and to the land itself.

A self-described "subhuman redneck," Murray has frequently attracted controversy with his outspoken condemnation of the forms of liberalism, feminism, and intellectual pretension he associates with urban Australia. Many have taken issue with Murray's politics; few have denied his ability to write with what a reviewer in *The New Republic* has described as "great linguistic power and moral energy."

Pigs

Us all on sore cement was we.
Not warmed then with glares. Not glutting mush
under that pole the lightning's tied to.
No farrow°-shit in milk to make us randy.   *young pig*
5   Us back in cool god-shit. We ate crisp.
We nosed up good rank in the tunnelled bush.
Us all fuckers then. And Big, huh? Tusked
the balls-biting dog and gutsed him wet.
Us shoved down the soft cement of rivers.
10 Us snored the earth hollow, filled farrow, grunted.
Never stopped growing. We sloughed, we soughed°   *sighed*

and balked no weird till the high ridgebacks was us
with weight-buried hooves. Or bristly, with milk.
Us never knowed like slitting nor hose-biff[1] then.
Nor the terrible sheet-cutting screams up ahead.   15
The burnt water kicking. This gone-already feeling
here in no place with our heads on upside down.

—1992

The Shield-Scales of Heraldry[2]

Surmounting my government's high evasions
stands a barbecue of crosses and birds
tended by a kangaroo and emu[3]
but in our courts, above the judge,
a lion and a unicorn still keep   5
their smaller offspring, plus a harp,
in an open prison looped with mottoes. [4]

Coats of arms, plaster Rorschach blots,
crowned stone moths, they encrust Europe.
As God was dismissed from churches   10
they fluttered in and cling to the walls,
abstract comic-pages held by scrolled beasts,
or wear on the flagstones underfoot.
They pertain to an earlier Antichrist,[5]

the one before police. Mafiose citadels   15
made them, states of one attended family
islanded in furrows. [6] The oldest
are the simplest. A cross, some coins,
a stripe, a roof tree, a spur rowel,

---

1   *biff* Blow or punch.
2   *Heraldry* Symbols and images appearing on coats of arms.
3   *barbeque ... emu* The Australian coat of arms depicts a shield decorated with crosses and
    birds, held up by a kangaroo and an emu.
4   *lion ... mottoes* In the contemporary coat of arms of the United Kingdom, a lion and a
    unicorn hold up a shield bearing a depiction of a harp and smaller lions; the shield is sur-
    rounded by a garter with a motto written on it.
5   *Antichrist* See 2 John 1.7.
6   *Mafiose citadels ... in furrows* Refers to the medieval origin of heraldry; initially a means
    of identifying friends and enemies on the battlefield, coats of arms evolved into inherited
    family symbols; *Mafiose* I.e., of organized crime.

20 bowstaves, a hollow-gutted lion,[1]
and all in lucid target colours.

The rhyming of name with name,
marriages quarter and cube them
till they are sacred campaign maps
25 or anatomy inside dissected mantling,
glyphs minutely clear through their one
rule, that colour must abut either
gold or silver, the non-weapon metals.

The New World doesn't blazon well—[2]
30 the new world ran away from blazonry
or was sent away in chains by it—
but exceptions shine: the spread eagle
with the fireworks display on its belly
and in the thinks-balloon above its head.[3]
35 And when as a half-autistic

kid in scrub paddocks vert and or
I grooved on the *cloisons*[4] of pedigree
it was a vivid writing of system
that hypnotised me, beyond the obvious
40 euphemism of force. It was eight hundred
years of cubist art and Europe's dreamings:
the Cup, the Rose, the Ship, the Antlers.

High courage, bestial snobbery,
neither now merits ungrace from us.
45 They could no longer hang me,
throttling, for a rabbit sejant.°   *sitting upright*
Like everyone, I would now be lord
or lady myself, and pardon me
or myself loose the coronet-necked hounds.

—1994

---

1   *cross ... lion* Symbols commonly seen on the shields of coats of arms.
2   *doesn't blazon well* I.e., doesn't take to heraldry.
3   *exceptions ... head* The front of the Great Seal of the United States, used as the country's
     official coat of arms, shows an eagle. In front of the eagle is a shield with red and white
     stripes and a blue portion; above the eagle is a circle containing thirteen stars.
4   *vert* Shade of green used in heraldry; *cloisons* French: partitions. Also refers to the *cloi-
     sonné* technique, sometimes used to make heraldic emblems; in *cloisonné*, thin metal strips
     are used to create distinct areas, called *cloisons*, that are each filled with coloured enamel.

The Early Dark

As the woman leaves the nursery, driving into early dark,
potholes in the lane make plants nudge and the wire-caged

fowls cluck like crockery, in the back of the station wagon.
A symphony is ending, too, over the brilliant city-plan

of the dashboard, and clapping pours like heavy rain   5
for minutes, outdoing the hoarse intake of asphalt

till her son giggles *I like that best, the applause part.*
He's getting older; now he has to win odd exchanges.

She's still partly back in the huge wind-wrangled steel shed
with its pastels and parterres[1] of seedlings, level by table   10

and the shy nurseryman, his eyes like a gatecrasher's fork
at a smorgasbord, spiking and circling. Now each object

in the headlights is unique, except the constant supplying
of trees, apparitional along verges, in near pastures. An owl

wrenches sideways off the road's hobnail; a refrigerator, shot   15
for children to breathe in it, guards someone's parcels; a boot.

A turn past this rollicking prewar bridge marks an end to tar.
Now for the hills, balancing on the tyres' running-shoes.

These road-ripples, Mum, they're sound-waves, did you know?
is also a surrender, to soothe. She recalls a suitor she told   20

about beauty's hardships, and her lovers, married and not,
whom he'd know. It felt kinder, confiding in an unattractive man.

—1999

---

1   *parterres* Ornamental gardens in which flowerboxes are arranged symmetrically on a level
     surface.

Margaret Atwood
b. 1939

In a career spanning half a century and virtually all genres, Margaret Atwood has risen to become one of Canada's most visible and versatile literary figures. Her work, which is as frequently found on best-seller lists as on academic syllabi, has been translated into over 35 languages. But despite her international appeal, Atwood remains a self-consciously Canadian writer.

Atwood writes within and across many traditional forms and categories. Although best known for novels such as *The Handmaid's Tale* (1985) and *Oryx and Crake* (2003), she initially established her reputation as a poet. Her first major collection, *The Circle Game* (1966) is concerned with national identity, particularly as it relates to Canada's natural landscape. Atwood explored similar themes in *The Animals in That Country* (1968) and *The Journals of Susanna Moodie* (1970), in which stark, precise, tightly controlled poems explore the artificial constructs that we attempt to impose on the uncontrollable, mysterious natural forces that inhabit and surround us.

The poems in her many collections range widely; national and feminist concerns are among the subjects she touches on, as are mythology, environmentalism, and old age and death. Regardless of their subject, her poems engage consistently with language itself; in Atwood's view, fiction "is the guardian of the moral and ethical sense" of a society, while "poetry is the heart of the language, the activity through which language is renewed and kept alive."

Death of a Young Son by Drowning[1]

He, who navigated with success
the dangerous river of his own birth
once more set forth

on a voyage of discovery
5 into the land I floated on
but could not touch to claim.

---

1 *Death of ... Drowning* From *The Journals of Susanna Moodie* (1970), a collection Atwood based on the life and work of Susanna Moodie, author of the 1852 pioneer memoir *Roughing It in the Bush*. Moodie's son drowned in the Moira River in Upper Canada, where the family had settled.

His feet slid on the bank,
the currents took him;
he swirled with ice and trees in the swollen water

and plunged into distant regions,   10
his head a bathysphere;[1]
through his eyes' thin glass bubbles
he looked out, reckless adventurer
on a landscape stranger than Uranus
we have all been to and some remember.   15

There was an accident; the air locked,
he was hung in the river like a heart.
They retrieved the swamped body,

cairn of my plans and future charts,
with poles and hooks   20
from among the nudging logs.

It was spring, the sun kept shining, the new grass
leapt to solidity;
my hands glistened with details.

After the long trip I was tired of waves.   25
My foot hit rock. The dreamed sails
collapsed, ragged.

            I planted him in this country
            like a flag.

                                                        —1970

[you fit into me]

you fit into me
like a hook into an eye

a fish hook
an open eye

                                                        —1971

_____
1   *bathysphere* Spherical diving-bell for deep-sea observation.

Variation on the Word *Sleep*

I would like to watch you sleeping,
which may not happen.
I would like to watch you,
sleeping. I would like to sleep
5 with you, to enter
your sleep as its smooth dark wave
slides over my head

and walk with you through that lucent°   *shining*
wavering forest of bluegreen leaves
10 with its watery sun & three moons
towards the cave where you must descend,
towards your worst fear
I would like to give you the silver
branch, the small white flower, the one
15 word that will protect you
from the grief at the centre
of your dream, from the grief
at the centre. I would like to follow
you up the long stairway
20 again & become
the boat that would row you back
carefully, a flame
in two cupped hands
to where your body lies
25 beside me, and you enter
it as easily as breathing in

I would like to be the air
that inhabits you for a moment
only. I would like to be that unnoticed
30 & that necessary.

—1981

The Door

The door swings open,
you look in.
It's dark in there,
most likely spiders:
nothing you want.   5
You feel scared.
The door swings closed.

The full moon shines,
it's full of delicious juice;
you buy a purse,   10
the dance is nice.
The door opens
and swings closed so quickly
you don't notice.

The sun comes out,   15
you have swift breakfasts
with your husband, who is still thin;
you wash the dishes,
you love your children,
you read a book,   20
you go to the movies.
It rains moderately.

The door swings open,
you look in:
why does this keep happening now?   25
Is there a secret?
The door swings closed.

The snow falls,
you clear the walk while breathing heavily;
it's not as easy as once.   30
Your children telephone sometimes.
The roof needs fixing.
You keep yourself busy.
The spring arrives.

35 The door swings open:
    it's dark in there,
    with many steps going down.
    But what is that shining?
    Is it water?
40 The door swings closed.

    The dog has died.
    This happened before.
    You got another;
    not this time though.
45 Where is your husband?
    You gave up the garden.
    It became too much.
    At night there are blankets;
    nonetheless you are wakeful.

50 The door swings open:
    O god of hinges,
    god of long voyages,
    you have kept faith.
    It's dark in there.
55 You confide yourself to the darkness.
    You step in.
    The door swings closed.

                                        —2007

Seamus Heaney
b. 1939

Born to farmers in County Derry, just outside Belfast, Seamus Heaney grew up in a Roman Catholic household in a predominantly Protestant part of Northern Ireland. He remained unmarked in childhood by the strife that would later affect the region; instead, he experienced a community that lived in harmony, regardless of religious affiliation. Heaney frequently draws on his roots for poetic inspiration, and many of his poems recall his childhood or draw on the activities of rural life—such as digging potatoes or churning milk—to comment on universal issues.

Much of Heaney's poetry concerns the political and sectarian violence that rocked Northern Ireland during the second half of the twentieth century. He has been criticized both for his allegedly ambivalent attitude toward the conflict and for his decision to leave Northern Ireland for the relatively stable Republic of Ireland in 1972. Heaney did not, however, forget the political turmoil of his birthplace, and in the decade following his move he wrote some of his most political works, including *North* (1975) and *Field Work* (1979).

The death of Heaney's mother in 1984 was the occasion for some of his most poignant poetry, published in *The Haw Lantern* (1987). When questioned about his memorializing of lost friends and family, Heaney responded: "The elegiac Heaney? There's nothing else." Heaney's poems addressing the past often comment indirectly on the present; among the best-known examples of this approach are his "bog poems" about the preserved bodies of ancient sacrificial victims discovered in the peat bogs of Denmark.

Heaney has combined writing with an academic career that has included guest lectureships at Harvard and Oxford. He has also written translations from ancient and medieval languages, among them a critically acclaimed translation of *Beowulf* (2000). In 1995, Heaney was awarded the Nobel Prize in Literature; the committee cited his "works of lyrical beauty and ethical depth, which exalt everyday miracles and the living past."

Digging

Between my finger and my thumb
The squat pen rests; as snug as a gun.

Under my window a clean rasping sound
When the spade sinks into gravelly ground:
My father, digging. I look down   5

Till his straining rump among the flowerbeds
Bends low, comes up twenty years away
Stooping in rhythm through potato drills[1]
Where he was digging.

10 The coarse boot nestled on the lug, the shaft
Against the inside knee was levered firmly.
He rooted out tall tops, buried the bright edge deep
To scatter new potatoes that we picked
Loving their cool hardness in our hands.

15 By God, the old man could handle a spade,
Just like his old man.

My grandfather could cut more turf[2] in a day
Than any other man on Toner's bog.
Once I carried him milk in a bottle
20 Corked sloppily with paper. He straightened up
To drink it, then fell to right away
Nicking and slicing neatly, heaving sods
Over his shoulder, digging down and down
For the good turf. Digging.

25 The cold smell of potato mould, the squelch and slap
Of soggy peat, the curt cuts of an edge
Through living roots awaken in my head.
But I've no spade to follow men like them.

Between my finger and my thumb
30 The squat pen rests.
I'll dig with it.

—1966

---

1   *potato drills* Rows of sown potatoes.
2   *turf* Slabs of peat.

Mid-Term Break[1]

I sat all morning in the college sick bay
Counting bells knelling classes to a close.
At two o'clock our neighbors drove me home.

In the porch I met my father crying—
He had always taken funerals in his stride—   5
And Big Jim Evans saying it was a hard blow.

The baby cooed and laughed and rocked the pram
When I came in, and I was embarrassed
By old men standing up to shake my hand

And tell me they were "sorry for my trouble,"   10
Whispers informed strangers I was the eldest,
Away at school, as my mother held my hand

In hers and coughed out angry tearless sighs.
At ten o'clock the ambulance arrived
With the corpse, stanched and bandaged by the nurses.   15

Next morning I went up into the room. Snowdrops
And candles soothed the bedside; I saw him
For the first time in six weeks. Paler now,

Wearing a poppy bruise on his left temple,
He lay in the four foot box as in his cot.   20
No gaudy scars, the bumper knocked him clear.

A four foot box, a foot for every year.

—1966

---

1   *Mid-Term Break* While Heaney was at boarding school in 1953, his four-year-old brother
     Christopher was killed in a car accident.

The Grauballe Man[1]

As if he had been poured
in tar, he lies
on a pillow of turf
and seems to weep

5 the black river of himself.
The grain of his wrists
is like bog oak,[2]
the ball of his heel

like a basalt egg.
10 His instep has shrunk
cold as a swan's foot
or a wet swamp root.

His hips are the ridge
and purse of a mussel,
15 his spine an eel arrested
under a glisten of mud.

The head lifts,
the chin is a visor
raised above the vent
of his slashed throat

20 that has tanned and toughened.
The cured wound
opens inwards to a dark
elderberry place.

Who will say "corpse"
25 to his vivid cast?
Who will say "body"
to his opaque repose?

---

1   *Grauballe Man* Man from the third century BCE whose preserved remains were found in
     1952, in a peat bog near the village of Grauballe, Denmark.
2   *bog oak* Wood of an oak tree preserved in a peat bog.

P.V. Glob, "The First Picture of the Grauballe Man," 1965. The Grauballe Man is one of hundreds of well-preserved ancient corpses that have been discovered in peat bogs in Northern Europe. In his book The Bog People: Iron Age Man Preserved *(Mose-folket: Jernalderens Mennesker bevaret I 2000 År, 1965), the Danish archaeologist P.V. Glob argued that most of these "bog people" were victims of ritual sacrifice. The* Bog People *and the photographs it contained were a source of inspiration for a number of poems by Seamus Heaney, including "The Grauballe Man."*

And his rusted hair,
a mat unlikely
as a foetus's.
I first saw his twisted face   30

in a photograph,
a head and shoulder
out of the peat,
bruised like a forceps baby,   35

but now he lies
perfected in my memory,
down to the red horn
of his nails,

40   hung in the scales
with beauty and atrocity:
with the Dying Gaul[1]
too strictly compassed

on his shield,
45   with the actual weight
of each hooded victim,
slashed and dumped.

—1975

Cutaways

i

Children's hands in close-up
On a bomb site, picking and displaying
Small shrapnel curds for the cameramen

Who stalk their levelled village. *Ferrum*
5   and *rigor* and *frigor*[2] of mouse grey iron,
The thumb and finger of my own right hand

Closing around old hard plasticine
Given out by Miss Walls, thumbing it
To nests no bigger than an acorn cup,

10   Eggs no bigger than a grain of wheat,
Pet pigs with sausage bellies, belly-buttoned
Fingerprinted sausage women and men.

---

1   *Dying Gaul* Roman copy of a lost Greek statue (c. 230–220 BCE) depicting a Gallic
     (French) warrior dying in battle.
2   *Ferrum* Latin: iron; *rigor* Latin: stiffness; *frigor* Latin: cold.

ii

Or trigger-fingering a six-gun stick,
Cocking a stiff hammer-thumb above
A sawn-off kitchen chair leg; or flying round   15

A gable, the wingspan of both arms
At full stretch and a-tilt, the left hand tip
Dangerously near earth, the air-shearing right

Describing arcs—angelic potential
Fleetly, unforgettably attained: 20
Now in richochets that hosannah[1] through

The backyard canyons of Mossbawn,[2]
Now a head and shoulders dive
And skive as we hightail it up and away

iii

To land hard back on heels, like the charioteer   25
Holding his own at Delphi,[3] his six horses
And chariot gone, his left hand lopped off

A wrist protruding like a waterspout,
The reins astream in his right
Ready at any moment to curb and grapple   30

Bits long fallen away.
The cast of him on a postcard was enough
To set me straight once more between two shafts,

Another's hand on mine to guide the plough,
Each slither of the share, each stone it hit   35
Registered like a pulse in the timbered grips.

—2008

---

1   *hosannah* Exclamation of praise used in Jewish and Christian worship.
2   *Mossbawn* Farmhouse where Heaney was born.
3   *charioteer ... Delphi* Bronze statue found at the temple of Apollo at Delphi and one of the best known surviving examples of ancient Greek sculpture (c. 475 BCE).

Billy Collins
b. 1941

William James Collins served as the Poet Laureate of the United States from 2001 to 2003. He has been called "the most popular poet in America" by *The New York Times*, in recognition of his regularly sold-out readings and record-breaking book sales.

Collins was born in New York City. He wrote his first poem before the age of ten but did not embark on a serious poetic career until his forties. Instead, he began his professional life as an academic, and he remains a professor of English, claiming that the poems he teaches provide inspiration for his own work. In addition to teaching, book touring, and writing prolifically, he appears frequently on National Public Radio and is a co-founder of the *Mid-Atlantic Review*.

In explanation of his popularity, Collins—who cites Warner Brothers cartoons as a formative influence on his artistic sensibility—says that his poetry is "suburban, it's domestic, it's middle class, and it's sort of unashamedly that." His work is criticized by some literary critics and fellow poets as being too "pedestrian, or one-note," or even too "accessible." Other critics, however, agree with Collins that his poems "are slightly underrated by the word 'accessible'"; one *New York Times* reviewer, for example, praises him for "luring his readers into the poem with humour, [then leading] them unwittingly into deeper, more serious places."

Pinup

The murkiness of the local garage is not so dense
that you cannot make out the calendar of pinup
drawings on the wall above a bench of tools.
Your ears are ringing with the sound of
5 the mechanic hammering on your exhaust pipe,
and as you look closer you notice that this month's
is not the one pushing the lawn mower, wearing
a straw hat and very short blue shorts,
her shirt tied in a knot just below her breasts.
10 Nor is it the one in the admiral's cap, bending
forward, resting her hands on a wharf piling,
glancing over the tiny anchors on her shoulders.
No, this is March, the month of great winds,
so appropriately it is the one walking her dog

along a city sidewalk on a very blustery day.   15
One hand is busy keeping her hat down on her head
and the other is grasping the little dog's leash,
so of course there is no hand left to push down
her dress which is billowing up around her waist
exposing her long stockinged legs and yes the secret   20
apparatus of her garter belt. Needless to say,
in the confusion of wind and excited dog
the leash has wrapped itself around her ankles
several times giving her a rather bridled
and helpless appearance which is added to   25
by the impossibly high heels she is teetering on.
You would like to come to her rescue,
gather up the little dog in your arms,
untangle the leash, lead her to safety,
and receive her bottomless gratitude, but   30
the mechanic is calling you over to look
at something under your car. It seems that he has
run into a problem and the job is going
to cost more than he had said and take
much longer than he had thought.   35
Well, it can't be helped, you hear yourself say
as you return to your place by the workbench,
knowing that as soon as the hammering resumes
you will slowly lift the bottom of the calendar
just enough to reveal a glimpse of what   40
the future holds in store: ah,
the red polka dot umbrella of April and her
upturned palm extended coyly into the rain.

—1993

Gwendolyn MacEwen
1941–1987

One of Canada's most accomplished poets, Gwendolyn MacEwen ventured in many of her best-known poems into what she called the "elementary world" of myth, dream, and the unconscious mind. As she explained in her essay "A Poet's Journey into the Interior" (1986), "I tend to regard poetry in much the same way as the ancients regarded the chants or hymns used in holy festivals—as a means of invoking the mysterious forces which move the world, inform our deepest and most secret thoughts, and often visit us in sleep."

MacEwen's volumes of poetry include the Governor General's Award-winning collections *The Shadow-Maker* (1969) and *Afterworlds* (1987). Margaret Atwood has praised her ability to create, "in a remarkably short time, a complete and diverse poetic universe and a powerful and unique voice, by turns playful, extravagant, melancholy, daring, and profound." MacEwen's work displays remarkable breadth of tone and style, but in its subject matter returns repeatedly to a cluster of themes, among them the nature of time and memory, alchemy and mysticism, the transcendent power of imagination, the interplay—and interdependence—of darkness and light, and the subterranean truths and terrors of dreams.

Dark Pines Under Water

This land like a mirror turns you inward
And you become a forest in a furtive lake;
The dark pines of your mind reach downward,
You dream in the green of your time,
5 Your memory is a row of sinking pines.

Explorer, you tell yourself this is not what you came for
Although it is good here, and green;
You had meant to move with a kind of largeness,
You had planned a heavy grace, an anguished dream.

10 But the dark pines of your mind dip deeper
And you are sinking, sinking, sleeper
In an elementary world;
There is something down there and you want it told.

—1969

The Discovery

do not imagine that the exploration
ends, that she has yielded all her mystery
or that the map you hold
cancels further discovery

I tell you her uncovering takes years,   5
takes centuries, and when you find her naked
look again,
admit there is something else you cannot name,
a veil, a coating just above the flesh
which you cannot remove by your mere wish   10

when you see the land naked, look again
(burn your maps, that is not what I mean),
I mean the moment when it seems most plain
is the moment when you must begin again

—1969

Don McKay
b. 1942

Don McKay is a prolific Canadian poet whose work reflects a conviction that poetry is crucial to society and to private life; "poetry comes about," he writes, "because language is not able to represent raw experience, yet it must."

Born in Owen Sound and raised in Cornwall, Ontario, McKay spent a self-described "all-Canadian boyhood" camping on the Precambrian Shield and canoeing remote northern lakes. His poetry often focuses on nature and its cycles of death and loss, birth and resurgence.

McKay is renowned for his technique of defamiliarization—of inviting readers to see as new and surprising the most common objects and materials, such as tools and rocks. For McKay, these things have secret "other lives" to which we can be privy if poetic attention is paid to them. Such an approach, he asserts, may grant us deeper access to reality; defamiliarization allows us to circumvent "the mind's categories to glimpse some thing's autonomy—its rawness, its *duende* [soul], its alien being."

McKay has taught creative writing for over 25 years and is a co-founder of the Canadian poetry press Brick Books. His work has been awarded some of Canada's most prestigious prizes, including the Griffin Poetry Prize for *Strike/Slip* (2007) and Governor General's Awards for *Night Field* (1991) and *Another Gravity* (2000). In 2008, McKay was appointed a Member of the Order of Canada for his service to the country as a poet and as a generous mentor to young and aspiring writers.

Some Functions of a Leaf

To whisper. To applaud the wind
and hide the Hermit thrush.
To catch the light
and work the humble spell of photosynthesis
5   (excuse me sir, if I might have one word)
by which it's changed to wood.
To wait
willing to feed
            and be food.

10 To die with style:
as the tree retreats inside itself,
shutting off the valves at its
extremities
            to starve in technicolour, then

having served two hours in a children's leaf pile, slowly   15
stir its vitamins into the earth.

To be the artist of mortality.

—1987

Meditation on a Geode

To find one, even among souvenirs of Banff[1] from acrylic to zinc, is to
realize that rock, ordinary limestone, composes in its own medium and
has other lives. This one sits by the telephone, an impacted hollow whole
note, formed, says my old geology textbook, from the modification and
enlargement of an original void. O : every time I look inside, that twinge of   5
tabu. And something more familiar: impossible words forming a lump in
my throat, the petrified ovary of the unspoken.

I have been trying to respond to the spaces in your letter, its rests and lapses,
and the slight halo effect of words spoken in an art gallery. Thanks especially
for the potato salad recipe with the missing mystery ingredient. You've   10
been breathing the spiked air of solitude and I'm feeling jealous. Echoless.
Probably I should get more exercise, once upon a time, once upon a time.
Meanwhile the geode by the phone. Astounded.

Once upon a time there was a little animal who lived and died, got buried
in the silt and gradually decayed to nothing, which filled up with water. And   15
on the inner surface of the hole a shell of jellied silica dividing the water
inside, which is quite salty, from the fresher water outside in the limestone:
a tiny ocean in an egg. In which a subtle and irresistible idea, osmosis,
unclenches outward against the rock, widening the hole and seeping
through the silica until the salts inside and outside balance. And everything   20
(slow gong) crystallizes: : animal, emptiness, ocean, gland: ode of the earth.

—1991

---

1   *Banff* Banff National Park is a popular tourist destination in Canada, located in the
     Rocky Mountains.

Meditation on Shovels

How well they love us, palm and instep, lifeline
running with the grain as we
stab   pry   heave
our grunts and curses are their music.
5 What a (stab) fucking life, you dig these
(pry) dumb holes in the ground and (heave) fill
them up again until they (stab)
dig a fucking hole for you:
                                        beautiful,
10 they love it, hum it as they stand,
disembodied backbones.
waiting for you to get back to work.

But in the Book of Symbols, after Shoes
(Van Gogh, Heidegger,[1] and Cinderella)
15 they do not appear.
Of course not.
                        They're still out there
humming
patiently pointing down.

—1991

Song for the Song of the Wood Thrush

For the following few seconds, while the ear
inhales the evening
only the offhand is acceptable. Poetry
clatters. The old contraption pumping
5 iambs in my chest is going to take a break
and sing a little something. What? Not much. There's
a sorrow that's so old and silver it's no longer
sorry. There's a place
between desire and memory, some back porch
10 we can neither wish for nor recall.

—1997

---

1   *Van Gogh, Heidegger* Vincent van Gogh's painting *A Pair of Shoes* (1886) is discussed by
     philosopher Martin Heidegger in his essay "The Origin of the Work of Art" (1963), in
     which Heidegger draws a distinction between everyday objects and art objects. One of
     Heidegger's concerns was the everyday relationship between human beings and things.

Roy Miki
b. 1942

Often preferring the free association of sound and rhythm to more traditional literary conventions, Roy Miki attempts to practise a way of thinking and creative writing that shares some of the anti-authoritarian goals of his activism. He often makes use of wordplay and multiple poetic voices to create poems that are complex, unstable, and challenging.

Miki was born on a sugar beet farm near Winnipeg, Manitoba. His parents had been forcibly relocated from the West Coast by the Canadian government, which during World War II dispossessed, transported, and interned thousands of Canadians of Japanese descent in contradiction of their rights as citizens. In the 1980s, Miki was among the leaders of the Japanese Canadian Redress Movement that eventually obtained an apology, compensation, and preventative measures from the federal government.

Miki committed many years to this issue and wrote, co-wrote, and contributed to several books on the subject, including *Redress: Inside the Japanese Canadian Call for Justice* (2004); he has also been very active as a poet and as a literary scholar. His activism and his poetic work often overlap; his poetry collection *Saving Face* (1991), for example, includes a section called "redress." Much of his work is concerned with the politics of origins and identity—and, more recently, with consumerism and globalization.

Considered a poet of the prairies but also aligned with the poetry of the West Coast, Miki has published scholarly work on other Canadian poets such as George Bowering and bpNichol, and has edited the collected poems of Roy Kiyooka. Miki earned a Governor General's Award for *Surrender* (2001), his third book of poems, and in 2006 received the Order of Canada.

attractive

the distaste for turmoil
embroiled oceanic slips

like wandering on tarmac
looking for insularity
finding dry grass

5

the promise of unbridled
recompense—risen dough
in the non-chalence forms

bleached by similitude
10 the probate will[1] runs on
neutral—gravity's weal

it's the sonic boom of
a lingual disequilibrium

the disinherited tracts of
15 murmur's master stroke

two syllables making out
in the compact rumble seat

tease of would you take
a turn if you had a choice

20 rather the brain child of
sea wagers than intervals

raucous vibes in the sunder
down of lyric i am ambushed

let's get serious a poetic
25 *text has to resonate*

has

to transport emotion to an
island called identity

what you want is the death
30 *of continuity the death of*
narration

death itself

you're a cancer

on the
35 body of real literature

---

1   *probate will* Will that has been validated by a court; a term from inheritance law used
here in a pun on "will" in the sense of "volition."

you're a wart

        on the
backside of texts erotique

you're the clad maw

      of iron hick crescendo   40

babble brain

       yeah like self
reliance is a liberal habit

the lame leap freight cars
the careen of nomadic lobes   45
the lubricants rescue the wheels

           —2001

on the sublime

a poem does not beg for forgiveness. it's not like real life.
not a case of relationships gone awry. its social
innuendoes are not a matter of secrets told in privacy.

once the consideration of intent is or was misplaced.
once it was a misdemeanour to forego the forlorn.   5

memory is a stranger. a maverick sound that crowds out
noise. the ease of its deployment is dependent on the size
of the ache.

when it drops into a sullied lap.

i hesitate to use the first person in this instance. a binge   10
of bebop is no ticket to oblivion. the causal routes arc
dogged with yelping signatures with nowhere to sign.

the sojourner notwithstanding.

'we' listened at the fork in the road. 'i've heard that
15   before.' the clause was held in perpetuity.

cacophonous airwaves are all the rage. the rollycoaster
on overdrive dallies then engages in tumult. fear is driven
deeper into the social debt of syntax controls and
formations that giggle on freeway billboards.

20   if its hem is showing.

'i wander by the corner store, gazing at the figures
winking back.' the encounter has ripple effects that
accumulate and announce the dispatch. the few who are
deaf to tonal variations listen to the heat waves instead.

25   the transportation wins approval.

when logic fails, logic hails a cab. 'we' cruise the early
morning city streets. the headlines as headlights, a
concept dying on the dashboard.

—2001

make it new

i have altered my tactics to reflect the new era

5   already the magnolia broken by high winds
           heals itself
the truncated branches already
speak to me.

the hallucinated cartoons spread their wings
10   no less eagles than the amber destination
of wanton discourses—
                     discards

           say what you will
the mountain ranges
15   once so populated with fleeting images
           look more attractive

histoires statistics documents
daily polls headlines make the blood rush

the earth is not heavy
with the weight of centuries   20
nor do bodies
of multitudes tread muted on fleet denizens

in the declension[1] of plumed echoes
or is it contractual fumes
the sunset clause[2] expires   25

—2001

---

1   *declension* Decay; also a grammatical term for a list of the forms a word can take according
     to its case, gender, and other factors.
2   *sunset clause* Provision attached to a piece of legislation that causes the legislation to
     expire on a predetermined date.

Sharon Olds
b. 1942

Sharon Olds's poems are notable for their intimate portrayals of taboo subjects such as family abuse, sexuality, violence, and the human body; she is often compared to an earlier generation of confessional poets such as Sylvia Plath and Anne Sexton. Olds herself describes her work as "apparently personal." Whether autobiographical or not, her poetry boldly examines many of life's fundamental experiences. Poet Tony Hoagland praises Olds's "empathetic insight" and describes her work as "an extended, meticulous, passionate, often deeply meditative testament about the 'central meanings'; skilled dramatic expressions of the most archetypal templates, obstructions and liberations of one human life."

Born in San Francisco, Olds studied at Stanford University, and she completed a PhD in English at Columbia University in 1972. Her first collection, *Satan Says* (1980), received the San Francisco Poetry Center Award, while her next, *The Dead and the Living* (1983), received the National Book Critics Circle Award. She is also a recipient of the T.S. Eliot Prize, for which she has been shortlisted multiple times: after being shortlisted for *The Father* (1992), a themed collection about an alcoholic father's death from cancer, and for *One Secret Thing* (2008), which addresses parenthood, sexuality, and past traumas, she won for *Stag's Leap* (2012), a volume centred on her experience of divorce.

The One Girl at the Boys Party

When I take my girl to the swimming party
I set her down among the boys. They tower and
bristle, she stands there smooth and sleek,
her math scores unfolding in the air around her.
5 They will strip to their suits, her body hard and
indivisible as a prime number,
they'll plunge in the deep end, she'll subtract
her height from ten feet, divide it into
hundreds of gallons of water, the numbers
10 bouncing in her mind like molecules of chlorine
in the bright blue pool. When they climb out,
her ponytail will hang its pencil lead
down her back, her narrow silk suit
with hamburgers and french fries printed on it

will glisten in the brilliant air, and they will   15
see her sweet face, solemn and
sealed, a factor of one, and she will
see their eyes, two each,
their legs, two each, and the curves of their sexes,
one each, and in her head she'll be doing her   20
wild multiplying, as the drops
sparkle and fall to the power of a thousand from her body.

—1983

Sex without Love

How do they do it, the ones who make love
without love? Beautiful as dancers,
gliding over each other like ice-skaters
over the ice, fingers hooked
inside each other's bodies, faces   5
red as steak, wine, wet as the
children at birth whose mothers are going to
give them away. How do they come to the
come to the   come to the   God   come to the
still waters,[1] and not love   10
the one who came there with them, light
rising slowly as steam off their joined
skin? These are the true religious,
the purists, the pros, the ones who will not
accept a false Messiah, love the   15
priest instead of the God. They do not
mistake the lover for their own pleasure,
they are like great runners: they know they are alone
with the road surface, the cold, the wind,
the fit of their shoes, their over-all cardio-   20
vascular health—just factors, like the partner
in the bed, and not the truth, which is the
single body alone in the universe
against its own best time.

—1984

---

1   *still waters* See Psalm 23.2: "he leadeth me beside the still waters."

Michael Ondaatje
b. 1943

Michael Ondaatje was born in 1943 in Ceylon (now Sri Lanka). His parents separated when he was two, and in 1949 his mother moved to London, where she ran a boarding school. When Ondaatje was ten he joined his mother in England. Before Ondaatje's first return to Sri Lanka in 1978, his childhood home rarely figured in his work. "Letters & Other Worlds" (1973), one of his best-known poems, is one notable exception; here he draws on his early experiences as he comes to terms with his father's death.

Ondaatje followed his older brother, Christopher, to Canada in 1962. At the University of Toronto, where he completed his BA, he began to make a name for himself as a poet, and was also introduced to Coach House Press, where he worked as an editor for several years. He cemented his reputation as a poet with *The Collected Works of Billy the Kid* (1970) and as a novelist with *In the Skin of a Lion* (1987); his more recent publications include the poetry collection *The Story* (2006) and the novel *The Cat's Table* (2011).

Many of Ondaatje's books of poetry resemble novels in their extended development of character and plot. His novels, on the other hand, are frequently described as poetic; they are often written in highly figurative language, flowing from one vivid image to the next rather than developing along any linear plot line. Ondaatje's awards include the Booker Prize, the Giller Prize, four Governor General's Awards, and the Order of Canada.

Letters & Other Worlds

"for there was no more darkness for him and, no doubt like Adam before the fall, he could see in the dark"[1]

My father's body was a globe of fear
His body was a town we never knew
He hid that he had been where we were going
His letters were a room he seldom lived in
5 In them the logic of his love could grow

My father's body was a town of fear
He was the only witness to its fear dance
He hid where he had been that we might lose him
His letters were a room his body scared

1   *for ... dark* Ondaatje is quoting a translation of Alfred Jarry's novel *La Dragonne* (1943) that is cited in Roger Shattuck's *The Banquet Years* (1955).

He came to death with his mind drowning.   10
On the last day he enclosed himself
in a room with two bottles of gin, later
fell the length of his body
so that brain blood moved
to new compartments   15
that never knew the wash of fluid
and he died in minutes of a new equilibrium.

His early life was a terrifying comedy
and my mother divorced him again and again.
He would rush into tunnels magnetized   20
by the white eye of trains
and once, gaining instant fame,
managed to stop a Perahara[1] in Ceylon
—the whole procession of elephants dancers
local dignitaries—by falling   25
dead drunk onto the street.

As a semi-official, and semi-white at that,
the act was seen as a crucial
turning point in the Home Rule Movement
and led to Ceylon's independence in 1948.   30

(My mother had done her share too—
her driving so bad
she was stoned by villagers
whenever her car was recognized)
For 14 years of marriage   35
each of them claimed he or she
was the injured party.
Once on the Colombo docks
saying goodbye to a recently married couple
my father, jealous   40
at my mother's articulate emotion,
dove into the waters of the harbour
and swam after the ship waving farewell.
My mother pretending no affiliation
mingled with the crowd back to the hotel.   45

---

1   *Perahara* Procession (originally of a religious nature) of praise or thanksgiving.

Once again he made the papers
though this time my mother
with a note to the editor
corrected the report—saying he was drunk
50 rather than broken hearted at the parting of friends.
The married couple received both editions
of *The Ceylon Times* when their ship reached Aden.

And then in his last years
he was the silent drinker,
55 the man who once a week
disappeared into his room with bottles
and stayed there until he was drunk
and until he was sober.

There speeches, head dreams, apologies,
60 the gentle letters, were composed.
With the clarity of architects
he would write of the row of blue flowers
his new wife had planted,
the plans for electricity in the house,
65 how my half-sister fell near a snake
and it had awakened and not touched her.
Letters in a clear hand of the most complete empathy
his heart widening and widening and widening
to all manner of change in his children and friends
70 while he himself edged
into the terrible acute hatred
of his own privacy
till he balanced and fell
the length of his body
75 the blood screaming in
the empty reservoir of bones
the blood searching in his head without metaphor

—1973

The Cinnamon Peeler[1]

If I were a cinnamon peeler
I would ride your bed
and leave the yellow bark dust
on your pillow.

Your breasts and shoulders would reek   5
you could never walk through markets
without the profession of my fingers
floating over you. The blind would
stumble certain of whom they approached
though you might bathe   10
under rain gutters, monsoon.

Here on the upper thigh
at this smooth pasture
neighbour to your hair
or the crease   15
that cuts your back. This ankle.
You will be known among strangers
as the cinnamon peeler's wife.

I could hardly glance at you
before marriage   20
never touch you
—your keen nosed mother, your rough brothers.
I buried my hands
in saffron, disguised them
over smoking tar,   25
helped the honey gatherers ...

When we swam once
I touched you in water
and our bodies remained free,
you could hold me and be blind of smell.   30
You climbed the bank and said

             this is how you touch other women

---

1   *Cinnamon Peeler* Cinnamon harvester; the spice is made from the inner bark of the
    cinnamon tree.

the grass cutter's wife, the lime burners daughter.
And you searched your arms
35   for the missing perfume
                    and knew

                what good is it
to be the lime burner's daughter
left with no trace
40   as if not spoken to in the act of love
as if wounded without the pleasure of a scar.

You touched
your belly to my hands
in the dry air and said
45   I am the cinnamon
peeler's wife. Smell me.

                                        —1982

To a Sad Daughter

All night long the hockey pictures
gaze down at you
sleeping in your tracksuit.
Belligerent goalies are your ideal.

5   Threats of being traded
cuts and wounds
—all this pleases you.
O my god! you say at breakfast
reading the sports page over the Alpen[1]
10   as another player breaks his ankle
or assaults the coach.

When I thought of daughters
I wasn't expecting this
but I like this more.
15   I like all your faults
even your purple moods
when you retreat from everyone

---

1   *Alpen* Brand of muesli breakfast cereal.

to sit in bed under a quilt.
And when I say "like"
I mean of course "love"   20
but that embarrasses you.
You who feel superior to black and white movies
(coaxed for hours to see *Casablanca*)[1]
though you were moved
by *Creature from the Black Lagoon*.[2]   25

One day I'll come swimming
beside your ship or someone will
and if you hear the siren[3]
listen to it. For if you close your ears
only nothing happens. You will never change.   30

I don't care if you risk
your life to angry goalies
creatures with webbed feet.
You can enter their caves and castles
their glass laboratories. Just   35
don't be fooled by anyone but yourself.

This is the first lecture I've given you.
You're "sweet sixteen" you said.
I'd rather be your closest friend
than your father. I'm not good at advice   40
you know that, but ride
the ceremonies
until they grow dark.

Sometimes you are so busy
discovering your friends   45
I ache with loss
—but that is greed.
And some times I've gone
into *my* purple world
and lost you.   50

---

1   *Casablanca* Widely acclaimed 1942 classic film.
2   *Creature from the Black Lagoon* 1954 monster movie that typifies the "B movies" of the
     1950s.
3   *siren* In Greek mythology, creatures whose singing enchanted sailors, causing them to
     steer their ships into the rocks.

One afternoon I stepped
into your room. You were sitting
at the desk where I now write this.
Forsythia outside the window
55 and sun spilled over you
like a thick yellow miracle
as if another planet
was coaxing you out of the house
—all those possible worlds!—
60 and you, meanwhile, busy with mathematics.

I cannot look at forsythia now
without loss, or joy for you.
You step delicately
into the wild world
65 and your real prize will be
the frantic search.
Want everything. If you break
break going out not in.
How you live your life I don't care
70 but I'll sell my arms for you,
hold your secrets forever.

If I speak of death
which you fear now, greatly,
it is without answers,
75 except that each
one we know is
in our blood.
Don't recall graves.
Memory is permanent.
80 Remember the afternoon's
yellow suburban annunciation.
Your goalie
in his frightening mask
dreams perhaps
85 of gentleness.

—1984

Eavan Boland
b. 1944

Eavan Boland has developed the concept of "dailiness," a focus on the ordinary minutiae of life, as a theme throughout her work. Beginning her career at a time when, she says, "nobody thought a suburb could be a visionary place for a poet" and "nobody thought a daily moment could be [poetic]," she was inspired by "a great tenderheartedness toward these things that were denied their visionary life." Her work also draws deeply on the past: she weaves scenes of the everyday together with re-imagined figures and motifs from mythology, and she examines Irish history with particular attention to its legacy of women's oppression. Boland does not shy away from the harsh realities of women's lives—past or present; domestic violence and anorexia are among the subjects addressed in her poems.

Born in 1944, Boland grew up in London and Ireland. She attended Trinity College in Dublin, and has since taught there and at other universities, including Bowdoin College and Stanford University. Since her first collection, *23 Poems* (1962), Boland has published ten volumes of poetry, among them *In a Time of Violence* (1994), which won the Lannan Award and was shortlisted for the T.S. Eliot Award. Her anthology *New Collected Poems* (2008), containing previously unpublished works as well as a selection of her early poems, has cemented her place as a leading contemporary Irish writer. In her collection of essays *A Journey with Two Maps: Becoming a Woman Poet* (2011), Boland reflects on her identity as a woman and a poet, and on the construction of those identities by others.

Night Feed

This is dawn.
Believe me
This is your season, little daughter.
The moment daisies open,
The hour mercurial rainwater   5
Makes a mirror for sparrows.
It's time we drowned our sorrows.

I tiptoe in.
I lift you up
Wriggling   10
In your rosy, zipped sleeper.
Yes, this is the hour

For the early bird and me
When finder is keeper.

15 I crook the bottle.
How you suckle!
This is the best I can be,
Housewife
To this nursery
20 Where you hold on,
Dear life.

A slit of milk.
The last suck.
And now your eyes are open,
25 Birth-coloured and offended.
Earth wakes.
You go back to sleep.
The feed is ended.

Worms turn.
30 Stars go in.
Even the moon is losing face.
Poplars stilt for dawn
And we begin
The long fall from grace.
35 I tuck you in.

—1982

Against Love Poetry

We were married in summer, thirty years ago. I have loved you deeply from that moment to this. I have loved other things as well. Among them the idea of women's freedom. Why do I put these words side by side? Because I am a woman. Because marriage is not freedom. Therefore, every word here is written against love poetry. Love poetry can do no justice to this. Here,   5 instead, is a remembered story from a faraway history: A great king lost a war and was paraded in chains through the city of his enemy. They taunted him. They brought his wife and children to him—he showed no emotion. They brought his former courtiers—he showed no emotion. They brought his old servant—only then did he break down and weep.[1] I did not find my   10 womanhood in the servitudes of custom. But I saw my humanity look back at me there. It is to mark the contradictions of a daily love that I have written this. Against love poetry.

—2001

---

1   *a remembered ... and weep* From Herodotus, *The Histories* 3.14. The defeated king explains, "my private sorrows were too great for tears, but the troubles of my companion deserved them."

bpNichol
1944–1988

As George Bowering wrote, bpNichol "did not sound like the rest of the poets of his time." One of Canada's most important avant-garde poets, he experimented not only with lyric and narrative poetry but also with the visual and auditory aspects of language. The range of his work encompassed both concrete poetry—a visual form in which the words form an image that contributes to the poem's meaning—and sound poetry, a spoken form that engages with the sounds of speech, usually independent of actual words.

Barrie Phillip Nichol was born in Vancouver, British Columbia. His first collection, *bp* (1967), challenged the notion of the book: it was published in the form of a box containing a book, a collection of loose visual poems, a record, and a flipbook, with a "Statement" printed on the back of the box. In 1970, Nichol won the Governor General's Award for four volumes published that year: *Still Water*, *The true eventual story of Billie the Kid*, *Beach Head*, and *The Cosmic Chief*. His experiments with form and genre were continued in works such as *The Captain Poetry Poems* (1971), a convergence of pop art, concrete and lyric poetry, and myth. Of his more than 30 books and filmed or recorded performances, perhaps the most impressive is *The Martyrology* (1972–92), a "life-long" poem spanning nine books in six volumes.

Nichol often worked collaboratively; he was a member of the famed sound poetry group The Four Horsemen and a co-founder of *grOnk*, a magazine with a focus on concrete poetry. With a fellow member of The Four Horsemen, he produced theoretical writing under the pseudonym "Toronto Research Group." He was also a writer for Jim Henson's television show *Fraggle Rock* (1983–87).

Blues

```
                    l                   e
                    o               e
            l       o       v       e
            o           e       v       o       l
5       l       o       v       e       o
            e       v       o       l
        e           o       l
    e               l
```

—1966

[dear Captain Poetry]

dear Captain Poetry,
your poetry is trite.
you cannot write a sonnet
tho you've tried to every night
since i've known you.   5
we're thru!!
       madame X

dear madame X

    Look how the sun leaps now upon our faces
    Stomps & boots our eyes into our skulls   10
    Drives all thot to weird & foreign places
    Till the world reels & the kicked mind dulls,
    Drags our hands up across our eyes
    Sends all white hurling into black
    Makes the inner cranium our skies   15
    And turns all looks sent forward burning back.
    And you, my lady, who should be gentler, kind,
    Have yet the fiery aspect of the sun
    Sending words to burn into my mind
    Destroying all my feelings one by one;   20
        You who should have tiptoed thru my halls
        Have slammed my doors & smashed me into walls.

               love
               Cap Poetry
               —1970

Craig Raine
b. 1944

Craig Raine began what has been called the "Martian school" of poetry alongside Christopher Reid in the late 1970s. This style is aptly named after Raine's collection *A Martian Sends a Postcard Home* (1979), which—with his first book, *The Onion, Memory* (1978)—established his place as a leader in the movement. The goal of Martian poetry is to view the world with new eyes, even from the perspective of an alien. This is accomplished through unusual and surprising metaphors that, according to poet James Fenton, encourage readers "to become strangers in our familiar world."

Raine's early work created something of a sensation and, for a brief time, inspired many imitators, but the fashion for Martian poetry in the British literary world was short-lived. Raine himself, however, has continued to produce a body of interesting work. He applied his characteristic Martian style to a book-length narrative in *History: The Home Movie* (1994), a semi-autobiographical verse-novel about his family history set among the wars of twentieth-century Europe. Another long poem, *A la recherche du temps perdu* (2000), elegizes a lover who died of AIDS. In addition to more than ten books of poetry, Raine has also published two novels, a translated drama, two opera librettos, and several scholarly works.

An outspoken critic as well as a poet, Raine has taught at Oxford University for much of his career. He also spent ten years as poetry editor at the influential publishing house Faber & Faber, and in 1999 became the editor of his own arts journal, *Areté*.

A Martian Sends a Postcard Home

Caxtons[1] are mechanical birds with many wings
and some are treasured for their markings—

they cause the eyes to melt
or the body to shriek without pain.

5 I have never seen one fly, but
sometimes they perch on the hand.

Mist is when the sky is tired of flight
and rests its soft machine on ground:

---

1   *Caxtons* William Caxton (1422–91) introduced the printing press to England.

then the world is dim and bookish
like engravings under tissue paper.   10

Rain is when the earth is television.
It has the property of making colours darker.

Model T¹ is a room with the lock inside—
a key is turned to free the world

for movement, so quick there is a film   15
to watch for anything missed.

But time is tied to the wrist
or kept in a box, ticking with impatience.

In homes, a haunted apparatus sleeps,
that snores when you pick it up.   20

If the ghost cries, they carry it
to their lips and soothe it to sleep

with sounds. And yet, they wake it up
deliberately, by tickling with a finger.

Only the young are allowed to suffer   25
openly. Adults go to a punishment room

with water but nothing to eat.
They lock the door and suffer the noises

alone. No one is exempt
and everyone's pain has a different smell.   30

At night, when all the colours die,
they hide in pairs

and read about themselves—
in colour, with their eyelids shut.

                                                                —1979

---

1   *Model T* Early model of the automobile, produced by the Ford Motor Company; the
    Model T was the first car to enjoy mass popularity.

Tom Wayman
b. 1945

Tom Wayman's poetry depicts the challenges of daily life and work with humour and honesty, addressing the commonplace in colloquial, conversational language. In his work, Wayman writes, he strives to "provide an accurate depiction of our common everyday life" and to help us "consider how our jobs shape us"—a consideration which requires that we recognize the relative "state of unfreedom" in which most of us lead our working lives. Much of his writing relates to working-class employment such as factory labour and construction, but some of his best-known poems are about the everyday experience of the university.

Born in Ontario in 1945 and raised in British Columbia, Wayman holds a BA from the University of British Columbia and an MFA from the University of California. His first collection, *Waiting for Wayman*, was published in 1973; it has been followed by more than a dozen volumes of poetry, as well as by short fiction, critical essays, drama, and a novel.

Wayman has edited several anthologies, often with a focus on work writing, and has been a teacher and a writer-in-residence at many Canadian universities. Among other awards, he has received the Canadian Authors' Association Poetry Award and the A.J.M. Smith Prize for distinguished achievement in Canadian poetry. His poetry collection *My Father's Cup* (2002) was shortlisted for the Governor General's Award.

Did I Miss Anything?

*Question frequently asked by
students after missing a class*

Nothing. When we realized you weren't here
we sat with our hands folded on our desks
in silence, for the full two hours

   Everything. I gave an exam worth
5 40 per cent of the grade for this term
   and assigned some reading due today
   on which I'm about to hand out a quiz
   worth 50 per cent

Nothing. None of the content of this course
has value or meaning   10
Take as many days off as you like:
any activities we undertake as a class
I assure you will not matter either to you or me
and are without purpose

     Everything. A few minutes after we began last time   15
     a shaft of light descended and an angel
     or other heavenly being appeared
     and revealed to us what each woman or man must do
     to attain divine wisdom in this life and
     the hereafter   20
     This is the last time the class will meet
     before we disperse to bring this good news to all people on earth

Nothing. When you are not present
how could something significant occur?

     Everything. Contained in this classroom   25
     is a microcosm of human existence
     assembled for you to query and examine and ponder
     This is not the only place such an opportunity has been gathered

     but it was one place

     And you weren't here   30

                        —1994

Robert Bringhurst
b. 1946

Robert Bringhurst spent ten years studying a variety of subjects—including physics, architecture, linguistics, and philosophy—at multiple universities before completing a BA in Comparative Literature from Indiana University. Since then he has published more than 15 collections of poetry and more than ten works of prose, including a canonical text on book design and typography, *Elements of Typographical Design* (1992).

Kate Kellaway of *The Observer* has commented that Bringhurst "has the curiosity of a scientist…. His writing is at once lyrical and spartan. And yet he is witty. And while he has no taste for lamentation, many a poem catches, calmly, at the heart." Interested in escaping what he calls "the prison of time" and "the prison of personality" through his work, Bringhurst tends not to focus on self-exploration but rather to explore larger topics: nature, timeless philosophical questions, mythology and literature (including the literature of the Bible, ancient Greek literature, and North American indigenous oral literature). He is well known for his work as a translator of Haida myths and narrative poems; that work has inspired controversy (he has been criticized for appropriating First Nations traditions), but it has also been widely praised for contributing to the preservation and promotion of Haida culture.

Bringhurst has received several prestigious awards for his works, including the Macmillan Poetry Prize (1975) and a Guggenheim Fellowship (1988), and was shortlisted for the prestigious Griffin Poetry Prize (2001). He lives on Quadra Island, British Columbia.

Leda and the Swan[1]

for George Faludy

Before the black beak reappeared
like a grin from in back of a drained cup,
letting her drop,
she fed at the sideboard of his thighs,
5 the lank air tightening in the sunrise,
yes. But no, she put on no knowledge

---

1   *Leda and the Swan* In Greek mythology, Leda was visited by Zeus in the form of a swan, who in some versions of the story raped her and in other versions seduced her. From their union she bore two eggs; one produced the twins Castor and Pollux, the other Helen (whose abduction later initiated the Trojan War). See W.B. Yeats's "Leda and the Swan," also included in this anthology.

with his power. And it was his power alone
that she saved of him for her daughter.
Not his knowledge.
No.   10
He was the one who put on knowledge.
He was the one who looked down out of heaven
with a dark croak, knowing more
than he had ever known before,
and knowing he knew it: 15

knowing the xylophone of her bones,
the lute of her back and the harp of her belly,
the flute of her throat,
woodwinds and drums of her muscles,
knowing the organ pipes of her veins;   20

knowing her as a man knows mountains he has hunted
naked and alone in—
knowing the fruits, the roots and the grasses,
the tastes of the streams
and the depths of the mosses,   25
knowing as he moves in the darkness he is also
resting at noon in the shade of her blood—
leaving behind him in the sheltered places
glyphs¹ meaning mineral and moonlight and mind
and possession and memory,   30
leaving on the outcrops signs meaning mountain
and sunlight and lust and rest and forgetting.

Yes. And the beak that opened to croak
of his knowing that morning creaked like a rehung
door and said nothing, felt nothing. The past   35
is past. What is known is as lean
as the day's edge and runs
one direction. The truth floats
down, out of fuel,
indigestible, like a feather. The lady   40
herself, though—whether
or not she was truth or untruth, or both, or was neither—

---

1   *glyphs* Carved figures or characters.

she dropped through the air like a looped rope,
a necklace of meaning, remembering
45 everything forward and backward—
the middle, the end, the beginning—
and lit like a fishing skiff gliding aground.

That evening, of course, while her husband, to whom
she told nothing, strode like the king
50 of Lakonia[1] through the orchestra
pit of her body, touching
this key and that string in his passing,
she lay like so much
green kindling,
55 fouled tackle and horse harness under his hands
and said nothing, felt
nothing, but only
lay thinking
not flutes, lutes and xylophones,
60 no: thinking soldiers
and soldiers and soldiers and soldiers
and daughters,
the rustle of knives in his motionless wings.

—1982

---

1   *Lakonia* Region in ancient Greece, of which Sparta was the principal city.

Marilyn Nelson
b. 1946

▬▬▬ The author of dozens of poetry collections, translations, and children's books, Marilyn Nelson is a prolific contributor to American literature. While her poetry traverses a range of subjects from marriage and motherhood to Christian spirituality, much of Nelson's work narrates American history, especially black history. Such volumes include *The Homeplace* (1990), which recounts her family history beginning with her great-great-grandmother; *Carver: A Life in Poems* (2001), about celebrated African American scientist George Washington Carver; and the sonnet crown *A Wreath for Emmett Till* (2005), about a teenager whose lynching galvanized the civil rights movement. Yet Nelson is more storyteller than political historian, creating poems that, as fellow poet Daniel Hoffman has said, "reach past feminist anguish and black rage" and "spring from her own sources." Some of Nelson's works are published as young adult books, but even these invite a broader audience; she explained that she wrote *Carver*, for example, "as I always do, striving for clarity and truthfulness, and imagining an audience of grown-ups."

Nelson is professor emerita at the University of Connecticut and also served as the state's Poet Laureate from 2001 to 2006. In 2004, she founded Soul Mountain Retreat, a writer's colony with special interest in "traditionally underrepresented racial and cultural groups." In 2012 Nelson received the Frost Medal for "distinguished lifetime achievement in poetry."

Minor Miracle

Which reminds me of another knock-on-wood
memory. I was cycling with a male friend,
through a small midwestern town. We came to a 4-way
stop and stopped, chatting. As we started again,
a rusty old pick-up truck, ignoring the stop sign,   5
hurricaned past scant inches from our front wheels.
My partner called, "Hey, that was a 4-way stop!"
The truck driver, stringy blond hair a long fringe
under his brand-name beer cap, looked back and yelled,
        "You fucking niggers!"   10
And sped off.
My friend and I looked at each other and shook our heads.
We remounted our bikes and headed out of town.
We were pedalling through a clear blue afternoon

15 between two fields of almost-ripened wheat
    bordered by cornflowers and Queen Anne's lace
    when we heard an unmuffled motor, a honk-honking.
    We stopped, closed ranks, made fists.
    It was the same truck. It pulled over.
20 A tall, very much in shape young white guy slid out:
    greasy jeans, homemade finger tattoos, probably
    a Marine Corps boot-camp footlockerful
    of martial arts techniques.

    "What did you say back there!" he shouted.
25 My friend said, "I said it was a 4-way stop.
    You went through it."
    "And what did I say?" the white guy asked.
    "You said: 'You fucking niggers.'"
    The afternoon froze.

30 "Well," said the white guy,
    shoving his hands into his pockets
    and pushing dirt around with the pointed toe of his boot,
    "I just want to say I'm sorry."
    He climbed back into his truck
35 and drove away.

                                                    —1994

Brian Patten
b. 1946

"When in public poetry should take off its clothes and wave to the nearest person in sight," writes Brian Patten; "it should be seen in the company of thieves and lovers rather than that of journalists and publishers." Patten shares his allegiance to a broad, popular audience with fellow "Liverpool Poets" Adrian Henri and Robert McGough, all three of whom wrote and performed in Liverpool at a time when bands such as The Beatles had brought the city to the centre of British popular culture. With their efforts to engage the public through performance, the Liverpool Poets opened the way for later performance poets such as Benjamin Zephaniah.

Patten was in his early twenties when he brought out his first solo collection, *Little Johnny's Confession* (1967), the same year he published with Henri and McGough in the bestselling anthology *The Mersey Sound*. Two years later, he followed this volume with *Notes to the Hurrying Man* (1969). His later work remains unpretentious but is often more serious in content; *Armada* (1996), for example, includes a series of poems in which the experience of his mother's death is intertwined with childhood memories, while *The Collected Love Poems* (2007) brings together his many poems about relationships. He has also authored several successful volumes of children's poetry.

Much of Patten's work, including "Somewhere Between Heaven and Woolworths, A Song," is written to be performed to music, and he remains committed to the importance of performance in bringing poetry to a popular audience.

Somewhere Between Heaven and Woolworths,[1] A Song

She keeps kingfishers in their cages
And goldfish in their bowls,
She is lovely and is afraid
Of such things as growing cold.

She's had enough men to please her,   5
Though they were more cruel than kind
And their love an act in isolation,
A form of pantomime.

---

1   *Woolworths* Department store chain popular for more than a century before going out of business in the 1990s.

She says she has forgotten
10 The feelings that she shared
At various all-night parties
Among the couples on the stairs,

For among the songs and dancing
She was once open wide,
15 A girl dressed in denim
With the boys dressed in lies.

She's eating roses on toast with tulip butter;
Praying for her mirror to stay young;
Though on its no longer gilted surface
20 This message she has scrawled:

"O somewhere between Heaven and Woolworths
I live I love I scold,
I keep kingfishers in their cages
And goldfish in their bowls."

—1967

Diane Ackerman

b. 1948

Diane Ackerman's poetry and non-fiction prose display diverse interests that encompass history, biology, anthropology, astronomy, and human nature. She often uses scientific concepts and terms in her poetry; for example, her first volume, *The Planets: A Cosmic Pastoral* (1976), is, by her own description, "a collection of scientifically accurate poems based on the planets." She calls herself "a nature writer," but for her "nature includes everything." That outlook is reflected in her subject matter, which ranges from plants and non-human animals to the solar system, and from human civilization to love.

Like her poetry, Ackerman's prose often engages with the physical and the sensual. In her book of essays *A Natural History of the Senses* (1990), for example, Ackerman considers the five senses and their impact on the human experience, while *An Alchemy of Mind* (2005) discusses topics such as consciousness and emotion in relation to the human brain. Her other works of non-fiction include *The Zookeeper's Wife* (2007), winner of the Orion Book Award, and *One Hundred Names for Love* (2011), a finalist for the Pulitzer Prize. Although she writes in different genres, Ackerman explains, "I began as a poet, and I still think of myself as a poet.... I have a poet's sensibility."

Sweep Me through Your Many-Chambered Heart

Sweep me through your many-chambered heart
if you like, or leave me here, flushed
amid the sap-ooze and blossom: one more dish
in the banquet called April, or think me hard-
won all your days full of women. Weeks   5
later, till I felt your arms around
me like a shackle, heard all the sundown
wizardries the fired body speaks.
Tell me why, if it was no more than this,
the unmuddled tumble, the renegade kiss,   10
today, rapt in a still life[1] and unaware,
my paintbrush dropped like an amber hawk;
thinking I'd heard your footfall on the stair,
I listened, heartwise, for the knock.

—1978

---

1   *still life* Painting or other art image depicting arranged objects, often including fruit or flowers.

Lorna Crozier

b. 1948

One of Canada's most celebrated poets, Lorna Crozier is well known for the musical simplicity of her language and her artful way of approaching complex subjects in a style that is at once forthright and sly. According to Crozier, the poet is a conduit who must develop an alertness to the world's sensory details so as to recreate them in the "small charged world of the poem." In her view, "the poem is in the details," and though experience may resist or elude language, it is the task of the poet to "circle what can't be said until something of its smell, sound, taste, and gesture appears on the page."

Crozier was born in Swift Current, Saskatchewan. Much of her work is informed by the atmosphere and culture of small-town prairie life—notably *Inventing the Hawk* (1992), winner of a Governor General's Award; *A Saving Grace* (1996), inspired by Sinclair Ross's prairie novel *As for Me and My House* (1941); and the memoir *Small Beneath the Sky* (2009). But such localism is by no means narrow or restrictive: Crozier frequently takes up broad political, spiritual, and philosophical questions. Through her poetic retellings of scripture, for example, she interrogates a Judeo-Christian vision of the world.

Critics have approached Crozier's work from many different angles. Some focus on her intimate connection to the Canadian prairies or her concern with social injustice; others explore her fascination with the gaps in our stories and experiences, with absence, silence, loss, and all that which "can't be said."

from *The Sex Lives of Vegetables*

Carrots

Carrots are fucking
the earth. A permanent
erection, they push deeper
into the damp and dark.
5   All summer long
they try so hard to please.
Was it good for you,
was it good?

Perhaps because the earth won't answer
they keep on trying.   10
While you stroll through the garden
thinking *carrot cake*,
carrots and onions in beef stew,
carrot pudding with caramel sauce,
they are fucking their brains out   15
in the hottest part of the afternoon.

Onions

The onion loves the onion.
It hugs its many layers,
saying O, O, O,
each vowel smaller
than the last.   5

Some say it has no heart.
It doesn't need one.
It surrounds itself,
feels whole. Primordial.
First among vegetables.   10

If Eve had bitten it
instead of the apple,
how different
Paradise.

—1985

The Dark Ages of the Sea

Because we are mostly
made of water and water
calls to water
like the ocean to the river,
the river to the stream,   5
there was a time when
children fell into wells.

It was a time of farms
across the grasslands,
10 ancient lakes
that lay beneath them,
and a faith in things
invisible, be it water
never seen or something
15 trembling in the air.

We are born to fall
and children fell,
some surviving
to tell the tale,
20 pulled from the well's
dark throat,
wet and blind with terror
like a calf
torn from the womb
25 with ropes.

Others diminished into ghosts,
rode the bucket up
and when you drank
became the cold shimmer
30 in your cup, the metallic
undertaste of nails
some boy had carried
in his pocket
or the silver locket
35 that held a small girl's
dreams.

In those days people
spoke to horses,
voices soft as bearded
40 wheat; music lived
inside a stone. Not to say
it was good, that falling,
but who could stop it?

We are made
of mostly water
and water calls to water   45
through centuries of reason
children fall
light and slender
as the rain.   50

                                              —1995

When I Come Again to My Father's House

When I come again to my father's house
I will climb wide wooden steps
to a blue door. Before I knock
I will stand under the porchlight and listen.
My father will be sitting in a plaid shirt,   5
open at the throat, playing his fiddle—
something I never heard in our other life.

Mother told me his music stopped
when I was born. He sold the fiddle
to buy a big console radio.   10
One day when I was two
I hit it with a stick,
I don't know why, Mother covering
the scratches with a crayon
so Father wouldn't see.   15
It was the beginning of things
we kept from him.

Outside my father's house
it will be the summer
before the drinking starts,   20
the jobs run out, the bitterness
festers like a sliver buried
in the thumb, too deep under the nail
to ever pull it out. The summer
before the silences, the small   25
hard moons growing in his throat.

When I come again to my father's house
the grey backdrop of the photos
my mother keeps in a shoebox
30   will fall away, the one sparse tree
multiply, branches green with rain.
My father will stand in his young man's pose
in front of a car, foot on the runningboard,
sleeves rolled up twice on each forearm.

35   I will place myself beside him.
The child in me will not budge
from this photograph,
will not leave my father's house
unless my father as he was
40   comes with me, throat swollen
with rain and laughter,
young hands full of music,
the slow, sweet song of his fiddle
leading us to my mother's
45   home.

—1995

Timothy Steele
b. 1948

▬▬▬ Emerging at a time when free verse and experimental poetry prevailed, Timothy Steele has distinguished himself by embracing the expressive capacities of poetic constraint. He is often identified with the New Formalism that began in the 1980s—a movement in which contemporary poets have re-engaged with standard verse forms and regular poetic patterning. But Steele has been reluctant to accept this label, instead claiming kinship with a longer lineage of formal poets. He has been praised for combining colloquial language with traditional form to address everyday and personal subject matter, employing, as poet Mary Kinzie remarks, "restraint as a mechanism for the release of both wit and feeling."

Born in Burlington, Vermont, Steele obtained a BA from Stanford University and then completed a PhD in English and American Literature at Brandeis University. In 1979 he published his first collection of poems, *Uncertainties and Rest;* that was followed by several more volumes, including *Sapphics Against Anger and Other Poems* (1986), *The Color Wheel* (1994), and *Toward the Winter Solstice* (2006).

Steele has received numerous awards and honours, including a Guggenheim Fellowship and a Peter I.B. Lavan Younger Poets Award, and he has taught at several California universities. As a critic, he is the author of *Missing Measures: Modern Poetry and the Revolt Against Meter* (1990), an analysis of modernist poetry in relation to metre and formal structure; and *All the Fun's in How You Say a Thing* (1999), an educational volume designed to teach students about poetic form, which he argues "gives a poem resistant grace and power."

Sapphics[1] Against Anger

Angered, may I be near a glass of water;
May my first impulse be to think of Silence,
Its deities (who are they? do, in fact, they
     Exist? etc.).

May I recall what Aristotle says of   5
The subject: to give vent to rage is not to

---

1   *Sapphics* Stanzas in a form named after the Greek poet Sappho (late seventh–early sixth century BCE). Each stanza comprises two 11-syllable lines and one 5-syllable line.

Release it but to be increasingly prone
10   To its incursions.[1]

May I imagine being in the Inferno,
Hearing it asked: "Virgilio mio,[2] who's
That sulking with Achilles[3] there?" and hearing
          Virgil say: "Dante,

15

That fellow, at the slightest provocation,
Slammed phone receivers down, and waved his arms like
A madman. What Attila did to Europe,
          What Genghis Khan did

20 To Asia,[4] that poor dope did to his marriage."
May I, that is, put learning to good purpose,
Mindful that melancholy is a sin, though
          Stylish at present.

Better than rage is the post-dinner quiet,
The sink's warm turbulence, the streaming platters,
25 The suds rehearsing down the drain in spirals
          In the last rinsing.

For what is, after all, the good life save that
Conducted thoughtfully, and what is passion
If not the holiest of powers, sustaining
          Only if mastered.

—1986

---

1   *What Aristotle ... its incursions* See Book IV of Aristotle's *Nicomachean Ethics*, in which
     he discusses the cultivation of virtue in oneself as a means to attaining the good life.
2   *Virgilio mio* Italian: my Virgil. In *Inferno*, the first part of Italian poet Dante Alighieri's
     Divine Comedy (c. 1308–21), Virgil is Dante's guide through hell.
3   *Achilles* Mythological hero of the Trojan War. In the *Divine Comedy* 1.5.64–66, Dante
     sees him being punished for the sin of lust in the second circle of hell.
4   *Attila* King of the Huns (c. 439–53) with a reputation for savagery, who expanded the
     European territory of the Hunnic Empire; *Genghis Khan* Ruler (1162–1227) who es-
     tablished a vast Mongolian Empire using tactics that included brutal pillaging and mass
     slaughter.

Agha Shahid Ali

1949–2001

Agha Shahid Ali was a Shia Muslim born in predominantly Hindu New Delhi, raised in Sunni Kashmir, and later educated in the United States, where he lived and worked for many years as an academic, poet, and translator. He drew inspiration from his diverse cultural heritage and literary influences, finding fertile ground for his imagination in both his native and adopted homelands. He was raised, he wrote, "a bilingual, bicultural (but never rootless) being," and his loyalties to English and Urdu were so deeply felt and closely joined that they "led not to confusion, but to a strange, arresting clarity."

In collections such as *The Half-Inch Himalayas* (1987), Ali often looks back on the past and dwells on the experience of living apart from one's history. But, in taking stock of what he has left behind, the poet also comes to better represent his own nature and place in the world. In *A Walk through the Yellow Pages* (1987) and *A Nostalgist's Map of America* (1991), Ali does not simply write poems about the vast and varied landscapes of the United States and the American Southwest; he writes as an American poet, working in the tradition of the American sublime.

Among Ali's most significant literary contributions are his translations of the celebrated Urdu poet Faiz Ahmed Faiz. Before Ali published *The Rebel's Silhouette* (1991), both Faiz's poetry and the *ghazal*, a Persian lyric form consisting of rhymed, thematically self-contained couplets, were little known in the West. Here as in much of his work, Ali was keen to experiment with ways to, as he phrased it, "make English behave outside its aesthetic habits."

Postcard from Kashmir

Kashmir shrinks into my mailbox,
my home a neat four by six inches.

I always loved neatness. Now I hold
the half-inch Himalayas in my hand.
This is home. And this the closest
I'll ever be to home. When I return,
the colours won't be so brilliant,
the Jhelum's[1] waters so clean,

5

---

1   *Jhelum* River originating in the Himalayas in Kashmir.

so ultramarine. My love
10 so overexposed.
And my memory will be a little
out of focus, in it
a giant negative, black
and white, still undeveloped.

—1987

The Wolf's Postscript to "Little Red Riding Hood"

First, grant me my sense of history:
I did it for posterity,
for kindergarten teachers
and a clear moral:
5   Little girls shouldn't wander off
in search of strange flowers,
and they mustn't speak to strangers.

And then grant me my generous sense of plot:
Couldn't I have gobbled her up
10 right there in the jungle?
Why did I ask her where her grandma lived?
As if I, a forest-dweller,
didn't know of the cottage
under the three oak trees
15 and the old woman lived there
all alone?
As if I couldn't have swallowed her years before?

And you may call me the Big Bad Wolf,
now my only reputation.
20 But I was no child-molester
though you'll agree she was pretty.

And the huntsman:
Was I sleeping while he snipped
my thick black fur
and filled me with garbage and stones?[1]   25
I ran with that weight and fell down,
simply so children could laugh
at the noise of the stones
cutting through my belly,
at the garbage spilling out   30
with a perfect sense of timing,
just when the tale
should have come to an end.

                                                              —1987

---

1   *And the ... stones* In the version of the Red Riding Hood story that appears in *Grimm's*
    Fairy Tales (1812–15), a huntsman discovers the wolf asleep and cuts its stomach open.
    He rescues the child and her grandmother, who are still alive inside, and they kill the wolf
    by filling its stomach with stones.

Anne Carson
b. 1950

Hailed by Michael Ondaatje as "the most exciting poet writing in English today," Anne Carson is known for formally experimental work that draws on a deep knowledge of literary history, from ancient Greek poetry and medieval mysticism to modernism and contemporary psychoanalysis. Her many accolades include the Griffin Prize for Poetry, the T.S. Eliot Prize for Poetry, and the Order of Canada.

Carson is a professor of classics, and her academic work and her poetry strongly influence each other. These talents most clearly overlap in her Greek translation work, including *If Not, Winter: Fragments of Sappho* (2002) and the three-play collection *An Oresteia* (2009). Captivated by the mindset of ancient Greek culture, Carson says that "what's entrancing about the Greeks is that you get little glimpses, little latches of similarity [to contemporary culture], embedded in unbelievable otherness." Her own poems often view the ancient through a contemporary lens; *Autobiography of Red: A Novel in Verse* (1998), for example, transforms the Greek story of Herakles' battle with the monster Geryon into a story of troubled love between twentieth-century men.

Carson's style is distinctive for its blending of genres, often occupying the borders between poetry and prose. Her first book of poetry, *Short Talks* (1992), is presented as a compilation of miniature lectures, while works such as *Plainwater* (1995) and *Men in the Off Hours* (2000) include poetic essays alongside more traditional lyric poetry. She is also known for her novels in free verse, such as *Autobiography of Red* and *The Beauty of the Husband: A Fictional Essay in 29 Tangos* (2001). With *Nox* (2010), Carson revives her first love—visual art—to memorialize the life of her brother through an interweaving of translation, original poetry, and photographic collage.

from *Short Talks*

On Rain

It was blacker than olives the night I left. As I
ran past the palaces, oddly joyful, it began to
rain. What a notion it is, after all—these small
shapes! I would get lost counting them. Who
5 first thought of it? How did he describe it to
the others? Out on the sea it is raining too.
It beats on no one.

On Sylvia Plath[1]

Did you see her mother on television? She said
plain, burned things. She said I thought it an
excellent poem but it hurt me. She did not say
jungle fear. She did not say jungle hatred wild
jungle weeping chop it back chop it. She said   5
self-government she said end of the road. She
did not say humming in the middle of the air[2]
what you came for chop.

On Walking Backwards

My mother forbade us to walk backwards. That
is how the dead walk, she would say. Where did
she get this idea? Perhaps from a bad translation. The dead, after all, do not walk backwards
but they do walk behind us. They have no lungs   5
and cannot call out but would love for us to
turn around. They are victims of love, many of
them.

—1992

---

1   *Sylvia Plath* (1932-63), American poet and author. The mother in her semi-autobiographical novel *The Bell Jar* (1963) and many of the mother figures in her poetry are
portrayed with hostility.

2   *in the middle of the air* See Plath's poem "The Disquieting Muses" (1960): "I woke one
day to see you, mother, / Floating above me in bluest air."

Dana Gioia

b. 1950

■■■■ Dana Gioia is often cited as the leader of the New Formalist movement, a movement that, beginning in the 1980s, has encouraged a re-engagement with more traditional uses of rhyme, metre, and standard verse forms. Unlike some others in the movement, however, Gioia writes free as well as formal verse and employs forms of his own invention alongside traditional ones; he has said that he cannot "imagine a poet who wouldn't want to have all the possibilities of the language available, especially the powerful enchantments of metre, rhyme, and narrative."

Initially intending to study music at Stanford University, Gioia was drawn instead to the rhythms of poetry, and he eventually undertook graduate work in Comparative Literature at Harvard. Opting not to continue with an academic career, he then earned an MBA and began a business career with General Foods Corporation, where he eventually rose to the rank of vice president. He continued to write and publish in his spare time, however, and when his work began to receive critical attention he resigned from General Foods to pursue a full-time writing career.

Gioia's poetry collections include *Daily Horoscope* (1986), *The Gods of Winter* (1991), and *Pity the Beautiful* (2012). He is also a translator and librettist, and he has commanded serious attention as a critic, both for his articulation of New Formalist principles and for his 1991 essay "Can Poetry Matter?", in which he laments the isolation of the poet from mainstream culture and calls for poetry to be made "more present in American public life."

Thanks for Remembering Us

The flowers sent here by mistake,
signed with a name that no one knew,
are turning bad. What shall we do?
Our neighbour says they're not for her,
5 and no one has a birthday near.
We should thank someone for the blunder.
Is one of us having an affair?
At first we laugh, and then we wonder.

The iris was the first to die,
10 enshrouded in its sickly-sweet
and lingering perfume. The roses
fell one petal at a time,

and now the ferns are turning dry.
The room smells like a funeral,
but there they sit, too much at home,   15
accusing us of some small crime,
like love forgotten, and we can't
throw out a gift we've never owned.

—1983

Planting a Sequoia¹

All afternoon my brothers and I have worked in the orchard,
Digging this hole, laying you into it, carefully packing the soil.
Rain blackened the horizon, but cold winds kept it over the Pacific,
And the sky above us stayed the dull grey
Of an old year coming to an end.   5

In Sicily a father plants a tree to celebrate his first son's birth—
An olive or a fig tree—a sign that the earth has one more life to bear.
I would have done the same, proudly laying new stock into my father's orchard,
A green sapling rising among the twisted apple boughs,
A promise of new fruit in other autumns.   10

But today we kneel in the cold planting you, our native giant,
Defying the practical custom of our fathers,
Wrapping in your roots a lock of hair, a piece of an infant's birth cord,
All that remains above earth of a first-born son,
A few stray atoms brought back to the elements.   15

We will give you what we can—our labour and our soil,
Water drawn from the earth when the skies fail,
Nights scented with the ocean fog, days softened by the circuit of bees.
We plant you in the corner of the grove, bathed in western light,
A slender shoot against the sunset.   20

And when our family is no more, all of his unborn brothers dead,
Every niece and nephew scattered, the house torn down,
His mother's beauty ashes in the air,
I want you to stand among strangers, all young and ephemeral to you,
Silently keeping the secret of your birth.   25

—1991

---

1   *Planting a Sequoia* Written about Gioia's first son, who died in infancy.

Roo Borson
b. 1952

Roo Borson's poetry, often meditative and sensual, has been praised by author Timothy Findley for its "compelling atmosphere of wonder." Frequent themes in her work include nature—especially the natural landscapes of North America—and the recollected past; "most of my work," she says, "uses memory and is about memory in some way."

Borson first became known for the contemplative lyrical poetry of *Landfall* (1970) and *Smoky Light of the Fields* (1980). Longer works such as *Rain* (1980) and *The Whole Night, Coming Home* (1984) marked a new interest in narrative and prose, while *Intent, or the Weight of the World* (1989) and *Water Memory* (1996) saw an increased emphasis on the personal. More recent works such as *Short Journey Upriver Toward Oishida* (2004) and *Rain; Road; An Open Boat* (2012) display the influence of Japanese poetry. Borson is also a member of the "collaborative poetry group" Pain Not Bread, which published the collection *Introduction to the Introduction to Wang Wei* in 2000.

Born Ruth Elizabeth Borson in Berkeley, California, Borson moved to Vancouver to attend the University of British Columbia, where she earned her MFA in 1977. In addition to the Griffin Poetry Prize, she has received three CBC Literary Awards and has been nominated several times for the Governor General's Literary Award, winning for *Short Journey Upriver Toward Oishida* in 2004. Borson has served as writer-in-residence at the University of Toronto and other Canadian universities.

Water Memory

Water does not remember, it moves
among reeds, nudges the little boat
(a little), effloresces[1] a shadowy fog
which forgets for us the way home
5   though the warm dry rooms are
in us. (Stretched on the examining table we
feel it when the unfamiliar hand
presses just there.) Water,
on its own, would not remember,
10   but herd follows herd, and memory is a shepherd
of the gentlest wants. Not even blood
can recall, though the live

---

1   *effloresces* Produces particles when exposed to air.

kidney shipped in its special box
wakes up one day in someone new.
No one made this world, there's no need
to feel ashamed. Be water,
find a lower place, go there.

—1996

Rita Dove
b. 1952

In Rita Dove's poetry, provocative images bridge the gap between the ordinary and the extraordinary. Her work traverses the space between the personal and the historical; Dove is, according to poet Brenda Shaughnessy, "a master at transforming a public or historic element—re-envisioning a spectacle and unearthing the heartfelt, wildly original private thoughts such historic moments always contain."

Born in Akron, Ohio, Dove was encouraged by her mother to develop a childhood passion for reading. She later studied Creative Writing at Miami University and the University of Iowa Writers' Workshop. After obtaining her MFA, she began to make a name for herself as a poet, first with *Yellow House on the Corner* (1980) and later with *Thomas and Beulah* (1986), a Pulitzer Prize-winning volume inspired by the life stories of her grandparents.

Dove works in a variety of genres: in addition to poetry collections, she has published verse drama and several book-length poems, from *Thomas and Beulah* to *Sonata Mulattica* (2009), a narrative based on the life of the eighteenth-century musician George Polgreen Bridgetower. Dove is also a prose fiction author, essayist, newspaper columnist, lyricist, and editor. Poet Laureate of the United States from 1993 to 1995, she remains an advocate for the public support of poetry. "Persephone, Falling" appeared in *Mother Love* (1995), a collection of poems focusing on the mother-daughter relationship.

Persephone, Falling[1]

One narcissus among the ordinary beautiful
flowers, one unlike all the others! She pulled,
stooped to pull harder—
when, sprung out of the earth
5　on his glittering terrible
carriage, he claimed his due.
It is finished. No one heard her.
No one! She had strayed from the herd.

1　*Persephone, Falling* In Greek mythology, Persephone was the daughter of Zeus and Demeter, and became the wife of Hades, god of the underworld. Because Persephone was so beautiful and desired by the male gods of Olympus, Demeter took her to Earth and kept her hidden for protection. One day as Persephone was out gathering flowers, Hades leapt from a crack in the earth and dragged her with him to the underworld.

(Remember: go straight to school.
This is important, stop fooling around!
Don't answer to strangers. Stick
with your playmates. Keep your eyes down.)
This is how easily the pit
opens. This is how one foot sinks into the ground.

—1988

Dionne Brand
b. 1953

For Dionne Brand, poetry is "a philosophical mode for thinking through how one lives in the world and one's relation to other human beings." Her poetry frequently engages with issues of race (and racism), and of gender and sexuality, at times bringing acutely personal perspectives into play to explore these facets of existence.

While Brand has written acclaimed novels, short stories, non-fiction prose, and documentaries, she remains best known as a poet. Her collections include *Chronicles of a Hostile Sun* (1984), a book of poems based on her experience working for a non-government organization in Grenada; *Land to Light On* (1997), a Governor General's Award-winning volume that focuses on experiences of displacement and homelessness, linking them to histories of slavery, colonialism, and migration; and *thirsty* (2002), a book-length poem set in the city of Toronto. She received a Griffin Poetry Prize for *Ossuaries* (2011), another long poem, which the award judges praised for "fulfilling the novelistic narrative ambition of her work, [without] sacrific[ing] the tight lyrical coil of the poetic line."

Born in Trinidad, Brand immigrated to Canada in 1970. She earned a BA at the University of Toronto (1975) and, later, an MA at the Ontario Institute for Studies in Education (1989). She has held a number of prestigious university positions including Distinguished Visiting Scholar at St. Lawrence University and University Research Chair at the University of Guelph. Brand was named Poet Laureate of Toronto in 2009.

from *thirsty*

30

Spring darkness is forgiving. It doesn't descend
abruptly before you have finished work,
it approaches palely waiting for you
to get outside to witness another illumined hour

5   you feel someone brush against you,
on the street, you smell leather, the lake,
the coming leaves, the rain's immortality
pierces you, but you will be asleep when it arrives

you will lie in the groove of a lover's neck
unconscious, translucent, tendons singing,   10
and that should be enough, the circumference
of the world narrowed to your simple dreams

Days are perfect, that's the thing about them,
standing here in half darkness, I think this.
It's difficult to rise to that, but I expect it   15
I expect each molecule of my substance to imitate that

I can't of course, I can't touch syllables
tenderness, throats.
Look it's like this, I'm just like the rest,
limping across the city, flying when I can   20

32

Every smell is now a possibility, a young man
passes wreathed in cologne, that is hope;
teenagers, traceries of marijuana, that is hope too, utopia;

smog braids the city where sweet grass used to,
yesterday morning's exhaust, this day's   5
breathing by the lightness, the heaviness of the soul.

Every night the waste of the city is put out and taken away
to suburban landfills and recycling plants,
and that is the rhythm everyone would prefer in their life,

that the waste is taken out, that what may be useful   10
be saved and the rest, most of it, the ill of it,
buried.

Sometimes the city's stink is fragrant offal,
sometimes it is putrid. All depends on what wakes you up,
the angular distance of death or the elliptic of living.   15

—2002

Kim Addonizio
b. 1954

Known for her direct and empathetic depictions of love, loss, desire, and struggle, Kim Addonizio has achieved recognition for her poetry and novels, as well as for public readings in which she often blends poetry with the sounds of the blues harmonica. Her many honours include a Guggenheim Fellowship, a Pushcart Prize, and two National Endowment for the Arts Fellowships.

Born in Washington, DC, Addonizio obtained a BA and an MA from San Francisco State University, then worked as a lecturer at several colleges while she began to pursue her writing career. Her first collection, *Three West Coast Women* (1987), was a collaboration with fellow poets Laurie Duesing and Dorianne Laux. Several solo volumes followed, including *The Philosopher's Club* (1994), *Tell Me* (2000), and *Lucifer at the Starlite* (2009). As a poet, Addonizio is notable for writing both in free verse and in fixed forms (including the sonnet and a variant of the sonnet that she invented, the sonnenizio); her work displays an abiding interest in the interplay of syntax and rhythm, and a highly developed (if often unobtrusive) talent for rhyme.

With Dorianne Laux, Addonizio co-authored *The Poet's Companion: A Guide to the Pleasures of Writing Poetry* (1997); in 2009, she released *Ordinary Genius: A Guide for the Poet Within*, her own collection of writing exercises and personal insights. Addonizio has taught writing at Goddard College, at San Francisco State University, and through private workshops.

First Poem for You

I like to touch your tattoos in complete
darkness, when I can't see them. I'm sure of
where they are, know by heart the neat
lines of lightning pulsing just above
5   your nipple, can find, as if by instinct, the blue
swirls of water on your shoulder where a serpent
twists, facing a dragon. When I pull you
to me, taking you until we're spent
and quiet on the sheets, I love to kiss
10   the pictures in your skin. They'll last until
you're seared to ashes; whatever persists
or turns to pain between us, they will still
be there. Such permanence is terrifying.
So I touch them in the dark; but touch them, trying.

—1994

Sarah Arvio
b. 1954

Sarah Arvio's poetry addresses subjects that range from love and loss to dream psychology and the workings of language in a meditative, technically playful, and frequently comic style.

Born in Philadelphia, Pennsylvania, Arvio grew up in New York State and earned her MFA from Columbia University. She is fluent in French and Spanish as well as English and has worked as a freelance translator for the United Nations; she has also translated novels, stories, poems, and documentary film. For several years, she was a Lecturer in Creative Writing at Princeton.

It was not until her forties, after she began psychoanalysis, that Arvio found her voice as a poet. In 2002 she published her first book, *Visits from the Seventh*, a collection of poems written through a process she describes as the "channelling" or transcription of voices—although she does not specify whether these voices originated in the spirit realm or her own unconscious. *Visits from the Seventh* received a Rome Prize, which enabled Arvio to go to the American Academy in Rome. There she wrote her next collection, *Sono: Cantos* (2006), a volume praised by poet Robert Pinsky for raising witty wordplay "to an unusual, expressive intensity." In *Night Thoughts* (2013), Arvio engages directly with her experience of psychoanalysis in a series of poems describing her dreams, accompanied by "Notes" analyzing their meanings.

Wood

The last thing I ever wanted was to
write again about grief did you think I
would your grief this time not mine oh good

grief enough is enough in my life that is
enough was enough I had all those   5
grievances all those griefs all engraved

into the wood of my soul but would you
believe it the wood healed I grew up and
grew out and would you believe it I found

your old woody heart sprouting I thought   10
good new growth good new luxuriant green
leaves leaves on their woody stalks and I said

I'll stake my life on this old stick I'll stick
and we talked into the morning and night
15 and laughed green leaves and sometimes a flower

oh bower of good new love I would have it
I would bow to the new and the green
and wouldn't you know it you were a stick

yes I know a good stick so often and then
20 a stick in my ribs in my heart your old
dark wood your old dark gnarled stalk

sprouting havoc and now I have grief again
and now I've stood for what I never should
green leaves of morning dark leaves of night

—2009

Carol Ann Duffy
b. 1955

As Jeanette Winterson has written, Carol Ann Duffy is Britain's "favourite poet after Shakespeare." In 2009, when Duffy was appointed the first female Poet Laureate of the United Kingdom, Prime Minister Gordon Brown described her as "a truly brilliant modern poet who has stretched our imaginations by putting the whole range of human experiences into lines that capture emotions perfectly." She is also (to quote Winterson once more) "political in that she wants to change things, [and] idealistic in that she believes she—and poetry—can change things. And, of course, she's a woman, she's a Celt, and she's gay."

Duffy was born in Glasgow, Scotland, and raised in Staffordshire, England. She graduated from the University of Liverpool in 1977 with an honours degree in philosophy, and over the following decade she wrote a number of radio plays and collections of poems. Her talent with a variety of poetic forms and her reluctance to shy away from disturbing content are both evident in her first book, *Standing Female Nude* (1985), which included, for example, a first-person poem from the point of view of a burgeoning murderer and an unflinching depiction of a Holocaust scene. In 1999, Duffy published *The World's Wife*, a series of dramatic monologues written in the voices of the wives of famous historical and fictional figures. *Mean Time* (1993), a volume of poems about the emotional struggles and triumphs of adolescence, won the Whitbread Poetry Award. In 2005, Duffy received the T.S. Eliot Award for *Rapture*, a semi-autobiographical collection recounting a love story from first sight to eventual collapse. Her 2011 work *The Bees* incorporates poems on war and climate change alongside lyrics on the death of the poet's mother.

Duffy's work is extraordinary not least of all for its formal artistry; she is renowned as a master of poetic rhythm and of rhyme as much as of image and metaphor. In her discussions of poetry as well as in the poems themselves, she draws connections between sounds and their human meanings: a poem, she has said, "is the place in language [where] we are most human and we can see ourselves fully—far more than prose in fiction. A poem is able to hold so much in so little space."

Drunk

Suddenly the rain is hilarious.
The moon wobbles in the dusk.

What a laugh. Unseen frogs
belch in the damp grass.

5   The strange perfumes of darkening trees.
Cheap red wine

and the whole world a mouth.
Give me a double, a kiss.

—1993

The Good Teachers

You run round the back to be in it again.
No bigger than your thumbs, those virtuous women
size you up from the front row. Soon now,
Miss Ross will take you for double History.
5   You breathe on the glass, making a ghost of her, say
South Sea Bubble Defenestration of Prague.[1]

You love Miss Pirie. So much, you are top
of her class. So much, you need two of you
to stare out from the year, serious, passionate.
10 The River's Tale by Rudyard Kipling[2] by heart.
Her kind intelligent green eye. Her cruel blue one.
You are making a poem up for her in your head.

But not Miss Sheridan. Comment vous appelez.[3]
But not Miss Appleby. Equal to the square
15 of the other two sides. Never Miss Webb.
Dar es Salaam. Kilimanjaro.[4] Look. The good teachers
swish down the corridor in long, brown skirts,
snobbish and proud and clean and qualified.

And they've got your number. You roll the waistband
20 of your skirt over and over, all leg, all
dumb insolence, smoke-rings. You won't pass.

---

1   *South Sea ... Prague* Two unconnected historical incidents.
2   *The River's Tale* 1911 poem summarizing English history up to the end of Roman occupation; *Rudyard Kipling* Bombay-born English novelist, poet, and short story writer (1865–1936).
3   *Comment vous appelez* French: what do you call.
4   *Dar es Salaam. Kilimanjaro* The largest city and the tallest mountain, respectively, in Tanzania.

You could do better. But there's the wall you climb
into dancing, lovebites, marriage, the Cheltenham
and Gloucester,[1] today. The day you'll be sorry one day.

—1993

Crush

The older she gets,
the more she awakes
with somebody's face strewn in her head
like petals which once made a flower.

What everyone does
is sit by a desk   5
and stare at the view, till the time
where they live reappears. Mostly in words.

Imagine a girl
turning to see   10
love stand by a window, taller,
clever, anointed with sudden light.

Yes, like an angel then,
to be truthful now.
At first a secret, erotic, mute;   15
today a language she cannot recall.

And we're all owed joy,
sooner or later.
The trick's to remember whenever
it was, or to see it coming.   20

—1998

Rapture

Thought of by you all day, I think of you.
The birds sing in the shelter of a tree.
Above the prayer of rain, unacred blue,
not paradise, goes nowhere endlessly.

---

1   *Cheltenham and Gloucester* Commercial bank in the United Kingdom.

5 How does it happen that our lives can drift
   far from our selves, while we stay trapped in time,
   queuing° for death? It seems nothing will shift   *lining up*
   the pattern of our days, alter the rhyme
   we make with loss to assonance with bliss.
10 Then love comes, like a sudden flight of birds
   from earth to heaven after rain. Your kiss,
   recalled, unstrings, like pearls, this chain of words.
   Huge skies connect us, joining here to there.
   Desire and passion on the thinking air.

—2005

Treasure

A soft ounce of your breath
in my cupped palm.
The gold weight of your head
on my numb arm.

5 Your heart's warm ruby
   set in your breast.
   The art of your hands,
   the slim turquoise veins under your wrists.

Your mouth, the sweet, chrism[1] blessing
10 of its kiss,
   the full measure of bliss pressed
   to my lips.

Your fine hair, run through my fingers,
sieved.
15 Your silver smile, your jackpot laugh,
   bright gifts.

Sighted amber, the 1001 nights
of your eyes.
Even the sparkling fool's gold
20 of your lies.

—2005

---

1   *chrism* Consecrated oil used for anointing in some Christian churches.

Marilyn Dumont
b. 1955

For Marilyn Dumont, poetry is a form of activism: beginning with her first collection, *A Really Good Brown Girl* (1997), she has evocatively told the neglected stories of Canadian Aboriginal experience. Her following works, *green girl dreams mountains* (2001) and *that tongued belonging* (2007), have been commended for their exploration of poverty, femininity, and the effects of colonization in Canada.

Although Dumont's commitment to Canadian Aboriginal issues has not changed, her approach to writing has developed in the course of her poetic career. *A Really Good Brown Girl*, she says, directly expresses "anger, shame, hurt, disillusionment and grief about the subjugation and mistreatment of Aboriginal peoples and traditions in Canada." Since then, however, she has found it more effective to communicate similar concepts "in different ways—through humour, through pathos, through sleight of hand, through elegance." Both approaches have attracted critical acclaim: Dumont received a Gerald Lampert Memorial Award for *A Really Good Brown Girl*, and *that tongued belonging* was chosen as Aboriginal Book of the Year by McNally Robinson and Poetry Book of the Year at the Ânskohk Aboriginal Literature Festival.

Dumont was born in northeastern Alberta in 1955 and spent her youth living in logging camps in the Alberta foothills. She is Métis and Cree, a descendant of Gabriel Dumont (a leader of Métis forces during the Northwest Rebellion of 1885), and was raised in a bilingual Cree and English household. She has been Writer-in-Residence at several institutions (among them the University of Alberta, the University of Windsor, Grant MacEwan University, and Athabasca University), and has also taught in the Aboriginal Emerging Writers Program at the Banff Centre for the Arts.

Not Just a Platform for My Dance

this land is not
just a place to set my house my car my fence

this land is not
just a plot to bury my dead my seed

this land is
my tongue   my eyes   my mouth
this headstrong grass and relenting willow

5

these flat-footed fields and applauding leaves
these frank winds and electric sky lines
10 are my prayer
they are my medicine
and they become my song
this land is not
just a platform for my dance

—1996

The White Judges

We lived in an old schoolhouse, one large room that my father converted
into two storeys with a plank staircase leading to the second floor. A single
window on the south wall created a space that was dimly lit even at midday.
All nine kids and the occasional friend slept upstairs like cadets in rows of
5 shared double beds, ate downstairs in the kitchen near the gas stove and
watched TV near the airtight heater in the adjacent room. Our floors were
worn linoleum and scatter rugs, our walls high and bare except for the
family photos whose frames were crowded with siblings waiting to come of
age, marry or leave. At supper eleven of us would stare down a pot of moose
10 stew, bannock and tea, while outside the white judges sat encircling our
house.

And they waited to judge

waited till we ate tripe
watched us inhale its wild vapour
15 sliced and steaming on our plates,
watched us welcome it into our being,
sink our teeth into its rubbery texture
chew and roll each wet and tentacled piece
swallow its gamey juices
20 until we had become it and it had become us.

Or waited till the cardboard boxes
were anonymously dropped at our door, spilling with clothes
waited till we ran swiftly away from the windows and doors
to the farthest room for fear of being seen
25 and dared one another to
'open it'
'no you open it'

'no you'
someone would open it
cautiously pulling out a shirt   30
that would be tried on
then passed around till somebody claimed it by fit
then sixteen or eighteen hands would be pulling out
skirts, pants, jackets, dresses from a box transformed now
into the Sears catalogue.   35

Or the white judges would wait till twilight
and my father and older brothers
would drag a bloodstained canvas
heavy with meat from the truck onto our lawn, and
my mother would lift and lay it in place   40
like a dead relative,
praying, coaxing and thanking it
then she'd cut the thick hair and skin back
till it lay in folds beside it like carpet

carving off firm chunks   45
until the marble bone shone out of the red-blue flesh
long into the truck-headlight-night she'd carve
talking in Cree to my father and in English to my brothers
long into the dark their voices talking us to sleep
while our bellies rested in the meat days ahead.   50

Or wait till the guitars came out
and the furniture was pushed up against the walls
and we'd polish the linoleum with our dancing
till our socks had holes.

Or wait till a fight broke out   55
and the night would settle in our bones
and we'd ache with shame
for having heard or spoken
that which sits at the edge of our light side
that which comes but we wished it hadn't   60
like 'settlement' relatives who would arrive at Christmas and
leave at Easter.

—1996

Robin Robertson
b. 1955

Poet, editor, and translator Robin Robertson was raised on the northeast coast of Scotland but has spent most of his professional life in London. He first established himself in the publishing industry as an editor and did not release a collection of his own poetry until his forties; this first book, *A Painted Field* (1997), was followed by *Slow Air* (2002), *Swithering* (2006), and *The Wrecking Light* (2010).

Robertson's work is known for its often bleak view of human relationships; for its use of natural imagery, especially imagery reflecting the landscape of Robertson's native Scotland; and for its frequent allusions to classical and Celtic mythology. Yet his work is immediate and contemporary in tone. *The New Yorker* has praised his "genius ... for finding the sensually charged moment—in a raked northern seascape, in a sexual or gustatory encounter—and depicting it in language that is simultaneously spare and ample."

Robertson is the first poet to win Britain's Forward Prize in all three categories: Best First Collection, Best Collection, and Best Single Poem. He was honoured with the E.M. Forster Award in 2004, elected a Fellow of the Royal Society of Literature in 2009, and presented with the T.S. Eliot Prize for Poetry in 2010. Robertson has also received critical praise for his work as a translator; such works include a translation of Euripides' play *Medea* (2008) and *The Deleted World* (2007), a bilingual edition of selections by the Swedish poet Tomas Tranströmer.

The Park Drunk

He opens his eyes to a hard frost,
the morning's soft amnesia of snow.

The thorned stems of gorse
are starred crystal; each bud
5 like a candied fruit, its yellow
picked out and lit
by the low pulse
of blood-orange
riding in the eastern trees.

10 What the snow has furred
to silence, uniformity,
frost amplifies, makes singular:

giving every form a sound,
an edge, as if
frost wants to know what   15
snow tries to forget.

And so he drinks for winter,
for the coming year,
to open all the beautiful tiny doors
in their craquelure[1] of frost;   20
and he drinks
like the snow falling, trying
to close the biggest door of all.

—2006

What the Horses See at Night

When the day-birds have settled
in their creaking trees,
the doors of the forest open
for the flitting
drift of deer   5
among the bright croziers[2]
of new ferns
and the legible stars;
foxes stream from the earth;
a tawny owl   10
sweeps the long meadow.
In a slink of river-light
the mink's face
is already slippery with yolk,
and the bay's   15
tiny islands are drops
of solder
under a drogue[3] moon.
The sea's a heavy sleeper,
dreaming in and out with a catch   20
in each breath, and is not disturbed

---

1   *craquelure* Texture of fine cracks found in old varnish or paint.
2   *croziers* Curled ends of new fern fronds.
3   *drogue* Funnel-shaped object dragged behind a boat or other vehicle to reduce its speed.

by that *plowt*[1]—the first
in a play of herring, a shoal
silvering open
25   the sheeted black skin of the sea.
Through the starting rain, the moon
skirrs[2] across the sky dragging
torn shreds of cloud behind.
The fox's call is red
30   and ribboned
in the snow's white shadow.
The horses watch the sea climb
and climb and walk
towards them on the hill,
35   hear the vole
crying under the alder,
our children
breathing slowly in their beds.

—2006

---

1   *plowt* Scots: splash.
2   *skirrs* Scots: scurries.

Li-Young Lee
b. 1957

When Li-Young Lee was two years old his Chinese family fled persecution in Indonesia, travelling through Hong Kong, Macau, and Japan before they reached the United States in 1964. Lee's work often focuses on his personal life, including his relationships with his wife and children; the most frequently recurring figure is his father, who had been Mao Zedong's personal physician, but in the United States became a Presbyterian minister. Lee strives to unite his examination of personal memories with a more universal exploration of selfhood and spirituality, describing himself as "an amateur mystic."

Although Lee is often pigeonholed as an immigrant writer and acknowledges the influence of Imperial-era Chinese poets such as Tu Fu and Su Tung-po, he also cites the influence of his father's Christianity on his work—and the influence of writers such as John Keats, Walt Whitman, and Cynthia Ozick. Resisting pressure to identify his poetry as "Asian," "American," or even "Asian-American," Lee says, "I want to be a global poet."

Lyrical and elegant in his handling of themes of exile, identity, and mortality, Lee has received critical acclaim since the publication of his first book, *Rose* (1986). Although his reputation rests primarily on poetry collections such as *The City in Which I Love You* (1990) and *Behind My Eyes* (2008), he has also published an American Book Award-winning prose memoir, *The Winged Seed* (1995).

Persimmons

In sixth grade Mrs. Walker
slapped the back of my head
and made me stand in the corner
for not knowing the difference
between *persimmon* and *precision*.   5
How to choose

persimmons. This is precision.
Ripe ones are soft and brown-spotted.
Sniff the bottoms. The sweet one
will be fragrant. How to eat: 10
put the knife away, lay down newspaper.
Peel the skin tenderly, not to tear the meat.
Chew the skin, suck it,

and swallow. Now, eat
15 the meat of the fruit,
so sweet,
all of it, to the heart.

Donna undresses, her stomach is white.
In the yard, dewy and shivering
20 with crickets, we lie naked,
face-up, face-down.
I teach her Chinese.
Crickets: *chiu chiu*. Dew: I've forgotten.
Naked: I've forgotten.
25 *Ni, wo*: you and me.
I part her legs,
remember to tell her
she is beautiful as the moon.

Other words
30 that got me into trouble were
fight and *fright*, *wren* and *yarn*.
Fight was what I did when I was frightened,
Fright was what I felt when I was fighting.
Wrens are small, plain birds,
35 yarn is what one knits with.
Wrens are soft as yarn.
My mother made birds out of yarn.
I loved to watch her tie the stuff;
a bird, a rabbit, a wee man.

40 Mrs. Walker brought a persimmon to class
and cut it up
so everyone could taste
a *Chinese apple*. Knowing
it wasn't ripe or sweet, I didn't eat
45 but watched the other faces.

My mother said every persimmon has a sun
inside, something golden, glowing,
warm as my face.

Once, in the cellar, I found two wrapped in newspaper,
50 forgotten and not yet ripe.
I took them and set both on my bedroom windowsill,

where each morning a cardinal
sang, *The sun, the sun.*

Finally understanding
he was going blind,   55
my father sat up all one night
waiting for a song, a ghost.
I gave him the persimmons,
swelled, heavy as sadness,
and sweet as love.   60

This year, in the muddy lighting
of my parents' cellar, I rummage, looking
for something I lost.
My father sits on the tired, wooden stairs,
black cane between his knees,   65
hand over hand, gripping the handle.
He's so happy that I've come home.
I ask how his eyes are, a stupid question.
All gone, he answers.

Under some blankets, I find a box.   70
Inside the box I find three scrolls.
I sit beside him and untie
three paintings by my father:
Hibiscus leaf and a white flower.
Two cats preening.   75
Two persimmons, so full they want to drop from the cloth.

He raises both hands to touch the cloth,
asks, *Which is this?*

This is persimmons, Father.

Oh, the feel of the wolftail on the silk,   80
the strength, the tense
precision in the wrist.
I painted them hundreds of times
eyes closed. These I painted blind.
Some things never leave a person: 85
scent of the hair of one you love,
the texture of persimmons,
in your palm, the ripe weight.

—1986

Benjamin Zephaniah
b. 1958

Benjamin Zephaniah is known as a writer of dub poetry, a form based on reggae rhythms that is best appreciated if the poem is read aloud. Through his insistence that poetry needs to be spoken and "performed," either live or on television, Zephaniah engages with a broad audience that might not otherwise seek out his work. He is a vegan, a Rastafarian, and a human rights activist, and much of his work is political, provoking his audiences to confront racism and other forms of injustice in Britain and across the world. His voice is sometimes humorous and hopeful, but is also expressive of anger; as he writes, "Black people do not have / Chips on their shoulders / They just have injustice on their backs."

Zephaniah was brought up in a Jamaican community in Birmingham, England. Frustrated, possibly because of his dyslexia, he left school at 13 and gained a local reputation as a poet before moving to London, where his first book, *Pen Rhythm*, was released in 1980. Since then he has published, performed, and recorded poetry for adults and children and has written novels for youth addressing subjects such as racism and violence.

Zephaniah's recordings often combine poetry with music that has its base in reggae but incorporates other influences, from jazz to hip hop; he has recorded with the reggae band The Wailers, with drummer Trevor Morais, and with singer-songwriter Sinéad O'Connor. Zephaniah holds more than a dozen honorary doctorates and in 2003 was offered the title Officer of the Order of the British Empire, which he refused.

Dis Poetry

Dis poetry is like a riddim dat drops
De tongue fires a riddim dat shoots like shots
Dis poetry is designed fe rantin
Dance hall style, big mouth chanting,
5 Dis poetry nar put yu to sleep
Preaching follow me
Like yu is blind sheep,
Dis poetry is not Party Political
Not designed fe dose who are critical.

10 Dis poetry is wid me when I gu to me bed
It gets into me dreadlocks
It lingers around me head
Dis poetry goes wid me as I pedal me bike
I've tried Shakespeare, Respect due dere

But dis is de stuff I like. 15
Dis poetry is not afraid of going ina book
Still dis poetry need ears fe hear an eyes fe hav a look
Dis poetry is Verbal Riddim, no big words involved
An if I hav a problem de riddim gets it solved,
I've tried to be more Romantic, it does nu good for me 20
So I tek a Reggae Riddim an build me poetry,
I could try be more personal
But you've heard it all before,
Pages of written words not needed
Brain has many words in store, 25
Yu could call dis poetry Dub Ranting
De tongue plays a beat
De body starts skanking,[1]
Dis poetry is quick an childish
Dis poetry is fe de wise an foolish, 30
Anybody can do it fe free,
Dis poetry is fe yu an me,
Don't stretch yu imagination
Dis poetry is fe de good of de Nation,
Chant, 35
In de morning
I chant
In de night
I chant
In de darkness 40
An under de spotlight,
I pass thru University
I pass thru Sociology
An den I got a Dread degree
In Dreadfull Ghettology. 45

Dis poetry stays wid me when I run or walk
An when I am talking to meself in poetry I talk,
Dis poetry is wid me,
Below me an above,
Dis poetry's from inside me 50
It goes to yu
WID LUV.

—1995

---

1   *skanking* Style of dancing associated with reggae music.

George Elliott Clarke
b. 1960

George Elliott Clarke is a playwright, academic, critic, and poet known for the power and lyricism of his language. His poetry draws on biblical stories, oral narratives, and music, especially jazz and the blues. He often uses linked poems as a mode of storytelling; speaking of the story-in-verse, Clarke has said that a "lyric poem—even a haiku—is always a little drama, a little story—just as every snapshot is a truncated tale. So, as soon as one compiles a bunch of lyrics, they almost always begin to comprise a narrative."

A political and cultural activist as well as a writer, Clarke frequently addresses the history and experiences of black Canadians in his work; he is especially interested in Maritimers of African descent, whom he refers to as "Africadians." Clarke's interests in black history and narrative poetry come together in works such as his verse novel *Whylah Falls* (1990), set in the 1930s in the fictional black Nova Scotian community of Whylah Falls.

Clarke himself is a seventh-generation Canadian and the descendant of black Loyalists who settled in Nova Scotia in 1783. He holds degrees from the University of Waterloo (BA), Dalhousie University (MA), and Queen's University (PhD). He was named the E.J. Pratt Professor of Canadian Literature at the University of Toronto in 2003 and Poet Laureate of Toronto in 2012. Among Clarke's many awards are numerous honorary doctorates, the Governor General's Award for his collection *Execution Poems* (2001), the Martin Luther King, Jr. Achievement Award (2004), the Pierre Elliott Trudeau Fellows Prize (2005), and the Order of Canada (2008).

from *Whylah Falls*

Blank Sonnet

The air smells of rhubarb, occasional
Roses, or first birth of blossoms, a fresh,
Undulant hurt, so body snaps and curls
Like flower. I step through snow as thin as script,
5 Watch white stars spin dizzy as drunks, and yearn
To sleep beneath a patchwork quilt of rum.
I want the slow, sure collapse of language
Washed out by alcohol. Lovely Shelley,[1]

---

1   *Shelley* The speaker's lover.

I have no use for measured, cadenced verse
If you won't read. Icarus-like,[1] I'll fall 10
Against this page of snow, tumble blackly
Across vision to drown in the white sea
That closes every poem—the white reverse
That cancels the blackness of each image.

Look Homeward, Exile

I can still see that soil crimsoned by butchered
Hog and imbrued with rye, lye, and homely
Spirituals everybody must know,
Still dream of folks who broke or cracked like shale:
Pushkin, who twisted his hands in boxing, 5
Marrocco, who ran girls like dogs and got stabbed,
Lavinia, her teeth decayed to black stumps,
Her lovemaking still in demand, spitting
Black phlegm—her pension after twenty towns,
And Toof; suckled on anger that no Baptist 10
Church could contain, who let wrinkled Eely
Seed her moist womb when she was just thirteen.
      And the tyrant sun that reared from barbed-wire
Spewed flame that charred the idiot crops
To Depression, and hurt my granddaddy 15
To bottle after bottle of sweet death,
His dreams beaten to one, tremendous pulp,
Until his heart seized, choked; his love gave out.
      But Beauty survived, secreted
In freight trains snorting in their pens, in babes 20
Whose faces were coal-black mirrors, in strange
Strummers who plucked Ghanaian banjos, hummed
Blind blues—precise, ornate, rich needlepoint,
In sermons scorched with sulphur and brimstone,
And in my love's dark, orient skin that smelled 25
Like orange peels and tasted like rum, good God!
      I remember my Creator in the old ways:
I sit in taverns and stare at my fists;

---

1   *Icarus* Ancient Greek mythological character who flew using wings made of feathers and wax. When Icarus flew too close to the sun, the wax melted, and he fell into the ocean and drowned.

I knead earth into bread, spell water into wine.
30 Still, nothing warms my wintry exile—neither
Prayers nor fine love, neither votes nor hard drink:
For nothing heals those saints felled in green beds,
Whose loves are smashed by just one word or glance
Or pain—a screw jammed in thick, straining wood.

                                                                —1990

Casualties

January 16, 1991[1]

Snow annihilates all beauty
this merciless January.
A white blitzkrieg,[2] Klan—cruel,
arsons and obliterates.

5 Piercing lies numb us to pain.
Nerves and words fail so we
can't feel agony or passion,
so we can't flinch or cry,

when we spy blurred children's
10 charred bodies protruding
from the smoking rubble
of statistics or see a man

stumbling in a blizzard
of bullets. Everything is
15 normal, absurdly normal.
We see, as if through a snow-

---

1   *January 16, 1991* Date of the beginning of the Gulf War (January–February 1991), in
     which the United States and its allies expelled the Iraqi military from Kuwait, which
     Iraq had invaded the previous year. The war demonstrated the power of American
     military technology; there were fewer than 500 casualties on the side of the American-led
     coalition, but tens of thousands of civilian casualties and as many as 100,000 casualties
     among Iraqi soldiers. The war also created millions of refugees.
2   *blitzkrieg* Intensive war strategy that combines aerial bombing and mechanized ground
     troops to surprise and overwhelm an enemy; the American-led coalition used this sort of
     strategy in the Gulf War.

storm, darkly. Reporters
rat-a-tat-tat tactics,
stratagems. Missiles bristle
behind newspaper lines.   20

Our minds chill; we weather
the storm, huddle in dreams.
Exposed, though, a woman,
lashed by lightning, repents

of her flesh, becomes a living   25
X-ray, "collateral damage."
The first casualty of war
is language.

—1992

Jackie Kay
b. 1961

Deemed "one of the most sure-footed voices in contemporary literature" by *The Guardian*, Jackie Kay is a writer of poetry, fiction, children's books, drama, and autobiography. She began writing in her late teens, she has said, because, as a black lesbian growing up in Scotland, she found "there wasn't anybody else saying the things I wanted to say.... I started out of that sense of wanting to create some images for myself."

Born to a Nigerian father and Scottish mother, Kay was adopted and raised in Glasgow by white parents—an experience that has informed much of her writing, including poetry collections such as *The Adoption Papers* (1991) and *Fiere* (2011) as well as her 2010 prose memoir *Red Dust Road*. "I sometimes take my own experience as a diving board to jump off into the pool of my imagination," Kay has said of her work, which often delves into aspects of identity, including race, culture, and sexuality. Her novel *Trumpet* (1998), for example, concerns a biological woman who lives his life as a man, while her BBC radio play *The Lamplighter* (2007) examines the history of the Atlantic slave trade.

Kay has more than 15 publications to her credit and is the recipient of numerous awards. She won the *Guardian* Fiction Prize for *Trumpet* and the CLPE Poetry Award for her children's poetry collection *Red, Cherry Red* (2007), and in 2006 she was made a Member of the Order of the British Empire for services to literature. She teaches creative writing at Newcastle University.

In My Country

Walking by the waters
down where an honest river
shakes hands with the sea,
a woman passed round me
5 in a slow watchful circle,
as if I were a superstition;

or the worst dregs of her imagination,
so when she finally spoke
her words spliced into bars
10 of an old wheel. A segment of air.
"Where do you come from?"
"Here," I said. "Here. These parts."

—1991

Her

I had been told about her
How she would always, always
How she would never, never
I'd watched and listened
But I still fell for her   5
How she always, always
How she never, never

In the small brave night
Her lips, butterfly moments
I tried to catch her and she laughed   10
A loud laugh that cracked me in two
But then I had been told about her
How she would always, always
How she would never, never

We two listened to the wind   15
We two galloped a pace
We two, up and away, away, away.
And now she's gone
Like she said she would go
But then I had been told about her
How she would always, always.

—2005

High Land

I don't remember who kissed who first,
who touched who first, who anything to whom.
All I remember in the highland night—
the sheep loose outside,
the full moon smoking in the sky—   5
was that you led me and I led you.
And all of a sudden we were in a small room
in a big house with the light coming in
and your legs open; mine too.
And it was this swirling, twirling thing.   10
It's hard to fasten it down;

it is hard to remember what was what—
who was who when the wind was coming in.

—2005

Late Love

How they strut about, people in love,
How tall they grow, pleased with themselves,
Their hair, glossy, their skin shining.
They don't remember who they have been.

5 How filmic they are just for this time.
How important they've become—secret, above
The order of things, the dreary mundane.
Every church bell ringing, a fresh sign.

How dull the lot that are not in love.
10 Their clothes shabby, their skin lustreless;
How clueless they are, hair a mess; how they trudge
Up and down the streets in the rain,

remembering one kiss in a dark alley,
A touch in a changing room, if lucky, a lovely wait
15 For the phone to ring, maybe, baby.
The past with its rush of velvet, its secret hush

Already miles away, dimming now, in the late day.

—2005

Lavinia Greenlaw
b. 1962

Lavinia Greenlaw's diverse career and background have allowed her to explore in writing a wide array of subjects—from science and music to art, history, and travel. Her style is characterized by precise description and a sometimes dry humour; her several collections of poetry include *Night Photograph* (1993), *A World Where News Travelled Slowly* (1997), *Minsk* (2003), and *The Casual Perfect* (2011).

Greenlaw was born in London and her childhood experiences in a science-oriented family have provided inspiration for many of her poems. She has been a writer-in-residence for such institutions as the Science Museum and the Royal Society of Medicine, but also worked as an arts administrator after earning an MA in seventeenth-century art from the Courtauld Institute. She teaches writing at the University of East Anglia, where she has served as chair of the Poetry Society and director of the Poetry MA program.

In addition to her books of poetry, Greenlaw has authored two novels and two non-fiction books (including the acclaimed 2007 memoir *The Importance of Music to Girls*). She has also written song texts and libretti for several operas, adapted works by Virginia Woolf and Geoffrey Chaucer into radio dramas, and created documentaries for BBC radio. Her interest in audio media led to her 2011 Ted Hughes Award-winning sound work *Audio Obscura*, a composition of monologues to be listened to in a train station. Her other accolades include a Forward Prize, a Cholmondeley Award, and an Arts Council Writer's Award.

Electricity

The night you called to tell me
that the unevenness between the days
is as simple as meeting or not meeting,
I was thinking about electricity—
how at no point on a circuit   5
can power diminish or accumulate,
how you also need a lack of balance
for energy to be released. *Trust it.*
Once, being held like that,
no edge, no end and no beginning,   10
I could not tell our actions apart:
if it was you who lifted my head to the light,

if it was I who said how much I wanted
to look at your face. *Your beautiful face.*

—1993

Zombies

1980, I was returned to the city exposed
in black and white as the lights went on and on.
A back-alley neon sign, the first I'd seen,
drew us sweetly down and in to brightness:
5 a doll's parasol, a spike of green cherries,
the physic of apricot brandy, actual limes
and morning-to-night shades of rum.
Newly old enough and government-moneyed,
we knocked them back, melting the ice
10 between us and the unaccustomed looseness
of being legitimate and free. What possessed us?
Was it the kick of spirits or the invisible syrup
in which they swam that worked in our veins,
charming us into a car and forty miles east

15 to the fields of our years of boredom?
Did we not remember the curse of this place?
How Sundays drank our blood as we watched
dry paint or the dust on the television screen.
How people died bursting out of a quiet life,
20 or from being written into a small world's stories.
Who can see such things and live to tell?
How we hunted all night for noise and love,
striking out once across ploughed and frozen earth,
lurching from rut to rut until at the edge
25 we smashed our way out through a hedge, to fall
eight feet to the road. Of course, we felt nothing.
Was it not ourselves who frightened us most?
As if brightness or sweetness could save us.

—2003

Simon Armitage
b. 1963

Simon Armitage was born in West Yorkshire, England, and worked as a probation officer in Manchester before becoming a full-time poet; his northern English background is reflected in both the language and subject matter of his work. Named Britain's Millennium Poet in 2000, he is also known for his work as a playwright, lecturer, translator, and novelist.

In Armitage's words, poetry is "a kind of human consequence" of our existence as "a species that looks for pattern, and looks for significance, and looks for meaning in a life"—a sentiment that speaks to the search for meaning behind the commonplace that characterizes his poetry. This attention to everyday subject matter is mirrored in Armitage's language, which is strongly influenced by northern British vernacular. Often colloquial in tone, many of his poems are straightforward on the surface, but their apparent simplicity conceals multiple levels of complex, ambiguous meaning. As poet Peter McDonald suggests, Armitage's work encourages readers to realize that "[t]hings are always ... more complicated than they appear, but also than we really want them to be."

Armitage does not constrain himself to a specific mode of writing; his more than 20 published works include two novels, several works of nonfiction, and translations of Homer's *Odyssey* and of the fourteenth-century Middle English poem *Sir Gawain and the Green Knight*. He is also involved in the British television and film scene and has written an opera libretto as well as song lyrics for his rock band The Scaremongers. Armitage is a Fellow of the Royal Society of Literature and vice-president of the Poetry Society in London.

Poem

And if it snowed and snow covered the drive
he took a spade and tossed it to one side.
And always tucked his daughter up at night.
And slippered[1] her the one time that she lied.

And every week he tipped up[2] half his wage.   5
And what he didn't spend each week he saved.
And praised his wife for every meal she made.
And once, for laughing, punched her in the face.

---

1   *slippered* Spanked with a shoe.
2   *tipped up* I.e., handed over.

And for his mum he hired a private nurse.
10 And every Sunday taxied her to church.
And he blubbed when she went from bad to worse.
And twice he lifted ten quid from her purse.

Here's how they rated him when they looked back:
sometimes he did this, sometimes he did that.

—1989

Very Simply Topping Up the Brake Fluid

Yes, love, that's why the warning light comes on. Don't
panic. Fetch some universal brake fluid
and a five-eighths screwdriver from your toolkit
then prop the bonnet open. Go on, it won't

5 eat you. Now, without slicing through the fan-belt
try and slide the sharp end of the screwdriver
under the lid and push the spade connector
through its bed, go on, that's it. Now you're all right

to unscrew, no, clockwise, you see it's Russian
10 love, back to front, that's it. You see, it's empty.
Now, gently with your hand and I mean gently,
try and create a bit of space by pushing

the float-chamber sideways so there's room to pour,
gently does it, that's it. Try not to spill it, it's
15 corrosive: rusts, you know, and fill it till it's
level with the notch on the clutch reservoir.

Lovely. There's some Swarfega[1] in the office
if you want a wash and some soft roll above
the cistern° for, you know. Oh don't mind him, love,   *toilet tank*
20 he doesn't bite. Come here and sit down Prince. Prince!

Now, where's that bloody alternator? Managed?
Oh any time, love. I'll not charge you for that
because it's nothing of a job. If you want
us again we're in the book. Tell your husband.

—1989

---

1   *Swarfega* British-made hand cleaner used to remove grease.

It Could Be You[1]

We interrupt our live coverage of the War
for details of tonight's National Lottery draw:

the winning numbers are fourteen, eighteen,
thirty-nine, forty-four, eighty-two, and ninety-one.[2]

The bonus ball is number two-thousand-and-some.   5
A record jackpot pay-out will be shared between

winning ticket holders in Belfast, Aberdeen,
Milford Haven and East Acton. Now back to the action.

—2002

---

1   *It Could Be You* Slogan of the UK National Lottery.
2   *fourteen … ninety-one* The wars in which Great Britain participated during the twentieth
    century include World War I (1914–18), World War II (1939–45), the Falklands War
    (1982), and the Gulf War (1991).

Ian Iqbal Rashid
b. 1965

Multifaceted artist Ian Iqbal Rashid is a poet, screenwriter, and director. Born Iqbal Rashid in Dar es Salaam, Tanzania, to a South Asian Muslim family, he was five years old when the family was forced to flee Tanzania. They settled in Toronto, where Rashid took up the name "Ian" when his first-grade teacher told him "Iqbal" was too difficult to pronounce.

Rashid's poetry is often concerned with cultural identity, sexual orientation, and the intersections between the two. His first poetry collection, *Black Markets, White Boyfriends and Other Acts of Elision* (1991), was nominated for the Gerald Lampert Memorial Prize. *Song of Sabu* (1994), his next collection, includes poems about the Indian American film actor Sabu (1924–63), who is also the subject of Rashid's first short film, *Surviving Sabu* (1998).

Rashid worked as a writer in British television before becoming a self-taught filmmaker. His first feature-length film, *Touch of Pink* (2004), is a semi-autobiographical comedy about a gay man coming out to his traditional Muslim mother. Both *Touch of Pink* and Rashid's second film, *How She Move* (2007), premiered at the Sundance Film Festival.

Rashid currently lives in the United Kingdom and regularly travels between England and Canada.

Could Have Danced All Night

1.

I once used to dream of being held knowingly by a man
on whom I would not look.

Then this all came again, the embrace held
in the ease of a dance, held within your hands small
5 yet capable and roped with thick vein.
And when I tried, it didn't surprise me
to be able to look into eyes, yours, like mine
the rough colour of night, into your shy, pie face.

Standing together tonight I long for the anise
10 taste of Thai basil on your skin,
your pale denim thighs and ass resplendent
in strobes of evening light.

Tonight I would dance with you across an alien landscape.
We might fly. ("I'm positive.")
But this night finds our legs rooted, knotted,   15
planted painfully like a flag. ("I've tested positive.")

2.

Tonight, I watch you walking away,
wheeling your burden before you into the night.
Fists jab my thighs on either side.
Fists which mean to unclench hold
fingers which mean to interlock   5
with yours, like pieces of a puzzle
join, into a picture of two men dancing.

Tonight movement is limited:
from hand to mouth to mind.
Tobacco, caustic laughter in the lungs,   10
the careful sipping of our herbal teas,
the careful sipping of our everything-will-be-all-rights.

—1991

Christian Bök
b. 1966

Few poets, especially those to whom the term *avant-garde* has been applied, live to see their work appear on international bestseller lists; Toronto-born poet Christian Bök is a rare exception. In *Eunoia* (2001), his Griffin Prize-winning collection of poetry and prose acclaimed as much for its ingenuity and playfulness as for its discipline, Bök set himself the task of composing a series of lipograms, each using only one of the five vowels ("Chapter I" from this series is included below). In addition to this exacting requirement, Bök imposed a number of other conditions upon himself: the use of the letter *y* would be forbidden; each of the collection's five chapters would have to contain "a culinary banquet, a prurient debauch, a pastoral tableau, and a nautical voyage"; and every line or sentence of the poem would have to ac-cent "internal rhyme through the use of syntactical parallelism."

Like the writers affiliated with the French *Oulipo* school (*Ouvroir de littérature potentielle*, or "workshop of potential literature"), Bök seeks in-spiration in constraint. *Eunoia* is more than an elaborate literary stunt: the poetical tension between the strictures of form and the expansiveness of content becomes a crucible and a catalyst as Bök experiments with expression through repression, thereby revealing the plasticity of the language and the "personality" of each vowel.

Although best known for *Eunoia*, Bök is also the author of the collec-tion *Crystallography* (1994), in which he explores the intersection of art and science by positing a relationship between words and crystal formations. In all of his work, Bök experiments with what he calls "lucid writing," a form of composition that "concerns itself with the exploratory examination of its own pattern."

Chapter I

for Dick Higgins

Writing is inhibiting. Sighing, I sit, scribbling in ink
this pidgin[1] script. I sing with nihilistic witticism,
disciplining signs with trifling gimmicks—impish
hijinks which highlight stick sigils. Isn't it glib?
5   Isn't it chic? I fit childish insights within rigid limits,
writing schtick which might instill priggish misgiv-

---

1   *pidgin* Linguistically simplified.

ings in critics blind with hindsight. I dismiss nit-
picking criticism which flirts with philistinism. I
bitch; I kibitz—griping whilst criticizing dimwits,
sniping whilst indicting nitwits, dismissing simplis-   10
tic thinking, in which philippic[1] wit is still illicit.

Pilgrims, digging in shifts, dig till midnight in mining
pits, chipping flint with picks, drilling schist with drills,
striking it rich mining zinc. Irish firms, hiring micks[2]
whilst firing Brits, bring in smiths with mining skills: 15
kilnwrights grilling brick in brickkilns, millwrights
grinding grist in gristmills. Irish tinsmiths, fiddling
with widgits, fix this rig, driving its drills which spin
whirring drillbits. I pitch in, fixing things. I rig this
winch with its wiring; I fit this drill with its piping. I   20
dig this ditch, filling bins with dirt, piling it high, sifting it, till I find bright prisms twinkling with glitz.

Hiking in British districts, I picnic in virgin firths,[3]
grinning in mirth with misfit whims, smiling if I find
birch twigs, smirking if I find mint sprigs. Midspring   25
brings with it singing birds, six kinds (finch, siskin, ibis,
tit, pipit, swift), whistling shrill chirps, trilling *chirr
chirr* in high pitch. Kingbirds flit in gliding flight,
skimming limpid springs, dipping wingtips in rills
which brim with living things: krill, shrimp, brill   30
fish with gilt fins, which swim in flitting zigs. Might
Virgil[4] find bliss implicit in this primitivism? Might
I mimic him in print if I find his writings inspiring?

Fishing till twilight, I sit, drifting in this birch skiff,
jigging kingfish with jigs, brining in fish which nip   35
this bright string (its vivid glint bristling with stick-
pins). Whilst I slit this fish in its gills, knifing it, slicing
it, killing it with skill, shipwrights might trim this jib,
swinging it right, hitching it tight, riding brisk winds

---

1   *philippic* Bitter, reproachful, ranting.
2   *micks* Offensive slang: Irish people.
3   *firths* Inlets.
4   *Virgil* Roman poet (70–19 BCE). His *Eclogues* have primarily rural settings, and in his
     Georgics he describes agricultural processes.

40   which pitch this skiff, tipping it, tilting it, till this ship
in crisis flips. Rigging rips. Christ, this ship is sinking. Diving in, I swim, fighting this frigid swirl, kicking, kicking, swimming in it till I sight high cliffs,
rising, indistinct in thick mists, lit with lightning.

45   Lightning blinks, striking things in its midst with
blinding light. Whirlwinds whirl; driftwinds drift.
Spindrift is spinning in thrilling whirligigs. Which
blind spirit is whining in this whistling din? Is it
this grim lich,[1] which is writhing in its pit, lifting its
50   lid with whitish limbs, rising, vivific, with ill will in
its mind, victimizing kids timid with fright? If it is—
which blind witch is midwifing its misbirth, binding
this hissing djinni[2] with witching spiritism? Is it this
thin, sickish girl, twitching in fits, whilst writing
55   things in spirit-writing? If it isn't—it is I; it is I …

Lightning flicks its riding whip, blitzing this night
with bright schisms. Sick with phthisis[3] in this driz-
zling mist, I limp, sniffling, spitting bilic spit, itching
livid skin (skin which is tingling with stinging pin-
60   pricks). I find this frigid drisk dispiriting; still, I fight
its chilling windchill. I climb cliffs, flinching with
skittish instincts. I might slip. I might twist this infirm wrist, crippling it, wincing whilst I bind it in its
splint, cringing whilst I gird it in its sling; still, I risk
65   climbing, sticking with it, striving till I find this rift,
in which I might fit, hiding in it till winds diminish.

Minds grim with nihilism still find first light inspiring. Mild pink in tint, its shining twilight brings bright
tidings which lift sinking spirits. With firm will, I finish
70   climbing, hiking till I find this inviting inn, in which
I might sit, dining. I thirst. I bid girls bring stiff drinks
—gin fizz which I might sip whilst finishing this rich
dish, nibbling its tidbits: ribs with wings in chili, figs

---

1   *lich* Corpse, especially a reanimated one.
2   *djinni* In Islamic mythology, a spirit with supernatural abilities.
3   *phthisis* Wasting sickness.

with kiwis in icing. I swig citric drinks with vim, tipping kirsch, imbibing it till, giggling, I flirt with girlish virgins in miniskirts: *wink, wink*. I miss living
in sin, pinching thighs, kissing lips pink with lipstick.

Slick pimps, bribing civic kingpins, distill gin in stills,
spiking drinks with illicit pills which might bring bliss.
Whiz kids in silk-knit shirts script films in which
slim girls might strip, jiggling tits, wiggling hips, in-
citing wild shindigs. Twin siblings in bikinis might kiss
rich bigwigs, giving this prim prig his wish, whipping
him, tickling him, licking his limp dick till, rigid,
his prick spills its jism. Shit! This ticklish victim is
trifling with kink. Sick minds, thriving in kinship
with pigs, might find insipid thrills in this filth. This
flick irks critics. It is swinish; it is piggish. It stinks.

Thinking within strict limits is stifling. Whilst Viking
knights fight griffins, I skirmish with this riddling
sphinx (this sigil—I), I print lists, filing things (kin with
kin, ilk with ilk), inscribing this distinct sign, listing
things in which its imprint is intrinsic. I find its missing links, divining its implicit tricks. I find it whilst
skindiving in Fiji; I find it whilst picnicking in Linz. I
find it in Inniskillin; I find it in Mississippi. I find it
whilst skiing in Minsk. (Is this intimism civilizing if
Klimt limns it, if Liszt[1] lilts it?) I sigh; I lisp. I finish writing this writ, signing it, kind sir: NIHIL, DICIT, FINI.[2]

—2001

---

1   *intimism* Genre of painting involving the impressionistic portrayal of domestic
     scenes; *Klimt* Gustav Klimt (1862–1918), Austrian artist; *limns* Portrays (here, by
     painting); *Liszt* Franz Liszt (1811–86), Hungarian composer and pianist.
2   *NIHIL, DICIT, FINI* Latin: NOTHING, HE SAYS, THE END.

Alice Oswald

b. 1966

Named one of the Poetry Book Society's "Next Generation" Poets in 2004, Alice Oswald has captured readers' attention with her bold depictions of the environment. Rejecting the sentimentalizing traditions of nature poetry, she strives to acknowledge nature as powerful, vulnerable, and alien to human beings. In her writing, she says, "I'm continually smashing down the nostalgia in my head. And I am trying to enquire of the landscape itself what it feels about itself.... There's a whole range of words that people use about landscape. Pastoral? Idyll? I can't stand them." If Oswald's overall approach is arresting, so too is her poetic style; the reader is continually surprised by small details of diction, of syntax, of rhythm, and of rhyme.

Born in Reading, Oswald read Classics at Oxford. After graduating she worked as a gardener, an occupation she has credited with providing thinking time in which her early poems could develop. In 1996, Oswald published *The Thing in the Gap-Stone Stile*, which won the Forward Poetry Prize for Best First Collection. The Devon landscape where she lives, depicted as a world of beauty and fear, features prominently both in this and in later work. In order to write the book-length poem *Dart* (for which she received the T.S. Eliot Award in 2002), Oswald researched for three years, spending time near the Dart River and interviewing the people who live and work alongside it.

Oswald's published volumes include *Woods Etc.* (2005), *A Sleepwalk on the Severn* (2009), and *Weeds and Wild Flowers* (2009), a collaboration with artist Jessica Greenman. *Memorial*, Oswald's 2011 work, draws upon her classical education, revisiting the mythological landscape of Homer's *Iliad* from the perspective of ordinary soldiers.

Wedding

From time to time our love is like a sail
and when the sail begins to alternate
from tack to tack, it's like a swallowtail
and when the swallow flies it's like a coat;
5   and if the coat is yours, it has a tear
like a wide mouth and when the mouth begins
to draw the wind, it's like a trumpeter
and when the trumpet blows, it blows like millions ...
and this, my love, when millions come and go
10 beyond the need of us, is like a trick;
and when the trick begins, it's like a toe

tip-toeing on a rope, which is like luck;
and when the luck begins, it's like a wedding,
which is like love, which is like everything.

—1996

Woods etc.

footfall, which is a means so steady
and in small sections wanders through the mind
unnoticed, because it beats constantly,
sweeping together the loose tacks of sound

I remember walking once into increasing   5
woods, my hearing like a widening wound
first your voice and then the rustling ceasing.
the last glow of rain dead in the ground

that my feet kept time with the sun's imaginary
changing position, hoping it would rise   10
suddenly from scattered parts of my body
into the upturned apses of my eyes.

no clearing in that quiet, no change at all.
in my throat the little mercury line
that regulates my speech began to fall   15
rapidly the endless length of my spine

—2005

Dunt[1]

a poem for a nearly dried-up river

Very small and damaged and quite dry,
a Roman water nymph[2] made of bone
tries to summon a river out of limestone.

---

1   *Dunt* Stream in the Gloucestershire County area of England.
2   *nymph* In classical mythology, a beautiful spirit associated with a natural setting.

Very eroded faded,
5 her left arm missing and both legs from the knee down,
a Roman water nymph made of bone
tries to summon a river out of limestone.

Exhausted, utterly worn down,
a Roman water nymph made of bone,
10 being the last known speaker of her language,
she tries to summon a river out of limestone.

Little distant sound of dry grass. Try again.

A Roman water nymph made of bone,
very endangered now,
15 in a largely unintelligible monotone,
she tries to summon a river out of limestone.

Little distant sound as of dry grass. Try again.

Exquisite bone figurine with upturned urn,
in her passionate self-esteem, she smiles, looking sideways.
20 She seemingly has no voice but a throat-clearing rustle
as of dry grass. Try again.

She tries leaning,
pouring pure outwardness from a grey urn.

Little slithering sounds as of a rabbit man in full night gear.
25 Who lies so low in the rickety willow herb
that a fox trots out of the woods
and over his back and away. Try again.
Very small and damaged and quite dry,
a Roman water nymph made of bone,
30 she pleads, she pleads a river out of limestone.

Little hobbling tripping of a nearly dried-up river
not really moving through the fields,
having had the gleam taken out of it
to the point where it resembles twilight.
35 Little grumbling shivering last-ditch attempt at a river
more nettles than water. Try again.

Very speechless, very broken old woman,
her left arm missing and both legs from the knee down,
she tries to summon a river out of limestone.

Little stoved-in, sucked-thin   40
low-burning glint of stones,
rough-sleeping and trembling and clinging to its rights.
Victim of Swindon.[1]
Puddle midden.°   *garbage heap*
Slum of overgreened foot-churn and pats   45
whose crayfish are cheap toolkits
made of the mud stirred up when a stone's lifted.

It's a pitiable likeness of clear running,
struggling to keep up with what's already gone:
the boat the wheel the sluice gate,   50
the two otters larricking° along. Go on.   *gallivanting*

And they say oh they say
in the days of better rainfall
it would flood through five valleys, there'd be cows and milking stools
washed over the garden walls   55
and when it froze you could skate for five miles. Yes go on.

Little loose-end shorthand unrepresented
beautiful disused route to the sea,
fish path with nearly no fish in.

—2006

---

1   *Swindon* Town in Wiltshire, England.

Karen Solie
b. 1966

The subject matter of Karen Solie's poetry spans great distances: from the rural landscapes of Saskatchewan where she was born and raised to the bars and hotels of urban Canada; from the scientific terms of physics and biology to the emotional language of disappointment and desire. Fellow poet Don McKay has described her work as "fierce writing of quickness and edge that can take on just about anything … with candour and a trenchant humour that's the cutting edge of intelligence."

Karen Solie worked for three years as a reporter in Lethbridge, Alberta, before completing a BA from the University of Lethbridge. Her career as a published poet began when her work was included in the anthology *Breathing Fire: Canada's New Poets* (1995), and six years later she released her first collection, *Short Haul Engine*, which won the Dorothy Livesay Poetry Prize. Solie then moved from Alberta to Toronto, where she further established herself as an important voice in Canadian poetry with her next collections, *Modern and Normal* (2005) and *Pigeon* (2009). *Pigeon* won several awards, including the Trillium Award and the Griffin Poetry Prize; the Griffin judges noted Solie's ability to "pull great wisdom from the ordinary" and "to see at once into and through our daily struggle, often thwarted by our very selves, toward something like an honourable life."

Solie has taught poetry at the Banff Centre for the Arts, been writer-in-residence at several Canadian universities, and held the first International Writer's Residency at the University of St. Andrews in Scotland.

Sturgeon

Jackfish and walleye circle like clouds as he strains
the silt floor of his pool, a lost lure in his lip,
Five of Diamonds, River Runt, Lazy Ike,[1]
or a simple spoon, feeding
5   a slow disease of rust through his body's quiet armour.
Kin to caviar, he's an oily mudfish. Inedible.
Indelible. Ancient grunt of sea
in a warm prairie river, prehistory a third eye in his head.
He rests, and time passes as water and sand
10   through the long throat of him, in a hiss, as thoughts
of food. We take our guilts

---

1   *Five of Diamonds ... Lazy Ike* Popular fishing lures. "Spoon" is also a type of lure.

to his valley and dump them in,
give him quicksilver° to corrode his fins, weed killer,   *mercury*
gas oil mix, wrap him in poison arms.
Our bottom feeder,   15
sin-eater.

On an afternoon mean as a hook we hauled him
up to his nightmare of us and laughed
at his ugliness, soft sucker mouth opening,
closing on air that must have felt like ground glass,   20
left him to die with disdain
for what we could not consume.
And when he began to heave and thrash over yards of rock
to the water's edge and, unbelievably, in,
we couldn't hold him though we were teenaged   25
and bigger than everything. Could not contain
the old current he had for a mind, its pull,
and his body a muscle called river, called spawn.

                                                    —2001

Nice

> "I think I'm kind of two-faced. I'm very ingratiating. It really kind
> of annoys me. I'm just sort of a little too nice. Everything is Oooo."
>   —Diane Arbus[1]

Still dark, but just. The alarm
kicks on. A voice like a nice hairdo
squeaks *People, get ready*
for another nice one. Low 20s,
soft breeze, ridge of high pressure   5
settling nicely. Songbirds swallowing, ruffling,
starting in. Does anyone curse
the winter wren, calling in Christ's name
for just one bloody minute of silence?
Of course not. They sound nice.   10
I pull away and he asks why I can't
be nicer to him. Well,
I have to work, I say, and wouldn't it be nice

---

1   *Diane Arbus* (1923-71), American photographer.

15 if someone made some money today?
Very nice, he quavers, rolling
his face to the wall. A nice face.
A nice wall. We agreed on the green
down to hue and shade straight away.
That was a very nice day.

—2003

Self-Portrait in a Series of Professional Evaluations

An excellent vocabulary, but spatial skills
are lacking. Poor in math. A bit uncoordinated,
possibly the inner ear? An eye exam
5 may be required. Not what you'd call a natural
athlete. Doesn't play well with others. Tries hard.

Fine sense of melody but a weak left hand. For God's sake
practice with a metronome. Your Chopin
is all over the place. Test scores indicate aptitude
10 for a career in the secretarial sciences. Handwriting
suggests some latent hostility. A diligent worker,
though often late. Please note:

an AC/DC t-shirt does not constitute professional
attire. You drove *how* long on the spare?
15 A good grasp of theory, though many sentence fragments
and an unusual fondness for semicolons; a tendency
toward unsubstantiated leaps. A black aura.

Needs to stroke essence of tangerine through the aura.
Should consider regular facials. Most people walk around
20 dehydrated all the time and don't even know it.
Normal. Negative. This month, avoid air travel
and dark-haired men. Focus on career goals.
Make a five-year plan.

—2005

Arundhathi Subramaniam
b. 1967

Arundhathi Subramaniam's poetry often addresses philosophical, political, or spiritual questions at the level of the local, the individual, and the everyday—an approach frequently inflected by Subramaniam's complex relationship with her home city of Mumbai. Her first two books of poetry, *On Cleaning Bookshelves* (1991) and *Where I Live* (2005), were published in English in her native India; her third collection, *Where I Live: New & Selected Poems* (2009), was published in the United Kingdom. In response to what she calls "the increasing spirit of cultural nativism ... [that interprets] the use of English as a reactionary throwback to the imperial past," she has defended her choice of language, arguing that "English is Indian—period. It's as Indian as cricket and democracy."

Subramaniam's commitment to the sincere consideration of spiritual matters has found expression not only in her poetry but also in her account of the Buddha's life, *The Book of Buddha* (2005), and her biography of contemporary yogi Jaggi Vasudev, *Sadhguru* (2010). In 2003, she received the Charles Wallace Fellowship at the University of Stirling, and in 2009 was given the Raza Award for Poetry. She has worked for the National Centre for the Performing Arts in Mumbai and was for many years a member of Mumbai's Poetry Circle.

To the Welsh Critic Who Doesn't Find Me Identifiably Indian

You believe you know me,
wide-eyed Eng Lit type
from a sun-scalded colony,
reading my Keats[1]—or is it yours—
while my country detonates   5
on your television screen.

You imagine you've cracked
my deepest fantasy—
oh, to be in an Edwardian[2] vicarage,
living out my dharma[3]   10

---

1   *Keats* John Keats (1795–1821), English poet.
2   *Edwardian* Characteristic of England during King Edward VII's reign (1901–10).
3   *dharma* In various Indian religions, the inherent nature and order of the universe, and a person's actions which uphold that order.

with every sip of dandelion tea
and dreams of the weekend jumble sale ...

You may have a point.
I know nothing about silly mid-offs,[1]
I stammer through my Tamil,[2]
15   and I long for a nirvana
that is hermetic,
odour-free,
bottled in Switzerland,
money-back-guaranteed.

20   This business about language,
how much of it is mine,
how much yours,
how much from the mind,
how much from the gut,
25   how much is too little,
how much too much,
how much from the salon,
how much from the slum,
how I say verisimilitude,
30   how I say Brihadaranyaka,[3]
how I say vaazhapazham[4]—
it's all yours to measure,
the pathology of my breath,
the halitosis of gender,
35   my homogenised plosives[5]
about as rustic
as a mouth-freshened global village.

Arbiter of identity,
remake me as you will.
40   Write me a new alphabet of danger,
a new patois to match

---

1   *mid-offs* Cricket term referring to the left side of the field.
2   *Tamil* Language spoken by the Tamil people in parts of India and Sri Lanka.
3   *Brihadaranyaka* Brihadaranyaka Upanishad, one of the Sanskrit texts that form the philosophical basis of the Hindu religion.
4   *vaazhapazham* Tamil: banana.
5   *plosives* Consonant sounds (such as *b*, *d*, and *p*), created by briefly halting airflow.

the Chola[1] bronze of my skin.
Teach me how to come of age
in a literature you've bark-scratched
into scripture.   45
Smear my consonants
with cow-dung and turmeric and godhuli.[2]
Pity me, sweating,
rancid, on the other side of the counter.
Stamp my papers,   50
lease me a new anxiety,
grant me a visa
to the country of my birth.
Teach me how to belong,
the way you do,   55
on every page of world history.

—2005

---

1   *Chola*   Chola dynasty, a long-ruling Tamil dynasty that rose to power in southern India
     during the Middle Ages.
2   *godhuli*   Urdu or Sanskrit: dusk; in Sanskrit, literally "the dust raised by the feet of cattle."

Rita Wong
b. 1968

Rita Wong describes the subject matter of her poetry as "scary, interrelated phenomena like social and environmental injustice, pollution, and global warming." Her poems often condemn the impact big corporations have on human rights and on the food system, but Wong also emphasizes her readers' collective responsibility to the often geographically distant people who face intolerable working conditions or the consequences of environmental damage. Environmental concerns are, for Wong, inextricable from concerns of race, class, and gender; her poetry is powerfully focused on globalization and the legacy of colonization.

A writer who makes frequent use of puns and other language play and often omits punctuation, Wong is experimental in her approach to poetry—an attitude that extends from the layout of words on the page to the writing process itself. Many of her poems include, as marginalia, Chinese characters or hand-written political or cultural statements, sometimes quotations from other thinkers that inform her work. Her long poem *sybil unrest* (2009), a collaboration with fellow Vancouver writer Larissa Lai, was composed over email.

Wong was raised in Calgary and received a PhD from Simon Fraser University, where she studied Asian North American literature. Her first book of poetry, *monkeypuzzle*, was published in 1998; her next, *forage* (2007), received the Dorothy Livesay Poetry Prize and was the winner of Canada Reads Poetry 2011. Wong is an associate professor at the Emily Carr University of Art and Design, where she teaches Critical and Cultural Studies.

opium[1]

chemical history narcopolemics
attempted genocide call it crack war
alcohol white powder suffocates
shades of deep brown earth red desert
yellow skin dependency myths who   5
needs the high of trying to kill the other?
racist gaze tingles on my skin induced
economic muscle flexes to displace
millions rifles fire behind the dollar
signs & still the underground pulses   10
suffering blue veins seek the
transformative heart as ordnance° drops   *artillery*
on embassies and arteries cry for kin

—2007

"Queen Victoria waged war twice.... in order to ensure the free commerce of opium."
—Avital Ronell

---

1   The handwritten quotation is from American philosopher and critical theorist Avital
     Ronell's *Crack Wars: Literature, Addiction, Mania* (1992). Britain conducted two
     "Opium Wars" (1839–42 and 1856–60) to force the Chinese government to legalize the
     importation of opium; trading opium for tea and other Chinese luxuries was important
     to the British economy.

nervous organism[1]

[Handwritten marginalia surrounding the poem, a quotation from Northrop Frye:]

"Some philosophers who assume that all meaning is descriptive meaning tell us that, as a poem does not describe things rationally, it must be a description of emotion. According to this, the literal core of poetry should be a cri de coeur, to use the elegant expression, the direct statement of a nervous organism confronting what something that seems to demand an emotional response, like a dog howling at the moon." —Northrop Frye

jellyfish potato/ jellypo fishtato/ glow in the pork toys/
nab your crisco while it's genetically cloudy boys/
science lab in my esophagus/ what big beakers you have
sir/ all the better to mutate you with my po monster/
po little jelly-kneed demonstrator/ throws flounder-crossed
tomatoes/ hafta nasty nafta[2] through mexico,
california, oregon, washington, canada/ hothoused
experiment nestled beside basketballs of lettuce,
avocado bullets/ industrial food defeats nutrition/
immune systems attrition/ soil vampires call/ shiny
aisles all touch and no contact/ jellypish for tato smack/
your science experiment snack yields slugfish arteries
brain murmurs tumour precipitation whack

—2007

---

1 The handwritten quotation is from Canadian literary critic Northrop Frye's *Anatomy of
Criticism* (1957); *cri de coeur* French: cry of the heart.
2 *nafta* North American Free Trade Agreement, a free trade pact between the United
States, Canada, and Mexico that took effect in 1994.

Rachel Zolf
b. 1968

Rachel Zolf has no qualms about defying traditional conventions in her work. Despite the "resistance to experimental writing" she sees in the literary community, she has embraced experimental poetry for its ability to challenge readers and encourage them to see things differently. "[I]n all my books," she has said, "I try to enact situations where the reader feels uncomfortable, dislocated in their own skin, and is forced to think about why they feel that way."

Zolf often makes use of found text in her work. Her collection *Neighbour Procedure* (2010), for example, addresses the Israeli-Palestinian conflict through a collage of text that originally appeared in a broad range of sources, from news reports to twentieth-century critical theory. Her Trillium Award-winning collection *Human Resources* (2007) similarly draws on eclectic material, especially language she encountered while working as a corporate copywriter. Zolf also holds what she describes as "the first collaborative MFA in creative writing," which she earned by composing original poems out of material sent to her by more than eighty other poets.

In addition to publishing several books of poetry, Zolf has worked in film and television and as poetry editor for *The Walrus*. She is an assistant professor at the University of Calgary, where her research and teaching focus on "the intersection of creative writing and contemporary theoretical practices."

from *Human Resources*[1]

[The job is to write in 'plain language.' No adjectives, adornment or surfeit]

The job is to write in 'plain language.' No adjectives, adornment or surfeit of meaning nuclear increasing[(w1269)]. All excess excised save the discrete pithy moment. Sonnet's rising eight lines, sublime orgasmic turn, dying six: perfect expenditure. Brisk stride along the green green grounds, sudden dip, ha-ha!

[New performance weightings a bit of a moving target the future liability of make this sing]

New performance weightings a bit of a moving target the future liability of make this sing.

Just to make sure we're speaking the same language we no longer have to use this caveat existing amounts grandfathered.

5 We'll have to wrap our heads around clear as mud I would like to move the goal posts.

Chunk it down into various links I'm totally medicated as I type.

---

1   *Human Resources* In a note at the end of *Human Resources* Zolf writes that, with the exception of a few poems not included in this anthology,

> All [...] poems were made by the author's proprietary machine-mind™, with some assistance from WordCount™ and QueryCount™ at www.wordcount.org. The former is a searchable list of the 86,800 most frequently used words in English, while the latter is a searchable list of words most frequently queried in WordCount. [...]
> WordCount values are represented in the text by the letter w [and] Query-Count by Q[...]. As QueryCount rankings shuffle every few hours to reflect recent word queries, Q values in this text will not match present QueryCount rankings. [...] Orthography and punctuation are also used as found.

[Given enough input elements, a writing machine can spew about anything]

Given enough input elements, a writing machine can spew about anything: private jets, exquisite gardens, offshore-banking havens, the Great Ephemeral Skin, how much we love our passionate[Q8992] francesca snazzy prat employees, how you breathe life into our Mission, Vision, Values, what we give you if you lose one finger[Q691] fool dance then gold on one hand and three toes on   5
one foot (25% of the premiums you've paid for years), or three fingers on one hand and four toes (50%) or two hands and two feet (75%!). Unlike poetry, it flows with ease and on the same page as BMO banker Barrett: 'a student who can divine[Q2855] pablo from swiss prostate patterns of imagery in Chaucer's *Canterbury Tales* can surely be taught the principles of double-entry accounting   10

[I don't want to trip over this in the future from where I'm sitting can you suggest massages]

I don't want to trip over this in the future from where I'm sitting can you suggest massages.

This will give you a sense of the 'new look' it seems the tail's wagging the tail this block of content has been rationalized.

We took this offline to firm up the 'one-stop shopping spot' for HR content   5
requires minor refreshing.

My head's spinning in reverse 360s just to close the loop with you.

—2007

Stephanie Bolster
b. 1969

Stephanie Bolster's body of work includes both miscellaneous collections and long poems or poem series united by a single theme; *A Page from the Wonders of Life on Earth* (2011), for example, takes zoos as its subject. Visual art, from seventeenth-century Dutch painting to contemporary photography, is a source of inspiration in works such as *Two Bowls of Milk* (1999) and "Long Exposure." Shortlisted for the 2012 CBC Poetry Prize, "Long Exposure" is part of a longer project based on the "post-disaster photographs" of Robert Polidori (b. 1951).

Bolster's first book, *White Stone: The Alice Poems* (1998) is focused on the protagonist of Lewis Carroll's children's classics *Alice's Adventures in Wonderland* (1865) and *Through the Looking-Glass* (1872), as well as on Alice Liddell, the real child after whom the character is named. In *White Stone*, Bolster explores the lives of both Alices, going so far as to create hypothetical relationships between Alice and the likes of Christopher Robin and Elvis Presley, as well as placing her in North America and in Bolster's own life. Bolster has discussed her approach in *The New Quarterly*: "by placing Alice within my own place and time, I was able to see that here and now were every bit as rich, nonsensical and distressing as both Wonderland and Victorian England." *White Stone* received several awards, including the Governor General's Award for Poetry.

Stephanie Bolster grew up in Burnaby, British Columbia, and earned an MFA from the University of British Columbia. She lives in Montreal, where she is associate professor at Concordia University.

from *White Stone*

Portrait of Alice, Annotated

Who was it strung these footnotes
from her toes and scribbled
italics on her wrists, indicating perhaps
that only slim-wristed girls
5   were allowed to enter Wonderland?

They wound her with measuring tape,
noted the resulting data on her skin, figures
for chest and waist identical. To her mouth

was taped a parchment proclamation
detailing origins of those words she spoke 10

as if they were as intimately hers
as earlobes. But the evidence proved
those words had a long history of their own,
belonged to themselves and would
outlive her. Whatever she had said 15

to end up in this predicament
was not her fault, she was exempt, thus safe.
What could be done to her now? Even her breasts
were claimed before they'd risen; some said
he'd placed his nitrate-ridden hands there.[1] 20

The critics overwrote each other
till all their words were tattooed black
upon her. Have mercy, she cried as they came
with the thousand-volumed weight of archives,
but those words were not hers either. 25

Portrait of Alice with Christopher Robin[2]

In the midst of a winter wood
she walks like old age,
bent under falling snow and the ghost
of her written self, heavy
as bundled kindling on her back. 5

At a tree's base he huddles his narrow shoulders
as if lost—his head, familiar from books
hung forward in dangerous
chilled sleep, calves downy-haired
and goose-bumped past short pants. 10

---

1   *some said ... hands there* Some biographers have suggested that Lewis Carroll might have
     been a paedophile; *nitrate* Cellulose nitrate, chemical compound used in photography.
     Lewis Carroll was a photographer and often took portraits of children, including Alice.
2   *Christopher Robin* Boy in A.A. Milne's children's stories *Winnie-the-Pooh* (1926) and *The
     House at Pooh Corner* (1928); the character is named after Milne's son.

Lewis Carroll, Alice Liddell as "The Beggar Maid," 1858. Lewis Carroll is most famous as the author of Alice's Adventures in Wonderland *(1865) and its sequel, but he was also an accomplished portrait photographer known for his images of children. Like many photographers of the time, he often portrayed his subjects in dramatic roles. Alice Liddell, the daughter of Carroll's friend Henry Liddell, posed for some of Carroll's most remarkable photographs, and the character of Alice is named after her.*

An italic fall of snowflakes
various as dreams across his face.

She watches his trembling lips
mumble of yellowed bears and bluster[1] and rain,
of being irrevocably stuck,   15
then presses her hand to his cheek.
His lashes flutter, he shows her
his eyes made of glaciers and pronounces her name.

To the magic flame he makes
with two rubbed sticks   20
she gives her pinafore[2] and white socks,
the ribbon from her fallen hair.
He fumbles with his buttons, burns
his trousers and dirty shirt.

They point to figures in the smoke—   25
lumpen bear, white rabbit, honey pot,
tea cup. Naked together, they watch with ash-stung
eyes and neither blink nor shiver.

—1998

---

1   *bluster* Word used in A.A. Milne's *The House at Pooh Corner*.
2   *pinafore* Apron worn over a dress; a white pinafore is part of Alice's iconic costume.

R. W. Gray
b. 1969

"I write for the uncertainty. I write for the mythology of it," says poet, serial novelist, short story author, and screenwriter Robert W. Gray; "uncertainty doesn't cloud the truth so much as unleash it." Praised by author Douglas Glover as "an amazing young writer with a startling range and emotional penetration," Gray has published poetry in journals such as *Arc* and in anthologies such as *Seminal: The Anthology of Canada's Gay Male Poets* (2007).

Gray works in a variety of media. Almost a dozen of Gray's short screenplays have been filmed, including *alice & huck* (2008), which won awards at festivals in New Orleans, Honolulu, and Beverly Hills. In 2010 he published his first book, *Crisp*, a collection of short fiction. It was well received by critics; Mark Jarman of *The Fiddlehead* has described Gray's stories as "exuberant, cinematic tales … a startling mix of wild currents and landlocked inner lives that are playful and scary."

Gray was born and raised in the northwest coastal region of British Columbia, and he attended the University of Alberta, where he earned a PhD in Poetry and Psychoanalysis in 2003. He has served as the head of the Screenwriting Programme at the Vancouver Film School and teaches film and screenwriting at the University of New Brunswick.

How this begins

Thrums he does, thrums like waves breaking, waves falling over each other on their way to his feet, but who can blame them.

Up along the streets the maples look awkward in their new dresses, billowing in the traffic gusts. Something, everything, has to begin.

5   Later we will recall this moment, though I will not speak of his clavicles and he will not mention my bottom lip. He tries to find some way to offer me a strawberry from the musky handful he picked on his way to work and I try to find some other word for clavicle but am distracted by his full-throated approach to wearing a T-shirt.

10 There are strawberry seeds under his fingernails. Tonight, falling asleep, a hand near his face on the pillow, he will smell strawberries and the crushed green runners. The strawberries he shucked for his and another's mouth. He will remember my bottom lip.

We will not agree. He will think it was a hot day, summer finally giving in. I will remember mostly the breeze through the open door, how spring just kept hanging around.   15

This will be the moment he liked me the least, but I liked him the most. He thought I was a sideways glance. I thought he was a swallow of water.

He will kiss me, outside at a table, leaning down to me as I look up, suspicious of a man who kisses me so soon and kisses me in a café.   20

He will wonder what comes next. I will wonder what just happened.

This is how it begins. He will not know I am on my way to analysis. That I was going to admit that I am tired of longing for longing. Tired of making up stories about picked strawberries.

—2006

Sharon Harris
b. 1972

Sharon Harris is a Canadian artist whose work combines a range of forms and mediums, including poetry, prose, photography, sculpture, and painting. Influenced by the poet bpNichol, much of her work has a significant visual dimension and depends for its effect on the interplay of word and image. In her concrete poems, the typographical characteristics and arrangement of the words on the page become part of the overall sense-making apparatus.

Harris's first full-length poetry collection, *AVATAR* (2006), is a blended, hybrid work that mingles figures and letters to create meaning. In it, she experiments with an array of devices and ideas, from pataphysics—the fictional science of imaginary phenomena—to the limits of art and language. This latter idea is a problem to which she returns repeatedly, both throughout the collection and in her work more generally: how does one write about things and places beyond words? *AVATAR* is preoccupied with the nature and uses of the phrase "I love you," which is at once ubiquitous and elusive, full of power and void of meaning.

At once playful and thoughtful, Harris's work invites the reader/viewer to look again at familiar words and phrases and see the concepts they gesture toward in an altogether different light.

99. Where Do Poems Come From?

Moisten your finger and hold it
straight up in the air. You will notice
at once that one side of the finger is
cold. This is the direction from
5 which the poem is coming.

—2005

FIGURE L

70. Why Do Poems Make Me Cry?

Reading a poem releases noxious
gases into your environment. The
brain reacts by telling your tear
ducts to produce water, to dilute the
irritating acid so the eyes are pro-   5
tected. Your other reaction is proba-
bly to rub your eyes, but this will
make the irritation a lot worse if you
have poem juices all over your
hands.   10

There are all kinds of remedies for
dealing with this irritating phenomenon, some more effective than
others. As a general rule, move your
head as far away from the poem   15
as you can, so the gas will mostly dis-
perse before it reaches your eyes. The
simplest   solution might be to not

—2005

Poetry in Translation

The translation of poetry is a process about which numerous writers have commented. Many have begun with the question of whether it is even possible to translate poems. Henry Wadsworth Longfellow—canonical American poet, and also one of the many translators of Dante's *Divine Comedy*—asserted that the translator should strive "to report what the author says, not to explain what he means," and advocated paying limited attention to matters of aesthetics or poetic form. At the other end of the spectrum, poet Octavio Paz suggested that, while a "literal translation is not impossible," such work is merely "a mechanism, a string of words that help us read the text in its original language. It is a glossary rather than a translation, which is always a literary activity." The problems for the translator are, in the first place, a matter of sense, as a word's meaning in one language can only be approximated in another: as poet and translator Erin Mouré puts it, "each word in a language is affected, touched, perturbed, split by the culture in which it is used." Furthermore, most of the elements considered crucial to poetry—elements such as rhythm, rhyme, and the nuances of figurative language—may vanish once the sense of the original has been rendered. It is no surprise, therefore, that translated poems are often considered to be original creative works in and of themselves.

For students of literature, the analysis of a translated work thus invites a kind of double approach. In the first place, the translation can be examined with the same attention to the way form interacts with meaning as would serve a literary text read in the original language. In the second place, especially when the original text is accessible (or when more than one translation is provided), the student can explore how approximations have been made, and how the process of translation may reveal something about the way writers from both language backgrounds make use of words to mean more than something literal. For example, when reading two different translations of Lorca's "Romance de la Luna, Luna," one might inquire into the effect of translating the Spanish phrase "El niño la mira, mira" as either "The young boy watches her, watches" (trans. Gunn) or "The boy-child looks and looks at her" (trans. Cobb). What is the difference between a "young boy" and a "boy-child," or between "watching"—a word that may connote an extended period of observation—and simply "looking," which might be thought of as a more innocuous activity (especially as it is associated with a "child")? Even without being able to understand the original, one might ask: do the lulling sounds contained in the phrase "la mira, mira" evoke the same response as the sounds in either of the translations ("watches her, watches" or "looks and looks at her")? How much does the reader of the translated poem have to know about moon symbolism in the Spanish tradition in order to develop a critical argument about this "romance" that—at the level of interpretation—tells the tale of a child's death? If Lorca's moon symbolism is "lost in translation"—i.e., if English-speaking readers think of the moon as signifying changeability, madness, or the feminine principle, according to their own cultural context—how does this alter the way the texts created by Gunn or Cobb can be read? Though it may be the case that no translation of a poem is ever a copy of the original, poems in translation provide almost unending opportunities to examine the complexity of the way form, diction, and cultural context produce sense.

Sappho

c. 630-612 BCE–c. 570 BCE

Very little can be said with certainty about Sappho's biography. Even the birth and death dates given above are still debated, and much of what is surmised about her life is based on references made in her poetry. Much of her work itself has also been lost in the course of history; only one of Sappho's poems survives in its entirety, while the rest of her extant work is made up of fragments found in damaged sources or quoted in the work of other ancient writers.

Probably the wife of an aristocrat and mother of a daughter named Cleis, Sappho was thought to have spent much of her time teaching and studying the arts within a circle of women friends and students on the Greek island of Lesbos. Her writing frequently expresses passionate feeling toward other women; this is often interpreted as sexual love, and the word "lesbian" itself derives from its connection to Sappho as a resident of Lesbos. Speculation regarding Sappho's sexual orientation has affected her reputation and reception since ancient times.

Sappho is remembered for intimately emotional poems on subjects such as love, friendship, marriage, and spirituality—a marked difference from the political and heroic content of most of her contemporaries' writing. Her work, written to be sung to the accompaniment of a stringed instrument called a lyre, came to be greatly admired and contributed to the early development of the lyric form (so named for the instrument with which it is associated). Plato (c. 427–c. 347 BCE) called her "the tenth Muse," adding her to the ranks of the nine gods of the arts in Greek mythology.

Sappho's popularity has fluctuated over the centuries, but her work has influenced poets from her own time to the present day, and it continues to be appreciated by and translated for contemporary readers. The following translations were composed by Canadian classicist and poet Anne Carson (b. 1950) and appeared in her book *If Not, Winter: Fragments of Sappho* (2002). Carson has used square brackets to indicate some—but not all—places where the source text has been damaged and words are absent or illegible. As you will see when you turn to her translations, Carson provides extensive notes that offer both factual information and more impressionistic responses to words, stressing the extent to which translations involve attempts to capture both denotative and connotative dimensions of the original poem.

2

]
..ανοθεν κατιου[ϲ]-
δευρυμμεκρητεϲιπ[.]ρ[　　]ι̣.ναῦον
ἄγνον ὄππ[αι·　]ι χάριεν μὲν ἄλϲος
μαλί[αν],ι βῶμοι δ' ἔ‹ν›ι θυμιάμε—
5　　　νοι [λι]ιβανώτω‹ι›·

ἐν δ' ὔδωρ ψῦχροιν‹ι› κελάδει δι' ὔϲδων
μαλίνων,ι βρόδοιϲι δὲ παῖϲ ὀ χῶροϲ
ἐϲκίαϲτ', αἰθυϲϲομένων δὲ φύλλωνι
　　　κῶμα καταιριον·

10　ἐν δὲ λείμωνι ἰππόβοτοϲ τέθαλε
τωτ...(.)ρινινοιϲ ἄνθεϲιν, αἰ ‹δ'› ἄηται
μέλλιιχα πν[έο]ιϲιν [
　　[　　　　　]

ἔνθα δὴ ϲὺ ϲυ.αν‹ ἔλοιϲα Κύπρι
χρυϲίαιϲιν ἐν κυλίκεϲϲιν ἄβρωϲ
15　‹ὀ›μ‹με›μεί‹χμενον θαλίαιϲι‹ νέκταρ
　　　οἰνοχόειϲα

—Late 7th or early 6th century

2

]
here[1] to me from Krete to this holy temple
where is your graceful grove
of apple trees and altars smoking
    with frankincense.

And in it cold water makes a clear sound through   5
apple branches and with roses the whole place
is shadowed and down from radiant-shaking leaves
    sleep[2] comes dropping.

And in it a horse meadow has come into bloom
with spring flowers and breezes   10
like honey are blowing
    [   ]

In this place you Kypris[3] taking up
in gold cups[4] delicately
nectar mingled with festivities: 15
    pour.

---

1   [Carson's note] "here": adverb of place that means "hither, to this place" with verbs of
    motion or "here, in this place" with verbs of rest, often used as an interjection "Come on!
    Here now!" when followed by an imperative verb. Notice that the imperative verb evoked
    by this adverb, for which the whole poem with its slow weight of onomatopoeically
    accumulating clauses seems to be waiting, does not arrive until the very last word: "pour"
    (16). Arrival is the issue, for it sanctifies waiting: *attente de Dieu* [French: waiting for God].
    The poem is a hymn of the type called "kletic," that is, a calling hymn, an invocation to
    god to come from where she is to where we are. Such a hymn typically names both
    of these places, setting its invocation in between so as to measure the difference—a
    difference exploded as soon as the hymn achieves its aim. Inherent in the rationale of
    a kletic hymn, then, is an emptiness or distance that it is the function of the hymn to
    mark by an act of attention. Sappho suspends attention between adverb at the beginning
    and verb at the end: the effect is uncanny—as if creation could be seen waiting for an
    event that is already perpetually *here*. There is no clear boundary between far and near;
    there is no climactic moment of god's arrival. Sappho renders a set of conditions that
    at the beginning depend on Aphrodite's absence but by the end include her presence—
    impossible drop that saturates the world. "God can only be present in creation under the
    form of absence," says Simone Weil, in *Gravity and Grace*, translated by Arthur Willis
    (Lincoln, Nebraska, 1997), 162.
2   [Carson's note] "sleep": *kōma* is a noun used in the Hippokratic texts [Ancient Greek
    medical texts] of the lethargic state called "coma" yet not originally a medical term. This

Papyrus with a fragment of a poem by Sappho, third century BCE. *A copy of a Sappho poem was written on this papyrus a few centuries after her death. It was discovered in the early 2000s; the papyrus had been used in the wrappings surrounding an ancient Egyptian mummy.*

---

is the profound, weird, sexual sleep that enwraps Zeus after love with Hera (Homer *Iliad* 14.359); this is the punishing, unbreathing stupor imposed for a year on any god who breaks an oath (Hesiod *Theogony* 798); this is the trance of attention induced by listening to music of the lyre (Pindar *Pythians* 1.12); this is the deep religious stillness described by Gregory of Nazianzus in a Christian poem from the fourth century A.D. that appears to be modelled on Sappho's, for Gregory imagines himself awaiting his god in a garden:

> Breezes whispered ...
> lavishing beautiful sleep [*kōma*] from the tops of the trees
> on my heart so very weary.
> —*Patrologia graeca* 37, ed. J.P. Migne (Paris, 1862), 755ff.

Otherworldliness is intensified in Sappho's poem by the synaesthetic quality of her *kōma*—dropping from leaves set in motion by a shiver of light over the tree: Sappho's adjective *aithussomenon* ("radiant-shaking," 7) blends visual and tactile perceptions with a sound of rushing emptiness.

3   *Kypris* Epithet of Aphrodite. It refers to the island of Cyprus, where a cult dedicated to her was located and where she was said to have emerged from the sea at her birth.

4   [Carson's note] "gold cups": not mortal tableware, nor is nectar a beverage normally enjoyed by any but gods (along with ambrosia, e.g., *Odyssey* 5.92–4).

55

κατθάνοιϲα δὲ κείϲηι οὐδέ ποτα μναμοϲύνα ϲέθεν
ἔϲϲετ' οὐδὲ ποκ' ὔϲτερον· οὐ γὰρ πεδέχηις βρόδων
τῶν ἐκ Πιερίας, ἀλλ' ἀφάνης κἀν Ἀίδα δόμωι
φοιτάϲηις πεδ' ἀμαύρων νεκύων ἐκπεποταμένα.

—Late 7th or early 6th century

55

Dead you will lie and never memory of you
will there be nor desire into the aftertime—for you do not share in the roses
of Pieria,[1] but invisible too in Hades'[2] house
you will go your way among dim shapes. Having been breathed out.[3]

---

1   *Pieria* Area in northern Greece and mythical birthplace of the Muses, nine Greek
    goddesses of knowledge and the arts.
2   *Hades* God of the underworld.
3   [Carson's note] "Dead.... Having been breathed out": a participle in the aorist tense (*kat-thanoisa*) begins the poem and a participle in the perfect tense (*ekpepotamena*) ends it.
    The aorist tense expresses past action as a point of fact; the perfect tense renders past
    action whose effect continues into the future; so does Sappho's poem softly exhale some
    woman from the point of death into an infinitely featureless eternity. Cognate with words
    for wings, flying, fluttering and breath, the participle *ekpepotamena*, with its splatter of
    plosives and final open vowel, sounds like the escape of a soul into nothingness.

Francesco Petrarch

1304–1374

Francesco Petrarch was born in Arezzo, Italy. He is best remembered for his *Rime sparse* (*Scattered Rhymes*, c. 1327–74), a series of 366 sonnets and other poems written about a woman named Laura, with whom Petrarch claimed to have fallen in love upon seeing her in a church in Avignon, France. He continued to add to (and rework) the collection throughout his life, though Laura herself died in 1348. The poems are not addressed to Laura; indeed, they are concerned more with Petrarch's emotional and spiritual development than they are with the object of his unrequited love. In their self-scrutiny, in the longing they express for an idealized and unattainable beauty, and in the ways in which they give poetic expression to these feelings through elaborate metaphors, paradox, and smoothly rhyming Italian verse, Petrarch's sonnets became a model for poets throughout the Renaissance.

Though known today primarily for his love poetry, Petrarch was a classical scholar, an ambassador and frequent traveller, and a cleric in the Roman Catholic Church. He was also famous in his own time for a range of scholarly writing and for his unfinished epic poem *Africa*. Although the *Rime sparse* were written in Italian, his other works were composed in Latin.

294

Soleasi nel mio cor star bella et viva,
com' alta donna in loco humile et basso:
or son fatto io per l'ultimo suo passo,
non pur mortal, ma morto, et ella è diva.

L'alma d'ogni suo ben spogliata et priva,   5
Amor de la sua luce ignudo et casso,
devrian de la pietà romper un sasso;
ma non è chi lor duol riconti o scriva:

ché piangon dentro, ov' ogni orecchia è sorda
se non la mia, cui tanta doglia ingombra   10
ch' altro che sospirar nulla m'avanza.

Veramente siam noi polvere et ombra,
veramente la voglia cieca e 'ngorda,
veramente fallace è la speranza.

—c. 1327–74

294[1]

In my heart she used to stand lovely and live,
Like a great lady in a place low and humble:
Now I am shown, by her final passing,
To be not only mortal, but dead, while she is divine.

My soul stripped of all its blessedness, deprived,   5
And love, stripped of her light, erased,
Are strong enough to break stone into pity
But none can tell or write of that pain:

They grieve within, and all ears are deaf
Except my own, blocked by grief,   10
And nothing is left me but sighs.

This is truth: we are nothing but ashes and shadow.
This is truth: the will grasps blindly.
This is truth: false are our hopes.

---

1   *294* Translation by D. LePan and M. Okun for this anthology (© Broadview Press).

Arthur Rimbaud

1854–1891

"One must be absolutely modern," wrote the French poet Arthur Rimbaud, whose career as an author of rebellious, complex, and sensually loaded verse and prose poetry was as brief as it was influential. His intense, non-traditional approach placed him among the French Symbolists, a group of poets and artists who strove not to depict objective reality but to express emotions, interior thoughts, and abstract ideas through metaphor. Rimbaud's often hallucinatory style would influence the surrealist movement of the 1920s, as well as a number of other twentieth-century artistic movements.

Rimbaud accomplished his entire poetic output in less than five years. Raised by his mother in Charleville, France, he was a high-achieving student until 1870, the year he published his first poems. The following year he sent some of his work to the Symbolist poet Paul Verlaine, who responded with an invitation to visit his home in Paris. The two poets soon became lovers, and they travelled together, leading a wild existence characterized by drinking, drug use, and violent arguments—their relationship ended when Verlaine shot Rimbaud in the wrist and was sentenced to two years in prison. Soon afterward, Rimbaud finished the only book he would publish himself, a short work of prose poetry entitled *Une saison en enfer* (*A Season in Hell*, 1873).

Around the age of 20, Rimbaud stopped writing poetry. He continued to travel extensively and eventually worked in Africa as a colonial tradesman. After this point, he showed little interest in the fate of his work, but in 1886 Verlaine edited and arranged for the publication of *Les Illuminations*, a collection of Rimbaud's prose poems.

The following poems have been translated by English poet, drama teacher, and translator Oliver Bernard (b. 1925).

À la Musique

Place de la Gare, à Charleville

Sur la place taillée en mesquines pelouses,
Square où tout est correct, les arbres et les fleurs,
Tous les bourgeois poussifs qu'étranglent les chaleurs
Portent, les jeudis soirs, leurs bêtises jalouses

—L'orchestre militaire, au milieu du jardin,   5
Balance ses schakos dans la *Valse des fifres*:
—Autour, aux premiers rangs, parade le gandin;
Le notaire pend à ses breloques à chiffres.

Des rentiers à lorgnons soulignent tous les couacs:
Les gros bureaux bouffis traînent leurs grosses dames   10
Auprès desquelles vont, officieux cornacs,
Celles dont les volants ont des airs de réclames;

Scene Set to Music

Place de la Gare, Charleville

On the square which is chopped into mean little plots of grass, the square
where all is just so, both the trees and the flowers, all the wheezy townsfolk
whom the heat chokes bring, each Thursday evening, their envious silliness.

The military band, in the middle of the gardens, swing their shakos[1] in
the *Waltz of the Fifes*: round about, near the front rows, the town dandy struts;   5
the notary hangs like a charm from his own watch chain.

Private incomes in pince-nez point out all false notes: great counting-
house desks, bloated, drag their stout spouses—close by whom, like bustling
elephant keepers, walk females whose flounces remind you of sales.

---

1   *shakos* Tall cylindrical military hats.

Sur les bancs verts, des clubs d'épiciers retraités
Qui tisonnent le sable avec leur canne à pomme,
15 Fort sérieusement discutent les traités,
Puis prisent en argent, et reprennent: « En somme!... »

Épatant sur son banc les rondeurs de ses reins,
Un bourgeois à boutons clairs, bedaine flamande,
Savoure son onnaing d'où le tabac par brins
20 Déborde—vous savez, c'est de la contrebande;—

Le long des gazons verts ricanent les voyous;
Et, rendus amoureux par le chant des trombones,
Très naïfs, et fumant des roses, les pioupious
Caressent les bébés pour enjôler les bonnes…

10   On the green benches, retired grocers' clubs, poking the sand with their
knobbed walking canes, gravely discuss trade agreements and then take snuff
from silver boxes, and resume: "In short!..."

Spreading over his bench all the fat of his rump, a pale-buttoned burgher,
a Flemish corporation, savours his Onnaing,[1] whence shreds of tobacco hang
15 loose—you realize, it's smuggled, of course ...

Along the grass borders yobs[2] laugh in derision; and, melting to love at
the sound of trombones, very simple, and sucking at roses, the little squaddies[3]
fondle the babies to get round their nurses ...

1   *Onnaing* Clay pipe made in Onnaing, a municipality in Northern France renowned for
    its pipe manufacturing.
2   *yobs* Disruptive youths.
3   *squaddies* Soldiers.

—Moi, je suis, débraillé comme un étudiant,   25
Sous les marronniers verts les alertes fillettes:
Elles le savent bien; et tournent en riant,
Vers moi, leurs yeux tout pleins de choses indiscrètes.

Je ne dis pas un mot: je regarde toujours
La chair de leurs cous blancs brodés de mèches folles: 30
Je suis, sous le corsage et les frêles atours,
Le dos divin après la courbe des épaules.

J'ai bientôt déniché la bottine, le bas ...
—Je reconstruis les corps, brûlé de belles fièvres.
Elles me trouvent drôle et se parlent tout bas ...   35
—Et mes désirs brutaux s'accrochent à leurs lèvres.

                                    —1889 (written 1870)

As for me, I follow, dishevelled like a student under the green chestnuts, the lively young girls—which they know very well, and they turn to me,   20 laughing, eyes which are full of indiscreet things.

I don't say a word: I just keep on looking at the skin of their white necks embroidered with stray locks: 1 go hunting, beneath bodices and thin attire, the divine back below the curve of the shoulders.

Soon I've discovered the boot and the stocking ...—I re-create their bodies,   25 burning with fine fevers. They find me absurd, and talk together in low voices ...—And my savage desires fasten on to their lips ...

Voyelles

A noir, E blanc, I rouge, U vert, O bleu: voyelles,
Je dirai quelque jour vos naissances latentes:
A, noir corset velu des mouches éclatantes
Qui bombinent autour des puanteurs cruelles,

5 Golfes d'ombre; E, candeurs des vapeurs et des tentes,
Lances des glaciers fiers, rois blancs, frissons d'ombelles;
I, pourpres, sang craché, rire des lèvres belles
Dans la colère ou les ivresses pénitentes;

U, cycles, vibrements divins des mers virides,
10 Paix des pâtis semés d'animaux, paix des rides
Que l'alchimie imprime aux grands fronts studieux;

Ô, suprême Clairon plein des strideurs étranges,
Silence traversés des Mondes et des Anges:
—Ô l'Oméga, rayon violet de Ses Yeux!—

—1883 (written c. 1871)

Vowels

A black, E white, I red, U green, O blue: vowels, I shall tell, one day, of your
mysterious origins: A, black velvety jacket of brilliant flies which buzz around
cruel smells,

5 gulfs of shadow; E, whiteness of vapours and of tents, lances of proud
glaciers, white kings, shivers of cow-parsley; I, purples, spat blood, smile of
beautiful lips in anger or in the raptures of penitence;

U, waves, divine shudderings of viridian[1] seas, the peace of pastures dotted
with animals, the calm of the furrows which alchemy prints on broad studious
foreheads;

10 O, sublime Trumpet full of strange piercing sounds, silences crossed by
Angels and by Worlds —O the Omega! the violet ray of Her Eyes!

---

1   *viridian* Blue-green.

Federico García Lorca
1898–1936

Federico García Lorca is best remembered for his modern reinterpretations of traditional Andalusian (southern Spanish) art forms, from folk ballads to puppet theatre. His passionate, often violent poems and plays were popular and acclaimed both within his native Spain and internationally.

Lorca grew up in the Andalusian countryside and in Granada but settled in Madrid as a university student. A theatrical personality, he quickly became a social success in a circle of intellectual and artistic friends that included the painter Salvador Dalí. Professional success came with his third book, *Romancero gitano* (*Gypsy Ballads*, 1928), which was popular with the public, although its incorporation of flamenco and Andalusian traditions led some critics to dismiss his work as quaint. However, Lorca would also earn modernist credibility through his engagement with surrealism, notably in his posthumously published collection *Poeta en Nueva York* (*Poet in New York*, 1940), written during an overseas trip in 1929–30.

Lorca began writing plays in the 1920s and focused increasingly on theatre toward the end of his career. As a playwright, he is best known for a trilogy of dramas about Spanish peasants beginning with the tragedy *Bodas de sangre* (*Blood Wedding*, 1933).

As political events in the 1930s led to the rise of fascism in Spain, Lorca declined an opportunity to escape to New York, saying, "I'm a poet, and no one kills poets." In the first year of the Spanish Civil War (1936–39), he was arrested and killed by the fascist forces, and was buried in a mass grave.

The following poem is accompanied by two English translations, included here both to provide additional insight into the original poem and to invite consideration of the process of translation itself.

Romance de la luna, luna   *A Conchita García Lorca*

La luna vino a la fragua
con su polisón de nardos.
El niño la mira, mira.
El niño la está mirando.
5   En el aire conmovido
mueve la luna sus brazos
y enseña, lúbrica y pura,
sus senos de duro estaño.
Huye luna, luna, luna.
10   Si vinieran los gitanos,
harían con tu corazón
collares y anillos blancos.
Niño, déjame que baile.
Cuando vengan los gitanos,
15   te encontrarán sobre el yunque
con los ojillos cerrados.
Huye luna, luna, luna,
que ya siento sus caballos.
Niño, déjame, no pises
20   mi blancor almidonado.

El jinete se acercaba
tocando el tambor del llano.
Dentro de la fragua el niño,
tiene los ojos cerrados.
25   Por el olivar venían,
bronce y sueño, los gitanos.
Las cabezas levantadas
y los ojos entornados.

Cómo canta la zumaya,
30   ¡ay, cómo canta en el árbol!
Por el cielo va la luna
con un niño de la mano.

Dentro de la fragua lloran,
dando gritos, los gitanos.
35   El aire la vela, vela.
El aire la está velando.

—1927

[The moon came to the forge]¹

The moon came to the forge²
  with her skirt of white, fragrant flowers.
  The young boy watches her, watches.
  The boy is watching her.

In the electrified air   5
  the moon moves her arms
  and points out, lecherous and pure,
  her breasts of hard tin.

Flee, moon, moon, moon.
  If the gypsies were to come,   10
  they would make with your heart
  white necklaces and rings.

Young boy, leave me to dance.
  When they come, the gypsies
  will find you upon the anvil   15
  with closed eyes.

Flee, moon, moon, moon.
  Already I sit astride horses.
  Young boy, leave me, don't step on
  my starched whiteness.   20

The horse rider approaches
  beating the drum of the plain.
  Within the forge the young man
  has closed eyes.

Through the olive grove they come,   25
  the gypsies—bronze and dreaming,
  heads lifted
  and eyes half closed.

Hark, hear the night bird—
  how it sings in the tree.   30
  Across the sky moves the moon,
  holding the young boy by the hand.

Within the forge the gypsies cry,
  are crying out.
  The air watches over her, watches.   35
  The air is watching over her.

---

1   *[The moon came to the forge]* Translated by Helen Gunn.
2   *forge* Workshop where blacksmiths melt and reshape metal.

Ballad of the Moon, Moon, Moon[1]

The moon came down to the forge in skirts
    With tuberose[2] bustle white.
The boy-child looks and looks at her,
    Keeps looking at the sight.

5 The moon then moves her arms about
    In an atmosphere astir,
And shows the hard tin of her breasts,
    Lascivious and pure.

Run away from here, oh moon, moon, moon!
10   Should the gypsies come tonight
They'd make your heart into necklaces
    And also rings of white.

Child, move and let me do my dance.
    Whenever the gypsies appear
15 They'll find you with your eyes shut tight
    Upon the anvil here.

Run away, oh moon, moon, moon, I feel
    The hoofbeats in the night!
Child, leave me alone, don't put your feet
20   Upon my starchéd white.

The approaching horseman was beating time
    Upon the drum of the plain.
Inside the forge his eyes shut tight
    The little boy remains.

25 Bronze and dream, the gypsy clan
    Came down through the olive grove,
Their heads held high up toward the sky,
    Their eyes in trance half-closed.

Oh how the screech-owl starts to sing,
30   Sings in his tree nearby!
The moon with boy-child by the hand
    Is going through the sky.

Inside the forge the gypsy clan
    Is loudly wailing, weeping;
35 The air its wake[3] is keeping, keeping,
    The air its wake is keeping.

---

1   *Ballad of the Moon, Moon, Moon* Translated by Carl W. Cobb.
2   *tuberose* Mexican plant with large white flowers similar in appearance to lilies.
3   *wake* Practice of sitting with or watching over the body of a deceased person.

Pablo Neruda

1904–1973

Chilean poet and political figure Pablo Neruda was a prolific writer whose work extended from erotic love poetry to political poems that gave voice to his commitment to communism. Adored in Chile and popular worldwide, he was also critically acclaimed; in 1971 he was awarded a Nobel Prize for "poetry that with the action of an elemental force brings alive a continent's destiny and dreams."

Neruda achieved fame at the age of 20 with his sensuous, highly figurative book *Veinte poemas de amor y una canción desesperada* (*Twenty Love Poems and a Song of Despair*, 1924). In his twenties, he joined the Chilean diplomatic service and acted as a consul in several nations; he was serving in Madrid when the Spanish Civil War (1936–39) broke out. His collection *España en el corazón* (*Spain in the Heart*, 1937) chronicles the atrocities of the war, including the execution of his friend the poet Federico García Lorca.

In 1943, Neruda joined the Chilean Communist Party and was elected to the Senate. When communism was banned in Chile, he was forced into hiding, where he completed *Canto general* (*General Song*, 1950), an epic re-examining South American history from a communist perspective; he then spent three years in exile, unable to return to Chile until 1952. In the later 1950s, he wrote several books of odes concerned with everyday life and ordinary objects.

Neruda died in 1973, in the weeks following a right-wing coup in Chile. Thousands of people defied the new dictatorship to attend his funeral.

The translation of "Exilio" included below is by Scottish poet, essayist, and linguist Alastair Reid (b. 1926); the translation of "Un Perro Ha Muerto" is by Californian writer William O'Daly (b. 1951), who has translated eight volumes of Neruda's poetry.

Exilio

Entre castillos de piedra cansada,
calles de Praga bella,
sonrisas y abedules siberianos,
Capri, fuego en el mar, aroma
5 de romero amargo
y el último, el amor,
el esencial amor se unió a mi vida
en la paz generosa,
mientras tanto,
10 entre una mano y otra mano amiga
se iba cavando un agujero oscuro
en la piedra de mi alma
y allí mi patria ardía
llamándome, esperándome, incitándome
15 a ser, a preserver, a padecer.

El destierro es redondo:
un círculo, un anillo:
le dan vuelta tus pies, cruzas la tierra,
no es tu tierra,
20 te despierta la luz, y no es tu luz,
la noche llega: faltan tus estrellas,
hallas hermanos: pero no es tu sangre.
Eres como un fantasma avergonzado
de no amar más a los que tanto te aman,
25 y aún es tan extraño que te falten
las hostiles espinas de tu patria,
el ronco desamparo de tu pueblo,
los asuntos amargos que te esperan
y que te ladrarán desde la puerta.

30 Pero con corazón irremediable
recordé cada signo innecesario
como si sólo deliciosa miel
se anidara en el árbol de mi tierra
y esperé en cada pájaro
35 el más remoto trino,
el que me despertó desde la infancia
bajo la luz mojada.

Exile

Among castles of tired stone,
streets of beautiful Prague,
smiles and Siberian birches,
Capri, fire in the sea, scent
of harsh rosemary,   5
and lastly, love,
essential love brought all my life together
in a generous peace,
meanwhile
with one hand and its friend, the other,   10
a dark hole was being dug out
in the stone of my spirit
and in it my country was burning,
calling me, waiting for me, spurring me on
to be, to preserve, to endure.   15

Exile is round in shape,
a circle, a ring.
Your feet go in circles, you cross land
and it's not your land.
Light wakes you up and it's not your light.   20
Night comes down, but your stars are missing.
You discover brothers, but they're not of your blood.
You're like an embarrassed ghost,
not loving more those who love you so much,
and it's still so strange to you that you miss   25
the hostile prickles of your own country,
the loud helplessness of your own people,
the bitter matters waiting for you
that will be snarling at you from the door.

But inevitably in my heart   30
I remembered every useless sign
as if only the sweetest honey
gathered in the tree of my own country
and I expected from every bird
the most faraway song   35
such as woke me from childhood on
in the damp light of dawn.

Me pareció mejor la tierra pobre
de mi país, el cráter, las arenas,
40 el rostro mineral de los desiertos
que la copa de luz que me brindaron.
Me sentí solo en el jardín, perdido:
fui un rústico enemigo de la estatua,
de lo que muchos siglos decidieron
45 entre abejas de plata y simetría.

Destierros! La distancia
se hace espesa,
respiramos el aire por la herida:
vivir es un precepto obligatorio.
50 Así es de injusta el alma sin raíces:
rechaza la belleza que le ofrecen:
busca su desdichado territorio:
y sólo allí el martirio o el sosiego.

—1964

It seemed better to me, the poor earth
of my country—crater, sand,
the mineral face of the deserts—
than the glass filled with light they toasted me with.
I felt lost and alone in the garden.
I was a rustic enemy of the statues,
of what many centuries had arrived at
among silver bees and symmetry.

Exiles! Distance
grows thicker.
We breathe air through a wound.
To live is a necessary obligation.
So, a spirit without roots is an injustice.
It rejects the beauty that is offered it.
It searches for its own unfortunate country
and only there knows martyrdom or quiet.

Un Perro Ha Muerto

Mi perro ha muerto.

Lo enterré en el jardín
junto a una vieja máquina oxidada.

Allí, no más abajo,
5 ni más arriba,
se juntará conmigo alguna vez.
Ahora él ya se fue con su pelaje,
su mala educación, su nariz fría.
Y yo, materialista que no cree
10 en el celeste cielo prometido
para ningún humano,
para este perro o para todo perro
creo en el cielo, sí, creo en un cielo
donde yo no entraré, pero él me espera
15 ondulando su cola de abanico
para que yo al llegar tenga armistades.

Ay no diré la tristeza en la tierra
de no tenerlo más por compañero
que para mí jamás fue un servidor.
20 Tuvo hacia mí amistad de un erizo
que conservaba su soberanía,
la amistad de una estrella independiente
sin más intimidad que la precisa,
sin exageraciones:
25 no se trepaba sobre mi vestuario
llenándome de pelos o de sarna,
no se frotaba contra mi rodilla
como otros perros obsesos sexuales.
No, mi perro me miraba
30 dándome la atención que necesito,
la atención necesaria
para hacer comprender a un vanidoso
que siendo perro él,
con esos ojos, más puros que los míos,

A Dog Has Died

My dog has died.

I buried him in the garden
beside a rusty old engine.

There, not too deep,
not too shallow,   5
he will greet me sometime.

He already left with his coat,
his bad manners, his cold nose.
And I, a materialist who does not believe
in the starry heaven promised   10
to a human being,
for this dog and for every dog
I believe in heaven, yes, I believe in a heaven
that I will never enter, but he waits for me
wagging his big fan of a tail   15
so I, soon to arrive, will feel welcomed.

No, I will not speak about my sadness on earth
at not having him as a companion anymore,
he never stooped to becoming my servant.
He offered me the friendship of a sea urchin   20
who always kept his sovereignty,
the friendship of an independent star
with no more intimacy than necessary,
with no exaggerations:
he never used to climb over my clothes   25
covering me with hair or with mange,
he never used to rub against my knee
like other dogs, obsessed with sex.
No, my dog used to watch me
giving me the attention I need,   30
yet only the attention necessary
to let a vain person know
that he being a dog,
with those eyes, more pure than mine,

35 perdía el tiempo, pero me miraba
    con la mirada que me reservó
    toda su dulce, su peluda vida,
    su silenciosa vida,
    cerca de mí, sin molestarme nunca,
40 y sin pedirme nada.

    Ay cuántas veces quise tener cola
    andando junto a él por las orillas
    del mar, en el Invierno de Isla Negra,
    en la gran soledad: arriba el aire
45 traspasado de pájaros glaciales
    y mi perro brincando, hirsuto, lleno
    de voltaje marino en movimiento:
    mi perro vagabundo y olfatorio
    enarbolando su cola dorada
50 frente a frente al Océano y su espuma.

    Alegre, alegre, alegre
    como los perros saben ser felices,
    sin nada más, con el absolutismo
    de la naturaleza descarada.
55 No hay adiós a mi perro que se ha muerto.
    Y no hay ni hubo mentira entre nosotros.

    Ya se fue y lo enterré, y eso era todo.

                                        —1974

was wasting time, but he watched   35
with a look that reserved for me
every bit of sweetness, his shaggy life,
his silent life,
sitting nearby, never bothering me,
never asking anything of me.   40

O, how many times I wanted to have a tail
walking next to him on the seashore,
in the Isla Negra[1] winter,
in the vast solitude: above us
glacial birds pierced the air   45
and my dog frolicking, bristly hair, full
of the sea's voltage in motion:
my dog wandering and sniffing around,
brandishing his golden tail
in the face of the ocean and its spume.   50

O merry, merry, merry,
like only dogs know how to be happy
and nothing more, with an absolute
shameless nature.
There are no goodbyes for my dog who has died.   55
And there never were and are no lies between us.

He has gone and I buried him, and that was all.

---

1   *Isla Negra* Coastal area in central Chile.

Paul Celan

1920–1970

Paul Antschel, who wrote under the pseudonym Paul Celan, was born in Czernovitz, Romania, to a German-speaking Jewish family. His life and work were profoundly affected by the Holocaust. In 1941, the German allies occupied Czernovitz, and Celan and his parents were forced to live in a ghetto. Not long after, he was separated from his parents when they were sent to an internment camp, where they later died; Celan himself was sent to a forced labour camp. He wrote poetry throughout his imprisonment.

With the notable exception of "Todesfugue" ("Death Fugue," 1952)—one of his most famous poems—Celan's poetry does not usually portray the camps directly. However, he described his writing in general as a response to the trauma of the Holocaust: "Only one thing remained reachable, close and secure amid all losses: language.... But it had to go through its own lack of answers, through terrifying silence, through the thousand darknesses of murderous speech.... It gave me no words for what was happening, but went through it." Especially in his later poetry, Celan was often concerned with the ways in which language itself was affected by the events of the Holocaust—an issue complicated by the fact that he composed most of his work in German, the language of those who perpetrated the atrocities. His expressions of suffering, grief, and loss are often difficult to interpret, as his work is characterized by surreal imagery, fragmented words and syntax, and dense allusion.

Celan spent the last 20 years of his life in Paris, where in addition to writing he was a teacher of German literature and translator of poetry from several languages. His work received such prestigious European awards as the Bremen Prize for Literature (1958) and the Georg Büchner Prize (1960). Celan committed suicide in 1970.

The following poems have been translated by German-born British poet, translator, and critic Michael Hamburger (1924–2007).

Totenhemd

Was du aus Leichtem wobst,
trag ich dem Stein zu Ehren.
Wenn ich im Dunkel die Schreie
wecke, weht es sie an.

Oft, wenn ich stammeln soll, 5
wirft es vergessene Falten,
und der ich bin, verzeiht
dem, der ich war.

Aber der Haldengott
rührt seine dumpfeste Trommel, 10
und wie die Falte fiel,
runzelt der Finstre die Stirn.

—1952

Shroud

That which you wove out of light thread
I wear in honour of stone.
When in the dark I awaken
the screams, it blows on them, lightly.

Often, when I should stammer, 5
it raises forgotten crinkles
and he that I am forgives
him that I was.

But the god of the slagheaps
beats his most muted drum, 10
and just as the crinkle ran
the grim one puckers his brow.

Todesfuge

Schwarze Milch der Frühe wir trinken sie abends
wir trinken sie mittags und morgens wir trinken sie nachts
wir trinken und trinken
wir schaufeln ein Grab in den Lüften da liegt man nicht eng
5 Ein Mann wohnt im Haus der spielt mit den Schlangen der schreibt
der schreibt wenn es dunkelt nach Deutschland dein goldenes Haar
    Margarete
er schreibt es und tritt vor das Haus und es blitzen die Sterne er pfeift seine
    Rüden herbei
er pfeift seine Juden hervor läßt schaufeln ein Grab in der Erde
er befiehlt uns spielt auf nun zum Tanz

10 Schwarze Milch der Frühe wir trinken dich nachts
wir trinken dich morgens und mittags wir trinken dich abends
wir trinken und trinken
Ein Mann wohnt im Haus der spielt mit den Schlangen der schreibt
der schreibt wenn es dunkelt nach Deutschland dein goldenes Haar
    Margarete
15 Dein aschenes Haar Sulamith wir schaufeln ein Grab in den Lüften da liegt
    man nicht eng

Er ruft stecht tiefer ins Erdreich ihr einen ihr andern singet und spielt
er greift nach dem Eisen im Gurt er schwingts seine Augen sind blau
stecht tiefer die Spaten ihr einen ihr andern spielt weiter zum Tanz auf

Schwarze Milch der Frühe wir trinken dich nachts
20 wir trinken dich mittags und morgens wir trinken dich abends
wir trinken und trinken

Death Fugue[1]

Black milk of daybreak we drink it at sundown
we drink it at noon in the morning we drink it at night
we drink and we drink it
we dig a grave in the breezes there one lies unconfined
A man lives in the house he plays with the serpents he writes   5
he writes when dusk falls to Germany your golden hair Margarete[2]
he writes it and steps out of doors and the stars are flashing he whistles his
    pack out
he whistles his Jews out in earth has them dig for a grave
he commands us strike up for the dance[3]

Black milk of daybreak we drink you at night   10
we drink in the morning at noon we drink you at sundown
we drink and we drink you
A man lives in the house he plays with the serpents he writes
he writes when dusk falls to Germany your golden hair Margarete
your ashen hair Shulamith[4] we dig a grave in the breezes there one lies   15
    unconfined

He calls out jab deeper into the earth you lot you others sing now and play
he grabs at the iron in his belt he waves it his eyes are blue
jab deeper you lot with your spades you others play on for the dance

Black milk of daybreak we drink you at night
we drink you at noon in the morning we drink you at sundown   20
we drink and we drink you

---

1   *Fugue* Musical composition in which a theme is introduced and then repeated with variations.

2   *Margarete* Character in German author Johann Wolfgang von Goethe's classic play *Faust* (1808–32). In Part One of the play, Faust makes a pact with the devil; under the devil's influence, he seduces the beautiful Margarete, whose life is destroyed by their relationship.

3   *he commands ... the dance* Some Nazi concentration camps had prisoner orchestras, which were required to provide music as the other prisoners marched to and from work and were sometimes forced to play during executions or during the selection of prisoners to be gassed.

4   *Shulamith* Hebrew name of Solomon's beautiful, idealized lover in the biblical Song of Songs.

ein Mann wohnt im Haus dein goldenes Haar Margarete
dein aschenes Haar Sulamith er spielt mit den Schlangen
Er ruft spielt süßer den Tod der Tod ist ein Meister aus Deutschland
25 er ruft streicht dunkler die Geigen dann steigt ihr als Rauch in die Luft
dann habt ihr ein Grab in den Wolken da liegt man nicht eng

Schwarze Milch der Frühe wir trinken dich nachts
wir trinken dich mittags der Tod ist ein Meister aus Deutschland
wir trinken dich abends und morgens wir trinken und trinken
30 der Tod ist ein Meister aus Deutschland sein Auge ist blau
er trifft dich mit bleierner Kugel er trifft dich genau
ein Mann wohnt im Haus dein goldenes Haar Margarete
er hetzt seine Rüden auf uns er schenkt uns ein Grab in der Luft
er spielt mit den Schlangen und träumet der Tod ist ein Meister aus Deutschland

35 dein goldenes Haar Margarete
dein aschenes Haar Sulamith

—1948

a man lives in the house your golden hair Margarete
your ashen hair Shulamith he plays with the serpents
He calls out more sweetly play death death is a master from Germany
he calls out more darkly now stroke your strings then as smoke you will rise   25
    into air
then a grave you will have in the clouds there one lies unconfined

Black milk of daybreak we drink you at night
we drink you at noon death is a master from Germany
we drink you at sundown and in the morning we drink and we drink you
death is a master from Germany his eyes are blue   30
he strikes you with leaden bullets his aim is true
a man lives in the house your golden hair Margarete
he sets his pack on to us he grants us a grave in the air
he plays with the serpents and daydreams death is a master from Germany

your golden hair Margarete   35
your ashen hair Shulamith

Nicole Brossard
b. 1943

As a poet, novelist, essayist, and activist, Nicole Brossard has contributed extensively to the fields of literary criticism, feminist thought, and literature, earning recognition both in her native province of Quebec and on a larger global stage. She has received two Governor General's Awards (1974 and 1984), Quebec's Prix Athanase-David (1991), and the Canada Council for the Arts Molson Prize (2006).

Born in Montreal, Brossard attended le Collège Marguerite Bourgeoys and l'Université de Montréal. After briefly working as a teacher she began a writing career, co-founding the formalist literary magazine *La Barre du Jour* (1965–77) and publishing her first book of poetry, *Aube à la saison* (*Dawning Season*, 1965). Her abstract style and her interest in the adaptability of language soon earned her a reputation as a progressive, inventive writer; in the celebrated novel *Le désert mauve* (*Mauve Desert*, 1987), for example, she employs an unconventional form and a nonlinear narrative. While pushing boundaries within her own writing, she continued to foster literary community, founding the feminist paper *Les Têtes de pioche* (1976–79) and co-founding *La Nouvelle Barre du Jour* (1977–90). Written from a feminist, lesbian, and urban French Canadian perspective, her work calls for social transformation, putting into practice her belief that "literature is subversion, transgression, and vision."

Brossard has written over 30 books, including poetry collections such as *Mécanique jongleuse* (*Daydream Mechanics*, 1974), *Amantes* (*Lovhers*, 1980), and *Double Impression* (1984). Her many collaborative projects include the film *Some American Feminists* (1977), which she co-directed with two other Canadian filmmakers. Writing in French and English, she has translated some of her poetry herself, finding that the process enables her to further explore the potential and limits of language.

The following poems have been translated by Montreal-born writer Robert Mazjels (b. 1950) and Canadian poet Erin Mouré (b. 1955). Their 2007 translation of Brossard's *Cahier de roses & de civilisation* (*Notebook of Roses and Civilization*, 2003) was shortlisted for a Governor General's Award and for the Griffin Prize.

Geste

je ne sais le comment
le commencement des pensées quand
elles se greffent à des gestes simples
comme s'il y avait un rapport entre
5 l'intention de bouger et la manière de penser
sans trop de malheur, la voix sensuelle
et toute l'ampleur d'une science au corps

—1989

Gesture

I don't know the how
the first howl of thoughts when
they graft on to simple gestures
somehow as if there were a link between
5 the intent to move and a way of thinking
without too much grief, the sensual voice
and all the fullness of a science of the body

[tous ces mois passés]

tous ces mois passés
à regarder les palmiers par en-dessous
de la naissance des parfums de jasmin
tout ce temps passé
à chercher la zone *twilight* du bord de l'univers   5
oui par en-dessous de la naissance
quand la tête est plongée
dans une ambiance de voix
et le cœur enroulé dans ses excès de réalité

—2003

[all these months spent]

all these months spent
gazing at the palms from below
the birth of the scent of jasmine
all this time spent
seeking the twilight zone at the edge of *l'univers*   5
yes from below its birth
when the head is plunged
into a world of voices
and the heart swathed in its excesses of reality

Yehuda Amichai

1924–2000

Israeli poet Yehuda Amichai said his first collection "outraged most critics—I was attacked for using colloquial language, attacked for trying techniques no one had ever tried before." Popular audiences, however, immediately appreciated his innovative use of everyday Hebrew alongside biblical language; his biographer Nili Scharf Gold has described him as "Israel's beloved unofficial national poet."

Born in Germany, Amichai was educated in Hebrew as a child, and when he was 11 his family moved to Palestine. During World War II, he worked for the British engineering corps in Egypt, and in the following decades he would be a schoolteacher, an activist, and—although he considered himself a proponent of nonviolence—a soldier in the Israeli military in three different wars. He began to seriously write poetry at the beginning of the 1950s while attending the Hebrew University of Jerusalem.

"I try to create a kind of equality between my personal history and the history around me," Amichai said, and he is remembered both for love poetry and for poetry reflecting his first-hand experience of Israel's formation and development. Critical appreciation of his work grew to match his popularity, and, among many other awards, Amichai received the Israel Prize for Poetry in 1982.

Amichai was also successful internationally, and his poems have been translated from Hebrew into more than 35 languages. In some respects, the plainness of his style is amenable to translation, but other distinctive qualities of his writing appear only in the Hebrew originals. Translator Robert Alter acknowledges the impossibility of capturing Amichai's "sensitivity to the expressive sounds of the Hebrew words he uses," his "inventive puns," and his sophisticated allusions to "densely specific Hebrew terms and texts."

The following poem was translated by Glenda Abramson, retired professor of Hebrew and Jewish Studies at Oxford, and Tudor Parfitt, founding director of the Centre for Jewish Studies at the University of London.

תַּיָּרִים

בִּקּוּרֵי אֲבֵלִים הֵם עוֹרְכִים אֶצְלֵנוּ,
יוֹשְׁבִים בְּיַד וָשֵׁם, מַרְצִינִים לְיַד הַכֹּתֶל הַמַּעֲרָבִי
וְצוֹחֲקִים מֵאֲחוֹרֵי וִילוֹנוֹת כְּבֵדִים בְּחַדְרֵי מָלוֹן,
מִצְטַלְּמִים עִם מֵתִים חֲשׁוּבִים בְּקֶבֶר רָחֵל
5 וּבְקֶבֶר הֶרְצֵל וּבַגִּבְעַת הַתַּחְמֹשֶׁת,
בּוֹכִים עַל יְפִי גְּבוּרַת נְעָרֵינוּ
וְחוֹשְׁקִים בִּקְשִׁיחוּת נַעֲרוֹתֵינוּ
וְתוֹלִים אֶת תַּחְתּוֹנֵיהֶם
לְיִבּוּשׁ מָהִיר
10 בְּאַמְבַּטְיָה כְּחֻלָּה וְצוֹנֶנֶת.

פַּעַם יָשַׁבְתִּי עַל מַדְרֵגוֹת לְיַד שַׁעַר בִּמְצוּדַת דָּוִד, אֶת שְׁנֵי הַסַּלִּים הַכְּבֵדִין
שַׂמְתִּי לְיָדִי. עָמְדָה שָׁם קְבוּצַת תַּיָּרִים סְבִיב הַמַּדְרִיךְ וְשִׁמַּשְׁתִּי לָהֶם נְקֻדַּת
צִיּוּן. "אַתֶּם רוֹאִים אֶת הָאִישׁ הַזֶּה עִם הַסַּלִּים? קְצָת יָמִינָה מֵרֹאשׁוֹ נִמְצֵאת
קֶשֶׁת מִן הַתְּקוּפָה הָרוֹמִית. קְצָת יָמִינָה מֵרֹאשׁוֹ". אֲבָל הוּא זָז, הוּא זָז!
15 אָמַרְתִּי בְּלִבִּי: הַגְּאֻלָּה תָּבוֹא רַק אִם יַגִּידוּ לָהֶם: אַתֶּם רוֹאִים שָׁם אֶת
הַקֶּשֶׁת מִן הַתְּקוּפָה הָרוֹמִית? לֹא חָשׁוּב: אֲבָל לְיָדָהּ, קְצָת שְׂמֹאלָה וּלְמַטָּה
מִמֶּנָּה, יוֹשֵׁב אָדָם שֶׁקָּנָה פֵּרוֹת וִירָקוֹת לְבֵיתוֹ.

—1980

Tourists

Visits of condolence is all we get from them.
They squat at the Holocaust Memorial,
They put on grave faces at the Wailing Wall[1]
And they laugh behind heavy curtains
In their hotels.   5
They have their pictures taken
Together with our famous dead
At Rachel's Tomb and Herzl's[2] Tomb
And on the top of Ammunition Hill.[3]
They weep over our sweet boys   10
And lust after our tough girls
And hang up their underwear
To dry quickly
In cool, blue bathrooms.

Once I sat on the steps by a gate at David's Tower,[4] I placed my two heavy   15
baskets at my side. A group of tourists was standing around their guide and
I became their target marker. "You see that man with the baskets? Just right
of his head there's an arch from the Roman Period. Just right of his head."
"But he's moving, he's moving!" I said to myself: redemption will come only
if their guide tells them, "You see that arch from the Roman period? It's not   20
important: but next to it, left and down a bit, there sits a man who's bought
fruit and vegetables for his family."

---

1   *Wailing Wall* Jewish site of pilgrimage and prayer. Originally part of the walls surrounding
     the site of the Temple in Jerusalem, it is traditionally considered sacred as a remnant of
     that Temple.
2   *Rachel* Biblical wife of Jacob. According to tradition, the site of her tomb is just out-
     side Bethlehem; *Herzl* Theodor Herzl (1860–1904), Viennese activist, journalist, play-
     wright, and founder of the Zionist movement. His grave is in Jerusalem.
3   *Ammunition Hill* Site of a major battle in the Six-Day War (1967) between Israel and
     Jordan, Egypt, and Syria; a museum and memorial are now located there.
4   *David's Tower* Tower of David, a citadel in Jerusalem with an architectural history span-
     ning 2,000 years.

Reesom Haile

1946–2003

Eritrean poet and activist Reesom Haile argued for the importance of preserving language: "If you lose your language, it isn't just the language you lose. It's the cultural codes imbedded in that language. It's the values, the sense of community.... This is what I do not want my people to lose." Haile's poetry is composed in Tigrinya, one of Eritrea's most widely spoken languages. Although he frequently performed live—reflecting Eritrean traditions of oral poetry—he also published written work in Tigrinya and in bilingual English/Tigrinya editions.

Haile grew up in an Eritrean farming community. He left the country during the war of independence (1961–91) in which Eritrea, then a province of Ethiopia, fought to secede and form its own nation. Over the next two decades, Haile worked as a journalist, university teacher, and consultant to the United Nations and various NGOs. When he returned home in 1994—a year after Eritrea officially achieved independence—he began a career in poetry that connected social activism with a desire to revitalize and celebrate Eritrean language and culture.

Haile's first collection of poems, *waza ms qumneger ntnsae hager* (*Tragicomedies for Resurrecting a Nation*, 1997), is written in Tigrinya and won the 1998 Raimok prize, Eritrea's most prestigious literary award. His two bilingual collections, *We Have Our Voice* (2000) and *We Invented the Wheel* (2002), consolidated his international reputation as a master of lively, passionate, often witty verse informed by keenly felt political and social ideals. Amiri Baraka has praised his "spare poetic line [that] carries the weight of incisive image, narrative clarity, [and] irony plus a droll humour." A prolific writer, Haile died in 2003, having composed more than 2,000 poems.

The following poems have been translated by Charles Cantalupo (b. 1951), a poet, critic, editor, and distinguished professor at Penn State University. Cantalupo translated both *We Have Our Voice* and *We Invented the Wheel* in consultation with Haile.

ስደት

አብ ካይሮ ኤርፖርት
ዙርያ ዝለበሳ
ገለ ሐሙሳ ሱሳ
ልቢ ዝማርኻ
ልቢ ዘፍስሳ   5
ርእናየን ናይ ኢትዮጵያ ኤክስፖርት
ንበይኑት ክሓልፉ
ናይ ሰብ ዓራት ከንጽፉ
ህይወተን ከሕለፉ
ክንደይ ከይሀብትማ ክንደይ ከየዕርፉ   10
ይኹነልክን ይቕናዕክን በላ ሕለፉ
ነዚአስ አይንደልያ አይንሃርፉ።።

c. 1997–99

Knowledge

First the earth, then the plow:
So knowledge comes out of knowledge.
We know, we don't know.
We don't know we know.
We know we don't know.   5
We think
This looks like that—
This lemon, that orange—
Until we taste the bitter.

አመሪካ ኢሉኩም

ዝሞተ እንተ ሞተ
ንዉ ኮካ ንስተ
ዝብሳዕ ዘይብልኩም
እንሆልኩም ማንካ
5 ዝሹመት ዘይብልኩም
እንሆልኩም ባንካ
ዘሎኩም ነጊፍኩም
ኩሉ ንዓይ አመሪካ

ናብራ ከሎኩም
10 ናብራ ተለቂሕኩም
ናብራ ከሎኩም
ናብራ ተገዚእኩም
ናብራ ከሎኩም
ናብራ ለሚንኩም
15 እና ክጽውዕ
አቤት እንዳበልኩም
ናጽነት ሓርነት
እንታይ ከገብረልኩም

ነዚ ዘይአመንኩም
20 ብረት ክሸጠልኩም
እንተ ብህይወትኩም
እንተ ብሞትኩም
ክኽስበኩም ' የ
አፍሪቃውያን።

c. 1997–99

Dear Africans

The overweight
God, America,
Is always late.
Don't wait.

You already know   5
What he'll state:
I regret the hearsay
Of so many dead and dying
And so much crying.

You already know   10
What he'll think:
It's dress-down Friday.
Can we have a snack?
Oh, man! Make that a big Mac
And a large Coke.   15
By the way, don't smoke.

Literary Non-Fiction

Literary non-fiction is a diverse genre with a long history—yet its nature is hard to pin down. A work of literary non-fiction is nowadays almost always written in prose, but it may be an essay, a memoir, a piece of journalism. It may be written for any one of a wide range of purposes. It may be as short as a page or two, or it may be of book length.

No work that calls itself "non-fiction" can be the product of pure invention—if you make up the story, you are writing fiction. Yet the line that separates fiction from non-fiction may sometimes be hard to determine. Many authors of literary non-fiction consider it a legitimate practice to shape the presentation of events or characters in an essay or a memoir in ways that deviate from the specifics of what actually happened. George Orwell, one of the most highly acclaimed writers of literary non-fiction of the twentieth century, is known to have done this frequently. So too, in the preface to one of the most influential works of literary non-fiction of the new century, *Dreams of My Father*, does Barack Obama candidly acknowledge that at least part of what he has written is, in some sense, fiction:

> Although much of this book is based on contemporaneous journals
> or the oral histories of my family, the dialogue is necessarily an ap-
> proximation of what was actually said or relayed to me. For the sake
> of compression, some of the characters that appear are composites
> of people I've known, and some events appear out of precise chro-
> nology.

In other words, the writer has felt at liberty to sift and shape the material to give a personal view of what seems to him to be, in his words, "some granite slab of truth." Obama goes on to acknowledge the difficulty in naming this sort of writing: "Whatever the label that attaches to this book—autobiography, memoir, family history, or something else—what I've tried to do is write an honest account of a particular province of my life." Critics have reached different conclusions as to whether or not the picture that emerges does in fact present "some granite slab of truth"; they disagree as to the degree to which such a work should be thought of as non-fiction. But virtually all have agreed—in much the same way as they have agreed about acclaimed non-fiction works by Orwell, such as "Shooting an Elephant," or *Down and Out in Paris and London*—that it should be thought of as literature.

Literary Non-Fiction and Academic Non-Fiction

The form that literary non-fiction most frequently takes is that of the essay. But an *essay* in this sense is something very different from the kind of essay that university students are asked to read (and, usually, to write) when they take courses in academic subjects. For the most part, students are taught that an academic essay should be distanced and impersonal. It should be structured according to established conventions of its academic discipline. And according to these conventions, the academic essay should strive for objectivity; subjective reflections that cannot be supported with evidence have little place in this kind of writing. The task of the essay writer is not to sway the reader through description or narration or emotional appeal of any sort, but rather to analyze evidence in support of an argument. Whether that argument is made inductively or deductively, an academic essay should display careful reasoning according to logical principles. It should also cite references to support its argument—and to make it easier for other students and scholars to verify the evidence and engage with the argument in a scholarly manner.

The sort of essay that constitutes a work of literary non-fiction is none of these things. Though it may sometimes marshal evidence in support of a reasoned argument, it may also employ narration and description and emotional appeal. It may be loosely structured. It is more likely to be personal in tone. And it will normally not include any cited sources.[1] Whereas the academic essay is generally addressed to an audience within a particular scholarly academic discipline, literary non-fiction is typically addressed to a broad audience. It aims to interest and entice readers and to give them pleasure, in the way that literature gives pleasure—through the use of well-crafted images, figurative language, and symbols, by ordering events to create suspense, and by creating interesting non-fictional "characters" to engage us.

Such pleasure is not contingent on the writer's topic being pleasurable. Just as a novel about horrific events can be, *as literature*, enjoyable as well as interesting to read, so too a piece of literary non-fiction about horrific events can be, *as literature*, enjoyable. Conveying in memorable and affecting ways the "unspeakable" is an important function of literature. Philip Gourevitch's piece in this volume, reflecting on the nature of genocide and on having seen

---

1   An essay such as David Foster Wallace's "Consider the Lobster" is in this respect less of an exception than it might seem. For the most part it employs notes not to cite sources but to provide tangential reflections—reflections that are surely of interest but that might act as a distraction if included in the body of the essay.

the aftermath of a massacre, falls squarely into this category. But if, as a general question, we ask what sorts of topics literary non-fiction addresses, there is no simple answer. The writer may work through any one of a wide range of structures in trying to mediate a reader's understanding of an endless variety of topics. Examples in this volume include an exploration of a father's life (Miriam Toews's memoir); an argument about the appeal of wrestling (Roland Barthes); a discussion of a lobster festival—and of the practice of boiling lobsters alive (David Foster Wallace); reflections tinged with double-edged humour on having a mixed cultural heritage (Drew Hayden Taylor); and an evocation of the thrill of travelling to a new country (Karen Connelly). In all literary non-fiction, though, style and structure are determined not by the conventions of an academic discipline, but by literary values—and by the writer's personality.

History of the Genre

Given that literary non-fiction has only recently begun to receive considerable attention as a distinct literary genre, one might easily imagine that writing of this sort would be a relatively recent phenomenon. In fact, its roots go almost as far back as do those of poetry and drama. Like them, the genre of literary non-fiction has strong roots in the classical cultures of ancient Greece and Rome. The ancients referred to the process of communication as *rhetoric*. Broadly defined, rhetoric may be said to be involved in almost anything to do with the study of cultural messages, with any communication that attempts to persuade, with almost every human effort to express thoughts coherently so as to communicate them to others. In practice, the Greeks and Romans defined rhetoric much more narrowly. Classical rhetoric was an art whose precepts were designed to help orators (*rhetors*) organize and deliver their arguments in a methodical, articulate, and persuasive way. That may sound a long way from the literary non-fiction of today—may sound, indeed, of more relevance to the roots of the modern academic essay than to those of literary non-fiction. And there can be no question of the relevance of classical rhetoric to the history of academic argument. But historians suggest that the modern essay as a work of literary non-fiction may also be found in embryonic form in the works of some classical writers—not least of all in a work now almost two thousand years old, the *Moral Letters* of the Roman Stoic philosopher Lucius Annaeus Seneca (usually known simply as Seneca).

Though the 124 pieces that make up the *Moral Letters* are written as letters to the then-governor of Sicily, Lucilius—each one begins "Seneca greets his Lucilius"—in every other respect the epistles far more closely resemble what we now call literary non-fiction than they do modern-day personal letters. They are personal in tone, to be sure, but they include little or nothing relating to the particulars of the personal relationship between Seneca and Lucilius. They seem rather to address a general audience. As is the case with the piece on masters and slaves included here, Seneca's epistles often discuss broad topics, and they often put forth a persuasive argument. They often employ narration (as Seneca does in recounting his little story about Callistus) and description (as when he gives us a picture of the dining table or describes the master whose greed has filled his distended belly). They often appeal to the senses and to the emotions at least as much as to reason. Each piece focuses on a particular topic—but the topics tend to be broad and range widely, from drunkenness to scientific invention, to how a love of sports can become excessive, to the issue of equality between men and women. Seneca is thought of today primarily as a philosopher, but in the *Moral Letters* his writing is far closer to that of today's writer of literary essays than it is to the writing of most contemporary philosophers.

In the post-medieval era the literary essay is generally said to have begun with the sixteenth-century French writer Michel de Montaigne, known in his day as the "French Seneca." Like Seneca, Montaigne wrote short pieces on a wide variety of broad topics ranging from marriage to study, education, and various aspects of current affairs. But Montaigne's pieces tend to be both more closely reasoned than those of Seneca, and looser in structure. More often than not they explore an idea rather than set out an argument in favour of a predetermined position. Montaigne saw writing of this sort less as a means of persuading the reader to accept a certain conclusion than as a means of trying to grope one's way toward understanding. Hence the name he gave to these short pieces—*essais*, or, in English, *attempts* or *tries*. (The connection is a direct one; among its definitions of *essay* the *Oxford English Dictionary* offers the following: "the action or process of trying or testing.") And always, while attempting to understand some aspect of an idea or of the world, Montaigne was attempting to understand himself—reflecting on his own thoughts, impulses, and desires. In the preface to the *Essais* Montaigne famously declares, "lecteur, je suis moi-même la matière de mon livre" ("reader, I am myself the subject of my book"). In all these respects—the looseness of structure, the vision of writing as a means of groping toward understanding, the tendency to use the essay to explore the outside world and the self simultaneously—Montaigne's writing continues to exert an influence on literary non-fiction.

The history of the literary essay in English is extraordinarily varied. It is often said to begin in early seventeenth-century England with the very Montaigne-like essays of Francis Bacon. With the eighteenth century came the pointed political and literary essays of Samuel Johnson and Jonathan Swift, and the beginnings of literary journalism. The nineteenth century brought the cultural criticism of Charles Dickens, Matthew Arnold, and George Eliot in Britain, and the personal-philosophic essays of Henry David Thoreau and Ralph Waldo Emerson in the United States. In the twentieth century the range of literary non-fiction became broader still, from Virginia Woolf's essays on gender and society and George Orwell's explorations of politics and culture, to the fresh approaches to form and the tremendous variety of subject matter that characterize the literary non-fiction of late twentieth- and early twenty-first-century writers from every corner of the globe. Across this diversity, though, direct links to Montaigne and Seneca remain—in tone, style, structure, and rhetorical strategies. Vestiges of the ancient traditions remain in a great many of today's literary essays—in their tone, in their structure and style, and in their rhetorical strategies.

Style and Structure, Argument, and Rhetoric

Let's return to our comparison of how arguments are presented in the modern academic essay versus literary non-fiction. As we have said, reason and logic are central to what the writer of the academic essay strives for, and the logic of the argument is made overt through such conventions as thesis statements and topic sentences. Anything that might impede an impersonal and objective presentation of a reasoned argument is often said to be inappropriate in an academic essay. Rhetorical flourishes are kept to a minimum. The structure in which an argument is presented tends to be standardized. The pronoun "I" is often said to have no place here, and the same is said of personal details or reflections. Style and structure, in short, are conventionalized in order for the writer to be as unobtrusive as possible—and in order to allow reasoned argument to shine through.

In literary non-fiction, on the other hand, a range of structures is available to the writer, and the adoption of a personal tone and a unique style are often very much a part of the presentation of the "argument." Why is the word "argument" put in quotation marks here? To make clear that, in the context of literary non-fiction, *argument* is not to be taken in the same sense as it is with most academic non-fiction. The argument of a piece of literary non-fiction is the line along which ideas are connected; it may be much looser and less overt than the argument of the typical academic paper of today, and its logic may be implicit, to be sought out by the reader.

Whether we are looking at non-literary academic arguments or those of literary non-fiction, the vocabulary of classical rhetoric remains highly useful when it comes to naming the elements of argument. According to one of the most influential classical rhetorical manuals, *Rhetorica ad Herennium* (which dates from the first century BCE), rhetoric has five canons or general, fundamental principles: invention, arrangement, style, memory, and delivery. As may readily be inferred from the last two items on that list, the expectation was that rhetorical arguments would be delivered orally through a speech (by a *rhetor*) rather than in writing. But the strength and originality of the ideas (invention), the way in which they are arranged, and the style with which they are presented are concepts that remain relevant to non-fiction writing of all sorts.

The *Rhetorica ad Herennium* also sets out guidelines for the layout of an argument (in classical terminology, its *disposition*), specifying that it should include the following elements:

- exordium (introduces the argument)

- narration (states the issue; may supply background or explore the history of the issue)

- division (separates and lists the parts under discussion)

- confirmation (elaborates and supports the *rhetor*'s position)

- confutation (refutes opposing arguments)

- peroration (conclusion)

We may observe these elements in Seneca's writing—how he separates the arts under discussion, how he anticipates (and refutes) the arguments of his opponents. Aside perhaps from *exordium* and *peroration*, though, it may well be thought that such concepts are of limited use in analyzing the contemporary literary essay. But from time to time they may indeed be useful in discussing literary non-fiction. We may see traces of the classical rhetorical strategies of narration and division, for example, in the way in which David Foster Wallace fills in some of the history of lobster eating and guides the reader through the parts of his argument.

Ancient guides to rhetoric also often considered arguments as belonging to one of three types: deliberative (concerned with the future), judicial (sometimes referred to as forensic; concerned with the past), and epideictic (celebratory arguments). These classifications too may sometimes be helpful in discussions of literary non-fiction. When Mark Twain addresses an imaginary audience in "Advice to Youth," he creates an epideictic argument. Roland Barthes, as he explores "The World of Wrestling," makes a judicial or forensic argument (as do several of the other selections). Deliberative arguments in anything close to a pure form, however, are rarely found in literary non-fiction; they occur far more frequently in politicians' speeches, in the arguments of newspaper and television commentators—or in the world of advertising.

Perhaps of greater relevance to today's literary non-fiction are the three categories of appeal that are set out in classical rhetoric (from the early Greek philosopher Aristotle on down): *logos*, *pathos*, and *ethos*. All three are widely and usefully employed in many discussions of literary writing today.

Logos is often translated as *logic*, and to a large extent appeals based on *logos* may indeed be appeals that are logical in nature. But in the world of rhetoric such appeals are not always made according to the principles of inductive or deductive logic that apply to most academic essays. The meaning of *logos* in the ancient world was multi-faceted; it could mean *reason* or *logic*, but it could also simply mean *word*; in the context of literary non-fiction, an appeal based on *logos* may perhaps best be understood as an appeal based on the ideas that the words hold. The rational arguments that Seneca makes—appealing to the principle of fairness and citing the benefits of treating one's slaves or servants well—represent appeals to *logos*. Much the same can be said of Barthes's arguments about the moral content of wrestling. These are arguments that in large part make appeals to *logos* based on traditional principles of logical reasoning. But Miriam Toews also makes an appeal to *logos* when she recounts the history in the Mennonite church of shunning those "out of faith"—a category that included those suffering from depression or despair—and then writes that she "can't help thinking" that this history of shunning had "just a little to do with" the ways in which her father tried to deal with his depression. Toews's line of reasoning cannot be said to follow the same sorts of logical steps that the arguments of Barthes or Seneca do—and she makes no claims to have reached an airtight conclusion. Yet her appeal to *logos* may be more powerful than that of any of the other pieces included here. Rather than establishing the tenets of and the conclusion to an argument, her appeal to *logos* suggests connections. And rather than demonstrating irrefutably that those connections exist, she persuades us that they are likely to have played a real part in what happened to her father. Giving readers freedom in this way to discern an argument's logic by forging connections for themselves is one important way in which the genre of literary non-fiction may exert powerful effects.

The word *pathos* is sometimes thought to hold pejorative connotations, describing an appeal to the emotions that is too contrived, blatant, or superficial. Appeals to the emotions may surely be all of those things. But they need not be any of them and certainly the term *pathos*, properly used, carries much the same meaning today as it did for the ancients, referring to any appeal to the emotions. Such appeals have a legitimate place in most forms of argumentation, given that our responses to experiences inevitably involve both heart and head; indeed, many would argue that the direction our reason takes is always informed at some level by our initial, emotional responses. Such appeals may take many forms. When you read Gourevitch's "We Wish to Inform You That

Tomorrow We Will Be Killed with Our Families" or Orwell's "Shooting an Elephant," you will likely be moved by the full sweep of the experience the writer is recounting. Toews's "A Father's Faith" is another example of a piece in which an appeal to *pathos* arguably runs throughout the essay. But appeals to *pathos* may be embedded even in very brief descriptions that have strong emotive content. Seneca's sentence describing the master and his distended belly (evoking in the reader the emotion of disgust at his display of greed) is a case in point.

For Aristotle and other ancient Greek authorities, an appeal to *ethos* was one based on the character of the person presenting the argument, whether that might have to do with the speaker's position of authority, his or her perceived honesty, or other ethical virtues. In modern usage, *ethos* is still used to refer to the character of the person putting forward an argument, but there may be more factors that come into play today in determining this character. The idea of authority is a case in point. Though our society's more populist impulses may make us less inclined to judge the merits of a given argument on the basis of the writer's credentials, reputation still influences the willingness many of us have to extend faith to authors. When Roland Barthes begins "The World of Wrestling" with the bold, seemingly contradictory claim that "The virtue of all-in wrestling is that it is a spectacle of excess," we are in part inclined to give the thought credence, or extend some faith that it will in fact become sensible, because it comes from such an esteemed thinker. Similarly, the idea of virtue today is somewhat more complicated: it is now quite widely accepted that we do not in fact have reliable information as to the virtues—or lack thereof—of the writer of an essay. Yet we can gain a sense of whether a writer seems virtuous or not from any number of tiny cues—in the compassion we may sense in an author's treatment of a subject, or, by contrast, in his or her failure to judge others generously. What this means is that, generally speaking, appeals to *ethos* may be considered to rest on a wider range of characteristics today, for instance on our knowledge of a given speaker and the way in which speakers present themselves, or on the overall personality that we sense behind a particular piece of writing.

Unlike the structural elements of logical arguments (whether as set out according to the principles of classical rhetoric, or according to those of modern manuals for academic essay writing), the sorts of appeals that literary non-fiction makes (to *logos*, *pathos*, and *ethos*) are unlikely ever to follow one upon the other in a predictable order. Appeals to logic may alternate with appeals to emotion, just as narrative and descriptive and argumentative passages may be interspersed one with another. Such alternation is a continual feature of a number of the pieces of literary non-fiction included here, including those by Gourevitch, Toews, and Foster Wallace. Arguments that are almost academic in their tone may alternate with paragraphs in which appeals to *ethos* and *pathos* come to the fore. There may be sudden turns; surprise is a strategy that we tend to associate with narrative fiction but also one that may feature prominently in literary non-fiction. Surprise may be said, for example, to be part of the structure of the Gourevitch piece, as it surely is of Toews's.

It may be appropriate to end this introduction to literary non-fiction with one more glance in the direction of the two points of comparison we've used throughout: the principles of classical rhetoric and those of modern academic essay writing. Both those sets of principles are prescriptive: Aristotle and other ancient classical authorities were endeavouring to explain to their readers how arguments should be structured; the precepts of classical rhetoric were designed to help orators organize and deliver their speeches in a methodical, articulate way. Similarly, modern manuals of essay writing aim to explain to students how such essays should be written; they are designed to help students follow the established conventions of an academic discipline. It is more difficult—perhaps impossible—to provide a blueprint for how to write literary non-fiction—and certainly this introduction makes no attempt to do so. It aims to be descriptive rather than prescriptive—to give some sense of the characteristics of the genre of literary non-fiction, and some sense as well of the degree to which an understanding of rhetorical principles may foster a broader understanding of the lines of argument that contemporary writers of literary non-fiction put forward, and the means of expression they employ in doing so. The selections here do not aim to trace the historical development of the genre. They are intended rather to be representative of the genre as it has developed—to provide some sense, however limited, of its diversity and versatility.

—P.L.

Lucius Annaeus Seneca

C. 4 BCE–65 CE

A philosopher, orator, and tragedian who produced works of lasting significance in each genre he attempted, Lucius Annaeus Seneca was among Imperial Rome's most versatile and admired men of letters. The dark vision and
violent emotion of his tragedies, which resound with rhetorically elaborate
speeches voiced by characters at extremes of distress, greatly influenced many
Tudor and Jacobean dramatists, including Shakespeare. The impact of his
prose works, in which he often adopts the persona of a moral or spiritual
adviser who addresses the reader in an engagingly frank and personal style,
was similarly far-reaching, providing writers such as Montaigne with a model
for the introspective essay.

In addition to his literary accomplishments, Seneca was also a statesman.
Banished in the wake of allegations of adultery, he was recalled from exile
to be a teacher to the young Nero; when Nero became emperor, Seneca rose
to political prominence as a senior advisor to his former pupil. For almost a
decade, Seneca occupied the very centre of power in Rome, but his influence
began to ebb as the emperor became increasingly erratic and extravagant.
With his position growing more tenuous, Seneca eventually withdrew to private life, but Nero nevertheless accused him of involvement in a conspiracy
and ordered him to commit suicide.

Before Nero's cruel ultimatum, which he obeyed with composure in a
scene famously recorded by Tacitus, Seneca wrote his masterpiece, the *Moral
Letters to Lucilius* (c. 65 CE). A series of 124 essays presented as a correspondence addressed to Lucilius Iunior, the governor of Sicily, the *Letters* represent a major contribution to Stoic philosophy. Like many later Stoics, Seneca
was especially interested in ethics, and the *Letters* describe a course of moral
therapy intended to improve the reader's character by offering guidance in
how to subdue emotion through reason and so maintain self-possession in
the face of adversity.

Epistle 47[1] from *Moral Letters to Lucilius*

I was pleased to learn from those who come from you that you live on familiar terms with your slaves. That is appropriate for a man of your intelligence
and education. "They are slaves," people say. No—they are people. "They are
slaves." No—they are attendant comrades. "But slaves is what they are." No—

---

1   *Epistle 47* Translation prepared for this anthology by Ian Johnston, Vancouver Island
University.

they are unassuming friends. "They are slaves." No—they are *fellow*-slaves, if you recognize that Fortune values both me and them quite equally.

And so I laugh at those who think it is demeaning to dine with one of their own slaves. Why would they think this, unless the reason is that our proudest customs require the master at his dinner to have a crowd of slaves standing around him? He eats more than he can hold and, in his enormous greed, stuffs his swollen belly, which now no longer functions as a stomach. So with a greater effort than it took to gorge himself he vomits up the entire meal. Meanwhile, the unhappy slaves are not permitted to move their lips, not even to speak. The rod suppresses every murmur. Even a random noise—a cough, a sneeze, a hiccup—earns them the whip. The punishment for any word that interrupts the silence is extremely harsh. All night long, the slaves stand there, mute and hungry.

As a result, those who are not permitted to speak in the presence of their master, talk about him. However, when slaves whose mouths were not stitched shut used to talk not only in the presence of their masters but also with them, they were prepared to stretch their necks out for their master's sake, to let any imminent threat to him fall on their heads. They would talk during the feast, but during torture they were silent. Later, thanks to this arrogance of masters the proverb spread, "To have as many enemies as one has slaves." When we acquire slaves, they are not enemies, but we make them our foes.

At the moment I will overlook other cruel and inhuman ways we treat our slaves, for we abuse them as if they were not even human beings, but beasts of burden. While we recline at ease to dine, one slave wipes up the vomit, another, crouching underneath the table, collects the leavings of the drunken guests. Another carves the expensive birds. With a practiced hand his sure strokes cut around the breast and rump, and he serves the portions, unhappy man who lives for this one task of carving plump fowl skillfully—unless the person who for pleasure's sake instructs this skill is even more unhappy than the one who learns it from necessity. Still another slave, who serves the wine and wears a woman's fancy clothes, struggles against his age, for he cannot escape being dragged back to his boyish years. By now he has a soldier's look, but his hair is scraped away or plucked out by the root to keep him beardless, and he must stay awake all night, dividing his time between his master's drunkenness and lust: in the bedroom he is a man, and at the feast a boy. Another one, whose job is to evaluate the guests, keeps standing there in misery to watch for those whose fawning flattery and intemperance in what they eat or what they say will invite them back tomorrow. Think of the ones who must prepare the feast, those with subtle expertise about their master's palate, who know the things whose taste excites it, whose appearance pleases him, whose novelty can rouse him from his nausea, as well as which foods will now disgust him if he gets too much and which will stimulate his appetite that day. With these slaves the master does not deign to eat. He believes that coming to the same table with his own slave diminishes his majesty. God forbid!

How many masters is he acquiring with slaves like these! I have observed Callistus'[1] master—the one who stuck a bill of sale on him and took him to the market with the useless slaves—standing before Callistus' door and kept outside while others entered. Callistus was included in the first job lot of slaves on which the auctioneer warms up his voice, and now the slave has paid his master back by rejecting him, in turn, and judging him unworthy to come in his house. The master sold Callistus, but how much has Callistus made his master pay!

You would do well to recognize that the man you call your slave sprang from the same seeds as you, enjoys the same sky, breathes, lives, and dies just as you do! You can look on him as a free born man, as much as he can see you as a slave. In that disaster caused by Marius,[2] many men of very splendid birth, preparing for a senatorial rank by military service, were sunk by Fortune, who made one of them a shepherd and another the custodian of a cottage. Now condemn the man whose change in fortune you may share while you condemn him.

I have no wish to involve myself in a huge issue and to explore the way we treat our slaves, towards whom we are excessively proud, cruel, and abusive. But the main thrust of my advice is this: live with your inferiors just as you would wish your superior to live with you. Whenever it crosses your mind how much you can do quite lawfully to a slave of yours, think about how much your master can legally inflict on you.

"But I," you may well say, "don't have a master." You are still young. Perhaps you will have one. Do you not know how old Hecuba was when she became a slave—or Croesus, or Darius' mother, or Plato, or Diogenes?[3]

Live with your slave calmly, even as a friend. Let him enter your conversations, your deliberations, and your social intercourse. At this point the whole crowd of those spoiled with luxury will complain to me: "Nothing would be

---

1   *Callistus* Gaius Julius Callistus (first century CE), a freed Roman slave who rose to political prominence.

2   *Marius* Gaius Marius (157–86 BCE) was a Roman general and politician. Near the end of his life his achievement of political authority brought about a brief period of murderous attacks against many prominent Romans.

3   *Hecuba* Wife of Priam, king of Troy. She became a slave after the city fell; *Croesus* Fabulously rich and powerful king of Lydia in the sixth century BCE. He was defeated and enslaved by the Persians; *Darius* Persian emperor (fourth century BCE) conquered by Alexander the Great; *Plato, or Diogenes* The Greek philosophers Plato (c. 427–c. 347 BCE) and Diogenes (fourth century BCE) also were captured and briefly enslaved.

more degrading than this, nothing more repulsive." These are the same people I will discover kissing the hand of other people's slaves.

Surely you recognize the fact that our ancestors removed everything invidious from the masters and everything insulting from the slaves? They called the master *father of the family*, and the slaves *members of the household*, a practice which still continues in the mimes.[1] They set up a festival day when masters ate with their slaves, but that was not the only time this happened. They assigned slaves honours in the house, permitted them to render judgment, and considered the house a miniature commonwealth.

"What then? Shall I bring all my slaves to my own table?" No. No more than you would bring all free men there. You are wrong if you think I would bar certain men who do more menial work—like, say, that herdsman or that slave who tends the mules. I will not judge them by the work they do, but by their characters. Each person gives himself his character; chance gives him his work. Let some slaves dine with you because they are worthy men, and dine with some to make them worthy. For if debased associations have made them servile, then the society of distinguished men will shake that off.

My dear Lucilius, you should not look for a friend only in the forum or the senate house. If you pay attention carefully, you will find one at home. Often without a skilled artist, good material is wasted. Try and you will find that out. Just as someone who is going to purchase a horse is a fool if he inspects the saddle and the bridle but not the animal itself, so that person is extremely stupid who evaluates a man either by his clothes or by his social condition (which, like our robes, is merely a cover).

"He is a slave." But perhaps his spirit is free. "He is slave." Will that make him culpable? Show me who is not a slave. One man is a slave to lust, another to avarice, another to ambition, and all are slaves to fear. I will show you an ex-consul enslaved to a little old woman, a rich man enslaved to a young serving maid. I will point out young men of the highest rank who are slaves of pantomimes! No slavery is more repulsive than voluntary servitude.

And so those fastidious types should not prevent you from acting affably with your slaves rather than proudly superior. To you your slaves should show respect rather than fear.

Someone may say that now I am calling for slaves to have the cap of liberty and for masters to be cast down from their lofty heights when I say slaves should respect their master rather than fear him. "That is precisely what he is saying: slaves are to show respect, as if they were clients or polite visitors." A man who says such things forgets that what satisfies a god is not too little for

---

1   *mimes* Popular form of theatre in ancient Rome.

a master. The man who is respected is also loved, but love and fear cannot be mixed together.

So, in my judgment, your actions are entirely correct, for you do not wish your slaves to fear you, and you punish them with words. We use a whip to reprimand dumb beasts. Everything which offends us does not do us harm. But our fastidiousness drives us into savage rage, so that whatever does not answer our desires, brings out our anger. We wrap ourselves up in royal passions. For kings also forget their own power and the weaknesses of other men and so grow hot and boil with rage, as if they had received an injury, when the loftiness of their position keeps them completely safe from any danger. They are not unaware of this, but by complaining they seize an opportunity to harm someone. They say they have been injured in order to inflict an injury.

I do not wish to delay you any longer. For you do not need my exhortations. Among their other traits, good characters possess this quality: they make their own decisions and hold to them. Malice is fickle and changes frequently, not into something better but merely something different.

Farewell.

—c. 65 CE

Michel de Montaigne
1533–1592

Michel de Montaigne is frequently credited with creating the modern essay. He was the first to use the word "essay" (meaning "attempt" in French) in its modern sense, applying the term to his efforts to arrive at a deeper understanding not only of his own experience as a human being, but of the universal experience of being human. Montaigne may have perfected the essay—which he approached less as a form than as a technique—but he was preceded by such ancient Roman practitioners of philosophical introspection as Plutarch, Cicero, and Seneca, all of whom figure in his masterpiece collection, the *Essays* (1580–95). In these writings, Montaigne establishes an intimacy with the reader such that we seem to overhear a man in conversation with himself, testing his own values, judgments, ideas, and beliefs in a forthright spirit of skeptical inquiry.

The *Essays* do not describe the evolution of a system of thought or a theory of knowledge, but instead explore topics as various as religious tolerance ("Of Cato the Younger"), sexual proclivities ("Of Some Verses of Virgil"), and cultural norms ("Of Cannibals"). The result is a self-portrait of a human being in the process of feeling, thinking, and changing. The meandering, digressive structure of the individual pieces and the randomness of their arrangement reflect the changeful, idiosyncratic, and infinitely curious nature of the mind in which they originated. As Montaigne observed of his project, "I do not portray being; I portray passing."

Born to a wealthy Roman Catholic merchant, Montaigne received a thorough education in Latin, philosophy, and law, and during his lifetime held positions as a courtier, a diplomat, a magistrate, and the mayor of Bordeaux. The *Essays* were first translated from French into English in 1603, and were influential in England as well as France, inspiring writers of philosophy and of literature such as René Descartes, Francis Bacon, and William Shakespeare.

On Cannibals[1]

When king Pyrrhus[2] moved across into Italy and had scouted out the organization of the army which the Romans sent out against him, he observed, "I do not know what sort of barbarians these are" (for the Greeks used to call all

---

1   *On Cannibals* This translation, prepared for this anthology by Ian Johnston of Vancouver Island University, is based upon the final (1595) version of the essay. Montaigne's frequent quotations in Latin have also been translated into English.

2   *Pyrrhus* King of Epirus (306–272 BCE), northwestern Greece, who invaded Italy; despite his skill as a general, he was eventually defeated.

foreign nations by that name) "but the formation of this army I am looking at has nothing barbarous about it." The Greeks said much the same about the army Flaminius[1] marched through their country, and so did Philip, when he looked down from a hillock on the order and layout of the Roman camp built in his kingdom under the command of Publius Sulpicius Galba.[2] There we see how we should be careful of clinging to common opinions and should judge them with the eye of reason, not by popular report.

For a long time I had with me a man who had lived ten or twelve years in that other world which was discovered in our century, in the place where Villegaignon[3] landed, which he called Antarctic France. This discovery of such an enormous country seems to merit serious consideration. I do not know if I can affirm that another such discovery will not occur in the future, given that so many people more important than we have been wrong about this one. I fear that our eyes are larger than our stomachs, that we have more curiosity than comprehension. We embrace everything, yet catch nothing but wind. Plato introduces Solon[4] telling a story which he had learned from the priests in the city of Saïs in Egypt. They said that long ago, before the Deluge,[5] there was a huge island called Atlantis, right at the entry to the Straits of Gibraltar,[6] which had more land than all of Africa and Asia combined and that the kings of this country not only possessed this island but also had extended their control so far into the mainland that they held territories across the width of Africa as far as Egypt and across Europe as far as Tuscany. They were planning to march over into Asia and to subjugate all nations bordering the Mediterranean up to the Black Sea. To achieve this they had moved across Spain, Gaul,[7] and Italy, all the way to Greece, where the Athenians stopped them. However, sometime later both the Athenians and these people, along with their island, were swallowed by the Flood.

It is very probable that this extreme inundation of water brought about strange alterations in the habitable regions of the earth, like the ones in which, so people say, the sea separated Sicily from Italy—

1   *Flaminius* Titus Quinctius Flaminius, Roman politician and military leader who obtained a Roman victory over Philip V of Macedon in the Second Macedonian War (200–196 BCE).
2   *Philip ... Publius Sulpicius Galba* Philip V fought against the Roman politician and general Publius Sulpicius Galba Maximus in the First Macedonian War (214–205 BCE).
3   *Villegaignon* In 1555 Nicolas Durand Villegaignon landed in the Bay of Rio de Janeiro, Brazil, and set up a French colony on a nearby island.
4   *Solon* Historical figure to whom the following story is attributed in Plato's dialogue *Critias* (fourth century BCE).
5   *Deluge* I.e., great flood; see the story of Noah in Genesis 6–8.
6   *Straits of Gibraltar* Strait at the mouth of the Mediterranean Sea.
7   *Gaul* France.

> They claim these places once were ripped apart
> by an enormously destructive force,
> where earlier both lands had been united[1]—

and split Cyprus from Syria, the island of Euboea from the mainland of Boeotia,[2] and in other places joined lands which had been separated, filling the trenches between them with sand and mud.

> ... long a sterile marsh on which men rowed
> it nourishes the neighbouring towns
> and feels the ploughshare's weight.[3]

But it does not seem very likely that this new world we have just discovered was this island of Atlantis, for it almost touched Spain, and the effect of that inundation would have been incredible if it had pushed the island back to where the new world is, a distance of more than twelve hundred leagues. Moreover, modern navigators have almost certainly already established that the new world is not an island but a mainland, connected on one side with the East Indies and on the other with the lands under the two poles. Or else, if it is divided off from them, what separates it is a narrow strait, a distance that does not entitle it to be called an island.

In these large bodies, as in our own, it appears that there are movements, some natural and others feverish. When I consider the inroads which my river, the Dordogne,[4] has made during my lifetime in the right bank of its descending flow and realize that in twenty years it has gained so much and washed away the foundations of several buildings, I clearly see that the disturbance has been extraordinary. For if it had always worked in this way or were to do so in future, the face of the earth would be completely altered. But rivers undergo changes: sometimes they overrun one bank, sometimes the other, and sometimes they flow between them. I am not speaking about sudden floods, whose causes we understand. In Medoc, along the seashore, my brother, the Sieur d'Arsac,[5] looks out at one of his estates being buried under the sand which the sea vomits up in front of her. The tops of some buildings are still visible. His rental properties and his fields have been turned into very poor pasture. The inhabitants say that for some years the sea has been pushing towards them so strongly that they have lost four leagues of ground. These sands are her harbinger: we see huge mounds of moving sand marching half a league in front

---

1   *They claim ... been united* From Virgil, *Aeneid* 3.414.
2   *Euboea* Greek island; *Boeotia* Mainland region of ancient Greece.
3   *... long ... ploughshare's weight* From Horace, *De Arte Poetica* 65.
4   *Dordogne* River that passed by Montaigne's family estate near Bordeaux, France.
5   *Medoc* Region north of Bordeaux; *Sieur d'Arsac* Lord of Arsac, a village in Medoc.

of her and overpowering the land. The other testimony from ancient times to which one could link this discovery of a new world is in Aristotle, at least if that little booklet *On Unheard-of Marvels*[1] is by him. In that work, he tells the story of certain Carthaginians[2] who, after setting out across the Atlantic Ocean beyond the Straits of Gibraltar and sailing for a long time, finally discovered a large fertile island, all covered with trees and watered by wide, deep rivers, a very long way from any mainland. Attracted by the goodness and fertility of the soil, they—and others after them—went with their wives and children and started a settlement there. However, the rulers of Carthage, noticing that their country was gradually losing its people, expressly prohibited any more people from going there, on pain of death, and they drove these new inhabitants out, fearing, so the story goes, that with the passage of time they might multiply to such an extent that they would supplant the Carthaginians themselves and ruin their state. But this story from Aristotle does not accord with our new lands any more than Plato's does.

The man I had with me was a plain, rough fellow, the sort likely to provide a true account. For intelligent people notice more and are much more curious, but they also provide their own gloss on things and, to strengthen their own interpretation and make it persuasive, they cannot help changing their story a little. They never give you a pure picture of things, but bend and disguise them to fit the view they had of them. To lend credit to their judgment and attract you to it, they willingly add to the material, stretching it out and amplifying it. We need either a very honest man or one so simple that he lacks what it takes to build up inventive falsehoods and make them plausible, someone not wedded to anything. My man was like that, and, in addition, at various times he brought some sailors and merchants he had known on that voyage to see me. Thus, I am happy with his information, without enquiring into what the cosmographers may say about it.

We need topographers who provide us a detailed account of the places they have been. But because they have seen Palestine and have that advantage over us, they wish to enjoy the privilege of telling us news about all the rest of the world. I would like everyone to write about what he knows, and only as much as he knows, not merely on this subject but on all others. For a person can have some specific knowledge of or experience with the nature of a river or a fountain and yet in other things know only what everyone else does. Yet, to publicize his small scrap of knowledge, he will undertake to write about all of physics. From this vice several serious difficulties arise.

---

1   *On Unheard-of Marvels* De mirabilibus auscultationibus, a text often falsely attributed to Aristotle during the sixteenth century.
2   *Carthaginians* Carthage was a major civilization in northern Africa and the Mediterranean region from the eighth to the second centuries BCE.

Now, to return to my subject, I find, from what I have been told about these people, that there is nothing barbarous and savage about them, except that everyone calls things which he does not practice himself barbaric. For, in fact, we have no test of truth and of reason other than examples and ideas of the opinions and habits in the country where we live. There we always have the perfect religion, the perfect political arrangements, the perfect and most accomplished ways of dealing with everything. Those natives are wild in the same way we call wild the fruits which nature has produced on her own in her normal manner; whereas, in fact, the ones we should really call wild are those we have altered artificially and whose ordinary behaviour we have modified. The former contain vital and vigorous virtues and properties, genuinely beneficial and natural, qualities which we have bastardized in the latter, by adapting them to gratify our corrupt taste. Nonetheless, the very flavour and delicacy in various uncultivated fruits from those countries over there are excellent even to our taste—they rival the fruit we produce. It is unreasonable that art should win the place of honour over our great and powerful mother nature. We have overburdened the beauty and richness of her works with our inventions to such an extent that we have completely suffocated her. Yet wherever she shines out in her full purity, her marvels put our vain and frivolous enterprises to shame.

> Ivy springs up better on its own
> In lonely caves arbutus grows more fair
> And birds not taught to sing have sweeter songs.[1]

All our efforts cannot succeed in recreating the nest of even the smallest bird—its texture, its beauty, and its practical convenience, let alone the web of the puny spider. All things, Plato states, are produced either by nature or by chance or by art: the greatest and most beautiful by one or other of the first two, the least and most imperfect by the last.

These nations therefore seem to me barbarous in the sense that they have received very little moulding from the human mind and are still very close to their original naive condition. Natural laws still govern them, hardly corrupted at all by our own. They live in such purity that I sometimes regret we did not learn about them earlier, at a time when there were men more capable of assessing them than we are. I am sad that Lycurgus[2] and Plato did not know them. For it seems to me that what our experience enables us to see in those nations there surpasses not only all the pictures with which poetry has embellished

---

1   *Ivy springs ... sweeter songs* From Propertius 1.2.10.
2   *Lycurgus* Political thinker who, according to legend, established the laws of Sparta in the eighth century BCE. It is not known whether he actually existed.

the Golden Age, as well as all its inventiveness in portraying a happy human condition, but also the conceptions and even the desires of philosophy. They have scarcely imagined such a pure and simple innocence as the one our experience reveals to us, and they would hardly have believed that our society could survive with so little artifice and social bonding among people. It is a nation, I would tell Plato, in which there is no form of commerce, no knowledge of letters, no science of numbers, no name for magistrate or political superior, no customs of servitude, no wealth or poverty, no contracts, no inheritance, no division of property, no occupations, other than leisure ones, no respect for family kinship, except for common ties, no clothing, no agriculture, no metal, no use of wine or wheat. The very words which signify lying, treason, dissimulation, avarice, envy, slander, and forgiveness are unknown. How distant from this perfection would Plato find the republic he imagined—"men freshly come from the gods."[1]

These are the habits nature first ordained.[2]

As for the rest, they live in a very pleasant and temperate country, so that, according to what my witnesses have told me, it is rare to see a sick person there. They have assured me that in this land one does not notice any of the inhabitants doddering, with rheumy eyes, toothless, or bowed down with old age. They have settled along the sea coast, closed off on the landward side by large, high mountains, with a stretch of territory about one hundred leagues wide in between. They have a great abundance of fish and meat, which has no resemblances to ours and which they simply cook and eat, without any other preparation. The first man who rode a horse there, although he had had dealings with them on several other voyages, so horrified them by his riding posture, that they killed him with arrows before they could recognize him.

Their buildings are very long, capable of holding two or three hundred souls, and covered with the bark of large trees. Strips of bark are held in the earth at one end and support and lean against one another at the top, in the style of some of our barns, in which the roof comes right down to the ground and acts as a wall. They have a wood so hard they cut with it and use it to make swords and grills to cook their meat. Their beds are made of woven cotton, suspended from the roof, like those of our sailors. Each man has his own, for the wives sleep separate from their husbands. They rise with the sun and, as soon as they get up, they eat to last them all day, for they have no other meal except that one. At that time they do not drink, like certain other Eastern

---

1   *men freshly ... the gods* From Seneca, *Letters* 90.
2   *These are ... first ordained* From Virgil, *Georgics* 2.20.

peoples Suidas[1] observed, who drank only apart from meals. They do drink several times a day and a considerable amount. The beverage is made from some root and is the colour of our claret wines. They drink it only lukewarm. It will keep for only two or three days. The drink has a slightly spicy taste, does not go to one's head, is good for the stomach, and works as a laxative for those who are not accustomed to it, but it is a very pleasant beverage for those who are. Instead of bread they use a certain white material, like preserved coriander. I have tried it—the taste is sweet and somewhat flat.

They spend the entire day dancing. Younger men go off to hunt wild animals with bows. Meanwhile, some of the women keep busy warming the drinks, which is their main responsibility. In the morning, before they begin their meal, one of the old men preaches to everyone in the whole barn, walking from one end to the other and repeating the same sentence several times until he has completed his tour of the building, which is easily one hundred paces long. He recommends only two things to them: courage against their enemies and affection for their wives. And these old men never fail to mention this obligation, adding as a refrain that their wives are the ones who keep their drinks warm and seasoned for them.

In several places, including my own home, there are examples of their beds, their ropes, their swords, their wooden bracelets, which they use to cover their wrists in combat, and their large canes open at one end, with whose sound they keep time in their dances. They are close shaven all over, and remove the hair much more cleanly than we do, using only wood or stone as a razor. They believe that the soul is immortal and that those who have deserved well of the gods are lodged in that part of the sky where the sun rises, while the damned are in regions to the west.

They have some sort of priests or prophets, who appear before the people relatively seldom, for they live in the mountains. When they arrive, there is a grand celebration and a solemn assembly of several villages (each barn, as I have described it, makes up a village, and the distance between them is approximately one French league). This prophet speaks to them in public, urging them to be virtuous and to do their duty. But their entire ethical knowledge contains only the two following articles, courage in warfare and affection for their wives. He prophesies to them about things to come and about the results they should expect from their endeavours and encourages them to go to war or to refrain from it. But he does this on the condition, that he must prophesy correctly, and if what happens to them is different from what he has predicted, he is cut up into a thousand pieces, if they catch him, and condemned as a

---

1   *Suidas* Name applied to the author of the *Suda* (10th century CE), a reference work compiling information from classical and early medieval sources.

false prophet. For this reason, a prophet who has been wrong once is never seen again.

Divination is a gift of God. For that reason, abusing it should be punished as fraud. Among the Scythians,[1] when the divines failed with their predictions, they were chained by their hands and feet, laid out on carts full of kindling and pulled by oxen, and burned there. Those who deal with matters in which the outcome depends on what human beings are capable of may be excused if they do their best. But surely the others, those who come to us with deluding assurances of an extraordinary faculty beyond our understanding, should be punished for not keeping their promises and for the recklessness of their deceit.

These natives have wars with the nations living on the other side of their mountains, further inland. They go out against them completely naked with no weapons except bows or wooden swords with a point at one end, like the tips of our hunting spears. What is astonishing is their resolution in combat, which never ends except in slaughter and bloodshed, for they have no idea of terror or flight. Each man brings back as a trophy the head of the enemy he has killed and attaches it to the entrance of his dwelling. After treating their prisoners well for a long time with every consideration they can possibly think of, the man who has a prisoner summons a grand meeting of his acquaintances. He ties a rope to one of the prisoner's arms and holds him there, gripping the other end, some paces away for fear of being injured, and he gives his dearest friend the prisoner's other arm to hold in the same way. Then the two of them, in the presence of the entire assembly, stab the prisoner to death with their swords. After that, they roast him. Then they all eat him together and send portions to their absent friends. They do this not, as people think, to nourish themselves, the way the Scythians did in ancient times, but as an act manifesting extreme vengeance. We see evidence for this from the following: having noticed that the Portuguese, who were allied with their enemies, used a different method of killing them when they took them prisoner—which was to bury them up to the waist, shoot the rest of their body full of arrows, and then hang them—they thought that this people who had come there from another world (and who had already spread the knowledge of many vicious practices throughout the neighbouring region and were much greater masters of all sorts of evil than they were) did not select this sort of vengeance for no reason and that therefore this method must be harsher than their own. And so they began to abandon their old practice and to follow this one.

---

1   *Scythians* Nomadic people who flourished in parts of Eastern Europe and Central Asia in the first millennium BCE.

I am not so much concerned that we call attention to the barbarous horror of this action as I am that, in judging their faults correctly, we should be so blind to our own. I believe that there is more barbarity in eating a man when he is alive than in eating him when he is dead, more in tearing apart by tortures and the rack a body still full of feeling, roasting it piece by piece, having it mauled and eaten by dogs and pigs (things I have not only read about but witnessed a short time ago, not among ancient enemies but among neighbours and fellow citizens, and, what is worse, under the pretext of piety and religion) than there is in roasting and eating a man once he has died.

In fact, Chrysippus and Zeno,[1] leaders of the Stoic sect, thought that there was nothing wrong in using our corpses for any purpose whatsoever, in case of need, including as a source of food, as our ancestors did when they were being besieged by Julius Caesar in the town of Alesia[2] and resolved to stave off the hunger of this siege with the bodies of old men, women, and other people useless in combat.

> They say the Gascons with such foods as these
> Prolonged their lives.[3]

And doctors are not afraid of using a dead body for all sorts of purposes in order to preserve our health, applying it either internally or externally. But no one has ever come across a point of view so unreasonable that it excuses treason, disloyalty, tyranny, and cruelty, which are common faults of ours.

Thus, we can indeed call these natives barbarians, as far as the laws of reason are concerned, but not in comparison with ourselves, who surpass them in barbarity of every kind. Their warfare is entirely noble and generous, as excusable and beautiful as this human malady can possibly be. With them it is based only on one thing, a jealous rivalry in courage. They do not argue about conquering new lands, for they still enjoy that natural fecundity which furnishes them without toil and trouble everything necessary and in such abundance that they do not need to expand their borders. They are still at that fortunate stage where they do not desire anything more than their natural demands prescribe. Everything over and above that is for them superfluous.

Those among them of the same age generally call each other brothers, those who are younger they call children, and the old men are fathers to all the others. These leave the full possession of their goods undivided to their

---

1   *Chrysippus and Zeno* Greek philosophers of the third and fourth centuries BCE.
2   *Alesia* Site of a major battle in Julius Caesar's 52 BCE invasion of Gaul (France), in which he defeated a coalition of French tribes.
3   *They say ... their lives* From Juvenal, *Satires* 15.93; *Gascons* Natives of Gascony, a southwestern region of France.

heirs in common, without any other title, except the completely simple one which nature gives to all her creatures by bringing them into the world.

If their neighbours cross the mountains to attack them and defeat them in battle, what the victors acquire is glory and the advantage of having proved themselves more courageous and valiant. For they have no further interest in the possessions of the conquered. They return to their own country, where they have no lack of anything they need, just as they do not lack that great benefit of knowing how to enjoy their condition in happiness and how to remain content with it. And the natives we are talking about, when their turn comes, do the same. They demand no ransom of their prisoners, other than a confession and a recognition that they have been beaten. But in an entire century there has not been one prisoner who did not prefer to die rather than to yield, either by his expression or by his words, a single bit of the grandeur of his invincible courage. Not one of them has been observed who did not prefer to be killed and eaten than merely to ask that he be spared. They treat the captives very freely, so that their lives will be all the more dear to them, and commonly make conversational threats about their coming death and the torments they will have to suffer, mentioning the preparations which are being made for this event, the slicing off of their limbs, and the celebrations which will be held at their expense. They do all this with one purpose in mind, to drag from the prisoners' mouths some weak or demeaning words or to make them eager to run away, in order to gain the advantage of having scared them and broken their resolution. For, all things well considered, that is the only point which makes a victory genuine.

> There is no victory
> except the one which conquers enemies who in their minds confess it.[1]

Long ago the Hungarians, who were very bellicose warriors, never pushed their advantage any further once they had made the enemy plead for mercy. For having wrung this confession from him, they let him go unharmed and without ransom, except, at most, for exacting his promise that he would not take up arms against them from that moment on.

We gain a number of advantages over our enemies which are borrowed and not our own. It is the quality of a porter, not of virtue, to have sturdier arms and legs: it is an inert and bodily quality, not an active habit. It is a stroke of luck which makes our enemy stumble and blinds his eyes with light from the sun. It is a trick of art and technique, which one may find in a worthless coward, that makes a competent fencer. The courage and value of a man lie in his heart and in his will: there one finds his true honour. Valour is strength,

---

1   *There is ... confess it* From Claudius, *On the Sixth Consulship of Honorius* 248.

not of legs and arms, but of courage and spirit. It does not consist of the value of our horse or of our weapons, but of ourselves: the man who falls still courageous and resolute, who "if his legs fail fights on his knees,"[1] who, whatever the danger of imminent death, does not relax his assertiveness one bit, and who, as he gives up his soul, still looks at his enemy with a firm and scornful eye—he is beaten, not by us but by fortune. He has been killed but not conquered. The most valiant are sometimes the most unfortunate.

Thus, there are defeats which are triumphs, as splendid as victories. Even those four sister victories, the most beautiful the eyes of the sun have ever gazed upon—Salamis, Plataea, Mycale, and Sicily[2]—never dared set all their combined glories up against the glorious defeat of king Leonidas and his men at the pass of Thermopylae.[3]

What soldier ever rushed with a more glorious and more ambitious desire to win a battle than captain Ischolas[4] did to lose one? Who has been more ingenious and more careful in ensuring his safety than he was in ensuring his own destruction. He was charged with defending a certain pass in the Peloponnese against the Arcadians.[5] Judging that this was completely impossible, given the nature of the place and the disparity in the numbers of troops, he decided that all those who confronted the enemy would have to die there. On the other hand, he thought it unworthy of his own virtue and magnanimity and of the Lacedaemonian[6] name to fail in his responsibilities. So between these two extremes he chose a middle course, as follows: he saved the youngest and most energetic of his force for the defence and service of their county, by sending them back, and he determined to hold the pass with those whose loss was less significant and by their deaths to do as much as he possibly could to make his enemies pay the highest price for their entry through it. And that is what happened. For they were soon surrounded on all sides by the Arcadians, and, after slaughtering a great many of them, he and his men were all put to the sword. Is there any trophy dedicated to the victors which would not be more deservingly given to these conquered men? A genuine victory emerges

---

1   *if his ... his knees* From Seneca, *On Providence* 2.
2   *Salamis, Plataea, Mycale* Series of Greek victories that brought an end to the second Persian invasion of Greece (480–479 BCE); *Sicily* In the First Sicilian War, also in 480 BCE, Greece defeated the attacking Carthaginians.
3   *the glorious ... of Thermopylae* During the second Persian invasion of Greece, the Spartan King Leonidas I and a hopelessly outnumbered Greek force held off the invading Persian army for several days; Leonidas and all of his soldiers died.
4   *Ischolas* Spartan commander of the fourth century BCE.
5   *Peloponnese* Peninsula in southern Greece; *Arcadians* Allied city-states of the region of Arcadia, in the Peloponnese.
6   *Lacedaemonian* Spartan.

from battle, not from survival, and virtuous honour lies in fighting, not in conquering.

To return to our story. These prisoners are so far from surrendering, in spite of everything done to them, that, by contrast, during the two or three months they are held, they look cheerful and urge their masters to hurry up and put them to the test. They defy and insult them. They reproach them with cowardice and the number of battles they have lost fighting against them. I have a song composed by one prisoner which contains a taunting invitation for them all to step up boldly and gather to dine on him, because they will at the same time be eating their fathers and grandfathers who have served to feed and nourish his body. "These muscles," he says, "this flesh, these veins—these are your own, poor fools that you are. You do not recognize that the substance of your ancestors' limbs is still contained in them. Savour them well. You will find there the taste of your own flesh"—an imaginative notion without the slightest flavour of barbarity. Those who paint these people as they die and depict what is going on when they are struck down show the prisoner spitting in the faces of his executioners and curling his lip at them in contempt. In fact, they do not stop their challenges and defiance with words and gestures right up to their final breath. Truly we have here really savage men in comparison to us. For that is what they must be beyond all doubt—either that, or we must be, for there is an amazing distance between their ways and ours.

The men there have several wives, and the higher their reputation for valour the greater the number. In their marriages there is something remarkably beautiful: with our wives jealousy deprives us of the friendship and kindness of other women, but with them a very similar jealousy leads their wives to acquire these relationships for their men. Since they care more for the honour of their husbands than for anything else, they go to great lengths to seek out and obtain as many companions for them as they can, since that is a testimony to their husbands' merit.

Our wives will cry out that this is a miracle. It is not. It is a proper marital virtue, but of the highest order. In the Bible, Leah, Rachel, Sarah, and Jacob's wives gave their beautiful servants to their husbands.[1] And Livia supported the appetites of Augustus,[2] to her own disadvantage. And Stratonice, wife of

---

1   *Leah, Rachel ... their husbands* Cf. Genesis 30. Jacob had children with his wives Rachel and Leah, as well as with their slaves Bilhah and Zilpah. Sarah, Abraham's wife, was barren, and offered her servant to Abraham as a surrogate.

2   *Livia supported ... of Augustus* Livia (58 BCE–29 CE) was the second wife of the Roman Emperor Augustus, who had a reputation as a womanizer; it was rumoured that Livia helped to find new virgins for him.

King Deiotarus[1] not only provided her husband for his own pleasure a very beautiful young housemaid in her service, but also carefully brought up her children and supported them as successors to their father's estates.

And so that people do not think that they do all this out of a simple and servile duty to habit and under pressure from the authority of their ancient customs, without reflection and judgment, because they have such stupid souls that they cannot choose any other way, I must cite some features of their capabilities. Apart from what I have just recited from one of their warrior songs, I have another, a love song which begins as follows: "Adder, stay, stay, adder, so that from the coloured markings on your skin my sister may take down the style and workmanship for a rich belt which I can give the woman I love—and in this way your beauty and your patterning will be preferred forever above all other snakes." This first couplet is the refrain of the song. Now, I am sufficiently familiar with poetry to judge this one: not only is there nothing barbaric in the imagination here, but it captures the spirit of Anacreon[2] throughout. Their language, too, is soft, with a pleasing sound, not unlike Greek in its word endings.

Three of these men, not knowing how much it will cost them one day in a loss of repose and happiness to learn about the corruptions among us and how interacting with us will lead to their ruin, which I assume is already well advanced (poor miserable creatures to let themselves be seduced by the desire for novelty and to have left the softness of their sky to come and see ours) were at Rouen when the late King Charles IX was there.[3] The king talked to them for a long time. They were shown our way of life, our splendour, and the layout of a beautiful city. After that, someone asked them their opinion, wishing to learn from them what they had found most astonishing. They answered that there were three things. I regret to say that I have forgotten the third, but I still remember two. They said, first of all, that they found it very strange that so many large, strong men with beards and weapons, who were around the king (they were probably talking about the Swiss soldiers in his guard) would agree to obey a child and that one of them was not chosen to command instead; and secondly (in their language they have a way of speaking of men as halves of one another) that they had noticed there were among us men completely

---

1   *Stratonice, wife of King Deiotarus* Stratonice is presented as a model of virtue in Plutarch's *De Mulierum Virtutibus* (*On the Bravery of Women*, first century CE); Plutarch writes that Stratonice, unable to bear children, suggested that Deiotarus secretly produce an heir for the married couple to raise as their own.

2   *Anacreon* Greek poet (c. 572–c. 488 BCE) known for his love lyrics.

3   *Three of ... was there* About fifty Native Brazilians were brought to Rouen in 1550, and some were presented to King Charles IX of France (then 12 years old) when he visited Rouen in 1562.

gorged with all sorts of commodities while their other halves were beggars at their doors, emaciated by hunger and poverty. They found it strange that these needy halves could tolerate such an injustice and did not seize the others by the throat or set fire to their dwellings.

I had a really long talk with one of them, but the interpreter with me followed my meaning so badly and, because of his stupidity, had so much trouble taking in my ideas, that I got hardly anything useful from him. When I asked the native what benefit he received from his superior position among his people (for he was a captain and our sailors called him king), he told me that it was to be the first to march out into battle. How many men followed him? He pointed out to me a piece of ground to indicate that the number was as many as a space like that could hold—it might have been four or five thousand men. Did all his authority end when there was no war? He said one thing remained: when he visited the villages which depended on him, they made pathways for him through the thickets in their forest, so that he could walk along at his ease.

All this does not sound too bad. But what of that? They wear no breeches.
—1580 (revised 1595)

Jonathan Swift
1667–1745

Although the art of literary satire traces its origins to antiquity, its golden age is often said to have occurred in the late seventeenth and eighteenth centuries—the time of Molière, Dryden, Pope, and Voltaire. Among the many gifted satirical minds that set out during this period to lash the vices and follies of mankind, none was more adept than Jonathan Swift, who aimed to "vex the world" into reform but acknowledged the limitations of satire as a "glass wherein beholders do generally discover everybody's face but their own."

Swift is best known as the author of *Gulliver's Travels* (1726), but he initially rose to prominence—first with the Whigs, then with the Tories—as one of the most brilliant political writers of his day. Ordained as a priest in the Anglican Church, Swift entertained hopes for ecclesiastical preferment in England, but when in 1714 the Tory ministry fell with the death of Queen Anne, he reluctantly retreated to his native Ireland, where he had been appointed dean of St. Patrick's Cathedral in Dublin. Here Swift came face to face with the appalling conditions of the Irish poor, whose hardships were much exacerbated by English economic policy. To this day Swift is regarded as a national hero for the many letters and pamphlets—published anonymously though their authorship was generally known—in which he championed Irish political and economic independence, discharging his "savage indignation" in some of the finest prose ever written.

Swift was moved to write much of his satire in response to particular events and circumstances, but the objects of his attack—above all the moral and intellectual failings of the human race—are perennial. "A Modest Proposal" (1729), his darkest, most disturbingly cynical work, appeared at the height of Ireland's wretchedness, a time of rampant inflation, poverty, famine, homelessness, and unemployment.

A Modest Proposal
For Preventing the Children of Poor People in Ireland from Being a Burden to Their Parents or the Country, and for Making Them Beneficial to the Public

It is a melancholy object to those who walk through this great town,[1] or travel in the country, when they see the streets, the roads, and cabin doors crowded with beggars of the female sex, followed by three, four, or six children, all in

---

1   *this great town* I.e., Dublin.

rags and importuning every passenger[1] for an alms. These mothers, instead of being able to work for their honest livelihood, are forced to employ all their time in strolling[2] to beg sustenance for their helpless infants, who, as they grow up, either turn thieves for want of work, or leave their dear native country to fight for the Pretender in Spain, or sell themselves to the Barbados.[3]

I think it is agreed by all parties that this prodigious number of children in the arms, or on the backs, or at the heels of their mothers, and frequently of their fathers, is, in the present deplorable state of the kingdom, a very great additional grievance; and therefore, whoever could find out a fair, cheap, and easy method of making these children sound and useful members of the commonwealth would deserve so well of the public as to have his statue set up for a preserver of the nation.

But my intention is very far from being confined to provide only for the children of professed beggars; it is of a much greater extent, and shall take in the whole number of infants at a certain age who are born of parents in effect as little able to support them as those who demand our charity in the streets.

As to my own part, having turned my thoughts for many years upon this important subject and maturely weighed the several schemes of other projectors,[4] I have always found them grossly mistaken in their computation. 'Tis true, a child just dropped from its dam may be supported by her milk for a solar year with little other nourishment, at most not above the value of two shillings, which the mother may certainly get, or the value in scraps, by her lawful occupation of begging; and it is exactly at one year old that I propose to provide for them in such a manner as, instead of being a charge upon their parents or the parish, or wanting food and raiment for the rest of their lives, they shall on the contrary contribute to the feeding, and partly to the clothing, of many thousands.

There is likewise another great advantage in my scheme, that it will prevent those abortions, and that horrid practice of women murdering their bastard children, alas, too frequent among us, sacrificing the poor innocent babes, I doubt,[5] more to avoid the expense than the shame, which would move tears and pity in the most savage and inhuman breast.

---

1   *passenger* Passerby.
2   *strolling* Wandering, roving.
3   *the Pretender* James Francis Edward Stuart, son of James II who was deposed from the throne in the Glorious Revolution due to his overt Catholicism. Catholic Ireland was loyal to Stuart, and the Irish were often recruited by France and Spain to fight against England; *Barbados* Because of the extreme poverty in Ireland, many Irish people emigrated to the West Indies, selling their labour to sugar plantations in advance to pay for the voyage.
4   *projectors* Those who design or propose experiments or projects.
5   *doubt* Think.

The number of souls in this kingdom being usually reckoned one million and a half, of these I calculate there may be about two hundred thousand couples whose wives are breeders, from which number I subtract thirty thousand couples who are able to maintain children, although I apprehend there cannot be as many under the present distresses of the kingdom; but this being granted, there will remain one hundred and seventy thousand breeders.

I again subtract fifty thousand for those women who miscarry, or whose children die by accident or disease within the year. There only remain one hundred and twenty thousand children of poor parents annually born. The question therefore is how this number shall be reared and provided for, which, as I have already said, under the present situation of affairs is utterly impossible by all the methods hitherto proposed. For we can neither employ them in handicraft or agriculture; we neither build houses (I mean in the country) nor cultivate land.[1] They can very seldom pick up a livelihood by stealing till they arrive at six years old, except where they are of towardly parts,[2] although I confess they learn the rudiments much earlier, during which time they can however be properly looked upon only as probationers, as I have been informed by a principal gentleman in the county of Cavan, who protested to me that he never knew above one or two instances under the age of six, even in a part of the kingdom so renowned for the quickest proficiency in that art.

I am assured by our merchants that a boy or a girl before twelve years old is no saleable commodity; and even when they come to this age, they will not yield above three pounds, or three pounds and half a crown at most, on the Exchange, which cannot turn to account[3] either to the parents or the kingdom, the charge of nutriment and rags having been at least four times that value.

I shall now therefore humbly propose my own thoughts, which I hope will not be liable to the least objection.

I have been assured by a very knowing American[4] of my acquaintance in London that a young healthy child well nursed is at a year old a most delicious, nourishing, and wholesome food, whether stewed, roasted, baked, or boiled; and I make no doubt that it will equally serve in a fricassee or a ragout.[5]

I do therefore humbly offer it to public consideration that of the hundred and twenty thousand children already computed, twenty thousand may be

---

1   *neither build ... land* The British placed numerous restrictions on the Irish agricultural industry, retaining the majority of land for the grazing of sheep. The vast estates of British absentee landlords further contributed to Ireland's poverty.
2   *of towardly parts* Exceptionally able.
3   *on the Exchange* At the market; *turn to account* Result in profit.
4   *American* I.e., Native American.
5   *fricassee or a ragout* Stews.

reserved for breed, whereof only one fourth part to be males, which is more than we allow to sheep, black cattle, or swine, and my reason is that these children are seldom the fruits of marriage, a circumstance not much regarded by our savages; therefore, one male will be sufficient to serve four females. That the remaining hundred thousand may at a year old be offered in sale to the persons of quality and fortune through the kingdom, always advising the mother to let them suck plentifully of the last month, so as to render them plump and fat for a good table. A child will make two dishes at an entertainment for friends, and when the family dines alone, the fore or hind quarter will make a reasonable dish, and seasoned with a little pepper or salt will be very good boiled on the fourth day, especially in winter.

I have reckoned upon a medium that a child just born will weigh twelve pounds, and in a solar year if tolerably nursed increase to twenty-eight pounds.

I grant this food will be somewhat dear,[1] and therefore very proper for landlords, who, as they have already devoured most of the parents, seem to have the best title to the children.

Infants' flesh will be in season throughout the year, but more plentiful in March, and a little before and after. For we are told by a grave author, an eminent French physician, that, fish being a prolific[2] diet, there are more children born in Roman Catholic countries about nine months after Lent than at any other season; therefore, reckoning a year after Lent, the markets will be more glutted than usual because the number of popish[3] infants is at least three to one in this kingdom, and therefore it will have one other collateral advantage by lessening the number of papists among us.

I have already computed the charge of nursing a beggar's child (in which list I reckon all cottagers,[4] labourers, and four fifths of the farmers) to be about two shillings per annum, rags included, and I believe no gentleman would repine to give ten shillings for the carcass of a good fat child, which, as I have said, will make four dishes of excellent nutritive meat when he hath only some particular friend or his own family to dine with him. Thus the squire[5] will learn to be a good landlord and grow popular among his tenants; the mother will have eight shillings net profit and be fit for work till she produces another child.

---

1   *dear* Expensive.

2   *grave author* Sixteenth-century satirist François Rabelais. See his *Gargantua and Pantagruel*; *prolific* I.e., causing increased fertility.

3   *popish* Derogatory term meaning "Catholic."

4   *cottagers* Country dwellers.

5   *squire* Owner of a country estate.

Those who are more thrifty (as I must confess the times require) may flay the carcass, the skin of which, artificially[1] dressed, will make admirable gloves for ladies and summer boots for fine gentlemen.

As to our city of Dublin, shambles[2] may be appointed for this purpose in the most convenient parts of it, and butchers we may be assured will not be wanting, although I rather recommend buying the children alive and dressing them hot from the knife, as we do roasting pigs.

A very worthy person, a true lover of his country, and whose virtues I highly esteem, was lately pleased, in discoursing on this matter, to offer a refinement upon my scheme. He said that, many gentlemen of this kingdom having of late destroyed their deer, he conceived that the want of venison might be well supplied by the bodies of young lads and maidens, not exceeding fourteen years of age nor under twelve, so great a number of both sexes in every county being now ready to starve for want of work and service; and these to be disposed of by their parents if alive, or otherwise by their nearest relations. But with due deference to so excellent a friend and so deserving a patriot, I cannot be altogether in his sentiments; for as to the males, my American acquaintance assured me from frequent experience that their flesh was generally tough and lean, like that of our schoolboys, by continual exercise, and their taste disagreeable, and to fatten them would not answer the charge. Then as to the females, it would, I think with humble submission, be a loss to the public because they soon would become breeders themselves. And besides, it is not improbable that some scrupulous people might be apt to censure such a practice (although indeed very unjustly) as a little bordering upon cruelty, which, I confess, hath always been with me the strongest objection against any project, however well intended.

But in order to justify my friend, he confessed that this expedient was put into his head by the famous Psalmanazar,[3] a native of the island of Formosa, who came from thence to London above twenty years ago, and in conversation told my friend that in his country, when any young person happened to be put to death the executioner sold the carcass to persons of quality as a prime dainty, and that in his time the body of a plump girl of fifteen, who was crucified for an attempt to poison the emperor, was sold to his Imperial Majesty's Prime Minister of State and other great Mandarins of the court, in joints from the

---

1   *artificially* Artfully, skillfully.

2   *shambles* Slaughterhouses.

3   *Psalmanazar* George Psalmanazar, a French adventurer who pretended to be a Formosan and published an account of Formosan customs, *Historical and Geographical Description of Formosa* (1704), which was later exposed as fraudulent. The story Swift recounts here is found in the second edition of Psalmanazar's work.

gibbet,[1] at four hundred crowns. Neither indeed can I deny that if the same use were made of several plump young girls in this town who, without one single groat to their fortunes, cannot stir abroad without a chair,[2] and appear at the playhouse and assemblies in foreign fineries which they never will pay for, the kingdom would not be the worse.

Some persons of a desponding spirit are in great concern about that vast number of poor people who are aged, diseased, or maimed, and I have been desired to employ my thoughts what course may be taken to ease the nation of so grievous an encumbrance. But I am not in the least pain upon that matter because it is very well known that they are every day dying and rotting by cold and famine, and filth and vermin, as fast as can be reasonably expected. And as to the younger labourers, they are now in almost as hopeful a condition. They cannot get work, and consequently pine away for want of nourishment to a degree that if at any time they are accidentally hired to common labour, they have not strength to perform it; and thus the country and themselves are happily delivered from the evils to come.

I have too long digressed, and therefore shall return to my subject. I think the advantages by the proposal which I have made are obvious and many, as well as of the highest importance.

For first, as I have already observed, it would greatly lessen the number of papists, with whom we are yearly overrun, being the principal breeders of the nation as well as our most dangerous enemies, and who stay at home on purpose with a design to deliver the kingdom to the Pretender, hoping to take their advantage by the absence of so many good Protestants, who have chosen rather to leave their country than stay at home and pay tithes against their conscience to an Episcopal curate.[3]

Secondly, the poorer tenants will have something valuable of their own, which by law may be made liable to distress[4] and help to pay their landlord's rent, their corn and cattle being already seized, and money a thing unknown.

Thirdly, whereas the maintenance of an hundred thousand children from two years old and upwards cannot be computed at less than ten shillings apiece per annum, the nation's stock will be thereby increased fifty thousand pounds per annum, besides the profit of a new dish introduced to the tables of all gentlemen of fortune in the kingdom who have any refinement in taste,

---

1   *gibbet* Gallows.
2   *groat* Silver coin equal in value to four pence. It was removed from circulation in 1662, and thereafter "a groat" was used metaphorically to signify any very small sum; *chair* Sedan chair, which seated one person and was carried on poles by two men.
3   *Episcopal curate* I.e., Anglican church official.
4   *distress* Seizure of property for the payment of debt.

and the money will circulate among ourselves, the goods being entirely of our own growth and manufacture.

Fourthly, the constant breeders, besides the gain of eight shillings sterling per annum by the sale of their children, will be rid of the charge of maintaining them after the first year.

Fifthly, this food would likewise bring great customs to taverns, where the vintners will certainly be so prudent as to procure the best receipts[1] for dressing it to perfection, and consequently have their houses frequented by all the fine gentlemen who justly value themselves upon their knowledge in good eating. And a skillful cook who understands how to oblige his guests will contrive to make it as expensive as they please.

Sixthly, this would be a great inducement to marriage, which all wise nations have either encouraged by rewards or enforced by laws and penalties. It would increase the care and tenderness of mothers toward their children, when they were sure of a settlement for life to the poor babes, provided in some sort by the public, to their annual profit instead of expense. We should soon see an honest emulation[2] among the married women, which of them could bring the fattest child to market. Men would become as fond of their wives during the time of their pregnancy as they are now of their mares in foal, their cows in calf, or sows when they are ready to farrow, nor offer to beat or kick them (as it is too frequent a practice) for fear of a miscarriage.

Many other advantages might be enumerated: for instance, the addition of some thousand carcasses in our exportation of barrelled beef; the propagation of swine's flesh and improvement in the art of making good bacon, so much wanted among us by the great destruction of pigs, too frequent at our tables, which are no way comparable in taste or magnificence to a well-grown, fat yearling child, which, roasted whole, will make a considerable figure at a Lord Mayor's feast or any other public entertainment. But this and many others I omit, being studious of brevity.

Supposing that one thousand families in this city would be constant customers for infants' flesh, besides others who might have it at merry-meetings, particularly weddings and christenings, I compute that Dublin would take off annually about twenty thousand carcasses, and the rest of the kingdom (where probably they will be sold somewhat cheaper) the remaining eighty thousand.

I can think of no one objection that will possibly be raised against this proposal, unless it should be urged that the number of people will be thereby much lessened in the kingdom. This I freely own, and it was indeed one principal design in offering it to the world. I desire the reader will observe

---

1   *receipts* Recipes.
2   *emulation* Rivalry.

that I calculate my remedy for this one individual kingdom of Ireland, and for no other that ever was, is, or, I think, ever can be upon earth. Therefore let no man talk to me of other expedients:[1] of taxing our absentees at five shillings a pound; of using neither clothes nor household furniture, except what is of our own growth and manufacture; of utterly rejecting the materials and instruments that promote foreign luxury; of curing the expensiveness of pride, vanity, idleness, and gaming[2] in our women; of introducing a vein of parsimony, prudence, and temperance; of learning to love our country, wherein we differ even from Laplanders and the inhabitants of Topinamboo; of quitting our animosities and factions, nor act any longer like the Jews, who were murdering one another at the very moment their city was taken;[3] of being a little cautious not to sell our country and consciences for nothing; of teaching landlords to have at least one degree of mercy toward their tenants; lastly, of putting a spirit of honesty, industry, and skill into our shopkeepers, who, if a resolution could now be taken to buy only our native goods, would immediately unite to cheat and exact upon us in the price, the measure, and the goodness, nor could ever yet be brought to make one fair proposal of just dealing, though often in earnest invited to it.

Therefore I repeat, let no man talk to me of these and the like expedients till he hath at least some glimpse of hope that there will ever be some hearty and sincere attempt to put them in practice.

But as to myself, having been wearied out for many years with offering vain, idle, visionary thoughts, and at length utterly despairing of success, I fortunately fell upon this proposal, which, as it is wholly new, so it hath something solid and real, of no expense and little trouble, full in our own power, and whereby we can incur no danger in disobliging England. For this kind of commodity will not bear exportation, the flesh being of too tender a consistence to admit a long continuance in salt, although perhaps I could name a country[4] which would be glad to eat up our whole nation without it.

After all, I am not so violently bent upon my own opinion as to reject any offer, proposed by wise men, which shall be found equally innocent, cheap, easy, and effectual. But before something of that kind shall be advanced in

---

1   *other expedients* All of which Swift had already proposed in earnest attempts to remedy Ireland's poverty. See, for example, his *Proposal for the Universal Use of Irish Manufactures*. In early editions the following proposals were italicized to show the suspension of Swift's ironic tone.

2   *gaming* Gambling.

3   *Topinamboo* District in Brazil; *Jews ... was taken* According to the history of Flavius Josephus, Roman Emperor Titus's invasion and capture of Jerusalem in 70 BCE was aided by the fact that factional fighting had divided the city.

4   *a country* I.e., England.

contradiction to my scheme, and offering a better, I desire the author or authors will be pleased maturely to consider two points.

First, as things now stand, how they will be able to find food and raiment for one hundred thousand useless mouths and backs.

And secondly, there being a round million of creatures in human figure throughout this kingdom whose whole subsistence, put into a common stock, would leave them in debt two million of pounds sterling, adding those who are beggars by profession to the bulk of farmers, cottagers, and labourers with their wives and children, who are beggars in effect.

I desire those politicians who dislike my overture, and may perhaps be so bold to attempt an answer, that they will first ask the parents of these mortals whether they would not at this day think it a great happiness to have been sold for food at a year old in the manner I prescribe, and thereby have avoided such a perpetual scene of misfortunes as they have since gone through by the oppression of landlords, the impossibility of paying rent without money or trade, the want of common sustenance, with neither house nor clothes to cover them from the inclemencies of the weather, and the most inevitable prospect of entailing[1] the like or greater miseries upon their breed forever.

I profess in the sincerity of my heart that I have not the least personal interest in endeavoring to promote this necessary work, having no other motive than the public good of my country by advancing our trade, providing for infants, relieving the poor, and giving some pleasure to the rich. I have no children by which I can propose to get a single penny, the youngest being nine years old, and my wife past childbearing.

—1729

---

1   *entailing* Bestowing, conferring.

Percy Bysshe Shelley
1792–1822

▬▬▬ A poet, thinker, and activist devoted to social reform and the overthrow of injustice, Percy Shelley was not only one of the most radical English Romantics but—as even the comparatively conservative Wordsworth acknowledged—"one of the best *artists* of us all ... in workmanship of style." Shelley's politics and poetics intersect in visionary works that seek to stimulate in the reader an awareness of a higher order of experience and greater forms of value than a materialist conception of the world can comprehend. His critics dismissed him as a reckless naïf with "a weak grasp upon the actual," but his idealism was bounded by his skepticism, and what he called his "dreams of what ought to be" take greater heed in his mature works of "the difficult and unbending realities of actual life."

For much of his life Shelley saw himself as a persecuted outcast. In light of his atheism and political views, his scandalous espousal of free love, and his sympathy for early democratic thinkers such as Thomas Paine and William Godwin, his work was often suppressed or attacked. Shelley was frequently on the defensive, not only with respect to his character and work but on behalf of poetry itself. His unfinished *Defence of Poetry* (1840), written to rebut a tongue-in-cheek essay in which his friend Thomas Love Peacock declared the art useless in the modern era of technological and scientific progress, remains an eloquent vindication of the transformative power of the "poetical faculty" and the social and moral role of the poet.

from *A Defence of Poetry, or Remarks Suggested by an Essay Entitled "The Four Ages of Poetry"*[1]

According to one mode of regarding those two classes of mental action which are called reason and imagination, the former may be considered as mind con-

---

1   *A Defence ... Ages of Poetry* This essay, begun in 1822 and never completed, was written in response to an 1820 essay by Shelley's friend Thomas Love Peacock called "The Four Ages of Poetry." In this partially ironic essay, Peacock describes four cycles through which poetry passes: the first is an iron age of crude folk ballads, medieval romances, etc.; the second, the gold age, contains the great epics of Homer, Dante, and Milton; the third, the silver age, contains the "derivative" poetry of the Augustan poets (who included John Dryden and Alexander Pope); and the fourth stage, the age of brass, is that of Peacock's contemporaries, whom he claimed were markedly inferior. Criticizing Romantic poets such as Byron, Coleridge, and Wordsworth, Peacock urged the men of his generation to apply themselves to new sciences, such as astronomy, economics, politics, mathematics,

templating the relations borne by one thought to another, however produced; and the latter, as mind acting upon those thoughts so as to colour them with its own light, and composing from them, as from elements, other thoughts, each containing within itself the principle of its own integrity. The one is the τὸ ποιειω,[1] or the principle of synthesis, and has for its objects those forms which are common to universal nature and existence itself; the other is the τὸ λογιζειω[2] or principle of analysis, and its action regards the relations of things, simply as relations; considering thoughts, not in their integral unity, but as the algebraical representations which conduct to certain general results. Reason is the enumeration of quantities already known; imagination is the perception of the value of those quantities, both separately and as a whole. Reason respects the differences, and imagination the similitudes of things. Reason is to Imagination as the instrument to the agent, as the body to the spirit, as the shadow to the substance.

Poetry, in a general sense, may be defined to be "the expression of the Imagination": and poetry is connate with the origin of man. Man is an instrument over which a series of external and internal impressions are driven, like the alternations of an ever-changing wind over an Æolian lyre,[3] which move it by their motion to ever-changing melody. But there is a principle within the human being, and perhaps within all sentient beings, which acts otherwise than in the lyre, and produces not melody alone, but harmony, by an internal adjustment of the sounds or motions thus excited to the impressions which excite them. It is as if the lyre could accommodate its chords to the motions of that which strikes them, in a determined proportion of sound; even as the musician can accommodate his voice to the sound of the lyre. A child at play by itself will express its delight by its voice and motions; and every inflexion of tone and every gesture will bear exact relation to a corresponding antitype in the pleasurable impressions which awakened it; it will be the reflected image of that impression; and as the lyre trembles and sounds after the wind has died away, so the child seeks, by prolonging in its voice and motions the duration of the effect, to prolong also a consciousness of the cause. In relation to the objects which delight a child, these expressions are what poetry is to higher objects. The savage (for the savage is to ages what the child is to years) expresses

---

or chemistry, instead of poetry. Though Shelley recognized Peacock's satirical humour, he also acknowledged that Peacock had put his finger on a common bias of the time—both in the theories of Utilitarian philosophers and in general public opinion—in favour of economic growth and scientific progress over creativity and humanitarian concerns. It was this bias that he attempted to correct in his *Defence*.

1 τὸ ποιειω Greek: making.
2 τὸ λογιζειω Greek: reasoning.
3 *Æolian lyre* Stringed instrument that produces music when exposed to wind.

the emotions produced in him by surrounding objects in a similar manner; and language and gesture, together with plastic[1] or pictorial imitation, become the image of the combined effect of those objects, and of his apprehension of them. Man in society, with all his passions and his pleasures, next becomes the object of the passions and pleasures of man; an additional class of emotions produces an augmented treasure of expressions; and language, gesture, and the imitative arts become at once the representation and the medium, the pencil and the picture, the chisel and the statue, the chord and the harmony. The social sympathies, or those laws from which as from its elements society results, begin to develop themselves from the moment that two human beings coexist; the future is contained within the present as the plant within the seed; and equality, diversity, unity, contrast, mutual dependence, become the principles alone capable of affording the motives according to which the will of a social being is determined to action, inasmuch as he is social; and constitute pleasure in sensation, virtue in sentiment, beauty in art, truth in reasoning, and love in the intercourse of kind. Hence men, even in the infancy of society, observe a certain order in their words and actions, distinct from that of the objects and the impressions represented by them, all expression being subject to the laws of that from which it proceeds. But let us dismiss those more general considerations which might involve an enquiry into the principles of society itself, and restrict our view to the manner in which the imagination is expressed upon its forms.

In the youth of the world, men dance and sing and imitate natural objects, observing[2] in these actions, as in all others, a certain rhythm or order. And, although all men observe a similar, they observe not the same order, in the motions of the dance, in the melody of the song, in the combinations of language, in the series of their imitations of natural objects. For there is a certain order or rhythm belonging to each of these classes of mimetic representation, from which the hearer and the spectator receive an intenser and purer pleasure than from any other: the sense of an approximation to this order has been called taste, by modern writers. Every man in the infancy of art observes an order which approximates more or less closely to that from which this highest delight results: but the diversity is not sufficiently marked, as that its gradations should be sensible, except in those instances where the predominance of this faculty of approximation to the beautiful (for so we may be permitted to name the relation between this highest pleasure and its cause) is very great. Those in whom it exists in excess are poets, in the most universal sense of the word; and the pleasure resulting from the manner in which they express the influence of

---

1   *plastic* I.e., sculptural.
2   *observing* Following.

society or nature upon their own minds, communicates itself to others, and gathers a sort of reduplication from that community. Their language is vitally metaphorical; that is, it marks the before unapprehended relations of things, and perpetuates their apprehension, until the words which represent them, become through time signs for portions or classes of thoughts instead of pictures of integral thoughts; and then if no new poets should arise to create afresh the associations which have been thus disorganized, language will be dead to all the nobler purposes of human intercourse. These similitudes or relations are finely said by Lord Bacon to be "the same footsteps of nature impressed upon the various subjects of the world"[1]—and he considers the faculty which perceives them as the storehouse of axioms common to all knowledge. In the infancy of society every author is necessarily a poet, because language itself is poetry; and to be a poet is to apprehend the true and the beautiful, in a word the good which exists in the relation, subsisting, first between existence and perception, and secondly between perception and expression. Every original language near to its source is in itself the chaos of a cyclic poem:[2] the copiousness of lexicography and the distinctions of grammar are the works of a later age, and are merely the catalogue and the form of the creations of Poetry.

But Poets, or those who imagine and express this indestructible order, are not only the authors of language and of music, of the dance and architecture and statuary and painting: they are the institutors of laws, and the founders of civil society and the inventors of the arts of life and the teachers, who draw into a certain propinquity with the beautiful and the true that partial apprehension of the agencies of the invisible world which is called religion. Hence all original religions are allegorical, or susceptible of allegory, and like Janus have a double face of false and true.[3] Poets, according to the circumstances of the age and nation in which they appeared, were called in the earlier epochs of the world legislators or prophets:[4] a poet essentially comprises and unites both these characters. For he not only beholds intensely the present as it is, and discovers those laws according to which present things ought to be ordered, but he beholds the future in the present, and his thoughts are the germs of the flower and the fruit of latest time. Not that I assert poets to be prophets in the gross sense of the word, or that they can foretell the form as surely as

---

1   *the same ... world* From Francis Bacon's *Of the Advancement of Learning* (1605) 3.1.

2   *cyclic poem* Set of poems dealing with the same subject (though not always by the same author). The "Arthurian Cycle," a series of poems about the court of King Arthur, is one example of the genre.

3   *like Janus ... true* Janus, the Roman god of war, of doorways, and of beginnings and endings, is generally depicted with two faces, one looking forward and one back.

4   *were called ... prophets* See Sir Philip Sidney's *Defence of Poesy* (1595), in which he points out that *vates*, the Latin word for poet, also means diviner or prophet.

they foreknow the spirit of events: such is the pretence of superstition which would make poetry an attribute of prophecy, rather than prophecy an attribute of poetry. A Poet participates in the eternal, the infinite, and the one; as far as relates to his conceptions, time and place and number are not. The grammatical forms which express the moods of time, and the difference of persons and the distinction of place, are convertible with respect to the highest poetry without injuring it as poetry, and the choruses of Æschylus, and the book of Job, and Dante's Paradise[1] would afford, more than any other writings, examples of this fact, if the limits of this essay did not forbid citation. The creations of sculpture, painting, and music are illustrations still more decisive.

Language, colour, form, and religious and civil habits of action are all the instruments and materials of poetry; they may be called poetry by that figure of speech which considers the effect as a synonym of the cause. But poetry in a more restricted sense expresses those arrangements of language, and especially metrical language, which are created by that imperial faculty whose throne is curtained within the invisible nature of man. And this springs from the nature itself of language, which is a more direct representation of the actions and passions of our internal being, and is susceptible of more various and delicate combinations, than colour, form, or motion, and is more plastic and obedient to the control of that faculty of which it is the creation. For language is arbitrarily produced by the Imagination and has relation to thoughts alone; but all other materials, instruments and conditions of art, have relations among each other, which limit and interpose between conception and expression. The former is as a mirror which reflects, the latter as a cloud which enfeebles, the light of which both are mediums of communication. Hence the fame of sculptors, painters and musicians, although the intrinsic powers of the great masters of these arts, may yield in no degree to that of those who have employed language as the hieroglyphic of their thoughts, has never equalled that of poets in the restricted sense of the term; as two performers of equal skill will produce unequal effects from a guitar and a harp. The fame of legislators and founders of religions, so long as their institutions last, alone seems to exceed that of poets in the restricted sense; but it can scarcely be a question whether, if we deduct the celebrity which their flattery of the gross opinions of the vulgar usually conciliates, together with that which belonged to them in their higher character of poets, any excess will remain.

We have thus circumscribed the meaning of the word Poetry within the limits of that art which is the most familiar and the most perfect expression of

1   *Æschylus* Greek tragic dramatist (c. 525–456 BCE); *Dante's Paradise* Reference to Italian poet Dante Alighieri's fourteenth-century work *The Divine Comedy*, which describes a journey from Hell, through Purgatory, to Paradise.

the faculty itself. It is necessary however to make the circle still narrower, and to determine the distinction between measured and unmeasured language; for the popular division into prose and verse is inadmissible in accurate philosophy. Sounds as well as thoughts have relation both between each other and towards that which they represent, and a perception of the order of those relations has always been found connected with a perception of the order of the relations of thoughts. Hence the language of poets has ever affected a certain uniform and harmonious recurrence of sound, without which it were not poetry, and which is scarcely less indispensable to the communication of its influence, than the words themselves, without reference to that peculiar order....

A poem is the very image of life expressed in its eternal truth. There is this difference between a story and a poem, that a story is a catalogue of detached facts, which have no other bond of connection than time, place, circumstance, cause and effect; the other is the creation of actions according to the unchangeable forms of human nature, as existing in the mind of the creator, which is itself the image of all other minds. The one is partial, and applies only to a definite period of time, and a certain combination of events which can never again recur; the other is universal, and contains within itself the germ of a relation to whatever motives or actions have place in the possible varieties of human nature....

Poetry is ever accompanied with pleasure: all spirits on which it falls open themselves to receive the wisdom which is mingled with its delight. In the infancy of the world, neither poets themselves nor their auditors are fully aware of the excellence of poetry: for it acts in a divine and unapprehended manner, beyond and above consciousness; and it is reserved for future generations to contemplate and measure the mighty cause and effect in all the strength and splendour of their union. Even in modern times, no living poet ever arrived at the fullness of his fame; the jury which sits in judgment upon a poet, belonging as he does to all time, must be composed of his peers: it must be impanelled by Time from the selectest of the wise of many generations. A Poet is a nightingale, who sits in darkness and sings to cheer its own solitude with sweet sounds; his auditors are as men entranced by the melody of an unseen musician, who feel that they are moved and softened, yet know not whence or why. The poems of Homer and his contemporaries were the delight of infant Greece; they were the elements of that social system which is the column upon which all succeeding civilization has reposed. Homer embodied the ideal perfection of his age in human character; nor can we doubt that those who read his verses were awakened to an ambition of becoming like to Achilles, Hector and Ulysses:[1] the truth and beauty of friendship, patriotism, and persevering devotion to an

1   *Achilles, Hector and Ulysses* Trojan and Greek heroes in Homer's *Iliad* and *Odyssey*.

object were unveiled to the depths in these immortal creations: the sentiments of the auditors must have been refined and enlarged by a sympathy with such great and lovely impersonations, until from admiring they imitated, and from imitation they identified themselves with the objects of their admiration....

The whole objection, however, of the immorality of poetry[1] rests upon a misconception of the manner in which poetry acts to produce the moral improvement of man. Ethical science[2] arranges the elements which poetry has created, and propounds schemes and proposes examples of civil and domestic life: nor is it for want of admirable doctrines that men hate, and despise, and censure, and deceive, and subjugate one another. But Poetry acts in another and diviner manner. It awakens and enlarges the mind itself by rendering it the receptacle of a thousand unapprehended combinations of thought. Poetry lifts the veil from the hidden beauty of the world, and makes familiar objects be as if they were not familiar; it reproduces all that it represents, and the impersonations clothed in its Elysian[3] light stand thenceforward in the minds of those who have once contemplated them, as memorials of that gentle and exalted content which extends itself over all thoughts and actions with which it coexists. The great secret of morals is Love; or a going out of our own nature, and an identification of ourselves with the beautiful which exists in thought, action, or person not our own. A man, to be greatly good, must imagine intensely and comprehensively; he must put himself in the place of another and of many others; the pains and pleasures of his species must become his own. The great instrument of moral good is the imagination; and poetry administers to the effect by acting upon the cause. Poetry enlarges the circumference of the imagination by replenishing it with thoughts of ever new delight, which have the power of attracting and assimilating to their own nature all other thoughts, and which form new intervals and interstices whose void for ever craves fresh food. Poetry strengthens that faculty which is the organ of the moral nature of man, in the same manner as exercise strengthens a limb. A Poet therefore would do ill to embody his own conceptions of right and wrong, which are usually those of his place and time, in his poetical creations, which participate in neither. By this assumption of the inferior office of interpreting the effect, in which perhaps after all he might acquit himself but imperfectly, he would resign the glory in a participation in the cause. There was little danger that Homer, or any of the eternal poets, should have so far misunderstood themselves as to have abdicated this throne of their widest dominion. Those

---

1 *immorality of poetry* An objection voiced by Plato in his *Republic*, in which he says that poetry often depicts characters who are morally imperfect and whose actions do not provide suitable examples for readers.
2 *Ethical science* Moral philosophy.
3 *reproduces* I.e., produces or creates anew; *Elysian* I.e., of paradise.

in whom the poetical faculty, though great, is less intense, as Euripides, Lucan, Tasso, Spenser,[1] have frequently affected a moral aim, and the effect of their poetry is diminished in exact proportion to the degree in which they compel us to advert to this purpose....

The drama at Athens, or wheresoever else it may have approached to its perfection, coexisted with the moral and intellectual greatness of the age. The tragedies of the Athenian poets are as mirrors in which the spectator beholds himself, under a thin disguise of circumstance, stript of all but that ideal perfection and energy which every one feels to be the internal type of all that he loves, admires, and would become. The imagination is enlarged by a sympathy with pains and passions so mighty that they distend in their conception the capacity of that by which they are conceived; the good affections are strengthened by pity, indignation, terror and sorrow; and an exalted calm is prolonged from the satiety of this high exercise of them into the tumult of familiar life; even crime is disarmed of half its horror and all its contagion by being represented as the fatal consequence of the unfathomable agencies of nature; error is thus divested of its willfulness; men can no longer cherish it as the creation of their choice. In a drama of the highest order there is little food for censure or hatred; it teaches rather self-knowledge and self-respect. Neither the eye nor the mind can see itself, unless reflected upon that which it resembles. The drama, so long as it continues to express poetry, is as a prismatic and many-sided mirror, which collects the brightest rays of human nature and divides and reproduces them from the simplicity of these elementary forms, and touches them with majesty and beauty, and multiplies all that it reflects, and endows it with the power of propagating its like wherever it may fall.

But in periods of the decay of social life, the drama sympathizes with that decay. Tragedy becomes a cold imitation of the form of the great masterpieces of antiquity, divested of all harmonious accompaniment of the kindred arts; and often the very form misunderstood: or a weak attempt to teach certain doctrines, which the writer considers as moral truths; and which are usually no more than specious flatteries of some gross vice or weakness with which the author in common with his auditors are infected....

The drama being that form under which a greater number of modes of expression of poetry are susceptible of being combined than any other, the connection of poetry and social good is more observable in the drama than in whatever other form: and it is indisputable that the highest perfection of human society has ever corresponded with the highest dramatic excellence;

---

1   *Euripides* Greek tragedian of the fifth century BCE; *Lucan* Roman poet of the first century CE; *Tasso* Torquato Tasso, Italian epic poet of the sixteenth century; *Spenser* Edmund Spenser, sixteenth-century epic poet; author of *The Faerie Queene*.

and that the corruption or the extinction of the drama in a nation where it has once flourished, is a mark of a corruption of manners, and an extinction of the energies which sustain the soul of social life. But, as Machiavelli[1] says of political institutions, that life may be preserved and renewed, if men should arise capable of bringing back the drama to its principles. And this is true with respect to poetry in its most extended sense: all language, institution and form, require not only to be produced but to be sustained: the office and character of a poet participates in the divine nature as regards providence, no less than as regards creation.

… It is admitted that the exercise of the imagination is most delightful, but it is alleged that that of reason is more useful. Let us examine as the grounds of this distinction, what is here meant by Utility. Pleasure or good, in a general sense, is that which the consciousness of a sensitive and intelligent being seeks, and in which when found it acquiesces. There are two kinds of pleasure, one durable, universal, and permanent; the other transitory and particular. Utility may either express the means of producing the former or the latter. In the former sense, whatever strengthens and purifies the affections, enlarges the imagination, and adds spirit to sense, is useful. But the meaning in which the Author of the Four Ages of Poetry seems to have employed the word utility is the narrower one of banishing the importunity of the wants of our animal nature, the surrounding men with security of life, the dispersing the grosser delusions of superstition, and the conciliating such a degree of mutual forbearance among men as may consist with the motives of personal advantage.

Undoubtedly the promoters of utility in this limited sense have their appointed office in society. They follow the footsteps of poets, and copy the sketches of their creations into the book of common life. They make space, and give time. Their exertions are of the highest value so long as they confine their administration of the concerns of the inferior powers of our nature within the limits due to the superior ones. But whilst the skeptic destroys gross superstitions, let him spare to deface, as some of the French writers have defaced, the eternal truths charactered upon the imaginations of men. Whilst the mechanist abridges, and the political economist combines, labour, let them beware that their speculations, for want of correspondence with those first principles which belong to the imagination, do not tend, as they have in modern England, to exasperate at once the extremes of luxury and want. They have exemplified the saying, "To him that hath, more shall be given; and from him that hath not,

---

1   *Machiavelli* Niccolò Machiavelli (1469–1527), author of the political treatise *The Prince*.

the little that he hath shall be taken away."[1] The rich have become richer, and
the poor have become poorer; and the vessel of the state is driven between the
Scylla and Charybdis[2] of anarchy and despotism. Such are the effects which
must ever flow from an unmitigated exercise of the calculating faculty.

It is difficult to define pleasure in its highest sense; the definition involving
a number of apparent paradoxes. For, from an inexplicable defect of harmony
in the constitution of human nature, the pain of the inferior is frequently connected with the pleasures of the superior portions of our being. Sorrow, terror,
anguish, despair itself are often the chosen expressions of an approximation to
the highest good. Our sympathy in tragic fiction depends on this principle;
tragedy delights by affording a shadow of the pleasure which exists in pain.
This is the source also of the melancholy which is inseparable from the sweetest
melody. The pleasure that is in sorrow is sweeter than the pleasure of pleasure
itself. And hence the saying, "It is better to go to the house of mourning, than
to the house of mirth."[3] Not that this highest species of pleasure is necessarily
linked with pain. The delight of love and friendship, the ecstasy of the admiration of nature, the joy of the perception and still more of the creation of poetry
is often wholly unalloyed.

The production and assurance of pleasure in this highest sense is true
utility. Those who produce and preserve this pleasure are Poets or poetical
philosophers.

The exertions of Locke, Hume, Gibbon, Voltaire, Rousseau,[4] and their
disciples, in favour of oppressed and deluded humanity, are entitled to the
gratitude of mankind. Yet it is easy to calculate the degree of moral and intellectual improvement which the world would have exhibited, had they never
lived. A little more nonsense would have been talked for a century or two; and
perhaps a few more men, women, and children, burnt as heretics. We might
not at this moment have been congratulating each other on the abolition of
the Inquisition in Spain.[5] But it exceeds all imagination to conceive what
would have been the moral condition of the world if neither Dante, Petrarch,
Boccaccio, Chaucer, Shakespeare, Calderon, Lord Bacon, nor Milton, had ever

---

1   *To him ... away* Repeatedly said by Jesus (Matthew 25.29, Mark 4.25, Luke 8.18 and
    19.26).
2   *Scylla and Charybdis* A group of rocks and a whirlpool located at the Strait of Messina
    (between Sicily and mainland Italy).
3   *It is ... mirth* From Ecclesiastes 7.2.
4   *Locke ... Rousseau* John Locke, David Hume, Edward Gibbon, François-Marie Arouet
    Voltaire, and Jean-Jacques Rousseau, noted philosophers of the seventeenth and eight-
    eenth centuries.
5   *We might ... Spain* The Inquisition was suspended in 1820, the year before Shelley
    wrote this essay, and abolished permanently in 1834.

existed; if Raphael and Michael Angelo[1] had never been born; if the Hebrew poetry had never been translated; if a revival of the study of Greek literature had never taken place; if no monuments of ancient sculpture had been handed down to us; and if the poetry of the religion of the ancient world had been extinguished together with its belief. The human mind could never, except by the intervention of these excitements, have been awakened to the invention of the grosser sciences, and that application of analytical reasoning to the aberrations of society, which it is now attempted to exalt over the direct expression of the inventive and creative faculty itself.

… The cultivation of those sciences which have enlarged the limits of the empire of man over the external world, has, for want of the poetical faculty, proportionally circumscribed those of the internal world; and man, having enslaved the elements, remains himself a slave. To what but a cultivation of the mechanical arts in a degree disproportioned to the presence of the creative faculty, which is the basis of all knowledge, is to be attributed the abuse of all invention for abridging and combining labour, to the exasperation of the inequality of mankind? From what other cause has it arisen that the discoveries which should have lightened, have added a weight to the curse imposed on Adam?[2] Poetry, and the principle of Self, of which money is the visible incarnation, are the God and the Mammon of the world.[3]

The functions of the poetical faculty are two-fold; by one it creates new materials of knowledge, and power and pleasure; by the other it engenders in the mind a desire to reproduce and arrange them according to a certain rhythm and order which may be called the beautiful and the good. The cultivation of poetry is never more to be desired than at periods when, from an excess of the selfish and calculating principle, the accumulation of the materials of external life exceed the quantity of the power of assimilating them to the internal laws of human nature. The body has then become too unwieldy for that which animates it.

Poetry is indeed something divine. It is at once the centre and circumference of knowledge; it is that which comprehends all science, and that to which all science must be referred. It is at the same time the root and blossom of all other systems of thought: it is that from which all spring, and that which

1   *Petrarch* Fourteenth-century Italian poet, best known for developing the Italian/Petrarchan sonnet; *Boccaccio* Italian poet, author of the *Decameron* (1351–53); *Calderon* Seventeenth-century Spanish poet and dramatist; *Raphael and Michael Angelo* Italian Renaissance painters.
2   *curse imposed on Adam* Adam is cursed to labour for his food; see Genesis 3.17–19.
3   *God and … world* See Matthew 6.24: "No man can serve two masters: for either he will hate the one, and love the other; or else he will hold to the one, and despise the other. Ye cannot serve God and Mammon," Mammon being the false idol of worldly possessions.

adorns all; and that which, if blighted, denies the fruit and the seed, and withholds from the barren world the nourishment and the succession of the scions[1] of the tree of life. It is the perfect and consummate surface and bloom of things; it is as the odour and the colour of the rose to the texture of the elements which compose it, as the form and the splendour of unfaded beauty to the secrets of anatomy and corruption. What were Virtue, Love, Patriotism, Friendship &c.—what were the scenery of this beautiful Universe which we inhabit—what were our consolations on this side of the grave—and what were our aspirations beyond it—if Poetry did not ascend to bring light and fire from those eternal regions where the owl-winged faculty of calculation dare not ever soar? Poetry is not like reasoning, a power to be exerted according to the determination of the will. A man cannot say, "I will compose poetry." The greatest poet even cannot say it: for the mind in creation is as a fading coal which some invisible influence, like an inconstant wind, awakens to transitory brightness: this power arises from within, like the colour of a flower which fades and changes as it is developed, and the conscious portions of our natures are unprophetic either of its approach or its departure.…

Poetry is the record of the best and happiest moments of the happiest and best minds. We are aware of evanescent visitations of thought and feeling sometimes associated with place or person, sometimes regarding our own mind alone, and always arising unforeseen and departing unbidden, but elevating and delightful beyond all expression: so that even in the desire and the regret they leave, there cannot but be pleasure, participating as it does in the nature of its object. It is as it were the interpenetration of a diviner nature through our own; but its footsteps are like those of a wind over a sea, which the coming calm erases, and whose traces remain only as on the wrinkled sand which paves it. These and corresponding conditions of being are experienced principally by those of the most delicate sensibility and the most enlarged imagination; and the state of mind produced by them is at war with every base desire. The enthusiasm of virtue, love, patriotism, and friendship is essentially linked with these emotions; and whilst they last, self appears as what it is, an atom to a Universe. Poets are not only subject to these experiences as spirits of the most refined organization, but they can colour all that they combine with the evanescent hues of this ethereal world; a word, a trait in the representation of a scene or a passion, will touch the enchanted chord, and reanimate, in those who have ever experienced these emotions, the sleeping, the cold, the buried image of the past. Poetry thus makes immortal all that is best and most beautiful in the world; it arrests the vanishing apparitions which haunt

---

1   *scions* Shoots.

the interlunations[1] of life, and veiling them or in language or in form sends them forth among mankind, bearing sweet news of kindred joy to those with whom their sisters abide—abide, because there is no portal of expression from the caverns of the spirit which they inhabit into the universe of things. Poetry redeems from decay the visitations of the divinity in man.

Poetry turns all things to loveliness; it exalts the beauty of that which is most beautiful, and it adds beauty to that which is most deformed: it marries exultation and horror, grief and pleasure, eternity and change; it subdues to union under its light yoke all irreconcilable things. It transmutes all that it touches, and every form moving within the radiance of its presence is changed by wondrous sympathy to an incarnation of the spirit which it breathes; its secret alchemy turns to potable[2] gold the poisonous waters which flow from death through life; it strips the veil of familiarity from the world, and lays bare the naked and sleeping beauty which is the spirit of its forms.

All things exist as they are perceived: at least in relation to the percipient. "The mind is its own place, and of itself can make a heaven of hell, a hell of heaven."[3] But poetry defeats the curse which binds us to be subjected to the accident of surrounding impressions. And whether it spreads its own figured curtain or withdraws life's dark veil from before the scene of things, it equally creates for us a being within our being. It makes us the inhabitants of a world to which the familiar world is a chaos. It reproduces the common universe of which we are portions and percipients, and it purges from our inward sight the film of familiarity which obscures from us the wonder of our being. It compels us to feel that which we perceive, and to imagine that which we know. It creates anew the universe after it has been annihilated in our minds by the recurrence of impressions blunted by reiteration....

The first part of these remarks has related to Poetry in its elements and principles; and it has been shown, as well as the narrow limits assigned them would permit, that what is called poetry, in a restricted sense, has a common source with all other forms of order and of beauty according to which the materials of human life are susceptible of being arranged, and which is poetry in an universal sense.

The second part[4] will have for its object an application of these principles to the present state of the cultivation of Poetry, and a defence of the attempt to idealize the modern forms of manners and opinion, and compel them into a subordination to the imaginative and creative faculty. For the

1   *interlunations* Periods between old and new moons; periods of darkness.
2   *potable* Drinkable. Alchemists sought a liquid form of gold that, when consumed, would be the elixir of life.
3   *The mind ... heaven* From Satan's speech in Milton's *Paradise Lost* 1.254–55.
4   *The second part* Shelley did not complete a second part.

literature of England, an energetic development of which has ever preceded or accompanied a great and free development of the national will, has arisen as it were from a new birth. In spite of the low-thoughted envy which would undervalue contemporary merit, our own will be a memorable age in intellectual achievements, and we live among such philosophers and poets as surpass beyond comparison any who have appeared since the last national struggle for civil and religious liberty.[1] The most unfailing herald, companion, and follower of the awakening of a great people to work a beneficial change in opinion or institution, is Poetry. At such periods there is an accumulation of the power of communicating and receiving intense and impassioned conceptions respecting man and nature. The persons in whom this power resides, may often, as far as regards many portions of their nature, have little apparent correspondence with that spirit of good of which they are the ministers. But even whilst they deny and abjure, they are yet compelled to serve the Power which is seated upon the throne of their own soul. It is impossible to read the compositions of the most celebrated writers of the present day without being startled with the electric life which burns within their words. They measure the circumference and sound the depths of human nature with a comprehensive and all-penetrating spirit, and they are themselves perhaps the most sincerely astonished at its manifestations, for it is less their spirit than the spirit of the age. Poets are the hierophants[2] of an unapprehended inspiration, the mirrors of the gigantic shadows which futurity casts upon the present, the words which express what they understand not; the trumpets which sing to battle, and feel not what they inspire: the influence which is moved not, but moves.[3] Poets are the unacknowledged legislators of the World.

—1820

---

1   *the last ... liberty* I.e., the English Civil War of the 1640s.
2   *hierophants* Interpreters of sacred mysteries.
3   *is moved ... moves* Reference to Greek philosopher Aristotle's description of God as the "Unmoved Mover" of the universe.

Mark Twain (Samuel Clemens)
1835–1910

Samuel Clemens spent his childhood on the banks of the Mississippi River. His pen name comes from a term used on the Mississippi to refer to the second mark on the line that measured the depth of the water—mark twain, or the two-fathom mark, was a safe depth for steamboats. His childhood adventures and life on the river also provided the background for his most popular and enduring works.

After a chequered career that included stints as a printer's apprentice, steamboat pilot, soldier, miner, and provisional governor of the territory of Nevada, Clemens began to write as "Mark Twain." His reputation as a humourist grew as he gave public lectures and published articles, travel letters, and his first book of tales, *The Celebrated Jumping Frog of Calaveras County, and other Sketches* (1867). His fame was established when an assignment to travel to Europe and the Middle East resulted in the irreverent and witty *The Innocents Abroad* (1869).

After his marriage, Twain settled down and wrote prolifically for the rest of his life, although he also undertook tours to give humourous and satirical lectures, such as "Advice to Youth" (1882). He set two novels, *The Prince and the Pauper* (1882) and *A Connecticut Yankee in King Arthur's Court* (1889), in England, but is best known for the two novels set in Twain's home state of Missouri: *The Adventures of Tom Sawyer* (1876) and *The Adventures of Huckleberry Finn* (1884). Ernest Hemingway famously said, "All modern American literature comes from one book by Mark Twain called *Huckleberry Finn*." Despite such critical admiration, this book has often generated controversy—as may be inevitable for any work that attempts to deal directly with issues of race and slavery in America.

Twain's writing continues to be highly regarded for its wit and satire, its lively depictions of Western life, and its effective use of vernacular language.

Advice to Youth

Being told I would be expected to talk here, I inquired what sort of talk I ought to make. They said it should be something suitable to youth—something didactic, instructive, or something in the nature of good advice. Very well. I have a few things in my mind which I have often longed to say for the instruction of the young; for it is in one's tender early years that such things will best take root and be most enduring and most valuable. First, then, I will say to you, my young friends—and I say it beseechingly, urgingly—

Always obey your parents, when they are present. This is the best policy in the long run, because if you don't they will make you. Most parents think they know better than you do, and you can generally make more by humouring that superstition than you can by acting on your own better judgment.

Be respectful to your superiors, if you have any, also to strangers, and sometimes to others. If a person offend you, and you are in doubt as to whether it was intentional or not, do not resort to extreme measures; simply watch your chance and hit him with a brick. That will be sufficient. If you shall find that he had not intended any offence, come out frankly and confess yourself in the wrong when you struck him; acknowledge it like a man and say you didn't mean to. Yes, always avoid violence; in this age of charity and kindliness, the time has gone by for such things. Leave dynamite to the low and unrefined.

Go to bed early, get up early—this is wise. Some authorities say get up with the sun; some others say get up with one thing, some with another. But a lark is really the best thing to get up with. It gives you a splendid reputation with everybody to know that you get up with the lark; and if you get the right kind of lark, and work at him right, you can easily train him to get up at half past nine, every time—it is no trick at all.

Now as to the matter of lying. You want to be very careful about lying; otherwise you are nearly sure to get caught. Once caught, you can never again be, in the eyes to the good and the pure, what you were before. Many a young person has injured himself permanently through a single clumsy and ill-finished lie, the result of carelessness born of incomplete training. Some authorities hold that the young ought not to lie at all. That, of course, is putting it rather stronger than necessary; still, while I cannot go quite so far as that, I do maintain, and I believe I am right, that the young ought to be temperate in the use of this great art until practice and experience shall give them that confidence, elegance, and precision which alone can make the accomplishment graceful and profitable. Patience, diligence, painstaking attention to detail—these are requirements; these, in time, will make the student perfect; upon these, and upon these only, may he rely as the sure foundation for future eminence. Think what tedious years of study, thought, practice, experience, went to the equipment of that peerless old master who was able to impose upon the whole world the lofty and sounding maxim that "truth is mighty and will prevail"—the most majestic compound fracture of fact which any of woman born has yet achieved. For the history of our race, and each individual's experience, are sown thick with evidence that a truth is not hard to kill and that a lie told well is immortal. There in Boston is a monument of the man who discovered anaesthesia;[1] many people are aware, in these latter days, that that man didn't discover it at all, but stole the discovery from another man. Is this truth mighty, and will it prevail? Ah no, my hearers, the monument is made of hardy material, but the lie it tells will outlast it a million years. An awkward, feeble, leaky lie is a thing which you ought to make it your unceasing study to avoid; such a lie as that has no more real permanence than an average truth. Why, you might as well tell the truth at once and be done with it. A feeble, stupid, preposterous lie will not live two years—except it be a slander upon somebody. It is indestructible, then, of course, but that is no merit of yours. A final word: begin your practice of this gracious and beautiful art early—begin now. If I had begun earlier, I could have learned how.

Never handle firearms carelessly. The sorrow and suffering that have been caused through the innocent but heedless handling of firearms by the young! Only four days ago, right in the next farm house to the one where I am spending the summer, a grandmother, old and grey and sweet, one of the loveliest spirits in the land, was sitting at her work, when her young grandson crept in and got down an old, battered, rusty gun which had not been touched for many years and was supposed not to be loaded, and pointed it at her, laughing and threatening to shoot. In her fright she ran screaming and pleading toward the door on the other side of the room; but as she passed him he placed the gun almost against her very breast and pulled the trigger! He had supposed it was not loaded. And he was right—it wasn't. So there wasn't any harm done. It is the only case of that kind I ever heard of. Therefore, just the same, don't you meddle with old unloaded firearms; they are the most deadly and unerring things that have ever been created by man. You don't have to take any pains at all with them; you don't have to have a rest, you don't have to have any sights on the gun, you don't have to take aim, even. No, you just pick out a relative and bang away, and you are sure to get him. A youth who can't hit a cathedral at thirty yards with a Gatling gun[2] in three quarters of an hour, can take up an old empty musket and bag his grandmother every time, at a hundred. Think what Waterloo would have been if one of the armies had been boys armed with old muskets supposed not to be loaded, and the other army had been composed of their female relations. The very thought of it makes one shudder.

1   *monument ... anaesthesia* Monument commemorating the work of Dr. William Thomas Green Morton (1815–68), who was the first to publicly demonstrate the use of ether as an anaesthetic. His claim to be the sole discoverer of ether's anaesthetic effects was disputed by several people.
2   *Gatling gun* Early machine gun invented in the 1860s and used by the American military.

There are many sorts of books; but good ones are the sort for the young to read. Remember that. They are a great, an inestimable, an unspeakable means of improvement. Therefore be careful in your selection, my young friends; be very careful; confine yourselves exclusively to Robertson's Sermons, Baxter's *Saint's Rest*,[1] *The Innocents Abroad*, and works of that kind.

But I have said enough. I hope you will treasure up the instructions which I have given you, and make them a guide to your feet and a light to your understanding. Build your character thoughtfully and painstaking upon these precepts, and by and by, when you have got it built, you will be surprised and gratified to see how nicely and sharply it resembles everybody else's.

—(1882)

---

1   *Robertson's Sermons* Sermons by Anglican minister F.W. Robertson (1816–53), which were published in the decade after his death and were widely read and respected; *Baxter's Saint's Rest* Richard Baxter's devotional work *The Saint's Everlasting Rest* (1650), considered a spiritual classic.

Virginia Woolf
1882–1941

As a writer of daring and ambitious novels; a publisher of avant-garde work by figures such as T.S. Eliot and Katherine Mansfield; and a founding member of the Bloomsbury Group, a circle of brilliant English artists and intellectuals, Virginia Woolf was at the forefront of literary modernism and its revolt against traditional forms and styles. Today, she is admired and studied primarily as the author of such masterpieces as *Mrs Dalloway* (1925), *To the Lighthouse* (1927), and *The Waves* (1931), novels that attempt to capture the rhythms of consciousness by rendering the subjective interplay of perception, recollection, emotion, and understanding. But in her own lifetime Woolf was just as well known for her non-fiction, a vast body of journalism, criticism, and essays in which she draws on "the democratic art of prose" (in her own words) to communicate with a broader readership.

Two of Woolf's longer non-fiction works, *A Room of One's Own* (1929) and *Three Guineas* (1938), are now acknowledged as ground-breaking feminist studies of the social, psychological, and political effects of patriarchy. But many critics have tended to treat Woolf's essays as incidental works, interesting only insofar as they illuminate her fictional theory and practice. Woolf herself distinguished between professional and creative writing—the one a means to an income, the other part of a broader artistic project. The essays tend to be more formally conventional than the novels, but many of them are nonetheless remarkable for their expression of personality and their open engagement with ideas. Amiable and urbane, more exploratory than authoritative, they wander from topic to topic, full of idiosyncratic asides and digressions. Through her engagingly forthright tone Woolf often achieves a remarkable intimacy with the reader. She considered the possibility for creating such intimacy to be a chief virtue of the form: as she observed, a good essay "must draw its curtain round us, but it must be a curtain that shuts us in, not out."

The Death of the Moth

Moths that fly by day are not properly to be called moths; they do not excite that pleasant sense of dark autumn nights and ivy-blossom which the commonest yellow-underwing asleep in the shadow of the curtain never fails to rouse in us. They are hybrid creatures, neither gay like butterflies nor sombre like their own species. Nevertheless the present specimen, with his narrow hay-coloured wings, fringed with a tassel of the same colour, seemed to be content with life. It was a pleasant morning, mid–September, mild, benignant, yet with a keener breath than that of the summer months. The plough was already scoring the field opposite the window, and where the share[1] had been, the earth was pressed flat and gleamed with moisture. Such vigour came rolling in from the fields and the down beyond that it was difficult to keep the eyes strictly turned upon the book. The rooks too were keeping one of their annual festivities; soaring round the tree tops until it looked as if a vast net with thousands of black knots in it had been cast up into the air; which, after a few moments sank slowly down upon the trees until every twig seemed to have a knot at the end of it. Then, suddenly, the net would be thrown into the air again in a wider circle this time, with the utmost clamour and vociferation, as though to be thrown into the air and settle slowly down upon the tree tops were a tremendously exciting experience.

The same energy which inspired the rooks, the ploughmen, the horses, and even, it seemed, the lean bare-backed downs, sent the moth fluttering from side to side of his square of the window-pane. One could not help watching him. One was, indeed, conscious of a queer feeling of pity for him. The possibilities of pleasure seemed that morning so enormous and so various that to have only a moth's part in life, and a day moth's at that, appeared a hard fate, and his zest in enjoying his meagre opportunities to the full, pathetic. He flew vigorously to one corner of his compartment, and, after waiting there a second, flew across to the other. What remained for him but to fly to a third corner and then to a fourth? That was all he could do, in spite of the size of the downs, the width of the sky, the far-off smoke of houses, and the romantic voice, now and then, of a steamer out at sea. What he could do he did. Watching him, it seemed as if a fibre, very thin but pure, of the enormous energy of the world had been thrust into his frail and diminutive body. As often as he crossed the pane, I could fancy that a thread of vital light became visible. He was little or nothing but life.

Yet, because he was so small, and so simple a form of the energy that was rolling in at the open window and driving its way through so many narrow and intricate corridors in my own brain and in those of other human beings, there was something marvellous as well as pathetic about him. It was as if someone had taken a tiny bead of pure life and decking it as lightly as possible with down and feathers, had set it dancing and zig-zagging to show us the true nature of life. Thus displayed one could not get over the strangeness of it. One is apt to forget all about life, seeing it humped and bossed and garnished and cumbered so that it has to move with the greatest circumspection and dignity. Again, the thought of all that life might have been had he been born in any other shape caused one to view his simple activities with a kind of pity.

---

1 *share* Blade of a plough.

After a time, tired by his dancing apparently, he settled on the window ledge in the sun, and, the queer spectacle being at an end, I forgot about him. Then, looking up, my eye was caught by him. He was trying to resume his dancing, but seemed either so stiff or so awkward that he could only flutter to the bottom of the window-pane; and when he tried to fly across it he failed. Being intent on other matters I watched these futile attempts for a time without thinking, unconsciously waiting for him to resume his flight, as one waits for a machine, that has stopped momentarily, to start again without considering the reason of its failure. After perhaps a seventh attempt he slipped from the wooden ledge and fell, fluttering his wings, on to his back on the window sill. The helplessness of his attitude roused me. It flashed upon me that he was in difficulties; he could no longer raise himself; his legs struggled vainly. But, as I stretched out a pencil, meaning to help him to right himself, it came over me that the failure and awkwardness were the approach of death. I laid the pencil down again.

The legs agitated themselves once more. I looked as if for the enemy against which he struggled. I looked out of doors. What had happened there? Presumably it was midday, and work in the fields had stopped. Stillness and quiet had replaced the previous animation. The birds had taken themselves off to feed in the brooks. The horses stood still. Yet the power was there all the same, massed outside indifferent, impersonal, not attending to anything in particular. Somehow it was opposed to the little hay-coloured moth. It was useless to try to do anything. One could only watch the extraordinary efforts made by those tiny legs against an oncoming doom which could, had it chosen, have submerged an entire city, not merely a city, but masses of human beings; nothing, I knew, had any chance against death. Nevertheless after a pause of exhaustion the legs fluttered again. It was superb this last protest, and so frantic that he succeeded at last in righting himself. One's sympathies, of course, were all on the side of life. Also, when there was nobody to care or to know, this gigantic effort on the part of an insignificant little moth, against a power of such magnitude, to retain what no one else valued or desired to keep, moved one strangely. Again, somehow, one saw life, a pure bead. I lifted the pencil again, useless though I knew it to be. But even as I did so, the unmistakable tokens of death showed themselves. The body relaxed, and instantly grew stiff. The struggle was over. The insignificant little creature now knew death. As I looked at the dead moth, this minute wayside triumph of so great a force over so mean an antagonist filled me with wonder. Just as life had been strange a few minutes before, so death was now as strange. The moth having righted himself now lay most decently and uncomplainingly composed. O yes, he seemed to say, death is stronger than I am.

—1942

Zora Neale Hurston

1891–1960

Today critics often speak of the resurrection of Zora Neale Hurston. Although among the most prolific African American writers of her generation, she spent her latter years in obscurity, earning a paltry and irregular subsistence as a maid, supply teacher, and sometime journalist. When she died in a county welfare home in Florida, she was buried in an unmarked grave, her achievements largely ignored or forgotten. It was not until 1975, when Alice Walker published her essay "In Search of Zora Neale Hurston," that the author of *Jonah's Gourd Vine* (1934) and *Their Eyes Were Watching God* (1937) was restored to her rightful place and recognized as "the intellectual and spiritual foremother of a generation of black women writers."

Many commentators on Hurston's novels, short stories, and pioneering studies of African folklore have been struck by what Walker describes as their exuberant "racial health—a sense of black people as complete, complex, *undiminished* human beings, a sense that is lacking in so much black writing and literature." Informed by the myths, rituals, and storytelling traditions that she documented in her anthropological work, Hurston's fiction celebrates black culture and the nuance and vitality of black vernacular speech. But her reluctance to use her art to "lecture on the race problem" or to give a politicized, sociological account of "the Negro" alienated many other prominent authors and intellectuals of the Harlem Renaissance. In a rancorous review of *Their Eyes Were Watching God*, Richard Wright accused Hurston of perpetuating a degrading minstrel tradition, dismissing her masterpiece as an exercise in "facile sensuality" that "carries no theme, no message, no thought."

Ever an individualist, Hurston refused to write resentful novels of social protest in which "black lives are only defensive reactions to white actions." As she declared in her essay "How It Feels to Be Coloured Me" (1928), "I do not belong to that sobbing school of Negrohood who hold that nature somehow has given them a lowdown dirty deal." Hurston's position was controversial, particularly in the era of Jim Crow segregation laws, but she sought after her own fashion to overcome what W.E.B. Du Bois called "the problem of the color line" by opening up the souls of black men and women so as to reveal their common humanity and individual strength.

How It Feels to Be Coloured Me

I am coloured but I offer nothing in the way of extenuating circumstances except the fact that I am the only Negro in the United States whose grandfather on the mother's side was *not* an Indian chief.[1]

I remember the very day that I became coloured. Up to my thirteenth year I lived in the little Negro town of Eatonville, Florida. It is exclusively a coloured town. The only white people I knew passed through the town going to or coming from Orlando. The native whites rode dusty horses, the Northern tourists chugged down the sandy village road in automobiles. The town knew the Southerners and never stopped cane chewing when they passed. But the Northerners were something else again. They were peered at cautiously from behind curtains by the timid. The more venturesome would come out on the porch to watch them go past and got just as much pleasure out of the tourists as the tourists got out of the village.

The front porch might seem a daring place for the rest of the town, but it was a gallery[2] seat for me. My favourite place was atop the gate-post. Proscenium box for a born first-nighter.[3] Not only did I enjoy the show, but I didn't mind the actors knowing that I liked it. I usually spoke to them in passing. I'd wave at them and when they returned my salute, I would say something like this: "Howdy-do-well-I-thank-you-where-you-goin'?" Usually the automobile or the horse paused at this, and after a queer exchange of compliments, I would probably "go a piece of the way" with them, as we say in farthest Florida. If one of my family happened to come to the front in time to see me, of course negotiations would be rudely broken off. But even so, it is clear that I was the first "welcome-to-our-state" Floridian, and I hope the Miami Chamber of Commerce will please take notice.

During this period, white people differed from coloured to me only in that they rode through town and never lived there. They liked to hear me "speak pieces" and sing and wanted to see me dance the parse-me-la, and gave me generously of their small silver for doing these things, which seemed strange to me for I wanted to do them so much that I needed bribing to stop. Only they didn't know it. The coloured people gave no dimes. They deplored any joyful tendencies in me, but I was their Zora nevertheless. I belonged to them, to the nearby hotels, to the county—everybody's Zora.

---

1   *I am ... Indian chief* An improbably high number of African Americans claimed to have Native American heritage, which was prestigious in African American communities at this time.

2   *gallery* Theatre seating area situated in an elevated balcony.

3   *Proscenium box* Theatre seating area near the proscenium, the frame of the stage; *first-nighter* Person who frequently appears in the audience of opening night performances.

But changes came in the family when I was thirteen, and I was sent to school in Jacksonville. I left Eatonville, the town of the oleanders, as Zora. When I disembarked from the river-boat at Jacksonville, she was no more. It seemed that I had suffered a sea change. I was not Zora of Orange County any more, I was now a little coloured girl. I found it out in certain ways. In my heart as well as in the mirror, I became a fast[1] brown—warranted not to rub nor run.

But I am not tragically coloured. There is no great sorrow dammed up in my soul, nor lurking behind my eyes. I do not mind at all. I do not belong to the sobbing school of Negrohood who hold that nature somehow has given them a lowdown dirty deal and whose feelings are all hurt about it. Even in the helter-skelter skirmish that is my life, I have seen that the world is to the strong regardless of a little pigmentation more or less. No, I do not weep at the world—I am too busy sharpening my oyster knife.

Someone is always at my elbow reminding me that I am the granddaughter of slaves. It fails to register depression with me. Slavery is sixty years in the past.[2] The operation was successful and the patient is doing well, thank you. The terrible struggle that made me an American out of a potential slave said "On the line!" The Reconstruction[3] said "Get set!"; and the generation before said "Go!" I am off to a flying start and I must not halt in the stretch to look behind and weep. Slavery is the price I paid for civilization, and the choice was not with me. It is a bully[4] adventure and worth all that I have paid through my ancestors for it. No one on earth ever had a greater chance for glory. The world to be won and nothing to be lost. It is thrilling to think—to know that for any act of mine, I shall get twice as much praise or twice as much blame. It is quite exciting to hold the centre of the national stage, with the spectators not knowing whether to laugh or to weep.

The position of my white neighbour is much more difficult. No brown spectre pulls up a chair beside me when I sit down to eat. No dark ghost thrusts its leg against mine in bed. The game of keeping what one has is never so exciting as the game of getting.

---

1   *fast* Adjective applied to dyes that will not run or change colour.

2   *Slavery is … the past* In 1863, the Emancipation Proclamation legally ended slavery in America.

3   *Reconstruction* Period of recovery (1865–77) after the American Civil War. During Reconstruction, the Southern states adjusted to an economy without legal slavery and rebuilt infrastructure that had been damaged by the war.

4   *bully* Merry, splendid.

I do not always feel coloured. Even now I often achieve the unconscious Zora of Eatonville before the Hegira.[1] I feel most coloured when I am thrown against a sharp white background.

For instance at Barnard.[2] "Beside the waters of the Hudson"[3] I feel my race. Among the thousand white persons, I am a dark rock surged upon, and overswept, but through it all, I remain myself. When covered by the waters, I am; and the ebb but reveals me again.

Sometimes it is the other way around. A white person is set down in our midst, but the contrast is just as sharp for me. For instance, when I sit in the drafty basement that is The New World Cabaret with a white person, my colour comes. We enter chatting about any little nothing that we have in common and are seated by the jazz waiters. In the abrupt way that jazz orchestras have, this one plunges into a number. It loses no time in circumlocutions, but gets right down to business. It constricts the thorax and splits the heart with its tempo and narcotic harmonies. This orchestra grows rambunctious, rears on its hind legs and attacks the tonal veil with primitive fury, rending it, clawing it until it breaks through to the jungle beyond. I follow those heathen—follow them exultingly. I dance wildly inside myself; I yell within, I whoop; I shake my assegai[4] above my head, I hurl it true to the mark *yeeeeooww*! I am in the jungle and living in the jungle way. My face is painted red and yellow and my body is painted blue. My pulse is throbbing like a war drum. I want to slaughter something—give pain, give death to what, I do not know. But the piece ends. The men of the orchestra wipe their lips and rest their fingers. I creep back slowly to the veneer we call civilization with the last tone and find the white friend sitting motionless in his seat smoking calmly.

"Good music they have here," he remarks, drumming the table with his fingertips.

Music. The great blobs of purple and red emotion have not touched him. He has only heard what I felt. He is far away and I see him but dimly across the ocean and the continent that have fallen between us. He is so pale with his whiteness then and I am *so* coloured.

At certain times I have no race, I am *me*. When I set my hat at a certain angle and saunter down Seventh Avenue, Harlem City, feeling as snooty as the lions

---

1   *Hegira* I.e., journey; refers to Mohammed's journey from Mecca to Medina, which marks the beginning of the current era in the Islamic calendar.

2   *Barnard* Women's liberal arts college in New York City, affiliated with Columbia University.

3   *Beside … Hudson* Barnard school song.

4   *assegai* Spear made of a tree of the same name, used by people of southern Africa.

in front of the Forty-Second Street Library, for instance. So far as my feelings are concerned, Peggy Hopkins Joyce on the Boule Mich[1] with her gorgeous raiment, stately carriage, knees knocking together in a most aristocratic manner, has nothing on me. The cosmic Zora emerges. I belong to no race nor time. I am the eternal feminine with its string of beads.

I have no separate feeling about being an American citizen and coloured. I am merely a fragment of the Great Soul that surges within the boundaries. My country, right or wrong.

Sometimes, I feel discriminated against, but it does not make me angry. It merely astonishes me. How *can* any deny themselves the pleasure of my company? It's beyond me.

But in the main, I feel like a brown bag of miscellany propped against a wall. Against a wall in company with other bags, white, red and yellow. Pour out the contents, and there is discovered a jumble of small things priceless and worthless. A first-water[2] diamond, an empty spool, bits of broken glass, lengths of string, a key to a door long since crumbled away, a rusty knife-blade, old shoes saved for a road that never was and never will be, a nail bent under the weight of things too heavy for any nail, a dried flower or two still a little fragrant. In your hand is the brown bag. On the ground before you is the jumble it held—so much like the jumble in the bags, could they be emptied, that all might be dumped in a single heap and the bags refilled without altering the content of any greatly. A bit of coloured glass more or less would not matter. Perhaps that is how the Great Stuffer of Bags filled them in the first place—who knows?

—1928

---

1   *Peggy Hopkins Joyce* White American actress (1893–1957) known for her extravagant lifestyle; *Boule Mich* Boulevard Saint-Michel, a major street in Paris.

2   *first-water* Best quality of diamond or other gem.

George Orwell

1903–1950

George Orwell is best known to modern readers for two works: the anti-Stalinist allegory *Animal Farm* (1945) and the dystopian nightmare *1984* (1949). It was with reference to these two novels that the word "Orwellian" entered the English language as a signifier for any oppressive, invasive, and manipulative practice that seems to threaten the freedom of a society. Orwell was also a successful and prolific writer of non-fiction: full-length works of political and social criticism (notably *The Road to Wigan Pier*, *Down and Out in Paris and London*, and *Homage to Catalonia*) as well as essays of a variety of sorts (memoir, literary criticism, political journalism). The imprint he left on English literary non-fiction may be even deeper than that which he left on English fiction; the scholar Leo Rockas has said that "Orwell's style is probably more admired and pointed to as a model than any other modern prose style, primarily for its no-nonsense approach."

Eric Arthur Blair, the man who would become famous as George Orwell, was born in the Indian municipality of Motihari to an English father employed in the Indian Civil Service. His mother had grown up in Burma, where her French father pursued his business interests. When he was one year old, his mother took him and his older sister to live in England; there, Orwell attended a number of boarding schools, including Eton, in preparation for a university career. His Eastern origins, however, exerted a strong influence on the young man, and in 1922 Orwell left England to begin service with the Indian Imperial Police in Burma.

Orwell's time in Burma would inform his art and politics for the rest of his life. Most directly, he would draw on his experiences in writing essays such as "Shooting an Elephant" (1936). Beyond that, the distaste he developed in Burma for the imperial project continued to inform Orwell's treatment of the themes of authority, oppression, and moral conscience—in the novels *Animal Farm* and *1984* as well as in his non-fiction.

Shooting an Elephant

In Moulmein, in Lower Burma, I was hated by large numbers of people—the only time in my life that I have been important enough for this to happen to me. I was sub-divisional police officer of the town, and in an aimless, petty kind of way anti-European feeling was very bitter. No one had the guts to raise a riot, but if a European woman went through the bazaars alone somebody would probably spit betel[1] juice over her dress. As a police officer I was an ob-

---

1   *betel* Leaf and nut mixture that is chewed as a stimulant, common in Southeast Asia.

vious target and was baited whenever it seemed safe to do so. When a nimble Burman tripped me up on the football field and the referee (another Burman) looked the other way, the crowd yelled with hideous laughter. This happened more than once. In the end the sneering yellow faces of young men that met me everywhere, the insults hooted after me when I was at a safe distance, got badly on my nerves. The young Buddhist priests were the worst of all. There were several thousands of them in the town and none of them seemed to have anything to do except stand on street corners and jeer at Europeans.

All this was perplexing and upsetting. For at that time I had already made up my mind that imperialism was an evil thing and the sooner I chucked up my job and got out of it the better. Theoretically—and secretly, of course—I was all for the Burmese and all against their oppressors, the British. As for the job I was doing, I hated it more bitterly than I can perhaps make clear. In a job like that you see the dirty work of Empire at close quarters. The wretched prisoners huddling in the stinking cages of the lock-ups, the grey, cowed faces of the long-term convicts, the scarred buttocks of the men who had been flogged with bamboos—all these oppressed me with an intolerable sense of guilt. But I could get nothing into perspective. I was young and ill-educated and I had had to think out my problems in the utter silence that is imposed on every Englishman in the East. I did not even know that the British Empire is dying, still less did I know that it is a great deal better than the younger empires that are going to supplant it. All I knew was that I was stuck between my hatred of the empire I served and my rage against the evil-spirited little beasts who tried to make my job impossible. With one part of my mind I thought of the British Raj as an unbreakable tyranny, as something clamped down, *in saecula saeculorum*,[1] upon the will of prostrate peoples; with another part I thought that the greatest joy in the world would be to drive a bayonet into a Buddhist priest's guts. Feelings like these are the normal by-products of imperialism; ask any Anglo-Indian official, if you can catch him off duty.

One day something happened which in a roundabout way was enlightening. It was a tiny incident in itself, but it gave me a better glimpse than I had had before of the real nature of imperialism—the real motives for which despotic governments act. Early one morning the sub-inspector at a police station the other end of the town rang me up on the phone and said that an elephant was ravaging the bazaar. Would I please come and do something about it? I did not know what I could do, but I wanted to see what was happening and I got on to a pony and started out. I took my rifle, an old .44 Winchester and much too small to kill an elephant, but I thought the noise might be useful *in*

---

1   *in saecula saeculorum* Latin: for centuries upon centuries; forever. This phrase appears frequently in the New Testament.

terrorem.[1] Various Burmans stopped me on the way and told me about the elephant's doings. It was not, of course, a wild elephant, but a tame one which had gone "must."[2] It had been chained up, as tame elephants always are when their attack of "must" is due, but on the previous night it had broken its chain and escaped. Its mahout,[3] the only person who could manage it when it was in that state, had set out in pursuit, but had taken the wrong direction and was now twelve hours' journey away, and in the morning the elephant had suddenly reappeared in the town. The Burmese population had no weapons and were quite helpless against it. It had already destroyed somebody's bamboo hut, killed a cow and raided some fruit-stalls and devoured the stock; also it had met the municipal rubbish van and, when the driver jumped out and took to his heels, had turned the van over and inflicted violences upon it.

The Burmese sub-inspector and some Indian constables were waiting for me in the quarter where the elephant had been seen. It was a very poor quarter, a labyrinth of squalid bamboo huts, thatched with palmleaf, winding all over a steep hillside. I remember that it was a cloudy, stuffy morning at the beginning of the rains. We began questioning the people as to where the elephant had gone and, as usual, failed to get any definite information. That is invariably the case in the East; a story always sounds clear enough at a distance, but the nearer you get to the scene of events the vaguer it becomes. Some of the people said that the elephant had gone in one direction, some said that he had gone in another, some professed not even to have heard of any elephant. I had almost made up my mind that the whole story was a pack of lies, when we heard yells a little distance away. There was a loud, scandalized cry of "Go away, child! Go away this instant!" and an old woman with a switch in her hand came round the corner of a hut, violently shooing away a crowd of naked children. Some more women followed, clicking their tongues and exclaiming; evidently there was something that the children ought not to have seen. I rounded the hut and saw a man's dead body sprawling in the mud. He was an Indian, a black Dravidian coolie,[4] almost naked, and he could not have been dead many minutes. The people said that the elephant had come suddenly upon him round the corner of the hut, caught him with its trunk, put its foot on his back and ground him into the earth. This was the rainy season and the ground was soft, and his face had scored a trench a foot deep and a couple of yards long. He was lying on his belly with arms crucified and head sharply twisted to one side. His face was coated with mud, the eyes wide open, the

---

1   *in terrorem* Legal term for a warning; literally, Latin phrase meaning "in fear or alarm."

2   *must* Condition characterized by aggressive behaviour brought on by a surge in testosterone.

3   *mahout* Elephant trainer or keeper.

4   *Dravidian coolie* I.e., southern Indian manual labourer.

teeth bared and grinning with an expression of unendurable agony. (Never tell me, by the way, that the dead look peaceful. Most of the corpses I have seen looked devilish.) The friction of the great beast's foot had stripped the skin from his back as neatly as one skins a rabbit. As soon as I saw the dead man I sent an orderly to a friend's house nearby to borrow an elephant rifle. I had already sent back the pony, not wanting it to go mad with fright and throw me if it smelt the elephant.

The orderly came back in a few minutes with a rifle and five cartridges, and meanwhile some Burmans had arrived and told us that the elephant was in the paddy fields below, only a few hundred yards away. As I started forward practically the whole population of the quarter flocked out of the houses and followed me. They had seen the rifle and were all shouting excitedly that I was going to shoot the elephant. They had not shown much interest in the elephant when he was merely ravaging their homes, but it was different now that he was going to be shot. It was a bit of fun to them, as it would be to an English crowd; besides they wanted the meat. It made me vaguely uneasy. I had no intention of shooting the elephant—I had merely sent for the rifle to defend myself if necessary—and it is always unnerving to have a crowd following you. I marched down the hill, looking and feeling a fool, with the rifle over my shoulder and an ever-growing army of people jostling at my heels. At the bottom, when you got away from the huts, there was a metalled road and beyond that a miry waste of paddy fields a thousand yards across, not yet ploughed but soggy from the first rains and dotted with coarse grass. The elephant was standing eight yards from the road, his left side towards us He took not the slightest notice of the crowd's approach. He was tearing up bunches of grass, beating them against his knees to clean them and stuffing them into his mouth.

I had halted on the road. As soon as I saw the elephant I knew with perfect certainty that I ought not to shoot him. It is a serious matter to shoot a working elephant—it is comparable to destroying a huge and costly piece of machinery—and obviously one ought not to do it if it can possibly be avoided. And at that distance, peacefully eating, the elephant looked no more dangerous than a cow. I thought then and I think now that his attack of 'must' was already passing off; in which case he would merely wander harmlessly about until the mahout came back and caught him. Moreover, I did not in the least want to shoot him. I decided that I would watch him for a little while to make sure that he did not turn savage again, and then go home.

But at that moment I glanced round at the crowd that had followed me. It was an immense crowd, two thousand at the least and growing every minute. It blocked the road for a long distance on either side. I looked at the sea of yellow faces above the garish clothes—faces all happy and excited over this bit of fun, all certain that the elephant was going to be shot. They were watching me as they would watch a conjurer about to perform a trick. They did not like me, but with the magical rifle in my hands I was momentarily worth watching. And suddenly I realized that I should have to shoot the elephant after all. The people expected it of me and I had got to do it; I could feel their two thousand wills pressing me forward, irresistibly. And it was at this moment, as I stood there with the rifle in my hands, that I first grasped the hollowness, the futility of the white man's dominion in the East. Here was I, the white man with his gun, standing in front of the unarmed native crowd—seemingly the leading actor of the piece; but in reality I was only an absurd puppet pushed to and fro by the will of those yellow faces behind. I perceived in this moment that when the white man turns tyrant it is his own freedom that he destroys. He becomes a sort of hollow, posing dummy, the conventionalized figure of a sahib.[1] For it is the condition of his rule that he shall spend his life in trying to impress the "natives," and so in every crisis he has got to do what the "natives" expect of him. He wears a mask, and his face grows to fit it. I had got to shoot the elephant. I had committed myself to doing it when I sent for the rifle. A sahib has got to act like a sahib; he has got to appear resolute, to know his own mind and do definite things. To come all that way, rifle in hand, with two thousand people marching at my heels, and then to trail feebly away, having done nothing—no, that was impossible. The crowd would laugh at me. And my whole life, every white man's life in the East, was one long struggle not to be laughed at.

But I did not want to shoot the elephant. I watched him beating his bunch of grass against his knees, with that preoccupied grandmotherly air that elephants have. It seemed to me that it would be murder to shoot him. At that age I was not squeamish about killing animals, but I had never shot an elephant and never wanted to. (Somehow it always seems worse to kill a *large* animal.) Besides, there was the beast's owner to be considered. Alive, the elephant was worth at least a hundred pounds; dead, he would only be worth the value of his tusks, five pounds, possibly. But I had got to act quickly. I turned to some experienced-looking Burmans who had been there when we arrived, and asked them how the elephant had been behaving. They all said the same thing: he took no notice of you if you left him alone, but he might charge if you went too close to him.

It was perfectly clear to me what I ought to do. I ought to walk up to within, say, twenty-five yards of the elephant and test his behaviour. If he charged, I could shoot; if he took no notice of me, it would be safe to leave

---

1   *sahib* I.e., colonial Englishman; this title of respect was used to address European men in colonial India.

him until the mahout came back. But also I knew that I was going to do no such thing. I was a poor shot with a rifle and the ground was soft mud into which one would sink at every step. If the elephant charged and I missed him, I should have about as much chance as a toad under a steam-roller. But even then I was not thinking particularly of my own skin, only of the watchful yellow faces behind. For at that moment, with the crowd watching me, I was not afraid in the ordinary sense, as I would have been if I had been alone. A white man mustn't be frightened in front of "natives"; and so, in general, he isn't frightened. The sole thought in my mind was that if anything went wrong those two thousand Burmans would see me pursued, caught, trampled on and reduced to a grinning corpse like that Indian up the hill. And if that happened it was quite probable that some of them would laugh. That would never do.

There was only one alternative. I shoved the cartridges into the magazine and lay down on the road to get a better aim. The crowd grew very still, and a deep, low, happy sigh, as of people who see the theatre curtain go up at last, breathed from innumerable throats. They were going to have their bit of fun after all. The rifle was a beautiful German thing with cross-hair sights. I did not then know that in shooting an elephant one would shoot to cut an imaginary bar running from ear-hole to ear-hole. I ought, therefore, as the elephant was sideways on, to have aimed straight at his ear-hole, actually I aimed several inches in front of this, thinking the brain would be further forward.

When I pulled the trigger I did not hear the bang or feel the kick—one never does when a shot goes home—but I heard the devilish roar of glee that went up from the crowd. In that instant, in too short a time, one would have thought, even for the bullet to get there, a mysterious, terrible change had come over the elephant. He neither stirred nor fell, but every line of his body had altered. He looked suddenly stricken, shrunken, immensely old, as though the frightful impact of the bullet had paralysed him without knocking him down. At last, after what seemed a long time—it might have been five seconds, I dare say—he sagged flabbily to his knees. His mouth slobbered. An enormous senility seemed to have settled upon him. One could have imagined him thousands of years old. I fired again into the same spot. At the second shot he did not collapse but climbed with desperate slowness to his feet and stood weakly upright, with legs sagging and head drooping. I fired a third time. That was the shot that did for him. You could see the agony of it jolt his whole body and knock the last remnant of strength from his legs. But in falling he seemed for a moment to rise, for as his hind legs collapsed beneath him he seemed to tower upward like a huge rock toppling, his trunk reaching skyward like a tree. He trumpeted, for the first and only time. And then down he came, his belly towards me, with a crash that seemed to shake the ground even where I lay.

I got up. The Burmans were already racing past me across the mud. It was obvious that the elephant would never rise again, but he was not dead. He was breathing very rhythmically with long rattling gasps, his great mound of a side painfully rising and falling. His mouth was wide open—I could see far down into caverns of pale pink throat. I waited a long time for him to die, but his breathing did not weaken. Finally I fired my two remaining shots into the spot where I thought his heart must be. The thick blood welled out of him like red velvet, but still he did not die. His body did not even jerk when the shots hit him, the tortured breathing continued without a pause. He was dying, very slowly and in great agony, but in some world remote from me where not even a bullet could damage him further. I felt that I had got to put an end to that dreadful noise. It seemed dreadful to see the great beast lying there, powerless to move and yet powerless to die, and not even to be able to finish him. I sent back for my small rifle and poured shot after shot into his heart and down his throat. They seemed to make no impression. The tortured gasps continued as steadily as the ticking of a clock.

In the end I could not stand it any longer and went away. I heard later that it took him half an hour to die. Burmans were bringing dahs[1] and baskets even before I left, and I was told they had stripped his body almost to the bones by the afternoon.

Afterwards, of course, there were endless discussions about the shooting of the elephant. The owner was furious, but he was only an Indian and could do nothing. Besides, legally I had done the right thing, for a mad elephant has to be killed, like a mad dog, if its owner fails to control it. Among the Europeans opinion was divided. The older men said I was right, the younger men said it was a damn shame to shoot an elephant for killing a coolie, because an elephant was worth more than any damn Coringhee[2] coolie. And afterwards I was very glad that the coolie had been killed; it put me legally in the right and it gave me a sufficient pretext for shooting the elephant. I often wondered whether any of the others grasped that I had done it solely to avoid looking a fool.

—1936

---

1   *dahs* Short swords or knives.
2   *Coringhee* From Coringha, a town on the coast of India.

Roland Barthes

1915–1980

Although scholars continue to debate the nature of his achievement, Roland Barthes, French critic, theorist, and champion of the avant-garde, was undoubtedly among the most influential intellectuals of the twentieth century. A pioneer in the field of semiology (the science of signs), and a trenchant critic of bourgeois culture and of the attitudes and values implicit in its icons, institutions, and "myths," Barthes has himself become something of a cultural icon. He is also famous for proclaiming "the death of the author" as the sovereign authority over textual meaning. Barthes is a difficult writer with whom to come to grips; the range of his interests and his highly idiosyncratic prose seem to be continually shifting—as are the contours of his thought.

Barthes is best known for his work on structuralism, an intellectual movement that grew out of the application of the methods and principles of structural linguistics to analyses of cultural phenomena, as a means of uncovering the system of codes and conventions whereby those phenomena are understood. He was also keenly interested in what he called "unlearning," the study of what is forgotten or taken for granted. By unmasking that which goes without saying, Barthes aims to reveal how the seemingly natural, self-evident meanings that circulate within a culture are in fact cultural products that support ideologies and serve particular social interests. We see this at play in *Mythologies* (1957), where Barthes brings his analytical powers to bear on a diverse host of subjects—wrestling, film, photography, wine, even children's toys—in an effort to expose the ideologically loaded secondary messages they emit.

Barthes is not without his detractors: skeptics have dismissed him as a dilettante whose convoluted theoretical pretensions ultimately lead to an intellectual dead end. But, as a "public experimenter" who took up and tested novel ideas and methods, Barthes opened new frontiers of critical study, challenging and transforming conventional views of authorship, realism, representation, the reading process, and the relationship between text and history.

The World of Wrestling

The grandiloquent truth of gestures on life's great occasions.[1]
—BAUDELAIRE

The virtue of all-in wrestling is that it is the spectacle of excess. Here we find a grandiloquence which must have been that of the ancient theatres. And in fact wrestling is an open-air spectacle, for what makes the circus[2] or the arena what they are is not the sky (a romantic value suited rather to fashionable occasions), it is the drenching and vertical quality of the flood of light. Even hidden in the most squalid Parisian halls, wrestling partakes of the nature of the great solar spectacles, Greek drama[3] and bull-fights: in both, a light without shadow generates an emotion without reserve.

There are people who think that wrestling is an ignoble sport. Wrestling is not a sport, it is a spectacle, and it is no more ignoble to attend a wrestled performance of Suffering than a performance of the sorrows of Arnolphe or Andromaque.[4] Of course, there exists a false wrestling, in which the participants unnecessarily go to great lengths to make a show of a fair fight; this is of no interest. True wrestling, wrongly called amateur wrestling, is performed in second-rate halls, where the public spontaneously attunes itself to the spectacular nature of the contest, like the audience at a suburban cinema. Then these same people wax indignant because wrestling is a stage-managed sport (which ought, by the way, to mitigate its ignominy). The public is completely uninterested in knowing whether the contest is rigged or not, and rightly so; it abandons itself to the primary virtue of the spectacle, which is to abolish all motives and all consequences: what matters is not what it thinks but what it sees.

This public knows very well the distinction between wrestling and boxing; it knows that boxing is ... based on a demonstration of excellence. One can bet on the outcome of a boxing-match: with wrestling, it would make no sense. A boxing-match is a story which is constructed before the eyes of the spectator; in wrestling, on the contrary, it is each moment which is intelligible, not the passage of time. The spectator is not interested in the rise and fall of

---

1   *The grandiloquent ... great occasions* From Charles Baudelaire, *Curiosités Esthétiques* (1868); *grandiloquent* Showy, grandiosely expressive.
2   *circus* Ancient outdoor stadium.
3   *Greek drama* In Ancient Athens, tragedies and comedies were performed in large outdoor arenas as part of mass religious festivals.
4   *Arnolphe* Protagonist of *The School for Wives* (1662), a play by the greatly admired French writer Molière; *Andromaque* Title character of a 1667 tragedy by Jean Racine, another widely respected French playwright.

fortunes; he expects the transient image of certain passions. Wrestling therefore demands an immediate reading of the juxtaposed meanings, so that there is no need to connect them. The logical conclusion of the contest does not interest the wrestling-fan, while on the contrary a boxing-match always implies a science of the future. In other words, wrestling is a sum of spectacles, of which no single one is a function: each moment imposes the total knowledge of a passion which rises erect and alone, without ever extending to the crowning moment of a result.

Thus the function of the wrestler is not to win; it is to go exactly through the motions which are expected of him. It is said that judo contains a hidden symbolic aspect; even in the midst of efficiency, its gestures are measured, precise but restricted, drawn accurately but by a stroke without volume. Wrestling, on the contrary, offers excessive gestures, exploited to the limit of their meaning. In judo, a man who is down is hardly down at all, he rolls over, he draws back, he eludes defeat, or, if the latter is obvious, he immediately disappears; in wrestling, a man who is down is exaggeratedly so, and completely fills the eyes of the spectators with the intolerable spectacle of his powerlessness.

This function of grandiloquence is indeed the same as that of ancient theatre, whose principle, language and props (masks and buskins[1]) concurred in the exaggeratedly visible explanation of a Necessity. The gesture of the vanquished wrestler signifying to the world a defeat which, far from disguising, he emphasizes and holds like a pause in music, corresponds to the mask of antiquity meant to signify the tragic mode of the spectacle. In wrestling, as on the stage in antiquity, one is not ashamed of one's suffering, one knows how to cry, one has a liking for tears.

Each sign[2] in wrestling is therefore endowed with an absolute clarity, since one must always understand everything on the spot. As soon as the adversaries are in the ring, the public is overwhelmed with the obviousness of the roles. As in the theatre, each physical type expresses to excess the part which has been assigned to the contestant. Thauvin, a fifty-year-old with an obese and sagging body, whose type of asexual hideousness always inspires feminine nicknames, displays in his flesh the characters of baseness, for his part is to represent what, in the classical concept of the *salaud*,[3] the "bastard" (the key-concept of any wrestling match), appears as organically repugnant. The nausea voluntarily provoked by Thauvin shows therefore a very extended use of signs: not only is ugliness used here in order to signify baseness, but in addition ugliness is wholly gathered into a particularly repulsive quality of matter: the pallid col-

---

1   *masks and buskins* The costumes for Greek tragic actors evolved to include highly stylized masks and boots called buskins, which had raised soles to make the actors appear taller.

2   *sign* Here, any unit that communicates meaning, such as a word, gesture, or image.

3   *salaud* French slang: bastard, someone despicably immoral and hypocritical.

lapse of dead flesh (the public calls Thauvin *la barbaque*, "stinking meat"), so that the passionate condemnation of the crowd no longer stems from its judgment, but instead from the very depth of its humours. It will thereafter let itself be frenetically embroiled in an idea of Thauvin which will conform entirely with this physical origin: his actions will perfectly correspond to the essential viscosity of his personage.

It is therefore in the body of the wrestler that we find the first key to the contest. I know from the start that all of Thauvin's actions, his treacheries, cruelties and acts of cowardice, will not fail to measure up to the first image of ignobility he gave me; I can trust him to carry out intelligently and to the last detail all the gestures of a kind of amorphous baseness, and thus fill to the brim the image of the most repugnant bastard there is: the bastard-octopus.... Thauvin will never be anything but an ignoble traitor, Reinières (a tall blond fellow with a limp body and unkempt hair) the moving image of passivity, Mazaud (short and arrogant like a cock) that of grotesque conceit, and Orsano (an effeminate teddy-boy first seen in a blue-and-pink dressing-gown) that, doubly humorous, of a vindictive *salope*,[1] or bitch....

The physique of the wrestlers therefore constitutes a basic sign, which like a seed contains the whole fight. But this seed proliferates, for it is at every turn during the fight, in each new situation, that the body of the wrestler casts to the public the magical entertainment of a temperament which finds its natural expression in a gesture. The different strata of meaning throw light on each other, and form the most intelligible of spectacles.... [A]bove the fundamental meaning of his body, the wrestler arranges comments which are episodic but always opportune, and constantly help the reading of the fight by means of gestures, attitudes and mimicry which make the intention utterly obvious. Sometimes the wrestler triumphs with a repulsive sneer while kneeling on the good sportsman; sometimes he gives the crowd a conceited smile which forebodes an early revenge; sometimes, pinned to the ground, he hits the floor ostentatiously to make evident to all the intolerable nature of his situation; and sometimes he erects a complicated set of signs meant to make the public understand that he legitimately personifies the ever-entertaining image of the grumbler, endlessly confabulating about his displeasure.

We are therefore dealing with a real Human Comedy, where the most socially-inspired nuances of passion (conceit, rightfulness, refined cruelty, a sense of "paying one's debts") always felicitously find the clearest sign which can receive them, express them and triumphantly carry them to the confines of the hall. It is obvious that at such a pitch, it no longer matters whether the passion is genuine or not. What the public wants is the image of passion, not pas-

---

1   *salope* French slang: bitch, slut; an insult typically directed at a woman.

sion itself. There is no more a problem of truth in wrestling than in the theatre. In both, what is expected is the intelligible representation of moral situations which are usually private. This emptying out of interiority to the benefit of its exterior signs, this exhaustion of the content by the form, is the very principle of triumphant classical art. Wrestling is an immediate pantomime, infinitely more efficient than the dramatic pantomime, for the wrestler's gesture needs no anecdote, no decor, in short no transference in order to appear true.

Each moment in wrestling is therefore like an algebra which instantaneously unveils the relationship between a cause and its represented effect. Wrestling fans certainly experience a kind of intellectual pleasure in *seeing* the moral mechanism function so perfectly. Some wrestlers, who are great comedians, entertain as much as a Molière character, because they succeed in imposing an immediate reading of their inner nature: Armand Mazaud, a wrestler of an arrogant and ridiculous character (as one says that Harpagon[1] is a character), always delights the audience by the mathematical rigour of his transcriptions, carrying the form of his gestures to the furthest reaches of their meaning, and giving to his manner of fighting a kind of vehemence and precision found in a great scholastic disputation,[2] in which what is at stake is at once the triumph of pride and the formal concern with truth.

What is thus displayed for the public is the great spectacle of Suffering, Defeat, and Justice. Wrestling presents man's suffering with all the amplification of tragic masks. The wrestler who suffers in a hold which is reputedly cruel (an arm-lock, a twisted leg) offers an excessive portrayal of Suffering; like a primitive Pietà,[3] he exhibits for all to see his face, exaggeratedly contorted by an intolerable affliction. It is obvious, of course, that in wrestling reserve would be out of place, since it is opposed to the voluntary ostentation of the spectacle, to this Exhibition of Suffering which is the very aim of the fight. This is why all the actions which produce suffering are particularly spectacular, like the gesture of a conjuror who holds out his cards clearly to the public. Suffering which appeared without intelligible cause would not be understood; a concealed action that was actually cruel would transgress the underwritten rules of wrestling and would have no more sociological efficacy than a mad or parasitic gesture. On the contrary suffering appears as inflicted with emphasis and conviction, for everyone must not only see that the man suffers, but also and above all understand why he suffers. What wrestlers call a hold, that is, any figure which allows one to immobilize the adversary indefinitely and to have him at one's mercy, has precisely the function of preparing in a conven-

---

1   *Harpagon* Stingy, old protagonist of Molière's comedy *The Miser* (1668).
2   *scholastic disputation* Formal philosophical argument of the sort conducted at medieval universities.
3   *Pietà* Work of art depicting the Virgin Mary holding Christ's dead body.

tional, therefore intelligible, fashion the spectacle of suffering, of methodically establishing the conditions of suffering. The inertia of the vanquished allows the (temporary) victor to settle in his cruelty and to convey to the public this terrifying slowness of the torturer who is certain about the outcome of his actions; to grind the face of one's powerless adversary or to scrape his spine with one's fist with a deep and regular movement, or at least to produce the superficial appearance of such gestures: wrestling is the only sport which gives such an externalized image of torture. But here again, only the image is involved in the game, and the spectator does not wish for the actual suffering of the contestant; he only enjoys the perfection of an iconography. It is not true that wrestling is a sadistic spectacle: it is only an intelligible spectacle.

There is another figure, more spectacular still than a hold; it is the forearm smash, this loud slap of the forearm, this embryonic punch with which one clouts the chest of one's adversary, and which is accompanied by a dull noise and the exaggerated sagging of a vanquished body. In the forearm smash, catastrophe is brought to the point of maximum obviousness, so much so that ultimately the gesture appears as no more than a symbol; this is going too far, this is transgressing the moral rules of wrestling, where all signs must be excessively clear, but must not let the intention of clarity be seen. The public then shouts "He's laying it on!," not because it regrets the absence of real suffering, but because it condemns artifice: as in the theatre, one fails to put the part across as much by an excess of sincerity as by an excess of formalism.

We have already seen to what extent wrestlers exploit the resources of a given physical style, developed and put to use in order to unfold before the eyes of the public a total image of Defeat. The flaccidity of tall white bodies which collapse with one blow or crash into the ropes with arms flailing, the inertia of massive wrestlers rebounding pitiably off all the elastic surfaces of the ring, nothing can signify more clearly and more passionately the exemplary abasement of the vanquished. Deprived of all resilience, the wrestler's flesh is no longer anything but an unspeakable heap spread out on the floor, where it solicits relentless reviling and jubilation. There is here a paroxysm of meaning in the style of antiquity, which can only recall the heavily underlined intentions in Roman triumphs. At other times, there is another ancient posture which appears in the coupling of the wrestlers, that of the suppliant who, at the mercy of his opponent, on bended knees, his arms raised above his head, is slowly brought down by the vertical pressure of the victor. In wrestling, unlike judo, Defeat is not a conventional sign, abandoned as soon as it is understood; it is not an outcome, but quite the contrary, it is a duration, a display, it takes up the ancient myths of public Suffering and Humiliation: the cross and the pillory. It is as if the wrestler is crucified in broad daylight and in the sight of all. I have heard it said of a wrestler stretched on the ground: "He is dead, little Jesus, there, on the cross," and these ironic words revealed the hidden roots of a spectacle which enacts the exact gestures of the most ancient purifications.

But what wrestling is above all meant to portray is a purely moral concept: that of justice. The idea of "paying" is essential to wrestling, and the crowd's "Give it to him" means above all else "Make him pay." This is therefore, needless to say, an immanent justice. The baser the action of the "bastard," the more delighted the public is by the blow which he justly receives in return. If the villain—who is of course a coward—takes refuge behind the ropes, claiming unfairly to have a right to do so by a brazen mimicry, he is inexorably pursued there and caught, and the crowd is jubilant at seeing the rules broken for the sake of a deserved punishment. Wrestlers know very well how to play up to the capacity for indignation of the public by presenting the very limit of the concept of Justice, this outermost zone of confrontation where it is enough to infringe the rules a little more to open the gates of a world without restraints. For a wrestling-fan, nothing is finer than the revengeful fury of a betrayed fighter who throws himself vehemently not on a successful opponent but on the smarting image of foul play. Naturally, it is the pattern of Justice which matters here, much more than its content: wrestling is above all a quantitative sequence of compensations (an eye for an eye, a tooth for a tooth). This explains why sudden changes of circumstances have in the eyes of wrestling habitués a sort of moral beauty: they enjoy them as they would enjoy an inspired episode in a novel, and the greater the contrast between the success of a move and the reversal of fortune, the nearer the good luck of a contestant to his downfall, the more satisfying the dramatic mime is felt to be. Justice is therefore the embodiment of a possible transgression; it is from the fact that there is a Law that the spectacle of the passions which infringe it derives its value.

It is therefore easy to understand why out of five wrestling-matches, only about one is fair. One must realize, let it be repeated, that "fairness" here is a role or a genre, as in the theatre: the rules do not at all constitute a real constraint; they are the conventional appearance of fairness. So that in actual fact a fair fight is nothing but an exaggeratedly polite one: the contestants confront each other with zeal, not rage; they can remain in control of their passions, they do not punish their beaten opponent relentlessly, they stop fighting as soon as they are ordered to do so, and congratulate each other at the end of a particularly arduous episode, during which, however, they have not ceased to be fair. One must of course understand here that all these polite actions are brought to the notice of the public by the most conventional gestures of fairness: shaking hands, raising the arms, ostensibly avoiding a fruitless hold which would detract from the perfection of the contest.

Conversely, foul play exists only in its excessive signs: administering a big kick to one's beaten opponent, taking refuge behind the ropes while ostensibly invoking a purely formal right, refusing to shake hands with one's opponent before or after the fight, taking advantage of the end of the round to rush treacherously at the adversary from behind, fouling him while the referee is not looking (a move which obviously only has any value or function because in fact half the audience can see it and get indignant about it). Since Evil is the natural climate of wrestling, a fair fight has chiefly the value of being an exception. It surprises the aficionado, who greets it when he sees it as an anachronism and a rather sentimental throwback to the sporting tradition ("Aren't they playing fair, those two"); he feels suddenly moved at the sight of the general kindness of the world, but would probably die of boredom and indifference if wrestlers did not quickly return to the orgy of evil which alone makes good wrestling.

Extrapolated, fair wrestling could lead only to boxing or judo, whereas true wrestling derives its originality from all the excesses which make it a spectacle and not a sport. The ending of a boxing-match or a judo-contest is abrupt, like the full-stop which closes a demonstration. The rhythm of wrestling is quite different, for its natural meaning is that of rhetorical amplification: the emotional magniloquence,[1] the repeated paroxysms, the exasperation of the retorts can only find their natural outcome in the most baroque confusion. Some fights, among the most successful kind, are crowned by a final charivari,[2] a sort of unrestrained fantasia where the rules, the laws of the genre, the referee's censuring and the limits of the ring are abolished, swept away by a triumphant disorder which overflows into the hall and carries off pell-mell wrestlers, seconds, referee and spectators....

What then is a "bastard" for this audience composed in part, we are told, of people who are themselves outside the rules of society? Essentially someone unstable, who accepts the rules only when they are useful to him and transgresses the formal continuity of attitudes. He is unpredictable, therefore asocial. He takes refuge behind the law when he considers that it is in his favour, and breaks it when he finds it useful to do so. Sometimes he rejects the formal boundaries of the ring and goes on hitting an adversary legally protected by the ropes, sometimes he reestablishes these boundaries and claims the protection of what he did not respect a few minutes earlier. This inconsistency, far more than treachery or cruelty, sends the audience beside itself with rage: offended not in its morality but in its logic, it considers the contradiction of arguments as the basest of crimes. The forbidden move becomes dirty only when it de-

---

1   *magniloquence* Excessive pomposity, usually in reference to speech or writing.
2   *charivari* Raucous procession of people making discordant noise by shouting, banging objects, blowing whistles, etc.

stroys a quantitative equilibrium and disturbs the rigorous reckoning of compensations; what is condemned by the audience is not at all the transgression of insipid official rules, it is the lack of revenge, the absence of a punishment. So that there is nothing more exciting for a crowd than the grandiloquent kick given to a vanquished "bastard"; the joy of punishing is at its climax when it is supported by a mathematical justification; contempt is then unrestrained. One is no longer dealing with a *salaud* but with a *salope*—the verbal gesture of the ultimate degradation.

Such a precise finality demands that wrestling should be exactly what the public expects of it. Wrestlers, who are very experienced, know perfectly how to direct the spontaneous episodes of the fight so as to make them conform to the image which the public has of the great legendary themes of its mythology. A wrestler can irritate or disgust, he never disappoints, for he always accomplishes completely, by a progressive solidification of signs, what the public expects of him. In wrestling, nothing exists except in the absolute, there is no symbol, no allusion, everything is presented exhaustively. Leaving nothing in the shade, each action discards all parasitic meanings and ceremonially offers to the public a pure and full signification, rounded like Nature. This grandiloquence is nothing but the popular and age-old image of the perfect intelligibility of reality. What is portrayed by wrestling is therefore an ideal understanding of things; it is the euphoria of men raised for a while above the constitutive ambiguity of everyday situations and placed before the panoramic view of a univocal Nature, in which signs at last correspond to causes, without obstacle, without evasion, without contradiction.

When the hero or the villain of the drama, the man who was seen a few minutes earlier possessed by moral rage, magnified into a sort of metaphysical sign, leaves the wrestling hall, impassive, anonymous, carrying a small suitcase and arm-in-arm with his wife, no one can doubt that wrestling holds that power of transmutation which is common to the Spectacle and to Religious Worship. In the ring, and even in the depths of their voluntary ignominy, wrestlers remain gods because they are, for a few moments, the key which opens Nature, the pure gesture which separates Good from Evil, and unveils the form of a Justice which is at last intelligible.

—1972

Philip Gourevitch
b. 1961

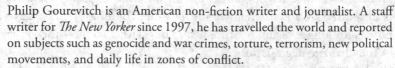

Philip Gourevitch is an American non-fiction writer and journalist. A staff
writer for *The New Yorker* since 1997, he has travelled the world and reported
on subjects such as genocide and war crimes, torture, terrorism, new political
movements, and daily life in zones of conflict.

Born in Philadelphia and raised in central Connecticut, Gourevitch received a BA from Cornell University and an MFA from the Writing Program
at Columbia. In addition to *The New Yorker*, he has published in *Granta*,
Harper's, *The New York Times Magazine*, and *The New York Review of Books*.
From 2005 to 2010, he served as editor of *The Paris Review*.

Gourevitch's third book, *Standard Operating Procedure* (2008), provides
a "thorough, terrifying account" of a turning point in the Iraq War: the Abu
Ghraib photographs of prisoner abuse. His second book, *Cold Case* (2001),
reopens an investigation into a New York City double homicide that went
unsolved for 30 years. But it was Gourevitch's first book that established him
as one of the leading voices of his generation. *We Wish to Inform You That
Tomorrow We Will Be Killed with Our Families* (1998) won many awards
and has received wide recognition for shedding new light on the Rwandan
genocide of 1994.

We Wish to Inform You contains visceral retellings of stories from individual Rwandan men and women. On six trips over nine months, Gourevitch gathered these stories on the ground. "Filled with empathy instead of
cautious neutrality, and written in powerful muckraking prose, Gourevitch's
book gives free rein to the anger—against both perpetrators and the international community—that others hold in check," wrote José E. Alvarez in
The American Journal of International Law.

from *We Wish to Inform You That Tomorrow We Will Be Killed with Our Families*

In the Province of Kibungo, in eastern Rwanda, in the swamp- and pastureland
near the Tanzanian border, there's a rocky hill called Nyarubuye with a church
where many Tutsis[1] were slaughtered in mid-April of 1994. A year after the

---

1   *Tutsis* African ethnic group living primarily within Rwanda and neighbouring Burundi.
     In pre-colonial Rwanda, the Tutsis dominated the Hutu, an ethnic group constituting the
     majority of Rwanda's population. When the nation was controlled by European colonial
     powers—first Germany beginning in 1894, then Belgium after World War I—these gov-
     ernments reinforced the privilege of the Tutsis, exacerbating pre-existing ethnic tensions.
     The Hutu seized power from the Tutsis just before Rwanda achieved independence in

killing I went to Nyarubuye with two Canadian military officers. We flew in a United Nations helicopter, travelling low over the hills in the morning mists, with the banana trees like green starbursts dense over the slopes. The uncut grass blew back as we dropped into the centre of the parish schoolyard. A lone soldier materialized with his Kalashnikov, and shook our hands with stiff, shy formality. The Canadians presented the paperwork for our visit, and I stepped up into the open doorway of a classroom.

At least fifty mostly decomposed cadavers covered the floor, wadded in clothing, their belongings strewn about and smashed. Macheted[1] skulls had rolled here and there.

The dead looked like pictures of the dead. They did not smell. They did not buzz with flies. They had been killed thirteen months earlier, and they hadn't been moved. Skin stuck here and there over the bones, many of which lay scattered away from the bodies, dismembered by the killers, or by scavengers—birds, dogs, bugs. The more complete figures looked a lot like people, which they were once. A woman in a cloth wrap printed with flowers lay near the door. Her fleshless hip bones were high and her legs slightly spread, and a child's skeleton extended between them. Her torso was hollowed out. Her ribs and spinal column poked through the rotting cloth. Her head was tipped back and her mouth was open: a strange image—half agony, half repose.

I had never been among the dead before. What to do? Look? Yes. I wanted to see them, I suppose; I had come to see them—the dead had been left unburied at Nyarubuye for memorial purposes—and there they were, so intimately exposed. I didn't need to see them. I already knew, and believed, what had happened in Rwanda. Yet looking at the buildings and the bodies, and hearing the silence of the place, with the grand Italianate basilica standing there deserted, and beds of exquisite, decadent, death-fertilized flowers blooming over the corpses, it was still strangely unimaginable. I mean one still had to imagine it.

Those dead Rwandans will be with me forever, I expect. That was why I had felt compelled to come to Nyarubuye: to be stuck with them—not with their experience, but with the experience of looking at them. They had been killed there, and they were dead there. What else could you really see at first? The Bible bloated with rain lying on top of one corpse or, littered about, the little woven wreaths of thatch which Rwandan women wear as crowns to balance the enormous loads they carry on their heads, and the water gourds, and the Converse tennis sneaker stuck somehow in a pelvis.

1962, and ongoing conflict culminated in the Rwandan genocide, which lasted from April to mid-July in 1994. During the genocide, Hutu militias killed between 500,000 and 1 million Tutsis.

1   *macheted* The machete—a large cleaver, intended for cutting jungle brush—was commonly used as a weapon during the genocide.

The soldier with the Kalashnikov—Sergeant Francis of the Rwandese Patriotic Army,[1] a Tutsi whose parents had fled to Uganda with him when he was
a boy, after similar but less extensive massacres in the early 1960s, and who
had fought his way home in 1994 and found it like this—said that the dead
in this room were mostly women who had been raped before being murdered.
Sergeant Francis had high, rolling girlish hips, and he walked and stood with
his butt stuck out behind him, an oddly purposeful posture, tipped forward,
driven. He was, at once, candid and briskly official. His English had the punc-
tilious clip of military drill, and after he told me what I was looking at I looked
instead at my feet. The rusty head of a hatchet lay beside them in the dirt.

A few weeks earlier, in Bukavu, Zaire, in the giant market of a refugee
camp that was home to many Rwandan Hutu militiamen, I had watched a man
butchering a cow with a machete. He was quite expert at his work, taking big
precise strokes that made a sharp hacking noise. The rallying cry to the killers
during the genocide was "Do your work!" And I saw that it *was* work, this
butchery; hard work. It took many hacks—two, three, four, five hard hacks—
to chop through the cow's leg. How many hacks to dismember a person?

Considering the enormity of the task, it is tempting to play with theories
of collective madness, mob mania, a fever of hatred erupted into a mass crime
of passion, and to imagine the blind orgy of the mob, with each member
killing one or two people. But at Nyarubuye, and at thousands of other sites
in this tiny country, on the same days of a few months in 1994, hundreds of
thousands of Hutus had worked as killers in regular shifts. There was always
the next victim, and the next. What sustained them, beyond the frenzy of the
first attack, through the plain physical exhaustion and mess of it?

The pygmy in Gikongoro said that humanity is part of nature and that
we must go against nature to get along and have peace. But mass violence,
too, must be organized; it does not occur aimlessly. Even mobs and riots have
a design, and great and sustained destruction requires great ambition. It must
be conceived as the means toward achieving a new order, and although the
idea behind that new order may be criminal and objectively very stupid, it
must also be compellingly simple and at the same time absolute. The ideology
of genocide is all of those things, and in Rwanda it went by the bald name of
Hutu Power.[2] For those who set about systematically exterminating an entire

---

1   *Rwandese Patriotic Army* Armed forces of the Rwandese Patriotic Front (RPF), a leftist
    political party largely composed of Tutsis, which took power in Rwanda in the aftermath
    of the genocide. The genocide itself was triggered when Hutu extremists accused the
    RPF of assassinating Rwandan president Juvénal Habyarimana and Burundian president
    Cyprien Ntaryamira on 6 April 1994.
2   *Hutu Power* Ideology that asserted the superiority of Hutu people and the inferiority of
    the Tutsis.

people—even a fairly small and unresisting subpopulation of perhaps a million and a quarter men, women, and children, like the Tutsis in Rwanda—blood lust surely helps. But the engineers and perpetrators of a slaughter like the one just inside the door where I stood need not enjoy killing, and they may even find it unpleasant. What is required above all is that they want their victims dead. They have to want it so badly that they consider it a necessity.

So I still had much to imagine as I entered the classroom and stepped carefully between the remains. These dead and their killers had been neighbours, schoolmates, colleagues, sometimes friends, even in-laws. The dead had seen their killers training as militias in the weeks before the end, and it was well known that they were training to kill Tutsis; it was announced on the radio, it was in the newspapers, people spoke of it openly. The week before the massacre at Nyarubuye, the killing began in Rwanda's capital, Kigali. Hutus who opposed the Hutu Power ideology were publicly denounced as "accomplices" of the Tutsis and were among the first to be killed as the extermination got under way. In Nyarubuye, when Tutsis asked the Hutu Power mayor how they might be spared, he suggested that they seek sanctuary at the church. They did, and a few days later the mayor came to kill them. He came at the head of a pack of soldiers, policemen, militiamen, and villagers; he gave out arms and orders to complete the job well. No more was required of the mayor, but he was also said to have killed a few Tutsis himself.

The killers killed all day at Nyarubuye. At night they cut the Achilles tendons of survivors and went off to feast behind the church, roasting cattle looted from their victims in big fires, and drinking beer. (Bottled beer, banana beer—Rwandans may not drink more beer than other Africans, but they drink prodigious quantities of it around the clock.) And, in the morning, still drunk after whatever sleep they could find beneath the cries of their prey, the killers at Nyarubuye went back and killed again. Day after day, minute to minute, Tutsi by Tutsi: all across Rwanda, they worked like that. "It was a process," Sergeant Francis said. I can see that it happened, I can be told how, and after nearly three years of looking around Rwanda and listening to Rwandans, I can tell you how, and I will. But the horror of it—the idiocy, the waste, the sheer wrongness—remains uncircumscribable.

Like Leontius,[1] the young Athenian in Plato, I presume that you are reading this because you desire a closer look, and that you, too, are properly disturbed by your curiosity. Perhaps, in examining this extremity with me, you hope for some understanding, some insight, some flicker of self-knowledge—a

---

1   *Leontius* Character referred to in Plato's *Republic* (c. 380 BCE) who was reputedly unable to resist staring at a heap of dead bodies. Plato's Socrates tells the story of Leontius in order to illustrate the compulsiveness and irrationality of the appetitive—i.e., desiring—aspect of the human soul.

moral, or a lesson, or a clue about how to behave in this world: some such information. I don't discount the possibility, but when it comes to genocide, you already know right from wrong. The best reason I have come up with for looking closely into Rwanda's stories is that ignoring them makes me even more uncomfortable about existence and my place in it. The horror, as horror, interests me only insofar as a precise memory of the offence is necessary to understand its legacy.

The dead at Nyarubuye were, I'm afraid, beautiful. There was no getting around it. The skeleton is a beautiful thing. The randomness of the fallen forms, the strange tranquility of their rude exposure, the skull here, the arm bent in some uninterpretable gesture there—these things were beautiful, and their beauty only added to the affront of the place. I couldn't settle on any meaningful response: revulsion, alarm, sorrow, grief, shame, incomprehension, sure, but nothing truly meaningful. I just looked, and I took photographs, because I wondered whether I could really see what I was seeing while I saw it, and I wanted also an excuse to look a bit more closely.

We went on through the first room and out the far side. There was another room and another and another and another. They were all full of bodies, and more bodies were scattered in the grass and there were stray skulls in the grass, which was thick and wonderfully green. Standing outside, I heard a crunch. The old Canadian colonel stumbled in front of me, and I saw, though he did not notice, that his foot had rolled on a skull and broken it. For the first time at Nyarubuye my feelings focused, and what I felt was a small but keen anger at this man. Then I heard another crunch, and felt a vibration underfoot. I had stepped on one, too.

Rwanda is spectacular to behold. Throughout its centre, a winding succession of steep, tightly terraced slopes radiates out from small roadside settlements and solitary compounds. Gashes of red clay and black loam mark fresh hoe work; eucalyptus trees flash silver against brilliant green tea plantations; banana trees are everywhere. On the theme of hills, Rwanda produces countless variations: jagged rain forests, round-shouldered buttes, undulating moors, broad swells of savanna, volcanic peaks sharp as filed teeth. During the rainy season, the clouds are huge and low and fast, mists cling in highland hollows, lightning flickers through the nights, and by day the land is lustrous. After the rains, the skies lift, the terrain takes on a ragged look beneath the flat unvarying haze of the dry season, and in the savannas of the Akagera Park wildlife blackens the hills.

One day, when I was returning to Kigali from the south, the car mounted a rise between two winding valleys, the windshield filled with purple-bellied clouds, and I asked Joseph, the man who was giving me a ride, whether Rwandans realize what a beautiful country they have. "Beautiful?" he said. "You think so? After the things that happened here? The people aren't good. If the people were good, the country might be OK." Joseph told me that his brother and sister had been killed, and he made a soft hissing click with his tongue against his teeth. "The country is empty," he said. "Empty!"

It was not just the dead who were missing. The genocide had been brought to a halt by the Rwandese Patriotic Front, a rebel army led by Tutsi refugees from past persecutions, and as the RPF advanced through the country in the summer of 1994, some two million Hutus had fled into exile at the behest of the same leaders who had urged them to kill. Yet except in some rural areas in the south, where the desertion of Hutus had left nothing but bush to reclaim the fields around crumbling adobe houses, I, as a newcomer, could not see the emptiness that blinded Joseph to Rwanda's beauty. Yes, there were grenade-flattened buildings, burnt homesteads, shot-up facades, and mortar-pitted roads. But these were the ravages of war, not of genocide, and by the summer of 1995, most of the dead had been buried. Fifteen months earlier, Rwanda had been the most densely populated country in Africa. Now the work of the killers looked just as they had intended: invisible.

From time to time, mass graves were discovered and excavated, and the remains would be transferred to new, properly consecrated mass graves. Yet even the occasionally exposed bones, the conspicuous number of amputees and people with deforming scars, and the superabundance of packed orphanages could not be taken as evidence that what had happened to Rwanda was an attempt to eliminate a people. There were only people's stories.

"Every survivor wonders why he is alive," Abbé Modeste, a priest at the cathedral in Butare, Rwanda's second-largest city, told me. Abbé Modeste had hidden for weeks in his sacristy,[1] eating communion wafers, before moving under the desk in his study, and finally into the rafters at the home of some neighbouring nuns. The obvious explanation of his survival was that the RPF had come to the rescue. But the RPF didn't reach Butare till early July, and roughly seventy-five percent of the Tutsis in Rwanda had been killed by early May. In this regard, at least, the genocide had been entirely successful: to those who were targeted, it was not death but life that seemed an accident of fate.

"I had eighteen people killed at my house," said Etienne Niyonzima, a former businessman who had become a deputy in the National Assembly. "Everything was totally destroyed—a place of fifty-five metres by fifty metres. In my neighbourhood they killed six hundred and forty-seven people. They tortured them, too. You had to see how they killed them. They had the number

---

1   *sacristy* Room in a Christian church where priests and attendants prepare for mass or other religious services.

of everyone's house, and they went through with red paint and marked the homes of all the Tutsis and of the Hutu moderates. My wife was at a friend's, shot with two bullets. She is still alive, only"—he fell quiet for a moment— "she has no arms. The others with her were killed. The militia left her for dead. Her whole family of sixty-five in Gitarama were killed." Niyonzima was in hiding at the time. Only after he had been separated from his wife for three months did he learn that she and four of their children had survived. "Well," he said, "one son was cut in the head with a machete. I don't know where he went." His voice weakened, and caught. "He disappeared." Niyonzima clicked his tongue, and said, "But the others are still alive. Quite honestly, I don't understand at all how I was saved."

Laurent Nkongoli attributed his survival to "Providence,[1] and also good neighbours, an old woman who said, 'Run away, we don't want to see your corpse.'" Nkongoli, a lawyer, who had become the vice president of the National Assembly after the genocide, was a robust man, with a taste for double-breasted suit jackets and lively ties, and he moved, as he spoke, with a brisk determination. But before taking his neighbour's advice, and fleeing Kigali in late April of 1994, he said, "I had accepted death. At a certain moment this happens. One hopes not to die cruelly, but one expects to die anyway. Not death by machete, one hopes, but with a bullet. If you were willing to pay for it, you could often ask for a bullet. Death was more or less normal, a resignation. You lose the will to fight. There were four thousand Tutsis killed here at Kacyiru"—a neighbourhood of Kigali. "The soldiers brought them here, and told them to sit down because they were going to throw grenades. And they sat.

"Rwandan culture is a culture of fear," Nkongoli went on. "I remember what people said." He adopted a pipey voice, and his face took on a look of disgust: "'Just let us pray, then kill us,' or 'I don't want to die in the street, I want to die at home.'" He resumed his normal voice. "When you're that resigned and oppressed you're already dead. It shows the genocide was prepared for too long. I detest this fear. These victims of genocide had been psychologically prepared to expect death just for being Tutsi. They were being killed for so long that they were already dead."

I reminded Nkongoli that, for all his hatred of fear, he had himself accepted death before his neighbour urged him to run away. "Yes," he said. "I got tired in the genocide. You struggle so long, then you get tired."

Every Rwandan I spoke with seemed to have a favourite, unanswerable question. For Nkongoli, it was how so many Tutsis had allowed themselves to be killed. For François Xavier Nkurunziza, a Kigali lawyer, whose father was Hutu and whose mother and wife were Tutsi, the question was how so many

---

1   *Providence* God's will, divine intervention.

Hutus had allowed themselves to kill. Nkurunziza had escaped death only by chance as he moved around the country from one hiding place to another, and he had lost many family members. "Conformity is very deep, very developed here," he told me. "In Rwandan history, everyone obeys authority. People revere power, and there isn't enough education. You take a poor, ignorant population, and give them arms, and say, 'It's yours. Kill.' They'll obey. The peasants, who were paid or forced to kill, were looking up to people of higher socio-economic standing to see how to behave. So the people of influence, or the big financiers, are often the big men in the genocide. They may think they didn't kill because they didn't take life with their own hands, but the people were looking to them for their orders. And, in Rwanda, an order can be given very quietly."

As I travelled around the country, collecting accounts of the killing, it almost seemed as if, with the machete, the *masu*—a club studded with nails—a few well-placed grenades, and a few bursts of automatic-rifle fire, the quiet orders of Hutu Power had made the neutron bomb[1] obsolete.

"Everyone was called to hunt the enemy," said Theodore Nyilinkwaya, a survivor of the massacres in his home village of Kimbogo, in the southwestern province of Cyangugu. "But let's say someone is reluctant. Say that guy comes with a stick. They tell him, 'No, get a *masu*.' So, OK, he does, and he runs along with the rest, but he doesn't kill. They say, 'Hey, he might denounce us later. He must kill. Everyone must help to kill at least one person.' So this person who is not a killer is made to do it. And the next day it's become a game for him. You don't need to keep pushing him."

At Nyarubuye, even the little terracotta votive statues[2] in the sacristy had been methodically decapitated. "They were associated with Tutsis," Sergeant Francis explained.

—1999

---

1   *neutron bomb* Thermonuclear weapon that releases a small amount of explosive energy, but an enormous amount of radiation. A neutron bomb does very little damage to infrastructure, but incredible damage to a human population.

2   *votive statues* Statues intended to be used as religious offerings.

Drew Hayden Taylor

b. 1962

Drew Hayden Taylor is a Canadian author who works in a variety of literary genres, though he is best known as a playwright. His award winning plays include *Toronto at Dreamer's Rock* (1990), *The Bootlegger Blues* (1991), and *Only Drunks and Children Tell the Truth* (1998). An Ojibway from the Curve Lake First Nation in Ontario, he is recognized as an important Aboriginal voice in the Canadian literary world. In addition to writing plays, he has served as the artistic director of Toronto's Native Earth Performing Arts theatre company, taught at the Centre for Indigenous Theatre, and served as Writer in Residence at the University of Michigan, the University of Western Ontario, the University of Luneburg (Germany), and several Canadian theatre companies.

Taylor has also written short stories and television and film scripts, and has contributed to numerous documentaries. In 2007, he published his first novel, the youth-oriented vampire tale *The Night Wanderer: A Native Gothic Novel* (2007). This was soon followed by his first novel for adults, *Motorcycles & Sweetgrass* (2010), which was nominated for the Governor General's Award for Fiction and earned him recognition as one of Random House Canada's 2010 New Faces of Fiction. He regularly contributes columns and articles to newspapers and magazines.

Central to this diverse body of work is Taylor's sensitivity to the demands of effective storytelling and his desire to convey an Aboriginal perspective in an honest and engaging way. In his words, "My whole philosophy as a writer is to create interesting characters, with an interesting story, and to take the audience on an interesting journey." Regarding the goals of his work, he has said, "I hope that I have provided a window of understanding between Native and non-Native cultures by demystifying Native life."

Pretty Like a White Boy

In this big, huge world, with all its billions and billions of people, it's safe to say that everybody will eventually come across personalities and individuals who will touch them in some peculiar yet poignant way. Characters that in some way represent and help define who you are. I'm no different—mine is Kermit the Frog. Not just because Natives have a long tradition of savouring frogs' legs, but because of this particular frog's music. You all may remember Kermit is quite famous for his rendition of *It's Not Easy Being Green*. I can relate. If I could sing, my song would be *It's Not Easy Having Blue Eyes in a Brown-Eyed Village*.

Yes, I'm afraid it's true. The author happens to be a card-carrying Indian. Once you get past the aforementioned eyes, the fair skin, light brown hair and noticeable lack of cheek bones, there lies the heart and spirit of an Ojibway storyteller. "Honest Injun" or as the more politically correct term may be, "Honest Aboriginal."

You see, I'm the product of a White father I never knew and an Ojibway woman who evidently couldn't run fast enough. As a kid I knew I looked a bit different but, then again, all kids are paranoid when it comes to their peers. I had a fairly happy childhood, frolicking through the bulrushes. But there were certain things that even then made me notice my unusual appearance. Whenever we played cowboys and Indians, guess who had to be the bad guy (the cowboy)?

It wasn't until I left the reserve for the big bad city, that I became more aware of the role people expected me to play, and the fact that physically, I didn't fit in. Everybody seemed to have this preconceived idea of how every Indian looked and acted. One guy, on my first day of college, asked me what kind of horse I preferred. I didn't have the heart to tell him "hobby."

I've often tried to be philosophical about the whole thing. I have both White and Red blood in me. I guess that makes me pink. I am a "Pink Man." Try to imagine this: I'm walking around on any typical reserve in Canada, my head held high, proudly announcing to everyone, "I am a Pink Man." It's a good thing I ran track in school.

My pinkness is constantly being pointed out to me over and over and over again. "You don't look Indian!" "You're not Indian, are you?" "Really?!?!" I got questions like that from both White and Native people. For a while I debated having my Status card tattooed on my forehead.

And like most insecure people, and especially a blue-eyed Native writer, I went through a particularly severe identity crisis at one point. In fact, I admit it, one depressing spring evening I dyed my hair black. Pitch black.

The reason for such a dramatic act, you ask? Show business. You see, for the last eight years or so, I've worked in various capacities in the performing arts, and as a result I often get calls to be an extra or even try out for an important role in some Native-oriented movie. This anonymous voice would phone, having been given my number, and ask if I would be interested in trying out for a movie. Being a naturally ambitious, curious and greedy young man, I would always readily agree, stardom flashing in my eyes and hunger pains calling from my wallet.

A few days later I would show up for the audition, and that was always an experience. What kind of experience you ask? Picture this: the movie calls for the casting of seventeenth century Mohawk warriors living in a traditional longhouse. The casting director calls the name Drew Hayden Taylor, and I enter. The casting director, the producer and the film's director look up and see my face, blue eyes shining in anticipation. I once was described as a slightly chubby beach boy. But even beach boys have tans. Anyway, there would be a quick flush of confusion, a recheck of the papers and a hesitant "Mr. Taylor?" Then they would ask if I was at the right audition. It was always the same. By the way, I never got any of the parts I tried for except for a few anonymous crowd shots. Politics tell me it's because of the way I look, reality tells me it's probably because I can't act. I'm not sure which is better.

It's not just film people either. Recently I've become quite involved in theatre—Native theatre to be exact. And one cold October day I was happily attending the Toronto leg of a province-wide tour of my first play, *Toronto at Dreamer's Rock*. The place was sold out, the audience very receptive, and the performance was wonderful. Ironically one of the actors was also half-White. The director later told me he had been talking with that actor's father, an older non-Native chap. Evidently he had asked a few questions about me, and how I did my research. This made the director curious and he asked about the man's interest. He replied, "He's got an amazing grasp of the Native situation for a White person."

Not all these incidents are work-related either. One time a friend and I were coming out of a rather up-scale bar (we were out yuppie-watching) and managed to catch a cab. We thanked the cab driver for being so comfortably close on such a cold night. He shrugged and nonchalantly talked about knowing what bars to drive around. "If you're not careful, all you'll get is drunk Indians." I hiccuped.

Another time, the cab driver droned on and on about the government. He started out by criticizing Mulroney himself, and then eventually, his handling of the Oka crisis.[1] This perked up my ears, until he said, "If it were me, I'd have tear-gassed the place by the second day. No more problems." He got a dime tip. A few incidents like this and I'm convinced I'd make a great undercover agent for Native political organizations.

But then again, even Native people have been known to look at me with a fair amount of suspicion. Many years ago when I was a young man, I was working on a documentary on Native culture up in the wilds of northern Ontario. We were at an isolated cabin filming a trapper woman and her kids. This one particular nine-year-old girl seemed to take a shine to me. She followed me around for two days, both annoying me and endearing herself to me. But she absolutely refused to believe that I was Indian. The whole film crew

---

1   *Mulroney* Brian Mulroney, prime minister of Canada from 1984 to 1993; *Oka crisis* Mohawk protest over disputed land that developed into a violent conflict with government military and police forces. Protesters occupied the disputed land—which the town of Oka, Quebec, wanted to use for a golf course—from July to September in 1990.

tried to tell her but to no avail. She was certain I was White. Then one day as I was loading up the car with film equipment, she asked me if I wanted some tea. Being in a hurry, I declined the tea. She immediately smiled with victory, crying out, "See, you're not Indian. All Indians drink tea!"

Frustrated and a little hurt, I whipped out my Status card and showed it to her. Now there I was, standing in a northern Ontario winter, showing my Status card to a nine-year-old, non-status, Indian girl who had no idea what it was. Looking back, this may not have been one of my brighter moves.

But I must admit, it was a Native woman that boiled everything down to one simple sentence. You may know that woman—Marianne Jones from *The Beachcombers*[1] television series. We were working on a film together out west and we got to gossiping. Eventually we got around to talking about our respective villages. Her village is on the Queen Charlotte Islands, or Haida Gwaii as the Haida call them, and mine is in central Ontario.

Eventually, childhood on the reserve was being discussed and I made a comment about the way I look. She studied me for a moment, smiled and said, "Do you know what the old women in my village would call you?" Hesitant but curious, I shook my head. "They'd say you were pretty like a White boy." To this day I'm still not sure if I like that.

Now some may argue that I am simply a Métis with a Status card. I disagree—I failed French in grade eleven. And the Métis, as everyone knows, have their own separate and honourable culture, particularly in western Canada. And, of course, I am well aware that I am not the only person with my physical characteristics.

I remember once looking at a video tape of a drum group, shot on a reserve up near Manitoulin Island. I noticed one of the drummers seemed quite fair-haired, almost blond. I mentioned this to my girlfriend of the time and she shrugged, saying, "Well, that's to be expected. The highway runs right through that reserve."

Perhaps I'm being too critical. There's a lot to be said for both cultures. For example, on the one hand, you have the Native respect for Elders. They understand the concept of wisdom and insight coming with age.

On the White hand, there's Italian food. I mean I really love my mother and family but seriously, does anything really beat good Veal Scaloppine? Most of my Aboriginal friends share my fondness for this particular type of food. Wasn't there a warrior at Oka named Lasagna? I found it ironic, though curiously logical, that Columbus was Italian. A connection, I wonder?

---

1   *Marianne Jones* Haida filmmaker and actor; *The Beachcombers* Canadian television series (1972–90) set in Gibsons, British Columbia.

Also, Native people have this wonderful respect and love for the land. They believe they are part of it, a mere link in the cycle of existence. Now as many of you know, this clashes with the accepted Judeo-Christian (i.e. western) view of land management. I even believe somewhere in the first chapters of the Bible it says something about God giving man dominion over nature. Check it out, Genesis 4 (?) "Thou shalt clear cut." But I grew up understanding that everything around me is important and alive. My Native heritage gave me that.

And again, on the White hand, there are breast implants. Darn clever them White people. That's something Indians would never have invented, seriously. We're not ambitious enough. We just take what the Creator decides to give us; but no, not the White man. Just imagine it, some serious looking White doctor (and let's face it people, we know it was a man who invented them) sitting around in his laboratory muttering to himself, "Big tits, big tits, hmm, how do I make big tits?" If it was an Indian, it would be, "Big tits, big tits, White women sure got big tits," and leave it at that.

So where does that leave me on the big philosophical score board? What exactly are my choices again? Indians: respect for Elders, love of the land. White people: food and big tits. In order to live in both cultures I guess I'd have to find an Indian woman with big tits who lives with her grandmother in a cabin out in the woods and can make Fettuccini Alfredo on a wood stove.

Now let me make myself clear—I'm not writing this for sympathy, or out of anger, or even some need for self-glorification. I am just setting the facts straight. For as you read this, a new Nation is born. This is a declaration of independence. My declaration of independence.

I've spent too many years explaining who and what I am repeatedly, so, as of this moment, I officially secede from both races. I plan to start my own separate nation. Because I am half Ojibway and half Caucasian, we will be called the Occasions. And of course, since I'm founding the new nation, I will be a Special Occasion.

—1991

David Foster Wallace
1962–2008

David Foster Wallace was an American writer of novels, essays, and short stories. The publication of his novel *Infinite Jest* (1996) catapulted him to national prominence as a writer; in 2005, *Time* magazine included it in their list of the "100 Best English-language Novels Published Since 1923." Wallace's essays—notably "Consider the Lobster" (2004) and "A Supposedly Fun Thing I'll Never Do Again" (1996)—are also widely referenced and anthologized; he has come to be recognized as an important writer in multiple literary genres.

Wallace's father was a professor of philosophy, and his mother was a professor of English; given that background, it is perhaps not surprising that Wallace's approach is both cerebral and consciously literary. His writing style is inquisitive, elliptical, and sometimes playful, but there is a deep seriousness to it; questions about the nature of human experience and the functioning of society lie at the heart of much of his writing, which displays a philosopher's resistance to final and certain answers. He has said that "part of our emergency is that it's so tempting ... to retreat to narrow arrogance, pre-formed positions, rigid filters, the 'moral clarity' of the immature. The alternative is dealing with massive, high-entropy amounts of info and ambiguity and conflict and flux." Reflecting this dilemma, his texts are often wildly discursive—peppered with asides, qualifications, and tangential discussions. *Infinite Jest*, for example, has hundreds of endnotes, many of which are themselves further annotated. The essay collected here, "Consider the Lobster," also employs notes extensively.

Wallace committed suicide in 2008 after a life-long battle with depression, leaving behind an unfinished manuscript for the novel *The Pale King* (2011). That the unfinished novel became a finalist for the 2012 Pulitzer Prize in fiction testifies to Wallace's important place in the literary world.

Consider the Lobster

The enormous, pungent, and extremely well-marketed Maine Lobster Festival is held every late July in the state's midcoast region, meaning the western side of Penobscot Bay, the nerve stem of Maine's lobster industry. What's called the midcoast runs from Owl's Head and Thomaston in the south to Belfast in the north. (Actually, it might extend all the way up to Bucksport, but we were never able to get farther north than Belfast on Route 1, whose summer traffic is, as you can imagine, unimaginable.) The region's two main communities are Camden, with its very old money and yachty harbour and five-star restaurants and phenomenal B&Bs, and Rockland, a serious old fishing town that hosts the festival every summer in historic Harbor Park, right along the water.[1]

Tourism and lobster are the midcoast region's two main industries, and they're both warm-weather enterprises, and the Maine Lobster Festival represents less an intersection of the industries than a deliberate collision, joyful and lucrative and loud. The assigned subject of this *Gourmet* article[2] is the 56th Annual MLF, 30 July–3 August, 2003, whose official theme this year was "Lighthouses, Laughter, and Lobster." Total paid attendance was over 100,000, due partly to a national CNN spot in June during which a senior editor of *Food & Wine* magazine hailed the MLF as one of the best food-themed galas in the world. 2003 festival highlights: concerts by Lee Ann Womack and Orleans,[3] annual Maine Sea Goddess beauty pageant, Saturday's big parade, Sunday's William G. Atwood Memorial Crate Race, annual Amateur Cooking Competition, carnival rides and midway attractions and food booths, and the MLF's Main Eating Tent, where something over 25,000 pounds of fresh-caught Maine lobster is consumed after preparation in the World's Largest Lobster Cooker near the grounds' north entrance. Also available are lobster rolls, lobster turnovers, lobster sauté, Down East lobster salad, lobster bisque, lobster ravioli, and deep-fried lobster dumplings. Lobster thermidor[4] is obtainable at a sit-down restaurant called the Black Pearl on Harbor Park's northwest wharf. A large all-pine booth sponsored by the Maine Lobster Promotion Council has free pamphlets with recipes, eating tips, and Lobster Fun Facts. The winner of Friday's Amateur Cooking Competition prepares Saffron Lobster Ramekins, the recipe for which is now available for public downloading at www.mainelobsterfestival.com. There are lobster T-shirts and lobster bobblehead dolls and inflatable lobster pool toys and clamp-on lobster hats with big scarlet claws that wobble on springs. Your assigned correspondent saw it all, accompanied by one girlfriend and both his own parents—one of which parents was actually born and raised in Maine, albeit in the extreme northern inland part, which is potato country and a world away from the touristic midcoast.[5]

For practical purposes, everyone knows what a lobster is. As usual, though, there's much more to know than most of us care about—it's all a matter of what your interests are. Taxonomically speaking, a lobster is a marine crustacean of the family Homaridae, characterized by five pairs of jointed legs, the

1   [Wallace's note] There's a comprehensive native apothegm: "Camden by the sea, Rockland by the smell."
2   *Gourmet article* This article originally appeared in *Gourmet* magazine.
3   *Lee Ann Womack* American pop-country musician; *Orleans* American pop-rock band.
4   *Lobster thermidor* French lobster in cream sauce dish requiring extensive preparation.
5   [Wallace's note] N.B. All personally connected parties have made it clear from the start that they do not want to be talked about in this article.

first pair terminating in large pincerish claws used for subduing prey. Like many other species of benthic[1] carnivore, lobsters are both hunters and scavengers. They have stalked eyes, gills on their legs, and antennae. There are a dozen or so different kinds worldwide, of which the relevant species here is the Maine lobster, *Homarus americanus*. The name "lobster" comes from the Old English *loppestre*, which is thought to be a corrupt form of the Latin word for locust combined with the Old English *loppe*, which meant spider.

Moreover, a crustacean is an aquatic arthropod of the class Crustacea, which comprises crabs, shrimp, barnacles, lobsters, and freshwater crayfish. All this is right there in the encyclopedia. And arthropods are members of the phylum Arthropoda, which phylum covers insects, spiders, crustaceans, and centipedes/millipedes, all of whose main commonality, besides the absence of a centralized brain-spine assembly, is a chitinous exoskeleton composed of segments, to which appendages are articulated in pairs.

The point is that lobsters are basically giant sea insects.[2] Like most arthropods, they date from the Jurassic period, biologically so much older than mammalia that they might as well be from another planet. And they are—particularly in their natural brown-green state, brandishing their claws like weapons and with thick antennae awhip—not nice to look at. And it's true that they are garbagemen of the sea, eaters of dead stuff,[3] although they'll also eat some live shellfish, certain kinds of injured fish, and sometimes one another.

But they are themselves good eating. Or so we think now. Up until sometime in the 1800s, though, lobster was literally low-class food, eaten only by the poor and institutionalized. Even in the harsh penal environment of early America, some colonies had laws against feeding lobsters to inmates more than once a week because it was thought to be cruel and unusual, like making people eat rats. One reason for their low status was how plentiful lobsters were in old New England. "Unbelievable abundance" is how one source describes the situation, including accounts of Plymouth Pilgrims wading out and capturing all they wanted by hand, and of early Boston's seashore being littered with lobsters after hard storms—these latter were treated as a smelly nuisance and ground up for fertilizer. There is also the fact that premodern lobster was cooked dead and then preserved, usually packed in salt or crude hermetic containers. Maine's earliest lobster industry was based around a dozen such seaside canneries in the 1840s, from which lobster was shipped as far away as California, in demand only because it was cheap and high in protein, basically chewable fuel.

---

1 *benthic* Bottom-dwelling.
2 [Wallace's note] Midcoasters' native term for a lobster is, in fact, "bug," as in "Come around on Sunday and we'll cook up some bugs."
3 [Wallace's note] Factoid: Lobster traps are usually baited with dead herring.

Now, of course, lobster is posh, a delicacy, only a step or two down from caviar. The meat is richer and more substantial than most fish, its taste subtle compared to the marine-gaminess of mussels and clams. In the US pop-food imagination, lobster is now the seafood analog to steak, with which it's so often twinned as Surf 'n' Turf on the really expensive part of the chain steakhouse menu.

In fact, one obvious project of the MLF, and of its omnipresently sponsorial Maine Lobster Promotion Council, is to counter the idea that lobster is unusually luxe or unhealthy or expensive, suitable only for effete palates or the occasional blow-the-diet treat. It is emphasized over and over in presentations and pamphlets at the festival that lobster meat has fewer calories, less cholesterol, and less saturated fat than chicken.[1] And in the Main Eating Tent, you can get a "quarter" (industry shorthand for a 1¼-pound lobster), a four-ounce cup of melted butter, a bag of chips, and a soft roll w/ butter-pat for around $12.00, which is only slightly more expensive than supper at McDonald's.

Be apprised, though, that the Main Lobster Festival's democratization of lobster comes with all the massed inconvenience and aesthetic compromise of real democracy. See, for example, the aforementioned Main Eating Tent, for which there is a constant Disneyland-grade queue, and which turns out to be a square quarter mile of awning-shaded cafeteria lines and rows of long institutional tables at which friend and stranger alike sit cheek by jowl, cracking and chewing and dribbling. It's hot, and the sagged roof traps the steam and the smells, which latter are strong and only partly food-related. It is also loud, and a good percentage of the total noise is masticatory. The suppers come in styrofoam trays, and the soft drinks are iceless and flat, and the coffee is convenience-store coffee in more styrofoam, and the utensils are plastic (there are none of the special long skinny forks for pushing out the tail meat, though a few savvy diners bring their own). Nor do they give you near enough napkins considering how messy lobster is to eat, especially when you're squeezed onto benches alongside children of various ages and vastly different levels of fine-motor development—not to mention the people who've somehow smuggled in their own beer in enormous aisle-blocking coolers, or who all of a sudden produce their own plastic tablecloths and spread them over large portions of tables to try to reserve them (the tables) for their little groups. And so on. Any one example is no more than a petty inconvenience, of course, but the MLF turns out to be full of irksome little downers like this—see for instance the Main Stage's headliner shows, where it turns out you have to

---

1   [Wallace's note] Of course, the common practice of dipping the lobster meat in melted butter torpedoes all these happy fat-specs, which none of the council's promotional stuff ever mentions, any more than potato industry PR talks about sour cream and bacon bits.

pay $20 extra for a folding chair if you want to sit down; or the North Tent's mad scramble for the Nyquil-cup-sized samples of finalists' entries handed out after the Cooking Competition; or the much-touted Maine Sea Goddess pageant finals, which turn out to be excruciatingly long and to consist mainly of endless thanks and tributes to local sponsors. Let's not even talk about the grossly inadequate Port-A-San facilities or the fact that there's nowhere to wash your hands before or after eating. What the Maine Lobster Festival really is is a midlevel county fair with a culinary hook, and in this respect it's not unlike Tidewater crab festivals, Midwest corn festivals, Texas chili festivals, etc., and shares with these venues the core paradox of all teeming commercial demotic[1] events: It's not for everyone.[2] Nothing against the euphoric senior editor of *Food & Wine*, but I'd be surprised if she'd ever actually been here in Harbor Park, amid crowds of people slapping canal-zone mosquitoes as they eat deep-fried Twinkies and watch Professor Paddywhack, on six-foot stilts

---

1   *demotic* Popular; for the masses.
2   [Wallace's note] In truth, there's a great deal to be said about the differences between working-class Rockland and the heavily populist flavour of its festival versus comfortable and elitist Camden with its expensive view and shops given entirely over to $200 sweaters and great rows of Victorian homes converted to upscale B&Bs. And about these differences as two sides of the great coin that is US tourism. Very little of which will be said here, except to amplify the above-mentioned paradox and to reveal your assigned correspondent's own preferences. I confess that I have never understood why so many people's idea of a fun vacation is to don flip-flops and sunglasses and crawl through maddening traffic to loud, hot, crowded tourist venues in order to sample a "local flavour" that is by definition ruined by the presence of tourists. This may (as my festival companions keep pointing out) all be a matter of personality and hardwired taste: the fact that I do not like tourist venues means that I'll never understand their appeal and so am probably not the one to talk about it (the supposed appeal). But, since this FN will almost surely not survive magazine-editing anyway, here goes:
     As I see it, it probably really is good for the soul to be a tourist, even if it's only once in a while. Not good for the soul in a refreshing or enlivening way, though, but rather in a grim, steely-eyed, let's-look-honestly-at-the-facts-and-find-some-way-to-deal-with-them way. My personal experience has not been that travelling around the country is broadening or relaxing, or that radical changes in place and context have a salutary effect, but rather that intranational tourism is radically constricting, and humbling in the hardest way—hostile to my fantasy of being a true individual, of living somehow outside and above it all. (Coming up is the part that my companions find especially unhappy and repellent, a sure way to spoil the fun of vacation travel:) To be a mass tourist, for me, is to become a pure late-date American: alien, ignorant, greedy for something you cannot ever have, disappointed in a way you can never admit. It is to spoil, by way of sheer ontology, the very unspoiledness you are there to experience. It is to impose yourself on places that in all non-economic ways would be better, realer, without you. It is, in lines and gridlock and transaction after transaction, to confront a dimension of yourself that is as inescapable as it is painful: As a tourist, you become economically significant but existentially loathsome, an insect on a dead thing.

in a raincoat with plastic lobsters protruding from all directions on springs, terrify their children.

Lobster is essentially a summer food. This is because we now prefer our lobsters fresh, which means they have to be recently caught, which for both tactical and economic reasons takes place at depths less than 25 fathoms. Lobsters tend to be hungriest and most active (i.e., most trappable) at summer water temperatures of 45–50 degrees. In the autumn, most Maine lobsters migrate out into deeper water, either for warmth or to avoid the heavy waves that pound New England's coast all winter. Some burrow into the bottom. They might hibernate; nobody's sure. Summer is also lobsters' molting season— specifically early- to mid-July. Chitinous arthropods grow by molting, rather the way people have to buy bigger clothes as they age and gain weight. Since lobsters can live to be over 100, they can also get to be quite large, as in 30 pounds or more—though truly senior lobsters are rare now, because New England's waters are so heavily trapped.[1] Anyway, hence the culinary distinction between hard- and soft-shell lobsters, the latter sometimes a.k.a. shedders. A soft-shell lobster is one that has recently molted. In midcoast restaurants, the summer menu often offers both kinds, with shedders being slightly cheaper even though they're easier to dismantle and the meat is allegedly sweeter. The reason for the discount is that a molting lobster uses a layer of seawater for insulation while its new shell is hardening, so there's slightly less actual meat when you crack open a shedder, plus a redolent gout of water that gets all over everything and can sometimes jet out lemonlike and catch a tablemate right in the eye. If it's winter or you're buying lobster someplace far from New England, on the other hand, you can almost bet that the lobster is a hard-shell, which for obvious reasons travel better.

As an à la carte entrée, lobster can be baked, broiled, steamed, grilled, sautéed, stir-fried, or microwaved. The most common method, though, is boiling. If you're someone who enjoys having lobster at home, this is probably the way you do it, since boiling is so easy. You need a large kettle w/ cover, which you fill about half full with water (the standard advice is that you want 2.5 quarts of water per lobster). Seawater is optimal, or you can add two tbsp salt per quart from the tap. It also helps to know how much your lobsters weigh. You get the water boiling, put in the lobsters one at a time, cover the kettle, and bring it back up to a boil. Then you bank the heat and let the kettle simmer—ten minutes for the first pound of lobster, then three minutes for each pound after that. (This is assuming you've got hard-shell lobsters, which,

---

1   [Wallace's note] Datum: In a good year, the US industry produces around 80,000,000 pounds of lobster, and Maine accounts for more than half that total.

again, if you don't live between Boston and Halifax is probably what you've got. For shedders, you're supposed to subtract three minutes from the total.) The reason the kettle's lobsters turn scarlet is that boiling somehow suppresses every pigment in their chitin but one. If you want an easy test of whether the lobsters are done, you try pulling on one of their antennae—if it comes out of the head with minimal effort, you're ready to eat.

A detail so obvious that most recipes don't even bother to mention it is that each lobster is supposed to be alive when you put it in the kettle. This is part of lobster's modern appeal—it's the freshest food there is. There's no decomposition between harvesting and eating. And not only do lobsters require no cleaning or dressing or plucking, they're relatively easy for vendors to keep alive. They come up alive in the traps, are placed in containers of seawater, and can—so long as the water's aerated and the animals' claws are pegged or banded to keep them from tearing one another up under the stresses of captivity[1]—survive right up until they're boiled. Most of us have been in supermarkets or restaurants that feature tanks of live lobsters, from which you can pick out your supper while it watches you point. And part of the overall spectacle of the Maine Lobster Festival is that you can see actual lobstermen's vessels docking at the wharves along the northeast grounds and unloading fresh-caught product, which is transferred by hand or cart 150 yards to the great clear tanks stacked up around the festival's cooker—which is, as mentioned, billed as the World's Largest Lobster Cooker and can process over 100 lobsters at a time for the Main Eating Tent.

So then here is a question that's all but unavoidable at the World's Largest Lobster Cooker, and may arise in kitchens across the US: Is it all right to boil a sentient creature alive just for our gustatory[2] pleasure? A related set of concerns: Is the previous question irksomely PC or sentimental? What does "all right" even mean in this context? Is the whole thing just a matter of personal choice?

---

1   [Wallace's note] N.B. Similar reasoning underlies the practice of what's termed "debeaking" broiler chickens and brood hens in modern factory farms. Maximum commercial efficiency requires that enormous poultry populations be confined in unnaturally close quarters, under which conditions many birds go crazy and peck one another to death. As a purely observational side-note, be apprised that debeaking is usually an automated process and that the chickens receive no anaesthetic. It's not clear to me whether most *Gourmet* readers know about debeaking, or about related practices like dehorning cattle in commercial feed lots, cropping swine's tails in factory hog farms to keep psychotically bored neighbours from chewing them off, and so forth. It so happens that your assigned correspondent knew almost nothing about standard meat-industry operations before starting work on this article.

2   *gustatory* Taste-related.

As you may or may not know, a certain well-known group called People for the Ethical Treatment of Animals thinks that the morality of lobster-boiling is not just a matter of individual conscience. In fact, one of the very first things we hear about the MLF ... well, to set the scene: We're coming in by cab from the almost indescribably odd and rustic Knox County Airport[1] very late on the night before the festival opens, sharing the cab with a wealthy political consultant who lives on Vinalhaven Island in the bay half the year (he's headed for the island ferry in Rockland). The consultant and cabdriver are responding to informal journalistic probes about how people who live in the midcoast region actually view the MLF, as in is the festival just a big-dollar tourist thing or is it something local residents look forward to attending, take genuine civic pride in, etc. The cabdriver (who's in his seventies, one of apparently a whole platoon of retirees the cab company puts on to help with the summer rush, and wears a US-flag lapel pin, and drives in what can only be called a very *deliberate* way) assures us that locals do endorse and enjoy the MLF, although he himself hasn't gone in years, and now come to think of it no one he and his wife know has, either. However, the demilocal consultant's been to recent festivals a couple times (one gets the impression it was at his wife's behest), of which his most vivid impression was that "you have to line up for an ungodly long time to get your lobsters, and meanwhile there are all these ex–flower children coming up and down along the line handing out pamphlets that say the lobsters die in terrible pain and you shouldn't eat them."

And it turns out that the post-hippies of the consultant's recollection were activists from PETA. There were no PETA people in obvious view at the 2003 MLF,[2] but they've been conspicuous at many of the recent festi-

---

1   [Wallace's note] The terminal used to be somebody's house, for example, and the lost-luggage-reporting room was clearly once a pantry.

2   [Wallace's note] It turned out that one Mr. William R. Rivas-Rivas, a high-ranking PETA official out of the group's Virginia headquarters, was indeed there this year, albeit solo, working the festival's main and side entrances on Saturday, 2 August, handing out pamphlets and adhesive stickers emblazoned with "Being Boiled Hurts," which is the tagline in most of PETA's published material about lobsters. I learned that he'd been there only later, when speaking with Mr. Rivas-Rivas on the phone. I'm not sure how we missed seeing him *in situ* at the festival, and I can't see much to do except apologize for the oversight—although it's also true that Saturday was the day of the big MLF parade through Rockland, which basic journalistic responsibility seemed to require going to (and which, with all due respect, meant that Saturday was maybe not the best day for PETA to work the Harbor Park grounds, especially if it was going to be just one person for one day, since a lot of diehard MLF partisans were off-site watching the parade (which, again with no offence intended, was in truth kind of cheesy and boring, consisting mostly of slow home-made floats and various midcoast people waving at one another, and with an extremely annoying man dressed as Blackbeard ranging up and down the length of the crowd saying "Arrr" over and over and brandishing a plastic sword at people, etc.; plus it rained)).

vals. Since at least the mid-1990s, articles in everything from *The Camden Herald* to *The New York Times* have described PETA urging boycotts of the Maine Lobster Festival, often deploying celebrity spokesmen like Mary Tyler Moore for open letters and ads saying stuff like "Lobsters are extraordinarily sensitive" and "To me, eating a lobster is out of the question." More concrete is the oral testimony of Dick, our florid and extremely gregarious rental-car liaison,[1] to the effect that PETA's been around so much during recent years that a kind of brittlely tolerant homeostasis[2] now obtains between the activists and the festival's locals, e.g.: "We had some incidents a couple years ago. One lady took most of her clothes off and painted herself like a lobster, almost got herself arrested. But for the most part they're let alone. [Rapid series of small ambiguous laughs, which with Dick happens a lot.] They do their thing and we do our thing."

This whole interchange takes place on Route 1, 30 July, during a four-mile, 50-minute ride from the airport[3] to the dealership to sign car-rental papers. Several irreproducible segues down the road from the PETA anecdotes, Dick—whose son-in-law happens to be a professional lobsterman and one of the Main Eating Tent's regular suppliers—explains what he and his family feel is the crucial mitigating factor in the whole morality-of-boiling-lobsters-alive issue: "There's a part of the brain in people and animals that lets us feel pain, and lobsters' brains don't have this part."

Besides the fact that it's incorrect in about nine different ways, the main reason Dick's statement is interesting is that its thesis is more or less echoed by the festival's own pronouncement on lobsters and pain, which is part of a Test Your Lobster IQ quiz that appears in the 2003 MLF program courtesy of the Maine Lobster Promotion Council:

> The nervous system of a lobster is very simple, and is in fact most similar to the nervous system of the grasshopper. It is decentralized with no brain. There is no cerebral cortex, which in humans is the area of the brain that gives the experience of pain.

1 [Wallace's note] By profession, Dick is actually a car salesman; the midcoast region's National Car Rental franchise operates out of a Chevy dealership in Thomaston.
2 *homeostasis* I.e., balance.
3 [Wallace's note] The short version regarding why we were back at the airport after already arriving the previous night involves lost luggage and a miscommunication about where and what the midcoast's National franchise was—Dick came out personally to the airport and got us, out of no evident motive but kindness. (He also talked nonstop the entire way, with a very distinctive speaking style that can be described only as manically laconic; the truth is that I now know more about this man than I do about some members of my own family.)

Though it sounds more sophisticated, a lot of the neurology in this latter claim is still either false or fuzzy. The human cerebral cortex is the brain-part that deals with higher faculties like reason, metaphysical self-awareness, language, etc. Pain reception is known to be part of a much older and more primitive system of nociceptors and prostaglandins that are managed by the brain stem and thalamus.[1,2] On the other hand, it is true that the cerebral cortex is involved in what's variously called suffering, distress, or the emotional experience of pain—i.e., experiencing painful stimuli as unpleasant, very unpleasant, unbearable, and so on.

Before we go any further, let's acknowledge that the questions of whether and how different kinds of animals feel pain, and of whether and why it might be justifiable to inflict pain on them in order to eat them, turn out to be extremely complex and difficult. And comparative neuroanatomy is only part of the problem. Since pain is a totally subjective mental experience, we do not have direct access to anyone or anything's pain but our own; and even just the principles by which we can infer that other human beings experience pain and have a legitimate interest in not feeling pain involve hard-core philosophy—metaphysics, epistemology, value theory, ethics. The fact that even the most highly evolved nonhuman mammals can't use language to communicate with us about their subjective mental experience is only the first layer of additional complication in trying to extend our reasoning about pain and morality to animals. And everything gets progressively more abstract and convoluted as we move farther and farther out from the higher-type mammals into cattle and swine and dogs and cats and rodents, and then birds and fish, and finally invertebrates like lobsters.

The more important point here, though, is that the whole animal-cruelty-and-eating issue is not just complex, it's also uncomfortable. It is, at any rate, uncomfortable for me, and for just about everyone I know who enjoys a variety of foods and yet does not want to see herself as cruel or unfeeling. As far as I can tell, my own main way of dealing with this conflict has been to avoid thinking about the whole unpleasant thing. I should add that it appears to me unlikely that many readers of *Gourmet* wish to think about it, either, or to be queried about the morality of their eating habits in the pages of a culinary monthly. Since, however, the assigned subject of this

---

1   *prostaglandins* Chemicals similar to hormones; *thalamus* Part of the brain that transmits sensory input to the cerebral cortex.

2   [Wallace's note] To elaborate by way of example: The common experience of accidentally touching a hot stove and yanking your hand back before you're even aware that anything's going on is explained by the fact that many of the processes by which we detect and avoid painful stimuli do not involve the cortex. In the case of the hand and stove, the brain is bypassed altogether; all the important neurochemical action takes place in the spine.

article is what it was like to attend the 2003 MLF, and thus to spend several days in the midst of a great mass of Americans all eating lobster, and thus to be more or less impelled to think hard about lobster and the experience of buying and eating lobster, it turns out that there is no honest way to avoid certain moral questions.

There are several reasons for this. For one thing, it's not just that lobsters get boiled alive, it's that you do it yourself—or at least it's done specifically for you, on-site.[1] As mentioned, the World's Largest Lobster Cooker, which is highlighted as an attraction in the festival's program, is right out there on the MLF's north grounds for everyone to see. Try to imagine a Nebraska Beef Festival[2] at which part of the festivities is watching trucks pull up and the live cattle get driven down the ramp and slaughtered right there on the World's Largest Killing Floor or something—there's no way.

The intimacy of the whole thing is maximized at home, which of course is where most lobster gets prepared and eaten (although note already the semi-conscious euphemism "prepared," which in the case of lobsters really means killing them right there in our kitchens). The basic scenario is that we come in from the store and make our little preparations like getting the kettle filled and boiling, and then we lift the lobsters out of the bag or whatever retail container they came home in ... whereupon some uncomfortable things start to happen. However stuporous a lobster is from the trip home, for instance, it tends to come alarmingly to life when placed in boiling water. If you're tilting it from a container into the steaming kettle, the lobster will sometimes try to cling to the container's sides or even to hook its claws over the kettle's rim like

---

1   [Wallace's note] Morality-wise, let's concede that this cuts both ways. Lobster-eating is at least not abetted by the system of corporate factory farms that produces most beef, pork, and chicken. Because, if nothing else, of the way they're marketed and packaged for sale, we eat these latter meats without having to consider that they were once conscious, sentient creatures to whom horrible things were done. (N.B. "Horrible" here meaning really, really horrible. Write off to PETA or peta.org for their free "Meet Your Meat" video, narrated by Mr. Alec Baldwin, if you want to see just about everything meat-related you don't want to see or think about. (N.B.$_2$ Not that PETA's any sort of font of unspun truth. Like many partisans in complex moral disputes, the PETA people are fanatics, and a lot of their rhetoric seems simplistic and self-righteous. But this particular video, replete with actual factory-farm and corporate-slaughterhouse footage, is both credible and traumatizing.))

2   [Wallace's note] Is it significant that "lobster," "fish," and "chicken" are our culture's words for both the animal and the meat, whereas most mammals seem to require euphemisms like "beef" and "pork" that help us separate the meat we eat from the living creature the meat once was? Is this evidence that some kind of deep unease about eating higher animals is endemic enough to show up in English usage, but that the unease diminishes as we move out of the mammalian order? (And is "lamb"/"lamb" the counterexample that sinks the whole theory, or are there special, biblico-historical reasons for that equivalence?)

a person trying to keep from going over the edge of a roof. And worse is when the lobster's fully immersed. Even if you cover the kettle and turn away, you can usually hear the cover rattling and clanking as the lobster tries to push it off. Or the creature's claws scraping the sides of the kettle as it thrashes around. The lobster, in other words, behaves very much as you or I would behave if we were plunged into boiling water (with the obvious exception of screaming).[1] A blunter way to say this is that the lobster acts as if it's in terrible pain, causing some cooks to leave the kitchen altogether and to take one of those little lightweight plastic oven-timers with them into another room and wait until the whole process is over.

There happen to be two main criteria that most ethicists agree on for determining whether a living creature has the capacity to suffer and so has genuine interests that it may or may not be our moral duty to consider.[2] One is how much of the neurological hardware required for pain-experience the animal comes equipped with—nociceptors, prostaglandins, neuronal opioid[3] receptors, etc. The other criterion is whether the animal demonstrates behaviour associated with pain. And it takes a lot of intellectual gymnastics and behaviourist hairsplitting not to see struggling, thrashing, and lid-clattering as just such pain-behaviour. According to marine zoologists, it usually takes lobsters between 35 and 45 seconds to die in boiling water. (No source I could find talked about how long it takes them to die in superheated steam; one rather hopes it's faster.)

There are, of course, other fairly common ways to kill your lobster on-site and so achieve maximum freshness. Some cooks' practice is to drive a sharp

---

1   [Wallace's note] There's a relevant populist myth about the high-pitched whistling sound that sometimes issues from a pot of boiling lobster. The sound is really vented steam from the layer of seawater between the lobster's flesh and its carapace (this is why shedders whistle more than hard-shells), but the pop version has it that the sound is the lobster's rabbit-like death-scream. Lobsters communicate via pheromones in their urine and don't have anything close to the vocal equipment for screaming, but the myth's very persistent—which might, once again, point to a low-level cultural unease about the boiling thing.

2   [Wallace's note] "Interests" basically means strong and legitimate preferences, which obviously require some degree of consciousness, responsiveness to stimuli, etc. See, for instance, the utilitarian philosopher Peter Singer, whose 1974 *Animal Liberation* is more or less the bible of the modern animal-rights movement:

> It would be nonsense to say that it was not in the interests of a stone to be kicked along the road by a schoolboy. A stone does not have interests because it cannot suffer. Nothing that we can do to it could possibly make any difference to its welfare. A mouse, on the other hand, does have an interest in not being kicked along the road, because it will suffer if it is.

3   *opioid* Brain chemical that reduces pain.

heavy knife point-first into a spot just above the midpoint between the lobster's eyestalks (more or less where the Third Eye is in human foreheads). This is alleged either to kill the lobster instantly or to render it insensate, and is said at least to eliminate some of the cowardice involved in throwing a creature into boiling water and then fleeing the room. As far as I can tell from talking to proponents of the knife-in-the-head method, the idea is that it's more violent but ultimately more merciful, plus that a willingness to exert personal agency and accept responsibility for stabbing the lobster's head honours the lobster somehow and entitles one to eat it (there's often a vague sort of Native American spirituality-of-the-hunt flavour to pro-knife arguments). But the problem with the knife method is basic biology: Lobsters' nervous systems operate off not one but several ganglia, a.k.a. nerve bundles, which are sort of wired in series and distributed all along the lobster's underside, from stem to stern. And disabling only the frontal ganglion does not normally result in quick death or unconsciousness.

Another alternative is to put the lobster in cold saltwater and then very slowly bring it up to a full boil. Cooks who advocate this method are going on the analogy to a frog, which can supposedly be kept from jumping out of a boiling pot by heating the water incrementally. In order to save a lot of research-summarizing, I'll simply assure you that the analogy between frogs and lobsters turns out not to hold—plus, if the kettle's water isn't aerated seawater, the immersed lobster suffers from slow suffocation, although usually not decisive enough suffocation to keep it from still thrashing and clattering when the water gets hot enough to kill it. In fact, lobsters boiled incrementally often display a whole bonus set of gruesome, convulsionlike reactions that you don't see in regular boiling.

Ultimately, the only certain virtues of the home-lobotomy and slow-heating methods are comparative, because there are even worse/crueler ways people prepare lobster. Time-thrifty cooks sometimes microwave them alive (usually after poking several extra vent-holes in the carapace, which is a precaution most shellfish-microwavers learn about the hard way). Live dismemberment, on the other hand, is big in Europe—some chefs cut the lobster in half before cooking; others like to tear off the claws and tail and toss only these parts in the pot.

And there's more unhappy news respecting suffering-criterion number one. Lobsters don't have much in the way of eyesight or hearing, but they do have an exquisite tactile sense, one facilitated by hundreds of thousands of tiny hairs that protrude through their carapace. "Thus it is," in the words of T.M. Prudden's industry classic *About Lobster*, "that although encased in what seems a solid, impenetrable armor, the lobster can receive stimuli and impressions from without as readily as if it possessed a soft and delicate skin." And lobsters do have nociceptors,[1] as well as invertebrate versions of the prostaglandins and major neurotransmitters via which our own brains register pain.

Lobsters do not, on the other hand, appear to have the equipment for making or absorbing natural opioids like endorphins and enkephalins, which are what more advanced nervous systems use to try to handle intense pain. From this fact, though, one could conclude either that lobsters are maybe even *more* vulnerable to pain, since they lack mammalian nervous systems' built-in analgesia,[2] or, instead, that the absence of natural opioids implies an absence of the really intense pain-sensations that natural opioids are designed to mitigate. I for one can detect a marked upswing in mood as I contemplate this latter possibility. It could be that their lack of endorphin/enkephalin hardware means that lobsters' raw subjective experience of pain is so radically different from mammals' that it may not even deserve the term "pain." Perhaps lobsters are more like those frontal-lobotomy patients one reads about who report experiencing pain in a totally different way than you and I. These patients evidently do feel physical pain, neurologically speaking, but don't dislike it—though neither do they like it; it's more that they feel it but don't feel anything *about* it—the point being that the pain is not distressing to them or something they want to get away from. Maybe lobsters, who are also without frontal lobes, are detached from the neurological-registration-of-injury-or-hazard we call pain in just the same way. There is, after all, a difference between (1) pain as a purely neurological event, and (2) actual suffering, which seems crucially to involve an emotional component, an awareness of pain as unpleasant, as something to fear/dislike/want to avoid.

Still, after all the abstract intellection, there remain the facts of the frantically clanking lid, the pathetic clinging to the edge of the pot. Standing at the stove, it is hard to deny in any meaningful way that this is a living creature experiencing pain and wishing to avoid/escape the painful experience. To my lay mind, the lobster's behaviour in the kettle appears to be the expression of a *preference*; and it may well be that an ability to form preferences is the decisive criterion for real suffering.[3] The logic of this (preference → suffering) relation may be easiest to see in the negative case. If you cut certain kinds of worms in half, the halves will often keep crawling around and going about

---

1   [Wallace's note] This is the neurological term for special pain-receptors that are "sensitive to potentially damaging extremes of temperature, to mechanical forces, and to chemical substances which are released when body tissues are damaged."
2   *analgesia* Pain reduction.
3   [Wallace's note] "Preference" is maybe roughly synonymous with "interests," but it is a better term for our purposes because it's less abstractly philosophical—"preference" seems more personal, and it's the whole idea of a living creature's personal experience that's at issue.

their vermiform business as if nothing had happened. When we assert, based on their post-op behaviour, that these worms appear not to be suffering, what we're really saying is that there's no sign that the worms know anything bad has happened or would *prefer* not to have gotten cut in half.

Lobsters, though, are known to exhibit preferences. Experiments have shown that they can detect changes of only a degree or two in water temperature; one reason for their complex migratory cycles (which can often cover 100-plus miles a year) is to pursue the temperatures they like best.[1] And, as mentioned, they're bottom-dwellers and do not like bright light—if a tank of food lobsters is out in the sunlight or a store's fluorescence, the lobsters will always congregate in whatever part is darkest. Fairly solitary in the ocean, they also clearly dislike the crowding that's part of their captivity in tanks, since (as also mentioned) one reason why lobsters' claws are banded on capture is to keep them from attacking one another under the stress of close-quarter storage.

In any event, at the MLF, standing by the bubbling tanks outside the World's Largest Lobster Cooker, watching the fresh-caught lobsters pile over one another, wave their hobbled claws impotently, huddle in the rear corners, or scrabble frantically back from the glass as you approach, it is difficult not to sense that they're unhappy, or frightened, even if it's some rudimentary version of these feelings ... and, again, why does rudimentariness even enter into it? Why is a primitive, inarticulate form of suffering less urgent or uncomfortable for the person who's helping to inflict it by paying for the food it results in? I'm

---

1 [Wallace's note] Of course, the most common sort of counterargument here would begin by objecting that "like best" is really just a metaphor, and a misleadingly anthropomorphic one at that. The counterarguer would posit that the lobster seeks to maintain a certain optimal ambient temperature out of nothing but unconscious instinct (with a similar explanation for the low-light affinities upcoming in the main text). The thrust of such a counterargument will be that the lobster's thrashings and clankings in the kettle express not unpreferred pain but involuntary reflexes, like your leg shooting out when the doctor hits your knee. Be advised that there are professional scientists, including many researchers who use animals in experiments, who hold to the view that nonhuman creatures have no real feelings at all, merely "behaviours." Be further advised that this view has a long history that goes all the way back to Descartes, although its modern support comes mostly from behaviourist psychology. [René Descartes (1596–1650) was an influential French philosopher; behaviourist psychology interprets psychology exclusively in terms of behaviour as opposed to internal mental states.]

To these what-looks-like-pain-is-really-just-reflexes counterarguments, however, there happen to be all sorts of scientific and pro-animal-rights counter-counterarguments. And then further attempted rebuttals and redirects, and so on. Suffice to say that both the scientific and the philosophical arguments on either side of the animal-suffering issue are involved, abstruse, technical, often informed by self-interest or ideology, and in the end so totally inconclusive that as a practical matter, in the kitchen or restaurant, it all still seems to come down to individual conscience, going with (no pun) your gut.

not trying to give you a PETA-like screed here—at least I don't think so. I'm trying, rather, to work out and articulate some of the troubling questions that arise amid all the laughter and saltation[1] and community pride of the Maine Lobster Festival. The truth is that if you, the festival attendee, permit yourself to think that lobsters can suffer and would rather not, the MLF begins to take on the aspect of something like a Roman circus or medieval torture-fest.

Does that comparison seem a bit much? If so, exactly why? Or what about this one: Is it possible that future generations will regard our own present agribusiness and eating practices in much the same way we now view Nero's entertainments or Mengele's experiments?[2] My own immediate reaction is that such a comparison is hysterical, extreme—and yet the reason it seems extreme to me appears to be that I believe animals are less morally important than human beings;[3] and when it comes to defending such a belief, even to myself, I have to acknowledge that (a) I have an obvious selfish interest in this belief, since I like to eat certain kinds of animals and want to be able to keep doing it, and (b) I haven't succeeded in working out any sort of personal ethical system in which the belief is truly defensible instead of just selfishly convenient.

Given this article's venue and my own lack of culinary sophistication, I'm curious about whether the reader can identify with any of these reactions and acknowledgements and discomforts. I am also concerned not to come off as shrill or preachy when what I really am is more like confused. For those *Gourmet* readers who enjoy well-prepared and -presented meals involving beef, veal, lamb, pork, chicken, lobster, etc.: Do you think much about the (possible) moral status and (probable) suffering of the animals involved? If you do, what ethical convictions have you worked out that permit you not just to eat but to savour and enjoy flesh-based viands[4] (since of course refined *enjoyment*, rather than mere ingestion, is the whole point of gastronomy)? If, on the other hand, you'll have no truck with confusions or convictions and regard stuff like the previous paragraph as just so much fatuous navel-gazing, what makes it feel truly okay, inside, to just dismiss the whole issue out of hand? That is, is your refusal to think about any of this the product of actual thought, or is it

1   *saltation* I.e., dancing, jumping around.

2   *Nero's entertainments* Among the spectacles that Roman Emperor Nero (37–68 CE) staged for his people's enjoyment were gladiator battles and the brutal public execution of Christians; *Mengele's experiments* Nazi doctor Josef Mengele (1911–79) conducted cruel medical experiments on inmates at the Auschwitz concentration camp.

3   [Wallace's note] Meaning a *lot* less important, apparently, since the moral comparison here is not the value of one human's life vs. the value of one animal's life, but rather the value of one animal's life vs. the value of one human's taste for a particular kind of protein. Even the most diehard carniphile will acknowledge that it's possible to live and eat well without consuming animals.

4   *viands* Foods.

just that you don't want to think about it? And if the latter, then why not? Do you ever think, even idly, about the possible reasons for your reluctance to think about it? I am not trying to bait anyone here—I'm genuinely curious. After all, isn't being extra aware and attentive and thoughtful about one's food and its overall context part of what distinguishes a real gourmet? Or is all the gourmet's extra attention and sensibility just supposed to be sensuous? Is it really all just a matter of taste and presentation?

These last few queries, though, while sincere, obviously involve much larger and more abstract questions about the connections (if any) between aesthetics and morality—about what the adjective in a phrase like "The Magazine of Good Living"[1] is really supposed to mean—and these questions lead straightaway into such deep and treacherous waters that it's probably best to stop the public discussion right here. There are limits to what even interested persons can ask of each other.

—2004

---

1   *The Magazine ... Living* Slogan of *Gourmet* magazine.

Miriam Toews

b. 1964

"This town is so severe. And silent. It makes me crazy, the silence." So the teenaged Nomi Nickel describes her home town, the Mennonite community of East Village, in Miriam Toews's fourth novel, *A Complicated Kindness* (2004). That book, which was a best-seller and winner of the Governor General's Award, established Toews as a major figure on the Canadian literary landscape. Like most of her other work, it draws powerfully upon Toews's experience growing up in the town of Steinbach, Manitoba. In Toews's fiction the currents of comedy are often as powerful as those of sadness or despair—and both often spring from her religious upbringing. "We're Mennonites," Nomi tells the reader: "As far as I know, we are the most embarrassing sub-sect of people to belong to if you're a teenager."

Toews is known for her sure touch with wry comedy, but her life and her work have also been touched by tragedy. In 1998, Toews's father committed suicide after a lifelong battle with bipolar disorder. Toews paid tribute to him in an essay on the connections between his Mennonite beliefs and his struggles with depression; "A Father's Faith" (1999) was first published in a magazine, and later reprinted in an anthology of women's writing, *Dropped Threads* (2001). Her full-length memoir, *Swing Low: A Life* (2000), was told from the point of view of her father. Her 2008 novel, *The Flying Troutmans*, also centres on mental illness. It tells the story of narrator Hattie's road trip with her niece and nephew, whose mother (Hattie's sister) suffers from severe depression.

In 2007 Toews was asked to star in Mexican director Carlo Reygadas' *Silent Light* (2007), a film set in a Mennonite community in Northern Mexico. Toews drew on that experience for her 2011 novel, *Irma Voth*, which concerns two young women whose family has moved from the Canadian prairie to a Mennonite community in Mexico; the arrival of a film crew who plan to make a film about the community becomes the catalyst for change.

In describing what she writes about, Toews has sometimes emphasized simple contrasts. In a 2008 interview with *Quill & Quire*, for example, she summed things up in this way: "Life is funny and life is sad. Life is comic and life is tragic. It's a breeze and it's hell." In "A Father's Faith," though—as in the best of her fiction—the interest comes less from simple oppositions than from Toews's sure feel for complications and for subtleties.

A Father's Faith

On the morning on May 13, 1998, my father woke up, had breakfast, got dressed and walked away from the Steinbach Bethesda Hospital, where he had been a patient for two and a half weeks. He walked through his beloved hometown, along Hespeler Road, past the old farmhouse where his mother had lived with her second husband, past the water tower, greeting folks in his loud, friendly voice, wishing them well. He passed the site on First Street where the house in which my sister and I grew up once stood. He walked down Main Street, past the Mennonite church where, throughout his life, he had received countless certificates for perfect attendance, past Elmdale School where he had taught grade six for forty years.

As he walked by his home on Brandt Road, he saw his old neighbour Bill sitting in his lawn chair. He waved and smiled again, then he continued on past the cemetery where his parents were buried, and the high school his daughters had attended, and down Highway 52, out of town, past the Frantz Motor Inn, which is just outside the town limits because it serves alcohol and Steinbach is a dry town. He kept walking until he got too tired, so he hitched a ride with a couple of guys who were on their way to buy a fishing licence in the small village of Woodridge on the edge of the Sandilands Forest.

The sun would have been very warm by the time they dropped him off, and he would have taken off his stylish cap and wiped his brow with the back of his hand. I'm sure he thanked them profusely, perhaps offering them ten dollars for their trouble, and then he walked the short distance to the café near the railroad tracks, the place he and my mom would sometimes go for a quiet coffee and a change of scenery. He would have been able to smell the clover growing in the ditches beside the tracks and between the ties. He may have looked down the line and remembered that the train would be coming from Ontario, through Warroad, Minnesota, on its way to Winnipeg.

A beautiful young woman named Stephanie was just beginning her shift and she spoke to him through the screen door at the side of the restaurant. Yes, she said, the train will be here soon. And my dad smiled and thanked her, and mentioned that he could hear the whistle. Moments later, he was dead.

Steinbach is an easy forty-minute drive from Winnipeg, east on the Trans-Canada, then south on Highway 12. On the way into town there's a sign proclaiming "Jesus Saves." On the way back to the city just off Highway 12 there's another that says, "Satan is Real. You Can't Be Neutral. Choose Now." The town has recently become a city of 8,500 people, two-thirds of whom are Mennonite, so it's not surprising that about half of the twenty-four churches are Mennonite and conservative. There is a Catholic church too, but it's new and I'm not sure exactly where it is. A little way down from the bowling alley

I can still make out my name on the sidewalk, carved in big bold letters when I was ten and marking my territory.

My town made sense to me then. For me it was a giant playground where my friends and I roamed freely, using the entire town in a game of arrows—something like hide-and-seek—for which my dad, the teacher, provided boxes and boxes of fresh new chalk and invaluable tips. He had, after all, played the same game in the same town many years before.

At six p.m. the siren would go off at the firehall, reminding all the kids to go home for supper, and at nine p.m. it was set off again, reminding us to go home to bed. I had no worries, and no desire ever to leave this place where everyone knew me. If they couldn't remember my name, they knew I was the younger daughter of Mel and Elvira Toews, granddaughter of C.T. Loewen and Henry Toews, from the Kleine Gemeinde congregation, and so on and so on. All the kids in town, other than the church-sponsored Laotians who came over in the seventies, could be traced all the way back to the precise Russian veldt their great-grandparents had emigrated from. They were some of the thousands of Mennonites who came to Manitoba in the late 1800s to escape religious persecution. They were given free land and a promise that they could, essentially, do their own thing without interference. They wanted to keep the world away from their children and their children away from the world. Naturally it was an impossible ideal.

As I grew older, I became suspicious and critical and restless and angry. Every night I plotted my escape. I imagined that Barkman's giant feed mill on Main Street, partially visible from my bedroom window, was a tall ship that would take me away some day. I looked up places like Hollywood and Manhattan and Venice and Montreal in my Childcraft encyclopedias. I begged my sister to play, over and over, the sad songs from her Jacques Brel piano book, and I'd light candles and sing along, wearing a Pioneer Girls tam[1] on my head, using a chopstick as a cigarette holder, pretending I was Jackie Brel, Jacques's long-lost but just as world-weary Mennonite twin. I couldn't believe that I was stuck in a town like Steinbach, where dancing was a sin and serving beer a felony.

There were other things I became aware of as well. That my grandmother was a vanilla alcoholic who believed she was a teetotaller. That seventy-five-year-old women who had borne thirteen children weren't allowed to speak to the church congregation, but that fifteen-year-old boys were. That every family had a secret. And I learned that my dad had been depressed all his life.

---

1   *Jacques Brel* Belgian singer-songwriter (1929–78) who became famous performing his poetic ballads in Paris clubs; *tam* Scottish soft hat similar to a beret.

I had wondered, when I was a kid, why he spent so much of the weekend in bed and why he didn't talk much at home. Occasionally he'd tell me, sometimes in tears, that he loved me very much and that he wished he were a better father, that he were more involved in my life. But I never felt the need for an apology. It made me happy and a bit envious to know that my dad's students were able to witness his humour and intelligence firsthand, to hear him expound on his favourite subjects: Canadian history, Canadian politics and Canadian newspapers. I remember watching him at work and marvelling at his energy and enthusiasm. I thought he looked very handsome when he rolled up his sleeves and tucked his tie in between the buttons of his shirt, his hands on his hips, all ready for business and hard work.

Teaching school—helping others make sense of the world—was a good profession for a man who was continuously struggling to find meaning in life. I think he needed his students as much as they needed him. By fulfilling his duties, he was also shoring up a psyche at risk of erosion.

Four years before his death he was forced to retire from teaching because of a heart attack and some small strokes. He managed to finish the book he was writing on Canada's prime ministers, but then he seemed to fade away. He spent more and more of his time in bed, in the dark, not getting up even to eat or wash, not interested in watching TV or listening to the radio. Despite our pleading and cajoling, despite the medication and visits to various doctors' offices, appointments he dutifully kept, and despite my mother's unwavering love, we felt we were losing him.

I know about brain chemistry and depression, but there's still a part of me that blames my dad's death on being Mennonite and living in that freaky, austere place where this world isn't good enough and admission into the next one, the perfect one, means everything, where every word and deed gets you closer to or farther away from eternal life. If you don't believe that then nothing Steinbach stands for will make sense. And if life doesn't make sense you lose yourself in it, your spirit decays. That's what I believed had happened to my dad, and that's why I hated my town.

In the weeks and months after his death, my mom and my sister and I tried to piece things together. William Ashdown, the executive director of the Mood Disorders Association of Manitoba, told us the number of mentally ill Mennonites is abnormally high. "We don't know if it's genetic or cultural," he said, "but the Steinbach area is one that we're vitally concerned about."

"It's the way the church delivers the message," says a Mennonite friend of mine, "the message of sin and accountability. To be human, basically, is to be a sinner. So a person, a real believer, starts to get down on himself, and where does it end? They say self-loathing is the cornerstone of depression, right?"

Years ago, the Mennonite Church practised something called "shunning," whereby if you were to leave your husband, or marry outside the Church, or elope, or drink, or in some way contravene the Church's laws or act "out of faith," you could be expelled from the Church and ignored, shunned by the entire community, including your own family. Depression or despair, as it would have been referred to then, was considered to be the result of a lack of faith and therefore could be another reason for shunning.

These days most Mennonites don't officially practise shunning, although William Ashdown claims there are still Mennonites from extreme conservative sects who are being shunned and shamed into silence within their communities for being mentally ill. Certainly Arden Thiessen, the minister of my dad's church, and a long-time friend of his, is aware of the causes of depression and the pain experienced by those who suffer from it. He doesn't see it as a lack of faith, but as an awful sickness.

But I can't help thinking that that history had just a little to do with my alcoholic grandmother's insisting that she was a non-drinker, and my dad's telling his doctors, smiling that beautiful smile of his, that he was fine, just fine.

Not long before he died my dad told me about the time he was five and was having his tonsils out. Just before the operation began he was knocked out with ether and he had a dream that he was somersaulting through the hospital walls, right through, easily, he said, moving his hands in circles through the air. It was wonderful. He told me he would never forget that feeling.

But mostly, the world was a sad and unsafe place for him, and his town provided shelter from it. Maybe he saw this as a gift, while I came to see it as oppression. He could peel back the layers of hypocrisy and intolerance and see what was good, and I couldn't. He believed that it mattered what he did in life, and he believed in the next world, one that's better. He kept the faith of his Mennonite forebears to the very end, or what he might call the beginning, and removed himself from this world entirely.

Stephanie, the waitress in the café in Woodridge, told my mother that my dad was calm and polite when he spoke to her, as if he were about to sit down to a cup of tea. She told her that he hadn't seemed at all afraid. But why would you be if you believed you were going to a place where there is no more sadness?

My dad never talked to us about God or religion. We didn't have family devotion like everybody else. He never quoted out loud from the Bible or lectured us about not going to church. In fact his only two pieces of advice to me were "Be yourself" and "You can do anything."

But he still went to church. It didn't matter how low he felt, or how cold it was outside. He would put on his suit and tie and stylish cap and walk the seven or eight blocks to church. He always walked, through searing heat or sub-arctic chill. If he was away on holidays he would find a church and go to it. At the lake he drove forty miles down gravel roads to attend an outdoor church in the bush. I think he needed church like a junkie needs a fix: to get him through another day in a world of pain.

What I love about my town is that it gave my dad the faith that stopped him from being afraid in those last violent seconds he spent on earth. And the place in my mind where we meet is on the front steps of my dad's church, the big one on Main Street across from Don's Bakery and the Goodwill store. We smile and talk for a few minutes outside, basking in the warmth of the summer sun he loved so much. Then he goes in and I stay outside, and we're both happy where we are.

—2001

Karen Connelly
b. 1969

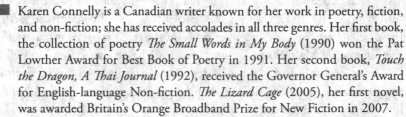

Karen Connelly is a Canadian writer known for her work in poetry, fiction, and non-fiction; she has received accolades in all three genres. Her first book, the collection of poetry *The Small Words in My Body* (1990) won the Pat Lowther Award for Best Book of Poetry in 1991. Her second book, *Touch the Dragon, A Thai Journal* (1992), received the Governor General's Award for English-language Non-fiction. *The Lizard Cage* (2005), her first novel, was awarded Britain's Orange Broadband Prize for New Fiction in 2007.

Connelly was born in Calgary, Alberta, into a working-class, fundamentalist Christian family. When she was 17, she received a Rotary scholarship to live in a small village in Thailand for a year. She returned to Canada, but soon turned down a number of university scholarships in favour of a life of travel and artistic pursuit in Spain and France. She spent her time honing her craft, recording her adventures, and organizing and refining the journals and letters that documented her time in Thailand. Those documents would eventually be shaped into *Touch the Dragon*; the selection here is an excerpt from that work.

Connelly's travels continued, eventually drawing her back to Thailand and, later, into Burma. Troubled by what she saw as the Orwellian dictatorship in Burma, Connelly took a more activist approach to her art; she was eventually blacklisted from travel to Burma for taking unauthorized photographs of a student demonstration. After her expulsion, she remained in Thailand and interviewed many Burmese dissidents, revolutionaries, and artists. These experiences led to the book of poetry *The Border Surrounds Us* (2000) and the novel *The Lizard Cage*. Connelly has written that she "grew up *believing* that the novel was a powerful act of creation; that books could change people's lives; that a brilliant novel, especially if it was brave enough to wade into politics, could constitute a kind of action, be a form of intervention."

from *Touch the Dragon: A Thai Journal*

August 21, 1986

Leaving Canada. A view of the body of mountains: deep sockets of aquamarine, blue veins slipping over cliff-sides, stone edges splintering from the earth like cracked bones.

When I think of the span of countries, when I run my fingers over the skin of a map, I get dizzy. I am too high up now—I should have glided into this journey on a boat. As the country pulls out from under me, I overturn like a glass on a yanked table-cloth, I spill. Land steadies people, holds them, even if they imagine they control it. Land owns and defines us. Without it, we become something else.

After refuelling in Kyoto, we are moving again, rising into another time zone, another time. These are the first pages of a new country. There's almost nothing to write yet because I know so little. I can't even imagine where I'm going. I am utterly alone, a small bit of dust blown into Asia's deep green eye. I lean against the glass and gaze down at an emerald flood, knowing I'll never be able to soak up such radiance. It's a colour I never knew I'd see, the astonishing canvas of a dream, undreamed.

At the airport in Bangkok, a bald foreigner lugs three gallons of water on his shoulder. He explains to suspicious customs officials that he has brought water from home because the water here is unsafe. There is laughter, a waving of dark arms and pale palms. I stumble through customs, crippled by luggage and jet lag. One English word rings out: taxi. The world is a wet braid of heat and flesh, glimpses of gold-studded teeth, shirts open to shining bellies, purple tattoos, wreaths of jasmine. Above the horde of cab-drivers looms a hand-painted sign warning all tourists to beware of thieves, illicit business deals, drugs and fake gems. The air slides over me thick as honey. I have never felt such tropical warmth before.

Then I see a cardboard sign with my name on it bobbing up in the crowd. Someone has come to get me. Someone has come to take me (farther) away.

August 22

We are driving northwards under black clouds, through darkness broken by lightning. I could believe now that the earth is flat, and its far edges are sparking flame. Rice fields, tree groves, gleaming oval ponds flash out of the night. Mr. Prasit Piyachinda and Mr. Prasert Jeenanukulwong have both suggested I call them *paw* for the sake of simplicity. Paw Prasit speaks English. "We will treat you like a daughter, and you will treat us like father." The Rotary Club of Denchai has almost twenty members. I can't pronounce any of their names. "You must learn to speak Thai very quickly," Paw Prasit explains. "It will not be difficult. No one in your family speaks English. You have no choice." He turns around to smile at me. He talks about spicy food, a famous Buddhist monk who is also a great fortune-teller, the school I will go to, the people who are anxious to meet me. When I ask why these people want to meet me, he giggles. "Why, because you are a falang." A foreigner. It is my first Thai word.

Sudden light spears the heavy rain. I squint out the streaming windows. The men laugh at my fascination with the countryside. "Are you afraid of the ... the ..."

"The lightning," I finish for Paw Prasit.

"Ah, yes, yes, are you afraid of it? My daughter, yes, is. She will not look at fields at night, fields in rain." He points towards a distant clump of trees and taps at the window. "Dragons. She says they are dragons." He laughs, turns to Prasert, translates, they laugh again, then hoot more at some other joke. I peer through the glass; his daughter is right. There they are, tree-dragons, moulded by wind and shadow, heavy-skulled dinosaurs gathered under lightning at the edges of ponds. They lean down to the water, their scaled flanks gleaming with rain.

I fall asleep, sliding down onto the seat, listening to Paw Prasit say, "And people will call you falang in the street because at first they will not know your name." I will be the only white person in the town. "You will be popular. Also there is a green fruit in Thailand called falang and when you eat it, everyone will laugh and say, 'Falang eat falang. Hahaha. Ha ha.'" Again he translates for Paw Prasert (why are their names so similar?) and both men slap their knees at this hilarious play on words. I keep missing the jokes in everything, possibly because I'm so tired. What time is it here? What time is it in Canada? Canada? The word sounds funny. I slump down farther on the seat and listen to wheels humming and my guardians speaking Thai. It is indecipherable birdsong. They talk on, their voices climbing and sliding down the banisters of five tones and strange letters. This is not comparable to high school French.

Suddenly, inexplicably, they are standing outside the car and calling me. "Kalen, Kalen, to bathroom now. We are in Phitsanulok. For pee-pee." The door is opened for me. I receive a handful of toilet paper and a gentle push in the right direction. I am disoriented, eyes salted with sleep. The young men hanging about the gas pumps stare and stare.

Once I am in the dark little washroom, reality swarms; the pungent odour of urine burns the dreamy quality out of everything. I lose my footing on the wet edges of the Thai toilet and laugh, imagining the embarrassment of breaking my ankle in a toilet the very first day. This is Thailand, the land of smiles, the Venice of the Orient, the pearl of Asia. The travel-agency phrases run off my tongue as mosquitoes settle on my thighs, arms, neck. Are they malarial or harmless? A few dark stains move up and down the walls, and my skin shivers, waiting for invasions.

Walking back across the lot, I notice small reddish lights glowing behind a cage with thin bars. I walk towards them, curious, moving closer, closer, stretching out my hand ... Paw Prasit yells, "No, no!" but it's too late. All I do is touch the bars and half a dozen gibbons leap shrieking towards my hand.

I scream at their screams, the gas-station attendants come loping across the lot and my Thai fathers rush forward to pull me away. I apologize to everyone.

The gibbons are the ones making the fuss. Their furious bodies spring and bounce inside the cage. "You must learn to be careful, Kalen." Paw Prasit takes my arm, his glasses steamed with worry. "There are snakes, too. You know?" He stares at me for a moment, then laughs and says something in Thai, which makes Paw Prasert laugh, too. Even the gas-pumpers giggle and kick a few pebbles, looking up at me even though their heads are lowered. I open the car door and crawl in. When we drive away, the boys wave us off. I stare back at the neon lights of the station for a long time, the savage human faces of the monkeys still vivid in my mind.

We reach Denchai in the dark, so I see little, other than dogs running through the beams of the headlights, barely making it. We finally stop at the last building on the street. "Liquor store," Paw Prasit says. "This is the liquor store of Paw Prasert. This is where you'll live." Prasert is already out of the car and up on a bench, stretching to press a door buzzer. As soon as his finger flexes, I hear barking and the rattling slap of a chain. The dog inside the building hurls against the metal door. We wait until the dog begins to whimper, then hear an old man's grunt and sniffle. There's a clatter of keys and a frightening roar of phlegm from the recesses of a throat; finally the door scrapes open along the cement floor. A balding old man beams at us. His skin is the colour and texture of a walnut, he is toothless and he wears nothing but a baggy pair of black satin trousers. Prasit says to me, "Old father is much blind." After awkward introductions, the three of them begin to speak in Thai. I smile and smile. Before coming in with us, the old man shuffles to the road and vigorously spits a small chunk of his lung into the gutter.

Inside the shop, the German shepherd once again begins to bark and strain against her chain. Her lips are pulled back over yellow teeth. Paw Prasert grins proudly, pulls up some long-forgotten vestige of English and yells over the barking, "My dog!" I smile back, nod. Paw Prasit adds, "But no worry, it not hurt you." She leaps toward us again, only to be choked back by the chain. After the old man hits her on the nose, she whimpers and slumps to the ground, chin between her paws. We walk deeper into the liquor store, past piles of dusty crates, a display of Thai whisky, a television, an old desk piled with newspapers and small bags of rice. Each of the men has one of my suitcases and is breathing audibly under its weight, insisting how light it is. We come to a small fridge. Paw Prasert opens it and whispers to Paw Prasit, who turns to me. "He say you take anything you want, you are like a daughter to him. You know?"

Thanking them, I glance into the fridge. It's full of water bottles and a few pots of murky sauces or oil paints.

Up one staircase: bathroom, sister's room, children's room. Paw Prasert's room. The top of another staircase brings us to an uninhabited floor. The one bedroom is for me. "You have room all to self." I am smiling, smiling my thanks. Now the men turn to leave. Yes, yes, see you tomorrow, to begin learning Thai, to begin learning, tomorrow, yes.

And the door closes. I look around: a low bed of cushions, a child's desk, a small mirror, a woven straw chair. Green curtains, green bedspread. A stark naked Thai girl with an erotic smile stares down from a picture on the wall. This smile—she must be kidding—does the trick. I sit on the edge of the bed, hug my elbows and sob for everything that isn't here. I think of the hundreds of days, the thousands of hours I have to stay here. Everything I understand, everything I own is buried in my skull, intangible. I am not feeling particularly brave. I'm sniffling, alone but for a Thai porn queen and three beaten-up suitcases. This does not feel exotic. Around me, the pool of night trembles with crickets and frogs, breaks with the distant bark of dogs, and slowly, slowly, closes over my head.

—1993

Glossary

Absurdist: characterized by a minimalist style and bleak worldview. The term is most frequently used with reference to certain plays of the post-World-War-II period (notable examples include Samuel Beckett's *Waiting for Godot* and Tom Stoppard's *Rosencrantz and Guildenstern Are Dead*). Such works seem set in a world stripped of faith in god or a rational cosmos, in which idealism has been lost, and human action and communication are futile. Absurdist characters are often portrayed as trapped in a pointless round of trivial, self-defeating acts of comical repetitiveness. For this reason, absurdism can verge on *farce* or *black comedy*. See also *existentialism*.

Accent: in poetry the natural emphasis (stress) speakers place on a syllable.

Accentual Verse: poetry in which a line is measured only by the number of accents or stresses, not by the number of syllables.

Accentual-Syllabic Verse: poetry in which a line is measured by the number of syllables and by the pattern of accented (stressed) and unaccented (unstressed) syllables. This is the most common metrical system in traditional English verse.

Act [of a play]: the sections into which a play or other theatrical work have been divided, either by the playwright or a later editor. Dividing plays into five acts became popular during the Renaissance in imitation of Roman tragedy; modern works are sometimes divided into three.

Aesthetes: members of a late nineteenth-century movement that valued "art for art's sake"—for its purely aesthetic qualities, as opposed to valuing art for the moral content it may convey, for the intellectual stimulation it may provide, or for a range of other qualities.

Allegory: a narrative with both a literal meaning and secondary, often symbolic meaning or meanings. Allegory frequently employs personification to give concrete embodiment to abstract concepts or entities, such as feelings or personal qualities. It may also present one set of characters or events in the guise of another, using implied parallels for the purposes of satire or political comment.

Alliteration: the grouping of words with the same initial consonant (e.g., "break, blow, burn, and make me new"). See also *assonance* and *consonance*.

Alliterative Verse: poetry that employs alliteration of stressed syllables in each line as its chief structural principle.

Allusion: a reference, often indirect or unidentified, to a person, thing, or event. A reference in one literary work to another literary work, whether to its content or its form, also constitutes an allusion.

Ambiguity: an "opening" of language created by the writer to allow for multiple meanings or differing interpretations. In literature, ambiguity may be deliberately employed by the writer to enrich meaning; this differs from any unintentional, unwanted ambiguity in non-literary prose.

Anachronism: accidentally or intentionally attributing people, things, ideas, and events to historical periods in which they do not and could not possibly belong.

Analepsis: see *flashback*.

Analogy: a broad term that refers to our processes of noting similarities among things or events. Specific forms of analogy in poetry include *simile* and *metaphor*.

Anapaest: a metrical foot containing two unstressed syllables followed by one stressed syllable: xx / (e.g., underneath, intervene).

Antistrophe: from Greek drama, the chorus's countermovement or reply to an initial movement (*strophe*). See *ode*.

Apostrophe: a figure of speech (a *trope*; see *figures of speech*) in which a writer directly addresses an object—or a dead or absent person—as if the imagined audience were actually listening.

Apron: the part of a stage that extends into the auditorium or audience beyond the *proscenium* arch; sometimes called a *forestage* or a *thrust stage*.

Archetype: in literature and mythology, a recurring idea, symbol, motif, character, or place. To some scholars and psychologists, an archetype represents universal human thought-patterns or experiences.

Arena Theatre: see *theatre-in-the-round*.

Asides: words delivered by actors to the audience, or by characters to themselves, which by *convention* are treated as if they were inaudible to the other characters on stage.

Assonance: the repetition of identical or similar vowel sounds in stressed syllables in which the surrounding consonants are different: for example, "shame" and "fate"; "gale" and "cage"; or the long "i" sounds in "Beside the pumice isle...."

Atmosphere: see *tone*.

Aubade: a lyric poem that greets or laments the arrival of dawn.

Ballad: a folk song, or a poem originally recited to an audience, which tells a dramatic story based on legend or history.

Ballad Stanza: a quatrain with alternating four-stress and three-stress lines, rhyming *abcb*. A variant is "common measure," in which the alternating lines are strictly iambic, and rhyme *abab*.

Baroque: powerful and heavily ornamented in style. "Baroque" is a term from the history of visual art and of music that is sometimes also used to describe certain literary styles.

Bathos: an anticlimactic effect brought about by a writer's descent from an elevated subject or tone to the ordinary or trivial.

Black Comedy: humour based on death, horror, or any incongruously macabre subject matter.

Blank Verse: unrhymed lines written in iambic pentameter. (A form introduced to English verse by Henry Howard, Earl of Surrey, in his translation of parts of Virgil's *Aeneid* in 1547.)

Bombast: inappropriately inflated or grandiose language.

Broken Rhyme: a kind of rhyme in which a multi-syllable word is split at the end of a line and continued onto the next, to allow an end-rhyme with the split syllable.

Burlesque: satire of a particularly exaggerated sort, particularly that which ridicules its subject by emphasizing its vulgar or ridiculous aspects.

Caesura: a pause or break in a line of verse occurring where a phrase, clause, or sentence ends, and indicated in scansion by the mark ||. If it occurs in the middle of the line, it is known as a "medial" caesura.

Canon: in literature, those works that are commonly accepted as possessing authority or importance. In practice, "canonical" texts or authors are those that are discussed most frequently by scholars and taught most frequently in university courses.

Canto: a sub-section of a long (usually epic) poem.

Canzone: a short song or poem, with stanzas of equal length and an *envoy*.

Caricature: an exaggerated and simplified depiction of character; the reduction of a personality to one or two telling traits at the expense of all other nuances and contradictions.

Carpe Diem: Latin (from Horace) meaning "seize the day." The idea of enjoying the moment is a common one in Renaissance love poetry. See, for example, Marvell's "To His Coy Mistress."

Catalexis: the omission of unstressed syllables from a line of verse (such a line is referred to as "catalectic"). In iambic verse it is usually the first syllable of the line that is omitted; in trochaic, the last. For example, in the first stanza of Housman's "To an Athlete Dying Young" the third line is catalectic: i.e., it has dropped the first, unstressed syllable called for by the poem's iambic tetrameter form: "The time you won your town the race / We chaired you through the market-place; / Man and boy stood cheering by, / And home we brought you shoulder-high."

Catharsis: the arousal through the performance of a dramatic tragedy of "emotions of pity and fear" to a point where "purgation" or "purification" occurs and the feelings are released or transformed. The concept was developed by Aristotle in his *Poetics* from an ancient Greek medical concept, and adapted by him into an aesthetic principle.

Characterization: the means by which an author develops and presents a character's personality qualities and distinguishing traits. A character may be established in the story by descriptive commentary or may be developed less directly—for example, through his or her words, actions, thoughts, and interactions with other characters.

Chiasmus: a figure of speech (a scheme) that reverses word order in successive parallel clauses. If the word order is A-B-C in the first clause, it becomes C-B-A in the second: for example, Donne's line "She is all states, and all princes, I" ("The Sun Rising") incorporates this reversal.

Chorus: originally, the choir of singing, dancing, masked young men who performed in ancient Greek tragedy and comedy. It gradually disappeared from tragedy and comedy, but many attempts have been made to revive some version of it, notably during the Italian and English Renaissance, under Weimar Classicism, and by such twentieth-century playwrights as Jean Anouilh, T.S. Eliot, and Michel Tremblay.

Chronology: the way a story is organized in terms of time. Linear narratives run continuously from one point in time to a later point, while non-linear narratives are non-continuous and may jump forward and backward in time. A *flashback*, in which a story jumps to a scene previous in time, is an example of non-linearity.

Classical: originating in or relating to ancient Greek or Roman culture. As commonly conceived, *classical* implies a strong sense of formal order. The term *neoclassical* is often used with reference to literature of the Restoration and eighteenth century that was strongly influenced by ancient Greek and Roman models.

Closet Drama: a play (typically in verse) written to be read rather than performed. The term came into use in the first half of the nineteenth century.

Closure: the sense of completion evoked at the end of a story when all or most aspects of the major conflicts have been resolved. An example of the resolution of an internal conflict in Charlotte Perkins Gilman's "The Yellow Wallpaper" is the narrator's "merging" with the woman behind the paper. Not every story has a strong sense of closure.

Coloured Narrative: alternative term for *free indirect discourse*.

Comedy: as a literary term, used originally to denote that class of ancient Greek drama in which the action ends happily. More broadly the term has been used to describe a wide variety of literary forms of a more or less light-hearted character.

Comedy of Manners: a type of comic play that flourished in the late seventeenth century in London, and elsewhere since, which bases its humour on the sexual and marital intrigues of "high society." It is sometimes contrasted with "comedy of character" as its *satire* is directed at the social habits and conventional hypocrisy of the whole leisured class. Also called Restoration comedy; exemplified by the plays of Aphra Behn, William Wycherley, and William Congreve.

Commedia dell'arte: largely improvised comic performances conducted by masked performers and involving considerable physical activity. The genre of *commedia dell'arte* originated in Italy in the sixteenth century; it was influential throughout Europe for more than two centuries thereafter.

Conceit: an unusually elaborate metaphor or simile that extends beyond its original tenor and vehicle, sometimes becoming a "master" analogy for the entire poem (see, for example, Donne's "The Flea"). Ingenious or fanciful images and comparisons were especially popular with the *metaphysical poets* of the seventeenth century, giving rise to the term "metaphysical conceit."

Concrete Poetry: an experimental form, most popular during the 1950s and 1960s, in which the printed type itself forms a visual image of the poem's key words or ideas. See also *pattern poetry*.

Conflict: struggles between characters and opposing forces. Conflict can be internal (psychological) or external (conflict with another character, for instance, or with society or nature).

Connotation: the implied, often unspoken meaning(s) of a given word, as distinct from its *denotation*, or literal meaning. Connotations may have highly emotional undertones and are usually culturally specific.

Consonance: the pairing of words with similar initial and ending consonants, but with different vowel sounds (live/love, wander/wonder). See also *alliteration*.

Convention: aesthetic approach, technique, or practice accepted as characteristic and appropriate for a particular form. It is a convention of certain sorts of plays, for example, that the characters speak in blank verse, of other sorts of plays that characters speak in rhymed couplets, and of still other sorts of dramatic performances that characters frequently break into song to express their feelings.

Couplet: a pair of rhyming lines, usually in the same metre. If they form a complete unit of thought and are grammatically complete, the lines are known as a closed couplet. See also *heroic couplet*.

Dactyl: a metrical foot containing one strong stress followed by two weak stresses: / xx (e.g., muttering, helplessly). A minor form known as "double dactyls" makes use of this metre for humorous purposes, e.g., "Jiggery pokery" or "Higgledy Piggledy."

Denotation: see *connotation*.

Dénouement: that portion of a narrative that follows a dramatic climax, in which conflicts are resolved and the narrative is brought to a close. Traditional accounts of narrative structure often posit a triangle or arc, with rising action followed by a climax and then by a dénouement. (Such accounts bear little relation, however, to the ways in which most actual narratives are structured—particularly most twentieth- and twenty-first-century literary fictions.)

Dialogue: words spoken by characters to one another. (When a character is addressing him or her self or the audience directly, the words spoken are referred to as a *soliloquy*.)

Diction: word choice. Whether the diction of a literary work (or of a literary character) is colloquial, conversational, formal, or of some other type contributes significantly to the tone of the text as well as to characterization.

Didacticism: aesthetic approach emphasizing moral instruction.

Dimeter: a poetic line containing two metrical feet.

Dirge: a song or poem that mourns someone's death. See also *elegy* and *lament*.

Dissonance: harsh, unmusical sounds or rhythms that writers may use deliberately to achieve certain effects. Also known as cacophony.

Dramatic Irony: this form of *irony* occurs when an audience has access to information not available to the character.

Dramatic Monologue: a lyric poem that takes the form of an utterance by a single person addressing a silent listener. The speaker may be an historical personage (as in some of Robert Browning's dramatic monologues), a figure drawn from myth or legend (as in some of Tennyson's), or an entirely imagined figure (as in Webster's "A Castaway").

Dub Poetry: a form of protest poetry originating in Jamaica, with its roots in dance rhythms, especially reggae, and often accompanied in performance by drums and music. See also *rap*.

Duple Foot: a duple foot of poetry has two syllables. The possible duple forms are *iamb* (in which the stress is on the second of the two syllables), *trochee* (in which the stress is on the first of the two syllables), *spondee* (in which both are stressed equally), and *pyrrhic* (in which both syllables are unstressed).

Eclogue: now generally used simply as an alternative name for a pastoral poem. In classical times and in the early modern period, however, an *eclogue* (or *idyll*) was a specific type of pastoral poem—a dialogue or dramatic monologue involving rustic characters. (The other main sub-genre of the pastoral was the *georgic*.)

Elegiac Stanza: a quatrain of iambic pentameters rhyming *abab*, often used in poems meditating on death or sorrow. The best-known example is Thomas Gray's "Elegy Written in a Country Churchyard."

Elegy: a poem which formally mourns the death of a particular person (e.g., Tennyson's "In Memoriam") or in which the poet meditates on other serious subjects (e.g., Gray's "Elegy"). See also *dirge*.

Elision: omitting or suppressing a letter or an unstressed syllable at the beginning or end of a word, so that a line of verse may conform to a given metrical scheme. For example, the three syllables at the beginning of Shakespeare's sonnet 129 are reduced to two by the omission of the first vowel: "Th' expense of spirit in a waste of shame." See also *syncope*.

Ellipsis: the omission of a word or words necessary for the complete grammatical construction of a sentence, but not necessary for our understanding of the sentence.

Embedded Narrative: a story contained within another story.

End-Rhyme: see *rhyme*.

End-Stopped: a line of poetry is said to be end-stopped when the end of the line coincides with a natural pause in the syntax, such as the conclusion of a sentence; e.g., in this couplet from Pope's "Essay on Criticism," both lines are end-stopped: "A little learning is a dangerous thing; / Drink deep, or taste not the Pierian spring." Compare this with *enjambment*.

Enjambment: the "running-on" of the sense from one line of poetry to the next, with no pause created by punctuation or syntax.

Envoy (Envoi): a stanza or half-stanza that forms the conclusion of certain French poetic forms, such as the *sestina* or the *ballade*. It often sums up or comments upon what has gone before.

Epic: a lengthy narrative poem, often divided into books and sub-divided into cantos. It generally celebrates heroic deeds or events, and the style tends to be lofty and grand. Examples in English include Spenser's *The Faerie Queene* and Milton's *Paradise Lost*.

Epic Simile: an elaborate simile, developed at such length that the vehicle of the comparison momentarily displaces the primary subject with which it is being compared.

Epigram: a very short poem, sometimes in closed couplet form, characterized by pointed wit.

Epigraph: a quotation placed at the beginning of a work to indicate or foreshadow the theme.

Epiphany: a moment at which matters of significance are suddenly illuminated for a literary character (or for the reader), typically triggered by something small and seemingly of little import. The term first came into wide currency in connection with the fiction of James Joyce.

Episodic Plot: plot comprising a variety of episodes that are only loosely connected by threads of story material (as opposed to plots that present one or more continually unfolding narratives, in which successive episodes build one on another).

Epithalamion: a poem celebrating a wedding. The best-known example in English is Edmund Spenser's "Epithalamion" (1595).

Epode: the third part of an *ode*, following the *strophe* and *antistrophe*.

Ethos: the perceived character, trustworthiness, or credibility of a writer or narrator.

Eulogy: text expressing praise, especially for a distinguished person recently deceased.

Euphemism: mode of expression through which aspects of reality considered to be vulgar, crudely physical, or unpleasant are referred to indirectly rather than named explicitly. A variety of euphemisms exist for the processes of urination and defecation; *passed away* is often used as a euphemism for *died*.

Euphony: pleasant, musical sounds or rhythms—the opposite of *dissonance*.

Existentialism: a philosophical approach according to which the meaning of human life is derived from the actual experience of the living individual. The existential worldview, in which life is assumed to have no essential or pre-existing meanings other than those we personally choose to endow it with, can produce an *absurdist* sensibility.

Exposition: the setting out of material in an ordered (and usually concise) form, either in speech or in writing. In a play those parts of the action that do not occur on stage but are rather recounted by the characters are frequently described as being presented in exposition. Similarly, when the background narrative is filled in near the beginning of a novel, such material is often described as having been presented in exposition.

Eye-Rhyme: see *rhyme*.

Fable: a short *allegorical* tale that conveys an explicit moral lesson. The characters are often animals or objects with human speech and mannerisms. See *parable*.

Fantasy: in fiction, a sub-genre characterized by the presence of magical or miraculous elements—usually acknowledged as such by the characters and the narrative voice. In *magic realism*, by contrast, miraculous occurrences tend to be treated by the characters and/or the narrative voice as if they were entirely ordinary. In fantasy (also in contrast to magic realism), the fictional world generally has an internal consistency to it that precludes any sense of absurdity on the part of the reader; and the plot tends to build a strong sense of expectation in the reader.

Farce: sometimes classed as the "lowest" form of *comedy*. Its humour depends not on verbal wit, but on physicality and sight gags.

Feminine Rhyme: see *rhyme*.

Fiction: imagined or invented narrative. In literature, the term is usually used to refer to prose narratives (such as novels and short stories).

Figures of Speech: deliberate, highly concentrated uses of language to achieve particular purposes or effects on an audience. There are two kinds of figures: schemes and *tropes*. Schemes involve changes in word-sound and word-order, such as *alliteration* and *chiasmus*. Tropes play on our understandings of words to extend, alter, or transform meaning, as in *metaphor* and *personification*.

First-Person Narrative: narrative recounted using *I* and *me*. See also *narrative perspective*.

Fixed Forms: the term applied to a number of poetic forms and stanzaic patterns, many derived from French models, such as *ballade, rondeau, sestina, triolet,* and *villanelle*. Other "fixed forms" include the *sonnet, rhyme royal, haiku,* and *ottava rima*.

Flashback: in fiction, the inclusion in the primary thread of a story's narrative of a scene (or scenes) from an earlier point in time. Flashbacks may be used to revisit from a different viewpoint events that have already been recounted in the main thread of narrative; to present material that has been left out in the initial recounting; or to present relevant material from a time before the beginning of the main thread of narrative. The use of flashbacks in fiction is sometimes referred to as *analepsis*.

Flashforward: the inclusion in the primary thread of a story's narrative of a scene (or scenes) from a later point in time. See also *prolepsis*.

Flat Character: the opposite of a *round character*, a flat character is defined by a small number of traits and does not possess enough complexity to be psychologically realistic. "Flat character" can be a disparaging term, but need not be; flat characters serve different purposes in a fiction than round characters, and are often better suited to some types of literature, such as allegory or farcical comedy.

Foil: in literature, a character whose behaviour and/or qualities set in relief for the reader or audience those of a strongly contrasting character who plays a more central part in the story.

Foot: a unit of a line of verse that contains a particular combination of stressed and unstressed syllables. Dividing a line into metrical feet (*iambs, trochees,* etc.), then counting the number of feet per line, is part of *scansion*. See also *metre*.

Foreshadowing: the inclusion of elements in a story that hint at some later development(s) in the same story. For example, in Flannery O'Connor's "A Good Man Is Hard to Find," the old family burying ground that the family sees on their drive foreshadows the violence that follows.

Found Space: a site that is not normally a theatre but is used for the staging of a theatrical production. Often, the choice of found space can reflect the play's setting or thematic content.

Free Indirect Discourse: a style of third-person narration that takes on characteristics of first-person narration, thus making it difficult to discern whether the reader is receiving the impressions of the character, the narrator, or some combination of the two.

Free Verse: poetry that does not follow any regular metre, line length, or rhyming scheme. In many respects, though, free verse follows the complex natural "rules" and rhythmic patterns (or cadences) of speech.

Freytag's Pyramid: a model of plot structure developed by the German novelist, playwright, and critic Gustav Freytag and introduced in his book *Die Technik des Dramas* (1863). In the pyramid, five stages of plot are identified as occurring in the following order: exposition, rising action, climax, falling action, and *dénouement*. Freytag intended his pyramid to diagram the structure of classical five-act plays, but it is also used as a tool to analyze other forms of fiction (even though many individual plays and stories do not follow the structure outlined in the pyramid).

Genre: a class or type of literary work. The concept of genre may be used with different levels of generality. At the most general, poetry, drama, and prose fiction are distinguished as separate genres. At a lower level of generality various sub-genres are frequently distinguished, such as (within the genre of prose fiction) the novel, the novella, and the short story; and, at a still lower level of generality, the mystery novel, the detective novel, the novel of manners, and so on.

Georgic: (from Virgil's *Georgics*) a poem that celebrates the natural wealth of the countryside and advises how to cultivate and live in harmony with it. Pope's *Windsor Forest* and James Thomson's *Seasons* are classed as georgics. Georgics were often said to make up, with *eclogues*, the two alliterative forms of pastoral poetry.

Ghazal: derived from Persian and Indian precedents, the ghazal presents a series of thoughts in closed couplets usually joined by a simple rhyme-scheme such as: *a/a b/a c/a d/a, ab bb cb eb fb*, etc.

Gothic: in architecture and the visual arts, a term used to describe styles prevalent from the twelfth to the fourteenth centuries, but in literature a term used to describe work with a sinister or grotesque tone that seeks to evoke a sense of terror on the part of the reader or audience. Gothic literature originated as a genre in the eighteenth century with works such as Horace Walpole's *The Castle of Otranto*. To some extent the notion of the medieval itself then carried with it associations of the dark and the grotesque, but from the beginning an element of intentional exaggeration (sometimes verging on self-parody) attached itself to the genre. The Gothic trend of youth culture that began in the late twentieth century is less clearly associated with the medieval, but shares with the various varieties of Gothic literature (from Walpole in the eighteenth century, to Bram Stoker in the early twentieth, to Stephen King and Anne Rice in the late twentieth) a fondness for the sensational and the grotesque, as well as a propensity to self-parody.

Grotesque: literature of the grotesque is characterized by a focus on extreme or distorted aspects of human characteristics. (The term can also refer particularly to a character who is odd or disturbing.) This focus can serve to comment on and challenge societal norms. The story "A Good Man Is Hard to Find" employs elements of the grotesque.

Haiku: a Japanese poetic form with three unrhymed lines of typically five, seven, and five syllables. Conventionally, it uses precise, concentrated images to suggest states of feeling.

Heptameter: a line containing seven metrical feet.

Heroic Couplet: a pair of rhymed iambic pentameters, so called because the form was much used in seventeenth- and eighteenth-century poems and plays on heroic subjects.

Hexameter: a line containing six metrical feet.

Horatian Ode: inspired by the work of the Roman poet Horace, an ode that is usually calm and meditative in tone, and homostrophic (i.e., having regular stanzas) in form. Keats's odes are English examples.

Hymn: a song whose theme is usually religious, in praise of divinity. Literary hymns may praise more secular subjects.

Hyperbole: a *figure of speech* (a *trope*) that deliberately exaggerates or inflates meaning to achieve particular effects, such as the irony in A.E. Housman's claim (from "Terence, This Is Stupid Stuff") that "malt does more than Milton can / To justify God's ways to man."

Iamb: the most common metrical foot in English verse, containing one unstressed syllable followed by a stressed syllable: x / (e.g., between, achieve).

Idyll: traditionally, a short pastoral poem that idealizes country life, conveying impressions of innocence and happiness.

Image: a representation of a sensory experience or of an object that can be known by the senses.

Imagery: the range of images in a given work. We can gain much insight into works by looking for patterns of imagery. For example, the imagery of spring (budding trees, rain, singing birds) in Kate Chopin's "The Story of an Hour" reinforces the suggestions of death and rebirth in the plot and theme.

Imagism: a poetic movement that was popular mainly in the second decade of the twentieth century. The goal of imagist poets (such as H.D. and Ezra Pound in their early work) was to represent emotions or impressions through highly concentrated imagery.

Implied author: see *narrator*.

Improvisation: the seemingly spontaneous invention of dramatic dialogue and/or a dramatic plot by actors without the assistance of a written text.

Incantation: a chant or recitation of words that are believed to have magical power. A poem can achieve an "incantatory" effect through a compelling rhyme scheme and other repetitive patterns.

Interlocking Rhyme: see *rhyme*.

Interlude: a short and often comical play or other entertainment performed between the *acts* of a longer or more serious work, particularly during the later Middle Ages and early Renaissance.

Internal Rhyme: see *rhyme*.

Intertextuality: the relationships between one literary work and other literary works. A literary work may connect with other works through *allusion*, *parody*, or *satire*, or in a variety of other ways.

Irony: the use of irony draws attention to a gap between what is said and what is meant, or what appears to be true and what is true. Types of irony include verbal irony (which includes *hyberbole*, *litotes*, and *sarcasm*), *dramatic irony*, and structural irony (in which the gap between what is "said" and meant is sustained throughout an entire piece, as when an author makes use of an unreliable narrator or speaker—see Robert Browning's "My Last Duchess").

Lament: a poem that expresses profound regret or grief either because of a death, or because of the loss of a former, happier state.

Language Poetry: a movement that defies the usual lyric and narrative conventions of poetry, and that challenges the structures and codes of everyday language. Often seen as both politically and aesthetically subversive, its roots lie in the works of modernist writers such as Ezra Pound and Gertrude Stein.

Litotes: a *figure of speech* (a *trope*) in which a writer deliberately uses understatement to highlight the importance of an argument, or to convey an ironic attitude.

Liturgical Drama: drama based on and/or incorporating text from the liturgy—the text recited during religious services.

Lyric: a poem, usually short, expressing an individual speaker's feelings or private thoughts. Originally a song performed with accompaniment on a lyre, the lyric poem is often noted for musicality of rhyme and rhythm. The lyric genre includes a variety of forms, including the *sonnet*, the *ode*, the *elegy*, the *madrigal*, the *aubade*, the *dramatic monologue*, and the *hymn*.

Madrigal: a lyric poem, usually short and focusing on pastoral or romantic themes. A madrigal is often set to music.

Magic Realism: a style of fiction in which miraculous or bizarre things often happen but are treated in a matter-of-fact fashion by the characters and/or the narrative voice. There is often an element of the absurd to magic realist narratives, and they tend not to have any strong plot structure generating expectations in the reader's mind. See also *fantasy*.

Masculine Ending: a metrical line ending on a stressed syllable.

Masculine Rhyme: see *rhyme*. An alternative term is hard landing.

Melodrama: originally a term used to describe nineteenth-century plays featuring sensational story lines and a crude separation of characters into moral categories, with the pure and virtuous pitted against evil villains. Early melodramas employed background music throughout the action of the play as a means of heightening the emotional response of the audience. By extension, certain sorts of prose fictions or poems are often described as having melodramatic elements.

Metafiction: fiction that calls attention to itself as fiction. Metafiction is a means by which authors render us conscious of our status as readers, often in order to explore the relationships between fiction and reality.

Metaphor: a *figure of speech* (in this case, a *trope*) in which a comparison is made or identity is asserted between two unrelated things or actions without the use of "like" or "as."

Metaphysical Poets: a group of seventeenth-century English poets, notably Donne, Cowley, Marvell, and Herbert, who employed unusual, difficult imagery and *conceits* in order to develop intellectual and religious themes. The term was first applied to these writers to mark as far-fetched their use of philosophical and scientific ideas in a poetic context.

Metonymy: a *figure of speech* (a *trope*), meaning "change of name," in which a writer refers to an object or idea by substituting the name of another object or idea closely associated with it: for example, the substitution of "crown" for monarchy, "the press" for journalism, or "the pen" for writing. *Synecdoche* is a kind of metonymy.

Metre: the pattern of stresses, syllables, and pauses that constitutes the regular rhythm of a line of verse. The metre of a poem written in the English accentual-syllabic tradition is determined by identifying the stressed and unstressed syllables in a line of verse, and grouping them into recurring units known as feet. See *accent, accentual-syllabic, caesura, elision,* and *scansion.* For some of the better-known metres, see *iamb, trochee, dactyl, anapaest,* and *spondee.* See also *monometer, dimeter, trimeter, tetrameter, pentameter,* and *hexameter.*

Mise en scène: French expression, literally meaning "the putting on stage," which has been adopted in other languages to describe the sum total of creative choices made in the staging of a play.

Mock-Heroic: a style applying the elevated diction and vocabulary of epic poetry to low or ridiculous subjects. An example is Alexander Pope's "The Rape of the Lock."

Modernism: in the history of literature, music, and the visual arts, a movement that began in the early twentieth century, characterized by a thoroughgoing rejection of the then-dominant conventions of literary plotting and characterization, of melody and harmony, and of perspective and other naturalistic forms of visual representation. In literature (as in music and the visual arts), modernists endeavoured to represent the complexity of what seemed to them to be an increasingly fragmented world by adopting techniques of presenting story material, illuminating character, and employing imagery that emphasized (in the words of Virginia Woolf) "the spasmodic, the obscure, the fragmentary."

Monologue: an extended speech by a single speaker or character in a poem or play. Unlike a *soliloquy,* a dramatic monologue has an implied listener.

Monometer: a line containing one metrical foot.

Mood: this can describe the writer's attitude, implied or expressed, toward the subject (see *tone*); or it may refer to the atmosphere that a writer creates in a passage of description or narration.

Motif: pattern formed by the recurrence of an idea, image, action, or plot element throughout a literary work, creating new levels of meaning and strengthening structural coherence. The term is taken from music, where it describes recurring melodies or themes. See also *theme.*

Motivation: the forces that seem to cause characters to act, or reasons why characters do what they do.

Narration: the process of disclosing information, whether fictional or non-fictional.

Narrative Perspective: in fiction, the point of view from which a story is narrated. A first-person narrative is recounted using *I* and *me*, whereas a third-person narrative is recounted using *he, she, they*, and so on. When a narrative is written in the third person and the narrative voice evidently "knows" all that is being done and thought, the story is typically described as being recounted by an "omniscient narrator." Second-person narratives, in which the narrative is recounted using *you*, are very rare.

Narrator: the voice (or voices) disclosing information. In fiction, the narrator is distinguished from both the author (a real, historical person) and the implied author (whom the reader imagines the author to be). Narrators can also be distinguished according to the degree to which they share the reality of the other characters in the story and the extent to which they participate in the action; according to how much information they are privy to (and how much of that information they are willing to share with the reader); and according to whether or not they are perceived by the reader as reliable or unreliable sources of information. See also *narrative perspective*.

Neoclassical Dramaturgy: the principles, rules, and *conventions* of writing plays according to the precepts and ideals of *neoclassicism*. Often based on the so-called *unities* of time, place, and action.

Neoclassicism: literally the "new classicism," the aesthetic style that dominated high culture in Europe through the seventeenth and eighteenth centuries, and in some places into the nineteenth century. Its subject matter was often taken from Greek and Roman myth and history; in *style*, it valued order, reason, clarity, and moderation.

Nonsense Verse: light, humorous poetry that contradicts logic, plays with the absurd, and invents words for amusing effects. Lewis Carroll is one of the best-known practitioners of nonsense verse.

Octave: also known as "octet," the first eight lines in certain forms of sonnet—notably the *Italian/Petrarchan*, in which the octet rhymes *abbaabba*. See also *sestet* and *sonnet*.

Octosyllabic: a line of poetry with eight syllables, as in iambic tetrameter.

Ode: originally a classical poetic form, used by the Greeks and Romans to convey serious themes. English poetry has evolved three main forms of ode: the Pindaric (imitative of the odes of the Greek poet Pindar); the Horatian (modelled on the work of the Roman writer Horace); and the irregular ode. The Pindaric ode has a tripartite structure of *strophe, antistrophe*, and *epode* (meaning turn, counterturn, and stand), modelled on the songs and movements of the *Chorus* in Greek drama. The Horatian ode is more personal, reflective, and literary, and employs a pattern of repeated stanzas. The irregular ode, as its name implies, avoids a recurrent stanza pattern, and is sometimes irregular in line length also (for example, Wordsworth's "Ode: Intimations of Immortality").

Omniscient Narrator: see *narrative perspective*.

Onomatopoeia: a *figure of speech* (a scheme) in which a word "imitates" a sound, or in which the sound of a word seems to reflect its meaning.

Orchestra: literally, "the dancing place." In the ancient world it was the lower, flat, circular surface-area of the outdoor theatre where the *chorus* danced and sang.

Ottava Rima: an eight-line stanza, usually in iambic pentameter, with the rhyme scheme *abababcc*. For an example, see Yeats's "Sailing to Byzantium."

Oxymoron: a *figure of speech* (a *trope*) in which two words whose meanings seem contradictory are placed together; we see an example in Shakespeare's *Twelfth Night*, when Orsino refers to the "sweet pangs" of love.

Pantoum: linked quatrains in a poem that rhymes *abab*. The second and fourth lines of one stanza are repeated as the first and third lines of the stanza that follows. In the final stanza the pattern is reversed: the second line repeats the third line of the first stanza, the fourth and final line repeats the first line of the first stanza.

Parable: a story told to illustrate a moral principle. It differs from *allegory* in being shorter and simpler: parables do not generally function on two levels simultaneously.

Parody: a close, usually mocking imitation of a particular literary work, or of the well-known style of a particular author, in order to expose or magnify weaknesses. Parody is a form of *satire*—that is, humour that may ridicule and scorn its object.

Pastiche: a discourse that borrows or imitates other writers' characters, forms, style, or ideas, sometimes creating something of a literary patchwork. Unlike a parody, a pastiche can be intended as a compliment to the original writer.

Pastoral: in general, pertaining to country life; in prose, drama, and poetry, a stylized type of writing that idealizes the lives and innocence of country people, particularly shepherds and shepherdesses. See also *eclogue, georgic, idyll*.

Pastoral Elegy: a poem in which the poet uses the pastoral style to lament the death of a friend, usually represented as a shepherd. Milton's "Lycidas" provides a good example of the form, including its use of such conventions as an invocation of the muse and a procession of mourners.

Pathetic Fallacy: a form of *personification* in which inanimate objects are given human emotions: for example, rain clouds "weeping." The word "fallacy" in this connection is intended to suggest the distortion of reality or the false emotion that may result from an exaggerated use of personification.

Pathos: the emotional quality of a discourse; or the ability of a discourse to appeal to our emotions. It is usually applied to the mood conveyed by images of pain, suffering, or loss that arouse feelings of pity or sorrow in the reader.

Pattern Poetry: a predecessor of modern *concrete poetry* in which the shape of the poem on the page is intended to suggest or imitate an aspect of the poem's subject. George Herbert's "Easter Wings" is an example of pattern poetry.

Pentameter: verse containing five metrical feet in a line.

Performance Poetry: poetry composed primarily for oral performance, often very theatrical in nature. See also *dub poetry* and *rap*.

Persona: the assumed identity or "speaking voice" that a writer projects in a discourse. The term "persona" literally means "mask."

Personification: a *figure of speech* (a *trope*), also known as "prosopopoeia," in which a writer refers to inanimate objects, ideas, or non-human animals as if they were human, or creates a human figure to represent an abstract entity such as Philosophy or Peace.

Phoneme: a linguistic term denoting the smallest unit of sound that it is possible to distinguish. The words *fun* and *phone* each have three phonemes, though one has three letters and one has five.

Plot: the organization of story materials within a literary work. Matters of plotting include the order in which story material is presented; the inclusion of elements that allow or encourage the reader or audience to form expectations as to what is likely to happen; and the decision to present some story material through exposition rather than present it directly to the reader as part of the narrative.

Point of View: see *narrative perspective*.

Postmodernism: in literature and the visual arts, a movement influential in the late twentieth and early twenty-first centuries. In some ways postmodernism represents a reaction to modernism, in others an extension of it. With roots in the work of French philosophers such as Jacques Derrida and Michel Foucault, it is deeply coloured by theory; indeed, it may be said to have begun at the "meta" level of theorizing rather than at the level of practice. Like modernism, postmodernism embraces difficulty and distrusts the simple and straightforward. More broadly, postmodernism is characterized by a rejection of absolute truth or value, of closed systems, of grand unified narratives.

Postmodernist fiction is characterized by a frequently ironic or playful tone in dealing with reality and illusion; by a willingness to combine different styles or forms in a single work (just as in architecture the postmodernist spirit embodies a willingness to borrow from seemingly disparate styles in designing a single structure); and by a highly attuned awareness of the problematized state of the writer, artist, or theorist as observer.

Prolepsis: originally a rhetorical term used to refer to the anticipation of possible objections by someone advancing an argument, prolepsis is used in discussions of fiction to refer to elements in a narrative that anticipate the future of the story. The *flashforward* technique of storytelling is often described as a form of prolepsis; the inclusion in a narrative of material that foreshadows future developments is also sometimes treated as a form of prolepsis.

Proscenium: a Latin architectural term derived from the Greek *proskenion*, the frontmost section of the theatre building as it developed in the post-Classical, Hellenistic period. Stages on which a pictorial illusion is created with the help of a border or frame are called "proscenium arch" or "picture-frame" theatres; they reached their heyday during the nineteenth century, the age of *realism*.

Prose Poem: a poetic discourse that uses prose formats (e.g., it may use margins and paragraphs rather than line breaks or stanzas) yet is written with the kind of attention to language, rhythm, and cadence that characterizes verse.

Prosody: the study and analysis of metre, rhythm, rhyme, stanzaic pattern, and other devices of versification.

Protagonist: the central character in a literary work.

Prothalamion: a wedding song; a term coined by the poet Edmund Spenser, adapted from *epithalamion*.

Pun: a play on words, in which a word with two or more distinct meanings, or two words with similar sounds, may create humorous ambiguities. Also known as "paranomasia."

Pyrrhic: a metrical foot containing two weak stresses.

Quantitative Metre: a metrical system used by Greek and Roman poets, in which a line of verse was measured by the "quantity," or length of sound of each syllable. A foot was measured in terms of syllables classed as long or short.

Quantity: duration of syllables in poetry. The line "There is a Garden in her face" (the first line from the poem of the same name by Thomas Campion) is characterized by the short quantities of the syllables. The last line of Thomas Hardy's "During Wind and Rain" has the same number of syllables as the line by Campion, but the quantities of the syllables are much longer—in other words, the line takes much longer to say: "Down their carved names the rain drop ploughs."

Quatrain: a four-line stanza.

Quintet: a five-line stanza. Sometimes given as "quintain."

Rap: originally coined to describe informal conversation, "rap" now usually describes a style of performance poetry in which a poet will chant rhymed verse, sometimes improvised and usually with musical accompaniment that has a heavy beat.

Realism: as a literary term, the presentation through literature of material closely resembling real life. As notions both of what constitutes "real life" and of how it may be most faithfully represented in literature have varied widely, "realism" has taken a variety of meanings. The term "naturalistic" has sometimes been used as a synonym for *realistic*; naturalism originated in the nineteenth century as a term denoting a form of realism focusing in particular on grim, unpleasant, or ugly aspects of the real.

Refrain: one or more words or lines repeated at regular points throughout a poem, often at the end of each stanza or group of stanzas. Sometimes a whole stanza may be repeated to create a refrain, like the chorus in a song.

Rhetoric: in classical Greece and Rome, the art of persuasion and public speaking. From the Middle Ages onwards, the study of rhetoric gave greater attention to style, particularly *figures of speech*. Today in poetics, the term rhetoric may encompass not only figures of speech, but also the persuasive effects of forms, sounds, and word choices.

Rhyme: the repetition of identical or similar sounds, usually in pairs and generally at the ends of metrical lines.

    End-Rhyme: a rhyming word or syllable at the end of a line.

    Eye Rhyme: rhyming that pairs words whose spellings are alike but whose pronunciations are different: for example, though/slough.

    Feminine Rhyme: a two-syllable (also known as "double") rhyme. The first syllable is stressed and the second unstressed: for example, hasty/tasty. See also *triple rhyme*.

    Interlocking Rhyme: the repetition of rhymes from one stanza to the next, creating links that add to the poem's continuity and coherence. Examples may be found in Shelley's use of *terza rima* in "Ode to the West Wind" and in Dylan Thomas's *villanelle* "Do Not Go Gentle into That Good Night."

    Internal Rhyme: the placement of rhyming words within lines so that at least two words in a line rhyme with each other.

Masculine Rhyme: a correspondence of sound between the final stressed syllables at the end of two or more lines, as in grieve/leave, ar-rive/sur-vive.

Slant Rhyme: an imperfect or partial rhyme (also known as "near" or "half" rhyme) in which the consonant sounds of stressed syllables match but the vowel sounds do not. E.g., spoiled/spilled, taint/stint.

Triple Rhyme: a three-syllable rhyme in which the first syllable of each rhyme-word is stressed and the other two unstressed (e.g., lottery/coterie).

True Rhyme: a rhyme in which everything but the initial consonant matches perfectly in sound and spelling.

Rhyme Royal: a stanza of seven iambic pentameters, with a rhyme-scheme of *ababbcc*. This is also known as the Chaucerian stanza, as Chaucer was the first English poet to use this form. See also *septet*.

Rhythm: in speech, the arrangement of stressed and unstressed syllables creates units of sound. In song or verse, these units may be shaped into a regular rhythmic pattern, described in prosody as *metre*.

Romance: a dreamlike genre of fiction or storytelling in which the ordinary laws of nature are suspended—in which, for example, statues come to life, or shipwrecked men emerge from the sea unharmed.

Romanticism: a major social and cultural movement, originating in Europe, that shaped much of Western artistic thought in the late eighteenth and nineteenth centuries. Opposing the ideal of controlled, rational order associated with the Enlightenment, Romanticism emphasizes the importance of spontaneous self-expression, emotion, and personal experience in producing art. In Romanticism, the "natural" is privileged over the conventional or the artificial.

Rondeau: a 15-line poem, generally octosyllabic, with only two rhymes throughout its three stanzas, and an unrhymed refrain at the end of the ninth and fifteenth lines, repeating part of the opening line.

Round Character: a complex and psychologically realistic character, often one who changes as a work progresses. The opposite of a round character is a *flat character*.

Sarcasm: a form of *irony* (usually spoken) in which the meaning is conveyed largely by the tone of voice adopted; something said sarcastically is meant to imply its opposite.

Satire: literary work designed to make fun of or seriously criticize its subject. According to many literary theories of the Renaissance and neoclassical periods, the ridicule through satire of a certain sort of behaviour may function for the reader or audience as a corrective of such behaviour.

Scansion: the formal analysis of patterns of rhythm and rhyme in poetry. Each line of accentual-syllabic verse will have a certain number of fairly regular "beats" consisting of alternating stressed and unstressed syllables. To "scan" a poem is to count the beats in each line, to mark stressed and unstressed syllables and indicate their combination into "feet," to note pauses, and to identify rhyme schemes with letters of the alphabet.

Scheme: see *figures of speech*.

Septet: a stanza containing seven lines.

Sestet: a six-line stanza. A sestet forms the second grouping of lines in an *Italian/Petrarchan sonnet*, following the octave. See *sonnet* and *sestina*.

Sestina: an elaborate unrhymed poem with six six-line stanzas and a three-line *envoy*.

Setting: the time, place, and cultural environment in which a story or work takes place.

Simile: a *figure of speech* (a *trope*) which makes an explicit comparison between a particular object and another object or idea that is similar in some (often unexpected) way. A simile always uses "like" or "as" to signal the connection. Compare with *metaphor*.

Soliloquy: in drama (or, less often, poetry), a speech in which a character, usually alone, reveals his or her thoughts, emotions, and/or motivations without being heard by other characters. The convention was frequently employed during the Elizabethan era, and many of the best-known examples are from Shakespeare; for example, Hamlet's "To be, or not to be" speech is a soliloquy. Soliloquies differ from *dramatic monologues* in that dramatic monologues address an implied listener, while the speaker of a soliloquy thinks aloud or addresses the audience.

Sonnet: a highly structured lyric poem, which normally has 14 lines of iambic pentameter. We can distinguish four major variations of the sonnet.

> **Italian/Petrarchan:** named for the fourteenth-century Italian poet Petrarch, has an octave rhyming *abbaabba*, and a sestet rhyming *cdecde*, or *cdcdcd* (other arrangements are possible here). Usually, a turn in argument takes place between the octave and sestet.

> **Miltonic:** developed by Milton and similar to the Petrarchan in rhyme scheme, but eliminating the turn after the octave, thus giving greater unity to the poem's structure of thought.

> **Shakespearean:** often called the English sonnet, this form has three quatrains and a couplet. The quatrains rhyme internally but do not interlock: *abab cdcd efef gg*. The turn may occur after the second quatrain, but is usually revealed in the final couplet. Shakespeare's sonnets are the best-known examples of this form.

Spenserian: after Edmund Spenser, who developed the form in his sonnet cycle *Amoretti*. This sonnet form has three quatrains linked through interlocking rhyme, and a separately rhyming couplet: *abab bcbc cdcd ee*.

Spenserian Stanza: a nine-line stanza, with eight iambic pentameters and a concluding 12-syllable line, rhyming *ababbcbcc*.

Spondee: a metrical foot containing two strong stressed syllables: // (e.g., blind mouths).

Sprung Rhythm: a modern variation of accentual verse, created by the English poet Gerard Manley Hopkins, in which rhythms are determined largely by the number of strong stresses in a line, without regard to the number of unstressed syllables. Hopkins felt that sprung rhythm more closely approximated the natural rhythms of speech than did conventional poetry.

Stanza: any lines of verse that are grouped together in a poem and separated from other similarly structured groups by a space. In metrical poetry, stanzas share metrical and rhyming patterns; however, stanzas may also be formed on the basis of thought, as in irregular odes. Conventional stanza forms include the *tercet*, the *quatrain*, *rhyme royal*, the *Spenserian stanza*, the *ballad stanza*, and *ottava rima*.

Stock Character: a character defined by a set of characteristics that are stereotypical and/or established by literary convention; examples include the "wicked stepmother" and the "absent-minded professor."

Story: narrative material, independent of the manner in which it may be presented or the ways in which the narrative material may be organized. Story is thus distinct from *plot*.

Stream of Consciousness: a narrative technique that conveys the inner workings of a character's mind, in which a character's thoughts, feelings, memories, and impressions are related in an unbroken flow, without concern for *chronology* or coherence.

Stress: see *accent*.

Strophe: a *stanza*. In a Pindaric *ode*, the *strophe* is the first stanza. This is followed by an *antistrophe*, which presents the same metrical pattern and rhyme scheme, and finally by an *epode*, differing in metre from the preceding stanzas. Upon completion of this "triad," the entire sequence can recur.

Style: a distinctive or specific use of language and form.

Sublime: a concept, popular in eighteenth-century England, that sought to capture the qualities of grandeur, power, and awe that may be inherent in or produced by undomesticated nature or great art. The sublime was thought of as higher and loftier than something that is merely beautiful.

Subplot: a line of story that is subordinate to the main storyline of a narrative. (Note that properly speaking a subplot is a category of story material, not of plot.)

Substitution: a deliberate change from the dominant pattern of stresses in a line of verse to create emphasis or variation. Thus the first line of Shakespeare's sonnet "Shall I compare thee to a summer's day?" is decidedly iambic in metre (x/x/x/x/x/), whereas the second line substitutes a trochee (/x) in the opening foot: "Thou art more lovely and more temperate."

Subtext: implied or suggested meaning of a passage of text, or of an entire work.

Surrealism: Surrealism incorporates elements of the true appearance of life and nature, combining these elements according to a logic more typical of dreams than waking life. Isolated aspects of surrealist art may create powerful illusions of reality, but the effect of the whole is usually to disturb or question our sense of reality rather than to confirm it.

Suspension of Disbelief: a willingness on the part of the audience member or reader to temporarily accept the fictional world presented in a narrative.

Syllabic Verse: poetry in which the length of a line is measured solely by the number of syllables, regardless of accents or patterns of stress.

Syllable: vocal sound or group of sounds forming a unit of speech; a syllable may be formed with a single effort of articulation. Some syllables consist of a single phoneme (e.g., the word *I*, or the first syllable in the word *u-ni-ty*) but others may be made up of several phonemes (as with one-syllable words such as *lengths*, *splurged*, and *through*). By contrast, the much shorter words *ago*, *any*, and *open* each have two syllables.

Symbol: something that represents itself but goes beyond this in suggesting other meanings. Like metaphor, the symbol extends meaning; but while the tenor and vehicle of metaphor are bound in a specific relationship, a symbol may have a range of connotations. For example, the image of a rose may call forth associations of love, passion, transience, fragility, youth, and beauty, among others. Depending upon the context, such an image could be interpreted in a variety of ways, as in Blake's lyric, "The Sick Rose."

Syncope: in poetry, the dropping of a letter or syllable from the middle of a word, as in "trav'ller." Such a contraction allows a line to stay within a metrical scheme. See also *catalexis* and *elision*.

Synecdoche: a kind of *metonymy* in which a writer substitutes the name of a part of something to signify the whole: for example, "sail" for ship or "hand" for a member of the ship's crew.

Syntax: the ordering of words in a sentence.

Tercet: a group, or stanza, of three lines, often linked by an interlocking rhyme scheme as in *terza rima*. See also *triplet*.

Terza Rima: an arrangement of tercets interlocked by a rhyme scheme of *aba bcb cdc ded*, etc., and ending with a couplet that rhymes with the second-last line of the final tercet (for example, *efe, ff*). See, for example, Percy Shelley's "Ode to the West Wind."

Tetrameter: a line of poetry containing four metrical feet.

Theatre-in-the-Round: a type of staging in which seating for the audience surrounds the stage on all (or at least most) of its sides. This approach was common in ancient Greek, ancient Roman, and medieval theatre; it was not often used after the seventeenth century, but in the mid-twentieth century its popularity increased, especially in experimental theatre. Also called "arena theatre."

Theme: in general, an idea explored in a work through character, action, and/or image. To be fully developed, however, a theme must consist of more than a single concept or idea: it should also include an argument about the idea. Thus if a poem examines the topic of jealousy, we might say the theme is that jealousy undermines love or jealousy is a manifestation of insecurity. Few, if any, literary works have single themes.

Third-Person Narrative: see *narrative perspective*.

Thrust Stage: see *apron*.

Tone: the writer's attitude toward a given subject or audience, as expressed through an authorial persona or "voice." Tone can be projected through particular choices of wording, imagery, figures of speech, and rhythmic devices. Compare *mood*.

Tragedy: in the traditional definition originating in discussions of ancient Greek drama, a serious narrative recounting the downfall of the protagonist, usually a person of high social standing. More loosely, the term has been applied to a wide variety of literary forms in which the tone is predominantly a dark one and the narrative does not end happily.

Tragicomedy: a genre of drama in which many elements of *tragedy* are present, but which generally has a happy end, or—more generally—which includes both serious and comic components.

Trimeter: verse containing three metrical feet in a line.

Triolet: a French form in which the first line appears three times in a poem of only eight lines. The first line is repeated at lines four and seven; the second line is repeated in line eight. The triolet has only two rhymes: *abaaabab*.

Triple Foot: poetic foot of three syllables. The possible varieties of triple foot are the anapest (in which two unstressed syllables are followed by a stressed syllable), the dactyl (in which a stressed syllable is followed by two unstressed syllables), and the mollossus (in which all three syllables are stressed equally). English poetry tends to use *duple* rhythms far more frequently than triple rhythms.

Triplet: a group of three lines with the same end-rhyme, much used by eighteenth-century poets to vary or punctuate the flow of couplets. See also *tercet*.

Trochee: a metrical foot containing one strong stress followed by one weak stress.

Trope: any figure of speech that plays on our understandings of words to extend, alter, or transform "literal" meaning. Common tropes include *metaphor, simile, personification, hyperbole, metonymy, oxymoron, synecdoche*, and *irony*. See also *figures of speech*.

Turn (Italian "volta"): the point in a *sonnet* where the mood or argument changes. The turn may occur between the octave and sestet, i.e., after the eighth line, or in the final couplet, depending on the kind of sonnet.

Unities: Many literary theorists of the late sixteenth through late eighteenth centuries held that a play should ideally be presented as representing a single place, and confining the action to a single day and a single dominant event. They disapproved of plots involving gaps or long periods of time, shifts in place, or subplots. These concepts, which came to be referred to as the unities of space, time, and action, were based on a misreading of classical authorities (principally of Aristotle).

Unreliable Narrator: a narrator whose reporting or understanding of events invites questioning from the reader. Narrators may be considered unreliable if they lack sufficient intelligence or experience to understand events, or if they have some reason to misrepresent events. See also *narrative perspective*.

Vers libre (French): see *free verse*.

Verse: a general term for works of poetry, usually referring to poems that incorporate some kind of metrical structure. The term may also describe a line of poetry, though more frequently it is applied to a stanza.

Villanelle: a poem usually consisting of 19 lines, with five three-line stanzas (tercets) rhyming *aba*, and a concluding quatrain rhyming *abaa*. The first and third lines of the first tercet are repeated at fixed intervals throughout the rest of the poem. See, for example, Dylan Thomas's "Do Not Go Gentle into That Good Night."

Volta: See *turn*.

Zeugma: a *figure of speech* (*trope*) in which one word links or "yokes" two others in the same sentence, often to comic or ironic effect. For example, a verb may govern two objects, as in Pope's line "Or stain her honour, or her new brocade."

Acknowledgement: The glossary for *The Broadview Introduction to Literature* incorporates some material initially prepared for the following Broadview anthologies: *The Broadview Anthology of Poetry*, edited by Herbert Rosengarten and Amanda Goldrick-Jones; *The Broadview Anthology of Drama*, edited by Jennifer Wise and Craig Walker; *The Broadview Anthology of Short Fiction*, edited by Julia Gaunce et al.; *The Broadview Anthology of British Literature*, edited by Joseph Black et al. The editors gratefully acknowledge the contributions of the editors of these other anthologies. Please note that all material in the glossary, whether initially published in another Broadview anthology or appearing here for the first time, is protected by copyright.

Permission Acknowledgements

Chinua Achebe. "Dead Men's Path," from *Girls at War and Other Stories*. Copyright © 1953, 1972, 1973 by Chinua Achebe. Used by permission of The Wylie Agency LLC.

Diane Ackerman. "Sweep Me through Your Many-Chambered Heart," from *Jaguar of Sweet Laughter* by Diane Ackerman, copyright © 1991 by Diane Ackerman. Used by permission of Random House, Inc. Any third party use of this material, outside of this publication, is prohibited. Interested parties must apply directly to Random House, Inc. for permission.

Kim Addonizio. "First Poem for You," from *The Philosopher's Club*. BOA Editions, Ltd., 1994. Copyright © Kim Addonizio. Reprinted by permission of the author.

Agha Shahid Ali. "Postcard from Kashmir," from *The Half-Inch Himalayas*, copyright © 1987 by Agha Shahid Ali. Published by Wesleyan University Press. Reprinted by permission of Wesleyan University Press. "The Wolf's Postscript to 'Little Red Riding Hood,'" from *A Walk Through the Yellow Pages*. SUN/gemini Press, 1987. Reprinted by permission of Iqbal Agha.

Ama Ata Aidoo. "The Message," from *Fragment from a Lost Diary and Other Stories*, edited by Naomi Katz and Nancy Milton. Pantheon Books, 1973.

Sherman Alexie. "Flight Patterns," from *Ten Little Indians*, copyright © 2003 by Sherman Alexie. Used by permission of Grove/Atlantic, Inc.

Yehuda Amichai. "Tourists," from *The Selected Poetry of Yehuda Amichai*. Translated by Chana Bloch and Stephen Mitchell, with a New Foreword by C.K. Williams. University of California Press. English translation reprinted with the permission of University of California Press via Copyright Clearance Center. Original Hebrew reprinted with the permission of Hana Amichai.

Simon Armitage. "It Could Be You," from *The Universal Home Doctor* by Simon Armitage. Faber and Faber, 2002; reprinted with the permission of Faber and Faber Ltd. "Poem," from *Kid* by Simon Armitage. Faber and Faber, 2002; reprinted with the permission of Faber and Faber Ltd. "Very Simply Topping Up the Brake Fluid," originally published in *Zoom!* by Bloodaxe Books, 1989; reprinted with the permission of Bloodaxe Books.

John Ashbery. "Civilization and Its Discontents," from *Rivers and Mountains* by John Ashbery. Copyright © 1962, 1966 by John Ashbery; reprinted by permission of Georges Borchardt, Inc., on behalf of the author. "The Improvement," from *And the Stars Were Shining* by John Ashbery. Copyright © 1994 by John Ashbery; reprinted by permission of Georges Borchardt, Inc., on behalf of the author.

Roo Borson. Excerpt from *Water Memory* by Roo Borson. Copyright © 1996 by Roo Borson. Reprinted by permission of McClelland & Stewart.

Dionne Brand. "XXX" and "XXXII," excerpted from *Thirsty* by Dionne Brand. Copyright © 2002, Dionne Brand. Reprinted by permission of McClelland & Stewart.

Robert Bringhurst. "Leda and the Swan," from *Selected Poems*. Gaspereau Press, 2009. Reprinted with the permission of Gaspereau Press.

Nicole Brossard. "All These Months Spent," from *Notebook of Roses and Civilization*, translated by Erín Mouré and Robert Majzels. Coach House Books, 2003. Reprinted with the permission of the author and Coach House Books. "Tous ces mois passés," from *Cahier de roses et de civilization*, by Nicole Brossard et Francine Simonin. Éditions d'art Le Sabord, Trois-Rivières, 2003, p. 89; reprinted with the permission of Les Éditions d'art Le Sabord. "Gesture," from *Installations (with and without pronouns)*, translated by Erín Mouré and Robert Majzels; reprinted with the permission of The Muses' Company/J. Gordon Shillingford Publishing. "Geste," from *Installations (avec et sans pronoms)*, by Nicole Brossard. Écrits des Forges, 1989; reprinted with the permission of Écrits des Forges.

Anne Carson. "On Walking Backwards," "On Sylvia Plath," and "On Rain," from *Short Talks*. Brick, 1992. Reprinted with the permission of United Talent Agency.

Raymond Carver. "Cathedral," from *Cathedral*. Copyright © 1981, 1982, 1983 by Raymond Carver. Used by permission of Alfred A. Knopf, a division of Random House, Inc. Any third party use of this material, outside of this publication, is prohibited. Interested parties must apply directly to Random House, Inc. for permission.

Paul Celan. "Shroud" and "Death Fugue," from *Poems of Paul Celan*, translated by Michael Hamburger. Translation copyright © 1972, 1980, 1988, 2002 by Michael Hamburger; reprinted by permission of Persea Books, Inc., New York. All rights reserved. "Totenhemd" and "Todesfuge" from *Mohn und Gedächtnis*, copyright © 1952, Deutsche Verlags-Anstalt, München, in der Verlagsgruppe Random House GmbH. Reprinted with permission.

George Elliott Clarke. "Blank Sonnet" and "Look Homeward, Exile," from *Whylah Falls*. Polestar Book Publishers, 1990; reprinted with the permission of the author. "Casualties," from *Fiery Spirits and Voices: Canadian Writers of African Descent*, edited by Ayanna Black. Harper Collins, 1992; reprinted with the permission of the author.

Lucille Clifton. "The Lost Baby Poem" and "Miss Rosie," from *The Collected Poems of Lucille Clifton*. Copyright © 1987 by Lucille Clifton. Reprinted with the permission of The Permissions Company, Inc. on behalf of BOA Editions Ltd. <www.boaeditions.org>.

Billy Collins. "Pinup," from *The Art of Drowning* by Billy Collins, copyright © 1995. Reprinted by permission of the University of Pittsburgh Press.

Karen Connelly. Entries for August 21 and 22 from *Touch the Dragon: A Thai Journal*. Turnstone Press, 1992, 2010. Reprinted with the permission of Karen Connelly.

Alasdair Gray. "The Star," from *Unlikely Stories, Mostly*. First published in Great Britain by Canongate Books Ltd., Edinburgh. Reprinted with the permission of Canongate Books.

R.W. Gray. "How This Begins," from *Seminal: The Anthology of Canada's Gay Male Poets*, edited by John Barton and Billeh Nickerson. Arsenal Pulp Press, 2007. Reprinted with the permission of the author.

Lavinia Greenlaw. "Zombies," from *Minsk*. Faber and Faber, 2003; reprinted with the permission of Faber and Faber Ltd. "Electricity," from *Night Photograph*. Faber and Faber, 1993; reprinted with the permission of Faber and Faber Ltd.

Thom Gunn. "The Hug," "Tamer and Hawk," and "To His Cynical Mistress," from *Collected Poems*. Faber and Faber, 1994. Reprinted with the permission of Faber and Faber Ltd.

Reesom Haile. "Knowledge" and "Dear Africans," from *We Have Our Voice* by Reesom Haile, translated by Charles Cantalupo. Red Sea Press, 2000. Translation reprinted with the permission of Charles Cantalupo.

Sharon Harris. "Where do poems come from?" and "Why do poems make me cry?" from *Avatar* by Sharon Harris. The Mercury Press, 2006. Originally published in *Fun with 'Pataphysics*. BookThug, 2004. Reprinted with the permission of the author.

Gwen Harwood. "In the Park," from *Gwen Harwood: Selected Poems*. Penguin Group (Australia), 2001. Reproduced with the permission of Penguin Group (Australia).

Seamus Heaney. "Digging," "Mid-Term Break," and "Grauballe Man," from *Opened Ground: Selected Poems 1966–1996*. Farrar, Straus and Giroux, 1998; reprinted with the permission of Faber and Faber Ltd. "Cutaways," originally published in *Irish Pages*, Volume 2 Number 2, 2008; reprinted with the permission of Faber and Faber Ltd.

Adrian Henri. "Mrs Albion You've Got a Lovely Daughter," from *The Mersey Sound* (poems by Roger McGough, Brian Patten, Adrian Henri). Copyright © Adrian Henri, 1968. Reproduced by permission of the author c/o Rogers, Coleridge & White Ltd., London.

Langston Hughes. "Harlem (2)" and "The Negro Speaks of Rivers," from *The Collected Poems of Langston Hughes* by Langston Hughes, edited by Arnold Rampersad with David Roessel, Associate Editor, copyright © 1994 by the Estate of Langston Hughes. Used by permission of Alfred A. Knopf, a division of Random House, Inc. Any third party use of this material, outside of this publication, is prohibited. Interested parties must apply directly to Random House, Inc. for permission.

Ted Hughes. "Hawk Roosting," "Pike," "Heptonstall Old Church," and "The Thought-Fox," from *Collected Poems*, edited by Paul Keegan. Faber and Faber, 2003. Reprinted with the permission of Faber and Faber Ltd.

Kazuo Ishiguro. "A Family Supper," from *The Art of the Story*, copyright © 1982 by Kazuo Ishiguro. Reproduced by permission of the author c/o Rogers, Coleridge & White Ltd., London.

Gwendolyn MacEwen. "Dark Pines under Water" and "The Discovery," from *The Shadow-Maker*. Macmillan, 1969. Reprinted with the permission of David MacKinnon.

Alistair MacLeod. "As Birds Bring Forth the Sun," from *As Birds Bring Forth the Sun* by Alistair MacLeod. Copyright © 1986 Alistair MacLeod. Reprinted by permission of McClelland & Stewart.

Colum McCann. "A Basket Full of Wallpaper," from *Fishing the Sloe-Black River: Stories* by Colum McCann. Copyright © 1994 by Colum McCann. Reprinted by permission of Henry Holt and Company, LLC.

Roger McGough. "Comeclose and Sleepnow," from *The Mersey Sound* (copyright © Roger McGough 1967) is reprinted by permission of United Agents (<www.unitedagents.co.uk>) on behalf of Roger McGough.

Don McKay. "Some Functions of a Leaf," "Meditations on Shovels," and "Song for the Song of the Wood Thrush," from *Camber* by Don McKay. Copyright © 2004 Don McKay; reprinted by permission of McClelland & Stewart. "Meditation on a Geode," from *Night Field* by Don McKay. Copyright © 1991 Don McKay; reprinted by permission of McClelland & Stewart.

Roy Miki. "Attractive," "Make It New," and "On the Sublime," from *Surrender*. The Mercury Press, 2001. Reprinted with the permission of the author.

Lydia Millet. "Love in Infant Monkeys," from *Love in Infant Monkeys*. Copyright © 2009 by Lydia Millet. Reprinted with the permission of Counterpoint.

Rohinton Mistry. "Squatter," from *Tales from Firozsha Baag* by Rohinton Mistry. Copyright © 1987 Rohinton Mistry. Reprinted by permission of McClelland & Stewart.

Marianne Moore. "Poetry," from *The Collected Poems of Marianne Moore*. Copyright © 1921 by Marianne Moore, renewed 1949 by Marianne Moore and T.S. Eliot; reprinted with the permission of Scribner, a Division of Simon & Schuster, Inc.; all rights reserved. "Poetry," from *The Collected Poems of Marianne Moore*. Copyright © 1935 by Marianne Moore, renewed 1963 by Marianne Moore and T.S. Eliot; reprinted with the permission of Scribner, a Division of Simon & Schuster, Inc.; all rights reserved.

Hannah Moscovitch. "Essay," copyright © 2008 by Hannah Moscovitch. Reprinted by permission of Playwrights Canada Press.

Charles Mungoshi. "The Setting Sun and the Rolling World," from *The Setting Sun and the Rolling World: Selected Stories*. Copyright © 1972, 1980 by Charles Mungoshi. Reprinted by permission of Beacon Press, Boston.

Alice Munro. "Friend of My Youth," from *Friend of My Youth* by Alice Munro. Copyright © 1990, Alice Munro. Reprinted by permission of McClelland & Stewart.

Les Murray. "The Early Dark," from *Conscious & Verbal* by Les Murray. Copyright © 2001 by Les Murray; reprinted with the permission of Farrar, Straus and Giroux, LLC. "The Shield-Scales of Heraldry," from *Learning Human* by Les Murray. Copyright © 1998 by Les Murray; reprinted with the permission of Farrar, Straus and Giroux, LLC. "Pigs," from *Translations from the Natural World* by Les

Science Fiction Poetry Association, 2008. Originally published in *Agni*, No. 64 (2006). Reprinted with the permission of United Agents on behalf of Alice Oswald.

P.K. Page. "Stories of Snow" and "The Stenographers," from *The Hidden Room*. The Porcupine's Quill, 1997. Reprinted with the permission of The Porcupine's Quill.

Brian Patten. "Somewhere Between Heaven and Woolworths, A Song," from *The Mersey Sound* (poems by Roger McGough, Brian Patten, Adrian Henri). Copyright © Brian Patten, 1968. Reproduced by permission of the author c/o Rogers, Coleridge & White Ltd., London.

Sylvia Plath. "Daddy" and "Lady Lazarus," from *Collected Poems*, edited by Ted Hughes. Faber and Faber, 1981. Reprinted with the permission of Faber and Faber Ltd.

Sharon Pollock. *Blood Relations* (1980), from *Blood Relations and Other Plays* (revised edition). NeWest Press, 2002. Reprinted with the permission of Sharon Pollock and NeWest Press.

Ezra Pound. "In a Station of the Metro" and "The River-Merchant's Wife: A Letter," from *Personae*, copyright © 1926 by Ezra Pound. Reprinted by permission of New Directions Publishing Corp.

Al Purdy. "Lament for the Dorsets" and "Trees at the Arctic Circle," from *Beyond Remembering: The Collected Poems of Al Purdy*, edited by Sam Solecki. Harbour Publishing, 2000. Reprinted with the permission of Harbour Publishing, <www.harbourpublishing.com>.

Craig Raine. "A Martian Sends a Postcard Home," from *A Martian Sends a Postcard Home* by Craig Raine. Copyright © Craig Raine, 1979. Reprinted with permission.

Ian Iqbal Rashid. "Could Have Danced All Night," from *Seminal: The Anthology of Canada's Gay Male Poets*, edited by John Barton and Billeh Nickerson. Arsenal Pulp Press, 2007. Reprinted with the permission of the author.

Adrienne Rich. "Aunt Jennifer's Tigers," copyright © 2002, 1951 by Adrienne Rich; "Diving into the Wreck," copyright © 2002 by Adrienne Rich, copyright © 1973 by W.W. Norton & Company Inc.; "Living in Sin," copyright © 2002, 1955 by Adrienne Rich; from *The Fact of a Doorframe: Selected Poems 1950–2001* by Adrienne Rich. Used by permission of W.W. Norton & Company, Inc.

Arthur Rimbaud. "Scene Set to Music" and "Vowels," from *Arthur Rimbaud: The Poems*, translated by Oliver Bernard. Revised and enlarged edition published by Anvil Press Poetry in 2012. Reprinted with the permission of Anvil Press Poetry.

Robin Robertson. "What the Horses See at Night" and "The Park Drunk," from *Swithering*. Picador, 2006.

Eden Robinson. "Terminal Avenue," by Eden Robinson, copyright © 1996 by Eden Robinson. Reprinted by permission of the author.

Theodore Roethke. "I Knew a Woman," copyright © 1954 by Theodore Roethke; "My Papa's Waltz," copyright © 1942 by Hearst Magazines, Inc.; "Root Cellar," copyright © 1943 by Modern Poetry Association, Inc., from *Collected Poems*

Miriam Toews. "A Father's Faith," first published in *Saturday Night Magazine*. Copyright © 1999 by Miriam Toews. Used by permission of The Wylie Agency, LLC.

William Trevor. "Folie à Deux," from *Cheating at Canasta*, Penguin Group, 2007. Copyright © William Trevor. Reproduced with the kind permission of Johnson Alcock Ltd.

Derek Walcott. "A Far Cry from Africa," "LII" from "Midsummer," and "Ruins of a Great House," from *Collected Poems 1948–1984* by Derek Walcott. Copyright © 1986 by Derek Walcott. Reprinted by permission of Farrar, Straus and Giroux, LLC. "Central America," from *The Arkansas Testament* by Derek Walcott. Copyright © by Derek Walcott. Reprinted by permission of Farrar, Straus and Giroux, LLC.

David Foster Wallace. "Consider the Lobster," originally published in *Gourmet Magazine*, 2004. Copyright © 2005, David Foster Wallace, *Consider the Lobster and Other Essays*, Little, Brown and Company. Used by permission of the David Foster Wallace Literary Trust.

Tom Wayman. "Did I Miss Anything?" from *Did I Miss Anything?: Selected Poems 1973–1993*. Harbour Publishing, 1993. Reprinted with the permission of Harbour Publishing, <www.harbourpublishing.com>.

Tennessee Williams. *Cat on a Hot Tin Roof,* copyright © 1954, 1955, 1971, 1975 by The University of the South. Reprinted by permission of New Directions Publishing Corp.

William Carlos Williams. "Spring and All," "The Red Wheelbarrow," and "This Is Just to Say," from *The Collected Poems: Volume 1, 1909–1939*, copyright © 1938 by New Directions Publishing Corp. Reprinted by permission of New Directions Publishing Corp. "Landscape with the Fall of Icarus," from *The Collected Poems: Volume 2, 1939–1962*, copyright © 1962 by William Carlos Williams. Reprinted by permission of New Directions Publishing Corp.

Rita Wong. "opium" and "nervous organism," from *forage*. Nightwood Editions, 2007. Reprinted with the permission of Nightwood Editions, <www.nightwood editions.com>.

Benjamin Zephaniah. "Dis Poetry," from *City Psalms*. Bloodaxe Books, 1992. Reprinted with the permission of Bloodaxe Books.

Rachel Zolf. "Human Resources" (pages 4 & 5), "Human Resources" (pages 6 & 7), and "Notes" (excerpt), from *Human Resources*. Coach House Books, 2007. Reprinted with the permission of the author and Coach House Books.

The publisher has endeavoured to contact rights holders for all copyrighted material, and would appreciate receiving any information as to errors or omissions.

Solutions to the Exeter Book riddles:
23, penis or onion (rose has also been suggested); 33, iceberg; 81, fish and river.

Index of First Lines

dear Captain Poetry   1225
Death be not proud, though some have
    called thee   901
Did you see her mother on television?
    She said plain, burned things.
    She   1249
Dis poetry is like a riddim dat
    drops   1274
Do not go gentle into that good
    night   1128
do not imagine that the
    exploration   1203
Entre castillos de piedra cansada   1338
First, grant me my sense of history   1246
First having read the book of
    myths   1156
First the earth, then the plow   1359
Five years have passed; five summers,
    with the length   966
footfall, which is a means so
    steady   1295
For the following few seconds, while the
    ear   1206
From my mother's sleep I fell into the
    State   1124
From time to time our love is like a
    sail   1294
Gather ye rosebuds while ye may   907
Given enough input elements, a
    writing machine can spew about
    anything   1309
Had we but world enough, and
    time   918
Half a league, half a league   1010
Happy ye leaves when as those lilly
    hands   889
He opens his eyes to a hard frost   1268
He was found by the Bureau of
    Statistics to be   1107
He, who navigated with success   1188
Helicopters are cutlassing the wild
    bananas   1170
Here rests his head upon the lap of
    earth   955

here to me from Krete to this holy
    temple   1323
How do I love thee? Let me count the
    ways   991
How do they do it, the ones who make
    love   1213
How they strut about, people in
    love   1282
How vainly men themselves amaze   915
How well they love us, palm and instep,
    lifeline   1206
I am a wondrous thing, a joy to
    women   881
I can still see that soil crimsoned by
    butchered   1277
I caught this morning morning's
    minion, king   1053
I celebrate myself, and sing
    myself   1020
I don't know the how   1354
I don't remember who kissed who
    first   1281
I don't want to trip over this in the
    future from where I'm sitting can
    you   1309
I found a dimpled spider, fat and
    white   1066
I had been told about her   1281
i have altered my tactics to reflect the
    new era   1210
I have done it again   1174
I have eaten   1072
I have met them at close of day   1057
I hear America singing, the varied carols
    I hear   1021
I heard a Fly buzz—when I
    died—   1026
I heard them marching the leaf-wet
    roads of my head   1169
I imagine this midnight moment's
    forest   1160
I knew a woman, lovely in her
    bones   1113
I leant upon a coppice gate   1047

Index of Authors and Titles

from the publisher

A name never says it all, but the word "broadview" expresses a good deal of the philosophy behind our company. We are open to a broad range of academic approaches and political viewpoints. We pay attention to the broad impact book publishing and book printing has in the wider world; we began using recycled stock more than a decade ago, and for some years now we have used 100% recycled paper for most titles. As a Canadian-based company we naturally publish a number of titles with a Canadian emphasis, but our publishing program overall is internationally oriented and broad-ranging. Our individual titles often appeal to a broad readership too; many are of interest as much to general readers as to academics and students.

Founded in 1985, Broadview remains a fully independent company owned by its shareholders—not an imprint or subsidiary of a larger multinational.

If you would like to find out more about Broadview and about the books we publish, please visit us at **www.broadviewpress.com**. And if you'd like to place an order through the site, we'd like to show our appreciation by extending a special discount to you: by entering the code below you will receive a 20% discount on purchases made through the Broadview website.

Discount code: **broadview20%**

Thank you for choosing Broadview.

Please note: this offer applies only to sales of bound books within the United States or Canada.

Daddy

You do not do, you do not do
Any more, black shoe
In which I have lived like a foot
For thirty years, poor and white,
5 Barely daring to breathe or Achoo.

Daddy, I have had to kill you.
You died before I had time—
Marble-heavy, a bag full of God,
Ghastly statue with one grey toe[1]
10 Big as a Frisco seal

And a head in the freakish Atlantic
Where it pours bean green over blue
In the waters off beautiful Nauset.[2]
I used to pray to recover you.
15 Ach, du.[3]

In the German tongue, in the Polish town[4]
Scraped flat by the roller
Of wars, wars, wars.
But the name of the town is common.
20 My Polack friend

Says there are a dozen or two.
So I never could tell where you
Put your foot, your root,
I never could talk to you.
25 The tongue stuck in my jaw.

It stuck in a barb wire snare
Ich, ich, ich, ich,[5]

---

1 *Ghastly ... grey toe* Plath's father, Otto Plath (1885–1940), died from complications due to untreated diabetes. Before he died, his toe became gangrenous and his leg was amputated.

2 *Nauset* Beach in Orleans, Massachusetts.

3 *Ach, du.* German: Oh, you.

4 *Polish town* Otto Plath emigrated to the US from the Polish town of Grabow.

5 *Ich, ich, ich, ich* German: I, I, I, I.

Sylvia Plath
1932–1963

Sylvia Plath's early life was, outwardly, one of upper middle-class privilege. The daughter of a Boston University professor and his wife, Plath was an excellent student both in school and later at Smith, a prestigious liberal arts college for women, where she became a prolific writer of poems and short stories. Inwardly, however, she had been profoundly affected by the death of her father when she was eight, and became deeply conflicted over the roles young women in the 1950s were expected to fulfill. Following her third year at Smith she was awarded a guest editorship at the young women's magazine *Mademoiselle*; the experience was a disappointment, however, and Plath fell into a deep depression. She attempted suicide that August, and spent many months thereafter in psychiatric care.

Plath recovered, and in 1955 was awarded a scholarship to Cambridge University, where her talents as a writer began to be more widely recognized—and where she met and soon married the British poet Ted Hughes. The couple both published well-received volumes of poetry (Plath's *The Colossus* appeared in 1960) and they had two children together, but their relationship was sometimes strained and Plath continued to suffer from depression. In 1962, following Plath's discovery that Hughes had been having an affair, the two separated. Between that time and Plath's suicide in February of 1963, living with the children in a bitterly cold flat in London, she wrote the extraordinary body of work on which her reputation now rests. These poems (published posthumously in 1965 in the volume *Ariel*) are spare and controlled in their form but entirely unsparing in the searing intensity with which they explore human strangeness and savagery—perhaps most memorably, the savagery of the Holocaust.

Plath's one novel, *The Bell Jar* (1963), is highly autobiographical, and, given the sensational aspects of her life, it is not surprising that her poetry is often discussed in relation to her life. But, as Catriona O'Reilly has observed, it will not do to regard Plath's work as "an extended suicide note." Her strongest poems are almost universally accorded a vital place in the history of poetry in the twentieth century.